World Drama

World Drama

Oscar G. Brockett

The University of Texas at Austin

Mark Pape

Holt, Rinehart and Winston
New York   Chicago   San Francisco   Philadelphia
Montreal   Toronto   London   Sydney
Tokyo   Mexico City   Rio de Janeiro   Madrid

Library of Congress Cataloging in Publication Data
Main entry under title:

World drama.

1. Drama—Collections.   I. Brockett, Oscar Gross,
date. II. Pape, Mark.
PN6112.W62   1984   808.82   82-15733
ISBN 0-03-057668-7

CBS COLLEGE PUBLISHING
Holt, Rinehart and Winston
The Dryden Press
Saunders College Publishing

Preface

This anthology is designed to assist students toward some partial achievement of one of the goals most commonly asserted in college and university catalogs: to provide students with a liberal education. Clearly, a collection of plays, however painstakingly selected and adroitly commented on, can be only one small part among the many parts in such an undertaking; but with it, the editors seek not only to present significant plays to be read and studied as works of literary and dramatic art, but also to stimulate interest in the historical contexts out of which the plays came and, thus, to encourage informed discussion of the issues of those times—the philosophical, political, ethical, and esthetic—which these plays raise.

To study plays in a liberal arts curriculum is certainly not an innovation. Literature, and drama as one form of literature, has long been a major component of liberal studies—along with history, philosophy, the arts, and other subjects that deal with mankind's recurring concern for values and the need to understand what responsible action is in public and private life. During the past fifty years, however, much of literary study has restrictingly focused on form, structure, and themes—all essential elements of the art of drama. Such study is valuable and will continue to be; indeed, these elements of the art of drama are major concerns in this anthology, as they must be if one seeks to understand a play primarily as a work of art. But this anthology seeks to enlarge on these artistic concerns by also viewing the plays within their historical and philosophical contexts. These supplementary views broaden our personal scope of understanding as they help to reveal the richness of meanings and implications of any play by reflections cast on its time and place in history as well as on its timeless artistic elements. These additional dimensions in perspective should enhance a reader's understanding of a play and of those concerns that characterize liberal studies.

More than by any other means, perhaps, we come to understand other civilizations and eras through their works of art. Indeed, critical understanding of a civilization depends in large measure on the art it has left behind. Those civilizations that have left behind no substantial art are little understood and certainly little valued. A people may have been militarily strong and materially wealthy; but unless it also permitted, and encouraged, intellectual inquiry, exploration of ethical and spiritual values, and the exercise of creative imagination, it is apt to be perceived by later generations as oppressive, limited, and less than it should and might have been. As one form of art, drama is a key to understanding both the civilizations of the past and of our own times.

In many ways drama is a record of the changing conceptions of being human, of human potential, and of human limitations. Its fullest study leads into almost all fields of inquiry, for drama is chiefly concerned, as Aristotle noted in his *Poetics*, with "man in action," a subject from which little can be excluded. "Man in action" reveals human motivations, human moral fiber, human intellectual strengths and weaknessess. "Man in action," in any time and place, requires that we concern ourselves with how a certain author, in a particular time and place, conceived of the reality in which the entire community existed; perceptions of causes related to effects determining the structure of events, conceptions of the dimensions of freedom of choice, of supernatural influences, of the power of societal customs and beliefs—the perception of mankind at that time in a total scheme of being. Drama also requires us "to feel our way into" what it would be like to live in other times and places and to be, empathically, someone other than ourselves (and also in addition to ourselves). It asks us to put ourselves imaginatively into the heart of those experiences that would otherwise be closed to us, thus grafting onto our own conscious awareness a warm and close sensitivity to the reality of the life of other people in other times and places.

In this anthology the plays are arranged chronologically, but they need not be read in that order. Similarly, the essays entitled "Drama and Its Structure" and "Form in Drama" may be studied whenever they seem most pertinent. Not every play, of course, lends itself to the same kind of study or yields equally rich results. Learning to recognize the kind of drama and that study of it most likely to be productive is also a part of the liberal educational process. In light of the goal the editors of this anthology have set, the essays related to the plays are necessarily limited in scope and suggest only a few of the ways to approach the study of drama. As in any vital learning situation, the great burden rests on the instructor, and also on the particular group of students, the library and other resources, and many other important factors too obvious and numerous to mention. The editors are convinced, however, of the almost unlimited educational potential of drama, within a liberal arts curriculum, when cogently and coherently studied; to encourage such study, the editors have assembled this anthology.

The editors wish to thank the following reviewers for their aid in preparing this book: Raymond Anschel, Normandale Community College; Dorothy Brown, Loyola University of the South; William Cook, Dartmouth College; Paul Davis, University of New Mexico; Tinsley Helton, University of Wisconsin; Cheryl Oreovitz, Purdue University; David Sauer, Spring Hill College; Arvin Sponberg, Valparaiso University; Frederick Stern, University of Illinois at Chicago Circle.

Austin, Texas **OGB**
MP

Contents

World Drama

Drama and
Its Structure

Drama is the representation of "man in action." When, in the fourth century B.C., Aristotle made this observation he had in mind Greek drama but his comment is true not only for the plays of Sophocles but also those of Shakespeare and, in our own time, of Harold Pinter and Samuel Beckett. By *action*, however, he did not mean only physical movement. Rather, in the largest sense, he thought of human action as including all those internal forces—emotional, intellectual, and ethical—which motivate, shape, and control human behavior. *Man in action*, then, embraces the entire range of feeling, thought, and judgment which gives rise to action and characterizes what kind of creatures human beings are—what they do and why they do it. Because the dramatic potential of human action is, in this perception, almost endless, no single play, obviously, can depict more than a small portion of possible human actions. Moreover, because each playwright's vision of human beings and the world they live in differs from that of others, each dramatist's works are, for that reason, unique. That uniqueness notwithstanding, plays, like all other recognizable phenomena, have sufficient points of likeness to justify some generalizations about them.

A play comes into being through the creative action of a human imagination. While a play may go through many revisions, once it is completed, it exists quite apart from its creator and may continue to exist long after its creator has disappeared. If a play is to achieve a significant autonomous existence (that is, if it is to survive for a considerable period of time as a meaningful work of art), it has probably adhered to five principles of effective dramatic action.

First, the play must be *complete and self-contained.* In other words, everything needed for understanding the play must be contained within it. The playwright will not always be available to explain what he has in mind and, even if he were, the play would be incomplete as a play if it required the author's ongoing commentary to be properly appreciated. This demand for completeness, however, must be tempered by our recognition that audiences other than those for whom the play was written may not immediately perceive what in actuality is in the play. A skillful writer does not belabor audiences with information already well known to them; he takes for granted that much information will be brought by the auditor or reader since this information is common knowledge in the society for which he is writing. Thus, Greek dramatists probably took it for granted that a mythological reference would trigger myriad associations, whereas a present-day reader may be mystified by the same reference and need to acquire the information generally known and understood by early Greek audiences. Most

1

playwrights prior to this century assumed that their audiences were familiar with Greek mythology, the Bible, major Western historical figures, numerous theological concepts, and certain other information that they could call on through allusions, without need for elaboration. But many of the great works of Western literature have come to seem remote because schools no longer acquaint students with the information most writers of the past took for granted. Consequently, to the statement that a good play is complete and self-contained, we must add: *if* the reader is sufficiently well informed to perceive what in actuality is contained in the play.

Second, a play should be *internally consistent*. This is the characteristic most persons have in mind when they speak of a play's "believability." But, believability does not depend on similarity to real life, for a play that depicts events impossible in reality may be judged believable if the incidents occur acceptably within the framework created by the writer. The opening section of any play begins to establish its frame of reference or system of logic. The audience expects the play to observe consistently the framework it has established; anything that violates a play's pattern of logic, however strange that pattern would be in real life, will seem out of place and inconsistent.

Third, a play's dramatic action is *organized to arouse a particular range of response*. In most instances, we are aware that the events in a play are intended to make us laugh, cry, arouse indignation, pity or fear, or to produce some other reasonably specific reaction. It is largely for this reason that we learn quickly to categorize plays into tragedies and comedies, those with serious and those with lighthearted intent. Occasionally, we find it difficult to determine purpose because intention seems to be mixed or to shift. This is especially true of contemporary drama, for which we often encounter such unusual labels as a *tragic farce* and an *anti-play*. Labels aside, however, all dramatic action arouses a response through its treatment of events and characters.

Fourth, dramatic action should be *unified*. Traditionally, the dominant source of unity in a play has been the cause-to-effect arrangement of incidents. With this method, the playwright sets up all the necessary elements in the opening scenes — the situation, the desires and motivations of the characters — out of which later events develop. The goals of one character may come into conflict with those of another or two conflicting desires within the same character may demand resolution. Attempts to surmount the obstacles make up the substance of the play, each scene growing out of the preceding ones. Less often, a dramatist uses a character as the principal source of unity, the incidents being held together chiefly because they center around one person. A playwright may also organize his material around a basic idea, with scenes linked largely as illustrative parts of a larger theme or argument. Much contemporary drama, for example, structurally resembles the theme-and-variations organization of many musical compositions as the play, too, introduces a theme or motif, then elaborates and improvises on it. Admittedly, any organizational pattern other than cause-to-effect is likely to seem loose because the play's incidents have no apparently direct cause and effect relation. In analyzing a play, however, it is essential to identify the source of unity, no matter how vague it may at first appear, for only then will the play build into a coherent whole rather than a random collection of unrelated happenings.

Fifth, within a unified dramatic action, there should be *variety*. A play can easily become monotonous if the tempo, for example, is not varied from one scene to another, or if the characters seem too much alike, or if the emotional tone remains the same for too long. Contrast and variety are as essential as unity in a play if the attention of the audience is to be captured and retained.

These five characteristics of effective dramatic action — complete and self-contained, internally consistent, organized to arouse specific responses, unity, and variety — are essential to all plays. Whether and how they have been achieved can be determined through a close study of the script. Analysis involves breaking a play down into parts and examining each carefully in order to discover how each part functions within and relates to the entire work.

The Analysis of Drama

Dramatic analysis is generally begun by examining the parts of a play: plot, character, thought, diction, music, and spectacle. To be sure, there are other approaches to analysis, but this one is sufficiently flexible and universally applicable to be useful with almost any type of play.

Plot is often considered to be merely the summary of a play's incidents. Although it includes the play's story line, it also refers to the play's organization so that plot includes the action and the specific organization of the action.

Most frequently the place, occasion, characters, mood, fundamental motifs, and the framework are established in the opening scenes of a play. *Exposition*, that is, information about earlier events, identity of characters, and events leading up to the present scene, begins but is not confined to the opening scenes because information about the past typically is revealed only gradually. The amount of exposition found at the beginning of most plays is determined in part by the *point of attack* — the moment at which the action starts. Shakespeare, for example, uses an early point of attack — that is, he begins the action very near the start of the story — and unfolds the events in chronological order. Consequently, he needs to provide relatively little information about prior occurrences. Greek tragic playwrights, however, use late points of attack, which require considerable exposition because the plays actually depict only the final parts of the story.

Most plays quickly focus attention on a question, conflict, or theme through what is sometimes called an *inciting incident* — an occurrence that sets the dramatic action into motion. In Sophocles' *Antigone*, Antigone's determination to bury her brother despite Creon's prohibition of the burial initiates the action and the thread that holds all the action together: the conflict between two opposing points of view.

At the opening of any play, the story has the potential of developing in almost any direction. Once action is set in motion, however, complications arise, narrowing the possibilities of action and thereby creating increasing suspense. A *complication* is any new element that alters the direction of the action. Usually, a complication is introduced by a *discovery*—of new information, opposition to a plan, identity of a character, an unforeseen dilemma, or some other new element. The steps taken to meet the new demands give rise to tensions and conflicts that often lead to a new discovery or revelation which may bring about a *reversal* of the situation through the unexpected outcome of some plan. As characters and events are more and more developed and as an increasing number of complications arise, alternative choices of action are progressively reduced. As a result, the audience comes to sense the specific or dominant direction of the action and, as possible actions are further and further narrowed, a feeling of imminent crisis approaches. Finally, a moment arrives when the alternatives have been so reduced that the next discovery will answer the major questions posed at the beginning of the play. This is the *crisis* or peak toward which the play builds, after which there is a gradual release of tension leading to the *resolution* (or *denouement*) of the action. The resolution creates a sense of completion and fulfillment, the audience now being able to see how the ending has come about even if it could not have predicted it.

Not all plays present a conflict or a clear-cut series of complications leading to a resolution. This is so because structure is related to the playwright's vision of reality. Until quite recently, most dramatists viewed the world as essentially orderly, a place where cause-to-effect principles operated everywhere and were discernible to those who observed carefully. The plays of these dramatists, therefore, reflected an orderly world view: a series of connected events which progressed in a pattern composing an easily perceivable pattern of beginning, middle, and end. But many contemporary dramatists view reality as chaotic, our world as a place of seemingly accidental events with little apparent relationship to each other. The structure of their plays, therefore, reflects this unpredictability and randomness. Such plays (those of Samuel Beckett, for example) are unified through idea or theme, for their fundamental subject is uncertainty and loss of direction—the nature of existence in a world that has lost its bearings.

Character is the primary element out of which plots are created because events evolve from the speech and actions of the dramatic persons. *Characterization* is the playwright's means of differentiating one person from another. To accomplish this differentiation of character, playwrights generally provide four types of information about them. The first type of information is *physical*, which is limited to external appearance—sex, age, size, color, and so on. Sometimes a script does not supply much physical information, but it is filled in when the play is produced, since actors necessarily give concrete form to the characters. The second type is *social*. It includes a character's economic status, profession or trade, family relationships and other factors that place him in his environment. The third type is *psychological*—the inner workings of the mind which precede action. Since drama most often arises from conflicting desires, psychological information is the most essential aspect of characterization. The fourth is *moral* or *ethical*. All plays have moral implications, but most plays keep moral elements at an implicit level. Serious plays, however, do emphasize a character's moral choice because of its dramatic consequences. More than any other kind of choice, moral decisions differentiate characters meaningfully since the choices they make when faced with ethical crises reveal significant aspects of character: selfish, honest, altruistic, hypocritical, etc. Moreover, a moral decision usually forces a character to examine his own motives and values, in the process of which his true nature is shown both to himself and to the audience.

Characterization is revealed through various other means: through description in *stage directions, prefaces,* or *other explanatory material* not part of the dialogue or action; through *what the character says;* through *what others say about the character;* and, most important, through *what the character does.* In assessing characterization, it is not enough merely to make a list of traits; it is also necessary to ask *how the character functions in the action.* For example, the audience needs to know little about the maid who appears only to announce dinner; any detailed characterization would be superfluous and distracting. The principal character in a serious play, however, will need to be drawn in great detail.

Neither in life nor in drama is it easy to perceive a person's true character since information in both cases is given in fragments over a considerable period of time. Many different and often contradictory pieces of information and concrete evidence of character may be given. Because the dramatist builds character through a composite of information, the audience must be attentive to all elements of characterization in order to decide which statements and actions are to be accepted as accurate revelations of character.

The third basic part of a play is *thought* (theme, argument, overall meaning, focus, or significance). Thought is more frequently implied than stated directly. A reader discovers it in the relationships among characters, the feelings associated with sympathetic and unsympathetic characters, the conflicts and their resolutions, and such elements as verbal imagery, spectacle, music, and song. Occasionally, a message is clearly stated in a drama, but this is rare. More often the meaning or meanings of a play are ambiguous and open to several interpretations. To many people, ambiguity is unsettling, and some people have used the diversity of interpretations of the same script to discount the value of all criticism. But, ambiguity is characteristic of practically all human experience; few, if any, experiences, have clear-cut, unarguable meanings. Life does not come so neatly wrapped. We are compelled to ponder our experiences, try to find meaning in them, and then, perhaps, to learn from them in order to act more wisely in the future. But we are seldom, if ever, certain that we have found *the* answer. Since human experience is the raw material of drama, the dramatist who sees no ambiguities in life will very likely create an oversimplified world in his plays, with quite superficial characters. Because the playwright is concerned with the patterns that underlie the infinite detail of life, he must eliminate what he considers unimportant. He selects, arranges, and shapes his material, and in so doing he creates implications, which may be few or many.

Dramatists have used many devices to project thought. Greek playwrights made extensive use of the *chorus;* those in later periods employed such devices as the *soliloquy, aside,* and *direct statement.* Still other dramatists have used *allegory* and *symbol.* But the most important means are dramatic action and character relationships.

Plot, character, and thought are the basic parts of drama; to convey these, the playwright must rely on *diction* or *language.* When a play is performed, music and spectacle are added, but in writing a play the dramatist depends almost entirely on dialogue and stage directions. Through language, the writer develops the dramatic action, characterizes the participants, implies ideas, establishes mood, tempo, and rhythm, and indicates the visual elements.

The diction of every play, no matter how realistic, is more carefully structured than that of ordinary conversation. A dramatist selects, arranges, and heightens language much more fully than we do in spontaneous speech. Consequently, even in a realistic play, although the dialogue may be modeled after everyday usage, the characters are more articulate and state their ideas and feelings more precisely than their real-life counterparts do. Realistic dialogue often retains the basic rhythms, tempos, and vocabulary of colloquial speech, but the dialogue of nonrealistic plays may deviate markedly from ordinary speech. Most frequently nonrealistic diction in drama employs a larger-than-life vocabulary, abandons the rhythms of conversation, and makes use of considerable imagery and metrical patterns. This permits a more precise choice of words, avoids the repetitiveness of colloquial speech, creates allusions and associations which enlarge or alter literal meanings, and permits more forceful expression when characters must transcend the ordinary and routine. Whether realistic or nonrealistic, the best diction is a mixture of the familiar and the strange: the familiar gives clarity, the strange adds variety.

When we read a play, we tend to restrict our attention to four elements: plot, character, thought, and diction. The final two parts—music and spectacle—are more closely associated with production, although the imaginative reader will supply them as they recreate the action in their minds.

Music, as ordinarily understood, is not a part of every play. But, if the term is extended to include all patterned sound, it is an important element in every production and imaginative reading of a play. It includes the actors' voices, songs, instrumental music, and sound effects.

A play is written to be performed on a stage by actors for an audience and is not fully a play—a work of dramatic art—until print is transformed into action and sound. Although the meaning of words may remain constant, their implications can be varied considerably by the voice. Note, for example, that by shifting the emphasis from one word to another or by altering the tone from anger to sarcasm to question to wonder, what numerous shades of meaning can be imparted to so simple a speech as, "You say he told her." The silent reader, like the actor, must seek appropriate emphasis and tone if he is to interpret a script properly.

The aural aspects of a play also include instrumental accompaniment and the musical notation for lyrics, neither of which ordinarily are included with a printed play text. It is easy for us to forget, therefore, that in many dramas the playwrights considered the musical element an integral part of the text. The authors of Greek tragedy and comedy, for example, expected that the choral passages would be sung and danced and that other portions of the plays would be sung or chanted to musical accompaniment. In Roman comedy, as many as two-thirds of the lines had musical accompaniment. Songs and instrumental music were prominent in many of Shakespeare's plays, and the melodramas of the nineteenth century utilized musical scores to enhance mood and atmosphere much as a film does today. We may read plays without making an attempt to imagine the musical element, but we are missing much when we do.

Along with sound, *spectacle*, the visual element, is a major means of expression. Usually, however, the author depends on others to supply spectacle when the play is produced. Until the nineteenth century, play scripts contained very few stage directions and both readers and performers had to deduce spectacle from the dialogue. (Most of the stage directions now found in older plays have been added by editors.)

Watching a live performance of a drama differs radically from reading a script of the same drama. In reading, only two elements are involved: the written word and the reader's capacity to understand and imaginatively envision what is conveyed through the written word. But a live performance is a director's translation of the written word into speech and concreteness of movement, setting, costume, lighting, atmosphere, and all else that otherwise would have to be imagined in a private reading.

A live performance is the concretization of a script by the specific vision of a director. If the performance is done effectively, it frees the spectator from the necessity of imagining the play for himself. The concretization of all the details (the actions of the characters, their physical appearance, the sounds of their voices, the setting, the lighting, the costumes, the music and other sounds, and so on) leaves the spectator free to concentrate on the developing action, the relationship among the characters, and the implications of action and character. In effect, the spectator is freed to observe the play as he would a scene from life, rather than, as in a silent reading, imaginatively to recreate every aspect of the entire play.

Nevertheless, performance has its drawbacks. The spectator must freely release himself on faith to be carried along at whatever pace the performers set. If he misses something he cannot go back and recover it. In the theatre there are no instant replays. A reader may proceed at his own pace, stop and start, turn back or look ahead. Play reading is more flexible and can be more thorough than play watching, although it can never be as satisfying as a truly great performance.

What a spectator sees and hears is also affected by the space in which he experiences a performance. It is important to know if the theatre has a proscenium arch stage, or a thrust stage, or an arena stage because the type of stage influences the dramatist's use of spectacle. It is also important to know how large or small the auditorium is and how its size will affect hearing and seeing. In reading plays, it is well to keep in mind that almost all scripts were written with a particular kind of theatre structure and theatrical conventions in mind, the better to imagine what is happening where and under what conditions. Full appreciation of a script depends partially on our knowledge of theatre history and theatre architecture. But most significantly, a satisfying production of any drama depends on the intelligence with which it has been produced, the level of knowledge and understanding of the audience, and the profound perception of character possessed by the performers.

Analyzing a play requires us to break it down and look at it bit by bit so we may see more fully how it is put together and what the author had in mind. Once that is done, however, we must go back and experience it as a whole once more, the parts reintegrated. But now the experience should be far more rewarding, for the insights gained through analysis should make the various ways in which a play means come together powerfully, both intellectually and emotionally.

Form in Drama

By definition and convention all literature is categorized by type: poetry, novel, short story, and drama. Like other literary forms, drama, too, is subdivided according to certain formal distinctions; the traditional subdivisions are tragedy, comedy, and tragicomedy.

Form is the shape given to something so it may serve a specific function. Tragedy, for example, is said to be structured so as to arouse pity and fear, whereas comedy is shaped to arouse joy, laughter, and ridicule.

Historically, form in drama has been approached through two major attitudes: form as fixed and form as organic. The idea that forms of drama are fixed and unchanging rests on the belief that the characteristics of dramatic types have been clearly isolated and defined more or less permanently. Many who have favored this view have also suggested that a play can be judged in part according to how well it adheres to the characteristics of the form to which it belongs. The idea of organic form is based on the belief that a play takes shape and grows much as a plant does, and that each play has been shaped to achieve its own purposes without regard to preexisting forms. Each of these two views is defensible. Most plays can be classified according to form and the major characteristics of each form can be listed. Furthermore, in studying a play it is useful to compare it with other works of a similar nature. Nevertheless, each play is unique in some respects and should be appreciated for its individuality. Often it is difficult to classify a play precisely according to form, and the attempt to label it may assume undue importance. When *Death of a Salesman* first appeared, there were numerous arguments over whether it could rightfully be called tragedy, the implication being that if it could its value would be enhanced. But one form is not *better* than another; each has only a different function. Furthermore, there are good and bad examples of each. Categorizing plays according to form, then, can be helpful; but this is only one step in understanding any play.

All labels used to describe dramatic forms can be related to one of three basic qualities: the serious, the comic, and the seriocomic. In turn, these three divisions are epitomized in three forms: tragedy, comedy, and tragicomedy (or melodrama or mixed form).

Tragedy

A tragedy presents a genuinely serious action and maintains a mood that underscores the play's serious intention (although there may be scenes of comic relief). It is concerned with significant issues or fundamental moral questions and leads to important insights and perceptions about human experiences.

9

Most tragedies prior to the modern period show the interaction between supernatural and natural forces: the involvement of a god, providence, or some moral power in the fate of human beings. Many tragedies imply that the protagonist has violated some moral order or divine principle that must be vindicated and reestablished. The presence of superhuman forces often makes the outcome of the action seem inevitable or predetermined.

During the eighteenth century, the supernatural element began to give way to concern for social and psychological forces, and conflicts were increasingly restricted to the human realm. Because this more recent drama has typically been concerned with everyday situations and less profound issues, many critics have refused to call it tragedy and have labeled such plays *drama*.

Most tragedies of the premodern period drew their major characters from the ruling class, but more recent drama has emphasized middle or lower class protagonists. This has led to much debate over whether the common man is a suitable protagonist for tragedy. Nevertheless, there seems little basis for relating social class to nobility of character and action. If tragedy has not fared well in modern times, it is in part owing to our revised estimate of man's place in the scheme of being, to our perceptions of human limitations, and most importantly, to a reexamination of what constitutes greatness in man especially by discounting position and class.

The protagonist of tragedy (the "tragic hero") is usually a person who arouses sympathy and admiration. Without being perfect, he is sufficiently superior to the average to inspire admiration while sufficiently imperfect to be partially responsible for the serious situation in which he finds himself. In his *Poetics*, Aristotle noted that the protagonist's downfall results from *hamartia*, a term which many critics have translated as *tragic flaw*, thereby implying that the tragic hero always has some deficiency which leads to his downfall. Undoubtedly, many tragic protagonists do have flaws: Lear's arrogance makes him believe that he can dispose of a kingdom as though it were private property and that he will still be obeyed as before. But many protagonists bring doom on themselves, as Antigone does, for example, in seeking to uphold a worthy principle. While Creon may call Antigone stubborn, he only proves that she will not compromise principle even when threatened with death. *Hamartia* may mean a flaw in character, but it can also be understood as an error in judgment (in *Antigone*, the error is Creon's) or mistake based upon lack of knowledge.

The tragic protagonist usually finds himself in a serious (often fatal) dilemma because, in pursuing a worthy aim, he violates some moral law which must be reaffirmed. A recurring motif of tragedy (as in *Hamlet*) is the imposition of a task, the performance of which will inevitably lead to loss of life, love, reputation, or peace of mind. The protagonist is faced, therefore, with choosing between two goals, each of which in other circumstances might have been good but which have been placed in seemingly irreconcilable conflict. Another recurring motif in tragedy is man's inability to control his own destiny. It is especially prominent in *King Lear*, and in *Iphigeneia at Aulis* we see it used ironically, for Agamemnon, Achilles, and Iphigeneia all believe that their actions will ensure their own fame and the future glory of Greece. Another frequent pattern is the failure to recognize the limits set on human power and the consequent attempt to assume power that belongs to the gods or to forces greater than the individual. In *Antigone*, Creon makes a decree that would negate a demand made by the gods, and furthermore he does so without the consent of the Theban people, thereby offending both the gods and men. This failure to recognize the limits was called *hubris* (overweening pride, excess) by the Greeks, and those guilty of it almost always had to pay a terrible price.

The emotional effect of tragedy is usually described as the arousal of pity and fear, but we must recognize that these two emotions subsume a wide range of others: compassion, admiration, apprehension, foreboding, dread, awe, and terror. Pity and fear are rooted in two instinctive human responses: fear is related to our desire for self-preservation; pity is based on our concern for others. Pity and fear are complementary emotions. To feel pity, we must perceive some likeness between ourselves and the character — we must be able to feel our way into his situation. The key to this feeling of likeness is fear, for it is the anxiety we would have for our own welfare if we were in the character's situation that allows the feelings of sympathy to develop. But, if fear for our own welfare becomes too great, we have no time to worry about others. A tempered fear, however, enables us to empathize with others. What begins with a selfish response (fear), then, is translated into generous concern (pity) and becomes a humanizing force which unites us with all humanity in its struggle for dignity.

Most tragedies end with the death of the protagonist, but some do not. All, however, have a sense of finality that is analogous to death. In most instances, the ending seems fated or inevitable in light of the events that have preceded. The ending also tends to calm or purge the emotions of pity and fear. Rather than leaving us emotionally unsettled, the resolution releases the tensions that have been aroused and brings us back to a state of equilibrium. It also usually leads us to recognize the implications of the dramatic action and into acceptance and reconciliation.

Comedy

The action of comedy is based on some deviation from normative behavior in action, character, thought, or speech. The deviation, however, must not pose a serious threat to us, and an "in fun" mood must be established and maintained. The normative behavior is not necessarily what the majority of persons would consider typical; rather, it is whatever the playwright presents as normative. He may well take what he believes to be the social norm and make it appear ridiculous, and in so doing he may establish another norm. His aim may be to ridicule the accepted patterns of behavior and to argue for some more desirable pattern. There is no subject, however trivial or weighty, that cannot be treated comically provided it is placed in a framework that emphasizes its incongruities.

Although a comedy arouses laughter, it may have a serious purpose, as Aristophanes so clearly demonstrates in *Lysistrata*, in which the sexual high jinks are used to point up the absurdity of war.

Whereas tragedy usually engages our sympathies, comedy demands distance or objectivity. Henri Bergson, in *Laughter*, states that comedy requires "an anesthesia of the heart" since it is difficult to laugh at anything with which we are too closely allied, either through sympathy or dislike. For example, we might find a man's pratfall amusing, but if we then discover that the man is a loved one just recovering from a serious operation, our concern will destroy laughter. Similarly, we may consider some behavior so morally reprehensible or socially pernicious that we cannot distance ourselves from it sufficiently to see humor in it.

Not everything in a comedy is laughable. The dramatist usually arouses acceptance for the norm he has established and ridicule for deviations from it. Part of comic pleasure comes from witnessing the eventual vindication of normative behavior, character, or idea over a threat from some deviation. Some plays include no normative characters. Rather, they may show a gallery of rogues seeking to outsmart each other. In Plautus' *Pseudolus*, for example, we see a slave use a series of clever devices to cheat a braggart soldier of a large sum of money and a pimp of a slave girl. But those he cheats are so dishonest or arrogant that we applaud the slave for his cleverness and for punishing those who so richly deserve it.

All comedy seeks to arouse emotions that lie in a range between joy and scorn. At one extreme, Shakespeare's romantic comedies (for example, *As You Like It*) elicit a response that can best be described as a feeling of well-being. It may arouse smiles but seldom boisterous laughter. At the other extreme, many comic scenes in the plays of Brecht become too painful for laughter. These extremes, from the gentlest teasing to the bitterest ridicule, mark the limits of the comic response.

Comedy seldom, except through implication, raises great moral questions, as does tragedy. Rather, it concentrates on man in his social relationships. It reaffirms the need for a society that allows adequate scope for acceptable human impulses while putting a check on deviations that distort or threaten what is acceptable by convention and custom. As social norms change from one era to another, so does the scope of comedy.

Because of its wide range, comedy (unlike tragedy) is often divided into numerous subtypes. All the classifications, however, can be related to three variables: the extent to which the action emphasizes situation, character, or thought; the degree of objectivity with which the protagonist is portrayed; and the nature and implications of the action. Consequently, the three basic types of comedy are (1) comedy of situation, (2) comedy of character, and (3) comedy of ideas. Each of these may in turn have several subdivisions.

A *comedy of situation* shows the ludicrous results of placing characters in unusual circumstances. For example, a number of characters are invited to a disreputable party, attendance at which might lead to numerous family or social repercussions. Each, nevertheless, would like to attend but would not like any of the others to know it. The devices used to elude each other, the attempts to avoid discovery when all turn up at the party, the reactions upon being recognized, and the eventual resolution make up the comic action. Character and idea are of little importance.

There is little to distinguish a comedy of situation from *farce*, a type which many critics consider to be a form entirely separate from comedy. Farce is often used as a classification for plays, or portions of plays, that rely principally on buffoonery, accident, and coincidence. Pies in the face, beatings, the naive or mistaken views of characters, the ludicrous situation arising from coincidence and circumstance exemplify the devices of farce. Often it seems a kind of inspired nonsense with situations so obviously contrived that a sensible word from any character would resolve the action. Farce is sometimes said to have no purpose beyond entertainment, and while it is true that most farces seem devoid of serious purpose, elements of farce have been important in many of the world's finest comedies, including those of Aristophanes and Molière.

A *comedy of character* grows out of the eccentricities of the protagonist. Some of Molière's finest plays are built around characters whose behavior is determined by hypochondria, miserliness, and hypocrisy.

Romantic comedy is closely related to the comedy of character, for it usually treats the struggles—often those centering around a love affair—of characters who are basically likable and admirable. It is perhaps best exemplified in such plays as Shakespeare's *Twelfth Night* and *As You Like It*. Any comic response they arouse is owing more to the ludicrous strategies they adopt in pursuing their goals and the misunderstandings that result than from any other source. We tend to smile upon them as we would upon a lovable but eccentric relative, small child, or pet. The more boisterous action is relegated to subplots involving minor but ridiculous characters.

A *comedy of ideas* has as its principal focus a conflict over a concept or way of thought. This type of comedy illustrates that, while laughter and ridicule may be weapons, they can be used for ultimately serious purposes. Aristophanes used comedy to make serious points about current issues, and Bernard Shaw used comedy to make audiences reconsider accepted views about a number of social problems and attitudes.

Social comedy is a variation on the comedy of ideas, for it explores social values, standards of behavior, or accepted ways of thought. If it aims at remedying society or behavior, it may be called *corrective comedy*, a label sometimes applied to a number of plays by Ben Jonson and George Bernard Shaw.

A *comedy of manners* is related to the comedy of ideas in that it exploits the incongruities that arise from misdirected adherence to an accepted code of behavior. The characters ridiculed are usually those who confuse outward appearance (such as fashionable dress or modes of speech) with the essence of the code. This type of comedy flourished most fully in England during the Restoration. It usually contrasts normative characters (who understand themselves and their society) with those would-be fashionable characters (who make fools of themselves). As a label, comedy of manners is often reserved for plays about aristocratic and sophisticated characters who indulge in sparkling and witty repartee and those who flock around them and imitate them unsuccessfully (the *in* crowd and the *would-be in* imitators). Because of the emphasis on witty dialogue, this type is also sometimes called *comedy of wit*.

Almost all comedy can be placed in one of these categories, but most have elements that relate them to more than one type. A comedy of character, for example, may use devices usually associated with farce, comedy of manners, or comedy of ideas. Labels, therefore, need to be used with some flexibility if they are to be helpful.

Seriocomic Forms

Not all plays are either tragic or comic. In the twentieth century, the majority is not. Rather, these plays are seriocomic. This type is not confined to the twentieth century, however; it has been common since ancient Greece, and in many eras it was among the most popular of theatrical fare. The nineteenth-century stage was dominated by one seriocomic type, *melodrama*, one which continues prominent today in television.

Melodrama. A melodrama deals with a temporarily serious action which is usually initiated and kept in motion by the malicious designs of a villain. A happy resolution is achieved by neutralizing or destroying the villain or his power. Melodrama depicts a world in which good and evil are sharply delineated. There is seldom any question as to where the audience's sympathies should lie.

The characters in melodrama are usually divided into those who are almost wholly sympathetic and those who are almost totally unsympathetic. There may also be, for the sake of variety, one or more eccentric, uninhibited, or simpleminded characters who provide comic relief. The unsympathetic characters usually set the complications in motion, while the sympathetic characters only seek to deal with the danger. The characters do not grow or change, since the moral nature of each is established at the beginning and remains constant throughout.

The action of melodrama usually develops a powerful threat against the well-being of a likable or innocent protagonist. It shows his entanglement in a web of circumstances and his eventual rescue from death, disgrace or ruin, usually at the last moment. Those who watch television dramas dealing with detectives seeking to outwit criminals will recognize the pattern.

The appeals of melodrama are strong and basic, since the incidents that build the most intense suspense create a desire to see wronged innocence vindicated and unchecked evil chastised. The emotions aroused by melodrama range from dread and concern for the good characters to strong dislike, even hatred, for the evil characters. Melodrama has a double ending in which poetic justice is meted out as the good characters are rescued and rewarded and the evil are detected and punished. Thus, melodrama is related to tragedy through the seriousness of its action and to comedy through its happy conclusion. It reassures us by showing that good triumphs over evil.

Tragicomedy. Not all seriocomic plays draw the line between good and evil so clearly as melodrama does. Tragicomedy, while sharing some characteristics with melodrama, is usually more complex. It originated with the Greeks, although they did not use the term since to them all serious plays were tragedies. A relatively large number of surviving serious Greek plays end happily. Some critics have labeled Euripides' *Iphigeneia at Aulis* a tragicomedy because a number of its characters are transparently petty, because no one achieves self-knowledge, and because the play seems to end happily. But, despite this happy ending, the play raises complex issues about love, friendship, cowardice, courage, and death, and the implications of the action are at times serious and at times ironically humorous.

Subsequent tragicomedies, such as those written by Beaumont and Fletcher in the early 1600s, often relied on concealed identity, misinformation, and coincidence to keep the action moving, and on accidental, last-minute revelations to resolve the action happily. More complex than melodrama in its characterizations and ideas, tragicomedy in this period nevertheless approaches melodrama. The intensification of these tendencies was to lead to the development of melodrama in the nineteenth century.

Many present-day critics have adopted tragicomedy as a label for much contemporary drama because many plays of the twentieth century do not fall neatly into any formal category. But these contemporary plays bear little resemblance to the tragicomedy of earlier periods, and to use the label tends to confuse rather than clarify.

Mixed Form. The labels applied by contemporary dramatists to their plays indicate how elements from various forms have been mingled. Eugène Ionesco has called one of his plays a tragic farce and another an anti-play; Michel de Ghelderode used such labels as *burlesque mystery* and *tragedy for the music hall;* and Harold Pinter's early plays have been called *comedies of menace.*

Such labels are indicative of a fundamental change from earlier times: a loss of belief in a clear-cut moral structure and uncertainty about the nature of reality. In twentieth-century thought, everything remains fluid, for we seem certain of nothing. Consequently, a single event may be seen almost simultaneously as serious, comic, threatening, or grotesque. Without fixity, tone may shift rapidly and firm action becomes difficult or meaningless. In such plays, elements associated with various dramatic forms may appear and disappear rapidly or be transformed into their opposites, thereby creating a mixture unlike that found in the dramatic forms of any previous era. As a result, form cannot be categorized with precision. Nevertheless, every play has form; it is up to us to perceive it in the individual work.

Other Forms. Much study of drama seems based on the assumption that learning to identify form is the goal. Frequently plays seem to have been chosen for study because they fit into two or three categories. As a result, a large portion of existing drama is ruled out, all too often because it cannot be categorized neatly. Consequently, centuries of playwriting may be leaped over, a treatment often accorded dramas of the Middle Ages, a period of some 500 years, perhaps because religious cycle plays and morality plays do not easily fit the traditional categories of forms. But these types may teach us much about the variety of form. A morality play usually shows a figure representative of all mankind being pulled in contrary directions by agents of good and evil; the protagonist, upon giving in to temptation, finds himself in danger of being eternally damned but is ultimately saved by God after He listens to the persuasive arguments of Mercy, Good Deeds, Faith, or some similar figure. The morality play is a form of serious didactic drama, the outcome of which resolves the most serious crisis a Christian can face — eternal salvation or eternal damnation.

Numerous similar subcategories of drama exist and, no doubt, will continue to be created. They should not prevent us from studying the traditional forms, but they should remind us that drama is more extensive than traditional forms suggest and that a play's failure to fit neatly into one of the traditional forms does not necessarily lessen its value as a play.

Drama in Classical Greece

Ancient Greece is critical in the development of drama for it was there that the basic forms of drama—tragedy and comedy—first evolved and were first described. It was also in Greece that drama first came to play a significant role in the artistic and social life of the people.

In Greece, drama was performed only at the festivals held in honor of Dionysus, god of fertility and wine, whose worship was closely associated with the recurring cycle of the seasons and of life itself (birth, maturity, death, and rebirth). Financed and supervised by the state, the festivals presented plays as offerings from the entire community to the god, whose goodwill was believed necessary to the continuing fertility of human beings and of the land. They placed so much value on the Dionysian festivals that, during them, the Greeks suspended all business activities and even freed prisoners from confinement so they might participate.

To have one's plays performed at the festivals was considered a great honor. For the principal festival—the City Dionysia—each tragic dramatist who wished to be represented was required to provide four plays: three tragedies and one satyr play (a short work which, taking its name from its chorus of satyrs, half-man/half-beast, poked fun at mythological subjects). Three tragic playwrights were chosen each year to compete for the prize offered for the best group of plays. During the festival one day was devoted to each playwright's work, performances beginning at daybreak and continuing without intermissions until completed.

To make sure that the plays were adequately mounted, the state paired each playwright with a *choregus*, a wealthy citizen who was required to finance the training and costuming of the chorus and to pay certain other expenses incurred in production. To serve as choregus was considered a civic duty of considerable importance, and any prize won by the plays was shared jointly by choregus and playwright.

One of the most distinctive features of ancient Greek drama was the chorus. The chorus connects drama to numerous rituals which had been sung and danced by masked and costumed performers for centuries prior to the development of drama. Aristotle stated that drama evolved out of improvisations in certain ritual performances, actors and episodes gradually being added to what had previously been wholly narrative and choral. The stories that came to be dramatized and combined with choral odes were for the most part drawn from epic poems which had been popular for some 200 years prior to the appearance of the first drama.

The chorus was more than a vestigial relic in drama, for once it entered on the stage following the prologue, it was present throughout the action of the play and served several functions. First, it was a participant in the action, expressing opinions, giving advice, and commenting on the events. Second, it often established an ethical or religious norm, in light of which the events were judged. Third, it sometimes served as the ideal spectator, reacting to events and characters in a way to lead audiences to respond as the author might wish. Fourth, the chorus helped to set the mood and heighten dramatic effect; it often voiced forebodings or helped to create powerful reversals by expressing joy just before some disastrous revelation. Fifth, it added considerable aural and visual appeal, as all choral odes were sung and danced to flute accompaniment. Sixth, it served an important structural function; not only did its presence throughout lend a kind of unity, but also the choral odes created retardations in the action during which the chorus looked forward or back, ruminated on events, enlarged the context of the action and thought. Without the chorus, the design of Greek drama would be incomplete.

Although the size of the tragic chorus may have changed from time to time, through most of the fifth century it included fifteen persons. At the same time, the number of actors was restricted to three, a convention probably adopted to make the contests as equitable as possible. The three-actor rule did not mean that there were only three characters in a play but that all speaking characters were played by three actors. Occasionally additional actors were permitted if they played mute roles or had only a line or two. In playing multiple roles, the actor was assisted by another convention: all performers wore masks which covered the entire head, thus making it possible to effect a change of role through a change of mask. All performers, actors and chorus, were male.

The size of the theatre also affected performance. All surviving Greek dramas were probably performed in the Theatre of Dionysus, an outdoor structure located on the slope of the Acropolis. Its seating capacity of approximately 17,000 persons makes it comparable to a sports arena of our time. The auditorium curved around an orchestra (or dancing place) about 65 feet in diameter where the chorus performed and in the middle of which was an altar *(thymele)* dedicated to Dionysus. Adjacent to the orchestra on the side away from the auditorium was a scene house *(skene)* which served as background for all plays. The skene had a large central doorway and two other smaller doors. Through the central doorway a platform *(eccyclema)* could be wheeled out to display the bodies of those who had died offstage. There probably were side wings *(paraskenia)* which jutted forward from the main building. The visual appearance may have been alterable through the addition of painted panels, but more probably it remained unchanged, the place of the action being established by references in the text. It is unclear whether there was a raised stage. If one existed, it was sufficiently low to permit the chorus and actors to intermingle freely. Between the skene and the auditorium there was on each side a passageway *(parados)* that served as entrance and exit to the orchestra.

The conditions of performance indicate that the overall effect of a Greek tragedy was quite different from what we experience in the theatre today. Among the conventions that affected performance were: the great size of the theatre and the consequent distance between performers and the audience; the shape of the theatre and the resulting physical relationship of audience to performer; the use of a chorus that spoke, sang, moved, and danced in unison or as two semichoruses; the use of flute accompaniment for much of the text; the all-male cast; the doubling of roles; and the use of masks with the consequent loss of changing facial expression. Despite these conventions, the plays create a sense of immediacy and reality, although they do so through a few telling strokes rather than through a multiplicity of detail. The nonessential was eliminated so the audience might experience the essential.

Although the Dionysian festivals continued for more than 500 years, few plays have survived. Of the tragedies, only 32 remain and these are the work of only three playwrights: seven plays by Aeschylus (525–456 B.C.), seven plays by Sophocles (496–406), and eighteen plays by Euripides (480–406). Though few in number, these plays are the foundation of the Western dramatic tradition. Two of these plays, Sophocles' *Antigone* and Euripides' *Iphigeneia at Aulis*, are included here for reading and discussion.

Antigone

by Sophocles / Translated by Dudley Fitts and Robert Fitzgerald

Sophocles (496–406 B.C.), the well-educated son of a wealthy Athenian, was the most admired playwright of the fifth century B.C. He began competing in the dramatic contests around 468, wrote some 120 plays (enough for 30 contests) and won first place in 24 contests, more than any other writer. He never placed lower than second. Only seven of his plays have survived. In addition to *Antigone*, they are *Ajax* (c.450–440), *Oedipus the King* (430–425), *Philoctetes* (409), *Electra* and *Trachiniae* (dates unknown), and *Oedipus at Colonus* (406).

Like the majority of surviving Greek tragedies, *Antigone* dramatizes material drawn from myths transmitted by Homer, Hesiod, and other poets who lived prior to the fifth century. Although *Antigone* (441 B.C.) is the earliest of the three plays Sophocles devoted to Oedipus and his family, it treats the final phase of the story. The first phase was not dramatized until Sophocles wrote *Oedipus the King* around 430. Briefly the story of Oedipus is this. Laius, King of Thebes, and his wife, Jocasta, are warned by an oracle that a son born to them will kill his father and marry his mother. When a child (Oedipus) is born, Laius has it exposed to die, but it is rescued and taken to Corinth where it is brought up as the son of the ruler. After he grows up, Oedipus consults an oracle that repeats the prophecy that had been told to Laius. In his desire to avoid this fate, Oedipus decides to flee Corinth. On the road he meets a traveler and in an ensuing argument he kills the man (later discovered to be Laius). He then proceeds to Thebes, where the city is being devastated by the Sphinx who kills those who cannot answer the riddle she poses. When Oedipus successfully answers, the Sphinx is destroyed and the Thebans in gratitude make him king and give him Jocasta in marriage. Oedipus and Jocasta live together quietly for many years and four children are born to them (Eteocles, Polyneices, Antigone, and Ismene). Then, a plague ravages the city and an oracle proclaims that the plague will cease only when Laius's murderer is discovered and banished. (It is at this point that Sophocles begins his play.) Oedipus vigorously pursues the murderer, having no suspicion that he is the guilty person. When the truth is revealed, Jocasta commits suicide, Oedipus puts out his eyes and is banished from Thebes by his brother-in-law, Creon, who has become the ruler.

Oedipus at Colonus (406), written when Sophocles was 90 years old, resumes the story. Many years have passed, during which Oedipus has wandered as an outcast shunned by all except Antigone. Meanwhile his sons have grown up and wrested power from Creon. They agree to alternate as rulers of Thebes, but when Eteocles' term ends he refuses to give up power. Polyneices flees to Argos, where he marries the daughter of the king and persuades six princes to join him in attacking Thebes. An oracle foretells that success will come to those having Oedipus's blessing while he lives and custody of his remains after he is dead. It is at this point that the play begins. Oedipus has arrived at Colonus, just outside Athens, and there Creon (representing Thebes) and Polyneices come to take possession of him, by force if necessary. Oedipus gains the protection of Theseus, ruler of Athens, and both Creon and Polyneices are sent away with Oedipus's curse. Oedipus then mysteriously vanishes into afterlife and his blessing falls on Athens.

Antigone relates the final part of the story. Before the action begins, Polyneices and his allies have attacked Thebes and have been defeated. Eteocles and Polyneices have killed each other and Creon has come to power once more. His first act is to bury Eteocles with honor and to decree that anyone who seeks to bury Polyneices will be killed. It is at this point that the action begins.

Much of the material in *Antigone* seems to have been invented by Sophocles, who, like other Greek writers, did not feel bound by the details of received myths but elaborated or altered them as dramatic need dictated. Among the events seemingly invented by Sophocles are: the quarrel between Antigone and Ismene; the love of Antigone and Haimon; the entombment of Antigone; the involvement of Teiresias; Creon's repentance; and the suicides of Antigone, Haimon, and Eurydice. One part of the story is barely hinted at: when the seige of Thebes began, an oracle foretold that the city could be saved only if Creon's son Megareus gave his life voluntarily, upon which Megareus sacrificed himself. In *Antigone*, nothing is made of this incident, perhaps because it might make Creon's decree seem motivated by personal revenge rather than by principle.

A portion of the material treated in *Antigone* had appeared earlier in Aeschylus' *Seven Against Thebes* (467 B.C.), which ended with the decree against Polyneices and with Antigone's determination to bury him. There the decree is attributed to the people of Thebes; Creon neither appears nor is named in the play. Sophocles takes up where Aeschylus leaves off and develops an action based on the conflict between two opposing demands.

PERSONS REPRESENTED

ANTIGONE
ISMENE
EURYDICE
CREON
HAIMON

TEIRESIAS
A SENTRY
A MESSENGER
CHORUS

SCENE:

Before the palace of Creon, King of Thebes.

TIME:

Dawn of the day after the repulse of the Argive army from the assault on Thebes.

PROLOGUE

(ANTIGONE *and* ISMENE *enter from the central door of the Palace.*)

ANTIGONE: Ismenê, dear sister,
  You would think that we had already
    suffered enough
  For the curse on Oedipus:
  I cannot imagine any grief
  That you and I have not gone through.
    And now—
  Have they told you of the new decree of
    our King Creon?
ISMENE: I have heard nothing: I know
  That two sisters lost two brothers, a double
    death
  In a single hour; and I know that the
    Argive army
  Fled in the night; but beyond this,
    nothing.
ANTIGONE: I thought so. And that is why I
    wanted you
  To come out here with me. There is
    something we must do.
ISMENE: Why do you speak so strangely?
ANTIGONE: Listen, Ismenê:
  Creon buried our brother Eteoclês
  With military honors, gave him a soldier's
    funeral,
  And it was right that he should; but
    Polyneicês,
  Who fought as bravely and died as
    miserably,—
  They say that Creon has sworn
  No one shall bury him, no one mourn for
    him,
  But his body must lie in the fields, a sweet
    treasure
  For carrion birds to find as they search for
    food.

That is what they say, and our good Creon
  is coming here
To announce it publicly; and the
    penalty—
Stoning to death in the public square!
                          There it is,
And now you can prove what you are:
A true sister, or a traitor to your family.
ISMENE: Antigonê, you are mad! What could
  I possibly do?
ANTIGONE: You must decide whether you
  will help me or not.
ISMENE: I do not understand you. Help you
  in what?
ANTIGONE: Ismenê, I am going to bury
  him. Will you come?
ISMENE: Bury him! You have just said the
  new law forbids it.
ANTIGONE: He is my brother. And he is
  your brother, too.
ISMENE: But think of the danger! Think
  what Creon will do!
ANTIGONE: Creon is not strong enough to
  stand in my way.
ISMENE: Ah sister!
  Oedipus died, everyone hating him
  For what his own search brought to light,
    his eyes
  Ripped out by his own hand; and Iocastê
    died,
  His mother and wife at once: she twisted
    the cords
  That strangled her life; and our two
    brothers died,
  Each killed by the other's sword. And we
    are left:
  But oh, Antigonê,
  Think how much more terrible than these
  Our own death would be if we should go
    against Creon
  And do what he has forbidden! We are
    only women,

We cannot fight with men, Antigonê!
The law is strong, we must give in to the law
In this thing, and in worse. I beg the Dead
To forgive me, but I am helpless: I must yield
To those in authority. And I think it is dangerous business
To be always meddling.

ANTIGONE: If that is what you think,
I should not want you, even if you asked to come.
You have made your choice, you can be what you want to be.
But I will bury him; and if I must die,
I say that this crime is holy: I shall lie down
With him in death, and I shall be as dear
To him as he to me.
It is the dead,
Not the living, who make the longest demands:
We die for ever . . .
You may do as you like,
Since apparently the laws of the gods mean nothing to you.

ISMENE: They mean a great deal to me; but I have no strength
To break laws that were made for the public good.

ANTIGONE: That must be your excuse, I suppose. But as for me,
I will bury the brother I love.

ISMENE: Antigonê,
I am so afraid for you!

ANTIGONE: You need not be:
You have yourself to consider, after all.

ISMENE: But no one must hear of this, you must tell no one!
I will keep it a secret, I promise!

ANTIGONE: Oh tell it! Tell everyone!
Think how they'll hate you when it all comes out
If they learn that you knew about it all the time!

ISMENE: So fiery! You should be cold with fear.

ANTIGONE: Perhaps. But I am doing only what I must.

ISMENE: But can you do it? I say that you cannot.

ANTIGONE: Very well: when my strength gives out, I shall do no more.

ISMENE: Impossible things should not be tried at all.

ANTIGONE: Go away, Ismenê:
I shall be hating you soon, and the dead will too,
For your words are hateful. Leave me my foolish plan:
I am not afraid of the danger; if it means death,
It will not be the worst of deaths — death without honor.

ISMENE: Go then, if you feel that you must.
You are unwise,
But a loyal friend indeed to those who love you.

(Exit into the Palace. ANTIGONE *goes off, L. Enter the* CHORUS.*)*

PÁRODOS

CHORUS: (STROPHE 1) Now the long blade of the sun, lying
Level east to west, touches with glory
Thebes of the Seven Gates. Open, unlidded
Eye of golden day! O marching light
Across the eddy and rush of Dircê's stream,
Striking the white shields of the enemy
Thrown headlong backward from the blaze of morning!

CHORAGOS: Polyneicês their commander
Roused them with windy phrases,
He the wild eagle screaming
Insults above our land,
His wings their shields of snow,
His crest their marshalled helms.

CHORUS: (ANTISTROPHE 1) Against our seven gates in a yawning ring
The famished spears came onward in the night;
But before his jaws were sated with our blood,

Or pinefire took the garland of our towers,
He was thrown back; and as he turned,
    great Thebes—
No tender victim for his noisy power—
Rose like a dragon behind him, shouting
    war.

CHORAGOS: For God hates utterly
    The bray of bragging tongues;
    And when he beheld their smiling,
    Their swagger of golden helms,
    The frown of his thunder blasted
    Their first man from our walls.

CHORUS: (STROPHE 2) We heard his shout of
    triumph high in the air
Turn to a scream; far out in a flaming arc
He fell with his windy torch, and the
    earth struck him.
And others storming in fury no less than
    his
Found shock of death in the dusty joy of
    battle.

CHORAGOS: Seven captains at seven gates
    Yielded their clanging arms to the god
    That bends the battle-line and breaks it.
    These two only, brothers in blood,
    Face to face in matchless rage,
    Mirroring each the other's death,
    Clashed in long combat.

CHORUS: (ANTISTROPHE 2) But now in the
    beautiful morning of victory
Let Thebes of the many chariots sing for
    joy!
With hearts for dancing we'll take leave of
    war:
Our temples shall be sweet with hymns of
    praise,
And the long night shall echo with our
    chorus.

SCENE I

CHORAGOS: But now at last our new King is
    coming:
Creon of Thebes, Menoikeus' son.
In this auspicious dawn of his reign
What are the new complexities
That shifting Fate has woven for him?
What is his counsel? Why has he
    summoned
The old men to hear him?

(Enter CREON *from the Palace, C. He addresses the*
CHORUS.*)*

CREON: Gentlemen, I have the honor to inform you that our Ship of State, which recent storms have threatened to destroy, has come safely to harbor at last, guided by the merciful wisdom of Heaven. I have summoned you here this morning because I know that I can depend upon you: your devotion to King Laïos was absolute; you never hesitated in your duty to our late ruler Oedipus; and when Oedipus died, your loyalty was transferred to his children. Unfortunately, as you know, his two sons, the princes Eteoclês and Polyneicês, have killed each other in battle; and I, as the next in blood, have succeeded to the full power of the throne.

I am aware, of course, that no Ruler can expect complete loyalty from his subjects until he has been tested in office. Nevertheless, I say to you at the very outset that I have nothing but contempt for the kind of Governor who is afraid, for whatever reason, to follow the course that he knows is best for the State; and as for the man who sets private friendship above the public welfare,—I have no use for him, either. I call God to witness that if I saw my country headed for ruin, I should not be afraid to speak out plainly; and I need hardly remind you that I would never have any dealings with an enemy of the people. No one values friendship more highly than I; but we must remember that friends made at the risk of wrecking our Ship are not real friends at all.

These are my principles, at any rate, and that is why I have made the following decision concerning the sons of Oedipus: Eteoclês, who died as a man should die, fighting for his country, is to be buried with full military honors, with all the ceremony that is usual when the greatest heroes die; but his brother Polyneicês, who broke his exile to come back with fire and sword against his native city and the shrines of his fathers' gods, whose one idea was to spill the blood of his blood and sell his own people into slavery—Polyneicês, I say, is to have no burial: no man is to touch him or say the least prayer for him; he shall lie on the plain, unburied; and the birds and the scavenging dogs can do with him whatever they like.

This is my command, and you can see the wisdom behind it. As long as I am King, no traitor is going to be honored with the loyal man. But whoever shows by word and deed that he is on the side of the State,—he shall have my respect while he is living, and my reverence when he is dead.

CHORAGOS: If that is your will, Creon son of Menoikeus,
You have the right to enforce it: we are yours.

CREON: That is my will. Take care that you do your part.

CHORAGOS: We are old men: let the younger ones carry it out.

CREON: I do not mean that: the sentries have been appointed.

CHORAGOS: Then what is it that you would have us do?

CREON: You will give no support to whoever breaks this law.

CHORAGOS: Only a crazy man is in love with death!

CREON: And death it is; yet money talks, and the wisest
Have sometimes been known to count a few coins too many.

(Enter SENTRY from L.)

SENTRY: I'll not say that I'm out of breath from running, King, because every time I stopped to think about what I have to tell you, I felt like going back. And all the time a voice kept saying, "You fool, don't you know you're walking straight into trouble?"; and then another voice: "Yes, but if you let somebody else get the news to Creon first, it will be even worse than that for you!" But good sense won out, at least I hope it was good sense, and here I am with a story that makes no sense at all; but I'll tell it anyhow, because, as they say, what's going to happen's going to happen, and—

CREON: Come to the point. What have you to say?

SENTRY: I did not do it. I did not see who did it. You must not punish me for what someone else has done.

CREON: A comprehensive defense! More effective, perhaps,
If I knew its purpose. Come: what is it?

SENTRY: A dreadful thing . . . I don't know how to put it—

CREON: Out with it!

SENTRY: Well, then;
The dead man—
                    Polyneicês—

(Pause. The SENTRY is overcome, fumbles for words. CREON waits impassively.)
                    out there—
                                        someone,—
New dust on the slimy flesh!
(Pause. No sign from CREON.)
Someone has given it burial that way, and Gone . . .
(Long pause. CREON finally speaks with deadly control:)

CREON: And the man who dared do this?

SENTRY: I swear I
Do not know! You must believe me!
                                        Listen:
The ground was dry, not a sign of digging, no,
Not a wheeltrack in the dust, no trace of anyone.
It was when they relieved us this morning: and one of them,
The corporal, pointed to it.
                    There it was,
The strangest—
            Look:
The body, just mounded over with light dust: you see?
Not buried really, but as if they'd covered it
Just enough for the ghost's peace. And no sign
Of dogs or any wild animal that had been there.
And then what a scene there was! Every man of us
Accusing the other: we all proved the other man did it,
We all had proof that we could not have done it.
We were ready to take hot iron in our hands,
Walk through fire, swear by all the gods,
It was not I!
I do not know who it was, but it was not I!
(CREON's rage has been mounting steadily, but the SENTRY is too intent upon his story to notice it.)
And then, when this came to nothing, someone said
A thing that silenced us and made us stare

Down at the ground: you had to be told
the news,
And one of us had to do it! We threw the
dice,
And the bad luck fell to me. So here I am,
No happier to be here than you are to
have me:
Nobody likes the man who brings bad
news.
CHORAGOS: I have been wondering, King:
can it be that the gods have done this?
CREON: *(Furiously)* Stop! Must you
doddering wrecks
Go out of your heads entirely? "The gods!"
Intolerable!
The gods favor this corpse? Why? How
had he served them?
Tried to loot their temples, burn their
images,
Yes, and the whole State, and its laws with
it!
Is it your senile opinion that the gods love
to honor bad men?
A pious thought! —
                    No, from the very
beginning
There have been those who have
whispered together,
Stiff-necked anarchists, putting their heads
together,
Scheming against me in alleys. These are
the men,
And they have bribed my own guard to do
this thing.
Money! *(Sententiously)*
There's nothing in the world so
demoralizing as money.
Down go your cities,
Homes gone, men gone, honest hearts
corrupted,
Crookedness of all kinds, and all for
money!
(To SENTRY*)*
              But you—!
I swear by God and by the throne of God,
The man who has done this thing shall
pay for it!
Find that man, bring him here to me, or
your death

Will be the least of your problems: I'll
string you up
Alive, and there will be certain ways to
make you
Discover your employer before you die;
And the process may teach you a lesson
you seem to have missed:
The dearest profit is sometimes all too
dear:
That depends on the source. Do you
understand me?
A fortune won is often misfortune.
SENTRY: King, may I speak?
CREON: Your very voice
distresses me.
SENTRY: Are you sure that it is my voice,
and not your conscience?
CREON: By God, he wants to analyze me
now!
SENTRY: It is not what I say, but what has
been done, that hurts you.
CREON: You talk too much.
SENTRY: Maybe; but I've
done nothing.
CREON: Sold your soul for some silver; that's
all you've done.
SENTRY: How dreadful it is when the right
judge judges wrong!
CREON: Your figures of speech
May entertain you now; but unless you
bring me the man,
You will get little profit from them in the
end.

(Exit CREON *into the Palace.)*

SENTRY: "Bring me the man"—!
I'd like nothing better than bringing him
the man!
But bring him or not, you have seen the
last of me here.
At any rate, I am safe!

(Exit SENTRY.*)*

ODE I

CHORUS: (STROPHE 1) Numberless are the
world's wonders, but none
More wonderful than man; the stormgray
sea

Yields to his prows, the huge crests bear
  him high;
Earth, holy and inexhaustible, is graven
With shining furrows where his plows
  have gone
Year after year, the timeless labor of
  stallions.
(ANTISTROPHE 1) The lightboned birds and
  beasts that cling to cover,
The lithe fish lighting their reaches of
  dim water,
All are taken, tamed in the net of his
  mind;
The lion on the hill, the wild horse
  windy-maned,
Resign to him; and his blunt yoke has
  broken
The sultry shoulders of the mountain bull.
(STROPHE 2) Words also, and thought as
  rapid as air,
He fashions to his good use; statecraft is
  his,
And his the skill that deflects the arrows
  of snow,
The spears of winter rain: from every
  wind
He has made himself secure—from all but
  one:
In the late wind of death he cannot stand.
(ANTISTROPHE 2) O clear intelligence, force
  beyond all measure!
O fate of man, working both good and
  evil!
When the laws are kept, how proudly his
  city stands!
When the laws are broken, what of his
  city then?
Never may the anárchic man find rest at
  my hearth,
Never be it said that my thoughts are his
  thoughts.

SCENE II

(*Re-enter* SENTRY *leading* ANTIGONE.)

CHORAGOS: What does this mean? Surely
  this captive woman
  Is the Princess, Antigonê. Why should she
  be taken?

SENTRY: Here is the one who did it! We
  caught her
  In the very act of burying him.—Where is
  Creon?
CHORAGOS: Just coming from the house.

(*Enter* CREON, *C.*)

CREON: What has
  happened?
  Why have you come back so soon?
SENTRY: (Expansively) O
                King,
  A man should never be too sure of
  anything:
  I would have sworn
  That you'd not see me here again: your
  anger
  Frightened me so, and the things you
  threatened me with;
  But how could I tell then
  That I'd be able to solve the case so soon?
  No dice-throwing this time: I was only too
  glad to come!
  Here is this woman. She is the guilty one:
  We found her trying to bury him.
  Take her, then; question her; judge her as
  you will.
  I am through with the whole thing now,
  and glád óf it.
CREON: But this is Antigonê! Why have you
  brought her here?
SENTRY: She was burying him, I tell you!
CREON: (Severely) Is this the truth?
SENTRY: I saw her with my own eyes. Can I
  say more?
CREON: The details: come, tell me quickly!
SENTRY: It was like this:
  After those terrible threats of yours, King,
  We went back and brushed the dust away
  from the body.
  The flesh was soft by now, and stinking,
  So we sat on a hill to windward and kept
  guard.
  No napping this time! We kept each other
  awake.
  But nothing happened until the white
  round sun
  Whirled in the center of the round sky
  over us:

Then, suddenly,
A storm of dust roared up from the earth,
    and the sky
Went out, the plain vanished with all its
    trees
In the stinging dark. We closed our eyes
    and endured it.
The whirlwind lasted a long time, but it
    passed;
And then we looked, and there was
    Antigonê!
I have seen
A mother bird come back to a stripped
    nest, heard
Her crying bitterly a broken note or
    two
For the young ones stolen. Just so, when
    this girl
Found the bare corpse, and all her love's
    work wasted,
She wept, and cried on heaven to damn
    the hands
That had done this thing.
                    And then she
    brought more dust
And sprinkled wine three times for her
    brother's ghost.
We ran and took her at once. She was not
    afraid,
Not even when we charged her with what
    she had done.
She denied nothing.
                    And this was a
    comfort to me,
And some uneasiness: for it is a good thing
To escape from death, but it is no great
    pleasure
To bring death to a friend.
                    Yet I always say
There is nothing so comfortable as your
    own safe skin!
CREON: (Slowly, dangerously) And you,
    Antigonê,
You with your head hanging,—do you
    confess this thing?
ANTIGONE: I do, I deny nothing.
CREON: (To SENTRY)   You may go.
    (Exit SENTRY.)
    (To ANTIGONE:)
Tell me, tell me briefly:

Had you heard my proclamation touching
    this matter?
ANTIGONE: It was public. Could I help
    hearing it?
CREON; And yet you dared defy the law.
ANTIGONE: I dared.
    It was not God's proclamation. That final
        Justice
    That rules the world below makes no such
        laws.
    Your edict, King, was strong,
    But all your strength is weakness itself
        against
    The immortal unrecorded laws of God.
    They are not merely now: they were, and
        shall be,
    Operative for ever, beyond man utterly.
    I knew I must die, even without your
        decree:
    I am only mortal. And if I must die
    Now, before it is my time to die,
    Surely this is no hardship: can anyone
    Living, as I live, with evil all about me,
    Think Death less than a friend? This
        death of mine
    Is of no importance; but if I had left my
        brother
    Lying in death unburied, I should have
        suffered.
    Now I do not.
                    You smile at me. Ah Creon,
    Think me a fool, if you like, but it may
        well be
    That a fool convicts me of folly.
CHORAGOS: Like father, like daughter: both
        headstrong, deaf to reason!
    She has never learned to yield.
CREON: She has
        much to learn.
    The inflexible heart breaks first, the
        toughest iron
    Cracks first, and the wildest horses bend
        their necks
    At the pull of the smallest curb.
                            Pride? In a
        slave?
    This girl is guilty of a double insolence,
    Breaking the given laws and boasting
        of it.
    Who is the man here,

She or I, if this crime goes unpunished?
Sister's child, or more than sister's child,
Or closer yet in blood — she and her sister
Win bitter death for this!
(To servants)

                  Go, some of you,
Arrest Ismenê. I accuse her equally.
Bring her: you will find her sniffling in
   the house there.
Her mind's a traitor: crimes kept in the
   dark
Cry for light, and the guardian brain
   shudders;
But how much worse than this
Is brazen boasting of barefaced anarchy!
ANTIGONE: Creon, what more do you want
   than my death?
CREON: Nothing.
   That gives me everything.
ANTIGONE: Then I beg you:
   kill me.
   This talking is a great weariness: your
     words
   Are distasteful to me, and I am sure that
     mine
   Seem so to you. And yet they should not
     seem so:
   I should have praise and honor for what I
     have done.
   All these men here would praise me
   Were their lips not frozen shut with fear
     of you.
   (Bitterly)
   Ah the good fortune of kings,
   Licensed to say and do whatever they
     please!
CREON: You are alone here in that opinion.
ANTIGONE: No, they are with me. But they
   keep their tongues in leash.
CREON: Maybe. But you are guilty, and they
   are not.
ANTIGONE: There is no guilt in reverence
   for the dead.
CREON: But Eteoclês — was he not your
   brother too?
ANTIGONE: My brother too.
CREON: And you insult
   his memory?
ANTIGONE: *(Softly)* The dead man would
   not say that I insult it.

CREON: He would: for you honor a traitor as
   much as him.
ANTIGONE: His own brother, traitor or not,
   and equal in blood.
CREON: He made war on his country.
   Eteoclês defended it.
ANTIGONE: Nevertheless, there are honors
   due all the dead.
CREON: But not the same for the wicked as
   for the just.
ANTIGONE: Ah Creon, Creon.
   Which of us can say what the gods hold
     wicked?
CREON: An enemy is an enemy, even
   dead.
ANTIGONE: It is my nature to join in love,
   not hate.
CREON: *(Finally losing patience)* Go join
   them, then; if you must have your
   love,
   Find it in hell
CHORAGOS: But see, Ismenê comes:
   (Enter ISMENE, *guarded)*
   Those tears are sisterly, the cloud
   That shadows her eyes rains down gentle
     sorrow.
CREON: You too, Ismenê,
   Snake in my ordered house, sucking my
     blood
   Stealthily — and all the time I never knew
   That these two sisters were aiming at my
     throne!
                Ismenê,
   Do you confess your share in this crime,
     or deny it?
   Answer me.
ISMENE: Yes, if she will let me say so. I am
   guilty.
ANTIGONE: *(Coldly)* No, Ismenê. You have
   no right to say so.
   You would not help me, and I will not
   have you help me.
ISMENE: But now I know what you meant;
   and I am here
   To join you, to take my share of
   punishment.
ANTIGONE: The dead man and the gods
   who rule the dead
   Know whose act this was. Words are not
   friends.

ISMENE: Do you refuse me, Antigonê? I want
to die with you:
I too have a duty that I must discharge to
the dead.

ANTIGONE: You shall not lessen my death
by sharing it.

ISMENE: What do I care for life when you
are dead?

ANTIGONE: Ask Creon. You're always
hanging on his opinions.

ISMENE: You are laughing at me. Why,
Antigonê?

ANTIGONE: It's a joyless laughter, Ismenê.

ISMENE: But can I do
nothing?

ANTIGONE: Yes. Save yourself. I shall not
envy you.
There are those who will praise you; I
shall have honor, too.

ISMENE: But we are equally guilty!

ANTIGONE: No more,
Ismenê.
You are alive, but I belong to Death.

CREON: (To the CHORUS) Gentlemen, I beg
you to observe these girls:
One has just now lost her mind; the other,
It seems, has never had a mind at all.

ISMENE: Grief teaches the steadiest minds to
waver, King.

CREON: Yours certainly did, when you
assumed guilt with the guilty!

ISMENE: But how could I go on living
without her?

CREON: You are.
She is already dead.

ISMENE: But your own son's
bride!

CREON: There are places enough for him to
push his plow.
I want no wicked women for my sons!

ISMENE: O dearest Haimon, how your father
wrongs you!

CREON: I've had enough of your childish
talk of marriage!

CHORAGOS: Do you really intend to steal
this girl from your son?

CREON: No; Death will do that for me.

CHORAGOS: Then she must
die?

CREON: (Ironically) You dazzle me.
                —But enough of
this talk!
(To GUARDS)
You there, take them away and guard
them well:
For they are but women, and even brave
men run
When they see Death coming.

(Exeunt ISMENE, ANTIGONE, and GUARDS.)

ODE II

CHORUS: (STROPHE 1) Fortunate is the man
who has never tasted God's vengeance!
Where once the anger of heaven has
struck, that house is shaken
For ever: damnation rises behind each
child
Like a wave cresting out of the black
northeast,
When the long darkness under sea roars
up
And bursts drumming death upon the
windwhipped sand.

(ANTISTROPHE 1) I have seen this gathering
sorrow from time long past
Loom upon Oedipus' children: generation
from generation
Takes the compulsive rage of the enemy
god.
So lately this last flower of Oedipus' line
Drank the sunlight! but now a passionate
word
And a handful of dust have closed up all
its beauty.

                (STROPHE 2) What mortal arrogance
                Transcends the wrath of Zeus?
Sleep cannot lull him, nor the effortless
long months
Of the timeless gods: but he is young for
ever,
And his house is the shining day of high
Olympos.
        All that is and shall be,
        And all the past, is his.
No pride on earth is free of the curse of
heaven.

(ANTISTROPHE 2) The straying dreams
of men
May bring them ghosts of joy:
But as they drowse, the waking embers
burn them;
Or they walk with fixed éyes, as blind
men walk.
But the ancient wisdom speaks for our
own time:
Fate works most for woe
With Folly's fairest show.
Man's little pleasure is the spring of
sorrow.

SCENE III

CHORAGOS: But here is Haimon, King, the
last of all your sons.
Is it grief for Antigonê that brings him
here,
And bitterness at being robbed of his
bride?

(Enter HAIMON.*)*

CREON: We shall soon see, and no need of
diviners.
—Son,
You have heard my final judgment on that
girl:
Have you come here hating me, or have
you come
With deference and with love, whatever I
do?
HAIMON: I am your son, father. You are my
guide.
You make things clear for me, and I obey
you.
No marriage means more to me than your
continuing wisdom.
CREON: Good. That is the way to behave:
subordinate
Everything else, my son, to your father's
will.
This is what a man prays for, that he may
get
Sons attentive and dutiful in his house,
Each one hating his father's enemies,
Honoring his father's friends. But if his
sons

Fail him, if they turn out unprofitably,
What has he fathered but trouble for
himself
And amusement for the malicious?
So you
are right
Not to lose your head over this woman.
Your pleasure with her would soon grow
cold, Haimon,
And then you'd have a hellcat in bed and
elsewhere
Let her find her husband in Hell!
Of all the people in this city, only she
Has had contempt for my law and broken
it.
Do you want me to show myself weak
before the people?
Or to break my sworn word? No, and I
will not.
The woman dies.
I suppose she'll plead "family ties." Well,
let her.
If I permit my own family to rebel,
How shall I earn the world's obedience?
Show me the man who keeps his house in
hand,
He's fit for public authority.
I'll have no
dealings
With law-breakers, critics of the
government:
Whoever is chosen to govern should be
obeyed—
Must be obeyed, in all things, great and
small,
Just and unjust! O Haimon,
The man who knows how to obey, and
that man only,
Knows how to give commands when the
time comes.
You can depend on him, no matter how
fast
The spears come: he's a good soldier, he'll
stick it out.
Anarchy, anarchy! Show me a greater
evil!
This is why cities tumble and the great
houses rain down,
This is what scatters armies!

No, no: good lives are made so by
  discipline.
We keep the laws then, and the
  lawmakers,
And no woman shall seduce us. If we
  must lose,
Let's lose to a man, at least! Is a woman
  stronger than we?
CHORAGOS: Unless time has rusted my
  wits,
What you say, King, is said with point and
  dignity.
HAIMON: (Boyishly earnest) Father:
  Reason is God's crowning gift to man, and
    you are right
  To warn me against losing mine. I cannot
    say —
  I hope that I shall never want to say! —
    that you
  Have reasoned badly. Yet there are other
    men
  Who can reason, too; and their opinions
    might be helpful.
  You are not in a position to know
    everything
  That people say or do, or what they feel:
  Your temper terrifies them — everyone
  Will tell you only what you like to hear.
  But I, at any rate, can listen; and I have
    heard them
  Muttering and whispering in the dark
    about this girl.
  They say no woman has ever, so
    unreasonably,
  Died so shameful a death for a generous
    act:
  "She covered her brother's body. Is this
    indecent?
  She kept him from dogs and vultures. Is
    this a crime?
  Death? — She should have all the honor
    that we can give her!"
  This is the way they talk out there in the
    city.
  You must believe me:
  Nothing is closer to me than your
    happiness.
  What could be closer? Must not any son
  Value his father's fortune as his father
    does his?

  I beg you, do not be unchangeable:
  Do not believe that you alone can be right.
  The man who thinks that,
  The man who maintains that only he has
    the power
  To reason correctly, the gift to speak, the
    soul —
  A man like that, when you know him,
    turns out empty.
  It is not reason never to yield to reason!
  In flood time you can see how some trees
    bend,
  And because they bend, even their twigs
    are safe,
  While stubborn trees are torn up, roots
    and all.
  And the same thing happens in sailing:
  Make your sheet fast, never slacken, — and
    over you go,
  Head over heels and under: and there's
    your voyage.
  Forget you are angry! Let yourself be
    moved!
  I know I am young; but please let me say
    this:
  The ideal condition
  Would be, I admit, that men should be
    right by instinct;
  But since we are all too likely to go astray,
  The reasonable thing is to learn from
    those who can teach.
CHORAGOS: You will do well to listen to
  him, King,
If what he says is sensible. And you,
  Haimon,
Must listen to your father. — Both speak
  well.
CREON: You consider it right for a man of
  my years and experience
  To go to school to a boy?
HAIMON: It is not right
  If I am wrong. But if I am young, and
    right,
  What does my age matter?
CREON: You think it right to stand up for an
  anarchist?
HAIMON: Not at all. I pay no respect to
  criminals.
CREON: Then she is not a criminal?
HAIMON: The City would deny it, to a man.

CREON: And the City proposes to teach me
　　how to rule?
HAIMON: Ah. Who is it that's talking like a
　　boy now?
CREON: My voice is the one voice giving
　　orders in this City!
HAIMON: It is no City if it takes orders from
　　one voice.
CREON: The State is the King!
HAIMON: 　　　　　　　　Yes, if the
　　State is a desert.

(Pause)

CREON: This boy, it seems, has sold out to a
　　woman.
HAIMON: If you are a woman: my concern
　　is only for you.
CREON: So? Your "concern"! In a public
　　brawl with your father!
HAIMON: How about you, in a public brawl
　　with justice?
CREON: With justice, when all that I do is
　　within my rights?
HAIMON: You have no right to trample on
　　God's right.
CREON: (Completely our of control) Fool,
　　adolescent fool! Taken in by a woman!
HAIMON: You'll never see me taken in by
　　anything vile.
CREON: Every word you say is for her!
HAIMON: 　　　　　　(Quietly, darkly)
　　　　　　　　And for you.
　　And for me. And for the gods under the
　　earth.
CREON: You'll never marry her while she
　　lives.
HAIMON: Then she must die. — But her
　　death will cause another.
CREON: Another?
　　Have you lost your senses? Is this an open
　　threat?
HAIMON: There is no threat in speaking to
　　emptiness.
CREON: I swear you'll regret this superior
　　tone of yours!
　　You are the empty one!
HAIMON: 　　　　　　If you were not my
　　father,
　　I'd say you were perverse.

CREON: You girlstruck fool, don't play at
　　words with me!
HAIMON: I am sorry. You prefer silence.
CREON: 　　　　　　　Now, by God —!
　　I swear, by all the gods in heaven above
　　us,
　　You'll watch it, I swear you shall!
　　　　　　　　(To the SERVANTS)
　　　　　　　　　Bring her out!
　　Bring the woman out! Let her die before
　　his eyes!
　　Here, this instant, with her bridegroom
　　beside her!
HAIMON: Not here, no; she will not die
　　here, King.
　　And you will never see my face again.
　　Go on raving as long as you've a friend to
　　endure you.

(Exit HAIMON.)

CHORAGOS: Gone, gone,
　　Creon, a young man in a rage is
　　dangerous!
CREON: Let him do, or dream to do, more
　　than a man can.
　　He shall not save these girls from death.
CHORAGOS: 　　　　　　These girls?
　　You have sentenced them both?
CREON: 　　　　　　　　No, you
　　are right.
　　I will not kill the one whose hands are
　　clean.
CHORAGOS: But Antigonê?
CREON: 　　　(Somberly) I will carry her
　　far away
　　Out there in the wilderness, and lock her
　　Living in a vault of stone. She shall have
　　food,
　　As the custom is, to absolve the State of
　　her death.
　　And there let her pray to the gods of hell:
　　They are her only gods:
　　Perhaps they will show her an escape from
　　death,
　　Or she may learn,
　　　　　　　　though late,
　　That piety shown the dead is pity in vain.

(Exit CREON.)

ODE III

CHORUS: (STROPHE) Love, unconquerable
    Waster of rich men, keeper
    Of warm lights and all-night vigil
    In the soft face of a girl:
    Sea-wanderer, forest-visitor!
    Even the pure Immortals cannot escape
        you,
    And mortal man, in his one day's dusk,
    Trembles before your glory.
    (ANTISTROPHE) Surely you swerve upon
        ruin
    The just man's consenting heart,
    As here you have made bright anger
    Strike between father and son—
    And none has conquered but Love!
    A girl's glánce wórking the will of heaven:
    Pleasure to her alone who mocks us,
    Merciless Aphroditê.[1]

SCENE IV

CHORAGOS: (As ANTIGONE enters guarded)
        But I can no longer stand in awe of
        this,
    Nor, seeing what I see, keep back my
        tears.
    Here is Antigonê, passing to that chamber
    Where all find sleep at last.
ANTIGONE: (STROPHE 1) Look upon me,
        friends, and pity me
    Turning back at the night's edge to say
    Good-by to the sun that shines for me no
        longer;
    Now sleepy Death
    Summons me down to Acheron,[2] that cold
        shore:
    There is no bridesong there, nor any
        music.
CHORUS: Yet not unpraised, not without a
        kind of honor,
    You walk at last into the underworld;
    Untouched by sickness, broken by no
        sword.
    What woman has ever found your way to
        death?

ANTIGONE: (ANTISTROPHE 1) How often I
        have heard the story of Niobê,[3]
    Tantalos' wretched daughter, how the
        stone
    Clung fast about her, ivy-close: and they
        say
    The rain falls endlessly
    And sifting soft snow; her tears are never
        done.
    I feel the loneliness of her death in mine.
CHORUS: But she was born of heaven, and
        you
    Are woman, woman-born. If her death is
        yours,
    A mortal woman's, is this not for you
    Glory in our world and in the world
        beyond?
ANTIGONE: (STROPHE 2) You laugh at me.
        Ah, friends, friends,
    Can you not wait until I am dead? O
        Thebes,
    O men many-charioted, in love with
        Fortune,
    Dear springs of Dircê, sacred Theban
        grove,
    Be witnesses for me, denied all pity,
    Unjustly judged! and think a word of love
    For her whose path turns
    Under dark earth, where there are no
        more tears.
CHORUS: You have passed beyond human
        daring and come at last
    Into a place of stone where Justice sits.
    I cannot tell
    What shape of your father's guilt appears
        in this.
ANTIGONE: (ANTISTROPHE 2) You have
        touched it at last: that bridal bed
    Unspeakable, horror of son and mother
        mingling:
    Their crime, infection of all our family!
    O Oedipus, father and brother!
    Your marriage strikes from the grave to
        murder mine.
    I have been a stranger here in my own
        land:
    All my life

[1] Aphrodite was goddess of love.
[2] Acheron was a river in Hades.
[3] Niobê was punished by the gods for her pride and eventually turned into a rock.

The blasphemy of my birth has followed
    me.
CHORUS: Reverence is a virtue, but strength
    Lives in established law: that must prevail.
    You have made your choice,
    Your death is the doing of your conscious
    hand.
ANTIGONE: (EPODE) Then let me go, since
    all your words are bitter,
    And the very light of the sun is cold to
    me.
    Lead me to my vigil, where I must have
    Neither love nor lamentation; no song, but
    silence.

    (CREON *interrupts impatiently.*)

CREON: If dirges and planned lamentations
    could put off death,
    Men would be singing for ever.
    (To the SERVANTS)   Take
    her, go!
    You know your orders: take her to the
    vault
    And leave her alone there. And if she lives
    or dies,
    That's her affair, not ours: our hands are
    clean.
ANTIGONE: O tomb, vaulted bride-bed in
    eternal rock,
    Soon I shall be with my own again
    Where Persephonê[4] welcomes the thin
    ghosts underground:
    And I shall see my father again, and you,
    mother,
    And dearest Polyneicês—
                     dearest indeed
    To me, since it was my hand
    That washed him clean and poured the
    ritual wine:
    And my reward is death before my time!
    And yet, as men's hearts know, I have
    done no wrong,
    I have not sinned before God. Or if I have,
    I shall know the truth in death. But if the
    guilt
    Lies upon Creon who judged me, then, I
    pray,
    May his punishment equal my own.

[4]Persephone was Queen of Hades.

CHORAGOS: O passionate heart,
    Unyielding, tormented still by the same
    winds!
CREON: Her guards shall have good cause to
    regret their delaying.
ANTIGONE: Ah! That voice is like the voice
    of death!
CREON: I can give you no reason to think
    you are mistaken.
ANTIGONE: Thebes, and you my fathers'
    gods,
    And rulers of Thebes, you see me now,
    the last
    Unhappy daughter of a line of kings,
    Your kings, led away to death. You will
    remember
    What things I suffer, and at what men's
    hands,
    Because I would not transgress the laws of
    heaven.
    (To the GUARDS, *simply)*
    Come: let us wait no longer.

    (Exit ANTIGONE, *L., guarded.)*

ODE IV

CHORUS: (STROPHE 1) All Danaê's[5] beauty
    was locked away
    In a brazen cell where the sunlight could
    not come:
    A small room, still as any grave, enclosed
    her.
    Yet she was a princess too,
    And Zeus in a rain of gold poured love
    upon her.
    O child, child.
    No power in wealth or war
    Or tough sea-blackened ships
    Can prevail against untiring Destiny!
    (ANTISTROPHE 1) And Dryas's son[6] also,
    that furious king,
    Bore the god's prisoning anger for his
    pride:

[5]Danae, a princess of Argos, was confined in a cell by her
father, but Zeus entered the cell in the form of a shower
of gold; she bore Zeus a son, Perseus.
[6]Dryas's son, Lykurgos, was driven mad by the god
Dionysos.

Sealed up by Dionysos in deaf stone,
His madness died among echoes.
So at the last he learned what dreadful
power
His tongue had mocked:
For he had profaned the revels,
And fired the wrath of the nine[7]
Implacable Sisters that love the sound of
the flute.
(STROPHE 2) And old men tell a half-
remembered tale[8]
Of horror done where a dark ledge splits
the sea
And a double surf beats on the gráy
shóres:
How a king's new woman, sick
With hatred for the queen he had
imprisoned,
Ripped out his two sons' eyes with her
bloody hands
While grinning Arês watched the shuttle
plunge
Four times: four blind wounds crying for
revenge,
(ANTISTROPHE 2) Crying, tears and blood
mingled. — Piteously born,
Those sons whose mother was of heavenly
birth!
Her father was the god of the North Wind
And she was cradled by gales,
She raced with young colts on the
glittering hills
And walked untrammeled in the open
light:
But in her marriage deathless Fate found
means
To build a tomb like yours for all her joy.

SCENE V

(Enter blind TEIRESIAS, led by a boy. The opening
speeches of TEIRESIAS should be in singsong
contrast to the realistic lines of CREON.)

TEIRESIAS: This is the way the blind man
comes, Princes, Princes,
Lock-step, two heads lit by the eyes of one.

[7]The nine Implacable Sisters were the Muses, who pre-
sided over the arts.
[8]This story, of which the details are given, is that of Phi-
neus, King of Thrace.

CREON: What new thing have you to tell us,
old Teiresias?
TEIRESIAS: I have much to tell you: listen to
the prophet, Creon.
CREON: I am not aware that I have ever
failed to listen.
TEIRESIAS: Then you have done wisely,
King, and ruled well.
CREON: I admit my debt to you. But what
have you to say?
TEIRESIAS: This, Creon: you stand once
more on the edge of fate.
CREON: What do you mean? Your words are
a kind of dread.
TEIRESIAS: Listen, Creon:
I was sitting in my chair of augury, at the
place
Where the birds gather about me. They
were all a-chatter,
As is their habit, when suddenly I heard
A stange note in their jangling, a scream, a
Whirring fury; I knew that they were
fighting,
Tearing each other, dying
In a whirlwind of wings clashing. And I
was afraid.
I began the rites of burnt-offering at the
altar,
But Hephaistos[9] failed me: instead of
bright flame,
There was only the sputtering slime of the
fat thigh-flesh
Melting: the entrails dissolved in gray
smoke,
The bare bone burst from the welter. And
no blaze!
This was a sign from heaven. My boy
described it,
Seeing for me as I see for others.
I tell you, Creon, you yourself have
brought
This new calamity upon us. Our hearths
and altars
Are stained with the corruption of dogs
and carrion birds
That glut themselves on the corpse of
Oedipus' son.
The gods are deaf when we pray to them,
their fire

[9]Hephaistos was the god of fire.

Recoils from our offering, their birds of
   omen
Have no cry of comfort, for they are
   gorged
With the thick blood of the dead.
                                    O my
                              son,
These are no trifles! Think: all men make
   mistakes,
But a good man yields when he knows his
   course is wrong,
And repairs the evil. The only crime is
   pride.
Give in to the dead man, then: do not
   fight with a corpse—
What glory is it to kill a man who is dead?
Think, I beg you:
It is for your own good that I speak as I do.
You should be able to yield for your own
   good.
CREON: It seems that prophets have made
   me their especial province.
All my life long
I have been a kind of butt for the dull
   arrows
Of doddering fortune-tellers!
                              No, Teiresias:
If your birds—if the great eagles of God
   himself
Should carry him stinking bit by bit to
   heaven,
I would not yield. I am not afraid of
   pollution:
No man can defile the gods.
                              Do what you
   will,
Go into business, make money, speculate
In India gold or that synthetic gold from
   Sardis,
Get rich otherwise than by my consent to
   bury him.
Teiresias, it is a sorry thing when a wise
   man
Sells his wisdom, lets out his words for
   hire!
TEIRESIAS: Ah Creon! Is there no man left in
   the world—
CREON: To do what?—Come, let's have the
   aphorism!
TEIRESIAS: No man who knows that wisdom
   outweighs any wealth?

CREON: As surely as bribes are baser than
   any baseness.
TEIRESIAS: You are sick, Creon! You are
   deathly sick!
CREON: As you say: it is not my place to
   challenge a prophet.
TEIRESIAS: Yet you have said my prophecy
   is for sale.
CREON: The generation of prophets has
   always loved gold.
TEIRESIAS: The generation of kings has
   always loved brass.
CREON: You forget yourself! You are
   speaking to your King.
TEIRESIAS: I know it. You are a king because
   of me.
CREON: You have a certain skill; but you
   have sold out.
TEIRESIAS: King, you will drive me to words
   that—
CREON: Say them, say them!
   Only remember: I will not pay you for
   them.
TEIRESIAS: No, you will find them too
   costly.
CREON: No doubt. Speak:
   Whatever you say, you will not change
   my will.
TEIRESIAS: Then take this, and take it to
   heart!
   The time is not far off when you shall pay
   back
   Corpse for corpse, flesh of your own flesh.
   You have thrust the child of this world
   into living night,
   You have kept from the gods below the
   child that is theirs:
   The one in a grave before her death, the
   other,
   Dead, denied the grave. This is your
   crime:
   And the Furies[10] and the dark gods of Hell
   Are swift with terrible punishment for
   you.
   Do you want to buy me now, Creon?
                              Not many days,
   And your house will be full of men and
   women weeping,
   And curses will be hurled at you from far

[10]Furies were goddesses of vengeance.

Cities grieving for sons unburied, left to
rot
Before the walls of Thebes.
These are my arrows, Creon: they are all
for you.
But come, child: lead me home.
(To BOY*)*
Let him waste his fine anger upon younger
men.
Maybe he will learn at last
To control a wiser tongue in a better head.

(Exit TEIRESIAS.*)*

CHORAGOS: The old man has gone, King,
but his words
Remain to plague us. I am old, too,
But I cannot remember that he was ever
false.
CREON: That is true. . . . It troubles me.
Oh it is hard to give in! but it is worse
To risk everything for stubborn pride.
CHORAGOS: Creon: take my advice.
CREON: What
shall I do?
CHORAGOS: Go quickly: free Antigonê from
her vault
And build a tomb for the body of
Polyneicês.
CREON: You would have me do this?
CHORAGOS: Creon,
yes!
And it must be done at once: God moves
Swiftly to cancel the folly of stubborn
men.
CREON: It is hard to deny the heart! But I
Will do it: I will not fight with destiny.
CHORAGOS: You must go yourself, you
cannot leave it to others.
CREON: I will go.
                    — Bring axes, servants:
Come with me to the tomb. I buried her, I
Will set her free.
                    Oh quickly!
My mind misgives —
The laws of the gods are mighty, and a
man must serve them
To the last day of his life!

(Exit CREON.*)*

PÆAN

CHORAGOS: God of many names[11]
*(*STROPHE *1)*
CHORUS: O Iacchos
son
of Kadmeian Sémelê
                          O born of the
Thunder!
Guardian of the West
                          Regent
of Eleusis' plain
                          O Prince of maenad
Thebes
and the Dragon Field by rippling Ismenos:
CHORAGOS: God of many names
*(*ANTISTROPHE *1)*
CHORUS: the flame
of torches
flares on our hills
                          the nymphs of Iacchos
dance at the spring of Castalia:
from the vine-close mountain
                          come ah
come in ivy:
Evohé evohé! sings through the streets of
Thebes
CHORAGOS: God of many names *(*STROPHE
2)
CHORUS: Iacchos of
Thebes
heavenly Child
                          of Sémelê bride of the
Thunderer!
The shadow of plague is upon us:
                                    come
with clement feet
                          oh come from Parnasos
down the long slopes
                          across the lamenting
water
CHORAGOS: *(*ANTISTROPHE *2)* Iô Fire!
Chorister of the throbbing stars!
O purest among the voices of the night!
Thou son of God, blaze for us!

---

[11]The god of many names is Dionysos, son of Zeus and
Semele, the Theban princess. Semele was the daughter of
Kadmos, from whom the Thebans were descended.

CHORUS: Come with choric rapture of
    circling Maenads
Who cry *Iô Iacche!*
                    God of many names!

ÉXODUS

(Enter MESSENGER, *L.)*

MESSENGER: Men of the line of Kadmos,
    you who live
Near Amphion's citadel:
                    I cannot say
Of any condition of human life "This is
    fixed,
This is clearly good, or bad." Fate raises
    up,
And Fate casts down the happy and
    unhappy alike:
No man can foretell his Fate.
                    Take the case
    of Creon:
Creon was happy once, as I count
    happiness:
Victorious in battle, sole governor of the
    land,
Fortunate father of children nobly born.
And now it has all gone from him! Who
    can say
That a man is still alive when his life's joy
    fails?
He is a walking dead man. Grant him
    rich,
Let him live like a king in his great house:
If his pleasure is gone, I would not give
So much as the shadow of smoke for all he
    owns.
CHORAGOS: Your words hint at sorrow:
    what is your news for us?
MESSENGER: They are dead. The living are
    guilty of their death.
CHORAGOS: Who is guilty? Who is dead?
    Speak!
MESSENGER: Haimon.
    Haimon is dead; and the hand that killed
    him
    Is his own hand.
CHORAGOS: His father's? or his own?
MESSENGER: His own, driven mad by the
    murder his father had done.

CHORAGOS: Teiresias, Teiresias, how clearly
    you saw it all!
MESSENGER: This is my news: you must
    draw what conclusions you can from it.
CHORAGOS: But look: Eurydicê, our Queen:
    Has she overheard us?

(Enter EURYDICE *from the Palace, C.)*

EURYDICE: I have heard something, friends:
    As I was unlocking the gate of Pallas'
    shrine,
For I needed her help today, I heard a
    voice
Telling of some new sorrow. And I fainted
There at the temple with all my maidens
    about me.
But speak again: whatever it is, I can bear
    it:
Grief and I are no strangers.
MESSENGER: Dearest Lady,
    I will tell you plainly all that I have
    seen.
I shall not try to comfort you: what is the
    use,
Since comfort could lie only in what is not
    true?
The truth is always best.
                    I went with
    Creon
To the outer plain where Polyneicês was
    lying,
No friend to pity him, his body shredded
    by dogs,
We made our prayers in that place to
    Hecatê[12]
And Pluto, that they would be merciful.
    And we bathed
The corpse with holy water, and we
    brought
Fresh-broken branches to burn what was
    left of it,
And upon the urn we heaped up a
    towering barrow
Of the earth of his own land.
                    When we
    were done, we ran

[12]Hecate was a goddess and Pluto was a god of the
underworld.

To the vault where Antigonê lay on her
    couch of stone.
One of the servants had gone ahead,
And while he was yet far off he heard a
    voice
Grieving within the chamber, and he
    came back
And told Creon. And as the King went
    closer,
The air was full of wailing, the words lost,
And he begged us to make all haste. "Am
    I a prophet?"
He said, weeping, "And must I walk this
    road,
The saddest of all that I have gone before?
My son's voice calls me on. Oh quickly,
    quickly!
Look through the crevice there, and tell
    me
If it is Haimon, or some deception of the
    gods!"
We obeyed; and in the cavern's farthest
    corner
We saw her lying:
She had made a noose of her fine linen
    veil
And hanged herself. Haimon lay beside
    her,
His arms about her waist, lamenting her,
His love lost under ground, crying out
That his father had stolen her away from
    him.
When Creon saw him the tears rushed to
    his eyes
And he called to him: "What have you
    done, child? Speak to me.
What are you thinking that makes your
    eyes so strange?
O my son, my son, I come to you on my
    knees!"
But Haimon spat in his face. He said not a
    word,
Staring —
        And suddenly drew his sword
And lunged. Creon shrank back, the blade
    missed; and the boy,
Desperate against himself, drove it half its
    length
Into his own side, and fell. And as he died

He gathered Antigonê close in his arms
    again,
Choking, his blood bright red on her
    white cheek.
And now he lies dead with the dead, and
    she is his
At last, his bride in the houses of the dead.

(Exit EURYDICE *into the Palace.)*

CHORAGOS: She has left us without a word.
    What can this mean?
MESSENGER: It troubles me, too; yet she
    knows what is best,
    Her grief is too great for public
    lamentation,
    And doubtless she has gone to her
    chamber to weep
    For her dead son, leading her maidens in
    his dirge.
CHORAGOS: It may be so: but I fear this
    deep silence

(Pause.)

MESSENGER: I will see what she is doing. I
    will go in.

(Exit MESSENGER *into the Palace. Enter* CREON *with
attendants, bearing* HAIMON'S *body.)*

CHORAGOS: But here is the King himself:
    oh look at him,
    Bearing his own damnation in his arms.
CREON: Nothing you say can touch me any
    more.
    My own blind heart has brought me
    From darkness to final darkness. Here you
    see
    The father murdering, the murdered
    son —
    And all my civic wisdom!
    Haimon my son, so young, so young to
    die,
    I was the fool, not you; and you died for
    me.
CHORAGOS: That is the truth; but you were
    late in learning it.
CREON: This truth is hard to bear. Surely a
    god
    Has crushed me beneath the hugest
    weight of heaven.

And driven me headlong a barbaric way
To trample out the thing I held most dear.
The pains that men will take to come to
pain!

(Enter MESSENGER *from the Palace.)*

MESSENGER: The burden you carry in your
hand is heavy,
But it is not all; you will find more in
your house.
CREON: What burden worse than this shall I
find there?
MESSENGER: The Queen is dead.
CREON: O port of death, deaf world,
Is there no pity for me? And you, Angel of
evil,
I was dead, and your words are death
again.
Is it true, boy? Can it be true?
Is my wife dead? Has death bred death?
MESSENGER: You can see for yourself.

(The doors are opened, and the body of EURYDICE
is disclosed within.)

CREON: Oh pity!
All true, all true, and more than I can
bear!
O my wife, my son!
MESSENGER: She stood before the altar, and
her heart
Welcomed the knife her own hand
guided,
And a great cry burst from her lips for
Megareus[13] dead,
And for Haimon dead, her sons; and her
last breath
Was a curse for their father, the murderer
of her sons.
And she fell, and the dark flowed in
through her closing eyes

[13]Megareus, son of Creon and Eurydice, sacrificed himself
after an oracle had declared his death necessary if Thebes
was to be saved in the war just ended.

CREON: O God, I am sick with fear.
Are there no swords here? Has no one a
blow for me?
MESSENGER: Her curse is upon you for the
deaths of both.
CREON: It is right that it should be. I alone
am guilty.
I know it, and I say it. Lead me in,
Quickly, friends.
I have neither life nor substance. Lead me
in.
CHORAGOS: You are right, if there can be
right in so much wrong.
The briefest way is best in a world of
sorrow.
CREON: Let it come,
Let death come quickly, and be kind to
me.
I would not ever see the sun again.
CHORAGOS: All that will come when it
will; but we, meanwhile,
Have much to do. Leave the future to
itself.
CREON: All my heart was in that prayer!
CHORAGOS: Then do not pray any more;
the sky is deaf.
CREON: Lead me away. I have been rash and
foolish.
I have killed my son and my wife.
I look for comfort; my comfort lies here
dead.
Whatever my hands have touched has
come to nothing.
Fate has brought all my pride to a thought
of dust.

(As CREON *is being led into the house, the*
CHORAGOS *advances and speaks directly to the*
audience.)

CHORAGOS: There is no happiness where
there is no wisdom;
No wisdom but in submission to the gods.
Big words are always punished,
And proud men in old age learn to be
wise.

This translation of *Antigone* clearly labels the characteristic divisions of Greek tragedy: a *prologue*, which establishes the current situation and foreshadows the conflict that will dominate the action; the *parados*, or entrance song of the chorus, which provides additional exposition, establishes mood, characterizes the chorus and explains its reason for being present; a series of *episodes* or *scenes* (the number may vary, but typically there are five); *choral odes* or *stasima* between scenes (the odes are often divided into *strophe* and *antistrophe*, indicative of responses between two semichoruses or of shifts in movement); and an *éxodos*, the final episode and exit of all the characters and the chorus.

These divisions are related to the structure of the dramatic action. In *Antigone*, the prologue, parados, and first episode clearly establish the situation and conflict through exposition about the present and immediate past. We learn that Creon, in his determination to discourage treason, has chosen to make an example of Polyneices by denying him burial — a terrible fate in Greek eyes, since without proper burial the dead could never find rest and peace. Creon considers obedience to his decree so important that he establishes death as the penalty for defiance. Undeterred, Antigone, believing it her sacred duty, is determined to bury her brother. By the end of the first scene, then, the conflict is established. Both Antigone and Creon have made it clear that they will not listen to any views contrary to their own.

The conflict is not only one between two persons but also one between two principles: the duty to accord certain sacred rites to the individual, regardless of what he has done, and the duty to establish and maintain order in the state by rewarding those who abide by its laws and punishing those who disobey. The dramatic action is unified by this conflict.

Sophocles has sharpened the dramatic issue by relating it to kinship. All the principal characters in the play are from the same family, the basic kinship unit. But in Greece, kinship extended from the family to the tribe, and it was the kinship relationship among a number of tribes that united them into a city state, or *polis*. In turn, all Greek city states considered themselves related through kinship, whereas all non-Greeks were called barbarians (a term which to the Greeks meant those content to believe without reason and to live without liberty). Greeks, nevertheless, accorded non-Greeks certain rights as was demonstrated when they buried the enemy dead following their victory over Persia in 480 B.C., even though the Persians were seeking to conquer Greece and deprive it of freedom. If Athenians were willing to bury barbarian enemies, they certainly would have hesitated to deprive a Greek of burial, especially one from their own *polis*, and still more especially one from their own family. Thus, Creon's decree would have seemed much more harsh to an Athenian audience than it does to us.

In scene two, the conflict intensifies when Creon discovers that Antigone, his niece, has defied his order. To Creon this seems a test of his integrity as a ruler: Will he uphold his decree or will he allow kinship to influence him? Since he has already decided on firmness, this discovery only hardens his resolve. So eager is he to demonstrate he cannot be swayed by kinship that he condemns Ismene along with Antigone.

Scene three shows Creon withstanding another attack on his authority from his son Haimon, who seeks to mediate between Antigone and Creon with reason and love. The exchanges between Haimon and Creon are crucial to the play's thought, for they concern differing conceptions of the state. Creon argues that a ruler has the right to make decrees without consulting anyone and that he should be obeyed unquestioningly. When Creon declares, "My voice is the one voice giving orders in this City!," Haimon replies, "It is no City if it takes order from one voice." Creon goes on to declare, "The State is the King," and is answered by Haimon, "Yes, if the State is a desert." These exchanges epitomize the distinctions between barbarian despotism and Athenian democracy. In Athens a decree had no authority unless it had been approved by the citizens. Creon favors a dictatorship and appears to see chaos as the alternative. Haimon, while acknowledging the need for order, makes it clear that the people of Thebes have not assented to Creon's decree and side with Antigone. But Creon is not open to reason, and Haimon leaves in despair.

By the end of the third scene, Antigone's and Creon's arguments have been made. It remains only for the consequences to be felt. Antigone's turn comes first. Throughout the first three scenes, the net around her has been tightening. In the fourth scene, she accepts her fate and goes off to die. Sophocles heightens the emotional power of this scene by making it a lyrical exchange between Antigone and the Chorus. Unfortunately, we can only imagine the impact of this song with its musical accompaniment (just as we must imagine the singing and dancing of the odes by the Chorus).

At the beginning of scene five, Creon seems to have triumphed, but in actuality it is only the beginning of retribution for him, signaled by the appearance of Teiresias. As seer or prophet, Teiresias argues the fallacy of Creon's actions from the religious point of view just as Haimon has from the political point of view. Teiresias declares that in not burying Polyneices, "You have kept from the gods below the child that is theirs," and that no god will listen to Thebes' prayers so long as the city is polluted by the unburied dead. When Creon accuses him of having been bribed, Teiresias leaves, foretelling of terrible retribution in store. Creon is sufficiently shaken that he sets out to undo his work by burying Polyneices and rescuing Antigone.

The final scene (or exodos) shows the destruction that results from the conflict: Antigone hangs herself, Haimon and Eurydice commit suicide, and, though he remains alive, Creon prays: "Let death come quickly." Most of these occurrences are narrated by the Messenger (a character common in Greek tragedy, in which deaths and scenes of violence most usually occurred offstage).

In the play's action, the choral odes may at first seem superfluous interruptions. But each ode contributes to the play's action or thought. Among other ideas, they suggest that human beings have been given intelligence, imagination, pride, and love, but that each of these may lead to good or evil depending upon how they are used and how well man conforms to the will of the gods. As the Chorus states at the end of the play: "There is no happiness where there is no wisdom;/ No wisdom but in submission to the gods." The Greek belief in the interaction of human and divine will is clearly indicated both in the choral odes and through the action of the entire play.

As is typical of Greek tragedy, in *Antigone* the characters are assigned only those few traits that are essential to the action. Information about physical, sociological, and psychological aspects of characterization is minimal. Most important are the moral choices made by the characters, especially by Antigone and Creon.

Some critics have tried to assign Antigone a tragic flaw — usually stubbornness. But surely no one would wish Antigone not to bury her brother or to give in to Creon when she is caught. It is much easier to assign Creon a flaw — pride (or *hubris*), which is seen in his attempt to assume all power and to deny what Antigone calls "the immortal unrecorded laws of God." At the end of the play Creon acknowledges his guilt: "Fate has brought all my pride to a thought of dust." Whether Antigone or Creon is the central character is a question often raised and an argument can be made for each. But the play's action requires two polar views and consequently attention is divided rather evenly between them.

Ultimately *Antigone* dramatizes a moral choice, one that has faced human beings from the beginning: how to reconcile man-made laws with demands derived from some higher authority (such as religion or morality). Such choices still confront us. Following World War II, the victorious Allies put a number of German officials on trial for war crimes. The officials maintained that they had merely followed the laws of their country and to have done otherwise would have been a crime under German law. But the prosecutors argued that what the Germans had done was so monstrous that it violated moral principles that outweigh the laws of any country, that it is the duty of human beings to assess the laws under which they live and to disobey those that violate universal moral standards. That one may rightfully disobey an unjust law also undergirded the civil disobedience in America during the 1950s and 1960s as various groups attempted to gain civil rights and to establish other claims. But we may prudently ask what situations justify disobedience of the law.

Antigone posed a question and provided an answer that was acceptable to Athenians: man-made law must be in accord with higher principles if disaster is to be avoided. While we may accede to this conclusion, it does not remove the problem, for people who live in a free society are continually faced with making judgments about situations specific to their own time — about how one is to define and verify a higher principle, about when a conflict has arisen between law and principle, and about how to resolve conflicts without risking disasters comparable to those of which Sophocles wrote. One of the principal purposes of education is to prepare us to make sound judgments on these and all the other issues constantly facing us in our personal as well as our civic lives. In their plays, the Greek dramatists addressed these problems and from them we can learn the importance of examining these problems as they are raised in our own times.

Iphigeneia at Aulis

by Euripides / Translated by W. S. Merwin and George E. Dimock, Jr.

Euripides (480–406 B.C.), son of a merchant, first competed in the contests in 455. He wrote approximately 92 plays (enough for 23 contests) but won the first prize only five times. If he was not always fully appreciated during his lifetime, he was valued above all other writers during the centuries immediately following his death. It is perhaps for this reason that eighteen of his tragedies have survived. Among these are *Alcestis* (438), *Medea* (431), *Hippolytus* (428), *The Trojan Women* (415), *Electra* (between 417 and 408), and *Bacchae* (406). Euripides also wrote the only complete satyr play that has survived, *Cyclops*. Near the end of his life, Euripides left Athens for Macedonia, where he died. *Iphigeneia at Aulis* was produced in Athens in the year following his death along with *Bacchae* and *Alcmaeon at Corinth* (now lost).

The relevant mythic context of *Iphigeneia at Aulis* is summarized by Agamemnon in the play's prologue. Another context is equally important: the war then underway between Athens and Sparta, for Euripides chooses myth not merely for its interest as story but for its ability to illuminate contemporary problems.

CHARACTERS

AGAMEMNON *King of Mycenae, leader of the Greek expedition against Troy*
OLD MAN *Clytemnestra's slave, attendant on Agamemnon*
CHORUS *of young women of Chalkis*
MENELAOS *brother of Agamemnon, husband of Helen of Troy*
FIRST MESSENGER *leader of Clytemnestra's escort*

SUPERNUMERARY CHORUS *of Clytemnestra's attendants*
CLYTEMNESTRA *Queen of Mycenae*
IPHIGENEIA *daughter of Agamemnon and Clytemnestra*
ORESTES *infant son of Agamemnon and Clytemnestra*
ACHILLES *hero-to-be of the Trojan War*
SECOND MESSENGER

SCENE:

In front of Agamemnon's tent, in the camp of the Greek armies by the bay at Aulis, where the ships are waiting. It is some time before dawn. As the light rises it will be perceived that the tent has a main entrance flanked by two side doors. AGAMEMNON *enters through the main door, a waxed tablet in his hand. He paces up and down before the tent in great indecision, then turns and calls in at the main door.*

AGAMEMNON: Come here, old man. In
    front of my tent.
OLD MAN: *(Inside)* I'm coming. Is there
    something new, King Agamemnon?
AGAMEMNON: Be quick about it!
OLD MAN: *(Entering)* I am quick. There's
    no sleep in me.
  My eyes won't stay shut now they're old.
AGAMEMNON: What star is that, what
    time
  crossing heaven?
OLD MAN: Sirius, pursuing the seven
    Pleiades,
  still traveling high at this hour.
AGAMEMNON: No bird-sound, no murmur
    from the sea.
  The winds are silent along these
  straits of Euripos.
OLD MAN: Then why are you up
  pacing outside your tent, King
    Agamemnon?
  There's not a voice stirring yet in Aulis.
  The watch is quiet
  up on the walls.
  Might we not go in?
AGAMEMNON: I envy you, old man. I envy
    any man
  whose life passes quietly, unnoticed by
    fame.
  I do not envy those in authority.
OLD MAN: But it is they who have the good
    of life.
AGAMEMNON: You call that good? It's a
    trap. Great honors
  taste sweet
  but they come bringing pain.
  Something goes wrong
  between a man and the gods
  and his whole life is overturned.
  At other times the notions of men, all
  different and all insatiable,
  grate it away by themselves.

OLD MAN: I don't like it, hearing a king
  talk that way. Atreus did not
  sire you, Agamemnon, into a world
  of pure happiness. You must expect
  to suffer as well as rejoice,
  since you're a man.
  And the gods will see to that, whether
  you like it or not.
  But you've lit your lamp. You've written
  some message. That's what you have in
    your hand.
  You keep putting on
  the seal and taking it off again.
  You write and then you
  rub out what you've written.
  You drop it to the ground, and tears
  stream down your face.
  From what I can see
  despair appears to be driving you
  out of your reason. Oh my king,
  Agamemnon, tell me what it is.
  I am a man of good will, I am
  loyal to you, you can trust me with it.
  I was in your
  wedding procession, don't you remember,
  back at the start. Tyndareos gave me
  to your wife as part of the dowry,
  because I could be trusted.
AGAMEMNON: Leda, the daughter of
    Thestios, had three
  girls of her own:
  Phoibe, and my wife Clytemnestra,
  and Helen.
  And the highest-born young men in
    Greece came
  asking to marry
  Helen.
  And threatened each other,
  looking for blood. Each of them said
  that if he himself did not get to marry her
  he would murder whoever did.
  So her father Tyndareos

could not think what he should do to
    avoid disaster.
Should he give her to one of them
or not let her marry at all?
Then he thought of a way.
The suitors would have to take an oath, all
    of them
together, a solemn oath, sealed
with a burnt offering,
swearing to defend whichever of them
should win Helen, Tyndareos' daughter,
    for his wife.
And if anyone
should ever carry her off, and keep
her husband from her bed, whether
he came from Greece or somewhere else,
    they would all
make war on his city and bring it to the
    ground.
So they swore. Old Tyndareos
was sharper than they were:
when it was over he left the choice to his
    daughter.
He said, "Now why shouldn't she marry
as the sweet breath of Aphrodite directs
    her?"
And her love fell—that's the pity of it—
on Menelaos.
It was later
that this Paris, who judged
the beauty of goddesses,[1]
as the Argives tell it,
came from Phrygia to Sparta. There were
    gold flowers
stitched onto his clothes,
he glittered with barbarian jewels,
he loved her.
She returned it. While Menelaos was away
he carried her off with him
to the summer pastures of Ida.[2]
Menelaos, stung by his fate, raged
through all Greece, reminding
everyone who had sworn that oath

that they were bound to come to his help
    now.
And the Greeks rushed to arms. And they
    have come
to the straits of Aulis
with their fighting gear, their ships, their
    shields,
their chariots, their horses.
And because Menelaos is my brother, they
    chose
me to be their general.
I wish they had saved the honor for
    someone else.
And when the whole army had mustered
here at Aulis,
the wind died. Calm. We still cannot sail.
There is only one hope of our going,
according to Kalchas,
the prophet. Iphigeneia, my daughter,
must be sacrificed to Artemis,
the deity of this place.
Then the wind will take us to Troy,
and the city will fall to us.
When I heard this I called Talthybios the
    herald
and said, "Sound the trumpet, sound it,
and tell them all to go home. I could never
make myself kill my own daughter."
But at that my brother started reasoning
    with me,
arguing, urging me
to commit this horror,
till I wrote a letter telling my wife
to send our daughter here
to be married to Achilles.
I told her
what a great man he is, and I said
he would not sail with us until a bride
from our own family
had been sent to his home in Phthia.
A story I made up
so that my wife would send the girl.
Among the Achaians the only ones who
    know
are Kalchas, Odysseus, and Menelaos.
And what I have done
is wrong, and I want to undo it. That is
    why
I wrote this second letter that you found
    me

[1]According to Greek myth, Paris was asked to choose one
of the goddesses Hera, Athena, or Aphrodite as the most
beautiful. Aphrodite, whom he chose, promised him the
most beautiful woman in the world—Helen.
[2]Mountain near Troy where Paris, although son of the
king, had been a shepherd.

sealing and unsealing. Take it. Go to
   Argos.
I will tell you what it says
since you are loyal to my wife and my
   house. *(Reads)*
"Clytemnestra, daughter of Leda,
I mean this letter to rule out the first one."
   (Pauses)
OLD MAN: Tell me the rest. Read it. Then I
   will be able
to repeat the message myself
as it is in the letter.
AGAMEMNON: *(Reads)* "Do not send your
   daughter
to this folded harbor of Euboia,
Aulis,
a shore where no waves come in.
We will find some other time for her
   marriage."
OLD MAN: But Achilles, when he learns
   there's no bride for him after all,
will he not blaze up
raging against you and your wife? That
frightens me. How will you deal with
   that?
AGAMEMNON: Only his name has been
   used. Achilles himself
knows nothing
of our plans, the marriage,
what I said about giving him my daughter
as his bride.
OLD MAN: Then you promised her to the
   son of a goddess
simply to fetch her here
to be a victim for the Argives! King
   Agamemnon,
your daring appalls me.
AGAMEMNON: I have lost the use of my
   reason! My ruin
is straight ahead of me. No. Go. Start.
Run. Never mind the age in your legs.
OLD MAN: I will lose no time, my lord.
AGAMEMNON: Do not pause at the springs
   in the shade,
nor stop to sleep.
OLD MAN: The gods keep me from it!
AGAMEMNON: When you get to where
   roads fork, take a sharp look
down all of them. Make sure
no chariot slips past you,

too fast or not noticed,
bringing my daughter here to the Greek
   ships.
OLD MAN: It shall be done.
AGAMEMNON: If she has left the palace
and you meet her and her escort
make them turn back. Take
the reins yourself and shake them loose
and urge on the horses to Mycenae
where the Cyclopes built the walls.
OLD MAN: One thing. What will make your
   wife
and your daughter trust me
when I tell them the message?
AGAMEMNON: This seal, on the letter.
Take it, and go now. Day
is breaking. Already the sun's
chariot of fire has sent
brightness into the sky. Go. Take up
your task. We must all suffer.

(The OLD MAN *goes off right.)*

No mortal
ever knows happiness and good fortune all
the way to the end.
Each one is born with his bitterness
   waiting for him.

(He goes in through the main door. The CHORUS *of
young Chalkidian women enters left.)*

CHORUS: I have crossed the narrows
of Euripos, I came sailing and I beached
at Aulis, on the sands. I left
Chalkis, my city, where the spring
of Arethousa wells up and runs flashing
down to the sea. I came
to see for myself this army of the
   Achaians,[3]
the oar-winged ships of the heroes,
the thousand galleys
which blond Menelaos and Agamemnon
   of the same
great lineage sent,
as our husbands tell us,
to fetch Helen again:
Helen.
Whom Paris the herdsman seized
from the reedy bank of the river Eurotas

[3]Achaians was a collective name for the Greeks.

where Aphrodite had led her for him,
  after
the goddess had bathed in the dewy
  fountain
and taken her place beside
Hera and Pallas Athene
for her beauty to be judged.
Through the grove
where the victims die on the altar
of Artemis I came
running, and I blushed for shyness
at my fever to see
the pitched strength of the Danaans, the
  tents[4]
hung with weapons, the clanging
press of armed horsemen.
Now I set eyes
on the two that are named Aias, I see
Oïleus' son and that son of Telamon
who is the hope of Salamis,
and with them Protesilaos,
and Palamedes, child of Poseidon's son,
hunched down, weaving
their cunning into a game of draughts.
Near them is Diomedes
delighting in throwing the discus,
  and Meriones, scion of Ares,
wonder of men. Laërtes' son
has come there from his craggy island,
and Nireus, most handsome of the
  Achaians.
I have seen wind-footed Achilles
in full armor racing over the sands:
Thetis' son, whom Cheiron reared,
and he was racing against horses,
four of them, and a chariot, on the curved
  track.
I saw the beauty of those horses, gold
worked into their bits and bridles,
the yoke pair dappled
gray with white in their manes, the trace
  horses
bays with dappled white fetlocks;
and Eumelos, the grandson of Pheres,
driving them, shouting,

[4]This choral ode is essentially a catalog of the Greek heroes who participated in the Trojan War, the different geographical divisions of Greece, and the might of the Greek forces.

goading them on faster, and they
hugged the turns, but Peleus' son
in all his armor stayed with them the
  whole way,
never falling behind the chariot rail and
  the axle,
and won.
And I came to where the ships lie. Even a
  god
would find no words for the way that
  sight
stirs a woman's eyes. Pleasure took my
  breath away.
The fleet of the Myrmidons from Phthia,
  fifty
lean vessels, lay to the right
bearing statues
of the sea-god's daughters, the Nereïds, in
  gold,
high on their sterns,
to show that those ships were Achilles'.
Next to them lay the galleys of the
  Argives,
their admiral
Mekisteus' son, whom Talaos
brought up to manhood;
and Sthenelos, Kapaneus' son, was there.
Then the sixty ships from Attica; the son
of Theseus is their commander, and their
  ensign
is Pallas Athene with her winged chariot
and its horses, a sign which lightens the
  hearts
of mariners.
Then the flotilla of fifty ships
from Boiotia with their ensign rising
from each of the sterns: Kadmos
holding a dragon of gold. Leïtos,
born of the earth,
is their admiral. And the same number
of ships from Lokris, commanded by the
  son
of Oïleus, who had come
from the famous city of Thronion
to moor beside them.
The son of Atreus had brought a hundred
  vessels
from Mycenae
where the Cyclopes built the walls. The
  king

his brother and companion-in-command,
sailed with him to bring vengeance
on the bride who had abandoned his house
to lie with a barbarian. I saw the ships
from Pylos, that Gerenian Nestor brought,
and their sign is the river
Alpheios, that flows
by his country, shown on his sterns
in the form of a bull. Then the twelve
Ainian vessels that obey King Gouneus,
and near them the lords of Elis, who are
    called
the Epeians: Eurytos commands
the ships that came with them.
And the white-oared Taphian galleys
    followed
King Meges, Phyleus' son, from the rocky
    islands
of Echinai that frighten sailors.
To the left
the twelve sleek galleys of Aias of Salamis
made up the end of the line
that ran back down the beach
without a break, beside the army. The
    barbarian
who joins battle with these should not
cling to his hopes of sailing home.
I have seen the whole fleet,
and when it is famous and they
tell of it where I live
I will remember.

(MENELAOS *and the* OLD MAN *enter right,
    quarreling.*)

OLD MAN: Menelaos, you have no right to
    do this!
MENELAOS: Get away! You are too loyal to
    your master.
OLD MAN: Your reproach does me honor.
MENELAOS: You'll be sorry if you go on
    meddling.
OLD MAN: You had no right
    to open the letter I was carrying.
MENELAOS: And you had no right to carry a
    letter
    that would harm the Greek cause.
OLD MAN: Argue with others about that.
    Give me the letter.
MENELAOS: I will not.
OLD MAN: (*Seizes him*) Then I won't let go.

MENELAOS: I'll bloody your head with my
    scepter.
OLD MAN: What greater glory than to die
    for my master?
MENELAOS: Let go! Your words are too big
    for a slave.
OLD MAN: (*Calling in at the main door of
    the tent*) Master! Help!
            This man
    snatched your letter out of my hand,
    Agamemnon! Mutiny!

(AGAMEMNON *enters from the main door.*)

AGAMEMNON: What is this? Brawling and
    arguing
    outside my tent door?
MENELAOS: My voice takes precedence
    here, I believe.

(*At a sign from* AGAMEMNON, *the* OLD MAN *goes in
    at the right-hand side door.*)

AGAMEMNON: How did you come to
    quarrel
    with this old man, Menelaos?
    And why were you so violent with him?
MENELAOS: Look at me, Agamemnon. Then
    I will
    start to tell you.
AGAMEMNON: Do you think I'm afraid
    to look you in the eye, Menelaos?
    I am a son of Atreus.
MENELAOS: Do you see this letter? It was
    meant
    to betray all of us.
AGAMEMNON: That letter—in the first
    place
    give it back to me.
MENELAOS: Not until I have told the
    Greeks what it says.
AGAMEMNON: You mean you broke the
    seal. So you know
    what you have no business knowing.
MENELAOS: Yes I broke the seal. And it's
    you
    who will suffer as a result, for acting
    behind our backs.
AGAMEMNON: How did you come to find
    him? Oh gods
    what shamelessness!

MENELAOS: I was watching for the arrival
of your daughter from Argos.
AGAMEMNON: You see? Shameless again!
What right have you
to spy on what concerns me?
MENELAOS: I chose to. I'm not your slave.
AGAMEMNON: This is beyond endurance!
Am I not to be allowed
to govern in my own house?
MENELAOS: No, because you're not to be
trusted.
You never were, you aren't to be trusted
now,
you never will be.
AGAMEMNON: How smooth you are with
your slanders.
I despise a nimble tongue.
MENELAOS: How do you feel about a mind
true to nothing and no one? It is you
who must answer for yourself. And don't
try
to shout down the truth
just because you're angry.
I won't be too harsh with you.
Have you forgotten the fever
of your ambition at the first thought
of leading an army against Troy?
You pretended
not to want the command but really
you'd have paid anything to be general.
You know how you humbled yourself
at the time. Touching hands,
keeping open house to the whole
citizenry,
making them all speak to you, one by one,
whether they wanted to or not.
Anything
to entice preferment out of the crowd.
But once you'd been chosen to command,
all that changed.
You dropped the friends you didn't need
any more.
It was hard to get to talk with you, you shut
yourself in.
Is one to admire a man
who changes as soon as he gets what he
wants
and turns from friends
the moment he's in a position to help
them?

That's the first point
in which I found you wanting,
Agamemnon.
Next, you led the combined armies
of the Hellenes[5] here to Aulis
and then at one stroke all your importance
collapsed
just because the wind fell.
You were nothing
if the gods would not fill your sails. And
the Danaans[5]
clamored for the ships to be sent home
and an end to these senseless efforts.
I haven't forgotten the sight
of your face when you heard that. What
anguish,
what gloom at the thought
that you might not sail in, after all,
lord
of a thousand ships
flooding Priam's beach with arms. Then
you asked me
to help you. "What shall I do? Isn't there
something I can do?" Anything
rather than lose the command
and the glory.
Then when Kalchas said, "Yes:
sacrifice your daughter to Artemis[6]
and the Greek ships
will be able to sail,"
how happy you were to promise.
And no one—admit it—forced you
to write to your wife
and tell her to send the girl here,
pretending that she would marry Achilles.
Then you change your mind,
you unburden yourself of a different
message
and it's discovered.
At this point you'd never murder your
daughter.
Well. This same sky
watched you speak otherwise. It's true
men find this happening to them
all the time. They sweat and clamber
for power until it's theirs,

[5]Hellenes and Danaans were collective names for Greeks.
[6]Artemis was goddess of wild animals and the young of
all creatures, especially humans.

then all at once they
fall back and amount to nothing again.
Sometimes it's the fault of the populace,
too stupid to know who's talking sense.
Other times it's richly deserved: the
  leaders
turn out not to be able
to keep the city safe.
I grieve above all
for Greece and her mortification.
She had set her heart on glory. Now
she will have nothing to answer
when the barbarian trash laugh at her,
thanks to you and your daughter.
Oh I would never put a man at the
  head
of a country or an army
just because of his connections.
A general needs to have a mind.
CHORUS: It is terrible when discord
  divides brothers
  and they fight each other with words.
AGAMEMNON: It's my turn now. And I'll
  keep my
reproach dignified: brief,
restrained.
Not staring wide, shamelessly, but with
modesty, remembering that you
are my brother. No man who amounts to
  anything
is without a sense of shame. You
come to me in a passion,
breathing hard, eyes
suffused with blood. Tell me, who
has wronged you? What do you want? Are
  you pining
for a virtuous wife? I'm afraid
I can't do much for you there. The one
  you had
is no credit to your government.
Am I, then, supposed to suffer
for your shortcomings
when they're no fault of mine? It's not
my ambition that is biting you.
You care about nothing,
nothing but holding a beautiful woman in
  your arms.
You've abandoned all decency, all sense.
The passions of a degraded man are
  degraded.

And if I was mistaken to start with, and
  later
was wise enough to change my mind,
is that madness? No, you're the one who's
  mad.
The gods in their kindness took a bad wife
  off your hands
and you're trying to get her back.
The suitors, it's true,
were so misguided
as to swear an oath to Tyndareos
while the lust was on them. In my view
some goddess—Hope, I imagine—
  accomplished that.
Not you in any case.
Still, lead them, by all means
to fight your war for you. They're foolish
  enough
to stick to their oaths. But the gods
will not be fooled. They can recognize
oaths that were set up as traps, and sworn
  to
under duress.
I will not kill my children.
There's no justice in things turning out
precisely the way you want them to—you
  get
your vengeance on a worthless wife—
while my days and nights melt
in tears, at the unholy
crimes I've committed against my own
  children.
These are the few things
I wanted to say to you once and for all.
You should be able to understand them.
You can refuse
to be sensible if you want to. But for my
  part
I will set straight my own affairs.
CHORUS: This is not what was said before.
  But the change
is for the better:
refusing to harm a child.
MENELAOS: Oh misery! Then I see I have
  no friends.
AGAMEMNON: When you have friends
  you try to destroy them.
MENELAOS: Is there no way that you will
  show
  that you are my father's son?

AGAMEMNON: I will share your reason,
    not your madness.
MENELAOS: You would share my troubles, if
    you were a brother and a friend.
AGAMEMNON: Say that when you have
    behaved like a brother and a friend to
    me,
  not when you are doing me harm.
MENELAOS: And Greece—you mean you'll
    abandon her now
  to her struggle?
AGAMEMNON: Greece has been driven
    mad by the same god
  who drove you out of your senses.
MENELAOS: Congratulate yourself on your
    scepter
  now that you've betrayed your own
    brother.
  I'll find some other way, other friends—

     (Enter a MESSENGER *right.)*

MESSENGER: Commander of all the armies
    of Greece, King
  Agamemnon, I have brought you,
  from home, your daughter
  whom you called Iphigeneia.
  And her mother, your Clytemnestra, is
    with her,
  and the boy Orestes. You've been away
    from home
  a long time, and the sight of them
  will be a joy to you.
  It's been a tiring journey, and they are
    resting
  now, bathing their soft feet
  at the flowing spring,
  and the horses are resting too;
  we turned them loose to graze there in the
    good pasture.
  I came on ahead to tell you,
  so that you would be ready. But rumor
  travels faster. The army knows
  your daughter is here. And they are
    running
  and crowding to get a look at the girl;
  everyone wants to catch a glimpse
  of those whom fortune has blessed.
  They say, "Is there going to be a wedding,
  or did King Agamemnon miss the child

so much that he sent for her?" Others say,
  "Offerings are being made
consecrating the child to Artemis,
goddess of Aulis,
as though for a wedding, but who
will be the bridegroom?" Come. Do
what comes next, Agamemnon. Bring the
    sacrificial
basket, and lead the procession
around the altar. Set the garlands on your
    heads.
King Menelaos, prepare
the marriage feast. Let the flute
trill within doors and the floor
resound with the dancing, for this is the
    day
that dawned to see your child made
    happy.
AGAMEMNON: Thank you. You may go
    inside. What is left to do
no doubt will turn out well, in the course
    of fate.
(The MESSENGER *goes in at the right-hand
    door.)*
Oh miserable creature that I am,
now what can I say? Where
can I begin in the face of this misery?
I have fallen into the snare of fate.
I laid my plan, but I was outwitted
from the start by the cunning of destiny.
How fortunate are the humbly born.
They can shed tears when they need to,
    they can tell
all their grief. But those of our station
are not allowed to appear
undignified. We are the slaves of the mob
    we lead,
molded by the pomp we must show in
    public.
I am ashamed
of my tears. But in the presence of this
enormity I am ashamed not to weep.
And my wife—
what words can I find, when I see her?
    How
will I greet her? With what eyes
will I welcome her? It was terrible
enough. Why did she have to come here
    too

when I never sent for her? But it is natural
for her to come here with her daughter,
to be present, the bride's mother,
to give her child in marriage.
And that's how she will learn of my
    treachery.
But the unhappy
girl. Girl? Why do I call her a girl?
When it seems that Hades
is about to make her his wife. Oh I
pity her. I can hear her
calling out to me, "Father!
Are you going to kill me? I hope that you
and everyone you love are married like
    this."
And Orestes will be there too, scarcely
old enough to walk, and he will
scream cries without words,
but my heart will know what they mean.
Oh what ruin Priam's son
Paris has brought me! All this he called
    down
by winning the love of Helen.
CHORUS: Grief lays hands on me too,
    though I am a stranger, and a woman, and
        these
    are a king's troubles.
MENELAOS: Brother, give me your hand.
AGAMEMNON: Here is my hand. You have
        won. I must bear
    the loss.
MENELAOS: I swear by Pelops, whom our
        father
    called "Father," and by Atreus himself
    who sired us both, that I will
    speak to you now openly, as I feel,
    without any hidden object in mind,
    but speaking from my heart. When I saw
        the tears
    running from your eyes
    I felt tears of my own
    and pity. I will not set myself against you
    any longer. I call back what I said before.
    I am with you now, and I add my voice
    to yours: do not
    kill your child, not for my sake.
    It cannot be just for you to suffer
    so that I can be satisfied,
    nor for your children to die
    while mine fill their eyes with the light.

What do I need after all? Could I not find
a wife who would do me credit
if I chose to marry again? Am I to lose
a brother, whom I should treasure, merely
    to win back
Helen,
buying evil with good?
I was rash. I behaved like a child, until
I came close to the thing itself
and saw what it means, to kill one's own
    child.
Then pity overcame me. For the girl
from my own family who was going to
    lose her life
because of my marriage. What has your
    daughter
to do with Helen? Let the army
break up and leave Aulis. Brother,
no more tears, now. Yours are the cause of
    mine.
Whatever the oracles say of your
    daughter,
from now on it concerns you, not me.
I give you my share in it. You can see how
    long
my threats lasted. I admit
I changed my mind. But that's
natural if a man loves his brother.
At every step I've tried to see
the right way to act.
That's not the vacillation of a weakling.
CHORUS: Your words are noble. They are
        worthy
    of your ancestors.
    Tantalos himself, the son of Zeus,
    might well have been proud of them.
AGAMEMNON: Menelaos, thank you. I
        never could have hoped
    that you would speak as you have spoken
        now.
    But what you have said is right
    and worthy of you. Discord
    flares up between brothers
    over love or the family estate.
    It is poisonous to both sides. I hate it.
    But I have reached a point where
        circumstances
    leave me no choice. I shall be
    forced to shed her blood,
    to kill my daughter.

MENELAOS: Forced? Who can make you kill
  the girl?
AGAMEMNON: The combined armies of
  the Achaians.
MENELAOS: Not if you've sent her home
  to Argos.
AGAMEMNON: I might be able to do that
  without anyone knowing. But
  afterwards—
MENELAOS: What? You're wrong
  to go in such dread of the mob.
AGAMEMNON: Kalchas will tell the whole
  army
  what was prophesied.
MENELAOS: Not if he's dead. And that's a
  simple matter.
AGAMEMNON: The tribe of prophets wants
  only to be important,
  the whole rotten crowd of them.
MENELAOS: When they don't prophesy
  they're useless, and when they do
  it does no good.
AGAMEMNON: But aren't you afraid of
  something,
  something I've just remembered?
MENELAOS: Not unless you tell me what it
  is.
AGAMEMNON: Someone else
  knows everything. The son of Sisyphos,
  Odysseus.
MENELAOS: There's no reason for Odysseus
  to do anything to injure you or me.
AGAMEMNON: He's cunning, and it always
  turns out
  that he and the crowd are on the same
  side.
MENELAOS: He loves power. A terrible love.
AGAMEMNON: Can't you see him rising
  to his feet in the middle of the Argives
  and repeating
  the oracles that Kalchas spelled out to us,
  telling how I promised
  to sacrifice to Artemis
  and then failed to keep my promise?
  Can't you see
  his words sweeping the whole army along
  with him
  when he tells them
  to kill you, kill me, and then sacrifice the
  girl themselves?

Even if I
could escape to Argos, they would follow
  me there.
They'd tear the city to the ground,
even the great walls that the Cyclopes
  built.
You see why I'm in despair. Almighty
  gods, how helpless
you have made me now!
There is nothing I can do. But you,
  Menelaos,
when you go back to the camp,
save me from one thing at least.
Take care that Clytemnestra
learns nothing of all this,
until I take my child and give her to
  Hades.
Let me suffer my ordeal
with as few tears as possible.
And you, women of Chalkis,
you will do well to say nothing.

(MENELAOS *goes off left.* AGAMEMNON *goes in at the*
  central door.)

CHORUS: Blessed are they
  who share the delights of Aphrodite
  and are not burned alive by them,
    moderate
  and happy,
  whom the passion has not stung into
    madness, at whom
  the archer with the golden hair,
  Eros, has not aimed
  desire in his two arrows, the one
  striking rapture, the other
  devastation. Oh Cyprian,[7]
  most beautiful of the goddesses, keep
  such wild flights from me.
  Let me know love
  within reason, and desire within
  marriage, and feel your presence
  not your rage.
  The natures of humans
  are various, and human ways of acting
  are different,
  but everyone knows what is right,
  and teaching
  inclines them at last to virtue.

[7]Cyprian is a name for Aphrodite, goddess of love.

Humility is wisdom,
making us see the right way
as something beautiful.
And from this beauty honor is born
and life earns immortal fame.
It is a great thing, the pursuit of virtue:
in women it is a stillness
in their love;
among men, multiplied
ten thousand times among citizens,
it makes a city great.
Oh Paris, they took you as a baby
to grow up herding white heifers on
    Mount Ida,
making on reeds a barbarous
music, a thin echo
of the Phrygian pipes of Olympos.
The milk-laden cattle
never stopped grazing when the goddesses
stood forth for you to judge their beauty.
You chose
madness, and madness brought you
here to Greece, to the palace
inlaid with ivory,
and to the eyes of Helen
that took your gaze full of love and
    returned it.
And from that rose the dispute that sends
the armed Greeks in their ships
to sack Troy.

(CLYTEMNESTRA, IPHIGENEIA, *and* ORESTES *enter in a
chariot escorted by the* CHORUS OF ATTENDANTS.)

CHORUS OF ATTENDANTS: Oh great is
        the fortune
    of the great!
    See, the king's daughter, Iphigeneia,
    my queen.
    And Tyndareos' daughter, Clytemnestra.
        How great
    were their ancestors! How momentous
    the occasion that brings them here!
    Those who excel in power and in wealth
    are gods, in the eyes
    of mortals less favored by fortune.
CHORUS OF WOMEN: *(Moving to the
        chariot)* Let us stand here, women of
        Chalkis,
    and hand the queen down from her
        chariot.

Make sure she does not stumble.
Gently, carefully, help with our hands,
let us help Agamemnon's
noble child to
descend unafraid for her first steps in
    Aulis.
(To the occupants of the chariot) We too
    are strangers here. Gently, quietly,
we welcome the strangers from Argos.
CLYTEMNESTRA: I think your kind
        greeting is a good omen.
    I have come here bringing
    this girl, as I hope, to a happy marriage.
    (To the ATTENDANTS.*)*
    Take from the chariot
    the gifts I brought with her, her dowry.
    Carry them in and set them down
        carefully.
    (The ATTENDANTS *carry the gifts into the
        tent.)*
    Daughter, come from the chariot, alight
    on your delicate feet. And you,
    young women, give her your arms, help
        her down.
    Someone do the same for me,
    as I step from the chariot. Someone stand
    in front of the horses' yoke.
    A colt's eye takes fright
    if there is no one to reassure it.
    This is Agamemnon's son. The baby
    Orestes. Take him.
    Are you still asleep, my child,
    lulled by the rocking of the chariot?
    When you wake, wake happily. This is
        your sister's
    wedding day. You had
    noble forebears, you will have
    a noble kinsman: the sea-nymph's son
    who is like his ancestors the gods.[8]
    *(*CLYTEMNESTRA *hands* ORESTES *to a member
        of the* CHORUS, *descends, takes* ORESTES
        *again, and sets him down at her feet.
        As she speaks the next lines*
        AGAMEMNON *enters through the main
        door.)*
    Sit here by my feet, child. Iphigeneia,
    come to your mother. Stand close

---

[8]The sea-nymph's son is Achilles, greatest of Greek
heroes.

and show these strangers
what reason I have to be happy. Now
here comes your dear father. Greet him.
IPHIGENEIA: *(Starts to run to* AGAMEMNON,
   then turns to CLYTEMNESTRA.) Mother,
   don't be angry
if I run from you
to be the first to embrace him.
CLYTEMNESTRA: *(Speaking at the same
   time)* Oh most revered in my eyes,
   Agamemnon, King,
you commanded us to come, and we are
   here.
IPHIGENEIA: *(Running to* AGAMEMNON*)* I
   want to run and put my arms around
   you,
Father, after such a long time!
How I have missed your face! Don't be
   angry!
CLYTEMNESTRA: It's as it should be, child.
   You were always,
of all the children I bore him, the one
who loved your father most.
IPHIGENEIA: Father, how happy I am to see
   you.
It has been so long.
AGAMEMNON: And I am happy to see you,
   Iphigeneia.
The same words rise to my lips.
IPHIGENEIA: Oh, if you could be as happy
   as I am! Father,
what a wonderful thing
to have brought me here to you.
AGAMEMNON: Perhaps my child. Perhaps.
IPHIGENEIA: How troubled your eyes look,
   yet you say
you are happy to see me.
AGAMEMNON: A king and a general
has many burdens.
IPHIGENEIA: Oh forget them, forget them
   for now. I am here.
Put them aside and be with me.
AGAMEMNON: I am with you. I am
   nowhere else.
IPHIGENEIA: Then don't frown any more.
I want those lines to leave your face.
AGAMEMNON: See. How happy I am to
   look at you.
IPHIGENEIA: But your eyes are overflowing
   with tears.

AGAMEMNON: We will be separated
   for so long.
IPHIGENEIA: I don't understand what you
   mean.
Dear father, I don't understand.
AGAMEMNON: If you understood I would
   feel even worse.
IPHIGENEIA: Then we'll talk and I won't
   understand,
if that will make you happier.
AGAMEMNON: Oh! *(Aside)* I can't contain
   my suffering!
(Aloud) Thank you.
IPHIGENEIA: Stay home, Father. Stay with
   your children.
AGAMEMNON: I want to. But I can't do
   what I
want to
and it makes me unhappy.
IPHIGENEIA: Oh I wish there were no more
   spears, no more
of this grievance that's come to Menelaos!
AGAMEMNON: Before they are done
they will destroy others as they have me.
IPHIGENEIA: Father, how long you've been
   shut away in Aulis!
AGAMEMNON: And even now something
   prevents me from sending the army on its
   way.
IPHIGENEIA: Where do they say
the Trojans live, Father?
AGAMEMNON: In the country where Priam
   has a son,
a son named Paris
who I wish had never been born.
IPHIGENEIA: You are going all that way,
   Father,
leaving me behind.
AGAMEMNON: Now you see
what you did not understand before.
IPHIGENEIA: Oh if only it were proper for
   me to go with you!
AGAMEMNON: You will think of your
   father
on your own long voyage.
IPHIGENEIA: Will my mother come with
   me
or will I be alone?
AGAMEMNON: Neither father nor mother.
   Alone.

IPHIGENEIA: You won't make me live
    somewhere else, will you, Father?
AGAMEMNON: I have said enough. Too
    much. Girls
are not meant to know about such things.
IPHIGENEIA: When you have finished what
    you have to do
at Troy, Father,
sail straight home to me.
AGAMEMNON: Before that
I must make a sacrifice. Here in Aulis.
IPHIGENEIA: Sacrifices are to find out
how we may please the gods.
AGAMEMNON: You will see. You will
    stand by the font
of purifying water.
IPHIGENEIA: Will we dance around the
    altar?
AGAMEMNON: How I envy you, knowing
    nothing!
Now go in. It's better
for young girls not to be seen.
Give me a kiss, and your right hand.
You will soon be far away from your
    father,
and for a long time.
Oh breast, cheeks, oh blonde head,
what a crushing weight
Helen and the Trojan city
have called down upon you!
I must not touch you any more.
it sets the tears flowing. Go in.
(IPHIGENEIA *goes in at the left-hand door.*)
Daughter of Leda, forgive me
for this access of grief
at giving my child in marriage to Achilles.
Partings such as these are happy, of course,
but when a father must send
his daughter to the house of another
after all his years of watching over her
it cuts into the heart.
CLYTEMNESTRA: I feel it too. I'm not so
    foolish as to reproach you
for grieving. I will feel just the same,
you know, when I lead the child
out into the marriage hymns,
so I don't blame you.
But time will heal the sadness. It's the
    custom and
we will get used to it. Tell me

about his ancestors, and where he was born.
    All I know is his name.
AGAMEMNON: To Asopos
a daughter was born, named Aigina.
CLYTEMNESTRA: Who married her? A
    mortal, a god?
AGAMEMNON: Zeus himself. And she bore
    him a son,
Aiakos, king of the island of Oinone.
CLYTEMNESTRA: And which of his
    children succeeded him?
AGAMMENON: Peleus. He married one of
    the daughters
of Nereus, the sea-god.
CLYTEMNESTRA: With her father's
    blessings, or did Peleus
take her in defiance of the gods?
AGAMEMNON: Zeus made the betrothal,
    and gave her in marriage.
He has the authority.
CLYTEMNESTRA: Where were they
    married?
Under the waves of the ocean?
AGAMEMNON: At the foot of Pelion,
    the sacred mountain where Cheiron lives.[9]
CLYTEMNESTRA: In the country where
    they say the centaurs live?
AGAMEMNON: There all the gods came to
    the marriage of Peleus
and the wedding feast.
CLYTEMNESTRA: And was it Thetis or his
    father Peleus
who brought Achilles up?
AGAMEMNON: It was Cheiron,
    to keep him from learning the evil ways of
    men.
CLYTEMNESTRA: Wise teacher! And Peleus
    was wiser still,
sending the boy to him.
AGAMEMNON: Such is the man who will
    be your daughter's husband.
CLYTEMNESTRA: He sounds acceptable.
    Where in Geece is he from?
AGAMEMNON: From Phthia, on the river
    Apidanos.
CLYTEMNESTRA: And that is where he will
    take our daughter?

[9]Cheiron was a centaur (half man, half horse) who served
as tutor to several Greek heroes.

AGAMEMNON: That is for him to decide.

CLYTEMNESTRA: May it be a happy
marriage!
When will it take place?

AGAMEMNON: At the full moon.
That is the most propitious time.

CLYTEMNESTRA: Have you made our
daughter's
sacrifice to the goddess?

AGAMEMNON: I will. We had just come to
that.

CLYTEMNESTRA: And afterwards you will
have the marriage feast?

AGAMEMNON: When I have offered the
gods
the sacrifice they require of me.

CLYTEMNESTRA: And where shall I
prepare the women's banquet?

AGAMEMNON: Here. By the high sterns of
the ships from Argos.

CLYTEMNESTRA: Here? Well, there is no
choice. I hope
good fortune comes of it.

AGAMEMNON: Do you know what you
should do?
Please do it.

CLYTEMNESTRA: What do you want? You
know I'm not in the habit
of disobeying you.

AGAMEMNON: Then here, in the presence
of the bridegroom,
we men will—

CLYTEMENESTRA: You? Will I not be there
for the things a bride's mother must do?

AGMEMNON: I will give away your child.
The army and I.

CLYTEMNESTRA: And where will I be
when that happens?

AGAMEMNON: In Argos, taking care of
your daughters.

CLYTEMNESTRA: Leaving my child here?
And who
will raise the bridal torch?

AGAMEMNON: I will provide the light, all
the light
proper for the bridal pair.

CLYTEMNESTRA: That is wrong, wrong.
And such things are important.

AGAMEMNON: It is not right for you to
stay here

jostling among the soldiers.

CLYTEMNESTRA: It is right that I should
give
my children in marriage. I am their
mother.

AGAMEMNON: It is not right for our
daughters at home
to be left alone.

CLYTEMNESTRA: They are well looked
after,
safe in their part of the palace.

AGAMEMNON: Please do it.

CLYTEMNESTRA: No, by the goddess who
reigns in Argos.
You see to the things outside
that concern you. I'll go in
and see to the preparations for my
daughter's wedding.

(She goes in at the left-hand door.)

AGAMEMNON: Oh, it was no use. I tried
but I failed
to send my wife out of my sight.
I contrive plots, I lay plans to deceive
those dearest to me
and it all comes to nothing.
Now I must arrange with Kalchas, who
performs
our sacrifices,
the thing which the goddess demands
and I hate the thought of.
I owe it to Greece.
A wise man supports in his house
a good and faithful wife. Or no wife at all.

(He goes off left.)

CHORUS: Now they will sail
to Simoïs where the waters spin silver,[10]
the Greeks in pride of numbers,
of ships, of weapons. They will come
to Ilion, to the plains below Troy[11]
shining in the blessing of Apollo,
where Kassandra, they say, flings[12]
like sunlight the blonde falls of her hair

[10]Simois was a Trojan river.

[11]Ilion was the citadel of Troy.

[12]Kassandra was the daughter of King Priam of Troy. She was given the power of prophecy by Apollo but was cursed in that no one believed her prophecies.

from under the green laurel when the god
grips her and she shakes
and sees what is to come.
At Troy on the ramparts, on the circling
walls, drawn up,
the Trojans will be waiting
as Ares in his bronze battle gear[13]
comes nearer with the falling oars,
the hanging prows riffling the estuary
    mouths
of Simoïs. What he will want
is Helen, the sister
of the twin sons of Zeus, the Dioskouroi,
who are stars in heaven.
To possess her again out of Priam's
    kingdom,
the prize
of the Achaians' spears, shields, labors in
    battle,
and bring her once more into Greece.
The god will girdle with slaughter
the stone-cased stronghold
of Pergamos, the Phrygians' city. He will
    see[14]
Priam's head hewn from its shoulders
and every house in Troy
smashed and rummaged. Then what a
    crying
from the girls and from Priam's queen.
And Helen herself, the daughter of Zeus,
will taste tears for the day she left her
    husband.
Oh may such anguish never befall us,
women of Chalkis, nor our children's
    children,
as shall then work through the Lydian
    women[15]
for all their gold,
and through the wives of Phrygia so that
    they
stand by the looms saying, "Who now
will wrap his wrist in my swaying hair
    and uproot me

out of my ruined home,
dragging me through my tears?
It is all thanks to you, daughter
of the swan with the sinuous neck, whose
    wings
hid Zeus from Leda,[16]
if that is true.
It is still you
even if that is no more than a story
out of the books of the Muses,
with no meaning."

(Enter ACHILLES *left, unarmed and dressed with
ostentatious simplicity. He looks about twenty-
five years old.)*

ACHILLES: Where is the commander of the
    Achaians?
Will one of his servants tell him that
    Peleus' son
Achilles is standing at his door?
It is not the same for all of us
having to wait here
by the straits. Some of us,
who have no wives, sit here by the shore,
    having left
empty houses at home. Others, who are
    married,
still have no children.
Such is the frenzy that has seized Greece
for this war,
not without the consent of the gods.
With things at this pass, let me say
what is due to me. Anyone else who
    wants to
may speak in his own behalf. I came away
from Pharsalia, I left Peleus,[17]
to be kept waiting for
a wind, beside the straits,
trying to keep my men quiet, my
    Myrmidons:
day after day they come up to me and say,
    "Achilles,
what is keeping us here? How much more
time must we waste on this expedition to
    Troy?

[13]Ares was god of war.
[14]Pergamos was another name for the Trojan citadel;
Phrygia is the name of the country in which Troy is
located.
[15]Lydia was a country adjacent to Phrygia and allied with
it.

[16]Helen was the daughter of Leda by Zeus, who appeared
to Leda in the guise of a swan.
[17]Pharsalia was a city in the area of Greece called
Thessaly.

Do what you came here to do
or else lead the army home.
Don't wait for the sons of Atreus."

(CLYTEMNESTRA *enters from the left-hand door.*)

CLYTEMNESTRA: Son of the Nereïd, I
heard your voice
and came out to greet you.
ACHILLES: Oh sacred modesty, who
is this beautiful woman?
CLYTEMNESTRA: You could hardly expect
to recognize me
since you never saw me before,
but your regard for modesty is
commendable.
ACHILLES: Who are you? And why have you
come
to the camp of the Greek army,
you a woman, here among the shields?
CLYTEMNESTRA: I am the daughter of Leda,
Clytemnestra. Agamemnon is my
husband.
ACHILLES: Brief and to the point.
But it is not seemly for me
to be seen talking with women.

(*He starts to go off left.*)

CLYTEMNESTRA: Wait. Why do you run
away? (*Following him*)
Give me your right hand—here is mine:
a happy beginning to this betrothal of
ours!
ACHILLES: (*Turns politely, then recoils in
horror*) Do you know what you are
saying? Touch
your hand? How could I face Agamemnon
if I touch what heaven forbids me to
touch?
CLYTEMNESTRA: Why do you say heaven
forbids it,
son of Thetis the sea-nymph,
when you are about to marry my
daughter?
ACHILLES: Marry? Lady, what do you mean?
I am left with no answer. Has some
delusion
led your mind astray?
CLYTEMNESTRA: I know it is natural
for men to be shy, faced with new kin
and the talk of marriage.

ACHILLES: Lady, I have never courted your
daughter,
and the sons of Atreus have not spoken
one word to me about marriage.
CLYTEMNESTRA: What does this mean?
Indeed my words must be as shocking
to you
as your words are shocking to me.
ACHILLES: We must both find the
explanation. There must be
some truth under what we both said.
CLYTEMNESTRA: I have been deceived. It
seems
I have been preparing a marriage
that exists only in my mind.
I am filled with shame.
ACHILLES: Perhaps someone is amusing
himself
with both of us.
Ignore it. It doesn't matter.
CLYTEMNESTRA: I will take my leave. I am
humiliated.
I have been made to lie.
I can no longer look you in the face.

(*She starts to go in at the left-hand door.*)

ACHILLES: Lady, good-bye. I shall go in
to see your husband.

*He starts to go in at the main entrance, then
pauses as he hears the* OLD MAN *call through the
right-hand door.* CLYTEMNESTRA *pauses also.*)

OLD MAN: (*Off*) Wait, stranger! Grandson
of Aiakos,
son of the goddess, you
I'm calling, and you, daughter of Leda.
ACHILLES: Who is that, shouting through
the doorway?
How shaken he sounds!
OLD MAN: I am a slave. That's the truth,
why not say it?
Fate has given me no choice.
ACHILLES: Whose slave? Not mine,
certainly, here
among Agamemnon's possessions.
OLD MAN: That lady's, in front of the tent.
I was given to her by Tyndareos, her
father.
ACHILLES: Well, here I am. Why did you
want me to stay?

OLD MAN: Is there no one else here
  besides you and her?
ACHILLES: We are alone. Come out from the
  king's tent. Speak.
OLD MAN: What I most feared has come to
  pass. Oh destiny,
  (Entering) spare those I pray for!
ACHILLES: Your words sound ominous,
  and the message, it seems, is important.
CLYTEMNESTRA: Don't wait to kiss my
  hand. What did you want to tell me?
OLD MAN: You know me, lady. You know
  my
  devotion to you and your children.
CLYTEMNESTRA: I know you've been a
  servant in the palace
  for a long time.
OLD MAN: I came to King Agamemnon
  as part of your dowry.
CLYTEMNESTRA: Yes, you came with us to
  Argos
  and you've always belonged to me.
OLD MAN: I have. And I put your interests
  ahead of your husband's.
CLYTEMNESTRA: Now tell us. What is
  your secret?
OLD MAN: Your daughter. Her father
  is going to kill her.
  With his own hand.
CLYTEMNESTRA: What? I spit against what
  you say, old man!
  You're out of your senses!
OLD MAN: He will plunge a blade into her
  white throat.
CLYTEMNESTRA: Oh, torment! Has he gone
  mad?
OLD MAN: No, he is sane about everything
  except you
  and your child. There he's lost his
  reason.
CLYTEMNESTRA: Why? What demon could
  prompt him to such a thing?
OLD MAN: The oracle. According to
  Kalchas. Saying
  what must happen before the fleet can
  sail.
CLYTEMNESTRA: What horror is coming to
  me, and the child
  whose father will kill her! Sail where?

OLD MAN: To the country of Dardanos,[18] for
  Menelaos
  to bring back Helen.
CLYTEMNESTRA: So the fates have woven
  Iphigeneia's death
  into Helen's homecoming?
OLD MAN: Now you know it all. He intends
  to sacrifice your daughter to Artemis.
CLYTEMNESTRA: And the talk of marriage,
  which brought me here?
OLD MAN: The king knew you would bring
  her, and gladly,
  to marry Achilles.
CLYTEMNESTRA: Oh daughter, you have
  come here
  to your death, and your mother with you.
OLD MAN: The child's fate is terrible. So is
  yours.
  It is a monstrous decision, Agamemnon's.
CLYTEMNESTRA: I am helpless. I am lost.
  Whatever I do
  the tears come.
OLD MAN: If losing a child is painful, you
  have
  reason for tears.
CLYTEMNESTRA: But where did you learn
  all this, old man?
  How did it come to your ears?
OLD MAN: I was sent to you with a second
  letter
  about the first one.
CLYTEMNESTRA: Telling me again to bring
  the girl here
  to die, or warning me not to?
OLD MAN: Warning you not to. At that
  moment
  your husband was in his right mind.
CLYTEMNESTRA: If you had such a letter
  for me
  why was it not delivered?
OLD MAN: Menelaos took it from me.
  All your troubles come from him.
CLYTEMNESTRA: Son of Thetis and Peleus,
  have you heard this?
ACHILLES: I have heard the cause of your
  grief,

[18]Dardanos was the son of Zeus and founder of the Trojan
royal line.

and I do not take lightly
the way I have been involved in the
matter.
CLYTEMNESTRA: They are going to kill my
child.
They tricked her with this talk of
marrying you.
ACHILLES: I too blame Agamemnon,
and not only for the reasons you speak of.
CLYTEMNESTRA: *(Dropping to her knees
and embracing* ACHILLES' *legs)* Son of a
goddess, I, a mortal,
am not ashamed to clasp your knees. What
good
would pride do me now? What matters
more to me
than my daughter's life?
Son of a goddess, save us: me
in my wretchedness,
and Iphigeneia, who they said was your
betrothed,
even though it was not true.
I myself put the bridal wreath on her head
for you,
I brought her here to be married,
and now I am leading her to her death.
You will be blamed if you do nothing to
defend her.
(She rises, puts her left hand to ACHILLES'
*cheek and takes his right hand in her
own.)*
Even though you were never married to
her
you were called her husband.
I implore you by your beard, by your right
hand,
by your own mother. Your name,
Achilles,
destroyed me; now you must clear it.
(Kneels and takes his knees again.)
There is no altar where I can take refuge,
none except your knees.
No friend smiles on me here. You have
heard
of Agamemnon's raw heartlessness.
Nothing is sacred to him.
And I am a woman, come
into a camp of sailors, hard to control
and ripe for any crime — though they can be
useful enough when they want to be.
If you can bring yourself to stretch out
your hand over me, we are saved.
If not, we are lost.
CHORUS: Giving birth is a mystery. It casts
a powerful spell over mothers. All, all of
them
without exception
will risk any suffering
for the sake of one of their children.
ACHILLES: Pride rises up in me
and draws me on. But I have learned
to curb my grief in adversity, and my joy
in triumph.
Mortals who have learned this
can hope to live by reason. There are
moments
when it is good not to be too wise,
but there are times too when taking
thought is useful.
I was brought up in the house of Cheiron,
the most righteous of men,
and he taught me to act from a simple
heart.
If the commands of the sons of Atreus
are just, I will obey them. If not,
I will refuse. But whether here
or in Troy, I will remain free,
and in my fighting will bring credit on the
war god
with my whole strength. As for you,
you have been treated cruelly
by those closest to you,
and as far as is proper for me, I shall
extend
my pity to cover you. Never shall your
daughter,
who has been called my betrothed,
be slaughtered by her father. He shall not
use
me in his manipulations.
That way my name would be her butcher
as surely as if it had drawn the sword.
Your husband is the cause of this, but my
own
body would be defiled
if through me that girl were to die,
horribly, brutally used, as she
has been. It fills me with rage

to think how she has been treated. I would be
the lowest of the Argives, a nothing,
and Menelaos a hero,
I would be no son of Peleus, but some
demon's offspring, if I
let my name do your husband's killing for him
I swear by Nereus, whom the waves cradled, father
of Thetis who gave me birth,
King Agamemnon shall not touch your daughter
nor so much as graze her gown
with his finger-tips,
or that barbarous settlement in Lydia,
Sipylos, where his sires
first saw the light,
is a Grecian city,
and no one has heard of Phthia.
This Kalchas, their prophet, will find
a bitter taste in the barley
and the lustral water before that sacrifice.
What is a prophet? Someone
who utters one truth in a flock of lies,
if he's lucky, and if he's not
everybody forgets.
I'm not saying this to earn a bride.
There are thousands I could marry.
But I will not suffer this insult from King Agamemnon.
He should have asked my permission
if he wanted to use me to lure the girl here
into his snare,
since it was to see her married to me
that Clytemnestra would have brought her most willingly.
I would have lent the use of my name
to the Greeks,
so that the ships could sail to Ilion.
I am here with the others. It is the same war.
I would not have refused to help.
But I have been treated by these commanders
as though I were nobody. They accord me their
honor or they ignore me as they please.

My sword may decide that. Blood will color it
before we sail to Phrygia
if anyone thinks to take your daughter from me.
Be calm. In your time of danger, suddenly
I appeared to you as if I were some great god.
I am not. But to save the girl,
I will be.
CHORUS: Son of Peleus, what you have said is worthy
of you, worthy of the proud sea-goddess
and her son.
CLYTEMNESTRA: How can I find the right praise,
neither cloying with flattery, nor so meager
that it offends you? Men of worth
have a way of hating those who praise them too much.
I am ashamed to enlarge on my sufferings.
They are mine, they do not concern you. Still,
even if their afflictions are not his, a good man
may help those in trouble. Take pity on us.
Our plight deserves it. First I thought
you would be my son—an empty hope, as I learned.
Now my child is threatened with death:
a bad augury for your marriage one day,
unless you take steps to protect yourself.
But why do I urge you? From beginning to end
you have spoken nobly. My child
will be saved, if you can save her. Would it please you
if she came and embraced your knees as a suppliant?
True, it is not seemly for a girl to do so,
but if you wished she would come
with dignity, and eyes cast down. And yet
if my supplication alone
can move you
I would rather she were not called.
She is over-timid, perhaps. But all forms

of modesty
are worth respecting.
ACHILLES: Do not bring your daughter
    here for me to see. Why should we incur
    the comments of the ignorant?
    An army crowded together, loosed from
        work at home,
    will gossip and spread foul stories.
    Whether you supplicate me or not, you
        come
    to the same end. For me
    the one thing of importance
    is to save you from disaster.
    And this you may count on: I never lie.
    May I die if I deceive you. And live
    only if she does.
CLYTEMNESTRA: May you be blessed all
    your days
    for helping those who are unhappy.
ACHILLES: We must lay plans. Listen.
CLYTEMNESTRA: Go on. I need no urging
    to listen to you.
ACHILLES: Let us try to make her father see
    reason.
CLYTEMNESTRA: He is too cowardly. He is
    afraid of the army.
ACHILLES: Arguments can beat down
    arguments.
CLYTEMNESTRA: A cold hope. But what do
    you want me to do?
ACHILLES: First, plead with him not to kill
    his daughter.
    If he refuses you, then you can come to
        me,
    but you may persuade him
    by yourself.
    Then there would be no need for my help.
    You are safe, in any case. And there would
        be
    no breach, then, in my friendship with
        Agamemnon,
    no cause for the army to reproach me,
    no weapon used to bring it about,
    only reason. So it would turn out well for
        you
    and those dear to you
    and I would not be forced to act.
CLYTEMNESTRA: How wise you are! I will
    do as you say. But suppose

something goes wrong: where
and how will I see you again?
Shall I come, in my misery, searching
for your hand to rescue us?
ACHILLES: I will be watching, in the right
    place.
    You will not have to be stared at
    hunting through the troops to find me. Do
        nothing
    that would disgrace your fathers.
    Tyndareos should not suffer shame.
    He was a great man in Greece.
CLYTEMNESTRA: You are right. Lead me. I
    ask only
    to be your slave.
    If there are gods the gods will reward your
        goodness.
    If there are none what does anything
        matter?

(CLYTEMNESTRA *goes in at the left door, the* OLD
MAN *at the right.* ACHILLES *goes off left.*)

CHORUS: Oh what a sound of Libyan flutes,
    of lyres leading the dance, of reeling
    reeds raised the marriage hymn
    on Pelion, when the Muses
    came robed in their bright hair to the
        banquet
    with the gods, and their gold
    sandals stamped the ground
    on the way to the marriage of Peleus,
    and their voices
    carried over the centaurs' slopes, and
        through
    the woods of Pelion, praise
    of Thetis and Aiakos' son.
    There Dardanos' child,
    Trojan Ganymede, the darling of Zeus,
        poured out
    mixed wine from the deep bowls of gold,
    and in celebration the fifty
    daughters of Nereus turned
    their braided dance on the white sand
    of the shore.
    And the centaurs came
    riding, with pine spears and crowned with
        leaves,
    to the feast of the gods, and the bowl

that Bakchos filled, and they cried,
  "Daughter
of Nereus, great
is the son you will bear:
a light and a splendor to Thessaly,
as Cheiron, who knows
the oracles of Apollo, foretells,
saying that your child will sail with an
  army
of Myrmidons, and their spears, to the
  land of Troy
to burn King Priam's glorious city,
his limbs traced
in gold armor wrought for him
by the god Hephaistos,
the gift of his mother Thetis, the sea-
  goddess."
So the gods celebrated the marriage of
  Peleus
and the first-born of the Nereïds.
But you, Iphigeneia, on your
lovely hair the Argives will set
a wreath, as on the brows
of a spotted heifer, led down
from caves in the mountains
to the sacrifice,
and the knife will open the throat
and let the blood of a girl.
And you were not
brought up to the sound of the shepherd's
  pipe
and the cries of the herdsmen,
but nurtured by your mother
to be a bride for one of great Inachos'
  sons.[19]
Oh where is the noble face
of modesty, or the strength of virtue, now
that blasphemy is in power
and men have put justice
behind them, and there is no law but
  lawlessness,
and none join in fear of the gods?

(CLYTEMNESTRA *enters from the left-hand door.*)

CLYTEMNESTRA: I have come out looking
  for my husband.

---

[19]Inachos was the river god, king, and ancestor of the people of Argos.

He has been away from here for some
  time. My daughter,
poor child, has learned
of the death her father plans for her.
One minute she is shaken with sobbing
and the next the tears
flow almost in silence.
But it was Agamemnon I named: here he
  is.
He will soon stand convicted
of planning a crime against his own child.

(AGAMEMNON *enters left, alone.*)

AGAMEMNON: Daughter of Leda, I am glad
  that we meet out here,
for I must speak to you now of things that
  a bride
should not hear.
CLYTEMNESTRA: It's a good moment for
  that.
AGAMEMNON: Call the child out to her
  father.
The libations are ready, and the barley
  grains
ready to be thrown into the purifying
  flame,
and the calves that must loose
to Artemis their dark blood
to bless the marriage.
CLYTEMNESTRA: You find innocent words
  to describe it
but there are no words
for what you have decided. (*She calls in at
  the left door.*) Come, child.
You know what your father means to do.
Wrap the baby Orestes
in your robe and bring him with you.

(IPHIGENEIA *enters from the left door, carrying*
ORESTES. *With her free hand she covers her face
with her robe.* CLYTEMNESTRA *too keeps her face
turned from* AGAMEMNON.)

Here she is, obedient to your command.
For the rest,
I will answer for us both.
AGAMEMNON: Why are you crying, child?
  Aren't you still happy
to see me? Why are you holding your robe
in front of your eyes,
with your face turned to the ground?

CLYTEMNESTRA: I cannot think where
 to start my bitter story,
 for its beginning is grief,
 its middle is grief,
 its end
 is grief.
AGAMEMNON: What is it? Why are all
 three of you
 afraid to look at me?
CLYTEMNESTRA: My husband,
 find the honesty of a man
 and answer me with it.
AGAMEMNON: There is no need for you to
 speak that way.
 Ask me your question.
CLYTEMNESTRA: Do you intend to kill
 your daughter?
AGAMEMNON: What a horrible thing to
 ask? What a vile suspicion!
CLYTEMNESTRA: Simply answer the
 question.
AGAMEMNON: Any reasonable question I
 would answer.
CLYTEMNESTRA: This question. This is the
 only one I care about.
AGAMEMNON: Oh immovable law of
 heaven! Oh my
 anguish, my relentless fate!
CLYTEMNESTRA: Yours? Mine. Hers. No
 relenting for any of us.
AGAMEMNON: How have you been
 wronged?
CLYTEMNESTRA: How can you ask? What
 a question
 for a man of sense!
AGAMEMNON: *(To himself)* I am lost.
 Someone has betrayed me.
CLYTEMNESTRA: I know the whole story. I
 have found out
 what you mean to do to me.
 Your silence itself is a confession.
 So is your sighing. No need to waste
 words.
AGAMEMNON: Then I will say nothing.
 What good would it do
 to lie, and add shamelessness to my
 troubles?
CLYTEMNESTRA: Listen to me, then. I will
 use plain words, and not
 talk in riddles. In the first place

you took me by force, you married me
against my will.
You killed the husband I had, Tantalos.
You ripped from my breast
my baby, still
living, you smashed it on the ground.
Then when my brothers, the sons
of Zeus, on their shining horses,
bore down on you bringing war,
you came on your knees to my old father
Tyndareos, and he saved you.
So you got me for your wife, again.
I came to love you. Admit
that as your wife I have deserved no
 reproach.
My demands in love have been modest. I
 have done
what I could to increase your house
so that you would be glad to come home,
 and you went out
proud and at peace. It is not often
that a man acquires a good wife.
There is no end of the other kind. And I
 bore you
this son, and three daughters, and now
you have the cruelty
to take one of these from me.
And if anyone asks you
why you intend to kill her, what will you
 say?
Shall I answer for you? So that Menelaos
can have Helen back. Strange
bargain: you'll pay your child's life
as the price of a worthless woman.
We'll buy back our own harm
with what is most dear to us.
Now I want you to think of this. You'll
 sail
to the war, and I'll be left in the house.
You may be gone for years. There I'll be.
And with what heart, do you imagine, I
 will pass
my days in those halls, finding
all her places empty,
her girl's room empty of her forever, and
finding myself alone
with nothing but my tears and the endless
grieving at her fate: "My child,
it was your own father who killed you.
No one else. That was his hand,

no one else's. That was his reward for
  love.
And after that, he will come home again."
Then almost any occasion
would serve, for my other children and
  me
to give you the welcome you will have
  earned.
In the name of the gods, don't force me to
  turn
against you. Don't wrong me yourself.
As you kill our child what prayers will
  you be saying?
What blessing can you ask
as you have cut her throat? A bad voyage
  home,
since your setting out was the consequence
  of a crime?
And in justice, could I give you my
  blessing?
We would have to think the gods had no
  minds,
to pray for murderers.
And when you come back to Argos
will you kiss your children? It will be
  forbidden
by the gods. And which of the children
will dare even to look at you? They will
  be afraid
that you will kiss them only to kill them.
Did any of that ever cross your mind? Or
  do you
think of nothing but waving scepters
and leading armies? Would it not have
  been fair
to say to the Achaians, "Men of Argos,
you want to sail to Troy. Draw lots. Let us
  see
whose daughter will die." That way would
  have had
its justice. There is none
in your offering up your daughter
as a victim for the army. Or let Menelaos,
to whom it matters most, after all, cut his
  own
daughter's throat: Hermione's, for the sake
of her mother. But it is my own child
who is to be torn from me, when I have
  been
faithful to you,

while she who dishonored her husband's
  bed will find
her daughter safe at home, in Sparta,
and be happy. Now answer me,
tell me if one thing I've said is not true.
But if there is justice and truth
in what I say, do not kill your daughter
  and mine.
Turn back, be wise.
CHORUS: Do as she asks, Agamemnon.
  It is good when people help each other,
  to save children. Who can deny that?

(IPHIGENEIA *hands* ORESTES *to her mother, then
kneels and clasps* AGAMEMNON's *knees.)*

IPHIGENEIA: If I had the tongue of Orpheus,
    Father, whose song
  could charm stones so that they followed
    after him,
  if my words could persuade
  whoever I wished to whatever I wished, I
    would use
  all my arts now. But all that I know how
    to do
  at this moment is cry. I offer you my tears.
  I press against your knees
  like a suppliant's torn branch, my body
  which my mother bore you. Do not send
    me
  into death before my time. It is sweet to
    see
  the light. Do not make me look
  at what is under the earth.
  I was the first who called you father, the
    first
  you called your child,
  the first to climb on your knees, and we
  held each other, we loved each other. You
    said,
  "Will I see you living in your husband's
    house,
  enjoying the happiness that is my
    daughter's right?"
  And I answered, touching your beard, as I
    do now—
  but now as the gesture
  of a suppliant—, "And what will I do for
    you
  then, Father? When you are old
  will you come to live with me,

and let me nurse your age, in return
for what you have done for me?"
I remember what we said, but you have
    forgotten.
And now you want to kill me. Oh, in the
    name
of Pelops, of your father
Atreus, of my mother, suffering here
again as at my birth, do not let it happen.
What have I to do with Paris
and Helen, and what they have done?
Why should Paris' coming to Argos mean
    that I
must die? Look at me. In my eyes. Kiss
    me,
so that at least I may remember that
when I am dying,
if you will not listen to what I say.
*(AGAMEMNON and IPHIGENEIA kiss. As she
    speaks the following lines IPHIGENEIA
    takes ORESTES from CLYTEMNESTRA and
    holds him up to AGAMEMNON.)*
My brother, you are so small
to have to help your friends. But cry
with me, cry to your father, beg him
not to kill your sister. See,
even babies sense the dread of evil to
    come.
Even without being able to speak, he cries
    to you,
begging. Take pity on me.
Respect your daughter's life. Both of us,
your own blood, touch your beard,
imploring you: a baby,
a grown girl. In three words I can say it
    all:
the sweetest thing
we ever see is this daylight. Under the
    ground
there is nothing.
Only the mad choose to be dead. The
    meanest life
is better than the most glorious death.

(She hands ORESTES to CLYTEMNESTRA.)

CHORUS: Oh reckless Helen, now from you
    and your marriage
a deadly struggle begins
between the sons of Atreus and their
    children.

AGAMEMNON: I know when pity is due,
    and when it is not.
I love my children. Only the mad do not.
Wife, it is terrible to me
to bring myself to do this,
and terrible if I do not.
For I am forced to do it. *(To IPHIGENEIA)*
    Look: how many ships,
the war fleet, assembled here, the proud
    men of Greece
and their bronze battle-gear, and they
cannot sail to the towers
of Ilion, and seize
the famous citadel, Troy,
according to Kalchas the prophet, unless I
sacrifice you.
Some strange Aphrodite has crazed
the whole Greek army with a passion to
    sail at once
to the barbarians' own country
and end this piracy of Greek marriage.
If I disobey the goddess, if I ignore
the oracle, then the army will sail to
    Argos,
they will kill you and me, and your sisters
who are still at home. I have not become
Menelaos' creature. I am not guided by
    him.
It is *Greece* that compels me
to sacrifice you, whatever I wish.
We are in stronger hands than our own.
Greece must be free
if you and I can make her so. Being
    Greeks,
we must not be subject to barbarians,
we must not let them carry off our wives.

(He goes off left.)

CLYTEMNESTRA: Oh strangers, oh my
    daughter, now I see
your death! Your father is running away
    from you,
after giving you up to Hades.
IPHIGENEIA: Oh mother, how can I bear it?
The same lamenting song
falls to us both, our fate.
I must say good-bye to the light. I will not
see the sun any more. Oh unlucky
valley of Phrygia, filled with snow,
oh high slopes of Ida where Priam

once left a baby, torn from its mother,
to die: Paris, his own child, known
in time as the son of Ida,
Paris of Ida,
among the Phrygians. If only the
    herdsman
had not brought him up with the flocks,
not reared him, Paris, Alexander,[20]
to watch his flock by the clear
springs where the nymphs rise,
and the rich pastures starred
with roses and hyacinths
for the goddesses to gather.
It was there that Pallas came,
and seductive Cypris, and Hera, and with
    them
Hermes, the gods' messenger:
Cypris proud of the desires she wakens,
Pallas proud of her spear,
Hera proud of the bed of Zeus,
came for the fatal judgment, vying in
    beauty,
whose issue is my death,
oh my friends,
whatever glory it brings to the Argives.
For I am to be the first sacrifice
to Artemis for the passage to Ilion.
And he who begot me has betrayed me
    and left me,
and I curse in my despair,
I curse the day that ever I saw you, Helen,
for I am to be murdered, I am to fall
to my ungodly father's
ungodly knife. Oh if only
Aulis had never opened
her folded bay to the bronze-beaked
    galleys,
the fir keels that will ferry them to Troy,
or the breath of Zeus had not blown fair
    up the current
of Euripos. Sweetly he blows
on this man's sails and on that man's,
    making those men
happy. To others he brings
bad luck, bitter compulsion.
Some can set out on voyages, and some
can make port. Others must wait. Truly

[20]Alexander was one of Paris's names.

we are creatures
of labor and suffering, and nothing for
    long.
Labor and suffering,
and the plain sight
of our destiny is the cruelest thing of all.
CHORUS: Oh daughter of Tyndareos, what
    anguish,
what bitter sorrows
you have called down on Greece!
    (To IPHIGENEIA)
I pity you. You do not deserve your fate.
IPHIGENEIA: (Looking offstage, left)
    Mother, mother! I see men coming.
CLYTEMNESTRA: (Looking in the same
    direction) Achilles too, child, the son
    of the goddess,
in whose name you were brought here.
IPHIGENEIA: (Running to the left door and
    calling to the servants inside) Women,
    open the doors so that I can hide.
CLYTEMNESTRA: Why, child?
IPHIGENEIA: I would be ashamed to see
    him.
CLYTEMNESTRA: Why?
IPHIGENEIA: I am ashamed of my unlucky
    marriage.
CLYTEMNESTRA: There is no time now for
    delicacy. Stay here.
    Do not be shy. We must do what we can.

(Enter ACHILLES left, followed by attendants
bearing his shield, spears, sword, breastplate,
        greaves, and helmet.)

ACHILLES: Unhappy daughter of Leda.
CLYTEMNESTRA: Unhappy is what I am.

    (Noise of shouting offstage.)

ACHILLES: The Argives are shouting.
    They want a terrible thing.
CLYTEMNESTRA: What are they shouting?
ACHILLES: About your daughter.
CLYTEMNESTRA: Your words have an
    unhappy beginning.
ACHILLES: They say she must be sacrificed.
CLYTEMNESTRA: And will no one speak
    against them?
ACHILLES: They shouted about me, too.
CLYTEMNESTRA: What did they say?

ACHILLES: "Stone him to death!"

CLYTEMNESTRA: For trying to save my
   daughter?

ACHILLES: For that.

CLYTEMNESTRA: Who would have dared
   to raise a hand against you?

ACHILLES: Every Greek there.

CLYTEMNESTRA: But your own army of
   Myrmidons,
   surely they took your side?

ACHILLES: They were the first to threaten
   me.

CLYTEMNESTRA: Oh my child, we are lost.

ACHILLES: They said I was foolish about this
   marriage.

CLYTEMNESTRA: What did you answer?

ACHILLES: That they were not to kill my
   bride.

CLYTEMNESTRA: Good.

ACHILLES: Whom her father had promised
   to me.

CLYTEMNESTRA: And brought here from
   Argos.

(More shouting offstage, left.)

ACHILLES: Their voices drowned me out.

CLYTEMNESTRA: The mob. An infernal
   thing!

ACHILLES: But I will defend you.

CLYTEMNESTRA: You alone? Against the
   whole army?

(ACHILLES *points to the armor-bearers.)*

ACHILLES: See. These men are carrying my
   armor.

CLYTEMNESTRA: May heaven reward your
   courage.

ACHILLES: Heaven will.

CLYTEMNESTRA: And my daughter will
   not be sacrificed?

ACHILLES: Not if I can stop it.

CLYTEMNESTRA: Will they come here to
   take the girl?

ACHILLES: Thousands of them,
   led by Odysseus.

CLYTEMNESTRA: The son of Sisyphos?

ACHILLES: That one.

CLYTEMNESTRA: Did he offer to do it, or
   did the army choose him?

ACHILLES: They chose him, but the choice
   pleased him.

CLYTEMNESTRA: A vile choice: to be the
   accomplice
   in a murder.

ACHILLES: I will stop him.

CLYTEMNESTRA: Is he going to drag her
   away aginst her will?

ACHILLES: By her blonde hair.

CLYTEMNESTRA: And what should I do
   then?

ACHILLES: Hold on to her.

CLYTEMNESTRA: You mean that will stop
   them
   from killing her?

ACHILLES: That is what it will come to.

IPHIGENEIA: Mother, both of you, listen to
   me.
   I see now that you are wrong
   to be angry with your husband.
   It is hard to hold out against the
     inevitable.
   The stranger deserves to be thanked
   for being willing to help us, but on no
     account
   must we let the army be stirred up against
     him.
   It would not help us, and he might come
     to harm.
   Now mother, listen to the conclusion
   that I have reached. I have made up my
     mind to die.
   I want to come to it
   with glory, I want to have thrown off
   all weak and base thoughts. Mother,
   look at it with my eyes,
   and see how right I am.
   All the people, all the strength of Greece
   have turned to me. All those ships,
   whether they sail, whether Troy falls,
   depend on me. I will be the one
   to protect our women, in the future,
   if ever the barbarians dare to come near.
   When they have paid for the ruin
   of Helen, whom Paris carried away,
   they will never again be so bold as to
     ravish
   well-born wives out of Greece.
   All these good things I can win by dying.

Because of me, Greece
will be free, and my name will be blessed
    there.
I must not cling to life too dearly.
You brought me into the world for the
    sake
of everyone in my country,
and not just for your own.
Thousands of men have slung shield on
    shoulder, thousands
have taken hold of the oars
when they saw their country wronged.
And each of them will strike and, if need
    be, die
for Greece. And shall my one life
stand in the way of it all?
What justice would there be in that? What
    answer
could I make to those who are ready to
    die?
There is another thing. It would not
be right for this man
to join battle with the whole of the army
and die for the sake of a woman.
If it means that one man can see the
    sunlight
what are the lives of thousands of women
in the balance? And if Artemis
demands the offering of my body,
I am a mortal: who am I
to oppose the goddess? It is not to be
considered. I give my life to Greece.
Take me, kill me,
and bring down Troy. That will be my
    monument
for ages to come. That will be my
    wedding,
my children, the meaning of my life.
Mother, it is the Greeks
who must rule the barbarians,
not the barbarians the Greeks.
They are born to be slaves; we
to be free.
CHORUS: Young woman, what you have said
    is noble.
It is the role of destiny, in this,
and the role of the goddess,
that are sick.
ACHILLES: Daughter of Agamemnon, if I
    could win you

for my wife, it would prove that some god
wanted to make me happy. I envy
Greece because you are hers, and you
because she is yours. What you have said
is beautiful, and worthy
of your country. You are no match
for the gods, and you have given up
the struggle against them. You have
    reconciled
what should be with what must be.
But as for me, the more clearly I see your
    spirit
the more I long to have
so noble a woman for my bride. Look. I
    want
to save you. To take you home with me.
I call Thetis my mother to witness: now
    more
than anything it would grieve me
not to pit myself against all the Danaans
and save you.
Think. Death is awesome. Something
    terrible.
IPHIGENEIA: I say what I am about to say
with no regard for anyone.
Tyndareos' daughter,
Helen, will bring on enough fighting,
    enough
death, for the sake of her body. As for you,
    stranger,
do not die for me,
and do not kill.
Let me save Greece if that is what I can
    do.
ACHILLES: Oh noble spirit! After that
what is there for me to say? You have
    chosen.
A splendor in your soul has led you—
why should a man not say it?
But later you may think differently. I
    want you
to know how I keep my word. I will have
    these arms
lying by the altar, ready
not to join in your death but to prevent it.
Even when the knife is almost at your
    neck
it will not be too late to accept my offer.
Turn, and I will not let you die
because of a moment's recklessness.

I will go now to the goddess's temple, with
these arms,
and wait there until you come.

(ACHILLES *goes off, left, followed by his armor-
bearers.*)

IPHIGENEIA: You are silent. But the tears
keep falling.
Mother, why these tears for me?
CLYTEMNESTRA: I have reason enough,
with this ache in my heart.
IPHIGENEIA: No more of that. Do not take
my own courage from me.
Will you do one thing for me?
CLYTEMNESTRA: Speak. How could I fail
you in anything, child?
IPHIGENEIA: Do not cut off a lock of your
hair
as is done for the dead.
Put on no mourning for me.
CLYTEMNESTRA: What do you mean,
child? I am losing you . . .
IPHIGENEIA: No. I am saved. My name will
be your glory.
CLYTEMNESTRA: I don't understand. I am
not to mourn for you?
IPHIGENEIA: No. I shall have no grave.
CLYTEMNESTRA: What of that? It is not
the grave we mourn,
but the dead.
IPHIGENEIA: The altar of the goddess, the
daughter of Zeus,
will be my grave. Tears are forbidden
there.
CLYTEMNESTRA: My daughter, what you
say is true.
I will obey you.
IPHIGENEIA: For I am blessed by fortune. It
was I
who could bring help to Greece.
CLYTEMNESTRA: And what shall I say to
your sisters?
IPHIGENEIA: Do not dress them in
mourning either.
CLYTEMNESTRA: Have you some message
of love to send them?
IPHIGENEIA: Say good-bye to them for me.
And bring up
Orestes to be a man
for my sake.

CLYTEMNESTRA: (*Holding* ORESTES *up to*
IPHIGENEIA) Put your arms around him
since you are looking at him for the last
time.
IPHIGENEIA: (*Hugging him*) Dear child, you
did what you could for those you love.
CLYTEMNESTRA: Is there something I can
do in Argos,
something that would give you pleasure?
IPHIGENEIA: Don't hate my father. He is
your husband.
CLYTEMNESTRA: He will not like the
course he must face because of you.
IPHIGENEIA: He destroyed me for the sake
of Greece
against his will.
CLYTEMNESTRA: But he used lies,
low schemes unworthy of Atreus.
IPHIGENEIA: Who will lead me to the place
so that they don't need to touch my hair?
CLYTEMNESTRA: I will go with you . . .
IPHIGENEIA: (*Interrupting*) No. That would
not be right.
CLYTEMNESTRA: . . . holding on to your
gown.
IPHIGENEIA: Mother, listen to me. It is
better for both of us
if you stay here. One of my father's
servants here can lead me to the meadow
where I am to be killed.

(*An attendant comes forward and takes*
IPHIGENEIA'S *hand.*)

CLYTEMNESTRA: My child, you are
going . . .
IPHIGENEIA: And I shall never come back.
CLYTEMNESTRA: Leaving your mother.
IPHIGENEIA: As you see. Not because I
deserve it.
CLYTEMNESTRA: Wait. Do not leave
me . . .
IPHIGENEIA: Now there must be no tears.
And you, young women,
join in my hymn to Artemis the virgin,
and celebrate my fate.
Let silence
descend on the army of the Argives.
Let the basket be brought,
light the fire of purification,
bring the barley. Father

must lead the procession around the altar.
I am coming bringing salvation for Greece,
and victory. Lead me.
(The attendant begins to lead IPHIGENEIA
offstage left while she sings her
triumphant lament.)
I who will conquer Troy
and bring down the city of Ilion.
Set the wreath on my head.
Bring the purifying waters.
Around the temple of Artemis, around
the altar of blessed Artemis,
in honor of the goddess begin
the dance. I will wash away
with my own blood the spell
that the oracle revealed.
CHORUS: Oh noble and revered mother,
we may not shed our tears for you.
The gods are not worshipped that way.
IPHIGENEIA: Young women, sing with me
now
glory to Artemis the goddess
whose temple faces Chalkis
where the ships wait, and
the passion for war is burning,
here in the narrows of Aulis,
because of me. Oh Pelasgia where I was
born,
Mycenae,
home!
CHORUS: Are you invoking the city of
Perseus
which the Cyclopes built?
IPHIGENEIA: You brought me up
to the light of Greece.
Dying, I can say it.
CHORUS: Your glory will not die.
IPHIGENEIA: Oh light that brings the day,
splendor
of Zeus, I am going
from this world to another destiny,
another home. Good-bye
light that I love.

(She goes out left, singing. CLYTEMNESTRA *carries*
ORESTES *inside the left door of the tent.)*

CHORUS: See, she is going. She who will
conquer
Troy and bring down the city of Ilion.

She leans her head for the victim's
garland,
for the sacred water. She goes
to drench with her blood the altar
of the divine goddess,
to the sword that will cut
her lovely throat. Your father is waiting
with the pure libations, and the Achaians
are waiting to sail to Troy.
But let us raise our voices to Artemis,
daughter
of Zeus, to ask
for a happy destiny. Awesome goddess,
pleased by this human sacrifice, send now
to Phrygia, to the land of deceitful Troy,
the armies of Greece.
There let Agamemnon
wreathe the Achaian weapons with
garlands
of victory, and himself win
a crown of unfading glory.
MESSENGER: *(Enters left and calls at the*
left door) Daughter of Tyndareos,
Clytemnestra,
come out and hear my message.
CLYTEMNESTRA: *(Enters, carrying* ORESTES*)*
I heard your voice. Here I am,
distraught, shaking with terror,
for fear that you have brought some new
disaster
to add to the grief I have.
MESSENGER: It is about your daughter. I
have
something miraculous to tell.
CLYTEMNESTRA: Tell me, tell me at once.
MESSENGER: Beloved mistress, you shall
hear everything
as it happened, from the beginning,
unless the seething of my mind
confuses my words. When we had come to
the grove
sacred to the daughter of Zeus,
and the flowered meadow of Artemis,
leading your child
to the place where the army
was ordered to assemble,
the Argives ran, all crowding to the spot.
and King Agamemnon, when he saw his
daughter

coming through the grove to the place of
     sacrifice,
groaned aloud and turned his head, hiding
his eyes and their tears with his robe.
But she came up to her father and said,
     "Father,
here I am. And I give my body
willingly as a sacrifice
for my country, for all of Greece.
Lead me to the altar
if this is what destiny has decreed.
For my part, I hope
it turns out well for all of you.
May the spoils of victory be yours,
and then the sight of your homes again.
Let none of the Argives lay hands on me.
I will offer my neck in silence,
I will not flinch." That is what she said,
and everyone who heard marvelled
at the girl's bravery and nobility.
Then the herald Talthybios, whose office
     it was,
called out from among them, to the army,
for the sacred silence,
and the prophet Kalchas drew from its
     sheath
the whetted knife, and laid it
in the basket worked with gold,
and set the crown upon her head. And
     Peleus' son
took the basket and the lustral water
and circled the altar, calling out,
"Daughter of Zeus, who bring death
to the wild creatures, who turn
your gleaming star through the darkness,
     accept
this sacrifice offered to you by us, the
     army
of the Achaians, and King Agamemnon,
this pure blood
from the throat of a beautiful girl. Now let
     our
war fleet embark on a smooth voyage
and our weapons bring down the walls of
     Troy."
Then the sons of Atreus and the whole
     army stood
with their eyes fixed on the ground, and
     the priest

took up the knife,
praying, and looked for the place
to plunge it. Pain welled up in me
at that, and I dropped my eyes.
And the miracle happened. Everyone
distinctly heard the sound of the knife
striking, but no one could see
the girl. She had vanished.
The priest cried out, and the whole army
echoed him, seeing
what some god had sent, a thing,
nobody could have prophesied. There it
     was,
we could see it, but we could scarcely
believe it: a deer
lay there gasping, a large
beautiful animal, and its blood ran
streaming over the altar of the goddess.
Then Kalchas, with
such joy as you can imagine, shouted,
     "Commanders
of the assembled armies of Greece, look:
the goddess has placed this victim
on her altar, a deer from the mountains,
and she accepts this instead of the girl,
rather than stain her altar with noble
     blood.
With this she is happy, and now she
     blesses
our voyage to attack Ilion.
Therefore let everyone who is to sail
take heart and go down to his ship,
for today we must leave the hollow gulf of
     Aulis,
and cross the Aegean Sea."
Then when Hephaistos' flame had left
     nothing
of the victim but ashes, he offered
the customary prayer for the army's safe
     return.
Agamemnon sent me to say this,
to tell you of this
destiny which the gods have sent
and of the glory which he has won
among the Greeks. I saw it myself. I was
     there.
It is plain that your daughter
has been taken up into heaven.
Let this quiet your grief

and put an end to your anger against your
husband.
No man living can tell what the gods will
do,
but they save those whom they love.
This same day has seen
your daughter dead and brought to life
again.

CHORUS: With what joy for your sake
I hear the messenger's words! Showing
how the girl is alive in heaven with the
gods.

CLYTEMNESTRA: Oh child, what deity has
carried you off?
How may I address you? How can I be sure,
how can I know,
that this is not a lie, made up
to silence my bitter grieving?

CHORUS: Here comes King Agamemnon. He
will tell you
the same thing.

(AGAMEMNON *enters left, attended by generals,
priests with the paraphernalia of sacrifice, soldiers,*
*camp-followers, sailors, and others taking part in
the expedition to Troy.*)

AGAMEMNON: Lady, as for your daughter,
we have reason to be happy. For truly
she has the gods for company.
Now you must take this young calf here
(*Indicates* ORESTES)
and travel home. The army is preparing to
sail.
Good-bye. My greetings will be slow
in reaching you from Troy. May you be
happy.

CHORUS: Son of Atreus, sail
with a light heart to the land of Phrygia,
and return with a light heart
and heavy spoils
from Troy.

(AGAMEMNON, *generals, etc., go off left, followed
by the* CHORUS. CLYTEMNESTRA, *carrying* ORESTES,
*goes in the main door of the tent. She does not
look back.*)

Although the translators of *Iphigeneia at Aulis* have not labeled its divisions,
the play follows the organizational pattern typical of Greek tragedy: prologue,
parados, episodes, choral odes, and exodos. The plot of *Iphigeneia* is among the
most complex and suspenseful of surviving Greek tragedies, filled as it is with
reversals that create and destroy hopes that Iphigeneia will be saved from sacrifice. However interesting the plot, it is to the characters—their motives, ration-
alizations, and self-deceptions—that we must look if we are to appreciate the play
fully. The characters are unreliable witnesses, and what they say cannot be
accepted at face value. We must continually be on the lookout, therefore, for half-
truths, contradictions, and unconscious revelations.

All of the major characters are linked through self-centered concerns for
honor and glory. Agamemnon may lament his burdens as leader of the Greek
army, but Menelaos reveals that Agamemnon has actively campaigned for the
post and, when the ships could not sail, was so concerned about losing his position
that he eagerly accepted the sacrifice of Iphigeneia as the price for continuing in
power. In his turn, Menelaos argues the necessity of restoring the honor of Greece
by destroying Troy, but Agamemnon accuses him of being motivated almost
solely by passion for Helen. And, although Achilles swears he will never permit
Iphigeneia to be sacrificed because his honor was compromised when his name

was used in summoning Iphigeneia to Aulis, he then admits he would willingly have gone along with the deception if only he had been asked.

Euripides extends this picture of self-serving reasoning to almost all Greeks. The Greek army has been assembled because of an oath extracted by Tyndareos from those princes who had sought to marry Helen: that they would join together to punish anyone who should take her from her husband. Once the suitors had sworn, Tyndareos had allowed Helen to make her own choice of husband, Menelaos. But Helen then fell in love with the Trojan prince, Paris, and willingly ran away with him. Although through this action Helen has made herself despicable to most Greeks, they have agreed, in the name of honor, to launch a major war to rescue her. Nevertheless, when the play begins the army is less than enthusiastic about the war and has on several occasions demanded to be sent home. It is only after it is told of Artemis's promise that it will take and sack Troy if Iphigeneia is sacrificed that the Greek Army shows any real concern for honor. They then consider Iphigeneia's sacrifice so necessary that they threaten to kill their own leaders if the sacrifice does not take place.

On the surface, Iphigeneia seems the only unselfish character because she eventually decides to die for Greece. But her unselfish decision is clouded by her jingoistic rhetoric through which she comes to see herself as a glorious heroine destined to save Greece and its honor. When she announces her decision, Agamemnon and Achilles, who supposedly have been seeking to save her, are overjoyed and actively participate in her sacrifice. They appear to see no moral barrier to sacrifice if the victim consents, and they eagerly accept a solution that will permit them to pursue their own glory by destroying Troy. Even the gods' seal of approval appears to be placed on the decision when Artemis, at the moment of sacrifice, supposedly snatches Iphigeneia away and substitutes a deer. What has actually happened remains quite unclear.

At the end of the play the Chorus sings "sail/with a light heart to the land of Phrygia,/and return with a light heart/and heavy spoils/from Troy." This passage is characteristic of the play as a whole, for it both indicates how unperceptive the characters are and how ironic words can be. A Greek audience would have been thoroughly familiar with the myths connected with the Trojan War. They would have known that this war, which the Greeks seem so eager to wage, would drag on for eleven years; that during it Achilles would be killed; that by defiling Troy's temples the Greeks would bring down disastrous retribution on themselves; that when Agamemnon returned home from the war he would be murdered by Clytemnestra giving as her reason the sacrifice of Iphigeneia; that Odysseus, who plays an important offstage role in getting the army to demand Iphigeneia's sacrifice, would on his way home from Troy wander the seas for years and lose all his ships and men. The choral farewell, then, though blithely optimistic about the future would have carried other, less pleasant, import for a Greek audience.

Athenians in Euripides' own time were often confused or angered by his treatment of the myths because, by delving into the moral implications of actions, he demythologized those figures traditionally considered the greatest of Greek heroes. In *Iphigeneia at Aulis* Euripides demonstrates his view of men who would sacrifice a young girl so they might wage war over a runaway wife. Also, because of his treatment of the gods, he was accused of blasphemy, for he approached the gods much as he did the heroes—emphasizing the gods' pettinesses, jealousies, infidelities, and revenges as depicted in the received myths. He seems to ask what kind of supernatural beings would act as they do. Euripides did not reject the gods so much as question the adequacy of the traditional picture of them. In *Iphigeneia*, Artemis appears more barbarous than the human beings—*if* she actually has demanded the sacrifice of Iphigeneia. Kalchas's statements are the only evidence that Artemis has made such a demand, and ultimately Artemis apparently rescues Iphigeneia. Does this mean that Artemis changed her mind? that it was not she who made the demand? that she has tested the Greeks to see how far they are willing to go in their desire to pursue war? The answer is uncertain. The play contains several passages casting doubt on the trustworthiness of Kalchas and all oracles; at the end of the play, Clytemnestra even questions whether the report of Iphigeneia's rescue may not be another of Agamemnon's deceptions.

In *Iphigeneia*, Euripides' ultimate concern is war. The play was written against the background of the Peloponnesian War, which had by then been going on for some twenty-five years. As in Euripides' play, there had been many opportunities to stop the war, but the participants had always found excuses for renewing it. And, just as the Greek army is roused to fight by the prophecy that they will win if Iphigeneia is sacrificed, the Peloponnesian War had been kept going in part by ambiguous oracles. In both Athens and Sparta, honor was invoked as a major issue. Like many leaders in Euripides' time, Agamemnon depicts himself as the slave of public opinion. Thus, instead of showing himself to be a leader, Agamemnon becomes in actuality a follower of the mob. Agamemnon also does in actuality what the Greeks of Euripides' day were doing less directly: sacrificing their children to a questionable cause. Furthermore, in the character of Iphigeneia, Euripides depicts youth as acquiescing in its own sacrifice and as being indoctrinated to see itself as savior of the people.

Several critics have argued that *Iphigeneia* is not a tragedy but a tragicomedy. (One critic even calls it a "melodramatic heroic comedy" because of its suspenseful story about threatened innocence and its happy outcome based on a heroic act.) Certainly it differs in many respects from tragedy as embodied in Sophocles' *Antigone*, but it is not for that reason any the less serious. Sophocles wrote tragedies concerning individual moral choices based on faith in higher principles, such as the good of the state or reverence for divine law. Euripides also wrote tragedies concerning individual moral choices, but rather than basing them on faith in higher principles he showed characters following their own desires and then offering excuses or voicing high sounding motives to justify their choices. Sophocles is reported to have said that he showed human beings as they should be, whereas Euripides showed them as they are.

In *Iphigeneia at Aulis*, Euripides raises serious questions about human motivations and about the human tendency to rationalize behavior. He also stimulates thought about the relationship of war to the concept of honor and about the tendency to glorify war and self-sacrifice. The play also implies questions about what kinds of situations, if any, justify war. Euripides seems to suggest that the issues in *Iphigeneia at Aulis* are petty excuses, but he does not deal with the question as to whether there are limits beyond which a nation cannot be pushed without retaliating and how we can define those limits. Issues similar to those treated by Euripides face us as individuals in our daily lives, for war among nations is like violence among individuals. We cannot escape concern for war and violence. Euripides' play does not provide answers as to how we can deal with these concerns so much as it stimulates us to think about problems we cannot avoid and must face. He leaves little doubt, however, implicit as it is throughout *Iphigeneia at Aulis*, that the answer does not lie in deceiving either oneself or others.

Lysistrata

by Aristophanes / Translated by Charles T. Murphy

Comedy developed later than tragedy, but throughout most of the fifth century B.C. it was a regular feature at the City Dionysia, where each of five dramatists presented one play. After 442, a second Dionysian festival, the *Lenaia*, began to include plays and to emphasize comedy. As at the City Dionysia, one comedy by each of five writers was presented at the Lenaia each year and the best was awarded a prize.

Comedy was produced in the same theatre as tragedy. Consequently, performance conditions were similar. Nevertheless, some conventions differed. The chorus of comedy had 24 members. Unlike tragedy, in which the members were all of the same sex, age, and appearance, in comedy the chorus might include both male and female characters (as in *Lysistrata*) or be quite varied in appearance (as in the *Birds* where the chorus represents several species of birds), or be quite fanciful (as is the chorus of *Clouds*). The comic chorus also indulged in more athletic and varied movement than tragic choruses did. As in tragedy, all performers were male and wore masks.

Aristotle states that comedy evolved out of phallic ceremonies. Certainly the comedy of Greece, more so than its tragedy, was obviously allied to Dionysian worship with its emphasis on fertility and its association with human sexuality and especially the male sexual organ *(phallus)*. In comedy, the male characters usually wore a visible phallus of exaggerated size, and the dialogue included numerous explicit sexual references. When female characters appeared, there was much talk about their sexual attributes and they, even more than the male characters, seemed preoccupied with sexual matters. Although the ultimate concerns in the plays might be serious, the argument for any line of action almost always promised more sex, food, and drink, and the characters almost always found this argument persuasive. Unlike tragedy, comedy used invented stories, borrowing only rarely from received myths.

All of the surviving comedies from the fifth century are by a single author, Aristophanes (c.448–c.380). He probably wrote about 40 plays, but only eleven survive: *Acharnians* (425), *Knights* (424), *Clouds* (423), *Wasps* (422), *Peace* (421), *Birds* (414), *Lysistrata* (411), *Thesmophoriazusae* (411), *Frogs* (405), *Ecclesiazusae* (392), and *Plutus* (388). Probably the most noteworthy characteristic of Aristophanic comedy is its commentary on contemporary society, politics, literature, war, or persons. The plays are organized around a ruling theme embodied in a happy idea (as in *Lysistrata* where the women decide to use a sex strike to end war). The parallels between the play's events, no matter how fantastic, and those of Athenian life are abundantly clear and the exaggerations only serve to point up the absurdity of their real-life counterparts. Other typical features include some of the most beautiful lyrics and some of the most obscene passages in Greek literature.

The basic structural pattern of Aristophanic comedy is simple. A happy idea is introduced, debated, and eventually adopted. The results are shown in a series of loosely connected episodes separated by choral odes. The play concludes with a reconciliation and an exit to feasting and revelry. Near the middle there usually is a *parabasis* (a choral ode in which the fictional framework is abandoned and the audience is addressed directly on some social or political problem, or alternatively on the author's worthiness or the need for the audience's support).

Of all Greek comedies, the best known is *Lysistrata*, probably because its basic premise is the most easily understood.

CHARACTERS

LYSISTRATA *an Athenian woman*
CALONICE *an Athenian woman*
MYRRHINE *an Athenian woman*
LAMPITO *a Spartan woman*
LEADER OF CHORUS OF OLD MEN
CHORUS OF OLD MEN
LEADER OF CHORUS OF OLD WOMEN
CHORUS OF OLD WOMEN
ATHENIAN MAGISTRATE

THREE ATHENIAN WOMEN
CINESIAS *an Athenian, husband of Myrrhine*
SPARTAN HERALD
SPARTAN AMBASSADORS
ATHENIAN AMBASSADORS
TWO ATHENIAN CITIZENS
CHORUS OF ATHENIANS
CHORUS OF SPARTANS

SCENE

In Athens, beneath the Acropolis. In the center of the stage is the propylaea, or gateway to the Acropolis; to one side is a small grotto, sacred to Pan. The orchestra represents a slope leading up to the gate-way. It is early in the morning. LYSISTRATA *is pacing impatiently up and down.*

LYSISTRATA: If they'd been summoned to worship the God of Wine, or Pan, or to visit the Queen of Love, why, you couldn't have pushed your way through the streets for all the timbrels. But now there's not a single woman here—except my neighbour; here she comes.

(Enter CALONICE*)*

Good day to you, Calonice.
CALONICE: And to you, Lysistrata. *(Noticing* LYSISTRATA'S *impatient air.)* But what ails you? Don't scowl, my dear; it's not becoming to you to knit your brows like that.

LYSISTRATA: *(Sadly)* Ah, Calonice, my heart aches; I'm so annoyed at us women. For among men we have a reputation for sly trickery—
CALONICE: And rightly too, on my word!
LYSISTRATA: —but when they were told to meet here to consider a matter of no small importance, they lie abed and don't come.

CALONICE: Oh, they'll come all right, my dear. It's not easy for a woman to get out, you know. One is working on her husband, another is getting up the maid, another has to put the baby to bed, or wash and feed it.

LYSISTRATA: But after all, there are other matters more important than all that.

CALONICE: My dear Lysistrata, just what is this matter you've summoned us women to consider! What's up? Something big?

LYSISTRATA: Very big.

CALONICE: (Interested) Is it stout, too?

LYSISTRATA: (Smiling) Yes indeed—both big and stout.

CALONICE: What? And the women still haven't come?

LYSISTRATA: It's not what you suppose; they'd have come soon enough for *that*. But I've worked up something, and for many a sleepless night I've turned it this way and that.

CALONICE: (In mock disappointment) Oh, I guess it's pretty fine and slender, if you've turned it this way and that.

LYSISTRATA: So fine that the safety of the whole of Greece lies in us women.

CALONICE: In us women? It depends on a very slender reed then.

LYSISTRATA: Our country's fortunes are in our hands; and whether the Spartans shall perish—

CALONICE: Good! Let them perish, by all means.

LYSISTRATA: —and the Boeotians shall be completely annihilated.

CALONICE: Not completely! Please spare the eels.[1]

LYSISTRATA: As for Athens, I won't use any such unpleasant words. But you understand what I mean. But if the women will meet here—the Spartans, the Boeotians, and we Athenians—then all together we will save Greece.

CALONICE: But what could women do that's clever or distinguished? We just sit around all dolled up in silk robes, looking pretty in our sheer gowns and evening slippers.

LYSISTRATA: These are just the things I hope will save us; these silk robes, perfumes, evening slippers, rouge, and our chiffon blouses.

CALONICE: How so?

LYSISTRATA: So never a man alive will lift a spear against the foe—

CALONICE: I'll get a silk gown at once.

LYSISTRATA: —or take up his shield—

CALONICE: I'll put on my sheerest gown!

LYSISTRATA: or sword.

CALONICE: I'll buy a pair of evening slippers.

LYSISTRATA: Well then, shouldn't the women have come?

CALONICE: Come? Why, they should have *flown* here.

LYSISTRATA: Well, my dear, just watch: they'll act in true Athenian fashion—everything too late! And now there's not a woman here from the shore or from Salamis.

CALONICE: They're coming, I'm sure; at daybreak they were laying—to their oars to cross the straits.

LYSISTRATA: And those I expected would be the first to come—the women of Acharnae—they haven't arrived.

CALONICE: Yet the wife of Theagenes means to come; she consulted Hecate about it. (Seeing a group of women approaching.) But look! Here come a few. And there are some more over here. Hurrah! Where do they come from?

LYSISTRATA: From Anagyra.

CALONICE: Yes indeed! We've raised up quite a stink from Anagyra anyway.[2]

(Enter MYRRHINE *in haste, followed by several other women.*)

MYRRHINE: (Breathlessly) Have we come in time, Lysistrata? What do you say? Why so quiet?

LYSISTRATA: I can't say much for you, Myrrhine, coming at this hour on such important business.

MYRRHINE: Why, I had trouble finding my girdle in the dark. But if it's so important, we're here now; tell us.

LYSISTRATA: No. Let's wait a little for the women from Boeotia and the Peloponnesus.

MYRRHINE: That's a much better suggestion. Look! Here comes Lampito now.

(Enter LAMPITO *with two other women.*)

LYSISTRATA: Greetings, my dear Spartan

---

[1]Boeotia was noted for seafood, especially eels.

[2]A pun based on Anagyra's name, which was taken from a foul-smelling plant.

friend. How pretty you look, my dear. What a smooth complexion and well-developed figure! You could throttle an ox.

LAMPITO: Faith, yes, I think I could. I take exercises and kick my heels against my bum.

(She demonstrates with a few steps of the Spartan "bottom-kicking" dance.)

LYSISTRATA: And what splendid breasts you have.

LAMPITO: La! You handle me like a prize steer.

LYSISTRATA: And who is this young lady with you?

LAMPITO: Faith, she's an Ambassadress from Boeotia.

LYSISTRATA: Oh yes, a Boeotian, and blooming like a garden too.

CALONICE: *(Lifting up her skirt)* My word! How neatly her garden's weeded![3]

LYSISTRATA: And who is the other girl?

LAMPITO: Oh, she's a Corinthian swell.

MYRRHINE: *(After a rapid examination)* Yes indeed. She swells very nicely *(Pointing)* here and here.

LAMPITO: Who has gathered together this company of women?

LYSISTRATA: I have.

LAMPITO: Speak up, then. What do you want?

MYRRHINE: Yes, my dear, tell us what this important matter is.

LYSISTRATA: Very well, I'll tell you. But before I speak, let me ask you a little question.

MYRRHINE: Anything you like.

LYSISTRATA: *(Earnestly)* Tell me: don't you yearn for the fathers of your children, who are away at the wars? I know you all have husbands abroad.

CALONICE: Why, yes; mercy me! my husband's been away for five months in Thrace keeping guard on — Eucrates.[4]

MYRRHINE: And mine for seven whole months in Pylus.

LAMPITO: And mine, as soon as ever he returns from the fray, readjusts his shield and flies out of the house again.

LYSISTRATA: And as for lovers, there's not even a ghost of one left. Since the Milesians revolted from us, I've not even seen an eight-inch dingus to be a leather consolation for us widows. Are you willing, if I can find a way, to help me end the war?

MYRRHINE: Goodness, yes! I'd do it, even if I had to pawn my dress and — get drunk on the spot!

CALONICE: And I, even if I had to let myself be split in two like a flounder.

LAMPITO: I'd climb up Mt. Taygetus if I could catch a glimpse of peace.[5]

LYSISTRATA: I'll tell you, then, in plain and simple words. My friends, if we are going to force our men to make peace, we must do without—

MYRRHINE: Without what? Tell us.

LYSISTRATA: Will you do it?

MYRRHINE: We'll do it, if it kills us.

LYSISTRATA: Well then, we must do without sex altogether. *(General consternation)* Why do you turn away? Where go you? Why turn so pale? Why those tears? Will you do it or not? What means this hesitation?

MYRRHINE: I won't do it! Let the war go on.

CALONICE: Nor I! Let the war go on.

LYSISTRATA: So, my little flounder? Didn't you say just now you'd split yourself in half?

CALONICE: Anything else you like. I'm willing, even if I have to walk through fire. Anything rather than sex. There's nothing like it, my dear.

LYSISTRATA: *(To* MYRRHINE*)* What about you?

MYRRHINE: *(Sullenly)* I'm willing to walk through fire, too.

LYSISTRATA: Oh vile and cursed breed! No wonder they make tragedies about us: we're naught but "love-affairs and bassinets." But you, my dear Spartan friend, if you alone are with me, our enterprise might yet succeed. Will you vote with me?

LAMPITO: 'Tis cruel hard, by my faith, for a woman to sleep alone without her nooky; but for all that, we certainly do need peace.

LYSISTRATA: O my dearest friend! You're the only real woman here.

CALONICE: *(Wavering)* Well, if we do refrain from — *(Shuddering)* what you say (God forbid!), would that bring peace?

LYSISTRATA: My goodness, yes! If we sit at home all rouged and powdered, dressed in our sheerest gowns, and neatly depilated, our men will

---

[3]Her pubic hair has been removed.
[4]Athenian general reputed to be corrupt.

[5]Mt. Taygetus was a mountain near Sparta.

get excited and want to take us; but if you don't come to them and keep away, they'll soon make a truce.

LAMPITO: Aye; Menelaus caught sight of Helen's naked breast and dropped his sword, they say.

CALONICE: What if the men give us up?

LYSISTRATA: "Flay a skinned dog," as Pherecrates says.[6]

CALONICE: Rubbish! These make-shifts are not good. But suppose they grab us and drag us into the bedroom?

LYSISTRATA: Hold on to the door.

CALONICE: And if they beat us?

LYSISTRATA: Give in with a bad grace. There's no pleasure in it for them when they have to use violence. And you must torment them in every possible way. They'll give up soon enough; a man gets no joy if he doesn't get along with his wife.

MYRRHINE: If this is your opinion, we agree.

LAMPITO: As for our men, we can persuade them to make a just and fair peace; but what about the Athenian rabble? Who will persuade them not to start any more monkey-shines?

LYSISTRATA: Don't worry. We guarantee to convince them.

LAMPITO: Not while their ships are rigged so well and they have that mighty treasure in the temple of Athene.

LYSISTRATA: We've taken good care for that too: we shall seize the Acropolis today. The older women have orders to do this, and while we are making our arrangements, they are to pretend to make a sacrifice and occupy the Acropolis.

LAMPITO: All will be well then. That's a very fine idea.

LYSISTRATA: Let's ratify this, Lampito, with the most solemn oath.

LAMPITO: Tell us what oath we shall swear.

LYSISTRATA: Well said. Where's our Policewoman? (To a Scythian slave) What are you gaping at? Set a shield upside-down here in front of me, and give me the sacred meats.

CALONICE: Lysistrata, what sort of an oath are we to take?

LYSISTRATA: What oath? I'm going to slaughter a sheep over the shield, as they do in Aeschylus.[7]

CALONICE: Don't, Lysistrata! No oaths about peace over a shield.

LYSISTRATA: What shall the oath be, then?

CALONICE: How about getting a white horse somewhere and cutting out its entrails for the sacrifice?

LYSISTRATA: White horse indeed!

CALONICE: Well then, how shall we swear?

MYRRHINE: I'll tell you: let's place a large black bowl upside-down and then slaughter—a flask of Thasian wine. And then let's swear—not to pour in a single drop of water.

LAMPITO: Lord! How I like that oath!

LYSISTRATA: Someone bring out a bowl and a flask.

(A slave brings the utensils for the sacrifice.)

CALONICE: Look, my friends! What a big jar! Here's a cup that 'twould give me joy to handle. (She picks up the bowl.)

LYSISTRATA: Set it down and put your hands on our victim. (As CALONICE places her hands on the flask) O Lady of Persuasion and dear Loving Cup, graciously vouchsafe to receive this sacrifice from us women. (She pours the wine into the bowl)

CALONICE: The blood has a good colour and spurts out nicely.

LAMPITO: Faith, it has a pleasant smell, too.

MYRRHINE: Oh, let me be the first to swear, ladies!

CALONICE: No, by our Lady! Not unless you're allotted the first turn.

LYSISTRATA: Place all your hands on the cup, and one of you repeat on behalf of all what I say. Then all will swear and ratify the oath. *I will suffer no man, be he husband or lover,*

CALONICE: *I will suffer no man, be he husband or lover,*

LYSISTRATA: *To approach me all hot and horny.* (As CALONICE hesitates) Say it!

CALONICE: (Slowly and painfully) *To approach me all hot and horny.* O Lysistrata, I feel so weak in the knees!

LYSISTRATA: *I will remain at home unmated,*

---

[6]Meaning uncertain, but usually taken to mean, "We'll have to take care of ourselves."

[7]Reference to a scene in *Seven Against Thebes.*

CALONICE: *I will remain at home unmated,*

LYSISTRATA: *Wearing my sheerest gown and carefully adorned,*

CALONICE: *Wearing my sheerest gown and carefully adorned,*

LYSISTRATA: *That my husband may burn with desire for me,*

CALONICE: *That my husband may burn with desire for me,*

LYSISTRATA: *And if he takes me by force against my will,*

CALONICE: *And if he takes me by force against my will,*

LYSISTRATA: *I shall do it badly and keep from moving.*

CALONICE: *I shall do it badly and keep from moving.*

LYSISTRATA: *I will not stretch my slippers toward the ceiling,*

CALONICE: *I will not stretch my slippers toward the ceiling,*

LYSISTRATA: *Nor will I take the posture of the lioness on the knife-handle.*[8]

CALONICE: *Nor will I take the posture of the lioness on the knife-handle,*

LYSISTRATA: *If I keep this oath, may I be permitted to drink from this cup,*

CALONICE: *If I keep this oath, may I be permitted to drink from this cup,*

LYSISTRATA: *But if I break it, may the cup be filled with water.*

CALONICE: *But if I break it, may the cup be filled with water.*

LYSISTRATA: Do you all swear to this?

ALL: I do, so help me!

LYSISTRATA: Come then, I'll just consummate this offering.

(She takes a long drink from the cup.)

CALONICE: *(Snatching the cup away)* Shares, my dear! Let's drink to our continued friendship.

(A shout is heard from off-stage.)

LAMPITO: What's that shouting?

LYSISTRATA: That's what I was telling you: the women have just seized the Acropolis. Now, Lampito, go home and arrange matters in Sparta;

[8]Crouching on all fours.

and leave these two ladies here as hostages. We'll enter the Acropolis to join our friends and help them lock the gates.

CALONICE: Don't you suppose the men will come to attack us?

LYSISTRATA: Don't worry about them. Neither threats nor fire will suffice to open the gates, except on the terms we've stated.

CALONICE: I should say not! Else we'd belie our reputation as unmanageable pests.

(LAMPITO leaves the stage. The other women retire and enter the Acropolis through the Propylaea. Enter the CHORUS OF OLD MEN, carrying fire-pots and a load of heavy sticks.)

LEADER OF MEN: Onward, Draces, step by step,
　　though your shoulder's aching.
　　Cursed logs of olive-wood, what a load you're
　　making!

FIRST SEMI-CHORUS OF OLD MEN:
　　(Singing)

Aye, many surprises await a man who lives to a ripe old age;
For who could suppose, Strymodorus my lad, that the women we've nourished (alas!),
Who sat at home to vex our days,
Would seize the holy image here,
And occupy this sacred shrine,
With bolts and bars, with fell design,
To lock the Propylaea?

LEADER OF MEN: Come with speed, Philourgus, come! to the temple hast'ning.
　　There we'll heap these logs about in a circle round them,
　　And whoever has conspired, raising this rebellion,
　　Shall be roasted, scorched, and burnt, all without exception,
　　Doomed by one unanimous vote—but first the wife of Lycon.[9]

SECOND SEMI-CHORUS: *(Singing)*
No, no! by Demeter, while I'm alive, no woman shall mock at me.

[9]Athenian woman noted for her loose morals.

Not even the Spartan Cleomenes, our citadel first
    to seize,
  Got off unscathed; for all his pride
  And haughty Spartan arrogance;
  He left his arms and sneaked away,
  Stripped to his shirt, unkempt, unshav'd,
With six years' filth still on him.
      LEADER OF MEN: I besieged that hero bold,
          sleeping at my station,
        Marshalled at these holy gates sixteen
            deep against him.
        Shall I not these cursed pests punish for
            their daring,
        Burning these Euripides-and-God-detested
            women?
        Aye! or else may Marathon overturn my
            trophy.
      FIRST SEMI-CHORUS: (Singing)
There remains of my road
  Just this brow of the hill;
  There I speed on my way.
Drag the logs up the hill, though we've got no ass
    to help.
(God! my shoulder's bruised and sore!)
  Onward still must we go.
  Blow the fire! Don't let it go out
Now we're near the end of our road.
      ALL: (Blowing on the fire-pots) Whew!
Whew! Drat the smoke!
      SECOND SEMI-CHORUS: (Singing)
Lord, what smoke rushing forth
  From the pot, like a dog
  Running mad, bites my eyes!
This must be Lemnos-fire. What a sharp and
    stinging smoke![10]
  Rushing onward to the shrine
  Aid the gods. Once for all
  Show your mettle, Laches my boy!
  To the rescue hastening all!
      ALL: (Blowing on the fire-pots) Whew!
Whew! Drat the smoke!

*(The CHORUS has now reached the edge of the
Orchestra nearest the stage, in front of the
propylaea. They begin laying their logs and fire-
pots on the ground.)*

[10]Lemnos-fire is a pun based on the similarity of sound
for the name of the Greek island and the Greek word for
sore eyes.

LEADER OF MEN: Thank heaven, this fire is
still alive. Now let's first put down these logs here
and place our torches in the pots to catch; then let's
make a rush for the gates with a battering-ram. If
the women don't unbar the gate at our summons,
we'll have to smoke them out.

Let me put down my load. Ouch! That hurts!
(To the audience) Would any of the generals in
Samos like to lend a hand with this log? *(Throwing
down a log)* Well, *that* won't break my back any
more, at any rate. *(Turning to his fire-pot)* Your job,
my little pot, is to keep those coals alive and furnish
me shortly with a red-hot torch.

O mistress Victory, be my ally and grant me to
rout these audacious women in the Acropolis.

(While the MEN *are busy with their logs and fires,
the* CHORUS OF OLD WOMEN *enters, carrying pitchers
of water.)*

      LEADER OF WOMEN: What's this I see?
          Smoke and flames? Is that a fire
          ablazing?
        Let's rush upon them. Hurry up! They'll
          find us women ready.
      FIRST SEMI-CHORUS OF OLD WOMEN:
          (Singing)
  With wingèd foot onward I fly,
  Ere the flames consume Neodice;
  Lest Critylla be overwhelmed
By a lawless, accurst herd of old men.
I shudder with fear. Am I too late to aid them?
At break of the day filled we our jars with water
Fresh from the spring, pushing our way straight
        through the crowds.
  Oh, what a din!
Mid crockery crashing, jostled by slave-girls,
Sped we to save them, aiding our neighbours,
Bearing this water to put out the flames.
      SECOND SEMI-CHORUS OF OLD WOMEN:
(Singing)
    Such news I've heard; doddering fools
    Come with logs, like furnace-attendants,
    Loaded down with three hundred pounds,
  Breathing many a vain, blustering threat,
  That all these abhorred sluts will be burnt to
        charcoal.
O goddess, I pray never may they be kindled;
Grant them to save Greece and our men, madness
        and war help them to end.

With this as our purpose, golden-plumed
    Maiden,[11]
Guardian of Athens, seized we thy precinct.
Be my ally, Warrior-maiden,
'Gainst these old men, bearing water with me.

(The WOMEN *have now reached their position in the Orchestra, and their* LEADER *advances toward the* LEADER OF THE MEN.*)*

LEADER OF WOMEN: Hold on there! What's this, you utter scoundrels? No decent, God-fearing citizens would act like this.

LEADER OF MEN: Oho! Here's something unexpected: a swarm of women have come out to attack us.

LEADER OF WOMEN: What, do we frighten you? Surely you don't think we're too many for you. And yet there are ten thousand times more of us whom you haven't seen.

LEADER OF MEN: What say, Phaedria? Shall we let these women wag their tongues? Shan't we take our sticks and break them over their backs?

LEADER OF WOMEN: Let's set our pitchers on the ground; then if anyone lays a hand on us, they won't get in our way.

LEADER OF MEN: By God! If someone gave them two or three smacks on the jaw, like Bupalus, they wouldn't talk so much!

LEADER OF WOMEN: Go on, hit me, somebody! Here's my jaw! But no other bitch will bite a piece out of you before me.

LEADER OF MEN: Silence! or I'll knock out your—senility!

LEADER OF WOMEN: Just lay one finger on Stratyllis, I dare you!

LEADER OF MEN: Suppose I dust you off with this fist? What will you do?

LEADER OF WOMEN: I'll tear the living guts out of you with my teeth.

LEADER OF MEN: No poet is more clever than Euripides: "There is no beast so shameless as a woman."

LEADER OF WOMEN: Let's pick up our jars of water, Rhodippe.

LEADER OF MEN: Why have you come here with water, you detestable slut?

LEADER OF WOMEN: And why have you

come with fire, you funeral vault? To cremate yourself?

LEADER OF MEN: To light a fire and singe your friends.

LEADER OF WOMEN: And I've brought water to put out your fire.

LEADER OF MEN: What? You'll put out my fire?

LEADER OF WOMEN: Just try and see!

LEADER OF MEN: I wonder: shall I scorch you with this torch of mine?

LEADER OF WOMEN: If you've got any soap, I'll give you a bath.

LEADER OF MEN: Give *me* a bath, you stinking hag?

LEADER OF WOMEN: Yes—a bridal bath!

LEADER OF MEN: Just listen to her! What crust!

LEADER OF WOMEN: Well, I'm a free citizen.

LEADER OF MEN: I'll put an end to your brawling.

(The MEN *pick up their torches.)*

LEADER OF WOMEN: You'll never do jury-duty again.

(The WOMEN *pick up their pitchers.)*

LEADER OF MEN: Singe her hair for her!

LEADER OF WOMEN: Do your duty, water!

(The WOMEN *empty their pitchers on the* MEN.*)*

LEADER OF MEN: Ow! Ow! For heaven's sake!

LEADER OF WOMEN: Is it too hot?

LEADER OF MEN: What do you mean "hot"? Stop! What are you doing?

LEADER OF WOMEN: I'm watering you, so you'll be fresh and green.

LEADER OF MEN: But I'm all withered up with shaking.

LEADER OF WOMEN: Well, you've got a fire; why don't you dry yourself?

(Enter an ATHENIAN MAGISTRATE, *accompanied by* FOUR SCYTHIAN POLICEMEN.*)*

MAGISTRATE: Have these wanton women flared up again with their timbrels and their continual worship of Sabazius? Is this another Adonisdirge

---

[11]Invocation to Athena, patron goddess of Athens.

upon the roof-tops—which we heard not long ago in the Assembly? That confounded Demonstratus was urging us to sail to Sicily, and the whirling women shouted, "Woe for Adonis!" And then Demonstratus said we'd best enroll the infantry from Zacynthus, and a tipsy woman on the roof shrieked, "Beat your breasts for Adonis!" And that vile and filthy lunatic forced his measure through. Such license do our women take.[12]

LEADER OF MEN: What if you heard of the insolence of these women here? Besides their other violent acts, they threw water all over us, and we have to shake out our clothes just as if we'd leaked in them.

MAGISTRATE: And rightly, too, by God! For we ourselves lead the women astray and teach them to play the wanton; from these roots such notions blossom forth. A man goes into the jeweler's shop and says, "About that necklace you made for my wife, goldsmith: last night, while she was dancing, the fastening-bolt slipped out of the hole. I have to sail over to Salamis today; if you're free, do come around tonight and fit in a new bolt for her." Another goes to the shoemaker, a strapping young fellow with manly parts, and says, "See here, cobbler, the sandal-strap chafes my wife's little—toe; it's so tender. Come around during the siesta and stretch it a little, so she'll be more comfortable." Now we see the results of such treatment: here I'm a special Councillor and need money to procure oars for the galleys; and I'm locked out of the Treasury by these women.

But this is no time to stand around. Bring up crow-bars there! I'll put an end to their insolence. *(To one of the policemen)* What are you gaping at, you wretch! What are you staring at? Got an eye out for a tavern, eh? Set your crow-bars here to the gates and force them open. *(Retiring to a safe distance)* I'll help from over here.

(The gates are thrown open and LYSISTRATA comes out followed by several other WOMEN.)

LYSISTRATA: Don't force the gates; I'm coming out of my own accord. We don't need crow-bars here. What we need is good sound common-sense.

MAGISTRATE: Is that so, you strumpet?

Where's my policeman? Officer, arrest her and tie her arms behind her back.

LYSISTRATA: By Artemis, if he lays a finger on me, he'll pay for it, even if he is a public servant.

(The POLICEMAN retires in terror.)

MAGISTRATE: You there, are you afraid? Seize her round the waist—and you, too. Tie her up, both of you!

FIRST WOMAN: *(As the SECOND POLICEMAN approaches LYSISTRATA)* By Pandrosus, if you but touch her with your hand, I'll kick the stuffings out of you.[13]

(The SECOND POLICEMAN retires in terror.)

MAGISTRATE: Just listen to that: "kick the stuffings out." Where's another policeman? Tie *her* up first, for her chatter.

SECOND WOMAN: By the Goddess of the Light, if you lay the tip of your finger on her, you'll soon need a doctor.[14]

(The THIRD POLICEMAN retires in terror.)

MAGISTRATE: What's this? Where's my policemen? Seize *her* too. I'll soon stop your sallies.

THIRD WOMAN: By the Goddess of Tauros, if you go near her, I'll tear out your hair until it shrieks with pain.[14]

(The FOURTH POLICEMAN retires in terror.)

MAGISTRATE: Oh, damn it all! I've run out of policemen. But women must never defeat us. Officers, let's charge them all together. Close up your ranks!

(The POLICEMEN rally for a mass attack.)

LYSISTRATA: By heaven, you'll soon find out that we have four companies of warrior-women, all fully equipped within!

MAGISTRATE: *(Advancing)* Twist their arms off, men!

LYSISTRATA: *(Shouting)* To the rescue, my valiant women!
O sellers-of-barley-green-stuffs-and-eggs,
O sellers-of-garlic, ye keepers-of-taverns, and vendors-of-bread,

---

[12]This speech refers to incidents related to the disastrous expedition to Sicily. The women's dirge was considered an evil omen.

[13]Pandrosus was goddess of dew.
[14]Goddess of Light and Goddess of Tauros were titles given to Artemis, goddess of the moon and the hunt.

Grapple! Smite! Smash!

Won't you heap filth on them? Give them
a tongue-lashing!

(The WOMEN *beat off the* POLICEMEN.*)*

Halt! Withdraw! No looting on the field.

MAGISTRATE: Damn it! My police-force has
put up a very poor show.

LYSISTRATA: What did you expect? Did you
think you were attacking slaves?

Didn't you know that women are filled
with passion?

MAGISTRATE: Aye, passion enough—for a
good strong drink!

LEADER OF MEN: O chief and leader of this
land, why spend your words in vain?

Don't argue with these shameless beasts.
You know not how we've fared:

A soapless bath they've given us; our
clothes are soundly soaked.

LEADER OF WOMEN: Poor fool! You never
should attack or strike a peaceful girl.

But if you do, your eyes must swell. For I
am quite content

To sit unmoved, like modest maids, in
peace and cause no pain;

But let a man stir up my hive, he'll find
me like a wasp.

CHORUS OF MEN: *(Singing)*

O God, whatever shall we do with creatures like
Womankind?

This can't be endured by any man alive. Question
them!

Let us try to find out what this means.

To what end have they seized on this shrine,

This steep and rugged, high and holy,

Undefiled Acropolis?

LEADER OF MEN: Come, put your questions;
don't give in, and probe her every statement.

For base and shameful it would be to leave this
plot untested.

MAGISTRATE: Well then, first of all I wish
to ask her this: for what purpose have you barred us
from the Acropolis?

LYSISTRATA: To keep the treasure safe, so
you won't make war on account of it.

MAGISTRATE: What? Do we make war on
account of the treasure?

LYSISTRATA: Yes, and you cause all our other
troubles for it, too. Peisander and those greedy office-
seekers keep things stirred up so they can find occa-

sions to steal. Now let them do what they like:
they'll never again make off with any of this
money.[15]

MAGISTRATE: What will you do?

LYSISTRATA: What a question! We'll administer it ourselves.

MAGISTRATE: *You* will administer the
treasure?

LYSISTRATA: What's so strange in that? Don't
we administer the household money for you?

MAGISTRATE: That's different.

LYSISTRATA: How is it different?

MAGISTRATE: We've got to make war with
this money.

LYSISTRATA: But that's the very first thing:
you mustn't make war.

MAGISTRATE: How else can we be saved?

LYSISTRATA: We'll save you.

MAGISTRATE: *You?*

LYSISTRATA: Yes, we!

MAGISTRATE: God forbid!

LYSISTRATA: We'll save you, whether you
want it or not.

MAGISTRATE: Oh! This is terrible!

LYSISTRATA: You don't like it, but we're
going to do it none the less.

MAGISTRATE: Good God! it's illegal!

LYSISTRATA: We *will* save you, my little
man!

MAGISTRATE: Suppose I don't want you to?

LYSISTRATA: That's all the more reason.

MAGISTRATE: What business have you with
war and peace?

LYSISTRATA: I'll explain.

MAGISTRATE: *(Shaking his fist)* Speak up, or
you'll smart for it.

LYSISTRATA: Just listen, and try to keep your
hands still.

MAGISTRATE: I can't. I'm so mad I can't stop
them.

FIRST WOMAN: Then you'll be the one to
smart for it.

MAGISTRATE: Croak to yourself, old hag! *(to*
LYSISTRATA*)* Now then, speak up.

LYSISTRATA: Very well. Formerly we
endured the war for a good long time with our usual
restraint, no matter what you men did. You
wouldn't let us say "boo," although nothing you did

[15]Peisander was an Athenian politician.

suited us. But we watched you well, and though we stayed at home we'd often hear of some terribly stupid measure you'd proposed. Then, though grieving at heart, we'd smile sweetly and say, "What was passed in the Assembly today about writing on the treaty-stone?" "What's that to you?" my husband would say. "Hold your tongue!" And I held my tongue.

FIRST WOMAN: But I wouldn't have — not I!

MAGISTRATE: You'd have been soundly smacked, if you hadn't kept still.

LYSISTRATA: So I kept still at home. Then we'd hear of some plan still worse than the first; we'd say, "Husband, how could you pass such a stupid proposal!" He'd scowl at me and say, "If you don't mind your spinning, your head will be sore for weeks. *War shall be the concern of men.*"[16]

MAGISTRATE: And he was right, upon my word!

LYSISTRATA: Why right, you confounded fool, when your proposals were so stupid and we weren't allowed to make any suggestions?

"There's not a *man* left in the country," says one. "No, not one," says another. Therefore all we women have decided in council to make a common effort to save Greece. How long should we have waited? Now, if you're willing to listen to our excellent proposals and keep silence for us in your turn, we still may save you.

MAGISTRATE: We men keep silence for you? That's terrible; I won't endure it!

LYSISTRATA: Silence!

MAGISTRATE: Silence for *you*, you wench, when you're wearing a snood? I'd rather die!

LYSISTRATA: Well, if that's all that bothers you — here! Take my snood and tie it round your head. (*During the following words the* WOMEN *dress up the* MAGISTRATE *in women's garments.*) And *now* keep quiet! Here, take this spinning-basket, too, and card your wool with robes tucked up, munching on beans. *War shall be the concern of Women!*

LEADER OF WOMEN: Arise and leave your
    pitchers, girls; no time is this to falter.
    We too must aid our loyal friends; our
      turn has come for action.

CHORUS OF WOMEN: (*Singing*)

I'll never tire of aiding them with song and dance;
    never may
Faintness keep my legs from moving to and fro
    endlessly.
  For I yearn to do all for my friends;
    They have charm, they have wit, they have
      grace,
      With courage, brains, and best of virtues —
        Patriotic sapience.

LEADER OF WOMEN: Come, child of manliest ancient dames, offspring of stinging nettles,

Advance with rage unsoftened; for fair breezes speed you onward.

LYSISTRATA: If only sweet Eros and the Cyprian Queen of Love shed charm over our breasts and limbs and inspire our men with amorous longing and priapic spasms, I think we may soon be called Peacemakers among the Greeks.

MAGISTRATE: What will you do?

LYSISTRATA: First of all, we'll stop those fellows who run madly about the Marketplace in arms.

FIRST WOMAN: Indeed we shall, by the Queen of Paphos.[17]

LYSISTRATA: For now they roam about the market, amid the pots and greenstuffs, armed to the teeth like Corybantes.

MAGISTRATE: That's what manly fellows ought to do!

LYSISTRATA: But it's so silly: a chap with a Gorgon-emblazoned shield buying pickled herring.

FIRST WOMAN: Why, just the other day I saw one of those long-haired dandies who command our cavalry ride up on horseback and pour into his bronze helmet the egg-broth he'd bought from an old dame. And there was a Thracian slinger too, shaking his lance like Tereus; he'd scared the life out of the poor fig-peddler and was gulping down all her ripest fruit.

MAGISTRATE: How can you stop all the confusion in the various states and bring them together?

LYSISTRATA: Very easily.

MAGISTRATE: Tell me how.

LYSISTRATA: Just like a ball of wool, when it's confused and snarled: we take it thus, and draw out a thread here and a thread there with our spindles; thus we'll unsnarl this war, if no one prevents

---

[16]Quotation from Homer's *Iliad*.

[17]Aphrodite, goddess of love.

us, and draw together the various states with embassies here and embassies there.

MAGISTRATE: Do you suppose you can stop this dreadful business with balls of wool and spindles, you nit-wits?

LYSISTRATA: Why, if *you* had any wits, you'd manage all affairs of state like our woolworking.

MAGISTRATE: How so?

LYSISTRATA: First you ought to treat the city as we do when we wash the dirt out of a fleece: stretch it out and pluck and thrash out of the city all those prickly scoundrels; aye, and card out those who conspire and stick together to gain office, pulling off their heads. Then card the wool, all of it, into one fair basket of goodwill, mingling in the aliens residing here, any loyal foreigners, and anyone who's in debt to the Treasury; and consider that all our colonies lie scattered round about like remnants; from all of these collect the wool and gather it together here, wind up a great ball, and then weave a good stout cloak for the democracy.

MAGISTRATE: Dreadful! Talking about thrashing and winding balls of wool, when you haven't the slightest share in the war!

LYSISTRATA: Why, you dirty scoundrel, we bear more than twice as much as you. First, we bear children and send off our sons as soldiers.

MAGISTRATE: Hush! Let bygones be bygones!

LYSISTRATA: Then, when we ought to be happy and enjoy our youth, we sleep alone because of your expeditions abroad. But never mind us married women: I grieve most for the maids who grow old at home unwed.

MAGISTRATE: Don't men grow old, too?

LYSISTRATA: For heaven's sake! That's not the same thing. When a man comes home, no matter how grey he is, he soon finds a girl to marry. But woman's bloom is short and fleeting; if she doesn't grasp her chance, no man is willing to marry her and she sits at home a prey to every fortune-teller.

MAGISTRATE: *(Coarsely)* But if a man can still get it up—

LYSISTRATA: See here, you: what's the matter? Aren't you dead yet? There's plenty of room for you. Buy yourself a shroud and I'll bake you a honey-cake. *(Handing him a copper coin for his passage across the Styx.)* Here's your fare! Now get yourself a wreath.

(During the following dialogue the WOMEN *dress up the* MAGISTRATE *as a corpse.)*

FIRST WOMAN: Here, take these fillets.
SECOND WOMAN: Here, take this wreath.
LYSISTRATA: What do you want? What's lacking? Get moving; off to the ferry! Charon is calling you; don't keep him from sailing.[18]

MAGISTRATE: Am I to endure these insults? By God! I'm going straight to the magistrates to show them how I've been treated.

LYSISTRATA: Are you grumbling that you haven't been properly laid out? Well, the day after tomorrow we'll send around all the usual offerings early in the morning.

(The MAGISTRATE *goes out still wearing his funeral decorations.* LYSISTRATA *and the* WOMEN *retire into the Acropolis.)*

LEADER OF MEN: Wake, ye sons of freedom, wake! 'Tis no time for sleeping. Up and at them, like a man! Let us strip for action.

(The CHORUS OF MEN *remove their outer cloaks.)*

CHORUS OF MEN: *(Singing)*
Surely there is something here greater than meets
    the eye;
For without a doubt I smell Hippias's tyranny.[19]
Dreadful fear assails me lest certain bands of
    Spartan men,
Meeting here with Cleisthenes, have inspired
    through treachery[20]
All these god-detested women secretly to seize
Athens' treasure in the temple, and to stop that
    pay
Whence I live at my ease.

LEADER OF MEN: Now isn't it terrible for them to advise the state and chatter about shields, being mere women?

And they think to reconcile us with the Spartans—men who hold nothing sacred any more than hungry wolves. Surely this is a web of deceit, my friends, to conceal an attempt at tyranny. But they'll

[18]Charon was the ferryman who rowed dead souls across the river Styx to Hades.
[19]Hippias was the tyrant ruler of Athens just before it became a democracy in 510 B.C.
[20]Cleisthenes was a well-known homosexual; often referred to in Aristophanes' plays.

never lord it over me; I'll be on my guard from now on,

"The blade I bear, A myrtle spray shall wear."

I'll occupy the market under arms and stand next to Aristogeiton.

Thus I'll stand beside him *(He strikes the pose of the famous statue of the tyrannicides, with one arm raised.)* And here's my chance to take this accurst old hag and— *(Striking the* LEADER OF WOMEN*)* smack her on the jaw!

LEADER OF WOMEN: You'll go home in such a state your Ma won't recognize you!

Ladies all, upon the ground let us place these garments.

(The CHORUS OF WOMEN *remove their outer garments.)*

CHORUS OF WOMEN: *(Singing)*
Citizens of Athens, hear useful words for the state.
Rightly; for it nurtured me in my youth royally.
As a child of seven years carried I the sacred box;
Then I was a Miller-maid, grinding at Athene's
  shrine;
Next I wore the saffron robe and played
  Brauronia's Bear;
And I walked as a Basket-bearer, wearing chains of
  figs,
  As a sweet maiden fair.[21]

LEADER OF WOMEN: Therefore, am I not bound to give good advice to the city?

Don't take it ill that I was born a woman, if I contribute something better than our present troubles. I pay my share; for I contribute MEN. But you miserable old fools contribute nothing, and after squandering our ancestral treasure, the fruit of the Persian Wars, you make no contribution in return. And now, all on account of you, we're facing ruin.

What, muttering, are you? If you annoy me, I'll take this hard, rough slipper and— *(Striking the* LEADER OF MEN*)* smack you on the jaw!

CHORUS OF MEN: *(Singing)*
This is outright insolence! Things go from bad to
  worse.
If you're men with any guts, prepare to meet the
  foe.
Let us strip our tunics off! We need the smell of
  male

Vigour. And we cannot fight all swaddled up in
  clothes.
(They strip off their tunics.)
Come then, my comrades, on to the battle, ye once
  to Leipsydrion came;[22]
  Then ye were MEN. Now call back your
    youthful vigour.
With light, wingèd footstep advance,
  Shaking old age from your frame.

LEADER OF MEN: If any of us give these wenches the slightest hold, they'll stop at nothing; such is their cunning.

They will even build ships and sail against us, like Artemisia. Or if they turn to mounting, I count our Knights as done for: a woman's such a tricky jockey when she gets astraddle, with a good firm seat for trotting. Just look at those Amazons that Micon painted, fighting on horseback against men!

But we must throw them all in the pillory— *(Seizing and choking the* LEADER OF WOMEN*)* grabbing hold of yonder neck!

CHORUS OF WOMEN: *(Singing)*
'Ware my anger! Like a boar 'twill rush upon you
  men.
Soon you'll bawl aloud for help, you'll be so
  soundly trimmed!
Come, my friends, let's strip with speed, and lay
  aside these robes;
Catch the scent of women's rage. Attack with
  tooth and nail!
(They strip off their tunics.)
Now then, come near me, you miserable man!
  You'll never eat garlic or black beans again.
And if you utter a single hard word, in rage I will
  "nurse" you as once
  The beetle requited her foe.[23]

LEADER OF WOMEN: For you don't worry me; no, not so long as my Lampito lives and our Theban friend, the noble Ismenia.

You can't do anything, not even if you pass a dozen—decrees! You miserable fool, all our neighbours hate you. Why, just the other day when I was holding a festival for Hecate, I invited as playmate from our neighbours the Boeotians a charming,

[21]This speech refers to various positions of honor at religious festivals.

[22]Leipsydrion was a mountain where Athenian patriots fought Hippias.
[23]According to Aesop's fable, the beetle retaliated against the eagle by ruining its eggs.

wellbred Copaic—eel. But they refused to send me one on account of your decrees.

And you'll never stop passing decrees until I grab your foot and— *(Tripping up the* LEADER OF MEN*)* toss you down and break your neck!

(Here an interval of five days is supposed to elapse. LYSISTRATA *comes out from the Acropolis.)*

LEADER OF WOMEN: *(Dramatically)*
 Empress of this great emprise and
  undertaking,
 Why come you forth, I pray, with
  frowning brow?

LYSISTRATA: Ah, these cursèd women! Their deeds and female notions make me pace up and down in utter despair.

LEADER OF WOMEN: Ah, what sayest thou?

LYSISTRATA: The truth, alas! the truth.

LEADER OF WOMEN: What dreadful tale hast thou to tell thy friends?

LYSISTRATA: 'Tis shame to speak, and not to speak is hard.

LEADER OF WOMEN: Hide not from me whatever woes we suffer.

LYSISTRATA: Well then, to put it briefly, we want—laying!

LEADER OF WOMEN: O Zeus, Zeus!

LYSISTRATA: Why call on Zeus? That's the way things are. I can no longer keep them away from the men, and they're all deserting. I caught one wriggling through a hole near the grotto of Pan, another sliding down a rope, another deserting her post; and yesterday I found one getting on a sparrow's back to fly off to Orsilochus,[24] and had to pull her back by the hair. They're digging up all sorts of excuses to get home. Look, here comes one of them now.

(A WOMAN *comes hastily out of the Acropolis.)*

Here you! Where are you off to in such a hurry?

FIRST WOMAN: I want to go home. My very best wool is being devoured by moths.

LYSISTRATA: Moths? Nonsense! Go back inside.

FIRST WOMAN: I'll come back; I swear it. I just want to lay it out on the bed.

---

[24]Orsilochus kept a brothel.

LYSISTRATA: Well, you won't lay it out, and you won't go home, either.

FIRST WOMAN: Shall I let my wool be ruined?

LYSISTRATA: If necessary, yes.

*(*ANOTHER WOMAN *comes out.)*

SECOND WOMAN: Oh, dear! Oh, dear! My precious flax! I left it at home all unpeeled.

LYSISTRATA: Here's another one, going home for her "flax." Come back here!

SECOND WOMAN: But I just want to work it up a little and then I'll be right back.

LYSISTRATA: No indeed! If you start this, all other women will want to do the same.

(A THIRD WOMAN *comes out.)*

THIRD WOMAN: O Eilithyia, goddess of travail, stop my labour till I come to a lawful spot!

LYSISTRATA: What's this nonsense?

THIRD WOMAN: I'm going to have a baby— right now!

LYSISTRATA: But you weren't even pregnant yesterday.

THIRD WOMAN: Well, I am today. O Lysistrata, do send me home to see a midwife, right away.

LYSISTRATA: What are you talking about? *(Putting her hand on her stomach)* What's this hard lump here?

THIRD WOMAN: A little boy.

LYSISTRATA: My goodness, what have you got there? It seems hollow; I'll just find out. *(Pulling aside her robe)* Why, you silly goose, you've got Athene's sacred helmet there. And you said you were having a baby!

THIRD WOMAN: Well, I *am* having one, I swear!

LYSISTRATA: Then what's this helmet for?

THIRD WOMAN: If the baby starts coming while I'm still in the Acropolis, I'll creep into this like a pigeon and give birth to it there.

LYSISTRATA: Stuff and nonsense! It's plain enough what you're up to. You just wait here for the christening of this—helmet.

THIRD WOMAN: But I can't sleep in the Acropolis since I saw the sacred snake.

FIRST WOMAN: And I'm dying for lack of sleep: the hooting of owls keep me awake.

LYSISTRATA: Enough of these shams, you

wretched creatures. You want your husbands, I suppose. Well, don't you think they want us? I'm sure they're spending miserable nights. Hold out, my friends, and endure for just a little while. There's an oracle that we shall conquer, if we don't split up. *(Producing a roll of paper)* Here it is.

FIRST WOMAN: Tell us what it says.

LYSISTRATA: Listen.

"When in the length of time the Swallows
    shall gather together,
Fleeing the Hoopoe's amorous flight and
    the Cockatoo shunning,
Then shall your woes be ended and Zeus
    who thunders in heaven
Set what's below on top—"

FIRST WOMAN: What? Are we going to be on top?

LYSISTRATA: "But if the Swallows rebel and
    flutter away from the temple,
Never a bird in the world shall seem more
    wanton and worthless."

FIRST WOMAN: That's clear enough, upon my word!

LYSISTRATA: By all that's holy, let's not give up the struggle now. Let's go back inside. It would be a shame, my dear friends, to disobey the oracle.

(The WOMEN *all retire to the Acropolis again.)*

CHORUS OF MEN: *(Singing)*
I have a tale to tell,
Which I know full well.
    It was told me
    In the nursery.

Once there was a likely lad,
    Melanion they name him;
The thought of marriage made him mad,
    For which I cannot blame him.

So off he went to mountains fair;
    (No women to upbraid him!)
A mighty hunter of the hare,
    He had a dog to aid him.

He never came back home to see
    Detested women's faces.
He showed a shrewd mentality.
    With him I'd fain change places!

ONE OF THE MEN: *(to* ONE OF THE WOMEN*)*
Come here, old dame; give me a kiss.

WOMAN: You'll ne'er eat garlic, if you dare!

MAN: I want to kick you—just like this!

WOMAN: Oh, there's a leg with bushy hair!

MAN: Myronides and Phormio[25]
Were hairy—and they thrashed the foe.

CHORUS OF WOMEN: *(Singing)*
I have another tale,
With which to assail
    Your contention
    'Bout Melanion.

Once upon a time a man
    Named Timon left our city,
To live in some deserted land.
    (We thought him rather witty.)

He dwelt alone amidst the thorn;
    In solitude he brooded.
From some grim Fury he was born:
    Such hatred he exuded.

He cursed you men, as scoundrels through
    And through, till life he ended.
He couldn't stand the sight of you!
    But women he befriended.

WOMAN: *(to* ONE OF THE MEN) I'll smash your face in, if you like.

MAN: Oh no, please don't! You frighten me.

WOMAN: I'll lift my foot—and thus I'll strike.

MAN: Aha! Look there! What's that I see?

WOMAN: Whate'er you see, you cannot say
That I'm not neatly trimmed today.

*(*LYSISTRATA *appears on the wall of the Acropolis.)*

LYSISTRATA: Hello! Hello! Girls, come here quick!

*(*SEVERAL WOMEN *appear beside her.)*

WOMAN: What is it? Why are you calling?

LYSISTRATA: I see a man coming: he's in a dreadful state. He's mad with passion. O Queen of Cyprus, Cythera, and Paphos, just keep on this way!

WOMAN: Where is the fellow?

[25]Victorious military leaders.

LYSISTRATA: There beside the shrine of Demeter.

WOMAN: Oh yes, so he is. Who is he?

LYSISTRATA: Let's see. Do any of you know him?

MYRRHINE: Yes indeed. That's my husband, Cinesias.

LYSISTRATA: It's up to you, now: roast him, rack him, fool him, love him—and leave him! Do everything, except what our oath forbids.

MYRRHINE: Don't worry; I'll do it.

LYSISTRATA: I'll stay here to tease him and warm him up a bit. Off with you.

(The OTHER WOMEN *retire from the wall. Enter* CINESIAS *followed by* A SLAVE *carrying a baby.* CINESIAS *is obviously in great pain and distress.)*

CINESIAS: *(Groaning)* Oh-h! Oh-h-h! This is killing me! O God, what tortures I'm suffering!

LYSISTRATA: *(From the wall)* Who's that within our lines?

CINESIAS: Me.

LYSISTRATA: A *man?*

CINESIAS: *(Pointing)* A *man,* indeed!

LYSISTRATA: Well, go away!

CINESIAS: Who are you to send me away?

LYSISTRATA: The captain of the guard.

CINESIAS: Oh, for heaven's sake, call out Myrrhine for me.

LYSISTRATA: Call Myrrhine? Nonsense! Who are you?

CINESIAS: Her husband, Cinesias of Paionidai.

LYSISTRATA: *(Appearing much impressed)* Oh, greetings, friend. Your name is not without honour here among us. Your wife is always talking about you, and whenever she takes an egg or an apple, she says, "Here's to my dear Cinesias!"

CINESIAS: *(Quivering with excitement)* Oh, ye gods in heaven!

LYSISTRATA: Indeed she does! And whenever our conversations turn to men, your wife immediately says, "All others are mere rubbish compared with Cinesias."

CINESIAS: *(Groaning)* Oh! Do call her for me.

LYSISTRATA: Why should I? What will you give me?

CINESIAS: Whatever you want. All I have is yours—and you see what I've got.

LYSISTRATA: Well then, I'll go down and call her. *(She descends.)*

CINESIAS: And hurry up! I've had no joy of life ever since she left home. When I go in the house, I feel awful: everything seems so empty and I can't enjoy my dinner. I'm in such a state all the time!

MYRRHINE: *(From behind the wall)* I *do* love him so. But he won't let me love him. No, no! Don't ask me to see him!

CINESIAS: O my darling, O Myrrhine honey, why do you do this to me?

*(*MYRRHINE *appears on the wall.)*

Come down here!

MYRRHINE: No, I won't come down.

CINESIAS: Won't you come, Myrrhine, when I call you?

MYRRHINE: No; you don't want me.

CINESIAS: *Don't want you?* I'm in agony!

MYRRHINE: I'm going now.

CINESIAS: Please don't. At least, listen to your baby. *(To the baby)* Here you, call your mamma! *(Pinching the baby.)*

BABY: Ma-ma! Ma-ma! Ma-ma!

CINESIAS: *(To* MYRRHINE*)* What's the matter with you? Have you no pity for your child, who hasn't been washed or fed for five whole days?

MYRRHINE: Oh, poor child; your father pays no attention to you.

CINESIAS: Come down then, you heartless wretch, for the baby's sake.

MYRRHINE: Oh, what it is to be a mother! I've got to come down, I suppose.

(She leaves the wall and shortly reappears at the gate.)

CINESIAS: *(To himself)* She seems much younger, and she has such a sweet look about her. Oh, the way she teases me! And her pretty, provoking ways make me burn with longing.

MYRRHINE: *(Coming out of the gate and taking the baby)* O my sweet little angel. Naughty papa! Here, let Mummy kiss you, Mamma's little sweetheart!

(She fondles the baby lovingly.)

CINESIAS: *(In despair)* You heartless creature, why do you do this? Why follow these other women and make both of us suffer so?

(He tries to embrace her.)

MYRRHINE: Don't touch me!

CINESIAS: You're letting all our things at home go to wrack and ruin.

MYRRHINE: I don't care.

CINESIAS: You don't care that your wool is being plucked to pieces by the chickens?

MYRRHINE: Not in the least.

CINESIAS: And you haven't celebrated the rites of Aphrodite for ever so long. Won't you come home?

MYRRHINE: Not on your life, unless you men make a truce and stop the war.

CINESIAS: Well, then, if that pleases you, we'll do it.

MYRRHINE: Well then, if that pleases *you*, I'll come home — afterwards! Right now I'm on oath not to.

CINESIAS: Then just lie down here with me for a moment.

MYRRHINE: No — *(In a teasing voice)* and yet I won't say I don't love you.

CINESIAS: You love me? Oh, do lie down here, Myrrhine dear!

MYRRHINE: What, you silly fool! in front of the baby?

CINESIAS: *(Hastily thrusting the baby at the slave)* Of course not. Here — home! Take him, Manes! *(The* SLAVE *goes off with the baby.)* See, the baby's out of the way. Now won't you lie down?

MYRRHINE: But where, my dear?

CINESIAS: Where? The grotto of Pan's a lovely spot.

MYRRHINE: How could I purify myself before returning to the shrine?

CINESIAS: Easily: just wash here in the Clepsydra.

MYRRHINE: And then, shall I go back on my oath?

CINESIAS: On my head be it! Don't worry about the oath.

MYRRHINE: All right, then. Just let me bring out a bed.

CINESIAS: No, don't. The ground's all right.

MYRRHINE: Heavens, no! Bad as you are, I won't let you lie on the bare ground.

(She goes into the Acropolis.)

CINESIAS: Why, she really loves me; it's plain to see.

MYRRHINE: *(Returning with a bed)* There! Now hurry up and lie down. I'll just slip off this dress. But — let's see: oh yes, I must fetch a mattress.

CINESIAS: Nonsense! No mattress for me.

MYRRHINE: Yes indeed! It's not nice on the bare springs.

CINESIAS: Give me a kiss.

MYRRHINE: *(Giving him a hasty kiss)* There!

(She goes.)

CINESIAS: *(In mingled distress and delight)* Oh-h! Hurry back!

MYRRHINE: *(Returning with a mattress)* Here's the mattress; lie down on it. I'm taking my things off now — but — let's see: you have no pillow.

CINESIAS: I don't *want* a pillow.

MYRRHINE: But I do.

(She goes.)

CINESIAS: Cheated again, just like Heracles and his dinner!

MYRRHINE: *(Returning with a pillow)* Here, lift your head. *(To herself, wondering how else to tease him)* Is that all?

CINESIAS: Surely that's all! Do come here, precious!

MYRRHINE: I'm taking off my girdle. But remember: don't go back on your promise about the truce.

CINESIAS: I hope to die, if I do.

MYRRHINE: You don't have a blanket.

CINESIAS: *(Shouting in exasperation) I don't want one!* I WANT TO—

MYRRHINE: Sh-h! There, there, I'll be back in a minute.

(She goes.)

CINESIAS: She'll be the death of me with these bedclothes.

MYRRHINE: *(Returning with a blanket)* Here, get up.

CINESIAS: I've got *this* up!

MYRRHINE: Would you like some perfume?

CINESIAS: Good heavens, no! I won't have it!

MYRRHINE: Yes, you shall, whether you want it or not.

(She goes.)

CINESIAS: O lord! Confound all perfumes anyway!

MYRRHINE: *(Returning with a flask)* Stretch out your hand and put some on.

CINESIAS: *(Suspiciously)* By God, I don't much like this perfume. It smacks of shilly-shallying, and has no scent of the marriage-bed.

MYRRHINE: Oh dear! This is Rhodian perfume I've brought.

CINESIAS: It's quite all right, dear. Never mind.

MYRRHINE: Don't be silly!

(She goes out with the flask.)

CINESIAS: Damn the man who first concocted perfumes!

MYRRHINE: *(Returning with another flask)* Here, try this flask.

CINESIAS: I've got another one all ready for you. Come, you wretch, lie down and stop bringing me things.

MYRRHINE: All right; I'm taking off my shoes. But, my dear, see that you vote for peace.

CINESIAS: *(Absently)* I'll consider it.

(MYRRHINE runs away to the Acropolis.) I'm ruined! The wench has skinned me and run away! *(Chanting, in tragic style)* Alas! Alas! Deceived, deserted by this fairest of women, whom shall I—lay? Ah, my poor little child, how shall I nurture thee? Where's Cynalopex? I needs must hire a nurse![26]

LEADER OF MEN: *(Chanting)* Ah, wretched man, in dreadful wise beguiled, bewrayed, thy soul is sore distressed. I pity thee, alas! What soul, what loins, what liver could stand this strain? How firm and unyielding he stands, with naught to aid him of a morning.

CINESIAS: O lord! O Zeus! What tortures I endure!

LEADER OF MEN: This is the way she's treated you, that vile and cursèd wanton.

LEADER OF WOMEN: Nay, not vile and cursèd, but sweet and dear.

LEADER OF MEN: Sweet, you say? Nay, hateful, hateful!

[26]Cynalopex was a pimp. His child is his phallus.

CINESIAS: Hateful indeed! O Zeus, Zeus!
Seize her and snatch her away,
Like a handful of dust, in a mighty,
Fiery tempest! Whirl her aloft, then let her drop
Down to the earth, with a crash, as she falls—
On the point of this waiting Thingummybob!

(He goes out. Enter a SPARTAN HERALD *in an obvious state of excitement, which he is doing his best to conceal.)*

HERALD: Where can I find the Senate or the Prytanes? I've got an important message.

(The Athenian MAGISTRATE *enters.)*

MAGISTRATE: Say there, are you a man or Priapus?[27]

HERALD: *(In annoyance)* I'm a herald, you lout! I've come from Sparta about the truce.

MAGISTRATE: Is that a spear you've got under your cloak?

HERALD: No, of course not!

MAGISTRATE: Why do you twist and turn so? Why hold your cloak in front of you. Did you rupture yourself on the trip?

HERALD: By gum, the fellow's an old fool.

MAGISTRATE: *(Pointing)* Why, you dirty rascal, you're excited.

HERALD: Not at all. Stop this tom-foolery.

MAGISTRATE: Well, what's that I see?

HERALD: A Spartan message-staff.

MAGISTRATE: Oh, certainly! That's just the kind of message-staff I've got. But tell me the honest truth: how are things going in Sparta?

HERALD: All the land of Sparta is up in arms—and our allies are up, too. We need Pellene.[28]

MAGISTRATE: What brought this trouble on you? A sudden Panic?

HERALD: No, Lampito started it and then all the other women in Sparta with one accord chased their husbands out of their beds.

MAGISTRATE: How do you feel?

[27]Fertility god usually represented with unusually large sexual organs.
[28]Pellene was a small state allied with Sparta. The point of the reference here is uncertain.

HERALD: Terrible. We walk around the city bent over like men lighting matches in a wind. For our women won't let us touch them unil we all agree and make peace throughout Greece.

MAGISTRATE: This is a general conspiracy of the women; I see it now. Well, hurry back and tell the Spartans to send ambassadors here with full powers to arrange a truce. And I'll go tell the Council to choose ambassadors from here; I've got something here that will soon persuade them!

HERALD: I'll fly there; for you've made an excellent suggestion.

(The HERALD *and the* MAGISTRATE *depart on opposite sides of the stage.)*

LEADER OF MEN: No beast or fire is harder than womankind to tame,
  Nor is the spotted leopard so devoid of shame.
LEADER OF WOMEN: Knowing this, you dare provoke us to attack?
  I'd be your steady friend, if you'd but take us back.
LEADER OF MEN: I'll never cease my hatred keen of womankind.
LEADER OF WOMEN: Just as you will. But now just let me help you find
  That cloak you threw aside. You look so silly there
  Without your clothes. Here, put it on and don't go bare.
LEADER OF MEN: That's very kind, and shows you're not entirely bad.
  But I threw off my things when I was good and mad.
LEADER OF WOMEN: At last you seem a man, and won't be mocked, my lad.
  If you'd been nice to me, I'd take this little gnat
  That's in your eye and pluck it out for you, like that.
LEADER OF MEN: So that's what bothered me and bit my eye so long!
  Please dig it out for me. I own that I've been wrong.
LEADER OF WOMEN: I'll do so, though you've been a most ill-natured brat.
  Ye gods! See here! A huge and monstrous little gnat!

LEADER OF MEN: Oh, how that helps! For it was digging wells in me.
  And now it's out, my tears can roll down hard and free.
LEADER OF WOMEN: Here, let me wipe them off, although you're such a knave,
  And kiss me.
LEADER OF MEN: No!
LEADER OF WOMEN: Whate'er you say, a kiss I'll have.

(She kisses him.)

LEADER OF MEN: Oh, confound these women! They've a coaxing way about them.
  He was wise and never spoke a truer word, who said,
  "We can't live with women, but we cannot live without them."
  Now I'll make a truce with you. We'll fight no more; instead,
  I will not injure you if you do me no wrong.
  And now let's join our ranks and then begin a song.
COMBINED CHORUS: *(Singing)*
Athenians, we're not prepared,
To say a single ugly word
About our fellow-citizens.
  Quite the contrary: we desire but to say and to do
  Naught but good. Quite enough are the ills now on hand.
Men and women, be advised:
  If anyone requires
Money — minae two or three —
  We've got what he desires.

My purse is yours, on easy terms:
  When Peace shall reappear,
Whate'er you've borrowed will be due.
  So speak up without fear.

You needn't pay me back, you see,
If you can get a cent from me!

We're about to entertain
  Some foreign gentlemen;
We've soup and tender, fresh-killed pork.
  Come round to dine at ten.

Come early; wash, and dress with care,
   And bring the children, too.
Then step right in, no "by your leave."
   We'll be expecting you.

Walk in as if you owned the place.
You'll find the door—shut in your face!

(Enter a group of SPARTAN AMBASSADORS; *they are
in the same desperate condition as the* HERALD *in
the previous scene.)*

LEADER OF CHORUS: Here comes the
envoys from Sparta, sprouting long beards and looking for the world as if they were carrying pig-pens
in front of them.
   Greetings, gentlemen of Sparta. Tell me, in
what state have you come?
   SPARTAN: Why waste words? You can
plainly see what state we've come in!
   LEADER OF CHORUS: Wow! You're in a
pretty highstrung condition, and it seems to be getting worse.
   SPARTAN: It's indescribable. Won't someone
please arrange a peace for us—in any way you like.
   LEADER OF CHORUS: Here come our own,
native ambassadors, crouching like wrestlers and
holding their clothes in front of them; this seems an
athletic kind of malady.

(Enter several Athenian AMBASSADORS.)

ATHENIAN: Can anyone tell us where Lysistrata is? You see our condition.
   LEADER OF CHORUS: Here's another case of
the same complaint. Tell me, are the attacks worse
in the morning?
   ATHENIAN: No, we're always afflicted this
way. If someone doesn't soon arrange this truce,
you'd better not let me get my hands on—
Cleisthenes![29]
   LEADER OF CHORUS: If you're smart, you'll
arrange your cloaks so none of these fellows who
smashed the Hermae can see you.[30]

[29]See note 20 above.
[30]Athenians used statues of Hermes, depicted with large
phallus, as protectors of their homes. Just before the Sicilian invasion, vandals had broken the phalluses off many
of the statues.

ATHENIAN: Right you are; a very good
suggestion.
   SPARTAN: Aye, by all means. Here, let's
hitch up our clothes.
   ATHENIAN: Greetings, Spartan. We've suffered dreadful things.
   SPARTAN: My dear fellow, we'd have suffered still worse if one of those fellows had seen us
in this condition.
   ATHENIAN: Well, gentlemen, we must get
down to business. What's your errand here?
   SPARTAN: We're ambassadors about peace.
   ATHENIAN: Excellent; so are we. Only Lysistrata can arrange things for us; shall we summon
her?
   SPARTAN: Aye, and Lysistratus too, if you
like.
   LEADER OF CHORUS: No need to summon
      her, it seems. She's coming out of her
      own accord.
      (Enter LYSISTRATA *accompanied by a statue
       of a nude female figure, which
       represents Reconciliation.)*
      Hail, noblest of women; now must thou be
      A judge shrewd and subtle, mild and
       severe,
      Be sweet yet majestic: all manners employ.
      The leaders of Hellas, caught by thy love-
       charms,
      Have come to thy judgment, their charges
       submitting.
   LYSISTRATA: This is no difficult task, if one
catch them still in amorous passion, before they've
resorted to each other. But I'll soon find out.
Where's Reconciliation? Go, first bring the Spartans
here, and don't seize them rudely and violently, as
our tactless husbands used to do, but as befits a
woman, like an old, familiar friend; if they won't
give you their hands, take them however you can.
Then go fetch these Athenians here, taking hold of
whatever they offer you. Now then, men of Sparta,
stand here beside me, and you Athenians on the
other side, and listen to my words.
   I am a woman, it is true, but I have a mind;
I'm not badly off in native wit, and by listening to
my father and my elders, I've had a decent
schooling.
   Now I intend to give you a scolding which you
both deserve. With one common font you worship
at the same altars, just like brothers, at Olympia, at

Thermopylae, at Delphi — how many more might I name, if time permitted; — and the Barbarians stand by waiting with their armies; yet you are destroying the men and towns of Greece.

ATHENIAN: Oh, this tension is killing me!

LYSISTRATA: And now, men of Sparta, — to turn to you — don't you remember how the Spartan Pericleidas came here once as a suppliant, and sitting at our altar, all pale with fear in his crimson cloak, begged us for an army? For all Messene had attacked you and the god sent an earthquake too? Then Cimon went forth with four thousand hoplites and saved all Lacedaemon. Such was the aid you received from Athens, and now you lay waste the country which once treated you so well.

ATHENIAN: (Hotly) They're in the wrong, Lysistrata, upon my word, they are!

SPARTAN: (Absently, looking at the statue of Reconciliation) We're in the wrong. What hips! How lovely they are!

LYSISTRATA: Don't think I'm going to let you Athenians off. Don't you remember how the Spartans came in arms when you were wearing the rough, sheepskin cloak of slaves and slew the host of Thessalians, the comrades and allies of Hippias? Fighting with you on that day, alone of all the Greeks, they set you free and instead of a sheepskin gave your folk a handsome robe to wear.

SPARTAN: (Looking at LYSISTRATA) I've never seen a more distinguished woman.

ATHENIAN: (Looking at Reconciliation) I've never seen a more voluptuous body!

LYSISTRATA: Why then, with these many noble deeds to think of, do you fight each other? Why don't you stop this villainy? Why not make peace? Tell me, what prevents it?

SPARTAN: (Waving vaguely at Reconciliation) We're willing, if you're willing to give up your position on yonder flank.

LYSISTRATA: What position, my good man?

SPARTAN: Pylus, we've been panting for it for ever so long.

ATHENIAN: No, by God! You shan't have it!

LYSISTRATA: Let them have it, my friend.

ATHENIAN: Then what shall we have to rouse things up?

LYSISTRATA: Ask for another place in exchange.

ATHENIAN: Well, let's see: first of all (Point-ing to various parts of Reconciliation's anatomy) give us Echinus here, this Maliac Inlet in back there, and these two Megarian legs.

SPARTAN: No, by heavens! You can't have everything, you crazy fool!

LYSISTRATA: Let it go. Don't fight over a pair of legs.

ATHENIAN: (Taking off his cloak) I think I'll strip and do a little planting now.

SPARTAN: (Following suit) And I'll just do a little fertilizing, by gosh!

LYSISTRATA: Wait until the truce is concluded. Now if you've decided on this course, hold a conference and discuss the matter with your allies.

ATHENIAN: Allies? Don't be ridiculous. They're in the same state we are. Won't our allies want the same thing we do — to jump in bed with their women?

SPARTAN: Ours will, I know.

ATHENIAN: Especially the Carystians, by God!

LYSISTRATA: Very well. Now purify yourselves, that your wives may feast and entertain you in the Acropolis; we've provisions by the basketfull. Exchange your oaths and pledges there, and then each of you may take his wife and go home.

ATHENIAN: Let's go at once.

SPARTAN: Come on, where you will.

ATHENIAN: For God's sake, let's hurry!

(They all go into the Acropolis.)

CHORUS: (Singing)
Whatever I have of coverlets
  And robes of varied hue
And golden trinkets, — without stint
  I offer them to you.

Take what you will and bear it home,
  Your children to delight,
Or if your girl's a Basket-maid;
  Just choose whate'er's in sight.

There's naught within so well secured
  You cannot break the seal
And bear it off; just help yourselves;
  No hesitation feel.

But you'll see nothing, though you try,
Unless you've sharper eyes than I!

If anyone needs bread to feed
   A growing family,
I've lots of wheat and full-grown loaves;
   So just apply to me.

Let every poor man who desires
   Come round and bring a sack
To fetch the grain; my slave is there
   To load it on his back.

But don't come near my door, I say:
Beware the dog, and stay away!

(An ATHENIAN *enters carrying a torch; he knocks
at the gate.)*

ATHENIAN: Open the door! *(To the* CHORUS,
which is clustered around the gate) Make way,
won't you! What are you hanging around for? Want
me to singe you with this torch? *(To himself)* No;
it's a stale trick, I won't do it! *(To the audience)* Still
if I've got to do it to please *you*, I suppose I'll have
to take the trouble.

(A SECOND ATHENIAN *comes out of the gate.)*

SECOND ATHENIAN: And I'll help you.
FIRST ATHENIAN: *(Waving his torch at the*
CHORUS*)* Get out! Go bawl your heads off! Move on
there, so the Spartans can leave in peace when the
banquet's over.

(They brandish their torches until the CHORUS
leaves the Orchestra.)

SECOND ATHENIAN: I've never seen such a
pleasant banquet: the Spartans are charming fellows, indeed they are! And we Athenians are very
witty in our cups.
FIRST ATHENIAN: Naturally: for when
we're sober we're never at our best. If the Athenians
would listen to me, we'd always get a little tipsy on
our embassies. As things are now, we go to Sparta
when we're sober and look around to stir up trouble.
And then we don't hear what they say—and as for
what they *don't* say, we have all sorts of suspicions.
And then we bring back varying reports about the

mission. But this time everything is pleasant; even
if a man should sing the Telamon-song when he
ought to sing "Cleitagorus," we'd praise him and
swear it was excellent.[31]

(The two CHORUSES *return, as a* CHORUS OF
ATHENIANS *and a* CHORUS OF SPARTANS.*)*

Here they come back again. Go to the devil,
you scoundrels!
SECOND ATHENIAN: Get out, I say! They're
coming out from the feast.

(Enter the SPARTAN *and* ATHENIAN ENVOYS,
followed by LYSISTRATA *and all the* WOMEN.*)*

SPARTAN: *(To one of his fellow-envoys)* My
good fellow, take up your pipes; I want to do a fancy
two-step and sing a jolly song for the Athenians.
ATHENIAN: Yes, do take your pipes, by all
means. I'd love to see you dance.
SPARTAN: *(Singing and dancing with the*
CHORUS OF SPARTANS*)*
   These youths inspire
To song and dance, O Memory;
Stir up my Muse, to tell how we
And Athens' men, in our galleys clashing
At Artemisium, 'gainst foremen dashing in godlike
   ire,
Conquered the Persian and set Greece free.

   Leonidas
Led on his valiant warriors
Whetting their teeth like angry boars.
Abundant foam on their lips was flow'ring,
A stream of sweat from their limbs was show'ring.
   The Persian was
Numberless as the sand on the shores.

O Huntress who slayest the beasts in the glade,[32]
O Virgin divine, hither come to our truce,
Unite us in bonds which all time will not loose.
Grant us to find in this treaty, we pray,
An unfailing source of true friendship today,
And all of our days, helping us to refrain

---

[31]Reference to a banquet custom of capping one song with
another appropriate one.
[32]The Huntress is Artemis.

From weaseling tricks which bring war in their
    train.
  Then hither, come hither! O huntress maid.

    LYSISTRATA: Come then, since all is fairly
done, men of Sparta, lead away your wives, and you,
Athenians, take yours. Let every man stand beside
his wife, and every wife beside her man, and then,
to celebrate our fortune, let's dance. And in
the future, let's take care to avoid these
misunderstandings.
    CHORUS OF ATHENIANS: *(Singing and
dancing)*
Lead on the dances, your graces revealing.
Call Artemis hither, call Artemis' twin,
Leader of dances, Apollo the Healing,
Kindly God—hither! Let's summon him in!
  Nysian Bacchus call,
Who with his Maenads, his eyes flashing fire,
  Dances, and last of all
Zeus of the thunderbolt flaming, the Sire,
    And Hera in majesty,
    Queen of prosperity.
    Come, ye Powers who dwell above
    Unforgetting, our witnesses be
Of Peace with bonds of harmonious love—
The Peace which Cypris has wrought for me.[33]
    Alleluia! Io Paean!
    Leap in joy—hurrah! hurrah!
    'Tis victory—hurrah! hurrah!
    Euoi! Euoi! Euai! Euai!

    LYSISTRATA: *(to the* SPARTANS*)* Come now,
    sing a new song to cap ours.

CHORUS OF ATHENIANS: *(Singing and
dancing)*
Leaving Taygetus fair and renown'd[34]
Muse of Laconia, hither come:
Amyclae's god in hymns resound.
Athene of the Brazen Home,
And Castor and Pollux, Tyndareus' sons,
Who sport where Eurotas murmuring runs.
  On with the dance! Heia! Ho!
    All leaping along,
  Mantles a-swinging as we go!
    Of Sparta our song.
There the holy chorus ever gladdens,
There the beat of stamping feet,
As our winsome fillies, lovely maidens,
Dance, beside Eurotas, banks a-skipping,—
Nimbly go to and fro
Hast'ning, leaping feet in measures tripping,

Like the Bacchae's revels, hair a-streaming.
Leda's child, divine and mild,
Leads the holy dance, her fair face beaming.
  On with the dance! as your hand
    Presses the hair
  Streaming away unconfined.
    Leap in the air
  Light as the deer; footsteps resound
    Aiding our dance, beating the ground.
Praise Athene, Maid divine, unrivalled in her
    might,
Dweller in the Brazen Home, unconquered in the
    fight.

    (All go out singing and dancing.)

[33]Cypris is Aphrodite.

[34]The choral passage that follows contains numerous references to places and persons associated with Sparta.

    Lysistrata has a question as its basis: How can the Peloponnesian War be
brought to an end? Aristophanes had already devoted two plays—*Acharnians*
(425) and *Peace* (421)—to this general subject. *Lysistrata* (411) was produced
when Athens' fortunes were near their lowest ebb. The city had recently sent an
expedition against the Greek settlements in Sicily, both because of their riches
and because they were the principal suppliers of food to Sparta. This expedition
ended with Athens' vast navy destroyed and all survivors enslaved. Since Athens'

power depended on its navy, the defeat in Sicily was a signal for allies to desert and enemies to attack.

Athens was in an especially vulnerable position because its preeminence in Greece was based on a contradiction: Athens was the most democratic of the Greek states, but its power and wealth derived from its domination of an empire of subject states. This empire had come into being only gradually. Following the defeat of Persia around 480 B.C., primarily owing to the Athenian navy, Athens had assumed the role of protector for the Greek states of the eastern Mediterranean. In the beginning its role was benign, since its sea power made commerce safe and military attack unwise. From each of its protectorates, Athens received annual payments. But, once its position of power was secure, Athens increased at will the sums tributary states had to pay, and it refused to let states withdraw, going so far as to annihilate some cities and execute their male citizens. Thus, the alliance was no longer voluntary, and resentment against Athens grew. With the monies it received from the empire, Athens kept its navy strong, but it also drew on the funds to beautify Athens, perhaps most notably with the Parthenon and other buildings on the Acropolis. Much of the Athenian art that we so admire was made possible by the subjugation of other Greek states. The Peloponnesian War originated in the desire of some states to withdraw and of others to evade Athens' attempt to force them into its empire. These states secured the support of Sparta, Athens' major rival among Greek states.

When the Athenian navy was destroyed in Siciliy, Athens' unwilling allies seized the opportunity to withdraw from the empire, and Sparta capitalized on Athens' weakness by seizing territory that cut Athens off from its major overland food supply and access to its silver mines, which were crucial to regaining its wealth. Nevertheless, Athens was able to build a new navy quickly, to fend off its enemies, and to regain many of its lost territories. But it was never to recover fully.

It is against this background that *Lysistrata* was written and performed. Lysistrata (whose name can be translated "She who disbands the armies") has hit upon a sex strike as a final desperate attempt to bring the men of Greece to their senses. No one in the play ever discusses the issues underlying the war or seeks to assess the rightness or wrongness of either side; although some specific events are referred to, most are merely cited as examples of male ineptitude. Aristophanes tends to depict the war as a family quarrel by drawing parallels between the divisions among Greek states and the divisions among husbands and wives that result from the sex strike. Thus, reconciliation demands that not only individual families but also all Greeks be reconciled. The sex strike, then, is used not merely for its comic possibilities but also to represent the divisions among Greek city-states.

The play's structure resembles that of other Old Comedies. In the *prologue*, Lysistrata presents her plan for ending the war, which, after some initial opposition, is adopted. When the plan is discussed, Lysistrata instructs the women to go home, dress and act provocatively to arouse their husbands sexually, and then to thwart their husbands' desires until they agree to peace. But, in actuality the women take over the Acropolis, the center of government, since it contains the temple of the goddess Athena (the religious center of the state) and the treasury (the financial basis of government). The women, in blocking access to the treasury, emulate Sparta, which had blocked Athenian access to its silver mines. The *parodos* graphically illustrates the division between male and female by its use of two semichoruses, one of old men, the other of old women. The emphasis in the choral passages, however, is not on sex but on physical and verbal combativeness.

Another typical feature of Old Comedy, the *agon* (or debate over the rightness or wrongness of the happy idea) occurs during the first *episode*—but only after the women have routed the police. The debate between Lysistrata and the Commissioner is rather one-sided, since he is never allowed to present his arguments. Nevertheless, just as the play as a whole shows the need for unity among Greeks, this scene argues the need for women to participate in decisions that affect them. Lysistrata effectively argues that through their exclusion from governmental decisions, women become the victims of male insensitivity and ineptitude. She also shows that the women are more sensible than the men, as well as more able to defend themselves. Although the Commissioner does not concede defeat, he is forced to retire, and the women's triumph is further established during the choral ode that follows.

The remainder of the play is composed of scenes showing the results of putting Lysistrata's plan into effect. Several days seem to have elapsed when the second episode begins. We see first the effect on the women, whose sexual frustrations lead them to try to escape to their husbands. Then comes the most famous and most amusing of the play's scenes: Kinesias's attempts to get his wife Myrrhine into bed and his hopeless frustration. (The names Kinesias and Myrrhine are given sexual connotations in the Greek text.) After the Spartan Herald demonstrates that all Greece is near the breaking point, he is sent back to summon delegates to a peace conference.

The reconciliation then begins, first with the Chorus as the Old Women seek to comfort the Old Men. In this choral section we also find the remnant of a *parabasis*, which otherwise is omitted from *Lysistrata*. During the peace conference Lysistrata makes eloquent appeals for compromise and understanding, although the men are more interested in the anatomy of Reconciliation than in the issues. The *exodos* shows the feasting, drinking, and merrymaking that come with peacemaking. It also includes beautiful lyrics that praise Sparta and Athens, their alliance in the past, and the promise of future harmony. The play ends with husbands and wives, Spartans and Athenians (and indeed all Greeks) united.

Although Aristophanes writes of current events and refers often to specific persons or happenings, he avoids realism. Instead, he adopts the techniques of the tall tale. In characterizing his men and women, he draws on popular stereotypes and pushes them to the extreme: his women are primarily concerned with sex, wine, finery, gossip, and troublemaking; his men are inept male chauvinists who leap to conclusions about public affairs and look condescendingly on family relationships. Character differentiations depend on age and a few psychological traits. Moral traits are almost wholly absent. Aristophanes also draws on stereotypes in depicting his Spartans as country bumpkins who (from the Athenian point of view) spoke a strange Greek dialect.

Lysistrata may be classified as a comedy of ideas, for, though plot and character are significant elements, it is the happy idea and the results of putting it into effect that unify the action. As in most of Aristophanes' plays, in *Lysistrata* the characters resist all persuasion except that which promises more sex, food, and drink. Subtlety of thought is not a trait of the characters. In arguing with the Commissioner, the program proposed by Lysistrata to set Athens' affairs straight foreshadows the promises made by present-day office seekers: she would rid the government of graft, establish a sound fiscal policy, mend relationships with friendly states, and use diplomacy to end quarrels with enemies. These may be worthy goals but they are not so easily achieved as Lysistrata seems to suggest. But, it is unwise to expect characters in plays to propose workable schemes to remedy real-life situations. Like Brecht in the twentieth century, Aristophanes seeks through his plays to stimulate audiences to think about problems in real life and to seek solutions to them. Although Aristophanes resolves his dramatic conflict within the framework of *Lysistrata*, he points to a real-life conflict beyond the play upon whose resolution the welfare of all Greece depends.

It was, of course, easier for Aristophanes to point out the need for an end to the war than it was to bring it about. When *Lysistrata* was presented, Athens' enemies were not inclined to favor peace since they seemed to be winning, and Athens itself was so disunified that before a year had passed its form of government had been changed three times: the democracy was overthrown and replaced by an oligarchy; the oligarchy was replaced by a blend of democracy and oligarchy; and finally democracy was reinstated. The war dragged on until Athens surrendered in 404 B.C.

The defeat of Athens coincided with the end of Athens' greatness in dramatic writing. Both Sophocles and Euripides had died in 406 and were to have no outstanding successors in tragic writing. Aristophanes continued to write for another 15 years, but with the defeat of Athens went his freedom to deal forthrightly with political and social issues. Athens soon regained its position as the artistic and intellectual center of Greece, and drama continued to be presented at the Dionysian festivals for several hundred years, but the achievements of the fifth century were never matched by later Greek dramatists. The plays that have survived from the fifth century established a standard of excellence seldom equaled in the history of Western civilization.

Pseudolus

by Plautus / Translated by Lionel Casson

During the 250 years preceding the birth of Christ, Rome gradually replaced Greece as the major power in Europe; it was to remain dominant until about 500 A.D. When the Romans encountered Greek culture, they assimilated much of it, including drama. The first regular comedy and tragedy were performed in Rome in 240 B.C., and thereafter dramatic entertainments remained prominent in Roman life.

If the Romans borrowed much, they also changed much. Like the Greeks, they performed their dramas at religious festivals, but whereas the Greeks had reserved plays for those festivals honoring Dionysus, the Romans presented plays at the festivals of several gods. Furthermore, in Rome drama was only one among many events offered at each festival. Others included chariot races, boxing matches, tightrope walking, and juggling; eventually gladiatorial combats, mock sea battles, and fights among animals or between men and animals were added. Drama had to compete with these events and it is probably for this reason that the drama of Rome lacks the profundity of that written in Greece. All events at a festival were offered free to audiences, who, like Americans switching from one television channel to another, moved from one attraction to another. If, over a period of time, a feature of the festival ceased to interest a sizable audience, it was dropped. Thus, there was a clear incentive to cater to audience tastes.

Regular comedy and tragedy did not retain their popularity for long. They flourished primarily in the years between 240 and 140 B.C. and thereafter were replaced by minor dramatic forms such as short farces, mimes, and variety entertainment (singing, dancing, acrobatics, and dramatic skits emphasizing sex and violence). But the Roman plays that survived—28 comedies and 10 tragedies— were to be among the most influential ever written, for when in the Renaissance interest in drama revived, dramatists turned to Rome for models to imitate and the new plays established traditions that have continued to the present.

All surviving Roman comedies are the work of two writers—Plautus (c.254–c.184 B.C.) and Terence (c.195–159 B.C.)—and all are based on Greek New Comedy. Since none of the Greek plays on which the adaptations are based has survived, it is difficult to judge the originality of Roman comic writers. Typically, a Roman comedy concerns a young man who seeks to rescue a young woman from the clutches of a pimp and save her from a life of slavery or prostitution; the young man's plans are usually discovered by his disapproving father, who seeks to thwart them; the young man turns to a trusted slave to assist him, and there follows a series of intrigues and complications that are most often resolved when objections to the young man's plans are removed by the discovery that the girl is the long-lost daughter of a well-to-do Athenian merchant. The Greek settings are retained as are Greek costumes and masks. The characters usually fall into a few conventionalized types: the obstinate father, the love-sick son, the clever slave, the pimp, and the braggart soldier. Few respectable women appear on stage, but they may figure prominently in the offstage action. All roles were played by men. A major change from Greek New Comedy was the abandonment of the chorus. The musical element, which in Greek drama is associated with the chorus, is in Roman comedy integrated into the episodes. Roman plays include a number of songs, and, in the original productions, up to two-thirds of the lines were accompanied by an on-stage flutist. Thus, Roman comedies bear a close resemblance to our musicals.

The theatres in which the plays were produced resembled those of Greece but differed in many details. They seated from 10,000 to 20,000 persons. The stage, raised about five feet above a semicircular orchestra, was long (100–300 feet) and deep (20–40 feet); it was backed by a facade (decorated with columns, statues, and niches) with three doors, which in comedy represented entrances to separate houses fronting a street (the stage); the exit at one end of the stage was treated as leading to the country, and that at the other end was treated as leading to the town. In seeking to envision a Roman comedy as originally presented, we need to keep in mind the festive occasion, large audience, massive theatre, stereotyped characters, conventionalized costumes and masks, and the extended musical accompaniment.

Of all Roman playwrights, Plautus was the most popular. Twenty-two of his plays, written between 205 and 185 B.C., have survived. From among these, *Pseudolus* (produced in 191 B.C.) has been chosen to represent Roman comedy. Although it is not one of the best known of the surviving plays, it embodies most of the characteristic features of Roman comedy. To those familiar with *A Funny Thing Happened on the Way to the Forum*, *Pseudolus* will seem familiar for it served as a principal source for that Broadway musical.

DRAMATIS PERSONAE

PSEUDOLUS *servant of Simo (slave)*

CALIDORUS *a young man about town, son of Simo*

BALLIO *a pimp*

SIMO *an elderly gentleman, father of Calidorus*

CALLIPHO *an elderly gentleman, neighbor of Simo*

HARPAX *orderly of an officer in the Macedonian army (slave)*

CHARINUS *friend of Calidorus*

A SLAVE BOY OF BALLIO

A COOK

MONKEY (SIMIA) *servant belonging to Charinus's family (slave)*

SERVANTS AND COURTESANS

SCENE

A street in Athens. Three houses front on it: stage left SIMO's, *center* CALLIPHO's, *right* BALLIO's. *The exit on stage left leads downtown, that on stage right to the country.*

PROLOGUE

You'd better get up and stretch your legs. There's a play by Plautus coming on, and it's a long one.[1]

ACT I

(The door of CALIDORUS' *house opens, and* CALIDORUS *and* PSEUDOLUS *walk out.* CALIDORUS, *"beauty's gift," is ancient comedy's traditional rich man's son: handsome, well-dressed, empty-headed, and unemployable. At the moment he is in a ludicrously blank state of despair, staring wordlessly at a set of waxed wooden tablets bound with cord (the ancient equivalent of folded sheets of paper) which he clutches with both hands.*

If CALIDORUS *has no brains,* PSEUDOLUS, *"tricky," the family servant, has enough for both. These are encased in an enormous head, which, along with a bulging belly and a pair of oversize feet, give* PSEUDOLUS *a most deceptively clownlike appearance.)*

PSEUDOLUS: If I could figure out from this silence of yours what's the misery that's making you miserable, I'd have the pleasure of saving two men trouble: me of asking you questions and you of answering them. But I can't, so I've got to put the question. Tell me, what's the matter? For days now you've been going around more dead than alive, holding that letter in your hands, washing it down with tears, and not confiding in anyone. Talk, will you! I'm in the dark; share the light with me.

CALIDORUS: *(Dully)* I'm miserable. Miserably miserable.

PSEUDOLUS: God forbid!

CALIDORUS: God has no jurisdiction in my case. I'm serving a sentence from Love, not God.

PSEUDOLUS: Am I allowed to know what it's all about? After all, up to now I was Accessory-in-Chief to all your projects.

CALIDORUS: I haven't changed.

[1]The original prologue has been lost.

PSEUDOLUS: Then let me in on what's ailing you. *(Importantly)* Resources, services, or good advice at your disposal.

CALIDORUS: *(Handing him the tablets)* Take this letter. Then you can recite yourself the story of the worry and woe that's wasting me away.

PSEUDOLUS: *(Taking the tablets)* Anything to make you happy. *(Turning them every which way and holding them at various distances from his eyes)* Hey, what's this?

CALIDORUS: What's what?

PSEUDOLUS: If you ask me, the letters here want to have babies: each one's mounting the other.

CALIDORUS: *(Bitterly)* Got to have your joke, don't you?

PSEUDOLUS: *(Still turning and twisting the tablets)* Maybe our Lady of the Riddles can read them, but I swear nobody else can.

CALIDORUS: *(Choking up)* Why are you so cruel to the lovely letters of this lovely letter written in such a lovely hand?

PSEUDOLUS: Damn it all, I ask you now: do hens have hands? Because, believe me, some hen scribbled these letters.

CALIDORUS: *(Exasperated)* You make me sick! *(Reaching for the tablets)* Either read it or hand it back.

PSEUDOLUS: *(Holding them out of reach)* Oh no. I'll read it to the bitter end. Listen, and keep your mind on what I say.

*   *   *

CALIDORUS: *(Impatiently)* Get going, will you!

PSEUDOLUS: *(Reading aloud)* "Dear sweetheart Calidorus. With tears in my eyes and tremors in my mind and heart and soul, . . . I send you my best wishes for *your* well-being—and my prayers for your help with *mine.*"

CALIDORUS: *(Frenzied)* Pseudolus! I'm lost! I'll never get what I need to help with hers!

PSEUDOLUS: What do you need?

CALIDORUS: *(Dolefully)* Gold.

PSEUDOLUS: *(Sticking the tablets in front of* CALIDORUS' *nose)* She sends best wishes in wood, and you want to answer in gold? Watch what you're doing, will you!

CALIDORUS: *(Dully)* Just go on reading. You'll find out soon enough how urgent it is that I get my hands on some gold.

PSEUDOLUS: *(Resuming his reading)* "The pimp has sold me for five thousand dollars to a foreigner, a major from Macedon. He's already left for home, after putting up a deposit of four thousand; all that's holding matters up is a mere one thousand dollars. To arrange payment of this, the major left behind as means of identification his own picture stamped by his seal ring on a wax seal; the pimp is to hand me over to whoever arrives with an identical seal. And the date fixed for my departure is this coming Dionysus Day."

CALIDORUS: *(Miserably)* That's tomorrow. My end is practically upon me—unless you can help.

PSEUDOLUS: *(Impatiently)* Let me finish reading.

CALIDORUS: Go ahead. *(Starry-eyed)* It makes me feel I'm talking with her. Read on; now you'll mix in some sweet for me along with the bitter.

PSEUDOLUS: *(Reading)* "Now our love, our life, the things we shared, our jokes and play and talks and soft-sweet kisses, the tight embrace of impassioned bodies in love, the soft pressure of parted lips meeting tenderly, the burgeoning of my breasts under the sweet caress of your hand—all these joys will be taken away, torn away, trampled away—for you as well as for me—if you do not come to my rescue and I to yours. I have done my share; now you know all that I know. I shall soon find out whether your love is real or pretended. Your loving Rosy."

CALIDORUS: *(Sobbing)* A piece of writing to make a man miserable, Pseudolus.

PSEUDOLUS: *(Glancing at the handwriting again)* Oh yes. Absolutely miserable.

CALIDORUS: *(Reproachfully)* Then why aren't you crying?

PSEUDOLUS: My eyes are made out of sand. I can't get them to squirt a single tear.

CALIDORUS: How come?

PSEUDOLUS: *(Dryly)* Chronic dryness of the eyes. Runs through the whole family.

CALIDORUS: *(Dismayed)* You don't have the heart to help me?

PSEUDOLUS: *(Shrugging disinterestedly)* What do you expect from me?

* * *

CALIDORUS: *(Resigned)* Then it's all over with me today. Could you please lend me two dollars? I'll pay you back tomorrow.

PSEUDOLUS: I couldn't raise that much even if I put my own self in hock. What are you going to do with two dollars, anyway?

CALIDORUS: Buy myself a rope.

PSEUDOLUS: What for?

CALIDORUS: To turn myself into a pendulum. I've decided to darken my eyes before dark today.

PSEUDOLUS: Then who'll pay me back my two dollars if I lend it to you? *(Suspiciously)* Are you deliberately planning to hang yourself just to do me out of two dollars if I lend it to you?

CALIDORUS: *(Starting to sob again)* I simply can't go on living if she's taken away from me and carried far, far away.

PSEUDOLUS: Stop crying, you dumb cluck! You'll live.

CALIDORUS: Why shouldn't I cry? I don't have a penny in my pocket and not the slightest prospect of borrowing anything from anybody.

PSEUDOLUS: *(Impatiently)* As I gather from this letter, unless you can cry some cash for her, all this shedding of tears to demonstrate your affections does about as much good as using a sieve for a cistern. *(As* CALIDORUS *starts wailing louder than ever)* But stop worrying, fond lover; I won't desert you. I'm a good operator; I have high hopes of finding salvation for you somewhere—financial salvation. Where am I going to get it? I can't tell you where; I don't know where. But I'll get it all right: I have a hunch today's my lucky day.

CALIDORUS: *(Hopelessly)* You say you can do it—if only you can do what you say!

PSEUDOLUS: *(Hurt)* Why, you know darn well the kind of ruckus I can raise once I start my hocus-pocus.

CALIDORUS: *(Desperately)* My life depends on you! You're my only hope!

PSEUDOLUS: *(Airily)* I'll arrange either to get you the girl or the five thousand. Will that satisfy you?

CALIDORUS: *(Doubtfully)* Yes—if you'll do it.

PSEUDOLUS: *(In the best lawyerlike fashion)*

Now put in a formal request for five thousand so I can prove I perform what I promise. *(CALIDORUS stares at him blankly)* For god's sake, ask, will you! I'm dying to make you a promise.

CALIDORUS: *(His heart not in it)* Do you hereby agree to give me five thousand in cash today?

PSEUDOLUS: I hereby agree. And now stop bothering me. And, just so you won't tell me later that I didn't tell you, I'm telling you in advance: if I can't get it from anyone else, I'll hit your father up for it.

CALIDORUS: *(Fervently)* God bless you! *(Becoming very grave)* But I want to be a dutiful son, so, if possible, put the touch on my mother too.

PSEUDOLUS: *(Confidently)* You're all set. Go to bed . . . *(Turning to the audience; in the tones of a town crier)* And now, so no one will say I didn't warn him, I hereby give public notice to everybody, voters, citizens, all my friends and acquaintances: watch out for me all day long! Don't trust me!

CALIDORUS: Shh! Keep quiet! Please!

PSEUDOLUS: *(Surprised)* What's up?

CALIDORUS: The pimp's door handle just twisted.

PSEUDOLUS: I wish to god it was his neck.

CALIDORUS: And there he is, the dirty double-crosser. He's coming out.

(The two move to an unobtrusive spot off to the side. The door swings open, and BALLIO, *"tosser around," the pimp, steps out, hefting a mean-looking whip.*

BALLIO *is a businessman in a thoroughly unpleasant business: he owns a bevy of slave girls whom he supplies to those with the wherewithal to hire them or buy them outright. A straggly beard on his chin, a permanent snarl on his lips, an avaricious glint in his eye, and a filthy miserly get-up make him as unappetizing in appearance as in métier.)*

(Song)

BALLIO: *(Turning and shouting through the open door)*
Come out of the house, good-for-nothings, come out!
What a mistake to have bought you and kept you about!
(Six terrified slave boys—miserable, underfed specimens in rags—scamper out of the door
and huddle in front of it; one holds a shopping basket and a purse, another a jug, another an ax. BALLIO eyes them distastefully, then turns to the audience)*
Not a one in the lot ever got the idea
To do anything good.
(Brandishing the whip)
        Without using this here,
They're all useless. To put them to use takes abuse.
And I've never seen hides more like donkeys', I swear:
They've been drubbed so, they've even grown calluses there;
Why, to thrash them takes less out of them than of you.
To be wear-the-whip-outers comes natural to
    The whole breed. The one thought in their heads
        Is to snatch, steal,
        Grab, make hay,
        Gorge, swill,
        And run away.
It's their one, single purpose in life. Why, I say
I'd as soon let a wolf guard my sheep any day,
As let these watch my house any time I'm away.
    (BALLIO glares at them. They summon up sickly smiles. He turns back to the audience.)
    Oh, their faces look fine; you can't go by their looks.
    It's at work that they pull every trick in the books.
    (He swings around abruptly and starts flailing with the whip.)
    Get the sleep from your eyes! Get the sloth from your brain!
    (Lowers the whip. Importantly)
    Pay attention. I'll shortly begin to explain
    The orders of the day.
    Listen hard or I'll batter your butts till they turn
    Every color, as gay
    As a highly embroidered Neapolitan shawl
    Or a Persian brocade with its beasties and all.
    (Shifts to a deadly menacing tone)
    I issued orders yesterday assigning each of you
    A station and official list of things he had to do.

You're such a bunch of loafers, though,
  such inborn stinkers that
(Shaking the whip)
You've forced me to remind you of your
  duties with this cat!
(Wearily lowering the whip)
My whip and I admit defeat; the victory's
  yours instead.
And it's all because of the way you're
  made—so hard in hide and head!
*(As the slaves visibly relax, he suddenly
  flails about madly with the whip, and
  they all make a wild scramble for
  safety. He addresses the audience with
  mock exasperation, gesturing toward
  the cowering slaves who are paying far
  more attention to the arc described by
  the whip than to him.)*
Now look at that, if you please! You see
  the way their minds will stray?
(Turning back to the slaves)
You mind me now, you hear! You tune
  those ears to what I say.
You stinkers, born and bred with special
  whip-proof back and side,
Remember that my rawhide's always
  harder than your hide.
*(Lunges suddenly and lands a blow on the
  nearest one, who lets out a howl.)*
What's up? It hurts? It's what I give a slave
  who's snotty to
His master. Now come here; face me, and
  hear what you're to do.
*(The slaves line up, keeping a wary eye
  on the whip.* BALLIO *addresses the one
  who is carrying a jug.)*
First you who's got the jug. Get water and
  fill the cooking pot.
(He turns to the one carrying an ax.)
And you with the ax I appoint my Chief
  of Fuel Supply.
        SLAVE: *(Timidly showing the ax)*
But it's not
Got an edge, it's too dull to use!
        BALLIO: *(Grinning like a hyena)*
So what?
*(Gesturing toward the whole cowering
  group)*
The whip's dulled your edge too.
Doesn't make the slightest difference to
  me—I keep using all of you.

*(*BALLIO *turns to the third)*
You make that whole house shine. You've
  got your job, now hop, you lout!
(To the fourth)
And you're Official Chair-Man.
(To the fifth)
And you clean silver and lay it out.
(To all of them)
Once I'm back from shopping, mind I find
  that everything's done—
Sweeping, setting, cleaning, shining—no
  chore undone, not one!
*(Switching to a tone of bloodcurdling
  enthusiasm)*
It's my birthday today. You must help
  celebrate.
Put the pig in the pot, from the trotters to
  pate.
Is that clear? I'm inviting big names; a big
  splash
Is the thing—make them think that I
  squander the cash.
Now go in and get going so there'll be no
  delay
When the chef makes it here. Because *I'm*
  on my way
To the market; I'm off on a fish-buying
  jag.
*(To the slave carrying a basket under one
  arm and a purse over one shoulder)*
Go in front. I'm back here to keep thieves
  from that bag.
*(They start walking off, while the others
  race inside.* BALLIO *suddenly stops
  short.)*
Wait a second. I almost forgot. I'm not
  through.
*(Goes to the doorway and calls through
  it)*
Can you hear me, you girls? I've an
  announcement for you.
*(Four flashily dressed, heavily made-up
  girls step out and line up sullenly in
  front of him. He gives them his hyena
  grin, and then addresses them.)*
You're all living in clover, my sweet little
  sprites.
You're all girls with a name, and the
  town's leading lights
Are your clients. Today I'll find out what
  you're at.

Do you work to get free? Or to gorge and
　　get fat?
To acquire a nest egg? Or sleep until three?
Yes, today I'll work out who I think will
　　get free
Or I think will wind up being sold for a
　　whore.
(Rubbing his hands, his eyes gleaming)
Have your clients bring in birthday
　　presents galore!
For today we lay in one year's bread,
　　drink, and meat
Or tomorrow I'll have you out walking the
　　street.
Now, you know it's my birthday. Well,
　　have them kick in,
All the boy friends for whom you've been
　　"Doll," "Bunnykin,"
"Cutie-pie," "Honeybunch," Sweetheart,"
　　and "Pet,"
"Snookle-puss," "Babykins," "Ducky," et cet.
Make their slaves, bearing gifties, come by
　　in brigades!
(Glaring at them)
All the jewelry, money, the clothes and
　　brocades
That I've had to provide — what's it got
　　me, I say?
Not a dime, only woe, from you bitches
　　today!
All your passion's for drink, to tank up,
　　whereas I
Have to live my whole life with a gullet
　　bone dry!
(He paces up and down a few seconds in a
　　rage. Then, in calmer tones)
And now, I'll call you up by name and
　　give you each the word.
This plan's the best since no one then can
　　claim she hadn't heard.
So, all of you,
Here's what you do.
I'll start with Sweetsie, darling of the men
　　who market grain.
Since each one stocks a good-sized hill,
　　you're please to make them rain
Enough on me to give our house a year's
　　supply to eat,
A flood so big my name will change from
　　"Pimp" to "King of Wheat."

PSEUDOLUS: (Sotto voce, to CALIDORUS)
Do you hear the rat talk? Like a pretty big
　　dealer,
Don't you think?
CALIDORUS: (Sotto voce, to PSEUDOLUS)
　　　　　　Good god, yes! And a
　　pretty big stealer.
Now shut up. Pay attention to what he
　　says next.
BALLIO: (Turning to the second girl)
Now listen, Golddig. You're the girl the
　　butchers all adore.
(They're like us pimps: they take their
　　cut — their pound of flesh and more!)
You bring me in three meathooks loaded
　　down with beef today
Or tomorrow you play Dirce — and her
　　story goes this way:
Her stepsons squared accounts with her by
　　hitching her to a bull.
Well, you I'll stretch on a meathook, see —
　　and that's a bull with pull!
PSEUDOLUS: (Aside, raging)
You hear him talk? I'm burning up — he's
　　got me hopping mad!
How can you, Youth of Athens, patronize
　　a man this bad?
Come out here, all you youngsters who've
　　been buying love from pimps,
Let's gather altogether, boys, and everyone
　　take part
To rid the citizen body of this canker at its
　　heart!
(Shakes his head gloomily, all his
　　excitement suddenly drained from
　　him.)
Pseudolus, you've got to learn,
Pseudolus, you've got no brains.
Why, sex makes youngsters all behave
Toward any pimp just like his slave
And rush to do his every whim.
And you want them to be so brave
They'll up and do away with him!
CALIDORUS: (Sotto voce, wildly)
Oh, shut your trap! You give me a pain —
　　you're drowning out what he's saying!
　　　　　*　　　*　　　*
BALLIO: (Turning to the third girl)
Your turn. Now listen, Olive, sweetheart
　　of the oil-trade crew.

When it comes to ready stock on hand,
    your lovers keep beaucoup.
I want a load of jugs of oil, and you'll
    produce tout' suite,
Or tomorrow *you'll* get boiled in oil and
    dumped out on the street;
I'll set a bed for you out there, where *you*
    won't get much rest
Though you'll be plenty tired—why say
    more? By now you've guessed.
You've got a mob of boy friends who just
    roll in oil, but you
Couldn't give your fellow slaves today a
    drop for their shampoo
Or give your lord and master some for
    juicing up his stew.
I know the reason too:
You don't have very much use for oil—
Your anointing's done with alcohol!
(Glaring at all of them)
All right! You carry out the orders that
    I've given you today,
(Shaking the whip)
Or, gad, I'll let you have it, all at once and
    in one way!
(He turns to the last girl, by far the best
looking of the four. It is Phoenicium,
"Rosy," CALIDORUS' inamorata.)
And now the girl always just about to buy
    her freedom and dash.
You're good at promising payment—but
    no good at raising cash.
Now, heartthrob of the upper crust, to you
    I've this to say.
Your boy friends, Rosy, own big farms; so
    you produce today
A load of all the stuff they raise or
    tomorrow *you* will pay;
I'll have you walking streets, my dame,
Your hide tanned brighter than your
    name.

(BALLIO and his marketing attendant remain where
they are. The girls, shuffling despondently, start
filing into the house under BALLIO's baleful gaze.
He does not hear the following conversation
which CALIDORUS and PSEUDOLUS hold sotto voce.)

CALIDORUS: *(Agonized)*
    Pseudolus! Hear what he says?

PSEUDOLUS: *(Mimicking his tone)*
                       Calidorus! I
    heard.
(Thoughtfully)
    And I'm thinking it out.
CALIDORUS: *(As before)*
                    What ideas have
    you got
Of a gift I can send so he'll weaken and
    not
Make a whore of my girl.
PSEUDOLUS: *(Patting his back*
    encouragingly)
                    Don't you worry.
    Don't be blue.
(Tapping his breast importantly)
Because *I'll* do the worrying for me and for
    you.

CALIDORUS: *(Hopelessly)*
    What's the use?
PSEUDOLUS: *(Taking him by the arm and*
    starting to haul him off)
                Won't you please run
    along? You just go.
And get thinking about something else.
CALIDORUS: *(Stubbornly resisting the*
    pulling)
                 Whoa there, whoa!
PSEUDOLUS: *(Tugging harder)*
    No there, no!
CALIDORUS: *(Almost in tears)*
    But I'm heartbroken!
PSEUDOLUS: *(Still hauling, though without*
    much effect)
               Harden your heart.
CALIDORUS: *(Piteously)*
    No, impossible
PSEUDOLUS: *(As before)*
             Do the impossible. Start.
CALIDORUS: *(Dumbly)*
    I'm to start the impossible? How?
PSEUDOLUS: *(As before)*
               Fight your heart.
Turn your mind to what's good. Heart's in
    tears? Close your ears!
CALIDORUS: *(Sadly and thoughtfully)*
    Oh, that's nonsense. A lover must act like
    a fool.
    Otherwise it's no fun.

PSEUDOLUS: *(Giving up the hauling and throwing up his hands in digust)*
           Since you won't stop
this drool—

     *   *   *

(At this moment the last of the girls shuffles inside, and BALLIO *turns around.)*

BALLIO: *(To his marketing attendant)*
We should go for that fish.
Time's awasting. Lead on.
CALIDORUS: *(Catching sight of them going off, frantically)*
          Hey, he's off!
Call him back!

(He wheels about to go after BALLIO. PSEUDOLUS *grabs him.)*

PSEUDOLUS: *(Calmly)*
Easy boy! What's the hurry?
CALIDORUS: *(Frantically)*
           Because, if
we're slack
He'll be gone
BALLIO: *(To his slave boy, kicking him brutally)*
        So you're taking it easy, boy,
eh?
PSEUDOLUS: *(Calling in dulcet tones)*
May I speak with you, birthday boy?
Birthday boy! Hey!
Turn around and look back, will you
please? Yes, we know
That you're rushed but we *must* hold you
up, even so.
(As BALLIO *keeps walking)*
Hey there, stop, will you! Look, there's
some people here who
Are most anxious to talk over matters with
you.
BALLIO: *(Stopping—but not turning; exasperated)*
It's just when I'm rushed that these
goddam yahoos
Hold me up! What's the matter? Who is it?
PSEUDOLUS: *(Dramatically)*
          One who's
Spent his life making sure that you
prosper and thrive!

BALLIO: *(As if to himself, muttering)*
Spent his life? Then he's dead. I prefer one
who's alive.
PSEUDOLUS:
Don't be snooty, there, you!
BALLIO:
            Don't annoy
me, there, you!

(BALLIO, *still without turning around, starts walking again.)*

CALIDORUS: *(To* PSEUDOLUS, *frantically)*
Hurry up! Hold him back!
BALLIO: *(Over his shoulder to his slave who is standing goggle-eyed)*
          Get a move on,
you, too!
PSEUDOLUS: *(To* CALIDORUS)
Hey, come this way! Don't let him
through!

(The two race around and stand blocking BALLIO'S *way.)*

BALLIO: *(To* PSEUDOLUS)
Whoever you are, I'll see you in
hell!
PSEUDOLUS: *(His voice carefully maintaining the ambiguity)*
I'd like to see you.
BALLIO *(To* CALIDORUS)
        And you as well.
(Over his shoulder to his slave as he charges off on a different tack.)
This way!
PSEUDOLUS: *(Nimbly barring the way again)* There's some things I'd like to
clear.
BALLIO:
But *I* wouldn't.
PSEUDOLUS: *(Wheedling)*
        Things you'll like to
hear.
BALLIO: *(Beginning to lose his temper)*
Will you let me go or not?
PSEUDOLUS: *(Grabbing his arm)*
          At ease!
BALLIO *(Thundering)*
Hands off!

CALIDORUS: *(Grabbing the other arm, desperately)*
>But, Ballio, listen, please!

BALLIO: *(Contemptuously)*
I'm deaf to boys who talk hot air.

CALIDORUS: *(Humbly)*
I gave while I had.

BALLIO: *(Grinning evilly)*
>>And I took. That's fair.

CALIDORUS: *(As before)*
When I get, I'll give.

BALLIO: *(As before)*
>>>When you do, I'll
give too.

CALIDORUS: *(Tearing his hair)*
Oh my god! All the money and gifts that I gave!
And to think how I lost it! All gone to the grave!

BALLIO: *(Airily)*
With your cash dead and buried, you're just talking for fun.
You're a fool if you try to go over what's done.

PSEUDOLUS: *(To BALLIO, trying bluster and pointing importantly to CALIDORUS)*
Let me tell you, at least, who he happens to be —

BALLIO: *(Contemptuously)*
Oh, I've known all along who he was.
And now he
Can just know who he is by himself, without me.
(He wheels about and starts to stomp off, calling over his shoulder to his slave.)
Shake a leg, will you!

PSEUDOLUS: *(Slyly)*
>>>Ballio, turn around,
please;
Turn around just this once, and you'll pocket some fees!

(BALLIO stops in his tracks and swivels about.)

BALLIO: *(To the audience)* For that price I'll turn around. I could be praying to god almighty, I could have the holy offerings in my hand ready to give to him, and if a chance to make a buck came along, I'd forget all about religion. No matter what,

the almighty dollar's one religion there's no resisting.

PSEUDOLUS: *(To the audience)* We bend the knees to heaven — and he snaps his finger at it.

BALLIO: *(To the audience, rubbing his hands)* I'll have a talk with them. *(To PSEUDOLUS)* Greetings, stinkingest slave in Athens!

PSEUDOLUS: *(With radiant benevolence)* Heaven put its blessing upon you and give you what *(Winking to CALIDORUS)* this boy and I wish for you. *(Switching to moral sternness)* But, if you deserve otherwise, may it put its curse upon you!

BALLIO: *(Blandly)* How're you doing, Calidorus?

CALIDORUS: I'm dying. Perishing for love — and dead broke.

BALLIO: I'd have some pity — if I could feed my household on pity.

PSEUDOLUS: *(Breaking in impatiently)* Look, we know what you're like, so you can skip the speeches. Do you know what we're here for?

BALLIO: *(Grinning)* Just about. To see me in hell.

PSEUDOLUS: That plus what we just called you back for. Now listen carefully.

BALLIO: *(Brusquely)* I'm listening. But whatever it is you're after, make it short, I'm busy now.

PSEUDOLUS: *(Gravely)* This boy here promised you five thousand for his girl, he promised it for a certain day, he hasn't paid it yet, and he feels terribly sorry about it all.

BALLIO: *(Snarling)* Feeling sorry is a lot easier for a fellow than feeling sore. He feels sorry because he didn't pay; I feel sore because I didn't get paid.

PSEUDOLUS: *(Earnestly)* He'll pay; he'll find a way. Just hold everything these next few days. You see, he's afraid you'll sell his girl because you have it in for him.

BALLIO: *(Sullenly)* He had the chance to give me my money a long time ago — *if* he had really wanted to.

CALIDORUS: *(Helplessly)* What if I didn't have it?

BALLIO: *(To CALIDORUS, contemptuously)* If you were really in love you'd have negotiated a loan — gone to a moneylender, given him his few pennies interest, and then stolen it all back from your father.

PSEUDOLUS: *(With histrionic rage)* He steal

from his father? You have a nerve! No chance of *your* ever giving lessons in honesty.

BALLIO: *(Grinning)* I'm a pimp. That's not my job.

CALIDORUS: *(Bitterly)* How could I steal anything from my father? He's always so careful! *(Suddenly remembering himself, in ringing tones)* What's more, even if I could, I wouldn't. Filial duty, you know.

BALLIO: *(Disgustedly)* I hear you. Then snuggle up to that filial duty of yours at night instead of Rosy. So filial duty is more important to you than your love life, is it? All right, then: is every man in the world your father? Isn't there anyone you can hit up for a loan?

CALIDORUS: *(Miserably)* Loan? There's no such word any more.

PSEUDOLUS: *(To* BALLIO, *confidentially)* Listen, ever since that gang of fakers finished tanking up at the till . . . all the moneylenders have been playing it safe, they're not trusting anyone.

* * *

CALIDORUS: *(Dumbly)* So you won't take pity on me?

BALLIO: Money talks—and you're here with empty pockets. *(Assuming a funereal expression and shaking his head mournfully)* Yet I'd have liked to see you alive and well.

PSEUDOLUS: Hey! He's not dead yet!

BALLIO: Whatever he is, when he talks the way he's been talking, believe me, to me he's dead. The minute a lover begins to plead with a pimp, life's over for him. *(To* CALIDORUS*)* When you come running to me, come with tears that clink. For example, this sob story of yours about not having any money. You're weeping on a stepmother's shoulders, boy!

PSEUDOLUS: Well! And just when did *you* marry his father?

BALLIO: *(Irascibly)* God forbid!

PSEUDOLUS: *(Earnestly, in a last stab at persuasion)* Do what we're asking, Ballio, please! If you're afraid to give *him* credit, trust me. Somewhere, on land or sea, I'll excavate the cash for you.

BALLIO: *(In astonishment)* I trust *you?*

PSEUDOLUS: *(Stoutly)* Why not?

BALLIO: Good god, I'd sooner tie up a runaway dog with a string of sausages than trust you.

CALIDORUS: *(Bitterly)* Is this the thanks I deserve from you? I act nice and you act nasty?

BALLIO: *(Savagely)* What do you want now, anyway?

CALIDORUS: Just hold everything for the next six days or so. Don't sell her. *(Tragically)* Don't destroy the man who loves her!

BALLIO: *(Suddenly effusively affable)* Don't worry. I'll even hold off for the next six months.

CALDORUS: *(In a transport of delight)* That's wonderful! Ballio, you're terrific!

BALLIO: *(Expansively)* Now that you're so happy, would you like me to make you even happier?

CALIDORUS: What do you mean?

BALLIO: *(Beaming)* Rosy's not even for sale now.

CALIDORUS: *(His jaw dropping)* She's not?

BALLIO: Nosirree!

* * *

CALIDORUS: *(To* BALLIO, *deadly serious)* Listen, I've got a question to ask you, and I want a serious answer. Do I understand that Rosy is not for sale?

BALLIO: She most certainly is not. *(Flashing his hyena grin)* You see, I've already sold her.

CALIDORUS: *(Stunned)* How?

BALLIO: *(Deadpan)* Garments excluded; just the carcass, guts and all.

CALIDORUS: *(As before)* You sold *my* girl?

BALLIO: *(Cheerfully)* That's right. For five thousand dollars.

CALIDORUS: *(Gulping)* Five thousand?

BALLIO: *(As before)* Let's say five times one thousand, if you prefer. To a major from Macedon. And I've already collected four thousand.

* * *

CALIDORUS: *(As before)* And you dared to do a thing like that?

BALLIO: *(Shrugging)* I felt like it. She was my property.

* * *

CALIDORUS: *(To* BALLIO*)* Listen here, you dirtiest double-crosser that ever walked the face of the earth, didn't you give me your solemn word you'd sell her to nobody but me?

BALLIO: *(Blandly)* I admit it.

CALIDORUS: Didn't you even cross your heart?

BALLIO: *(As before)* I crossed my fingers *too.*

CALIDORUS: *(Thundering)* You filthy liar, you went back on your word!

BALLIO: *(As before)* But I came into my money. *(Contemptuously)* I'm a filthy liar, but now I've got money to burn tucked away. You're a model son, you come from the right family — and you don't have a dime.

CALIDORUS: Pseudolus! Stand on the other side of him and cuss him out!

PSEUDOLUS: *(Racing around)* Right! I'm covering ground faster than I would en route to City Hall for my emancipation proclamation.

(The two take up positions on either side of BALLIO. CALIDORUS, breathing fire, and PSEUDOLUS, champing at the bit, face each other; BALLIO, standing unconcerned between them, faces the audience.)

CALIDORUS *(To PSEUDOLUS)* Give it to him! Pile it on!

PSEUDOLUS: *(To BALLIO)* Now I'm going to tear you to tatters. With my tongue. *(At the top of his lungs)* Good-for-nothing!

BALLIO: *(Nodding agreeably)* That's right.

PSEUDOLUS: *(As before)* Dirty rat!

BALLIO: *(As before)* It's the truth.

PSEUDOLUS: Jailbait!

BALLIO: Naturally.

PSEUDOLUS: Grave robber!

BALLIO: Of course.

PSEUDOLUS: Skunk!

BALLIO: *(Admiringly)* Very good!

PSEUDOLUS: You'd rob your best friend!

BALLIO: Yes, I'd do that.

PSEUDOLUS: And kill your father!

BALLIO: *(To CALIDORUS, enthusiastically)* Now you take a turn.

CALIDORUS: Church-robber!

BALLIO: I admit it.

CALIDORUS: Dirty double-crosser!

BALLIO: *(Reproachfully)* Old hat. You sang that song before.

*   *   *

PSEUDOLUS: Jailbreaker!

BALLIO: Voici!

CALIDORUS: Lawbreaker!

BALLIO: Obviously.

PSEUDOLUS: Crook!

CALIDORUS: Lousy —

PSEUDOLUS: —pimp!

CALIDORUS: Scum!

BALLIO: *(Bursting into a round of applause)* In fine voice, both of you!

CALIDORUS: *(Losing steam)* You beat your father and mother.

BALLIO: *(Imperturbably)* What's more, I killed them sooner than pay for their upkeep. Nothing wrong in that, was there?

PSEUDOLUS: *(To CALIDORUS, disgusted)* We're pouring into a punctured pot. We're wasting our breath.

BALLIO: *(Making preparations to move on)* Any further comments you would like to make?

CALIDORUS: *(Weakly)* Aren't you ashamed of anything?

BALLIO: *(Angrily)* Aren't *you* ashamed of turning out to be a lover as broke as a nutshell? *(Starts to leave, then suddenly turns around.)* In spite of all the nasty names you've called me, I'll do this for you. Today's the last day for payment; if before tonight that major hasn't handed over the thousand he owes, I think I'll be in a position to do my duty.

CALIDORUS: What's that?

BALLIO: If you pay me first, I'll break my promise to him. *(With his hyena grin)* That's doing my duty. Well, if there was anything in it for me, I'd go on with this chat, but, without any cash, you're just kidding yourself if you think I'll have any pity on you. That's my considered opinion, so you can start figuring out what you're going to do next.

(BALLIO turns and stalks off, stage left, his attendant at his heels.)

CALIDORUS: *(In alarm)* Leaving already?

BALLIO: *(Over his shoulder)* I'm busy every minute right now.

PSEUDOLUS: *(Shaking his fist at the retreating back)* You'll be even busier a little later! *(To himself)* That fellow's my meat, unless god and man both desert me. I'll fillet him just the way a cook fillets an eel. *(To CALIDORUS)* Calidorus, I want your help now.

CALIDORUS: *(Promptly)* At your orders, sir!

PSEUDOLUS: *(Gesturing toward BALLIO's house, thoughtfully)* I want this town besieged and taken by storm before tonight. For this we need a cagey, clever, careful, competent man capable of carrying out orders, who won't go to sleep on his feet.

CALIDORUS: Tell me—what are you up to?

PSEUDOLUS: I'll let you know when the time comes. I don't want to go over it twice. (*Grinning at the audience*) Plays are long enough as is.

* * *

CALIDORUS: (*Enthusiastically*) I'll have him here right away.

PSEUDOLUS: (*Pushing him off*) Can't you get going? All this talk is holding you up.

(CALIDORUS *dashes off, stage left,* PSEUDOLUS *stands where he is, meditating.*

PSEUDOLUS: (*To himself, despondently*) Well, Pseudolus, he's gone off, and you're here on your own. What are you going to do now after all the big talk you handed him? What's going to happen to those promises of yours? You haven't even the shred of a plot in mind. You'd like to weave one, but you don't have a beginning to start from or an end to finish at . . . I told the boy a long time ago that I'd come up with the money for him. I wanted to get it out of the old man but somehow or other he always caught wise first. (*Looking toward the wings, stage left*) But I've got to turn off the talk and shut up! Look who I see coming—our Simo and his neighbor, Callipho. (*Gesturing derisively toward* SIMO) This is the grave I'm going to rob today for the five thousand I need for his son. (*Going over to an unobtrusive spot off to one side*) I'll just move over here where I can listen in on what they say.

(*Two graybeards, deep in conversation, totter in, leaning heavily on their sticks.*
SIMO, CALIDORUS' *father and* PSEUDOLUS' *owner, has the face you would expect on a man who all his life has been a canny, tightfisted businessman; a card shark would look benevolent in comparison.* CALLIPHO *is the exact opposite; his round, innocent countenance exudes goodness and implicit faith in his fellow man.*
From the waggling of the head and other gesticulating, it is clear that SIMO *is in a foul mood.*)

SIMO: (*Angrily*) If we decided to pick a spendthrift or a rake for Governor of Athens, no one, I swear, would be any competition for that son of mine. He's the one topic of conversation in the whole town, how he's got his heart set on freeing

his girl friend and is hunting for the money to do it. I've been getting reports from all sides. But I had smelled something fishy and knew all about it a long time ago; I just pretended I didn't.

PSEUDOLUS: (*Aside, dismayed*) . . . The campaign's collapsed, the offensive's stuck in a rut. There's a tight roadblock across the route I wanted to take to the cash depot . . .

CALLIPHO: (*Indignantly*) If I had my way, people who babble gossip or listen to it would all hang—babblers by the tongue and listeners by the ears. Why, these reports that you're getting, that your son has a love affair and wants to steal from you, may be all just talk, a pack of lies. But even if every word is true, the way people behave these days, what's he done that's so out of the ordinary? What's so odd about a young fellow falling in love and setting his girl friend free?

PSEUDOLUS: (*Aside*) What a nice old man!

SIMO: (*Snarling*) Well, I'm an old fellow, and I don't want it!

CALLIPHO: (*Smiling indulgently*) It won't do you the slightest good not to want it. It *might* have, if you hadn't behaved the same way when you were young. Only a parent who was a paragon can expect his son to be better than he was. And you—the money you threw away and the affairs you had could have taken care of every single solitary male in the city, barring none! Is it any wonder that the son takes after the father?

PSEUDOLUS: (*To himself—but good and loud*) Mon dieu! How few of you decent people there are in this world. Now, *there's* the kind of father a father should be to a son!

SIMO: (*Whirling around*) Who's that talking? (*To* CALLIPHO, *disgusted*) It's my servant Pseudolus. He's the archcriminal who's corrupted my son: he's his guide and mentor. I'd like to see him at the end of a rope!

CALLIPHO: (*Sotto voce*) Now that's very silly of you, to show how angry you are. You'll get much further by being nice to him and finding out whether those reports you're getting are true. . . .

SIMO: (*Sotto voce*) All right. I'll take your advice.

(*The two oldsters start walking toward* PSEUDOLUS.)

PSEUDOLUS: (*To himself*) The offensive's under way, Pseudolus! Have some fast talk ready for the old man. *(As they draw near, beaming)* Greetings to you first, master, as is only right and proper. And if any are left over, *(With a respectful bow to* CALLIPHO) greetings to the neighbors.

SIMO: Greetings. *(All affability)* Well, now, how are we doing?

PSEUDOLUS: *(Leaning back negligently and grinning)* Oh, we're just standing here this way.

SIMO: *(Reverting immediately to type, to* CALLIPHO) Look at that pose, will you? His lordship!

CALLIPHO: I think his pose is very nice. *(Nodding approvingly)* Self-confident.

PSEUDOLUS: *(Virtuously)* If a servant is honest and his conscience is clear, he *should* hold his head high, especially in front of his master.

CALLIPHO: *(Beaming on* PSEUDOLUS) We have a few things we'd like to ask you about. Some rumors we've been hearing that we're a bit vague about.

SIMO: *(To* CALLIPHO, *disgusted)* He'll talk you to death. You'll think it's Socrates and not Pseudolus you're talking to.

PSEUDOLUS: *(To* SIMO, *pathetically)* Yes, you haven't thought very well of me for quite some time now, I can see it. I know — you don't have very much faith in me. *(Squaring his jaw)* You'd like to see me bad and wicked, but, in spite of you, I'm going to be honest and decent!

SIMO: *(Resignedly)* Pseudolus, will you kindly vacate the rooms in your ears so some things I have to say can move in?

PSEUDOLUS: *(Gravely)* Even though I'm very annoyed with you, you go right ahead, say whatever you like.

SIMO: *(Staring at him)* You annoyed with me? The servant annoyed with the master?

PSEUDOLUS: *(Haughtily)* And does that seem so strange to you?

SIMO: My god, the way you talk, I'd better watch out you don't get angry with me. *(Eyeing him narrowly)* You're thinking of giving me a beating, aren't you? And *not* the kind I'm accustomed to give you! *(To* CALLIPHO) What's your idea?

CALLIPHO: *(Vehemently)* I really think he has every right to be angry. After all, you *don't* have much faith in him.

SIMO: *(Sneering)* Well, let him be angry. I'll see to it he does me no damage. *(To* PSEUDOLUS, *brusquely)* Listen, you. What about the things I want to find out?

PSEUDOLUS: *(All co-operation)* Anything you want to know, just ask. And consider whatever you hear from me an oracle from heaven.

SIMO: *(Curtly)* Then pay attention and don't forget your promise. Listen, are you aware that my son is having an affair with a certain chorus girl?

PSEUDOLUS: *(Like an oracle from heaven)* Yea, verily.

SIMO: And that he wants to set her free?

PSEUDOLUS: Yea, verily to that too.

SIMO: And that you're getting your stunts and smart schemes set to steal a certain five thousand dollars from me?

PSEUDOLUS: *(Wide-eyed)* I steal from *you?*

SIMO: *(Grimly)* That's right. To give to my son so he can set the girl free. *(Impatiently, as* PSEUDOLUS *hesitates)* Admit it, just say "Yea, verily to that too."

PSEUDOLUS: *(Meekly)* Yea, verily to that too.

CALLIPHO: *(In shocked surprise)* He admits it!

SIMO: *(To* CALLIPHO, *smugly)* I told you so, all along.

CALLIPHO: *(Sadly)* Yes, I remember.

SIMO: *(To* PSEUDOLUS, *angrily)* Why didn't you tell me the minute you heard instead of hiding it from me? Why didn't *I* hear about it?

PSEUDOLUS: *(Readily)* I'll tell you why. I didn't want to be the one to start a bad precedent — this business of a servant carrying tales about one master to another.

SIMO: *(To* CALLIPHO, *snarling)* He should have been hauled off by the heels to the mill wheel!

CALLIPHO: *(Anxiously)* He didn't do anything wrong, did he?

SIMO: Anything? Everything!

PSEUDOLUS: *(To* CALLIPHO) Don't, Callipho. I know how to handle my own affairs. I deserve the blame. *(To* SIMO) Now listen carefully. Why did I keep you in the dark about your son's love affair? Because he had the mill wheel all set for me if I talked.

SIMO: And you didn't know *I'd* have it all set for you if you kept quiet?

PSEUDOLUS: I knew that.

SIMO: *(Menacingly)* Then why wasn't I told?

PSEUDOLUS: *(Glibly)* Because one evil was in front of me and the other a little farther on. His was right there; with yours I had a teensy breathing spell.

(SIMO glares at him. PSEUDOLUS looks him in the eye serenely.)

SIMO: *(Deciding to accept the explanation)* What are you two going to do now? After all, you can't get any money out of me; I know everything. And I'm going to pass the word right now to everyone in town not to lend you a dime.

PSEUDOLUS: *(Blandly)* Believe me, I'm not going to go begging. Not as long as *you're* alive. Because, by god, *you're* going to give me the money. I'm going to get it from you.

SIMO: *(Superciliously)* So you're going to get it from me, eh?

PSEUDOLUS: And how!

SIMO: Well, by god, you can poke my eyes out if I ever give you that money!

PSEUDOLUS: *(Airily)* You will. I'm telling you about it right now so you'll be on your guard.

SIMO: One thing I'm sure of: if you do pull it off, you deserve a citation for the sensation of the century.

PSEUDOLUS: *(Casually)* I will.

SIMO: *(Ghoulishly)* Suppose you don't?

PSEUDOLUS: *(Promptly)* Whip me to shreds. But suppose I do?

SIMO: *(Promptly)* As god's my witness, I won't lay a finger on you and you can keep the money all your life.

PSEUDOLUS: *(Pointing a warning finger at him)* Don't you forget that.

SIMO: *(Taken aback by PSEUDOLUS' cocksureness, uneasily)* How can you possibly catch me off guard, now that I've been forewarned?

PSEUDOLUS: I gave you fair warning to be on your guard. And I'm telling you now, in so many words: be on your guard. BE ON YOUR GUARD! *(Pointing to SIMO's hands)* Watch out — today, with those two hands, you're going to give me the money.

CALLIPHO: *(Goggle-eyed)* The man's a virtuoso, a maestro, if he keeps his word!

PSEUDOLUS: *(To CALLIPHO, in ringing tones)* Carry me off and make me your slave if I don't!

SIMO: Very nice and friendly of you — but don't you happen to be *my* slave at the moment?

PSEUDOLUS: *(Ignoring the last remark)* Would you like to hear something that'll amaze the both of you even more?

CALLIPHO: *(Enthusiastically)* Oh yes! I'm dying to hear it. I love listening to you.

PSEUDOLUS: *(Turning to SIMO)* Before I conduct my campaign against you, I'm going to fight still another glorious and memorable campaign.

SIMO: What campaign?

PSEUDOLUS: *(Gesturing toward BALLIO's house)* Against the pimp who lives next door. You watch — with my stunts and smart schemes I'm going to pluck that chorus girl your son's pining for plunk from under his pimpish nose.

SIMO: What's that you say?

PSEUDOLUS: *(Triumphantly)* And I'll have both jobs done by tonight!

SIMO: *(Dubiously)* Well, if you make good on all this big talk, you're a better man than Alexander the Great. *(Sternly)* But, if you don't, is there any reason why I shouldn't have you shut up in the mill, pronto?

PSEUDOLUS: *(Promptly)* And not just for one day. For every day of my life as long as I live. But, if I do, will you, of your own free will, give me money for the pimp, pronto?

CALLIPHO: *(As SIMO hesitates)* That's a fair proposition. Tell him you will.

SIMO: *(Clutching CALLIPHO's arm)* You know what I just thought of. Supposing those two have a deal on! Suppose they're in cahoots and have a scheme cooked up to do me out of the money?

PSEUDOLUS: *(Laughing off the suggestion)* Even *I* wouldn't have the nerve to pull a stunt like that! No, Simo, it's not that way at all. *(Earnestly)* If he and I have any deal on, or if we ever had a single meeting or discussion about any deal, you can take a rawhide pen and scribble over my whole hide just as if you were filling up a page with writing.

SIMO: *(Shrugging in acquiescence)* You can announce your act now, whenever you want.

PSEUDOLUS: *(To CALLIPHO)* Callipho, would you please help me and not get tied up in any other business? It's just for today.

CALLIPHO: *(Hesitating)* But I've had everything set up since yesterday to go off to the country . . .

PSEUDOLUS: Well, please dismantle the setup, will you?

CALLIPHO: *(Suddenly making up his mind)* All right. I've decided to stay, for your sake. *(His* eyes glistening) I'm dying to watch your act, Pseudolus. And, if I hear that *(Gesturing toward* SIMO*)* he won't pay you the money he promised, I'll pay it myself rather than see you lose out.

SIMO: *(Muttering)* I won't go back on my word.

PSEUDOLUS: *(To* SIMO, *promptly)* Darned right — because, if you don't come across, I'll dun you, and the din will be long and loud. Now out of here, both of you; get inside and leave the field clear for my hocus-pocus.

CALLIPHO: *(Moving off toward his house)* Right. Anything you say.

PSEUDOLUS: *(Calling to him)* Now I don't want you to leave the house, you hear?

CALLIPHO: Of course. Glad to oblige.

SIMO: *(To* PSEUDOLUS*)* But I have to go downtown. I'll be back right away.

PSEUDOLUS: *(Warningly)* Then hurry.

(CALLIPHO goes into his house, and SIMO leaves, stage left. PSEUDOLUS walks downstage and addresses the audience.)

PSEUDOLUS: I suspect that you suspect that I've made all these big promises . . . and that I'm not going to do the things I said I'd do. *(Mimicking* SIMO*'s tones)* "I won't go back on my word." *(Gaily)* So far as I can see, I can't see how I'm going to do it — but, if there's one thing I *can* see, it's that I *will* do it . . . *(Moving off toward* SIMO*'s house)* And now I'd like to step inside here for a minute while I carry out a mental mobilization of my underhand forces. I won't keep you long; I'm coming right out. Our flutist will entertain you . . . in the meantime.

(PSEUDOLUS races into SIMO*'s house, leaving the stage empty. . . . The flutist . . . plays an entr'-acte.)*

ACT II

(The door of SIMO'S *house flies open.* PSEUDOLUS *bursts out and races downstage to address the audience.)*

Song

PSEUDOLUS: *(Excitedly)*
Holy mackerel! It's marvelous! Everything I try
    Works out just like a charm.
(Tapping his brow)
Up in here is a scheme I can certify
    Is guaranteed free of harm.
(Importantly)
When your eye's on the big things, it's madness, I
    say,
To proceed in a timid or half-hearted way.

    The way that the things work out
    Is completely up to you.
    You want to do big things?
    Then think and act big too!

You take *me*. Why, up here in this head,
    Standing by for the fray,
Are my armies — plus ambush, intrigue,
    Dirty deals, and foul play.

With the courage inherited from a long line of
    heroes,
    With the double-cross serving as shining shield,
The enemy's mine wherever I'll meet him —
    I'll phony my foemen from the field!

    Just watch me now. I'm set to go,
    To fight the man who's our common foe,
    To rally-oh,
    And sally-oh
      'Gainst Ballio!
(Pointing to BALLIO*'s house)*
Here's the fortress I want to lay siege to today.
So I'll draw up my forces in battle array,
And I'll take it by storm — to the joy of the
    nation —
And then quickly re-form for the next operation,

(Pointing to SIMO*'s house)*
To lay siege to the doddering fort over here.
Here I'll load my allies and myself with such
    plunder

I'll be hailed as the scourge of my foes, as a wonder.

(Puffing out his chest)

> I was born to be great;
> It's a family trait —
> To fight battles victorious,
> Memorable, glorious.

(Suddenly looking toward the wings, stage right)

Someone's coming this way. Who's this man that I
    spy?
Who's this stranger so suddenly in the way of my
    eye?
What's he want with that cutlass there, *I'd* like to
    know.
What's his business here? Pseudolus! Ambush the
    foe!

*(*PSEUDOLUS *moves to an unobtrusive spot off to
the side, and, a second later,* HARPAX, *"snatcher,"
enters.* HARPAX *has a sort of primitive cunning and
suspicion in his makeup but, aside from that, is
not very bright. He is an officer's orderly; he wears
a uniform and carries a sword. In one hand he
clutches a purse, obviously well-filled.
The hesitant way in which he walks along,
stopping to peer at the doorways, reveals
immediately that he is a stranger in town).*

HARPAX: *(To himself)*
The report of my eyes confirms, I can see,
The report my commander imparted to me,
    Here's the district and quarter he meant.
Seven blocks from the entrance to town I should
    spot
The pimp's house, where the master said leave the
    whole lot,
    Both this cash and the seal that he sent.
But I'd like to see someone come by who'd make
    clear
If a pimp, name of Ballio, lives around here.
PSEUDOLUS: *(To himself)*
Not a sound! Not a word! Unless heaven and men
    All desert me, this man is my meat!
But I need a new gambit since all of a sudden
    A new path has appeared at my feet.
All the plans I worked out must be jettisoned now;
    In my new start I'll concentrate here.
        (Pointing to HARPAX*)*
So you've come as an errand boy, *mon général?*
    Watch me soon stand you up on your ear!

*(*HARPAX *walks up to* BALLIO's *house and raises his
hand to knock.)*

HARPAX: *(To himself)* I'll knock on the door
and get someone to come out.
PSEUDOLUS: *(Calling)* Hey, whoever you are,
I wish you'd cut out that knocking. You see, I'm
patron protecter of portals. Popped out here for a
precautionary peep.
HARPAX: *(Dubiously)* Are you Ballio?
PSEUDOLUS: *(Importantly)* Not exactly. I'm
Vice-Ballio.
HARPAX: What's that mean?
PSEUDOLUS: *(As before)* Chief layer-outer
and layer-inner. Lord of the larder.
HARPAX: *(Impressed)* You mean to say you're
the major-domo?
PSEUDOLUS: Me? I give orders to the major-
domo!
HARPAX: *(Puzzled, unable to square* PSEUDO-
LUS' *tones with his slave's get-up)* Are you a slave
or aren't you?
PSEUDOLUS: *(Deflated)* Well, for the
moment, still a slave.
HARPAX: *(Inflated)* You look it. You don't
look the type to be anything but.
PSEUDOLUS: *(Promptly)* Ever take a look at
yourself before making cracks about others?
HARPAX: *(To the audience, gesturing toward*
PSEUDOLUS*)* Must be a bad egg, this one here.
PSEUDOLUS: *(To the audience, gesturing
toward* HARPAX*)* Well, look what heaven sent me!
A nest all my own — I'll hatch plenty of schemes in
it today!
HARPAX: *(To himself, suspiciously)* What's
he talking to himself about?
PSEUDOLUS: *(Calling)* Hey, mister!
HARPAX: What?
PSEUDOLUS: Are you from that Macedonian
major? Servant of the fellow who bought a girl from
us and paid my master four thousand and still owes
him a thousand?
HARPAX: *(Surprised)* That's right. But where
in the world do you know me from? Where did you
ever see me or talk to me, anyway? I never set foot
in Athens before and never laid eyes on you till this
minute.
PSEUDOLUS: *(Studiedly offhand)* You looked
as if you came from him. After all, when he left he

agreed on today as the last day for payment, and he hasn't yet made good.

HARPAX: *(Hefting the purse)* Oh, no. It's here.

PSEUDOLUS: *(Affecting surprise)* You brought it?

HARPAX: *(Importantly)* I certainly did.

PSEUDOLUS: *(Reaching for the purse, as if in a considerable hurry)* What are you waiting for? Hand it over.

HARPAX: *(Jerking the purse out of his reach)* Hand it over to who? You?

PSEUDOLUS: Certainly to me. I'm in charge of Ballio's books. I handle the cash — receive all receivables, pay all payables.

HARPAX: *(Grimly)* Certainly *not* to you. You could be cashier for god almighty and all the treasures of heaven, but I'm not trusting you with a cent.

PSEUDOLUS: *(Ignoring the last remark, all business)* Why, in two shakes of a lamb's tail, we could have the whole thing done.

HARPAX: *(As before, showing the tightly bound purse)* I'd rather keep it *undone.*

PSEUDOLUS: You go to the devil! So you've come here to blacken my good name, eh? As if people don't trust me personally with a thousand times that much money!

HARPAX: *(Stubbornly)* Others can think that way. Doesn't mean *I* have to trust you.

PSEUDOLUS: *(Working himself up)* You mean to say I'm trying to do you out of your money?

HARPAX: Oh, no. *You* mean to say it. I mean to say I have my suspicions. What's your name, anyway?

PSEUDOLUS: *(To the audience)* The pimp has a servant named Syrus. That's who I'll say I am. *(To* HARPAX*)* Syrus.

HARPAX: Syrus, eh?

PSEUDOLUS: That's my name.

HARPAX: *(Impatiently)* Enough talk. Listen, whatever your name is, if your master's home, call him out so I can do what I was sent here to do.

PSEUDOLUS: *(Apologetically)* If he *were* here, I'd call him out. *(Earnestly)* But don't you want to give it to me? *(Innocently)* You'll be relieved of the whole business — more so than if you gave it to him in person.

HARPAX: *(Contemptuously)* You don't get the point. The commander gave it to me to pay with, not play with. Oh, I can see you're practically running a fever because you can't dig your claws into it. I don't hand over a cent to a soul except to Ballio in person.

PSEUDOLUS: He's tied up right now. In court on a case.

HARPAX: Well, I hope he wins. I'll come back when I figure he'll be at home. *(Pulling out a letter and handing it to* PSEUDOLUS*)* Here, take this letter and give it to him. It's got the identification seal my master agreed on with yours in this deal for the girl.

PSEUDOLUS: *(Taking it, studiedly casual)* Yes, I know. The major told us what he wanted: we're to send the girl off with a fellow who'd bring the money and a seal with his picture. He left a duplicate with us, you know.

HARPAX: *(Impressed, is spite of himself)* You know everything, don't you?

PSEUDOLUS: *(With a shrug, carelessly)* Why shouldn't I?

HARPAX: *(Pointing to the letter)* So you give him that identification.

PSEUDOLUS: Right. What's your name, anyway?

HARPAX: Snatcher.

PSEUDOLUS: *(Pretending fright)* On your way, Snatcher boy, I don't like you. You're not coming inside this house, believe me; I want none of your snatching there.

HARPAX: *(Puffing out his chest)* I take my enemies alive, right out of the front line. That's how I got the name.

PSEUDOLUS: If you ask me, you take the silverware right out of the front rooms.

HARPAX: *(Loftily)* No, sir! *(Struck by a thought)* Say, Syrus, you know what I'd like to ask you to do?

PSEUDOLUS: Tell me and I'll know.

HARPAX: I'm staying at the third inn outside the city gate. The one run by that old buttertub, Chrysis, the lame dame.

PSEUDOLUS: What do you want?

HRAPAX: Come and pick me up there when your master gets back.

PSEUDOLUS: Sure. Anything you say.

HARPAX: I'm tired from the trip. Want to get some rest.

PSEUDOLUS: *(Nodding vigorously)* Very

smart. Good idea. But don't make me go looking all over the place when I come to get you.

HARPAX: Oh, no. After a bite to eat, a nap is all I'm interested in.

PSEUDOLUS: (As before) I'll bet.

HARPAX: (Preparing to leave) Well, anything I can do for you?

PSEUDOLUS: You go take that nap.

HARPAX: I'm going. (Starts walking off, stage right.)

PSEUDOLUS: (Calling after him, solicitiously) Snatcher! Listen! Use plenty of blankets. You get a good sweat up, and you'll feel tiptop.

(HARPAX leaves. The minute he is out of earshot, PSEUDOLUS races downstage and addresses the audience.)

PSEUDOLUS: (Exultantly)
Ye gods! That fellow saved my life by
turning up, I swear!
I was heading wrong, he set me right—
and he's to pay the fare!
Lady Luck herself could never have come
at a luckier time, you see,
Than when I had this lucky letter luckily
left with me.
(Brandishing the letter)
He's handed me a horn of plenty, in here's
what I want and more:
Embezzlement, swindle, double-cross, dirty
tricks, shady deals galore,
The cash we're after plus that girl the boy
is crazy for.
And now I'll show my generous soul; my
name and fame shall soar!
(Shaking his head wonderingly)
My army of plans had been mobilized,
was at stations, was all set —
The way I'd go about the job, approach the
pimp and get
The girl away from him. It all was in my
head, but it seems
Lady Luck by herself can overturn a
hundred wise men's schemes.
The fact is that, when we're doing well,
and people say we're smart,
We owe it all to just how much Lady
Luck has taken our part.
We hear that someone's plans have
worked out; "He's a genius!" all of us
chime.
We hear that someone's plans went wrong;
"What a fool!" we chime this time.
Why, we're the fools—we're unaware
how wasted is our whole
Benighted, greedy struggle toward any
particular goal,
As if the right path's ever known to any
human soul!
The bird in hand we always leave to go for
those in the bush;
And then 'mid all our sweat and strain,
enter Death to give his push!

(Suddenly snapping his fingers) But enough of this philosophizing . . . (Gleefully) Ye gods! That brain storm I suddenly got a little while ago, to bluff and say I belonged to the pimp, is worth a fortune! Now, with this letter, I'll double-cross the three of them, master, pimp, and letter giver. (His attention suddenly caught, looks toward the wings, stage left.) Well, look at that! Something else I wanted is happening, just as good as this. Here comes Calidorus, and he's got somebody with him.

(CALIDORUS and his friend CHARINUS [pronounced ka-RYEnus], "charitable," enter so deep in conversation they don't notice PSEUDOLUS.)

CALIDORUS: So I've told you everything, the sweet and the bitter. You know my toils, my troubles, my financial tribulations.

CHARINUS: (Nodding) I have everything in mind. Now just tell me what you want me to do.

CALIDORUS: Pseudolus gave me orders to bring someone who can get things done and who'd be willing to do me a good turn.

CHARINUS: You carry out orders to the letter: you're bringing a good friend ready to do you a good turn. But who's this Pseudolus? He's new to me.

CALIDORUS: (Enthusiastically) The greatest virtuoso alive, my maestro of miracles. He's the one who told me he was going to do all the things I told you about.

PSEUDOLUS: (To himself, importantly) I'll go up and greet him in the grand manner.

CALDIORUS: (His attention caught) Whose voice is that?

PSEUDOLUS: (Adopting the tones and gestures of a character in grand opera)
'Tis thee I seek, Your Majesty, yea thee

Whom thy servant Pseudolus serves. 'Tis
    thee I seek
To give thee thrice, in triplewise, in form
Threefold, three thrice-deserved delights
    derived
From dumbbells three and by devices three:
Deceit, deception, and double-cross.
(Waving the letter)
Delights that I bring thee signed and sealed
In this here paltry piece of paper.

CALIDORUS: *(To* CHARINUS, *excitedly)* That's
the fellow!

CHARINUS: *(Admiringly)* The devil's better
than an opera star!

PSEUDOLUS: *(Walking toward them, as
    before)*
Advance thy step as I do mine and boldly
Extend to me thy hand and welcome
    words.

CALIDORUS:
To welcome rescue true — or welcome *words?*

PSEUDOLUS: *(Dropping the act and grinning)*
Both!

CALIDORUS: *(With great relief)* Welcome,
words and rescue! *(Tensely)* What happened?

PSEUDOLUS: *(Amused)* What are you so nervous about?

CALIDORUS: *(Pointing to* CHARINUS, *proudly)*
I've produced your man.

PSEUDOLUS: What's this "produced"
business?

CALIDORUS: *(Meekly)* I mean I've brought
him here.

PSEUDOLUS: *(Looking* CHARINUS *over)* Who
is he?

CALIDORUS: Charinus.

PSEUDOLUS: Bravo!
               No man named Charinus
               Will ever malign us.

CHARINUS: *(Energetically)* What do you
need done? Step up and give me my orders.

PSEUDOLUS: *(Playing disinterested to test his
man's interest)* Thanks just the same and all the
best to you, Charinus, but we really don't want to
put you to any trouble.

CHARINUS: *(Promptly)* You won't put me to
any trouble. Not a bit.

PSEUDOLUS: *(Promptly)* Then stick around.
(Ostentatiously examines the letter.)

CALIDORUS: What's that?

PSEUDOLUS: *(Triumphantly)* I've just inter-
cepted this letter and this identification!

CALIDORUS: Identification? What identification?

PSEUDOLUS: The one the major just sent. His
servant, the fellow who came to take your girl
away, brought it along with the one thousand dollars — *(Grinning)* and did I make a monkey out of
him just now!

CALIDORUS: How?

PSEUDOLUS: *(Gesturing toward the audi-
ence)* Look, this play's being given for the benefit of
these people. And they were here, they know all
about it. I'll tell you two later.

CALIDORUS: What do we do now?

PSEUDOLUS: *(In ringing tones)* By tonight
you'll have your girl friend in your arms — and
she'll be a free woman!

CALIDORUS: *(Dumbfounded)* I?

PSEUDOLUS: Yes, you. I say — if I manage to
stay alive. Provided, however, you two find me a
man in a hurry.

CHARINUS: What kind of man?

PSEUDOLUS: A good-for-nothing. But one
who's slick and smart enough, once he's been given
a start, to figure out what to do next on his own.
And it mustn't be anyone too well known around
here.

CHARINUS: Does it matter if he's a slave?

PSEUDOLUS: *(In a what-a-silly-question tone
of voice)* On the contrary, I prefer a slave.

CHARINUS: I think I have the man for you.
He's a good-for-nothing, he's smart, and my father
just sent him here from overseas. He came to Athens only yesterday, and he hasn't been out of the
house yet.

PSEUDOLUS: *(To* CHARINUS, *nodding)* That'll
be a great help. *(Frowning in thought)* Now I've got
to borrow a thousand dollars which I'll need just till
tonight. *(Gesturing toward* CALIDORUS, *grinning)*
His father owes me money.

CHARINUS: *(Expansively)* Oh, I'll give it to
you. Don't bother going to anyone else.

PSEUDOLUS: My lifesaver! *(Thoughtful
again)* But I also need a uniform and a sword.

CHARINUS: I've got some to spare.

PSEUDOLUS: *(Exultantly)* Ye gods! This
Charinus is all plus and no minus! Now, about that
servant of yours who's just arrived — is he strong in
the head?

CHARINUS: No, just under the armpits.

PSEUDOLUS: He ought to wear long sleeves. Is he tough? Does he have the old vinegar in the veins?

CHARINUS: As sour as it comes.

PSEUDOLUS: Suppose he has to give out with the old sweetness, instead? Has he got it in him?

CHARINUS: Has he! Honey, sugar, syrup—he once tried to run a grocery in his guts.

PSEUDOLUS: *(Grinning)* Touché, Charinus: beat me at my own game. But what's this servant of yours called?

CHARINUS: Monkey.

PSEUDOLUS: Can he do a good turn?

CHARINUS: Like a top.

PSEUDOLUS: Does he grasp things easily?

CHARINUS: All the time—other people's things.

PSEUDOLUS: Suppose he's caught in the act?

CHARINUS: He slips out. He's an eel.

PSEUDOLUS: Has he got any sense?

CHARINUS: More sense than the Board of Censors.

PSEUDOLUS: Well, from what you say he sounds like a good man.

CHARINUS: You have no idea how good! Why, the minute he sees you he'll tell *you* what you want him for. What have you got in mind, anyway?

PSEUDOLUS: I'll tell you. When I'm done dressing your man up, I want him to impersonate the major's orderly. He'll take this identification along with a thousand dollars to the pimp and make off with the girl. There, now you know the whole plot. The mechanics of how to do it I'll save for our impersonator.

CALIDORUS: *(Impatiently)* Well, what are we standing around for?

PSEUDOLUS: I'm off to the Aeschinus Loan Company. You two dress your man in dress uniform and bring him to me there. But hurry!

CHARINUS: We'll be there before you will.

PSEUDOLUS: Then you'd better shake a leg! *(As* CALIDORUS *and* CHARINUS *dash off, stage left, he turns and addresses the audience.)*

> It's left my mind, it's gone away, the last
>   shred of doubt and fear
> I'd had before. My mind's been scoured,
>   the road ahead is clear.
>
> *   *   *
>
> But first downtown to hand a load of sage
>   advice to Monk:
> Tell him what to do so he plays it smart
>   and doesn't go kerplunk.
> And then to storm Castle Pimp itself—and
>   the enemy's cause is sunk!

*(*PSEUDOLUS *dashes off triumphantly, stage left, and the stage is empty.)*

ACT III

(The door of BALLIO'S *house opens, and* BALLIO'S *catamite steps out, a repulsive little boy with an ugly face as heavily made up as any whore's. He minces downstage and addresses the audience.)*

BOY: When Fate makes a boy a slave in a pimp's home and, on top of that, makes him homely, believe me, as I can tell from my feelings right now, she's made him plenty of toil and trouble. Take me—that's the kind of slavery that came my way; I'm the sole support of all sorts of sorrows, small and large. *(Whimpering)* And I can't find any lover boy to love me and care for me so that for once in my life things would be a teeny bit brighter.

(Whimpers a second or so longer, then continues worriedly) Today is this pimp's birthday, and he's laid down the law to everyone in the house from the lowest to the highest: whoever doesn't get him a gift today gets the life tortured out of him tomorrow. In the position I'm in, what in heaven's name can I do? *I* can't give what people who can give usually give. And, if I don't give the pimp a gift today, tomorrow he'll empty the chamber pots down my throat. *(Blubbering)* I'm still too small for things like that!

(Getting his blubbering under control) Golly, poor me, I'm so scared of swilling slops, *(leering)* if someone slipped something into my palm to give it a little weight, *(archly)* I think I could somehow grit my teeth and bear it even though it makes a person cry hard—*(innocently)* so they tell me.

(His attention caught, looks toward the wings, stage left) But right now I have to shut my mouth and bear it—there's Ballio coming back bringing a cook with him.

(The boy hurries into the house. A second later BALLIO *enters, at his heels his slave boy, and at his side an enormously fat cook behind whom trails a long line of young assistants.)*

BALLIO: *(To the world at large)* And people, the damn fools, say the market is where you hire cooks! It's where you hire crooks, not cooks! I tell you, if I had actually taken an oath to find a worse cook than the one I've got here, I couldn't have done it. Useless, brainless, a blowhard and a blabbermouth! I know why he never died and went below: so he could be on hand here to cater funeral feasts: he's the only one who can cook what a corpse would eat.

COOK: *(Unabashed)* If you really think I'm the type you tell me I am, why did you hire me?

BALLIO: Shortage. There was no one else. If you're such a great cook, why were all the others already gone from the square and you were still sitting there all by yourself?

COOK: *(With a great air of candor)* I'll tell you. I'm considered a poorer cook. Not through any fault of my own, mind you. Through human greed.

BALLIO: How's that?

COOK: *(As before)* I'll tell you. It's because, when people come to hire a cook, they never go after the best who'll cost the most; they'd rather hire the cook who costs the least. That's why I was sitting in sole possession of the square today. *(Contemptuously)* Let those other poor devils cook their five-buck feeds. *(Pounding his chest)* Nobody gets me off my seat for less than ten. I don't do a dinner like other cooks. They pile up plates with potted pasture, that's what they do. They make cattle out of the guests—feed 'em fodder! And even the fodder they season with still more fodder. Inside they put coriander, fennel, garlic, celery. Outside they put cabbage, beets, sorrel, spinach. On top of it all, they throw in a pound of asafetida. Then they'll grate in that damned mustard, which has the graters' eyes going at a great rate before they're done grating. When these cooks cook a meal and it comes to the seasoning, they don't season with seasonings, they season with vultures—gives 'em a chance to get at the easy livers around the table while still alive.

That's why people hereabouts don't live very long: they bloat their bellies with all this fodder that's horrible to mention let alone eat. Fodder a cow wouldn't eat, a person will.

BALLIO: *(Snarling)* What about yourself? If you sneer at these seasonings, what do you use? Seasonings from heaven to make people live longer?

COOK: *(Promptly)* You can say that again. If people ate regularly the meals I prepare, they could live to even two hundred. Once I drop some clovidoopus in a pan, or some dillipoopus, or a dash of fathead or cutathroat, right away the pan starts sizzling on its own. *(Becoming the maître d'hôtel)* Now, these seasonings are for your dishes made from the finny tribe. For your dishes made from the earthy tribes I season with nutmegoopus. Or tenus tenerus or even muvius fluvius.

BALLIO: *(Exploding)* You and your seasoning can go plumb to hell! And take all your damned lies with you!

COOK: *(Unruffled)* Will you kindly allow me to continue?

BALLIO: Continue—and then go to hell!

COOK: When every pot is hot, I uncover every one, and *(Closing his eyes in rapture)* the aroma flies to heaven with feet outspread.

BALLIO: The aroma with feet outspread, eh?

COOK: *(Apologetically)* Made a slip. Didn't realize it.

BALLIO: How's that?

COOK: *(Straight-faced)* With arms outspread, I meant to say. *(Resuming his rapture)* The lord in heaven sups nightly on this aroma.

BALLIO: *(Sarcastically)* And if you don't happen to be cooking anywhere, what in the world does the lord in heaven sup on?

COOK: *(Promptly)* He goes to bed unsupped.

BALLIO: *(Roaring)* And you go to hell! *(Indicating by a contempestuous wave of the hand all the cook's big talk)* So for all this I'm supposed to pay you ten dollars today, am I!

COOK: *(Smugly)* Oh, I admit I'm a very expensive cook. But I make sure the people get their money's worth in any house I go to cook in.

BALLIO: To rob in, you mean.

COOK: *(Shrugging)* You think you can find a cook who doesn't have a pair of claws like a vulture?

BALLIO: And you think you can go just anywhere to cook and not pull those claws in while you're cooking? *(Turning to his slave boy)* Now listen, you, you're on my side, so I'm giving you orders right now to get everything that belongs to us out of sight in a hurry. And after that you keep your eyes on *(Gesturing toward the cook)* his. Wherever he looks, you look too. If he takes a step in any direction, you take a step in the same direction. If he reaches a hand in any direction, you reach a hand in the same direction. If he takes hold of anything that's his, you let him. If he takes hold of anything that's ours, you take hold of the other end. If he moves, you move. If he stands, you stand. If he squats, you squat. *(Looking down the line of the cook's assistants)* And I'm appointing personal watchmen for these assistants of his too.

COOK: *(Soothingly)* Now you just stop worrying.

BALLIO: I ask you, just show me how I can stop worrying when I'm bringing *you* into my house?

COOK: *(Heartily)* Because I'll make a concoction for you today that'll do for you what Medea did for Pelias when she cooked the old fellow up. They say that by using her poisonous potions she turned the old fellow back into a young one. Well, I'll do the same for you.

BALLIO: So you poison people, do you?

COOK: No sir. On the contrary. I cure them.

BALLIO: Look here, how much will you charge to teach me that one recipe?

COOK: Which?

BALLIO: The one that'll cure me from your stealing.

COOK: *(Promptly)* If you trust me, ten dollars; if you don't, even five hundred's not enough. *(Thinking for a moment)* This dinner you're giving, is it for friends or enemies?

BALLIO: My god! For my friends, of course.

COOK: *(Enthusiastically)* Why don't you invite your enemies instead? I'll do your diners such a dinner, make such deliciously delicious dishes, that, as soon as they pick up something and taste it, they'll chomp off their fingers in the process.

BALLIO: Please do me a favor, will you? Before you serve anything to any of my guests, you first take a taste and let your assistants taste too—so all of you can chomp off those thieving hands of yours.

COOK: *(Innocently)* Maybe you don't believe what I'm telling you?

BALLIO: *(Impatiently)* Now don't be a nuisance, please! I've had enough of your cackling. Shut up! *(Gesturing toward his house)* Look, there's where I live. Go on in and cook dinner. And get a move on!

(The cook stalks in, BALLIO's *slave boy scampers in in his wake, and the line of assistants follows. The last boy in line turns and calls out to* BALLIO.*)*

ASSISTANT: *(Like a butler making an announcement)* Kindly take your place at the table and call your guests. Dinner's now being—spoiled! *(Disappears into the house.)*

BALLIO: *(To the audience)* Look at that, will you! What a breed! *(Gesturing toward the boy who has just gone in)* That Chief Dishlicker there is already a full-fledged good-for-nothing. *(Shaking his head)* I honestly don't know which to keep an eye on first: I've got thieves inside my house and *(Gesturing toward* PSEUDOLUS' *house)* a bandit next door. You see, just a few minutes ago while downtown, my neighbor here, Calidorus' father, warned me over and over to watch out for his servant Pseudolus, not to trust him. Says Pseudolus is out to pull a fast one and get the girl away from me if he can. Claims Pseudolus swore up and down that he was going to sneak Rosy away from me. I'll go in now and warn the household that none of them is to trust that Pseudolus one bit.

*(*BALLIO *enters his house, and the stage is now empty.)*

ACT IV

(Enter PSEUDOLUS, *stage left, walking on air.)*

Song

PSEUDOLUS: *(As if to* MONKEY *who he assumes is at his heels)*
If Fate has ever felt an urge to help a mortal out,

She feels it now for the boy and me, of that I have no doubt:
If she's produced an assistant like you, with brains and education,

Then she wants to see the saving of us, and the
  pimp's extermination.

(Turns to face MONKEY—*and discovers there is no*
* *MONKEY *to face.)*
  Where is he? I'm talking to myself
    Like someone not all there!
  By god, he's put one over on me
    And left me flat, I'll swear
  For one crook dealing with another,
    I've been caught off guard for fair.

If Monk's made off, my goose is cooked. The job I
  wanted done
I'll never be able to do today. But wait, I see
  someone—
There he is. He's coming now, our answer to a
  hangman's prayer.
And look at the way he steps along. Quite a strut
  our boy has there!

(Enter MONKEY, *resplendent in a uniform*
somewhat like HARPAX'S, *and swaggering along as*
* magnificently as a major general.)*

PSEUDOLUS: *(Calling to him, petulantly)*
  Hey, I've been looking all over for you.
  Damned scared you'd run out on me.
MONKEY: *(Haughtily)*
  And if I'd been acting the way that I
    should
  I damned well would, I agree.
PSEUDOLUS: *(As before)*
  Well, where did you stop?
MONKEY: *(Coolly)*
                  Where I wanted
    to be.
PSEUDOLUS: *(Peevishly)*
  I know that.
MONKEY: *(Shrugging)*
          You do? Then why ask me?
PSEUDOLUS: *(Hastily changing the subject)*
  I wanted to give you this warning to—
MONKEY: *(Interrupting)*
  Don't warn me, I'm warning *you!*
PSEUDOLUS: *(Resentfully)*
  Now you look here. You're treating me
  Like dirt, and I don't like it, see?
MONKEY: *(Ostentatiously adjusting his hat*
  and sword, distastefully)
  A holder of the *croix de guerre*
  Be nice to you? I wouldn't dare!

PSEUDOLUS: *(Throwing a worried look at*
  BALLIO'S *door)*
  We've started something, and now I'd like
  To do the job.
MONKEY: *(Drawing his sword and trying a*
  few practice thrusts)
              For the love of Mike,
  Just what do you think I'm doing, eh?
PSEUDOLUS: *(As before)*
  Then shake a leg. Don't take all day!
MONKEY: *(Ambling along with maddening*
  slowness)
  I do things in a leisurely way.
PSEUDOLUS: *(Urgently, gesturing toward*
  BALLIO'S *house)*
  Here's our chance! While our soldier boy
    snores,
  I want *you* to be first through those doors.
MONKEY: *(Lazily)*
  What's your hurry?
  Take it easy, don't worry,
  The good lord can let
  That soldier be set
  On *this* same spot, right here with me.
  Whatever's the name
  Of this fellow who came,
  I'll make a better Snatcher than he!
  So don't worry, I'll see
  That it's done, one two three.
  I'll bamboozle him so,
  With my lying, I'll throw
  Such a scare in our foe
  He'll deny that he really is he
  And declare that he really is me!
PSEUDOLUS: *(Doubtfully)*
  Yes, but how?
MONKEY: *(Working himself up)*
             All these questions I get!
  Oh, you *will* be the death of me yet!
PSEUDOLUS: *(Sweetly)*
  You're so gracious and charming, my pet.
MONKEY: *(Snarling)*
  Now there's something I'd like you to
    know:
  I admit you're my boss in this show,
  But in cheating and double-cross you
  Can't come close to the things I can do.
PSEUDOLUS: *(All innocent gratitude)*
  Oh, god bless you! For my sake.
MONKEY: *(With gracious condescension)*
                   No, mine.

(Squaring his shoulders and straightening his uniform)
Look me over now, please. Does the line
Of this uniform suit me this way?

PSEUDOLUS: *(Enthusiastically)*
Oh, it's perfect, it's great!

MONKEY: *(Condescendingly)*
Then okay.

PSEUDOLUS: . . . *(To the audience, gesturing toward* MONKEY*)*
The lowest, sneakiest good-for-nothing I
ever laid eyes upon.

MONKEY: *(Menacingly)*
You'd say a thing like that to me?

PSEUDOLUS: *(Swiftly switching back to humility)*
My lips are sealed from now on.
(Clamps his lips shut—and manages to stay that way for five full seconds at least; then, bursting out—)
You do a careful job for me and what gifts
you'll get!

MONKEY: *(Snarling)*
Shut up!
Remind a man who remembers things,
and you'll make the man forget
The things he has to remember. I've got it
all by heart, it's set
(Tapping his head)
In here. My tricks are all worked out—
and worked out trickily.

PSEUDOLUS: *(To the audience, admiringly)*
This man is good.

MONKEY: *(To the audience, gesturing toward* PSEUDOLUS*)*
And this one's not—and the same is true
for me.

PSEUDOLUS: *(Worriedly)*
Now watch your step.

MONKEY:
Oh, shut your mouth.

PSEUDOLUS:
I swear, so help me god—

MONKEY: *(Interrupting witheringly)*
Help you? Not he! You're set to spout the
lies and spout them hard!

PSEUDOLUS: *(Unruffled)*
—by my love and fear and vast respect for
your consummate treachery—

MONKEY: *(As before)*

I teach that sort of thing to others. *You*
can't soft-soap *me.*

PSEUDOLUS: *(As before)*
—you pull this job successfully, and I'll
see you have things nice—

MONKEY:
Some joke!

PSEUDOLUS: *(Gathering momentum)*
—nice wine, hors d'oeuvres and food, a
regular paradise,
Plus a nice little girl to make things nice
with kiss upon kiss upon kiss.

MONKEY: *(Acidly)*
You're too nice to me.

PSEUDOLUS: *(Rising to a climax)*
You pull this job, and the word you'll use
is bliss!

*(*MONKEY *stares at him for a full ten seconds, deadpan and without batting an eyelash. Suddenly he breaks into a broad grin and slaps him resoundingly on the back.)*

MONKEY: *(Enthusiastically)*
If *I* don't do
This job for you,
Tell the torturer to
Give me rack and screw!

*(*MONKEY *sets his hat firmly on his head, adjusts his sword and, girded for action, turns to* PSEUDOLUS*.)*

MONKEY: *(All business)* All right, hurry and show me where I enter the jaws of the pimp's house.

PSEUDOLUS: *(Pointing)* The third this way.

(The "jaws" suddenly open, and BALLIO *appears on the threshold.)*

MONKEY: Shh! They've opened wide.

PSEUDOLUS: If you ask me, the house has a bellyache.

MONKEY: Why?

PSEUDOLUS: It's throwing up the pimp.

MONKEY: Is that the fellow?

PSEUDOLUS: That's the fellow.

MONKEY: *(Distastefully)* Rotten piece of merchandise, that.

PSEUDOLUS: *(As* BALLIO *sidles out the door)* Look, will you? He walks sideways, not frontwards. Like a crab!

(PSEUDOLUS *and* MONKEY *move off to the side where they can overhear without being seen.* BALLIO *sidles downstage and addresses the audience.*)

BALLIO: He wasn't as bad as I thought, that cook I hired. All he's made off with so far is a cup and a jug.

PSEUDOLUS: (*To* MONKEY, *sotto voce*) Hey! Now's our chance!

MONKEY: (*To* PSEUDOLUS, *sotto voce*) My feelings exactly.

PSEUDOLUS: (*To* MONKEY, *sotto voce*) On your way and play it smart. I'll stay here in ambush.

(MONKEY *steps into the street while* BALLIO's *back is turned, and walks slowly along, acting as if he is looking for some house.*)

MONKEY: (*To himself—but good and loud*) I kept count carefully: this is the sixth street from the town gate, and this is where he told me to turn in. But how many houses he said, I can't for the life of me remember.

BALLIO: (*Swiveling about at the sound of a voice, to himself*) Who's this fellow in uniform? Where does he come from? Who's he looking for? Looks like a stranger; I don't recognize the face.

MONKEY: (*Turning and assuming an expression of pleased surprise at seeing* BALLIO; *to the world at large*) Well, here's someone who certainly can relieve my uncertainty.

BALLIO: (*To himself*) He's heading straight for me. Now where in the world could he be from?

MONKEY: (*Like a top sergeant*) Hey, you standing there, you with the beard like a billy goat, I have a question for you.

BALLIO: (*Snappishly*) Just like that, eh, without even a "Good afternoon"?

MONKEY: Anything good I don't give away.

BALLIO: (*Snarling*) Then, damn it all, the same goes for me!

PSEUDOLUS: (*Aside, shaking his head despairingly*) Doing just great, right from the start!

MONKEY: Know anybody who lives in this street? (*As* BALLIO *remains stubbornly silent*) How about it, you?

BALLIO: (*Sullenly*) Me? Sure, myself.

MONKEY: Aren't many who can say that. Downtown there isn't one in ten who really knows himself.

PSEUDOLUS: (*Aside, sarcastically*) I'm safe—now he's become a philosopher!

MONKEY: I'm looking for someone around here—a nasty, filthy, low-down, lawbreaking liar.

BALLIO: (*Aside, promptly*) He's looking for me. Those are all my titles. Now, if he'd only mention the name—(*To* MONKEY) What's the fellow's name?

MONKEY: Ballio. A pimp.

BALLIO: (*Aside*) I knew it! (*To* MONKEY, *tapping himself on the chest*) Mister, the man you're looking for is right here.

MONKEY: (*Incredulously*) You're Ballio?

BALLIO: Sure I'm Ballio.

MONKEY: (*Eying the unappetizing get-up*) From the clothes I'd say you're a pickpocket.

BALLIO: (*Promptly*) So when *you* hold me up some dark night, you won't bother to put your thieving hands on them.

MONKEY: (*Getting down to business*) My master wants me to give you his best regards. (*Taking out the letter*) Here, take this letter; I have orders to give it to you.

BALLIO: Orders from whom?

PSEUDOLUS: (*Aside, clutching his hair*) I'm a goner! My man's in a jam—he doesn't know the name! We're stuck!

BALLIO: (*Noticing* MONKEY *hesitate, sharply*) Who do you say sent this to me?

MONKEY: (*In his best top sergeant's manner, pointing to the seal*) Identify that picture, and then *you* tell me his name. I want to make sure you're really Ballio.

BALLIO: Give me the letter.

MONKEY: (*Handing it over*) Here. Now identify the seal.

BALLIO: (*Taking a quick look, to himself*) Major I. Kutall Hedzoff to the life. I recognize him. (*To* MONKEY) Hey, his name is I. Kutall Hedzoff.

MONKEY: (*Dryly*) Well, now that you've told me his name is I. Kutall Hedzoff, I know I gave the letter to the right man.

BALLIO: What's he doing these days, anyway?

MONKEY: (*Striking a military pose*) What any brave, honest soldier does, by god! (*Relaxing*) Now get a move on and read the letter through—that's first on the docket—then take the money and deliver the girl, and make it snappy. Because if I'm not in Sicyon by today, I'm in my coffin by tomorrow. That's the way the major operates.

BALLIO: *(Nodding understandingly)* Don't I know! You're talking to someone who knows him.

MONKEY: *(Curtly)* Then get a move on and read the letter.

BALLIO: Just keep quiet and I will. *(Opens the letter and starts reading)* "Letter of Major I. Kutall Hedzoff to Pimp Ballio sealed with picture as provided by previous mutual agreement."

MONKEY: *(Pointing)* It's the seal on the letter.

BALLIO: I see it. I recognize it. But does he always write letters this way? With no salutation?

MONKEY: *(Sternly)* Standard military procedure, Ballio. They send greetings to friends *(Saluting)* with the hand—and *(Going through the motions of a saber cut)* destruction to enemies with ditto. But keep on with the reading. Go ahead, find out what the letter says.

BALLIO: Then listen. *(Reading)* "This is my orderly Harpax who has come to you—" *(Looking up)* Are you Harpax?

MONKEY: That's me—the Snatcher in the flesh.

BALLIO: *(Resuming his reading)* "—and who is delivering this letter. I want you to accept payment of the money from him and at the same time send the girl off with him. Deserving people deserve a letter with a salutation. If I thought you were deserving, I'd have sent one."

MONKEY: *(As BALLIO looks up)* What do we do now?

BALLIO: *(Promptly)* You hand over the money and take the girl.

MONKEY: *(Impatiently)* Well, who's holding up who?

BALLIO: *(Going toward his door)* Follow me in, then.

MONKEY: I'm following.

(The two go into BALLIO's house. The minute the door closes behind them, PSEUDOLUS bursts out of his hiding place.)

PSEUDOLUS: *(To the audience, excitedly)* I swear to god, never in all my life have I seen a dirty rat as fiendishly clever as that fellow! I'm afraid of him. I'm really scared of him. He might pull the same sort of dirty trick on me he pulled *(Gesturing toward BALLIO's house)* on him. With things going so well, he might lower his horns and charge *me*, if he ever gets the chance to do me dirt. And that's

something I would not like—because *(Smiling)* I like the guy!

(Shaking his head despairingly) Right now I've got three good reasons to be scared stiff. First of all, I'm scared that that colleague of mine will desert me and defect to the enemy. Next, I'm scared that Simo will be back any minute from downtown: we'll capture the loot, and *he'll* capture the looters. And, along with all these scares, I'm scared *(Gesturing in the direction of the town gate)* that *that* Harpax will get here before *this* Harpax gets out of here with the girl.

(Staring intently at the door) This is killing me! They're taking so long to come out! My heart's all ready with its bags packed: if he doesn't come out of there with the girl, it's saying good-by to my chest and taking off for good. *(The door opens and MONKEY and ROSY step out.)* I win! My guards were all on their guard, and I beat them all!

(MONKEY walks from the door dragging a reluctant ROSY who is dissolved to tears.)

MONKEY: *(Earnestly)* Please don't cry, Rosy. You don't understand what's happening. I promise you, you'll find out very soon, at the party. I'm not taking you to that snaggle-toothed monster of a major from Macedon, who's making you cry this way. I'm taking you to the one man you want to belong to most of all. I promise you, in a little while you'll be giving Calidorus a big hug.

PSEUDOLUS: *(Frantically)* What were you hanging around inside there for? My heart's been pounding in my chest so long, it's all bruised!

MONKEY: *(Angrily)* Damn you, a fine time you pick to cross-examine me, in the middle of an enemy ambush! Out of here on the double!

PSEUDOLUS: *(Swiveling about)* You're a good-for-nothing but, so help me, you have good ideas. *(Shouting)* Hip, hip, hooray! Forward march! Straight for that jug, men!

(They dash off, stage left, dragging the bewildered ROSY after them. A second later the door of BALLIO's house opens, and BALLIO sidles out. He looks positively gay for a change.)

BALLIO: *(To the audience)* Whew! My mind's finally at rest, now that that fellow's gone and taken the girl away. Now let that dirty rat of a Pseudolus come and try to sneak her away from me!

There's one thing I know for sure: I'd sooner commit perjury under oath a thousand times than have him pull a fast one and get the laugh on me. Now I'll have the laugh on him, if I ever meet him. You ask me, though, the only thing he'll be meeting is his deserts—on a mill wheel. I wish Simo would come along so he could enjoy some of my joy.

(At this point SIMO *conveniently enters, stage left.)*

SIMO: *(To himself)* I've come to see what that Ulysses of mine has accomplished. Whether he's stolen the statue from Fort Ballio yet.[2]

BALLIO: *(Heartily)* Hey, lucky fellow, let me shake that lucky hand.

SIMO: *(Taken aback by the strange phenomenon of a genial* BALLIO*)* What's the matter?

BALLIO: *(Deliberately)* There is no longer—

SIMO: *(Impatiently)* No longer what?

BALLIO: —anything for you to be afraid of.

SIMO: What's happened? Has he been to your house?

BALLIO: *(Smiling beatifically)* Nope.

SIMO: *(Sourly)* Then what's happened that's so good?

BALLIO: *(As before)* That five thousand Pseudolus solemnly swore he'd get out of you today is safe and sound.

SIMO: *(Fervently)* God, do I wish it!

BALLIO: *(Cockily)* If he gets his hands on that girl today or gives her to your son today, the way he said he would, you get the five thousand from *me.* Do me a favor: let's make it official. I'm dying to do it that way just to prove that there's absolutely no chance for a slip-up anywhere. I'll even throw in the girl as a gift, too.

SIMO: *(Shrugging)* I can't see a thing I've got to lose by taking you up. All right—do you hereby agree to give me five thousand dollars on those terms?

BALLIO: *(Airily)* I hereby agree.

SIMO: *(Finally convinced, rubbing his hands delightedly)* Well, this isn't a bad turn of affairs at all. Did you run into him?

BALLIO: Into the both of them, as a matter of fact.

[2]Ulysses in the *Iliad* stole the sacred statue of Athena from the citadel of Troy.

SIMO: *(Eagerly)* What did he say? What did he tell you? What kind of story did he give you?

BALLIO: *(Shrugging)* The nonsense you hear on the stage. The stuff they always say about pimps in comedies, stuff any schoolboy knows by heart. He told me I was a dirty, filthy double-crosser.

SIMO: Believe me, he wasn't lying.

BALLIO: *(Grinning)* I wasn't the least bit sore. What difference do insults make to a fellow who doesn't give a damn or bother to deny them?

SIMO: But why don't I have to be afraid of him? That's what I want to hear.

BALLIO: *(Gleefully)* Because he'll never get the girl away from me. He can't! Remember I told you a little while ago that I had sold her to a major from Macedon?

SIMO: Yes.

BALLIO: *(Deliberately drawing his story out)* Well, his orderly brought me the money plus a sealed letter with identification—

SIMO: *(Impatiently)* Yes, yes.

BALLIO: *(Not to be hurried)* —which he and I had agreed on between us. *(Triumphantly)* Well, just a few minutes ago, the orderly took the girl away with him!

SIMO: *(Excitedly)* Is this the truth you're telling me? On your honor?

BALLIO: *(Grinning)* Where would *I* get any honor?

SIMO: *(Doubtfully)* Just watch out that he hasn't pulled some fancy stunt on you.

BALLIO: *(Cockily)* The letter and the picture make me absolutely certain. I tell you, he just left the city with her. He's headed for Sicyon.

SIMO: *(Jubilantly)* Well done, by god! Why don't I have Pseudolus put his name down for immigration to Treadmill Town this minute? *(His attention caught, looks toward the wings, stage right.)* Who's this fellow in uniform?

BALLIO: *(Following* SIMO's *gaze)* I don't know. Let's watch where he goes and what he does.

(Enter Harpax looking a bit worried. He walks downstage and addresses the audience.)

Song

HARPAX:
The servant who doesn't give a damn for the
    orders a master's issued
Is a dirty good-for-nothing, that's a fact.

And *I* don't give a damn for the kind whose
    memory's so short
They need a second warning before they'll
    act.

    And those who think they're emancipated
    The minute they find themselves located
    Out of the master's sight, and drink and
        whore
    And go through every cent they've saved
        and more,
    Will bear the name of slave
    To the grave.
    There's nothing good in them — unless you
        add
    The knack to stay alive by being bad.

Now *I* won't mix or be seen with this ilk; I cut
    them dead on the spot.
When *I* get orders, and the master's away, I act as
    if he's not.

    It's when he's gone I start to fear —
    In order not to when he's near.

*(Holds up the purse and continues more
    agitatedly.)*
    Here's a job that I'd better begin.
    Up till now I've been out at the inn,
    Where that Syrus — the fellow that I
    Gave the documents to — let me lie.
    There I stayed, since he told me to stay:
    He'd come back and he'd fetch me away,
    So he said, when the pimp had come home.
    When he didn't show up, on my own
I came here to find out what the matter could be,
And not give him a chance to get funny with me!

(Walking up to the pimp's door)
    The best I can do is knock right here and
        find someone who's free;
    I want the pimp to take this cash, and
        send the girl with me.
BALLIO: *(To* SIMO *sotto voce, his eyes
    glistening)*
    Hey, Simo!
SIMO: *(sotto voce)*
    What?
BALLIO: *(As before)*
    He's mine!

SIMO:
            How's that?
BALLIO: *(Smacking his lips)*
    Because this man's my meat.
    He wants a wench, he's got the cash — I'm
        dying to start to eat!
SIMO: *(Incredulously)*
    You'll eat him up this minute?
BALLIO: *(As before)*
    Fresh and hot and nicely brown
    And served you on a platter thus, that's
        the time to gulp them down.
    (Flashing his hyena grin)
    All decent people let me starve, but the
        sinners don't, you see;
    The solid citizen slaves for the state — and
        the sinner slaves for me!
SIMO: *(Disgusted)*
    You're such a rat, when the good lord acts,
        what tortures he'll decree!

HARPAX: *(To himself)* I'm wasting time. I'll
knock on the door this minute and find out
whether Ballio's in or not.

BALLIO: *(To* SIMO, *sotto voce, gleefully)* These
blessings come to me from Lady Love. She brings
them here, these people who run away from profit
to chase after loss by spending their lives having a
good time. They eat, they drink, they whore, *(Eyeing* SIMO *distastefully)* they have different ideas
from the likes of you, who won't let yourself have
a good time and begrudge those who do.

HARPAX: *(Banging on the door and shouting)*
Hey, where is everybody?

BALLIO: *(To* SIMO, *sotto voce, rubbing his
hands)* The fellow's coming straight at me by the
straightest route.

HARPAX: *(Shouting even louder)* Hey, where
are you people?

BALLIO: *(Calling to* HARPAX*)* Hey, mister,
someone in there owe you money? *(To* SIMO, *sotto
voce)* I'll get a good haul out of him. I can tell this
is my lucky day.

HARPAX: *(Not hearing, despairingly)* Isn't
anyone going to open this door?

BALLIO: *(Calling louder)* Hey, soldier, someone in there owe you money?

HARPAX: *(Finally looking up and seeing the
two of them)* I'm looking for the master of the
house. Ballio, the pimp.

BALLIO: Mister, you can cut your looking short, whoever you are.

HARPAX: Why?

BALLIO: Because you are personally in the flesh looking at him personally in the flesh.

HARPAX: *(Pointing to* SIMO*)* You're Ballio?

SIMO: *(Visibly shuddering and shaking his stick)* Soldier, you watch your step or you'll be in trouble from this stick. Point that finger at *him;* he's your pimp.

BALLIO: *(To* HARPAX, *with a contemptuous gesture in* SIMO*'s direction)* Oh yes, *he's* an honest man. *(To* SIMO, *sneering)* And you, my honest man, every time you go downtown you get plenty of dunning from your creditors since you don't have a cent outside of what said pimp helps you out with.

HARPAX: *(Impatiently)* Would you mind talking to me?

BALLIO: *(Leaving* SIMO*'s side and walking up to* HARPAX*)* I am. What's on your mind?

HARPAX: *(Holding out the purse)* Take this money.

BALLIO: *(Whipping his hand out)* I've had my hand out for hours ready for you to hand over.

HARPAX: *(Handing it over)* Take it: exactly one thousand dollars, every coin full weight. Major I. Kutall Hedzoff, my master, gave me orders to deliver it—it's the balance he owes—and take Rosy away with me.

BALLIO: *(Studying him closely)* Your master?

HARPAX: That's right.

BALLIO: A major?

HARPAX: That's correct.

BALLIO: From Macedon maybe?

HARPAX: Exactly.

BALLIO: I. Kutall Hedzoff sent you to me, eh?

HARPAX: Precisely.

BALLIO: To give me this money?

HARPAX: If you're Ballio the pimp.

BALLIO: And to take the girl away with you?

HARPAX: Right.

BALLIO: Rosy he said her name was?

HARPAX: You've got a good memory.

BALLIO: Wait a second. I'll be right back. *(Turns and rushes over to* SIMO.*)*

HARPAX: *(Calling after him)* But hurry, because *I'm* in a hurry. You can see for yourself how late it is.

BALLIO: *(Calling back)* I see, all right. I want to consult with this man here. You just wait there. I'll be right with you. *(To* SIMO, *sotto voce, glee-* fully*)* What's next, Simo? What do we do now? This fellow who's brought the money—I've caught him in the act!

SIMO: *(Sotto voce, blankly)* What do you mean?

BALLIO: *(Sotto voce, chuckling)* Don't you know what this is all about?

SIMO: *(As before)* I haven't the slightest idea.

BALLIO: *(Sotto voce, triumphantly)* That Pseudolus of yours has sent this fellow to make believe he's from the major!

*(*BALLIO *grins delightedly. An answering grin gradually spreads over* SIMO*'s face as the import sinks in. They continue talking, sotto voce.)*

SIMO: *(His eyes gleaming)* Did you get the money from him?

BALLIO: *(Hefting the purse)* Do you have to ask? Can't you see?

SIMO: *(Quickly)* Just remember to hand over half of that loot to me. It's only right we share it.

BALLIO: *(His grin widening)* Why the hell not? It all comes from you!

HARPAX: *(Calling impatiently)* When are you going to take care of me?

BALLIO: *(Calling back, meaningfully)* I am right now! *(To* SIMO*)* What do you suggest I do now?

SIMO: *(Excitedly)* Let's have some fun with our spy, the faker! And let's keep it up till he catches on we're making fun of him.

BALLIO: Let's go. *(The two walk up together to* HARPAX.*)* So you're the major's orderly, eh?

HARPAX: Of course.

BALLIO: *(Sneering)* How much did you cost him?

HARPAX: *(Drawing himself up)* Every ounce of strength he had, to win me in battle. I'll have you know I was commander in chief of the armed forces back in my homeland.

BALLIO: *(As before)* Your homeland? When did the major ever capture a jail?

HARPAX: *(Sharply)* You pass any nasty cracks and you'll hear some yourself.

BALLIO: How long did it take you to get here from Sicyon?

HARPAX: Day and a half.

BALLIO: Pretty fast traveling, that.

SIMO: *(To* BALLIO*)* Oh this fellow's quick, all right. One look at those legs and you can see they're just the kind for—carrying shackles, extra-heavy shackles.

BALLIO: (To HARPAX) Tell me, when you were a boy, did you used to (Leering) play around with girls?

SIMO: (To BALLIO, eyeing HARPAX distastefully) Of course he did.

BALLIO: (To HARPAX) And did you used to— (Leering) you know what I'm going to say?

SIMO: (To BALLIO, with alacrity) Of course he did.

HARPAX: (Looking from one to the other blankly) Are you two in your right mind?

BALLIO: Answer me this. When the major stood watch at night and you used to go along with him, (Making an obscene gesture) did his sword fit in your scabbard?

HARPAX: (Losing his temper) You go to the devil!

BALLIO: (Unruffled) You can go there yourself. Today. Very soon today.

HARPAX: (Grimly) Are you going to give me the girl? If not, hand back the money. (Reaches for the purse.)

BALLIO: (Quickly putting it behind his back) Wait a second.

HARPAX: Why should I?

BALLIO: (Mockingly) Tell me, how much did it cost to hire that uniform?

HARPAX: What are you talking about?

SIMO: (To HARPAX) And how much for the sword?

HARPAX: (To himself) These fellows need a dose of hellebore![3]

BALLIO: (To HARPAX, reaching for his cap) Hey—

HARPAX: (Pulling back) Hands off!

BALLIO: (To HARPAX) —how much is that headpiece earning for its owner?

HARPAX: (Bewildered) What do you mean, owner? What are you two dreaming about? Everything I'm wearing belongs to me, bought with my own money.

BALLIO: (Leering) Sure—earned by the sweat of your thighs.

HARPAX: (To himself, grimly, as he girds for action) This pair has had the steam bath. Now what they're asking for is a good old-fashioned massage.

BALLIO: (Promptly backing away, and changing his tune) In all seriousness now, I ask you: how

much are you getting out of this? What's the pittance Pseudolus is paying you?

HARPAX: (Blankly) Pseudolus? who's Pseudolus?

BALLIO: Your trainer, the fellow who coached you in this swindle so you could swindle the girl away from me.

HARPAX: (As before) What Pseudolus? What's this swindle you're talking about? I don't know the man, never saw hide nor hair of him.

BALLIO: (Wearily) Why don't you just be on your way. There's no pickings for any crooks around here today. You tell Pseudolus that someone else made off with the loot, that Harpax beat him to it.

HARPAX: (Angrily) God damn it, I'm Harpax!

BALLIO: (Sneering) God damn it, you mean you wish you were! (To SIMO) This man's a crook, plain as the nose on your face.

HARPAX: (Heatedly) Listen, I just now gave you the money and a little while ago, the minute I arrived, right in front of this door I handed your servant the identification, the letter sealed with the major's picture.

BALLIO: (Taken aback) You handed a letter to my servant? What servant?

HARPAX: Syrus.

BALLIO: (To SIMO, nervously) He lacks confidence. Not very good at being a crook, this fellow here: hasn't even thought up a good story. Damn that good-for-nothing Pseudolus! He sure figured out a smart stunt: he gave this fellow the exact amount of money the major owed and dressed him all up so he could do me out of the girl. (With great assurance—as if to convince himself) As a matter of fact, this letter he's talking about was delivered to me by the real Harpax himself.

HARPAX: (Frantically) I'm Harpax! I'm the major's orderly! I'm not trying any tricks or pulling any swindles! I haven't the faintest idea who that Pseudolus of yours is, I never heard of him in my life!

(There is a dead silence as BALLIO and SIMO stare at each other.)

SIMO: (Slowly and emphatically) Pimp, unless I am very much mistaken, you are out one girl.

BALLIO: (Nodding gloomily) Damn it all, the more I hear, the more I'm afraid of just that. Damn it all, I got cold shivers a second ago from that there

[3]The standard ancient remedy for mental illness.

Syrus who took this fellow's identification. I wouldn't be at all surprised if it was Pseudolus. *(To* HARPAX*)* Listen, that fellow you gave the identification to before, what did he look like?

HARPAX: Red hair, pot belly, piano legs, big head, pointy eyes, darkish skin, red face, and whopping big feet.

BALLIO: *(Groaning)* The minute you mentioned those feet, you did for me! It was Pseudolus, all right. *(To* SIMO*)* Simo, it's all over with me. I'm a dead man!

HARPAX: *(Promptly)* I'm not letting you do any dying until I get my money back—five thousand dollars.

SIMO: *(Blandly)* And another five thousand for me.

BALLIO: *(Reproachfully)* You mean you'd actually take a bonus like that from me when I promised it just for a joke?

SIMO: *(Archly)* It's a man's duty to take bonuses—or booty—from crooks.

BALLIO: *(Between his teeth)* At least hand Pseudolus over to me.

SIMO: *(Shrugging)* I hand Pseudolus over to you? What crime did he commit? Didn't I tell you a thousand times to watch out for him?

BALLIO: *(Desperately)* He's killed me!

SIMO: And hit me for a forfeit of a measly five thousand.

BALLIO: *(As before)* What do I do now?

HARPAX: Pay me back my money, and you can go hang yourself.

BALLIO: *(To* HARPAX*)* Damn your hide! *(Turns and starts walking off, stage left.)* All right, follow me downtown and I'll settle up.

HARPAX: *(Falling in behind with alacrity)* I'm following.

SIMO: *(Calling after him)* What about me?

BALLIO: *(Stopping)* Aliens today, citizens tomorrow. *(To the audience)* Pseudolus practically held a session of the Supreme Court and got a death sentence against me when he sent that fellow today to sneak off my girl. *(To* HARPAX*)* Follow me, you. *(To the audience, gesturing toward the street)* Don't think I'm coming back by this street here. The way things have worked out, I've decided to use the back alleys.

HARPAX: *(Impatiently)* If you did as much walking as talking, you'd be downtown by now.

BALLIO: *(Starting to trudge off, forlornly)* I've decided to change today from my birthday to my deathday. *(He exits, stage left, with* HARPAX *at his heels.)*

SIMO: *(To the audience)* I made a monkey out of him for fair—and my servant made a monkey out of his worst enemy for fair.

(After a moment's thought) I've decided not to spring on Pseudolus what they always do in comedies. No whips, no canes. I'm going in now to get the five thousand I promised him if he pulled off this stunt. I'll hand it over to him without waiting to be dunned. *(Shaking his head admiringly)* There's a fellow who's really smart, really tricky, a real scoundrel. He did better than Ulysses and the Trojan Horse, that Pseudolus, I'll go in now, bring out the money, and spring my surprise on him.

(Simo enters his house, and the stage is now empty.)

ACT V

(Enter PSEUDOLUS, *stage left. He has just left a wild party at* CHARINUS' *house—and looks it; he has a chaplet askew on his head, is grinning drunkenly from ear to ear, and is staggering along, combating, with not too much success, a certain rubberiness in shanks and feet.)*

Song

PSEUDOLUS:
What's goin' on? What a way to act!
Hey, feet, will *you* stand up or not?
You want to leave me lying here
Till someone heaves me from the spot?
If *I* go into a somersault,
Believe you me, it's all your fault!
(Makes a wild lurch)
Insist on keeping at it, eh?
I'll have to tell you off today!
(Finally makes the center of the stage and stands there weaving)

'At's the trouble with wine. Always wrestles
    unfair;
First thing in the ring, has your feet in the air.
(Grins blissfully)
I'm as drunk as a lord, I'm loaded, I'm high!
What with elegance fit for the gods in the sky,
    And the choicest of foods for us all,
And a spot just as gala as a room for a ball,
    Boy, oh boy, did *we* have a ball!
(With drunken gravity)
    Now, why should I beat about the bush?
        This is why we stay alive,
        This is where all pleasure lies,
        This is where all joys derive —
        And *my* view is — it's paradise!
(Rapturously)
    When a man takes a girl in his arms,
    When he presses his mouth against hers,
    When the two, without trying to hide,
    Hold on fast, tongue on tongue — neither
        stirs,
    When her bosom is pressed to his breast,
    Or their bodies, if they choose, become
        one —
    Ah, that's when the time is the best
    To take from a dainty white hand
    A full glass, and to drink — it's just grand!
    It's the time when we're all out for fun,
    And the feelings are good all around,
    And the talk isn't just empty sound . . .
(Working himself up)
    Let's not spare the bouquets or perfume!
    Or the stuff for the looks of the room!
    And the cooking and all of the rest —
    No need asking: only the best!

(Breaks off and smiles blissfully. Then continues a
    little more matter-of-factly.)
    That's how we spent the rest of the day,
    The boy and I; we were *gai, très gai,*
    When once I'd done my job as planned
    And driven off the enemy band.
(Gesturing drunkenly toward the wings, stage
    left)
    I left them gorging, guzzling, whoring,
    (Left my own girl too), all getting roaring
    Drunk and happy. When I stood up,
    They asked me please to do a dance.
(Lumbering through a few weird steps)
    I gave them this, performed, of course,

    With all my usual elegance.
    The steps I did were the very best kinds —
    I've had lessons, you know, in bumps and
        grinds.
(More lumbering)
    Then I put on my coat and gave them one
    That goes like this — but just for fun.
    They stamped, they clapped, they yelled
        "encore."
    And called me back to give them more.
(Still lumbering)

                *   *   *

    So then I try to get on my feet,
        And — whoops — all over my coat!
    I hand them a laugh with that — and get
        The jug as antidote.
    I take a drink, I change my coat,
        I leave the old one there,
    I come out here to clear my head
        By getting a breath of air.

   (Lurching up to SIMO's *door)*
    I've left the son to see the father, and put a
        word in his ear
    About our deal.
   (Shouting)
                Open up! Tell Simo,
    Pseudolus is here!

(He pounds like a madman, then lurches a few
feet away. A second later the door opens, and
SIMO *appears clutching a purse.)*

SIMO: *(As he comes out)*
    It's the voice of that scoundrel that's
        brought me out here.
   (Catching sight of PSEUDOLUS *advancing*
    boozily)
    But what's *this* that I see? And how come?
        Very queer!
PSEUDOLUS: *(Affably)*
    It's your Pseudolus, fresh from a party —
        and tight.
SIMO:
    From loose living, by god. Look at that!
        What a sight!
    That your master's right here doesn't scare
        you one bit.
   (To himself)
    What's this call for? Sweet reason or
        throwing a fit?

(Caressing the purse, ruefully)
Ah, but *this* which I'm holding rules out
  being rough,
(Gesturing contemptuously toward
  PSEUDOLUS*)*
If I have any hopes out of *that* for this
  stuff.
PSEUDOLUS: *(In the grand manner)*
Common sinner comes calling on saint
  nonpareil.
SIMO: *(Grimly managing a smile and going
  up to him)*
Hearty greetings, dear Pseudolus—
(As PSEUDOLUS *belches resoundingly)*
                                      you go
  to hell!
PSEUDOLUS: *(Trying hard to keep his
  balance, as* SIMO *gives him a shove.)*
Hey, what's that for?
SIMO: *(Snarling)*
                        Just what do you
  mean, you disgrace,
By belching your drunken breath in my
  face?
PSEUDOLUS: *(Grabbing him for support,
  reproachfully)*
Take it easy! Hey, hold me and spare me
  more spills—
Can't you see that I'm tight? I'm soused to
  the gills!
SIMO: *(Holding him up, grimly)*
You sure have a nerve going around in
  this way—
As drunk as a lord in the broad light of
  day!
PSEUDOLUS: *(Grinning fatuously)*
I just felt I'd like doing it.

                  *   *   *

SIMO: *(Disgustedly)*
I swear, you could swill in an hour
All the alcohol Italy's manpower,
Using bumper crops only, could press
In four years.
PSEUDOLUS: *(Grinning)*
                  Not an hour. Much
  less.
SIMO: *(Nodding tight-lipped)*
Guess you're right. Here's a point I've
  ignored:

At what dock was this load put aboard?
PSEUDOLUS: *(Carelessly)*
With your son. We've been boozing away.
(Gleefully)
I sure gave it to Ballio, eh?
I did what I told you I would!
SIMO: *(Unhappily)*
You're a model of stinkerhood.
PSEUDOLUS:
It's the girl's fault, you know. She's been
  freed,
And she's there with your son at the feed.
SIMO: *(Wearily)*
Oh, I've heard a complete résumé.
PSEUDOLUS: *(Stoutly)*
Then what's holding things up? Where's
  my pay?
SIMO: *(Summoning up a ghastly smile,
  holding out the purse)*
It's your right. I agree. Here you are.
PSEUDOLUS: *(Unable to believe his eyes)*
You said you'd never come across—and
  here I get my pay!
*(He grins from ear to ear. Then, like a
  master ordering his slave, he points to
  his shoulder.)*
Well, load it on this shoulder, boy, and
  follow me this way.
SIMO: *(Shocked)*
You're asking *me* to put this there?
PSEUDOLUS: *(Grinning)*
You will, and I know why.
SIMO: *(To the world at large)*
He takes my money and then gets
  funny—what can I do with this guy?
PSEUDOLUS: *(As before)*
The victor gets the spoils, they say.
SIMO: *(Grimly)*
Then bend that shoulder down.
PSEUDOLUS:
                                      Okay.

                  *   *   *

SIMO: *(Managing to work up an ingratiating
  smile)*
Now my boy, would you rob your old
  master of this treasure?
PSEUDOLUS: *(Promptly)*
You're damned right. There's nothing
  would give me more pleasure.

SIMO: *(Wheedling)*

    Won't you please, as a favor, leave me
      some little part?

PSEUDOLUS:

    I will not! Go on, call me a miser at heart,
    But you'll never be richer by a penny
      from me.
    Had my plans not worked out so
      successfully, I'd
    Have got damned little pity out of *you* for
      my hide.

SIMO: *(Losing control and shaking his stick)*

    Just as sure as I live, I'll get even, you'll
      see!

PSEUDOLUS: *(Shrugging)*

    With the hide that I've got, do you think
      you scare me?

SIMO: *(Turning away and walking off*
     baffled)

    All right, then. Good-by!

PSEUDOLUS: *(Calling)*

                Hey, come back!

SIMO: *(In high dudgeon)*

    I come back? And what for?

PSEUDOLUS:

               Just come
  back.
    I won't fool you.

SIMO: *(Walking back, suspiciously)*

             I'm back.

PSEUDOLUS: *(Taking his arm and starting*
    to pull him, gaily)

              Well, just
  think—
    Here's the two of us off for a drink!

SIMO: *(Trying to hold back as* PSEUDOLUS *tugs*
    energetically)

    For a drink?

PSEUDOLUS: *(Holding up the purse*
    enticingly)

    You just do as I say
    And I promise you half of this pay—
    Maybe more.

SIMO: *(Suddenly giving up all resistance)*

    Show the way and I'll go
    Any place that you want.

PSEUDOLUS: *(Innocently)*

                Is that so?
    You're not angry at me or your son
    On account of these things that I've done?

SIMO: *(Eying the purse hungrily)*

    Not at all.

PSEUDOLUS: *(Starting to walk off, stage*
    left)

               Come this way.

SIMO: *(Following him)*

                I'm behind.
    (Stopping and pointing to the audience)
    Let's invite the whole crowd. Do you
      mind?

PSEUDOLUS: *(Stopping and eying the*
    audience)

    Lord, they and I have never exchanged
    A single invitation.
    (To the audience)
    But if you're willing to give a hand,
    A loud and warm ovation.
    To all our actors and their play—
    I invite you all—but not today!

    The title *Pseudolus* may very appropriately be translated as *The Trickster* or *The Cheat,* for it depicts the machinations of one of comedy's most familiar character types: the clever rogue who outwits less clever rogues. Such comedy requires that moral concerns be kept at a distance, that the audience's attention be directed to how goals are to be achieved rather than to their ethical implications. In another framework, the situation in *Pseudolus* would appear sordid, dealing as it does with pimps and prostitutes, con men and con games. So well is our attention diverted that we may not at first recognize that the girl Calidorus is seeking to rescue is a prostitute and that he does not expect to marry her; his goal is merely to buy her from the pimp before someone else does.

Plautus focuses our attention on Pseudolus' attempts to assist his rather dim-witted master. His trickery is made acceptable (even admirable) by the behavior of those he sets out to dupe. Ballio, the pimp, is shown to be so unscrupulous and mean-spirited that we can take pleasure in seeing him outwitted; to rescue anyone from his clutches would be praiseworthy. The other characters also deserve their defeat for they complacently believe that they cannot be outsmarted. The trickery is made even more enjoyable by Pseudolus' insistence on warning everyone of his intentions.

The play's focus is not always on the intrigue. Some scenes (such as that between Ballio and the Cook and the final scene) are devoted primarily to verbal banter. Occasionally Pseudolus makes comments to the audience about the play's action or about playwriting conventions.

Pseudolus also includes a number of false leads. For example, the elderly Callipho, after being enlisted as a helper by Pseudolus, is never heard of again. Similarly, Calidorus' friend Charinus appears in one scene and then disappears from the play. Even Calidorus is absent during the last half of the action. But these apparent lapses are more obvious to the analytical reader than to a theatre audience. A more coherent arrangement would have all the characters reappear in the final scene, but Plautus was apparently more concerned with entertaining an audience than with achieving structural unity.

To seek profundity in *Pseudolus* would be futile. Like other types of popular entertainment, which have persisted from ancient times to the present, it manipulates accepted values and social attitudes without questioning them. *Pseudolus* treats slavery and the abuses accompanying it, for example, as being as much a commonplace of daily life as the unionization of workers is in our television dramas.

If *Pseudolus* is not profound, it nevertheless illustrates an issue that has been debated since ancient times. Are plays which countenance or view humorously such subjects as cheating, sex, and violence potential threats to a society's moral fiber? Those who answer affirmatively argue that the influence of such plays may not be immediately apparent but that gradually they condition audiences to accept behavior that they would otherwise condemn. They also often find popular entertainment (such as *Pseudolus*) to be especially pernicious because it is considered by most viewers to be mere diversion and therefore harmless. Does *Pseudolus* argue indirectly that it is all right to cheat those we disapprove of or those who are dishonest or unreasonable?

Many people have rejected the views of those who would censor what we may see or read. Common counter arguments are that plays reflect life and that familiarity with a wide range of behavior and values is essential to sound judgment and that censorship constitutes a threat far greater than that posed by freedom of expression. Anyone familiar with current events knows that the debate still continues, often virulently, not only about plays but also about television programming, textbook selection, library holdings, and educational curricula.

Those who wish to see a connection between popular entertainment and moral climate have always pointed to Rome as an example. They see the decline and fall of Rome (some 600–700 years after *Pseudolus* was written) as intimately connected with the debasement of popular entertainment as the taste grew for gladiatorial contests, fights to the death between men and wild animals, and skits about sexual exploits. Since Roman times, moralists have typically sought to bolster their indictments of popular entertainments by pointing to the fall of Rome as a graphic example of the likely outcome if the perceived evils are not curbed.

Everyman

Anonymous

Following the disintegration of the Roman Empire during the fifth and sixth centuries A.D., organized dramatic activity virtually ceased in Western Europe for several hundred years. The lavish state-financed festivals, which had been typical in both Greece and Rome, gave way to storytelling and songs by individual performers, short playlets by small traveling troupes, and entertainment by itinerant jugglers, acrobats, and exhibitors of trained animals.

Not until the tenth century did drama take on new life when short plays began to be used in church services to dramatize episodes from the Bible. During the following centuries, drama steadily gained in popularity and by the fifteenth century some religious plays had become extremely long, requiring many days to perform. By that time, they also were being presented out of doors with casts of hundreds and with elaborate scenery and costumes. The stage used for these spectacles reflected the contemporary view of the universe. Heaven, located at one end of the long platform, was opposed by Hell, located at the opposite end; earthly locales were situated between Heaven and Hell. Thus, the temporal was framed by the eternal. Locales were suggested, rather than fully depicted, by scenic structures (or mansions) set up along the rear of the platform. In performance, the location of a scene was indicated by placing the characters within or alongside the appropriate mansion; as the scene progressed, the performers moved out from the mansion, utilizing as much of the stage space as the action required. Time and space, then, were easily transformable and could be telescoped or expanded as needed in plays which frequently included episodes ranging from the Creation to the Last Judgment.

By the fifteenth century, religious and civic authorities were once more financing productions and providing the populace with lavish, free entertainments. Such spectacular drama remained common until the mid-sixteenth century, and some (most notably the Passion Play at Oberammergau) are still performed.

Until the sixteenth century, most plays were based on religious sources, although by the late thirteenth century plays based on purely secular themes had begun to appear. From 1300 onward, secular dramas steadily increased in number and popularity. Farces (depicting hypocrisy, trickery, and knavery of all sort) were especially popular.

A third type, the morality play, originated in the fourteenth century and flourished between 1400 and 1550. It occupies a place between the religious and the secular dramas, for unlike the religious plays, which featured biblical characters or saints, and unlike the secular plays, which treated ordinary human beings and their frailties, the morality play showed mankind caught in a struggle between the temptations of the world and the demands of religious doctrine. This struggle was made fully evident through allegory. Characters on the side of virtue were given such names as Good Counsel, Mercy, Charity, Knowledge, and Good Deeds; those on the side of evil were given such names as Bad Counsel, Lust, Greed, Ignorance, and Bad Deeds. The protagonist, the representative human being, was called Mankind, Prince of Life, or Everyman. He was easily tempted into forgetfulness of his duty and risked eternal damnation, but at the end of the play he usually returned to the path of righteousness and achieved salvation.

Most of the surviving morality plays are long and cover lengthy periods of time, but the most admired of the morality plays, *Everyman* (c. 1500), treats only the final portion of life: the summoning of Everyman by Death to account to God for his life.

MESSENGER	KNOWLEDGE
GOD *Adonai*	CONFESSION
DEATH	BEAUTY
EVERYMAN	STRENGTH
FELLOWSHIP	DISCRETION
COUSIN	FIVE WITS
KINDRED	ANGEL
GOODS	DOCTOR
GOOD DEEDS	

Here beginneth a treatise how the High Father of Heaven sendeth Death to summon every creature to come and give account of their lives in this world, and is in manner of a moral play.

(Enter MESSENGER *to speak Prologue.)*

MESSENGER: I pray you all give your
    audience,
And hear this matter with reverence,
By figure a moral play —
The *Summoning of Everyman* called it is,
That of our lives and ending shows
How transitory we be all day.
This matter is wondrous precious,
But the intent of it is more gracious,
And sweet to bear away.
The story saith: Man, in the beginning,
Look well, and take good heed to the
    ending,

Be you never so gay!
Ye think sin in the beginning full sweet,
Which in the end causeth the soul to
    weep,
When the body lieth in clay.
Here shall you see how Fellowship and
    Jollity,
Both Strength, Pleasure, and Beauty,
Will fade from thee as flower in May.
For ye shall hear how our Heaven King
Calleth Everyman to a general reckoning.
Give audience, and hear what he doth say.

(Exit)

*(*GOD *speaketh from above)*

GOD: I perceive, here in my majesty,
How that all creatures be to me unkind,
Living without dread in wordly prosperity.
Of ghostly[1] sight the people be so blind,
Drowned in sin, they know me not for
their God.
In wordly riches is all their mind,
They fear not my rightwiseness, the sharp
rod;
My love that I showed when I for them
died
They forget clean, and shedding of my
blood red;
I hanged between two, it cannot be denied;
To get them life I suffered to be dead;
I healed their feet, with thorns hurt was
my head.
I could do no more that I did, truly;
And now I see the people do clean forsake
me.
They use the seven deadly sins damnable;
As pride, covetise, wrath, and lechery,
Now in the world be made commendable;
And thus they leave of angels the
heavenly company.
Every man liveth so after his own
pleasure,
And yet of their life they be nothing sure.
I see the more that I them forbear
The worse they be from year to year;
All that liveth appaireth[2] fast.
Therefore I will, in all the haste,
Have a reckoning of every man's person;
For, and[3] I leave the people thus alone
In their life and wicked tempests,
Verily they will become much worse than
beasts;
For now one would by envy another up
eat;
Charity they all do clean forget.
I hoped well that every man
In my glory should make his mansion,
And thereto I had them all elect;
But now I see, like traitors deject,
They thank me not for the pleasure that I
to them meant,
Not yet for their being that I them have
lent.
I proffered the people great multitude of
mercy,
And few there be that asketh it heartily;
They be so cumbered with worldly riches,
That needs on them I must do justice,
On every man living, without fear.
Where are thou, Death, thou mighty
messenger?

(Enter DEATH.*)*

DEATH: Almighty God, I am here at your
will,
Your commandment to fulfil.
GOD: Go thou to Everyman,
And show him, in my name,
A pilgrimage he must on him take,
Which he in no wise may escape;
And that he bring with him a sure
reckoning
Without delay or any tarrying.
DEATH: Lord, I will in the world go run over
all
And cruelly out search both great and
small. (GOD *withdraws.*)
Every man will I beset that liveth beastly
Out of God's laws, and dreadeth not folly.
He that loveth riches I will strike with my
dart,
His sight to blind, and from heaven to
depart,
Except that alms be his good friend,
In hell for to dwell, world without end.
Lo, yonder I see Everyman walking;
Full little he thinketh on my coming;
His mind is on fleshly lusts and his
treasure;
And great pain it shall cause him to
endure
Before the Lord, Heaven King.
Everyman, stand still! Whither art thou
going
Thus gaily? Hast thou thy Maker forgot?
EVERYMAN: Why askest thou?
Wouldst thou wete?[4]
DEATH: Yea, sir, I will show you;
In great haste I am sent to thee

[1]Spiritual.
[2]Is impaired.
[3]If (thus frequently throughout the play).
[4]Know.

From God out of his Majesty.

EVERYMAN: What, sent to me?

DEATH: Yea, certainly.

Though thou have forgot him here,

He thinketh on thee in the heavenly
sphere,

As, ere we depart, thou shalt know.

EVERYMAN: What desireth God of me?

DEATH: That shall I show thee;

A reckoning he will needs have

Without any longer respite.

EVERYMAN: To give a reckoning longer
leisure I crave;

This blind matter troubleth my wit.

DEATH: On thee thou must take a long
journey;

Therefore thy book of count with thee
thou bring;

For turn again thou can not by no way.

And look thou be sure of thy reckoning.

For before God thou shalt answer and
show

Thy many bad deeds, and good but a few,

How thou hast spent thy life, and in what
wise,

Before the Chief Lord of paradise.

Have ado[5] that we were in that way.

For, wete thou well, thou shalt make none
attorney.

EVERYMAN: Full unready I am such
reckoning to give.

I know thee not. What messenger art
thou?

DEATH: I am Death, that no man dreadeth.

For every man I 'rest, and no man spareth;

For it is God's commandment

That all to me should be obedient.

EVERYMAN: O Death! thou comest when I
had thee least in mind!

In thy power it lieth me to save,

Yet of my goods will I give thee, if thou
will be kind;

Yea, a thousand pound shalt thou have,.

If thou defer this matter till another day.

DEATH: Everyman, it may not be, by no
way!

I set not by gold, silver, nor riches,

[5]Get ready.

Nor by pope, emperor, king, duke, nor
princes.

For, and I would receive gifts great,

All the world I might get;

But my custom is clean contrary.

I give thee no respite. Come hence, and
not tarry.

EVERYMAN: Alas! shall I have no longer
respite?

I may say Death giveth no warning.

To think on thee, it maketh my heart
sick,

For all unready is my book of reckoning.

But twelve year and I might have abiding,

My counting-book I would make so clear,

That my reckoning I should not need to
fear.

Wherefore, Death, I pray thee, for God's
mercy,

Spare me till I be provided of remedy.

DEATH: Thee availeth not to cry, weep, and
pray;

But haste thee lightly that thou were gone
that journey,

And prove thy friends if thou can.

For wete thou well the tide abideth no man;

And in the world each living creature

For Adam's sin must die of nature.

EVERYMAN: Death, if I should this
pilgrimage take,

And my reckoning surely make,

Show me, for saint charity,

Should I not come again shortly?

DEATH: No, Everyman; and thou be once
there,

Thou mayst never more come here,

Trust me verily.

EVERYMAN: O gracious God, in the high
seat celestial,

Have mercy on me in this most need!

Shall I have no company from this vale
terrestrial

Of mine acquaintance that way me to
lead?

DEATH: Yea, if any be so hardy,

That would go with thee and bear thee
company.

Hie thee that thou were gone to God's
magnificence,

Thy reckoning to give before his presence.
What! weenest thou thy life is given thee,
And thy worldly goods also?
EVERYMAN: I had weened so, verily.
DEATH: Nay, nay; it was but lent thee;
For, as soon as thou art gone,
Another a while shall have it, and then go
therefrom
Even as thou hast done.
Everyman, thou art mad! Thou hast thy
wits five,
And here on earth will not amend thy
life;
For suddenly I do come.
EVERYMAN: O wretched caitiff! whither
shall I flee,
That I might 'scape endless sorrow?
Now, gentle Death, spare me till tomorrow,
That I may amend me
With good advisement.
DEATH: Nay, thereto I will not consent,
Nor no man will I respite,
But to the heart suddenly I shall smite
Without any advisement
And now out of thy sight I will me hie;
See thou make thee ready shortly,
For thou mayst say this is the day
That no man living may 'scape away.

(Exit DEATH.*)*

EVERYMAN: Alas! I may well weep with
sighs deep.
Now have I no manner of company
To help me in my journey and me to
keep;
And also my writing is full unready.
How shall I do now for to excuse me?
I would to God I had never been gete![6]
To my soul a full great profit it had be;
For now I fear pains huge and great.
The time passeth; Lord, help, that all
wrought.
For though I mourn it availeth naught.
The day passeth, and is almost a-go;
I wot not well what for to do.
To whom were I best my complaint to
make?

What if I to Fellowship thereof spake,
And showed him of this sudden chance?
For in him is all mine affiance,[7]
We have in the world so many a day
Been good friends in sport and play.
I see him yonder, certainly;
I trust that he will bear me company;
Therefore to him will I speak to ease my
sorrow.
Well met, good Fellowship, and good
morrow!

*(*FELLOWSHIP *speaketh.)*

FELLOWSHIP: Everyman, good morrow, by
this day!
Sir, why lookest thou so piteously?
If any thing be amiss, I pray thee me say,
That I may help to remedy.
EVERYMAN: Yea, good Fellowship, yea,
I am in great jeopardy.
FELLOWSHIP: My true friend, show to me
your mind;
I will not forsake thee to my life's end
In the way of good company.
EVERYMAN: That was well spoken, and
lovingly.
FELLOWSHIP: Sir, I must needs know your
heaviness;
I have pity to see you in any distress;
If any have you wronged, ye shall
revenged be,
Though I on the ground be slain for thee,
Though that I know before that I should
die.
EVERYMAN: Verily, Fellowship, gramercy.
FELLOWSHIP: Tush! by thy thanks I set not
a straw!
Show me your grief, and say no more.
EVERYMAN: If I my heart should to you
break,
And then you to turn your mind from me,
And would not me comfort when you
hear me speak,
Then should I ten times sorrier be.
FELLOWSHIP: Sir, I say as I will do, indeed.
EVERYMAN: Then be you a good friend at
need;

----

[6]Born.

[7]Trust.

I have found you true here before.

FELLOWSHIP: And so ye shall evermore;
    For, in faith, and thou go to hell.
    I will not forsake thee by the way!

EVERYMAN: Ye speak like a good friend. I
    believe you well;
    I shall deserve it, and I may.

FELLOWSHIP: I speak of no deserving, by
    this day!
    For he that will say and nothing do
    Is not worthy with good company to go;
    Therefore show me the grief of your
    mind,
    As to your friend most loving and kind.

EVERYMAN: I shall show you how it is:
    Commanded I am to go a journey.
    A long way, hard and dangerous,
    And give a strict count without delay
    Before the high judge, Adonai.
    Wherefore, I pray you, bear me company,
    As ye have promised, in this journey.

FELLOWSHIP: That is matter indeed! Promise
    is duty;
    But, and I should take such a voyage on
    me,
    I know it well, it should be to my pain.
    Also it maketh me afeared, certain.
    But let us take counsel here as well as we
    can,
    For your words would fright a strong man.

EVERYMAN: Why, ye said if I had need,
    Ye would me never forsake, quick nor
    dead,
    Though it were to hell, truly.

FELLOWSHIP: So I said, certainly,
    But such pleasures be set aside, the sooth
    to say.
    And also, if we took such a journey,
    When should we come again?

EVERYMAN: Nay, never again till the day of
    doom.

FELLOWSHIP: In faith, then will not I come
    there!
    Who hath you these tidings brought?

EVERYMAN: Indeed, Death was with me
    here.

FELLOWSHIP: Now, by God that all hath
    bought,
    If Death were the messenger,

For no man that is living today
    I will not go that loath journey—
    Not for the father that begat me!

EVERYMAN: Ye promised otherwise, pardie.[8]

FELLOWSHIP: I wot well I said so, truly;
    And yet if thou wilt eat, and drink, and
    make good cheer,
    Or haunt to women the lusty company,
    I would not forsake you while the day is
    clear,
    Trust me verily!

EVERYMAN: Yea, thereto ye would be
    ready;
    To go to mirth, solace, and play.
    Your mind will sooner apply
    Than to bear me company in my long
    journey.

FELLOWSHIP: Now, in good faith, I will not
    that way,
    But and thou wilt murder, or any man
    kill,
    In that I will help thee with a good will!

EVERYMAN: O, that is a simple advice
    indeed!
    Gentle fellow, help me in my necessity;
    We have loved long, and now I need,
    And now, gentle Fellowship, remember
    me!

FELLOWSHIP: Whether ye have loved me or
    no,
    By Saint John, I will not with thee go.

EVERYMAN: Yet, I pray thee, take the labor,
    and do so much for me
    To bring me forward, for saint charity,
    And comfort me till I come without the
    town.

FELLOWSHIP: Nay, and thou would give me
    a new gown,
    I will not a foot with thee go;
    But, and thou had tarried, I would not
    have left thee so.
    And as now God speed thee in thy
    journey.
    For from thee I will depart as fast as I may.

EVERYMAN: Whither away, Fellowship?
    Will you forsake me?

[8]*Par dieu*; indeed.

FELLOWSHIP: Yea, by my fay, to God I
    betake[9] thee.
EVERYMAN: Farewell, good Fellowship! For
    thee my heart is sore;
  Adieu for ever! I shall see thee no more.
FELLOWSHIP: In faith, Everyman, farewell
    now at the end!
  For you I will remember that parting is
    mourning.

        (Exit FELLOWSHIP.*)*

EVERYMAN: Alack! shall we thus depart
    indeed
  (Ah, Lady, help!) without any more
    comfort;
  Lo, Fellowship forsaketh me in my most
    need.
  For help in this world whither shall I
    resort?
  Fellowship here before with me would
    merry make,
  And now little sorrow for me doth he
    take.
  It is said, "In prosperity men friends may
    find,
  Which in adversity be full unkind."
  Now whither for succor shall I flee,
  Sith that Fellowship hath forsaken me?
  To my kinsmen I will, truly,
  Praying them to help me in my necessity;
  I believe that they will do so,
  For "kind will creep where it may not
    go."[10]
  I will go say,[11] for yonder I see them go.
  Where be ye now, my friends and
    kinsmen?

    (Enter KINDRED *and* COUSIN.*)*

KINDRED: Here be we now, at your
    commandment.
  Cousin, I pray you show us your intent
  In any wise, and do not spare.
COUSIN: Yea, Everyman, and to us declare
  If ye be disposed to go any whither,

For, wete you well, we will live and die
    together.
KINDRED: In wealth and woe we will with
    you hold,
  For over his kin a man may be bold.
EVERYMAN: Gramercy, my friends and
    kinsmen kind.
  Now shall I show you the grief of my
    mind.
  I was commanded by a messenger
  That is a high king's chief officer;
  He bade me go a pilgrimage, to my pain,
  And I know well I shall never come again;
  Also I must give a reckoning straight,
  For I have a great enemy that hath me in
    wait,[12]
  Which intendeth me for to hinder.
KINDRED: What account is that which ye
    must render?
  That would I know.
EVERYMAN: Of all my works I must show
  How I have lived, and my days spent;
  Also of ill deeds that I have used
  In my time, sith life was me lent;
  And of all virtues that I have refused.
  Therefore I pray you go thither with me,
  To help to make mine account, for saint
    charity.
COUSIN: What, to go thither? Is that the
    matter?
  Nay, Everyman, I had liefer fast bread and
    water
  All this five year and more.
EVERYMAN: Alas, that ever I was bore!
  For now shall I never be merry
  If that you forsake me.
KINDRED: Ah, sir, what! Ye be a merry
    man!
  Take good heart to you, and make no
    moan.
  But one thing I warn you, by Saint Anne,
  As for me, ye shall go alone.
EVERYMAN: My Cousin, will you not with
    me go?
COUSIN: No, by our Lady! I have the cramp
    in my toe.

[9]Commit.
[10]Walk.
[11]Try.

[12]Lies in wait.

Trust not to me; for, so God me speed,
I will deceive you in your most need.
KINDRED: It availeth not us to tice.[13]
Ye shall have my maid with all my heart;
She loveth to go to feasts, there to be
nice,[14]
And to dance, and abroad to start;
I will give her leave to help you in that
journey,
If that you and she may agree.
EVERYMAN: Now show me the very effect
of your mind.
Will you go with me, or abide behind?
KINDRED: Abide behind? Yea, that will I,
and I may!
Therefore farewell till another day.

(Exit KINDRED.*)*

EVERYMAN: How should I be merry or
glad?
For fair promises men to me make,.
But when I have most need, they me
forsake.
I am deceived; that maketh me sad.
COUSIN: Cousin Everyman, farewell now,
For verily I will not go with you;
Also of mine own life an unready
reckoning
I have to account; therefore I make
tarrying.
Now, God keep thee, for now I go.

(Exit COUSIN.*)*

EVERYMAN: Ah, Jesus! is all come hereto?
Lo, fair words maketh fools fain;[15]
They promise and nothing will do certain.
My kinsmen promised me faithfully
For to abide with me steadfastly,
And now fast away do they flee.
Even so Fellowship promised me.
What friend were best me of to provide?
I lose my time here longer to abide.
Yet in my mind a thing there is;
All my life I have loved riches;
If that my Goods now help me might,
He would make my heart full light.

I will speak to him in this distress.
Where art thou, my Goods and riches?
GOODS: *(From within)* Who calleth me?
Everyman? What, hast thou haste?
I lie here in corners, trussed and piled so
high,
And in chests I am locked so fast,
Also sacked in bags — thou mayst see with
thine eye —
I cannot stir; in packs low I lie.
What would ye have? Lightly me say.
EVERYMAN: Come hither, Goods, in all the
haste thou may.
For of counsel I must desire thee.

(Enter GOODS.*)*

GOODS: Sir, and ye in the world have sorrow
or adversity,
That can I help you to remedy shortly.
EVERYMAN: It is another disease that
grieveth me;
In this world it is not, I tell thee so.
I am sent for another way to go,
To give a strict count general
Before the highest Jupiter of all;
And all my life I have had joy and
pleasure in thee;
Therefore I pray thee go with me,
For, peradventure, thou mayst before God
Almighty
My reckoning help to clean and purify;
For it is said ever among,
That "money maketh all right that is
wrong."
GOODS: Nay, Everyman; I sing another song,
I follow no man in such voyages;
For, and I went with thee,
Thou shouldst fare much the worse for
me;
For because on me thou did set thy mind,
Thy reckoning I have made blotted and
blind,
That thine account thou cannot make
truly;
And that hast thou for the love of me.
EVERYMAN: That would grieve me full
sore,
When I should come to that fearful
answer.
Up, let us go thither together.

[13]Entice, coax.
[14]Wanton.
[15]Glad.

GOODS: Nay, not so! I am too brittle, I may
    not endure;
  I will follow no man one foot, be ye sure.
EVERYMAN: Alas! I have thee loved, and
    had great pleasure
  All my life-days on goods and treasure.
GOODS: That is to thy damnation, without
    lesing![16]
  For my love is contrary to the love
    everlasting.
  But if thou had me loved moderately
    during,
  As to the poor to give part of me,
  Then shouldst thou not in this dolor be,
  Nor in this great sorrow and care.
EVERYMAN: Lo, now was I deceived ere I
    was ware,
  And all I may wyte[17] my spending of time.
GOODS: What, weenest thou that I am thine?
EVERYMAN: I had weened so.
GOODS: Nay, Everyman, I say no;
  As for a while I was lent thee,
  A season thou hast had me in prosperity.
  My condition is man's soul to kill;
  If I save one, a thousand I do spill;
  Weenest thou that I will follow thee
  From this world? Nay, verily.
EVERYMAN: I had weened otherwise.
GOODS: Therefore to thy soul Goods is a
    thief;
  For when thou art dead, this is my
    guise —[18]
  Another to deceive in the same wise
  As I have done thee, and all to his soul's
    reprief.[19]
EVERYMAN: O false Goods, curséd thou be!
  Thou traitor to God, that hast deceived me
  And caught me in thy snare.
GOODS: Marry! thou brought thyself in care,
  Whereof I am right glad.
  I must needs laugh, I cannot be sad.
EVERYMAN: Ah, Goods, thou hast had long
    my heartly love;
  I gave thee that which should be the
    Lord's above.

  But wilt thou not go with me indeed?
  I pray thee truth to say.
GOODS: No, so God me speed!
  Therefore farewell, and have good day.

     (Exit GOODS.*)*

EVERYMAN: O, to whom shall I make my
    moan
  For to go with me in that heavy journey?
  First Fellowship said he would with me
    gone;
  His words were very pleasant and gay,
  But afterward he left me alone.
  Then spake I to my kinsmen, all in
    despair,
  And also they gave me words fair,
  They lacked no fair speaking,
  But all forsook me in the ending.
  Then went I to my Goods, that I loved
    best,
  In hope to have comfort, but there had I
    least;
  For my Goods sharply did me tell
  That he bringeth many into hell.
  Then of myself I was ashamed,
  And so I am worthy to be blamed;
  Thus may I well myself hate.
  Of whom shall I now counsel take?
  I think that I shall never speed
  Till that I go to my Good Deeds.
  But alas! she is so weak
  That she can neither go nor speak.
  Yet will I venture on her now.
  My Good Deads, where be you?

  *(*GOOD DEEDS *speaks from the ground.)*

GOOD DEEDS: Here I lie, cold in the ground.
  Thy sins hath me sore bound,
  That I cannot stir.
EVERYMAN: O Good Deeds! I stand in fear;
  I must you pray of counsel,
  For help now should come right well.
GOOD DEEDS: Everyman, I have
    understanding
  That ye be summoned account to make
  Before Messias, of Jerusalem King;
  And you do by me,[20] that journey with
    you will I take.

[16]Lying.
[17]Blame to.
[18]Practice, trick.
[19]Reproof.

[20]Act by my advice.

EVERYMAN: Therefore I come to you my
    moan to make;
  I pray you that ye will go with me.
GOOD DEEDS: I would full fain, but I
    cannot stand, verily.
EVERYMAN: Why, is there anything on you
    fall?
GOOD DEEDS: Yea, sir, I may thank you of
    all;
  If ye had perfectly cheered[21] me,
  Your book of count full ready had be.
  Look, the books of your works and deeds
    eke;
  Ah, see how they lie under the feet,
  To your soul's heaviness.
EVERYMAN: Our Lord Jesus help me!
  For one letter here I can not see.
GOOD DEEDS: There is a blind reckoning in
    time of distress!
EVERYMAN: Good Deeds, I pray you, help
    me in this need,
  Or else I am for ever damned indeed;
  Therefore help me to make my reckoning
  Before the Redeemer of all thing,
  That King is, and was, and ever shall.
GOOD DEEDS: Everyman, I am sorry of your
    fall,
  And fain would I help you, and I were
    able.
EVERYMAN: Good Deeds, your counsel I
    pray you give me.
GOOD DEEDS: That shall I do verily;
  Though that on my feet I may not go,
  I have a sister that shall with you also,
  Called Knowledge, which shall with you
    abide,
  To help you to make that dreadful
    reckoning.

(Enter KNOWLEDGE.*)*

KNOWLEDGE: Everyman, I will go with
    thee, and be thy guide
  In thy most need to go by thy side.
EVERYMAN: In good condition I am now in
    every thing,
  And am wholly content with this good
    thing;
  Thanked be God my Creator.

GOOD DEEDS: And when he hath brought
    thee there,
  Where thou shalt heal thee of thy smart,
  Then go you with your reckoning and
    your Good Deeds together
  For to make you joyful at heart
  Before the blessèd Trinity.
EVERYMAN: My Good Deeds, gramercy!
  I am well content, certainly,
  With your words sweet.
KNOWLEDGE: Now go we together lovingly
  To Confession, that cleansing river.
EVERYMAN: For joy I weep; I would we
    were there!
  But, I pray you, give me cognition
  Where dwelleth that holy man,
    Confession.
KNOWLEDGE: In the house of salvation;
  We shall find him in that place,
  That shall us comfort, by God's grace.
  (KNOWLEDGE *leads* EVERYMAN *to*
  CONFESSION.*)*
  Lo, this is Confession. Kneel down and ask
    mercy,
  For he is in good conceit[22] with God
    almighty.
EVERYMAN: *(Kneeling)* O glorious fountain,
    that all uncleanness doth clarify,
  Wash from me the spots of vice unclean,
  That on me no sin may be seen.
  I come, with Knowledge, for my
    redemption,
  Redempt with hearty and full contrition;
  For I am commanded a pilgrimage to take,
  And great accounts before God to make.
  Now, I pray you, Shrift, mother of
    salvation.
  Help my Good Deeds for my piteous
    exclamation.
CONFESSION: I know your sorrow well,
    Everyman.
  Because with Knowledge ye come to me,
  I will you comfort as well as I can,
  And a precious jewel I will give thee,
  Called penance, voider of adversity;
  Therewith shall your body chastised be,
  With abstinence, and perseverance in
    God's service.

[21]Cherished.

[22]Esteem.

Here shall you receive that scourge of me.
(*Gives* EVERYMAN *a scourge*)
Which is penance strong, that ye must
endure
To remember thy Savior was scourged for
thee
With sharp scourges, and suffered it
patiently;
So must thou ere thou 'scape that painful
pilgrimage.
Knowledge, keep him in this voyage,
And by that time Good Deeds will be
with thee.
But in any wise be seeker of mercy,
For your time draweth fast, and ye will
saved be;
Ask God mercy, and He will grant truly;
When with the scourge of penance man
doth him bind,
The oil of forgiveness then shall he find.

(*Exit* CONFESSION.)

EVERYMAN: Thanked be God for his
gracious work!
For now I will my penance begin;
This hath rejoiced and lighted my heart,
Though the knots be painful and hard
within.
KNOWLEDGE: Everyman, look your
penance that ye fulfil,
What pain that ever it to you be,
And Knowledge shall give you counsel at
will
How your account ye shall make clearly.

(EVERYMAN *kneels.*)

EVERYMAN: O eternal God! O heavenly
figure!
O way of rightwiseness! O goodly vision!
Which descended down in a virgin pure
Because he would Everyman redeem,
Which Adam forfeited by his
disobedience.
O blesséd Godhead! elect and high divine,
Forgive me my grievous offence;
Here I cry thee mercy in this presence.
O ghostly treasure! O ransomer and
redeemer!
Of all the world hope and conductor,
Mirror of joy, and founder of mercy,

Which illumineth heaven and earth
thereby,
Hear my clamorous complaint, though it
late be.
Receive my prayers; unworthy in this
heavy life.
Though I be a sinner most abominable,
Yet let my name be written in Moses'
table.
O Mary! pray to the Maker of all thing,
Me for to help at my ending,
And save me from the power of my
enemy,
For Death assaileth me strongly.
And, Lady, that I may by means of thy
prayer
Of your Son's glory to be partner,
By the means of his passion I it crave;
I beseech you, help my soul to save.
(*He rises*)
Knowledge, give me the scourge of
penance.
My flesh therewith shall give a quittance.
I will now begin, if God give me grace.
KNOWLEDGE: Everyman, God give you
time and space.
Thus I bequeath you in the hands of our
Savior,
Now may you make your reckoning sure.
EVERYMAN: In the name of the Holy
Trinity,
My body sore punished shall be.
(*Scourges himself.*)
Take this, body, for the sin of the flesh;
Also thou delightest to go gay and fresh,
And in the way of damnation thou did me
bring;
Therefore suffer now strokes of punishing.
Now of penance I will wade the water
clear,
To save me from purgatory, that sharp
fire.

(GOOD DEEDS *rises from floor.*)

GOOD DEEDS: I thank God, now I can walk
and go,
And am delivered of my sickness and woe.
Therefore with Everyman I will go, and
not spare;
His good works I will help him to declare.

KNOWLEDGE: Now, Everyman, be merry
    and glad!
    Your Good Deeds cometh now, ye may
      not be sad;
    Now is your Good Deeds whole and
      sound,
    Going upright upon the ground.
EVERYMAN: My heart is light, and shall be
    evermore.
    Now will I smite faster than I did before.
GOOD DEEDS: Everyman, pilgrim, my
    special friend,
    Blesséd be thou without end.
    For thee is prepared the eternal glory.
    Ye have me made whole and sound,
    Therefore I will bide by thee in every
      stound.[23]
EVERYMAN: Welcome, my Good Deeds;
    now I hear thy voice,
    I weep for very sweetness of love.
KNOWLEDGE: Be no more sad, but ever
    rejoice;
    God seeth thy living in his throne above.
    Put on this garment to thy behoof,
    Which is wet with your tears,
    Or else before God you may it miss,
    When you to your journey's end come
      shall.
EVERYMAN: Gentle Knowledge, what do ye
    it call?
KNOWLEDGE: It is the garment of sorrow;
    From pain it will you borrow;
    Contrition it is
    That getteth forgiveness;
    It pleaseth God passing well.
GOOD DEEDS: Everyman, will you wear it
    for your heal?

(EVERYMAN puts on garment of contrition.)

EVERYMAN: Now blesséd be Jesu, Mary's
    Son,
    For now have I on true contrition.
    And let us go now without tarrying;
    Good Deeds, have we clear our reckoning?
GOOD DEEDS: Yea, indeed I have it here.
EVERYMAN: Then I trust we need not fear.
    Now, friends, let us not part in twain.

KNOWLEDGE: Nay, Everyman, that will we
    not, certain.
GOOD DEEDS: Yet must thou lead with thee
    Three persons of great might.
EVERYMAN: Who should they be?
GOOD DEEDS: Discretion and Strength they
    hight,[24]
    And thy Beauty may not abide behind.
KNOWLEDGE: Also ye must call to mind
    Your Five Wits as for your counselors.
GOOD DEEDS: You must have them ready at
    all hours.
EVERYMAN: How shall I get them hither?
KNOWLEDGE: You must call them all
    together,
    And they will hear you incontinent.
EVERYMAN: My friends, come hither and
    be present;
    Discretion, Strength, my Five Wits, and
    Beauty.

(Enter DISCRETION, STRENGTH, FIVE WITS, and
        BEAUTY.)

BEAUTY: Here at your will we be all ready.
    What will ye that we should do?
GOOD DEEDS: That ye would with
    Everyman go,
    And help him in his pilgrimage.
    Advise you, will ye with him or not in
    that voyage?
STRENGTH: We will bring him all thither,
    To his help and comfort, ye may believe
    me.
DISCRETION: So will we go with him all
    together.
EVERYMAN: Almighty God, lovéd may
    thou be!
    I give thee laud that I have hither brought
    Strength, Discretion, Beauty, and Five
    Wits. Lack I naught;
    And my Good Deeds, with Knowledge
    clear,
    All be in company at my will here.
    I desire no more to my business.
STRENGTH: And I, Strength, will by you
    stand in distress,
    Though thou would in battle fight on the
    ground.

[23]Always.

[24]Are called.

FIVE WITS: And though it were through the world round,
We will not depart for sweet nor sour.
BEAUTY: No more will I, unto death's hour,
Whatsoever thereof befall.
DISCRETION: Everyman, advise you first of all;
Go with a good advisement and deliberation.
We all give you virtuous monition
That all shall be well.
EVERYMAN: My friends, hearken what I will tell;
I pray God reward you in his heavenly sphere.
Now hearken, all that be here,
For I will make my testament
Here before you all present:
In alms half my goods I will give with my hands twain
In the way of charity, with good intent,
And the other half still shall remain;
I it bequeath to be returned there it ought to be.
This I do in despite of the fiend of hell,
To go quite out of his peril
Ever after and this day.
KNOWLEDGE: Everyman, hearken what I say;
Go to Priesthood, I you advise,
And receive of him in any wise
The holy sacrament and ointment together;
Then shortly see ye turn again hither;
We will all abide you here.
FIVE WITS: Yea, Everyman, hie you that ye ready were.
There is no emperor, king, duke, nor baron,
That of God hath commission
As hath the least priest in the world being;
For of the blessèd sacraments pure and benign
He beareth the keys, and thereof hath the cure
For man's redemption—it is ever sure—
Which God for our soul's medicine
Gave us out of his heart with great pain,
Here in this transitory life, for thee and me.

The blessèd sacraments seven there be:
Baptism, confirmation, with priesthood good,
And the sacrament of God's precious flesh and blood,
Marriage, the holy extreme unction, and penance.
These seven be good to have in remembrance,
Gracious sacraments of high divinity.
EVERYMAN: Fain would I receive that holy body
And meekly to my ghostly[25] father I will go.
FIVE WITS: Everyman, that is the best that ye can do.
God will you to salvation bring,
For priesthood exceedeth all other thing;
To us Holy Scripture they do teach,
And converteth man from sin, heaven to reach;
God hath to them more power given,
Than to any angel that is in heaven.
With five words he may consecrate
God's body in flesh and blood to make,
And handleth his Maker between his hands.
The priest bindeth and unbindeth all bands,
Both in earth and in heaven;
Thou ministers all the sacraments seven;
Though we kissed thy feet, thou wert worthy;
Thou art the surgeon that cureth sin deadly;
No remedy we find under God
But all only priesthood.
Everyman, God gave priests that dignity,
And setteth them in his stead among us to be;
Thus be they above angels, in degree.

(Exit EVERYMAN.*)*

KNOWLEDGE: If priests be good, it is so, surely.
But when Jesus hanged on the cross with great smart,
There he gave out of his blessèd heart

[25]Spiritual.

The same sacrament in great torment.
He sold them not to us, that Lord
  omnipotent.
Therefore Saint Peter the Apostle doth say
That Jesus' curse hath all they
Which God their Savior do buy or sell,
Or they for any money do take or tell.
Sinful priests giveth the sinners example
  bad;
Their children sitteth by other men's fires,
  I have heard;
And some haunteth women's company
With unclean life, as lusts of lechery.
These be with sin made blind.
FIVE WITS: I trust to God no such may we
  find.
Therefore let us priesthood honor,
And follow their doctrine for our souls'
  succor.
We be their sheep, and they shepherds be
By whom we all be kept in surety.
Peace! for yonder I see Everyman come,
Which hath made true satisfaction.
GOOD DEEDS: Methinketh it is he indeed.

(Re-enter EVERYMAN.*)*

EVERYMAN: Now Jesu be your alder
  speed.[26]
I have received the sacrament for my
  redemption,
And then mine extreme unction.
Blesséd be all they that counseled me to
  take it!
And now, friends, let us go without longer
  respite.
I thank God that ye have tarried so long.
Now set each of you on this rod[27] your
  hand,
And shortly follow me.
I go before, there I would be. God be our
  guide.
STRENGTH: Everyman, we will not from
  you go,
Till ye have done this voyage long.
DISCRETION: I, Discretion, will bide by you
  also.

KNOWLEDGE: And though this pilgrimage
  be never so strong,
I will never part you fro.
Everyman, I will be as sure by thee
As ever I did by Judas Maccabee.

(They go together to the grave.)

EVERYMAN: Alas! I am so faint I may not
  stand,
My limbs under me do fold.
Friends, let us not turn again to this land,
Not for all the world's gold;
For into this cave must I creep
And turn to earth, and there to sleep.
BEAUTY: What, into this grave? Alas!
EVERYMAN: Yea, there shall you consume,
  more and less.
BEAUTY: And what, should I smother here?
EVERYMAN: Yea, by my faith, and never
  more appear.
In this world live no more we shall,
But in heaven before the highest Lord of
  all.
BEAUTY: I cross out all this; adieu, by Saint
  John!
I take my cap in my lap and am gone.
EVERYMAN: What, Beauty, whither will ye?
BEAUTY: Peace! I am deaf. I look not behind
  me,
Not and thou would give me all the gold
  in thy chest.

(Exit BEAUTY.*)*

EVERYMAN: Alas, whereto may I trust?
Beauty goeth fast away from me;
She promised with me to live and die.
STRENGTH: Everyman, I will thee also
  forsake and deny.
Thy game liketh me not at all.
EVERYMAN: Why, then ye will forsake me
  all?
Sweet Strength, tarry a little space.
STRENGTH: Nay, sir, by the rood of grace,
I will hie me from thee fast,
  Though thou weep till thy heart to-brast.[28]
EVERYMAN: Ye would ever bide by me, ye
  said.

---

[26]Succor of all of you.
[27]Cross.
[28]Break into pieces.

STRENGTH: Yea, I have you far enough
 conveyed.
 Ye be old enough, I understand.
 Your pilgrimage to take on hand.
 I repent me that I hither came.
EVERYMAN: Strength, you to displease I am
 to blame;
 Yet promise is debt, this ye well wot.
STRENGTH: In faith, I care not!
 Thou art but a fool to complain.
 You spend your speech and waste your
 brain;
 Go, thrust thee into the ground.

(Exit STRENGTH.*)*

EVERYMAN: I had weened surer I should
 you have found.
 He that trusteth in his Strength
 She him deceiveth at the length.
 Both Strength and Beauty forsaketh me,
 Yet they promised me fair and lovingly.
DISCRETION: Everyman, I will after
 Strength be gone;
 As for me I will leave you alone.
EVERYMAN: Why, Discretion, will ye
 forsake me?
DISCRETION: Yea, in faith, I will go from
 thee;
 For when Strength goeth before
 I follow after evermore.
EVERYMAN: Yet, I pray thee, for the love of
 the Trinity,
 Look in my grave once piteously.
DISCRETION: Nay, so nigh will I not come.
 Farewell, every one!

(Exit DISCRETION.*)*

EVERYMAN: O all thing faileth, save God
 alone —
 Beauty, Strength, and Discretion;
 For when Death bloweth his blast,
 They all run from me full fast.
FIVE WITS: Everyman, my leave now of thee
 I take;
 I will follow the other, for here I thee
 forsake.
EVERYTHING: Alas! then may I wail and
 weep,
 For I took you for my best friend.

FIVE WITS: I will no longer thee keep;
 Now farewell, and there an end.

(Exit FIVE WITS.*)*

EVERYMAN: O Jesu, help! All hath forsaken
 me!
GOOD DEEDS: Nay, Everyman; I will bide
 with thee,
 I will not forsake thee indeed;
 Thou shalt find me a good friend at need.
EVERYMAN: Gramercy, Good Deeds! Now
 may I true friends see.
 They have forsaken me, every one;
 I loved them better than my Good Deeds
 alone.
 Knowledge, will ye forsake me also?
KNOWLEDGE: Yea, Everyman, when ye to
 death shall go;
 But not yet, for no manner of danger.
EVERYMAN: Gramercy, Knowledge, with all
 my heart.
KNOWLEDGE: Nay, yet I will not from
 hence depart
 Till I see where ye shall be come.
EVERYMAN: Methink, alas, that I must be
 gone
 To make my reckoning and my debts pay,
 For I see my time is nigh spent away.
 Take example, all ye that this do hear or
 see,
 How they that I loved best do forsake me,
 Except my Good Deeds that bideth truly.
GOOD DEEDS: All earthly things is but
 vanity.
 Beauty, Strength, and Discretion do man
 forsake,
 Foolish friends and kinsmen, that fair
 spake,
 All fleeth save Good Deeds, and that am I.
EVERYMAN: Have mercy on me, God most
 mighty;
 And stand by me, thou Mother and Maid,
 holy Mary!
GOOD DEEDS: Fear not, I will speak for thee.
EVERYMAN: Here I cry God mercy!
GOOD DEEDS: Short our end, and 'minish
 our pain.
 Let us go and never come again.

EVERYMAN: Into thy hands, Lord, my soul I
commend.
Receive it, Lord, that it be not lost.
As thou me boughtest, so me defend,
And save me from the fiend's boast,
That I may appear with that blesséd host
That shall be saved at the day of doom.
In manus tuas — of might's most
For ever — *commendo spiritum meum*.[29]

(EVERYMAN *and* GOOD DEEDS *descend into the
grave.*)

KNOWLEDGE: Now hath he suffered that
we all shall endure;
The Good Deeds shall make all sure.
Now hath he made ending.
Methinketh that I hear angels sing
And make great joy and melody
Where Everyman's soul received shall be.
ANGEL: *(Within)* Come, excellent elect
spouse to Jesu!
Here above thou shalt go
Because of thy singular virtue.
Now the soul is taken the body fro,
Thy reckoning is crystal clear.
Now shalt thou into the heavenly sphere,
Unto the which all ye shall come
That liveth well before the day of doom.

(Exit KNOWLEDGE. *Enter* DOCTOR *for Epilogue.)*

DOCTOR: This moral men may have in
mind;
Ye hearers, take it of worth, old and
young,
And forsake Pride, for he deceiveth you in
the end,
And remember Beauty, Five Wits,
Strength, and Discretion,
They all at the last do Everyman forsake,
Save his Good Deeds there doth he take.
But beware, and they be small
Before God he hath no help at all.
None excuse may be there for Everyman.
Alas, how shall he do then?
For, after death, amends may no man make,
For then mercy and pity doth him forsake.
If his reckoning be not clear when he doth
come,
God will say, *"Ite, maledicti, in ignem
aeternum."*[30]
And he that hath his account whole and
sound,
High in heaven he shall be crowned,
Unto which place God bring us all
thither,
That we may live body and soul together.
Thereto help the Trinity!
Amen, say ye, for saint charity.

THUS ENDETH THIS MORAL PLAY OF *EVERYMAN*.

[29]"Into thy hands I commend my spirit."

[30]"Go cursed ones, into eternal fire."

Everyman treats a subject of universal interest: death. No one sufficiently old
to be aware of the world can avoid awareness of death, even if one resists thoughts
of one's own death. *Everyman* is also concerned with another universal subject:
how best to lead one's life, since it is a prelude to death. It has been argued that
human beings, unlike other creatures, are aware that they must die and that it is
this awareness that leads them to speculate about the significance of human
existence.

In Western civilization ideas about life and death have been shaped most
fully by Judeo-Christian concepts that depict death as the gateway through which

one passes into another life, the nature of which depends in large part upon how closely one has adhered to biblical teachings and church doctrines.

Everyman is based in Christianity and especially the teachings of the Catholic church. It depicts mankind as prone to a thoughtless search for pleasure (forgetful that death awaits when least expected) and ungrateful to God for His love. Unready when summoned by Death, Everyman begs for more time in which to prepare himself, not recognizing that his entire life should have been a time of preparation. Unable to avoid the inevitable, he goes to his boon companions— Fellowship, Kindred, Cousin, and Goods—expecting that they will willingly accompany him on his journey just as they have gladly participated in his revels. And they all lightly promise to go with him—until they learn the destination. All then find many reasons why they cannot go: Kindred has a cramp in his toe; Cousin offers to send his maid in his place; Goods says that his presence will only condemn Everyman for not sharing his wealth with the poor. Only Good Deeds is willing to go but, having been long neglected, he is unable to stand.

Perceiving his danger at last, Everyman acknowledges his need for instruction that will rescue him. Knowledge agrees to serve as guide through the steps required for forgiveness: confession, contrition, penance, abstinence, and perseverance. When Everyman has undertaken these steps, Good Deeds is restored to strength.

Everyman then encounters a new set of characters (Discretion, Strength, Five Wits, and Beauty) who personify personal endowments just as Fellowship, Kindred, Cousin, and Goods have personified societal relationships. Everyman then leaves the stage (the only time he does so during the action), to seek Priesthood, who holds the keys to redemption—the seven sacraments. During Everyman's absence, Knowledge denounces the misuse of priestly office, no doubt intending to call attention to the kind of abuses that shortly would motivate Protestant secessions from the Catholic church.

Everyman returns in a state of grace, having received the sacraments of bread and wine and extreme unction. He and his companions proceed to the grave, but only Good Deeds will enter it with Everyman. Even Knowledge must remain behind, for excepting Good Deeds, all else in life is vanity. As the action ends, an Angel welcomes Everyman to his reward.

The didacticism of *Everyman* is unmistakable not only in the allegory but also in the prologue and epilogue. This apparent overemphasis on teaching a lesson is attributable in large part to the time when the play was written. The Middle Ages was preoccupied with the problem of salvation, the goal that gave meaning to existence. Since mankind was considered to be weak and forgetful of his goal, he needed to be reminded frequently and forcefully of the right path and of the dangers of going astray.

Its allegory and archaic language may distance *Everyman* from today's reader, but its subject is of as much interest now as in 1500. Our intense concern for the topic is manifested in the proliferation of courses on death offered by American colleges and universities and in the number of books about death published each year. In our time, death frequently delivers its summons in the form of terminal illness, heart attack, or stroke — bringing with it awareness of imminent death but leaving time to consider how life has been spent. Or, the sudden death of a young, vital, and likable person who seemed destined for outstanding success may bring us suddenly face to face with our own mortality and the need to question whether we are living our own lives wisely and fully. Thus, though we voice our concerns about death in terms that differ from those of *Everyman*, we remain intensely interested in this universal topic.

Matsukaze

by Kanze Kiyotsugu Kan'ami, Revised by Kanze Motokiyo Zeami /
Translated by Royall Tyler

During the Middle Ages, a drama quite unlike that of Europe — the Noh —
was evolving in Japan. Noh drama had its origins in rituals and popular entertainments of the eleventh century and assumed its distinctive form in the fourteenth and fifteenth centuries under the protection of the *shogunate.* In 1192 the
emperor of Japan ceded his secular power to a *shogun* (military dictator), a title
that became hereditary, although new families won possession of the title from
time to time in civil wars. This arrangement continued until 1868, when secular
power was returned to the emperor.

Under the shogunate, Japan developed a strict feudal system within which
each social class had its assigned dress, manners, and diversions. Numerous ceremonies, performed with reverence and precision, helped to give form and meaning to daily life. It was within this context that Noh developed.

In the period from the fourteenth to the sixteenth centuries, the arts flourished under the patronage and encouragement of the shogunate, then held by the
Ashikaga family. Around 1375 the reigning shogun took Kanze Kiyotsugu
Kan'ami (1333–1384) and his son Kanze Motokiyo Zeami (1363–1444) under his
patronage, and it was they who gave Noh its distinctive form. Zeami not only
wrote three treatises in which he summed up Noh's aesthetic goals but also wrote
a large number of plays that established Noh's characteristic style. With Zeami,
Noh drama achieved its highest level of literary distinction.

A major influence on Noh was Zen Buddhism, from which Zeami concluded
that true beauty lies in suggestion, simplicity, subtlety, and restraint. Owing
largely to Zeami's theory and practice, most Noh drama seeks, through retrospec-
tion about some past event, to evoke an emotional state or mood; it is not essentially storytelling. The written script is very short by Western standards, but it
may consume two or more hours in performance. A Noh play usually culminates
in a dance, and the dialogue which precedes the dance serves primarily to clarify
the circumstances that have motivated it. While the actor dances, a chorus sings
his lines; it also narrates many events during the remainder of the play. Most of
the lines are sung or intoned, and even the spoken passages are recited in a highly
conventionalized manner.

Noh plays are classified into five types: plays about gods, plays about warriors,
plays about women, miscellaneous plays (most often about mad persons or spirits),
and plays about demons and similar supernatural beings. Traditionally, a perfor-

Reprinted by permission of Royall Tyler.

161

mance includes one play of each type in the order named above. Today, it is common to see programs composed of only two or three plays.

The number of roles in a Noh drama is small. Each play includes a *shite* (principal character) and a *waki* (supporting character). Each of these characters may have one or more companions *(tsure)*. All of the performers are male. Costumes, rich in color and design, are based on the feudalistic clothing of several centuries ago. They are often changed or adjusted on stage with the help of stage assistants, whose presence the audience ignores. The *shite* and his companion also wear masks made of painted wood.

The Noh stage has long been standardized. The two principal areas, the stage proper *(butai)* and the bridge *(hashigakari)* are both roofed like the shrines from which they are derived. The stage roof is supported by four columns, each with its own name and use. At the upstage right column *(shitebashira,* or principal character's pillar) characters pause at the naming place to state their names and the places from which they have come. While reciting these speeches, they face the pillar at the downstage right corner *(metsuke-bashira* or gazing pillar). The pillar at the downstage left corner is called *wakibashira* because of its association with the secondary character, and the upstage left pillar is called *fuebashira* (flute pillar) because the flute player sits by it. The area outlined by the four pillars is about eighteen feet square; under the stage floor sounding jars are placed so as to amplify the rhythmic stamping of the actors. In back of the upstage pillars is an area occupied by the orchestra of two or three drums and a flute. To stage left of the pillars is the space occupied by the chorus of six to ten members. The principal entrance to the stage is the railed gangway or bridge which leads from the dressing room. In front of the bridge are three pine trees symbolizing heaven, earth, and man. On the wall behind the musicians, a pine tree and bamboo are painted. There is no scenery. Stage properties are simple; a miniature wooden or bamboo structure may represent a house, mountain, cart, or boat. Hand properties are also few and conventionalized. The fan is the most important, since it can be used to suggest the blowing of the wind, ripple of water, rising moon, falling rain, and many subtle emotional responses.

A Noh performance is perhaps the most precisely controlled in the world. Every movement of hands and feet and every intonation of voice follows a set rule. Every episode is drawn out to great length so as to extract the full flavor of the ritualized action. The orchestra supplies a musical setting and controls the timing.

The following play, *Matsukaze,* written by Kan'ami and revised by Zeami, has been chosen to represent Noh drama. It is classified as a play about women. In the translation used here, the sung portions are rendered in verse.

PERSONS

AN ITINERANT PRIEST *(waki)*   MATSUKAZE *(shite)*
A VILLAGER   MURASAME *(tsure)*

PLACE

Suma Bay in Settsu Province

TIME

Autumn, the ninth month

(The stage assistant places a stand with a pine sapling set into it at the front of the stage. The PRIEST *enters and stands at the naming-place. He carries a rosary.)*

PRIEST: I am a priest who travels from province to province. Lately I have been in the Capital. I visited the famous sites and ancient ruins, not missing a one. Now I intend to make a pilgrimage to the western provinces. *(He faces forward.)* I have hurried, and here I am already at the Bay of Suma in Settsu Province. *(His attention is caught by pine tree.)* How strange! That pine on the beach has a curious look. There must be a story connected with it. I'll ask someone in the neighborhood. *(He faces the bridgeway.)* Do you live in Suma?

(The VILLAGER *comes down the bridgeway to the first pine. He wears a short sword.)*

VILLAGER: Perhaps I am from Suma; but first tell me what you want.

PRIEST: I am a priest and I travel through the provinces. Here on the beach I see a solitary pine tree with a wooden tablet fixed to it, and a poem slip hanging from the tablet. Is there a story connected with the tree? Please tell me what you know.

VILLAGER: The pine is linked with the memory of two fisher girls, Matsukaze and Murasame. Please say a prayer for them as you pass.

PRIEST: Thank you. I know nothing about them, but I will stop at the tree and say a prayer for them before I move on.

VILLAGER: If I can be of further service, don't hesitate to ask.

PRIEST: Thank you for your kindness.

VILLAGER: At your command, sir.

(The VILLAGER *exits. The* PRIEST *goes to stage center and turns toward the pine tree.)*

PRIEST: So, this pine tree is linked with the memory of two fisher girls, Matsukaze and Murasame. It is sad! Though their bodies are buried in the ground, their names linger on. This lonely pine tree lingers on also, ever green and untouched by autumn, their only memorial. Ah! While I have been chanting sutras and invoking Amida Buddha for their repose, the sun, as always on autumn days, has quickly set. That village at the foot of the mountain is a long way. Perhaps I can spend the night in this fisherman's salt shed.

(He kneels at the waki-position. The stage assistant brings out the prop, a miniature cart for carrying pails of brine, and sets it by the gazing-pillar. He places a pail on the cart. MURASAME *enters and comes down the bridgeway as far as the first pine. She wears the tsure mask.* MATSUKAZE *follows her and stops at the third pine. She wears the shite mask. Each carries a water pail. They face each other.)*

MATSUKAZE AND MURASAME: A brine
    cart wheeled along the beach
    Provides a meager livelihood:
    The sad world rolls
    Life by quickly and in misery!
MURASAME: Here at Suma Bay
    The waves shatter at our feet,
    And even the moonlight wets our sleeves
    With its tears of loneliness.

*(*MURASAME *goes to stage center while* MATSUKAZE *moves to the* shite-*position.)*

MATSUKAZE: The autumn winds are sad.
    When the Middle Counselor Yukihira
    Lived here back a little from the sea,
    They inspired his poem,
    "Salt winds blowing from the mountain
        pass. . . ."
    On the beach, night after night,
    Waves thunder at our door;
    And on our long walks to the village
    We've no companion but the moon.[1]

---

[1]A modified quotation from a poem by Hōkyō Chūmei.

Our toil, like all of life, is dreary,
But none could be more bleak than ours.
A skiff cannot cross the sea,
Nor we this dream world.
Do we exist, even?
Like foam on the salt sea,
We draw a cart, friendless and alone,
Poor fisher girls whose sleeves are wet
With endless spray, and tears
From our hearts' unanswered longing.
CHORUS: Our life is so hard to bear
  That we envy the pure moon[2]
  Now rising with the tide.
  But come, let us dip brine,
  Dip brine from the rising tide!
  Our reflections seem to shame us!
  *(They look down as if catching a glimpse
    of their reflections in the water. The
    movement of their heads "clouds" the
    expression on their masks, making it
    seem sad.)*
  Yes, they shame us!
  Here, where we shrink from men's eyes,
  Drawing our timorous cart;
  The withdrawing tide
  Leaves stranded pools behind.
  How long do they remain?
  If we were the dew on grassy fields,
  We would vanish with the sun.
  But we are sea tangle,
  Washed up on the shore,
  Raked into heaps by the fishermen,
  Fated to be discarded, useless,
  Withered and rotting,
  Like our trailing sleeves,
  Like our trailing sleeves.
  (They look down again.)
  Endlessly familiar, still how lovely
  The twilight at Suma![3]
  The fishermen call out in muffled voices;
  At sea, the small boats loom dimly.
  Across the faintly glowing face of the
    moon
  Flights of wild geese streak,
  And plovers flock below along the shore.

Fall gales and stiff sea winds:
These are things, in such a place,
That truly belong to autumn.
But oh, the terrible, lonely nights!

(They hide their faces.)

MATSUKAZE: Come, dip the brine
MURASAME: Where the seas flood and fall.
  Let us tie our sleeves back to our shoulders
MATSUKAZE: Think only, "Dip the brine."
MURASAME: We ready ourselves for the
  task,
MATSUKAZE: But for women, this cart is
  too hard.
CHORUS: While the rough breakers surge
  and fall,
  *(MURASAME moves upstage to stand beside
    MATSUKAZE.)*
  While the rough breakers surge and fall,
  And cranes among the reeds
  Fly up with sharp cries.
  The four winds add their wailing.
  How shall we pass the cold night?
  (They look up.)
  The late moon is so brilliant—
  What we dip is its reflection!
  Smoke from the salt fires
  May cloud the moon—take care!
  Are we always to spend only
  The sad autumns of fishermen?
  At Ojima in Matsushima[4]
  *(MATSUKAZE half-kneels by the brine cart
    and mimes dipping with her fan.)*
  The fisherfolk, like us,
  Delight less in the moon
  Than in the dipping of its reflection;
  There they take delight in dipping
  Reflections of the moon.
  (MATSUKAZE returns to the shite-position.)
  We haul our brine from afar,
  As in far-famed Michinoku[5]
  And at the salt kilns of Chika—
  Chika, whose name means "close by."

[2]From a poem by Fujiwara Takamitsu.
[3]The following description is inspired by a chapter from a novel, *The Tale of Genji.*

[4]Ojima is an island at Matsushima, a place noted for scenic beauty and associated in poetry with fisherwomen.
[5]This and the names that follow in this passage are place names associated with the sea as well as allusions and play on words.

MATSUKAZE: Humble folk hauled wood for
    salt fires
    At the ebb tide on Akogi Shore;
CHORUS: On Ise Bay there's Twice-See
    Beach —
    Oh, could I live my life again!

(MATSUKAZE looks off into the distance.)

MATSUKAZE: On days when pine groves
    stand hazy,
    And the sea lanes draw back
    From the coast at Narumi —
CHORUS: You speak of Narumi; this is
    Naruo,
    Where pines cut off the moonlight
    From the reed-thatched roofs of Ashinoya.
MATSUKAZE: Who is to tell of our
    unhappiness
    Dipping brine at Nada?
    With boxwood combs set in our hair,[6]
    From rushing seas we draw the brine,
    Oh look! I have the moon in my pail!

*(MURASAME kneels before the brine cart and places
her pail on it. MATSUKAZE, still standing, looks
into her pail.)*

MATSUKAZE: In my pail too I hold the
    moon!
CHORUS: How lovely! A moon here too!

*(MURASAME picks up the rope tied to the cart and
gives it to MATSUKAZE, then moves to the shite-
position. MATSUKAZE looks up.)*

MATSUKAZE: The moon above is one;
    Below it has two, no, three reflections
    (She looks into both pails.)
    Which shine in the flood tide tonight,
    *(She pulls the cart to a spot before the
    musicians.)*
    And on our cart we load the moon!
    No, life is not all misery
    Here by the sea lanes.

*(She drops the rope. The stage assistant removes
the cart. MATSUKAZE sits on a low stool and
MURASAME kneels beside her, a sign that the two
women are resting inside their hut. The PRIEST
rises.)*

[6]This passage is derived from an earlier Japanese poem.

PRIEST: The owner of the salt shed has
returned. I shall ask for a night's lodging. *(To MAT-
SUKAZE and MURASAME)* I beg your pardon. Might I
come inside?
MURASAME: *(Standing and coming forward
a little)* Who might you be?
PRIEST: A traveler, overtaken by night on my
journey. I should like to ask lodging for the night.
MURASAME: Wait here. I must ask the
owner. *(She kneels before MATSUKAZE.)* A traveler
outside asks to come in and spend the night.
MATSUKAZE: That is little enough, but our
hut is so wretched we cannot ask him in. Please tell
him so.
MURASAME: *(Standing, to the PRIEST)* I have
spoken to the owner. She says the house is too
wretched to put anyone up.
PRIEST: I understand those feelings perfectly,
but poverty makes no difference at all to me. I am
only a priest. Please say I beg her to let me spend
the night.
MURASAME: No, we really cannot put you
up.
MATSUKAZE: *(To MURASAME)* Wait!
    I see in the moonlight
    One who has renounced the world.
    He will not mind a fisherman's hut,
    With its rough pine pillars and bamboo
      fence;
    I believe it is very cold tonight,
    So let him come in and warm himself
    At our sad fire of rushes.
    You may tell him that.
MURASAME: Please come in.
PRIEST: Thank you very much. Forgive me
    for intruding.

*(He takes a few steps forward and kneels.
MURASAME goes back beside MATSUKAZE.)*

MATSUKAZE: I wished from the beginning
to invite you in, but this place is so poor I felt I must
refuse.
PRIEST: You are very kind. I am a priest and a
traveler, and never stay anywhere very long. Why
prefer one lodging to another? In any case, what sensitive person would not prefer to live here at Suma,
in the quiet solitude. Yukihira wrote,
    "If ever anyone
    Chances to ask for me,

Say I live alone,
Soaked by the dripping seaweed
On the shore of Suma Bay."
(He looks at the pine tree.) A while ago I asked someone the meaning of that solitary pine on the beach. I was told it grows there in memory of two fisher girls, Matsukaze and Murasame. There is no connection between them and me, but I went to the pine anyway and said a prayer for them. *(MATSU-KAZE and MURASAME weep. The PRIEST stares at them.)* This is strange! They seem distressed at the mention of Matsukaze and Murasame. Why?

MATSUKAZE AND MURASAME: Truly,
    when a grief is hidden,
    Still, signs of it will show.
    His poem, "If ever anyone
    Chances to ask for me,"
    Filled us with memories which are far too
        fond.
    Tears of attachment to the world
    Wet our sleeves once again.

PRIEST: Tears of attachment to the world? You speak as though you are no longer of the world. Yukihira's poem overcame you with memories. More and more bewildering! Please, both of you, tell me who you are.

MATSUKAZE AND MURASAME: We
    would tell you our names,
    But we are too ashamed!
    No one, ever,
    Has chanced to ask for us,
    Long dead as we are,
    And so steeped in longing
    For the world by Suma Bay
    That pain has taught us nothing.
    Ah, the sting of regret!
    But having said this,
    Why should we hide our names any
        longer?
    At twilight you said a prayer
    By a mossy grave under the pine
    For two fisher girls,
    Matsukaze and Murasame.
    We are their ghosts, come to you.
    When Yukihira was here he whiled away
    Three years of weary exile
    Aboard his pleasure boat,
    His heart refreshed
    By the moon of Suma Bay.
    There were, among the fisher girls

Who hauled brine each evening,
    Two sisters whom he chose for his favors.
    "Names to fit the season!"
    He said, calling us
    Pine Wind and Autumn Rain.
    We had been Suma fisher girls,
    Accustomed to the moon,
    But he changed our salt makers' clothing
    To damask robes,
    Burnt with the scent of faint perfumes.[7]

MATSUKAZE: Then, three years later,
    Yukihira
    Returned to the Capital.

MURASAME: Soon, we heard he had died,
    oh so young!

MATSUKAZE: How we both loved him!
    Now the message we pined for
    Would never, never come.

CHORUS: Pine Wind and Autumn Rain
    Both drenched their sleeves with the tears
    Of hopeless love beyond their station,
    Fisher girls of Suma.
    Our sin is deep, o priest.
    Pray for us, we beg of you!
    *(They press their palms together in
        supplication.)*
    Our love grew rank as wild grasses;
    Tears and love ran wild.
    It was madness that touched us.
    Despite spring purification,
    Performed in our old robes,
    Despite prayers inscribed on paper
        streamers,[8]
    The gods refused us their help.
    We were left to melt away
    Like foam on the waves,
    And, in misery, we died.
    *(MATSUKAZE looks down, shading her
        mask.)*
    Alas! How the past evokes our longing!
    Yukihira, the Middle Counselor,
    *(The stage assistant puts a man's cloak
        and court hat in MATSUKAZE'S left
        hand.)*
    Lived three years here by Suma Bay.
    Before he returned to the Capital,

[7]Derived from a poem by Fujiwara Tameuji.
[8]Reference to a traditional ceremony. The streamers were conventional Shinto offerings.

He left us these keepsakes of his stay:
A court hat and a hunting cloak.
Each time we see them,
(*She looks at the cloak.*)
Our love grows again,
And gathers like dew
On the tip of a leaf
So that there's no forgetting,
Not for an instant.
Oh endless misery!
(*She places the cloak in her lap.*)
"This keepsake
Is my enemy now;
For without it
(*She lifts the cloak.*)
I might forget."[9]
(*She stares at the cloak.*)
The poem says that
And it's true:
My anguish only deepens.
(*She weeps.*)
MATSUKAZE: "Each night before I go to
    sleep,
I take off the hunting cloak
CHORUS: And hang it up . . ."[10]
(*The keepsakes in her hand, she stands
    and, as in a trance, takes a few steps
    toward the gazing-pillar.*)
I hung all my hopes
On living in the same world with him,
But being here makes no sense at all
And these keepsakes are nothing.
(*She starts to drop the cloak, only to
    cradle it in her arms and press it to
    her.*)
I drop it, but I cannot let it lie;
So I take it up again
To see his face before me yet once more.
(*She turns to her right and goes toward
    the naming-place, then stares down the
    bridgeway as though something were
    coming after her.*)
"Awake or asleep,
From my pillow, from the foot of my bed,
Love rushes in upon me."[11]

Helplessly I sink down,
Weeping in agony.
(*She sits at the* shite-*position, weeping. The stage
assistant helps her take off her outer robe and
replace it with the cloak. He also helps tie on the
court hat.*)
MATSUKAZE: The River of Three Fords[12]
Has gloomy shallows
Of never-ending tears;
I found, even there,
An abyss of wildest love.
Oh joy! Look! Over there!
Yukihira has returned!
(*She rises, staring at the pine tree.*)
He calls me by my name, Pine Wind!
I am coming!
(*She goes to the tree.* MURASAME *hurriedly
    rises and follows. She catches*
    MATSUKAZE'S *sleeve.*)
MURASAME: For shame! For such thoughts
    as these
You are lost in the sin of passion.
All the delusions that held you in life—
None forgotten!
(*Both step back from the tree.*)
That is a pine tree.
And Yukihira is not here.
MATSUKAZE: You are talking nonsense!
(*She looks at the pine tree.*)
This pine *is* Yukihira!
"Though we may part for a time,
If I hear you are pining for me,
I'll hurry back."[13]
Have you forgotten those words he wrote?
MURASAME: Yes, I had forgotten!
He said, "Though we may part for a time,
If you pine, I will return to you."
MATSUKAZE: I have not forgotten.
And I wait for the pine wind
To whisper word of his coming.
MURASAME: If that word should ever come,
My sleeves for a while
Would be wet with autumn rain.

[9]Quotation from an anonymous Japanese poem.
[10]First part of a poem by Ki no Tomomori.
[11]Quotation from another anonymous Japanese poem.

[12]The river of the afterworld.
[13]This and the other quotations on this page are from a poem by Ariwara no Yukihira (818–893), a famous poet whose poem about his exile to Suma seems to have inspired *Matsukaze*.

MATSUKAZE: So we await him. He will
    come,
  Constant ever, green as a pine.
MURASAME: Yes, we can trust
MATSUKAZE: his poem:
CHORUS: "I have gone away

*(MURASAME, weeping, kneels before the flute
player. MATSUKAZE goes to the first pine on the
bridgeway, then returns to the stage and dances.)*

MATSUKAZE: Into the mountains of Inaba,
  Covered with pines,
  But if I hear you pine,
  I shall come back at once."
  Those are the mountain pines
  Of distant Inaba,
  (She looks up the bridgeway.)
  And these are the pines
  On the curving Suma shore.
  Here our dear prince once lived.
  If Yukihira comes again,
  I shall go stand under the tree
  (She approaches the tree.)
  Bent by the sea-wind,
  And, tenderly, tell him

(She stands next to the tree.)
I love him still!

*(She steps back a little and weeps. Then she
circles the tree, her dancing suggesting madness.)*

CHORUS: Madly the gale howls through the
    pines,
  And breakers crash in Suma Bay;
  Through the frenzied night
  We have come to you
  In a dream of deluded passion.
  Pray for us! Pray for our rest!
  *(At stage center, MATSUKAZE presses her
    palms together in supplication.)*
  Now we take our leave. The retreating
    waves
  Hiss far away, and a wind sweeps down
  From the mountain to Suma Bay.
  The cocks are crowing on the barrier road.
  Your dream is over. Day has come.
  Last night you heard the autumn rain;
  This morning all that is left
  Is the wind in the pines,
  The wind in the pines.

As *Matsukaze* illustrates, Noh drama calls into question most Western conceptions of dramatic effectiveness. In it, there is little concern for story, character development, or dramatic action. It emphasizes atmosphere rather than personality, one prevailing emotion rather than conflict.

The structure of *Matsukaze* resembles that of music. First, there is an introduction in which the prevailing theme and atmosphere are established. In it, the *waki* sets out on a journey, arrives at a new place, and asks a question about an unexpected sight. This section is written in a mixture of poetry and prose. It also establishes time in terms of season (here it is autumn) and the mood and imagery are entirely in keeping with that season. Second, comes the development, during which the *shite* is drawn back to this world by a deep, unsatisfied longing which is gradually revealed in poetic narrative and dialogue. The initial appearance of the two fisherwomen is subdued and the poetry not deeply emotional, but as the tempo and complexity increase, the poetic effect is heightened. Last, there is a climactic dance which epitomizes the emotions of the *shite* and during which the play's most moving poetry occurs.

In Noh, a number of devices serve to distance the spectator. Time and space are infinitely variable: in *Matsukaze* the *waki* completes his opening journey in a few steps; time often changes during a single line; and many years are leaped over in a retrospective passage. The stylized language also serves a distancing function. It greatly reduces realism of characterization, since two fisherwomen are depicted as speaking exquisite poetry which might seem more appropriate to highborn or well-educated characters. Furthermore, numerous quotations from earlier poets are embedded within the script, and lines of dialogue are divided in several ways (a single thought may be divided between the *shite* and her companion or between the *shite* and the chorus; the *shite* sometimes speaks of herself in the third person and the chorus frequently speaks the *shite*'s lines, especially when she is dancing).

Imagery is very important in Noh drama. In *Matsukaze*, the moon, a symbol of Buddhist enlightenment, is said to be one in the sky but many when reflected in the waters below; thus, it represents the unity behind apparent multiplicity. The names of the sisters also serve imagistically. *Matsukaze* means wind in the pines and *Murasame* means autumn rain. Thus, not only do they represent the ghosts of girls who have lived long ago, but also natural forces into which they are absorbed at the end of the play. The names also add to the atmosphere of autumnal melancholy which dominates the play.

The young women in *Matsukaze* are condemned to linger as ghosts because of sins that may not be readily apparent to a Western audience. According to Buddhist thought, they have sinned by giving themselves up so completely to the passion of love, and their agony is prolonged because they are unable to reconcile themselves to their loss. Consequently, they must linger in the world of pain because they still desire earthly joy and have not achieved resignation and renunciation, through which peace comes.

Matsukaze raises questions about the degree to which standards of artistic excellence are culturally conditioned. It tends to contradict most Western ideas about drama, but its power also raises questions about the adequacy of those ideas. For those able to enter into the play, *Matsukaze* can open a path to understanding Japanese culture, one markedly different from our own. Such understanding is desirable because it bridges divisions that are all too numerous in the contemporary world; equally important, the more we understand other cultures, the more we understand our own through contrast. For example, Americans place considerable emphasis on novelty, change, and progress, and consequently they expect to see new plays each year performed in various production styles. In contrast, the Japanese seek to maintain unchanged many of their art forms, among them Noh drama. Consequently, essentially the same repertory of Noh plays is performed each year with production techniques that have remained fixed for centuries, having been passed down through hereditary schools of Noh acting. These fundamental attitudes about change and fixity (along with many others equally divergent) are crucial to our understanding of the two cultures and their differences.

King Lear

by William Shakespeare

During the sixteenth century, Europe was wracked with religious controversy as a growing number of dissident groups sought to reform the Catholic church. The results were secessions by Protestant sects, bitter partisanship, and, in some instances, war. Because drama, since the tenth century, had been associated with religion, it was perhaps inevitable that it would become a weapon in the religious controversy and be used to depict the supporters of a group as soldiers of God and the opponents as instruments of the Devil. Seeking to restore order, both church and state around 1550 made a determined effort to suppress religious plays as one cause of disorder. Consequently, by 1600 both religious dramas and morality plays had virtually disappeared in most parts of Europe. Therefore, playwrights were restricted to secular, nonpolitical subjects.

These developments strengthened forces that had given rise to the Renaissance, which had begun in Italy during the 1300s and had gradually spread to the rest of Western Europe. The Renaissance marked a turning away from the preoccupation with theological matters, which had characterized the Middle Ages, and a trend toward concern for the worthiness of human beings and their earthly lives, not merely as preparation for eternity but as valuable in themselves. It drew inspiration from the classical world and stimulated renewed interest in Greece and Rome. Following the introduction of movable type and the printing press around 1450, the pace of the Renaissance quickened, for printing made possible a more rapid and wider dissemination of ideas. Among other works, the surviving Greek and Roman plays were printed and, after 1500, many were translated into the vernacular languages.

The influence of the Renaissance was not extensive in England until the sixteenth century, when the study and performance of Roman (and to a lesser extent, Greek) plays became common in the schools and universities of England. By the time Elizabeth I came to the throne in 1558, knowledge of Greek and Roman plays was extensive among the educated classes.

During the same period, the theatre was beginning to undergo a significant change as it was increasingly professionalized. In Greece, Rome, and medieval Europe, the theatre, in its most characteristic form, had enjoyed the active support of governmental and religious bodies. It had also been ceremonial and occasional, essentially a community offering used to celebrate significant holidays. When religious drama was suppressed in the sixteenth century, theatre was deprived of its celebratory function and thereafter had to fight for recognition on commercial and artistic grounds. The clergy, town councils and trade guilds, who had sponsored and financed the elaborate religious spectacles, withdrew their support, making a clear distinction between productions motivated by religious and civic pride and the work of professional actors seeking to entertain for pay. Many of these former supporters became enemies of the theatre actively seeking to suppress it.

If the theatre was to become self-supporting, it had to undergo many changes. Performances could not be reserved for special occasions but had to be given regularly if they were to provide a living wage for the theatre's personnel. Since performances could no longer be given free, spaces had to be found or constructed that would ensure that no one could enter without paying an admission fee. A repertory of constantly changing plays had to be offered so as to keep audiences coming back. The new arrangements created a greatly enlarged demand for professional actors and dramatists.

The English professional theatre, after a precarious beginning, had by 1576 engendered enough confidence in James Burbage that he erected England's first permanent theatre, which he called simply The Theatre. By 1615, eight other theatres of a similar type had been built in the London area. The best known of these is The Globe because of its close association with Shakespeare's work.

These Elizabethan theatre structures were not identical in details, but they did have a number of common features. A large central unroofed space, called the pit or yard, was enclosed by three tiers of roofed galleries that formed the outside perimeter of the building. A raised and roofed stage extended to the center of the yard. This large platform was the principal acting area. Spectators could stand around three sides, and the galleries commanded a view from three sides. At the rear of the stage there was a multileveled facade. On the stage level, at least two large doors served as entrances and exits. On this level there may also have been another area (the discovery space) equipped with curtains that could be opened to reveal persons or objects and drawn to conceal them. Another acting area was located on the second level of the facade, and on the third level there may have been a gallery for musicians. This stage permitted a continuous flow of action: as the performers left the main stage by one door at the end of a scene, another group might enter at the other door to begin the next scene; or, a scene on the main platform might be followed by one on the second level; one scene flowed into another without pause.

The mounting of plays was simple. There was little scenery, place usually being established through lines in the play. Furniture was used only if essential to the action. Trap doors in the stage floor served as graves, entrances for ghosts, or for such special effects as fire and smoke. Costumes, usually contemporary dress, were often expensive and colorful. Since performances took place during the afternoon, stage lighting was unimportant. Both the stage and staging conventions were derived from those of the medieval theatre.

Acting companies consisted of from ten to twenty adults and three to five apprentices (boys who played most of the female roles). All performers were male, and doubling of roles was common. The company changed its bill daily, repeating a play at regular intervals during the season. When a play ceased to be popular, it was dropped and another took its place. Thus, the demand for new plays was constant.

In the early years of the English professional theatre, the plays were crude and still essentially medieval in form. After The Theatre was built in 1576, a conscious effort seems to have been made to obtain plays of a higher quality, and in the 1580s a number of university-educated playwrights came to prominence. Usually called the "University Wits," their most prominent members were Thomas Kyd (1558–1594), whose *The Spanish Tragedy* (c.1587), the most popular play of the century, established the vogue for revenge tragedy (of which *Hamlet* was to be the outstanding example), and Christopher Marlowe (1564–1593), who popularized blank verse as the medium for English drama through such plays as *Tamburlaine*, parts I and II (1587–1588) and *Doctor Faustus* (c.1588), and whose *Edward II* (1592) played a crucial role in developing the history (or chronicle) play. Perhaps most importantly, the University Wits were able to synthesize their knowledge of classical form and structure with subjects of contemporary interest to create a distinctively new drama. From the 1580s until the 1640s, England enjoyed one of the most productive periods the theatre has known.

From among the many English playwrights of this period, William Shakespeare (1564–1616) stands out as the acknowledged master and as probably the greatest playwright the world has known. In addition to being a playwright, he was an actor and a shareholder in acting companies and theatres; he was directly involved in more aspects of the theatre than any other playwright of his day. He is credited with 38 plays, which, like the work of his contemporaries, borrowed heavily from novels, older plays, history, mythology, and other sources. His plays are usually divided into three groups: histories, comedies, and tragedies. In the histories (or chronicle plays), he dealt with the English past, especially the War of the Roses. Such plays as *Richard II*, *Henry IV*, Parts I and II, *Henry V*, and *Richard III* show his skill at reducing large masses of material to the demands of the stage. His comedies represent a wide range of types. *The Comedy of Errors* (based on Plautus's *The Menaechmi*) and *The Taming of the Shrew* emphasize farce; *A Midsummer Night's Dream*, *As You Like It*, and *Twelfth Night* are romantic comedies; *All's Well That Ends Well* and *Measure for Measure* are usually referred to as dark comedies because their serious aspects mute any comic effect. But it was in tragedy that Shakespeare excelled. *Romeo and Juliet*, *Hamlet*, *Macbeth*, *Othello*, and *King Lear* are ranked among the greatest tragedies ever written. Near the end of his career Shakespeare also wrote several tragicomedies, among them *Cymbeline* and *The Winter's Tale*. Whatever the dramatic type, Shakespeare entered into all situations sympathetically and made them appear truthful representations of human action and not mere stage invention. His penetrating insights into human behavior have remained valid for all succeeding generations. He was by far the most comprehensive, sensitive, and dramatically effective playwright of his day.

DRAMATIS PERSONAE

LEAR *King of Britain*
KING OF FRANCE
DUKE OF BURGUNDY
DUKE OF CORNWALL
DUKE OF ALBANY
EARL OF KENT
EARL OF GLOUCESTER
EDGAR *son of Gloucester*
EDMUND *bastard son of Gloucester*
CURAN *a courtier*
OSWALD *steward to Goneril*
OLD MAN *tenant of Gloucester*

DOCTOR
FOOL *to Lear*
A CAPTAIN *under Edmund*
GENTLEMAN *attendant on Cordelia*
HERALD
SERVANTS *to Cornwall*
GONERIL ⎫
REGAN ⎬ *daughters of Lear*
CORDELIA ⎭
KNIGHTS *attending on Lear,* GENTLEMEN,
MESSENGERS, SOLDIERS, *and* ATTENDANTS.

SCENE

Britain.

ACT I

SCENE I

King Lear's palace

(Enter KENT, GLOUCESTER, *and* EDMUND.)

KENT: I thought the King had more affected the Duke of Albany than Cornwall.

GLOUCESTER: It did always seem so to us. But now in the division of the kingdom it appears not which of the dukes he values most, for equalities are so weighed, that curiosity in neither can make choice of either's moiety.

KENT: Is not this your son, my lord?

GLOUCESTER: His breeding, sir, hath been at my charge. I have so often blushed to acknowledge him, that now I am brazed to't.

KENT: I cannot conceive you.

GLOUCESTER: Sir, this young fellow's mother could; whereupon she grew round-wombed, and had indeed, sir, a son for her cradle, ere she had a husband for her bed. Do you smell a fault?

KENT: I cannot wish the fault undone, the issue of it being so proper.

GLOUCESTER: But I have a son, sir, by order of law, some year elder than this, who yet is no dearer in my account, though this knave came something saucily to the world before he was sent for. Yet was his mother fair; there was good sport at his making, and the whoreson must be acknowledged. Do you know this noble gentleman, Edmund?

EDMUND: No, my lord.

GLOUCESTER: My lord of Kent. Remember him hereafter as my honourable friend.

EDMUND: My services to your lordship.

KENT: I must love you, and sue to know you better.

EDMUND: Sir, I shall study deserving.

GLOUCESTER: He hath been out nine years, and away he shall again. The King is coming.

(Sennet. Enter one bearing a coronet, LEAR, CORNWALL, ALBANY, GONERIL, REGAN, CORDELIA, *and* ATTENDANTS.)

LEAR: Attend the Lords of France and
 Burgundy, Gloucester.

(Exeunt GLOUCESTER *and* EDMUND.)

LEAR: Meantime we shall express our darker
 purpose.
 Give me the map there. Know that we
 have divided

In three our kingdom; and 'tis our fast
    intent
To shake all cares and business from our
    age,
Conferring them on younger strengths,
    while we
Unburdened crawl toward death. Our son
    of Cornwall,
And you our no less loving son of Albany,
We have this hour a constant will to
    publish
Our daughters' several dowers, that future
    strife
May be prevented now. The princes,
    France and Burgundy,
Great rivals in our youngest daughter's
    love,
Long in our Court have made their
    amorous sojourn,
And here are to be answered. Tell me my
    daughters—
Since now we will divest us both of rule,
Interest of territory. Cares of state—
Which of you shall we say doth love us
    most,
That we our largest bounty may extend
Where nature doth with merit challenge.
    Goneril,
Our eldest born, speak first.
GONERIL: Sir, I love you more than word
    can wield the matter,
Dearer than eyesight, space, and liberty,
Beyond what can be valued, rich or rare,
No less than life, with grace, health,
    beauty, honour,
As much as child e'er loved, or father
    found;
A love that makes breath poor, and speech
    unable—
Beyond all manner of so much I love you.
CORDELIA: (Aside) What shall Cordelia
    speak? Love, and be silent.
LEAR: Of all these bounds, even from this
    line to this,
With shadowy forests and with champains
    riched,
With plenteous rivers, and wide-skirted
    meads,
We make thee lady. To thine and
    Albany's issue

Be this perpetual. What says our second
    daughter?
Our dearest Regan, wife of Cornwall?
    Speak.
REGAN: I am made of that self metal as my
    sister,
And prize me at her worth. In my true
    heart,
I find she names my very deed of love.
Only she comes too short, that I profess
Myself an enemy to all other joys,
Which the most precious square of sense
    possesses,
And find I am alone felicitate
In your dear Highness' love.
CORDELIA: (Aside)   Then poor
    Cordelia—
And yet not so, since I am sure my love's
More ponderous than my tongue.
LEAR: To thee, and thine hereditary ever,
    Remain this ample third of our fair
    kingdom,
No less in space, validity, and pleasure,
Than that conferred on Goneril. Now our
    joy,
Although our last and least, to whose
    young love
The vines of France and milk of Burgundy
Strive to be interest. What can you say, to
    draw
A third more opulent than your sisters?
    Speak.
CORDELIA: Nothing my lord.
LEAR: Nothing?
CORDELIA: Nothing.
LEAR: Nothing will come of nothing. Speak
    again.
CORDELIA: Unhappy that I am, I cannot
    heave
My heart into my mouth. I love your
    Majesty
According to my bond, no more nor less.
LEAR: How, how, Cordelia? Mend your
    speech a little,
Lest you may mar your fortunes.
CORDELIA: Good my
    lord,
You have begot me, bred me, loved me. I
Return those duties back as are right fit,
Obey you, love you, and most honour you.

Why have my sisters husbands, if they say
They love you all? Haply when I shall wed,
That lord whose hand must take my
    plight shall carry
Half my love with him, half my care, and
    duty.
Sure I shall never marry like my sisters,
To love my father all.
LEAR: But goes thy heart with this?
CORDELIA: Ay my
    good lord.
LEAR: So young, and so untender?
CORDELIA: So young my lord, and true.
LEAR: Let it be so, thy truth then be thy
    dower.
For by the sacred radiance of the sun,
The mysteries of Hecate and the night,
By all the operation of the orbs
From whom we do exist, and cease to be,
Here I disclaim all my paternal care,
Propinquity and property of blood,
And as a stranger to my heart and me
Hold thee from this for ever. The
    barbarous Scythian,
Or he that makes his generation messes
To gorge his appetite, shall to my bosom
Be as well neighboured, pitied, and
    relieved,
As thou my sometime daughter.
KENT: Good my
    liege —
LEAR: Peace Kent,
Come not between the dragon and his
    wrath.
I loved her most, and thought to set my
    rest
On her kind nursery. — Hence, and avoid
    my sight. —
So be my grave my peace, as here I give
Her father's heart from her. Call France.
    Who stirs?
Call Burgundy. Cornwall and Albany,
With my two daughters' dowers digest the
    third.
Let pride, which she calls plainness, marry
    her.
I do invest you jointly with my power,
Pre-eminence, and all the large effects
That troop with majesty. Ourself by
    monthly course,

With reservation of an hundred knights,
By you to be sustained, shall our abode
Make with you by due turn. Only we
    shall retain
The name, and all th' addition to a King.
The sway, revenue, execution of the rest,
Beloved sons, be yours, which to confirm,
This coronet part between you.
KENT: Royal Lear,
Whom I have ever honoured as my King,
Loved as my father, as my master
    followed,
As my great patron thought on in my
    prayers —
LEAR: The bow is bent and drawn, make
    from the shaft.
KENT: Let it fall rather, though the fork
    invade
The region of my heart. Be Kent
    unmannerly,
When Lear is mad. What wouldst thou do,
    old man?
Think'st thou that duty shall have dread
    to speak,
When power to flattery bows? To
    plainness honour's bound,
When majesty fall to folly. Reserve thy
    state,
And in thy best consideration check
This hideous rashness. Answer my life my
    judgement;
Thy youngest daughter does not love thee
    least,
Nor are those empty-hearted whose low
    sounds
Reverb no hollowness.
LEAR: Kent, on thy life no
    more.
KENT: My life I never held but as a pawn
To wage against thine enemies; ne'er
    feared to lose it,
Thy safety being motive.
LEAR: Out of my sight!
KENT: See better, Lear, and let me still
    remain
The true blank of thine eye.
LEAR: Now by Apollo —
KENT: Now by Apollo,
    King,
Thou swear'st thy gods in vain.

LEAR: O vassal!
   Miscreant!
ALBANY and CORNWALL: Dear sir,
   forbear.
KENT: Kill thy physician, and the fee bestow
   Upon the foul disease. Revoke thy gift,
   Or whilst I can vent clamour from my
      throat,
   I'll tell thee thou dost evil.
LEAR: Hear me
   recreant,
   On thine allegiance hear me.
   That thou hast sought to make us break
      our vow,
   Which we durst never yet, and with
      strained pride
   To come between our sentence and our
      power,
   Which nor our nature nor our place can
      bear,
   Our potency made good, take thy reward.
   Five days we do allot thee for provision
   To shield thee from disasters of the world,
   And on the sixth to turn thy hated back
   Upon our kingdom. If on the tenth day
      following
   Thy banished trunk be found in our
      dominions,
   The moment is thy death. Away! By
      Jupiter,
   This shall not be revoked.
KENT: Fare thee well, King; sith thus thou
   wilt appear,
   Freedom lives hence, and banishment is
      here.
   (To CORDELIA) The gods to their dear
      shelter take thee, maid,
   That justly think'st, and hast most rightly
      said.
   (To REGAN and GONERIL) And your large
      speeches may your deeds approve,
   That good effects may spring from words
      of love.
   Thus Kent, o princes, bids you all adieu;
   He'll shape his old course in a country
      new. (Exit)

(Flourish. Enter GLOUCESTER, with KING OF FRANCE,
   BURGUNDY, and ATTENDANTS.)

GLOUCESTER: Here's France and Burgundy,
   my noble lord.
LEAR: My Lord of Burgundy,
   We first address toward you, who with
      this King
   Hath rivalled for our daughter. What in
      the least
   Will you require in present dower with
      her,
   Or cease your quest of love?
BURGUNDY: Most royal
   Majesty,
   I crave no more than hath your Highness
      offered,
   Nor will you tender less.
LEAR: Right noble
   Burgundy,
   When she was dear to us, we did hold her
      so,
   But now her price is fallen. Sir, there she
      stands.
   If aught within that little-seeming
      substance,
   Or all of it, with our displeasure pieced,
   And nothing more, may fitly like your
      Grace,
   She's there, and she is yours.
BURGUNDY: I know no
   answer.
LEAR: Will you, with those infirmities she
   owes,
   Unfriended, new adopted to our hate,
   Dowered with our curse, and strangered
      with our oath,
   Take her, or leave her?
BURGUNDY: Pardon me royal sir,
   Election makes not up in such conditions.
LEAR: Then leave her sir, for by the power
   that made me,
   I tell you all her wealth. (To FRANCE) For
      you, great King,
   I would not from your love make such a
      stray,
   To match you where I hate, therefore
      beseech you,
   T' avert your liking a more worthier way
   Than on a wretch whom nature is
      ashamed
   Almost t' acknowledge hers.

KING OF FRANCE: This is most strange,
That she whom even but now was your best object,
The argument of your praise, balm of your age,
The best, the dearest, should in this trice of time
Commit a thing so monstrous, to dismantle
So many folds of favour. Sure her offence
Must be of such unnatural degree,
That monsters it; or your fore-vouched affection
Fall into taint, which to believe of her,
Must be a faith that reason without miracle
Should never plant in me.

CORDELIA: I yet beseech your Majesty—
If for I want that glib and oily art,
To speak and purpose not; since what I well intend,
I'll do't before I speak—that you make known
It is no vicious blot, murder, or foulness,
No unchaste action, or dishonoured step,
That hath deprived me of your grace and favour;
But even for want of that for which I am richer,
A still-soliciting eye, and such a tongue
That I am glad I have not, though not to have it
Hath lost me in your liking.

LEAR: Better thou
Hadst not been born, than not t' have pleased me better.

KING OF FRANCE: Is it but this? A tardiness in nature
Which often leaves the history unspoke
That it intends to do? My Lord of Burgundy,
What say you to the lady? Love's not love
When it is mingled with regards that stands
Aloof from the entire point. Will you have her?
She is herself a dowry.

BURGUNDY: Royal King,
Give but that portion which yourself proposed,
And here I take Cordelia by the hand,
Duchess of Burgundy.

LEAR: Nothing. I have sworn, I am firm.

BURGUNDY: I am sorry then you have so lost a father,
That you must lose a husband.

CORDELIA: Peace be with Burgundy.
Since that respects of fortune are his love,
I shall not be his wife.

KING OF FRANCE: Fairest Cordelia, that art most rich being poor,
Most choice forsaken, and most loved despised,
Thee and thy virtues here I seize upon.
Be it lawful I take up what's cast away.
Gods, gods! 'Tis strange that from their cold'st neglect
My love should kindle to inflamed respect.
Thy dowerless daughter, King, thrown to my chance,
Is Queen of us, of ours, and our fair France.
Not all the dukes of wat'rish Burgundy
Can buy this unprized precious maid of me.
Bid them farewell, Cordelia, though unkind;
Thou losest here, a better where to find.

LEAR: Thou hast her France, let her be thine, for we
Have no such daughter, nor shall ever see
That face of hers again. Therefore be gone,
Without our grace, our love, our benison.
Come noble Burgundy.

(Flourish. Exeunt LEAR, BURGUNDY, CORNWALL, ALBANY, GLOUCESTER, and ATTENDANTS.)

KING OF FRANCE: Bid farewell to your sisters.

CORDELIA: The jewels of our father, with washed eyes
Cordelia leaves you. I know you what you are,
And like a sister am most loth to call

Your faults as they are named. Love well
    our father.
To your professed bosoms I commit him,
But yet alas, stood I within his grace,
I would prefer him to a better place.
So farewell to you both.
REGAN: Prescribe not us our duty.
GONERIL: Let your
    study
Be to content your lord, who hath received
    you
At fortune's alms. You have obedience
    scanted,
And well are worth the want that you
    have wanted.
CORDELIA: Time shall unfold what plighted
    cunning hides,
Who covers faults, at last with shame
    derides.
Well may you prosper.
KING OF FRANCE: Come my fair
    Cordelia.

(Exeunt KING OF FRANCE *and* CORDELIA.*)*

GONERIL: Sister, it is not little I have to say of
what most nearly appertains to us both. I think our
father will hence to-night.

REGAN: That's most certain, and with you;
next month with us.
GONERIL: You see how full of changes his age
is; the observation we have made of it hath not been
little. He always loved our sister most, and with
what poor judgement he hath now cast her off
appears too grossly.
REGAN: 'Tis the infirmity of his age; yet he
hath ever but slenderly known himself.
GONERIL: The best and soundest of his time
hath been but rash, then must we look from his age
to receive not alone the imperfections of long-
ingrafted condition, but therewithal the unruly
waywardness that infirm and choleric years bring
with them.
REGAN: Such unconstant starts are we like to
have from him, as this of Kent's banishment.
GONERIL: There is further compliment of
leave-taking between France and him. Pray let us
hit together; if our father carry authority with such
disposition as he bears, this last surrender of his will
but offend us.
REGAN: We shall further think of it.
GONERIL: We must do something, and i' th'
heat. *(Exeunt)*

SCENE II

GLOUCESTER's castle

(Enter EDMUND, *with a letter.)*

EDMUND: Thou, Nature, art my goddess, to
    thy law
My services are bound. Wherefore
    should I
Stand in the plague of custom, and permit
The curiosity of nations to deprive me,
For that I am some twelve or fourteen
    moonshines
Lag of a brother? Why bastard? Wherefore
    base,
When my dimensions are as well compact,
My mind as generous, and my shape as
    true,

As honest madam's issue? Why brand they
    us
With base? With baseness? Bastardy? Base,
    base!
Who in the lusty stealth of nature take
More composition, and fierce quality,
Than doth within a dull, stale, tired bed
Go to th' creating a whole tribe of fops,
Got 'tween asleep and wake? Well then,
Legitimate Edgar, I must have your land.
Our father's love is to the bastard Edmund
As to th' legitimate. Fine word—
    legitimate!
Well, my legitimate, if this letter speed,
And my invention thrive, Edmund the base

Shall to th' legitimate. I grow, I prosper.
Now gods, stand up for bastards.

(*Enter* GLOUCESTER.)

GLOUCESTER: Kent banished thus! And
    France in choler parted!
And the King gone to-night! Prescribed his
    power,
Confined to exhibition! All this done
Upon the gad. Edmund, how now! What
    news?

EDMUND: So please your lordship, none.

GLOUCESTER: Why so earnestly seek you to put up that letter?

EDMUND: I know no news, my lord.

GLOUCESTER: What paper were you reading?

EDMUND: Nothing my lord.

GLOUCESTER: No? What needed then that terrible dispatch of it into your pocket? The quality of nothing hath not such need to hide itself. Let's see. Come, if it be nothing, I shall not need spectacles.

EDMUND: I beseech you, sir, pardon me; it is a letter from my brother, that I have not all o'er-read; and for so much as I have perused, I find it not fit for your o'er-looking.

GLOUCESTER: Give me the letter, sir.

EDMUND: I shall offend either to detain or give it. The contents, as in part I understand them, are to blame.

GLOUCESTER: Let's see, let's see.

EDMUND: I hope, for my brother's justification, he wrote this but as an essay or taste of my virtue.

GLOUCESTER: (*Reads*) *This policy, and reverence of age, makes the world bitter to the best of our times; keeps our fortunes from us, till our oldness cannot relish them. I begin to find an idle and fond bondage in the oppression of aged tyranny, who sways not as it hath power, but as it is suffered. Come to me, that of this I may speak more. If our father would sleep till I waked him, you should enjoy half his revenue for ever, and live the beloved of your brother. Edgar.*

Hum! Conspiracy!—*Sleep till I waked him, you should enjoy half his revenue*—My son Edgar! Had he a hand to write this? A heart and brain to breed it in? When came this to you? Who brought it?

EDMUND: It was not brought me, my lord; there's the cunning of it. I found it thrown in at the casement of my closet.

GLOUCESTER: You know the character to be your brother's?

EDMUND: If the matter were good, my lord, I durst swear it were his; but in respect of that, I would fain think it were not.

GLOUCESTER: It is his.

EDMUND: It is his hand, my lord. But I hope his heart is not in the contents.

GLOUCESTER: Has he never before sounded you in this business?

EDMUND: Never my lord. But I have heard him oft maintain it to be fit, that sons at perfect age, and fathers declined, the father should be as ward to the son, and the son manage his revenue.

GLOUCESTER: O villain, villain—his very opinion in the letter. Abhorred villain, unnatural, detested, brutish villain; worse than brutish! Go sirrah, seek him: I'll apprehend him. Abominable villain, where is he?

EDMUND: I do not well know my lord. If it shall please you to suspend your indignation against my brother, till you can derive from him better testimony of his intent, you should run a certain course; where, if you violently proceed against him, mistaking his purpose, it would make a great gap in your own honour, and shake in pieces the heart of his obedience. I dare pawn down my life for him, that he hath writ this to feel my affection to your honour, and to no other pretence of danger.

GLOUCESTER: Think you so?

EDMUND: If your honour judge it meet, I will place you where you shall hear us confer of this, and by an auricular assurance have your satisfaction, and that without any further delay than this very evening.

GLOUCESTER: He cannot be such a monster.

EDMUND: Nor is not sure.

GLOUCESTER: To his father, that so tenderly and entirely loves him—heaven and earth! Edmund, seek him out; wind me into him, I pray you. Frame the business after your own wisdom. I would unstate myself, to be in a due resolution.

EDMUND: I will seek him, sir, presently; convey the business as I shall find means, and acquaint you withal.

GLOUCESTER: These late eclipses in the sun

and moon portend no good to us; though the wisdom of nature can reason it thus, and thus, yet nature finds itself scourged by the sequent effects. Love cools, friendship falls off, brothers divide. In cities, mutinies; in countries, discord; in palaces, treason; and the bond cracked 'twixt son and father. This villain of mine comes under the prediction, there's son against father; the King falls from bias of nature, there's father against child. We have seen the best of our time. Machinations, hollowness, treachery, and all ruinous disorders, follow us disquietly to our graves. Find out this villain, Edmund; it shall lose thee nothing, do it carefully. And the noble and true-hearted Kent banished; his offence, honesty. 'Tis strange.

(Exit)

EDMUND: This is the excellent foppery of the world, that when we are sick in fortune, often the surfeits of our own behavior, we make guilty of our disasters the sun, the moon, and stars, as if we were villains on necessity, fools by heavenly compulsion, knaves, thieves, and treachers by spherical predominance; drunkards, liars, and adulterers by an enforced obedience of planetary influence; and all that we are evil in, by a divine thrusting on. An admirable evasion of whoremaster man, to lay his goatish disposition on the charge of a star. My father compounded with my mother under the dragon's tail, and my nativity was under ursa major, so that it follows, I am rough and lecherous. Fut, I should have been that I am, had the maidenliest star in the firmament twinkled on my bastardizing.

(Enter EDGAR)

Edgar! Pat. He comes like the catastrophe of the old comedy. My cue is villainous melancholy, with a sigh like Tom o' Bedlam. —O these eclipses do portend these divisions. Fa, sol, la, mi.

EDGAR: How now, brother Edmund, what serious contemplation are you in?

EDMUND: I am thinking, brother, of a prediction I read this other day, what should follow these eclipses.

EDGAR: Do you busy yourself with that?

EDMUND: I promise you, the effects he writes of succeed unhappily; as of unnaturalness between the child and the parent; death, dearth, dissolutions of ancient amities, divisions in state, menaces and maledictions against king and nobles; needless diffidences, banishment of friends, dissipation of cohorts, nuptial breaches, and I know not what.

EDGAR: How long have you been a sectary astronomical?

EDMUND: Come, come, when saw you my father last?

EDGAR: The night gone by.

EDMUND: Spake you with him?

EDGAR: Ay, two hours together.

EDMUND: Parted you in good terms? Found you no displeasure in him, by word, nor countenance?

EDGAR: None at all.

EDMUND: Bethink yourself wherein you may have offended him; and at my entreaty forbear his presence until some little time hath qualified the heat of his displeasure, which at this instant so rageth in him, that with the mischief of your person it would scarcely allay.

EDGAR: Some villain hath done me wrong.

EDMUND: That's my fear. I pray you, have a continent forbearance till the speed of his rage goes slower; and as I say, retire with me to my lodging, from whence I will fitly bring you to hear my lord speak. Pray ye go, there's my key. If you do stir abroad, go armed.

EDGAR: Armed, brother?

EDMUND: Brother, I advise you to the best; I am no honest man if there be any good meaning toward you. I have told you what I have seen, and heard—but faintly—nothing like the image and horror of it. Pray you away.

EDGAR: Shall I hear from you anon?

EDMUND: I do serve you in this business.

(Exit EDGAR.)

A credulous father, and a brother noble,
Whose nature is so far from doing harms,
That he suspects none; on whose foolish honesty
My practices ride easy. I see the business.
Let me, if not by birth, have lands by wit;
All with me's meet, that I can fashion fit.

(Exit)

SCENE III
ALBANY'S *palace*

(Enter GONERIL *and* OSWALD.*)*

GONERIL: Did my father strike my
    gentleman for chiding of his fool?
OSWALD: Ay madam.
GONERIL: By day and night, he wrongs me;
    every hour
He flashes into one gross crime or other,
That sets us all at odds. I'll not endure it.
His knights grow riotous, and himself
    upbraids us
On every trifle. When he returns from
    hunting,
I will not speak with him, say I am sick;
If you come slack of former services,
You shall do well; the fault of it I'll
    answer.

(Horns within.)

OSWALD: He's coming madam, I hear him.
GONERIL: Put on what weary negligence
    you please,
    You and your fellows—I'd have it come to
    question.

If he distaste it, let him to my sister,
Whose mind and mine I know in that are
    one.
Not to be over-ruled. Idle old man,
That still would manage those authorities
That he hath given away. Now by my
    life,
Old fools are babes again, and must be
    used
With checks as flatteries, when they are
    seen abused.
Remember what I have said.
OSWALD: Well madam.
GONERIL: And let his knights have colder
    looks among you.
What grows of it no matter, advise your
    fellows so.
I would breed from hence occasions, and I
    shall,
That I may speak. I'll write straight to my
    sister
To hold my very course. Prepare for
    dinner. *(Exeunt)*

SCENE IV
The same

(Enter KENT, *disguised.)*

KENT: If but as well I other accents borrow,
That can my speech defuse, my good
    intent
May carry through itself to that full issue
For which I razed my likeness. Now
    banished Kent,
If thou canst serve where thou dost stand
    condemned,
So may it come, thy master whom thou
    lov'st
Shall find thee full of labours.

(Horns within. Enter LEAR, KNIGHTS, *and*
ATTENDANTS.*)*

LEAR: Let me not stay a jot for dinner, go get
it ready.

(Exit an ATTENDANT.*)*

How now, what art thou?
    KENT: A man sir.
    LEAR: What dost thou profess? What wouldst
thou with us?
    KENT: I do profess to be no less than I seem;
to serve him truly that will put me in trust, to love
him that is honest, to converse with him that is
wise and says little, to fear judgement, to fight when
I cannot choose, and to eat no fish.
    LEAR: What art thou?

KENT: A very honest-hearted fellow, and as poor as the King.

LEAR: If thou beest as poor for a subject as he's for a King, thou are poor enough. What wouldst thou?

KENT: Service.

LEAR: Who wouldst thou serve?

KENT: You.

LEAR: Dost thou know me, fellow?

KENT: No sir, but you have that in your countenance which I would fain call master.

LEAR: What's that?

KENT: Authority.

LEAR: What services canst thou do?

KENT: I can keep honest counsel, ride, run, mar a curious tale in telling it, and deliver a plain message bluntly. That which ordinary men are fit for, I am qualified in, and the best of me is diligence.

LEAR: How old art thou?

KENT: Not so young sir, to love a woman for singing, nor so old to dote on her for any thing. I have years on my back forty-eight.

LEAR: Follow me, thou shalt serve me; if I like thee no worse after dinner, I will not part from thee yet. Dinner ho, dinner! Where's my knave? My fool? Go you and call my fool hither.

(Exit an ATTENDANT. *Enter* OSWALD.*)*

You, you sirrah, where's my daughter?

OSWALD: So please you— *(Exit)*

LEAR: What says the fellow there? Call the clotpoll back. *(Exit a* KNIGHT*)* Where's my fool, ho? I think the world's asleep.

(Enter KNIGHT*)*

How now? Where's that mongrel?

KNIGHT: He says, my lord, your daughter is not well.

LEAR: Why came not the slave back to me when I called him?

KNIGHT: Sir, he answered me in the roundest manner, he would not.

LEAR: He would not?

KNIGHT: My lord, I know not what the matter is, but to my judgement your Highness is not entertained with that ceremonious affection as you were wont; there's a great abatement of kindness appears as well in the general dependants, as in the duke himself also, and your daughter.

LEAR: Ha! Sayest thou so?

KNIGHT: I beseech you pardon me my lord, if I be mistaken, for my duty cannot be silent, when I think your Highness wronged.

LEAR: Thou but rememberest me of mine own conception. I have perceived a most faint neglect of late, which I have rather blamed as mine own jealous curiosity than as a very pretence and purpose of unkindness; I will look further into't. But where's my fool? I have not seen him this two days.

KNIGHT: Since my young lady's going into France sir, the fool hath much pined away.

LEAR: No more of that, I have noted it well. Go you and tell my daughter I would speak with her. *(Exit an* ATTENDANT*)* Go you, call hither my fool.

(Exit another ATTENDANT. *Enter* OSWALD.*)*

O, you sir, you, come you hither, sir. Who am I, sir?

OSWALD: My lady's father.

LEAR: My lady's father? My lord's knave! You whoreson dog, you slave, you cur!

OSWALD: I am none of these, my lord, I beseech your pardon.

LEAR: Do you bandy looks with me, you rascal? *(Strikes him)*

OSWALD: I'll not be strucken, my lord.

KENT: Nor tripped neither, you base football player. *(Trips up his heels)*

LEAR: I thank thee, fellow. Thou serv'st me, and I'll love thee.

KENT: Come, sir, arise, away, I'll teach you differences. Away, away! If you will measure your lubber's length again, tarry. But away! Go to, have you wisdom? So. *(Pushes* OSWALD *out)*

LEAR: Now, my friendly knave, I thank thee, there's earnest of thy service. *(Gives* KENT *money)*

(Enter FOOL.*)*

FOOL: Let me hire him too, here's my coxcomb. *(Offers* KENT *his cap)*

LEAR: How now, my pretty knave, how dost thou?

FOOL: Sirrah, you were best take my coxcomb.

KENT: Why, fool?

FOOL: Why for taking one's part that's out of favour. Nay an thou canst not smile as the wind sits, thou'lt catch cold shortly; there, take my coxcomb. Why this fellow has banished two on's daughters, and did the third a blessing against his will; if thou follow him, thou must needs wear my coxcomb.

How now nuncle? Would I had two coxcombs, and two daughters.

LEAR: Why, my boy?

FOOL: If I gave them all my living, I'd keep my coxcombs myself. There's mine, beg another of thy daughters.

LEAR: Take heed, sirrah — the whip.

FOOL: Truth's a dog must to kennel; he must be whipped out, when the Lady Brach may stand by th'fire and stink.

LEAR: A pestilent gall to me.

FOOL: Sirrah, I'll teach thee a speech.

LEAR: Do.

FOOL: Mark it, nuncle.

> Have more than thou showest,
> Speak less than thou knowest,
> Lend less than thou owest,
> Ride more than thou goest,
> Learn more than thou trowest,
> Set less than thou throwest;
> Leave thy drink and thy whore,
> And keep in-a-door,
> And thou shalt have more
> Than two tens to a score.

KENT: This is nothing, fool.

FOOL: Then 'tis the breath of an unfeed lawyer, you gave me nothing for't. Can you make no use of nothing, nuncle?

LEAR: Why no, boy, nothing can be made out of nothing.

FOOL: (To KENT) Prithee tell him, so much the rent of his land comes to; he will not believe a fool.

LEAR: A bitter fool.

FOOL: Dost thou know the difference, my boy, between a bitter fool, and a sweet one?

LEAR: No, lad, teach me.

FOOL: That lord that counselled thee
> To give away thy land,
> Come place him here by me,
> Do thou for him stand.
> The sweet and bitter fool
> Will presently appear;
> The one in motley here,
> The other found out there.

LEAR: Dost thou call me fool, boy?

FOOL: All thy other titles thou hast given away, that thou wast born with.

KENT: This is not altogether fool my lord.

FOOL: No, faith, lords and great men will not let me; if I had a monopoly out, they would have part an't; and ladies too, they will not let me have all the fool to myself; they'll be snatching, Nuncle, give men an egg and I'll give thee two crowns.

LEAR: What two crowns shall they be?

FOOL: Why, after I have cut the egg i' th' middle and eat up the meat, the two crowns of the egg. When thou clovest thy crown i' th' middle, and gav'st way both parts, thou bor'st thine ass on thy back o'er the dirt. Thou hadst little wit in thy bald crown, when thou gav'st thy golden one away. If I speak like myself in this, let him be whipped that first finds it so.

> Fools had ne'er less grace in a year,
> For wise men are grown foppish,
> And know not how their wits to wear,
> Their manners are so apish.

LEAR: When were you wont to be so full of songs, sirrah?

FOOL: I have used it, nuncle, ever since thou mad'st thy daughters thy mothers, for when thou gav'st them the rod, and put'st down thine own breeches —

> Then they for sudden joy did weep,
> And I for sorrow sung,
> That such a king should play bo-peep,
> And go the fools among.

> Prithee, nuncle, keep a schoolmaster that can
> teach thy fool to lie —
> I would fain learn to lie.

LEAR: An you lie, sirrah, we'll have you whipped.

FOOL: I marvel what kin thou and thy daughters are, they'll have me whipped for speaking true, thou'lt have me whipped for lying, and sometimes I am whipped for holding my peace. I had rather be any kind o' thing than a fool, and yet I would not be thee, nuncle; thou hast pared thy wit o' both sides, and left nothing i' th' middle —

(Enter GONERIL*)*

Here comes one o' the parings.

LEAR: How now, daughter, what makes that
> frontlet on?
> You are too much of late i' th' frown.

FOOL: Thou wast a pretty fellow when thou hadst no need to care for her frowning; now thou art an O without a figure. I am better than thou art now; I am a fool, thou art nothing. *(To* GONERIL*)* Yes forsooth, I will hold my tongue; so your face bids me, though you say nothing.

Mum, mum.
He that keeps nor crust nor crumb,
Weary of all, shall want some.
That's a shealed peascod.
   GONERIL: Not only, sir, this your all-
      licensed fool,
   But other of your insolent retinue
   Do hourly carp and quarrel, breaking forth
   In rank and not-to-be-endured riots. Sir,
   I had thought by making this well known
      unto you,
   To have found a safe redress, but now
      grow fearful,
   By what yourself too late have spoke and
      done,
   That you protect this course, and put it on
   By your allowance; which if you should,
      the fault
   Would not 'scape censure, nor the
      redresses sleep,
   Which in the tender of a wholesome weal,
   Might in their working do you that
      offence,
   Which else were shame, that then
      necessity
   Will call discreet proceeding.
   FOOL: For you know, nuncle,
   The hedge-sparrow fed the cuckoo so long,
   That it's had its head bit off by its young.
So out went the candle, and we were left darkling.
   LEAR: Are you our daughter?
   GONERIL: I would you would make use of
      your good wisdom,
   Whereof I know you are fraught, and put
      away
   These dispositions, which of late transport
      you
   From what you rightly are.
   FOOL: May not an ass know when the cart
draws the horse? Whoop, Jug, I love thee.
   LEAR: Does any here know me? This is not
      Lear.
   Does Lear walk thus? Speak thus? Where
      are his eyes?
   Either his notion weakens, his discernings
   Are lethargied. Ha, waking? 'Tis not so.
   Who is it that can tell me who I am?
   FOOL: Lear's shadow.
   LEAR: I would learn that, for by the marks of

sovereignty, knowledge, and reason, I should be
false persuaded I had daughters.
   FOOL: Which they will make an obedient
father.
   LEAR: Your name, fair gentlewoman?
   GONERIL: This admiration, sir, is much o'
      th' savour
   Of other your new pranks. I do beseech
      you
   To understand my purposes aright,
   As you are old, and reverend, should be
      wise.
   Here do you keep a hundred knights and
      squires,
   Men so disordered, so deboshed, and bold,
   That this our court infected with their
      manners,
   Shows like a riotous inn; epicurism and
      lust
   Makes it more like a tavern, or a brothel,
   Than a graced palace. The shame itself
      doth speak
   For instant remedy. Be then desired
   By her, that else will take the thing she
      begs,
   A little to disquantity your train;
   And the remainders that shall still depend,
   To be such men as may besort your age,
   Which know themselves and you.
   LEAR: Darkness and
      devils!
   Saddle my horses; call my train together.
   Degenerate bastard, I'll not trouble thee.
   Yet have I left a daughter.
   GONERIL: You strike my people, and your
      disordered rabble
   Make servants of their betters.
   LEAR: Woe, that too late repents.

          (Enter ALBANY.*)*

   O sir, are you come?
   Is it your will? Speak, sir. Prepare my
      horses.
   Ingratitude, thou marble-hearted fiend,
   More hideous when thou show'st thee in a
      child,
   Than the sea-monster.
   ALBANY: Pray, sir, be patient.
   LEAR: *(To* GONERIL*)* Detested kite, thou liest.

My train are men of choice and rarest
  parts,
That all particulars of duty know,
And in the most exact regard support
The worships of their name. O most small
  fault,
How ugly didst thou in Cordelia show,
Which like an engine wrenched my frame
  of nature
From the fixed place; drew from my heart
  all love,
And added to the gall. O Lear, Lear, Lear!
Beat at this gate that let thy folly in,
  (Strikes his head)
And thy dear judgement out. Go, go, my
  people.
ALBANY: My lord, I am guiltless, as I am
  ignorant
  Of what hath moved you.
LEAR: It may be so, my
  lord.
  Hear Nature, hear, dear goddess, hear.
  Suspend thy purpose, if thou didst intend
  To make this creature fruitful.
  Into her womb convey sterility,
  Dry up in her the organs of increase,
  And from her derogate body never spring
  A babe to honour her. If she must teem,
  Create her child of spleen, that it may live
  And be a thwart disnatured torment to
  her.
  Let it stamp wrinkles in her brow of
  youth,
  With cadent tears fret channels in her
  cheeks,
  Turn all her mother's pains and benefits
  To laughter, and contempt, that she may
  feel
  How sharper than a serpent's tooth it is
  To have a thankless child. Away, away!
  (Exit.)
ALBANY: Now, gods that we adore, whereof
  comes this?
GONERIL: Never afflict yourself to know
  more of it;
  But let his disposition have that scope
  As dotage gives it.

(Enter LEAR)

LEAR: What, fifty of my followers at a clap?
  Within a fortnight?
ALBANY: What's the matter sir?
LEAR: I'll tell thee. (To GONERIL) Life and
  death, I am ashamed
  That thou hast power to shake my
  manhood thus,
  That these hot tears, which break from me
  perforce,
  Should make thee worth them. Blasts and
  fogs upon thee!
  Th' untented woundings of a father's curse
  Pierce every sense about thee. Old fond
  eyes,
  Beweep this cause again, I'll pluck ye out,
  And cast you with the waters that you
  loose
  To temper clay. Ha, is't come to this?
  Let it be so, I have another daughter,
  Who I am sure is kind and comfortable.
  When she shall hear this of thee, with her
  nails
  She'll flay thy wolvish visage. Thou shalt
  find,
  That I'll resume the shape which thou
  dost think
  I have cast off for ever.

(Exeunt LEAR, KENT, and ATTENDANTS.)

GONERIL: Do you mark that?
ALBANY: I cannot be so partial, Goneril,
  To the great love I bear you—
GONERIL: Pray you, content. What Oswald,
  ho!
  (To FOOL) You sir, more knave than fool,
  after your master.
FOOL: Nuncle Lear, nuncle Lear, tarry, take
  the fool with thee.
  A fox, when one has caught her,
  And such a daughter,
  Should sure to the slaughter,
  If my cap would buy a halter;
  So the fool follows after. (Exit)
GONERIL: This man hath had good counsel.
  A hundred knights!
  'Tis politic, and safe, to let him keep
  At point a hundred knights—yes, that on
  every dream,

Each buzz, each fancy, each complaint,
  dislike,
He may enguard his dotage with their
  powers,
And hold our lives in mercy. Oswald, I
  say!
ALBANY: Well, you may fear too far.
GONERIL: Safer
    than trust too far.
Let me still take away the harms I fear,
Not fear still to be taken. I know his
  heart.
What he hath uttered I have writ my
  sister.
If she sustain him, and his hundred
  knights,
When I have showed th' unfitness—

        (Enter OSWALD.)
              How now, Oswald?

What, have you writ that letter to my
  sister?
OSWALD: Ay, madam.
GONERIL: Take you some company, and
    away to horse.
Inform her full of my particular fear,
And thereto add such reasons of your own,
As may compact it more. Get you gone,
And hasten your return. *(Exit* OSWALD*)*
    No, no, my lord,
This milky gentleness and course of yours,
Though I condemn not, yet under pardon,
You are much more ataxed for want of
  wisdom,
Than praised for harmful mildness.
ALBANY: How far your eyes may pierce I
    cannot tell;
Striving to better, oft we mar what's well.
GONERIL: Nay then—
ALBANY: Well, well, th' event. *(Exeunt)*

SCENE V

Before ALBANY'S *palace*

(Enter LEAR, KENT, *and* FOOL.)

LEAR: Go you before to Gloucester with these letters. Acquaint my daughter no further with any thing you know than comes from her demand out of the letter. If your diligence be not speedy, I shall be there afore you.

KENT: I will not sleep, my lord, till I have delivered your letter. *(Exit)*

FOOL: If a man's brains were in's heels, were't not in danger of kibes?

LEAR: Ay, boy.

FOOL: Then I prithee be merry, thy wit shall not go slipshod.

LEAR: Ha, ha, ha!

FOOL: Shalt see thy other daughter will use thee kindly, for though she's as like this, as a crab's like an apple, yet I can tell what I can tell.

LEAR: What canst tell, boy?

FOOL: She will taste as like this as a crab does to a crab. Thou canst tell why one's nose stands i' th' middle on's face?

LEAR: No.

FOOL: Why to keep one's eyes of either side's nose, that what a man cannot smell out, he may spy into.

LEAR: I did her wrong.

FOOL: Canst tell how an oyster makes his shell?

LEAR: No.

FOOL: Nor I neither; but I can tell why a snail has a house.

LEAR: Why?

FOOL: Why to put's head in; not to give it away to his daughters, and leave his horns without a case.

LEAR: I will forget my nature. So kind a father. Be my horses ready?

FOOL: Thy asses are gone about 'em. The reason why the seven stars are no more than seven, is a pretty reason.

LEAR: Because they are not eight?

FOOL: Yes indeed, thou wouldst make a good fool.

LEAR: To take't again perforce. Monster ingratitude.

FOOL: If thou wert my fool, nuncle, I'd have thee beaten for being old before thy time.

LEAR: How's that?

FOOL: Thou shouldst not have been old, till thou hadst been wise.

LEAR: O let me not be mad, not mad, sweet
    heaven.
    Keep me in temper, I would not be mad.
    (Enter GENTLEMAN*)*
    How now, are the horses ready?

GENTLEMAN: Ready, my lord.

LEAR: Come, boy.

    (Exeunt LEAR *and* GENTLEMAN.*)*

FOOL: She that's a maid now, and laughs at
    my departure,
    Shall not be a maid long, unless things be
    cut shorter. *(Exit)*

ACT II

SCENE I

Before GLOUCESTER'S *castle*

(Enter EDMUND *and* CURAN, *at several doors.)*

EDMUND: Save thee, Curan.

CURAN: And you, sir. I have been with your father, and given him notice that the Duke of Cornwall, and Regan his duchess, will be here with him this night.

EDMUND: How comes that?

CURAN: Nay, I know not. You have heard of the news abroad, I mean the whispered ones, for they are yet but ear-kissing arguments?

EDMUND: Not I. Pray you what are they?

CURAN: Have you heard of no likely wars toward, 'twixt the Dukes of Cornwall and Albany?

EDMUND: Not a word.

CURAN: You may do then in time. Fare you well, sir. *(Exit)*

EDMUND: The duke be here to-night? The
    better. Best.
    This weaves itself perforce into my
      business.
    My father hath set guard to take my
      brother,
    And I have one thing of a queasy question
    Which I must act. Briefness and fortune
      work.
    (Enter EDGAR*)*
    Brother, a word; descend. Brother, I say!
    My father watches. O sir, fly this place,
    Intelligence is given where you are hid;
    You have now the good advantage of the
      night.
    Have you not spoken 'gainst the Duke of
      Cornwall?
    He's coming hither, now i' th' night, i' th'
      haste,
    And Regan with him; have you nothing
      said
    Upon his party 'gainst the Duke of
      Albany?
    Advise yourself.

EDGAR: I am sure on't, not a word.

EDMUND: I hear my father coming. Pardon
    me,
    In cunning, I must draw my sword upon
      you.
    Draw, seem to defend yourself; now quit
      you well—
    Yield, come before my father. Light ho,
      here!—
    Fly, brother—Torches, torches!—So
      farewell.
    (Exit EDGAR*)*
    Some blood drawn on me would beget
      opinion
    Of my more fierce endeavour. *(Stabs his
      arm)*
    I have seen drunkards
    Do more than this in sport. Father, father!
    Stop, stop! No help?

(Enter GLOUCESTER, *and* SERVANTS *with torches.)*

GLOUCESTER: Now, Edmund,
      where's the villain?

EDMUND: Here stood he in the dark, his
    sharp sword out,
    Mumbling of wicked charms, conjuring
      the moon
    To stand's auspicious mistress.

GLOUCESTER: But where is
    he?

EDMUND: Look sir, I bleed.

GLOUCESTER: Where is the
    villain, Edmund?

EDMUND: Fled this way, sir. When by no
    means he could—

GLOUCESTER: Pursue him, ho! Go after.
    (Exeunt SERVANTS*)* By no means what?

EDMUND: Persuade me to the murder of
    your lordship;
    But that I told him the revenging gods
    'Gainst parricides did all their thunders
      bend,
    Spoke with how manifold and strong a
      bond
    The child was bound to th' father; sir, in
      fine,
    Seeing how loathly opposite I stood
    To his unnatural purpose, in fell motion,
    With his prepared sword, he charges home
    My unprovided body, latched mine arm;
    And when he saw my best alarumed
      spirits
    Bold in the quarrel's right, roused to th'
      encounter,
    Or whether gasted by the noise I made,
    Full suddenly he fled.

GLOUCESTER: Let him fly far.
    Not in this land shall he remain uncaught;
    And found—dispatch. The noble duke my
      master,
    My worthy arch and patron, comes to-
      night.
    By his authority I will proclaim it,
    That he which finds him shall deserve our
      thanks,
    Bringing the murderous coward to the
      stake;
    He that conceals him, death.

EDMUND: When I dissuaded him from his
    intent,
    And found him pight to do it, with curst
      speech
    I threatened to discover him; he replied,
    Thou unpossessing bastard, dost thou
      think,
    If I would stand against thee, would the
      reposal
    Of any trust, virtue, or worth in thee,
    Make thy words faithed? No, what I
      should deny—

    As this I would, ay though thou didst
      produce
    My very character—I'd turn it all
    To thy suggestion, plot, and damned
      practice.
    And thou must make a dullard of the
      world,
    If they not thought the profits of my
      death
    Were very pregnant and potential spirits
    To make thee seek it.

GLOUCESTER: O strange and
    fastened villain,
    Would he deny his letter?—I never got
    him.
    (Tucket within)
    Hark, the duke's trumpets; I know not
      why he comes.
    All ports I'll bar; the villain shall not
      'scape,
    The duke must grant me that. Besides, his
      picture
    I will send far and near, that all the
      kingdom
    May have due note of him; and of my
      land,
    Loyal and natural boy, I'll work the means
    To make thee capable.

(Enter CORNWALL, REGAN *and* ATTENDANTS.*)*

CORNWALL: How now, my noble friend.
    Since I came hither,
    Which I can call but now—I have heard
      strange news.

REGAN: If it be true, all vengeance comes
    too short
    Which can pursue th' offender. How dost,
      my lord?

GLOUCESTER: O madam, my old heart is
    cracked, it's cracked.

REGAN: What, did my father's godson seek
    your life?
    He whom my father named, your Edgar?

GLOUCESTER: O lady, lady, shame would
    have it hid.

REGAN: Was he not companion with the
    riotous knights
    That tend upon my father?

GLOUCESTER: I know not madam; 'tis too
    bad, too bad.

EDMUND: Yes, madam, he was of that
  consort.
REGAN: No marvel then, though he were ill
  affected.
  'Tis they have put him on the old man's
    death,
  To have th' expense and waste of his
    revenues.
  I have this present evening from my sister
  Been well informed of them, and with
    such cautions,
  That if they come to sojourn at my house,
  I'll not be there.
CORNWALL: Nor I, assure thee Regan.
  Edmund, I hear that you have shown your
    father
  A child-like office.
EDMOND: It was my duty, sir.
GLOUCESTER: He did bewray his practice,
    and received
  This hurt you see, striving to apprehend
    him.
CORNWALL: Is he pursued?
GLOUCESTER: Ay, my good
    lord.
CORNWALL: If he be taken, he shall never
    more
  Be feared of doing harm. Make your own
    purpose,
  How in my strength you please. For you,
    Edmund,

Whose virtue and obedience doth this
  instant
So much commend itself, you shall be
  ours.
Natures of such deep trust we shall much
  need.
You we first seize on.
EDMUND: I shall serve you, sir,
  Truly, however else.
GLOUCESTER: For him I thank your
  Grace.
CORNWALL: You know not why we came
  to visit you?
REGAN: Thus out of season, threading dark-
  eyed night.
  Occasions, noble Gloucester, of some poise,
  Wherein we must have use of your advice.
  Our father he hath writ, so hath our sister,
  Of differences, which I best thought it fit
  To answer from our home; the several
    messengers
  From hence attend dispatch. Our good old
    friend,
  Lay comforts to your bosom, and bestow
  Your needful counsel to our businesses,
  Which craves the instant use.
GLOUCESTER: I serve you,
  madam.
  Your Graces are right welcome. *(Exeunt)*

SCENE II
The same

(Enter KENT *and* OSWALD, *at several doors.)*

OSWALD: Good dawning to thee, friend, art of
this house?
  KENT: Ay.
  OSWALD: Where may we set our horses?
  KENT: I' th' mire.
  OSWALD: Prithee, if thou lov'st me, tell me.
  KENT: I love thee not.
  OSWALD: Why then I care not for thee.
  KENT: If I had thee in Lipsbury pinfold, I
would make thee care for me.
  OSWALD: Why dost thou use me thus? I
know thee not.

KENT: Fellow, I know thee.
  OSWALD: What dost thou know me for?
  KENT: A knave, a rascal, an eater of broken
meats, a base, proud, shallow, beggarly, three-suited,
hundred pound, filthy worsted-stocking knave, a
lily-livered, action-taking, whoreson glass-gazing
super-serviceable finical rogue, one trunk-inheriting
slave, one that wouldst be a bawd in way of good
service, and art nothing but the composition of a
knave, beggar, coward, pandar, and the son and heir
of a mongrel bitch; one whom I will beat into clamorous whining, if thou deny'st the least syllable of
thy addition.

OSWALD: Why, what a monstrous fellow art thou, thus to rail on one that is neither known of thee, nor knows thee.

KENT: What a brazen-faced varlet art thou, to deny thou knowest me. Is it two days since I tripped up thy heels, and beat thee before the King? Draw, you rogue, for though it be night, yet the moon shines; I'll make a sop o' th' moonshine of you, you whoreson cullionly barbermonger. Draw. *(Draws his sword)*

OSWALD: Away, I have nothing to do with thee.

KENT: Draw, you rascal, you come with letters against the King, and take Vanity the puppet's part against the royalty of her father. Draw, you rogue, or I'll so carbonado your shanks—draw, you rascal, come your ways.

OSWALD: Help, ho, murder, help!

KENT: Strike, you slave; stand, rogue, stand you neat slave, strike. *(Beats him.)*

OSWALD: Help ho! murder, murder!

(Enter EDMUND, *with his rapier drawn,* GLOUCESTER, CORNWALL, REGAN *and* SERVANTS.*)*

EDMUND: How now, what's the matter? Part!

KENT: With you, goodman, boy, if you
    please; come,
    I'll flesh ye; come on, young master.

GLOUCESTER: Weapons? Arms? What's the
    matter here?

CORNWALL: Keep peace upon your lives;
    He dies that strikes again. What is the
    matter?

REGAN: The messengers from our sister, and the King.

CORNWALL: What is your difference, speak.

OSWALD: I am scarce in breath, my lord.

KENT: No marvel, you have so bestirred your valour. You cowardly rascal, nature disclaims in thee. A tailor made thee.

CORNWALL: Thou art a strange fellow. A tailor make a man?

KENT: A tailor, sir; a stone-cutter, or a painter, could not have made him so ill, though they had been but two years o' th' trade.

CORNWALL: Speak yet, how grew your quarrel?

OSWALD: This ancient ruffian, sir, whose life I have spared at suit of his gray beard—

KENT: Thou whoreson zed, thou unnecessary letter—my lord, if you will give me leave, I will tread this unbolted villain into mortar, and daub the wall of a jakes with him. Spare my gray beard, you wagtail?

CORNWALL: Peace, sirrah!
    You beastly knave, know you no
    reverence?

KENT: Yes sir, but anger hath a privilege.

CORNWALL: Why art thou angry?

KENT: That such a slave as this should wear
    a sword,
    Who wears no honesty. Such smiling
    rogues as these
    Like rats oft bite the holy cords atwain
    Which are too intrinse t' unloose; smooth
    every passion
    That in the natures of their lords rebel,
    Bring oil to fire, snow to their colder
    moods;
    Renege, affirm, and turn their halcyon
    beaks
    With every gale and vary of their masters,
    Knowing naught, like dogs, but following.
    A plague upon your epileptic visage,
    Smile you my speeches, as I were a fool?
    Goose, if I had you upon Sarum plain,
    I'd drive ye cackling home to Camelot.

CORNWALL: What, art thou mad, old
    fellow?

GLOUCESTER: How fell you out, say that.

KENT: No contraries hold more antipathy
    Than I and such a knave.

CORNWALL: Why dost thou call him
    knave? What is his fault?

KENT: His countenance likes me not.

CORNWALL: No more perchance does mine,
    nor his, nor hers.

KENT: Sir, 'tis my occupation to be plain;
    I have seen better faces in my time
    Than stands on any shoulder that I see
    Before me, at this instant.

CORNWALL: This is some
    fellow,
    Who having been praised for bluntness,
    doth affect
    A saucy roughness, and constrains the garb
    Quite from his nature. He cannot flatter,
    he;
    An honest mind and plain; he must speak
    truth;

An they will take it, so; if not, he's plain.
These kind of knaves I know, which in
    this plainness
Harbour more craft, and more corrupter
    ends,
Than twenty silly ducking observants
That stretch their duties nicely.
KENT: Sir, in good faith, in sincere verity,
    Under th' allowance of your great aspect,
    Whose influence like the wreath of
        radiant fire
    On flickering Phœbus' front—
CORNWALL: What
    mean'st by this?
KENT: To go out of my dialect, which you dis-
commend so much. I know, sir, I am no flatterer; he
that beguiled you in plain accent was a plain knave,
which for my part I will not be, though I should
win your displeasure to entreat me to't.
CORNWALL: What was th' offence you gave
him?
OSWALD: I never gave him any.
    It pleased the King his master very late
    To strike at me, upon his misconstruction;
    When he compact, and flattering his
        displeasure,
    Tripped me behind; being down, insulted,
        railed,
    And put upon him such a deal of man,
    That worthied him, got praises of the King
    For him attempting who was self-subdued,
    And in the fleshment of this dread exploit,
    Drew on me here again.
KENT: None of these
    rogues and cowards
    But Ajax is their fool.
CORNWALL: Fetch forth the
    stocks.
    You stubborn ancient knave, you reverend
        braggart,
    We'll teach you.
KENT: Sir, I am too old to learn.
    Call not your stocks for me; I serve the
        King,
    On whose employment I was sent to you.
    You shall do small respect, show too bold
        malice
    Against the grace and person of my
        master,
    Stocking his messenger.

CORNWALL: Fetch forth the stocks. As I
    have life and honour,
    There shall he sit till noon.
REGAN: Till noon? Till night my lord, and
    all night too.
KENT: Why, madam, if I were your father's
    dog,
    You should not use me so.
REGAN: Sir, being his
    knave, I will.
CORNWALL: This is a fellow of the self-
    same colour
    Our sister speaks of. Come, bring away the
    stocks.

(Stocks discovered in the inner stage.)

GLOUCESTER: Let me beseech your Grace
    not to do so.
    His fault is much, and the good King his
        master
    Will check him for't; your purposed low
        correction
    Is such as basest and contemned'st
        wretches
    For pilferings and most common
        trespasses
    Are punished with. The King must take it
        ill,
    That he, so slightly valued in his
        messenger,
    Should have him thus restrained.
CORNWALL: I'll
    answer that.
REGAN: My sister may receive it much more
    worse,
    To have her gentleman abused, assaulted,
    For following her affairs. Put in his legs.
    Come my good lord, away.

(Exeunt all but GLOUCESTER *and* KENT.*)*

GLOUCESTER: I am sorry for thee, friend,
    'tis the duke's pleasure,
    Whose disposition, all the world well
        knows,
    Will not be rubbed nor stopped. I'll entreat
        for thee.
KENT: Pray do not, sir. I have watched, and
    travelled hard;
    Some time I shall sleep out, the rest I'll
        whistle.

A good man's fortune may grow out at
    heels.
Give you good morrow.
GLOUCESTER: The duke's to blame in this,
    'twill be ill taken. *(Exit)*
KENT: Good King, that must approve the
    common saw,
Thou out of heaven's benediction com'st
To the warm sun.
Approach thou beacon to this under globe,
That by thy comfortable beams I may
Peruse this letter. Nothing almost sees
    miracles

But misery. I know 'tis from Cordelia,
Who hath most fortunately been informed
Of my obscured course — *(Reads) and shall
find time
From this enormous state, seeking to give
Losses their remedies.* — All weary and
    o'erwatched,
Take vantage heavy eyes, not to behold
This shameful lodging.
Fortune, good night; smile once more, turn
    thy wheel.

(Sleeps. Curtains drawn.)

SCENE III

The open country

(Enter EDGAR.)

EDGAR: I heard myself proclaimed,
    And by the happy hollow of a tree
Escaped the hunt. No port is free, no
    place,
That guard, and most unusual vigilance,
Does not attend my taking. Whiles I may
    'scape,
I will preserve myself; and am bethought
To take the basest and most poorest shape
That ever penury in contempt of man
Brought near to beast; my face I'll grime
    with filth,
Blanket my loins, elf all my hairs in knots,
And with presented nakedness outface
The winds and persecutions of the sky.

The country gives me proof and precedent
Of Bedlam beggars, who with roaring
    voices,
Strike in their numbed and mortified bare
    arms
Pins, wooden pricks, nails, sprigs of
    rosemary;
And with this horrible object, from low
    farms,
Poor pelting villages, sheep cotes, and
    mills,
Sometime with lunatic bans, sometime
    with prayers,
Enforce their charity. Poor Turlygod, poor
    Tom!
That's something yet. Edgar I nothing am.
    (Exit)

SCENE IV

Before GLOUCESTER'S castle

---

*(KENT discovered in the stocks. Enter LEAR, FOOL,
and GENTLEMAN.)*

LEAR: 'Tis strange that they should so depart
    from home,
And not send back my messenger.
GENTLEMAN: As I learned,

The night before there was no purpose in
    them
Of this remove.
KENT: Hail to thee, noble master.
LEAR: Ha!
    Mak'st thou this shame thy pastime?
KENT: No, my lord.

FOOL: Ha, ha, he wears cruel garters. Horses are tied by the heads, dogs and bears by th' neck, monkeys by th' loins, and men by th' legs. When a man's over-lusty at legs, then he wears wooden netherstocks.

LEAR: What's he that hath so much thy
      place mistook
    To set thee here?

KENT: It is both he and she,
    Your son and daughter.

LEAR: No.

KENT: Yes.

LEAR: No, I say.

KENT: I say, yea.

LEAR: By Jupiter, I swear, no.

KENT: By Juno, I swear, ay.

LEAR: They durst not
    do't;
    They could not, would not do't; 'tis worse
      than murder,
    To do upon respect such violent outrage.
    Resolve me with all modest haste, which
      way
    Thou mightst deserve, or they impose this
      usage,
    Coming from us.

KENT: My lord; when at their
              home
    I did commend your Highness' letters to
      them,
    Ere I was risen from the place that showed
    My duty kneeling, came there a reeking
      post,
    Stewed in his haste, half breathless,
      panting forth
    From Goneril his mistress salutations;
    Delivered letters, spite of intermission,
    Which presently they read; on whose
      contents
    They summoned up their meiny, straight
      took horse,
    Commanded me to follow, and attend
    The leisure of their answer, gave me cold
      looks;
    And meeting here the other messenger,
    Whose welcome I perceived had poisoned
      mine,
    Being the very fellow which of late
    Displayed so saucily against your
      Highness,

    Having more man than wit about me,
      drew.
    He raised the house, with loud and coward
      cries;
    Your son and daughter found this trespass
      worth
    The shame which here it suffers.

FOOL: Winter's not gone yet, if the wild geese fly that way.
    Fathers that wear rags
    Do make their children blind,
    But fathers that bear bags
    Shall see their children kind.
    Fortune, that arrant whore,
    Ne'er turns the key to th' poor.
But for all this thou shalt have as many dolours for thy daughters as thou canst tell in a year.

LEAR: O how this mother swells up toward
      my heart!
    Hysterica passio, down thou climbing
      sorrow,
    Thy element's below. Where is this
      daughter?

KENT: With the earl, sir, here within.

LEAR: Follow
    me not;
    Stay here. *(Exit)*

GENTLEMAN: Made you no more offence but what you speak of?

KENT: None.

How chance the King comes with so small a number?

FOOL: An thou hadst been set i' th' stocks for that question, thou'dst well deserved it.

KENT: Why fool?

FOOL: We'll set thee to school to an ant, to teach thee there's no labouring i' th' winter. All that follow their noses are led by their eyes but blind men, and there's not a nose among twenty but can smell him that's stinking. Let go thy hold when a great wheel runs down a hill, lest it break thy neck with following. But the great one that goes upward, let him draw thee after. When a wise man gives thee better counsel, give me mine again; I would have none but knaves follow it, since a fool gives it.
    That sir, which serves and seeks for gain,
    And follows but for form
    Will pack when it begins to rain,
    And leave thee in the storm.

But I will tarry, the fool will stay,
And let the wise man fly.
The knave turns fool that runs away;
The fool no knave perdy.
KENT: Where learned you this, fool?
FOOL: Not i' th' stocks, fool.

(Enter LEAR *with* GLOUCESTER.*)*

LEAR: Deny to speak with me? They are sick,
   they are weary,
   They have travelled all the night! Mere
      fetches,
   The images of revolt and flying off.
   Fetch me a better answer.
GLOUCESTER: My dear lord,
   You know the fiery quality of the duke,
   How unremovable and fixed he is
   In his own course.
LEAR: Vengeance, plague, death, confusion!
   Fiery? What quality? Why Gloucester,
      Gloucester,
   I'd speak with the Duke of Cornwall, and
      his wife.
GLOUCESTER: Well my good lord, I have
   informed them so.
LEAR: Informed them? Dost thou understand
   me, man?
GLOUCESTER: Ay, my good lord.
LEAR: The King would speak with Cornwall;
   the dear father
   Would with his daughter speak,
      commands their service.
   Are they informed of this? My breath and
      blood!
   Fiery? The fiery duke? Tell the hot duke
      that—
   No, but not yet, may be he is not well;
   Infirmity doth still neglect all office
   Whereto our health is bound; we are not
      ourselves,
   When nature being oppressed, commands
      the mind
   To suffer with the body; I'll forbear,
   And am fallen out with my more headier
      will,
   To take the indisposed and sickly fit
   For the sound man. Death on my state!
      Wherefore
   Should he sit here? This act persuades me,
   That this remotion of the duke and her

Is practice only. Give me my servant forth.
Go tell the duke and's wife I'd speak with
   them.
Now, presently. Bid them come forth and
   hear me,
Or at their chamber door I'll beat the drum,
Till it cry sleep to death.
GLOUCESTER: I would have all well betwixt
you. *(Exit)*
LEAR: O me, my heart! My rising heart! But
down.
FOOL: Cry to it, nuncle, as the cockney did to
the eels, when she put 'em i' th' paste alive; she
knapped 'em o' th' coxcombs with a stick, and cried,
down wantons, down. 'Twas her brother, that in
pure kindness to his horse buttered his hay.

(Enter CORNWALL, REGAN, GLOUCESTER, *and*
SERVANTS.*)*

LEAR: Good morrow to you both.
CORNWALL: Hail to your
   Grace.

*(*KENT *is set at liberty.)*

REGAN: I am glad to see your Highness.
LEAR: Regan, I think you are. I know what
   reason
   I have to think so. If thou shouldst not be
      glad,
   I would divorce me from thy mother's
      tomb,
   Sepulchring an adultress. *(To* KENT*)* O are
      you free?
   Some other time for that.—Beloved Regan,
   Thy sister's naught. O Regan, she hath
      tied
   Sharp-toothed unkindness, like a vulture,
      here. *(Points to his heart)*
   I can scarce speak to thee; thou'lt not
      believe
   Of how depraved a quality—O Regan.
REGAN: I pray you, sir, take patience; I have
   hope
   You less know how to value her desert
   Than she to scant her duty.
LEAR: Say—how is
   that?
REGAN: I cannot think my sister in the least
   Would fail her obligation. If, sir,
      perchance

She have restrained the riots of your
    followers,
'Tis on such ground, and to such
    wholesome end,
As clear her from all blame.
LEAR: My curses on her.
REGAN: O sir, you are old;
    Nature in you stands on the very verge
    Of his confine. You should be ruled, and
       led
    By some discretion that discerns your state
    Better than you yourself. Therefore I pray
      you,
    That to our sister you do make return;
    Say you have wronged her.
LEAR: Ask her
    forgiveness?
    Do you but mark how this becomes the
      house—
    Dear daughter, I confess that I am old;
    Age is unnecessary, on my knees I beg
    That you'll vouchsafe me raiment, bed,
      and food. *(Kneels)*
REGAN: Good sir, no more; these are
    unsightly tricks.
    Return you to my sister.
LEAR: *(Rises)*   Never, Regan.
    She hath abated me of half my train;
    Looked black upon me, struck me with
      her tongue
    Most serpent-like, upon the very heart.
    All the stored vengeances of heaven fall
    On her ingrateful top. Strike her young
      bones,
    You taking airs, with lameness.
CORNWALL: Fie, sir, fie!
LEAR: You nimble lightnings, dart your
    blinding flames
    Into her scornful eyes. Infect her beauty,
    You fen-sucked fogs, drawn by the
      powerful sun,
    To fall and blister her.
REGAN: O the blessed gods,
    So will you wish on me when the rash
      mood—
LEAR: No, Regan, thou shalt never have my
    curse.
    Thy tender-hefted nature shall not give
    Thee o'er to harshness. Her eyes are fierce,
      but thine

Do comfort, and not burn. 'Tis not in thee
To grudge my pleasures, to cut off my
    train,
To bandy hasty words, to scant my sizes,
And in conclusion, to oppose the bolt
Against my coming in. Thou better
    know'st
The offices of nature, bond of childhood,
Effects of courtesy, dues of gratitude.
Thy half o' th' kingdom hast thou not
    forgot,
Wherein I thee endowed.
REGAN: Good sir, to th'
    purpose.
LEAR: Who put my man i' th' stocks?
(Tucket within)
CORNWALL: What trumpet's
    that?

(Enter OSWALD.*)*

REGAN: I know't—my sister's. This approves
    her letter,
    That she would soon be here.—Is your
      lady come?
LEAR: This is a slave, whose easy-borrowed
    pride
    Dwells in the fickle grace of her he
      follows.
    Out varlet, from my sight.
CORNWALL: What means
    your Grace?
LEAR: Who stocked my servant? Regan, I
    have good hope
    Thou didst not know on't.

(Enter GONERIL.*)*

               Who comes
    here? O heavens,
    If you do love old men, if your sweet sway
    Allow obedience, if you yourselves are old,
    Make it your cause. Send down, and take
      my part.
    (To GONERIL*)* Art not ashamed to look
      upon this beard?
    O Regan, will you take her by the hand?
GONERIL: Why not by th' hand, sir? How
    have I offended?
    All's not offence that indiscretion finds,
    And dotage terms so.

LEAR: O sides, you are too
    tough.
    Will you yet hold? How came my man i'
        th' stocks?
CORNWALL: I set him there, sir. But his
        own disorders
Deserved much less advancement.
LEAR: You?
    Did you?
REGAN: I pray you, father, being weak, seem
    so.
    If till the expiration of your month,
    You will return and sojourn with my
        sister,
    Dismissing half your train, come then to
        me.
    I am now from home, and out of that
        provision
    Which shall be needful for your
        entertainment.
LEAR: Return to her? And fifty men
        dismissed?
    No, rather I abjure all roofs, and choose
    To wage against the enmity o' th' air,
    To be a comrade with the wolf and owl,
    Necessity's sharp pinch. Return with her?
    Why the hot-blooded France, that
        dowerless took
    Our youngest born, I could as well be
        brought
    To knee his throne, and squire-like
        pension beg
    To keep base life afoot. Return with her?
    Persuade me rather to be slave and
        sumpter
    To this detested groom.
GONERIL: At your choice, sir.
LEAR: I prithee, daughter, do not make me
        mad.
    I will not trouble thee, my child; farewell.
    We'll no more meet, no more see one
        another.
    But yet thou art my flesh, my blood, my
        daughter;
    Or rather a disease that's in my flesh,
    Which I must needs call mine. Thou art a
        boil,
    A plague-sore, or embossed carbuncle
    In my corrupted blood. But I'll not chide
        thee;

Let shame come when it will, I do not call
    it;
I do not bid the thunder-bearer shoot,
Nor tell tales of thee to high-judging Jove.
Mend when thou canst, be better at thy
    leisure;
I can be patient, I can stay with Regan,
I and my hundred knights.
REGAN: Not altogether
    so:
    I looked not for you yet, nor am provided
    For your fit welcome. Give ear, sir, to my
        sister,
    For those that mingle reason with your
        passion
    Must be content to think you old, and
        so—
    But she knows what she does.
LEAR: Is this well
    spoken?
REGAN: I dare avouch it, sir. What, fifty
        followers?
    Is it not well? What should you need of
        more?
    Yea or so many, sith that both charge and
        danger
    Speak 'gainst so great a number? How in
        one house
    Should many people, under two
        commands,
    Hold amity? 'Tis hard, almost impossible.
GONERIL: Why might not you, my lord,
        receive attendance
    From those that she calls servants, or from
        mine?
REGAN: Why not, my lord? If then they
        chanced to slack ye,
    We could control them. If you will come
        to me—
    For now I spy a danger—I entreat you
    To bring but five and twenty; to no more
    Will I give place or notice.
LEAR: I gave you all.
REGAN: And in good time you
    gave it.
LEAR: Made you my guardians, my
        depositaries,
    But kept a reservation to be followed
    With such a number. What, must I come
        to you

With five and twenty? Regan, said you
  so?
REGAN: And speak't again, my lord; no more
  with me.
LEAR: Those wicked creatures yet do look
  well-favoured,
  When others are more wicked; not being
  the worst
  Stands in some rank of praise. *(To*
  GONERIL*)* I'll go with thee;
  Thy fifty yet doth double five and twenty,
  And thou art twice her love.
GONERIL: Hear me, my
  lord;
  What need you five and twenty? Ten? Or
  five?
  To follow in a house where twice so many
  Have a command to tend you?
REGAN: What need
  one?
LEAR: O reason not the need. Our basest
  beggars
  Are in the poorest thing superfluous.
  Allow not nature more than nature needs,
  Man's life is cheap as beast's. Thou art a
  lady;
  If only to go warm were gorgeous,
  Why nature needs not what thou gorgeous
  wear'st,
  Which scarcely keeps thee warm but for
  true need.
  You heavens, give me that patience,
  patience I need.
  You see me here, you gods, a poor old
  man,
  As full of grief as age, wretched in both.
  If it be you that stirs these daughters'
  hearts
  Against their father, fool me not so much
  To bear it tamely; touch me with noble
  anger,
  And let not women's weapons, water-
  drops,
  Stain my man's cheeks. No, you unnatural
  hags,
  I will have such revenges on you both,
  That all the world shall—I will do such
  things;
  What they are, yet I know not, but they
  shall be

The terrors of the earth. You think I'll
  weep.
No, I'll not weep. *(Storm and tempest)*
I have full cause of weeping; but this heart
Shall break into a hundred thousand flaws
Or e'er I'll weep. O fool, I shall go mad.

(Exeunt LEAR, GLOUCESTER, KENT, *and* FOOL.*)*

CORNWALL: Let us withdraw, 'twill be a
  storm.
REGAN: This house is little; the old man
  and's people
  Cannot be well bestowed.
GONERIL: 'Tis his own blame; hath put
  himself from rest,
  And must needs taste his folly.
REGAN: For his particular, I'll receive him
  gladly,
  But not one follower.
GONERIL: So am I purposed.
  Where is my Lord of Gloucester?
CORNWALL: Followed the old man forth—

(Enter GLOUCESTER.*)*

            He is returned.
GLOUCESTER: The King is in high rage.
CORNWALL: Whither is he
  going?
GLOUCESTER: He calls to horse, but will I
  know not whither.
CORNWALL: 'Tis best to give him way, he
  leads himself.
GONERIL: My lord, entreat him by no
  means to stay.
GLOUCESTER: Alack, the night comes on,
  and the high winds
  Do sorely ruffle; for many miles about
  There's scarce a bush.
REGAN: O sir, to wilful men
  The injuries that they themselves procure
  Must be their schoolmasters. Shut up your
  doors,
  He is attended with a desperate train,
  And what they may incense him to, being
  apt
  To have his ear abused, wisdom bids fear.
CORNWALL: Shut up your doors my lord,
  'tis a wild night.
  My Regan counsels well. Come out o' th'
  storm. *(Exeunt)*

ACT III

SCENE I

A heath. Storm still

(*Enter* KENT *and* GENTLEMAN, *at several doors.*)

KENT: Who's there, besides foul weather?
GENTLEMAN: One minded like the
    weather, most unquietly.
KENT: I know you. Where's the King?
GENTLEMAN: Contending with the fretful
    elements;
  Bids the wind blow the earth into the sea,
  Or swell the curled waters 'bove the main,
  That things might change or cease; tears
    his white hair,
  Which the impetuous blasts with eyeless
    rage
  Catch in their fury, and make nothing of;
  Strives in his little world of man to
    outstorm
  The to and fro conflicting wind and rain.
  This night, wherein the cub-drawn bear
    would couch,
  The lion, and the belly-pinched wolf
  Keep their fur dry, unbonneted he runs,
  And bids what will take all.
KENT: But who is
    with him?
GENTLEMAN: None but the fool, who
    labours to outjest
  His heart-struck injuries.
KENT: Sir, I do know
    you,
  And dare upon the warrant of my note
  Commend a dear thing to you. There is
    division,
  Although as yet the face of it is covered
  With mutual cunning, 'twixt Albany and
    Cornwall;
  Who have — as who have not, that their
    great stars
  Throned and set high — servants, who
    seem no less,
  Which are to France the spies and
    speculations
  Intelligent of our state. What hath been
    seen,
  Either in snuffs and packings of the dukes,
  Or the hard rein which both of them hath
    borne
  Against the old kind King, or something
    deeper,
  Whereof perchance these are but
    furnishings —
  But true it is, from France there comes a
    power
  Into this scattered kingdom, who already,
  Wise in our negligence, have secret feet
  In some of our best ports, and are at point
  To show their open banner. Now to you.
  If on my credit you dare build so far
  To make your speed to Dover, you shall
    find
  Some that will thank you, making just
    report
  Of how unnatural and bemadding sorrow
  The King hath cause to plain.
  I am a gentleman of blood and breeding,
  And from some knowledge and assurance,
    offer
  This office to you.
GENTLEMAN: I will talk further with you.
KENT: No, do not.
  For confirmation that I am much more
  Than my out-wall, open this purse, and
    take
  What it contains. If you shall see Cordelia,
  As fear not but you shall, show her this
    ring,
  And she will tell you who that fellow is
  That yet you do not know. Fie on this
    storm!
  I will go seek the King.
GENTLEMAN: Give me your hand. Have
    you no more to say?
KENT: Few words, but to effect more than all
    yet,
  That when we have found the King — in
    which your pain
  That way, I'll this — he that first lights on
    him
  Holla the other.

(*Exeunt at several doors*)

SCENE II

The same. Storm still

(Enter LEAR *and* FOOL.*)*

LEAR: Blow winds, and crack your cheeks.
    Rage, blow,
  You cataracts, and hurricanoes, spout
  Till you have drenched our steeples,
    drowned the cocks.
  You sulphurous and thought-executing
    fires,
  Vaunt-couriers of oak-cleaving
    thunderbolts,
  Singe my white head. And thou all-
    shaking thunder,
  Strike flat the thick rotundity o' th' world,
  Crack nature's moulds, all germens spill at
    once,
  That makes ingrateful man.
FOOL: O nuncle, Court holy water in a dry
house is better than this rainwater out o' door. Good
nuncle, in, ask thy daughters' blessing; here's a
night pities neither wise men, nor fools.
LEAR: Rumble thy bellyful. Spit fire, spout
    rain.
  Nor rain, wind, thunder, fire, are my
    daughters;
  I tax not you, you elements, with
    unkindness.
  I never gave you kingdom, called you
    children;
  You owe me no subscription. Then let
    fall
  Your horrible pleasure. Here I stand your
    slave,
  A poor, infirm, weak, and despised old
    man.
  But yet I call you servile ministers,
  That will with two pernicious daughters
    join
  Your high-engendered battles 'gainst a
    head
  So old and white. O, oho, 'tis foul.
FOOL: He that has a house to put's head in has
a good head-piece.
  The codpiece that will house,
  Before the head has any,
  The head and he shall louse;

So beggars marry many.
  The man that makes his toe,
  What he his heart should make,
  Shall of a corn cry woe,
  And turn his sleep to wake.
For there was never yet fair woman, but she made
mouths in a glass.
LEAR: No, I will be the pattern of all
    patience,
  I will say nothing.

(Enter KENT.*)*

KENT: Who's there?
FOOL: Marry here's grace, and a codpiece;
    that's a wise man, and a fool.
KENT: Alas sir are you here? Things that
    love night
  Love not such nights as these. The
    wrathful skies
  Gallow the very wanderers of the dark,
  And make them keep their caves. Since I
    was man,
  Such sheets of fire, such bursts of horrid
    thunder,
  Such groans of roaring wind, and rain, I
    never
  Remember to have heard. Man's nature
    cannot carry
  Th' affliction, nor the fear.
LEAR: Let the great
    gods
  That keep this dreadful pudder o'er our
    heads
  Find out their enemies now. Tremble,
    thou wretch,
  That hast within thee undivulged crimes,
  Unwhipped of justice. Hide thee, thou
    bloody hand;
  Thou perjured, and thou simular of virtue
  That art incestuous. Caitiff, to pieces
    shake,
  That under covert and convenient seeming
  Has practised on man's life. Close pent-up
    guilts,
  Rive your concealing continents, and cry

These dreadful summoners grace. I am a
man
More sinned against, than sinning.
KENT: Alack, bare-
headed!
Gracious my lord, hard by here is a hovel,
Some friendship will it lend you 'gainst
the tempest.
Repose you there, while I to this hard
house —
More harder than the stones whereof 'tis
raised,
Which even but now, demanding after
you,
Denied me to come in — return, and force
Their scanted courtesy.
LEAR: My wits begin to
turn.
Come on my boy. How dost, my boy? Art
cold?
I am cold myself. Where is this straw, my
fellow?
The art of our necessities is strange
That can make vile things precious. Come,
your hovel.
Poor fool and knave, I have one part in my
heart
That's sorry yet for thee.

FOOL: (Sings)
He that has and a little tiny wit,
    With hey, ho, the wind and the rain,
Must make content with his fortunes fit,
    Though the rain it raineth every day.
LEAR: True, boy. Come bring us to this
hovel.

(Exeunt LEAR and KENT.)

FOOL: This is a brave night to cool a courtezan.
I'll speak a prophecy ere I go:
    When priests are more in word than matter;
    When brewers mar their malt with water;
    When nobles are their tailors' tutors;
    No heretics burned, but wenches' suitors;
    When every case in law is right;
    No squire in debt, nor no poor knight;
    When slanders do not live in tongues;
    Nor cutpurses come not to throng;
    When usurers tell their gold i' th' field,
    And bawds and whores do churches build,
    Then shall the realm of Albion
    Come to great confusion.
    Then comes the time, who lives to see't,
    That going shall be used with feet.
This prophecy Merlin shall make, for I live before
his time. (Exit)

SCENE III

GLOUCESTER'S *castle*

(Enter GLOUCESTER and EDMUND.)

GLOUCESTER: Alack, alack Edmund, I like
not this unnatural dealing. When I desired their
leave that I might pity him, they took from me the
use of mine own house, charged me on pain of perpetual displeasure neither to speak of him, entreat
for him, nor any way sustain him.
EDMUND: Most savage and unnatural.
GLOUCESTER: Go to; say you nothing. There
is division between the dukes, and a worse matter
than that. I have received a letter this night — 'tis
dangerous to be spoken — I have locked the letter in
my closet; these injuries the King now bears will be
revenged home. There is part of a power already
footed; we must incline to the King. I will look him,
and privily relieve him; go you and maintain talk
with the duke, that my charity be not of him perceived. If he ask for me, I am ill, and gone to bed.
If I die for it, as no less is threatened me, the King
my old master must be relieved. There is strange
things toward, Edmund, pray you be careful. (Exit)
EDMUND: This courtesy, forbid thee, shall
the duke
Instantly know, and of that letter too.
This seems a fair deserving, and must
draw me
That which my father loses — no less than
all.
The younger rises when the old doth fall.
(Exit)

SCENE IV
The heath, before a hovel

(Enter LEAR, KENT, *and* FOOL.*)*

KENT: Here is the place, my lord; good my
    lord, enter.
    The tyranny of the open night's too rough
    For nature to endure.

(Storm still.)

LEAR: Let me alone.
KENT: Good my lord, enter here.
LEAR: Wilt break
    my heart?
KENT: I had rather break mine own. Good
    my lord, enter.
LEAR: Thou think'st 'tis much that this
    contentious storm
    Invades us to the skin; so 'tis to thee,
    But where the greater malady is fixed,
    The lesser is scarce felt. Thou'dst shun a
    bear,
    But if thy flight lay toward the roaring sea,
    Thou'dst meet the bear i' th' mouth.
        When the mind's free,
    The body's delicate; this tempest in my
    mind
    Doth from my senses take all feeling else
    Save what beats there. Filial ingratitude,
    Is it not as this mouth should tear this
    hand
    For lifting food to't? But I will punish
    home.
    No, I will weep no more. In such a night
    To shut me out! Pour on, I will endure.
    In such a night as this! O Regan,
        Goneril—
    Your old kind father, whose frank heart
        gave all—
    O that way madness lies, let me shun that.
    No more of that.
KENT: Good my lord, enter here.
LEAR: Prithee go in thyself, seek thine own
    ease.
    This tempest will not give me leave to
    ponder
    On things would hurt me more. But I'll go
    in.

    In boy, go first.—You houseless poverty—
    Nay, get thee in. I'll pray, and then I'll
    sleep.

(Exit FOOL *into the hovel.)*

    Poor naked wretches, wheresoe'er you are,
    That bide the pelting of this pitiless storm,
    How shall your houseless heads, and unfed
    sides,
    Your looped and windowed raggedness,
    defend you
    From seasons such as these? O I have ta'en
    Too little care of this! Take physic, pomp;
    Expose thyself to feel what wretches feel,
    That thou mayst shake the superflux to
    them,
    And show the heavens more just.
EDGAR: *(Within)* Fathom and half, fathom
    and half!
    Poor Tom!

(Enter FOOL *from the hovel.)*

    FOOL: Come not in here, nuncle, here's a
spirit. Help me, help me.
    KENT: Give me thy hand. Who's there?
    FOOL: A spirit, a spirit, he says his name's poor
Tom.
    KENT: What art thou that dost grumble there
i' th' straw? Come forth.

(Enter EDGAR *from the hovel, disguised as a
madman.)*

    EDGAR: Away, the foul fiend follows me.
Through the sharp hawthorn blow the winds.
Hum, go to thy cold bed and warm thee.
    LEAR: Didst thou give all to thy daughters?
And art thou come to this?
    EDGAR: Who gives any thing to poor Tom,
whom the foul fiend hath led through fire, and
through flame, through ford and whirlpool, o'er bog
and quagmire, that hath laid knives under his pillow, and halters in his pew, set ratsbane by his por-
ridge, made him proud of heart to ride on a bay trot-
ting-horse over four-inched bridges, to course his
own shadow for a traitor. Bless thy five wits, Tom's
a-cold. O do, de, do, de, do, de. Bless thee from

whirlwinds, star-blasting, and taking, do poor Tom some charity, whom the foul fiend vexes. There could I have him now—and there—and there again, and there.

(Storm still.)

LEAR: What, has his daughters brought him to this pass?

Couldst thou save nothing? Wouldst thou give 'em all?

FOOL: Nay, he reserved a blanket, else we had been all shamed.

LEAR: Now all the plagues that in the pendulous air

Hang fated o'er men's faults light on thy daughters.

KENT: He hath no daughters, sir.

LEAR: Death, traitor; nothing could have subdued nature

To such a lowness but his unkind daughters.

Is it the fashion, that discarded fathers Should have thus little mercy on their flesh?

Judicious punishment; 'twas this flesh begot

Those pelican daughters.

EDGAR: Pillicock sat on Pillicock-hill. Alow; alow, loo, loo!

FOOL: This cold night will turn us all to fools, and madmen.

EDGAR: Take heed o' th' foul fiend, obey thy parents, keep thy words justly, swear not, commit not with man's sworn spouse; set not thy sweet heart on proud array. Tom's a-cold.

LEAR: What hast thou been?

EDGAR: A servingman, proud in heart and mind; that curled my hair, wore gloves in my cap; served the lust of my mistress' heart, and did the act of darkness with her; swore as many oaths as I spake words, and broke them in the sweet face of heaven; one that slept in the contriving of lust, and waked to do it. Wine loved I deeply, dice dearly; and in woman out-paramoured the Turk. False of heart, light of ear, bloody of hand; hog in sloth, fox in stealth, wolf in greediness, dog in madness, lion in prey. Let not the creaking of shoes, nor the rustling of silks, betray thy poor heart to woman; keep thy foot out of brothels, thy hand out of plackets, thy pen from lenders' books, and defy the foul fiend.

Still through the hawthorn blows the cold wind; says suum, mun, nonny. Dolphin my boy, boy sessa, let him trot by.

(Storm still.)

LEAR: Thou wert better in a grave, than to answer with thy uncovered body this extremity of the skies. Is man no more than this? Consider him well. Thou ow'st the worm no silk, the beast no hide, the sheep no wool, the cat no perfume. Ha? Here's three on's are sophisticated. Thou art the thing itself; unaccommodated man is no more but such a poor, bare, forked animal as thou art. Off, off, you lendings! Come, unbutton here. *(Pulls at his clothes)*

FOOL: Prithee, nuncle, be contented, 'tis a naughty night to swim in. Now a little fire in a wild field were like an old lecher's heart, a small spark, all the rest on's body cold.

(Enter GLOUCESTER, *with a torch.)*

Look, here comes a walking fire.

EDGAR: This is the foul Flibbertigibbet; he begins at curfew, and walks till the first cock; he gives the web and the pin, squints the eye, and makes the hare-lip; mildews the white wheat, and hurts the poor creature of earth.

Swithold footed thrice the 'old;

He met the night-mare, and her nine-fold;

Bid her alight,

And her troth plight,

And, aroint thee, witch, aroint thee!

GLOUCESTER: How fares your Grace?

LEAR: What's he?

KENT: Who's there? What is't you seek?

GLOUCESTER: What are you there? Your names?

EDGAR: Poor Tom, that eats the swimming frog, the toad, the tadpole, the wall-newt and the water; that in the fury of his heart, when the foul fiend rages, eats cow-dung for sallets; swallows the old rat and the ditch-dog; drinks the green mantle of the standing pool; who is whipped from tithing to tithing, and stock-punished, and imprisoned; who hath had three suits to his back, six shirts to his body,

Horse to ride, and weapons to wear;

But mice, and rats, and such small deer,

Have been Tom's food, for seven long year.

Beware my follower. Peace, Smulkin, peace, thou
fiend.

    GLOUCESTER: What, hath your Grace no bet-
ter company?

    EDGAR: The prince of darkness is a gentle-
man. Modo he's called, and Mahu.

    GLOUCESTER: Our flesh and blood, my lord,
        is grown so vile,
    That it doth hate what gets it.

    EDGAR: Poor Tom's a-cold.

    GLOUCESTER: Go in with me; my duty
        cannot suffer
    T' obey in all your daughters' hard
        commands.
    Though their injunction be to bar my
        doors,
    And let this tyrannous night take hold
        upon you,
    Yet have I ventured to come seek you out,
    And bring you where both fire and food is
        ready.

    LEAR: First let me talk with this
        philosopher.
    What is the cause of thunder?

    KENT: Good my lord take his offer, go into
        the house.

    LEAR: I'll talk a word with this same learned
        Theban.
    What is your study?

    EDGAR: How to prevent the fiend, and to
        kill vermin.

    LEAR: Let me ask you one word in private.

    KENT: Importune him once more to go, my
        lord,
    His wits begin t' unsettle.

(Storm still.)

    GLOUCESTER: Canst thou
        blame him?
    His daughters seek his death. Ah, that
        good Kent,
    He said it would be thus—poor banished
        man.
    Thou sayst the King grows mad; I'll tell
        thee, friend,
    I am almost mad myself. I had a son,
    Now outlawed from my blood; he sought
        my life
    But lately, very late. I loved him, friend,
    No father his son dearer. True to tell thee,
    The grief hath crazed my wits. What a
        night's this!
    I do beseech your Grace—

    LEAR: O cry you
        mercy, sir.
    Noble philosopher, your company.

    EDGAR: Tom's a-cold.

    GLOUCESTER: In fellow, there, into the
        hovel; keep thee warm.

    LEAR: Come, let's in all.

    KENT: This way, my lord.

    LEAR: With him;
    I will keep still with my philosopher.

    KENT: Good my lord, soothe him; let him
        take the fellow.

    GLOUCESTER: Take him you on.

    KENT: Sirrah, come on; go along with us.

    LEAR: Come, good Athenian.

    GLOUCESTER: No words, no words, hush.

    EDGAR: Child Rowland to the dark tower
        came,
    His word was still, fie, foh, and fum,
    I smell the blood of a British man.

    (Exeunt)

SCENE V

GLOUCESTER'S *castle*

(Enter CORNWALL *and* EDMUND.*)*

    CORNWALL: I will have my revenge ere I
depart his house.

    EDMUND: How, my lord, I may be censured,
that nature thus gives way to loyalty, something
fears me to think of.

    CORNWALL: I now perceive, it was not alto-
gether your brother's evil disposition made him
seek his death; but a provoking merit set awork by
a reproveable badness in himself.

    EDMUND: How malicious is my fortune, that

I must repent to be just. This is the letter he spoke of, which approves him an intelligent party to the advantages of France. O heavens, that this treason were not, or not I the detector!

CORNWALL: Go with me to the duchess.

EDMUND: If the matter of this paper be certain, you have mighty business in hand.

CORNWALL: True or false, it hath made thee Earl of Gloucester. Seek out where thy father is, that he may be ready for our apprehension.

EDMUND: (Aside) If I find him comforting the King, it will stuff his suspicion more fully.—I will persevere in my course of loyalty, though the conflict be sore between that and my blood.

CORNWALL: I will lay trust upon thee; and thou shalt find a dearer father in my love. (Exeunt)

SCENE VI

An outbuilding of the castle

(Enter KENT *and* GLOUCESTER.)

GLOUCESTER: Here is better than the open air, take it thankfully. I will piece out the comfort with what addition I can. I will not be long from you.

KENT: All the power of his wits have given way to his impatience. The gods reward your kindness.

(Exit GLOUCESTER. *Enter* LEAR, EDGAR, *and* FOOL.)

EDGAR: Frateretto calls me, and tells me Nero is an angler in the lake of darkness. Pray, innocent, and beware the foul fiend.

FOOL: Prithee, nuncle, tell me, whether a madman be a gentleman or a yeoman?

LEAR: A king, a king.

FOOL: No, he's a yeoman that has a gentleman to his son; for he's a mad yeoman that sees his son a gentleman before him.

LEAR: To have a thousand with red burning spits
Come hissing in upon 'em—

EDGAR: The foul fiend bites my back.

FOOL: He's mad that trusts in the tameness of a wolf, a horse's health, a boy's love, or a whore's oath.

LEAR: It shall be done; I will arraign them straight.
(*To* EDGAR) Come, sit thou here, most learned Justice.
(*To the* FOOL) Thou, sapient sir, sit here.—
Now, you she-foxes!

EDGAR: Look where he stands and glares.—

Want'st thou eyes at trial, madam?
Come o'er the bourn Bessy to me.

FOOL: Her boat hath a leak,
And she must not speak,
Why she dares not come over to thee.

EDGAR: The foul fiend haunts poor Tom in the voice of a nightingale. Hopdance cries in Tom's belly for two white herring. Croak not, black angel, I have no food for thee.

KENT: How do you, sir? Stand you not so amazed.
Will you lie down and rest upon the cushions?

LEAR: I'll see their trial first. Bring in their evidence.
Thou robed man of justice, take thy place;
And thou his yoke-fellow of equity,
Bench by his side. (*To* KENT) You are o' th' commission,
Sit you too.

EDGAR: Let us deal justly.
Sleepest or wakest thou, jolly shepherd?
Thy sheep be in the corn,
And for one blast of thy minikin mouth
Thy sheep shall take no harm.
Purr. The cat is gray.

LEAR: Arraign her first; 'tis Goneril. I here take my oath before this honourable assembly, she kicked the poor King her father.

FOOL: Come hither, mistress. Is your name Goneril?

LEAR: She cannot deny it.

FOOL: Cry you mercy, I took you for a joint-stool.

LEAR: And here's another whose warped looks proclaim
What store her heart is made on. Stop her there!
Arms, arms, sword, fire! Corruption in the place!
False justicer, why hast thou let her 'scape?

EDGAR: Bless thy five wits.

KENT: O pity! Sir, where is the patience now
That you so oft have boasted to retain?

EDGAR: *(Aside)* My tears begin to take his part so much,
They mar my counterfeiting.

LEAR: The little dogs and all,
Tray, Blanch, and Sweetheart, see, they bark at me.

EDGAR: Tom will throw his head at them.
Avaunt you curs!
Be thy mouth or black or white,
Tooth that poisons if it bite;
Mastiff, greyhound, mongrel grim,
Hound or spaniel, brach or lym,
Or bobtail tike or trundle-tail,
Tom will make him weep and wail;
For with throwing thus my head,
Dogs leapt the hatch, and all are fled.
Do de, de, de. Sessa! Come, march to wakes and fairs and market towns. Poor Tom, thy horn is dry.

LEAR: Then let them anatomize Regan. See what breeds about her heart. Is there any cause in nature that makes these hard hearts? *(To* EDGAR*)* You sir, I entertain for one of my hundred; only I do not like the fashion of your garments. You will say they are Persian; but let them be changed.

KENT: Now, good my lord, lie here, and rest awhile.

LEAR: Make no noise, make no noise, draw the curtains.
So, so, we'll go to supper i' th' morning.

FOOL: And I'll go to bed at noon.

(Enter GLOUCESTER.*)*

GLOUCESTER: Come hither, friend. Where is the King my master?

KENT: Here, sir, but trouble him not, his wits are gone.

GLOUCESTER: Good friend, I prithee take him in thy arms;
I have o'erheard a plot of death upon him.
There is a litter ready, lay him in't,
And drive toward Dover, friend, where thou shalt meet
Both welcome and protection. Take up thy master.
If thou shouldst dally half an hour, his life,
With thine, and all that offer to defend him,
Stand in assured loss. Take up, take up;
And follow me, that will to some provision
Give thee quick conduct.

KENT: Oppressed nature sleeps.
This rest might yet have balmed thy broken sinews,
Which, if convenience will not allow,
Stand in hard cure. *(To* FOOL*)* Come help to bear thy master;
Thou must not stay behind.

GLOUCESTER: Come, come away.

(Exeunt KENT, GLOUCESTER, *and* FOOL, *bearing off* LEAR.*)*

EDGAR: When we our betters see bearing our woes,
We scarcely think our miseries our foes.
Who alone suffers, suffers most i' th' mind,
Leaving free things and happy shows behind;
But then the mind much sufferance doth o'erskip,
When grief hath mates, and bearing fellowship.
How light and portable my pain seems now,
When that which makes me bend, makes the King bow —
He childed as I fathered. Tom, away!
Mark the high noises; and thy self bewray,
When false opinion, whose wrong thoughts defile thee,
In thy just proof repeals and reconciles thee.
What will hap more to-night, safe 'scape the King.
Lurk, lurk.
(Exit)

SCENE VII

GLOUCESTER'S *castle*

(*Enter* CORNWALL, REGAN, GONERIL, EDMUND, *and* SERVANTS.)

CORNWALL: Post speedily to my lord your husband; show him this letter—the army of France is landed—seek out the traitor Gloucester.

REGAN: Hang him instantly.

GONERIL: Pluck out his eyes.

CORNWALL: Leave him to my displeasure. Edmund, keep you our sister company; the revenges we are bound to take upon your traitorous father are not fit for your beholding. Advise the duke where you are going, to a most festinate preparation; we are bound to the like. Our posts shall be swift and intelligent betwixt us. Farewell, dear sister; farewell, my Lord of Gloucester.

(*Enter* OSWALD.)

How now? Where's the King?

OSWALD: My Lord of Gloucester hath
  conveyed him hence.
 Some five or six and thirty of his knights,
 Hot questrists after him, met him at gate,
 Who with some other of the lords
  dependants,
 Are gone with him toward Dover; where
  they boast
 To have well armed friends.

CORNWALL: Get horses for
 your mistress.

GONERIL: Farewell, sweet lord, and sister.

CORNWALL: Edmund, farewell.

(*Exeunt* GONERIL, EDMUND, *and* OSWALD.)

        Go seek the
 traitor Gloucester,
 Pinion him like a thief, bring him before
 us.

(*Exeunt* SERVANTS.)

Though well we may not pass upon his
 life
Without the form of justice; yet our power
Shall do a court'sy to our wrath, which
 men
May blame, but not control.

(*Enter* GLOUCESTER, *brought in by* SERVANTS.)

         Who's there?
 The traitor?

REGAN: Ingrateful fox, 'tis he.

CORNWALL: Bind fast his corky arms.

GLOUCESTER: What means your Graces?
  Good my friends, consider
 You are my guests. Do me no foul play,
  friends.

CORNWALL: Bind him, I say.

REGAN: Hard, hard. (*She helps bind him.*) O filthy traitor!

GLOUCESTER: Unmerciful lady as you are, I'm none.

CORNWALL: To this chair bind him. Villain, thou shalt find— (REGAN *plucks his beard.*)

GLOUCESTER: By the kind gods, 'tis most
  ignobly done
 To pluck me by the beard.

REGAN: So white, and such a traitor

GLOUCESTER: Naughty
 lady,
 These hairs which thou dost ravish from
  my chin
 Will quicken, and accuse thee. I am your
  host;
 With robbers' hands my hospitable favours

 You should not ruffle thus. What will you
  do?

CORNWALL: Come, sir, what letters had you
 late from France?

REGAN: Be simple-answered, for we know
 the truth.

CORNWALL: And what confederacy have
 you with the traitors
 Late footed in the kingdom?

REGAN: To whose hands you have sent the
 lunatic King. Speak.

GLOUCESTER: I have a letter guessingly set
 down,
 Which came from one that's of a neutral
 heart,
 And not from one opposed.

CORNWALL: Cunning.

REGAN: And
   false.
CORNWALL: Where hast thou sent the
   King?
GLOUCESTER: To Dover.
REGAN: Wherefore to Dover? Wast thou not
   charged at peril—
CORNWALL: Wherefore to Dover? Let him
   answer that.
GLOUCESTER: I am tied to th' stake, and I
   must stand the course.
REGAN: Wherefore to Dover?
GLOUCESTER: Because I would not see thy
   cruel nails
   Pluck out his poor old eyes; nor thy fierce
   sister
   In his anointed flesh stick boarish fangs.
   The sea, with such a storm as his bare
   head
   In hell-black night endured, would have
   buoyed up
   And quenched the stelled fires;
   Yet, poor old heart, he help the heavens to
   rain.
   If wolves had at thy gate howled that stern
   time,
   Thou shouldst have said, good porter turn
   the key.
   All cruels else subscribe—but I shall see
   The winged vengeance overtake such
   children.
CORNWALL: See't shalt thou never. Fellows
   hold the chair.
   Upon these eyes of thine I'll set my foot.
GLOUCESTER: He that will think to live till
   he be old,
   Give me some help!—O cruel!—O you
   gods!
REGAN: One side will mock another—th'
   other too.
CORNWALL: If you see vengeance—
FIRST SERVANT: Hold
   your hand, my lord.
   I have served you ever since I was a child;
   But better service have I never done you
   Than now to bid you hold.
REGAN: How now, you
   dog!
FIRST SERVANT: If you did wear a beard
   upon your chin,

I'd shake it on this quarrel. What do you
   mean?
CORNWALL: My villain! *(Draws)*
FIRST SERVANT: Nay, then come on, and
   take the chance of anger.

(Draws. CORNWALL *is wounded.)*

REGAN: Give me thy sword. A peasant stand
   up thus?

(Takes a sword from another SERVANT *and stabs*
FIRST SERVANT.*)*

FIRST SERVANT: O I am slain! My lord, you
   have one eye left
   To see some mischief on him. O! *(Dies.)*
CORNWALL: Lest it see more, prevent it—
   out vile jelly!
   Where is thy lustre now?
GLOUCESTER: All dark and comfortless.
   Where's my son Edmund?
   Edmund, enkindle all the sparks of nature
   To quit this horrid act.
REGAN: Out, treacherous
   villain!
   Thous call'st on him that hates thee. It
   was he
   That made the overture of thy treasons to
   us;
   Who is too good to pity thee.
GLOUCESTER: O my follies!
   Then Edgar was abused.
   Kind gods, forgive me that, and prosper
   him.
REGAN: Go thrust him out at gates, and let
   him smell
   His way to Dover.

(Exit SERVANT *with* GLOUCESTER.*)*

How is't, my lord? How look you?
CORNWALL: I have received a hurt. Follow
   me, lady.
   Turn out that eyeless villain. Throw this
   slave
   Upon the dunghill. Regan, I bleed apace.
   Untimely comes this hurt. Give me your
   arm.

(Exit CORNWALL, *led by* REGAN.*)*

SECOND SERVANT: I'll never care what
    wickedness I do,
    If this man come to good.
THIRD SERVANT: If she live long,
    And in the end meet the old course of
    death,
    Women will all turn monsters.
SECOND SERVANT: Let's follow the old
    earl, and get the bedlam

To lead him where he would; his roguish
    madness
Allows itself to any thing.
THIRD SERVANT: Go thou. I'll fetch some
    flax and whites of eggs
To apply to his bleeding face. Now heaven
    help him.

(Exeunt separately.)

ACT IV

SCENE I
The heath

(Enter EDGAR.)

EDGAR: Yet better thus, and known to be
    contemned,
    Than still contemned and flattered. To be
    worst,
    The lowest and most dejected thing of
    fortune,
    Stands still in esperance, lives not in fear.
    The lamentable change is from the best:
    The worst returns to laughter. Welcome
    then,
    Thou unsubstantial air that I embrace.
    The wretch that thou hast blown unto the
    worst
    Owes nothing to thy blasts.

(Enter GLOUCESTER, led by OLD MAN.)

                 But who comes
    here?
    My father, poorly led? World, world, o
    world!
    But that thy strange mutations make us
    hate thee,
    Life would not yield to age.
OLD MAN: O my good
    lord,
    I have been your tenant, and your father's
    tenant,
    These fourscore years.
GLOUCESTER: Away, get thee away; good
    friend, be gone.
    Thy comforts can do me no good at all;
    Thee they may hurt.

OLD MAN: You cannot see your
    way.
GLOUCESTER: I have no way, and therefore
    want no eyes.
    I stumbled when I saw. Full oft 'tis seen,
    Our means secure us, and our mere defects
    Prove our commodities. O dear son Edgar,
    The food of thy abused father's wrath;
    Might I but live to see thee in my touch,
    I'd say I had eyes again.
OLD MAN: How now? Who's
    there?
EDGAR: *(Aside)* O gods! Who is't can say, I
    am at the worst?
    I am worse than e'er I was.
OLD MAN: 'Tis poor mad
    Tom.
EDGAR: *(Aside)* And worse I may be yet.
    The worst is not
    So long as we can say, this is the worst.
OLD MAN: Fellow, where goest?
GLOUCESTER: Is it a
    beggar-man?
OLD MAN: Madman and beggar too.
GLOUCESTER: He has some reason, else he
    could not beg.
    I' th' last night's storm, I such a fellow
    saw;
    Which made me think a man a worm.
    My son
    Came then into my mind, and yet my
    mind
    Was then scarce friends with him. I have
    heard more since.

As flies to wanton boys, are we to the gods;
They kill us for their sport.

EDGAR: *(Aside)* How should
  this be?
Bad is the trade that must play fool to
  sorrow,
Ang'ring itself and others.—Bless thee,
  master.

GLOUCESTER: Is that the naked fellow?

OLD MAN: Ay, my lord.

GLOUCESTER: Then prithee get thee away,
  if for my sake
Thou wilt o'ertake us hence a mile or
  twain
I' th' way toward Dover, do it for ancient
  love,
And bring some covering for this naked
  soul,
Which I'll entreat to lead me.

OLD MAN: Alack sir, he
  is mad.

GLOUCESTER: 'Tis the times' plague, when
  madmen lead the blind.
Do as I bid thee, or rather do thy pleasure.
Above the rest, be gone.

OLD MAN: I'll bring him the best 'parel that
  I have,
Come on't what will. *(Exit)*

GLOUCESTER: Sirrah, naked fellow.

EDGAR: Poor Tom's a-cold. *(Aside)* I cannot
daub it further.

GLOUCESTER: Come hither, fellow.

EDGAR: *(Aside)* And yet I must. Bless thy
sweet eyes, they bleed.

GLOUCESTER: Know'st thou the way to
Dover?

EDGAR: Both stile, and gate; horse-way, and
footpath. Poor Tom hath been scared out of his good
wits. Bless thee, good man's son, from the foul fiend.
Five fiends have been in poor Tom at once; of lust,
as Obidicut; Hobbididence prince of dumbness;
Mahu of stealing; Modo of murder; and Flibbertigibbet of mopping and mowing, who since possesses
chambermaids and waiting-women. So, bless thee,
master.

GLOUCESTER: Here, take this purse, thou
  whom the heavens' plagues
Have humbled to all strokes. That I am
  wretched
Makes thee the happier. Heavens, deal so
  still.
Let the superfluous and lust-dieted man,
That slaves your ordinance, that will not
  see
Because he does not feel, feel your power
  quickly;
So distribution should undo excess,
And each man have enough. Dost thou
  know Dover?

EDGAR: Ay, master.

GLOUCESTER: There is a cliff, whose high
  and bending head
Looks fearfully in the confined deep.
Bring me but to the very brim of it,
And I'll repair the misery thou dost bear
With something rich about me. From that
  place
I shall no leading need.

EDGAR: Give me thy arm;
  Poor Tom shall lead thee. *(Exeunt)*

SCENE II

Before ALBANY'S *palace*

(Enter GONERIL *and* EDMUND.*)*

GONERIL: Welcome, my lord, I marvel our
  mild husband
Not met us on the way.

(Enter OSWALD.*)*
    Now, where's your
master?

OSWALD: Madam, within; but never man so
  changed.
I told him of the army that was landed;
He smiled at it. I told him you were
  coming;
His answer was, the worse. Of Gloucester's
  treachery,
And of the loyal service of his son,

When I informed him, then he called me
   sot,
And told me I had turned the wrong side
   out.
What most he should dislike, seems
   pleasant to him;
What like, offensive.
GONERIL: *(To* EDMUND*)* Then shall you go
   no further.
Is it the cowish terror of his spirit,
That dares not undertake. He'll not feel
   wrongs,
Which tie him to an answer. Our wishes
   on the way
May prove effects. Back, Edmund, to my
   brother.
Hasten his musters, and conduct his
   powers,
I must change names at home, and give
   the distaff
Into my husband's hands. This trusty
   servant
Shall pass between us; ere long you are
   like to hear,
If you dare venture in your own behalf,
A mistress's command. Wear this; spare
   speech, *(Gives a favour)*
Decline your head. This kiss, if it durst
   speak,
Would stretch thy spirits up into the air.
Conceive, and fare thee well.
EDMUND: Yours, in the ranks of death.
GONERIL: My most dear
   Gloucester.

       (Exit EDMUND.*)*
O, the difference of man and man! To thee
A woman's services are due; my fool
Usurps my body.
OSWALD: Madam, here comes my
   lord. *(Exit)*

      (Enter ALBANY.*)*

GONERIL: I have been worth the whistle.
ALBANY: O Goneril,
   You are not worth the dust which the
     rude wind
   Blows in your face. I fear your disposition.
   That nature which contemns its origin
   Cannot be bordered certain in itself;

   She that herself will sliver and disbranch
   From her material sap, perforce must
     wither,
   And come to deadly use.
GONERIL: No more; the text is foolish.
ALBANY: Wisdom and goodness to the vile
     seem vile,
   Filths savour but themselves. What have
     you done?
   Tigers, not daughters, what have you
     performed?
   A father, and a gracious aged man,
   Whose reverence even the head-lugged
     bear would lick,
   Most barbarous, most degenerate, have you
     madded.
   Could my good brother suffer you to do it?
   A man, a Prince, by him so benefited.
   If that the heavens do not their visible
     spirits
   Send quickly down to tame these vile
     offences,
   It will come,
   Humanity must perforce prey on itself,
   Like monsters of the deep.
GONERIL: Milk-livered
   man,
   That bear'st a cheek for blows, a head for
     wrongs,
   Who hast not in thy brows an eye
     discerning
   Thine honour from thy suffering, that not
     know'st
   Fools do those villains pity who are
     punished
   Ere they have done their mischief.
     Where's thy drum?
   France spreads his banners in our noiseless
     land
   With plumed helm. Thy state begins to
     threat,
   Whilst thou a moral fool sits still and
     cries,
   Alack why does he so?
ALBANY: See thyself, devil.
   Proper deformity shows not in the fiend
   So horrid as in woman.
GONERIL: O vain fool.
ALBANY: Thou changed and self-covered
     thing, for shame

Be-monster not thy feature. Were't my
    fitness
To let these hands obey my blood,
They are apt enough to dislocate and tear
Thy flesh and bones. Howe'er thou art a
    fiend,
A woman's shape doth shield thee.
GONERIL: Marry, your manhood—mew!

(Enter MESSENGER.*)*

ALBANY: What news?
MESSENGER: O my good lord, the Duke of
    Cornwall's dead,
Slain by his servant, going to put out
The other eye of Gloucester.
ALBANY: Gloucester's
    eyes!
MESSENGER: A servant that he bred, thrilled
    with remorse,
Opposed against the act; bending his sword
To his great master, who thereat enraged,
Flew on him, and amongst them felled
    him dead,
But not without that harmful stroke
    which since
Hath plucked him after..
ALBANY: This shows you
    are above,
You justicers, that these our nether crimes
So speedily can venge. But, o poor
    Gloucester,
Lost he his other eye?

MESSENGER: Both, both, my lord.
This letter, madam, craves a speedy
    answer;
'Tis from your sister.
GONERIL: *(Aside)* One way I like this well.
But being widow, and my Gloucester with
    her,
May all the building in my fancy pluck
Upon my hateful life. Another way
The news is not so tart.—I'll read, and
    answer. *(Exit)*
ALBANY: Where was his son, when they did
    take his eyes?
MESSENGER: Come with my lady hither.
ALBANY: He is not here.
MESSENGER: No, my good lord, I met him
    back again.
ALBANY: Knows he the wickedness?
MESSENGER: Ay, my good lord; 'twas he
    informed against him,
And quit the house on purpose that their
    punishment
Might have the freer course.
ALBANY: Gloucester, I
    live
To thank thee for the love thou show'dst
    the King,
And to revenge thine eyes. Come hither
    friend,
Tell me what more thou know'st.
    (Exeunt)

SCENE III

The French camp, near Dover

(Enter KENT *and* GENTLEMAN.*)*

KENT: Why the King of France is so suddenly
gone back, know you no reason?
GENTLEMAN: Something he left imperfect
in the state, which since his coming forth is thought
of; which imports to the kingdom so much fear and
danger, that his personal return was most required
and necessary.
KENT: Who hath he left behind him general?
GENTLEMAN: The Marshal of France Monsieur La Far.

KENT: Did your letters pierce the Queen to
any demonstration of grief?
GENTLEMAN: Ay, sir, she took them, read
    them in my presence,
And now and then an ample tear trilled
    down
Her delicate cheek; it seemed she was a
    queen
Over her passion, who most rebel-like,
Sought to be king o'er her.
KENT: O then it moved
    her.

GENTLEMAN: Not to a rage; patience and
    sorrow strove
  Who should express her goodliest. You
    have seen
  Sunshine and rain at once; her smiles and
    tears
  Were like a better way; those happy
    smilets
  That played on her ripe lip seemed not to
    know
  What guests were in her eyes, which
    parted thence
  As pearls from diamonds dropped. In brief,
  Sorrow would be a rarity most beloved,
  If all could so become it.
KENT: Made she no
    verbal question?
GENTLEMAN: Faith, once or twice she
    heaved the name of father
  Pantingly forth, as if it pressed her heart;
  Cried, sisters, sisters, shame of ladies,
    sisters!
  Kent! Father! Sisters! What, i' th' storm? I'
    th' night?
  Let pity not be believed. There she shook
  The holy water from her heavenly eyes,
  And clamour-moistened; then away she
    started
  To deal with grief alone.
KENT: It is the stars,
  The stars above us govern our conditions,
  Else one self mate and make could not
    beget
  Such different issues. You spoke not with
    her since?
GENTLEMAN: No.

KENT: Was this before the King returned?
GENTLEMAN: No, since.
KENT: Well, sir, the poor distressed Lear's i'
    th' town,
  Who sometime in his better tune
    remembers
  What we are come about, and by no
    means
  Will yield to see his daughter.
GENTLEMAN: Why, good
    sir?
KENT: A sovereign shame so elbows him; his
    own unkindness
  That stripped her from his benediction,
    turned her
  To foreign casualties, gave her dear rights
  To his dog-hearted daughters, these things
    sting
  His mind so venomously that burning
    shame
  Detains him from Cordelia.
GENTLEMAN: Alack poor
    gentleman!
KENT: Of Albany's and Cornwall's powers
    you heard not?
GENTLEMAN: 'Tis so, they are afoot.
KENT: Well, sir, I'll bring you to our master
    Lear,
  And leave you to attend him. Some dear
    cause
  Will in concealment wrap me up awhile;
  When I am known aright you shall not
    grieve,
  Lending me this acquaintance. I pray you
    go
  Along with me. *(Exeunt)*

SCENE IV
The same

(Enter, with drum and colours, CORDELIA, DOCTOR,
and SOLDIERS.)

CORDELIA: Alack, 'tis he; why he was met
    even now
  As mad as the vexed sea, singing aloud,
  Crowned with rank fumiter and furrow-
    weeds,

With hardocks, hemlock, nettles, cuckoo-
    flowers,
Darnel, and all the idle weeds that grow
In our sustaining corn. A century send
    forth;
Search every acre in the high-grown field,
And bring him to our eye. *(Exit* OFFICER*)*
  What can man's wisdom

In the restoring his bereaved sense?
He that helps him take all my outward
  worth.
DOCTOR: There is means, madam.
  Our foster-nurse of nature is repose,
  The which he lacks; that to provoke in
    him
  Are many simples operative, whose power
  Will close the eye of anguish.
CORDELIA: All blessed
    secrets,
  All you unpublished virtues of the earth,
  Spring with my tears, be aidant and
    remediate
  In the good man's distress. Seek, seek for
    him,
  Lest his ungoverned rage dissolve the life
  That wants the means to lead it.

(Enter MESSENGER.*)*

MESSENGER: News,
    madam;
  The British powers are marching
    hitherward.
CORDELIA: 'Tis known before. Our
    preparation stands
  In expectation of them. O dear father,
  It is thy business that I go about;
  Therefore great France
  My mourning and importuned tears hath
    pitied.
  No blown ambition doth our arms incite,
  But love, dear love, and our aged father's
    right.
  Soon may I hear, and see him. *(Exeunt)*

SCENE V

GLOUCESTER'S *castle*

(Enter REGAN *and* OSWALD.*)*

REGAN: But are my brother's powers set
    forth?
OSWALD: Ay, madam.
REGAN: Himself in person there?
OSWALD: Madam,
    with much ado.
  Your sister is the better soldier.
REGAN: Lord Edmund spake not with your
    lord at home?
OSWALD: No, madam.
REGAN: What might import my sister's
    letter to him?
OSWALD: I know not, lady.
REGAN: Faith, he is posted hence on serious
    matter.
  It was great ignorance, Gloucester's eyes
    being out,
  To let him live. Where he arrives, he
    moves
  All hearts against us. Edmund, I think, is
    gone,
  In pity of his misery, to dispatch
  His nighted life; moreover to descry

The strength o' th' enemy.
OSWALD: I must needs after him, madam,
    with my letter.
REGAN: Our troops set forth to-morrow, stay
    with us.
  The ways are dangerous.
OSWALD: I may not, madam.
  My lady charged my duty in this business.
REGAN: Why should she write to Edmund?
    Might not you
  Transport her purposes by word? Belike,
  Something, I know not what—I'll love
    thee much,
  Let me unseal the letter.
OSWALD: Madam, I had
    rather—
REGAN: I know your lady does not love her
    husband,
  I am sure of that; and at her late being
    here
  She gave strange œillades and most
    speaking looks
  To noble Edmund. I know you are of her
    bosom.
OSWALD: I, madam?

REGAN: I speak in understanding; y'are, I know't,
Therefore I do advise you take this note.
My lord is dead; Edmund and I have talked,
And more convenient is he for my hand
Than for your lady's. You may gather more.
If you do find him, pray you give him this;
And when your mistress hears thus much from you,
I pray, desire her call her wisdom to her.
So fare you well.
If you do chance to hear of that blind traitor,
Preferment falls on him that cuts him off.
OSWALD: Would I could meet him, madam, I should show
What party I do follow.
REGAN: Fare thee well.
(Exeunt)

SCENE VI

The country near Dover

(Enter GLOUCESTER, and EDGAR dressed like a peasant.)

GLOUCESTER: When shall I come to th' top of that same hill?
EDGAR: You do climb up it now. Look how we labour.
GLOUCESTER: Methinks the ground is even.
EDGAR: Horrible steep.
Hark, do you hear the sea?
GLOUCESTER: No, truly.
EDGAR: Why then your other senses grow imperfect
By your eyes' anguish.
GLOUCESTER: So may it be indeed.
Methinks thy voice is altered, and thou speak'st
In better phrase and matter than thou didst.
EDGAR: Y'are much deceived. In nothing am I changed
But in my garments.
GLOUCESTER: Methinks y'are better spoken.
EDGAR: Come on, sir, here's the place; stand still. How fearful
And dizzy 'tis, to cast one's eyes so low.
The crows and choughs that wind the midway air
Show scarce so gross as beetles. Half way down
Hangs one that gathers samphire —
dreadful trade.
Methinks he seems no bigger than his head.
The fishermen, that walk upon the beach,
Appear like mice; and yond tall anchoring bark,
Diminished to her cock; her cock, a buoy
Almost too small for sight. The murmuring surge,
That on th' unnumbered idle pebble chafes,
Cannot be heard so high. I'll look no more,
Lest my brain turn, and the deficient sight
Topple down headlong.
GLOUCESTER: Set me where you stand.
EDGAR: Give me your hand. You are now within a foot
Of th' extreme verge. For all beneath the moon
Would I not leap upright.
GLOUCESTER: Let go my hand.
Here, friend, 's another purse; in it a jewel
Well worth a poor man's taking. Fairies and gods
Prosper it with thee. Go thou further off,
Bid me farewell, and let me hear thee going.
EDGAR: Now fare ye well, good sir.
GLOUCESTER: With all my heart.
EDGAR: *(Aside)* Why I do trifle thus with his despair,
Is done to cure it.

GLOUCESTER: *(Kneels)* O you mighty gods!
This world I do renounce, and in your sights
Shake patiently my great affliction off.
If I could bear it longer, and not fall
To quarrel with your great opposeless wills,
My snuff and loathed part of nature should
Burn itself out. If Edgar live, o bless him.
Now fellow, fare thee well.
EDGAR: Gone sir—farewell.
(GLOUCESTER *falls forward*)
(Aside) And yet I know not how conceit may rob
The treasury of life, when life itself
Yields to the theft. Had he been where he thought,
By this had thought been past. Alive or dead?—
Ho, you sir! Friend! Hear you sir, speak.
(Aside) Thus might he pass indeed; yet he revives.—
What are you, sir?
GLOUCESTER: Away, and let me die.
EDGAR: Hadst thou been aught but gossamer, feathers, air,
So many fathom down precipitating,
Thou'dst shivered like an egg; but thou dost breathe.
Hast heavy substance, bleed'st not, speak'st, art sound.
Ten masts at each make not the altitude
Which thou hast perpendicularly fell.
Thy life's miracle. Speak yet again.
GLOUCESTER: But have I fall'n or no?
EDGAR: From the dread summit of this chalky bourn.
Look up a height, the shrill-gorged lark so far
Cannot be seen or heard; do but look up.
GLOUCESTER: Alack, I have no eyes.
Is wretchedness deprived that benefit
To end itself by death? 'Twas yet some comfort,
When misery could beguile the tyrant's rage,
And frustrate his proud will.
EDGAR: Give me your arm.

Up. So. How is't? Feel you your legs? You stand.
GLOUCESTER: Too well, too well.
EDGAR: This is above all strangeness.
Upon the crown o' th' cliff, what thing was that
Which parted from you?
GLOUCESTER: A poor unfortunate beggar.
EDGAR: As I stood here below, methought his eyes
Were two full moons; he had a thousand noses,
Horns whelked and waved like the enridged sea.
It was some fiend. Therefore thou happy father,
Think that the clearest gods, who make them honours
Of men's impossibilities, have preserved thee.
GLOUCESTER: I do remember now; henceforth I'll bear
Affliction, till it do cry out itself,
Enough, enough, and die. That thing you speak of,
I took it for a man; often 'twould say,
The fiend, the fiend; he led me to that place.
EDGAR: Bear free and patient thoughts.

(Enter LEAR, his hat bedecked with weeds and flowers.)
                              But who comes here?
The safer sense will ne'er accommodate
His master thus.
LEAR: No, they cannot touch me for coming;
I am the King himself.
EDGAR: *(Aside)* O thou side-piercing sight!
LEAR: Nature's above art in that respect.
There's your press-money. That fellow handles his
bow like a crow-keeper; draw me a clothier's yard.
Look, look, a mouse! Peace, peace, this piece of
toasted cheese will do't. There's my gauntlet, I'll
prove it on a giant. Bring up the brown bills. O well
flown, bird; i' th' clout, i' th' clout. Hewgh! Give
the word.
EDGAR: Sweet marjoram.
LEAR: Pass.

GLOUCESTER: I know that voice.

LEAR: Ha! Goneril with a white beard! They flattered me like a dog, and told me I had white hairs in my beard, ere the black ones were there. To say ay, and no, to everything that I said! Ay, and no too, was no good divinity. When the rain came to wet me once, and the wind to make me chatter; when the thunder would not peace at my bidding; there I found 'em, there I smelt 'em out. Go to, they are not men o' their words; they told me I was every thing. 'Tis a lie, I am not ague-proof.

GLOUCESTER: The trick of that voice I do
    well remember;
  Is't not the King?

LEAR: Ay, every inch a King:
  When I do stare, see how the subject
    quakes.
  I pardon that man's life. What was thy
    cause?
  Adultery?
  Thou shalt not die. Die for adultery? No,
  The wren goes to't, and the small gilded
    fly
  Does lecher in my sight.
  Let copulation thrive; for Gloucester's
    bastard son
  Was kinder to his father than my
    daughters
  Got 'tween the lawful sheets.
  To't luxury pell-mell, for I lack soldiers.
  Behold yond simpering dame,
  Whose face between her forks presages
    snow,
  That minces virtue, and does shake the
    head
  To hear of pleasure's name—
  The fitchew nor the soiled horse goes to't
  With a more riotous appetite.
  Down from the waist they are centaurs,
  Though women all above;
  But to the girdle do the gods inherit,
  Beneath is all the fiends';
  There's hell, there's darkness, there is the
    sulphurous pit,
  Burning, scalding, stench, consumption.
    Fie, fie, fie; pah, pah! Give me an ounce
    of civet; good apothecary, sweeten my
    imagination.
  There's money for thee.

GLOUCESTER: O let me kiss that hand.

LEAR: Let me wipe it first, it smells of mortality.

GLOUCESTER: O ruined piece of nature; this
    great world
  Shall so wear out to naught. Dost thou
    know me?

LEAR: I remember thine eyes well enough. Dost thou squint at me? No, do thy worst, blind Cupid, I'll not love. Read thou this challenge; mark but the penning of it.

GLOUCESTER: Were all thy letters suns, I could not see one.

EDGAR: (Aside) I would not take this from
    report—it is,
  And my heart breaks at it.

LEAR: Read.

GLOUCESTER: What, with the case of eyes?

LEAR: O ho, are you there with me? No eyes in your head, nor no money in your purse? Your eyes are in a heavy case, your purse in a light, yet you see how this world goes.

GLOUCESTER: I see it feelingly.

LEAR: What, art mad? A man may see how this world goes, with no eyes. Look with thine ears. See how yond justice rails upon yond simple thief. Hark in thine ear. Change places; and handy-dandy, which is the justice, which is the thief? Thou hast seen a farmer's dog bark at a beggar?

GLOUCESTER: Ay sir.

LEAR: An the creature run from the cur,
    there thou mightst behold the great
    image of authority—a dog's obeyed in
    office.
  Thou, rascal beadle, hold thy bloody hand;
  Why dost thou lash that whore? Strip
    thine own back;
  Thou hotly lusts to use her in that kind
  For which thou whipst her. The usurer
    hangs the cozener.
  Through tattered clothes small vices do
    appear;
  Robes and furred gowns hide all. Plate sin
    with gold,
  And the strong lance of justice hurtless
    breaks.
  Arm it in rags, a pigmy's straw does pierce
    it.
  None does offend, none—I say, none; I'll
    able 'em.
  Take that of me, my friend, who have the
    power
  To seal the accuser's lips. Get thee glass
    eyes,

And like a scurvy politician, seem
 To see the things thou dost not.—Now,
  now, now, now.
 Pull off my boots; harder, harder; so.
EDGAR: *(Aside)* O matter and impertinency
  mixed;
 Reason in madness.
LEAR: If thou wilt weep my fortunes, take
  my eyes.
 I know thee well enough, thy name is
  Gloucester.
 Thou must be patient; we came crying
  hither.
 Thou know'st, the first time that we smell
  the air
 We wawl, and cry. I will preach to thee.
  Mark. *(Takes off his hat)*
GLOUCESTER: Alack, alack the day!
LEAR: When we are born, we cry that we are
  come
 To this great stage of fools.—This a good
  block;
 It were a delicate stratagem to shoe
 A troop of horse with felt. I'll put't in
  proof,
 And when I have stol'n upon these son-in-
  laws,
 Then, kill, kill, kill, kill, kill, kill!

(Enter GENTLEMAN, *with* ATTENDANTS.*)*

GENTLEMAN: O here he is; lay hand upon
  him. Sir,
 Your most dear daughter—
LEAR: No rescue? What, a prisoner? I am
  even
 The natural fool of fortune. Use me well,
 You shall have ransom. Let me have
  surgeons,
 I am cut to th' brains
GENTLEMAN: You shall have any
  thing.
LEAR: No seconds? All myself?
 Why, this would make a man a man of
  salt,
 To use his eyes for garden water-pots,
 Ay and laying autumn's dust.
GENTLEMAN: Good sir—
LEAR: I will die bravely, like a smug
  bridegroom. What!
 I will be jovial. Come, come, I am a King,
 My masters; know you that.

GENTLEMAN: You are a royal one, and we
  obey you.
LEAR: Then there's life in't. Come, an you
  get it, you shall get it by running. Sa,
  sa, sa, sa.

(Exit running. ATTENDANTS *follow.)*

GENTLEMAN: A sight most pitiful in the
  meanest wretch,
 Past speaking of in a King. Thou hast a
  daughter,
 Who redeems nature from the general
  curse
 Which twain have brought her to.
EDGAR: Hail, gentle sir.
GENTLEMAN: Sir, speed you.
 What's your will?
EDGAR: Do you hear aught, sir, of a battle
  toward?
GENTLEMAN: Most sure, and vulgar. Every
  one hears that,
 Which can distinguish sound.
EDGAR: But by your
  favour;
 How near's the other army?
GENTLEMAN: Near, and on speedy foot; the
  main descry
 Stands on the hourly thought.
EDGAR: I thank you
  sir, that's all.
GENTLEMAN: Though that the Queen on
  special cause is here,
 Her army is moved on.
EDGAR: I thank you, sir.

(Exit GENTLEMAN.*)*

GLOUCESTER: You ever gentle gods, take
  my breath from me;
 Let not my worser spirit tempt me again
 To die before you please.
EDGAR: Well pray you,
  father.
GLOUCESTER: Now good sir, what are you?
EDGAR: A most poor man, made tame to
  fortune's blows;
 Who, by the art of known and feeling
  sorrows,
 Am pregnant to good pity. Give me your
  hand,
 I'll lead you to some biding.

GLOUCESTER: Hearty thanks.
  The bounty and the benison of heaven
  To boot, and boot.

(Enter OSWALD.*)*

OSWALD: A proclaimed prize;
    most happy!
  That eyeless head of thine was first framed
    flesh
  To raise my fortunes. Thou old unhappy
    traitor,
  Briefly thyself remember — the sword is
    out
  That must destroy thee.
GLOUCESTER: Now let thy
    friendly hand
  Put strength enough to't.

*(*EDGAR *interposes.)*

OSWALD: Wherefore, bold
    peasant,
  Dar'st thou support a published traitor?
    Hence,
  Lest that th' infection of his fortune take
  Like hold on thee. Let go his arm.
EDGAR: Chill not let go zir, without vurther
'casion.
  OSWALD: Let go, slave, or thou diest.
  EDGAR: Good gentleman, go your gait, and let
poor volk pass. An chud ha' bin zwaggered out of
my life, 'twould not ha' bin zo long as 'tis, by a vort-
night. Nay, come not near th' old man; keep out che
vor ye, or ise try whether your costard or my ballow
be the harder; chill be plain with you.
  OSWALD: Out, dunghill! *(Thrusts at him)*
  EDGAR: Chill pick your teeth, zir; come, no
matter vor your foins.

(They fight. OSWALD *falls.)*

OSWALD: Slave, thou hast slain me. Villain,
    take my purse;
  If ever thou wilt thrive, bury my body,
  And give the letters which thou find'st
    about me
  To Edmund Earl of Gloucester; seek him
    out
  Upon the English party. O untimely
    death!
  Death! (Dies)
EDGAR: I know thee well. A serviceable
    villain,

As duteous to the vices of thy mistress
  As badness would desire.
GLOUCESTER: What, is he dead?
EDGAR: Sit down, father; rest you.
  Let's see these pockets; the letters that he
    speaks of
  May be my friends. He's dead; I am only
    sorry
  He had no other deathsman. Let us see.
  Leave, gentle wax; and manners, blame us
    not.
  To know our enemies' minds, we'd rip
    their hearts;
  Their papers is more lawful. *(Reads)*
Let our reciprocal vows be remembered. You
have many opportunities to cut him off: if your
will want not, time and place will be fruitfully
offered. There is nothing done, if he return the con-
queror: then am I the prisoner and his bed my gaol;
from the loathed warmth whereof deliver me, and
supply the place for your labour.
    Your—wife, so I would say—
      Affectionate servant,
        Goneril.
  O indistinguished space of woman's will!
  A plot upon her virtuous husband's life,
  And the exchange my brother. Here in
    the sands,
  Thee I'll rake up, the post unsanctified
  Of murderous lechers; and in the mature
    time,
  With this ungracious paper strike the sight
  Of the death-practised duke. For him 'tis
    well,
  That of thy death and business I can tell.
GLOUCESTER: The King is mad: how stiff is
    my vile sense,
  That I stand up, and have ingenious
    feeling
  Of my huge sorrows! Better I were distract;
  So should my thoughts be severed from
    my griefs,
  And woes, by wrong imaginations, lose
  The knowledge of themselves.

(Drum afar off.)

EDGAR: Give me
    your hand.
  Far off methinks I hear the beaten drum.
  Come, father, I'll bestow you with a
    friend. *(Exeunt)*

SCENE VII

Before a tent in the French camp

(Enter CORDELIA *and* KENT. DOCTOR *and* GENTLEMAN *follow.)*

CORDELIA: O thou good Kent, how shall I
    live and work,
    To match thy goodness? My life will be
    too short,
    And every measure fail me.
KENT: To be acknowledged madam, is
    o'erpaid.
    All my reports go with the modest truth;
    Nor more, nor clipped, but so.
CORDELIA: Be better
    suited;
    These weeds are memories of those worser
    hours.
    I prithee put them off.
KENT: Pardon, dear madam,
    Yet to be known shortens my made intent.
    My boon I make it, that you know me not
    Till time and I think meet.
CORDELIA: Then be't so, my good lord. *(To*
    DOCTOR*)* How does the King?
DOCTOR: Madam, sleeps still.
CORDELIA: O you kind gods,
    Cure this great breach in his abused
    nature.
    Th' untuned and jarring senses, o wind up
    Of this child-changed father.
DOCTOR: So please your
    Majesty
    That we may wake the King? He hath
    slept long.
CORDELIA: Be governed by your knowledge,
    and proceed
    I' th' sway of your own will. Is he arrayed?
GENTLEMAN: Ay, madam, in the heaviness
    of sleep
    We put fresh garments on him.
DOCTOR: Be by, good madam, when we do
    awake him.
    I doubt not of his temperance.
CORDELIA: Very well.
DOCTOR: Please you draw near.—Louder the
    music there.

(Music. DOCTOR *draws curtains.* LEAR *discovered on
a couch.)*

CORDELIA: O my dear father! Restoration
    hang
    Thy medicine on my lips, and let this kiss
    Repair those violent harms that my two
    sisters
    Have in thy reverence made.
KENT: Kind and dear
    Princess.
CORDELIA: Had you not been their father,
    these white flakes
    Did challenge pity of them. Was this a face
    To be opposed against the warring winds,
    To stand against the deep dread-bolted
    thunder,
    In the most terrible and nimble stroke
    Of quick, cross lightning, to watch—poor
    perdu—
    With this thin helm? Mine enemy's dog,
    Though he had bit me, should have stood
    that night
    Against my fire; and wast thou fain, poor
    father,
    To hovel thee with swine and rogues
    forlorn,
    In short and musty straw? Alack, alack,
    'Tis wonder that thy life and wits at once
    Had not concluded all. He wakes, speak to
    him.
DOCTOR: Madam, do you, 'tis fittest.
CORDELIA: How does my royal lord? How
    fares your Majesty?
LEAR: You do me wrong to take me out o' th'
    grave.
    Thou art a soul in bliss, but I am bound
    Upon a wheel of fire, that mine own tears
    Do scald like molten lead.
CORDELIA: Sir, do you know
    me?
LEAR: You are a spirit, I know; where did
    you die?
CORDELIA: Still, still, far wide.
DOCTOR: He's scarce awake, let him alone
    awhile.
LEAR: Where have I been? Where am I? Fair
    daylight?
    I am mightily abused; I should e'en die
    with pity,

To see another thus. I know not what to
  say.
I will not swear these are my hands; let's
  see—
I feel this pin prick. Would I were assured
Of my condition.
CORDELIA: O look upon me, sir.
And hold your hands in benediction o'er
  me—
No, sir, you must not kneel.
LEAR: Pray do not
  mock me.
I am a very foolish fond old man,
Fourscore and upward, not an hour more
  nor less;
And to deal plainly,
I fear I am not in my perfect mind.
Methinks I should know you, and know
  this man,
Yet I am doubtful. For I am mainly
  ignorant
What place this is; and all the skill I have
Remembers not these garments; nor I
  know not
Where I did lodge last night. Do not laugh
  at me,
For as I am a man, I think this lady
To be my child Cordelia.
CORDELIA: And so I am—I
  am.
LEAR: Be your tears wet? Yes, faith. I pray
  weep not.
If you have poison for me, I will drink it.
I know you do not love me, for your
  sisters
Have, as I do remember, done me wrong.
You have some cause, they have not.
CORDELIA: No cause, no
  cause.

LEAR: Am I in France?
KENT: In your own kingdom,
  sir.
LEAR: Do not abuse me.
DOCTOR: Be comforted, good madam, the
  great rage,
  You see, is killed in him: and yet it is
  danger
  To make him even o'er the time he has
  lost.
  Desire him to go in, trouble him no more
  Till further settling.
CORDELIA: Will't please your Highness
  walk?
LEAR: You must bear with me.
  Pray you now forget, and forgive; I am old
  and foolish.

(Exeunt all but KENT *and* GENTLEMAN.)*

GENTLEMAN: Holds it true, sir, that the
Duke of Cornwall was so slain?
KENT: Most certain, sir.
GENTLEMAN: Who is conductor of his
people?
KENT: As 'tis said, the bastard son of
Gloucester.
GENTLEMAN: They say Edgar his banished
son is with the Earl of Kent in Germany.
KENT: Report is changeable. 'Tis time to look
about, the powers of the kingdom approach apace.
GENTLEMAN: The arbitrement is like to be
bloody. Fare you well, sir. *(Exit)*
KENT: My point and period will be
  thoroughly wrought,
    Or well, or ill, as this day's battle's fought.
    (Exit)

ACT V

SCENE I
The British camp, near Dover

(Enter, with drum and colours, EDMUND, REGAN,
  GENTLEMEN, *and* SOLDIERS.)*

EDMUND: Know of the duke if this last
  purpose hold,
  Or whether since he is advised by aught

To change the course. He's full of
  alteration,
And self-reproving. Bring his constant
  pleasure.

(Exit GENTLEMAN.)*

REGAN: Our sister's man is certainly
    miscarried.
EDMUND: 'Tis to be doubted, madam.
REGAN: Now, sweet lord,
    You know the goodness I intend upon you:
    Tell me—but truly—but then speak the
      truth—
    Do you not love my sister?
EDMUND: In honoured
    love.
REGAN: But have you never found my
    brother's way,
    To the forfended place?
EDMUND: That thought
    abuses you.
REGAN: I am doubtful that you have been
    conjunct
    And bosomed with her, as far as we call
    hers.
EDMUND: No by mine honour, madam.
REGAN: I never shall endure her. Dear my
    lord,
    Be not familiar with her.
EDMUND: Fear me not,
    She and the duke her husband—

*(Enter, with drum and colours, ALBANY, GONERIL,
and SOLDIERS.)*

GONERIL: *(Aside)* I had rather lose the
    battle, than that sister
    Should loosen him and me.
ALBANY: Our very loving sister, well be-
    met.
    Sir, this I heard, the King is come to his
    daughter,
    With others whom the rigour of our state
    Forced to cry out. Where I could not be
    honest,
    I never yet was valiant. For this business,
    It touches us, as France invades our land,
    Not bolds the King, with others whom I
    fear
    Most just and heavy causes make oppose.
EDMUND: Sir, you speak nobly.
REGAN: Why is this
    reasoned?
GONERIL: Combine together 'gainst the
    enemy;
    For these domestic and particular broils
    Are not the question here.

ALBANY: Let's then
    determine
    With th' ancient of war on our proceeding.
EDMUND: I shall attend you presently at
    your tent.
REGAN: Sister, you'll go with us?
GONERIL: No.
REGAN: 'Tis most convenient, pray you go
    with us.
GONERIL: *(Aside)* O ho, I know the
    riddle.—I will go.

(As they are going out, enter EDGAR disguised.)

EDGAR: If e'er your Grace had speech with
    man so poor,
    Hear me one word.
ALBANY: I'll overtake you.—
    Speak.

(Exeunt all but ALBANY and EDGAR.)

EDGAR: Before you fight the battle, ope this
    letter.
    If you have victory, let the trumpet sound
    For him that brought it. Wretched though
    I seem,
    I can produce a champion that will prove
    What is avouched there. If you miscarry,
    Your business of the world hath so an end,
    And machination ceases. Fortune love you.
ALBANY: Stay till I have read the letter.
EDGAR: I was forbid it.
    When time shall serve, let but the herald
    cry,
    And I'll appear again.
ALBANY: Why fare thee well, I will o'erlook
    thy paper.

(Exit EDGAR. Enter EDMUND.)

EDMUND: The enemy's in view, draw up
    your powers.
    Here is the guess of their true strength and
    forces,
    By diligent discovery, but your haste
    Is now urged on you.
ALBANY: We will greet the
    time.

(Exit ALBANY.)

EDMUND: To both these sisters have I
    sworn my love;

Each jealous of the other, as the stung
Are of the adder. Which of them shall I
  take?
Both? One? Or neither? Neither can be
  enjoyed,
If both remain alive. To take the widow,
Exasperates, makes mad her sister Goneril,
And hardly shall I carry out my side,
Her husband being alive. Now then, we'll
  use

His countenance for the battle, which
  being done,
Let her who would be rid of him devise
His speedy taking off. As for the mercy
Which he intends to Lear and to Cordelia,
The battle done, and they within our
  power,
Shall never see his pardon; for my state
Stands on me to defend, not to debate.
  (Exit)

SCENE II

A field between the two camps

(Alarum within. Enter, with drum and colours,
LEAR, CORDELIA, *and* SOLDIERS *over the stage and
exeunt. Enter* EDGAR *and* GLOUCESTER.*)*

EDGAR: Here, father, take the shadow of this
  tree
  For your good host; pray that the right
    may thrive.
  If ever I return to you again,
  I'll bring you comfort.
GLOUCESTER: Grace go with you, sir.

(Exit EDGAR. *Alarum and retreat within. Enter*
EDGAR.*)*

EDGAR: Away old man, give me thy hand,
  away!
  King Lear hath lost, he and his daughter
    ta'en.
  Given me thy hand. Come on.
GLOUCESTER: No further, sir, a man may
  rot even here.
EDGAR: What, in ill thoughts again? Men
  must endure
  Their going hence, even as their coming
    hither;
  Ripeness is all. Come on.
GLOUCESTER: And that's true
  too. *(Exeunt)*

SCENE III

The British camp, near Dover

(Enter, in conquest, with drum and colours,
EDMUND; LEAR *and* CORDELIA *as prisoners;*
GENTLEMAN, CAPTAIN, *and* SOLDIERS.*)*

EDMUND: Some officers take them away;
  good guard,
  Until their greater pleasures first be
    known
  That are to censure them.
CORDELIA: We are not the
  first
  Who with best meaning have incurred the
    worst.
  For thee, oppressed King, am I cast down,
  Myself could else out-frown false fortune's
    frown.
  Shall we not see these daughters, and these
    sisters?

LEAR: No, no, no, no; come let's away to
  prison:
  We two alone will sing like birds i' th'
    cage.
  When thou dost ask me blessing, I'll kneel
    down,
  And ask of thee forgiveness. So we'll live,
  And pray, and sing, and tell old tales, and
    laugh
  At gilded butterflies; and hear poor rogues
  Talk of court news, and we'll talk with
    them too,
  Who loses, and who wins, who's in, who's
    out;
  And take upon's the mystery of things,
  As if we were God's spies. And we'll wear
    out

In a walled prison, packs and sects of great
    ones,
That ebb and flow by th' moon.
EDMUND: Take them
    away.
LEAR: Upon such sacrifices, my Cordelia,
    The gods themselves throw incense. Have
      I caught thee?
    He that parts us shall bring a brand from
      heaven,
    And fire us hence like foxes. Wipe thine
      eyes;
    The good-years shall devour them, flesh
      and fell,
    Ere they shall make us weep. We'll see
      'em starved first. Come.

    (Exeunt LEAR *and* CORDELIA, *guarded.)*

EDMUND: Come hither, captain, hark.
    Take thou this note, go follow them to
      prison.
    One step I have advanced thee, if thou
      dost
    As this instructs thee, thou dost make thy
      way
    To noble fortunes. Know thou this, that
      men
    Are as the time is; to be tender-minded
    Does not become a sword. Thy great
      employment
    Will not bear question; either say thou'lt
      do't,
    Or thrive by other means.
CAPTAIN: I'll do't, my lord.
EDMUND: About it, and write happy when
    th'hast done.
    Mark, I say instantly, and carry it so
    As I have set it down.
CAPTAIN: I cannot draw a cart, nor eat dried
    oats.
    If it be man's work, I'll do't. *(Exit)*

(Flourish. Enter ALBANY, GONERIL, REGAN,
    GENTLEMEN, *and* SOLDIERS.*)*

ALBANY: Sir, you have showed to-day your
    valiant strain,
    And fortune led you well; you have the
      captives
    Who were the opposites of this day's strife.
    We do require them of you, so to use
      them

As we shall find their merits and our
    safety
May equally determine.
EDMUND: Sir, I thought it fit
    To send the old and miserable King
    To some retention and appointed guard;
    Whose age has charms in it, whose title
      more,
    To pluck the common bosom on his side,
    And turn our impressed lances in our eyes
    Which do command them. With him I
      sent the Queen;
    My reason all the same; and they are
      ready
    To-morrow, or at further space, t' appear
    Where you shall hold your session. At this
      time
    We sweat and bleed; the friend hath lost
      his friend,
    And the best quarrels in the heat are
      cursed
    By those that feel their sharpness.
    The question of Cordelia and her father
    Requires a fitter place.
ALBANY: Sir, by your
    patience,
    I hold you but a subject of this war,
    Not as a brother.
REGAN: That's as we list to grace
    him.
    Methinks our pleasure might have been
      demanded,
    Ere you had spoke so far. He led our
      powers,
    Bore the commission of my place and
      person,
    The which immediately may well stand
      up
    And call itself your brother.
GONERIL: Not so hot.
    In his own grace he doth exalt himself,
    More than in your addition.
REGAN: In my rights
    By me invested, he compeers the best.
GONERIL: That were the most, if he should
    husband you.
REGAN: Jesters do oft prove prophets.
GONERIL: Holla,
    holla!
    That eye that told you so looked but a-
    squint.

REGAN: Lady, I am not well, else I should answer
From a full-flowing stomach. General,
Take thou my soldiers, prisoners, patrimony;
Dispose of them, of me, the walls is thine:
Witness the world, that I create thee here
My lord and master.
GONERIL: Mean you to enjoy him?
ALBANY: The let-alone lies not in your good will.
EDMUND: Nor in thine, lord.
ALBANY: Half-blooded fellow, yes.
REGAN: *(To* EDMUND*)* Let the drum strike, and prove my title thine.
ALBANY: Stay yet, hear reason. Edmund, I arrest thee
On capital treason; and in thy attaint,
This gilded serpent *(Points to* GONERIL*)*.
For your claim, fair sister,
I bar it in the interest of my wife;
'Tis she is sub-contracted to this lord,
And I her husband contradict your banns.
If you will marry, make your loves to me —
My lady is bespoke.
GONERIL: An interlude.
ALBANY: Thou art armed, Gloucester. Let the trumpet sound.
If none appear to prove upon thy person
Thy heinous, manifest, and many treasons,
There is my pledge *(Throws down a glove)*. I'll make it on thy heart,
Ere I taste bread, thou art in nothing less
Than I have here proclaimed thee.
REGAN: Sick, o sick!
GONERIL: *(Aside)* If not. I'll ne'er trust medicine.
EDMUND: There's my exchange *(Throws down a glove)*.
What in the world he is
That names me traitor, villain-like he lies.
Call by thy trumpet; he that dares approach,
On him, on you, who not, I will maintain
My truth and honour firmly.
ALBANY: A herald, ho!

EDMUND: A herald, ho, a herald!
ALBANY: Trust to thy single virtue, for thy soldiers,
All levied in my name, have in my name
Took their discharge.
REGAN: My sickness grows upon me.
ALBANY: She is not well, convey her to my tent.

(Exit REGAN. *Enter* HERALD.*)*

Come hither herald. Let the trumpet sound,
And read out this.

(A trumpet sounds.)

HERALD: *(Reads) If any man of quality or degree, within the lists of the army, will maintain upon Edmund, supposed Earl of Gloucester, that he is a manifold traitor, let him appear by the third sound of the trumpet: he is bold in his defence.*

(First trumpet.)

HERALD: Again!

(Second trumpet.)

Again!

(Third trumpet.)

(Trumpet answers within.)

(Enter EDGAR, *armed, a trumpet before him.)*

ALBANY: Ask him his purposes, why he appears
Upon this call o' th' trumpet.
HERALD: What are you?
Your name, your quality, and why you answer
This present summons?
EDGAR: Know, my name is lost,
By treason's tooth bare-gnawn and canker-bit,
Yet am I noble as the adversary
I come to cope.
ALBANY: Which is that adversary?
EDGAR: What's he that speaks for Edmund Earl of Gloucester?

EDMUND: Himself—what sayest thou to
　　him?
EDGAR:　Draw thy sword,
　　That if my speech offend a noble heart,
　　Thy arm may do thee justice; here is
　　　mine.
　　Behold, it is the privilege of mine honours,
　　My oath, and my profession. I protest—
　　Maugre thy strength, youth, place, and
　　　eminence,
　　Despite thy victor sword and fire-new
　　　fortune,
　　Thy valour and thy heart—thou art a
　　　traitor;
　　False to thy gods, thy brother, and thy
　　　father,
　　Conspirant 'gainst this high illustrious
　　　prince.
　　And from th' extremest upward of thy
　　　head,
　　To the descent and dust below thy foot,
　　A most toad-spotted traitor. Say thou no,
　　This sword, this arm, and my best spirits
　　　are bent
　　To prove upon thy heart, whereto I speak,
　　Thou liest.
EDMUND:　In wisdom I should ask thy
　　name,
　　But since thy outside looks so fair and
　　　warlike,
　　And that thy tongue some say of breeding
　　　breathes,
　　What safe and nicely I might well delay,
　　By rule of knighthood, I disdain and
　　　spurn.
　　Back do I toss these treasons to thy head;
　　With the hell-hated lie o'erwhelm thy
　　　heart;
　　Which—for they yet glance by, and
　　　scarcely bruise—
　　This sword of mine shall give them
　　　instant way,
　　Where they shall rest for ever. Trumpets
　　　speak!

　　(Alarums. They fight. EDMUND falls.)

ALBANY: Save him, save him.
GONERIL:　　　　　　　　This is
　　practice, Gloucester.

By the law of war, thou wast not bound to
　　answer
An unknown opposite; thou art not
　　vanquished,
But cozened, and beguiled.
ALBANY:　　　　　　　　Shut your
　　mouth dame,
　　Or with this paper shall I stop it. Hold sir,
　　Thou worse than any name, read thine
　　　own evil.
　　No tearing, lady, I perceive you know it.
　　　(Gives the letter to EDMUND)
GONERIL: Say if I do, the laws are mine, not
　　thine.
　　Who can arraign me for't?
ALBANY:　　　　　　　　Most monstrous!
　　O!
　　Know'st thou this paper?
GONERIL:　　　　　　　　Ask me not what
　　I know. *(Exit)*
ALBANY: Go after her, she's desperate,
　　govern her.

　　　　　　(Exit GENTLEMAN.)

EDMUND: What you have charged me with,
　　that have I done,
　　And more, much more; the time will
　　　bring it out.
　　'Tis past, and so am I. But what art thou
　　That hast this fortune on me? If thou'rt
　　　noble,
　　I do forgive thee.
EDGAR:　　　　　　Let's exchange charity.
　　I am no less in blood than thou art,
　　　Edmund;
　　If more, the more th'hast wronged me.
　　My name is Edgar, and thy father's son.
　　The gods are just, and of our pleasant vices
　　Make instruments to plague us.
　　The dark and vicious place where thee he
　　　got
　　Cost him his eyes.
EDMUND:　　　　　　Th'hast spoken right,
　　'tis true.
　　The wheel is come full circle; I am here.
ALBANY: Methought thy very gait did
　　prophesy
　　A royal nobleness. I must embrace thee.
　　Let sorrow split my heart, if ever I
　　Did hate thee, or thy father.

EDGAR: Worthy
    prince,
  I know't.
ALBANY: Where have you hid yourself?
  How have you known the miseries of your
    father?
EDGAR: By nursing them, my lord. List a
    brief tale;
  And when 'tis told, o that my heart would
    burst.
  The bloody proclamation to escape,
  That followed me so near—o our lives'
    sweetness,
  That we the pain of death would hourly
    die
  Rather than die at once—taught me to
    shift
  Into a madman's rags, t' assume a
    semblance
  That very dogs disdained, and in this habit
  Met I my father with his bleeding rings,
  Their precious stones new lost; became his
    guide,
  Led him, begged for him, saved him from
    despair.
  Never—o fault—revealed myself unto
    him,
  Until some half hour past, when I was
    armed;
  Not sure, though hoping of this good
    success,
  I asked his blessing, and from first to last
  Told him my pilgrimage. But his flawed
    heart,
  Alack too weak the conflict to support,
  'Twixt two extremes of passion, joy and
    grief,
  Burst smilingly.
EDMUND: This speech of yours hath
    moved me,
  And shall perchance do good, but speak
    you on;
  You look as you had something more to
    say.
ALBANY: If there be more, more woeful,
    hold it in,
  For I am almost ready to dissolve,
  Hearing of this.
EDGAR: This would have seemed a
    period

To such as love not sorrow; but another,
To amplify too much, would make much
    more,
And top extremity.
Whilst I was big in clamour, came there
    in a man,
Who having seen me in my worst estate,
Shunned my abhorred society, but then
    finding
Who 'twas that so endured, with his
    strong arms
He fastened on my neck, and bellowed out
As he'd burst heaven, threw him on my
    father,
Told the most piteous tale of Lear and him
That ever ear received: which in
    recounting
His grief grew puissant, and the strings of
    life
Began to crack. Twice then the trumpets
    sounded,
And there I left him tranced.
ALBANY: But who was
    this?
EDGAR: Kent, sir, the banished Kent, who in
    disguise
  Followed his enemy King and did him
    service
  Improper for a slave.

(Enter GENTLEMAN *with a bloody knife.)*

GENTLEMAN: Help, help; o help!
EDGAR: What kind
    of help?
ALBANY: Speak man.
EDGAR: What means this bloody knife?
GENTLEMAN: 'Tis hot, it smokes,
  It came even from the heart of—o she's
    dead!
ALBANY: Who dead? speak man.
GENTLEMAN: Your lady sir, your lady; and
    her sister
  By her is poisoned; she confesses it.
EDMUND: I was contracted to them both.
    All three
  Now marry in an instant.

(Enter KENT.*)*

EDGAR: Here comes
    Kent.

ALBANY: Produce the bodies, be they alive
    or dead.

(Exit GENTLEMAN.*)*

This judgement of the heavens, that
    makes us tremble,
Touches us not with pity.—O is this he?
The time will not allow the compliment
Which very manners urges.
KENT: I am come
    To bid my King and master aye good
    night.
    Is he not here?
ALBANY: Great thing of us forgot.
    Speak, Edmund, where's the King? And
    where's Cordelia?

(The bodies of GONERIL *and* REGAN *are brought in.)*

    Seest thou this object, Kent?
KENT: Alack, why thus?
EDMUND: Yet Edmund was
    beloved.
    The one the other poisoned for my sake,
    And after slew herself.
ALBANY: Even so. Cover their faces.
EDMUND: I pant for life. Some good I mean
    to do,
    Despite of mine own nature. Quickly
    send—
    Be brief in it—to the castle, for my writ
    Is on the life of Lear, and on Cordelia.
    Nay, send in time.
ALBANY: Run, run, o run.
EDGAR: To who my lord? Who has the
    office? Send
    Thy token of reprieve.
EDMUND: Well thought on, take my sword;
    Give it the captain.
ALBANY: Haste thee for thy life.

(Exit EDGAR.*)*

EDMUND: He hath commission from thy
    wife and me
    To hang Cordelia in the prison, and
    To lay the blame upon her own despair,
    That she fordid herself.
ALBANY: The gods defend her. Bear him
    hence awhile.

*(*EDMUND *is borne off.)*

(Enter LEAR, *with* CORDELIA *dead in his arms;*
    EDGAR, GENTLEMAN, *and others.)*

LEAR: Howl, howl, howl! O you are men of
    stones.
    Had I your tongues and eyes, I'd use them
    so
    That heaven's vault should crack. She's
    gone forever.
    I know when one is dead, and when one
    lives;
    She's dead as earth. Lend me a looking-
    glass;
    If that her breath will mist or stain the
    stone,
    Why then she lives.
KENT: Is this the promised
    end?
EDGAR: Or image of that horror?
ALBANY: Fall, and
    cease.
LEAR: This feather stirs, she lives; if it be so,
    It is a chance which does redeem all
    sorrows
    That ever I have felt.
KENT: O my good master.
LEAR: Prithee away.
EDGAR: 'Tis noble Kent your
    friend.
LEAR: A plague upon you, murderers.
    Traitors all.
    I might have saved her; now she's gone for
    ever.
    Cordelia, Cordelia, stay a little. Ha!
    What is't thou sayst?—Her voice was ever
    soft,
    Gentle, and low, an excellent thing in
    woman.
    I killed the slave that was a-hanging
    thee.
GENTLEMAN: 'Tis true my lords, he did.
LEAR: Did I not fellow?
    I have seen the day, with my good biting
    falchion
    I would have made them skip. I am old
    now,
    And these same crosses spoil me. Who are
    you?
    Mine eyes are not o' th' best, I'll tell you
    straight.

KENT: If fortune brag of two she loved and
    hated.
    One of them we behold.
LEAR: This is a dull sight. Are you not Kent?
KENT: The same.
    Your servant Kent. Where is your servant
    Caius?
LEAR: He's a good fellow, I can tell you that.
    He'll strike, and quickly too—he's dead
    and rotten.
KENT: No, my good lord, I am the very man—
LEAR: I'll see that straight.
KENT: That from your first of difference and
    decay,
    Have followed your sad steps.
LEAR: You are
    welcome hither.
KENT: Nor no man else. All's cheerless, dark,
    and deadly.
    Your eldest daughters have fordone
    themselves,
    And desperately are dead.
LEAR: Ay, so I think.
ALBANY: He knows not what he says, and
    vain is it
    That we present us to him.
EDGAR: Very bootless.

(Enter GENTLEMAN.*)*

    Edmund is dead, my lord.
ALBANY: That's but a trifle
    here.
    You lords and noble friends, know our
    intent.
    What comfort to this great decay may
    come
    Shall be applied. For us, we will resign,
    During the life of this old Majesty,
    To him our absolute power—(To EDGAR
    and KENT*)* you to your rights,
    With boot, and such addition as your
    honours
    Have more than merited. All friends shall
    taste

    The wages of their virtue, and all foes
    The cup of their deservings. O see, see!
LEAR: And my poor fool is hanged. No, no,
    no life?
    Why should a dog, a horse, a rat, have life,
    And thou no breath at all? Thou'lt come
    no more,
    Never, never, never, never, never.
    Pray you undo this button. Thank you, sir.
    Do you see this? Look on her, look her
    lips—
    Look there, look there— *(Dies)*
EDGAR: He faints. My lord,
    my lord!
KENT: Break heart, I prithee break.
EDGAR: Look up,
    my lord.
KENT: Vex not his ghost. O let him pass. He
    hates him,
    That would upon the rack of this tough
    world
    Stretch him out longer.
EDGAR: He is gone indeed.
KENT: The wonder is, he hath endured so
    long;
    He but usurped his life.
ALBANY: Bear them from hence. Our
    present business
    Is general woe. *(To* KENT *and* EDGAR*)*
    Friends of my soul, you twain
    Rule in this realm, and the gored state
    sustain.
KENT: I have a journey, sir, shortly to go.
    My master calls me, I must not say no.
EDGAR: The weight of this sad time we
    must obey,
    Speak what we feel, not what we ought to
    say.
    The oldest hath borne most; we that are
    young
    Shall never see so much, nor live so long.

    (Exeunt, with a dead march.)

If one were to reduce *King Lear* to its bare story, it would show a marked kinship to our television dramas about deception, violence, and sex and to a number of lurid melodramas of the nineteenth century. The villainy of Edmund, Goneril, and Regan is transparent, and few scenes in drama are more violent than that in which Gloucester's eyes are gouged out in a sadistic frenzy and, though sex plays little on-stage part, the sexual relationships of Goneril and Regan with Edmund are clearly noted. But Shakespeare's play is much more than its bare story, for he infuses the violent and sensational elements with such significance that violence and sensationalism are never the primary focus. His concern is not merely with events but with what events imply about human beings and their behavior. Thus, Shakespeare's play combines an interesting story with a philosophical concern for the significance of the story.

On the surface, *King Lear* is a drama about parent-child relationships (Lear and his daughters, Gloucester and his sons), but there are as well a number of other concerns of equal or greater importance. In part, *King Lear* is a play about power — its uses and abuses. The opening scene establishes Lear's position as that of an absolute monarch. He disposes of the kingdom as though it were his private property and he passes judgments on others without reference to any law other than his own whim. He expects his every desire to be met; he demands that his daughters make a public display of their love for him and disowns Cordelia when she will say no more than the truth. In this opening scene he acts both as ruler of a kingdom and as ruler of a family; public and private power are intertwined, and consequently Shakespeare seems to imply that a ruler is to his subjects what a father is to his family. But such absoluteness of power carries with it the need to guard against using it unjustly. It is Lear's abuse of power that sets the main plot in motion; given his example, it is not surprising that Goneril and Regan, upon acquiring power, use it against him. A variation on this motif is seen in the subplot about Gloucester and his sons. Edmund manipulates his father through flattery and feigned love, just as Goneril and Regan manipulate Lear, but he does so with a more sinister goal in mind — to provoke his father to disinherit the honest and loving son, much as Lear has disinherited Cordelia.

Against the abuse of power, what weapons do the innocent have? Love, honesty, and integrity. But these can have little effect if the wielders of power do not perceive them and recognize their value. Lear does not fully perceive his own errors until the storm scene, and Gloucester is not aware of his gullibility until his eyes are put out. By then, both have lost their power, and it is their powerlessness to resist the abuses of those now in power that forces Lear and Gloucester to reassess their own behavior and values. At the end of the play, the wicked have been punished and power has passed into the hands of Edgar, who, we are led to believe, will use it wisely, but the price has been high.

King Lear clearly suggests that power is corrupt when it is not used justly, but to use power justly one must recognize the difference between appearance and reality. Both Lear and Gloucester are deceived (on little evidence and without seeking to discover the truth) by an appearance of perfidy or lack of gratitude in children who are actually loyal and true, and both accept as truth the lies told by children who deliberately deceive them. Shakespeare draws a contrast between physical sight and spiritual blindness. After he has lost his eyes, Gloucester says, "I stumbled when I saw." And Lear's madness, the equivalent of blindness, leads him to discover truths he had ignored: "A man may see how this world goes with no eyes/ . . . Get thee glass eyes/ And, like a scurvy politician, seem/ To see things thou dost not." Both Lear and Gloucester must deal with the results of hasty, unjust decisions made on the basis of appearance.

Another motif in *King Lear* is the degree to which an individual is responsible for his own fate. For instance, Gloucester, early in the play, suggests that strange happenings in human affairs are caused by some dislocation in the planets, and later he says, "As flies to wanton boys are we to th'gods:/ They kill us for their sport." Fortune is also referred to as governing man's fate. In Shakespeare's time Fortune was often pictured as a goddess with a wheel, on which she raised people to the pinnacle of power and just as inexplicably dashed them down again. On the other hand, Edmund derides those who would blame Fortune or the stars for their behavior; and Edgar, in the final scene, concludes: "The gods are just, and of our pleasant vices / Make instruments to plague us."

These opposing views of human destiny are partially explained by the Renaissance conception of the universe. Humanity, as the final creation of God, was thought to be the center of God's concern, since God had made the earth and all its nonhuman inhabitants for human use. Furthermore, the entire universe was said to revolve around the immobile earth. The planets were thought to move in concentric spheres, one inside the other. Because all the parts of the universe were connected like the cogs of a machine, the well-being of the whole was affected by each part. Harmony among all created a "music of the spheres," but chaotic conditions reverberated unpleasantly throughout the system. This belief explains why physical manifestations of disorder play such a large part in Shakespeare's tragedies. The storm in *King Lear* is a metaphorical indication of the disruption of order. But if his characters state contrary views about fate and responsibility, Shakespeare seems to suggest that man is not a mere puppet but an intelligent being free to choose his own path. Consequently, he depicts human beings as frequently violating the divine order and suffering accordingly.

The implications of Shakespeare's plays are conveyed not only through the action and character relationships but also through Shakespeare's dramatic poetry, generally conceded to be the finest in any language. His basic medium is blank verse, which allows the flexibility of ordinary speech while elevating and formalizing it. Perhaps the most important element in Shakespeare's dialogue is figurative language, which sets up direct or indirect comparisons and associative patterns which enlarge significance without distracting attention from the action. For example, in the storm scene of *King Lear*, the storm is treated as an actual source of physical discomfort, but it is also associated with the cruelty of Lear's daughters and with divine displeasure. Thus, it both heightens Lear's immediate situation and places it in a much broader context.

A comparison of *King Lear* and *Antigone* can be very revealing. Both plays depict rulers who make rash and hasty decisions that lead to disasters in the state and in the family, and both rulers recognize their errors too late to rectify them.

Despite these and other similarities, these likenesses are probably less significant than the differences between the plays. *Antigone* is restricted in scope, focusing on a few characters in a compact action which occurs in one locale and within a few hours; *King Lear* introduces a large number of characters in a multifaceted action which occurs over a long period of time and in numerous places. Sophocles' play focuses on a clash between two principles, championed by Antigone and Creon, both with some claims to being right; Shakespeare's play divides its conflicts among many characters, but the clash between good and evil is ever-present. *Antigone* eliminates everything not essential to the action; *King Lear* includes much that is not essential but that adds texture and dimension to the action. Meanings and implications are more clearly evident in *Antigone* than in *King Lear*, perhaps because *Antigone* is more sharply focused. *Antigone* may be likened to a Greek temple in its carefully controlled symmetry, whereas *King Lear* may be likened to a Gothic cathedral with its sprawling structure and multiplicity of detail that create diversity within an ultimate unity.

A more detailed comparison would reveal many additional similarities and differences both between these two plays and between Greek and Elizabethan tragedy. Such comparisons can be very helpful, for they sharpen our perceptions both by making us aware of differences among plays and by making us see more clearly what is distinctive about each play.

The School for Wives

by Molière / Translated by Richard Wilbur

By the time Molière wrote *The School for Wives* in 1662, both theatre and drama had changed considerably since Shakespeare's day. The theatre had retreated indoors, where plays were performed on a stage framed by a proscenium arch and with settings painted in perspective on wings and drops. The auditorium reflected a class-conscious society: tiers of *boxes* (arranged so the well-to-do might attend the theatre without having to mingle with the general public) surrounded the *pit*, or large open space at ground level (favored by the man-about-town and the middle class), and surmounted by a *gallery* (located just under the roof and used primarily by the poor and working classes). Theatres usually had their own resident companies (which now included women) that performed a large number of plays each season in rotation. The bill changed almost daily.

During the 1630s, French critics and playwrights argued bitterly over the principles that should govern playwriting. This battle was eventually won by the proponents of a set of rather strict rules and precepts that made up what has come to be called the Neoclassical ideal and which were to dominate dramatic writing until the end of the eighteenth century. Under Neoclassicism, all regular drama had to be divided into five acts and was expected to observe the unity of time (according to which the entire dramatic action should occur within a 24-hour period), the unity of place (according to which all of the action should occur in the same place or in places sufficiently near each other as to be easily reached), and the unity of action (according to which the action should be restricted to a single plot or a main plot with closely related subplots). There were a number of additional rules, all said to be derived from Greek and Roman ideas or practices. During the course of the seventeenth century, Paris came to be considered the primary cultural center of Europe, and, largely because of the tragedies of Pierre Corneille (1606–1684) and Jean Racine (1639–1699) and the comedies of Molière, French drama came to be the standard against which dramatists elsewhere were measured.

Molière (Jean-Baptiste Poquelin, 1622–1673), son of a prosperous upholsterer, was given an excellent education and was destined for a position at court until he joined a theatre company in 1643. Unsuccessful in Paris, the company toured the provinces until 1658, when it was invited to perform for the king and was sufficiently well received to be awarded a subsidy and the use of a court theatre. In the years between 1658 and 1673, Molière was not only the leading writer of comedy in France but also head of a theatrical troupe and its principal actor.

Molière wrote many kinds of plays, including farces (such as *The Doctor in Spite of Himself* and *The Tricks of Scapin*), comedy ballets (having interludes of music and dance, as in *The Forced Marriage* and *The Princess of Elide*, all written for court entertainments), and spectacle plays (such as *Amphitryon* and *Psyché*). But he is best known for his comedies of character and manners, among them *The School for Wives, Tartuffe, The Misanthrope, The Miser*, and *The Imaginary Invalid*, each focusing on a central character with an all-consuming obsession and satirizing attitudes, ideas, and behavior of the times. Molière was also one of the most controversial dramatists of his century because he chose subjects of contemporary interest and questioned accepted conventions and entrenched prejudices. Fortunately, he enjoyed the favor of Louis XIV, who protected him against his most bitter foes.

Molière first stirred controversy with *The School for Wives*, which was judged to be dangerous because it questioned accepted views of marital infidelity, arranged marriages, the authority of parents or guardians over children, and the duty of wives to husbands. Molière wrote two additional plays in defense of this comedy: *The School for Wives Criticized* and *The Rehearsal at Versailles*. In these plays, he sought to clarify the attitudes expressed in *The School for Wives* and his ideas about the role of drama in society, about acting, and about a variety of other topics.

Molière did not exclude himself from his satire and often seemed to deal with his own problems in his plays. In 1662 he had married a woman 20 years his junior (his enemies spread the rumor that she was his own illegitimate daughter) and for the remainder of his life had to cope with a stormy marital relationship.

At this time in France acting was still considered an immoral profession, and the Catholic church denied actors its sacraments unless they first foreswore their profession. Because he would not give up acting, Molière could not receive many honors awarded lesser dramatists, and when he died he was denied a Christian burial until Louis XIV interceded and then he was given the briefest ceremony possible.

The School for Wives is written in a verse form that had been accepted as the standard for French drama — the Alexandrine, a line of 12 syllables and paired rhyming lines. The translation that follows has been widely acclaimed for capturing the essence of Molière's original text.

CHARACTERS

ARNOLPHE *also known as* MONSIEUR DE LA SOUCHE

AGNÈS *an innocent young girl, Arnolphe's ward*

HORACE *Agnès' lover, Oronte's son*

ALAIN *a peasant, Arnolphe's manservant*

GEORGETTE *a peasant woman, servant to Arnolphe*

CHRYSALDE *a friend of Arnolphe's*

ENRIQUE *Chrysalde's brother-in-law, Agnès' father*

ORONTE *Horace's father and Arnolphe's old friend*

A NOTARY

The scene is a square in a provincial city.

ACT I

SCENE I

CHRYSALDE, ARNOLPHE

CHRYSALDE: So, you're resolved to give this
    girl your hand?
ARNOLPHE: Tomorrow I shall marry her, as
    planned.
CHRYSALDE: We're quite alone here, and
    we can discuss
  Your case with no one overhearing us:
  Shall I speak openly, and as your friend?
  This plan — for your sake — troubles me no
    end.
  I must say that, from every point of view,
  Taking a wife is a rash step for you.
ARNOLPHE: You think so? Might it be,
    friend, that you base
  Your fears for me upon your own sad case?
  Cuckolds would have us think that all
    who marry
  Acquire a set of horns as corollary.
CHRYSALDE: Fate gives men horns, and fate
    can't be withstood;
  To fret about such matters does no good.

What makes me fear for you is the way
    you sneer
At every luckless husband of whom you
    hear.
You know that no poor cuckold, great or
    small,
Escapes your wit; you mock them one and
    all,
And take delight in making boisterous
    mention
Of all intrigues which come to your
    attention.
ARNOLPHE: Why not? What other town on
    earth is known
For husbands so long-suffering as our own?
Can we not all too readily bring to mind
Ill-treated dupes of every shape and kind?
One husband's rich; his helpmeet shares
    the wealth
With paramours who cuckold him by
    stealth;

Another, with a scarcely kinder fate,
Sees other men heap gifts upon his mate—
Who frees his mind of jealous insecurity
By saying that they're tributes to her
    purity.
One cuckold impotently storms and rants;
Another mildly bows to circumstance,
And when some gallant calls to see his
    spouse,
Discreetly takes his hat and leaves the
    house.
One wife, confiding in her husband,
    mentions
A swain who bores her with his warm
    attentions;
The husband smugly pities the poor swain
For all his efforts—which are *not* in vain.
Another wife explains her wealthy state
By saying that she's held good cards of
    late;
Her husband thanks the Lord and gives
    Him praise,
Not guessing what bad game she truly
    plays.
Thus, all about us, there are themes for
    wit;
May I not, as an observer, jest a bit?
May I not laugh at—
CHRYSALDE: Yes; but remember,
    do,
That those you mock may someday mock
    at you.
Now, I hear gossip, I hear what people say
About the latest scandals of the day,
But whatsoever I'm told, I never hear it
With wicked glee and in a gloating spirit.
I keep my counsel; and though I may
    condemn
Loose wives, and husbands who put up
    with them,
And though I don't propose, you may be
    sure,
To endure the wrongs which some weak
    men endure,
Still, I am never heard to carp and crow,
For tables have been known to turn, you
    know,
And there's no man who can predict, in
    fact,
How in such circumstances he would act.

In consequence, should fate bestow on me
What all must fear, the horns of
    cuckoldry,
The world would treat me gently, I
    believe,
And be content with laughing up its
    sleeve.
There are, in fact, some kindly souls who
    might
Commiserate me in my sorry plight.
But you, dear fellow, with you it's not the
    same.
I say once more, you play a dangerous
    game.
Since with your jeering tongue you plague
    the lives
Of men who are unlucky in their wives,
And persecute them like a fiend from
    Hell,
Take care lest someday you be jeered as
    well.
If the least whisper about your wife were
    heard,
They'd mock you from the housetops,
    mark my word.
What's more—
ARNOLPHE: Don't worry, friend; I'm
    not a fool.
I shan't expose myself to ridicule.
I know the tricks and ruses, shrewd and
    sly,
Which wives employ, and cheat their
    husbands by;
I know that women can be deep and
    clever;
But I've arranged to be secure forever:
So simple is the girl I'm going to wed
That I've no fear of horns upon my head.
CHRYSALDE: Simple! You mean to bind
    yourself for life—
ARNOLPHE: A man's not simple to take a
    simple wife.
Your wife, no doubt, is a wise, virtuous
    woman,
But brightness, as a rule, is a bad omen,
And I know men who've undergone much
    pain
Because they married girls with too much
    brain.
I want no intellectual, if you please,

Who'll talk of nothing but her Tuesday
    teas,
Who'll frame lush sentiments in prose and
    verse
And fill the house with wits, and fops, and
    worse,
While I, as her dull husband, stand about
Like a poor saint whose candles have gone
    out.
No, keep your smart ones; I've no taste for
    such.
Women who versify know far too much.
I want a wife whose thought is not
    sublime,
Who has no notion what it is to rhyme,
And who, indeed, if she were asked in
    some
Insipid parlor game, "What rhymes with
    drum?"
Would answer in all innocence, "A fife."
In short, I want an unaccomplished wife,
And there are four things only she must
    know:
To say her prayers, love me, spin, and sew.
CHRYSALDE: Stupidity's your cup of tea, I
    gather.
ARNOLPHE: I'd choose an ugly, stupid
    woman rather
Than a great beauty who was over-wise.
CHRYSALDE: But wit and beauty—
ARNOLPHE: Virtue is
    what I prize.
CHRYSALDE: But how can you expect an
    idiot
To know what's virtuous and what is not?
Not only would it be a lifelong bore
To have a senseless wife, but what is
    more,
I hardly think you could depend upon her
To guard her husband's forehead from
    dishonor.
If a bright woman breaks her wedding
    vow,
She knows what she is doing, anyhow;
A simpleton, however, can commit
Adultery without suspecting it.
ARNOLPHE: To that fine argument I can but
    say
What Pantagruel says in Rabelais:
Preach and harangue from now till
    Whitsuntide

Against my preference for a stupid bride;
You'll be amazed to find, when you have
    ceased,
That I've not been persuaded in the least.
CHRYSALDE: So be it.
ARNOLPHE: Each man has his own
    design
For wedded bliss, and I shall follow mine.
I'm rich, and so can take a wife who'll be
Dependent, in the least respect, on me—
A sweet, submissive girl who cannot claim
To have brought me riches or an ancient
    name.
The gentle, meek expression which she
    wore
Endeared Agnès to me when she was four;
Her mother being poor, I felt an urge
To make the little thing my ward and
    charge,
And the good peasant woman was most
    pleased
To grant my wish, and have her burden
    eased.
In a small convent, far from the haunts of
    man,
The girl was reared according to my plan:
I told the nuns what means must be
    employed
To keep her growing mind a perfect void,
And, God be praised, they had entire
    success.
As a grown girl, her simple-mindedness
Is such that I thank Heaven for granting
    me
A bride who suits my wishes to a T.
She's out of the convent now, and since
    my gate
Stands open to society, early and late,
I keep her here, in another house I own,
Where no one calls, and she can be alone:
And, to protect her artless purity,
I've hired two servants as naïve as she.
I've told you all this so that you'll
    understand
With what great care my marriage has
    been planned;
And now, to clinch my story, I invite
You, my dear friend, to dine with her
    tonight;
I want you to examine her, and decide
Whether or not my choice is justified.

CHRYSALDE: Delighted.

ARNOLPHE: You'll gain, I think, a lively sense
  Of her sweet person and her innocence.

CHRYSALDE: As to her innocence, what you've related
  Leaves little doubt —

ARNOLPHE: My friend, 't was understated.
  Her utter naïveté keeps me in stitches.
  I laugh so that I almost burst my breeches.
  You won't believe this, but the other day
  She came and asked me in a puzzled way,
  And with a manner touchingly sincere,
  If children are begotten through the ear.

CHRYSALDE: I'm happy indeed, Monsieur Arnolphe —

ARNOLPHE: For Shame!
  Why must you always use my former name?

CHRYSALDE: I'm used to it, I suppose.
  What's more, I find
  That *de la Souche* forever slips my mind.
  What in the devil has persuaded you
  To debaptize yourself at forty-two
  And take a lordly title which you base
  On an old tree stump at your country place?

ARNOLPHE: The name La Souche goes with the property
  And sounds much better than Arnolphe to me.

CHRYSALDE: But why forsake the name your fathers bore
  For one that's fantasy and nothing more?
  Yet lately that's become the thing to do.
  I am reminded — no offense to you —
  Of a peasant named Gros-Pierre, who owned a small
  Parcel of land, an acre or so in all;
  He dug a muddy ditch around the same
  And took Monsieur de l'Isle for his new name.

ARNOLPHE: I can dispense with stories of that kind.
  My name is de la Souche, if you don't mind.
  I like that title, and it's mine by right;
  To address me otherwise is impolite.

CHRYSALDE: Your new name is employed by few, at best;
  Much of your mail, I've noticed, comes addressed —

ARNOLPHE: I don't mind that, from such as haven't been told;
  But you —

CHRYSALDE: Enough. Enough. No need to scold.
  I hereby promise that, at our next meeting,
  "Good day, Monsieur de la Souche" shall be my greeting.

ARNOLPHE: Farewell. I'm going to knock now on my door
  And let them know that I'm in town once more.

CHRYSALDE: *(Aside, as he moves off)* The man's quite mad. A lunatic, in fact.

ARNOLPHE: *(Alone)* On certain subjects he's a trifle cracked.
  It's curious to see with what devotion
  A man will cling to some quite pointless notion.
  Ho, there!

SCENE II

ALAIN, GEORGETTE, ARNOLPHE

ALAIN: *(Within)* Who's knocking?

ARNOLPHE: Ho! *(Aside)* They'll greet me, after
  My ten day's trip, with smiles and happy laughter.

ALAIN: Who's there?

ARNOLPHE: It's I.

ALAIN: Georgette!

GEORGETTE: What?

ALAIN: Open below!

GEORGETTE: Do it yourself!

ALAIN: You do it!

GEORGETTE: I won't go!

ALAIN: I won't go either!
ARNOLPHE: Gracious servants,
    these,
    To leave me standing here. Ho! If you
        please!
GEORGETTE: Who's there?
ARNOLPHE: Your master.
GEORGETTE: Alain!
ALAIN: What?
GEORGETTE: Go lift the latch!
    It's him.
ALAIN: You do it.
GEORGETTE: I'm getting the fire to
    catch.
ALAIN: I'm keeping the cat from eating the
    canary.
ARNOLPHE: Whoever doesn't admit me, and
    in a hurry,
    Will get no food for four long days, and
        more. Aha!
GEORGETTE: I'll get it; what are you
    coming for?
ALAIN: Why you, not me? That's a sneaky
    trick to play!
GEORGETTE: Get out of the way.
ALAIN: No, *you*
    get out of the way.
GEORGETTE: I want to open that door.
ALAIN: I want to, too.
GEORGETTE: You won't.
ALAIN: And you won't
    either.
GEORGETTE: Neither
    will you.
ARNOLPHE: *(To himself)* My patience with
    these two amazes me.
ALAIN: I've opened the door, Sir.
GEORGETTE: No, I did it!
    See?
    'T was I.

ALAIN: If only the master, here, weren't
        present,
    I'd—
ARNOLPHE: *(Receiving a blow from* ALAIN,
    meant for GEORGETTE*)* Blast you!
ALAIN: Sorry,
    Sir.
ARNOLPHE: You clumsy
    peasant!
ALAIN: It's her fault too, Sir.
ARNOLPHE: Both of you,
    stop this row.
    I want to question you; no nonsense, now.
    Alain, is everything going smoothly here?
ALAIN: Well, Sir, we're—
    *(*ARNOLPHE *removes* ALAIN'S *hat;* ALAIN
        obliviously puts it back on.)
    Well, Sir—
    (Hat business again)
    Well, thank God, Sir, we're—
    *(*ARNOLPHE *removes* ALAIN'S *hat a third
        time, and throws it to the ground.)*
ARNOLPHE: Where did you learn, you lout,
    to wear a hat
    While talking to your master? Answer me
        that.
ALAIN: You're right, I'm wrong.
ARNOLPHE: *(To* GEORGETTE*)*
    Now, have Agnès come down.
    Was she unhappy while I was out of town?
GEORGETTE: Unhappy? No.
ARNOLPHE: No?
GEORGETTE: Yes.
ARNOLPHE: For what reason,
    then?
GEORGETTE: Well, she kept thinking you'd
    be back again,
    So that whatever passed on the avenue—
    Horse, mule, or ass—she thought it must
        be you.

SCENE III

AGNÈS, ALAIN, GEORGETTE, ARNOLPHE

ARNOLPHE: Her needlework in hand! That's
    a good sign.
    Well, well, Agnès, I'm back and feeling
        fine.
    Are you glad to see me?

AGNÈS: Oh, yes, Sir; thank
    the Lord.
ARNOLPHE: I'm glad to see you too, my
    little ward.
    I take it everything has been all right?

AGNÈS: Except for the fleas, which bothered
    me last night.
ARNOLPHE: Well, there'll be someone soon
    to drive them away.
AGNÈS: I shall be glad of that.
ARNOLPHE: Yes, I dare say.
    What are you making?
AGNÈS: A headpiece, Sir, for
    me;
    Your nightshirts are all finished, as you'll
    see.
ARNOLPHE: Excellent. Well, upstairs with
    you, my dear:

SCENE IV

HORACE, ARNOLPHE

ARNOLPHE: What does her lack of money
    matter to me?
    What matters—Oh! What's this? No! Can
    it be?
    I'm dreaming. Yes, it's he, my dear friend's
    boy. Well!
HORACE: Sir!
ARNOLPHE: Horace!
HORACE: Arnolphe!
ARNOLPHE: Ah, what a
    joy!
    How long have you been in town?
HORACE: Nine
    days.
ARNOLPHE: Ah, so.
HORACE: I called at your house, in vain, a
    week ago.
ARNOLPHE: I'd left for the country.
HORACE: Yes, you
    were three days gone.
ARNOLPHE: How quickly children grow!
    How time rolls on!
    I am amazed that you're so big and
    tall.
    I can remember when you were—
    *(He makes a gesture of measuring from
    the floor).*
                    that
    small.
HORACE: Yes, time goes by.
ARNOLPHE: But come now,
    tell me of

I'll soon come back and see you, never
    fear;
There's serious talk in which we must
    engage.
(Exeunt all but ARNOLPHE.)
O learned ladies, heroines of the age,
Gushers of sentiment, I say that you,
For all your verse, and prose, and billets-
    doux,
Your novels, and your bright
    accomplishments,
Can't match this good and modest
    ignorance.

Oronte, your father, whom I esteem and
    love:
How's my old friend? Still spry and full of
    zest?
In all that's his, I take an interest.
Alas, it's four years since I talked with him,
And we've not written in the interim.
HORACE: Seigneur Arnolphe, he's spry
    enough for two;
    He gave me this little note to give to you,
    But now he writes me that he's coming
    here
    Himself, for reasons not entirely clear.
    Some fellow-townsman of yours, whom
    you may know,
    Went to America fourteen years ago;
    He's come back rich. Do you know of
    whom I speak?
ARNOLPHE: No. Did the letter give his
    name?
HORACE: Enrique.
ARNOLPHE: No . . . no . . .
HORACE: My father writes
    as if I ought
    To recognize that name, but I do not.
    He adds that he and Enrique will soon set
    out
    On some great errand that he's vague
    about.
ARNOLPHE: I long to see your father, that
    sterling man.
    I'll welcome him as royally as I can.

(He reads the note from Oronte.)
A friendly letter needn't flatter and fuss.
All this politeness is superfluous,
And even without his asking, I'd have
    desired
To lend you any money you required.
HORACE: I'll take you at your word, Sir. Can
    you advance
Fifty *pistoles* or so, by any chance?
ARNOLPHE: I'm grateful that you let me be
    of use,
And what you ask, I happily can produce.
Just keep the purse.
HORACE: Here—
ARNOLPHE: Forget the
    I.O.U.
Now, how does our town impress you?
    Tell me, do.
HORACE: It's rich in people, sublime in
    architecture,
And full of fine amusements, I conjecture.
ARNOLPHE: There's pleasure here for every
    taste; and those
The world calls gallants, ladies' men, or
    beaux
Find here the sport on which their hearts
    are set,
Since every woman in town's a born
    coquette.
Our ladies, dark or fair, are pliant
    creatures;
Their husbands, likewise, have permissive
    natures;
Oh, it's a capital game; it's often made
Me double up with mirth to see it played.
But you've already broken some hearts, I'd
    guess;
Have you no gallant conquest to confess?
Cuckolds are made by such as you, young
    man,
And looks like yours buy more than
    money can.
HORACE: Well, since you ask, I'll lay my
    secrets bare.
I *have* been having a covert love affair—
Which, out of friendship, I shall now
    unveil.
ARNOLPHE: Good, good; 't will be another
    rakish tale
Which I can put into my repertory.

HORACE: Sir, I must beg you: don't divulge
    my story.
ARNOLPHE: Of course not.
HORACE: As you know, Sir,
    in these matters,
One word let slip can leave one's hopes in
    tatters.
To put the business plainly, then, my
    heart's
Been lost to a lady dwelling in these parts.
My overtures, I'm very pleased to state,
Have found her ready to reciprocate,
And not to boast, or slur her reputation,
I think I'm in a hopeful situation.
ARNOLPHE: *(Laughing)* Who is she?
HORACE: A girl whose
    beauty is past telling,
And yonder red-walled mansion is her
    dwelling.
She's utterly naïve, because a blind
Fool has sequestered her from humankind,
And yet, despite the ignorance in which
He keeps her, she has charms that can
    bewitch;
She's most engaging, and conveys a sense
Of sweetness against which there's no
    defense.
But you, perhaps, have seen this star of love
Whose many graces I'm enamoured of.
Her name's Agnès.
ARNOLPHE: *(Aside)* Oh, death!
HORACE: The man, I
    hear,
Is called La Zousse, La Source, or
    something queer;
I didn't pay much attention to the name.
He's rich, I gather, but his wits are lame,
And he's accounted a ridiculous fellow.
D'you know him?
ARNOLPHE: *(Aside)* Ugh, what a bitter pill
    to swallow!
HORACE: I said, do you know him?
ARNOLPHE: Yes, I do,
    in a way.
HORACE: He's a dolt, isn't he?
ARNOLPHE: Oh!
HORACE: What?
                                         What
    What did you say?
He is, I take it. And a jealous idiot, too?

An ass? I see that all they said was true.
Well, to repeat, I love Agnès, a girl
Who is, to say the least, an orient pearl,
And it would be a sin for such a treasure
To be subjected to that old fool's pleasure.
Henceforth, my thoughts and efforts shall
    combine
To break his jealous hold and make her
    mine;
This purse, which I made bold to borrow,
    will lend
Me great assistance toward that worthy end.
As you well know, whatever means one
    tries,
Money's the key to every enterprise,
And this sweet metal, which all men
    hanker for,
Promotes our conquests, whether in love
    or war.
You look disturbed, Sir; can it be that you
Do not approve of what I mean to do?

ARNOLPHE: No; I was thinking—

HORACE: I'm boring you.
    Farewell, then.
    I'll soon drop by, to express my thanks
    again.

ARNOLPHE: *(To himself)* How could this
    happen—

HORACE: *(Returning)* Again, Sir, I entreat
    You not to tell my secret; be discreet.
    (He leaves)

ARNOLPHE: *(To himself)* I'm
    thunderstruck.

HORACE: *(Returning)* Above all, don't
    inform
    My father; he might raise a dreadful
    storm.
    (He leaves.)

ARNOLPHE: *(He expects* HORACE *to return
    again; that not occurring, he talks to
    himself.)* Oh! . . . What I've suffered
    during this conversation!
No soul has ever endured such agitation.
With what imprudence, and how hastily
He came and told the whole affair . . . to
    me!
He didn't know I'd taken a new title;
Still, what a rash and blundering recital!
I should, however, have kept myself in
    hand,
So as to learn what strategy he's planned,
And prompt his indiscretion, and discover
To what extent he has become her lover.
Come, I'll catch up with him; he can't be
    far;
I'll learn from him precisely how things
    are.
Alas, I'm trembling; I fear some further
    blow;
One can discover more than one wants to
    know.

ACT II

SCENE I

ARNOLPHE

ARNOLPHE: It's just as well, no doubt, that I
    should fail
    To catch him—that I somehow lost his trail:
For I could not have managed to dissemble
The turbulence of soul which makes me
    tremble;
He'd have perceived my present near-
    despair,
Of which it's best that he be unaware.
But I'm not one to be resigned and meek
And turn this little fop the other cheek.
I'll stop him; and the first thing I must do

Is find out just how far they've gone, those
    two.
This matter involves my honor, which I
    prize;
The girl's my wife already, in my eyes;
If she's been tarnished, I am covered with
    shame,
And all she's done reflects on my good
    name.
Oh, why did I take that trip? Oh, dear, oh,
    dear.
(He knocks at his door.)

SCENE II

ALAIN, GEORGETTE, ARNOLPHE

ALAIN: Ah! *This* time, Sir—

ARNOLPHE: Hush! Both of
you come here.

This way, this way. Come, hurry! Do as
you're told!

GEORGETTE: You frighten me; you make
my blood run cold.

ARNOLPHE: So! In my absence, you have
disobeyed me!

The two of you, in concert, have betrayed
me!

GEORGETTE: *(Falling on her knees)* Don't
eat me, Sir; don't eat me alive, I beg.

ALAIN: *(Aside)* I'd swear some mad dog's
nipped him in the leg.

ARNOLPHE: *(Aside)* Oof! I'm too tense to
speak. I'd like to shed

These blasted clothes. I'm burning up
with dread.

(To ALAIN *and* GEORGETTE*)* You cursèd
scoundrels, while I was gone you let

A man into this house—

(To ALAIN, *who has made a move to flee)*
No, not just yet!

Tell me at once— *(To* GEORGETTE*)* Don't
move! I want you two

To tell me—Whff! I mean to learn from
you—

*(*ALAIN *and* GEORGETTE *rise and try to
escape.)*

If anyone moves, I'll squash him like a
louse.

Now tell me, how did that man get into
my house?

Well, speak! Come, hurry. Quickly! Time
is fleeting!

Let's hear it! Speak!

ALAIN and GEORGETTE: *(Falling on their
knees)* Oh! Oh!

GEORGETTE: My heart's
stopped beating.

ALAIN: I'm dying.

ARNOLPHE: *(Aside)*
I'm sweating, and I need
some air.

I must calm down. I'll walk around the
square.

When I saw him in his cradle, I didn't
know

What he'd grow up and do to me. O woe!

Perhaps—yes, I'd do better to receive

The truth from her own lips, I now believe.

I'll mute my rage as well as I know how;

Patience, my wounded heart! Beat softly,
now!

(To ALAIN *and* GEORGETTE*)*

Get up, and go inside, and call Agnès.

Wait. *(Aside)* That way her surprise
would be the less.

They'd warn her of my anger, I don't
doubt.

I'd best go in myself and bring her out.

(To ALAIN *and* GEORGETTE*)*

Wait here.

SCENE III

ALAIN, GEORGETTE

GEORGETTE: God help us, but his rage is
terrible!

The way he glared at me—it was
unbearable.

He's the most hideous Christian I ever did
see.

ALAIN: He's vexed about that man, as I said
he'd be.

GEORGETTE: But why does he order us,
with barks and roars,

Never to let the mistress go outdoors?

Why does he want us to conceal her here

From all the world, and let no man come
near?

ALAIN: It's jealousy that makes him treat her
so.

GEORGETTE: But how did he get like that,
I'd like to know?

ALAIN: It comes of being jealous, I assume.

GEORGETTE: But why is he jealous? Why
    must he rage and fume?
ALAIN: Well, jealousy—listen carefully,
    Georgette—
    Is a thing—a thing—which makes a man
    upset,
    And makes him close his doors to
    everyone.
    I'm going to give you a comparison,
    So that you'll clearly understand the word.
    Suppose you were eating soup, and it
    occurred
    That someone tried to take what you were
    eating:
    Wouldn't you feel like giving him a
    beating?
GEORGETTE: Yes, I see that.
ALAIN: Then grasp this,
    if you can.
    Womankind is, in fact, the soup of man,

And when a man perceives that others
    wish
    To dip their dirty fingers into his dish,
    His temper flares, and bursts into a flame.
GEORGETTE: Yes. But not everybody feels
    the same.
    Some husbands seem to be delighted
    when
    Their wives consort with fancy
    gentlemen.
ALAIN: Not every husband is the greedy
    kind
    That wants to have it all.
GEORGETTE: If I'm not blind.
    He's coming back.
ALAIN: It's he; your eyes are
    keen.
GEORGETTE: He's scowling.
ALAIN: That's because
    he's feeling mean.

SCENE IV

ARNOLPHE, ALAIN, GEORGETTE

ARNOLPHE: *(Aside)* A certain Greek
    presumed once to advise
    The great Augustus, and his words were
    wise:
    When you are vexed, he said, do not
    forget,
    Before you act, to say the alphabet,
    So as to cool your temper, and prevent
    Rash moves which later on you might
    repent.

In dealing with Agnès, I have applied
    That counsel, and I've bidden her come
    outside,
    Under the pretext of a morning stroll,
    So that I can relieve my jangled soul
    By seeking dulcetly to draw her out
    And learn the truth, and put an end to
    doubt.
    (Calling) Come out, Agnès. *(To* ALAIN *and*
    GEORGETTE*)* Go in.

SCENE V

ARNOLPHE, AGNÈS

ARNOLPHE: The weather's mild.
AGNÈS: Oh, yes.
ARNOLPHE: Most pleasant.
AGNÈS: Indeed!
ARNOLPHE: What news, my
    child?
AGNÈS: The kitten died.
ARNOLPHE: Too bad, but what
    of that?
    All men are mortal, my dear, and so's a cat.

While I was gone, no doubt it rained and
    poured?
AGNÈS: No
ARNOLPHE: You were bored, perhaps?
AGNÈS: I'm
    never bored.
ARNOLPHE: During my ten days' absence,
    what did you do?
AGNÈS: Six nightshirts, I believe; six
    nightcaps, too.

ARNOLPHE: *(After a pause)* My dear Agnès,
 this world's a curious thing.
 What wicked talk one hears, what
  gossiping!
 While I was gone, or so the neighbors
  claim,
 There was a certain strange young man
  who came
 To call upon you here, and was received.
 But such a slander's not to be believed,
 And I would wager that their so-called
  news—
AGNÈS: Heavens! Don't wager; you'd be sure
 to lose.
ARNOLPHE: What! Is it true, that a man—
AGNÈS: Oh, yes.
 In fact, he all but lived at this address.
ARNOLPHE: *(Aside)* That frank reply would
 seem to demonstrate
 That she's still free of guile, at any rate.
 (Aloud)
 But I gave orders, Agnès, as I recall,
 That you were to see no one, no one at all.
AGNÈS: I disobeyed you, but when I tell you
 why,
 You'll say that you'd have done the same
  as I.
ARNOLPHE: Perhaps; well, tell me how this
 thing occurred.
AGNÈS: It's the most amazing story you ever
 heard.
 I was sewing, out on the balcony, in the
  breeze,
 When I noticed someone strolling under
  the trees.
 It was a fine young man, who caught my
  eye
 And made me a deep bow as he went by.
 I, not to be convicted of a lack
 Of manners, very quickly nodded back.
 At once, the young man bowed to me
  again.
 I bowed to him a second time, and then
 It wasn't very long until he made
 A third deep bow, which I of course
  repaid.
 He left, but kept returning, and as he
  passed,
 He'd bow, each time, more gracefully than
  the last,

 While I, observing as he came and went,
 Gave each new bow a fresh
  acknowledgment.
 Indeed, had night not fallen, I declare
 I think that I might still be sitting there,
 And bowing back each time he bowed to
  me,
 For fear he'd think me less polite than he."
ARNOLPHE: Go on.
AGNÈS: Then an old woman
 came, next day,
 And found me standing in the entryway.
 She said to me, "May Heaven bless you,
  dear,
 And keep you beautiful for many a year.
 God, who bestowed on you such grace and
  charm,
 Did not intend those gifts to do men harm,
 And you should know that there's a heart
  which bears
 A wound which you've inflicted
  unawares."
ARNOLPHE: *(Aside)* Old witch! Old tool of
 Satan! Damn her hide!
AGNÈS: "You say I've wounded somebody?"
 I cried.
 "Indeed you have," she said. "The victim's
  he
 Whom yesterday you saw from the
  balcony."
 "But how could such a thing occur?" I
  said;
 "Can I have dropped some object on his
  head?"
 "No," she replied, "your bright eyes dealt
  the blow;
 Their glances are the cause of all his
  woe."
 "Good heavens, Madam," said I in great
  surprise,
 "Is there some dread contagion in my
  eyes?"
 "Ah, yes, my child," said she. "Your eyes
  dispense,
 Unwittingly, a fatal influence:
 The poor young man has dwindled to a
  shade;
 And if you cruelly deny him aid,
 I greatly fear," the kind old woman went
  on,

"That two days more will see him dead
    and gone."
"Heavens," I answered, "that would be sad
    indeed.
But what can I do for him? What help
    does he need?"
"My child," said she, "he only asks of you
The privilege of a little interview;
It is your eyes alone which now can save
    him,
And cure him of the malady they gave
    him."
"If that's the case," I said, "I can't refuse;
I'll gladly see him, whenever he may
    choose."
ARNOLPHE: *(Aside)* O "kind old woman"!
    O vicious sorceress!
May Hell reward you for your cleverness!
AGNÈS: And so I saw him, which brought
    about his cure.
You'll grant I did the proper thing, I'm
    sure.
How could I have the conscience to deny
The succor he required, and let him die —
I, who so pity anyone in pain,
And cannot bear to see a chicken slain?
ARNOLPHE: *(Aside)* It's clear that she has
    meant no wrong, and I
Must blame that foolish trip I took,
    whereby
I left her unprotected from the lies
That rascally seducers can devise.
Oh, what if that young wretch, with one
    bold stroke,
Has compromised her? That would be no
    joke.
AGNÈS: What's wrong? You seem a trifle
    irritated.
Was there some harm in what I just
    related?
ARNOLPHE: No, but go on. I want to hear it
    all.
What happened when the young man
    came to call?
AGNÈS: Oh, if you'd seen how happy he
    was, how gay,
And how his sickness vanished right
    away,
And the jewel-case he gave me — not to
    forget

The coins he gave to Alain and to
    Georgette,
You would have loved him also, and you
    too —
ARNOLPHE: And when you were alone,
    what did he do?
AGNÈS: He swore he loved me with a
    matchless passion,
And said to me, in the most charming
    fashion,
Things which I found incomparably
    sweet,
And never tire of hearing him repeat,
So much do they delight my ear, and start
I know not what commotion in my heart.
ARNOLPHE: *(Aside)* O strange interrogation,
    where each reply
Makes the interrogator wish to die!
(To AGNÈS*)*
Besides these compliments, these sweet
    addresses,
Were there not also kisses, and caresses?
AGNÈS: Oh, yes! He took my hands, and
    kissed and kissed
Them both, as if he never would desist.
ARNOLPHE: And did he not take —
    something else as well?
(He notes that she is taken aback.)
    Agh!
AGNÈS: Well, he —
ARNOLPHE: Yes?
AGNÈS: Took —
ARNOLPHE: What?
AGNÈS: I dare not
    tell.
I fear that you'll be furious with me.
ARNOLPHE: No.
AGNÈS: Yes.
ARNOLPHE: No, no.
AGNÈS: Then promise not to be.
ARNOLPHE: I promise.
AGNÈS: He took my — oh,
    you'll have a fit.
ARNOLPHE: No.
AGNÈS: Yes.
ARNOLPHE: No, no. The devil! Out
    with it!
What did he take from you?
AGNÈS: He took —
ARNOLPHE: *(Aside)*   God save me!

AGNÈS: He took the pretty ribbon that you
    gave me.
    Indeed, he begged so that I couldn't resist.
ARNOLPHE: *(Taking a deep breath)* Forget
    the ribbon. Tell me: once he'd kissed
    Your hands, what else did he do, as you
    recall?
AGNÈS: Does one do other things?
ARNOLPHE: No, not at
    all;
    But didn't he ask some further medicine
    For the sad state of health that he was in?
AGNÈS: Why, no. But had he asked, you
    may be sure
    I'd have done anything to speed his cure.
ARNOLPHE: *(Aside)* I've got off cheap this
    once, thanks be to God;
    If I slip again, let all men call me clod.
    (To AGNÈS)
    Agnès, my dear, your innocence is vast;
    I shan't reproach you; what is past is past.
    But all that trifler wants to do—don't
    doubt it—
    Is to deceive you, and then boast about it.
AGNÈS: Oh, no. He's often assured me
    otherwise.
ARNOLPHE: Ah, you don't know how that
    sort cheats and lies.
    But do grasp this: to accept a jewel-case,
    And let some coxcomb praise your pretty
    face,
    And be complaisant when he takes a notion
    To kiss your hands and fill you with
    "commotion"
    Is a great sin, for which your soul could
    die.
AGNÈS: A sin, you say! But please, Sir, tell
    me why.
ARNOLPHE: Why? Why? Because, as all
    authority states,
    It's just such deeds that Heaven
    abominates.
AGNÈS: Abominates! But why should
    Heaven feel so?
    It's all so charming and so sweet, you
    know!
    I never knew about this sort of thing
    Till now, or guessed what raptures it could
    bring.
ARNOLPHE: Yes, all these promises of love
    undying,

These sighs, these kisses, are most
    gratifying,
    But they must be enjoyed in the proper
    way;
    One must be married first, that is to say.
AGNÈS: And once you're married, there's no
    evil in it?
ARNOLPHE: That's right.
AGNÈS: Oh, let me marry,
    then, this minute!
ARNOLPHE: If that's what you desire, I feel
    the same;
    It was to plan your marriage that I came.
AGNÈS: What! Truly?
ARNOLPHE: Yes.
AGNÈS: How happy I shall
    be!
ARNOLPHE: Yes, wedded life will please
    you, I foresee.
AGNÈS: You really intend that we two—
ARNOLPHE: Yes, I do.
AGNÈS: Oh, how I'll kiss you if that dream
    comes true!
ARNOLPHE: And I'll return your kisses,
    every one.
AGNÈS: I'm never sure when people are
    making fun.
    Are you quite serious?
ARNOLPHE: Yes, I'm serious.
    Quite.
AGNÈS: We're to be married?
ARNOLPHE: Yes.
AGNÈS: But when?
ARNOLPHE: Tonight.
AGNÈS: *(Laughing)* Tonight?
ARNOLPHE: Tonight. It
    seems you're moved to laughter.
AGNÈS: Yes.
ARNOLPHE: Well, to see you happy is what
    I'm after.
AGNÈS: Oh, Sir, I owe you more than I can
    express!
    With him, my life will be pure happiness!
ARNOLPHE: With whom?
AGNÈS: With . . . him.
ARNOLPHE: With *him!* Well,
    think again.
    You're rather hasty in your choice of men.
    It's quite another husband I have in mind;
    And as for "him," as you call him, be so
    kind,

Regardless of his pitiable disease,
As never again to see him, if you please.
When next he calls, girl, put him in his
  place
By slamming the door directly in his face;
Then, if he knocks, go up and drop a brick
From the second-floor window. That
  should do the trick.
Do you understand, Agnès? I shall be hidden
Nearby, to see that you do as you are bidden.

AGNÈS: Oh, dear, he's so good-looking, so—
ARNOLPHE: Be still!
AGNÈS: I just won't have the heart—
ARNOLPHE: Enough; you will.
  Now go upstairs.
AGNÈS: How can you—
ARNOLPHE: Do as I
  say.
I'm master here; I've spoken; go, obey.

ACT III

SCENE I

ARNOLPHE, AGNÈS, ALAIN, GEORGETTE

ARNOLPHE: Yes. I'm most pleased; it
  couldn't have gone better.
By following my instructions to the letter,
You've put that young philanderer to flight:
See how wise generalship can set things
  right.
Your innocence had been abused, Agnès;
Unwittingly, you'd got into a mess,
And, lacking my good counsel, you were
  well
Embarked upon a course which leads to
  Hell.
Those beaux are all alike, believe you me:
They've ribbons, plumes, and ruffles at the
  knee,
Fine wigs, and polished talk, and brilliant
  teeth,
But they're all scales and talons
  underneath—
Indeed, they're devils of the vilest sort,
Who prey on women's honor for their sport.
However, owing to my watchful care,
You have emerged intact from this affair.
The firm and righteous way in which you
  threw

That brick at him, and dashed his hopes of
  you,
Persuades me that there's no cause to delay
The wedding which I promised you today.
But first, it would be well for me to make
A few remarks for your improvement's
  sake.
(To ALAIN, *who brings a chair*)
I'll sit here, where it's cool.
(To GEORGETTE) Remember, now—
GEORGETTE: Oh, Sir, we won't forget again,
  I vow.
That young man won't get round us any
  more.
ALAIN: I'll give up drink if he gets through
  that door.
Anyway, he's an idiot; we bit
Two coins he gave us, and they were
  counterfeit.
ARNOLPHE: Well, go and buy the food for
  supper, and then
One of you, as you're coming home again,
Can fetch the local notary from the
  square.
Tell him that there's a contract to prepare.

SCENE II

ARNOLPHE, AGNÈS

ARNOLPHE: (*Seated*) Agnès, stop knitting
  and hear what I have to say.
Lift up your head a bit, and turn this
  way.

(*Putting his finger to his forehead*)
Look at me *there* while I talk to you right
  there,
And listen to my every word with care.

My dear, I'm going to wed you, and you
    should bless
Your vast good fortune and your
    happiness.
Reflect upon your former low estate,
And judge, then, if my goodness is not
    great
In raising you, a humble peasant lass,
To be a matron of the middle class,
To share the bed and the connubial bliss
Of one who's shunned the married state
    till this,
Withholding from a charming score or
    two
The honor which he now bestows on you.
Be ever mindful, Agnès, that you would
    be,
Without this union, a nonentity;
And let that thought incline your heart to
    merit
The name which I shall lend you, and to
    bear it
With such propriety that I shall never
Regret my choice for any cause whatever.
Marriage, Agnès, is no light matter; the
    role
Of wife requires austerity of soul,
And I do not exalt you to that station
To lead a life of heedless dissipation.
Yours is the weaker sex, please realize;
It is the beard in which all power lies,
And though there are two portions of
    mankind,
Those portions are not equal, you will
    find:
One half commands, the other must obey;
The second serves the first in every way;
And that obedience which the soldier
    owes
His general, or the loyal servant shows
His master, or the good child pays his sire,
Or the stern abbot looks for in the friar,
Is nothing to the pure docility,
The deep submission and humility
Which a good wife must ever exhibit
    toward
The man who is her master, chief, and
    lord.
Should he regard her with a serious air,
She must avert her eyes, and never dare

To lift them to his face again, unless
His look should change to one of
    tenderness.
Such things aren't understood by women
    today,
But don't let bad example lead you astray.
Don't emulate those flirts whose
    indiscretions
Are told all over town at gossip-sessions,
Or yield to Satan's trickery by allowing
Young fops to please you with their smiles
    and bowing.
Remember that, in marrying, I confide
To you, Agnès, my honor and my pride;
That honor is a tender, fragile thing
With which there can be no light
    dallying;
And that all misbehaving wives shall
    dwell
In ever-boiling cauldrons down in Hell.
These are no idle lessons which I impart,
And you'll do well to get them all by
    heart.
Your soul, if you observe them, and abjure
Flirtation, will be lily-white and pure;
But deviate from honor, and your soul
Will forthwith grow as vile and black as
    coal;
All will abhor you as a thing of evil,
Till one day you'll be taken by the Devil,
And Hell's eternal fire is where he'll send
    you —
From which sad fate may Heaven's grace
    defend you.
Make me a curtsey. Now then, just as a
    novice,
Entering the convent, learns by heart her
    office,
So, entering wedlock, you should do the
    same.
(He rises)
I have, in my pocket, a book of no small
    fame
From which you'll learn the office of a
    wife.
'T was written by some man of pious life.
Study his teaching faithfully, and heed it.
Here, take the book; let's hear how well
    you read it.
AGNÈS: *(Reading)*

The Maxims of Marriage
or
*The Duties of a Married Woman,
Together with Her Daily Exercises.*

First Maxim:
A woman who in church has said
She'll love and honor and obey
Should get it firmly in her head,
Despite the fashions of the day,
That he who took her for his own
Has taken her for his bed alone.

ARNOLPHE: I shall explain that; doubtless
        you're perplexed.
    But, for the present, let us hear what's
    next.
AGNÈS: *(Continuing)*

Second Maxim:
She needs no fine attire
More than he may desire
Who is her lord and master.
To dress for any taste but his is vain;
    If others find her plain,
        'T is no disaster.

Third Maxim:
Let her not daub her face
With paint and patch and powder-base
And creams which promise beauty on the label.
It is not for their husbands' sake
But vanity's, that women undertake
The labors of the dressing table.

Fourth Maxim:
Let her be veiled whenever she leaves the house,
So that her features are obscure and dim.
If she desires to please her spouse,
She must please no one else but him.

Fifth Maxim:
Except for friends who call
To see her husband, let her not admit
    Anyone at all.
    A visitor whose end

Is to amuse the wife with gallant wit
    Is *not* the husband's friend.

Sixth Maxim:
To men who would confer kind gifts upon her,
She must reply with self-respecting nays.
Not to refuse would be to court dishonor.
Nothing is given for nothing nowadays.

Seventh Maxim:
She has no need, whatever she may think,
Of writing table, paper, pen, or ink.
In a proper house, the husband is the one
To do whatever writing's to be done.

Eighth Maxim:
    At those licentious things
    Called social gatherings,
Wives are corrupted by the worldly crowd.
Since, at such functions, amorous plots are laid
        And married men betrayed,
        They should not be allowed.

Ninth Maxim:
Let the wise wife, who cares for her good name,
Decline to play at any gambling game.
In such seductive pastimes wives can lose
Far more than coins, or bills, or I.O.U.'s.

Tenth Maxim:
    It is not good for wives
    To go on gay excursions,
    Picnics, or country drives.
    In all such light diversions,
    No matter who's the host,
    The husbands pay the most.

Eleventh Maxim—

ARNOLPHE: Good. Read the rest to yourself.
        I'll clarify
    Whatever may confuse you, by and by.
    I've just recalled some business I'd forgot;
    'T will only take a moment, like as not.
    Go in, and treat that precious book with
        care.
    If the notary comes, tell him to have a
        chair.

SCENE III

ARNOLPHE

ARNOLPHE: What could be safer than to
    marry her?
She'll do and be whatever I prefer.
She's like a lump of wax, and I can mold
    her
Into what shape I like, as she grows older.
True, she was almost lured away from me,
Whilst I was gone, through her simplicity;
But if one's wife must have some
    imperfection,
It's best that she should err in that
    direction.
Such faults as hers are easy to remove:
A simple wife is eager to improve,
And if she has been led astray, a slight
Admonitory talk will set her right.
But a clever wife's another kettle of fish:
One's at the mercy of her every wish;
What she desires, she'll have at any cost,
And reasoning with her is labor lost.
Her wicked wit makes virtues of her
    crimes,
Makes mock of principle, and oftentimes
Contrives, in furtherance of some wicked
    plan,
Intrigues which can defeat the shrewdest
    man.
Against her there is no defense, for she's
Unbeatable at plots and strategies,
And once she has resolved to amputate
Her husband's honor, he must bow to fate.
There's many a decent man could tell that
    story.
But that young fool will have no chance to
    glory
In my disgrace: he has too loose a tongue,
And that's a fault of Frenchmen, old or
    young.
When they are lucky in a love affair,
To keep the secret's more than they can
    bear;
A foolish vanity torments them, till
They'd rather hang, by Heaven, than be
    still.
What but the spells of Satan could incline
Women to favor men so asinine?
But here he comes; my feelings must not
    show
As I extract from him his tale of woe.

SCENE IV

HORACE, ARNOLPHE

HORACE: I've just been at your house, and I
    begin
To fear I'm fated never to find you in.
But I'll persist, and one day have the joy —
ARNOLPHE: Ah, come, no idle compliments,
    my boy.
All this fine talk, so flowery and so
    polished,
Is something I'd be glad to see abolished.
It's a vile custom: most men waste two-
    thirds
Of every day exchanging empty words.
Let's put our hats on, now, and be at ease.
Well, how's your love life going? Do tell
    me, please.
I was a bit distrait when last we met,
But what you told me I did not forget:
Your bold beginnings left me much
    impressed,
And now I'm all agog to hear the rest.
HORACE: Since I unlocked my heart to you,
    alas,
My hopes have come to an unhappy pass.
ARNOLPHE: Oh, dear! How so?
HORACE: Just now —
    alas — I learned
That my beloved's guardian has returned.
ARNOLPHE: That's bad.
HORACE: What's more, he's
    well aware that we've
Been meeting secretly, without his
    leave.

ARNOLPHE: But how could he so quickly
    find that out?
HORACE: I don't know, but he has, beyond a
    doubt.
    I went at my usual hour, more or less,
    To pay my homage to her loveliness,
    And found the servants changed in
      attitude.
    They barred my way; their words and
      looks were rude.
    "Be off!" they told me, and with no good
      grace
    They slammed the door directly in my
      face.
ARNOLPHE: Right in your face!
HORACE: Yes.
ARNOLPHE: Dreadful.
    Tell me more.
HORACE: I tried to reason with them
    through the door,
    But whatsoever I said to them, they cried,
    "The master says you're not to come
      inside."
ARNOLPHE: They wouldn't open it!
HORACE: No. And then Agnès,
    On orders from her guardian, as one could
      guess,
    Came to her window, said that she was
      sick
    Of my attentions, and threw down a brick.
ARNOLPHE: A brick, you say!
HORACE: A brick; and it
    wasn't small.
    Not what one hopes for when one pays a
      call.
ARNOLPHE: Confound it! That's no mild
    rebuff, my lad.
    I fear your situation's pretty bad.
HORACE: Yes, that old fool's return has
    spoiled my game.
ARNOLPHE: You have my deepest
    sympathy; it's a shame.
HORACE: He's wrecked my plans.
ARNOLPHE: Oh, come;
    you've lost some ground,
    But some means of recouping will be
      found.
HORACE: With a little inside help, I might
    by chance
    Outwit this jealous fellow's vigilance.

ARNOLPHE: That should be easy. The lady,
    as you say,
    Loves you.
HORACE: Indeed, yes.
ARNOLPHE: Then you'll find a
    way.
HORACE: I hope so.
ARNOLPHE: You must not be put to
    flight
    By that ungracious brick.
HORACE: Of course you're
    right.
    I knew at once that that old fool was back
    And secretly directing the attack.
    But what amazed me (you'll be amazed as
      well)
    Was something else she did, of which I'll
      tell—
    A daring trick one wouldn't expect to see
    Played by a girl of such simplicity.
    Love is indeed a wondrous master, Sir,
    Whose teaching makes us what we never
      were,
    And under whose miraculous tuition
    One suddenly can change one's
      disposition.
    It overturns our settled inclinations,
    Causing the most astounding
      transformations:
    The miser's made a spendthrift overnight,
    The coward valiant, and the boor polite;
    Love spurs the sluggard on to high
      endeavor,
    And moves the artless maiden to be clever.
    Well, such a miracle has changed Agnès.
    She cried, just now, with seeming
      bitterness,
    "Go! I refuse to see you, and don't ask
      why;
    To all your questions, here is my reply!"—
    And having made that statement, down
      she threw
    The brick I've mentioned, and a letter, too.
    Note how her words apply to brick *and*
      letter:
    Isn't that fine? Could any ruse be better?
    Aren't you amazed? Do you see what great
      effect
    True love can have upon the intellect?
    Can you deny its power to inspire

The gentlest heart with fortitude and fire?
How do you like that trick with the letter, eh?
A most astute young woman, wouldn't you say?
As for my jealous rival, isn't the role
He's played in this affair extremely droll?
Well?

ARNOLPHE:
      Yes, quite droll.

HORACE: Well, laugh, if that's the case!

(ARNOLPHE *gives a forced laugh*)

My, what a fool! He fortifies his place
Against me, using bricks for cannon balls,
As if he feared that I might storm the walls;
What's more, in his anxiety he rallies
His two domestics to repulse my sallies;
And then he's hoodwinked by the girl he meant
To keep forever meek and innocent!
I must confess that, though this silly man's
Return to town has balked my amorous plans,
The whole thing's been so comical that I find
That I'm convulsed whenever it comes to mind.
You haven't laughed as much as I thought you would.

ARNOLPHE: *(With a forced laugh)* I beg your pardon; I've done the best I could.

HORACE: But let me show you the letter she wrote, my friend.
What her heart feels, her artless hand has penned
In the most touching terms, the sweetest way,
With pure affection, purest naïveté;
Nature herself, I think, would so express
Love's first awakening and its sweet distress.

ARNOLPHE: *(Aside)* Behold what scribbling leads to! It was quite
Against my wishes that she learned to write.

HORACE: *(Reading)* I am moved to write to you, but I am much at a loss as to how to begin. I have thoughts which I should like you to know of; but I don't know how to go about telling them to you, and I mistrust my own words. I begin to perceive that I have always been kept in a state of ignorance, and so I am fearful of writing something I shouldn't, or of saying more than I ought. In truth, I don't know what you have done to me, but I know that I am mortally vexed by the harsh things I am made to do to you, that it will be the most painful thing in the world to give you up, and that I would be happy indeed to be yours. Perhaps it is rash of me to say that; but in any case I cannot help saying it, and I wish that I could have my desire without doing anything wrong. I am constantly told that all young men are deceivers, that they mustn't be listened to, and that all you have said to me is mere trickery; I assure you, however, that I have not yet been able to think that of you, and your words so touch me that I cannot believe them false. Please tell me frankly what you intend; for truly, since my own intentions are blameless, it would be very wicked of you to deceive me, and I think that I should die of despair.

ARNOLPHE: *(Aside)* The bitch!

HORACE: What's wrong?

ARNOLPHE: Oh, nothing: I was sneezing.

HORACE: Was ever a style so amiable, so pleasing?
Despite the tyranny she's had to bear,
Isn't her nature sweet beyond compare?
And is it not a crime of the basest kind
For anyone to stifle such a mind,
To starve so fine a spirit, and to enshroud
In ignorance a soul so well-endowed?
Love has begun to waken her, however,
And if some kind star favors my endeavor
I'll free her from that utter beast, that black
Villain, that wretch, that brute, that maniac—

ARNOLPHE: Good-bye.

HORACE: What, going?

ARNOLPHE: I've just recalled that I'm
Due somewhere else in a few minutes' time.

HORACE: Wait! Can you think of someone who might possess
An entrée to that house, and to Agnès?

I hate to trouble you, but do please lend
Whatever help you can, as friend to
    friend.
The servants, as I said, both man and
    maid,
Have turned against my cause, and can't
    be swayed.
Just now, despite my every blandishment,
They eyed me coldly, and would not
    relent.
I had, for a time, the aid of an old woman
Whose talent for intrigue was
    superhuman;
She served me, at the start, with much
    success,
But died four days ago, to my distress.
Don't you know someone who could help
    me out?
ARNOLPHE: I don't; but you'll find someone,
    I don't doubt.
HORACE: Farewell, then, Sir. You'll be
    discreet, I know.

SCENE V

ARNOLPHE

ARNOLPHE: In that boy's presence, what
    hell I undergo,
Trying to hide my anguish from his eye!
To think that an innocent girl should
    prove so sly!
Either she's fooled me, and never *was*
    naïve,
Or Satan's just now taught her to deceive.
That cursèd letter! I wish that I were dead.
Plainly that callow wretch has turned her
    head,
Captured her mind and heart, eclipsed me
    there,
And doomed me to distraction and despair.
The loss of her entails a double hell:
My honor suffers, and my love as well.
It drives me mad to see myself displaced,
And all my careful planning gone to
    waste.
To be revenged on her, I need but wait
And let her giddy passion meet its fate;
The upshot can't be anything but bad.
But oh, to lose the thing one loves is sad.
Good Lord! To rear her with such
    calculation,
And then fall victim to infatuation!
She has no funds, no family, yet she can
    dare
Abuse my lavish kindness and my care;
And what, for Heaven's sake, is my
    reaction?
In spite of all, I love her to distraction!
Have you no shame, fool? Don't you resent
    her crimes?
Oh, I could slap my face a thousand times!
I'll go inside for a bit, but only to see
How she will face me after her treachery.
Kind Heaven, let no dishonor stain my
    brow;
Or if it is decreed that I must bow
To that misfortune, lend me at least, I
    pray,
Such patient strength as some poor men
    display.

ACT IV

SCENE I

ARNOLPHE

ARNOLPHE: (*Entering from the house, alone*)
    I can't hold still a minute, I declare.
    My anxious thoughts keep darting here
        and there,
Planning defenses, seeking to prevent
That rascal from achieving his intent.
How calm the traitress looked when I
    went in!

Despite her crimes, she shows no sense of
sin,
And though she's all but sent me to my
grave,
How like a little saint she dares behave!
The more she sat there, cool and
unperturbed,
The less I thought my fury could be
curbed;
Yet, strange to say, my heart's increasing
ire
Seemed only to redouble my desire.
I was embittered, desperate, irate,
And yet her beauty had never seemed so
great.
Never did her bright eyes so penetrate me,
So rouse my spirit, so infatuate me;
Oh, it would break the heart within my
breast
Should fate subject me to this cruel jest.

What! Have I supervised her education
With loving care and long consideration,
Sheltered her since she was a tiny
creature,
Cherished sweet expectations for her
future,
For thirteen years molded her character
And based my hopes of happiness on her,
Only to see some young fool steal the prize
Of her affection, under my very eyes,
And just when she and I were all but wed?
Ah, no, young friend! Ah, no, young
chucklehead!
I mean to stop you; I swear that you shall
not
Succeed, however well you scheme and
plot,
And that you'll have no cause to laugh at
me.

SCENE II

THE NOTARY, ARNOLPHE

NOTARY: Ah, here you are, Sir! I am the
notary.
So, there's a contract which you'd have me
draw?
ARNOLPHE: *(Unaware of the notary)* How
shall I do it?
NOTARY: According to the law.
ARNOLPHE: *(Still oblivious)* I must be
prudent, and think what course is best.
NOTARY: I shall do nothing against your
interest.
ARNOLPHE: *(Oblivious)* One must
anticipate the unexpected.
NOTARY: In my hands, you'll be thoroughly
protected.
But do remember, lest you be betrayed,
To sign no contract till the dowry's paid.
ARNOLPHE: *(Oblivious)* I must act covertly;
if this thing gets out,
The gossips will have much to blab about.
NOTARY: If you're so anxious not to make a
stir,
The contract can be drawn in secret, Sir.
ARNOLPHE: *(Oblivious)* But how shall she
be dealt with? Can I condone—

NOTARY: The dowry is proportional to her
own.
ARNOLPHE: *(Oblivious)* It's hard to be strict
with one whom you adore.
NOTARY: In that case, you may wish to give
her more.
ARNOLPHE: *(Oblivious)* How should I treat
the girl? I must decide.
NOTARY: As a general rule, the husband
gives the bride
A dowry that's one-third the size of hers;
But he may increase the sum, if he prefers.
ARNOLPHE: *(Oblivious)* If—
NOTARY: (ARNOLPHE *now noticing him)*
                    As for property,
and its division
In case of death, the husband makes
provision
As he thinks best.
ARNOLPHE: Eh?
NOTARY: He can make certain
of
His bride's security, and show his love,
By jointure, or a settlement whereby
The gift is canceled should the lady die,

Reverting to her heirs, if so agreed;
Or go by common law; or have a deed
Of gift appended to the instrument,
Either by his sole wish, or by consent.
Why shrug your shoulders? Am I talking
    rot?
Do I know contracts, Sir, or do I not?
Who could instruct me? Who would be so
    bold?
Do I not know that spouses jointly hold
Goods, chattels, lands, and money in their
    two names,
Unless one party should renounce all
    claims?
Do I not know that a third of the bride's
    resources
Enters the joint estate —
ARNOLPHE: All that, of course,
    is

True. But who asked for all this pedantry?
NOTARY: You did! And now you sniff and
    shrug at me,
And treat my competence with ridicule.
ARNOLPHE: The devil take this ugly-
    featured fool!
Good day, good day. An end to all this
    chatter.
NOTARY: Did you not ask my aid in a legal
    matter?
ARNOLPHE: Yes, yes, but now the matter's
    been deferred.
When your advice is needed, I'll send
    word.
Meanwhile, stop blathering, you
    blatherskite!
NOTARY: He's mad, I judge; and I think my
    judgment's right.

SCENE III

THE NOTARY, ALAIN, GEORGETTE, ARNOLPHE

NOTARY: *(To* ALAIN *and* GEORGETTE*)* Your
    master sent you to fetch me, isn't that
    so?
ALAIN: Yes.
NOTARY: How you feel about him I don't
    know,

But I regard him as a senseless boor.
Tell him I said so.
GEORGETTE: We will, you may be
    sure.

SCENE IV

ALAIN, GEORGETTE, ARNOLPHE

ALAIN: Sir —
ARNOLPHE: Ah, come here, my good
    friends, tried and true:
You've amply proved that I may count on
    you.
ALAIN: The notary —
ARNOLPHE: Tell me later, will you
    not?
My honor's threatened by a vicious plot;
Think, children, what distress you'd feel,
    what shame,
If some dishonor touched your master's
    name!
You wouldn't dare to leave the house, for
    fear

That all the town would point at you, and
    sneer.
Since we're together, then, in this affair,
You must be ever watchful, and take care
That no approach that gallant may
    adopt —
GEORGETTE: We've learned our lesson, Sir;
    he shall be stopped.
ARNOLPHE: Beware his fine words and his
    flatteries.
ALAIN: Of course.
GEORGETTE: We can resist such talk
    with ease.
ARNOLPHE: *(To* ALAIN*)* What if he said,
    "Alain, for mercy's sake,

Do me a kindness" — what answer would
    you make?
ALAIN: I'd say, "You fool!"
ARNOLPHE: Good, good. *(To* GEORGETTE*)*
    "Georgette, my dear, I'm sure you're
    just as sweet as you appear."
GEORGETTE: "Fathead!"
ARNOLPHE: Good, good. *(To*
    ALAIN*)* "Come, let me in. You know
    That my intent is pure as the driven
    snow."
ALAIN: "Sir, you're a knave!"
ARNOLPHE: Well said. *(To*
    GEORGETTE*)* "Unless you take
    Pity on my poor heart, it's sure to break."
GEORGETTE: "You are an impudent ass!"
ARNOLPHE: Well said,
    Georgette.
    "I'm not the sort of person to forget
    A favor, or begrudge the *quid pro quo,*
    As these few coins, Alain, will serve to
    show.
    And you, Georgette, take this and buy a
    dress.
    (Both hold out their hands and take the
    money.)
    That's but a specimen of my largesse.
    And all I ask is that you grant to me

An hour of your young mistress'
    company."
GEORGETTE: *(Giving him a shove)* "You're
    crazy!"
ARNOLPHE: Good!
ALAIN: *(Shoving* ARNOLPHE*)* "Move on!"
ARNOLPHE: Good!
GEORGETTE: *(Shoving* ARNOLPHE*)*
         "Out of my sight!"
ARNOLPHE: Good, good — but that's enough.
GEORGETTE: Did I do it right?
ALAIN: Is that how we're to treat him?
ARNOLPHE: You were fine;
    Except for the money, which you should
    decline.
GEORGETTE: We didn't think, Sir. That was
    wrong indeed.
ALAIN: Would you like to do it over again?
ARNOLPHE: No need;
    Go back inside.
ALAIN: Sir, if you say the word,
    we —
ARNOLPHE: No, that will do; go in at once;
    you heard me.
    Just keep the money; I shall be with you
    shortly.
    Be on your guard, and ready to support
    me.

SCENE V

ARNOLPHE

ARNOLPHE: The cobbler at the corner is
    sharp of eye;
    I think that I'll enlist him as a spy.
    As for Agnès, I'll keep her under guard,
    And all dishonest women shall be barred —
    Hairdressers, glovers, handkerchief-makers,
    those
    Who come to the door with ribbons, pins,
    and bows,

And often, as a sideline to such wares,
Are go-betweens in secret love affairs.
I know the world, and the tricks that
    people use;
That boy will have to invent some brand-
    new ruse
If he's to get a message in to her.

SCENE VI

HORACE, ARNOLPHE

HORACE: What luck to find you in this
    quarter, Sir!
    I've just had a narrow escape, believe you
    me!

Just after I left you, whom did I chance to
    see
Upon her shady balcony, but the fair
Agnès, who had come out to take the air!

She managed, having signaled me to wait,
To steal downstairs and open the garden
    gate.
We went to her room, and were no sooner
    there
Than we heard her jealous guardian on
    the stair;
In which great peril I was thrust by her
Into a wardrobe where her dresses were.
He entered. I couldn't see him, but I heard
Him striding back and forth without a
    word,
Heaving deep sighs of woe again and again,
Pounding upon the tables now and then,
Kicking a little dog, who yipped in fright,
And throwing her possessions left and
    right.
What's more, to give his fury full release,
He knocked two vases off her mantelpiece.
Clearly the old goat had some vague,
    dismaying
Sense of the tricks his captive had been
    playing.
At last, when all his anger had been spent

On objects which were dumb and
    innocent,
The frantic man, without a word, went
    striding
Out of the room, and I came out of hiding.
Quite naturally, we didn't dare extend
Our rendezvous, because our jealous friend
Was still about; tonight, however, I
Shall visit her, quite late, and on the sly.
Our plan is this: I'll cough, three times,
    outside;
At that, the window will be opened wide;
Then, with a ladder and the assistance of
Agnès, I'll climb into our bower of love.
Since you're my only friend, I tell you
    this —
For telling, as you know, augments one's
    bliss.
However vast the joy, one must confide
In someone else before one's satisfied.
You share, I know, my happy
    expectations.
But now, farewell; I must make
    preparations.

SCENE VII

ARNOLPHE

ARNOLPHE: The evil star that's hounding
    me to death
Gives me no time in which to catch my
    breath!
Must I, again and again, be forced to see
My measures foiled through their
    complicity?
Shall I, at my ripe age, be duped, forsooth,
By a green girl and by a harebrained
    youth?
For twenty years I've sagely contemplated
The woeful lives of men unwisely mated,
And analyzed with care the slips whereby
The best-planned marriages have gone
    awry;
Thus schooled by others' failures, I felt
    that I'd
Be able, when I chose to take a bride,
To ward off all mischance, and be protected
From griefs to which so many are subjected.
I took, to that end, all the shrewd and wise
Precautions which experience could devise;

Yet, as if fate had made the stern decision
That no man living should escape derision,
I find, for all my pondering of this
Great matter, all my keen analysis,
The twenty years and more which I have
    spent
In planning to escape the embarrassment
So many husbands suffer from today,
That I'm as badly victimized as they.
But no, damned fate, I challenge your
    decree!
The lovely prize is in my custody,
And though her heart's been filched by
    that young pest,
I guarantee that he'll not get the rest,
And that this evening's gallant rendezvous
Won't go as smoothly as they'd like it to.
There's one good thing about my present
    fix —
That I'm forewarned of all my rival's tricks,
And that this oaf who's aiming to undo me
Confesses all his bad intentions to me.

SCENE VIII

CHRYSALDE, ARNOLPHE

CHRYSALDE: Well, shall we dine, and then
    go out for a stroll?
ARNOLPHE: No, no, the dinner's off.
CHRYSALDE: Well,
    well, how droll!
ARNOLPHE: Forgive me: there's a crisis I
    must face.
CHRYSALDE: Your wedding plans have
    changed? Is that the case?
ARNOLPHE: I have no need of your
    solicitude.
CHRYSALDE: Tell me your troubles, now,
    and don't be rude.
    I'd guess, friend, that your marriage
      scheme has met
    With difficulties, and that you're upset.
    To judge by your expression, I'd almost
      swear it.
ARNOLPHE: Whatever happens, I shall have
    the merit
    Of not resembling some in this
      community,
    Who let young gallants cheat them with
      impunity.
CHRYSALDE: It's odd that you, with your
    good intellect,
    Are so obsessive in this one respect,
    Measure all happiness thereby, and base
    On it alone men's honor or disgrace.
    Greed, envy, vice, and cowardice are not
    Important sins to you; the one grave blot
    You find on any scutcheon seems to be
    The crime of having suffered cuckoldry.
    Now, come: shall a man be robbed of his
      good name
    Through an ill chance for which he's not
      to blame?
    Shall a good husband lacerate his soul
    With guilt for matters not in his control?
    When a man marries, why must we scorn
      or praise him
    According to whether or not his wife
      betrays him?
    And if she does so, why must her husband
      see
    The fact as an immense catastrophe?
    Do realize that, to a man of sense,

    There's nothing crushing in such
      accidents;
    That, since no man can dodge the blows of
      fate,
    One's sense of failure should not be too
      great,
    And that there's no harm done, whatever
      they say,
    If one but takes things in the proper way.
    In difficulties of this sort, it seems,
    As always, wiser to avoid extremes.
    One shouldn't ape those husbands who
      permit
    Such scandal, and who take a pride in it,
    Dropping the names of their wives' latest
      gallants,
    Praising their persons, bragging of their
      talents,
    Professing warm regard for them,
      attending
    The parties that they give, and so
      offending
    Society, which properly resents
    Displays of laxity and impudence.
    Needless to say, such conduct will not do;
    And yet the other extreme's improper
      too.
    If men do wrong to flatter their wives'
      gallants,
    It's no less bad when, lacking tact and
      balance,
    They vent their grievances with savage
      fury,
    Calling the whole world to be judge and
      jury,
    And won't be satisfied till they acquaint
    All ears whatever with their loud
      complaint.
    Between these two extremes, my friend,
      there lies
    A middle way that's favored by the wise,
    And which, if followed, will preserve
      one's face
    However much one's wife may court
      disgrace.
    In short, then, cuckoldry need not be
      dreaded

Like some dire monster, fierce and many-
headed;
It can be lived with, if one has the wit
To take it calmly, and make the best of it.
ARNOLPHE: For that fine speech, the great
fraternity
Of cuckolds owes you thanks, your
Excellency;
And all men, if they heard your wisdom,
would
Make joyous haste to join the brotherhood.
CHRYSALDE: No, that I shouldn't approve.
But since it's fate
Whereby we're joined to one or another
mate,
One should take marriage as one takes
picquette,
In which, if one has made a losing bet,
One takes the setback calmly, and takes
pains
To do the best one can with what remains.
ARNOLPHE: In other words, eat hearty and
sleep tight,
And tell yourself that everything's all right.
CHRYSALDE: Laugh on, my friend; but I
can, in all sobriety,
Name fifty things which cause me more
anxiety,
And would, if they occurred, appall me
more
Than this misfortune which you so abhor.
Had I to choose between adversities,
I'd rather be a cuckold, if you please,
Than marry one of those good wives who
find
Continual reason to upbraid mankind,
Those virtuous shrews, those fiendish
paragons,
As violently chaste as Amazons,
Who, having had the goodness not to horn
us,
Accord themselves the right to nag and
scorn us,

And make us pay for their fidelity
By being as vexatious as can be.
Do learn, friend, that when all is said and
done,
Cuckoldry's what you make of it; that one
Might welcome it in certain situations,
And that, like all things, it has
compensations.
ARNOLPHE: Well, if you want it, may you
get your wish;
But, as for me, it's not at all my dish.
Before I'd let my brow be decked with
horn—
CHRYSALDE: Tut, tut! Don't swear, or you
may be forsworn.
If fate has willed it, your resolves will fail,
And all your oaths will be of no avail.
ARNOLPHE: I! I a cuckold?
CHRYSALDE: Don't let it fret you so.
It happens to the best of men, you know.
Cuckolds exist with whom, if I may be
frank,
You can't compare for person, wealth, or
rank.
ARNOLPHE: I have no wish to be compared
with such.
Enough, now, of your mockery; it's too
much.
You try my patience.
CHRYSALDE: So, you're annoyed
with me?
Ah, well. Good-bye. But bear in mind that
he
Who thumps his chest and swears upon
his soul
That he will never play the cuckold's role
Is studying for the part, and may well get
it.
ARNOLPHE: That won't occur, I swear; I
shall not let it.
I shall remove that threat this very minute.
(He knocks at his own gate.)

SCENE IX

ALAIN, GEORGETTE, ARNOLPHE

ARNOLPHE: My friends, the battle's joined,
and we must win it.

Your love for me, by which I'm touched
and moved,

Must now, in this emergency, be proved,
And if your deeds repay my confidence,
You may expect a handsome recompense.
This very night—don't tell a soul, my
    friends—
A certain rascal whom you know intends
To scale the wall and see Agnès; but we
Shall lay a little trap for him, we three.
You'll both be armed with clubs, and
    when the young
Villain has almost reached the topmost
    rung
(I meanwhile shall have flung the shutters
    wide),
You shall lean out and so lambaste his
    hide,
So bruise his ribs by your combined attack,
That he will never dream of coming back.
Don't speak my name while this is
    happening, mind you,

Or let him know that I am there behind
    you.
Have you the pluck to serve me in this
    action?
ALAIN: If blows are called for, we can give
    satisfaction.
I'll show you that this good right arm's not
    lame.
GEORGETTE: Mine looks less strong than
    his, but all the same
Our foe will know that he's been beaten
    by it.
ARNOLPHE: Go in, then; and, whatever you
    do, keep quiet.
    (Alone)
Tonight, I'll give a lesson to mankind.
If all endangered husbands took a mind
To greet their wives' intrusive gallants
    thus,
Cuckolds, I think, would be less numerous.

ACT V

SCENE I

ALAIN, GEORGETTE, ARNOLPHE

ARNOLPHE: You brutes! What made you be
    so heavy-handed?
ALAIN: But, Sir, we only did as you
    commanded.
ARNOLPHE: Don't put the blame on me;
    your guilt is plain.
    I wished him beaten; I didn't wish him
    slain.
    And furthermore, if you'll recall, I said
To hit him on the ribs, not on the head.
It's a ghastly situation in which I'm
    placed;

How is this young man's murder to be
    faced?
Go in, now, and be silent as the grave
About that innocent command I gave.
    (Alone)
It's nearly daybreak. I must take thought,
    and see
How best to cope with this dire tragedy.
God help me! What will the boy's father
    say
When this appalling story comes his way?

SCENE II

HORACE, ARNOLPHE

HORACE: Who's this, I wonder. I'd best
    approach with care.
ARNOLPHE: How could I have foreseen . . . I
    say, who's there?
HORACE: Seigneur Arnolphe?
ARNOLPHE: Yes—
HORACE: It's Horace, once
    more.

My, you're up early! I was heading for
Your house, to ask a favor.
ARNOLPHE: Oh, God, I'm
    dizzy.
Is he a vision? Is he a ghost? What is he?
HORACE: Sir, I'm in trouble once again, I
    fear.
It's providential that you should appear

Just at the moment when your help was
    needed.
My plans, I'm happy to tell you, have
    succeeded
Beyond all expectations, and despite
An incident which might have spoiled
    them quite.
I don't know how it happened, but
    someone knew
About our contemplated rendezvous;
For, just as I'd almost reached her window
    sill,
I saw some frightful figures, armed to kill,
Lean out above me, waving their clubs
    around.
I lost my footing, tumbled to the ground,
And thus, though rather scratched and
    bruised, was spared
The thumping welcome which they had
    prepared.
Those brutes (of whom Old Jealous, I
    suppose,
Was one) ascribed my tumble to their
    blows,
And since I lay there, motionless, in the
    dirt
For several minutes, being stunned and
    hurt,
They judged that they had killed me, and
    they all
Took fright at that, and so began to brawl.
I lay in silence, hearing their angry cries:
They blamed each other for my sad
    demise,
Then tiptoed out, in darkness and in
    dread,
To feel my body, and see if I were dead.
As you can well imagine, I played the part
Of a limp, broken corpse with all my
    heart.
Quite overcome with terror, they
    withdrew,
And I was thinking of withdrawing, too,
When young Agnès came hurrying, out of
    breath
And much dismayed by my supposèd
    death:
She had been able, of course, to overhear
All that my foes had babbled in their fear,
And while they were distracted and
    unnerved

She'd slipped from the house, entirely
    unobserved.
Ah, how she wept with happiness when
    she found
That I was, after all, both safe and sound!
Well, to be brief: electing to be guided
By her own heart, the charming girl
    decided
Not to return to her guardian, but to flee,
Entrusting her security to me.
What must his tyranny be, if it can force
So shy a girl to take so bold a course!
And think what peril she might thus
    incur,
If I were capable of wronging her.
Ah, but my love's too pure for that, too
    strong;
I'd rather die than do her any wrong;
So admirable is she that all I crave
Is to be with her even to the grave.
I know my father: this will much
    displease him,
But we shall manage somehow to appease
    him.
In any case, she's won my heart, and I
Could not desert her, even if I chose to try.
The favor I ask of you is rather large:
It's that you take my darling in your
    charge,
And keep her, if you will, for several days
In your own house, concealed from the
    world's gaze.
I ask your help in this because I'm bent
On throwing all pursuers off the scent;
Also because, if she were seen with me,
There might be talk of impropriety.
To you, my loyal friend, I've dared to
    impart,
Without reserve, the secrets of my heart,
And likewise it's to you I now confide
My dearest treasure and my future bride.
ARNOLPHE: I'm at your service; on that you
    may depend.
HORACE: You'll grant the favor that I ask,
    dear friend?
ARNOLPHE: Of course; most willingly. I'm
    glad indeed
That I can help you in your hour of need.
Thank Heaven that you asked me! There's
    no request
To which I could accede with greater zest.

HORACE: How kind you are! What gratitude I feel!

I feared you might refuse my rash appeal;

But you're a man of the world, urbane and wise,

Who looks upon young love with tolerant eyes.

My man is guarding her, just down the street.

ARNOLPHE: It's almost daylight. Where had we better meet?

Someone might see me, if you brought her here,

And should you bring her to my house, I fear

'T would start the servants talking. We must look

For some more shadowy and secluded nook.

That garden's handy; I shall await her there.

HORACE: You're right, Sir. We must act with the utmost care.

I'll go, and quickly bring Agnès to you,

Then seek my lodgings without more ado.

ARNOLPHE: *(Alone)* Ah, Fortune! This good turn will compensate

For all the tricks you've played on me of late.

(He hides his face in his cloak.)

SCENE III

AGNÈS, HORACE, ARNOLPHE

HORACE: Just come with me; there's no cause for alarm.

I'm taking you where you'll be safe from harm.

To stay together would be suicide:

Go in, and let this gentleman be your guide.

(ARNOLPHE, whom she does not recognize, takes her hand.)

AGNÈS: Why are you leaving me?

HORACE: Dear Agnès, I must.

AGNÈS: You'll very soon be coming back, I trust?

HORACE: I shall; my yearning heart will see to that.

AGNÈS: Without you, life is miserable and flat.

HORACE: When I'm away from you, I pine and grieve.

AGNÈS: Alas! If that were so, you wouldn't leave.

HORACE: You know how strong my love is, and how true.

AGNÈS: Ah, no, you don't love me as I love you.

(ARNOLPHE tugs at her hand.)

Why does he pull my hand?

HORACE: 'T would ruin us,

My dear, if we were seen together thus,

And therefore this true friend, who's filled with worry

About our welfare, urges you to hurry.

AGNÈS: But why must I go with him—a perfect stranger?

HORACE: Don't fret. In his hands you'll be out of danger.

AGNÈS: I'd rather be in *your* hands; that was why—

(To ARNOLPHE, who tugs her hand again)

Wait, wait.

HORACE: It's daybreak. I must go. Goodbye.

AGNÈS: When shall I see you?

HORACE: Very soon, I swear.

AGNÈS: Till that sweet moment, I'll be in despair.

HORACE: *(Leaving, to himself)* My happiness is assured; my fears may cease;

Praise be to Heaven, I now can sleep in peace.

SCENE IV

ARNOLPHE, AGNÈS

ARNOLPHE: *(Hiding his face in his cloak,*
and disguising his voice) Come, this is
not where you're to stay, my child;
It's elsewhere that you shall be domiciled.
You're going to a safe, sequestered place.
(Revealing himself, and using his normal
voice)
Do you know me?

AGNÈS *(Recognizing him)*
Aagh!

ARNOLPHE: You wicked girl!
My face
Would seem, just now, to give you rather
a fright.
Oh, clearly I'm a most unwelcome sight:
I interfere with your romantic plan.
*(*AGNÈS *turns and looks in vain for*
HORACE*)*
No use to look for help from that young
man;
He couldn't hear you now; he's gone too
far.
Well, well! For one so young, how sly you
are!
You ask—most innocently, it would
appear—
If children are begotten through the ear,
Yet you know all too well, I now discover,
How to keep trysts—at midnight—with a
lover!
What honeyed words you spoke to him
just now!
Who taught you such beguilements? Tell
me how,
Within so short a time, you've learned so
much!
You used to be afraid of ghosts and such;
Has your gallant taught you not to fear the
night?
You ingrate! To deceive me so, despite
The loving care with which you have
been blessed!
Oh, I have warmed a serpent at my breast
Until, reviving, it unkindly bit
The very hand that was caressing it!

AGNÈS: Why are you cross with me?

ARNOLPHE: Oh! So I'm unfair?

AGNÈS: I've done no wrong of which I am
aware.

ARNOLPHE: Was it right, then, to run off
with that young beau?

AGNÈS: He wants me for his wife; he's told
me so.
I've only done as you advised; you said
That, so as not to sin, one ought to wed.

ARNOLPHE: Yes, but I made it perfectly
clear that I'd
Resolved, myself, to take you as my bride.

AGNÈS: Yes; but if I may give my point of
view,
He'd suit me, as a husband, better than
you.
In all your talk of marriage, you depict
A state that's gloomy, burdensome, and
strict;
But, ah! when *he* describes the married
state,
It sounds so sweet that I can hardly wait.

ARNOLPHE: Ah! So you love him, faithless
girl!

AGNÈS: Why, yes.

ARNOLPHE: Have you the gall to tell me
that, Agnès?

AGNÈS: If it's the truth, what's wrong with
telling it?

ARNOLPHE: How dared you fall in love
with him, you chit?

AGNÈS: It was no fault of mine; he made me
do it.
I was in love with him before I knew it.

ARNOLPHE: You should have overcome
your amorous feeling.

AGNÈS: It's hard to overcome what's so
appealing.

ARNOLPHE: Didn't you know that I would
be put out?

AGNÈS: Why, no. What have you to
complain about?

ARNOLPHE: Nothing, of course! I'm wild
with happiness!
You don't, I take it, love me.

AGNÈS: Love you?

ARNOLPHE: Yes.

AGNÈS: Alas, I don't.

ARNOLPHE: You *don't?*

AGNÈS: Would you
      have me lie?

ARNOLPHE: Why don't you love me, hussy?
      Tell me why!

AGNÈS: Good heavens, it's not I whom you
      should blame.

   He made me love him; why didn't you do
      the same?

   I didn't hinder you, as I recall.

ARNOLPHE: I tried to make you love me; I
      gave my all;

   Yet all my pains and strivings were in
      vain.

AGNÈS: He has more aptitude than you,
      that's plain;

   To win my heart, he scarcely had to try.

ARNOLPHE: *(Aside)* This peasant girl can
      frame a neat reply!

   What lady wit could answer with more
      art?

   Either she's bright, or in what concerns
      the heart

   A foolish girl can best the wisest man.

   (To AGNÈS*)*

   Well, then, Miss Back-Talk, answer this if
      you can:

   Did I raise you, all these years, at such
      expense,

   For another's benefit? Does that make
      sense?

AGNÈS: No. But he'll gladly pay you for
      your trouble.

ARNOLPHE: *(Aside)* Such flippancy! It
      makes my rage redouble.

   (To AGNÈS*)*

   You minx! How could he possibly
      discharge

   Your obligations to me? They're too large.

AGNÈS: Frankly, they don't seem very large
      to me.

ARNOLPHE: Did I not nurture you from
      infancy?

AGNÈS: Yes, that you did. I'm deeply
      obligated.

   How wondrously you've had me educated!

   Do you fancy that I'm blind to what
      you've done,

And cannot see that I'm a simpleton?

Oh, it humiliates me; I revolt

Against the shame of being such a dolt.

ARNOLPHE: Do you think you'll gain the
      knowledge that you need

   Through that young dandy's tutelage?

AGNÈS: Yes, indeed.

   It's thanks to him I know what little I do;

   I owe far more to him than I do to you.

ARNOLPHE: What holds me back, I ask
      myself, from treating

   So insolent a girl to a sound beating?

   Your coldness irks me to the point of tears,

   And it would ease my soul to box your
      ears.

AGNÈS: Alas, then, beat me, if you so desire.

ARNOLPHE: *(Aside)* Those words and that
      sweet look dissolve my ire,

   Restoring to my heart such tender feeling

   As makes me quite forget her double-
      dealing.

   How strange love is! How strange that
      men, from such

   Perfidious beings, will endure so much!

   Women, as all men know, are frailly
      wrought:

   They're foolish and illogical in thought,

   Their souls are weak, their characters are
      bad,

   There's nothing quite so silly, quite so
      mad,

   So faithless; yet, despite these sorry
      features,

   What won't we do to please the wretched
      creatures?

   (To AGNÈS*)*

   Come, traitress, let us be at peace once
      more.

   I'll pardon you, and love you as before.

   Repay my magnanimity, and learn

   From my great love to love me in return.

AGNÈS: Truly, if I were able to, I would.

   I'd gladly love you if I only could.

ARNOLPHE: You can, my little beauty, if
      you'll but try.

   (He sighs)

   Just listen to that deep and yearning sigh!

   Look at my haggard face! See how it
      suffers!

   Reject that puppy, and the love he offers;

He must have cast a spell on you; with
    me,
You'll be far happier, I guarantee.
I know that clothes and jewels are your
    passion;
Don't worry: you shall always be in
    fashion.
I'll pet you night and day; you shall be
    showered
With kisses; you'll be hugged, caressed,
    devoured.
And you shall have your wish in every
    way.
I'll say no more; what further could I say?
(Aside)
Lord, what extremes desire will drive us
    to!
(To AGNÈS*)*
In short, no love could match my love for
    you.

Tell me, ungrateful girl, what proof do
    you need?
Shall I weep? Or beat myself until I bleed?
What if I tore my hair out—would that
    sway you?
Shall I kill myself? Command, and I'll
    obey you.
I'm ready, cruel one, for you to prove me.
AGNÈS: Somehow, your lengthy speeches fail
    to move me.
Horace, in two words, could be more
    engaging.
ARNOLPHE: Enough of this! Your
    impudence is enraging.
I have my plans for you, you stubborn
    dunce,
And I shall pack you out of town at once.
You've spurned my love, and baited me as
    well—
Which you'll repent of in a convent cell.

SCENE V

ALAIN, ARNOLPHE, AGNÈS

ALAIN: It's very strange, but Agnès has
    vanished, Sir.
I think that corpse has run away with
    her.
ARNOLPHE: She's here. Go shut her in my
    room, securely.
That's not where he'd come looking for
    her, surely,
And she'll be there but half an hour, at
    most.

Meanwhile I'll get a carriage, in which
    we'll post
To a safe retreat. Go now, and lock up
    tight,
And see that you don't let her out of sight.
(Alone)
Perhaps a change of scene and
    circumstance
Will wean her from this infantile
    romance.

SCENE VI

HORACE, ARNOLPHE

HORACE: Seigneur Arnolphe, I'm
    overwhelmed with grief,
And Heaven's cruelty is beyond belief;
It seems now that a brutal stroke of fate
May force my love and me to separate.
My father, just this minute, chanced to
    appear,
Alighting from his coach not far from here,
And what has brought him into town this
    morning

Is a dire errand of which I'd had no
    warning:
He's made a match for me, and, ready or
    not,
I am to marry someone on the spot.
Imagine my despair! What blacker curse
Could fall on me, what setback could be
    worse?
I told you, yesterday, of Enrique. It's he
Who's brought about my present misery;

He's come with Father, to lead me to the
  slaughter,
And I am doomed to wed his only
  daughter.
When they told me that, it almost made
  me swoon;
And, since my father spoke of coming
  soon
To see you, I excused myself, in fright,
And hastened to forewarn you of my
  plight.
Take care, Sir, I entreat you, not to let him
Know of Agnès and me; 't would much
  upset him.
And try, since he so trusts your judgment,
  to
Dissuade him from the match he has in
  view.

ARNOLPHE: I shall.
HORACE: That failing, you could
  be of aid
By urging that the wedding be delayed.
ARNOLPHE: Trust me.
HORACE: On you, my dearest
  hopes repose.
ARNOLPHE: Fine, fine.
HORACE: You're a father to me,
  Heaven knows.
Tell him that young men — Ah! He's
  coming! I spy him.
Here are some arguments with which to
  ply him.

*(They withdraw to a corner of the stage, and
  confer in whispers.)*

SCENE VII

ENRIQUE, ORONTE, CHRYSALDE, HORACE, ARNOLPHE

ENRIQUE: *(To* CHRYSALDE*)* No need for
  introductions, Sir. I knew
  Your name as soon as I set eyes on you.
  You have the very features of your late
  Sister, who was my well-belovèd mate;
  Oh, how I wish that cruel Destiny
  Had let me bring my helpmeet back with
  me,
  After such years of hardship as we bore,
  To see her home and family once more.
  But fate has ruled that we shall not again
  Enjoy her charming presence; let us, then,
  Find solace in what joys we may design
  For the sole offspring of her love and
  mine.
  You are concerned in this; let us confer,
  And see if you approve my plans for her.
  Oronte's young son, I think, is a splendid
  choice;
  But in this matter you've an equal voice.
CHRYSALDE: I've better judgment, Brother,
  than to question
So eminently worthy a suggestion.
ARNOLPHE: *(To* HORACE*)* Yes, yes, don't
  worry; I'll represent you well.
HORACE: Once more, don't tell him —

ARNOLPHE: I promise not to
  tell.

*(*ARNOLPHE *leaves* HORACE, *and crosses to embrace*
  ORONTE.*)*

ORONTE: Ah, my old friend: what a warm,
  hearty greeting!
ARNOLPHE: Oronte, dear fellow, what a
  welcome meeting!
ORONTE: I've come to town —
ARNOLPHE: You needn't
  say a word;
  I know what brings you.
ORONTE: You've already
  heard?
ARNOLPHE: Yes.
ORONTE: Good.
ARNOLPHE: Your son regards this match
  with dread;
  His heart rebels at being forced to wed,
  And I've been asked, in fact, to plead his
  case.
  Well, do you know what I'd do, in your
  place?
  I'd exercise a father's rightful sway
  And tie the wedding knot without delay.

What the young need, my friend, is
    discipline;
We only do them harm by giving in.
HORACE: *(Aside)* Traitor!
CHRYSALDE: If the prospect fills
    him with revulsion,
    Then surely we should not employ
        compulsion.
    My brother-in-law, I trust, would say the
        same.
ARNOLPHE: Shall a man be governed by his
    son? For shame!
    Would you have a father be so meek and
        mild
    As not to exact obedience from his child?
    At his wise age, 't would be grotesque
        indeed
    To see him led by one whom he should
        lead.
    No, no; my dear old friend is honor-bound;
    He's given his word, and he must not give
        ground.
    Let him be firm, as a father should, and
        force

His son to take the necessary course.
ORONTE: Well said: we shall proceed with
    this alliance,
    And I shall answer for my son's
        compliance.
CHRYSALDE: *(To* ARNOLPHE*)* It much
    surprises me to hear you press
    For this betrothal with such eagerness.
    What is your motive? I can't make you
        out.
ARNOLPHE: Don't worry, friend; I know
    what I'm about.
ORONTE: Indeed, Arnolphe—
CHRYSALDE: He finds that
    name unpleasant.
    Monsieur de la Souche is what he's called
        at present.
ARNOLPHE: No matter.
HORACE: What do I hear?
ARNOLPHE: *(Turning toward* HORACE*)*
    Well, now you know,
    And now you see why I have spoken so.
HORACE: Oh, what confusion—

SCENE VIII

GEORGETTE, ENRIQUE, ORONTE, CHRYSALDE, HORACE, ARNOLPHE

GEORGETTE: Sir, please come. Unless
    You do, I fear we can't restrain Agnès.
    The girl is frantic to escape, I swear,
    And might jump out of the window in
        despair.
ARNOLPHE: Bring her to me: I'll take her
    away from here
    Posthaste, this very minute.
    (To HORACE*)*
                Be of good
    cheer.

Too much good luck could spoil you; and,
    as they say
In the proverb, every dog must have his
    day.
HORACE: What man, O Heaven, was ever
    betrayed like this,
    Or hurled into so hopeless an abyss?
ARNOLPHE: *(To* ORONTE*)* Pray don't delay
    the nuptials—which, dear friend,
    I shall be most delighted to attend.
ORONTE: I shan't delay.

SCENE IX

AGNÈS, ALAIN, GEORGETTE, ORONTE, ENRIQUE, ARNOLPHE, HORACE, CHRYSALDE

ARNOLPHE: Come, come, my pretty child,
    You who are so intractable and wild.
    Here is your gallant: perhaps he should
        receive

A little curtsey from you, as you leave.
(To HORACE*)*
Farewell: your sweet hopes seem to have
    turned to gall;

But love, my boy, can't always conquer
all.

AGNÈS: Horace! Will you let him take me
away from you?

HORACE: I'm dazed with grief, and don't
know what to do.

ARNOLPHE: Come, chatterbox.

AGNÈS: No. Here I
shall remain.

ORONTE: Now, what's the mystery? Will
you please explain?

All this is very odd; we're baffled by it.

ARNOLPHE: When I've more time, I'll
gladly clarify it.

Till then, good-bye.

ORONTE: Where is it you mean
to go?

And why won't you tell us what we ask to
know?

ARNOLPHE: I've told you that, despite your
stubborn son,

You ought to hold the wedding.

ORONTE: It shall be
done.

But weren't you told that his intended
spouse

Is the young woman who's living in your
house—

The long-lost child of that dear Angélique
Who secretly was married to Enrique?

What, then, did your behavior mean just
now?

CHRYSALDE: His words amazed me, too, I
must allow.

ARNOLPHE: What? What?

CHRYSALDE: My sister married
secretly;

Her daughter's birth was kept from the
family.

ORONTE: The child was placed with an old
country dame,

Who reared her under a fictitious name.

CHRYSALDE: My sister's husband, beset by
circumstance,

Was soon obliged to take his leave of
France,

ORONTE: And undergo great trials and
miseries

In a strange, savage land beyond the seas,

CHRYSALDE: Where, through his labors, he
regained abroad

What here he'd lost through men's deceit
and fraud.

ORONTE: Returning home, he sought at
once to find

The nurse to whom his child had been
consigned,

CHRYSALDE: And the good creature told
him, as was true,

That she'd transferred her little charge to
you,

ORONTE: Because of your benevolent
disposition,

And the dire poverty of her condition.

CHRYSALDE: What's more, Enrique,
transported with delight,

Has brought the woman here to set things
right.

ORONTE: She'll join us in a moment, and
then we'll see

A public end to all this mystery.

CHRYSALDE: *(To* ARNOLPHE*)* I know that
you're in a painful state of mind;

Yet what the Fates have done is not
unkind.

Since your chief treasure is a hornless
head,

The safest course, for you, is not to wed.

ARNOLPHE: *(Leaving in a speechless
passion)* Oof!

ORONTE: Why is he rushing off without a
word?

HORACE: Father, a great coincidence has
occurred.

What in your wisdom you projected,
chance

Has wondrously accomplished in
advance.

The fact is, Sir, that I am bound already,

By the sweet ties of love, to this fair lady;

It's she whom you have come to seek, and
she

For whose sake I opposed your plans for
me.

ENRIQUE: I recognized her from the very
first,

With such deep joy, I thought my heart
would burst.

Dear daughter, let me take you in my
  embrace.
(He does so)
CHRYSALDE: I have the same urge, Brother,
  but this place
Will hardly do for private joys like these.
Let us go in, resolve all mysteries,

Commend our friend Arnolphe, and for
  the rest
With such deep joy, I thought my heart
  would burst.
Thank Heaven, which orders all things for
  the best.

As in several others of his plays, in *The School for Wives*, Molière has taken one trait (fear of cuckoldry) and made it an obsession with the protagonist. So fearful is Arnolphe of having an unfaithful wife that he has avoided marriage until (for that period) an unusually late age. He tends to see cuckoldry everywhere, and he takes great pleasure in ridiculing those who have unfaithful wives. Obsessed by the determination not to be cuckolded, Arnolphe has selected, 13 years before the play begins, a girl only four years old and has had her reared in a manner he thinks will guarantee her faithfulness after he marries her.

Arnolphe's idea of an appropriate education for a wife is to keep her as ignorant as possible by isolating her from society and to teach her only such fundamental skills as sewing, reading, and writing (and as little of the latter two as possible). Extreme as Arnolphe's ideas may seem, they were sufficiently near the typical education of middle-class girls of the time that Molière's criticism of the plan was attacked as a threat to chaste upbringing of young women.

Arnolphe's ideas of how·a woman should behave once married are summarized in *The Maxims of Marriage*, which he gives Agnès to study, memorize, and obey. It is clear from these maxims that, like a nun in a cloister, the wife is to remain at home cut off from the world, devoting herself entirely to the service of her master to the exclusion of all other interests. At no time does Arnolphe consider the rights of women or the duties of a husband. Nor does he see that concern only for himself has made Agnès a victim of his selfishness. As is typical in Molière's plays, such one-sidedness inevitably brings its own comic retribution.

Against Arnolphe's obsession with cuckoldry, Molière sets up contrasts through other characters. The most obvious contrast is provided by Chrysalde, a married man of Arnolphe's own age who seeks to follow a middle path between Arnolphe's extreme concern and that of men who countenance and cooperate in their wives' infidelities. Chrysalde argues that there is no way of guaranteeing that one's wife will be faithful, that one should not condone or encourage unfaithfulness but that to be cuckolded is not a matter of shame for the husband but for the wife, that there are many greater tribulations than cuckoldry, and that a man should bear cuckoldry philosophically. Some critics have argued that Molière did not mean Chrysalde's arguments to be taken seriously and that he is merely using these arguments to point up the ridiculousness of Arnolphe's obsession. Regardless of Molière's intentions, his detractors considered Chrysalde's speeches on cuckoldry to be blasphemous in seeming to condone adultery.

The most important contrasts to Arnolphe's ideas are provided by Agnès and Horace. Arnolphe's plans that have been 13 years in the making are overthrown in an instant by the young couple's instincts, which they neither understand nor can resist. Their lack of calculation contrasts sharply with Arnolphe's almost mathematical plan; and the absurdity of Arnolphe's attempt to make marriage the culmination of a coldly rational plan is made even more evident when he himself falls in love with Agnès when he sees her attracted to another. Additionally, the young couple's trusting confidences contrast tellingly with Arnolphe's self-serving deceptions. Furthermore, unlike Arnolphe, both Agnès and Horace become increasingly aware that love requires one to be concerned about the welfare of the loved one. Horace in the beginning tends to view his accidental acquaintance with Agnès as providing the potential for sexual conquest, but as his love surfaces so does his determination to ensure Agnès's welfare and to protect her reputation, and Agnès becomes increasingly aware that the ignorance imposed upon her by Arnolphe is preventing her from knowing how to act wisely and honorably both to Arnolphe and Horace. Thus, Arnolphe's school for wives teaches lessons quite different from those he had in mind. Molière argues that a marriage based on love and consideration is far better insurance against infidelity than isolation and ignorance and that knowledge and experience of the world provide a woman with a basis for appropriate behavior. Perhaps above all, Molière suggests that human beings cannot control events, as Arnolphe seeks to do, but that they can only deal with them common-sensically when they occur and accept philosophically what cannot be avoided.

The School for Wives, like many of Molière's plays, reflects the influence of Roman comedy, especially in the outdoor setting, the unplanned but fortuitous meetings of characters, and the complications created by love. Perhaps the most obvious influence is seen in the resolution when children and parents are reunited after a long separation and a happy ending is made possible. Although such an ending may seem contrived, it is understandable in Molière's plays for this reason: since the protagonist's obsession is the block to a happy ending, only a change in the character can bring about such an ending; but since Molière did not believe that character can be changed, some new element that takes the power of decision away from the protagonist is required if the play is to end happily. In *The School for Wives*, a long-vanished parent reappears, removes Agnès from Arnolphe's authority, and unites her with Horace. As Arnolphe storms from the scene, he gives no indication that he has learned anything from his experience.

The School for Wives raises issues that are still important. One concerns the attempt to censor a young person's education. Are standards of conduct more firmly implanted by protecting young people from certain kinds of information or by exposing them to a wide range of information in the hope that it will provide a basis for discriminating wisely among alternatives? Arnolphe takes pride in Agnès's total ignorance about sex and believes that this ignorance will keep her chaste. Molière appears to argue that sexual urges, being natural, will inevitably be aroused and that they can be dealt with more satisfactorily through knowledge than through ignorance. These points of view (or variations on them) are still common in the heated debates that center on such issues as sex education in schools, family planning, and the uses of sex in the mass media. Other questions raised by Molière's play include: What conditions make for happy (and unhappy) marriages? What sorts of plans for the future can one make and realistically expect to carry out?

Although Molière never advocated equal rights for women, he certainly was sensitive to many inequities in the treatment of women. In Molière's day, women were not educated for any professions other than marriage and motherhood. If they rebelled, the alternatives were few indeed, for parents had absolute legal power over their children, just as husbands did over their wives. Parents considered it a duty to see that their children married well, and they arranged marriages for them, often without even consulting the child involved. Love was not considered a sound basis for marriage; rather, it might blind one to the necessity of assuring financial security. Molière opposed arranged marriages on the grounds that they were a primary cause of unfaithfulness and unhappiness. But he did not propose radical changes in social customs. Instead, he seemed to suggest that rather than following custom blindly, each situation should be handled according to the dictates of common sense.

The Recruiting Officer

by George Farquhar

During the hundred years that separated Shakespeare's *King Lear* (1606) from Farquhar's *The Recruiting Officer* (1706), English drama and theatre underwent numerous changes. Many of these changes were related to political events and foreign influence. When in 1642 civil war broke out between the supporters of Charles I and his Puritan opponents, Parliament closed all theatres and kept them closed until Charles II was restored to the throne in 1660. During these years the royal family took refuge in France, where the Neoclassical ideal had recently triumphed and where proscenium-arch theatres with wing-and-drop scenery were standard. (Stages and scenery of this type had been used in England before the civil war for royal entertainments, but they had not yet been introduced into the public theatres.)

When English theatres reopened in 1660, they were strongly influenced both by French practices and by prewar English practices. Thus, although the English public stage was now given a proscenium arch and perspective scenery painted on wings and drops, it differed from its French counterpart in having a forestage that jutted into the auditorium some 12 or more feet forward of the proscenium arch. Furthermore, doors on either side of this forestage served as exits and entrances, while the scenery back of the proscenium served primarily as background. Thus, the English stage combined features of the prewar public theatres and the contemporary French stage.

In drama, while the Neoclassical ideal gradually triumphed after 1660, the English, probably because of the continuing popularity of Shakespeare and other prewar dramatists, never insisted on rules as strict as those adhered to by the French. Unlike the French, who favored a single setting, a single plot, and a time lapse of no more than 24 hours, the English permitted one or more subplots (so long as all were related and were brought together in the play's resolution) and any number of locales so long as they were near enough to each other that moving among them would not violate the 24-hour rule. Therefore, English Neoclassicism sometimes seemed nearer to the practices of Shakespeare than to those of Molière and Racine.

For the years between 1660 and 1700 (commonly referred to as the Restoration) English drama is now remembered primarily for comedy and above all for its comedy of manners, which focused on London's fashionable set, who reveled in behavior removed as far as possible from that of the austere Puritans. In Restoration comedy, the principal characters, drawn primarily from the aristocracy, are preoccupied with seduction, advantageous marriage, witty conversation, and fashion. The young men prefer sexual conquests that do not involve marriage and consider it bad form to be thought in love; the young women frequent fashionable gatherings in search of gossip, diversion, and flirtation. The butt of jokes and derision are those who seek to be part of the "in" crowd but who never fully understand the rules of the game; they include those whose attempts at wit only make them appear foolish, aging men and women who try to appear youthful and to attract young lovers, anyone from the country, or anyone who takes anything too seriously. The settings are the fashionable spots of London—parks, coffee houses, and drawing rooms.

Restoration comedies have often been accused of condoning morally reprehensible behavior. Some may do so, but they also imply that sophisticated people, though aware of foolish or immoral behavior, maintain their aplomb and do not become indignant about it. Admirable behavior consists in living up to the maxim "Know thyself," and avoiding those things apt to arouse ridicule. The plays satirize those who have not achieved this ideal and are either self-deceived or are attempting to deceive others. Restoration comedy is seen at its best in such plays as George Etherege's *The Man of Mode* (1676), William Wycherley's *The Country Wife* (1675), and William Congreve's *The Way of the World* (1700).

The tone of English life began to change after 1690 under William III and Mary II. As the merchant class gained power and attended the theatre in increased numbers, their taste influenced the choice of plays. The rise of the middle class also coincided with a resurgence of Puritan protests against the theatre, culminating in Jeremy Collier's *A Short View of the Immorality and Profaneness of the English Stage* (1698). In this work, Collier chose as his special target the comedies of manners. Many dramatists sought to defend themselves, but they were victims of the Neoclassical view of drama to which they subscribed: most were on record as acknowledging that the purposes of drama are moral instruction and pleasure. Most of the playwrights found it difficult to point out the moral lessons of their plays, and it did not occur to them to question whether moral teaching is the prime purpose of drama. The bitter controversy dragged on for several years; by the time it ended in the early eighteenth century, drama was already in a state of transition.

The plays that best illustrate the transition from Restoration comedy to the more sedate and sentimental comedy of the eighteenth century are *The Recruiting Officer* (1706) and *The Beaux' Stratagem* (1707) by George Farquhar (1678–1707). Farquhar retained many of the Restoration's favorite subjects (advantageous marriages, seductions, and, to a lesser degree, witty conversation) but he shifted the setting to the country and greatly softened the moral tone. The plays were extraordinarily successful and remained in the repertory throughout the eighteenth and nineteenth centuries. Both have been revived frequently in the twentieth century.

Following Farquhar's death, English comedy became increasingly sentimental, and by 1722 Sir Richard Steele, in the preface to his *The Conscious Lovers*, argued that the proper purpose of comedy was to draw forth a smile and a tear. During the remainder of the eighteenth century, with the exception of Oliver Goldsmith and Richard Brinsley Sheridan in the 1770s, few playwrights attempted laughing comedy.

DRAMATIS PERSONAE

MEN

MR. BALANCE *country squire and justice of the peace*
MR. SCALE *justice of the peace*
MR. SCRUPLE *justice of the peace*
MR. WORTHY *Shropshire gentleman*
CAPTAIN PLUME *recruiting officer*
CAPTAIN BRAZEN *recruiting officer*

KITE *sergeant to Plume*
BULLOCK *country lad*
COSTAR PEARMAIN *recruit*
THOMAS APPLETREE *recruit*
BUTCHER *recruit*
SMITH *recruit*
CONSTABLE

WOMEN

MELINDA *Shropshire lady of fortune*
SILVIA *daughter to Balance, in love with Plume*

LUCY *Melinda's maid*
ROSE *Bullock's sister*
RECRUITS, SERVANTS, ATTENDANTS, AND MOB

Scene:

Shrewsbury

ACT I

SCENE I
The marketplace

(Drum beats the Grenadier March. Enter SERGEANT KITE *followed by the* MOB.)

KITE: *(Making a speech)* If any gentlemen soldiers or others have a mind to serve her Majesty and pull down the French king, if any 'prentices have severe masters, any children have undutiful parents, if any servants have too little wages, or any husband too much wife, let them repair to the noble Sergeant Kite at the Sign of the Raven in this good town of Shrewbury and they shall receive present relief and entertainment.

Gentlemen, I don't beat my drums here to ensnare or inveigle any man; for you must know, gentlemen, that I am a man of honor. Besides, I don't beat up for common soldiers. No, I list only grenadiers, grenadiers, gentlemen. Pray, gentlemen, observe this cap. This is the cap of honor; it dubs a man a gentleman in the drawing of a tricker; and he that has the good fortune to be born six foot high was born to be a great man. *(To one of the* MOB) Sir, will you give me leave to try this cap upon your head?

MOB: Is there no harm in't? Won't the cap list me?

KITE: No, no, no more than I can. Come, let me see how it becomes you.

MOB: Are you sure there be no conjuration in it, no gunpowder plot upon me?

KITE: No, no, friend; don't fear, man.

MOB: My mind misgives me plaguely. Let me see it. (Going to put it on) It smells woundily of sweat and brimstone. Pray, Sergeant, what writing is this upon the face of it?

KITE: The crown,[1] or the bed of honor.

MOB: Pray now, what may be that same bed of honor?

KITE: Oh, a mighty large bed, bigger by half than the great bed of Ware. Ten thousand people may lie in't together and never feel one another.[2]

MOB: My wife and I would do well to lie in't, for we don't care for feeling one another. But do folk sleep sound in this same bed of honor?

KITE: Sound! Ay, so sound that they never wake.

MOB: Wauns! I wish again that my wife lay there.

KITE: Say you so? Then I find, brother—

MOB: Brother! Hold there, friend, I'm no kindred to you that I know of as yet. Look'e, Sergeant, no coaxing, no wheedling, d'ye'see. If I have a mind to list, why so; if not, why 'tis not so. Therefore, take your cap and your brothership back again, for I an't disposed at this present writing. No coaxing, no brothering me, faith.

KITE: I coax! I wheedle! I'm above it. Sir, I have served twenty campaigns. But, sir, you talk well, and I must own that you are a man every inch of you, a pretty, young, sprightly fellow. I love a fellow with a spirit, but I scorn to coax, 'tis base; though I must say that never in my life have I seen a better built man. How firm and strong he treads; he steps like a castle! But I scorn to wheedle any man. Come, honest lad, will you take share of a pot?

MOB: Nay, for that matter, I'll spend my penny with the best he that wears a head, that is begging you pardon, sir, and in a fair way.

KITE: Give me your hand then, and now, gentlemen, I have no more to say but this. Here's a purse of gold, and there is a tub of humming ale at my quarters; 'tis the Queen's money and the Queen's drink. She's a generous Queen and loves her subjects. I hope, gentlemen, you won't refuse the Queen's health?

ALL MOB: No, no, no.

KITE: Huzza then, huzza for the Queen and the honor of Shropshire.

ALL MOB: Huzza.

KITE: Beat drum.

(Exeunt, drum beating the Grenadier March)

(Enter PLUME *in a riding habit.)*

PLUME: By the Grenadier March that should be my drum and by that shout it should beat with success. Let me see. *(Looks on his watch.)* Four o'clock. At ten yesterday morning I left London. A hundred and twenty miles in thirty hours is pretty smart riding, but nothing to the fatigue of recruiting.

(Enter KITE.*)*

KITE: Welcome to Shrewsbury, noble Captain; from the banks of the Danube to the Severn side, noble Captain, you are welcome.[3]

PLUME: A very elegant reception indeed, Mr. Kite. I find you are fairly entered into your recruiting strain. Pray, what success?

KITE: I have been here but a week and I have recruited five.

PLUME: Five! Pray, what are they?

KITE: I have listed the strong man of Kent, the king of the gypsies, a Scotch peddler, a scoundrel attorney, and a Welsh parson.

PLUME: An attorney! Wer't thou mad? List a lawyer! Discharge him, discharge him this minute.

KITE: Why, sir?

PLUME: Because I will have nobody in my company that can write. A fellow that can write can draw petitions. I say, this minute discharge him.

KITE: And what shall I do with the parson?

PLUME: Can he write?

KITE: Umh.—He plays rarely upon the fiddle.

[1]The cap of the Grenadier Guards had a crown on it.
[2]The great bed of Ware was legendary and was said to accommodate 24 people.

[3]Plume has just come to Shrewsbury (located on the Severn River) from battles on the continent near the Danube River.

PLUME: Keep him, by all means. But how stands the country affected? Were the people pleased with the news of my coming to town?

KITE: Sir, the mob are so pleased with your honor and the justices and better sort of people are so delighted with me that we shall soon do our business. But, sir, you have got a recruit here that you little think of.

PLUME: Who?

KITE: One that you beat up for last time you were in the country. You remember your old friend Molly at the Castle?

PLUME: She's not with child, I hope.

KITE: No, no, sir. She was brought to bed yesterday.

PLUME: Kite, you must father the child.

KITE: Humph. And so her friends will oblige me to marry the mother.

PLUME: If they should, we'll take her with us. She can wash, you know, and make a bed upon occasion.

KITE: Ay, or unmake it upon occasion, but your honor knows that I'm married already.

PLUME: To how many?

KITE: I can't tell readily. I have set them down here upon the back of the muster roll. (Draws out the muster roll) Let me see. Imprimis, Mrs. Sheely Snickereyes; she sells potatoes upon Ormond-Key in Dublin; Peggy Guzzle, the brandy woman at the Horse-Guard at Whitehall; Dolly Waggon, the carrier's daughter in Hull; Mademoiselle Van-Bottomflat at the Buss. Then Jenny Oakam the ship-carpenter's widow at Portsmouth, but I don't reckon upon her, for she was married at the same time to two lieutenants of marines and a man of war's boatswain.

PLUME: A full company. You have named five. Come, make 'em half a dozen, Kite. Is the child a boy or a girl?

KITE: A chopping boy.

PLUME: Then set the mother down in your list and the boy in mine. Enter him a grenadier by the name of Francis Kite, absent upon furlough. I'll allow you a man's pay for his subsistence, and go comfort the wench in the straw.

KITE: I shall, sir.

PLUME: But hold, have you made any use of your German doctor's habit since you arrived?

KITE: Yes, yes, sir, and my fame's all about the country for the most famous fortune-teller that ever told a lie. I was obliged to let my landlord into the secret for the convenience of keeping it so, but he's an honest fellow and will be trusty to any roguery that is confided to him. This device, sir, will get you men and me money, which I think is all we want at present. But yonder comes your friend, Mr. Worthy. Has your honor any further commands?

PLUME: None at present.

(Exit KITE)

'Tis indeed the picture of Worthy, but the life's departed.

(Enter WORTHY.)

PLUME: What! Arms-across, Worthy! Methinks you should hold 'em open when a friend's so near. The man has got the vapors in his ears, I believe. I must expel this melancholy spirit.

Spleen, thou worst of fiends below,
Fly, I conjure thee by this magic blow.

(Slaps WORTHY on the shoulder.)

WORTHY: Plume! My dear Captain, welcome. Safe and sound returned?

PLUME: I 'scaped safe from Germany and sound, I hope, from London. You see I have lost neither leg, arm, nor nose. Then for my inside, 'tis neither troubled with sympathies nor antipathies, and I have an excellent stomach for roast beef.

WORTHY: Thou art a happy fellow; once I was so.

PLUME: What ails thee, man? No inundations nor earthquakes in Wales, I hope? Has your father rose from the dead and reassumed his estate?

WORTHY: No.

PLUME: Then you are married surely?

WORTHY: No.

PLUME: Then you are mad or turning Quaker.

WORTHY: Come, I must out with it. Your once gay, roving friend is dwindled into an obsequious, thoughtful, romantic, constant coxcomb.

PLUME: And pray, what is all this for?

WORTHY: For a woman.

PLUME: Shake hands, brother, if you go to that. Behold me as obsequious, as thoughtful, and as constant a coxcomb as your worship.

WORTHY: For whom?

PLUME: For a regiment. But for a woman, 'sdeath, I have been constant to fifteen at one time, but never melancholy for one. And can the love of one bring you into this pickle? Pray, who is this miraculous Helen?

WORTHY: A Helen indeed, not to be won under a ten years' siege; as great a beauty and as great a jilt.

PLUME: A jilt! Pho, is she as great a whore?

WORTHY: No, no.

PLUME: 'Tis ten thousand pities. But who is she? Do I know her?

WORTHY: Very well.

PLUME: Impossible. I know no woman that will hold out a ten years' siege.

WORTHY: What think you of Melinda?

PLUME: Melinda! Why she began to capitulate this time twelve-month, and offered to surrender upon honorable terms. And I advised you to propose a settlement of five hundred pound a year to her before I went last abroad.

WORTHY: I did, and she hearkened to't, desiring only one week to consider, when beyond her hopes the town was relieved and I forced to turn my siege into a blockade.

PLUME: Explain, explain.

WORTHY: My Lady Richly, her aunt in Flintshire, dies and leaves her at this critical time twenty thousand pound.

PLUME: Oh, the devil, what a delicate woman was there spoiled! But by the rules of war now, Worthy, your blockade was foolish. After such a convoy of provisions was entered the place, you could have no thought of reducing it by famine. You should have redoubled your attacks, taken the town by storm, or have died upon the breach.

WORTHY: I did make one general assault and pushed it with all my forces, but I was so vigorously repulsed that, despairing of ever gaining her for a mistress, I have altered my conduct, given my addresses the obsequious and distant turn, and court her now for a wife.

PLUME: So, as you grew obsequious, she grew haughty, and because you approached her as a goddess, she used you like a dog.

WORTHY: Exactly.

PLUME: 'Tis the way of 'em all. Come Worthy, your obsequious and distant airs will never bring you together. You must not think to surmount her pride by your humility. Would you bring her to better thoughts of you, she must be reduced to a meaner opinion of herself. Let me see. The very first thing that I would do should be to lie with her chambermaid and hire three or four wenches in the neighborhood to report that I had got them with child. Suppose we lampooned all the pretty women in town and left her out? Or what if we made a ball and forgot to invite her, with one or two of the ugliest?

WORTHY: These would be mortifications, I must confess. But we live in such a precise, dull place that we can have no balls, no lampoons, no—

PLUME: What! No bastards! And so many recruiting officers in town. I thought 'twas a maxim among them to leave as many recruits in the country as they carried out.

WORTHY: Nobody doubts your good will, noble Captain, in serving your country with your best blood. Witness our friend Molly at the Castle. There have been tears in town about that business, Captain.

PLUME: I hope Silvia has not heard of't.

WORTHY: Oh, sir, have you thought of her? I began to fancy you had forgot poor Silvia.

PLUME: Your affairs had put my own quite out of my head. 'Tis true Silvia and I had once agreed to go to bed together, could we have adjusted preliminaries, but she would have the wedding before consummation and I was for consummation before the wedding. We could not agree. She was a pert, obstinate fool and would lose her maidenhead her own way so she may keep it for Plume.

WORTHY: But do you intend to marry upon no other conditions?

PLUME: Your pardon, sir, I'll marry upon no conditions at all. If I should, I'm resolved never to bind myself to a woman for my whole life till I know whether I shall like her company for half an hour. Suppose I married a woman that wanted a leg? Such a thing might be, unless I examined the goods beforehand. If people would but try one another's constitutions before they engaged, it would prevent all these elopements, divorces, and the devil knows what.

WORTHY: Nay, for that matter, the town did not stick to say that—

PLUME: I hate country towns for that reason. If your town has a dishonorable thought of Silvia, it deserves to be burned to the ground. I love Silvia, I admire her frank, generous disposition. There's something in that girl more than woman. Her sex is but a foil to her. The ingratitude, dissimulation, envy, pride, avarice, and vanity of her sister females do but set off their contraries in her. In short, were I once a general, I would marry her.

WORTHY: Faith, you have reason, for were you but a corporal, she would marry you. But my Melinda coquets it with every fellow she sees. I lay fifty pound she makes love to you.

PLUME: I'll lay fifty pound that I return it if she does. Look'e, Worthy, I'll win her and give her to you afterwards.

WORTHY: If you win her, you shall wear her, faith. I would not give a fig for the conquest without the credit of the victory.

(Enter KITE.*)*

KITE: Captain, Captain, a word in your ear.

PLUME: You may speak out; here are none but friends.

KITE: You know, sir, that you sent me to comfort the good woman in the straw, Mrs. Molly, my wife, Mr. Worthy.

WORTHY: Oho, very well. I wish you joy, Mr. Kite.

KITE: Your worship very well may, for I have got both a wife and a child in half an hour, but as I was a-saying, you sent me to comfort Mrs. Molly, my wife, I mean. But what d'ye think, sir? She was better comforted before I came.

PLUME: As how?

KITE: Why, sir, a footman in a blue livery had brought her ten guineas to buy her baby clothes.

PLUME: Who in the name of wonder could send them?

KITE: Nay, sir, I must whisper that. *(Whispers* PLUME*)* Mrs. Silvia.

PLUME: Silvia! Generous creature!

WORTHY: Silvia! Impossible.

KITE: Here be the guineas, sir. I took the gold as part of my wife's portion. Nay farther, sir, she sent word that the child should be taken all imaginable care of, and that she intended to stand godmother. The same footman, as I was coming to you with this news, called after me and told me that his lady would speak with me. I went, and upon hearing that you were come to town, she gave me half a guinea for the news and ordered me to tell you that Justice Balance, her father, who is just come out of the country, would be glad to see you.

PLUME: There's a girl for you, Worthy. Is there anything of woman in this? No, 'tis a noble and generous, manly friendship. Show me another woman that would lose an inch of her prerogative that way, without tears, fits, and reproaches. The common jealousy of her sex, which is nothing but their avarice of pleasure, she despises, and can part with the lover though she dies for the man. Come, Worthy. Where's the best wine? For there I'll quarter.

WORTHY: Horton has a fresh pipe of choice Barcelona which I would not let him pierce before because I reserved the maidenhead of it for your welcome to town.

PLUME: Let's away then. Mr. Kite, wait on the lady with my humble service and tell her that I shall only refresh a little, and wait on her.

WORTHY: Hold, Kite. Have you seen the other recruiting captain?

KITE: No, sir.

PLUME: Another? Who is he?

WORTHY: My rival in the first place, and the most unaccountable fellow. But I'll tell you more as we go. *(Exeunt)*

SCENE II

An apartment

(Enter; MELINDA *and* SILVIA *meeting.)*

MELINDA: Welcome to town, cousin Silvia. *(Salute)* I envied you your retreat in the country, for Shrewsbury, methinks, and all your heads of shires, are the most irregular places for living. Here we have smoke, noise, scandal, affectation, and pre-

tension, in short, everything to give the spleen and nothing to divert it. Then the air is intolerable.

SILVIA: Oh, madam, I have heard the town commended for its air.

MELINDA: But you don't consider, Silvia, how long I have lived in it; for I can assure you that to a lady the least nice in her constitution, no air can be good above half a year. Change of air I take to be the most agreeable of any variety in life.

SILVIA: As you say, cousin Melinda, there are several sorts of airs: airs in conversation, airs in behavior, airs in dress. Then we have our quality airs, our sickly airs, our reserved airs, and sometimes our impudent airs.

MELINDA: Pshaw, I talk only of the air we breathe, or more properly, of that we taste. Have not you, Silvia, found a vast difference in the taste of airs?

SILVIA: Pray, cousin, are not vapors a sort of air? Taste air? You may as well tell me I might feed upon air. But prithee, my dear Melinda, don't put on such airs to me. Your education and mine were just the same, and I remember the time when we never troubled our heads about air, but when the sharp air from the Welsh mountains made our noses drop in a cold morning at the boarding school.

MELINDA: Our education, cousin, was the same, but our temperaments had nothing alike. You have the constitution of a horse.

SILVIA: So far as to be troubled with neither spleen, colic, nor vapors. I need no salt for my stomach, no hartshorn for my head, nor wash for my complexion. I can gallop all the morning after the hunting horn and all the evening after a fiddle. In short, I can do everything with my father but drink and shoot flying, and I'm sure I can do everything my mother could, were I put to the trial.

MELINDA: You are in a fair way of being put to't, for I'm told your captain is come to town.

SILVIA: Ay, Melinda, he is come, and I'll take care he shan't go without a companion.

MELINDA: You're certainly mad, cousin.

SILVIA: And there's a pleasure sure in being mad, Which none but madmen know.

MELINDA: Thou poor, romantic Quixote. Hast thou the vanity to imagine that a young, sprightly officer that rambles over half the globe in half a year can confine his thoughts to the little daughter of a country justice in an obscure corner of the world?

SILVIA: Pshaw! What care I for his thoughts? I should not like a man with confined thoughts; it shows a narrowness of soul. Constancy is but a dull, sleepy quality at best; they will hardly admit it among the manly virtues. Nor do I think it deserves a place with bravery, knowledge, policy, justice, and some other qualities that are proper to that noble sex. In short, Melinda, I think a petticoat a mighty simple thing, and I'm heartily tired of my sex.

MELINDA: That is, you are tired of an appendix to our sex that you can't so handsomely get rid of in petticoats as if you were in breeches. O'my conscience, Silvia, hadst thou been a man, thou hadst been the greatest rake in Christendom.

SILVIA: I should endeavor to know the world, which a man can never do thoroughly without half a hundred friendships and as many amours. But now I think on't, how stands your affair with Mr. Worthy?

MELINDA: He's my aversion.

SILVIA: Vapors!

MELINDA: What do you say, madam?

SILVIA: I say that you should not use that honest fellow so inhumanely. He's a gentleman of parts and fortune, and beside that he's my Plume's friend, and by all that's sacred, if you don't use him better, I shall expect satisfaction.

MELINDA: Satisfaction! You begin to fancy yourself in breeches in good earnest. But to be plain with you, I like Worthy the worse for being so intimate with your captain, for I take him to be a loose, idle, unmannerly coxcomb.

SILVIA: Oh, madam. You never saw him, perhaps, since you were mistress of twenty thousand pound. You only knew him when you were capitulating with Worthy for a settlement which might encourage him to be a little loose and unmannerly with you.

MELINDA: What do you mean, madam?

SILVIA: My meaning needs no interpretation, madam.

MELINDA: Better it had, madam, for methinks you're too plain.

SILVIA: If you mean the plainness of my person, I think your ladyship as plain as me to the full.

MELINDA: Were I assured of that, I should be glad to take up with a rakely officer as you do.

SILVIA: Again! Look'e, madam, you're in your own house.

MELINDA: And if you had kept in yours, I should have excused you.

SILVIA: Don't be troubled, madam. I shan't desire to have my visit returned.

MELINDA: The sooner therefore you make an end of this, the better.

SILVIA: I'm easily advised to follow my inclinations. So, madam, your humble servant. *Exit.*

MELINDA: Saucy thing!

(Enter LUCY.*)*

LUCY: What's the matter, madam?

MELINDA: Did not you see the proud nothing, how she swells upon the arrival of her fellow?

LUCY: Her fellow has not been long enough arrived to occasion any great swelling, madam. I don't believe she has seen him yet.

MELINDA: Nor shan't if I can help it. Let me see. I have it. Bring me pen and ink. Hold, I'll go write in my closet.

LUCY: An answer to this letter, I hope, madam. *(Presents a letter.)*

MELINDA: Who sent it?

LUCY: Your captain, madam.

MELINDA: He's a fool, and I'm tired of him. Send it back unopened.

LUCY: The messenger's gone, madam.

MELINDA: Then how shall I send an answer? Call him back immediately, while I go write. *(Exeunt severally.)*

ACT II

SCENE I

An apartment.

Enter JUSTICE BALANCE *and* PLUME.

BALANCE: Look'e, Captain, give us but blood for our money and you shan't want men. I remember that for some years of the last war we had no blood nor wounds but in the officers' mouths, nothing for our millions but newspapers not worth a reading. Our armies did nothing but play at prison bars, and hide and seek with the enemy, but now ye have brought us colors and standards and prisoners. Odmylife, Captain, get us but another Marshal of France and I'll go myself for a soldier.[4]

PLUME: Pray, Mr. Balance, how does your fair daughter?

BALANCE: Ah, Captain, what is my daughter to a Marshal of France. We're upon a nobler subject. I want to have a particular description of the battle of Hochstadt.

PLUME: The battle, sir, was a very pretty battle as one should desire to see, but we were all so intent upon victory that we never minded the battle. All that I know of the matter is, our general commanded us to beat the French and we did so, and if he pleases to say the word, we'll do't again. But pray, sir, how does Mrs. Silvia?

BALANCE: Still upon Silvia! For shame, Captain. You're engaged already, wedded to the war.

[4]The English captured a French Marshal (one of the highest ranking officers in the army) at the battle of Hochstadt (now usually referred to as the battle at Blenheim).

War is your mistress, and it is below a soldier to think of any other.

PLUME: As a mistress, I confess, but as a friend, Mr. Balance?

BALANCE: Come, come, Captain, never mince the matter. Would not you debauch my daughter if you could?

PLUME: How, sir! I hope she is not to be debauched.

BALANCE: Faith, but she is, sir, and any woman in England of her age and complexion, by a man of your youth and vigor. Look'e, Captain, once I was young and once an officer as you are, and I can guess at your thoughts now by what mine were then, and I can remember very well that I would have given one of my legs to have deluded the daughter of an old, plain country gentleman, as like me as I was then like you.

PLUME: But, sir, was that country gentleman your friend and benefactor?

BALANCE: Not much of that.

PLUME: There the comparison breaks; the favors, sir, that—

BALANCE: Pho, I hate speeches. If I have done you any service, Captain, 'twas to please myself, for I love thee, and if I could part with my girl, you should have her as soon as any young fellow I know. But I hope you have more honor than to quit the service, and she more prudence than to follow the camp. But she's at her own disposal; she has fifteen hundred pound in her pocket, and so, Silvia, Silvia. *(Calls)*

Enter SILVIA.

SILVIA: There are some letters, sir, come by the post from London; I left them upon the table in your closet.

BALANCE: And here is a gentleman from Germany. *(Presents* PLUME *to her)* Captain, you'll excuse me; I'll go read my letters and wait on you. *(Exit)*

SILVIA: Sir, you're welcome to England.

PLUME: Blessings in heaven we should receive in a prostrate posture; let me receive my welcome thus. *(Kneels and kisses her hand)*

SILVIA: Pray, rise, sir, I'll give you fair quarter.

PLUME: All quarter I despise; the height of conquest is to die at your feet.
(Kissing her hand again)

SILVIA: Well, well, you shall die at my feet, or where you will, but first let me desire you to make your will; perhaps you'll leave me something.

PLUME: My will, madam, is made already, and there it is. *(Gives her a parchment)* And if you please to open that parchment, which was drawn the evening before the battle of Blenheim, you will find whom I left my heir.

*(*SILVIA *opens the will and reads.)*

SILVIA: Mrs. Silvia Balance. Well, Captain, this is a handsome and a substantial compliment, but I can assure you I am much better pleased with the bare knowledge of your intention than I should have been in the possession of your legacy. But methinks, sir, you should have left something to your little boy at the Castle.

PLUME: *(Aside)* That's home. — My little boy! Lackaday, madam, that alone may convince you 'twas none of mine. Why the girl, madam, is my sergeant's wife, and so the poor creature gave out that I was father in hopes that my friends might support her in case of necessity; that was all, madam. My boy, no, no.

(Enter SERVANT.*)*

SERVANT: Madam, my master has received some ill news from London and desires to speak with you immediately, and he begs the Captain's pardon that he can't wait on him as he promised.

PLUME: Ill news! Heavens avert it; nothing could touch me nearer than to see that generous, worthy gentleman afflicted. I'll leave you to comfort him, and be assured that if my life and fortune can be any way serviceable to the father of my Silvia, she shall freely command both.

SILVIA: The necessity must be very pressing that would engage me to do either. *(Exeunt severally.)*

SCENE II
Scene changes to another apartment.

(Enter BALANCE *and* SILVIA.*)*

SILVIA: Whilst there is life there is hope, sir; perhaps my brother may recover.

BALANCE: We have but little reason to expect it. Dr. Kilman acquaints me here that before this comes to my hands he fears I shall have no son. Poor Owen! But the decree is just. I was pleased with the death of my father because he left me an estate, and now I'm punished with the loss of an heir to inherit mine. I must now look upon you as the only hopes of my family, and I expect that the augmentation of your fortune will give you fresh thoughts and new prospects.

SILVIA: My desire of being punctual in my obedience requires that you would be plain in your commands, sir.

BALANCE: The death of your brother makes you sole heiress to my estate, which three or four years hence will amount to twelve hundred pound per annum. This fortune gives you a fair claim to quality and a title. You must set a just value upon yourself and, in plain terms, think no more of Captain Plume.

SILVIA: You have often commended the gentleman, sir.

BALANCE: And I do still; he's a very pretty fellow. But though I liked him well enough for a bare son-in-law, I don't approve of him for an heir to my estate and family. Fifteen hundred pound, indeed, I might trust in his hands, and it might do the young fellow a kindness, but odsmylife, twelve hundred pound a year would ruin him, quite turn his brain. A Captain of Foot worth twelve hundred pound a year! 'Tis a prodigy in nature. Besides this, I have five or six thousand pounds in woods upon my estate. Oh, that would make him stark mad, for you must know that all captains have a mighty aversion to timber. They can't endure to see trees standing. Then I should have some rogue of a builder by the help of his damned magic art transform my noble oaks and elms into cornices, portals, sashes, birds, breasts, gods, and devils, to adorn some maggoty, new-fashioned bauble upon the Thames. And then you should have a dog of a gardener bring a *habeus corpus* for my *terra firma*, remove it to Chelsea or Twitnam,[5] and clap it into grassplots and gravel walks.

(Enter a SERVANT.*)*

SERVANT: Sir, here's one below with a letter for your worship, but he will deliver it into no hands but your own.

BALANCE: Come show me the messenger. *(Exit with* SERVANT.*)*

SILVIA: Make the dispute between love and duty, and I am Prince Prettyman exactly.[6] If my brother dies, ah, poor brother; if he lives, ah, poor sister. 'Tis bad both ways. I'll try again. Follow my own inclinations and break my father's heart, or obey his commands and break my own. Worse and worse. Suppose I take thus—a moderate fortune, a pretty fellow and a pad,[7] or a fine estate, a coach-and-six, and an ass. That will never do neither.

(Enter BALANCE *and* SERVANT.*)*

BALANCE: Put four horses into the coach. *(To the* SERVANT, *who goes out.)* Silvia.

SILVIA: Sir.

BALANCE: How old were you when your mother died?

SILVIA: So young that I don't remember I ever had one. And you have been so careful, so indulgent to me since, that indeed I never wanted one.

[5]Two suburbs of London.
[6]Character in a play torn between love and duty.
[7]A riding horse.

BALANCE: Have I ever denied you anything you asked of me?

SILVIA: Never, that I remember.

BALANCE: Then, Silvia, I must beg that once in your life you would grant me a favor.

SILVIA: Why should you question it, sir?

BALANCE: I don't, but I would rather counsel than command. I don't propose this with the authority of a parent, but with the advice of your friend, that you would take the coach this moment and go into the country.

SILVIA: Does this advice proceed from the contents of the letter you received just now?

BALANCE: No matter. I shall be with you in three or four days and then give you my reasons. But before you go, I expect you will make me one solemn promise.

SILVIA: Propose the thing, sir.

BALANCE: That you will never dispose of yourself to any man without my consent.

SILVIA: I promise.

BALANCE: Very well, and to be even with you, I promise that I will never dispose of you without your own consent. And so, Silvia, the coach is ready. Farewell. *(Leads her to the door and returns)* Now she's gone, I'll examine the contents of this letter a little nearer. *(Reads)*

"Sir,

My intimacy with Mr. Worthy has drawn a secret from him that he had from his friend, Captain Plume, and my friendship and relation to your family oblige me to give you timely notice of it. The captain has dishonorable designs upon my cousin Silvia. Evils of this nature are more easily prevented than amended, and that you would immediately send my cousin into the country is the advice of,

Sir, your humble servant,
Melinda."

Why, the devil's in the young fellows of this age! They're ten times worse than they were in my time. Had he made my daughter a whore and foreswore it like a gentleman, I could have almost pardoned it, but to tell tales beforehand is monstrous! Hang it, I can fetch down a woodcock or snipe, and why not a hat and feather? I have a case of good pistols and have a good mind to try.

(Enter WORTHY.*)*

BALANCE: Worthy, your servant.

WORTHY: I'm sorry, sir, to be the messenger of ill news.

BALANCE: I apprehend it, sir. You have heard that my son Owen is past recovery.

WORTHY: My advices say he's dead, sir.

BALANCE: He's happy, and I am satisfied. The strokes of heaven I can bear, but injuries from men, Mr. Worthy, are not so easily supported.

WORTHY: I hope, sir, you are under no apprehension of wrong from anybody?

BALANCE: You know I ought to be.

WORTHY: You wrong my honor, sir, in believing I could know anything to your prejudice without resenting it as much as you should.

BALANCE: This letter, sir, which I tear in pieces to conceal the person that sent it, informs me that Plume has a design upon Silvia and that you are privy to't.

WORTHY: Nay then, sir, I must do myself justice and endeavor to find out the author. *(Takes up a piece of the letter)* Sir, I know the hand, and if you refuse to discover the contents, Melinda shall tell me. *(Going)*

BALANCE: Hold, sir, the contents I have told you already, only with this circumstance, that her intimacy with Mr. Worthy has drawn the secret from him.

WORTHY: Her intimacy with me! Dear sir, let me pick up the pieces of this letter. 'Twill give me such a hank upon her pride to have her own an intimacy under her hand. 'Twas the luckiest accident. *(Gathering up the letter)* The aspersion, sir, was nothing but malice, the effect of a little quarrel between her and Mrs. Silvia.

BALANCE: Are you sure of that, sir?

WORTHY: Her maid gave me the history of part of the battle just now, as she overheard it.

BALANCE: 'Tis probable. I am satisfied.

WORTHY: But I hope, sir, your daughter has suffered nothing upon the account?

BALANCE: No, no. Poor girl, she is so afflicted with the news of her brother's death that to avoid company she begged leave to be gone into the country.

WORTHY: And is she gone?

BALANCE: I could not refuse her; she was so pressing. The coach went from the door the minute before you came.

WORTHY: So pressing to be gone, sir. I find her fortune will give her the same airs with Melinda, and then Plume and I may laugh at one another.

BALANCE: Like enough. Women are as subject to pride as we are, and why mayn't great women as well as great men forget their old acquaintance? But come, where's this young fellow? I love him so well it would break the heart of me to think him a rascal. *(Aside)* I'm glad my daughter's gone fairly off though. — Where does the captain quarter?

WORTHY: At Horton's. I'm to meet him there two hours hence, and we should be glad of your company.

BALANCE: Your pardon, dear Worthy. I must allow a day or two to the death of my son. The decorum of mourning is what we owe the world because they pay it to us. Afterwards, I'm yours over a bottle, or how you will.

WORTHY: Sir, I'm your humble servant. *(Exeunt severally.)*

SCENE III
The street

(KITE enters with one of the MOB in each hand, drunk.)

KITE: *(Sings)*
Our prentice Tom may now refuse
To wipe his scoundrel master's shoes,
For now he's free to sing and play,

Over the hills and far away.
Over the hills, &c. *(The MOB sing the chorus.)*
We all shall lead more happy lives
By getting rid of brats and wives,
That scold and brawl both night and day,
Over the hills and far away.
Over the hills, &c.

Hey, boys. Thus we soldiers live, drink, dance, play; we live, as one should say. We live. 'Tis impossible to tell how we live. We're all princes. Why, why, you're a king. You're an emperor, and I'm a prince. Now, an't we?

1 MOB: No, Sergeant, I'll be no emperor.

KITE: No?

1 MOB: No, I'll be a justice of peace.

KITE: A justice of peace, man?

1 MOB: Ay, wauns will I, for since this pressing act they are greater than any emperor under the sun.

KITE: Done, you're a justice of peace, and you're a king, and I'm a duke, and a rum duke, an't I?

2 MOB: No, but I'll be no king.

KITE: What then?

2 MOB: I'll be a queen.

KITE: A queen!

2 MOB: Ay, Queen of England.[8] That's greater than any king of 'em all.

KITE: Bravely said, faith! Huzza for the Queen! (All huzza) But hear'e, you Mr. Justice, and you Mr. Queen, did you ever see the Queen's picture?

1 AND 2 MOB: No, no.

KITE: I wonder at that; I have two of 'em set in gold, and as like Her Majesty, God bless the mark. (He takes two broad pieces out of his pocket.)[9] See here, they're set in gold. (Gives one to each)

1 MOB: (Looking earnestly upon the piece) The wonderful works of nature!

2 MOB: What's this written about? Here's a posy, I believe. Ca ro lus—what's that, Sergeant?

KITE: Oh, Carolus, why Carolus is Latin for Queen Anne, that's all.

2 MOB: 'Tis a fine thing to be a scollard, Sergeant. Will you part with this? I'll buy it on you if it come within the compass of a crown.

KITE: A crown! Never talk of buying. 'Tis the same thing among friends, you know. I present them to you both; you shall give me as good a thing. Put them up and remember your old friend, when I'm over the hills and far away. (Singing)

[8]At this time, England was ruled by Queen Anne.

[9]Broad pieces were twenty-shilling coins from the reign of Charles I. Subsequent jokes deal with Carolus (Charles, in Latin); thus the coin does not have the Queen's picture on it.

(They sing and put up the money.)

(Enter PLUME singing.)

PLUME:
Over the hills, and o're the main,
To Flanders, Portugal, or Spain;
The Queen commands, and we'll obey,
Over the hills and far away.
Come on ye men of mirth, away with it. I'll make one among ye. Who are these hearty lads?

KITE: Off with your hats, wauns, off with your hats. This is the captain, the captain.

1 MOB: We have seen captains before now, mun.

2 MOB: Ay, and lieutenant captains too; flesh, I'se keep on my nab.

1 MOB: And I'se scarcely doff mine for any captain in England. My vether's a freeholder.

PLUME: Who are these jolly lads, Sergeant?

KITE: A couple of honest, brave fellows that are willing to serve the Queen. I have entertained them just now as volunteers under your honor's command.

PLUME: And good entertainment they shall have. Volunteers are the men I want; those are the men fit to make soldiers, captains, generals.

2 MOB: Wauns, Tummas, what's this? Are you listed?

1 MOB: Flesh, not I. Are you, Costar?

2 MOB: Wauns, not I.

KITE: What, not listed? Ha, ha, ha, a very good jest, faith.

2 MOB: Come, Tummas, we'll go whome.

1 MOB: Ay, ay, come.

KITE: Home! For shame, gentlemen, behave yourselves better before your captain. Dear Tummas, honest Costar—

2 MOB: No, no, we'll be gone. (Going.)

KITE: Nay, then I command you to stay. I place you both sentinels in this place for two hours to watch the motion of St. Mary's clock you, and you the motion of St. Chad's. And he that dare stir from his post till he be relieved shall have my sword in his guts the next minute.

PLUME: What's the matter, Sergeant? I'm afraid you're too rough with these gentlemen.

KITE: I'm too mild, sir. They disobey command, sir, and one of them should be shot for an example to the other.

2 MOB: Shot, Tummas!

PLUME: Come, gentlemen, what is the matter?

1 MOB: We don't know. The noble sergeant is pleased to be in a passion, sir, but—

KITE: They disobey command; they deny their being listed.

2 MOB: Nay, Sergeant, we don't downright deny it neither; that we dare not do for fear of being shot, but we humbly conceive in a civil way, and begging your worship's pardon, that we may go home.

PLUME: That's easily known. Have either of you received any of the Queen's money?

1 MOB: Not a brass farthing, sir.

KITE: Sir, they have each of them received three and twenty shillings and sixpence and 'tis now in their pockets.[10]

1 MOB: Wauns, if I have a penny in my pocket but a bent sixpence, I'll be content to be listed, and shot into the bargain.

2 MOB: And I, look'e here, sir.

1 MOB: Ay, here's my stock too, nothing but the Queen's picture that the sergeant gave me just now.

KITE: See there, a broad piece, three and twenty shillings and sixpence. The t'other has the fellow on't.

PLUME: The case is plain, gentlemen, the goods are found upon you. Those pieces of gold are worthy three and twenty and sixpence each.

2 MOB: So it seems that *Carolus* is three and twenty shillings and sixpence in Latin.

1 MOB: 'Tis the same thing in the Greek, for we are listed.

2 MOB: Flesh, but we an't, Tummas. I desire to be carried before the mayar, Captain.

(While they talk, the CAPTAIN *and* SERGEANT *whisper.)*

PLUME: 'Twill never do, Kite; your damned tricks will ruin me at last. I won't lose the fellows though, if I can help it. Well, gentlemen, there must be some trick in this. My sergeant offers here to take his oath that you're fairly listed.

1 MOB: Why, Captain, we know that you soldiers have more liberty of conscience than other folks, but for me or neighbor Costar here to take such an oath 'twould be downright perjuration.

[10]The twenty-shilling broadpiece from the reign of Charles I was, by 1706, worth 23 shillings and 6 pence.

PLUME: Look'e, you rascal, you villain, if I find that you have imposed upon these two honest fellows, I'll trample you to death, you dog. Come, how was't?

1 MOB: Nay, then we will speak. Your sergeant, as you say, is a rogue, begging your worship's pardon, and—

2 MOB: Nay, Tummas, let me speak. You know I can read. And so, sir, he gave us those two pieces of money for pictures of the Queen by way of a present.

PLUME: How! By way of a present! The son of a whore! I'll teach him to abuse honest fellows like you. Scoundrel, rogue, villain! *(Beats the* SERGEANT *off the stage and follows him out)*

BOTH MOB: O brave, noble Captain! Huzza, a brave captain, faith!

2 MOB: Now, Tummas, *Carolus* is Latin for a beating. This is the bravest captain I ever saw. Wauns, I have a month's mind to go with him.

(Re-enter PLUME.)

PLUME: A dog, to abuse two such pretty fellows as you! Look'e, gentlemen, I love a pretty fellow. I come among you here as an officer to list soldiers, not as a kidnapper to steal slaves.

2 MOB: Mind that, Tummas.

PLUME: I desire no man to go with me but as I went myself. I went a volunteer, as you or you may go, for a little time carried a musket, and now I command a company.

1 MOB: Mind that, Costar, a sweet gentleman.

PLUME: 'Tis true, gentlemen, I might take an advantage of you; the Queen's money was in your pockets; my sergeant was ready to take his oath that you were listed, but I scorn to do a base thing. You are both of you at your liberty.

2 MOB: Thank you, noble Captain. I cod, I cannot find in my heart to leave him, he talks so finely.

1 MOB: Ay, Costar, would he always hold in this mind?

PLUME: Come, my lads, one thing more I'll tell you. You're both young, tight fellows and the army is the place to make you men forever. Every man has his lot, and you have yours. What think you now of a purse full of French gold out of a monsieur's pocket, after you have dashed out his brains with the butt of your firelock, eh?

2 MOB: Wauns, I'll have it. Captain, give me a shilling; I'll follow you to the end of the world.

1 MOB: Nay, dear Costar, duna; be advised.

PLUME: Here, my hero, here are two guineas for thee as earnest of what I'll do farther for thee.

1 MOB: Duna take it, duna, dear Costar. *(Cries and pulls back his arm)*

2 MOB: I wull, I wull. Wauns, my mind gives me that I shall be a captain myself. I take your money, sir, and now I'm a gentlemen.

PLUME: Give me thy hand. And now you and I will travel the world o'er and command wherever we tread. *(Aside)* Bring your friend with you if you can.

2 MOB: Well, Tummas, must we part?

1 MOB: No, Costar, I cannot leave thee. Come, Captain *(crying)*, I'll e'en go along too, and if you have two honester, simpler lads in your company than we twa been — I'll say no more.

PLUME: Here, my lad. *(Gives him money)* Now your name.

1 MOB: Thummas Appletree.

PLUME: And yours?

2 MOB: Costar Pearmain.

PLUME: Born where?

1 MOB: Both in Herefordshire.

PLUME: Very well. Courage, my lads. Now we will sing over the hills and far away.

Courage, boys, 'tis one to ten,
But we return all gentlemen, &c. *(Exeunt)*

ACT III

SCENE I
The marketplace.

(Enter PLUME and WORTHY.)

WORTHY: I cannot forbear admiring the equality of our two fortunes. We loved two ladies; they met us halfway, and just as we were upon the point of leaping into their arms, fortune drops into their laps, pride possesses their hearts, a maggot fills their heads, madness takes 'em by the tail; they snort, kick up their heels, and away they run.

PLUME: And leave us here to mourn upon the shore, a couple of poor, melancholy monsters. What shall we do?

WORTHY: I have a trick for mine, the letter, you know, and the fortune-teller.

PLUME: And I have a trick for mine.

WORTHY: What is't?

PLUME: I'll never think of her again.

WORTHY: No!

PLUME: No, I think myself above administering to the pride of any woman, were she worth twelve thousand a year, and I haven't the vanity to believe I shall even gain a lady worth twelve hundred. The generous, good-natured Silvia in her smock I admire, but the haughty, scornful Silvia with her fortune I despise.

A Song

1.

Come, fair one, be kind
You never shall find
A fellow so fit for a lover.
The world shall view
My passion for you,
But never your passion discover.

2.

I still will complain
Of your frowns and disdain,
Though I revel through all your charms.
The world shall declare
That I die with despair,
When I only die in your arms.

3.

I still will adore
And love more and more,
But, by Jove, if you chance to prove cruel,
I'll get me a miss
That freely will kiss,
Though I afterwards drink water gruel.

What, sneak out o'town and not so much as a word,

a line, a compliment! 'Sdeath, how far off does she live? I'd go and break her windows.

WORTHY: Ha, ha, ha. Ay, and the window bars too to come at her. Come, come, friend, no more of your rough military airs.

(Enter KITE.*)*

KITE: Captain, sir, look yonder; she's a-coming this way; 'tis the prettiest, cleanest little tit.

PLUME: Now, Worthy, to show you how much I'm in love. Here she comes, and what is that great country fellow with her?

KITE: I can't tell, sir.

(Enter ROSE *and her brother* BULLOCK, ROSE *with a basket on her arm crying chickens.)*

ROSE: Buy chickens, young and tender; young and tender chickens.

PLUME: Here, you chickens.

ROSE: Who calls?

PLUME: Come hither, pretty maid.

ROSE: Will you please to buy, sir?

WORTHY: Yes, child, we'll both buy.

PLUME: Nay, Worthy, that's not fair; market for yourself. Come, my child, I'll buy all you have.

ROSE: Then all I have is at your service. *(Curtsies)*

WORTHY: Then I must shift for myself, I find. *(Exit* WORTHY*)*

PLUME: Let me see. Young and tender, you say? *(Chucks her under the chin)*

ROSE: As ever you tasted in your life, sir. *(Curtsies)*

PLUME: Come, I must examine your basket to the bottom, my dear.

ROSE: Nay, for that matter, put in your hand; feel, sir. I warrant my ware as good as any in the market.

PLUME: And I'll buy it all, child, were it ten times more.

ROSE: Sir, I can furnish you.

PLUME: Come then; we won't quarrel about the price; they're fine birds. Pray what's your name, pretty creature?

ROSE: Rose, sir. My father is a farmer within three short mile o' th' town. We keep this market; I sell chickens, eggs, and butter, and my brother Bullock there sells corn.

BULLOCK: Come, sister, hast ye; we shall be

liate a whome. *(All this while* BULLOCK *whistles about the stage)*

PLUME: Kite! *(He tips the wink upon* KITE, *who returns it)* Pretty Mrs. Rose, you have, let me see, how many?

ROSE: A dozen, sir, and they are richly worth a crown.

BULLOCK: Come, Ruose, Ruose, I sold fifty stracke[11] o'barley today in half this time, but will you higgle and higgle for a penny more than the commodity is worth.

ROSE: What's that to you, oaf? I can make as much out of a groat as you can out of fourpence, I'm sure. The gentlemen bids fair, and when I meet with a chapman,[12] I know how to make the best on him. And so, sir, I say for a crown piece the bargain is yours.

PLUME: Here's a guinea, my dear.

ROSE: I can't change your money, sir.

PLUME: Indeed, indeed but you can. My lodging is hard by. You shall bring home the chickens and we'll make change there.

*(PLUME *goes off; she follows him.)*

KITE: So, sir, as I was telling you, I have seen one of these hussars eat up a ravelin[13] for his breakfast and afterwards pick his teeth with a palisado.[14]

BULLOCK: Ay, you soldiers see very strange things. But pray, sir, what is a ravelin?

KITE: Why 'tis like a modern minced pie, but the crust is confounded hard and the plums are somewhat hard of digestion.

BULLOCK: Then your palisado, pray what may he be? — Come, Ruose, pray ha' done.

KITE: Your palisado is a pretty sort of bodkin about the thickness of my leg.

BULLOCK: *(Aside)* That's a fib, I believe. Eh, where's Ruose? Ruose, Ruose, 'sflesh, where's Ruose gone?

KITE: She's gone with the captain.

BULLOCK: The captain! Wauns, there's no pressing of women, sure?[15]

KITE: But there is, sir.

[11]Stracke are bushels.
[12]A chapman is a haggler.
[13]A ravelin is an angled wall of a fortification.
[14]A palisado is one of a row of large, pointed stakes used to make a fence for a fortification.
[15]A pressing is impressing or forcibly enlisting.

BULLOCK: If the captain should press Ruose, I should be ruined. Which way went she? Oh, the devil take your rablins and palisaders.

(Exit BULLOCK*)*

KITE: You shall be better acquainted with them, honest Bullock, or I shall miss of my aim.

(Enter WORTHY.*)*

WORTHY: Why thou'rt the most useful fellow in nature to your captain, admirable in your way, I find.

KITE: Yes, sir, I understand my business, I will say it. You must know, sir, I was born a gypsy and bred among that crew till I was ten year old. There I learned canting and lying. I was bought from my mother, Cleopatra, by a certain nobleman for three pistoles, who, liking my beauty, made me his page. There I learned impudence and pimping. I was turned off for wearing my lord's linen and drinking my lady's brandy, and then turned bailiff's follower. There I learned bullying and swearing. I at last got into the army, and there I learned whoring and drinking. So that if your worship pleases to cast up the whole sum, *viz.*, canting, lying, impudence, pimping, bullying, swearing, whoring, drinking, and a halberd,[16] you will find the sum total will amount to a recruiting sergeant.

WORTHY: And pray, what induced you to turn soldier?

KITE: Hunger and ambition. The fears of starving and hopes of a truncheon[17] led me along to a gentleman with a fair tongue and fair periwig who loaded me with promises, but I gad 'twas the lightest load that I ever felt in my life. He promised to advance me, and indeed he did so, to a garret in the Savoy. I asked him why he put me in prison; he called me lying dog and said I was in garrison, and indeed 'tis a garrison that may hold out till doomsday before I should desire to take it again. But here comes Justice Balance.

(Enter BALANCE *and* BULLOCK.*)*

BALANCE: Here, you Sergeant, where's your captain? Here's a poor, foolish fellow comes clamoring to me with a complaint that your master has pressed his sister. Do you know anything of this matter, Worthy?

WORTHY: Ha, ha, ha. I know his sister is gone with Plume to his lodgings to sell him some chickens.

BALANCE: Is that all? The fellow's a fool.

BULLOCK: I know that, an't please you, but if your worship pleases to grant me a warrant to bring her before you for fear o' th' worst.

BALANCE: Thou art a mad fellow! Thy sister's safe enough.

KITE: *(Aside)* I hope so too.

WORTHY: Hast thou no more sense, fellow, than to believe that the captain can list women?[18]

BULLOCK: I know not whether they list them, or what they do with them, but I'm sure they carry as many women as men with them out of the country.

BALANCE: But how came you not to go along with your sister?

BULLOCK: Luord, sir, I thought no more of her going than I do of the day I shall die, but this gentleman, here, not suspecting any hurt neither, I believe. You thought no harm, friend, did ye?

KITE: Lack-a-day, sir, not I. *(Aside)* Only that I believe I shall marry her tomorrow.

BALANCE: I begin to smell powder. Well, friend, but what did that gentleman with you?

BULLOCK: Why, sir, he entertained me with a fine story of a great fight between the Hungarians, I think it was, and the Irish. And so, sir, while we were in the heat of the battle, the captain carried off the baggage.

BALANCE: Sergeant, go along with this fellow to your captain. Give him my humble service, and I desire him to discharge the wench, though he has listed her.

BULLOCK: Ay, and if he ben't free for that, he shall have another man in her place.

KITE: Come, honest friend. *(Aside)* You shall go to my quarters instead of the captain's.

(Exeunt KITE *and* BULLOCK.*)*

BALANCE: We must get this mad captain his compliment of men and send him a-packing, else he'll over-run the country.

WORTHY: You see, sir, how little he values your daughter's disdain.

BALANCE: I like him the better; I was much such another fellow at his age. I never set my heart upon any woman so much as to make me uneasy at

---

[16]A halberd is a battle weapon, a combined spear and axe.
[17]A truncheon is a baton signifying authority.

[18]List means enlist here.

the disappointment. But what was most surprising both to myself and friends, I changed o' th' sudden from the most fickle lover to be the most constant husband in the world. But how goes your affair with Melinda?

WORTHY: Very slowly. Cupid had formerly wings, but I think in this age he goes upon crutches, or I fancy Venus had been dallying with her cripple Vulcan when my amour commenced, which has made it go on so lamely. My mistress has got a captain too, but such a captain! As I live, yonder he comes.

BALANCE: Who? That bluff fellow in the sash? I don't know him.

WORTHY: But I engage he knows you, and everybody at first sight. His impudence were a prodigy were not his ignorance proportionable. He has the most universal acquaintance of any man living, for he won't be alone, and nobody will keep him company twice. Then he's a Caesar among the women: *veni, vidi, vici*, that's all. If he has but talked with the maid, he swears he has lain with the mistress, but the most surprising part of his character is his memory, which is the most prodigious and the most trifling in the world.

BALANCE: I have met with such men, and I take this good-for-nothing memory to proceed from a certain contexture of the brain, which is purely adapted to impertinencies, and they lodge secure, the owner having no thoughts of his own to disturb them. I have known a man as perfect as a chronologer as to the day and year of the most important transactions, but be altogether ignorant of the causes, springs, or consequences of any one thing of moment. I have known another acquire so much by travel as to tell you the names of most places in Europe, with their distances of miles, leagues, or hours as punctually as a post-boy, but for anything else, as ignorant as the horse that carries the mail.

WORTHY: This is your man, sir. Add but the traveler's privilege of lying, and even that he abuses. This is the picture, behold the life!

(Enter BRAZEN.*)*

BRAZEN: Mr. Worthy, I'm your servant, and so forth. Heark'e, my dear.

WORTHY: Whispering, sir, before company is not manners, and when nobody's by, 'tis foolish.

BRAZEN: Company! *Mort de ma vie*, I beg the gentleman's pardon. Who is he?

WORTHY: Ask him.

BRAZEN: So I will. My dear, I'm your servant, and so forth. Your name, my dear?

BALANCE: Very laconic, sir.

BRAZEN: Laconic, a very good name truly. I have known several of the Laconics abroad. Poor Jack Laconic, he was killed at the battle of Landen. I remember that he had a blue ribband in his hat that very day, and after he fell, we found a piece of neat's tongue in his pocket.

BALANCE: Pray, sir, did the French attack us or we them at Landen?

BRAZEN: The French attack us! Wauns, sir, are you a Jacobite?[19]

BALANCE: Why that question?

BRAZEN: Because none but a Jacobite could think that the French durst attack us. No, sir, we attacked them on the—I have reason to remember the time, for I had two-and-twenty horses killed under me that day.

WORTHY: Then, sir, you rid mighty hard.

BALANCE: Or perhaps, sir, like my countryman, you rid upon half a dozen horses at once.

BRAZEN: What d'e mean, gentlemen. I tell you they were killed, all torn to pieces by cannon shot, except six that I staked to death upon the enemy's *chevaux de frise*.[20]

BALANCE: Noble Captain, may I crave your name?

BRAZEN: Brazen, at your service.

BALANCE: Oh, Brazen, a very good name. I have known several of the Brazens abroad.

WORTHY: Do you know Captain Plume, sir?

BRAZEN: Is he anything related to Frank Plume in Northamptonshire? Honest Frank! Many, many a dry bottle have we cracked hand to fist. You must have known his brother Charles that was concerned in the India Company. He married the daughter of old Tongue-Pad, the Master in Chancery, a very pretty woman, only squinted a little. She died in childbed of her first child, but the child survived. 'Twas a daughter, but whether 'twas called Margaret or Marjory, upon my soul I can't remember. But, gentlemen *(Looking on his watch)*,

---

[19] A Jacobite is a supporter of the Stuart pretender to the English throne—the son of James II, who had been forced to abdicate in 1688.

[20] A chevaux de frise is a row of sharp spikes angled toward the enemy as a protection against cavalry charges.

I must meet a lady, a twenty-thousand pounder, presently, upon the walk by the water. Worthy, your servant; Laconic, yours.

(Exit BRAZEN*)*

BALANCE: If you can have so mean an opinion of Melinda as to be jealous of this fellow, I think she ought to give you cause to be so.

WORTHY: I don't think she encourages him so much for gaining herself a lover as to set me up a rival. Were there any credit to be given to his words, I should believe Melinda had made him this assignation. I must go see. Sir, you'll pardon me.

BALANCE: Ay, ay, sir, you're a man of business. *(Exit* WORTHY*)* But what have we got here?

(Enter ROSE *singing.)*

ROSE: And I shall be a lady, a captain's lady, and ride single upon a white horse with a star upon a velvet sidesaddle, and I shall go to London and see the tombs and the lions and the Queen. Sir, an't please your worship, I have often seen your worship ride through our grounds a-hunting, begging your worship's pardon. Pray, what may this lace be worth a yard? *(Showing some lace)*

BALANCE: Right Mechlin,[21] by this light! Where did you get this lace, child?

ROSE: No matter for that, sir, I come honestly by't.

BALANCE: I question it much.

ROSE: And see here, sir, a fine turkey-shell snuff box, and fine mangeree,[22] see here. *(She takes snuff affectedly)* The captain learnt me how to take it with an air.

BALANCE: Oho, the captain! Now the murder's out. And so the captain taught you to take it with an air?

ROSE: Yes, and give it with an air too. Will your worship please to taste my snuff? *(Offers the snuff affectedly)*

[21]Mechlin is expensive Belgian lace.
[22]Mangaree is Rose's corruption of orangeree, an orange-flavored snuff.

BALANCE: You're a very apt scholar, pretty maid, and pray what did you give the captain for these fine things?

ROSE: He's to have my brother for a soldier; and two or three sweethearts that I have in the country, they shall all go with the captain. Oh, he's the finest man and the humblest withal. Would you believe it, sir, he carried me up with him to his own chamber with as much gallantry as if I had been the best lady in the land.

BALANCE: Oh, he's a mighty familiar gentleman as can be.

ROSE: But I must beg your worship's pardon. I must go seek out my brother Bullock. *(ROSE runs off singing)*

BALANCE: If all officers took the same method of recruiting with this gentleman, they might come in time to be fathers as well as captains of their companies.

(Enter PLUME *singing.)*

PLUME:
But it is not so
With those that go
Through frost and snow
Most apropo,
My maid with the milking pail
(Takes hold on ROSE *who has returned)*
How, the justice! Then I'm arraigned, condemned, and executed.

BALANCE: Oh, my noble Captain.

ROSE: And my noble captain too, sir.

PLUME: 'Sdeath, child, are you mad? Mr. Balance, I am so full of business about my recruits that I ha'n't a moment's time to—I have just now three or four people to—

BALANCE: Nay, Captain, I must speak to you.

ROSE: And so must I too, Captain.

PLUME: Any other time, sir; I cannot for my life, sir—

BALANCE: Pray, sir.

PLUME: Twenty thousand things—I would but—now, sir, pray—devil take me—I cannot—I must—

(Breaks away)

BALANCE: Nay, I'll follow you.

ROSE: And I too.

SCENE II

The walk by the Severn side.

(Enter MELINDA *and her maid* LUCY.*)*

MELINDA: And pray, was it a ring or buckle or pendants or knots, or in what shape was the almighty gold transformed that has bribed you so much in his favor?

LUCY: Indeed, madam, the last bribe I had was from the captain, and that was only a small piece of Flanders edging for pinners.[23]

MELINDA: Ay, Flanders lace is as constant a present from officers to their women as something else is from their women to them. They every year bring over a cargo of lace to cheat the Queen of her duty and her subjects of their honesty.

LUCY: They only barter one sort of prohibited goods for another, madam.

MELINDA: Has any of them been bartering with you, Mrs. Pert, that you talk so like a trader?

LUCY: Madam, you talk as peevishly to me as if it were my fault. The crime is none of mine though I pretend to excuse it. Though he should not see you this week can I help it? But as I was saying, madam, his friend, Captain Plume, has so taken him up these two days—

MELINDA: Pshaw! Would his friend, the captain, were tied on his back. I warrant he has never been sober since that confounded captain came to town. The devil take all officers, I say; they do the nation more harm by debauching us at home than they do good by defending us abroad. No sooner a captain comes to town, but all the young fellows flock about him, and we can't keep a man to ourselves.

LUCY: One would imagine, madam, by your concern for Worthy's absence, that you should use him better when he's with you.

MELINDA: Who told you, pray, that I was concerned for his absence? I'm only vexed that I've had nothing said to me these two days. One may like the love and despise the lover, I hope, as one may love the treason and hate the traitor. Oh, here comes another captain, and a rogue that has the confidence to make love to me; but indeed, I don't won-

der at that when he has the assurance to fancy himself a gentleman.

LUCY: *(Aside)* If he should speak o' th' assignation, I should be ruined.

(Enter BRAZEN.*)*

BRAZEN: True to the touch, faith. *(Aside)* I'll draw up all my compliments into one grand platoon and fire upon her at once.

Thou peerless princess of Salopian plains,
Envied by nymphs and worshipped by the
swains,
Behold how humbly does the Severn glide,
To greet thee, princess of the Severn side.

Madam, I'm your humble servant and all that, madam. A fine river this same Severn; do you love fishing, madam?

MELINDA: 'Tis a pretty melancholy amusement for lovers.

BRAZEN: I'll go buy hooks and lines presently; for you must know, madam, that I have served in Flanders against the French, in Hungary against the Turks, and in Tangier against the Moors, and I was never so much in love before. And split me, madam, in all the campaigns I ever made I have not seen so fine a woman as your ladyship.

MELINDA: And from all the men I ever saw I never had so fine a compliment, but you soldiers are the best-bred men, that we must allow.

BRAZEN: Some of us, madam, but there are brutes among us too, very sad brutes. For my own part, I have always had the good luck to prove agreeable. I have had very considerable offers, madam. I might have married a German princess worth fifty thousand crowns a year, but her stove disgusted me. The daughter of a Turkish bashaw fell in love with me too, when I was prisoner among the infidels. She offered to rob her father of his treasure and make her escape with me, but I don't know how, my time was not come. Hanging and marriage, you know, go by destiny. Fate has reserved me for a Shropshire lady with twenty thousand pound. Do you know any such person, madam?

MELINDA: Extravagant coxcomb! To be sure,

---

[23]Pinners are headdresses.

a great many ladies of that fortune would be proud of the name of Mrs. Brazen.

BRAZEN: Nay, for that matter, madam, there are women of very good quality of the name of Brazen.

(Enter WORTHY.)

MELINDA: Oh, are you there, gentleman? Come, Captain, we'll walk this way; give me your hand.

BRAZEN: My hand, heart's blood, and guts are at your service. Mr. Worthy, your servant, my dear. *Exit leading* MELINDA.

WORTHY: Death and fire! This is not to be borne.

(Enter PLUME.)

PLUME: No more it is, faith.

WORTHY: What?

PLUME: The March beer at the Raven. I have been doubly serving the Queen, raising men and raising the excise. Recruiting and elections are good friends to the excise.[24]

WORTHY: You an't drunk?

PLUME: No, no, whimsical only; I could be mighty foolish and fancy myself mighty witty. Reason still keeps its throne, but it nods a little, that's all.

WORTHY: Then you're just fit for a frolic.

PLUME: As fit as close pinners for a punk in the pit.[25]

WORTHY: There's your play then; recover me that vessel from that Tangerine.

PLUME: She's well rigged, but how is she manned?

WORTHY: By Captain Brazen that I told you of today. The frigate is called the Melinda, a first rate I can assure you. She sheered off with him just now on purpose to affront me, but according to your advice I would take no notice, because I would seem to be above a concern for her behavior. But have a care of a quarrel.

PLUME: No, no, I never quarrel with anything in my cups but with an oyster wench or a cook maid, and if they ben't civil, I knock 'em down. But

[24]Excise is sales tax.
[25]"Close pinners for a punk in the pit" refers to a head-dress with flaps to conceal the identity of a prostitute in the pit (orchestra) of a theatre.

hark'e, my friend, I will make love, and I must make love. I tell'e what, I'll make love like a platoon.

WORTHY: A platoon! How's that?

PLUME: I'll kneel, stoop, and stand, faith. Most ladies are gained by platooning.

WORTHY: Here they come; I must leave you. (Exit WORTHY)

PLUME: So, now I must look as sober and demure as a whore at a christening.

(Enter BRAZEN and MELINDA.)

BRAZEN: Who's that, madam?

MELINDA: A brother officer of yours, I suppose.

BRAZEN: Ay! My dear. (To PLUME)

PLUME: My dear!

(They run and embrace)

BRAZEN: My dear boy, how is't? Your name, my dear. If I be not mistaken, I have seen your face.

PLUME: I never see yours in my life, my dear. But there's a face well known as the sun's, that shines on all and is by all adored.

BRAZEN: Have you any pretensions, sir?

PLUME: Pretensions?

BRAZEN: That is, sir, have you ever served abroad?

PLUME: I have served at home, sir, for ages served this cruel fair. And that will serve the turn, sir.

MELINDA: So, between the fool and the rake I shall bring a fine spot of work upon my hands. (Aside) I see Worthy yonder; I could be content to be friends with him would he come this way.

BRAZEN: Will you fight for the lady, sir?

PLUME: No, sir, but I'll have her notwithstanding.

Thou peerless princess of Salopian plains,
Envied by nymphs and worshipped by the
swains.

BRAZEN: Wauns, sir, not fight for her!

PLUME: Prithee be quiet, I shall be out.

Behold how humbly does the Severn glide
To greet thee, princess of the Severn side.

BRAZEN: Don't mind him, madam. If he were not so well dressed, I should take him for a poet, but I'll show you the difference presently. Come, madam, we'll place you between us, and now the longest sword carries her. (Draws, MELINDA shrieks)

(Enter WORTHY.)

MELINDA: Oh, Mr. Worthy, save me from these madmen.

*(*MELINDA *runs off with* WORTHY.)

PLUME: Ha, ha, ha. Why don't you follow, sir, and fight the bold ravisher?

BRAZEN: No, sir, you're my man.

PLUME: I don't like the wages, and I won't be your man.

BRAZEN: Then you're not worth my sword.

PLUME: No, pray what did it cost?

BRAZEN: It cost my enemies thousands of lives, sir.

PLUME: Then they had a dear bargain.

(Enter SILVIA *dressed in man's apparel.)*

SILVIA: Save ye, save ye, gentlemen.

BRAZEN: My dear, I'm yours.

PLUME: Do you know the gentleman?

BRAZEN: No, but I will presently. Your name, my dear?

SILVIA: Wilful, Jack Wilful at your service.

BRAZEN: What! The Kentish Wilfuls or those of Staffordshire?

SILVIA: Both sir, both; I'm related to all the Wilfuls in Europe, and I'm head of the family at present.

PLUME: Do you live in the country, sir?

SILVIA: Yes, sir, I live where I should. I have neither home, house, nor habitation beyond this spot of ground.

BRAZEN: What are you, sir?

SILVIA: A rake.

PLUME: In the army, I presume.

SILVIA: No, but I intend to list immediately. Look'e gentlemen, he that bids me fairest shall have me.

BRAZEN: Sir, I'll prefer you; I'll make you a corporal this minute.

PLUME: A corporal! I'll make you my companion; you shall eat with me.

BRAZEN: You shall drink with me.

PLUME: You shall lie with me, you young rogue. *(Kisses her)*

BRAZEN: You shall receive your pay and do no duty.

SILVIA: Then you must make me a field officer.

PLUME: Pho, pho, I'll do more than all this.

I'll make you a corporal and give you a brevet for sergeant.

BRAZEN: Can you read and write, sir?

SILVIA: Yes.

BRAZEN: Then your business is done. I'll make you chaplain to the regiment.

SILVIA: Your promises are so equal that I'm at a loss to choose. There is one Plume that I hear much commended in town; pray which of you is Captain Plume?

PLUME: I'm Captain Plume.

BRAZEN: No, no, I am Captain Plume.

SILVIA: Hey day!

PLUME: Captain Plume, I'm your servant, my dear.

BRAZEN: Captain Brazen, I'm yours. The fellow dare not fight.

(Enter KITE, *goes to whisper* PLUME.)

KITE: Sir, if you please —

PLUME: No, no, there's your captain. Captain Plume, your sergeant here has got so drunk he mistakes me for you.

BRAZEN: He's an incorrigible sot. Here, my Hector of Holbourn, forty shillings for you.

PLUME: I forbid the banns. Look'e, friend, you shall list with Captain Brazen.

SILVIA: I will see Captain Brazen hanged first. I will list with Captain Plume. I'm a freeborn Englishman and will be a slave my own way. Look'e, sir, will you stand by me? *(To* BRAZEN*)*

BRAZEN: I warrant you, my lad.

SILVIA: Then I will tell you, Captain Brazen *(to* PLUME*)*, that you are an ignorant, pretending, impudent coxcomb.

BRAZEN: Ay, ay, a sad dog.

SILVIA: A very sad dog. Give me the money, noble Captain Plume.

PLUME: Hold, hold, then you won't list with Captain Brazen?

SILVIA: I won't.

BRAZEN: Never mind him, child. I'll end the dispute presently. Heark'e, my dear. *(Takes* PLUME *to one side of the stage and entertains him in dumb show.)*

KITE: Sir, he in the plain coat is Captain Plume; I'm his sergeant and will take my oath on't.

SILVIA: What, are you Sergeant Kite?

KITE: At your service.

SILVIA: Then I would not take your oath for a farthing.

KITE: A very understanding youth of his age. Pray, sir, let me look you full in the face.

SILVIA: Well, sir, what have you to say to my face?

KITE: The very image and superscription of my brother. Two bullets of the same caliber were never so like. Sure it must be Charles, Charles.

SILVIA: What d'ye mean by Charles?

KITE: The voice too, only a little variation in effa ut flat.[26] My dear brother, for I must call you so, if you should have the fortune to enter into the most noble society of the sword, I bespeak you for a comrade.

SILVIA: No, sir, I'll be your captain's comrade if anybody's.

KITE: Ambition. There again, 'tis a noble passion for a soldier; by that I gained this glorious halberd. Ambition! I see a commission in his face already. Pray, noble Captain, give me leave to salute you. *(Offers to kiss her)*

SILVIA: What, men kiss one another!

KITE: We officers do; 'tis our way. We live together like man and wife, always either kissing or fighting. But I see a storm a-coming.

SILVIA: Now, Sergeant, I shall see who is your captain by your knocking down the t'other.

KITE: My captain scorns assistance, sir.

BRAZEN: How dare you contend for anything and not dare to draw your sword? But you're a young fellow and have not been much abroad; I

---

excuse that, but prithee resign the man, prithee do. You're a very honest fellow.

PLUME: You lie, and you're a son of a whore. *(Draws and makes up to BRAZEN)*

BRAZEN: *(Retiring)* Hold, hold, did not you refuse to fight for the lady?

PLUME: I always do, but for a man I'll fight knee deep, so you lie again.

(PLUME and BRAZEN fight. SILVIA draws and is held by KITE, who takes SILVIA in his arms and carries her off the stage.)

BRAZEN: Hold! Where's the man?

PLUME: Gone.

BRAZEN: Then what do we fight for? *(Puts up)* Now let's embrace, my dear.

PLUME: With all my heart, my dear. *(Puts up)* I suppose Kite has listed him by this time. *(They embrace)*

BRAZEN: You're a brave fellow. I always fight with a man before I make him my friend, and if once I find he will fight, I never quarrel with him afterwards. And now I'll tell you a secret, my dear friend. That lady that we frighted out o'the walk just now I found in bed this morning, so beautiful, so inviting. I presently locked the door. But I'm a man of honor. But I believe I shall marry her nevertheless; her twenty thousand pound, you know, will be a pretty convenience. I had an assignation with her here, but your coming spoiled my sport, curse ye, my dear. But don't do so again.

PLUME: No, no, my dear. Men are my business at present. *(Exeunt)*

---

[26]"Effa ut flat," a designation of the musical note F.

ACT IV

SCENE I

The walk by the Severn side.

(Enter ROSE and BULLOCK meeting.)

ROSE: Where have you been, you great booby? You're always out o'th' way in the time of preferment.

BULLOCK: Preferment. Who should prefer me?

ROSE: I would prefer you. Who should prefer

a man but a woman? Come throw away that great club, hold up your head, cock your hat, and look big.

BULLOCK: Ah, Ruose, Ruose, I fear somebody will look big sooner than folk think of. This genteel breeding never comes into the country without a train of followers. Here has been Cartwheel, your sweetheart. What will become o' him?

ROSE: Look'e, I'm a great woman and will provide for my relations. I told the captain how finely he could play upon the tabor and pipe, so he has set him down for a drum major.

BULLOCK: Nay, sister, why did not you keep that place for me? You know I always loved to be a-drumming, if it were but on a table or on a quart pot.

(Enter SILVIA.)

SILVIA: Had I but a commission in my pocket, I fancy my breeches would become me as well as any ranting fellow of 'em all, for I take a bold step, a rakish toss, a smart cock, and an impudent air to be the principal ingredients in the composition of a captain. What's here? Rose, my nurse's daughter. I'll go and practice. Come, child, kiss me at once. *(Kisses ROSE.)* And her brother too. Well, honest Dungfork, do you know the difference between a horse cart and a cart horse, eh?

BULLOCK: I presume that your worship is a captain by your clothes and your courage.

SILVIA: Suppose I were, would you be contented to list, friend?

ROSE: No, no, though your worship be a handsome man, there be others as fine as you. My brother is engaged to Captain Plume.

SILVIA: Plume! Do you know Captain Plume?

ROSE: Yes, I do, and he knows me. He took the very ribbands out of his shirtsleeves and put them into my shoes. See there. I can assure that I can do anything with the captain.

BULLOCK: That is, in a modest way, sir. Have a care what you say, Ruose; don't shame your parentage.

ROSE: Nay, for that matter I am not so simple as to say that I can do anything with the captain but what I may do with anybody else.

SILVIA: So. And pray what do you expect from this captain, child?

ROSE: I expect, sir, I expect, but he ordered me to tell nobody. But suppose that he should promise to marry me?

SILVIA: You should have a care, my dear. Men will promise anything beforehand.

ROSE: I know that, but he promised to marry me afterwards.

BULLOCK: Wauns, Ruose, what have you said?

SILVIA: Afterwards! After what?

ROSE: After I had sold him my chickens. I hope there's no harm in that, though there be an ugly song of chickens and 'sparagus.

(Enter PLUME.)

PLUME: What, Mr. Wilful, so close with my market woman!

SILVIA: *(Aside)* I'll try if he loves her. — Close, sir, ay, and closer yet, sir. Come, my pretty maid, you and I will withdraw a little.

PLUME: No, no, friend, I han't done with her yet.

SILVIA: Nor have I begun with her, so I have as good a right as you have.

PLUME: Thou art a bloody, impudent fellow. Let her go, I say.

SILVIA: Do you let her go.

PLUME: *Entendez-vous français, mon petit garçon?*[27]

SILVIA: *Oui.*

PLUME: *Si vous voulez donc vous enroller dans ma companie, la demoiselle sera à vous.*

SILVIA: *Avez-vous couché avec elle?*

PLUME: *Non.*

SILVIA: *Assurement?*

PLUME: *Ma foi.*

SILVIA: *C'est assez. Je serai votre soldat.*

PLUME: *La prenez donc.* I'll change a woman for a man at any time.

ROSE: But I hope, Captain, you won't part with me. *(Cries)* I have heard before that you captains used to sell your men.

BULLOCK: *(Crying)* Pray, Captain, don't send Ruose to the West Indies.

PLUME: Ha, ha, ha, West Indies! No, no, my honest lad, give me thy hand. Nor you nor she shall move a step farther than I do. This gentleman is one of us and will be kind to you, Mrs. Rose.

ROSE: But will you be so kind to me, sir, as the captain would?

SILVIA: I can't be altogether so kind to you. My circumstances are not so good as the captain's, but I'll take care of you, upon my word.

[27]The English translation of the following exchange is: P. Do you understand French, my young man? S. Yes. P. If you wish to enroll in my company, the young woman is yours. S. Have you slept with her? P. No. S. Truly? P. On my honor. S. That's good enough. I will be your soldier. P. Agreed then.

PLUME: Ay, ay, we'll all take care of her. She shall live like a princess, and her brother here shall be—what would you be?

BULLOCK: Ah, sir, if you had not promised the place of drum major.

PLUME: Ay, that is promised, but what think ye of barrack master? You're a person of understanding, and barrack master you shall be. But what's become of this same Cartwheel you told me of, my dear?

ROSE: We'll go fetch him. Come, brother barrack master. We shall find you at home, noble Captain.

(Exit ROSE *and* BULLOCK.*)*

PLUME: Yes, yes. And now, sir, here are your forty shillings.

SILVIA: Captain Plume, I despise your listing money. If I do serve, 'tis purely for love, of that wench I mean, for you must know that among my other sallies, I have spent the best part of my fortune in search of a maid, and could never find one hitherto. So you may be assured that I won't sell my freedom under a less purchase than I did my estate. So before I list I must be certified that this girl is a virgin.

PLUME: Mr. Wilful, I can't tell how you can be certified in that point till you try, but upon my honor she may be a vestal for ought that I know to the contrary. I gained her heart, indeed, by some trifling presents and promises, and knowing that the best security for a woman's soul is her body, I would have made myself master of that too, had not the jealousy of my impertinent landlady interposed.

SILVIA: So you want only an opportunity for accomplishing your designs upon her?

PLUME: Not at all. I have already gained my ends, which were only the drawing in one or two of her followers. The women, you know, are the loadstones everywhere. Gain the wives and you're caressed by the husbands; please the mistresses and you are valued by their gallants; secure an interest with the finest women at court and you procure the favor of the greatest men. So, kiss the prettiest country wenches and you are sure of listing the lustiest fellows. Some people may call this artifice, but I term it stratagem, since it is so main a part of the service. Besides, the fatigue of recruiting is so intolerable that unless we could make ourselves some

pleasure amidst the pain, no mortal would be able to bear it.

SILVIA: Well, sir, I'm satisfied as to the point in debate. But now let me beg you to lay aside your recruiting airs, put on the man of honor, and tell me plainly what usage I must expect when I'm under your command.

PLUME: You must know in the first place, then, that I hate to have gentlemen in my company, for they are always troublesome and expensive, sometimes dangerous; and 'tis a constant maxim among us that those who know the least obey the best. Notwithstanding all this, I find something so agreeable about you that engages me to court your company, and I can't tell how it is, but I should be uneasy to see you under the command of anybody else. Your usage will chiefly depend upon your behavior. Only this you must expect, that if you commit a small fault I will excuse it, if a great one, I'll discharge you, for something tells me I shall not be able to punish you.

SILVIA: And something tells me that if you do discharge me 'twill be the greatest punishment you will inflict, for were we this moment to go upon the greatest dangers in your profession, they would be less terrible to me than to stay behind you. And now your hand. This lists me, and now you are my captain.

PLUME: Your friend. *(Kisses her)* 'Sdeath, there's something in this fellow that charms me.

SILVIA: One favor I must beg. This affair will make some noise, and I have some friends that would censure my conduct if I threw myself into the circumstances of a private sentinel of my own head. I must, therefore, take care to be impressed by the Act of Parliament. You shall leave that to me.

PLUME: What you please as to that. Will you lodge at my quarters in the meantime? You shall have part of my bed.

SILVIA: Oh, fie, lie with a common soldier? Would not you rather lie with a common woman?

PLUME: No, faith, I am not that rake that the world imagines. I have got an air of freedom which people mistake for lewdness in me as they mistake formality in others for religion. The world is all a cheat, only I take mine which is undesigned to be more excusable than theirs, which is hypocritical. I hurt nobody but myself, but they abuse all mankind. Will you lie with me?

SILVIA: No, no, Captain, you forget Rose. She's to be my bedfellow, you know.

PLUME: I had forgot; pray be kind to her. *(Exeunt severally.)*

(Enter MELINDA *and* LUCY.*)*

MELINDA: 'Tis the greatest misfortune in nature for a woman to want a confidante. We are so weak that we can do nothing without assistance, and then a secret racks us worse than the colic. I'm at this minute so sick of a secret that I'm ready to faint away. Help me, Lucy.

LUCY: Bless me, madam, what's the matter?

MELINDA: Vapors only. I begin to recover. If Silvia were in town, I could heartily forgive her faults for the ease of discovering my own.

LUCY: You're thoughtful, madam. Am not I worthy to know the cause?

MELINDA: You're a servant, and a secret would make you saucy.

LUCY: Not unless you should find fault without a cause, madam.

MELINDA: Cause or no cause, I must not lose the pleasure of chiding when I please. Women must discharge their vapors somewhere, and before we get husbands, our servants must expect to bear with 'em.

LUCY: Then, madam, you had better raise me to a degree above a servant. You know my family, and that five hundred pound would set me upon the foot of a gentlewoman and make me worthy the confidence of any lady in the land. Besides, madam, 'twill extremely encourage me in the great design that I now have in hand.

MELINDA: I don't find that your design can be of any great advantage to you. 'Twill please me, indeed, in the humor I have of being revenged on the fool for his vanity of making love to me, so I don't much care if I do promise you five hundred pound the day of my marriage.

LUCY: That is the way, madam, to make me diligent in the vocation of a confidante, which I think is generally to bring people together.

MELINDA: Oh, Lucy, I can hold my secret no longer. You must know that, hearing of the famous fortune-teller in town, I went disguised to satisfy a curiosity which has cost me dear. That fellow is certainly the devil or one of his bosom favorites; he has told me the most surprising things of my past life.

LUCY: Things past, madam, can hardly be reckoned surprising because we know them already. Did he tell you anything surprising that was to come?

MELINDA: One thing very surprising; he said I should die a maid.

LUCY: Die a maid! Come into the world for nothing! Dear madam, if you should believe him, it might come to pass, for the bare thought on't might kill one in four-and-twenty hours. And did you ask him any questions about me?

MELINDA: You, why I passed for you.

LUCY: So, 'tis I that am to die a maid. But the devil was a liar from the beginning; he can't make me die a maid; I have put it out of his power already.

MELINDA: I do but jest. I would have passed for you and called myself Lucy, but he presently told me my name, my quality, my fortune, and gave me the whole history of my life. He told me of a lover I had in this country and described Worthy exactly, but in nothing so well as in his present indifference. I fled to him for refuge here today. He never so much as encouraged me in my fright, but coldly told me that he was sorry for the accident because it might give the town cause to censure my conduct, excused his not waiting on me home, made me a careless bow, and walked off. 'Sdeath, I could have stabbed him, or myself, 'twas the same thing. Yonder he comes. I will so slave him.

LUCY: Don't exasperate him. Consider what the fortune-teller told you. Men are scarce, and as times go, it is not impossible for a woman to die a maid.

(Enter WORTHY.*)*

MELINDA: No matter.

WORTHY: I find she's warmed. I must strike while the iron is hot. — You have a great deal of courage, madam, to venture into the walks where you were so late frighted.

MELINDA: And you have a quantity of impudence to appear before me, that you have so lately affronted.

WORTHY: I had no design to affront you, nor appear before you either, madam. I left you here because I had business in another place, and came hither thinking to meet another person.

MELINDA: Since you find yourself disappointed, I hope you'll withdraw to another part of the walk.

WORTHY: The walk is as free for me as you, madam, and broad enough for us both. *(They walk one by another)* Will you please to take snuff, madam?

(He offers her his box; she strikes it out of his hand. While he is gathering it up, enter BRAZEN, *who takes* MELINDA *about the middle; she cuffs him.)*

BRAZEN: What, here before me, my dear!

MELINDA: What means this insolence?

LUCY: *(runs to* BRAZEN*)* Are you mad? Don't you see Mr. Worthy?

BRAZEN: No, no, I'm struck blind. Worthy. Adso, well turned. My mistress has wit at her finger's ends. Madam, I ask your pardon; 'tis our way abroad. Mr. Worthy, you're the happy man?

WORTHY: I don't envy your happiness very much if the lady can afford no other sort of favors but what she has bestowed upon you.

MELINDA: I'm sorry the favor miscarried, for it was designed for you, Mr. Worthy, and be assured, 'tis the last and only favor you must expect at my hands. Captain, I ask your pardon. *(Exit with* LUCY*.)*

BRAZEN: I grant it. You see, Mr. Worthy, 'twas only a random shot; it might ha' taken off your head as well as mine. Courage, my dear, 'tis the fortune of war. But the enemy has thought fit to withdraw, I think.

WORTHY: Withdraw! Wauns, sir, what d'ye mean by withdraw?

BRAZEN: I'll show you. *(Exit* BRAZEN*)*

WORTHY: She's lost, irrecoverably lost, and Plume's advice has ruined me. 'Sdeath, why should I that knew her haughty spirit be ruled by a man that is a stranger to her pride.

(Enter PLUME.*)*

PLUME: Ha, ha, ha, a battle royal. Don't frown so, man, she's your own, I tell'e. I saw the fury of her love in the extremity of her passion. The wildness of her anger is a certain sign that she loves you to madness. That rogue, Kite, began the battle with abundance of conduct and will bring you off victorious, my life on't. He plays his part admirably; she's to be with him again presently.

WORTHY: But what could be the meaning of Brazen's familiarity with her?

PLUME: You are no logician if you pretend to draw consequences from the actions of fools. There's no arguing by the rule of reason upon a science without principles, and such is their conduct. Whim, unaccountable whim hurries them on like a man drunk with brandy before ten o'clock in the morning. But we lost our sport; Kite has opened above an hour ago. Let's away.

Exeunt.

SCENE II
A chamber, a table with books and globes

KITE, *disguised in a strange habit, and sitting at the table.*

KITE: *(Rising)* By the position of the heavens, gained from my observation upon these celestial globes, I find that Luna was a tidewaiter,[28] Sol a surveyor, Mercury a thief, Venus a whore, Saturn an alderman, Jupiter a rake, and Mars a sergeant of grenadiers. And this is the system of Kite the conjurer.

(Enter PLUME *and* WORTHY.*)*

[28]A tidewaiter is a customs official.

PLUME: Well, what success?

KITE: I have sent away a shoemaker and a tailor already; one's to be a captain of marines and the other a major of dragoons. I am to manage them at night. Have you seen the lady, Mr. Worthy?

WORTHY: Ay, but it won't do. Have you showed her her name that I tore off from the bottom of the letter?

KITE: No, sir, I reserve that for the last stroke.

PLUME: What letter?

WORTHY: One that I would not let you see for fear you should break Melinda's windows in good earnest. *(Knocking at the door)*

KITE: Officers to your post. *(Exeunt* WORTHY *and* PLUME*)* Tycho, mind the door.

(Servant opens the door and enter a SMITH*.)*

SMITH: Well, master, are you the cunning man?

KITE: I am the learned Copernicus.

SMITH: Well, Master Coppernose, I'm but a poor man and I can't afford above a shilling for my fortune.

KITE: Perhaps that is more than 'tis worth.

SMITH: Look'e, Doctor, let me have something that's good for my shilling, or I'll have my money again.

KITE: If there be faith in the stars, you shall have your shilling forty fold. Your hand, countryman. You are by trade a smith.

SMITH: How the devil should you know that?

KITE: Because the devil and you are brother tradesmen. You were born under Forceps.[29]

SMITH: Forceps, what's that?

KITE: One of the signs. There's Leo, Sagitarius, Forceps, Furns, Dixmude, Namur, Brussels, Charleroy, and so forth. Twelve[30] of 'em. Let me see. Did you ever make any bombs or cannon's bullets?

SMITH: Not I.

KITE: You either have or will. The stars have decreed that you shall be—I must have more money, sir, your fortune's great.

SMITH: Faith, Doctor, I have no more.

KITE: Oh, sir, I'll trust you and take it out of your arrears.

SMITH: Arrears! What arrears?

KITE: The five hundred pound that's owing to you from the government.

SMITH: Owing me!

KITE: Owing you, sir. Let me see your t'other hand. I beg your pardon; it will be owing to you, and the rogue of an agent will demand fifty per cent for a fortnight's advance.

SMITH: I'm in the clouds, Doctor, all this while.

KITE: So am I, sir, among the stars. In two years, three months, and two hours, you will be

made Captain of the Forges to the Grand Train of Artillery, and will have ten shillings a day and two servants. 'Tis the decree of the stars, and of the fixed stars, that are as immovable as your anvil. Strike, sir, while the iron is hot. Fly, sir, be gone.

SMITH: What would you have me do, Doctor? I wish the stars put me in a way for this fine place.

KITE: The stars do. Let me see. Ay, about an hour hence walk carelessly into the market place and you'll see a tall, slender gentleman cheapening a pen'worth of apples, with a cane hanging upon his button. This gentleman will ask you what's o'clock. He's your man and the maker of your fortune. Follow him, follow him. And now go home and take leave of your wife and children. An hour hence exactly is your time.

SMITH: A tall, slender gentleman, you say, with a cane. Pray, what sort of a head has the cane?

KITE: An amber head with a black ribband.

SMITH: But pray, of what employment is the gentleman?

KITE: Let me see. He's either a collector of the excise, a plenipotentiary, or a captain of grenadiers. I can't tell exactly which. But he'll call you honest—Your name is?

SMITH: Thomas.

KITE: Right, he'll call you honest Tom.

SMITH: But how the devil should he know my name?

KITE: Oh, there are several sorts of Toms. Tom a Lincoln, Tom-tit, Tom Telltroth, Tom o' Bedlam, Tom Fool. *(Knocking at the door.)* Be gone. An hour hence precisely.

SMITH: You say he'll ask me what's o'clock?

KITE: Most certainly, and you'll answer you don't know, but be sure to look at St. Mary's dial, for the sun won't shine, and if it should, you won't be able to tell the figures.

SMITH: I will, I will. *(Exit* SMITH*)*

PLUME: *(Behind)* Well done, conjurer, go on and prosper.

KITE: As you were.

(Enter a BUTCHER*.)*

KITE: *(Aside)* What, my old friend Pluck, the butcher. I offered the surly bulldog five guineas this morning and he refused it.

BUTCHER: So, Master Conjurer, here's half a crown. And now you must understand—

---

[29]Forceps are fire tongs.
[30]Kite's mangling of the names of the zodiac signs is used humorously to show how little he knows of fortune-telling.

KITE: Hold, friend, I know your business beforehand.

BUTCHER: You're devilish cunning then, for I don't well know it myself.

KITE: I know more than you, friend. You have a foolish saying that such a one knows no more than the man in the moon. I tell you the man in the moon knows more than all the men under the sun; don't the moon see all the world?

BUTCHER: All the world see the moon, I must confess.

KITE: Then she must see all the world, that's certain. Give me your hand. You are by trade either a butcher or a surgeon.

BUTCHER: True, I am a butcher.

KITE: And a surgeon you will be. The employments differ only in the name. He that can cut up an ox may dissect a man, and the same dexterity that cracks a marrow bone will cut off a leg or an arm.

BUTCHER: What d'ye mean, Doctor, what d'ye mean?

KITE: Patience, patience, Mr. Surgeon General. The stars are great bodies and move slowly.

BUTCHER: But what d'ye mean by Surgeon General, Doctor?

KITE: Nay, sir, if your worship won't have patience, I must beg the favor of your worship's absence.

BUTCHER: My worship, my worship! But why my worship?

KITE: Nay, then I have done. (Sits)

BUTCHER: Pray, Doctor.

KITE: Fire and fury sir. (Rises in a passion) Do you think the stars will be hurried? Do the stars owe you any money, sir, that you dare to dun their lordships at this rate? Sir, I am porter to the stars, and I am ordered to let no dun come near their doors.

BUTCHER: Dear Doctor, I never had any dealings with the stars; they don't owe me a penny. But since you are the porter, please to accept of this half crown to drink their healths, and don't be angry.

KITE: Let me see your hand then, once more. Here has been gold, five guineas, my friend, in this very hand this morning.

BUTCHER: Nay, then he is the devil. Pray, Doctor, were you born of a woman or did you come into the world of your own head?

KITE: That's a secret. This gold was offered you by a proper, handsome man called Hawk or Buzzard or—

BUTCHER: Kite, you mean.

KITE: Ay, ay, Kite.

BUTCHER: As errant a rogue as ever carried a halberd. The impudent rascal would have decoyed me for a soldier.

KITE: A soldier! A man of your substance for a soldier! Your mother has a hundred pound in hard money lying at this minute in the hands of a mercer, not forty yards from this place.

BUTCHER: Wauns, and so she has, but very few know so much.

KITE: I know it, and that rogue, what's his name, Kite, knew it, and offered you five guineas to list because he knew your poor mother would give the hundred for your discharge.

BUTCHER: There's a dog now. 'Flesh, Doctor, I'll give you t'other half crown, and tell me that this same Kite will be hanged.

KITE: He's in as much danger an any man in the county of Salop.

BUTCHER: There's your fee, but you have forgot the Surgeon General all this while.

KITE: You put the stars in a passion. (Looks on his books) But now they're pacified again. Let me see. Did you never cut off a man's leg?

BUTCHER: No.

KITE: Recollect, pray.

BUTCHER: I say no.

KITE: That's strange, wonderful strange, but nothing is strange to me, such wonderful changes have I seen. The second or third, ay, the third campaign that you make in Flanders, the leg of a great officer will be shattered by a great shot. You will be there accidentally and with your cleaver chop off the limb at a blow. In short, the operation will be performed with so much dexterity that with the general applause you will be made Surgeon General of the whole army.

BUTCHER: Nay, for the matter of cutting off a limb, I'll do't. I'll do't with any surgeon in Europe, but I have no thoughts of making a campaign.

KITE: You have no thoughts! What matter for your thoughts? The stars have decreed it, and you must go.

BUTCHER: The stars decree it. Wauns, sir, the justices can't press me.

KITE: Nay, friend, 'tis none of my business; I

ha' done. Only mind this, you'll know more an hour and a half hence. That's all. Farewell. *(Going)*

BUTCHER: Hold, hold, Doctor, Surgeon General! Pray, what is the place worth, pray?

KITE: Five hundred pound a year, beside guineas for claps.

BUTCHER: Five hundred pound a year! An hour and half hence you say?

KITE: Prithee, friend, be quiet, don't be so troublesome. Here's such a work to make a booby butcher accept of five hundred pound a year. But if you must hear it, I tell you in short, you'll be standing in your stall an hour and half hence, and a gentleman will come by with a snuff box in his hand and the tip of his handkerchief hanging out of his right pocket. He'll ask you the price of a loin of veal, and at the same time stroke your great dog upon the head and call him Chopper.

BUTCHER: Mercy upon us; Chopper is the dog's name.

KITE: Look'e there; what I say is true. Things that are to come must come to pass. Get you home; sell off your stock. Don't mind the whining and the sniveling of your mother and your sister; women always hinder preferment. Make what money you can and follow that gentleman. His name begins with a P. Mind that. There will be the barber's daughter, too, that you promised marriage to; she will be pulling and hauling you to pieces.

BUTCHER: What, know Sally too! He's the devil, and he needs must go that the devil drives. *(Going)* The tips of his handkerchief out of his left pocket?

KITE: No, no, his right pocket. If it be the left, 'tis none of the man.

BUTCHER: Well, well, I'll mind him.

PLUME: *(Behind with his pocket book)* The right pocket, you say?

KITE: I hear the rustling of silks. *(Knocking)* Fly, sir, 'tis Madam Melinda.

(Enter MELINDA *and* LUCY.*)*

KITE: Tycho, chairs for the ladies.

MELINDA: Don't trouble yourself. We shan't stay, Doctor.

KITE: Your ladyship is to stay much longer than you imagine.

MELINDA: For what?

KITE: For a husband. *(To* LUCY.*)* For your part, madam, you won't stay for a husband.

LUCY: Pray, Doctor, do you converse with the stars or with the devil?

KITE: With both. When I have the destinies of men in search, I consult the stars; when the affairs of women come under my hand, I advise with my t'other friend.

MELINDA: And have you raised the devil upon my account?

KITE: Yes, madam, and he's now under the table.

LUCY: Oh, heavens protect us! Dear madam, let us be gone.

KITE: If you be afraid of him, why do you come to consult him?

MELINDA: Don't fear, fool. Do you think, sir, that because I'm a woman I'm to be fooled out of my reason or frighted out of my senses? Come, show me this devil.

KITE: He's a little busy at present, but when he has done he shall wait on you.

MELINDA: What is he doing?

KITE: Writing your name in his pocket book.

MELINDA: Ha, ha, ha, my name! Pray, what have you or he to do with my name?

KITE: Look'e, fair lady, the devil is a very modest person. He seeks nobody unless they seek him first. He's chained up like a mastiff and cannot stir unless he be let loose. You come to me to have your fortune told. Do you think, madam, that I can answer you of my own head? No, madam, the affairs of women are so irregular that nothing less than the devil can give any account of 'em. Now to convince you of your incredulity, I'll show you a trial of my skill. Here, you, *Caco-demon del fuego,* exert your power. Draw me this lady's name, the word Melinda in the proper letters and character of her own handwriting. Do it at three motions: one, two, three. 'Tis done. Now, madam, will you please send your maid to fetch it.

LUCY: I fetch it! The devil fetch me if I do.

MELINDA: My name in my own handwriting; that would be convincing indeed.

KITE: Seeing's believing. *(Goes to the table, lifts up the carpet)*[31] Here Tre, Tre, poor Tre, give me the bone, sirrah.

---

[31]A carpet is a tablecloth here.

(He puts his hand under the table. PLUME *steals to the other side of the table and catches him by the hand.)*

Oh, oh, the devil, the devil in good earnest. My hand, my hand, the devil, my hand!

*(*MELINDA *and* LUCY *shriek and run to a corner of the stage.* KITE *discovers* PLUME *and gets away his hand.)*

A plague o' your pincers; he has fixed his nails in my very flesh. Oh, madam, you put the demon into such a passion with your scruples that it has almost cost me my hand.

MELINDA: It has cost us our lives almost. But have you got the name?

KITE: Got it, ay, madam, I have got it here. I'm sure the blood comes. But there's your name upon that square piece of paper. Behold.

MELINDA: 'Tis wonderful. My very letters to a tittle.

LUCY: 'Tis like your hand, madam, but not so like your hand neither; and now I look nearer, 'tis not like your hand at all.

KITE: Here's a chambermaid now that will out-lie the devil.

LUCY: Look'e, madam, they shan't impose upon us. People can't remember their hands no more than they can their faces. Come, madam, let us be certain; write your name upon this paper. *(Takes out paper and folds it.)* Then we'll compare the two names.

KITE: Anything for your satisfaction, madam. Here's pen and ink.

*(*MELINDA *writes and* LUCY *holds the paper.)*

LUCY: Let me see it, madam. 'Tis the same, the very same. *(Aside)* But I'll secure one copy for my own affairs.

MELINDA: This is demonstration.

KITE: 'Tis so, madam. The word demonstration comes from demon, the father of lies.

MELINDA: Well, Doctor, I'm convinced, and now pray what account can you give me of my future fortune?

KITE: Before the sun has made one course round this earthly globe, your fortune will be fixed for happiness or misery.

MELINDA: What, so near the crisis of my fate!

KITE: Let me see. About the hour of ten tomor-row you will be saluted by a gentleman who will come to take his leave of you, being designed for travel. His intention of going abroad is sudden, and the occasion a woman. Your fortune and his are like the bullet and the barrel; one runs plump into t'other. In short, if the gentleman travels, he will die abroad; and if he does, you will die before he comes home.

MELINDA: What sort of man is he?

KITE: Madam, he is a fine gentleman and a lover, that is, a man of very good sense and a very great fool.

MELINDA: How is that possible, Doctor?

KITE: Because, madam, because it is so. A woman's reason is the best for a man's being a fool.

MELINDA: Ten o'clock, you say?

KITE: Ten, about the hour of tea drinking throughout the kingdom.

MELINDA: Here, Doctor. *(Gives him money)* Lucy, have you any questions to ask?

LUCY: Oh, madam, a thousand.

KITE: I must beg your patience till another time, for I expect more company this minute; besides, I must discharge the gentleman under the table.

LUCY: Pray, sir, discharge us first.

KITE: Tycho, wait on the ladies downstairs.

(Exit MELINDA *and* LUCY*)*

(Enter PLUME *and* WORTHY *laughing.)*

KITE: Ay, you may well laugh, gentlemen. Not all the cannon of the French army could have frighted me so much as that grip you gave me under the table.

PLUME: I think, Mr. Doctor, I out-conjured you that bout.

KITE: I was surprised, for I should not have taken a captain for a conjurer.

PLUME: No more than I should a sergeant for a wit.

KITE: Mr. Worthy, you were pleased to wish me joy today; I hope to be able to return the compliment tomorrow.

WORTHY: I'll make it the best compliment to you that you ever made in your life if you do, but I must be a traveler, you say?

KITE: No farther than the chops of the Channel, I presume, sir.

PLUME: That we have concerted already. *(Knocking hard)* Hey day. You don't profess midwifery, Doctor?

KITE: Away to your ambuscade.

(Exeunt PLUME and WORTHY)

(Enter BRAZEN.)

BRAZEN: Your servant, servant, my dear.

KITE: Stand off. I have my familiar already.

BRAZEN: Are you bewitched, my dear?

KITE: Yes, my dear, but mine is a peaceable spirit and hates gunpowder. Thus I fortify myself. *(Draws a circle round him.)* And now, Captain, have a care how you force my lines.

BRAZEN: Lines! What dost talk of lines? You have something like a fishing rod there, indeed, but I come to be acquainted with you, man. What's your name, my dear?

KITE: Conundrum.

BRAZEN: Conundrum. Rat me, I know a famous doctor in London of your name. ·Where were you born?

KITE: I was born in Algebra.

BRAZEN: Algebra! 'Tis no country in Christendom I'm sure, unless it be some pitiful place in the Highlands of Scotland.

KITE: Right, I told you I was bewitched.

BRAZEN: So am I, my dear. I'm going to be married. I've had two letters from a lady of fortune that loves me to madness, fits, colic, spleen, and vapors. Shall I marry her in four and twenty hours, ay or no?

KITE: I must have the year and the day o'th' month when these letters were dated.

BRAZEN: Why you old bitch, did you ever hear of love letters dated with the year and day o'th' month? Do you think *billets doux* are like bank bills?

KITE: They are not so good. But if they bear no date, I must examine the contents.

BRAZEN: Contents, that you shall, old boy; here they be both.

KITE: Only the last you received, if you please. *(Takes the letter)* Now, sir, if you please to let me consult my books for a minute, I'll send this letter enclosed to you with the determination of the stars upon it to your lodgings.

BRAZEN: With all my heart, I must give him— *(Puts his hand in's pocket)* Algebra! I fancy, Doctor, 'tis hard to calculate the place of your nativity. Here. *(Gives him money)* And if I succeed, I'll build a watchtower upon the top of the highest mountain in Wales for the study of astrology and the benefit of Conundrums. *(Exit BRAZEN)*

(Enter PLUME and WORTHY.)

WORTHY: Oh, Doctor, that letter's worth a million. Let me see it. And now I have it, I'm afraid to open it.

PLUME: Pho, let me see it. *(Opening the letter)* If she be a jilt, damn her, she is one. There's her name at the bottom on't.

WORTHY: How! Then I will travel in good earnest. By all my hopes, 'tis Lucy's hand!

PLUME: Lucy's!

WORTHY: Certainly; 'tis no more like Melinda's character than black is to white.

PLUME: Then 'tis certainly Lucy's contrivance to draw in Brazen for a husband. But are you sure 'tis not Melinda's hand?

WORTHY: You shall see. Where's the bit of paper I gave you just now that the devil writ Melinda upon?

KITE: Here, sir.

PLUME: 'Tis plain; they're not the same. And is this the malicious name that was subscribed to the letter which made Mr. Balance send his daughter into the country?

WORTHY: The very same. The other fragments I showed you just now. I once intended it for another use, but I think I have turned it now to better advantage.

PLUME: But 'twas barbarous to conceal this so long and to continue me so many hours in the pernicious heresy of believing that angelic creature could change. Poor Silvia!

WORTHY: Rich Silvia, you mean, and poor Captain. Ha, ha, ha. Come, come, friend, Melinda is true and shall be mine. Silvia is constant and may be yours.

PLUME: No, she's above my hopes, but for her sake, I'll recant my opinion of her sex.

By some the sex is blam'd without design,
Light, harmless censure such as yours or mine,
Sallies of wit and vapors of our wine.
Others the justice of the sex condemn,
And wanting merit to create esteem,

Would hide their own defects by cens'ring them.
But they, secure in their all-conqu'ring charms,
Laugh at the vain efforts of false alarms;

He magnifies their conquests who complains,
For none would struggle were they not in chains.
(Exeunt)

ACT V

SCENE I

An antechamber, with a periwig, hat, and sword upon the table

---

(Enter SILVIA *in her nightcap.)*

SILVIA: I have rested but indifferently, and I believe my bedfellow was as little pleased. Poor Rose. Here she comes.

(Enter ROSE.*)*

Good morrow, my dear, how d'ye this morning?

ROSE: Just as I was last night, neither better nor worse for you.

SILVIA: What's the matter? Did you not like your bedfellow?

ROSE: I don't know whether I had a bedfellow or not.

SILVIA: Did not I lie with you?

ROSE: No. I wonder you could have the conscience to ruin a poor girl for nothing.

SILVIA: I have saved thee from ruin, child. Don't be melancholy. I can give you as many fine things as the captain can.

ROSE: But you can't, I'm sure. *(Knocking at the door)*

SILVIA: Odso, my accoutrements. *(Puts on her periwig, hat, and sword)* Who's at the door?

WITHOUT: Open the door or we'll break it down.

SILVIA: Patience a little. *(Opens the door)*

(Enter CONSTABLE *and mob.)*

CONSTABLE: We have 'em, we have 'em, the duck and the mallard both in the decoy.

SILVIA: What means this plot? Stand off. *(Draws)* The man dies that comes within reach of my point.

CONSTABLE: That is not the point, master. Put up your sword or I shall knock you down, and so I command the Queen's peace.

SILVIA: You are some blockhead of a constable?

CONSTABLE: I am so, and have a warrant to apprehend the bodies of you and your whore there.

ROSE: Whore! Never was poor woman so abused.

(Enter BULLOCK *unbuttoned.)*

BULLOCK: What's matter now? Oh, Mr. Bridewell, what brings you abroad so early?

CONSTABLE: This, sir. *(Lays hold of* BULLOCK.*)* You're the Queen's prisoner.

BULLOCK: Wauns, you lie, sir; I'm the Queen's soldier.

CONSTABLE: No matter for that. You shall go before Justice Balance.

SILVIA: Balance, 'tis what I wanted. Here, Mr. Constable, I resign my sword.

ROSE: Can't you carry us before the captain, Mr. Bridewell?

CONSTABLE: Captain! Ha'n't you got your belly full of captains yet? Come, come, make way there. *Exeunt.*

SCENE II

JUSTICE BALANCE'S *house*

(Enter BALANCE *and* SCALE.*)*

SCALE: I say 'tis not to be borne, Mr. Balance.

BALANCE: Look'e, Mr. Scale, for my own part I shall be very tender in what regards the officers of the army. They expose their lives to so many dangers for us abroad that we may give them some grains of allowance at home.

SCALE: Allowance! This poor girl's father is my tenant, and if I mistake not, her mother nursed a child for you. Shall they debauch our daughters to our faces?

BALANCE: Consider, Mr. Scale, that were it not for the bravery of these officers we should have French dragoons among us that would leave us neither liberty, property, wife, nor daughter. Come, Mr. Scale, the gentlemen are vigorous and warm, and may they continue so. The same heat that stirs them up to love spurs them on to battle. You never knew a great general in your life that did not love a whore. This I only speak in reference to Captain Plume, for the other spark I know nothing of.

SCALE: Nor can I hear of anybody that does. Oh, here they come.

(Enter SILVIA, BULLOCK, ROSE—*prisoners,* CONSTABLE *and mob.)*

CONSTABLE: May it please your worships, we took them in the very act, *re infecta,*[32] sir. The gentleman indeed behaved like a gentleman, for he drew his sword and swore, and afterwards laid it down and said nothing.

BALANCE: Give the gentleman his sword again. Wait you without.

(Exit CONSTABLE *and mob)*

(To SILVIA*)* I'm sorry, sir, to know a gentleman upon such terms that the occasion of our meeting should prevent the satisfaction of an acquaintance.

SILVIA: Sir, you need make no apology for your warrant, nor more than I shall do for my behavior. My innocence is upon an equal foot with your authority.

SCALE: Innocence! Have you not seduced that young maid?

SILVIA: No, Mr. Goosecap, she seduced me.

BULLOCK: So she did, I'll swear, for she proposed marriage first.

BALANCE: What, then you're married, child?

(To ROSE*)*

ROSE: Yes, sir, to my sorrow.

BALANCE: Who was the witness?

BULLOCK: That was I. I danced, threw the stocking, and spoke jokes by their bedside, I'm sure.

BALANCE: Who was the minister?

BULLOCK: Minister! We are soldiers and want

no ministers. They were married by the Articles of War.

BALANCE: Hold thy prating, fool. Your appearance, sir, promises some understanding. Pray, what does this fellow mean?

SILVIA: He means marriage, I think, but that, you know, is so odd a thing that hardly any two people under the sun agree in the ceremony. Some make it a sacrament, others a convenience, and others make it a jest, but among soldiers 'tis most sacred. Our sword, you know, is our honor. That we lay down; the hero jumps over it first and the amazon after. Leap rogue, follow whore. The drum beats a ruff and so to bed, that's all. The ceremony is concise.

BULLOCK: And the prettiest ceremony, so full of pastime and prodigality.

BALANCE: What, are you a soldier?

BULLOCK: Ay, that I am. Will your worship lend me your cane and I'll show you how I can exercise.

BALANCE: Take it. *(Strikes him over the head)* Pray, sir, what commission may you bear? *(To Silvia)*

SILVIA: I'm called Captain, sir, by all the coffeemen, drawers, whores, and groom porters in London, for I wear a red coat, a sword *bien troussée,*[33] a martial twist in my cravat, a fierce knot in my periwig, a cane upon my button, piquet in[34] my head, and dice in my pocket.

SCALE: Your name, pray, sir.

SILVIA: Captain Pinch. I cock my hat with a pinch; I take snuff with a pinch, pay my whores with a pinch. In short, I can do anything at a pinch but fight and fill my belly.

BALANCE: And pray, sir, what brought you into Shropshire?

SILVIA: A pinch, sir. I knew that you country gentlemen want wit, and you know that we town gentlemen want money, and so—

BALANCE: I understand you, sir. Here, Constable.

(Enter CONSTABLE.*)*

Take this gentleman into custody till further orders.

ROSE: Pray, your worship, don't be uncivil to

---

[32]*Re infecta*—the act not having been completed.

[33]*Bien troussée*—well turned.
[34]Piquet is a card game.

him, for he did me no hurt. He's the most harmless man in the world, for all he talks so.

SCALE: Come, come, child, I'll take care of you.

SILVIA: What, gentlemen, rob me of my freedom and my wife at once. 'Tis the first time they ever went together.

BALANCE: Heark'e, Constable. *(Whispers the* CONSTABLE*)*

CONSTABLE: It shall be done, sir. Come along, sir. *(Exeunt* CONSTABLE, BULLOCK, *and* SILVIA*)*

BALANCE: Come, Mr. Scale, we'll manage the spark presently. *(Exeunt* BALANCE *and* SCALE*)*

SCENE III

Scene changes to MELINDA'S *apartment.*

(Enter MELINDA *and* WORTHY.*)*

MELINDA: *(Aside)* So far the prediction is right. 'Tis ten exactly. — And pray, sir, how long have you been in this traveling humor?

WORTHY: 'Tis natural, madam, for us to avoid what disturbs our quiet.

MELINDA: Rather the love of change, which is more natural, may be the occasion of it.

WORTHY: To be sure, madam, there must be charms in variety, else neither you nor I should be so fond of it.

MELINDA: You mistake, Mr. Worthy. I am not so fond of variety as to travel for it, nor do I think it prudence in you to run yourself into a certain expense and danger in hopes of precarious pleasures which at best never answer expectation, as 'tis evident from the example of most travelers that long more to return to their own country than they did to go abroad.

WORTHY: What pleasures I may receive abroad are indeed uncertain, but this I am sure of, I shall meet with less cruelty among the most barbarous nations than I have found at home.

MELINDA: Come, sir, you and I have been jangling a great while. I fancy if we made up our accounts we should the sooner come to an agreement.

WORTHY: Sure, madam, you won't dispute your being in my debt. My fears, sighs, vows, promises, assiduities, anxieties, jealousies have run on for a whole year without any payment.

MELINDA: A year. Oh, Mr. Worthy, what you owe to me is not to be paid under a seven years' servitude. How did you use me the year before, when taking the advantage of my innocence and

necessity, you would have made me your mistress, that is, your slave? Remember the wicked insinuations, artful baits, deceitful arguments, cunning pretenses? Then your impudent behavior, loose expressions, familiar letters, rude visits, remember those, those, Mr. Worthy?

WORTHY: *(Aside)* I do remember and am sorry I made no better use of 'em. — But you may remember, madam, that —

MELINDA: Sir, I'll remember nothing. 'Tis your interest that I should forget. You have been barbarous to me; I have been cruel to you. Put that and that together and let one balance the other. Now if you will begin upon a new score, lay aside your adventuring airs, and behave yourself handsomely till Lent be over, here's my hand. I'll use you as a gentleman should be.

WORTHY: And if I don't use you as a gentlewoman should be, may this be my poison. *(Kissing her hand)*

(Enter SERVANT.*)*

SERVANT: Madam, the coach is at the door.

MELINDA: I'm going to Mr. Balance's country house to see my cousin Silvia. I have done her an injury and can't be easy till I have asked her pardon.

WORTHY: I dare not hope for the honor of wating on you.

MELINDA: My coach is full, but if you will be so gallant as to mount your own horses and follow us, we shall be glad to be overtaken. And if you bring Captain Plume with you, we shan't have the worse reception.

WORTHY: I'll endeavor it.

(Exit WORTHY *leading* MELINDA*)*

SCENE IV

The marketplace

(Enter PLUME *and* KITE.)

PLUME: A baker, a tailor, a smith, and a butcher. I believe the first colony planted at Virginia had not more trades in their company than I have in mine.

KITE: The butcher, sir, will have his hands full, for we have two sheep stealers among us. I hear of a fellow, too, committed just now for stealing of horses.

PLUME: We'll dispose of him among the dragoons. Have we never a poulterer among us?

KITE: Yes, sir, the king of the gypsies is a very good one. He has an excellent hand at a goose or a turkey. Here's Captain Brazen. Sir, I must go look after the men. *(Exit* KITE*)*

(Enter BRAZEN *reading a letter.)*

BRAZEN: Um, um, um, the canonical hour. Um, um, very well. My dear Plume, give me a buss.

PLUME: Half a score if you will, my dear. What hast got in thy hand, child?

BRAZEN: 'Tis a project for laying out a thousand pound.

PLUME: Were it not requisite to project first how to get in?

BRAZEN: You can't imagine, my dear, that I want twenty-thousand pound. I have spent twenty times as much in the service. Now, my dear, pray advise me. My head runs much upon architecture. Shall I build a privateer or a playhouse?

PLUME: An odd question. A privateer or a playhouse! 'Twill require some consideration. Faith, I'm for a privateer.

BRAZEN: I'm not of your opinion, my dear, for in the first place a privateer may be ill-built.

PLUME: And so may a playhouse.

BRAZEN: But a privateer may be ill-mannered.

PLUME: And so may a playhouse.

BRAZEN: But a privateer may run upon the shallows.

PLUME: Not so often as a playhouse.

BRAZEN: But, you know, a privateer may spring a leak.

PLUME: And I know that a playhouse may spring a great many.

BRAZEN: But suppose the privateer come home with a rich booty; we should never agree about our shares.

PLUME: 'Tis just so in a playhouse. So, by my advice, you shall fix upon the privateer.

BRAZEN: Agreed. But if this twenty thousand should not be in specie.

PLUME: What twenty thousand?

BRAZEN: Heark'e. *(Whispers)*

PLUME: Married!

BRAZEN: Presently. We're to meet about half a mile out of town at the waterside. And so forth. *(Reads)* "For fear I should be known by any of Worthy's friends, you must give me leave to wear my mask till after the ceremony, which will make me ever yours."—Look'e there, my dear dog. *(Shows the bottom of the letter to* PLUME*)*

PLUME: Melinda. And by this light, her own hand! Once more, if you please, my dear. Her hand exactly! Just now you say?

BRAZEN: This minute I must be gone.

PLUME: Have a little patience and I'll go with you.

BRAZEN: No, no, I see a gentleman coming this way that may be inquisitive. 'Tis Worthy; do you know him?

PLUME: By sight only.

BRAZEN: Have a care; the very eyes discover secrets. *(Exit* BRAZEN*)*

(Enter WORTHY.)

WORTHY: To boot and saddle, Captain, you must mount.

PLUME: Whip and spur, Worthy, or you won't mount.

WORTHY: But I shall. Melinda and I are agreed. She is gone to visit Silvia; we are to mount and follow, and could we carry a parson with us, who knows what might be done for us both?

PLUME: Don't trouble your head. Melinda has secured a parson already.

WORTHY: Already! Do you know more than I?

PLUME: Yes, I saw it under her hand. Brazen and she are to meet half a mile hence at the waterside, there to take boat, I suppose, to be ferried over to the Elysian fields, if there be any such thing in matrimony.

WORTHY: I parted with Melinda just now. She assured me she hated Brazen and that she resolved to discard Lucy for daring to write letters to him in her name.

PLUME: Nay, nay, there's nothing of Lucy in this. I tell ye, I saw Melinda's hand as surely as this is mine.

WORTHY: But I tell you, she's gone this minute to Justice Balance's country house.

PLUME: But I tell you, she's gone this minute to the waterside.

(Enter a SERVANT.*)*

SERVANT: *(To* WORTHY*)* Madam Melinda has sent word that you need not trouble yourself to follow her because her journey to Justice Balance's is put off, and she's gone to take the air another way. *(Exit)*

WORTHY: How! Her journey put off?

PLUME: That is, her journey was a put-off to you.

WORTHY: 'Tis plain, plain. But how, where, when is she to meet Brazen?

PLUME: Just now I tell you, half a mile hence at the waterside.

WORTHY: Up or down the water?

PLUME: That I don't know.

WORTHY: I'm glad my horses are ready. Jack, get 'em out.

PLUME: Shall I go with you?

WORTHY: Not an inch. I shall return presently. *(Exit* WORTHY*)*

PLUME: You'll find me at the hall. The justices are sitting by this time and I must attend them. *(Exit* PLUME*)*

SCENE V

A court of justice

---

*(*BALANCE, SCALE, SCRUPLE *upon the bench.* CONSTABLE, KITE, *mob in attendance.* KITE *and* CONSTABLE *advance to the front of the stage.)*

KITE: Pray, who are those honorable gentlemen upon the bench?

CONSTABLE: He in the middle is Justice Balance, he on the right is Justice Scale, and he on the left is Justice Scruple, and I am Mr. Constable. Four very honest gentlemen.

KITE: Oh, dear sir, I'm your most obedient servant. *(Saluting the* CONSTABLE.*)* I fancy, sir, that your employment and mine are much the same, for my business is to keep people in order, and if they disobey, to knock 'em down. And then we're both staff officers.

CONSTABLE: Nay, I'm a sergeant myself, of the militia. Come, brother, you shall see me exercise. Suppose this a musket now. *(He puts his staff on his right shoulder.)* Now I'm shouldered.

KITE: Ay, you're shouldered pretty well for a constable's staff, but for a musket you must put it on t'other shoulder, my dear.

CONSTABLE: Adso, that's true. Come now, give the word o'command.

KITE: Silence.

CONSTABLE: Ay, ay, so we will. We will be silent.

KITE: Silence, you dog, silence. *(Strikes him over the head with his halberd.)*

CONSTABLE: That's the way to silence a man with a witness. What d'ye mean, friend.

KITE: Only to exercise you, sir.

CONSTABLE: Your exercise differs so from ours that we shall ne'er agree about it. If my own captain had given me such a rap, I had taken the law of him.

(Enter PLUME.*)*

BALANCE: Captain, you're welcome.

PLUME: Gentlemen, I thank'e.

SCRUPLE: Come, honest Captain, sit by me. *(*PLUME *ascends and sits upon the bench.)* Now produce your prisoners. Here, that fellow there, set him up. Mr. Constable, what have you to say against this man?

CONSTABLE: I have nothing to say against him, an't please ye.

BALANCE: No? What made you bring him hither?

CONSTABLE: I don't know, an't please your worship.

SCRUPLE: Did not the contents of your warrant direct you what sort of men to take up?

CONSTABLE: I can't tell, an't please ye. I can't read.

SCRUPLE: A very pretty constable truly! I find we have no business here.

KITE: May it please the worshipful bench, I desire to be heard in this case, as being counsel for the Queen.

BALANCE: Come, Sergeant, you shall be heard since nobody else will speak. We won't come here for nothing.

KITE: This man is but one man. The country may spare him and the army wants him. Besides he's cut out by nature for a grenadier: he's five foot ten inches high; he shall box, wrestle, or dance the Cheshire Round with any man in the county; he gets drunk every sabbath day; and he beats his wife.

WIFE: You lie, sirrah, you lie an't please your worship. He's the best-natured, painstaking man in the parish. Witness my five poor children.

SCRUPLE: A wife and five children! You, Constable, you, rogue, how durst you impress a man that has a wife and children?

SCALE: Discharge him, discharge him.

BALANCE: Hold, gentlemen. Hark'e, friend, how do you maintain your wife and children?

PLUME: They live upon wild fowl and venison, sir. The husband keeps a gun and kills all the hares and partridges within five miles around.

BALANCE: A gun! Nay, if he be so good at gunning he shall have enough on't. He may be of use against the French, for he shoots flying to be sure.

SCRUPLE: But his wife and children, Mr. Balance.

WIFE: Ay, ay, that's the reason you would send him away. You know I have a child each year and you're afraid they should come upon the parish at last.

PLUME: Look'e there, gentlemen, the honest woman has spoke it at once. The parish had better maintain five children this year than six or seven the next. That fellow upon his high feeding may get you two or three beggars at a birth.

WIFE: Look'e, Mr. Captain, the parish shall get nothing by sending him away, for I won't lose my teeming time if there be a man left in the parish.

BALANCE: Send that woman to the house of correction. And the man—

KITE: I'll take care o' him, if you please. *(Takes the man down)*

SCALE: Here, you Constable, the next. Set up that black-faced fellow. He has a gunpowder look. What can you say against this man, Constable?

CONSTABLE: Nothing but that he's a very honest man.

PLUME: Pray, gentlemen, let me have one honest man in my company for the novelty's sake.

BALANCE: What are you, friend?

MOB: A collier; I work in the coal pits.

SCRUPLE: Look'e, gentlemen, this fellow has a trade, and the Act of Parliament here expresses that we are to impress no man that has any visible means of a livelihood.

KITE: May it please your worships, this man has no visible means of a livelihood, for he works underground.

PLUME: Well said, Kite. Besides, the army wants miners.

BALANCE: Right. And had we an order of government for't, we could raise you in this and the neighboring county of Stafford five hundred colliers that would run you underground like moles and do more service in a siege than all the miners in the army.

SCRUPLE: Well, friend, what have you to say for yourself?

MOB: I'm married.

KITE: Lackaday, so am I.

MOB: Here's my wife, poor woman.

BALANCE: Are you married, good woman?

WOMAN: I'm married in conscience.

KITE: May it please your worship, she's with child in conscience.

SCALE: Who married you, mistress?

WOMAN: My husband. We agreed that I should call him husband to avoid passing for a whore, and that he should call me wife to shun going for a soldier.

SCRUPLE: A very pretty couple. Pray, Captain, will you take 'em both.

PLUME: What say you, Mr. Kite? Will you take care of the woman?

KITE: Yes, sir, she shall go with us to the seaside, and there, if she has a mind to drown herself, we'll take care that nobody shall hinder her.

BALANCE: Here, Constable, bring in my man. (*Exit* CONSTABLE)

Now, Captain, I'll fit you with a man such as you ne'er listed in your life.

(*Enter* CONSTABLE *and* SILVIA.)

Oh, my friend Pinch, I'm very glad to see you.

SILVIA: Well, sir, and what then?

SCALE: What then! Is that your respect to the bench?

SILVIA: Sir, I don't care a farthing for you nor your bench neither.

SCRUPLE: Look'e, gentlemen, that's enough. He's a very impudent fellow, and fit for a soldier.

SCALE: A notorious rogue, I say, and very fit for a soldier.

CONSTABLE: A whoremaster, I say, and therefore fit to go.

BALANCE: What think you, Captain?

PLUME: I think he's a very pretty fellow, and therefore fit to serve.

SILVIA: Me for a soldier! Send your own lazy, lubberly sons at home, fellows that hazard their necks every day in pursuit of a fox, yet dare not peep abroad to look an enemy in the face.

CONSTABLE: May it please your worships, I have a woman at the door to swear a rape against this rogue.

SILVIA: Is it your wife or daughter, booby? I ravished 'em both yesterday.

BALANCE: Pray, Captain, read the Articles of War. We'll see him listed immediately.

(PLUME *reads Articles of War against mutiny and desertion.*)[35]

SILVIA: Hold, sir. Once more, gentlemen, have a care what you do, for you shall severely smart for any violence you offer to me. And you, Mr. Balance, I speak to you particularly; you shall heartily repent it.

PLUME: Look'e, young spark, say but one word more and I'll build a horse for you as high as the ceiling, and make you ride the most tiresome journey that ever you made in your life.

SILVIA: You have made a fine speech, good Captain Huffcap, but you had better be quiet. I shall find a way to cool your courage.

PLUME: Pray, gentlemen, don't mind him; he's distracted.

SILVIA: 'Tis false. I'm descended of as good a family as any in your county. My father is as good a man as any upon your bench, and I am heir to twelve hundred pounds a year.

BALANCE: He's certainly mad. Pray, Captain, read the Articles of War.

SILVIA: Hold once more. Pray, Mr. Balance, to you I speak. Suppose I were your child, would you use me at this rate?

BALANCE: No, faith, were you mine, I would send you to Bedlam[36] first and into the army afterwards.

SILVIA: But consider. My father, sir, he's as good, as generous, as brave, as just a man as ever served his country. I'm his only child; perhaps the loss of me may break his heart.

BALANCE: He's a very great fool if it does. Captain, if you don't list him this minute, I'll leave the court.

PLUME: Kite, do you distribute the levy money to the men whilst I read.

KITE: Ay, sir. Silence, gentlemen.

(PLUME *reads the Articles of War.*)

BALANCE: Very well. Now, Captain, let me beg the favor of you not to discharge this fellow upon any account whatsoever. Bring in the rest.

CONSTABLE: There are no more, an't please your worship.

BALANCE: No more! There were five two hours ago.

SILVIA: 'Tis true, sir, but this rogue of a constable let the rest escape for a bribe of eleven shillings a man because he said that the Act allows him but ten, so the odd shilling was clear gains.

ALL JUSTICES: How!

SILVIA: Gentlemen, he offered to let me get away for two guineas, but I had not so much about me. This is truth and I'm ready to swear it.

---

[35]Reading to a recruit the Articles of War and the Mutiny Acts completed his official enlistment.

[36]Bedlam was a hospital for the insane.

KITE: And I'll swear it; give me the book. 'Tis for the good of the service.

MOB: May it please your worship, I gave him half a crown to say that I was an honest man, and now that your worships have made me a rogue, I hope I shall have my money again.

BALANCE: 'Tis my opinion that this constable be put into the captain's hands, and if his friends don't bring four good men for his ransom by tomorrow night, Captain, you shall carry him to Flanders.

SCALE. SCRUPLE: Agreed, agreed.

PLUME: Mr. Kite, take the constable into custody.

KITE: Ay, ay, sir. (To the CONSTABLE.) Will you please to have your office taken from you, or will you handsomely lay down your staff as your betters have done before you?

(The CONSTABLE drops his staff.)

BALANCE: Come, gentlemen, there needs no great ceremony in adjourning this court. Captain, you shall dine with me.

KITE: Come, Mr. Militia Sergeant, I shall silence you now, I believe, without your taking the law of me.

(Exeunt omnes)

SCENE VI
Scene changes to the fields

(BRAZEN *leading in* LUCY *masked.*)

BRAZEN: The boat is just below here.

(Enter WORTHY *with a case of pistols under his arm, parts* BRAZEN *and* LUCY.)

WORTHY: Here, sir, take your choice. (Offering the pistols)

BRAZEN: What, pistols! Are they charged, my dear?

WORTHY: With a brace of bullets each.

BRAZEN: But I'm a foot officer, my dear, and never use pistols. The sword is my way, and I won't be put out of my road to please any man.

WORTHY: Nor I either, so have at you. (Cocks one pistol)

BRAZEN: Look'e, my dear, I do not care for pistols. Pray oblige me and let us have a bout at sharps. Dam't, there's no parrying these bullets.

WORTHY: Sir, if you han't your belly full of these, the swords shall come in for second course.

BRAZEN: Why then, fire and fury. I have eaten smoke from the mouth of a cannon, sir. Don't think I fear powder, for I live upon't. Let me see. (Takes a pistol) And now, sir, how many paces distant shall we fire?

WORTHY: Fire when you please; I'll reserve my shot till I be sure of you.

BRAZEN: Come, where's your cloak?

WORTHY: Cloak. What d'ye mean?

BRAZEN: To fight upon; I always fight upon a cloak. 'Tis our way abroad.

LUCY: Come, gentlemen, I'll end the strife. (Pulls off her mask)

WORTHY: Lucy! Take her.

BRAZEN: The devil take me if I do. Huzza! (Fires his pistol.) D'ye hear, d'ye hear, you plaguey harridan, how those bullets whistle. Suppose they had been lodged in my gizzard now?

LUCY: Pray, sir, pardon me.

BRAZEN: I can't tell, child, till I know whether my money be safe. (Searching his pockets) Yes, yes, I do pardon you, but if I had you in the Rose Tavern, Covent Garden, with three or four hearty rakes, and three or four smart napkins, I would tell you another story, my dear. (Exit BRAZEN)

WORTHY: And was Melinda Privy to this?

LUCY: No, sir. She wrote her name upon a piece of paper at the fortune-teller's last night, which I put in my pocket, and so writ above it to the captain.

WORTHY: And how came Melinda's journey put off?

LUCY: At the town's end she met Mr. Balance's steward, who told her that Mrs. Silvia was gone from her father's, and nobody could tell whither.

WORTHY: Silvia gone from her father's! This will be news to Plume. Go home and tell your lady how near I was being shot for her. (Exeunt)

SCENE VII

(BALANCE'S *house*)

(Enter BALANCE *with a napkin in his hand as risen from dinner, talking with his* STEWARD.)

STEWARD: We did not miss her till the evening, sir, and then searching for her in the chamber that was my young master's, we found her clothes there, but the suit that your son left in the press when he went to London was gone.

BALANCE: The white, trimmed with silver?

STEWARD: The same.

BALANCE: You han't told that circumstance to anybody?

STEWARD: To none but your worship.

BALANCE: And be sure you don't. Go into the dining room and tell Captain Plume that I beg to speak with him.

STEWARD: I shall.

BALANCE: Was ever man so imposed upon? I had her promise indeed that she should never dispose of herself without my consent. I have consented with a witness, given her away as my act and deed. And this, I warrant, the captain thinks will pass. No, I shall never pardon him the villainy, first of robbing me of my daughter, and then the mean opinion he must have of me to think that I could be so wretchedly imposed upon. Her extravagant passion might encourage her in the attempt, but the contrivance must be his. I'll know the truth presently.

(Enter PLUME.)

Pray, Captain, what have you done with your young gentleman soldier?

PLUME: He's at my quarters, I suppose, with the rest of my men.

BALANCE: Does he keep company with the common soldiers?

PLUME: No, he's generally with me.

BALANCE: He lies with you, I presume.

PLUME: No, faith, I offered him part of my bed, but the young rogue fell in love with Rose and has lain with her, I think, since he came to town.

BALANCE: So that between you both, Rose has been finely managed.

PLUME: Upon my honor, sir, she had no harm from me.

BALANCE: All's safe, I find. Now, Captain, you must know that the young fellow's impudence in court was well grounded. He said that I should heartily repent his being listed, and I do from my soul.

PLUME: Ay! For what reason?

BALANCE: Because he is no less than what he said he was, born of as good a family as any in the county, and is heir to twelve hundred pound a year.

PLUME: I'm very glad to hear it, for I wanted but a man of that quality to make my company a perfect representative of the whole commons of England.

BALANCE: Won't you discharge him?

PLUME: Not under a hundred pound sterling.

BALANCE: You shall have it, for his father is my intimate friend.

PLUME: Then you shall have him for nothing.

BALANCE: Nay, sir, you shall have your price.

PLUME: Not a penny, sir. I value an obligation to you much above a hundred pound.

BALANCE: Perhaps, sir, you shan't repent your generosity. Will you please to write his discharge in my pocket book. (Gives his book) In the meantime, we'll send for the gentleman. Who waits there?

(Enter SERVANT.)

Go to the captain's lodgings and inquire for Mr. Wilful. Tell him his captain wants him here immediately.

SERVANT: Sir, the gentleman's below at the door inquiring for the captain.

PLUME: Bid him come up. Here's the discharge, sir.

BALANCE: Sir, I thank you. (Aside) 'Tis plain he had no hand in't.

(Enter SILVIA.)

SILVIA: I think, Captain, you might have used me better than to leave me yonder among your swearing, drunken crew. And you, Mr. Justice, might have been so civil as to have invited me to dinner, for I have eaten with as good a man as your worship.

PLUME: Sir, you must charge our want of respect upon our ignorance of your quality. But now you're at liberty. I have discharged you.

SILVIA: Discharged me!

BLAANCE: Yes, sir, and you must once more go home to your father.

SILVIA: My father. Then I'm discovered! Oh, sir, I expect no pardon. *(Kneeling)*

BALANCE: Pardon. No, no, child, your crime shall be your punishment. Here, Captain, I deliver her over to the conjugal power for her chastisement. Since she will be a wife, be you a husband, a very husband. When she tells you of her love, upbraid her with her folly. Be modishly ungrateful because she has been unfashionably kind. And use her worse than you would anybody else, because you can't use her so well as she deserves.

PLUME: And are you Silvia in good earnest?

SILVIA: Earnest. I have gone too far to make it a jest, sir.

PLUME: And do you give her to me in good earnest?

BALANCE: If you please to take her, sir.

PLUME: Why then, I have saved my legs and arms and lost my liberty; secure from wounds I'm prepared for the gout. Farewell subsistence and welcome taxes. Sir, my liberty and hopes of being a general are much dearer to me than your twelve hundred pound a year, but to your love, madam, I resign my freedom, and to your beauty, my ambition, greater in obeying at your feet than commanding at the head of an army.

(Enter WORTHY.*)*

WORTHY: I'm sorry to hear, Mr. Balance, that your daughter is lost.

BALANCE: So am not I, sir, since an honest gentleman has found her.

(Enter MELINDA.*)*

MELINDA: Pray, Mr. Balance, what's become of my cousin Silvia?

BALANCE: Your cousin Silvia is talking yonder with your cousin Plume.

MELINDA and WORTHY: How!

SILVIA: Do you think it strange, cousin, that a woman should change? But, I hope, you'll excuse a change that has proceeded from constancy. I altered my outside because I was the same within, and only laid by the woman to make sure of my man. That's my history.

MELINDA: Your history is a little romantic, cousin, but since success has crowned your adventures, you will have the world o' your side, and I shall be willing to go with the tide, provided you pardon an injury I offered you in the letter to your father.

PLUME: That injury, madam, was done to me, and the reparation I expect shall be made to my friend. Make Mr. Worthy happy, and I shall be satisfied.

MELINDA: A good example, sir, will go a great way. When my cousin is pleased to surrender, 'tis probable I shan't hold out much longer.

(Enter BRAZEN.*)*

BRAZEN: Gentlemen, I am yours. Madam, I am not yours.

MELINDA: I'm glad on't, sir.

BRAZEN: So am I. You have got a pretty house here, Mr. Laconic.

BALANCE: 'Tis time to right all mistakes. My name, sir, is Balance.

BRAZEN: Balance. Sir, I'm your most obedient. I know your whole generation. Had not you an uncle that was governor of the Leeward Islands some years ago?

BALANCE: Did you know him?

BRAZEN: Intimately, sir. He played at billiards to a miracle. You had a brother, too, that was captain of a fireship. Poor Dick, he had the most engaging way with him of making punch, and then his cabin was so neat. But his boy Jack was the most comical bastard, ha, ha, ha, a pickled dog. I shall never forget him.

PLUME: Well, Captain, are you fixed in your project yet? Are you still for the privateer?

BRAZEN: No, no, I had enough of a privateer just now. I had like to have been picked up by a cruiser under false colors, and a French picaroon for ought I know.

PLUME: But have you got your recruits, my dear?

BRAZEN: Not a stick, my dear.

PLUME: Probably I shall furnish you.

(Enter ROSE *and* BULLOCK.*)*

ROSE: Captain, Captain, I have got loose once more and have persuaded my sweetheart Cartwheel to go with us, but you must promise not to part with me again.

SILVIA: I find Mrs. Rose has not been pleased with her bedfellow.

ROSE: Bedfellow! I don't know whether I had a bedfellow or not.

SILVIA: Don't be in a passion, child. I was as little pleased with your company as you could be with mine.

BULLOCK: Pray, sir, dunna be offended at my sister. She's something underbred. But if you please, I'll lie with you in her stead.

PLUME: I have promised, madam, to provide for this girl. Now will you be pleased to let her wait upon you, or shall I take care of her?

SILVIA: She shall be my charge, sir. You may find it business enough to take care of me.

BULLOCK: Ay, and of me, Captain, for wauns, if ever you lift your hand against me, I'll desert.

PLUME: Captain Brazen shall take care o'that. My dear, instead of the twenty thousand pound you talked of, you shall have the twenty brave recruits that I have raised, at the rate they cost me. My commission I lay down to be taken up by some braver fellow that has more merit and less good fortune, while I endeavor by the example of this worthy gentleman to serve my Queen and country at home.

With some regret I quit the active field,
Where glory full reward for life does
  yield;
But the recruiting trade with all its train,
Of lasting plague, fatigue, and endless
  pain,
I gladly quit, with my fair spouse to stay,
And raise recruits the matrimonial way.

The Recruiting Officer develops three intertwined plot strands: Captain Plume's efforts to recruit soldiers; Plume's courtship of Silvia; and Worthy's courtship of Melinda. They are linked through Plume's involvement in all.

The first strand forms a backdrop for the other two. Originally, part of the play's appeal was its topicality, for it was based on Farquhar's experience as a lieutenant assigned to recruit soldiers for a war still underway when the play was first performed. (The War of Spanish Succession, 1701–1714, pitted several European countries against France, which was attempting to place Louis XIV's grandson on the throne of Spain.) Farquhar's subject was also novel, for no previous play had treated recruiting so extensively. This comedy tells much about the varied methods then in use for securing soldiers. One law provided that debtors and convicted criminals could be released from prison if they would serve in the army or navy. Another law allowed Justices of the Peace (of which Balance is one) forcibly to enlist (or *impress*) any man without a lawful calling or visible means of support. Farquhar shows how the final provision could be twisted when he has Plume suggest that Balance impress a coal miner because working underground does not constitute a *visible* means of support. But much of Farquhar's humor stems from a third method of securing soldiers—enlisting them, either voluntarily or unwittingly. Since a man was considered to have joined the army if he accepted money from the recruiter, Sergeant Kite tricks two bumpkins into accepting the Queen's picture—that is, a coin showing the ruler's image. Another recruiting device, apparently one of Plume's most effective ones, is the basis of a continuing thread of the subplot—seducing an attractive young woman (in this case, Rose) and then getting her to persuade relatives and boyfriends to enlist. Still another inducement is the lure of money and great honors, exploited especially by Kite's disguise as a fortune-teller (he even convinces a butcher that he is destined to become Surgeon General of the Army).

The second plot strand — Plume's courtship of Silvia — is much less novel than the first, since it is a variation on a stock situation of comedy: obstacles to the fulfillment of love. In the beginning, the obstacle has been created by the lovers themselves, or as Plume explains it to Worthy: "'Tis true Silvia and I had once agreed to go to bed together, could we have adjusted the preliminaries, but she would have the wedding before the consummation and I was for consummation before the wedding. We could not agree." In addition to establishing the relationship between Plume and Silvia, this speech typifies the rakish tone underlying much of the play. It also tells much about Silvia's character, since she is sufficiently frank to discuss sex but sufficiently firm in her standards of conduct that she will not violate them. She also accepts without indignation Plume's sexual adventures with other women, although she tries to mitigate the results — as when she sends money to a serving woman who has borne Plume a child and when she tries to protect Rose from being seduced. It is this combination of frankness, integrity, and understanding in Silvia that endears her to Plume.

The obstacles in the path of Plume and Silvia soon become more complex, for when Justice Balance's son dies Silvia becomes his sole heir and thus, so wealthy that Plume is no longer considered to be a suitable match for her. This too is a familiar theme of comedy — the opposition of a parent to a suitor solely on the basis of lack of wealth. In this, Justice Balance is merely responding according to the custom of his day. The law of primogeniture required that the bulk of a family's estate pass to the firstborn son. Balance had provided that Silvia would be given 1,500 pounds as her inheritance, and he saw no reason to oppose her marriage to Plume should they reach an agreement. Plume is a gentleman and promises to rise in the army and to increase his income considerably. Once Silvia becomes heiress to a fortune, however, Balance views Plume as a fortune hunter. Knowing Silvia to be headstrong, Balance makes her promise that she will not marry without his consent. (Elopements and secret marriages were possible, although they often brought on disinheritance.) In turn, Balance promises Silvia that he will not marry her off without her consent.

The device that Silvia uses to win Plume and her father's consent to marry Plume involves still another familiar comic device — to disguise herself as a man. Breeches roles (women in men's clothing) were popular with male theatregoers because male clothing revealed the actress' legs, which were usually entirely concealed by the floor-length dresses of the time. Consequently, exposing a woman's legs in that period would be comparable to exposing her breasts today. Thus, Silvia's disguise adds another slightly risqué note. The complications that arise from Silvia's disguise eventually convince Balance that his daughter will love no one except Plume and that Plume is an honorable man worthy of her. Apparently, now that Silvia is rich, Plume no longer insists on sleeping with her before he will marry her.

The third plot strand—Worthy's courtship of Melinda—serves as a contrast to the second. Some time prior to the opening of the play, Melinda, having no fortune or prospect of an advantageous marriage, was on the verge of becoming Worthy's mistress in return for a sizable gift of money; then she unexpectedly inherited a fortune. When the play begins, Melinda is making Worthy miserable by seeming to take seriously the attention being paid her by Captain Brazen (whose character is summed up in his name). Eventually she consents to marry Worthy, but it tells much about the period that Worthy has come to consider the wealthy Melinda a highly desirable wife whereas he thought the penniless Melinda suitable only as a mistress. Farquhar seems to see nothing unusual in this change of attitude.

All three plot strands come together in the final scene, during which the two couples agree to marry and Plume decides to give up his commission and turn over his recruits to Brazen.

Farquhar's greatest innovation was to locate the action of his play in the country rather than in London, which had been the usual setting of Restoration comedy. This change removes the action from the rarified atmosphere of London's aristocracy and reduces the emphasis on witty conversation and fashion. But even here it is the upper class that serves as the norm and the lower class as the butt of humor.

The Recruiting Officer is considered to be a transitional play because of the way it sets up a dubious moral tone in the opening acts and then wholly dispels it in the final act. Thus, the tone of the first part resembles that of Restoration comedy and the tone of the ending foreshadows that of the sentimental comedy to come.

It can be revealing to compare *The Recruiting Officer* with *Pseudolus* and *The School for Wives* to see what each implies about normative attitudes and standards of morality. *Pseudolus* suggests that money and power are the primary controlling forces in society, but that cleverness can sometimes overcome them. It also suggests that those with power and money are cruel, insensitive, or stupid. The most admirable character is a slave, whose only resource is his sharp mind; he violates conventional morality but in a good cause. Still, the play does not attack the social structure or advocate reforms. It is a comedy of situation, emphasizing the humor of intrigue rather than character, ideas, or manners.

The School for Wives implies that nature and common sense are normative and that any attempt to subvert them is mistaken. We see an obsessed character (Arnolphe) ignore nature in his attempt to meet his own needs, but, as Horace and Agnès demonstrate, natural instinct will exert itself; and, as Chrysalde argues, human beings should learn to accept what is beyond their control and use common sense as a guide in dealing with it. The play combines attributes of comedies of character (in its emphasis on Arnolphe's obsessiveness as the basis of the dramatic action), comedies of ideas (in its concern for the education of women), and comedies of manners (in its demonstration of how manners and customs influence behavior). It implies that all aspects of society not in accord with reason and nature are flawed.

In *The Recruiting Officer* normative behavior is that of the aristocracy as embodied in Plume and Silvia. This norm includes a demand for personal integrity and tolerance for the shortcomings of others; it accepts imperfections as inevitable and acknowledges custom as a necessary guide for behavior. Thus, in *The Recruiting Officer* there is a relaxed attitude about morality and no suggestion that social customs should be changed, since justified exceptions (as in the case of Plume's and Silvia's marriage) can be made without threatening accepted standards. The comedy is based primarily on the manners and customs of the time, whether they relate to marriage or to recruiting. It depicts a world in which the characters can laugh at the flaws they see without becoming morally incensed and in which things ultimately work out for the best.

Such comparisons not only should help us to see differences among various kinds of comedy but also should provoke us to think about the standards that underlie our own behavior. Our assumptions, conscious or unconscious, about the norms of our world determine which standards we accept and which we think it justified to ignore; they also influence what we think to be essential to survival or prosperity and which persons we should admire or dislike. Thus, the study of plays may help us understand varied standards of human behavior, not only those depicted in the plays but also, through comparison, those of our own group.

Uncle Tom's Cabin or Life Among the Lowly

by George L. Aiken / Adapted from the novel by Harriet Beecher Stowe

In the late eighteenth century, the hold of Neoclassicism weakened, and in the early nineteenth century it was broken altogether. It was succeeded by another ideal — Romanticism — under which Shakespeare's plays were considered the model for dramatic writing. The unities of time and place were rejected and the unity of action was enlarged to permit any number of plot strands; the serious and the comic were intermingled in the same play. Spectacle was assigned an ever-increasing role, and audiences came to expect that they would see plays performed with settings and costumes that recreated the places and dress of the period when the action occurred; they marveled at the realistic simulation of earthquakes, volcanic eruptions, burning buildings, collapsing bridges, and other spectacular effects. Whereas the Neoclassical stage had reduced everything to essentials, the nineteenth-century stage sought to depict the infinite variety and complexity of the world.

In no genre was the new taste more evident than in melodrama, the most popular form of the nineteenth century. The dominance of melodrama may be explained in part by its appeal to a new audience that came into the theatre at this time. The Industrial Revolution, which began in the late eighteenth century and accelerated in the nineteenth, motivated an enormous increase in the population of cities and industrial towns as factories were erected. This enlarged population created an expanding demand for entertainment and diversions. Since there were virtually no professionalized sports events and since a large proportion of the population could not read, the theatre provided the most readily available entertainment. Theatre owners were eager to meet the tastes of this large and growing audience, even though this meant altering the traditional repertory by curtailing performances of plays by Shakespeare and other standard dramatists and increasing the proportion of melodramas and variety entertainments. Many sophisticated theatregoers, disdaining the new repertory, ceased attending; not until the last half of the nineteenth century did theatre owners recognize that it was possible to prosper with a repertory of limited range aimed at one segment of the audience rather than the general populace. Consequently, around 1875 theatres began to specialize in the classics, in comedy, in musicals, in vaudeville or music hall entertainment. This specialization permitted audiences to choose theatres that catered to their tastes.

The great popularity of melodrama with unsophisticated audiences is probably explained by its strong emotional appeals and lack of moral complexity. Melodrama depicts a world in which moral distinctions are clear-cut; it does not ask audiences to choose among characters whose motives are diverse and whose morality is complex; it makes clear from the beginning which characters are good and which are bad and where the audience's sympathies should lie. It is a reassuring form, for it shows the triumph of virtue and the defeat of vice. Its emotional appeals are basic: pity and indignation at the wrongful treatment of good people and intense dislike for oppression and oppressors. In the nineteenth century these emotional appeals were underlined by a musical score much as they are in movies in the twentieth century. Melodrama also appealed through its variety. In addition to strong and suspenseful stories, it provided comic relief through minor characters, usually rather simpleminded or overly frank ones. Most melodramas also included incidental songs and dances which, according to the capabilities of the cast, could be expanded or contracted as the talent permitted.

Melodrama came to the fore around 1800 primarily through the work of two playwrights, August Friedrich Ferdinand von Kotzebue (1761–1819) in Germany, and René Charles Guilbert de Pixérécourt (1773–1844) in France. A craze for their works swept Europe and America, bringing full houses for managers who sought to keep the audiences coming back by offering other plays of the same general type. In this favorable climate, melodrama flourished.

The most popular melodrama of the nineteenth century was *Uncle Tom's Cabin*, an adaptation of Harriet Beecher Stowe's novel (published in 1852). A number of adaptations for the stage were made, but that of George L. Aiken was to be the most popular. His adaptation was first produced in 1852 and originally consisted of two separate three-act plays, the first ending with the death of Little Eva, the second with the death of Uncle Tom. These two plays were combined into a six-act version in 1853, and it was this script that became phenomenally popular, enjoying an initial run in New York of 325 performances, an enormous number at a time before long runs became common. At one time, five theatres in New York and five in London were presenting *Uncle Tom's Cabin* simultaneously. Although the craze died down by 1860, it revived in the 1870s, when some 50 traveling companies were performing it; by 1899 this number had grown to 500. Companies vied to see which could provide the most spectacular production. In 1901 a production in New York used numerous horses and bloodhounds, 200 singers and dancers, and 18 gigantic settings. The play's popularity continued into the twentieth century. In 1927 there were still 12 touring companies that performed nothing but this play, and at least 12 movie versions of this melodrama have been made since 1900. *Uncle Tom's Cabin* also enjoyed enormous popularity throughout Western Europe and in some Asian countries. It became a major factor in the fight against slavery in the United States. In the South, Mrs. Stowe was vilified, but in the North her work was considered strong evidence for the need to free the slaves. The impact on society of *Uncle Tom's Cabin* has been equaled by few other plays of any period.

CAST OF CHARACTERS

GEORGE SHELBY *slave owner*
UNCLE TOM *slave owned by Shelby*
CHLOE *his wife*
ELIZA *slave owned by Shelby*
GEORGE HARRIS *slave, husband to Eliza*
HARRY *child of Eliza and George*
HALEY *a slave trader*
PHINEAS FLETCHER *former slave owner, now a Quaker*
MARKS *lawyer, pursuer of runaway slaves*
TOM LOKER *his partner*
THREE MEN *their helpers*
WAITER
ST. CLARE *slave owner, purchaser of Uncle Tom*
MARIE *his wife*

EVA *his daughter*
OPHELIA *his sister, from Vermont*
TOPSY *slave child given to Ophelia*
WILSON *owner of a bagging factory*
GUMPTION CUTE *"relative" of Ophelia*
SKEGGS *slave auctioneer*
ADOLF *slave, valet to St. Clare*
MANN *purchaser of Adolf*
EMMELINE *quadroon, owned by St. Clare, bought by Simon Legree*
SIMON LEGREE *slave owner, purchaser of Uncle Tom and Emmeline*
CASSY ⎫
SAMBO ⎬ *slaves owned by Legree*
QUIMBO ⎭
DEACON PERRY *Vermonter, suitor to Ophelia*

ACT I

SCENE I

Plain chamber. (Enter ELIZA, R.H., *meeting* GEORGE, L.H.*)*

ELIZA: Ah! George, is it you? Well, I am so glad you've come. (GEORGE *regards her mournfully*) Why don't you smile, and ask after Harry?

GEORGE: *(Bitterly)* I wish he'd never been born!—I wish I'd never been born myself!

ELIZA: *(Sinking her head upon his breast and weeping)* Oh George!

GEO.: There now, Eliza, it's too bad for me to make you feel so. Oh! how I wish you had never seen me—you might have been happy!

ELIZA: George! George! how can you talk so?

What dreadful thing has happened, or is going to happen? I'm sure we've been very happy till lately.

GEO.: So we have, dear. But oh! I wish I'd never seen you, nor you me.

ELIZA: Oh, George! how can you?

GEO.: Yes, Eliza, it's all misery! misery! The very life is burning out of me! I'm a poor, miserable, forlorn drudge! I shall only drag you down with me, that's all! What's the use of our trying to do anything—trying to know anything—trying to be anything? I wish I was dead!

ELIZA: Oh! now, dear George, that is really wicked. I know how you feel about losing your place in the factory, and you have a hard master; but pray be patient—

GEO: Patient! Haven't I been patient? Did I say a word when he came and took me away—for no earthly reason—from the place where everybody was kind to me? I'd paid him truly every cent of my earnings, and they all say I worked well.

ELIZA: Well, it *is* dreadful; but, after all, he is your master, you know.

GEO: My master! And who made him my master? That's what I think of? What right has he to me? I'm as much a man as he is. What right has he to make a drayhorse of me?—to take me from things I can do better than he can, and put me to work that any horse can do? He tries to do it; he says he'll bring me down and humble me, and he puts me to just the hardest, meanest and dirtiest work on purpose.

ELIZA: Oh, George! George! you frighten me. Why, I never heard you talk so. I'm afraid you'll do something dreadful. I don't wonder at your feelings at all; but oh! do be careful—for my sake, for Harry's.

GEO: I have been careful, and I have been patient, but it's growing worse and worse—flesh and blood can't bear it any longer. Every chance he can get to insult and torment me he takes. He says that though I don't say anything, he sees that I've got the devil in me, and he means to bring it out; and one of these days it will come out, in a way that he won't like, or I'm mistaken.

ELIZA: Well, I always thought that I must obey my master and mistress, or I couldn't be a Christian.

GEO: There is some sense in it in your case. They have brought you up like a child—fed you, clothed you and taught you, so that you have a good education—that is some reason why they should claim you. But I have been kicked and cuffed and sworn at, and what do I owe? I've paid for all my keeping a hundred times over. I won't bear it!—no, I *won't!* Master will find out that I'm one whipping won't tame. My day will come yet, if he don't look out!

ELIZA: What are you going to do? Oh! George, don't do anything wicked; if you only trust in heaven and try to do right, it will deliver you.

GEO: Eliza, my heart's full of bitterness. I can't trust in heaven. Why does it let things be so?

ELIZA: Oh, George! we must all have faith. Mistress says that when all things go wrong to us, we must believe that heaven is doing the very best.

GEO: That's easy for people to say who are sitting on their sofas and riding in their carriages; but let them be where I am—I guess it would come some harder. I wish I could be good; but my heart burns and can't be reconciled. You couldn't, in my place, you can't now, if I tell you all I've got to say; you don't know the whole yet.

ELIZA: What do you mean?

GEO: Well, lately my master has been saying that he was a fool to let me marry off the place—that he hates Mr. Shelby and all his tribe—and he says he won't let me come here any more, and that I shall take a wife and settle down on his place.

ELIZA: But you were married to *me* by the minister, as much as if you had been a white man.

GEO: Don't you know I can't hold you for my wife if he chooses to part us? That is why I wish I'd never seen you—it would have been better for us both—it would have been better for our poor child if he had never been born.

ELIZA: Oh! but my master is so kind.

GEO: Yes, but who knows?—he may die, and then Harry may be sold to nobody knows who. What pleasure is it that he is handsome and smart and bright? I tell you, Eliza, that a sword will pierce through your soul for every good and pleasant thing your child is or has. It will make him worth too much for you to keep.

ELIZA: Heaven forbid!

GEO: So, Eliza, my girl, bear up now, and good by, for I'm going.

ELIZA: Going, George! Going where?

GEO: To Canada; and when I'm there I'll buy you—that's all the hope that's left us. You have a kind master, that won't refuse to sell you. I'll buy you and the boy—heaven helping me, I will!

ELIZA: Oh, dreadful! If you should be taken?

GEO: I won't be taken, Eliza—I'll *die* first! I'll be free, or I'll die.

ELIZA: You will not kill yourself?

GEO: No need of that; they will kill me, fast enough. I will never go down the river alive.

ELIZA: Oh, George! for my sake, do be careful. Don't lay hands on yourself, or anybody else. You are tempted too much, but don't. Go, if you must, but go carefully, prudently, and pray heaven to help you!

GEO: Well, then, Eliza, hear my plan. I'm

going home quite resigned, you understand, as if all was over. I've got some preparations made, and there are those that will help me; and in the course of a few days I shall be among the missing. Well, now, good by.

ELIZA: A moment—our boy.

GEO: *(Choked with emotion)* True I had forgotten him; one last look, and then farewell!

ELIZA: And heaven grant it be not forever! *(Exeunt, R.H.)*

SCENE II

A dining room. Table and chairs. Dessert, wine, etc., on table. SHELBY *and* HALEY *discovered at table.*

SHEL: That is the way I should arrange the matter.

HAL: I can't make trade that way—I positively can't, Mr. Shelby. *(Drinks)*

SHEL: Why, the fact is, Haley, Tom is an uncommon fellow! He is certainly worth that sum anywhere—steady, honest, capable, manages my whole farm like a clock!

HAL: You mean honest, as niggers go. *(Fills glass)*

SHEL: No; I mean, really, Tom is a good, steady, sensible, pious fellow. He got religion at a camp-meeting, four years ago, and I believe he really did get it. I've trusted him since then, with everything I have—money, house, horses, and let him come and go round the country, and I always found him true and square in everything.

HAL: Some folks don't believe there is pious niggers, Shelby, but *I* do. I had a fellow, now, in this yer last lot I took to Orleans—'twas as good as a meetin' now, really, to hear that critter pray; and he was quite gentle and quiet like. He fetched me a good sum, too for I bought him cheap of a man that was 'bliged to sell out, so I realized six hundred on him. Yes, I consider religion a valeyable thing in a nigger, when it's the genuine article and no mistake.

SHEL: Well, Tom's got the real article, if ever a fellow had. Why last fall I let him go to Cincinnati alone, to do business for me and bring home five hundred dollars. "Tom," says I to him, "I trust you, because I think you are a Christian—I know you wouldn't cheat." Tom comes back sure enough, I knew he would. Some low fellows, they say, said to him—"Tom, why don't you make tracks for Canada?" "Ah, master trusted me, and I couldn't," was his answer. They told me all about it. I am sorry to part with Tom, I must say. You ought to let him cover the whole balance of the debt and you would, Haley, if you had any conscience.

HAL: Well, I've got just as much conscience as any man in business can afford to keep, just a little, you know, to swear by, as twere; and then I'm ready to do anything in reason to 'blige friends, but this yer, you see, is a leetle too hard on a fellow—a leetle too hard! *(Fills glass again)*

SHEL: Well, then, Haley, how will you trade?

HAL: Well, haven't you a boy or a girl that you could throw in with Tom?

SHEL: Hum! none that I could well spare; to tell the truth, it's only hard necessity makes me willing to sell at all. I don't like parting with any of my hands, that's a fact. *(*HARRY *runs in R.H.)* Hulloa! Jim Crow! *(Throws a bunch of raisins towards him)* Pick that up now! *(*HARRY *does so)*

HAL: Bravo, little 'un! *(Throws an orange, which* HARRY *catches. He sings and dances around the stage.)* Hurrah! Bravo! What a young 'un! That chap's a case, I'll promise. Tell you what, Shelby, fling in that chap, and I'll settle the business. Come, now, if that ain't doing the thing up about the rightest!

*(*ELIZA *enters R.H.—Starts on beholding* HALEY, *and gazes fearfully at* HARRY, *who runs and clings to her dress, showing the orange, etc.)*

SHEL: Well, Eliza?

ELIZA: I was looking for Harry, please, sir.

SHEL: Well, take him away, then.

*(*ELIZA *grasps the child eagerly in her arms, and casting another glance of apprehension at* HALEY, *exits hastily, R.H.)*

HAL: By Jupiter! there's an article, now. You might make your fortune on that ar gal in Orleans any day. I've seen over a thousand in my day, paid down for gals not a bit handsomer.

SHEL: I don't want to make my fortune on her. Another glass of wine. *(Fills the glasses)*

HAL: *(Drinks and smacks his lips)* Capital wine—first chop. Come, how will you trade about the gal? What shall I say for her? What'll you take?

SHEL: Mr. Haley, she is not to be sold. My wife wouldn't part with her for her weight in gold.

HAL: Ay, ay! women always say such things, 'cause they hain't no sort of calculation. Just show 'em how many watches, feathers and trinkets one's weight in gold would buy, and that alters the case, I reckon.

SHEL: I tell you, Haley, this must not be spoken of—I say no, and I mean no.

HAL: Well, you'll let me have the boy tho'; you must own that I have come down pretty handsomely for him.

SHEL: What on earth can you want with the child?

HAL: Why, I've got a friend that's going into this yer branch of the business—wants to buy up handsome boys to raise for the market. Well, what do you say?

SHEL: I'll think the matter over and talk with my wife.

HAL: Oh, certainly, by all means; but I'm in a devil of a hurry and shall want to know as soon as possible, what I may depend on.

(Rises and puts on his overcoat, which hangs on a chair. Takes hat and whip.)

SHEL: Well, call up this evening, between six and seven, and you shall have my answer.

HAL: All right. Take care of yourself, old boy! *(Exit* L.H.*)*

SHEL: If anybody had ever told me that I should sell Tom to those rascally traders, I should never have believed it. Now it must come for aught I see, and Eliza's child too. So much for being in debt, heigho! The fellow sees his advantage and means to push it. *(Exit* R.H.*)*

SCENE III

Snowy landscape. UNCLE TOM'S *Cabin,* L.U.E. *Snow on roof.—Practical door and window. Dark Stage. Music. Enter* ELIZA *hastily,* R.U.E. *with* HARRY *in her arms.)*

ELIZA: My poor boy! they have sold you, but your mother will save you yet!

(Goes to Cabin and taps on window. AUNT CHLOE *appears at window with a large white night-cap on.)*

CHLOE: Good Lord! what's that? My sakes alive if it ain't Lizy! Get on your clothes, old man, quick! I'm gwine to open the door.

(The door opens and CHLOE *enters followed by* UNCLE TOM *in his shirt sleeves holding a tallow candle.* TOM *crosses to* C.*)*

TOM: (C. *Holding the light towards* ELIZA) Lord bless you! I'm skeered to look at ye, Lizy! Are ye tuck sick, or what's come over ye?

ELIZA: (R.) I'm running away, Uncle Tom and Aunt Chloe, carrying off my child! Master sold him!

TOM and CHLOE: (L.) Sold him!

ELIZA: Yes, sold him! I crept into the closet by mistress' door tonight and heard master tell mistress that he had sold my Harry and you, Uncle Tom, both, to a trader, and that the man was to take possession to-morrow.

CHLOE: The good lord have pity on us! Oh! it don't seem as if it was true. What has he done that master should sell *him?*

ELIZA: He hasn't done anything—it isn't for that. Master don't want to sell, and mistress—she's always good. I heard her plead and beg for us, but he told her 'twas no use—that he was in this man's debt, and he had got the power over him, and that if he did not pay him off clear, it would end in his having to sell the place and all the people and move off.

CHLOE: Well, old man, why don't you run away, too? Will you wait to be toted down the river, where they kill niggers with hard work and starving? I'd a heap rather die than go there, any day! There's time for ye, be off with Lizy — you've got a pass to come and go any time. Come, bustle up, and I'll get your things together.

TOM: No, no — I ain't going. Let Eliza go — it's her right. I wouldn't be the one to say no — 'tain't in natur for her to stay; but you heard what she said? If I must be sold, or all the people on the place, and everything go to rack, why, let me be sold. I s'pose I can bar it as well as any one. Mas'r always found me on the spot — he always will. I never have broken trust, nor used my pass no ways contrary to my word, and I never will. It's better for me to go alone, than to break up the place and sell all. Mas'r ain't to blame, and he'll take care of you and the poor little 'uns! *(Overcome)*

CHLOE: Now, old man, what is you gwine to cry for? Does you want to break this old woman's heart? *(Crying)*

ELIZA: I saw my husband only this afternoon, and I little knew then what was to come. He told me he was going to run away. Do try, if you can, to get word to him. Tell him how I went and why I went, and tell him I'm going to try and find Canada. You must give my love to him, and tell him if I never see him again on earth, I trust we shall meet in heaven!

TOM: Dat is right, Lizy, trust in the Lord — he is our best friend — our only comforter.

ELIZA: You won't go with me, Uncle Tom?

TOM: No; time was when I would, but the Lord's given me a work among these yer poor souls, and I'll stay with 'em and bear my cross with 'em till the end. It's different with you — it's more'n you could stand, and you'd better go if you can.

ELIZA: Uncle Tom, I'll try it!

TOM: Amen! The lord help ye!

(Exit ELIZA *and* HARRY, R. *1* E.*)*

CHLOE: What is you gwine to do, old man! What's to become of you?

TOM: *(Solemnly)* Him that saved Daniel in the den of lions — that saved the children in the fiery furnace — Him that walked on the sea and bade the winds be still — He's alive yet! and I've faith to believe he can deliver me.

CHLOE: You is right, old man.

TOM: The Lord is good unto all that trust him, Chloe *(Exeunt into Cabin)*

SCENE IV

Room in tavern by the river side. A large window in flat, through which the river is seen, filled with floating ice. Moon light. Table and chairs brought on. Enter PHINEAS, L.H.

PHINEAS: Chaw me up into tobaccy ends! how in the name of all that's onpossible am I to get across that yer pesky river? It's a reg'lar blockade of ice! I promised Ruth to meet her to-night, and she'll be into my har if I don't come. *(Goes to window)* Thar's a conglomerated prospect for a loveyer! What in creation's to be done? That thar river looks like a permiscuous ice-cream shop come to an awful state of friz. If I war on the adjacent bank, I wouldn't care a teetotal atom. Rile up, you old varmit, and shake the ice off your back!

(Enter ELIZA *and* HARRY, L.H.*)*

ELIZA: Courage, my boy — we have reached the river. Let it but roll between us and our pursuers, and we are safe! *(Goes to window)* Gracious powers! the river is choked with cakes of ice!

PHIN: Holloa, gal! — what's the matter? You look kind of streaked.

ELIZA: Is there any ferry or boat that takes people over now?

PHIN: Well, I guess not; the boats have stopped running.

ELIZA: *(In dismay)* Stopped running?

PHIN: Maybe you're wanting to get over — anybody sick? Ye seem mighty anxious.

ELIZA: I — I — I've got a child that's very dangerous. I never heard of it till last night, and I've walked quite a distance to-day, in hopes to get to the ferry.

PHIN: Well, now, that's onlucky; I'm re'lly consarned for ye. Thar's a man, a piece down here, that's going over with some truck this evening, if he duss to; he'll be in here to supper to-night, so you'd better set down and wait. That's a smart little chap. Say, young'un have a chaw tobaccy? *(Takes out a large plug and a bowie-knife)*

ELIZA: No, no! not any for him.

PHIN: Oh! he don't use it, eh? Hain't come to it yet? Well, I have. *(Cuts off a large piece, and returns the plug and knife to pocket)* What's the matter with the young'un? He looks kind of white in the gills!

ELIZA: Poor fellow! he is not used to walking, and I've hurried him on so.

PHIN: Tuckered, eh? Well, there's a little room there, with a fire in it. Take the babby in there, make yourself comfortable till that thar ferryman shows his countenance—I'll stand the damage.

ELIZA: How shall I thank you for such kindness to a stranger?

PHIN: Well, if you don't know how, why, don't try; that's the teetotal. Come, vamose! *(Exit ELIZA and HARRY, R.H.D.)* Chaw me into sassage meat, if that ain't a perpendicular fine gal! she's a reg'lar A No. 1 sort of female! How'n thunder am I to get across this refrigerated stream of water? I can't wait for that ferryman. *(Enter MARKS L.H.)* Halloa! what sort of a critter's this? *(Advances)* Say, stranger, will you have something to drink?

MARKS: You are excessively kind: I don't care if I do.

PHIN: Ah! he's a human. Holloa, thar! bring us a jug of whisky instantaneously, or expect to be teetotally chawed up! Squat yourself, stranger, and go in for enjoyment. *(They sit at table)* Who are you, and what's your name?

MARKS: I am a lawyer, and my name is Marks.

PHIN: A land shark, eh? Well, I don't think no worse on you for that. The law is a kind of necessary evil; and it breeds lawyers just as an old stump does fungus. Ah! here's the whisky. *(Enter WAITER, with jug and tumblers, L.H.—Places them on table)* Here, you—take that shin-plaster. *(Gives bill)* I

don't want any change—thar's a gal stopping in that room—the balance will pay for her—d'ye hear?—vamose! *(Exit WAITER, L.H.—Fills glass)* Take hold, neighbor Marks—don't shirk the critter. Here's hoping your path of true love may never have an ice-choked river to cross! *(They drink)*

MARKS: Want to cross the river, eh?

PHIN: Well, I do, stranger. Fact is, I'm in love with the teetotalist pretty girl, over on the Ohio side, that ever wore a Quaker bonnet. Take another swig, neighbor. *(Fills glasses, and they drink)*

MARKS: A Quaker, eh?

PHIN: Yes—kind of strange, ain't it? The way of it was this:—I used to own a grist of niggers—had 'em to work on my plantation, just below here. Well, stranger, do you know I fell in with that gal—of course I was considerably smashed—knocked into a pretty conglomerated heap—and I told her so. She said she wouldn't hear a word from me so long as I owned a nigger!

MARKS: You sold them, I suppose?

PHIN: You're teetotally wrong, neighbor. I gave them all their freedom, and told 'em to vamose!

MARKS: Ah! yes—very noble, I dare say but rather expensive. This act won you your lady-love, eh?

PHIN: You're off the track again, neighbor. She felt kind of pleased about it, and smiled, and all that; but she said she could never be mine unless I turned Quaker! Thunder and earth! what do you think of that? You're a lawyer—come, now, what's your opinion? Don't you call it a knotty point?

MARKS: Most decidedly. Of course you refused.

PHIN: Teetotally; but she told me to think better of it, and come to-night and give her my final conclusion. Chaw me into mince meat, if I haven't made up my mind to do it!

MARKS: You astonish me!

PHIN: Well, you see, I can't get along without that gal;—she's sort of fixed my flint, and I'm sure to hang fire without her. I know I shall make a queer sort of Quaker, because you see, neighbor, I ain't precisely the kind of material to make a Quaker out of.

MARKS: No, not exactly.

PHIN: Well, I can't stop no longer. I must try to get across that candaverous river some way. It's getting late — take care of yourself, neighbor lawyer. I'm a teetotal victim to a pair of black eyes. Chaw me up to feed hogs, if I'm not in a ruinatious state! *(Exit* L.H.*)*

MARKS: Queer genius, that, very! *(Enter* TOM LOKER, L.H.*)* So you've come at last.

LOKER: Yes. *(Looks into jug)* Empty! Waiter! more whisky!

*(*WAITER *enters,* L.H., *with jug, and removes the empty one. Enter* HALEY, L.H.*)*

HAL: By the land! if this yer ain't the nearest, now, to what I've heard people call Providence! Why, Loker, how are ye?

LOKER: The devil! What brought you here, Haley?

HAL: *(Sitting at table)* I say, Tom, this yer's the luckiest thing in the world. I'm in a devil of a hobble, and you must help me out!

LOKER: Ugh! aw! like enough. A body may be pretty sure of that when you're glad to see 'em, or can make something off of 'em. What's the blow now?

HAL: You've got a friend here — partner, perhaps?

LOKER: Yes, I have. Here, Marks — here's that ar fellow that I was with in Natchez.

MARKS: *(Grasping* HALEY'S *hand)* Shall be pleased with his acquaintance. Mr. Haley, I believe?

HAL: The same, sir. The fact is, gentlemen, this morning I bought a young 'un of Shelby up above here. His mother got wind of it, and what does she do but cut her lucky with him; and I'm afraid by this time that she has crossed the river, for I tracked her to this very place.

MARKS: So, then, ye're fairly sewed up, ain't ye? He! he! he! it's neatly done, too.

HAL: This young 'un business makes lots of trouble in the trade.

MARKS: Now, Mr. Haley, what is it? Do you want us to undertake to catch this gal?

HAL: The gal's no matter of mine — she's Shel-

by's — it's only the boy. I was a fool for buying the monkey.

LOKER: You're generally a fool!

MARKS: Come now, Loker, none of your huffs; you see, Mr. Haley's a-puttin' us in a way of a good job. I reckon: just hold still — these yer arrangements are my forte. This yer gal, Mr. Haley — how is she? — what is she?

*(*ELIZA *appears, with* HARRY, R.H.D., *listening.)*

HAL: Well, white and handsome — well brought up. I'd have given Shelby eight hundred or a thousand, and then made well on her.

MARKS: White and handsome — well brought up! Look here now, Loker, a beautiful opening. We'll do a business here on our own account. We does the catchin'; the boy, of course, goes to Mr. Haley — we takes the gal to Orleans to speculate on. Ain't it beautiful? *(They confer together)*

ELIZA: Powers of mercy, protect me! How shall I escape these human blood-hounds? Ah! the window — the river of ice! That dark stream lies between me and liberty! Surely the ice will bear my trifling weight. It is my only chance of escape — better sink beneath the cold waters, with my child locked in my arms, than have him torn from me and sold into bondage. He sleeps upon my breast — Heaven, I put my trust in thee! *(Gets out of window)*

MARKS: Well, Tom Loker, what do you say?

LOKER: It'll do!

(Strikes his hand violently on the table. ELIZA *screams. They all start to their feet.* ELIZA *disappears. Music, chord.)*

HAL: By the land, there she is now! *(They all rush to the window.)*

MARKS: She's making for the river!

LOKER: Let's after her!

(Music. They all leap through the window. ·Change.)

SCENE V

Snow landscape. Music. Enter ELIZA, *with* HARRY, *hurriedly*, L. 1 E.

ELIZA: They press upon my footsteps—the river is my only hope. Heaven grant me strength to reach it, ere they overtake me! Courage, my child!—we will be free—or perish! *(Rushes off*, R.H. *Music continued.)*

(Enter LOKER, HALEY *and* MARKS, L. *1* E.*)*

HAL: We'll catch her yet; the river will stop her!

MARKS: No, it won't, for look! she has jumped upon the ice! She's a brave gal, anyhow!

LOKER: She'll be drowned!

HAL: Curse that young 'un! I shall lose him, after all.

LOKER: Come on, Marks, to the ferry!

HAL: Aye, to the ferry!—a hundred dollars for a boat!

(Music. They rush off, R.H.*)*

SCENE VI

The entire depth of stage, representing the Ohio River filled with Floating Ice. Set bank on R.H. *and in front.* ELIZA *appears, with* HARRY, R.H., *on a cake of ice, and floats slowly across to* L.H. HALEY, LOKER, *and* MARKS, *on bank* R.H., *observing.* PHINEAS *on opposite.*

ACT II

SCENE I

A handsome parlor. MARIE *discovered reclining on a sofa*, R.H.

MARIE: *(Looking at a note)* What can possibly detain St. Clare? According to this note he should have been here a fortnight ago. *(Noise of carriage without)* I do believe he has come at last.

*(*EVA *runs in*, L. 1 E.*)*

EVA: Mamma! *(Throws her arms around* MARIE'S *neck, and kisses her.)*

MARIE: That will do—take care, child—don't you make my head ache! *(Kisses her languidly)*

(Enter ST. CLARE, OPHELIA, *and* TOM, *nicely dressed,* L. *1* E.*)*

ST. CLARE: Well, my dear Marie, here we are at last. The wanderers have arrived, you see. Allow me to present my cousin, Miss Ophelia, who is about to undertake the office of our housekeeper.

MARIE: *(Rising to a sitting posture)* I am delighted to see you. How do you like the appearance of our city?

EVA: *(Running to* OPHELIA*)* Oh! is it not beautiful? My own darling home!—is it not beautiful?

OPHELIA: Yes, it is a pretty place, though it looks rather old and heathenish to me.

ST. C: Tom, my boy, this seems to suit you?

TOM: Yes, mas'r, it looks about the right thing.

ST. C: See here, Marie, I've brought you a coachman, at last, to order. I tell you, he is a regular hearse for blackness and sobriety, and will drive you like a funeral, if you wish. Open your eyes, now, and look at him. Now, don't say I never think about you when I'm gone.

MARIE: I know he'll get drunk.

ST. C: Oh! no he won't. He's warranted a pious and sober article.

MARIE: Well, I hope he may turn out well; it's more than I expect, though.

ST. C: Have you no curiosity to learn how and where I picked up Tom?

EVA: *Uncle* Tom, papa; that's his name.

ST. C: Right, my little sunbeam!

TOM: Please, mas'r, that ain't no 'casion to say nothing bout me.

ST. C: You are too modest, my modern Hannibal. Do you know, Marie, that our little Eva took a fancy to Uncle Tom — whom we met on board the steamboat — and persuaded me to buy him.

MARIE: Ah! she is so odd.

ST. C: As we approached the landing, a sudden rush of the passengers precipitated Eva into the water —

MARIE: Gracious heavens!

ST. C: A man leaped into the river, and, as she rose to the surface of the water, grasped her in his arms, and held her up until she could be drawn on the boat again. Who was that man, Eva?

EVA: Uncle Tom! *(Runs to him. He lifts her in his arms. She kisses him.)*

TOM: The dear soul!

OPH: *(Astonished)* How shiftless!

ST. C: *(Overhearing her)* What's the matter now, pray?

OPH: Well, I want to be kind to everybody, and I wouldn't have anything hurt, but as to kissing —

ST. C: Niggers! that you're not up to, hey?

OPH: Yes, that's it — how can she?

ST. C: Oh! bless you, it's nothing when you are used to it!

OPH: I could never be so shiftless!

EVA: Come with me, Uncle Tom, and I will show you about the house. *(Crosses to* R.H. *with* TOM*)*

TOM: Can I go, mas'r?

ST. C: Yes, Tom; she is your little mistress — your only duty will be to attend to her! *(*TOM *bows and exits,* R. 1 E.*)*

MARIE: Eva, my dear!

EVA: Well, mamma?

MARIE: Do you exert yourself too much!

EVA: No, mamma! *(Runs out,* R.H.*)*

OPH: *(Lifting up her hands)* How shiftless!

*(*ST. CLARE *sits next to* MARIE *on sofa.* — OPHELIA *next to* ST. CLARE.*)*

ST. C: Well, what do you think of Uncle Tom, Marie?

MARIE: He is a perfect behemoth!

ST. C: Come, now, Marie, be gracious, and say something pretty to a fellow!

MARIE: You've been gone a fortnight beyond the time!

ST. C: Well, you know I wrote you the reason.

MARIE: Such a short, cold letter!

ST. C: Dear me! the mail was just going, and it had to be that or nothing.

MARIE: That's just the way; always something to make your journeys long and letters short!

ST. C: Look at this. *(Takes an elegant velvet case from his pocket)* Here's a present I got for you in New York — a Daguerreotype of Eva and myself.

MARIE: *(Looks at it with a dissatisfied air)* What made you sit in such an awkward position?

ST. C: Well, the position may be a matter of opinion, but what do you think of the likeness?

MARIE: *(Closing the case snappishly)* If you don't think anything of my opinion in one case, I suppose you wouldn't in another.

OPH: *(Sententiously, aside)* How shiftless!

ST. C: Hang the woman! Come, Marie, what do you think of the likeness? Don't be nonsensical now.

MARIE: It's very inconsiderate of you, St. Clare, to insist on my talking and looking at things. You know I've been lying all day with the sick headache, and there's been such a tumult made ever since you came, I'm half dead!

OPH: You're subject to the sick headache, ma'am?

MARIE: Yes, I'm a perfect martyr to it!

OPH: Juniper-berry tea is good for sick headache; at least, Molly, Deacon Abraham Perry's wife, used to say so; and she was a great nurse.

ST. C: I'll have the first juniper-berries that get ripe in our garden by the lake brought in for that especial purpose. Come, cousin, let us take a stroll in the garden. Will you join us, Marie?

MARIE: I wonder how you can ask such a question, when you know how fragile I am. I shall retire to my chamber, and repose till dinner time. *(Exit R. 2 E.)*

OPH: *(Looking after her)* How shiftless!

ST. C: Come, cousin! *(As he goes out)* Look out for the babies! If I step upon any body, let them mention it.

OPH: Babies under foot! How shiftless! *(Exeunt L. 1 E.)*

SCENE II

A Garden.

TOM *discovered, seated on a bank,* R.U.E., *with* EVA *on his knee, his button-holes are filled with flowers, and* EVA *is hanging a wreath around his neck. Music at opening of scene. Enter* ST. CLARE *and* OPHELIA, L.U.E., *observing.*

EVA: Oh, Tom! you look so funny.

TOM: *(Sees* ST. CLARE *and puts* EVA *down)* I begs pardon, mas'r, but the young missis would do it. Look yer, I'm like the ox, mentioned in the good book, dressed for the sacrifice.

ST. C: I say, what do you think, Pussy? Which do you like the best—to live as they do at your uncle's, up in Vermont, or to have a house-full of servants, as we do?

EVA: Oh! of course our way is the pleasantest.

ST. C: *(Patting her head)* Why so?

EVA: Because it makes so many more round you to love, you know.

OPH: Now, that's just like Eva—just one of her odd speeches.

EVA: Is it an odd speech, papa?

ST. C: Rather, as this world goes, Pussy. But where has my little Eva been?

EVA: Oh! I've been up in Tom's room, hearing him sing.

ST. C: Hearing Tom sing, hey?

EVA: Oh, yes! he sings such beautiful things, about the new Jerusalem, and bright angels, and the land of Canaan.

ST. C: I dare say; it's better than the opera, isn't it?

EVA: Yes; and he's going to teach them to me.

ST. C: Singing lessons, hey? You are coming on.

EVA: Yes, he sings for me, and I read to him in my Bible, and he explains what it means. Come, Tom. *(She takes his hand and they exit,* R.U.E*)*

ST. C: *(Aside)* Oh, Evangeline! Rightly named; hath not heaven made thee an evangel to me?

OPH: How shiftless! How can you let her?

ST. C: Why not?

OPH: Why, I don't know; it seems so dreadful.

ST. C: You would think no harm in a child's caressing a large dog even if he was black; but a crea-ture that can think, reason and feel, and is immortal, you shudder at. Confess it, cousin. I know the feeling among some of you Northerners well enough. Not that there is a particle of virtue in our not having it, but custom with us does what Christianity ought to do: obliterates the feeling of personal prejudice. You loathe them as you would a snake or a toad, yet you are indignant at their wrongs. You would not have them abused but you don't want to have anything to do with them yourselves. Isn't that it?

OPH: Well, cousin, there may be some truth in this.

ST. C: What would the poor and lowly do without children? Your little child is your only true democrat. Tom, now, is a hero to Eva; his stories are wonders in her eyes; his songs and Methodist hymns are better than an opera, and the traps and little bits of trash in his pockets a mine of jewels, and he the most wonderful Tom that ever wore a black skin. This is one of the roses of Eden that the Lord has dropped down expressly for the poor and lowly, who get few enough of any other kind.

OPH: It's strange, cousin; one might almost think you was a *professor*, to hear you talk.

ST. C.: A professor?

OPH: Yes, a professor of religion.

ST. C: Not at all; not a professor as you town folks have it, and, what is worse, I'm afraid, not a *practicer*, either.

OPH: What makes you talk so, then?

ST. C: Nothing is easier than talking. My forte lies in talking, and yours, cousin, lies in doing. And speaking of that puts me in mind that I have made a purchase for your department. There's the article now. Here, Topsy! *(Whistles)*

(TOPSY *runs on,* L.U.E., *down* C.)

OPH: Good gracious! what a heathenish, shiftless looking object! St. Clare, what in the world have you brought that thing here for?

ST. C: For you to educate, to be sure, and train in the way she should go. I thought she was rather a funny specimen in the Jim Crow line. Here,

Topsy, give us a song, and show us some of your dancing. (TOPSY *sings a verse and dances a breakdown*)

OPH: *(Paralyzed)* Well, of all things! If I ever saw the like!

ST. C: *(Smothering a laugh)* Topsy, this is your new mistress—I'm going to give you up to her. See now that you behave yourself.

TOP: Yes, mas'r.

ST. C: You're going to be good, Topsy, you understand?

TOP: Oh, yes, mas'r.

OPH: Now, St. Clare, what upon earth is this for? Your house is so full of these plagues now, that a body can't set down their foot without treading on 'em. I get up in the morning and find one asleep behind the door, and see one black head poking out from under the table—one lying on the door mat, and they are moping and mowing and grinning between all the railings, and tumbling over the kitchen floor! What on earth did you want to bring this one for?

ST. C: For you to educate—didn't I tell you? You're always preaching about educating, I thought I would make you a present of a fresh caught specimen, and let you try your hand on her and bring her up in the way she should go.

OPH: I don't want her, I am sure; I have more to do with 'em now than I want to.

ST. C: That's you Christians, all over. You'll get up a society, and get some poor missionary to spend all his days among just such heathen; but let me see one of you that would take one into your house with you, and take the labor of their conversion upon yourselves.

OPH: Well, I didn't think of in that light. It might be a real missionary work. Well, I'll do what I can. *(Advances to* TOPSY*)* She's dreadful dirty and shiftless! How old are you, Topsy?

TOP: Dunno, missis.

OPH: How shiftless! Don't know how old you are? Didn't anybody ever tell you? Who was your mother?

TOP: *(Grinning)* Never had none.

OPH: Never had any mother? What do you mean? Where was you born?

TOP: Never was born.

OPH: You musn't answer me in that way. I'm not playing with you. Tell me where you was born, and who your father and mother were?

TOP: Never was born, tell you; never had no father, nor mother, nor nothin'. I war raised by a speculator, with lots of others. Old Aunt Sue used to take car on us.

ST. C: She speaks the truth, cousin. Speculators buy them up cheap, when they are little, and get them raised for the market.

OPH: How long have you lived with your master and mistress?

TOP: Dunno, missis.

OPH: How shiftless! Is it a year, or more, or less?

TOP: Dunno, missis.

ST. C: She does not know what a year is; she don't even know her own age.

OPH: Have you ever heard anything about heaven, Topsy? *(*TOPSY *looks bewildered and grins)* Do you know who made you?

TOP: Nobody, as I knows on, he, he, he! I spect I growed. Don't think nobody never made me.

OPH: The shiftless heathen! What can you do? What did you do for your master and mistress?

TOP: Fetch water—and wash dishes—and rub knives—and wait on folks—and dance breakdowns.

OPH: I shall break down, I'm afraid, in trying to make anything of you, you shiftless mortal!

ST. C: You find virgin soil there, cousin; put in your own ideas—you won't find many to pull up. *(Exit, laughing* R. 1 E.*)*

OPH: *(Takes out her handkerchief. A pair of gloves falls.* TOPSY *picks them up slyly and puts them in her sleeve.)* Follow me, you benighted innocent!

TOP: Yes, missis.

(As OPHELIA *turns her back to her, she seizes the end of the ribbon she wears around her waist, and twitches it off.* OPHELIA *turns and sees her as she is putting it in her other sleeve.* OPHELIA *takes ribbon from her.)*

OPH: What's this? You naughty, wicked girl, you've been stealing this?

TOP: Laws! why, that ar's missis' ribbon, a'nt it? How could it got caught in my sleeve?

OPH: Topsy, you naughty girl, don't you tell me a lie—you stole that ribbon!

TOP: Missis, I declare for't, I didn't—never seed it till dis yer blessed minnit.

OPH: Topsy, don't you know it's wicked to tell lies?

TOP: I never tells no lies, missis; it's just de truth I've been telling now and nothing else.

OPH: Topsy, I shall have to whip you, if you tell lies so.

TOP: Laws missis, if you's to whip all day, couldn't say no other way. I never seed dat ar—it must a got caught in my sleeve. *(Blubbers)*

OPH: *(Seizes her by the shoulders)* Don't you tell me that again, you barefaced fibber! *(Shakes her. The gloves fall on Stage.)* There you, my gloves too—you outrageous young heathen! *(Picks them up)* Will you tell me, now, you didn't steal the ribbon?

TOP: No, missis; stole de gloves, but didn't steal de ribbon. It was permiskus.

OPH: Why, you young reprobate!

TOP: Yes—I's know I's wicked!

OPH: Then you know you ought to be punished. *(Boxes her ears)* What do you think of that?

TOP: He, he, he! De Lord, missis; dat wouldn't kill a 'skeeter. *(Runs off laughing,* R.U.E.—OPHELIA *follows indignantly,* R.U.E.*)*

SCENE III

The tavern by the river. Table and chairs. Jug and glasses on table. On flat is a printed placard, headed: "Four Hundred Dollars Reward—Runaway—George Harris!" PHINEAS *is discovered, seated at table.*

PHIN: So yer I am; and pretty business I've undertook to do. Find the husband of the gal that crossed the river on the ice two or three days ago. Ruth said I must do it, and I'll be teetotally chawed up if I don't do it. I see they've offered a reward for him, dead or alive. How in creation am I to find the varmint? He isn't likely to go round looking natural, with a full description of his hide and figure staring him in the face. *(Enter* MR. WILSON, L. 1 E.*)* I say, stranger, how are ye? *(Rises and comes forward,* R.*)*

WIL: Well, I reckon.

PHIN: Any news? *(Takes out plug and knife)*

WIL: Not that I know of.

PHIN: *(Cutting a piece of tobacco and offering it)* Chaw?

WIL: No, thank ye—it don't agree with me.

PHIN: Don't eh? *(Putting it in his own mouth)* I never felt any the worse for it.

WIL: *(Sees placard)* What's that?

PHIN: Nigger advertised. *(Advances towards it and spits on it.)* There's my mind upon that.

WIL: Why, now, stranger, what's that for?

PHIN: I'd do it all the same to the writer of that ar paper, if he was here. Any man that owns a boy like that, and can't find any better way of treating him, than branding him on the hand with the letter H, as that paper states, *deserves* to lose him. Such papers as this ar' a shame to old Kaintuck! that's my mind right out, if anybody wants to know.

WIL: Well, now, that's a fact.

PHIN: I used to have a gang of boys, sir—that was before I fell in love—and I just told em:—"Boys," says I, "run now! Dig! put! jest when you want to. I never shall come to look after you!" That's the way I kept mine. Let 'em know they are free to run any time, and it jest stops their wanting to. It stands to reason it should. Treat 'em like men, and you'll have men's work.

WIL: I think you are altogether right, friend, and this man described here is a fine fellow—no mistake about that. He worked for me some half dozen years in my bagging factory, and he was my best hand, sir. He is an ingenious fellow, too; he invented a machine for the cleaning of hemp—a really valuable affair; it's gone into use in several factories. His master holds the patent of it.

PHIN: I'll warrant ye; holds it, and makes money out of it, and then turns round and brands the boy in his right hand! If I had a fair chance, I'd mark him, I reckon, so that he'd carry it *one* while!

(Enter GEORGE HARRIS, *disguised,* L. 1 E.*)*

GEO: *(Speaking as he enters)* Jim, see to the trunks. *(Sees* WILSON.*)* Ah! Mr. Wilson here?

WIL: Bless my soul, can it be?

GEO: *(Advances and grasps his hand)* Mr. Wilson, I see you remember me, Mr. Butler, of Oaklands. Shelby county.

WIL: Ye—yes—yes—sir.

PHIN: Holloa! there's a screw loose here somewhere. That old gentleman seems to be struck into a pretty considerable heap of astonishment. May I be teetotally chawed up! if I don't believe that's the identical man I'm arter. *(Crosses to* GEORGE*) How are ye, George Harris?*

GEO: *(Starting back and thrusting his hands into his breast)* You know me?

PHIN: Ha, ha, ha! I rather conclude I do; but don't get riled, I an't a bloodhound in disguise.

GEO: How did you discover me?

PHIN: By a teetotal smart guess. You're the very man I want to see. Do you know I was sent after you?

GEO: Ah! by my master?

PHIN: No; by your wife.

GEO: My wife! Where is she?

PHIN: She's stopping with a Quaker family over on the Ohio side.

GEO: Then she is safe?

PHIN: Teetotally!

GEO: Conduct me to her.

PHIN: Just wait a brace of shakes and I'll do it. I've got to go and get the boat ready. 'Twon't take me but a minute—make yourself comfortable till I get back. Chaw me up! but this is what I call doing things in short order. *(Exit* L. 1 E.*)*

WIL: George!

GEO: Yes, George!

WIL: I couldn't have thought it!

GEO: I am pretty well disguised, I fancy; you see I don't answer to the advertisement at all.

WIL: George, this is a dangerous game you are playing; I could not have advised you to it.

GEO: I can do it on my own responsibility.

WIL: Well, George, I suppose you're running away—leaving your lawful master, George, (I don't wonder at it) at the same time, I'm sorry, George, yes, decidedly. I think I must say that it's my duty to tell you so.

GEO: Why are you sorry, sir?

WIL: Why to see you, as it were, setting yourself in opposition to the laws of your country.

GEO: *My* country! What country have *I,* but the grave? And I would to heaven that I was laid there!

WIL: George, you've got a hard master, in fact he is—well, he conducts himself reprehensibly—I can't pretend to defend him. I'm sorry for you, now; it's a bad case—very bad; but we must all submit to the indications of providence. George, don't you see?

GEO: I wonder, Mr. Wilson, if the Indians should come and take you a prisoner away from your wife and children, and want to keep you all your life hoeing corn for them, if you'd think it your duty to abide in the condition in which you were called? I rather imagine that you'd think the first stray horse you could find an indication of providence, shouldn't you?

WIL: Really, George, putting the case in that somewhat peculiar light—I don't know—under those circumstances—but what I might. But it seems to me you are running an awful risk. You can't hope to carry it out. If you're taken it will be worse with you than ever; they'll only abuse you, and half kill you, and sell you down river.

GEO: Mr. Wilson, I know all this. I *do* run a risk, but—*(Throws open coat and shows pistols and knife in his belt.)* There! I'm ready for them. Down South I never *will* go! no, if it comes to that, I can earn myself at least six feet of free soil—the first and last I shall ever own in Kentucky!

WIL: Why, George, this state of mind is awful—it's getting really desperate. I'm concerned. Going to break the laws of your country?

GEO: My country again! Sir, I haven't any country any more than I have any father. I don't want anything of *your* country, except to be left alone—to go peaceably out of it; but if any man tries to stop me, let him take care, for I am desperate. I'll fight for my liberty, to the last breath I breathe! You say your fathers did it, if it was right for them, it is right for me!

WIL: *(Walking up and down and fanning his face with a large yellow silk handkerchief)* Blast 'em all! Haven't I always said so—the infernal old cusses! Bless me! I hope I an't swearing now! Well, go ahead, George, go ahead. But be careful, my boy; don't shoot anybody, unless—well, you'd *better* not shoot—at least I wouldn't *hit* anybody, you know.

GEO: Only in self-defense.

WIL: Well, well. *(Fumbling in his pocket)* I suppose, perhaps, I an't following my judgement— hang it, I won't follow my judgement. So here, George. *(Takes out a pocket-book and offers* GEORGE *a roll of bills)*

GEO: No, my kind, good sir, you've done a great deal for me, and this might get you into trouble. I have money enough, I hope, to take me as far as I need it.

WIL: No; but you must, George. Money is a great help everywhere, can't have too much, if you get it honestly. Take it, *do take it*, *now* do, my boy!

GEO: *(Taking the money)* On condition, sir, that I may repay it at some future time, I will.

WIL: And now, George, how long are you going to travel in this way? Not long or far I hope? It's well carried on, but too bold.

GEO: Mr. Wilson, it is *so bold*, and this tavern is so near, that they will never think of it; they will look for me on ahead, and you yourself wouldn't know me.

WIL: But the mark on your hand?

GEO: *(Draws off his glove and shows scar)* That is a parting mark of Mr. Harris' regard. Looks interesting, doesn't it? *(Puts on glove again)*

WIL: I declare, my very blood runs cold when I think of it—your condition and your risks!

GEO: Mine has run cold a good many years; at present, it's about up to the boiling point.

WIL: George, something has brought you out wonderfully. You hold up your head, and move and speak like another man.

GEO: *(Proudly)* Because I'm a *freeman!* Yes, sir; I've said "master" for the last time to any man. *I'm free!*

WIL: Take care! You are not sure; you may be taken.

GEO: All men are free and equal *in the grave*, if it comes to that, Mr. Wilson.

(Enter PHINEAS, L. 1 E.)

PHIN: Them's my sentiment, to a teetotal atom, and I don't care who knows it! Neighbor, the boat is ready, and the sooner we make tracks the better. I've seen some mysterious strangers lurking about these diggings, so we'd better put.

GEO: Farewell, Mr. Wilson, and heaven reward you for the many kindnesses you have shown the poor fugitive!

WIL: *(Grasping his hand)* You're a brave fellow, George. I wish in my heart you were safe through, though—that's what I do.

PHIN: And ain't I the man of all creation to put him through, stranger? Chaw me up if I don't take him to his dear little wife, in the smallest possible quantity of time. Come, neighbor, let's vamose.

GEO: Farewell, Mr. Wilson. *(Crosses to L.H.)*

WIL: My best wishes go with you, George. *(Exit, R. 1 E.)*

PHIN: You're a trump, old Slow-and-Easy.

GEO: *(Looking off, R.H.)* Look! look!

PHIN: Consarn their picters, here they come! We can't get out of the house without their seeing us. We're teetotally treed!

GEO: Let us fight our way through them!

PHIN: No, that won't do; there are too many of them for a fair fight—we should be chawed up in no time. *(Looks round and sees trap door, C.)* Holloa! here's a cellar door. Just you step down here a few minutes, while I parley with them. *(Lifts trap)*

GEO: I am resolved to perish sooner than surrender! *(Goes down trap)*

PHIN: That's your sort! *(Closes trap and stands on it)* Here they are!

(Enter HALEY, MARKS, LOKER and three MEN, L. 1 E.)

HAL: Say, stranger, you haven't seen a runaway darkey about these parts, eh?

PHIN: What kind of a darkey?

HAL: A mulatto chap, almost as light-complexioned as a white man.

PHIN: Was he a pretty good-looking chap?

HAL: Yes.

PHIN: Kind of tall?

HAL: Yes.

PHIN: With brown hair?

HAL: Yes.

PHIN: And dark eyes?

HAL: Yes.

PHIN: Pretty well dressed?

HAL: Yes.

PHIN: Scar on his right hand?

HAL: Yes, yes.

PHIN: Well, I ain't seen him.

HAL: Oh, bother! Come, boys, let's search the house. *(Exeunt, R. 1 E.)*

PHIN: *(Raises trap)* Now, then, neighbor George. (GEORGE *enters, up trap)* Now's the time to cut your lucky.

GEO: Follow me, Phineas. *(Exit, L. 1 E.)*

PHIN. In a brace of shakes. *(Is closing trap as* HALEY, MARKS, LOKER, *etc., re-enter, R. 1 E.)*

HAL: Ah! he's down in the cellar. Follow me,

boys! *(Thrusts* PHINEAS *aside, and rushes down trap, followed by the others.* PHINEAS *closes trap and stands on it.)*

PHIN: Chaw me up! but I've got 'em all in a trap. *(Knocking below)* Be quiet, you pesky varmints! *(Knocking)* They're getting mighty oneasy.

(Knocking) Will you be quiet, you savagerous critters! *(The trap is forced open.* HALEY *and* MARKS *appear.* PHINEAS *seizes a chair and stands over trap—picture)* Down with you or I'll smash you into apple-fritters! *(Tableau—closed in)*

SCENE IV

A plain chamber.

TOP: *(Without,* L.H.*)* You go 'long. No more nigger dan you be! *(Enters,* L.H.*, shouts and laughter without, looks off)* You seem to think yourself white folks. You ain't nerry one—black nor white. I'd like to be one or turrer. Law! you niggers, does you know you's all sinners? Well, you is—everybody is. White folks is sinners too—Miss Feely says so—but I 'spects niggers is the biggest ones. But Lor! ye ain't any on ye up to me. I's so awful wicked there can't nobody do nothin' with me. I used to keep old missis a-swarin' at me ha' de time. I 'spects I's de wickedest critter in de world. *(Song and dance introduced. Enter* EVA, L. 1 E.*)*

EVA: Oh, Topsy! Topsy! you have been very wrong again.

TOP: Well, I 'spects I have.

EVA: What makes you do so?

TOP: I dunno; I 'spects it's cause I's so wicked.

EVA: Why did you spoil Jane's earrings?

TOP: 'Cause she's so proud. She called me a little black imp, and turned up her pretty nose at me 'cause she is whiter than I am. I was gwine by her room, and I seed her coral earrings lying on de table, so I threw dem on de floor, and put my foot on 'em, and scrunches 'em all to little bits—he! he! he! I's so wicked.

EVA: Don't you know that was very wrong?

TOP: I don't car'! I despises dem what sets up for fine ladies, when dey ain't nothing but cream-colored niggers! Dere's Miss Rosa—she gives me lots of 'pertinent remarks. T'other night she was gwine to a ball. She put on a beau'ful dress dat missis give her—wid her har curled, all nice and pretty. She hab to go down de back stairs—dem am dark—and I puts a pail of hot water on dem, and she put her foot into it, and den she go tumbling to de bottom of de stairs—and de water go all ober her, and spile her dress, and scald her dreadful bad! He! he! he! I's so wicked!

EVA: Oh! how could you!

TOP: Don't dey despise me cause I don't know nothing? Don't dey laugh at me 'cause I'm brack, and dey ain't?

EVA: But you shouldn't mind them.

TOP: Well, I don't mind dem; but when dey are passing under my winder, I trows dirty water on 'em, and dat spiles der complexions.

EVA: What does make you so bad, Topsy? Why won't you try and be good? Don't you love anybody, Topsy?

TOP: Can't recommember.

EVA: But you love your father and mother?

TOP: Never had none, ye know, I told ye that, Miss Eva.

EVA: Oh! I know; but hadn't you any brother, or sister, or aunt, or—

TOP: No, none on 'em—never had nothing nor nobody. I's brack—no one loves me!

EVA: Oh! Topsy, I love you! *(Laying her hand on* TOPSY'S *shoulder.)* I love you because you haven't had any father, or mother, or friends. I love you, I want you to be good. I wish you would try to be good for my sake. *(*TOPSY *looks astonished for a moment, and then bursts into tears.)* Only think of it, Topsy—you can be one of those spirits bright Uncle Tom sings about!

TOP: Oh! dear Miss Eva—dear Miss Eva! I will try—I will try. I never did care nothin' about it before.

EVA: If you try, you will succeed. Come with me. *(Crosses to* R. *and takes* TOPSY'S *hand.)*

TOP: I will try; but den, I's so wicked! *(Exit* EVA R.H.*, followed by* TOPSY, *crying.)*

SCENE IV

Chamber. Enter GEORGE, ELIZA *and* HARRY, R. *1* E.

GEO: At length, Eliza, after many wanderings, we are united.

ELIZA: Thanks to these generous Quakers, who have so kindly sheltered us.

GEO: Not forgetting our friend Phineas.

ELIZA: I do indeed owe him much. 'Twas he I met upon the icy river's bank, after that fearful, but successful attempt, when I fled from the slave-trader with my child in my arms.

GEO: It seems almost incredible that you could have crossed the river on the ice.

ELIZA: Yes, I did. Heaven helping me, I crossed on the ice, for they were behind me—right behind—and there was no other way.

GEO: But the ice was all in broken-up blocks, swinging and heaving up and down in the water.

ELIZA: I know it was—I know it; I did not think I should get over, but I did not care—I could but die if I did not! I leaped on the ice, but how I got across I don't know; the first I remember, a man was helping me up the bank—that man was Phineas.

GEO: My brave girl! you .deserve your freedom—you have richly earned it!

ELIZA: And when we get to Canada I can help you to work, and between us we can find something to live on.

GEO: Yes, Eliza, so long as we have each other, and our boy. Oh, Eliza, if these people only knew what a blessing it is for a man to feel that his wife and child belong to *him!* I've often wondered to see men that could call their wives and children *their own,* fretting and worrying about anything else. Why, I feel rich and strong, though we have nothing but our bare hands. If they will only let me alone now, I will be satisfied—thankful!

ELIZA: But we are not quite out of danger; we are not yet in Canada.

GEO: True, but it seems as if I smelt the free air, and it makes me strong!

(Enter PHINEAS, *dressed as a Quaker,* L. *1* E.)

PHIN: *(With a snuffle)* Verily, friends, how is it with thee?—hum!

GEO: Why, Phineas, what means this metamorphosis?

PHIN: I've become a Quaker, that's the meaning on't.

GEO: What—you?

PHIN: Teetotally! I was driven to it by a strong argument, composed of a pair of sparkling eyes, rosy cheeks, and pouting lips. Them lips would persuade a man to assassinate his grandmother! *(Assumes the Quaker tone again)* Verily, George, I have discovered something of importance to the interests of thee and thy party, and it were well for thee to hear it.

GEO: Keep us not in suspense!

PHIN: Well, after I left you on the road, I stopped at a little, lone tavern, just below here. Well, I was tired with hard driving, and after my supper I stretched myself down on a pile of bags in the corner, and pulled a buffalo hide over me—and what does I do but get fast asleep.

GEO: With one ear open, Phineas?

PHIN: No, I slept ears and all for an hour or two, for I was pretty well tired; but when I came to myself a little, I found that there were some men in the room, sitting round a table, drinking and talking; and I thought, before I made much muster, I'd just see what they were up to, especially as I heard them say something about the Quakers. Then I listened with both ears and found they were talking about you. So I kept quiet, and heard them lay off all their plans. They've got a right notion of the track we are going to-night, and they'll be down after us, six or eight strong. So, now, what's to be done?

ELIZA: What *shall* we do, George?

GEO: I know what I shall do! *(Takes out pistols)*

PHIN: Ay—ay, thou seest, Eliza, how it will work—pistols—phitz—poppers!

ELIZA: I see; but I pray it come not to that!

GEO: I don't want to involve any one with or for me. If you will lend me your vehicle, and direct me, I will drive alone to the next stand.

PHIN: Ah! well, friend, but thee'll need a driver for all that. Thee's quite welcome to do all the fighting thee knows; but I know a thing or two about the road that thee doesn't.

GEO: But I don't want to involve you.

PHIN: Involve me! Why, chaw me — that is to say — when thee does involve me, please to let me know.

ELIZA: Phineas is a wise and skillful man. You will do well, George, to abide by his judgment. And, oh! George, be not hasty with these — young blood is hot! *(Laying her hand on pistols)*

GEO: I will attack no man. All I ask of this country is to be left alone, and I will go out peaceably. But I'll fight to the last breath before they shall take from me my wife and son! Can you blame me?

PHIN: Mortal man cannot blame thee, neighbor George! Flesh and blood could not do otherwise. Woe unto the world because of offenses, but woe unto them through whom the offense cometh! That's gospel, teetotally!

GEO: Would not even you, sir, do the same, in my place?

PHIN: I pray that I be not tried; the flesh is weak — but I think my flesh would be pretty tolerably strong in such a case; I ain't sure, friend George, that I shouldn't hold a fellow for thee, if thee had any accounts to settle with him.

ELIZA: Heaven grant we be not tempted.

PHIN: But if we are tempted too much, why, consarn 'em! let them look out, that's all.

GEO: It's quite plain you was not born for a Quaker. The old nature has its way in you pretty strong yet.

PHIN. Well, I reckon you are pretty teetotally right.

GEO. Had we not better hasten our flight?

PHIN: Well, I rather conclude we had; we're full two hours ahead of them, if they start at the time they planned; so let's vamose. *(Exeunt R. 1 E.)*

SCENE VI

A rocky pass in the hills. Large set rock and platform, L.U.E.

PHIN: *(Without,* R.U.E.*)* Out with you in a twinkling, every one, and up into these rocks with me! run *now,* if you *ever* did run! *(Music.* PHINEAS *enters, with* HARRY *in his arms.* GEORGE *supporting* ELIZA, R.U.E.*)* Come up here; this is one of our old hunting dens. Come up. *(They ascend the rock)* Well, here we are. Let 'em get us if they can. Whoever comes here has to walk single file between those two rocks, in fair range of your pistols — d'ye see?

GEO: I do see. And now, as this affair is mine, let me take all the risk, and do all the fighting.

PHIN: Thee's quite welcome to do the fighting, George; but I may have the fun of looking on, I suppose. But see, these fellows are kind of debating down there, and looking up, like hens when they are going to fly up onto the roost. Hadn't thee better give 'em a word of advice, before they come up, just to tell 'em handsomely they'll be shot if they do.

(LOKER, MARKS, and three MEN enter, R. 2 E.)

MARKS: Well, Tom, your coons are fairly treed.

LOKER: Yes, I see 'em go up right here; and here's a path — I'm for going right up. They can't jump down in a hurry, and it won't take long to ferret 'em out.

MARKS: But, Tom, they might fire at us from behind the rocks. That would be ugly, you know.

LOKER: Ugh! always for saving your skin, Marks. No danger, niggers are too plaguy scared!

MARKS: I don't know why I shouldn't save my skin, it's the best I've got; and niggers do fight like the devil sometimes.

GEO: *(Rising on the rock)* Gentlemen, who are you down there and what do you want?

LOKER: We want a party of runaway niggers. One George and Eliza Harris, and their son. We've got the officers here, and a warrant to take 'em too. D'ye hear? An't you George Harris, that belonged to Mr. Harris, of Shelby county, Kentucky?

GEO: I am George Harris. A Mr. Harris, of Kentucky, did call me his property. But now I'm a freeman, standing on heaven's free soil! My wife and child I claim as mine. We have arms to defend ourselves and we mean to do it. You can come up if you like, but the first one that comes within range of our bullets is a dead man!

MARKS: Oh, come—come, young man, this ar no kind of talk at all for you. You see we're officers of justice. We've got the law on our side, and the power and so forth; so you'd better give up peaceably, you see—for you'll certainly have to give up at last.

GEO: I know very well that you've got the law on your side, and the power; but you haven't got us. We are standing here as free as you are, and by the great power that made us, we'll fight for our liberty till we die! *(During this,* MARKS *draws a pistol, and when he concludes fires at him.* ELIZA *screams.)* It's nothing, Eliza; I am unhurt.

PHIN: *(Drawing* GEORGE *down)* Thee'd better keep out of sight with thy speechifying; they're teetotal mean scamps.

LOKER: What did you do that for, Marks?

MARKS: You see, you get jist as much for him dead as alive in Kentucky.

GEO: Now, Phineas, the first man that advances I fire at; you take the second and so on. It won't do to waste two shots on one.

PHIN: But what if you don't hit?

GEO: I'll try my best.

PHIN: Creation! chaw me up if there a'nt stuff in you!

MARKS: I think I must have hit some on'em. I heard a squeal.

LOKER. I'm going right up for one. I never was afraid of niggers, and I an't a going to be now. Who goes after me?

(Music. LOKER *dashes up the rock.* GEORGE *fires. He staggers for a moment, then springs to the top.* PHINEAS *seizes him. A struggle.)*

PHIN: Friend, thee is not wanted here! *(Throws* LOKER *over the rock)*

MARKS: *(Retreating)* Lord help us—they're perfect devils!

(Music. MARKS *and* PARTY *run off* R. 2 E. GEORGE *and* ELIZA *kneel in an attitude of thanksgiving, with the* CHILD *between them.* PHINEAS *stands over them exulting. Tableau.)*

END OF ACT TWO

ACT III

SCENE I

Chamber. Enter ST. CLARE, *followed by* TOM, R. 1 E.

ST. C: *(Giving money and papers to* TOM*)* There, Tom, are the bills, and the money to liquidate them.

TOM: Yes, mas'r.

ST. C: Well, Tom, what are you waiting for? Isn't all right there?

TOM: I'm 'fraid not, mas'r.

ST. C: Why, Tom, what's the matter? You look as solemn as a judge.

TOM: I feel very bad, mas'r. I allays have thought that mas'r would be good to everybody.

ST. C: Well, Tom, haven't I been? Come, now, what do you want? There's something you haven't got, I suppose, and this is the preface.

TOM: Mas'r allays been good to me. I haven't nothing to complain of on that head; but there is one that mas'r isn't good to.

ST. C: Why, Tom, what's got into you? Speak out—what do you mean?

TOM: Last night, between one and two, I thought so. I studied upon the matter then—mas'r isn't good to *himself.*

ST. C: Ah! now I understand; you allude to the state in which I came home last night. Well, to tell the truth, I *was* slightly elevated—a little more champagne on board than I could comfortably carry. That's all, isn't it?

TOM: *(Deeply affected—clasping his hands and weeping)* All! Oh! my dear young mas'r, I'm 'fraid it will be *loss of all—all,* body and soul. The good book says "it biteth like a serpent and stingeth like an adder," my dear mas'r.

ST. C: You poor, silly fool! I'm not worth crying over.

TOM: Oh, mas'r! I implore you to think of it before it gets too late.

ST. C: Well, I won't go to any more of their cursed nonsense, Tom—on my honor, I won't. I don't know why I haven't stopped long ago; I've always despised *it*, and myself for it. So now, Tom, wipe up your eyes and go about your errands.

TOM: Bless you, mas'r. I feel much better now. You have taken a load from poor Tom's heart. Bless you!

ST. C: Come, come, no blessings; I'm not so wonderfully good, now. There, I'll pledge my honor to you, Tom, you don't see me so again. *(Exit* TOM, R. *1* E.*)* I'll keep my faith with him, too.

OPH: *(Without,* L. *1* E.*)* Come along, you shiftless mortal!

ST. C: What new witchcraft has Topsy been brewing? That commotion is of her raising, I'll be bound.

(Enter OPHELIA, *dragging in* TOPSY, L. *1* E.*)*

OPH: Come here now; I will tell your master.

ST. C: What's the matter now?

OPH: The matter is that I cannot be plagued with this girl any longer. It's past all bearing; flesh and blood cannot endure it. Here I locked her up and gave her a hymn to study; and what does she do but spy out where I put my key, and has gone to my bureau, and got a bonnet-trimming and cut it all to pieces to make dolls' jackets! I never saw anything like it in my life!

ST. C: What have you done to her?

OPH: What have I done? What haven't I done? Your wife says I ought to have her whipped till she couldn't stand.

ST. C: I don't doubt it. Tell me of the lovely rule of woman. I never saw above a dozen women that wouldn't half kill a horse or servant, either, if they had their own way with them—let alone a man.

OPH: I am sure, St. Clare, I don't know what to do. I've taught and taught—I've talked till I'm tired; I've whipped her, I've punished her in every way I could think of, and still she's just what she was at first.

ST. C: Come here, Tops, you monkey! *(*TOPSY *crosses to* ST. CLARE, *grinning)* What makes you behave so?

TOP: 'Spects it's my wicked heart—Miss Feely says so.

ST. C: Don't you see how much Miss Ophelia has done for you? She says she has done everything she can think of.

TOP: Lord, yes, mas'r! old missis used to say so, too. She whipped me a heap harder, and used to pull my ha'r, and knock my head agin the door; but it didn't do me no good. I 'spects if they's to pull every spear of ha'r out o' my head, it wouldn't do no good neither—I's so wicked! Laws! I's nothin' but a nigger, no ways! *(Goes up)*

OPH: Well, I shall have to give her up; I can't have that trouble any longer.

ST. C: I'd like to ask you one question.

OPH: What is it?

ST. C: Why, if your doctrine is not strong enough to save one heathen child, that you can have at home here, all to yourself, what's the use of sending one or two poor missionaries off with it among thousands of just such? I suppose this girl is a fair sample of what thousands of your heathen are.

OPH: I'm sure I don't know; I never saw such a girl as this.

ST. C: What makes you so bad, Tops? Why won't you try and be good? Don't you love any one, Topsy?

TOP: *(Comes down,* C.*)* Dunno nothing 'bout love; I loves candy and sich, that's all.

OPH: But, Topsy, if you'd only try to be good, you might.

TOP: Couldn't never be nothing but a nigger, if I was ever so good. If I could be skinned and come white, I'd try then.

ST. C: People can love you, if you are black, Topsy. Miss Ophelia would love you, if you were good. *(*TOPSY *laughs)* Don't you think so?

TOP: No, she can't b'ar me, 'cause I'm a nigger—she'd's soon have a toad touch her. There can't nobody love niggers, and niggers can't do nothin'! I don't car'! *(Whistles)*

ST. C: Silence, you incorrigible imp, and begone!

TOP: He! he! he! didn't get much out of dis chile! *(Exit,* L. *1* E.*)*

OPH: I've always had a prejudice against negroes, and it's a fact—I never could bear to have that child touch me, but I didn't think she knew it.

ST. C: Trust any child to find that out, there's no keeping it from them. But I believe all the trying in the world to benefit a child, and all the substantial favors you can do them, will never excite one emotion of gratitude, while that feeling of repugnance remains in the heart. It's a queer kind of a fact, but so it is.

OPH: I don't know how I can help it—they are disagreeable to me, this girl in particular. How can I help feeling so?

ST. C: Eva does, it seems.

OPH: Well, she's so loving. I wish I was like her. She might teach me a lesson.

ST. C: It would not be the first time a little child had been used to instruct an old disciple, if it were so. (Crosses to L.) Come, let us seek Eva, in her favorite bower by the lake.

OPH: Why the dew is falling, she mustn't be out there. She is unwell, I know.

ST. C: Don't be croaking, cousin—I hate it.

OPH: But she has that cough.

ST. C: Oh, nonsense, of that cough—it is not anything. She has taken a little cold, perhaps.

OPH: Well, that was just the way Eliza Jane was taken—and Ellen—

ST. C: Oh, stop these hobgoblin, nurse legends. You old hands get so wise, that a child cannot cough or sneeze, but you see desperation and ruin at hand. Only take care of the child, keep her from the night air, and don't let her play too hard, and she'll do well enough. (Exeunt L. 1 E.)

SCENE II

The flat represents the lake. The rays of the setting sun tinge the waters with gold. A large tree R. 3 E. *Beneath this a grassy bank, on which Eva (*L.*) and* TOM (*R.*) *are seated side by side.* EVA *has a Bible open on her lap. Music.*

TOM: Read dat passage again, please, Miss Eva?

EVA: (Reading) "And I saw a sea of glass, mingled with fire." (Stopping suddenly and pointing to lake) Tom, there it is!

TOM: What, Miss Eva?

EVA: Don't you see there? There's a "sea of glass mingled with fire."

TOM: True enough, Miss Eva. (Sings)

> Oh, had I the wings of the morning,
> I'd fly away to Canaan's shore;
> Bright angels should convey me home,
> To the New Jerusalem.

EVA: Where do you suppose New Jerusalem is, Uncle Tom?

TOM: Oh, up in the clouds, Miss Eva.

EVA: Then I think I see it. Look in those clouds, they look like great gates of pearl; and you can see beyond them—far, far off—it's all gold! Tom, sing about 'spirits bright.'

TOM: (Sings)

> I see a band of spirits bright,
> That taste the glories there;
> They are all robed in spotless white,
> And conquering palms they bear.

EVA: Uncle Tom, I've seen *them*.

TOM: To be sure you have; you are one of them yourself. You are the brightest spirit I ever saw.

EVA: They come to me sometimes in my sleep—those spirits bright—

> They are all robed in spotless white,
> And conquering palms they bear.

Uncle Tom, I'm going there.

TOM: Where, Miss Eva?

EVA: (Pointing to the sky) I'm going *there*, to the spirits bright, Tom; I'm going before long.

TOM: It's jest no use tryin' to keep Miss Eva here; I've allays said so. She's got the Lord's mark in her forehead. She wasn't never like a child that's to live—there was always something deep in her eyes. (Rises and comes forward R. EVA also comes forward C., leaving Bible on bank.)

(Enter ST. CLARE, L. 1 E.)

ST. C: Ah! my little pussy, you look as blooming as a rose! You are better now-a-days, are you not?

EVA: Papa, I've had things I wanted to say to you a great while. I want to say them now, before I get weaker.

ST. C: Nay, this is an idle fear, Eva; you know you grow stronger every day.

EVA: It's all no use, papa, to keep it to myself any longer. The time is coming that I am going to leave you, I am going, and never to come back.

ST. C: Oh, now, my dear little Eva! you've got nervous and low spirited; you mustn't indulge such gloomy thoughts.

EVA: No, papa, don't deceive yourself, I am *not* any better; I know it perfectly well, and I am going before long. I am not nervous—I am not low spirited. If it were not for you, papa, and my friends, I should be perfectly happy. I want to go — I long to go!

ST. C: Why, dear child, what has made your poor little heart so sad? You have everything to make you happy that could be given you.

EVA: I had rather be in heaven! There are a great many things here that makes me sad — that seem dreadful to me; I had rather be there; but I don't want to leave you — it almost breaks my heart!

ST. C: What makes you sad, and what seems dreadful, Eva?

EVA: I feel sad for our poor people; they love me dearly, and they are all good and kind to me. I wish, papa, they were all *free!*

ST. C: Why, Eva, child, don't you think they are well enough off now?

EVA: *(Not heeding the question)* Papa, isn't there a way to have slaves made free? When I am dead, papa, then you will think of me and do it for my sake?

ST. C: When you are dead, Eva? Oh, child, don't talk to me so. You are all I have on earth!

EVA: Papa, these poor creatures love their children as much as you do me. Tom loves his children. Oh, do something for them!

ST. C: There, there darling; only don't distress yourself, and don't talk of dying, and I will do anything you wish.

EVA: And promise me, dear father, that Tom shall have his freedom as soon as — *(Hesitating)* — I am gone!

ST. C: Yes, dear, I will do anything in the world — anything you could ask me to. There, Tom, take her to her chamber, this evening air is too chill for her. *(Music. Kisses her.* TOM *takes* EVA *in his arms, and exit* R.U.E. *Gazing mournfully after* EVA.*)* Has there ever been a child like Eva? Yes, there has been; but their names are always on grave-stones, and their sweet smiles, their heavenly eyes, their singular words and ways, are among the buried treasures of yearning hearts. It is as if heaven had an especial band of angels, whose office it is to sojourn for a season here, and endear to them the wayward human heart, that they might bear it upward with them in their homeward flight. When you see that deep, spiritual light in the eye when the little soul reveals itself in words sweeter and wiser than the ordinary words of children, hope not to retain that child; for the seal of heaven is on it, and the light of immortality looks out from its eyes! *(Music. Exit* R.U.E.*)*

SCENE III

A corridor. Proscenium doors on. Music. Enter TOM, L. 1 E., *he listens at* R. *door and then lies down. Enter* OPHELIA, L. 1 E., *with candle.*

OPH: Uncle Tom, what alive have you taken to sleeping anywhere and everywhere, like a dog, for? I thought you were one of the orderly sort, that liked to lie in bed in a Chrisitan way.

TOM: *(Rises. Mysteriously.)* I do, Miss Feely, I do, but now —

OPH: Well, what now?

TOM: We mustn't speak loud; Mas'r St. Clare won't hear on't; but Miss Feely, you know there must be somebody watchin' for the bridegroom.

OPH: What do you mean, Tom?

TOM: You know it says in Scripture, "At midnight there was a great cry made, behold, the bridegroom cometh!" That's what I'm spectin' now, every night, Miss Feely, and I couldn't sleep out of hearing, noways.

OPH: Why, Uncle Tom, what makes you think so?

TOM: Miss Eva, she talks to me. The Lord, he sends his messenger in the soul. I must be thar, Miss Feely; for when that ar blessed child goes into the kingdom, they'll open the door so wide, we'll all get a look in at the glory!

OPH: Uncle Tom, did Miss Eva say she felt more unwell than usual to-night?

TOM: No; but she telled me she was coming nearer — thar's them that tells it to the child, Miss Feely. It's the angels — it's the trumpet sound afore the break o' day!

OPH: Heaven grant your fears be vain! *(Crosses to* R.*)* Come in, Tom. *(Exeunt* R. 1 E.*)*

SCENE IV

EVA'S *Chamber.* EVA *discovered on a couch. A table stands near the couch with a lamp on it. The light shines upon* EVA'S *face, which is very pale. Scene half dark.* UNCLE TOM *is kneeling near the foot of the couch,* L.H. OPHELIA *stands at the head,* R.H. ST. CLARE *at back. Scene opens to plaintive music. After a strain enter* MARIE, *hastily,* L. 1 E.

MARIE: St. Clare! Cousin! Oh! what is the matter now?

ST. C: (*Hoarsely*) Hush! she is dying!

MARIE: (*Sinking on her knees, beside* TOM) Dying!

ST. C: Oh! if she would only wake and speak once more. (*Bending over* EVA) Eva, darling! (EVA *uncloses her eyes, smiles, raises her head and tries to speak.*) Do you know me, Eva?

EVA: (*Throwing her arms feebly about his neck*) Dear papa. (*Her arms drop and she sinks back*)

ST. C: Oh heaven! this is dreadful! Oh! Tom, my boy, it is killing me!

TOM: Look at her, mas'r. (*Points to* EVA)

ST. C: Eva! (*A pause*) She does not hear. Oh Eva! tell us what you see. What is it?

EVA: (*Feebly smiling*) Oh! love! joy! peace! (*Dies*)

TOM: Oh! bless the Lord! it's over, dear mas'r, it's over.

ST. C: (*Sinking on his knees*) Farewell, beloved child! the bright eternal doors have closed after thee. We shall see thy sweet face no more. Oh! wo for them who watched thy entrance into heaven when they shall wake and find only the cold, gray sky of daily life and thou gone forever. (*Solemn music, slow curtain.*)

END OF ACT THREE

ACT IV

SCENE I

A street in New Orleans. Enter GUMPTION CUTE R., *meeting* MARKS L.H.

CUTE: How do ye dew?

MARKS: How are you?

CUTE: Well, now, squire, it's a fact that I am dead broke and busted up.

MARKS: You have been speculating, I suppose!

CUTE: That's just it and nothing shorter.

MARKS: You have had poor success, you say?

CUTE: Tarnation bad, now I tell you. You see I came to this part of the country to make my fortune.

MARKS: And you did not do it?

CUTE: Scarcely. The first thing I tried my hand at was keeping school. I opened an academy for the instruction of youth in the various branches of orthography, geography, and other graphies.

MARKS: Did you succeed in getting any pupils?

CUTE: Oh, lots of 'em! and a pretty set of dunces they were too. After the first quarter, I called on the respectable parents of the juveniles, and requested them to fork over. To which they politely answered—don't you wish you may get it?

MARKS: What did you do then?

CUTE: Well, I kind of pulled up stakes and left those diggins. Well then I went into Spiritual Rappings for a living. That paid pretty well for a short time, till I met with an accident.

MARKS: An accident?

CUTE: Yes; a tall Yahoo called on me one day, and wanted me to summon the spirit of his mother—which, of course, I did. He asked me about a dozen questions which I answered to his satisfaction. At last he wanted to know what she died of— I said, Cholera. You never did see a critter so riled as he was. 'Look yere, stranger,' said he, 'it's my opinion that you're a pesky humbug! for my mother was blown up in a *Steamboat!*' with that he left the premises. The next day the people furnished me with a conveyance, and I rode out of town.

MARKS: Rode out of town?

CUTE: Yes; on a rail!

MARKS: I suppose you gave up the spirits, after that?

CUTE: Well, I reckon I did; it had such an effect on my spirits.

MARKS: It's a wonder they didn't tar and feather you.

CUTE: There was some mention made of that, but when they said *feathers*, I felt as if I had wings and flew away.

MARKS: You cut and run?

CUTE: Yes; I didn't like their company and I cut it. Well, after that I let myself out as an overseer on a cotton plantation. I made a pretty good thing of that, though it was dreadful trying to my feelings to flog the darkies; but I got used to it after a while, and then I used to lather 'em like Jehu. Well, the proprietor got the fever and ague and shook himself out of town. The place and all the fixings were sold at auction and I found myself adrift once more.

MARKS: What are you doing at present?

CUTE: I'm in search of a rich relation of mine.

MARKS: A rich relation?

CUTE: Yes, a Miss Ophelia St. Clare. You see, a niece of hers married one of my second cousins— that's how I came to be a relation of hers. She came on here from Vermont to be housekeeper to a cousin of hers, of the same name.

MARKS: I know him well.

CUTE: The deuce you do!—well, that's lucky.

MARKS: Yes, he lives in this city.

CUTE: Say, you just point out the locality, and I'll give him a call.

MARKS: Stop a bit. Suppose you shouldn't be able to raise the wind in that quarter, what have you thought of doing?

CUTE: Well, nothing particular.

MARKS: How should you like to enter into a nice, profitable business—one that pays well?

CUTE: That's just about my measure—it would suit me to a hair. What is it?

MARKS: Nigger catching.

CUTE: Catching niggers! What on airth do you mean?

MARKS: Why, when there's a large reward offered for a runaway darkey, we goes after him, catches him, and gets the reward.

CUTE: Yes, that's all right so far—but s'pose there ain't no reward offered?

MARKS: Why, then we catches the darkey on our own account, sells him, and pockets the proceeds.

CUTE: By chowder, that ain't a bad speculation!

MARKS: What do you say? I want a partner. You see, I lost my partner last year, up in Ohio—he was a powerful fellow.

CUTE: Lost him! How did you lose him?

MARKS: Well, you see, Tom and I—his name was Tom Loker—Tom and I were after a mulatto chap, called George Harris, that run away from Kentucky. We traced him through the greater part of Ohio, and came up with him near the Pennsylvania line. He took refuge among some rocks, and showed fight.

CUTE: Oh! then runaway darkies show fight, do they?

MARKS: Sometimes. Well, Tom—like a headstrong fool as he was—rushed up the rocks, and a Quaker chap, who was helping this George Harris, threw him over the cliff.

CUTE: Was he killed?

MARKS: Well, I didn't stop to find out. Seeing that the darkies were stronger than I thought, I made tracks for a safe place.

CUTE: And what became of this George Harris?

MARKS: Oh! he and his wife and child got away safe into Canada. You see, they will get away sometimes though it isn't very often. Now what do you say? You are just the figure for a fighting partner. Is it a bargain?

CUTE: Well, I rather calculate our teams won't hitch, no how. By chowder, I hain't no idea of setting myself up as a target for darkies to fire at—that's a speculation that don't suit my constitution.

MARKS: You're afraid, then?

CUTE: No, I ain't, it's against my principles.

MARKS: Your principles—how so?

CUTE: Because my principles are to keep a sharp lookout for No. 1. I shouldn't feel wholesome if a darkey was to throw me over that cliff to look after Tom Loker. (*Exeunt arm-in-arm*, L.H.)

SCENE II

Gothic Chamber. Slow music. ST. CLARE *discovered, seated on sofa,* R.H. TOM, L.H.

ST. C: Oh! Tom, my boy, the whole world is as empty as an egg shell.

TOM: I know it, mas'r, I know it. But oh! if mas'r could look up—up where our dear Miss Eva is—

ST. C: Ah, Tom! I do look up; but the trouble is, I don't see anything when I do. I wish I could. It seems to be given to children and poor, honest fellows like you, to see what we cannot. How comes it?

TOM: Thou hast hid from the wise and prudent, and revealed unto babes; even so, Father, for so it seemed good in thy sight.

ST. C: Tom, I don't believe—I've got the habit of doubting—I want to believe and I cannot.

TOM: Dear mas'r, pray to the good Lord: "Lord, I believe; help thou my unbelief."

ST. C: Who knows anything about anything? Was all that beautiful love and faith only one of the ever-shifting phases of human feeling, having nothing real to rest on, passing away with the little breath? And is there no more Eva—nothing?

TOM: Oh! dear mas'r, there is. I know it; I'm sure of it. Do, do, dear mas'r, believe it!

ST. C: How do you know there is, Tom? You never saw the Lord.

TOM: Felt Him in my soul, mas'r—feel Him now! Oh, mas'r! when I was sold away from my old woman and the children, I was jest a'most broken up—I felt as if there warn't nothing left—and then the Lord stood by me, and He says, "Fear not, Tom," and He brings light and joy into a poor fellow's soul—makes all peace; and I's so happy, and loves everybody, and feels willin' to be jest where the Lord wants to put me. I know it couldn't come from me, 'cause I's a poor, complaining creature—it comes from above, and I know He's willin' to do for mas'r.

ST. C: (*Grasping* TOM's *hand*) Tom, you love me!

TOM: I's willin' to lay down my life this blessed day for you.

ST. C: (*Sadly*) Poor, foolish fellow! I'm not worth the love of one good, honest heart like yours.

TOM: Oh, mas'r! there's more than me loves you—the blessed Saviour loves you.

ST. C: How do you know that, Tom?

TOM: The love of the Saviour passeth knowledge.

ST. C: (*Turns away*) Singular! that the story of a man who lived and died eighteen hundred years ago can affect people so yet. But He was no man. (*Rises*) No man ever had such long and living power. Oh! that I could believe what my mother taught me, and pray as I did when I was a boy! But, Tom, all this time I have forgotten why I sent for you. I'm going to make a freeman of you so have your trunk packed, and get ready to set out for Kentucky.

TOM: (*Joyfully*) Bless the Lord!

ST. C: (*Dryly*) You haven't had such very bad times here, that you need be in such a rapture, Tom.

TOM: No, no mas'r, 'tain't that; it's being a *freeman*—that's what I'm joyin' for.

ST. C: Why, Tom, don't you think, for your own part, you've been better off than to be free?

TOM: No, *indeed*, Mas'r St. Clare—no, indeed!

ST. C: Why, Tom, you couldn't possibly have earned, by your work, such clothes and such living as I have given you.

TOM: I know all that, Mas'r St. Clare—mas'r's been too good; but I'd rather have poor clothes, poor house, poor everything, and have 'em *mine*, than have the best, if they belong to somebody else. I had *so*, mas'r; I think it's natur', mas'r.

ST. C: I suppose so, Tom; and you'll be going off and leaving me in a month or so—though why you shouldn't no mortal knows.

TOM: Not while mas'r is in trouble. I'll stay with mas'r as long as he wants me, so as I can be any use.

ST. C: (*Sadly*) Not while I'm in trouble, Tom? And when will my trouble be over?

TOM: When you are a believer.

ST. C: And you really mean to stay by me till that day comes? (*Smiling and laying his hand on* TOM's *shoulder*) Ah, Tom! I won't keep you till that day. Go home to your wife and children, and give my love to all.

TOM: I's faith to think that day will come — the Lord has a work for mas'r.

ST. C: A work, hey? Well, now, Tom, give me your views on what sort of a work it is — let's hear.

TOM: Why, even a poor fellow like me has a work; and Mas'r St. Clare, that has larnin', and riches, and friends, how much he might do for the Lord.

ST. C: Tom, you seem to think the Lord needs a great deal done for him.

TOM: We does for him when we does for his creatures.

ST. C: Good theology, Tom. Thank you, my boy; I like to hear you talk. But go now, Tom, and leave me alone. *(Exit* TOM, L. 1 E.*)* That faithful fellow's words have excited a train of thoughts that almost bear me, on the strong tide of faith and feeling, to the gates of that heaven I so vividly conceive. They seem to bring me nearer to Eva.

OPH: *(Outside,* L. 1 E.*)* What are you doing there, you limb of Satan? You've been stealing something, I'll be bound.

*(*OPHELIA *drags in* TOPSY L. 1 E.*)*

TOP: You go 'long, Miss Feely, 'tain't none o' your business.

ST. C: Heyday! what is all this commotion?

OPH: She's been stealing.

TOP: *(Sobbing)* I hain't neither.

OPH: What have you got in your bosom?

TOP: I've got my hand dar.

OPH: But what have you got in your hand?

TOP: Nuffin'.

OPH: That's a fib, Topsy.

TOP: Well, I 'spects it is.

OPH: Give it to me, whatever it is.

TOP: It's mine — I hope I may die this bressed minute, if it don't belong to me.

OPH: Topsy, I order you to give me that article; don't let me have to ask you again. *(*TOPSY *reluctantly takes the foot of an old stocking from her bosom and hands it to* OPHELIA.*)* Sakes alive! what is all this? *(Takes from it a lock of hair, and a small book, with a bit of crape twisted around it.)*

TOP: Dat's a lock of ha'r dat Miss Eva give me — she cut it from her own beau'ful head herself.

ST. C: *(Takes book)* Why did you wrap *this* (*Pointing to crape)* around the book?

TOP: 'Cause — 'cause — 'cause 'twas Miss Eva's. Oh! don't take 'em away, please! *(Sits down on stage, and, putting her apron over her head, begins to sob vehemently.)*

OPH: Come, come, don't cry; you shall have them.

TOP: *(Jumps up joyfully and takes them)* I wants to keep 'em, 'cause dey makes me good; I ain't half so wicked as I used to was. *(Runs off,* L. 1 E.*)*

ST. C: I really think you can make something of that girl. Any mind that is capable of a *real sorrow* is capable of good. You must try and do something with her.

OPH: The child has improved very much: I have great hopes of her.

ST. C: I believe I'll go down the street, a few moments, and hear the news.

OPH: Shall I call Tom to attend you?

ST. C: No, I shall be back in an hour. *(Exit,* L. 1 E.*)*

OPH.: He's got an excellent heart, but then he's so dreadful shiftless! *(Exit,* R. 1 E.*)*

SCENE III

Front chamber. Enter TOPSY, L.H.

TOP: Dar's somethin' de matter wid me — I isn't a bit like myself. I haven't done anything wrong since poor Miss Eva went up in de skies and left us. When I's gwine to do anything wicked, I tinks of her, and somehow I can't do it. I's getting to be good, dat's a fact. I 'spects when I's dead I shall be turned into a little brack angel.

(Enter OPHELIA, L.H.*)*

OPH: Topsy, I've been looking for you; I've got something very particular to say to you.

TOP: Does you want me to say the catechism?

OPH: No, not now.

TOP: *(Aisde)* Golly! dat's one comfort.

OPH: Now, Topsy, I want you to try and understand what I am going to say to you.

TOP: Yes, missis, I'll open my ears drefful wide.

OPH: Mr. St. Clare has given you to me, Topsy.

TOP: Den I b'longs to you, don't I? Golly! I thought I always belong to you.

OPH: Not till to-day have I received any authority to call you my property.

TOP: I's your property, am I? Well, if you say so, I 'spects I am.

OPH: Topsy, I can give you your liberty.

TOP: My liberty?

OPH: Yes, Topsy.

TOP: Has you got 'um with you?

OPH: I have, Topsy.

TOP: Is it clothes or wittles?

OPH: How shiftless! Don't you know what your liberty is, Topsy?

TOP: How should I know when I never seed 'um?

OPH: Topsy, I am going to leave this place; I am going many miles away—to my own home in Vermont.

TOP: Den what's to become of dis chile?

OPH: If you wish to go, I will take you with me.

TOP: Miss Feely, I doesn't want to leave you no how, I loves you I does.

OPH: Then you shall share my home for the rest of your days. Come, Topsy.

TOP: Stop, Miss Feely; does dey hab any oberseers in Varmount?

OPH: No, Topsy.

TOP: Nor cotton plantations, nor sugar factories, nor darkies, nor whipping nor nothing?

OPH: No, Topsy.

TOP: By Golly! de quicker you is gwine de better den.

(Enter TOM, hastily, L.H.)

TOM: Oh, Miss Feely! Miss Feely!

OPH: Gracious me, Tom! what's the matter?

TOM: Oh, Mas'r St. Clare! Mas'r St. Clare!

OPH: Well, Tom, well?

TOM: They've just brought him home and I do believe he's killed.

OPH: Killed?

TOP: Oh dear! what's to become of de poor darkies now?

TOM: He's dreadful weak. It's just as much as he can do to speak. He wanted me to call you.

OPH: My poor cousin! Who would have thought of it? Don't say a word to his wife, Tom; the danger may not be so great as you think; it would only distress her. Come with me; you may be able to afford some assistance. (Exeunt, L. 1 E.)

SCENE IV

Handsome chamber. ST. CLARE *discovered seated on sofa.* OPHELIA R.H., TOM R.H., *and* TOPSY L., *are clustered around him.* DOCTOR *back of sofa feeling his pulse. Scene opens to slow music.*

ST. C: (Raising himself feebly) Tom—poor fellow!

TOM: Well, mas'r?

ST. C: I have received my death wound.

TOM: Oh, no, no, mas'r!

ST. C: I feel that I am dying—Tom, pray!

TOM: (Sinking on his knees) I do, pray, mas'r! I do pray!

ST. C: (After a pause) Tom, one thing preys upon my mind—I have forgotten to sign your freedom papers. What will become of you when I am gone?

TOM: Don't think of that, mas'r.

ST. C: I was wrong, Tom, very wrong, to neglect it. I may be the cause of much suffering to you hereafter. Marie, my wife—she—oh!—

OPH: His mind is wandering.

ST. C: (Energetically) No! it is coming *home* at last! (Sinks back) At last! at last! Eva, I come! (Dies. Music. Slow curtain)

END OF ACT FOUR

ACT V

SCENE I

An auction mart. UNCLE TOM *and* EMMELINE *at back—*ADOLF, SKEGGS, MARKS, MANN, *and various spectators discovered.* MARKS *and* MANN *come forward.*

MARKS: Hulloa, Alf! what brings you here?

MANN: Well, I was wanting a valet, and I heard that St. Clare's valet was going; I thought I'd just look at them.

MARKS: Catch me ever buying any of St. Clare's people. Spoiled niggers, every one—impudent as the devil.

MANN: Never fear that; if I get 'em, I'll soon have their airs out of them—they'll soon find that they've another kind of master to deal with than St. Clare. 'Pon my word, I'll buy that fellow—I like the shape of him. *(Pointing to* ADOLF.*)*

MARKS: You'll find it'll take all you've got to keep him—he's deucedly extravagant.

MANN: Yes, but my lord will find that he *can't* be extravagant with *me.* Just let him be sent to the calaboose a few times, and thoroughly dressed down, I'll tell you if it don't bring him to a sense of his ways. Oh! I'll reform him, up hill and down, you'll see. I'll buy him; that's flat.

(Enter LEGREE, L.H. *he goes up and looks at* ADOLF, *whose boots are nicely blacked.)*

LEGREE: A nigger with his boots blacked—bah! *(Spits on them)* Holloa, you! *(To* TOM*) Let's see your teeth. (Seizes* TOM *by the jaw and opens his mouth)* Strip up your sleeve and show your muscle. *(*TOM *does so)* Where was you raised?

TOM: In Kintuck, mas'r.

LEG: What have you done?

TOM: Had care of mas'r's farm.

LEG: That's a likely story. *(Turns to* EMMELINE*)* You're a nice-looking girl enough. How old are you? *(Grasps her arm)*

EMMELINE: *(Shrieking)* Ah! you hurt me.

SKEEGS: Stop that, you minx! No whimpering here. The sale is going to begin. *(Mounts the rostrum)* Gentlemen, the next article I shall offer you to-day is Adolf, late valet to Mr. St. Clare. How much am I offered? *(Various bids are made.* ADOLF *is knocked down to* MANN *for eight hundred dollars.)* Gentlemen, I now offer a prime article—the quadroon girl, Emmeline, only fifteen years of age, warranted in every respect. *(Business as before.* EMMELINE *is sold to* LEGREE *for one thousand dollars.)* Now, I shall close to-day's sale by offering you the valuable article known as Uncle Tom, the most useful nigger ever raised. Gentlemen in want of an overseer, now is the time to bid.

(Business as before. TOM *is sold to* LEGREE *for twelve hundred dollars.)*

LEG: Now look here, you two belong to me. *(*TOM *and* EMMELINE *sink on their knees)*

TOM: Heaven help us, then!

(Music. LEGREE *stands over them exulting. Picture—closed in.)*

SCENE II

The garden of MISS OPHELIA's *house in Vermont. Enter* OPHELIA *and* DEACON PERRY, L. 1 E.

DEACON: Miss Ophelia, allow me to offer you my congratulations upon your safe arrival in your native place. I hope it is your intention to pass the remainder of your days with us?

OPH: Well, Deacon, I have come here with that express purpose.

DEA: I presume you were not over-pleased with the South?

OPH: Well, to tell you the truth, Deacon, I wasn't; I liked the country very well, but the people there are so dreadful shiftless.

DEA: The result, I presume, of living in a warm climate.

OPH: Well, Deacon, what is the news among you all here?

DEA: Well, we live on in the same even jog-trot pace. Nothing of any consequence has happened—Oh! I forgot. *(Takes out his handkerchief)* I've lost my wife; my Molly has left me. *(Wipes his eyes)*

OPH: Poor soul! I pity you, Deacon.

DEA: Thank you. You perceive I bear my loss with resignation.

OPH: How you must miss her tongue!

DEA: Molly certainly was fond of talking. She always would have the last word—heigho!

OPH: What was her complaint, Deacon?

DEA: A very mild and soothing one, Miss Ophelia: she had a severe attack of the lockjaw.

OPH: Dreadful!

DEA: Wasn't it? When she found she couldn't use her tongue, she took it so much to heart that it struck to her stomach and killed her. Poor dear! Excuse my handkerchief; she's been dead only eighteen months.

OPH: Why, Deacon, by this time you ought to be setting your cap for another wife.

DEA: Do you think so, Miss Ophelia?

OPH: I don't see why you shouldn't—you are still a good-looking man, Deacon.

DEA: Ah! well, I think I do wear well—in fact, I may say remarkably well. It has been observed to me before.

OPH: And you are not much over fifty:

DEA: Just turned of forty, I assure you.

OPH: Hale and hearty?

DEA: Health excellent—look at my eye! Strong as a lion—look at my arm!! A No. 1 constitution—look at my leg!!!

OPH: Have you no thoughts of choosing another partner?

DEA: Well, to tell you the truth, I have.

OPH: Who is she?

DEA: She is not far distant. *(Looks at* OPHELIA *in an anguishing manner)* I have her in my eye at this present moment.

OPH: *(Aside)* Really, I believe he's going to pop. Why, surely, Deacon, you don't mean to—

DEA: Yes, Miss Ophelia, I do mean; and believe me, when I say— *(Looking off,* R. *1* E.*)* The Lord be good to us, but I believe there is the devil coming!

*(*TOPSY *runs on,* R. *1* E.*, with bouquet. She is now dressed very neatly.)*

TOP: Miss Feely, here is some flowers dat I hab been gathering for you. *(Gives bouquet)*

OPH: That's a good child.

DEA: Miss Ophelia, who is this young person?

OPH: She is my daughter.

DEA: *(Aside)* Her daughter! Then she must have married a colored man off South. I was not aware that you had been married, Miss Ophelia?

OPH: Married! Sakes alive! what made you think I had been married?

DEA: Good gracious, I'm getting confused. Didn't I understand you to say that this—somewhat tanned—young lady was your daughter?

OPH: Only by adoption. She is my adopted daughter.

DEA: O—oh! *(Aside)* I breathe again.

TOP: *(Aside)* By Golly! dat old man's eyes stick out of 'um head dre'ful. Guess he never seed anything like me afore.

OPH: Deacon, won't you step into the house and refresh yourself after your walk?

DEA: I accept your polite invitation. *(Offers his arm)* Allow me.

OPH: As gallant as ever, Deacon. I declare, you grow younger every day.

DEA: You can never grow old, madam.

OPH: Ah, you flatterer! *(Exeunt,* R. *1* E.*)*

TOP: Dar dey go, like an old goose and gander. Guess dat ole gemblemun feels kind of confectionary—rather sweet on my old missis. By Golly! she's been dre'ful kind to me ever since I come away from de South; and I loves her, I does, 'cause she takes such car' on me and gives me dese fine clothes. I tries to be good too, and I's getting 'long 'mazin' fast. I's not so wicked as I used to was. *(Looks out,* L. *1* E.*)* Holloa! dar's some one comin' here. I wonder what he wants now. *(Retires, observing)*

(Enter GUMPTION CUTE, L. *1* E.*, very shabby—a small bundle, on a stick, over his shoulder.)*

CUTE: By chowder, here I am again. Phew, it's a pretty considerable tall piece of walking between here and New Orleans, not to mention the wear of shoe-leather. I guess I'm about done up. If this streak of bad luck lasts much longer, I'll borrow sixpence to buy a rope, and hang myself right straight up! When I went to call on Miss Ophelia, I swow if I didn't find out that she had left for Vermont; so I kind of concluded to make tracks in that direction myself and as I didn't have any money left, why I had to foot it, and here I am in old Varmount once more. They told me Miss Ophelia lived up here. I wonder if she will remember the relationship. *(Sees* TOPSY*)* By chowder, there's a darkey. Look here, Charcoal!

TOP: *(Comes forward,* R.H.*)* My name isn't Charcoal—it's Topsy.

CUTE: Oh! your name is Topsy, is it, you juvenile specimen of Day & Martin?

TOP: Tell you I don't know nothin' 'bout Day & Martin. I's Topsy and I belong to Miss Feely St. Clare.

CUTE: I'm much obleeged to you, you small extract of Japan, for your information. So Miss Ophelia lives up there in the white house, does she? *(Points,* R. 1 E.*)*

TOP: Well, she don't do nothin' else.

CUTE: Well, then, just locomote your pins.

TOP: What—what's dat?

CUTE: Walk your chalks!

TOP: By Golly! dere ain't no chalk 'bout me.

CUTE: Move your trotters.

TOP: How you does spoke! What you mean by trotters?

CUTE: Why, your feet, Stove Polish.

TOP: What does you want me to move my feet for?

CUTE: To tell your mistress, you ebony angel, that a gentleman wishes to see her.

TOP: Does you call yourself a gentleman! By Golly! you look more like a scar'crow.

CUTE: Now look here, you Charcoal, don't you be sassy. I'm a gentleman in distress; a done-up speculator; one that has seen better days—long time ago—and better clothes too, by chowder! My creditors are like my boots—they've no soles. I'm a victim to circumstances. I've been through much and survived it. I've taken walking exercise for the benefit of my health; but as I was trying to live on air at the same time, it was a losing speculation, 'cause it gave me such a dreadful appetite.

TOP: Golly! you look as if you could eat an ox, horns and all.

CUTE: Well, I calculate I could, if he was roasted—it's a speculation I should like to engage in. I have returned like the fellow that run away in Scripture; and if anybody's got a fatted calf they want to kill, all they got to do is to fetch him along.

Do you know, Charcoal, that your mistress is a relation of mine?

TOP: Is she your uncle?

CUTE: No, no, not quite so near as that. My second cousin married her niece.

TOP: And does you want to see Miss Feely?

CUTE: I do. I have come to seek a home beneath her roof, and take care of all the spare change she don't want to use.

TOP: Den just you follow me, mas'r.

CUTE: Stop! By chowder, I've got a great idee. Say, you Day & Martin, how should you like to enter into a speculation?

TOP: Golly! I doesn't know what a spec—spec—cu—what-do-you-call-'um am.

CUTE: Well, now, I calculate I've hit upon about the right thing. Why should I degrade the manly dignity of the Cutes by becoming a beggar—expose myself to the chance of receiving the cold shoulder as a poor relation? By chowder, my blood biles as I think of it? Topsy, you can make my fortune, and your own, too. I've an idee in my head that is worth a million dollars.

TOP: Golly! is your head worth dat? Guess you wouldn't bring dat out South for de whole of you.

CUTE: Don't you be too severe, now, Charcoal; I'm a man of genius. Did you ever hear of Barnum?

TOP: Barnum! Barnum! Does he live out South?

CUTE: No, he lives in New York. Do you know how he made his fortin?

TOP: What is him fortin, hey? Is it something he wears?

CUTE: Chowder, how green you are!

TOP: *(Indignantly)* Sar, I hab you to know I's not green; I's brack.

CUTE: To be sure you are, Day & Martin. I calculate, when a person says another has a fortune, he means he's got plenty of money, Charcoal.

TOP: And did he make the money?

CUTE: Sartin sure, and no mistake.

TOP: Golly! now I thought money always growed.

CUTE: Oh, git out! You are too cute—you are cuterer than I am—and I'm Cute by name and cute by nature. Well, as I was saying, Barnum made his money by exhibiting a *woolly* horse; now wouldn't it be an all-fired speculation to show you as the woolly gal?

TOP: You want to make a sight of me?

CUTE: I'll give you half the receipts, by chowder!

TOP: Should I have to leave Miss Feely?

CUTE: To be sure you would.

TOP: Den you hab to get a woolly gal somewhere else, Mas'r Cute. (Runs off, R. 1 E.)

CUTE: There's another speculation gone to smash, by chowder! (Exit, R. 1 E.)

SCENE III

A Rude chamber. TOM *is discovered, in old clothes, seated on a stool,* C, *he holds in his hand a paper containing a curl of* EVA's *hair. The scene opens to the symphony of "Old Folks at Home."*

TOM: I have come to de dark places; I's going through de vale of shadows. My heart sinks at times and feels just like a big lump of lead. Den it gits up in my throat and chokes me till de tears roll out of my eyes; den I take out dis curl of little Miss Eva's hair, and the sight of it brings calm to my mind and I feels strong again. *(Kisses the curl and puts it in his breast—takes out a silver dollar, which is suspended around his neck by a string.)* Dere's de bright silver dollar dat Mas'r George Shelby gave me the day I was sold away from old Kentucky, and I've kept it ever since. Mas'r George must have grown to be a man by this time. I wonder if I shall ever see him again.

(Song "Old Folks at Home." Enter LEGREE,
EMMELINE, SAMBO *and* QUIMBO, L.H.)

LEG: Shut up, you black cuss! Did you think I wanted any of your infernal howling? *(Turns to* EMMELINE*)* We're home. *(*EMMELINE *shrinks from him. He takes hold of her ear.)* You didn't ever wear earrings?

EMME: *(Trembling)* No, master.

LEG: Well, I'll give you a pair, if you're a good girl. You needn't be so frightened; I don't mean to make you work very hard. You'll have fine times with me and live like a lady; only be a good girl.

EMME: My soul sickens as his eyes gaze upon me. His touch makes my very flesh creep.

LEG: *(Turns to* TOM, *and points to* SAMBO *and* QUIMBO*)* Ye see what ye'd get if ye'd try to run off. These yer boys have been raised to track niggers and they'd just as soon chaw one on ye up as eat their suppers; so mind yourself. *(To* EMMELINE*)* Come, mistress, you go in here with me. *(Taking* EMMELINE's *hand, and leading her towards* R.U.E.)

EMME: *(Withdrawing her hand, and shrinking back)* No, no! let me work in the fields; I don't want to be a lady.

LEG: Oh! you're going to be contrary, are you? I'll soon take all that out of you.

EMME: Kill me, if you will.

LEG: Oh! you want to be killed, do you? Now come here, you Tom, you see I told you I didn't buy you jest for the common work; I mean to promote you and make a driver of you, and to-night ye may jest as well begin to get yer hand in. Now ye jest take this yer gal, and flog her; ye've seen enough on't to know how.

TOM: I beg mas'rs pardon—hopes mas'r won't set me at that. It's what I a'nt used to—never did, and can't do—no way possible.

LEG: Ye'll larn a pretty smart chance of things ye never did know before I've done with ye. *(Strikes* TOM *with whip, three blows. Music chord each blow.)* There! now will ye tell me ye can't do it?

TOM: Yes, mas'r! I'm willing to work night and day, and work while there's life and breath in me; but this yer thing I can't feel it right to do, and, mas'r, I *never* shall do it, *never!*

LEG: What! ye black beast! tell *me* ye don't think it right to do what I tell ye! What have any of you cussed cattle to do with thinking what's right? I'll put a stop to it. Why, what do ye think ye are? May be ye think yer a gentleman, master Tom, to be telling your master what's right and what a'nt! So you pretend it's wrong to flog the gal?

TOM: I think so, mas'r; 'twould be downright cruel, and it's what I never will do, mas'r. If you mean to kill me, kill me; but as to raising my hand agin any one here, I never shall—I'll die first!

LEG: Well, here's a pious dog at last, let down

among us sinners—powerful holy critter he must be. Here, you rascal! you make believe to be so pious, didn't you never read out of your Bible, "Servants, obey your masters"? An't I your master? Didn't I pay twelve hundred dollars, cash, for all there is inside your cussed old black shell? An't you mine, body and soul?

TOM: No, no! My soul a'nt yours, mas'r; you haven't bought it—ye can't buy it; it's been bought and paid for by one that is able to keep it, and you can't harm it!

LEG: I can't? we'll see, we'll see! Here, Sambo! Quimbo! give this dog such a breaking in as he won't get over this month!

EMME: Oh, no! you will not be so cruel—have some mercy! (Clings to TOM.)

LEG: Mercy? you won't find any in this shop! Away with the black cuss! Flog him within an inch of his life!

(Music. SAMBO and QUIMBO seize TOM and drag him up stage. LEGREE seizes EMMELINE, and throws her round to R.H. She falls on her knees, with her hands lifted in supplication. LEGREE raises his whip, as if to strike TOM. Picture. Closed in.)

SCENE IV

Plain chamber. Enter OPHELIA, followed by TOPSY, L.H.

OPH: A person inquiring for me, did you say, Topsy?

TOP: Yes, missis.

OPH: What kind of a looking man is he?

TOP: By golly! he's very queer looking man, anyway; and den he talks so dre'ful funny. What does you think? yah! yah! he wanted to 'zibite me as de woolly gal! yah! yah!

OPH: Oh! I understand. Some cute Yankee, who wants to purchase you, to make a show of—the heartless wretch!

TOP: Dat's just him, missis; dat's just his name. He tole me dat it was Cute—Mr. Cute Speculashum—dat's him.

OPH: What did you say to him, Topsy?

TOP: Well, I didn't say much, it was brief and to the point—I tole him I wouldn't leave you, Miss Feely, no how.

OPH: That's right, Topsy; you know you are very comfortable here—you wouldn't fare quite so well if you went away among strangers.

TOP: By golly! I know dat; you takes care on me, and makes me good. I don't steal any now, and I don't swar, and I don't dance breakdowns. Oh! I isn't so wicked as I used to was.

OPH: That's right, Topsy; now show the gentleman, or whatever he is, up.

TOP: By golly! I guess he won't make much out of Miss Feely. (Crosses to R., and exit R. 1 E.)

OPH: I wonder who this person can be? Perhaps it is some old acquaintance, who has heard of my arrival, and who comes on a social visit.

(Enter CUTE, R. 1 E.)

CUTE: Aunt, how do ye do? Well, I swan, the sight of you is good for weak eyes. (Offers his hand)

OPH: (Coldly drawing back) Really, sir, I can't say that I ever had the pleasure of seeing you before.

CUTE: Well, it's a fact that you never did. You see I never happened to be in your neighborhood afore now. Of course you've heard of me? I'm one of the Cutes—Gumption Cute, the first and only son of Josiah and Maria Cute, of Oniontown, on the Onion river in the north part of this ere State of Varmount.

OPH: Can't say I ever heard the name before.

CUTE: Well then, I calculate your memory must be a little ricketty. I'm a relation of yours.

OPH: A relation of mine! Why, I never heard of any Cutes in our family.

CUTE: Well, I shouldn't wonder if you never did. Don't you remember your niece, Mary?

OPH: Of course I do. What a shiftless question!

CUTE: Well, you see my second cousin, Abijah Blake, married her. So you see that makes me a relation of yours.

OPH: Rather a distant one, I should say.

CUTE: By chowder! I'm near enough, just at present.

OPH: Well, you certainly are a sort of connection of mine.

CUTE: Yes, kind of sort of.

OPH: And of course you are welcome to my house, as long as you choose to make it your home.

CUTE: By chowder! I'm booked for the next six months—this isn't a bad speculation.

OPH: I hope you left all your folks well at home?

CUTE: Well, yes, they're pretty comfortably disposed of. Father and mother's dead, and Uncle Josh has gone to California. I am the only representative of the Cutes left.

OPH: There doesn't seem to be a great deal of *you* left. I declare, you are positively in rags.

CUTE: Well, you see, the fact is, I've been speculating—trying to get bank-notes—specie-rags, as they say—but I calculate I've turned out rags of another sort.

OPH: I'm sorry for your ill luck, but I am afraid you have been shiftless.

CUTE: By chowder! I've done all that a fellow could do. You see, somehow, everything I take hold of kind of bursts up.

OPH: Well, well, perhaps you'll do better for the future; make yourself at home. I have got to see to some household matters, so excuse me for a short time. *(Aside)* Impudent and shiftless. *(Exit L. 1 E.)*

CUTE: By chowder! I rather guess that this speculation will hitch. She's a good-natured old critter; I reckon I'll be a son to her while she lives, and take care of her valuables after she's a defunct departed. I wonder if they keep the vittles in this ere room? Guess not. I've got extensive accommodations for all sorts of eatables. I'm a regular vacuum, throughout—pockets and all. I'm chuck full of emptiness. *(Looks out, R.H.)* Holloa! who's this elderly individual coming up stairs? He looks like a compound essence of starch and dignity. I wonder if he isn't another relation of mine. I should like a rich old fellow now for an uncle.

(Enter DEACON PERRY, R. 1 E.)

DEA: Ha! a stranger here!

CUTE: How d'ye do?

DEA: You are a friend to Miss Ophelia, I presume?

CUTE: Well, I rather calculate that I am a lee-tle more than a friend.

DEA: *(Aside)* Bless me! what can he mean by those mysterious words? Can he be her—no I don't think he can. She said she wasn't—well, at all events, it's very suspicious.

CUTE: The old fellow seems kind of stuck up.

DEA: You are a particular friend to Miss Ophelia, you say?

CUTE: Well, I calculate I am.

DEA: Bound to her by any tender tie?

CUTE: It's something more than a tie—it's a regular double-twisted knot.

DEA: Ah! just as I suspected. *(Aside)* Might I inquire the nature of that tie?

CUTE: Well, it's the natural tie of relationship.

DEA: A relation—what relation?

CUTE: Why, you see, my second cousin, Abijah Blake, married her niece, Mary.

DEA: Oh! is that all?

CUTE: By chowder, ain't that enough?

DEA: Then you are not her husband?

CUTE: To be sure I ain't. What put that ere idee into your cranium?

DEA: *(Shaking him vigorously by the hand)* My dear sir, I'm delighted to see you.

CUTE: Holloa! you ain't going slightly insane, are you?

DEA: No, no fear of that; I'm only happy, that's all.

CUTE: I wonder if he's been taking a nipper?

DEA: As you are a relation of Miss Ophelia's, I think it proper that I should make you my confidant; in fact, let you into a little scheme that I have lately conceived.

CUTE: Is it a speculation?

DEA: Well, it is, just at present; but I trust before many hours to make it a surety.

CUTE: By chowder! I hope it won't serve you the way my speculations have served me. But fire away, old boy, and give us the prospectus.

DEA: Well, then, my young friend, I have been thinking, ever since Miss Ophelia returned to Vermont, that she was just the person to fill the place of my lamented Molly.

CUTE: Say, you, you couldn't tell us who your lamented Molly was, could you?

DEA: Why, the late Mrs. Perry, to be sure.

CUTE: Oh! then the lamented Molly was your wife?

DEA: She was.

CUTE: And now you wish to marry Miss Ophelia!

DEA: Exactly.

CUTE: *(Aside)* Consarn this old porpoise! if I let him do that he'll Jew me out of my living. By chowder! I'll put a spoke in his wheel.

DEA: Well, what do you say? will you intercede for me with your aunt?

CUTE: No! bust me up if I do!

DEA: No?

CUTE: No, I tell you. I forbid the bans. Now, ain't you a purty individual, to talk about getting married, you old superannuated Methuselah specimen of humanity! Why, you've got one foot in etarnity already, and t'other ain't fit to stand on. Go home and go to bed! have your head shaved, and send for a lawyer to make your will, leave your property to your heirs—if you hain't got any, why leave it to me—I'll take care of it, and charge nothing for the trouble.

DEA: Really, sir, this language to one of my standing, is highly indecorous—it's more, sir, than I feel willing to endure, sir. I shall expect an explanation, sir.

CUTE: Now, you see, old gouty toes, you're losing your temper.

DEA: Sir, I'm a deacon; I never lost my temper in all my life, sir.

CUTE: Now, you see, you're getting excited; you had better go; we can't have a disturbance here!

DEA: No, sir! I shall not go sir! I shall not go until I have seen Miss Ophelia. I wish to know if she will countenance this insult.

CUTE: Now keep cool, old stick-in-the-mud! Draw it mild, old timber-toes!

DEA: Damn it all, sir, what—

CUTE: Oh! only think, now, what would people say to hear a deacon swearing like a trooper?

DEA: Sir—I—you—this is too much, sir.

CUTE: Well, now, I calculate that's just about my opinion, so we'll have no more of it. Get out of this! start your boots, or by chowder! I'll pitch you from one end of the stairs to the other.

(Enter OPHELIA, *L.H.)*

OPH: *(Crossing to* C.) Hoity toity! What's the meaning of all these loud words?

CUTE: *(Together)* Well, you see, Aunt—
DEA: Miss Ophelia, I beg—

CUTE: Now, look here, you just hush your yap! How can I fix up matters if you keep jabbering?

OPH: Silence! for shame, Mr. Cute. Is that the way you speak to the deacon?

CUTE: Darn the deacon!

OPH: Deacon Perry, what is all this?

DEA: Madam, a few words will explain everything. Hearing from this person that he was your nephew, I ventured to tell him that I cherished hopes of making you my wife, whereupon he flew into a violent passion, and ordered me out of the house.

OPH: Does this house belong to you or me, Mr. Cute?

CUTE: Well, to you, I reckon.

OPH: Then how dare you give orders in it?

CUTE: Well, I calculated that you wouldn't care about marrying old half a century there.

OPH: That's enough; I will marry him; and as for you, *(Points* R.H.) get out.

CUTE: Get out?

OPH: Yes; the sooner the better.

CUTE: Darned if I don't serve him out first though.

(Music. CUTE *makes a dash at* DEACON, *who gets behind* OPHELIA. TOPSY *enters,* R.H., *with a broom and beats* CUTE *around stage.* OPHELIA *faints in* DEACON'S *arms.* CUTE *falls, and* TOPSY *butts him kneeling over him. Quick drop.)*

END OF ACT FIVE

ACT VI

SCENE I

Dark Landscape. An old, roofless shed, R.U.E. TOM *is discovered in shed, lying on some old cotton bagging.* CASSY *kneels by his side, holding a cup to his lips.*

CASSY: Drink all ye want. I knew how it would be. It isn't the first time I've been out in the night, carrying water to such as you.

TOM: *(Returning cup)* Thank you, missis.

CAS: Don't call me missis. I'm a miserable slave like yourself—a lower one than you can ever be! It's no use, my poor fellow, this you've been trying to do. You were a brave fellow. You had the right on your side; but it's all in vain for you to struggle. You are in the Devil's hands; he is the strongest, and you must give up.

TOM: Oh! how can I give up?

CAS: You see *you* don't know anything about it; I do. Here you are, on a lone plantation, ten miles from any other, in the swamps; not a white person here who could testify, if you were burned alive. There's no law here that can do you, or any of us, the least good; and this man! there's no earthly thing that he is not bad enough to do. I could make one's hair rise, and their teeth chatter, if I should only tell what I've seen and been knowing to here; and it's no use resisting! Did I *want* to live with him? Wasn't I a woman delicately bred? and he! — Father in Heaven! what was he and is he? And yet I've lived with him these five years, and cursed every moment of my life, night and day.

TOM: Oh heaven! have you quite forgot us poor critters?

CAS: And what are these miserable low dogs you work with, that you should suffer on their account? Every one of them would turn against you the first time they get a chance. They are all of them as low and cruel to each other as they can be; there's no use in your suffering to keep from hurting them?

TOM: What made 'em cruel? If I give out I shall get used to it and grow, little by little, just like 'em. No, no, Missis, I've lost everything, wife and children, and home, and a kind master, and he would have set me free if he'd only lived a day longer — I've lost everything in *this* world, and now I can't lose heaven, too: no I can't get to be wicked besides all.

CAS: But it can't be that He will lay sin to our account; he won't charge it to us when we are forced to it; he'll charge it to them that drove us to it. Can I do anything more for you? Shall I give you some more water?

TOM: Oh missis! I wish you'd go to Him who can give you living waters!

CAS: Go to him! Where is he? Who is he?

TOM: Our Heavenly Father!

CAS: I used to see the picture of him, over the altar, when I was a girl but *he isn't here!* there's nothing here but sin, and long, long despair! There, there, don't talk any more, my poor fellow. Try to sleep, if you can. I must hasten back, lest my absence be noted. Think of me when I am gone, Uncle Tom, and pray, pray for me.

(*Music. Exit* CASY, L.U.E. TOM *sinks back to sleep.*)

SCENE II

Street in New Orleans. Enter GEORGE SHELBY, R. *1* E.)

GEORGE: At length my mission of mercy is nearly finished, I have reached my journey's end. I have now but to find the house of Mr. St. Clare, repurchase old Uncle Tom, and convey him back to his wife and children, in old Kentucky. Some one approaches; he may, perhaps, be able to give me the information I require. I will accost him. (*Enter* MARKS, L. *1* E.) Pray, sir, can you tell me where Mr. St. Clare dwells?

MARKS: Where I don't think you'll be in a hurry to seek him.

GEO: And where is that?

MARKS: In the grave! (*Crosses to* R.)

GEO: Stay, sir! you may be able to give me some information concerning Mr. St. Clare.

MARKS: I beg pardon, sir, I am a lawyer; I can't afford to *give* anything.

GEO: But you would have no objections to selling it?

MARKS: Not the slightest.

GEO: What do you value it at?

MARKS: Well, say five dollars, that's reasonable.

GEO: There they are (*Gives money*) Now answer me to the best of your ability. Has the death of St. Clare caused his slaves to be sold?

MARKS: It has.

GEO: How were they sold?

MARKS: At auction — they went dirt cheap.

GEO: How were they bought — all in one lot?

MARKS: No, they went to different bidders.

GEO: Was you present at the sale?

MARKS: I was.

GEO: Do you remember seeing a negro among them called Tom?

MARKS: What, Uncle Tom?

GEO: The same — who bought him?

MARKS: A Mr. Legree.

GEO: Where is his plantation?

MARKS: Up in Louisiana, on the Red river; but a man never could find it, unless he had been there before.

GEO: Who could I get to direct me there?

MARKS: Well, stranger, I don't know of any one just at present 'cept myself, could find it for you; it's such an out-of-the-way sort of hole; and if you are a mind to come down handsomely, why, I'll do it.

GEO: The reward shall be ample.

MARKS: Enough said, stranger; let's take the steamboat at once. (*Exeunt* R. 1 E.)

SCENE III

A Rough chamber. Enter LEGREE, L.H. *Sits*

LEG: Plague on that Sambo, to kick up this yer row between Tom and the new hands. (CASSY *steals on* L.H., *and stands behind him.*) The fellow won't be fit to work for a week now, right in the press of the season.

CAS: (R.) Yes, just like you.

LEG: (L.) Hah! you she-devil! you've come back, have you? (*Rises*)

CAS: Yes, I have; come to have my own way, too.

LEG: You lie, you jade! I'll be up to my word. Either behave yourself, or stay down in the quarters and fare and work with the rest.

CAS: I'd rather, ten thousand times, live in the dirtiest hole at the quarters, than be under your hoof!

LEG: But you are under my hoof, for all that, that's one comfort; so sit down here and listen to reason. (*Grasps her wrist*)

CAS: Simon Legree, take care! (LEGREE *lets go his hold*) You're afraid of me, Simon, and you've reason to be; for I've got the Devil in me!

LEG: I believe to my soul you have. After all, Cassy, why can't you be friends with me, as you used to?

CAS: (*Bitterly*) Used to!

LEG: I wish, Cassy, you'd behave yourself decently.

CAS: *You* talk about behaving decently! and what have you been doing? You haven't even sense enough to keep from spoiling one of your best hands, right in the most pressing season, just for your devilish temper.

LEG: I was a fool, it's fact, to let any such brangle come up. Now when Tom set up his will he had to be broke in.

CAS: You'll never break *him* in.

LEG: Won't I? I'd like to know if I won't? He'd be the first nigger that ever come it round me! I'll break every bone in his body but he shall give up. (*Enter* SAMBO, L.H., *with a paper in his hand, stands bowing*) What's that, you dog?

SAM: It's a witch thing, mas'r.

LEG: A What?

SAM: Something that niggers gits from witches. Keep 'em from feeling when they's flogged. He had it tied round his neck with a black string.

(LEGREE *takes the paper and opens it. A silver dollar drops on the stage, and a long curl of light hair twines around his finger.*)

LEG: Damnation. (*Stamping and writhing, as if the hair burned him*) Where did this come from? Take it off! burn it up! burn it up! (*Throws the curl away*) What did you bring it to me for?

SAM: (*Trembling*) I beg pardon, mas'r; I thought you would like to see um.

LEG: Don't you bring me any more of your devilish things. (*Shakes his fist at* SAMBO *who runs off* L.H. LEGREE *kicks the dollar after him.*) Blast it! where did he get that? If it didn't look just like— whoo! I though I'd forgot that. Curse me if I think there's any such thing as forgetting anything, any how.

CAS: What is the matter with you, Legree? What is there in a simple curl of fair hair to appall a man like you—you who are familiar with every form of cruelty.

LEG: Cassy, to-night the past has been recalled to me—the past that I have so long and vainly striven to forget.

CAS: Has aught on this earth power to move a soul like thine?

LEG: Yes, for hard and reprobate as I now seem, there has been a time when I have been rocked on the bosom of mother, cradled with prayers and pious hymns, my now seared brow bedewed with the waters of holy baptism.

CAS: *(Aside)* What sweet memories of childhood can thus soften down that heart of iron?

LEG: In early childhood a fair-haired woman has led me, at the sound of Sabbath bells, to worship and to pray. Born of a hard-tempered sire, on whom that gentle woman had wasted a world of unvalued love, I followed in the steps of my father. Boisterous, unruly and tyrannical, I despised all her counsel, and would have none of her reproof, and, at an early age, broke from her to seek my fortunes on the sea. I never came home but once after that; and then my mother, with the yearning of a heart that must love something, and had nothing else to love, clung to me, and sought with passionate prayers and entreaties to win me from a life of sin.

CAS: That was your day of grace, Legree; then good angels called you, and mercy held you by the hand.

LEG: My heart inly relented; there was·a conflict, but sin got the victory, and I set all the force of my rough nature against the conviction of my conscience. I drank and swore, was wilder and more brutal than ever. And one night, when my mother, in the last agony of her despair, knelt at my feet, I spurned her from me, threw her senseless on the floor, and with brutal curses fled to my ship.

CAS: Then the fiend took thee for his own.

LEG: The next I heard of my mother was one night while I was carousing among drunken companions. A letter was put in my hands. I opened it, and a lock of long, curling hair fell from it, and twined about my fingers, even as that lock twined but now. The letter told me that my mother was dead, and that dying she blest and forgave me! *(Buries his face in his hands)*

CAS: Why did you not even then renounce your evil ways?

LEG: There is a dread, unhallowed necromancy of evil, that turns things sweetest and holiest to phantoms of horror and afright. That pale, loving mother,—her dying prayers, her forgiving love,—wrought in my demoniac heart of sin only as a damning sentence, bringing with it a fearful looking for of judgment and fiery indignation.

CAS: And yet you would not strive to avert the doom that threatened you.

LEG: I burned the lock of hair and I burned the letter; and when I saw them hissing and crackling in the flame, inly shuddered as I thought of everlasting fires! I tried to drink and revel, and swear away the memory; but often in the deep night, whose solemn stillness arraigns the soul in forced communion with itself, I have seen that pale mother rising by my bed-side, and felt the soft twining of that hair around my fingers, 'till the cold sweat would roll down my face, and I would spring from my bed in horror—horror! *(Falls in chair—after a pause)* What the devil ails me? Large drops of sweat stand on my forehead, and my heart beats heavy and thick with fear. I thought I saw something white rising and glimmering in the gloom before me, and it seemed to bear my mother's face! I know one thing; I'll let that fellow Tom alone, after this. What did I want with his cussed paper? I believe I am bewitched sure enough! I've been shivering and sweating ever since! Where did he get that hair? It couldn't have been that! I *burn'd* that up, I know I did! It would be a joke if hair could rise from the dead! I'll have Sambo and Quimbo up here to sing and dance one of their dances, and keep off these horrid notions. Here, Sambo! Quimbo! *(Exit L. 1 E.)*

CAS.: Yes, Legree, that golden tress was charmed; each hair had in it a spell of terror and remorse for thee, and was used by a mightier power to bind thy cruel hands from inflicting uttermost evil on the helpless! *(Exit R. 1 E.)*

SCENE IV

Street. Enter MARKS R. *1* E., *meeting* CUTE, *who enters* L. *1* E., *dressed in an old faded uniform.*

MARKS: By the land, stranger, but it strikes me that I've seen you somewhere before.

CUTE: By chowder! do you know now, that's just what I was a going to say?

MARKS: Isn't your name Cute?

CUTE: You're right, I calculate. Yours is Marks, I reckon.

MARKS: Just so.

CUTE: Well, I swow, I'm glad to see you. *(They shake hands)* How's your wholesome?

MARKS: Hearty as ever. Well, who would have thought of ever seeing you again. Why, I thought you was in Vermont?

CUTE: Well, so I was. You see I went there after that rich relation of mine — but the speculation didn't turn out well.

MARKS: How so?

CUTE: Why, you see, she took a shine to an old fellow — Deacon Abraham Perry — and married him.

MARKS: Oh, that rather put your nose out of joint in that quarter.

CUTE: Busted me right up, I tell you. The Deacon did the hand-some thing though, he said if I would leave the neighborhood and go out South again, he'd stand the damage. I calculate I didn't give him much time to change his mind, and so, you see, here I am again.

MARKS: What are you doing in that soldier rig?

CUTE: Oh, this is my sign.

MARKS: Your sign?

CUTE: Yes; you see, I'm engaged just at present in an all-fired good speculation, I'm a Fillibusterow.

MARKS: A What?

CUTE: A Fillibusterow! Don't you know what that is? It's Spanish for Cuban Volunteer; and means a chap that goes the whole perker for glory and all that ere sort of thing.

MARKS: Oh! you've joined the order of the Lone Star!

CUTE: You've hit it. You see I bought this uniform at a second hand clothing store, I puts it on and goes to a benevolent individual and I says to him, — appealing to his feelings, — I'm one of the fellows that went to Cuba and got massacred by the bloody Spaniards. I'm in a destitute condition — give me a trifle to pay my passage back, so I can whop the tyrannical cusses and avenge my brave fellow soger what got slewed there.

MARKS: How pathetic!

CUTE: I tell you it works up the feelings of benevolent individuals dreadfully. It draws tears from their eyes and money from their pockets. By chowder! one old chap gave me a hundred dollars to help on the cause.

MARKS: I admire a genius like yours.

CUTE: But I say, what are you up to?

MARKS: I am the traveling companion of a young gentleman by the name of Shelby, who is going to the plantation of a Mr. Legree of the Red River, to buy an old darkey who used to belong to his father.

CUTE: Legree — Legree? Well, now, I calculate I've heard that ere name afore.

MARKS: Do you remember that man who drew a bowie knife on you in New Orleans?

CUTE: By chowder! I remember the circumstance just as well as if it was yesterday; but I can't say that I recollect much about the man, for you see I was in something of a hurry about that time and didn't stop to take a good look at him.

MARKS: Well, that man was this same Mr. Legree.

CUTE: Do you know, now, I should like to pay that critter off!

MARKS: Then I'll give you an opportunity.

CUTE: Chowder! how will you do that?

MARKS: Do you remember the gentleman that interfered between you and Legree?

CUTE: Yes — well?

MARKS: He received the blow that was intended for you, and died from the effects of it. So, you see, Legree is a murderer, and we are only witnesses of the deed. His life is in our hands.

CUTE: Let's have him right up and make him dance on nothing to the tune of Yankee Doodle!

MARKS: Stop a bit, Don't you see a chance for a profitable speculation?

CUTE: A speculation! Fire away, don't be bashful, I'm the man for a speculation.

MARKS: I have made a deposition to the Governor of the state on all the particulars of that affair at Orleans.

CUTE: What did you do that for?

MARKS: To get a warrant for his arrest.

CUTE: Oh! and have you got it?

MARKS: Yes; here it is. *(Takes out paper)*

CUTE: Well, now , I don't see how you are going to make anything by that bit of paper?

MARKS: But I do. I shall say to Legree, I have got a warrant against you for murder; my friend, Mr. Cute, and myself are the only witnesses who can appear against you. Give us a thousand dollars, and we will tear the warrant and be silent.

CUTE: Then Mr. Legree forks over a thousand dollars, and your friend Cute pockets five hundred of it, is that the calculation?

MARKS: If you will join me in the undertaking.

CUTE: I'll do it, by chowder!

MARKS: Your hand to bind the bargain.

CUTE: I'll stick by you thro' thick and thin.

MARKS: Enough said.

CUTE: Then shake. *(They shake hands)*

MARKS: But I say, Cute, he may be contrary and show fight.

CUTE: Never mind, we've got the law on our side, and we're bound to stir him up. If he don't come down handsomely we'll present him with a neck-tie made of hemp!

MARKS: I declare you're getting spunky.

CUTE: Well, I reckon, I am. Let's go and have something to drink. Tell you what, Marks, if we don't get *him* we'll have his hide, by chowder! *(Exeunt, arm in arm, R. 1 E.)*

SCENE V

Rough chamber. Enter LEGREE, *followed by* SAMBO, L.H.

LEG: Go and send Cassy to me.

SAM: Yes, mas'r. *(Exit R.U.E.)*

LEG: Curse the woman! she's got a temper worse than the devil; I shall do her an injury one of these days, if she isn't careful. *(Re-enter SAMBO, R.U.E., frightened)* What's the matter with you, you black scoundrel?

SAM: S'help me, mas'r, she isn't dere.

LEG: I suppose she's about the house somewhere?

SAM: No, she isn't, mas'r; I's been all over de house and I can't find nothing of her nor Emmeline.

LEG: Bolted, by the Lord! Call out the dogs! saddle my horse. Stop! are you sure they really have gone?

SAM: Yes, mas'r; I's been in every room 'cept the haunted garret and dey wouldn't go dere.

LEG: I have it! Now, Sambo, you jest go and walk that Tom up here, right away! *(Exit SAMBO, L.U.E.)* The old cuss is at the bottom of this yer whole matter; and I'll have it out of his infernal black hide, or I'll know the reason why! I *hate* him—I *hate* him! And isn't he *mine?* Can't I do what I like with him? Who's to hinder, I wonder? *(TOM is dragged on by SAMBO and QUIMBO, L.U.E. LEGREE grimly confronting TOM.)* Well, Tom, do you know, I've made up my mind to *kill* you?

TOM: It's very likely, Mas'r.

LEG: *I—have—done—just—that—thing,* Tom, unless you'll tell me what do you know about these yer gals? *(TOM is silent)* D'ye hear? Speak!

TOM: I han't got anything to tell, mas'r.

LEG: Do you dare to tell me, you old black rascal, you don't know? Speak! Do you know anything?

TOM: I know, mas'r; but I can't tell anything. *I can die!*

LEG: Hark ye, Tom! ye think, 'cause I have let you off before, I don't mean what I say; but, this time, I have made *up my mind,* and counted the cost. You've always stood it out agin me; now, I'll *conquer ye or kill ye!* one or t'other. I'll count every drop of blood there is in you, and take 'em one by one, 'till ye give up!

TOM: Mas'r, if you was sick, or in trouble, or dying, and I could save, I'd *give* you my heart's blood; and, if taking every drop of blood in this poor old body would save your precious soul, I'd give 'em freely. Do the worst you can, my troubles will be over soon; but if you don't repent yours won't never end.

(LEGREE strikes TOM down with the butt of his whip.)

LEG: How do you like that?

SAM: He's most gone, mas'r!

TOM: *(Rises feebly on his hands)* There an't no more you can do. I forgive you with all my soul. *(Sinks back, and is carried off R.U.E. by SAMBO and QUIMBO.)*

LEG: I believe he's done for finally. Well, his mouth is shut up at last—that's one comfort. *(Enter GEORGE SHELBY, MARKS and CUTE, L. 1 E.)* Strangers! Well what do you want?

GEO: I understand that you bought in New Orleans a negro named Tom?

LEG: Yes, I did buy such a fellow, and a devil of a bargain I had of it, too! I believe he's trying to die, but I don't know as he'll make it out.

GEO: Where is he? Let me see him!

SAM: Dere he is! *(Points to TOM, R.U.E.)*

LEG: How dare you speak? *(Drives SAMBO and QUIMBO off L.U.E.—GEORGE exits, R.U.E.)*

CUTE: Now's the time to nab him.

MARKS: How are you, Mr. Legree?

LEG: What the devil brought you here?

MARKS: This little bit of paper. I arrest you for the murder of Mr. St. Clare. What do you say to that?

LEG: This is my answer! *(Makes a blow at* MARKS, *who dodges, and* CUTE *receives the blow— he cries out and runs off,* L.H. MARKS *fires at* LEGREE, *and follows* CUTE.) I am hit!—the game's up! *(Falls dead.* QUIMBO *and* SAMBO *return and carry him off laughing.)*

*(*GEORGE SHELBY *enters, supporting* TOM. *Music. They advance to front and* TOM *falls,* C.)

GEO: Oh! dear Uncle Tom! do wake—do speak once more! look up! Here's Master George—your own little Master George. Don't you know me?

TOM: *(Opening his eyes and speaking in a feeble tone)* Mas'r George! Bless de Lord! it's all I wanted! They hav'n't forgot me! It warms my soul; it does my old heart good! Now I shall die content!

GEO: You shan't die! you mustn't die, nor think of it. I have come to buy you, and take you home.

TOM: Oh, Mas'r George, you're too late. The Lord has bought me, and is going to take me home.

GEO: Oh! don't die. It will kill me—it will break my heart to think what you have suffered, poor, poor fellow!

TOM: Don't call me, poor fellow! I *have* been poor fellow; but that's all past and gone now. I'm right in the door, going into glory! Oh, Mas'r George! *Heaven has come!* I've got the victory, the Lord has given it to me! Glory be to his name! *(Dies)*

(Solemn music. GEORGE *covers* UNCLE TOM *with his cloak, and kneels over him. Clouds work on and conceal them, and then work off.)*

SCENE VII

Gorgeous clouds, tinted with sunlight. EVA, *robed in white, is discovered on the back of a milk-white dove, with expanded wings, as if just soaring upward. Her hands are extended in benediction over* ST. CLARE *and* UNCLE TOM *who are kneeling and gazing up to her. Expressive music. Slow curtain.*

THE END

Uncle Tom's Cabin is composed of a number of loosely connected stories divided into six acts and thirty scenes. The play is kept moving and its parts are related largely through the operation of coincidence—characters meet or turn up at just the right moment, and drastic, wholly unexpected reversals in the fortunes of key characters sharply alter the direction of the action. Variety and contrast are also major devices—George's rebelliousness contrasts with Uncle Tom's patience; Simon Legree's cruelty differs strikingly from Shelby's and St. Clare's gentleness as slave owners; Topsy's mischievousness serves as an antidote to Little Eva's perfection; comic and serious, quite and bustling scenes alternate; the action ranges through Kentucky, Ohio, Louisiana, and Vermont and from wealthy homes to rough cabins, from city streets to desolate country scenes, and from slave auctions to family gatherings.

Typically in melodrama, the action is set in motion and kept moving by the machinations of a villain, as the protagonist merely reacts by seeking to avoid or free himself from the traps set by the villain. In *Uncle Tom's Cabin*, while there are villainous characters such as Marks and Legree, the true villain is an institution—slavery. The play shows how families are divided by the sale of some members, how slaves are denied all civil rights, how slaves who run away are hunted down like wild animals, how slaves are degraded and mistreated by owners like Legree—how in general slaves are reduced to the status of livestock. While the play is careful to show that there are kind and well-meaning slave owners, it also shows that the good intentions of such owners are often subverted by conditions beyond their control. Shelby is forced to sell some of his slaves, including Uncle Tom, because of financial setbacks, and St. Clare's murder keeps him from signing papers that would have freed Uncle Tom.

In melodrama, a happy ending is usually brought about by exposing the villain and his machinations, but since *Uncle Tom's Cabin* could not show slavery being abolished, another type of happy ending had to be found for it—one intimately connected with a central theme of the play, the power of religion. (Mrs. Stowe was married to a clergyman and she was a member of the Beecher family, which was famous as theologians.) Uncle Tom is sustained throughout his trials by his faith in God—and it is his faith that is used to explain his trustworthiness and acceptance of his lot. He teaches Little Eva his religion, he aids in St. Clare's conversion, and he comforts Cassy with his picture of God's love. This thread culminates in the final tableau showing Little Eva, astride a "milk-white dove" among clouds bright with sunlight, welcoming St. Clare and Uncle Tom into Heaven. This tableau constitutes the play's happy ending, suggesting as it does that religious faith, patience, and goodness will lead to eternal salvation.

The power of human love is only slightly less important to the play than religion. Topsy is reclaimed by love, St. Clare is motivated to reform by his love for Little Eva, Eliza and George are kept strong by their love, and Phineas Fletcher frees his slaves and becomes an abolitionist out of love for a Quaker girl. In contrast, the evil characters are depicted as lacking in love for others.

Since the 1950s, *Uncle Tom's Cabin* has assumed a special place in American thought. In the intensified battle for civil rights the name *Uncle Tom* came to be used as a derogatory label for any black who cooperated with whites and seemed to accept the status quo—one who is subservient and assures his own position through his subservience. As a result, the play has also fallen into disfavor and has been avoided in schools out of fear that it may offend blacks. Consequently, many people who have not read it now believe they know what the play is about. But a reading of the play shows that the present-day use of the label *Uncle Tom* distorts the facts. The label may be defended if one reads only the first half of the play, but the second half alters the pciture considerably. In Act IV, scene 2, St. Clare suggests to Uncle Tom that he is better off as a slave than he would be as a free man. Tom replies: "being a *free man*—that's what I'm joyin' for. . . . I'd rather have poor clothes, poor house, poor everything, and have 'em *mine*, than have the best, if they belong to somebody else." Later, Tom is flogged unmercifully and ultimately killed by Simon Legree because he will not cooperate in Legree's mistreatment of other slaves. Tom's patience under other masters is attributed to his religion rather than to any attempt to curry favor. Throughout the play, he is depcited as a man of integrity and principle, and, interestingly, he is used to counteract the stereotyped views expressed by evil whites — that blacks are untrustworthy, devious, and lazy. The black character most nearly in accord with current ideas of the appropriate response to slavery is George Harris, who runs away from his owner, insists upon his dignity and rights as a human being, argues for the natural rights of man, and defends himself and his wife against his would-be captors, even killing one of them.

The issues raised by *Uncle Tom's Cabin* are for the most part clearly stated in the play. Obviously the overriding one is slavery, probably the most dehumanizing institution imaginable, both for those owned and for owners. The former are reduced to objects, pieces of property, and the latter accept that property rights are more important than human rights. Slavery has a long history. It was an accepted part of the ancient world; the economies of Greece and Rome were built on slavery. But it is especially ironic that slavery should have flourished in the United States, since its Declaration of Independence emphasizes this premise: "We hold these truths to be self-evident, that all men are created equal, that they are endowed by their Creator with certain unalienable Rights, that among these are Life, Liberty and the pursuit of Happiness." Perhaps it is even more ironic that the principal author of this Declaration, Thomas Jefferson, was himself a slave owner, as was George Washington. The framers of the Constitution had to accept slavery as legitimate in order to get the slaveholding states to join the union. Such property rights figure prominently in *Uncle Tom's Cabin*, since the action is initiated by Shelby's indebtedness, which forces him to sell a number of slaves to meet his debts. (It does not seem to occur to him that he might sell some other type of property.)

It has become common to speak of people as enslaved by circumstances other than actual slavery. People are said to have been reduced to the status of slaves by poverty (as Shaw's *Major Barbara* does), by sex (women as the property or servants of men, as in *The School for Wives* or *A Doll's House* by race (as in *Slave Ship*), or by ideology, social custom, one's job, or various other things. Some of these conditions are the results of inequitable laws or adverse economic conditions, others are psychological (inner compulsions as opposed to outer restraints).

Slavery, whether actual or symbolic, implies another condition: freedom. But, what does it mean to be free? Are any of us completely free? Why is it important that laws seek to guarantee equity? Why is it important for laws to impose restraints? How does the concept of natural law relate to man-made law?

Ultimately, there are few issues of greater importance than those raised by the concept of slavery, under which human beings are legally and forcibly restrained from becoming what they are capable of. Consequently, *Uncle Tom's Cabin*, if viewed in its historical and ethical context, can be seen as an attempt to deal with one of the most significant aspects of human existence.

A Doll's House

by Henrik Ibsen / Translated by William Archer

The Industrial Revolution that had been instrumental in creating audiences for melodrama also was crucial to the development of the artistic movement called Realism. The urbanization that accelerated with industrialization brought with it slums, overcrowding, poor sanitary conditions, crime, and poverty. At the same time, technological advances proliferated and each new invention increased admiration for science and engineering. This juxtaposition of vast social and economic problems with faith in science and technology soon gave rise to the idea that society's problems might be solved if only they were approached scientifically. Auguste Comte (1798–1857) proposed a new science — sociology — devoted to a systematic study of society's problems, and soon his disciples were seeking to apply scientific method to the complex issues of the day.

By the 1850s a number of artists and critics in France were arguing for a comparable approach to all forms of art — an approach they labeled Realism. The main premises of the new movement were: art must depict truthfully the real, physical world; truth can be perceived only through the five senses; only contemporary life and manners can be experienced directly; and the artist must strive to be impersonal and objective. Playwrights influenced by the new movement began to emphasize the details of contemporary life and to avoid historical subjects, the supernatural, and idealized human actions. Many writers turned to themes not previously treated on the stage, leading conservative critics to charge that the theatre had become little better than a tavern or a sewer. To these charges of immorality, the supporters of Realism replied that the plays, as truthful depictions of life, were moral, since truth is the highest form of morality, and that to present an idealized picture would be to elevate falsehood over truth. Furthermore, they went on, if audiences did not like the pictures of contemporary life shown on the stage, they should strive to change the society that had furnished the models rather than denounce the playwright who had merely reflected what he saw around him. A number of playwrights, most notably Alexandre Dumas *fils* (1824–1895) and Emile Augier (1820–1889), sought to implement the realistic mode, but it is to Ibsen that credit is usually given for its triumph.

Henrik Ibsen, *A Doll's House*, translated by William Archer, *The Collected Works of Henrik Ibsen*, Vol. VII (New York: Charles Scribner's Sons, 1906). Reprinted with the permission of Charles Scribner's Sons.

Henrik Ibsen (1828–1906), Norway's first important dramatist, began writing plays about 1850. His early work, much of it based on Norwegian legend or history, was written in verse. It was not until the late 1870s that he consciously abandoned his earlier methods and began to write prose plays about contemporary subjects. *A Doll's House* (1879) and *Ghosts* (1881) made Ibsen the most controversial dramatist in Europe, for the first appeared to attack the institutions of marriage and the family, and the second brought the taboo subject of syphilis to the stage. Because in European countries of this time plays had to be licensed for production by censors, *A Doll's House* was performed in some cities only after it was given a much softened ending, and *Ghosts* was denied production almost everywhere. Nevertheless, Ibsen's plays were widely read and discussed and were almost universally acknowledged to represent a new direction in drama. With Ibsen's prose plays, the modern drama is usually said to have begun.

Ibsen soon turned to other subjects and enlarged means. Beginning with *The Wild Duck* (1884) and continuing with such plays as *Rosmersholm* (1886), *Hedda Gabler* (1890), and *The Master Builder* (1892), Ibsen concentrated on personal relationships and made increasing use of symbolism. But despite changes in subject and techniques, Ibsen's basic theme remained constant: the struggle for integrity, the conflict between duty to oneself and duty to others.

Much of Ibsen's drama contributed to Realism. For the most part, he discarded asides and soliloquies, and he was careful to motivate all exposition and incidents. All scenes were causally related and culminated in a logical resolution. Each role was conceived as a personality whose behavior was explainable by heredity and environment. Dialogue, settings, costumes, and stage business were selected to reveal character and milieu and were clearly described in stage directions.

Ibsen's late plays were to exert great influence on subsequent nonrealistic plays primarily because of his use of symbolism, which enlarged the implications of the action and often suggested that fate or some supernatural force lay behind the events. Almost all later playwrights, whether Realists or not, were affected by Ibsen's conviction that drama should be a source of insight, a creator of discussion, a conveyor of ideas, something more than entertainment. He gave dramatists a new vision of their role.

DRAMATIS PERSONÆ

TORVALD HELMER	HELMER'S THREE YOUNG CHILDREN
NORA *his wife*	ANNE *their nurse*
DOCTOR RANK	A HOUSEMAID
MRS. LINDE	A PORTER
NILS KROGSTAD	

The action takes place in Helmer's house.

ACT I

SCENE.

A room furnished comfortably and tastefully but not extravagantly. At the back, a door to the right leads to the entrance-hall, another to the left leads to Helmer's study. Between the doors stands a piano. In the middle of the left-hand wall is a door, and beyond it a window. Near the window are a round table, armchairs and a small sofa. In the right-hand wall, at the farther end, another door; and on the same side, nearer the footlights, a stove, two easy chairs and a rocking-chair; between the stove and the door, a small table. Engravings on the walls; a cabinet with china and other small objects; a small book-case with well-bound books. The floors are carpeted, and a fire burns in the stove. It is winter.

A bell rings in the hall; shortly afterwards the door is heard to open. Enter NORA, *humming a tune and in high spirits. She is in out-door dress and carries a number of parcels; these she lays on the table to the right. She leaves the outer door open after her, and through it is seen a* PORTER *who is carrying a Christmas Tree and a basket, which he gives to the* MAID *who has opened the door.*

NORA: Hide the Christmas Tree carefully, Helen. Be sure the children do not see it till this evening, when it is dressed. *(To the* PORTER, *taking out her purse)* How much?

PORTER: Sixpence.

NORA: There is a shilling. No, keep the change. *(The* PORTER *thanks her, and goes out.* NORA *shuts the door. She is laughing to herself, as she takes off her hat and coat. She takes a packet of macaroons from her pocket and eats one or two; then goes cautiously to her husband's door and listens.)* Yes, he is in. *(Still humming, she goes to the table on the right.)*

HELMER: *(Calls out from his room)* Is that my little lark twittering out there?

NORA: *(Busy opening some of the parcels)* Yes, it is!

HELMER: Is it my little squirrel bustling about?

NORA: Yes!

HELMER: When did my squirrel come home?

NORA: Just now. *(Puts the bag of macaroons into her pocket and wipes her mouth)* Come in here, Torvald, and see what I have bought.

HELMER: Don't disturb me. *(A little later, he opens the door and looks into the room, pen in hand.)* Bought, did you say? All these things? Has my little spendthrift been wasting money again?

NORA: Yes, but, Torvald, this year we really can let ourselves go a little. This is the first Christmas that we have not needed to economise.

HELMER: Still, you know, we can't spend money recklessly.

NORA: Yes, Torvald, we may be a wee bit more reckless now, mayn't we? Just a tiny wee bit! You are going to have a big salary and earn lots and lots of money.

HELMER: Yes, after the New Year; but then it will be a whole quarter before the salary is due.

NORA: Pooh! we can borrow till then.

HELMER: Nora! *(Goes up to her and takes her playfully by the ear)* The same little featherhead! Suppose, now, that I borrowed fifty pounds to-day, and you spent it all in the Christmas week, and then on New Year's Eve a slate fell on my head and killed me, and—

NORA: *(Putting her hands over his mouth)* Oh! don't say such horrid things.

HELMER: Still, suppose that happened,—what then?

NORA: If that were to happen, I don't suppose I should care whether I owed money or not.

HELMER: Yes, but what about the people who had lent it?

NORA: They? Who would bother about them? I should not know who they were.

HELMER: That is like a woman! But seriously, Nora, you know what I think about that. No debt, no borrowing. There can be no freedom or beauty about a home life that depends on borrowing and debt. We two have kept bravely on the straight road so far, and we will go on the same way for the short time longer that there need be any struggle.

NORA: *(Moving towards the stove)* As you please, Torvald.

HELMER: *(Following her)* Come, come, my little skylark must not droop her wings. What is this! Is my little squirrel out of temper? *(Taking out his purse)* Nora, what do you think I have got here?

NORA: *(Turning round quickly)* Money!

HELMER: There you are. *(Gives her some money)* Do you think I don't know what a lot is wanted for housekeeping at Christmas-time?

NORA: *(Counting)* Ten shillings—a pound—two pounds! Thank you, thank you, Torvald; that will keep me going for a long time.

HELMER: Indeed it must.

NORA: Yes, yes, it will. But come here and let me show you what I have bought. And all so cheap! Look, here is a new suit for Ivar, and a sword; and a horse and a trumpet for Bob; and a doll and dolly's bedstead for Emmy,—they are very plain, but anyway she will soon break them in pieces. And here are dress-lengths and handkerchiefs for the maids; old Anne ought really to have something better.

HELMER: And what is in this parcel?

NORA: *(Crying out)* No, no! you mustn't see that till this evening.

HELMER: Very well. But now tell me, you extravagant little person, what would you like for yourself?

NORA: For myself? Oh, I am sure I don't want anything.

HELMER: Yes, but you must. Tell me something reasonable that you would particularly like to have.

NORA: No, I really can't think of anything—unless, Torvald—

HELMER: Well?

NORA: *(Playing with his coat buttons, and without raising her eyes to his)* If you really want to give me something, you might—you might—

HELMER: Well, out with it!

NORA: *(Speaking quickly)* You might give me money, Torvald. Only just as much as you can afford; and then one of these days I will buy something with it.

HELMER: But, Nora—

NORA: Oh, do! dear Torvald; please, please do! Then I will wrap it up in beautiful gilt paper and hang it on the Christmas Tree. Wouldn't that be fun?

HELMER: What are little people called that are always wasting money?

NORA: Spendthrifts—I know. Let us do as you suggest, Torvald, and then I shall have time to think what I am most in want of. That is a very sensible plan, isn't it?

HELMER: *(Smiling)* Indeed it is—that is to say, if you were really to save out of the money I give you, and then really buy something for yourself. But if you spend it all on the housekeeping and any number of unnecessary things, then I merely have to pay up again.

NORA: Oh but, Torvald—

HELMER: You can't deny it, my dear little Nora. *(Puts his arm around her waist)* It's a sweet little spendthrift, but she uses up a deal of money. One would hardly believe how expensive such little persons are!

NORA: It's a shame to say that. I do really save all I can.

HELMER: *(Laughing)* That's very true,—all you can. But you can't save anything!

NORA: *(Smiling quietly and happily)* You haven't any idea how many expenses we skylarks and squirrels have Torvald.

HELMER: You are an odd little soul. Very like your father. You always find some new way of wheedling money out of me, and, as soon as you have got it, it seems to melt in your hands. You never know where it has gone. Still, one must take you as you are. It is in the blood; for indeed it is true that you can inherit these things, Nora.

NORA: Ah, I wish I had inherited many of papa's qualities.

HELMER: And I would not wish you to be anything but just what you are, my sweet little skylark. But, do you know, it strikes me that you are looking rather—what shall I say—rather uneasy today?

NORA: Do I?

HELMER: You do, really. Look straight at me.

NORA: *(Looks at him)* Well?

HELMER: *(Wagging his finger at her)* Hasn't Miss Sweet-Tooth been breaking rules in town today?

NORA: No; what makes you think that?

HELMER: Hasn't she paid a visit to the confectioner's?

NORA: No, I assure you, Torvald—

HELMER: Not been nibbling sweets?

NORA: No, certainly not.

HELMER: Not even taken a bite at a macaroon or two?

NORA: No, Torvald, I assure you really—

HELMER: There, there, of course I was only joking.

NORA: (Going to the table on the right) I should not think of going against your wishes.

HELMER: No, I am sure of that; besides, you gave me your word— (Going up to her) Keep your little Christmas secrets to yourself, my darling. They will all be revealed to-night when the Christmas Tree is lit, no doubt.

NORA: Did you remember to invite Doctor Rank?

HELMER: No. But there is no need; as a matter of course he will come to dinner with us. However, I will ask him when he comes in this morning. I have ordered some good wine. Nora, you can't think how I am looking forward to this evening.

NORA: So am I! And how the children will enjoy themselves, Torvald!

HELMER: It is splendid to feel that one has a perfectly safe appointment, and a big enough income. It's delightful to think of, isn't it?

NORA: It's wonderful!

HELMER: Do you remember last Christmas? For a full three weeks beforehand you shut yourself up every evening till long after midnight, making ornaments for the Christmas Tree and all the other fine things that were to be a surprise to us. It was the dullest three weeks I ever spent!

NORA: I didn't find it dull.

HELMER: (Smiling) But there was precious little result, Nora.

NORA: Oh, you shouldn't tease me about that again. How could I help the cat's going in and tearing everything to pieces?

HELMER: Of course you couldn't, poor little girl. You had the best of intentions to please us all, and that's the main thing. But it is a good thing that our hard times are over.

NORA: Yes, it is really wonderful.

HELMER: This time I needn't sit here and be dull all alone, and you needn't ruin your dear eyes and your pretty little hands—

NORA: (Clapping her hands) No, Torvald, I needn't any longer, need I! It's wonderfully lovely to hear you say so! (Taking his arm) Now I will tell you how I have been thinking we ought to arrange things, Torvald. As soon as Christmas is over— (A bell rings in the hall) There's the bell. (She tidies the room a little) There's someone at the door. What a nuisance!

HELMER: If it is a caller, remember I am not at home.

MAID: (In the doorway) A lady to see you, ma'am,—a stranger.

NORA: Ask her to come in.

MAID: (To HELMER) The doctor came at the same time, sir.

HELMER: Did he go straight into my room?

MAID: Yes, sir.

(HELMER goes into his room. The MAID ushers in MRS. LINDE, who is in travelling dress, and shuts the door.)

MRS. LINDE: (In a dejected and timid voice) How do you do, Nora?

NORA: (Doubtfully) How do you do—

MRS. LINDE: You don't recognise me, I suppose.

NORA: No, I don't know—yes, to be sure, I seem to— (Suddenly) Yes! Christine! Is it really you?

MRS. LINDE: Yes, it is I.

NORA: Christine! To think of my not recognising you! And yet how could I— (In a gentle voice) How you have altered, Christine!

MRS. LINDE: Yes, I have indeed. In nine, ten long years—

NORA: Is it so long since we met? I suppose it is. The last eight years have been a happy time for me, I can tell you. And so now you have come into the town, and have taken this long journey in winter—that was plucky of you.

MRS. LINDE: I arrived by steamer this morning.

NORA: To have some fun at Christmas-time, of course. How delightful! We will have such fun together! But take off your things. You are not cold, I hope. (Helps her) Now we will sit down by the stove, and be cosy. No, take this arm-chair; I will sit here in the rocking-chair. (Takes her hands) Now you look like your old self again; it was only the first moment— You are a little paler, Christine, and perhaps a little thinner.

MRS. LINDE: And much, much older, Nora.

NORA: Perhaps a little older; very, very little; certainly not much. (Stops suddenly and speaks seriously) What a thoughtless creature I am, chattering away like this. My poor, dear Christine, do forgive me.

MRS. LINDE: What do you mean, Nora?

NORA: (Gently) Poor Christine, you are a widow.

MRS. LINDE: Yes; it is three years ago now.

NORA: Yes, I knew; I saw it in the papers. I assure you, Christine, I meant ever so often to write to you at the time, but I always put it off and something always prevented me.

MRS. LINDE: I quite understand, dear.

NORA: It was very bad of me, Christine. Poor thing, how you must have suffered. And he left you nothing?

MRS. LINDE: No.

NORA: And no children?

MRS. LINDE: No.

NORA: Nothing at all, then?

MRS. LINDE: Not even any sorrow or grief to live upon.

NORA: (Looking incredulously at her) But, Christine, is that possible?

MRS. LINDE: (Smiles sadly and strokes her hair) It sometimes happens, Nora.

NORA: So you are quite alone. How dreadfully sad that must be. I have three lovely children. You can't see them just now, for they are out with their nurse. But now you must tell me all about it.

MRS. LINDE: No, no; I want to hear about you.

NORA: No, you must begin. I mustn't be selfish to-day; to-day I must only think of your affairs. But there is one thing I must tell you. Do you know we have just had a great piece of good luck?

MRS. LINDE: No, what is it?

NORA: Just fancy, my husband has been made manager of the Bank!

MRS. LINDE: Your husband? What good luck!

NORA: Yes, tremendous! A barrister's profession is such an uncertain thing, especially if he won't undertake unsavoury cases; and naturally Torvald has never been willing to do that, and I quite agree with him. You may imagine how pleased we are! He is to take up his work in the Bank at the New Year, and then he will have a big salary and lots of commissions. For the future we can live quite differently—we can do just as we like. I feel so relieved and so happy, Christine! It will be splendid to have heaps of money and not need to have any anxiety, won't it?

MRS. LINDE: Yes, anyhow I think it would be delightful to have what one needs.

NORA: No, not only what one needs, but heaps and heaps of money.

MRS. LINDE: (Smiling) Nora, Nora, haven't you learnt sense yet? In our schooldays you were a great spendthrift.

NORA: (Laughing) Yes, that is what Torvald says now. (Wags her finger at her.) But "Nora, Nora" is not so silly as you think. We have not been in a position for me to waste money. We have both had to work.

MRS. LINDE: You too?

NORA: Yes; odds and ends, needlework, crochet-work, embroidery, and that kind of thing. (Dropping her voice) And other things as well. You know Torvald left his office when we were married? There was no prospect of promotion there, and he had to try and earn more than before. But during the first year he overworked himself dreadfully. You see, he had to make money every way he could, and he worked early and late; but he couldn't stand it, and fell dreadfully ill, and the doctors said it was necessary for him to go south.

MRS. LINDE: You spent a whole year in Italy, didn't you?

NORA: Yes. It was no easy matter to get away, I can tell you. It was just after Ivar was born; but naturally we had to go. It was a wonderfully beautiful journey, and it saved Torvald's life. But it cost a tremendous lot of money, Christine.

MRS. LINDE: So I should think.

NORA: It cost about two hundred and fifty pounds. That's a lot, isn't it?

MRS. LINDE: Yes, and in emergencies like that it is lucky to have the money.

NORA: I ought to tell you that we had it from papa.

MRS. LINDE: Oh, I see. It was just about that time that he died, wasn't it?

NORA: Yes; and just think of it, I couldn't go and nurse him. I was expecting little Ivar's birth every day and I had my poor sick Torvald to look after. My dear, kind father—I never saw him again,

Christine. That was the saddest time I have known since our marriage.

MRS. LNDE: I know how fond you were of him. And then you went off to Italy?

NORA: Yes; you see we had money then, and the doctors insisted on our going, so we started a month later.

MRS. LINDE: And your husband came back quite well?

NORA: As sound as a bell!

MRS. LINDE: But — the doctor?

NORA: What doctor?

MRS. LINDE: I thought your maid said the gentleman who arrived here just as I did, was the doctor?

NORA: Yes, that was Doctor Rank, but he doesn't come here professionally. He is our greatest friend, and comes in at least once every day. No, Torvald has not had an hour's illness since then, and our children are strong and healthy and so am I. *(Jumps up and claps her hands)* Christine! Christine! it's good to be alive and happy! — But how horrid of me; I am talking of nothing but my own affairs. *(Sits on a stool near her, and rests her arms on her knees)* You mustn't be angry with me. Tell me, is it really true that you did not love your husband? Why did you marry him?

MRS. LINDE: My mother was alive then, and was bedridden and helpless, and I had to provide for my two younger brothers; so I did not think I was justified in refusing his offer.

NORA: No, perhaps you were quite right. He was rich at that time, then?

MRS. LINDE: I believe he was quite well off. But his business was a precarious one; and, when he died, it all went to pieces and there was nothing left.

NORA: And then? —

MRS. LINDE: Well, I had to turn my hand to anything I could find — first a small shop, then a small school, and so on. The last three years have seemed like one long working-day, with no rest. Now it is at an end, Nora. My poor mother needs me no more, for she is gone; and the boys do not need me either; they have got situations and can shift for themselves.

NORA: What a relief you must feel it —

MRS. LINDE: No, indeed; I only feel my life unspeakably empty. No one to live for any more. *(Gets up restlessly)* That was why I could not stand the life in my little backwater any longer. I hope it may be easier here to find something which will busy me and occupy my thoughts. If only I could have the good luck to get some regular work — office work of some kind —

NORA: But, Christine, that is so frightfully tiring, and you look tired out now. You had far better go away to some watering-place.

MRS. LINDE: *(Walking to the window)* I have no father to give me money for a journey, Nora.

NORA: *(Rising)* Oh, don't be angry with me.

MRS. LINDE: *(Going up to her)* It is you that must not be angry with me, dear. The worst of a position like mine is that it makes one so bitter. No one to work for, and yet obliged to be always on the look-out for chances. One must live, and so one becomes selfish. When you told me of the happy turn your fortunes have taken — you will hardly believe it — I was delighted not so much on your account as on my own.

NORA: How do you mean? — Oh, I understand. You mean that perhaps Torvald could get you something to do.

MRS. LINDE: Yes, that was what I was thinking of.

NORA: He must, Christine. Just leave it to me; I will broach the subject very cleverly — I will think of something that will please him very much. It will make me so happy to be of some use to you.

MRS. LINDE: How kind you are, Nora, to be so anxious to help me! It is doubly kind in you, for you know so little of the burdens and troubles of life.

NORA: I —? I know so little of them?

MRS. LINDE: *(Smiling)* My dear! Small household cares and that sort of thing! You are a child, Nora.

NORA: *(Tosses her head and crosses the stage)* You ought not to be so superior.

MRS. LINDE: No?

NORA: You are just like the others. They all think that I am incapable of anything really serious —

MRS. LINDE: Come, come —

NORA: — that I have gone through nothing in this world of cares.

MRS. LINDE: But, my dear Nora, you have just told me all your troubles.

NORA: Pooh! — those were trifles. *(Lowering her voice)* I have not told you the important thing.

MRS. LINDE: The important thing? What do you mean?

NORA: You look down upon me altogether, Christine — but you ought not to. You are proud, aren't you, of having worked so hard and so long for your mother?

MRS. LINDE: Indeed, I don't look down on any one. But it is true that I am both proud and glad to think that I was privileged to make the end of my mother's life almost free from care.

NORA: And you are proud to think of what you have done for your brothers.

MRS. LINDE: I think I have the right to be.

NORA: I think so, too. But now, listen to this; I too have something to be proud and glad of.

MRS. LINDE: I have no doubt you have. But what do you refer to?

NORA: Speak low, Suppose Torvald were to hear! He mustn't on any account — no one in the world must know, Christine, except you.

MRS. LINDE: But what is it?

NORA: Come here. (Pulls her down on the sofa beside her) Now I will show you that I too have something to be proud and glad of. It was I who saved Torvald's life.

MRS. LINDE: "Saved"? How?

NORA: I told you about our trip to Italy. Torvald would never have recovered if he had not gone there —

MRS. LINDE: Yes, but your father gave you the necessary funds.

NORA: (Smiling) Yes, that is what Torvald and all the others think, but —

MRS. LINDE: But —

NORA: Papa didn't give us a shilling. It was I who procured the money.

MRS. LINDE: You? All that large sum?

NORA: Two hundred and fifty pounds. What do you think of that?

MRS. LINDE: But, Nora, how could you possibly do it? Did you win a prize in the Lottery?

NORA: (Contemptuously) In the Lottery? There would have been no credit in that.

MRS. LINDE: But where did you get it from, then?

NORA: (Humming and smiling with an air of mystery) Hm, hm! Aha!

MRS. LINDE: Because you couldn't have borrowed it.

NORA: Couldn't I? Why not?

MRS. LINDE: No, a wife cannot borrow without her husband's consent.

NORA: (Tossing her head) Oh, if it is a wife who has any head for business — a wife who has the wit to be a little bit clever —

MRS. LINDE: I don't understand it at all, Nora.

NORA: There is no need you should. I never said I had borrowed the money. I may have got it some other way. (Lies back on the sofa) Perhaps I got it from some other admirer. When anyone is as attractive as I am —

MRS. LINDE: You are a mad creature.

NORA: Now, you know you're full of curiosity, Christine.

MRS. LINDE: Listen to me, Nora dear. Haven't you been a little bit imprudent?

NORA: (Sits up straight) Is it imprudent to save your husband's life?

MRS. LINDE: It seems to me imprudent, without his knowledge, to —

NORA: But it was absolutely necessary that he should not know! My goodness, can't you understand that? It was necessary he should have no idea what a dangerous condition he was in. It was to me that the doctors came and said that his life was in danger, and that the only thing to save him was to live in the south. Do you suppose I didn't try, first of all, to get what I wanted as if it were for myself? I told him how much I should love to travel abroad like other young wives; I tried tears and entreaties with him; I told him that he ought to remember the condition I was in, and that he ought to be kind and indulgent to me; I even hinted that he might raise a loan. That nearly made him angry, Christine. He said I was thoughtless, and that it was his duty as my husband not to indulge me in my whims and caprices — as I believe he called them. Very well, I thought, you must be saved — and that was how I came to devise a way out of the difficulty —

MRS. LINDE: And did your husband never get to know from your father that the money had not come from him?

NORA: No, never. Papa died just at that time. I had meant to let him into the secret and beg him never to reveal it. But he was so ill then — alas, there never way any need to tell him.

MRS. LINDE: And since then have you never told your secret to your husband?

NORA: Good Heavens, no! How could you think so? A man who has such strong opinions about these things! And besides, how painful and humiliating it would be for Torvald, with his manly independence, to know that he owed me anything! It would upset our mutual relations altogether; our beautiful happy home would no longer be what it is now.

MRS. LINDE: Do you mean never to tell him about it?

NORA: (Meditatively, and with a half smile) Yes—some day, perhaps, after many years, when I am no longer as nice-looking as I am now. Don't laugh at me! I mean, of course, when Torvald is no longer as devoted to me as he is now; when my dancing and dressing-up and reciting have palled on him; then it may be a good thing to have something in reserve— (Breaking off) What nonsense! That time will never come. Now, what do you think of my great secret, Christine? Do you still think I am of no use? I can tell you, too, that this affair has caused me a lot of worry. It has been by no means easy for me to meet my engagements punctually. I may tell you that there is something that is called, in business, quarterly interest, and another thing called payment in instalments, and it is always so dreadfully difficult to manage them. I have had to save a little here and there, where I could, you understand. I have not been able to put aside much from my housekeeping money, for Torvald must have a good table. I couldn't let my children be shabbily dressed; I have felt obliged to use up all he gave me for them, the sweet little darlings!

MRS. LINDE: So it has all had to come out of your own necessaries of life, poor Nora?

NORA: Of course. Besides, I was the one responsible for it. Whenever Torvald has given me money for new dresses and such things, I have never spent more than half of it; I have always bought the simplest and cheapest things. Thank Heaven, any clothes look well on me, and so Torvald has never noticed it. But it was often very hard on me, Christine—because it is delightful to be really well dressed, isn't it?

MRS. LINDE: Quite so.

NORA: Well, then I have found other ways of earning money. Last winter I was lucky enough to get a lot of copying to do; so I locked myself up and sat writing every evening until quite late at night.

Many a time I was desperately tired; but all the same it was a tremendous pleasure to sit there working and earning money. It was like being a man.

MRS. LINDE: How much have you been able to pay off in that way?

NORA: I can't tell you exactly. You see, it is very difficult to keep an account of a business matter of that kind. I only know that I have paid every penny that I could scrape together. Many a time I was at my wits' end. (Smiles) Then I used to sit here and imagine that a rich old gentleman had fallen in love with me—

MRS. LINDE: What! Who was it?

NORA: Be quiet!—that he had died; and that when his will was opened it contained, written in big letters, the instruction: "The lovely Mrs. Nora Helmer is to have all I possess paid over to her at once in cash."

MRS. LINDE: But, my dear Nora—who could the man be?

NORA: Good gracious, can't you understand? There was no old gentleman at all; it was only something that I used to sit here and imagine, when I couldn't think of any way of procuring money. But it's all the same now; the tiresome old person can stay where he is, as far as I am concerned; I don't care about him or his will either, for I am free from care now. (Jumps up) My goodness, it's delightful to think of, Christine! Free from care! To be able to be free from care, quite free from care; to be able to play and romp with the children; to be able to keep the house beautifully and have everything just as Torvald likes it! And, think of it, soon the spring will come and the big blue sky! Perhaps we shall be able to take a little trip—perhaps I shall see the sea again! Oh, it's a wonderful thing to be alive and be happy. (A bell is heard in the hall)

MRS. LINDE: (Rising) There is the bell; perhaps I had better go.

NORA: No, don't go; no one will come in here; it is sure to be for Torvald.

SERVANT: (At the hall door) Excuse me, ma'am—there is a gentleman to see the master, and as the doctor is with him—

NORA: Who is it?

KROGSTAD: (At the door) It is I, Mrs. Helmer. (MRS. LINDE starts, trembles, and turns to the window)

NORA: (Takes a step towards him, and speaks

in a strained, low voice) You? What is it? What do you want to see my husband about?

KROGSTAD: Bank business—in a way. I have a small post in the Bank, and I hear your husband is to be our chief now—

NORA: Then it is—

KROGSTAD: Nothing but dry business matters, Mrs. Helmer; absolutely nothing else.

NORA: Be so good as to go into the study, then. *(She bows indifferently to him and shuts the door into the hall; then comes back and makes up the fire in the stove.)*

MRS. LINDE: Nora—who was that man?

NORA: A lawyer, of the name of Krogstad.

MRS. LINDE: Then it really was he.

NORA: Do you know the man?

MRS. LINDE: I used to—many years ago. At one time he was a solicitor's clerk in our town.

NORA: Yes, he was.

MRS. LINDE: He is greatly altered.

NORA: He made a very unhappy marriage.

MRS. LINDE: He is a widower now, isn't he?

NORA: With several children. There now, it is burning up. *(Shuts the door of the stove and moves the rockingchair aside)*

MRS. LINDE: They say he carries on various kinds of business.

NORA: Really! Perhaps he does; I don't know anything about it. But don't let us think of business: it is so tiresome.

DOCTOR RANK: *(Comes out of* HELMER'S *study. Before he shuts the door he calls to him)* No, my dear fellow, I won't disturb you; I would rather go in to your wife for a little while. *(Shuts the door and sees* MRS. LINDE*)* I beg your pardon; I am afraid I am disturbing you too.

NORA: No, not at all. *(Introducing him)* Doctor Rank, Mrs. Linde.

RANK: I have often heard Mrs. Linde's name mentioned here. I think I passed you on the stairs when I arrived, Mrs. Linde?

MRS. LINDE: Yes, I go up very slowly; I can't manage stairs well.

RANK: Ah! some slight internal weakness?

MRS. LINDE: No, the fact is I have been overworking myself.

RANK: Nothing more than that? Then I suppose you have come to town to amuse yourself with our entertainments?

MRS. LINDE: I have come to look for work.

RANK: Is that a good cure for overwork?

MRS. LINDE: One must live, Doctor Rank.

RANK: Yes, the general opinion seems to be that it is necessary.

NORA: Look here, Doctor Rank—you know you want to live.

RANK: Certainly. However wretched I may feel, I want to prolong the agony as long as possible. All my patients are like that. And so are those who are morally diseased; one of them, and a bad case too, is at this very moment with Helmer—

MRS. LINDE: *(Sadly).* Ah!

NORA: Whom do you mean?

RANK: A lawyer of the name of Krogstad, a fellow you don't know at all. He suffers from a diseased moral character, Mrs. Helmer; but even he began talking of its being highly important that he should live.

NORA: Did he? What did he want to speak to Torvald about?

RANK: I have no idea; I only heard that it was something about the Bank.

NORA: I didn't know this—what's his name—Krogstad had anything to do with the Bank.

RANK: Yes, he has some sort of appointment there. *(To* MRS. LINDE*)* I don't know whether you find also in your part of the world that there are certain people who go zealously snuffing about to smell out moral corruption, and, as soon as they have found some, put the person concerned into some lucrative position where they can keep their eye on him. Healthy natures are left out in the cold.

MRS. LINDE: Still I think the sick are those who most need taking care of.

RANK: *(Shrugging his shoulders)* Yes, there you are. That is the sentiment that is turning Society into a sickhouse.

*(*NORA, *who has been absorbed in her thoughts, breaks out into smothered laughter and claps her hands.)*

RANK: Why do you laugh at that? Have you any notion what Society really is?

NORA: What do I care about tiresome Society? I am laughing at something quite different, something extremely amusing. Tell me, Doctor Rank, are all the people who are employed in the Bank dependent on Torvald now?

RANK: Is that what you find so extremely amusing?

NORA: *(Smiling and humming)* That's my affair! *(Walking about the room)* It's perfectly glorious to think that we have—that Torvald has so much power over so many people. *(Takes the packet from her pocket)* Doctor Rank, what do you say to a macaroon?

RANK: What, macaroons? I thought they were forbidden here.

NORA: Yes, but these are some Christine gave me.

MRS. LINDE: What! I?—

NORA: Oh, well, don't be alarmed! You couldn't know that Torvald had forbidden them. I must tell you that he is afraid they will spoil my teeth. But, bah!—once in a way— That's so, isn't it, Doctor Rank? By your leave! *(Puts a macaroon into his mouth)* You must have one too, Christine. And I shall have one, just a little one—or at most two. *(Walking about)* I am tremendously happy. There is just one thing in the world now that I should dearly love to do.

RANK: Well, what is that?

NORA: It's something I should dearly love to say, if Torvald could hear me.

RANK: Well, why can't you say it?

NORA: No, I daren't; it's so shocking.

MRS. LINDE: Shocking?

RANK: Well, I should not advise you to say it. Still, with us you might. What is it you would so much like to say if Torvald could hear you?

NORA: I should just love to say—Well, I'm damned!

RANK: Are you mad?

MRS. LINDE: Nora, dear—!

RANK: Say it, here he is!

NORA: *(Hiding the packet)* Hush! Hush! Hush! *(HELMER comes out of his room, with his coat over his arm and his hat in his hand.)*

NORA: Well, Torvald dear, have you got rid of him?

HELMER: Yes, he has just gone.

NORA: Let me introduce you—this is Christine, who has come to town.

HELMER: Christine—? Excuse me, but I don't know—

NORA: Mrs. Linde, dear; Christine Linde.

HELMER: Of course. A school friend of my wife's, I presume?

MRS. LINDE: Yes, we have known each other since then.

NORA: And just think, she has taken a long journey in order to see you.

HELMER: What do you mean?

MRS. LINDE: No, really, I—

NORA: Christine is tremendously clever at book-keeping, and she is frightfully anxious to work under some clever man, so as to perfect herself—

HELMER: Very sensible, Mrs. Linde.

NORA: And when she heard you had been appointed manager of the Bank—the news was telegraphed, you know—she travelled here as quick as she could. Torvald, I am sure you will be able to do something for Christine, for my sake, won't you?

HELMER: Well, it is not altogether impossible. I presume you are a widow, Mrs. Linde?

MRS. LINDE: Yes.

HELMER: And have had some experience of bookkeeping?

MRS. LINDE: Yes, a fair amount.

HELMER: Ah! well, it's very likely I may be able to find something for you.

NORA: *(Clapping her hands)* What did I tell you? What did I tell you?

HELMER: You have just come at a fortunate moment, Mrs. Linde.

MRS. LINDE: How am I to thank you?

HELMER: There is no need. *(Puts on his coat)* But to-day you must excuse me—

RANK: Wait a minute; I will come with you. *(Brings his fur coat from the hall and warms it at the fire)*

NORA: Don't be long away, Torvald dear.

HELMER: About an hour, not more.

NORA: Are you going too, Christine?

MRS. LINDE: *(Putting on her cloak)* Yes, I must go and look for a room.

HELMER: Oh, well then, we can walk down the street together.

NORA: *(Helping her)* What a pity it is we are so short of space here; I am afraid it is impossible for us—

MRS. LINDE: Please don't think of it! Good-bye, Nora dear, and many thanks.

NORA: Good-bye for the present. Of course you will come back this evening. And you too, Dr. Rank. What do you say? If you are well enough? Oh, you must be! Wrap yourself up well. *(They go to the door all talking together. Children's voices are heard on the staircase)*

NORA: There they are. There they are! *(She*

runs to open the door. The NURSE comes in with the children.) Come in! Come in! (Stoops and kisses them) Oh, you sweet blessings! Look at them, Christine! Aren't they darlings?

RANK: Don't let us stand here in the draught.

HELMER: Come along, Mrs. Linde; the place will only be bearable for a mother now!

(RANK, HELMER, and MRS. LINDE go downstairs. The NURSE comes forward with the children; NORA shuts the hall door.)

NORA: How fresh and well you look! Such red cheeks!—like apples and roses. (The children all talk at once while she speaks to them.) Have you had great fun? That's splendid! What, you pulled both Emmy and Bob along on the sledge?—both at once?—that was good. You are a clever boy, Ivar. Let me take her for a little, Anne. My sweet little baby doll! (Takes the baby from the MAID and dances it up and down) Yes, yes, mother will dance with Bob too. What! Have you been snowballing? I wish I had been there too! No, no, I will take their things off, Anne; please let me do it, it is such fun. Go in now, you look half frozen. There is some hot coffee for you on the stove.

(The NURSE goes into the room on the left. NORA takes off the children's things and throws them about, while they all talk to her at once.)

NORA: Really! Did a big dog run after you? But it didn't bite you? No, dogs don't bite nice little dolly children. You mustn't look at the parcels, Ivar. What are they? Ah, I daresay you would like to know. No, no—it's something nasty! Come, let us have a game! What shall we play at? Hide and Seek? Yes, we'll play Hide and Seek. Bob shall hide first. Must I hide? Very well, I'll hide first. (She and the children laugh and shout, and romp in and out of the room; at last NORA hides under the table, the children rush in and look for her, but do not see her; they hear her smothered laughter, run to the table, lift up the cloth and find her. Shouts of laughter. She crawls forward and pretends to frighten them. Fresh laughter. Meanwhile there has been a knock at the hall door, but none of them has noticed it. The door is half opened, and KROGSTAD appears. He waits a little; the game goes on.)

KROGSTAD: Excuse me, Mrs. Helmer.

NORA: (With a stifled cry, turns round and gets up on to her knees) Ah! what do you want?

KROGSTAD: Excuse me, the outer door was ajar; I suppose someone forgot to shut it.

NORA: (Rising) My husband is out, Mr. Krogstad.

KROGSTAD: I know that.

NORA: What do you want here, then?

KROGSTAD: A word with you.

NORA: With me?— (To the children, gently) Go in to nurse. What? No, the strange man won't do mother any harm. When he has gone we will have another game. (She takes the children into the room on the left, and shuts the door after them.) You want to speak to me?

KROGSTAD: Yes, I do.

NORA: To-day? It is not the first of the month yet.

KROGSTAD: No, it is Christmas Eve, and it will depend on yourself what sort of a Christmas you will spend.

NORA: What do you want? To-day it is absolutely impossible for me—

KROGSTAD: We won't talk about that till later on. This is something different. I presume you can give me a moment?

NORA: Yes—yes, I can—although—

KROGSTAD: Good. I was in Olsen's Restaurant and saw your husband going down the street—

NORA: Yes?

KROGSTAD: With a lady.

NORA: What then?

KROGSTAD: May I make so bold as to ask if it was a Mrs. Linde?

NORA: It was.

KROGSTAD: Just arrived in town?

NORA: Yes, to-day.

KROGSTAD: She is a great friend of yours, isn't she?

NORA: She is. But I don't see—

KROGSTAD: I knew her too, once upon a time.

NORA: I am aware of that.

KROGSTAD: Are you? So you know all about it; I thought as much. Then I can ask you, without beating about the bush—is Mrs. Linde to have an appointment in the Bank?

NORA: What right have you to question me, Mr. Krogstad?—You, one of my husband's subordinates! But since you ask, you shall know. Yes, Mrs.

Linde *is* to have an appointment. And it was I who pleaded her cause, Mr. Krogstad, let me tell you that.

KROGSTAD: I was right in what I thought, then.

NORA: *(Walking up and down the stage)* Sometimes one has a tiny little bit of influence, I should hope. Because one is a woman, it does not necessarily follow that—. When anyone is in a subordinate position, Mr. Krogstad, they should really be careful to avoid offending anyone who—who—

KROGSTAD: Who has influence?

NORA: Exactly.

KROGSTAD: *(Changing his tone)* Mrs. Helmer, you will be so good as to use your influence on my behalf.

NORA: What? What do you mean?

KROGSTAD: You will be so kind as to see that I am allowed to keep my subordinate position in the Bank.

NORA: What do you mean by that? Who proposes to take your post away from you?

KROGSTAD: Oh, there is no necessity to keep up the pretence of ignorance. I can quite understand that your friend is not very anxious to expose herself to the chance of rubbing shoulders with me; and I quite understand, too, whom I have to thank for being turned off.

NORA: But I assure you—

KROGSTAD: Very likely; but, to come to the point, the time has come when I should advise you to use your influence to prevent that.

NORA: But, Mr. Krogstad, I *have* no influence.

KROGSTAD: Haven't you? I thought you said yourself just now—

NORA: Naturally I did not mean you to put that construction on it. I! What should make you think I have any influence of that kind with my husband?

KROGSTAD: Oh, I have known your husband from our student days. I don't suppose he is any more unassailable than other husbands.

NORA: If you speak slightingly of my husband, I shall turn you out of the house.

KROGSTAD: You are bold, Mrs. Helmer.

NORA: I am not afraid of you any longer. As soon as the New Year comes, I shall in a very short time be free of the whole thing.

KROGSTAD *(Controlling himself)* Listen to me, Mrs. Helmer. If necessary, I am prepared to fight for my small post in the Bank as if I were fighting for my life.

NORA: So it seems.

KROGSTAD: It is not only for the sake of the money; indeed, that weighs least with me in the matter. There is another reason—well, I may as well tell you. My position is this. I daresay you know, like everybody else, that once, many years ago, I was guilty of an indiscretion.

NORA: I think I have heard something of the kind.

KRAGSTAD: The matter never came into court; but every way seemed to be closed to me after that. So I took to the business that you know of. I had to do something; and, honestly, I don't think I've been one of the worst. But now I must cut myself free from all that. My sons are growing up; for their sake I must try and win back as much respect as I can in the town. This post in the Bank was like the first step up for me—and now your husband is going to kick me downstairs again into the mud.

NORA: But you must believe me, Mr. Krogstad; it is not in my power to help you at all.

KROGSTAD: Then it is because you haven't the will; but I have means to compel you.

NORA: You don't mean that you will tell my husband that I owe you money?

KROGSTAD: Hm!—suppose I were to tell him?

NORA: It would be perfectly infamous of you. *(Sobbing)* To think of his learning my secret, which has been my joy and pride, in such an ugly, clumsy way—that he should learn it from you! And it would put me in a horribly disagreeable position—

KROGSTAD: Only disagreeable?

NORA: *(Impetuously)* Well, do it, then!—and it will be the worse for you. My husband will see for himself what a blackguard you are, and you certainly won't keep your post then.

KROGSTAD: I asked you if it was only a disagreeable scene at home that you were afraid of?

NORA: If my husband does get to know of it, of course he will at once pay you what is still owing, and we shall have nothing more to do with you.

KROGSTAD: *(Coming a step nearer)* Listen to me, Mrs. Helmer. Either you have a very bad memory or you know very little of business. I shall be obliged to remind you of a few details.

NORA: What do you mean?

KROGSTAD: When your husband was ill, you came to me to borrow two hundred and fifty pounds.

NORA: I didn't know any one else to go to.

KROGSTAD: I promised to get you that amount—

NORA: Yes, and you did so.

KROGSTAD: I promised to get you that amount, on certain conditions. Your mind was so taken up with your husband's illness, and you were so anxious to get the money for your journey, that you seem to have paid no attention to the conditions of our bargain. Therefore it will not be amiss if I remind you of them. Now, I promised to get the money on the security of a bond which I drew up.

NORA: Yes, and which I signed.

KROGSTAD: Good. But below your signature there were a few lines constituting your father a surety for the money; those lines your father should have signed.

NORA: Should? He did sign them.

KROGSTAD: I had left the date blank; that is to say your father should himself have inserted the date on which he signed the paper. Do you remember that?

NORA: Yes, I think I remember—

KROGSTAD: Then I gave you the bond to send by post to your father. Is that not so?

NORA: Yes.

KROGSTAD: And you naturally did so at once, because five or six days afterwards you brought me the bond with your father's signature. And then I gave you the money.

NORA: Well, haven't I been paying it off regularly?

KROGSTAD: Fairly so, yes. But—to come back to the matter in hand—that must have been a very trying time for you, Mrs. Helmer?

NORA: It was, indeed.

KROGSTAD: Your father was very ill, wasn't he?

NORA: He was very near his end.

KROGSTAD: And died soon afterwards?

NORA: Yes.

KROGSTAD: Tell me, Mrs. Helmer, can you by any chance remember what day your father died?—on what day of the month, I mean.

NORA: Papa died on the 29th of September.

KROGSTAD: That is correct; I have ascertained it for myself. And, as that is so, there is a discrepancy *(Taking a paper from his pocket)* which I cannot account for.

NORA: What discrepancy? I don't know—

KROGSTAD: The discrepancy consists, Mrs. Helmer, in the fact that your father signed this bond three days after his death.

NORA: What do you mean? I don't understand—

KROGSTAD: Your father died on the 29th of September. But, look here; your father has dated his signature the 2nd of October. It is a discrepancy, isn't it? *(NORA is silent)* Can you explain it to me? *(NORA is still silent)* It is a remarkable thing, too, that the words "2nd of October," as well as the year, are not written in your father's handwriting but in one that I think I know. Well, of course it can be explained; your father may have forgotten to date his signature, and someone else may have dated it haphazard before they knew of his death. There is no harm in that. It all depends on the signature of the name; and *that* is genuine, I suppose, Mrs. Helmer? It was your father himself who signed his name here?

NORA: *(After a short pause, throws her head up and looks defiantly at him)* No, it was not. It was I that wrote papa's name.

KROGSTAD: Are you aware that is a dangerous confession?

NORA: In what way? You shall have your money soon.

KROGSTAD: Let me ask you a question; why did you not send the paper to your father?

NORA: It was impossible; papa was so ill. If I had asked him for his signature, I should have had to tell him what the money was to be used for; and when he was so ill himself I couldn't tell him that my husband's life was in danger—it was impossible.

KROGSTAD: It would have been better for you if you had given up your trip abroad.

NORA: No, that was impossible. That trip was to save my husband's life; I couldn't give that up.

KROGSTAD: But did it never occur to you that you were committing a fraud on me?

NORA: I couldn't take that into account; I didn't trouble myself about you at all. I couldn't bear you, because you put so many heartless difficulties in my way, although you knew what a dangerous condition my husband was in.

KROGSTAD: Mrs. Helmer, you evidently do not realise clearly what it is that you have been guilty of. But I can assure you that my one false step, which lost me all my reputation, was nothing more or nothing worse than what you have done.

NORA: You? Do you ask me to believe that you were brave enough to run a risk to save your wife's life?

KROGSTAD: The law cares nothing about motives.

NORA: Then it must be a very foolish law.

KROGSTAD: Foolish or not, it is the law by which you will be judged, if I produce this paper in court.

NORA: I don't believe it. Is a daughter not to be allowed to spare her dying father anxiety and care? Is a wife not to be allowed to save her husband's life? I don't know much about law; but I am certain that there must be laws permitting such things as that. Have you no knowledge of such laws — you who are a lawyer? You must be a very poor lawyer, Mr. Krogstad.

KROGSTAD: Maybe. But matters of business — such business as you and I have had together — do you think I don't understand that? Very well. Do as you please. But let me tell you this — if I lose my position a second time, you shall lose yours with me. *(He bows, and goes out through the hall)*

NORA: *(Appears buried in thought for a short time, then tosses her head)* Nonsense! Trying to frighten me like that! — I am not so silly as he thinks. *(Begins to busy herself putting the children's things in order)* And yet — ? No, it's impossible! I did it for love's sake.

THE CHILDREN *(In the doorway on the left)* Mother, the stranger man has gone out through the gate.

NORA: Yes, dears, I know. But, don't tell anyone about the stranger man. Do you hear? Not even papa.

CHILDREN: No, mother; but will you come and play again?

NORA: No no, — not now.

CHILDREN: But, mother, you promised us.

NORA: Yes, but I can't now. Run away in; I have such a lot to do. Run away in, my sweet little darlings. *(She gets them into the room by degrees and shuts the door on them; then sits down on the sofa, takes up a piece of needlework and sews a few stitches, but soon stops.)* No! *(Throws down the work, gets up, goes to the hall door and calls out)* Helen! bring the Tree in. *(Goes to the table on the left, opens a drawer, and stops again)* No, no! it is quite impossible!

MAID: *(Coming in with the Tree)* Where shall I put it, ma'am?

NORA: Here, in the middle of the floor.

MAID: Shall I get you anything else?

NORA: No, thank you. I have all I want.

(Exit MAID*)*

NORA: *(Begins dressing the tree)* A candle here — and flowers here — . The horrible man! It's all nonsense — there's nothing wrong. The Tree shall be splendid! I will do everything I can think of to please you. Torvald! — I will sing for you, dance for you — *(*HELMER *comes in with some papers under his arm.)* Oh! are you back already?

HELMER: Yes. Has anyone been here?

NORA: Here? No.

HELMER: That is strange. I saw Krogstad going out of the gate.

NORA: Did you? Oh yes, I forgot, Krogstad was here for a moment.

HELMER: Nora, I can see from your manner that he has been here begging you to say a good word for him.

NORA: Yes.

HELMER: And you were to appear to do it of your own accord; you were to conceal from me the fact of his having been here; didn't he beg that of you too?

NORA: Yes, Torvald, but —

HELMER: Nora, Nora, and you would be a party to that sort of thing? To have any talk with a man like that, and give him any sort of promise? And to tell me a lie into the bargain?

NORA: A lie — ?

HELMER: Didn't you tell me no one had been here? *(Shakes his finger at her)* My little song-bird must never do that again. A song-bird must have a clean beak to chirp with — no false notes! *(Puts his arm round her waist)* That is so, isn't it? Yes, I am sure it is. *(Lets her go.)* We will say no more about it. *(Sits down by the stove)* How warm and snug it is here! *(Turns over his papers)*

NORA: *(After a short pause, during which she busies herself with the Christmas Tree)* Torvald!

HELMER: Yes.

NORA: I am looking forward tremendously to the fancy dress ball at the Stenborgs' the day after to-morrow.

HELMER: And I am tremendously curious to see what you are going to surprise me with.

NORA: It was very silly of me to want to do that.

HELMER: What do you mean?

NORA: I can't hit upon anything that will do; everything I think of seems so silly and insignificant.

HELMER: Does my little Nora acknowledge that at last?

NORA: *(Standing behind his chair with her arms on the back of it)* Are you very busy, Torvald?

HELMER: Well —

NORA: What are all those papers?

HELMER: Bank business.

NORA: Already?

HELMER I have got authority from the retiring manager to undertake the necessary changes in the staff and in the rearrangement of the work; and I must make use of the Christmas week for that, so as to have everything in order for the new year.

NORA: Then that was why this poor Krogstad —

HELMER: Hm!

NORA: *(Leans against the back of his chair and strokes his hair)* If you hadn't been so busy I should have asked you a tremendously big favour, Torvald.

HELMER: What is that? Tell me.

NORA: There is no one has such good taste as you. And I do so want to look nice at the fancy-dress ball. Torvald, couldn't you take me in hand and decide what I shall go as, and what sort of a dress I shall wear?

HELMER: Aha! so my obstinate little woman is obliged to get someone to come to her rescue?

NORA: Yes, Torvald, I can't get along a bit without your help.

HELMER: Very well, I will think it over, we shall manage to hit upon something.

NORA: That *is* nice of you. *(Goes to the Christmas Tree. A short pause.)* How pretty the red flowers look —. But, tell me, was it really something very bad that this Krogstad was guilty of?

HELMER: He forged someone's name. Have you any idea what that means?

NORA: Isn't it possible that he was driven to do it by necessity?

HELMER: Yes; or, as in so many cases, by imprudence. I am not so heartless as to condemn a man altogether because of a single false step of that kind.

NORA: No you wouldn't, would you, Torvald?

HELMER: Many a man has been able to retrieve his character, if he has openly confessed his fault and taken his punishment.

NORA: Punishment —?

HELMER: But Krogstad did nothing of that sort; he got himself out of it by a cunning trick, and that is why he has gone under altogether.

NORA: But do you think it would —?

HELMER: Just think how a guilty man like that has to lie and play the hypocrite with everyone, how he has to wear a mask in the presence of those near and dear to him, even before his own wife and children. And about the children — that is the most terrible part of it all, Nora.

NORA: How?

HELMER: Because such an atmosphere of lies infects and poisons the whole life of a home. Each breath the children take in such a house is full of the germs of evil.

NORA: *(Coming nearer him)* Are you sure of that?

HELMER: My dear, I have often seen it in the course of my life as a lawyer. Almost everyone who has gone to the bad early in life has had a deceitful mother.

NORA: Why do you only say — mother?

HELMER: It seems most commonly to be the mother's influence, though naturally a bad father's would have the same result. Every lawyer is familiar with the fact. This Krogstad, now, has been persistently poisoning his own children with lies and dissimulation; that is why I say he has lost all moral character. *(Holds out his hands to her)* That is why my sweet little Nora must promise me not to plead his cause. Give me your hand on it. Come, come, what is this? Give me your hand. There now, that's settled. I assure you it would be quite impossible for me to work with him; I literally feel physically ill when I am in the company of such people.

NORA: *(Takes her hand out of his and goes to the opposite side of the Christmas Tree)* How hot it is in here; and I have such a lot to do.

HELMER: *(Getting up and putting his papers in order)* Yes, and I must try and read through some of these before dinner; and I must think about your costume, too. And it is just possible I may have something ready in gold paper to hang up on the

Tree. *(Puts his hand on her head)* My precious little singing-bird! *(He goes into his room and shuts the door after him)*

NORA: *(After a pause, whispers)* No, no—it isn't true. It's impossible; it must be impossible.

(The NURSE opens the door on the left.)

NURSE: The little ones are begging so hard to be allowed to come in to mamma.

NORA: No, no, no! Don't let them come in to me! You stay with them, Anne.

NURSE: Very well, ma'am. *(Shuts the door)*

NORA: *(Pale with terror)* Deprave my little children? Poison my home? *(A short pause. Then she tosses her head)* It's not true. It can't possibly be true.

ACT II

THE SAME SCENE.

The Christmas Tree is in the corner by the piano, stripped of its ornaments and with burnt-down candle-ends on its dishevelled branches. NORA'S cloak and hat are lying on the sofa. She is alone in the room, walking about uneasily. She stops by the sofa and takes up her cloak.

NORA: *(Drops the cloak)* Someone is coming now! *(Goes to the door and listens.)* No—it is no one. Of course, no one will come to-day, Christmas Day—nor tomorrow either. But, perhaps—*(Opens the door and looks out)* No, nothing in the letter-box; it is quite empty. *(Comes forward)* What rubbish! Of course he can't be in earnest about it. Such a thing couldn't happen; it is impossible—I have three little children.

(Enter the NURSE from the room on the left, carrying a big cardboard box.)

NURSE: At last I have found the box with the fancy dress.

NORA: Thanks; put it on the table.

NURSE: *(Doing so)* But it is very much in want of mending.

NORA: I should like to tear it into a hundred thousand pieces.

NURSE: What an idea! It can easily be put in order—just a little patience.

NORA: Yes, I will go and get Mrs. Linde to come and help me with it.

NURSE: What, out again? In this horrible weather? You will catch cold, ma'am, and make yourself ill.

NORA: Well, worse than that might happen. How are the children?

NURSE: The poor little souls are playing with their Christmas presents, but—

NORA: Do they ask much for me?

NURSE: You see, they are so accustomed to have their mamma with them.

NORA: Yes, but, nurse, I shall not be able to be so much with them now as I was before.

NURSE: Oh well, young children easily get accustomed to anything.

NORA: Do you think so? Do you think they would forget their mother if she went away altogether?

NURSE: Good heavens!—went away altogether?

NORA: Nurse, I want you to tell me something I have often wondered about—how could you have the heart to put your own child out among strangers?

NURSE: I was obliged to, if I wanted to be little Nora's nurse.

NORA: Yes, but how could you be willing to do it?

NURSE: What, when I was going to get such a good place by it? A poor girl who has got into trouble should be glad to. Besides, that wicked man didn't do a single thing for me.

NORA: But I suppose your daughter has quite forgotten you.

NURSE: No, indeed she hasn't. She wrote to me when she was confirmed, and when she was married.

NORA: *(Putting her arms around her neck)* Dear old Anne, you were a good mother to me when I was little.

NURSE: Little Nora, poor dear, had no other mother but me.

NORA: And if my little ones had no other mother, I am sure you would— What nonsense I am talking! *(Opens the box)* Go in to them. Now I must—. You will see to-morrow how charming I shall look.

NURSE: I am sure there will be no one at the ball so charming as you, ma'am. *(Goes into the room on the left)*

NORA: *(Begins to unpack the box, but soon pushes it away from her)* If only I dared go out. If only no one would come. If only I could be sure nothing would happen here in the meantime. Stuff and nonsense! No one will come. Only I mustn't think about it. I will brush my muff. What lovely, lovely gloves! Out of my thoughts, out of my thoughts! One, two, three, four, five, six— *(Screams)* Ah! there is someone coming—. *(Makes a movement towards the door, but stands irresolute)*

(Enter MRS. LINDE *from the hall, where she has taken off her cloak and hat.)*

NORA: Oh, it's you, Christine. There is no one else out there, is there? How good of you to come!

MRS. LINDE: I heard you were up asking for me.

NORA: Yes, I was passing by. As a matter of fact, it is something you could help me with. Let us sit down here on the sofa. Look here. To-morrow evening there is to be a fancy-dress ball at the Stenborgs', who live above us; and Torvald wants me to go as a Neapolitan fisher-girl, and dance the Tarantella that I learnt at Capri.

MRS. LINDE: I see; you are going to keep up the character.

NORA: Yes, Torvald wants me to. Look, here is the dress; Torvald had it made for me there, but now it is all so torn, and I haven't any idea—

MRS. LINDE: We will easily put that right. It is only some of the trimming come unsewn here and there. Needle and thread? Now then, that's all we want.

NORA: It *is* nice of you.

MRS. LINDE: *(Sewing)* So you are going to be dressed up to-morrow, Nora. I will tell you what— I shall come in for a moment and see you in your fine feathers. But I have completely forgotten to thank you for a delightful evening yesterday.

NORA: *(Gets up, and crosses the stage)* Well I don't think yesterday was as pleasant as usual. You ought to have come to town a little earlier, Christine. Certainly Torvald does understand how to make a house dainty and attractive.

MRS. LINDE: And so do you, it seems to me; you are not your father's daughter for nothing. But tell me, is Doctor Rank always as depressed as he was yesterday?

NORA: No; yesterday it was very noticeable. I must tell you that he suffers from a very dangerous disease. He has consumption of the spine, poor creature. His father was a horrible man who committed all sorts of excesses; and that is why his son was sickly from childhood, do you understand?

MRS. LINDE: *(Dropping her sewing)* But, my dearest Nora, how do you know anything about such things?

NORA: *(Walking about)* Pooh! When you have three children, you get visits now and then from—from married women, who know something of medical matters, and they talk about one thing and another.

MRS. LINDE: *(Goes on sewing. A short silence)* Does Doctor Rank come here every day?

NORA: Every day regularly. He is Torvald's most intimate friend, and a great friend of mine too. He is just like one of the family.

MRS. LINDE: But tell me this—is he perfectly sincere? I mean, isn't he the kind of man that is very anxious to make himself agreeable?

NORA: Not in the least. What makes you think that?

MRS. LINDE: When you introduced him to me yesterday, he declared he had often heard my name mentioned in this house; but afterwards I noticed that your husband hadn't the slightest idea who I was. So how could Doctor Rank—?

NORA: That is quite right, Christine. Torvald is so absurdly fond of me that he wants me absolutely to himself, as he says. At first he used to seem almost jealous if I mentioned any of the dear folk at home, so naturally I gave up doing so. But I often talk about such things with Doctor Rank, because he likes hearing about them.

MRS. LINDE: Listen to me, Nora. You are still very like a child in many things, and I am older than you in many ways and have a little more experience. Let me tell you this—you ought to make an end of it with Doctor Rank.

NORA: What ought I to make an end of?

MRS. LINDE: Of two things, I think. Yesterday you talked some nonsense about a rich admirer who was to leave you money—

NORA: An admirer who doesn't exist, unfortunately! But what then?

MRS. LINDE: Is Doctor Rank a man of means?

NORA: Yes, he is.

MRS. LINDE: And has no one to provide for?

NORA: No, no one; but—

MRS. LINDE: And comes here every day?

NORA: Yes, I told you so.

MRS. LINDE: But how can this well-bred man be so tactless?

NORA: I don't understand you at all.

MRS. LINDE: Don't prevaricate, Nora. Do you suppose I don't guess who lent you the two hundred and fifty pounds?

NORA: Are you out of your senses? How can you think of such a thing! A friend of ours, who comes here every day! Do you realise what a horribly painful position that would be?

MRS. LINDE: Then it really isn't he?

NORA: No, certainly not. It would never have entered into my head for a moment. Besides, he had no money to lend then; he came into his money afterwards.

MRS. LINDE: Well, I think that was lucky for you, my dear Nora.

NORA: No, it would never have come into my head to ask Doctor Rank. Although I am quite sure that if I had asked him—

MRS. LINDE: But of course you won't.

NORA: Of course not. I have no reason to think it could possibly be necessary. But I am quite sure that if I told Doctor Rank—

MRS. LINDE: Behind your husband's back?

NORA: I must make an end of it with the other one, and that will be behind his back too. I *must* make an end of it with him.

MRS. LINDE: Yes, that is what I told you yesterday, but—

NORA: *(Walking up and down)* A man can put a thing like that straight much easier than a woman—

MRS. LINDE: One's husband, yes.

NORA: Nonsense! *(Standing still)* When you pay off a debt you get your bond back, don't you?

MRS. LINDE: Yes, as a matter of course.

NORA: And can tear it into a hundred thousand pieces, and burn it up—the nasty dirty paper!

MRS. LINDE: *(Looks hard at her, lays down her sewing and gets up slowly)* Nora, you are concealing something from me.

NORA: Do I look as if I were?

MRS. LINDE: Something has happened to you since yesterday morning. Nora, what is it?

NORA: *(Going nearer to her)* Christine! *(Listens)* Hush! there's Torvald come home. Do you mind going in to the children for the present? Torvald can't bear to see dressmaking going on. Let Anne help you.

MRS. LINDE: *(Gathering some of the things together)* Certainly—but I am not going away from here till we have had it out with one another. *(She goes into the room on the left, as Helmer comes in from the hall)*

NORA: *(Going up to* HELMER*)* I have wanted you so much, Torvald dear.

HELMER: Was that the dressmaker?

NORA: No, it was Christine; she is helping me to put my dress in order. You will see I shall look quite smart.

HELMER: Wasn't that a happy thought of mine, now?

NORA: Splendid! But don't you think it is nice of me, too, to do as you wish?

HELMER: Nice?—because you do as your husband wishes? Well, well, you little rogue, I am sure you did not mean it in that way. But I am not going to disturb you; you will want to be trying on your dress, I expect.

NORA: I suppose you are going to work.

HELMER: Yes. *(Shows her a bundle of papers)* Look at that. I have just been into the bank. *(Turns to go into his room)*

NORA: Torvald.

HELMER: Yes.

NORA: If your little squirrel were to ask you for something very, very prettily—?

HELMER: What then?

NORA: Would you do it?

HELMER: I should like to hear what it is, first.

NORA: Your squirrel would run about and do all her tricks if you would be nice, and do what she wants.

HELMER: Speak plainly.

NORA: Your skylark would chirp about in every room, with her song rising and falling—

HELMER: Well, my skylark does that anyhow.

NORA: I would play the fairy and dance for you in the moonlight, Torvald.

HELMER: Nora—you surely don't mean that request you made of me this morning?

NORA: *(Going near him)* Yes, Torvald, I beg you so earnestly—

HELMER: Have you really the courage to open up that question again?

NORA: Yes, dear, you *must* do as I ask; you *must* let Krogstad keep his post in the bank.

HELMER: My dear Nora, it is his post that I have arranged Mrs. Linde shall have.

NORA: Yes, you have been awfully kind about that; but you could just as well dismiss some other clerk instead of Krogstad.

HELMER: This is simply incredible obstinacy! Because you chose to give him a thoughtless promise that you would speak for him, I am expected to—

NORA: That isn't the reason, Torvald. It is for your own sake. This fellow writes in the most scurrilous newspapers; you have told me so yourself. He can do you an unspeakable amount of harm. I am frightened to death of him—

HELMER: Ah, I understand; it is recollections of the past that scare you.

NORA: What do you mean?

HELMER: Naturally you are thinking of your father.

NORA: Yes—yes, of course. Just recall in your mind what these malicious creatures wrote in the papers about papa, and how horribly they slandered him. I believe they would have procured his dismissal if the Department had not sent you over to inquire into it, and if you had not been so kindly disposed and helpful to him.

HELMER: My little Nora, there is an important difference between your father and me. Your father's reputation as a public official was not above suspicion. Mine is, and I hope it will continue to be so, as long as I hold my office.

NORA: You never can tell what mischief these men may contrive. We ought to be so well off, so snug and happy here in our peaceful home, and have no cares—you and I and the children, Torvald! That is why I beg you so earnestly—

HELMER: And it is just by interceding for him that you make it impossible for me to keep him. It is already known at the Bank that I mean to dismiss Krogstad. Is it to get about now that the new manager has changed his mind at his wife's bidding—

NORA: And what if it did?

HELMER: Of course!—if only this obstinate little person can get her way! Do you suppose I am going to make myself ridiculous before my whole staff, to let people think that I am a man to be swayed by all sorts of outside influence? I should very soon feel the consequences of it, I can tell you! And besides, there is one thing that makes it quite impossible for me to have Krogstad in the bank as long as I am manager.

NORA: Whatever is that?

HELMER: His moral failings I might perhaps have overlooked, if necessary—

NORA: Yes, you could—couldn't you?

HELMER: And I hear he is a good worker, too. But I knew him when we were boys. It was one of those rash friendships that so often prove an incubus in after life. I may as well tell you plainly, we were once on very intimate terms with one another. But this tactless fellow lays no restraint on himself when other people are present. On the contrary, he thinks it gives him the right to adopt a familiar tone with me, and every minute it is "I say, Helmer, old fellow!" and that sort of thing. I assure you it is extremely painful for me. He would make my position in the bank intolerable.

NORA: Torvald, I don't believe you mean that.

HELMER: Don't you? Why not?

NORA: Because it is such a narrow-minded way of looking at things.

HELMER: What are you saying? Narrow-minded? Do you think I am narrow-minded?

NORA: No, just the opposite, dear—and it is exactly for that reason.

HELMER: It's the same thing. You say my point of view is narrow-minded, so I must be so too. Narrow-minded! Very well—I must put an end to this. *(Goes to the hall-door and calls)* Helen!

NORA: What are you going to do?

HELMER: *(Looking among his papers)* Settle it. *(Enter MAID)* Look here; take this letter and go downstairs with it at once. Find a messenger and tell him to deliver it, and be quick. The address is on it, and here is the money.

MAID: Very well, sir. *(Exit with the letter)*

HELMER: *(Putting his papers together)* Now then, little Miss Obstinate.

NORA: *(Breathlessly)* Torvald—what was that letter?

HELMER: Krogstad's dismissal.

NORA: Call her back, Torvald! There is still time. Oh Torvald, call her back! Do it for my sake—

for your own sake—for the children's sake! Do you hear me, Torvald? Call her back! You don't know what that letter can bring upon us.

HELMER: It's too late.

NORA: Yes, it's too late.

HELMER: My dear Nora, I can forgive the anxiety you are in, although really it is an insult to me. It is, indeed. Isn't it an insult to think that I should be afraid of a starving quill-driver's vengeance? But I forgive you nevertheless, because it is such eloquent witness to your great love for me. *(Takes her in his arms)* And that is as it should be, my own darling Nora. Come what will, you may be sure I shall have both courage and strength if they be needed. You will see I am man enough to take everything upon myself.

NORA: *(In a horror-stricken voice)* What do you mean by that?

HELMER: Everything, I say—

NORA: *(Recovering herself)* You will never have to do that.

HELMER: That's right. Well, we will share it, Nora, as man and wife should. That is how it shall be. *(Caressing her)* Are you content now? There! there!—not these frightened dove's eyes! The whole thing is only the wildest fancy!—Now, you must go and play through the Tarantella and practise with your tambourine. I shall go into the inner office and shut the door, and I shall hear nothing; you can make as much noise as you please. *(Turns back at the door)* And when Rank comes, tell him where he will find me. *(Nods to her, takes his papers and goes into his room, and shuts the door after him)*

NORA: *(Bewildered with anxiety, stands as if rooted to the spot, and whispers)* He was capable of doing it. He will do it. He will do it in spite of everything.—No, not that! Never, never! Anything rather than that! Oh, for some help, some way out of it! *(The door-bell rings)* Doctor Rank! Anything rather than that—anything, whatever it is! *(She puts her hands over her face, pulls herself together, goes to the door and opens it.* RANK *is standing without, hanging up his coat. During the following dialogue it begins to grow dark.)*

NORA: Good-day, Doctor Rank. I knew your ring. But you mustn't go into Torvald now; I think he is busy with something.

RANK: And you?

NORA: *(Brings him in and shuts the door after him)* Oh, you know very well I always have time for you.

RANK: Thank you. I shall make use of as much of it as I can.

NORA: What do you mean by that? As much of it as you can?

RANK: Well, does that alarm you?

NORA: It was such a strange way of putting it. Is anything likely to happen?

RANK: Nothing but what I have long been prepared for. But I certainly didn't expect it to happen so soon.

NORA: *(Gripping him by the arm)* What have you found out? Doctor Rank, you must tell me.

RANK: *(Sitting down by the stove)* It is all up with me. And it can't be helped.

NORA: *(With a sigh of relief)* Is it about yourself?

RANK: Who else? It is no use lying to one's self. I am the most wretched of all my patients, Mrs. Helmer. Lately I have been taking stock of my internal economy. Bankrupt! Probably within a month I shall lie rotting in the churchyard.

NORA: What an ugly thing to say!

RANK: The thing itself is cursedly ugly, and the worst of it is that I shall have to face so much more that is ugly before that. I shall only make one more examination of myself; when I have done that, I shall know pretty certainly when it will be that the horrors of dissolution will begin. There is something I want to tell you. Helmer's refined nature gives him an unconquerable disgust at everything that is ugly; I won't have him in my sick-room.

NORA: Oh, but, Doctor Rank—

RANK: I won't have him there. Not on any account. I bar my door to him. As soon as I am quite certain that the worst has come, I shall send you my card with a black cross on it, and then you will know that the loathsome end has begun.

NORA: You are quite absurd to-day. And I wanted you so much to be in a really good humour.

RANK: With death stalking beside me?—To have to pay this penalty for another man's sin! Is there any justice in that? And in every single family, in one way or another, some such inexorable retribution is being exacted—

NORA: *(Putting her hands over her ears)* Rubbish! Do talk of something cheerful.

RANK: Oh, it's a mere laughing matter, the whole thing. My poor innocent spine has to suffer for my father's youthful amusements.

NORA: *(Sitting at the table on the left)* I suppose you mean that he was too partial to asparagus and pâté de foie gras, don't you.

RANK: Yes, and to truffles.

NORA: Truffles, yes. And oysters too, I suppose?

RANK: Oysters, of course, that goes without saying.

NORA: And heaps of port and champagne. It is sad that all these nice things should take their revenge on our bones.

RANK: Especially that they should revenge themselves on the unlucky bones of those who have not had the satisfaction of enjoying them.

NORA: Yes, that's the saddest part of it all.

RANK: *(With a searching look at her)* Hm!—

NORA: *(After a short pause)* Why did you smile?

RANK: No, it was you that laughed.

NORA: No, it was you that smiled, Doctor Rank!

RANK: *(Rising)* You are a greater rascal than I thought.

NORA: I am in a silly mood to-day.

RANK: So it seems.

NORA: *(Putting her hands on his shoulders)* Dear, dear Doctor Rank, death mustn't take you away from Torvald and me.

RANK: It is a loss you would easily recover from. Those who are gone are soon forgotten.

NORA: *(Looking at him anxiously)* Do you believe that?

RANK: People form new ties, and then—

NORA: Who will form new ties?

RANK: Both you and Helmer, when I am gone. You yourself are already on the high road to it, I think. What did that Mrs. Linde want here last night?

NORA: Oho!—you don't mean to say you are jealous of poor Christine?

RANK: Yes, I am. She will be my successor in this house. When I am done for, this woman will—

NORA: Hush! don't speak so loud. She is in that room.

RANK: To-day again. There, you see.

NORA: She has only come to sew my dress for me. Bless my soul, how unreasonable you are! *(Sits down on the sofa)* Be nice now, Doctor Rank, and to-morrow you will see how beautifully I shall dance, and you can imagine I am doing it all for you—and for Torvald too, of course. *(Takes various things out of the box)* Doctor Rank, come and sit down here, and I will show you something.

RANK: *(Sitting down)* What is it?

NORA: Just look at those!

RANK: Silk stockings.

NORA: Flesh-coloured. Aren't they lovely? It is so dark here now, but to-morrow—. No, no, no! you must only look at the feet. Oh well, you may have leave to look at the legs too.

RANK: Hm!—

NORA: Why are you looking so critical? Don't you think they will fit me?

RANK: I have no means of forming an opinion about that.

NORA: *(Looks at him for a moment)* For shame! *(Hits him lightly on the ear with the stockings)* That's to punish you. *(Folds them up again)*

RANK: And what other nice things am I to be allowed to see?

NORA: Not a single thing more, for being so naughty. *(She looks among the things, humming to herself)*

RANK: *(After a short silence)* When I am sitting here, talking to you as intimately as this, I cannot imagine for a moment what would have become of me if I had never come into this house.

NORA: *(Smiling)* I believe you do feel thoroughly at home with us.

RANK: *(In a lower voice, looking straight in front of him)* And to be obliged to leave it all—

NORA: Nonsense, you are not going to leave it.

RANK: *(As before)* And not be able to leave behind one the slightest token of one's gratitude, scarcely even a fleeting regret—nothing but an empty place which the first comer can fill as well as any other.

NORA: And if I asked you now for a—? No!

RANK: For what?

NORA: For a big proof of your friendship—

RANK: Yes, yes!

NORA: I mean a tremendously big favour—

RANK: Would you really make me so happy for once?

NORA: Ah, but you don't know what it is yet.

RANK: No—but tell me.

NORA: I really can't, Doctor Rank. It is something out of all reason; it means advice, and help, and a favour—

RANK: The bigger a thing it is the better. I can't conceive what it is you mean. Do tell me. Haven't I your confidence?

NORA: More than anyone else. I know you are my truest and best friend, and so I will tell you what it is. Well, Doctor Rank, it is something you must help me to prevent. You know how devotedly, how inexpressibly deeply Torvald loves me; he would never for a moment hesitate to give his life for me.

RANK: *(Leaning towards her)* Nora—do you think he is the only one—?

NORA: *(With a slight start)* The only one—?

RANK: The only one who would gladly give his life for your sake.

NORA: *(Sadly)* Is that it?

RANK: I was determined you should know it before I went away, and there will never be a better opportunity than this. Now you know it, Nora. And now you know, too, that you can trust me as you would trust no one else.

NORA: *(Rises, deliberately and quietly)* Let me pass.

RANK: *(Makes room for her to pass him, but sits still)* Nora!

NORA: *(At the hall door)* Helen, bring in the lamp. *(Goes over to the stove)* Dear Doctor Rank, that was really horrid of you.

RANK: To have loved you as much as anyone else does? Was that horrid?

NORA: No, but to go and tell me so. There was really no need—

RANK: What do you mean? Did you know—? (MAID *enters with lamp, puts it down on the table, and goes out)* Nora—Mrs. Helmer—tell me, had you any idea of this?

NORA: Oh, how do I know whether I had or whether I hadn't? I really can't tell you— To think you could be so clumsy, Doctor Rank! We were getting on so nicely.

RANK: Well, at all events you know now that you can command me, body and soul. So won't you speak out?

NORA: *(Looking at him)* After what happened?

RANK: I beg you to let me know what it is.

NORA: I can't tell you anything now.

RANK: Yes, yes. You mustn't punish me in that way. Let me have permission to do for you whatever a man may do.

NORA: You can do nothing for me now. Besides, I really don't need any help at all. You will find that the whole thing is merely fancy on my part. It really is so—of course it is! *(Sits down in the rocking-chair, and looks at him with a smile.)* You are a nice sort of man, Doctor Rank!—don't you feel ashamed of yourself, now the lamp has come?

RANK: Not a bit. But perhaps I had better go—for ever?

NORA: No, indeed, you shall not. Of course you must come here just as before. You know very well Torvald can't do without you.

RANK: Yes, but you?

NORA: Oh, I am always tremendously pleased when you come.

RANK: It is just that, that put me on the wrong track. You are a riddle to me. I have often thought that you would almost as soon be in my company as in Helmer's.

NORA: Yes—you see there are some people one loves best, and others whom one would almost always rather have as companions.

RANK: Yes, there is something in that.

NORA: When I was at home, of course I loved papa best. But I always thought it tremendous fun if I could steal down into the maids' room, because they never moralised at all, and talked to each other about such entertaining things.

RANK: I see—it is *their* place I have taken.

NORA: *(Jumping up and going to him)* Oh, dear, nice Doctor Rank, I never meant that at all. But surely you can understand that being with Torvald is a little like being with papa—

(Enter MAID *from the hall.)*

MAID: If you please, ma'am. *(Whispers and hands her a card)*

NORA: *(Glancing at the card)* Oh! *(Puts it in her pocket)*

RANK: Is there anything wrong?

NORA: No, no, not in the least. It is only something—it is my new dress—

RANK: What? Your dress is lying there.

NORA: Oh, yes, that one; but this is another. I ordered it. Torvald mustn't know about it—

RANK: Oho! Then that was the great secret.

NORA: Of course. Just go in to him; he is sitting in the inner room. Keep him as long as—

RANK: Make your mind easy; I won't let him escape. *(Goes into* HELMER'S *room.)*

NORA: *(To the* MAID*)* And he is standing waiting in the kitchen?

MAID: Yes; he came up the back stairs.

NORA: But didn't you tell him no one was in?

MAID: Yes, but it was no good.

NORA: He won't go away?

MAID: No; he says he won't until he has seen you, ma'am.

NORA: Well, let him come in—but quietly. Helen, you mustn't say anything about it to anyone. It is a surprise for my husband.

MAID: Yes, ma'am, I quite understand. *(Exit)*

NORA: This dreadful thing is going to happen! It will happen in spite of me! No, no, no, it can't happen—it shan't happen! *(She bolts the door of* HELMER'S *room. The* MAID *opens the hall door for* KROGSTAD *and shuts it after him. He is wearing a fur coat, high boots and a fur cap.)*

NORA: *(Advancing towards him)* Speak low—my husband is at home.

KROGSTAD: No matter about that.

NORA: What do you want of me?

KROGSTAD: An explanation of something.

NORA: Make haste then. What is it?

KROGSTAD: You know, I suppose, that I have got my dismissal.

NORA: I couldn't prevent it, Mr. Krogstad. I fought as hard as I could on your side, but it was no good.

KROGSTAD: Does your husband love you so little, then? He knows what I can expose you to, and yet he ventures—

NORA: How can you suppose that he has any knowledge of the sort?

KROGSTAD: I didn't suppose so at all. It would not be the least like our dear Torvald Helmer to show so much courage—

NORA: Mr. Krogstad, a litle respect for my husband, please.

KROGSTAD: Certainly—all the respect he deserves. But since you have kept the matter so carefully to yourself, I make bold to suppose that you have a little clearer idea, than you had yesterday, of what it actually is that you have done?

NORA: More than you could ever teach me.

KROGSTAD: Yes, such a bad lawyer as I am.

NORA: What is it you want of me?

KROGSTAD: Only to see how you were, Mrs. Helmer. I have been thinking about you all day long. A mere cashier, a quill-driver, a—well, a man like me—even he has a little of what is called feeling, you know.

NORA: Show it, then; think of my little children.

KROGSTAD: Have you and your husband thought of mine? But never mind about that. I only wanted to tell you that you need not take this matter too seriously. In the first place there will be no accusation made on my part.

NORA: No, of course not; I was sure of that.

KROGSTAD: The whole thing can be arranged amicably; there is no reason why anyone should know anything about it. It will remain a secret between us three.

NORA: My husband must never get to know anything about it.

KROGSTAD: How will you be able to prevent it? Am I to understand that you can pay the balance that is owing?

NORA: No, not just at present.

KROGSTAD: Or perhaps that you have some expedient for raising the money soon?

NORA: No expedient that I mean to make use of.

KROGSTAD: Well, in any case, it would have been of no use to you now. If you stood there with ever so much money in your hand, I would never part with your bond.

NORA: Tell me what purpose you mean to put it to.

KROGSTAD: I shall only preserve it—keep it in my possession. No one who is not concerned in the matter shall have the slightest hint of it. So that if the thought of it has driven you to any desperate resolution—

NORA: It has.

KROGSTAD: If you had it in your mind to run away from your home—

NORA: I had.

KROGSTAD: Or even something worse—

NORA: How could you know that?

KROGSTAD: Give up the idea.

NORA: How did you know I had thought of *that?*

KROGSTAD: Most of us think of that at first. I did, too—but I hadn't the courage.

NORA: *(Faintly)* No more had I.

KROGSTAD: *(In a tone of relief)* No, that's it, isn't it—you hadn't the courage either?

NORA: No, I haven't—I haven't.

KROGSTAD: Besides, it would have been a great piece of folly. Once the first storm at home is over — . I have a letter for your husband in my pocket.

NORA: Telling him everything?

KROGSTAD: In as lenient a manner as I possibly could.

NORA: (Quickly) He mustn't get the letter. Tear it up. I will find some means of getting money.

KROGSTAD: Excuse me, Mrs. Helmer, but I think I told you just now —

NORA: I am not speaking of what I owe you. Tell me what sum you are asking my husband for, and I will get the money.

KROGSTAD: I am not asking your husband for a penny.

NORA: What do you want, then?

KROGSTAD: I will tell you. I want to rehabilitate myself, Mrs. Helmer; I want to get on; and in that your husband must help me. For the last year and a half I have not had a hand in anything dishonourable, and all that time I have been struggling in most restricted circumstances. I was content to work my way up step by step. Now I am turned out, and I am not going to be satisfied with merely being taken into favour again. I want to get on, I tell you. I want to get into the Bank again, in a higher position. Your husband must make a place for me —

NORA: That he will never do!

KROGSTAD: He will; I know him; he dare not protest. And as soon as I am in there again with him, then you will see! Within a year I shall be the manager's right hand. It will be Nils Krogstad and not Torvald Helmer who manages the Bank.

NORA: That's a thing you will never see!

KROGSTAD: Do you mean that you will — ?

NORA: I have courage enough for it now.

KROGSTAD: Oh, you can't frighten me. A fine, spoilt lady like you —

NORA: You will see, you will see.

KROGSTAD: Under the ice, perhaps? Down into the cold, coal-black water? And then, in the spring, to float up to the surface, all horrible and unrecognisable, with your hair fallen out —

NORA: You can't frighten me.

KROGSTAD: Nor you me. People don't do such things, Mrs. Helmer. Besides, what use would it be? I should have him completely in my power all the same.

NORA: Afterwards? When I am no longer —

KROGSTAD: Have you forgotten that it is I who have the keeping of your reputation? (Nora stands speechlessly looking at him) Well, now, I have warned you. Do not do anything foolish. When Helmer has had my letter, I shall expect a message from him. And be sure you remember that it is your husband himself who has forced me into such ways as this again. I will never forgive him for that. Good-bye, Mrs. Helmer. (Exit through the hall)

NORA: (Goes to the hall door, opens it slightly and listens) He is going. He is not putting the letter in the box. Oh no, no! that's impossible! (Opens the door by degrees) What is that? He is standing outside. He is not going downstairs. Is he hesitating? Can he — ? (A letter drops into the box; then KROGSTAD'S footsteps are heard, till they die away as he goes downstairs. NORA utters a stifled cry, and runs across the room to the table by the sofa. A short pause.)

NORA: In the letter-box. (Steals across to the hall-door) There it lies — Torvald, Torvald, there is no hope for us now!

(MRS. LINDE comes in from the room on the left, carrying the dress.)

MRS. LINDE: There, I can't see anything more to mend now. Would you like to try it on — ?

NORA: (In a hoarse whisper) Christine, come here.

MRS. LINDE: (Throwing the dress down on the sofa) What is the matter with you? You look so agitated!

NORA: Come here. Do you see that letter? There, look — you can see it through the glass in the letter-box.

MRS. LINDE: Yes, I see it.

NORA: That letter is from Krogstad.

MRS. LINDE: Nora — it was Krogstad who lent you the money!

NORA: Yes, and now Torvald will know all about it.

MRS. LINDE: Believe me, Nora, that's the best thing for both of you.

NORA: You don't know all. I forged a name.

MRS. LINDE: Good heavens — !

NORA: I only want to say this to you, Christine — you must be my witness.

MRS. LINDE: Your witness? What do you mean? What am I to — ?

NORA: If I should go out of my mind—and it might easily happen—

MRS. LINDE: Nora!

NORA: Or if anything else should happen to me—anything, for instance, that might prevent my being here—

MRS. LINDE: Nora! Nora! you are quite out of your mind.

NORA: And if it should happen that there were someone who wanted to take all the responsibility, all the blame, you understand—

MRS. LINDE: Yes, yes—but how can you suppose—?

NORA: Then you must be my witness, that it is not true, Christine. I am not out of my mind at all; I am in my right senses now, and I tell you no one else has known anything about it; I, and I alone, did the whole thing. Remember that.

MRS. LINDE: I will, indeed. But I don't understand all this.

NORA: How should you understand it? A wonderful thing is going to happen.

MRS. LINDE: A wonderful thing?

NORA: Yes, a wonderful thing!—But it is so terrible, Christine; it *mustn't* happen, not for all the world.

MRS. LINDE: I will go at once and see Krogstad.

NORA: Don't go to him; he will do you some harm.

MRS. LINDE: There was a time when he would gladly do anything for my sake.

NORA: He?

MRS. LINDE: Where does he live?

NORA: How should I know—? Yes *(Feeling in her pocket)* here is his card. But the letter, the letter—!

HELMER: *(Calls from his room, knocking at the door)* Nora!

NORA: *(Cries out anxiously)* Oh, what's that? What do you want?

HELMER: Don't be so frightened. We are not coming in; you have locked the door. Are you trying on your dress?

NORA: Yes, that's it. I look so nice, Torvald.

MRS. LINDE: *(Who has read the card)* I see he lives at the corner here.

NORA: Yes, but it's no use. It is hopeless. The letter is lying there in the box.

MRS. LINDE: And your husband keeps the key?

NORA: Yes, always.

MRS. LINDE: Krogstad must ask for his letter back unread, he must find some pretence—

NORA: But it is just at this time that Torvald generally—

MRS. LINDE: You must delay him. Go in to him in the meantime. I will come back as soon as I can. *(She goes out hurriedly through the hall door)*

NORA: *(Goes to* HELMER'S *door, opens it and peeps in)* Torvald!

HELMER: *(From the inner room)* Well? May I venture at last to come into my own room again? Come along, Rank, now you will see— *(Halting in the doorway)* But what is this?

NORA: What is what, dear?

HELMER: Rank led me to expect a splendid transformation.

RANK: *(In the doorway)* I understood so, but evidently I was mistaken.

NORA: Yes, nobody is to have the chance of admiring me in my dress until to-morrow.

HELMER: But, my dear Nora, you look so worn out. Have you been practising too much?

NORA: No, I have not practised at all.

HELMER: But you will need to—

NORA: Yes, indeed I shall, Torvald. But I can't get on a bit without you to help me; I have absolutely forgotten the whole thing.

HELMER: Oh, we will soon work it up again.

NORA: Yes, help me, Torvald. Promise that you will! I am so nervous about it—all the people—. You must give yourself up to me entirely this evening. Not the tiniest bit of business—you mustn't even take a pen in your hand. Will you promise, Torvald dear?

HELMER: I promise: This evening I will be wholly and absolutely at your service, you helpless little mortal. Ah, by the way, first of all I will just—
(Goes towards the hall-door.)

NORA: What are you going to do there?

HELMER: Only see if any letters have come.

NORA: No, no! don't do that, Torvald!

HELMER: Why not?

NORA: Torvald, please don't. There is nothing there.

HELMER: Well, let me look. *(Turns to go to the letterbox.* NORA, *at the piano, plays the first bars of the Tarantella.* HELMER *stops in the doorway.)* Aha!

NORA: I can't dance to-morrow if I don't practise with you.

HELMER: *(Going up to her)* Are you really so afraid of it, dear?

NORA: Yes, so dreadfully afraid of it. Let me practise at once; there is time now, before we go to dinner. Sit down and play for me, Torvald dear; criticise me, and correct me as you play.

HELMER: With great pleasure, if you wish me to. *(Sits down at the piano.)*

NORA: *(Takes out of the box a tambourine and a long variegated shawl. She hastily drapes the shawl round her. Then she springs to the front of the stage and calls out.)* Now play for me! I am going to dance!

(HELMER plays and NORA dances. RANK stands by the piano behind HELMER, and looks on.)

HELMER: *(As he plays)* Slower, slower!

NORA: I can't do it any other way.

HELMER: Not so violently, Nora!

NORA: This is the way.

HELMER: *(Stops playing)* No, no—that is not a bit right.

NORA: *(Laughing and swinging the tambourine).* Didn't I tell you so?

RANK: Let me play for her.

HELMER *(Getting up)* Yes, do. I can correct her better then.

(RANK sits down at the piano and plays. NORA dances more and more wildly. HELMER has taken up a position beside the stove, and during her dance gives her frequent instructions. She does not seem to hear him; her hair comes down and falls over her shoulders; she pays no attention to it, but goes on dancing. Enter MRS. LINDE.)

MRS. LINDE: *(Standing as if spell-bound in the doorway)* Oh!—

NORA: *(As she dances)* Such fun, Christine!

HELMER: My dear darling Nora, you are dancing as if your life depended on it.

NORA: So it does.

HELMER: Stop, Rank; this is sheer madness. Stop, I tell you! *(RANK stops playing, and NORA suddenly stands still. HELMER goes up to her.)* I could never have believed it. You have forgotten everything I taught you.

NORA: *(Throwing away the tambourine).* There, you see.

HELMER: You will want a lot of coaching.

NORA: Yes, you see how much I need it. You must coach me up to the last minute. Promise me that, Torvald!

HELMER: You can depend on me.

NORA: You must not think of anything but me, either to-day or to-morrow; you mustn't open a single letter—not even open the letter-box—

HELMER: Ah, you are still afraid of that fellow—

NORA: Yes, indeed I am.

HELMER: Nora, I tell from your looks that there is a letter from him lying there.

NORA: I don't know; I think there is; but you must not read anything of that kind now. Nothing horrid must come between us till this is all over.

RANK: *(Whispers to HELMER)* You mustn't contradict her.

HELMER: *(Taking her in his arms)* The child shall have her way. But to-morrow night, after you have danced—

NORA: Then you will be free. *(The MAID appears in the doorway to the right)*

MAID: Dinner is served, ma'am.

NORA: We will have champagne, Helen.

MAID: Very good, ma'am. *(Exit)*

HELMER: Hullo!—are we going to have a banquet?

NORA: Yes, a champagne banquet till the small hours. *(Calls out)* And a few macaroons, Helen—lots, just for once!

HELMER: Come, come, don't be so wild and nervous. Be my own little skylark, as you used.

NORA: Yes, dear, I will. But go in now and you too, Doctor Rank. Christine, you must help me to do up my hair.

RANK: *(Whispers to HELMER as they go out)* I suppose there is nothing—she is not expecting anything?

HELMER: Far from it, my dear fellow; it is simply nothing more than this childish nervousness I was telling you of. *(They go into the right-hand room)*

NORA: Well!

MRS. LINDE: Gone out of town.

NORA: I could tell from your face.

MRS. LINDE: He is coming home to-morrow evening. I wrote a note for him.

NORA: You should have let it alone; you must prevent nothing. After all, it is splendid to be waiting for a wonderful thing to happen.

MRS. LINDE: What is it that you are waiting for?

NORA: Oh, you wouldn't understand. Go in to them, I will come in a moment. *(MRS. LINDE goes into the dining-room. NORA stands still for a little while, as if to compose herself. Then she looks at her watch.)* Five o'clock. Seven hours till midnight; and then four-and-twenty hours till the next midnight. Then the Tarantella will be over. Twenty-four and seven? Thirty-one hours to live.

HELMER: *(From the doorway on the right)* Where's my little skylark?

NORA: *(Going to him with her arms outstretched)* Here she is!

ACT III

THE SAME SCENE.

The table has been placed in the middle of the stage, with chairs round it. A lamp is burning on the table. The door into the hall stands open. Dance music is heard in the room above. MRS. LINDE is sitting at the table idly turning over the leaves of a book; she tries to read, but does not seem able to collect her thoughts. Every now and then she listens intently for a sound at the outer door.

MRS. LINDE: *(Looking at her watch)* Not yet—and the time is nearly up. If only he does not—. *(Listens again)* Ah, there he is. *(Goes into the hall and opens the outer door carefully. Light footsteps are heard on the stairs. She whispers.)* Come in. There is no one here.

KROGSTAD: *(In the doorway)* I found a note from you at home. What does this mean?

MRS. LINDE: It is absolutely necessary that I should have a talk with you.

KROGSTAD: Really? And is it absolutely necessary that it should be here?

MRS. LINDE: It is impossible where I live; there is no private entrance to my rooms. Come in; we are quite alone. The maid is asleep, and the Helmers are at the dance upstairs.

KROGSTAD: *(Coming into the room)* Are the Helmers really at a dance to-night?

MRS. LINDE: Yes, why not?

KROGSTAD: Certainly—why not?

MRS. LINDE: Now, Nils, let us have a talk.

KROGSTAD: Can we two have anything to talk about.

MRS. LINDE: We have a great deal to talk about.

KROGSTAD: I shouldn't have thought so.

MRS. LINDE: No, you have never properly understood me.

KROGSTAD: Was there anything else to understand except what was obvious to all the world—a heartless woman jilts a man when a more lucrative chance turns up.

MRS. LINDE: Do you believe I am as absolutely heartless as all that? And do you believe that I did it with a light heart?

KROGSTAD: Didn't you?

MRS. LINDE: Nils, did you really think that?

KROGSTAD: If it were as you say, why did you write to me as you did at that time?

MRS. LINDE: I could do nothing else. As I had to break with you, it was my duty also to put an end to all that you felt for me.

KROGSTAD: *(Wringing his hands)* So that was it. And all this—only for the sake of money!

MRS. LINDE: You must not forget that I had a helpless mother and two little brothers. We couldn't wait for you, Nils; your prospects seemed hopeless then.

KROGSTAD: That may be so, but you had no right to throw me over for any one else's sake.

MRS. LINDE: Indeed I don't know. Many a time did I ask myself if I had the right to do it.

KROGSTAD: *(More gently)* When I lost you, it was as if all the solid ground went from under my feet. Look at me now—I am a shipwrecked man clinging to a bit of wreckage.

MRS. LINDE: But help may be near.

KROGSTAD: It *was* near; but then you came and stood in my way.

MRS. LINDE: Unintentionally, Nils. It was only to-day that I learnt it was your place I was going to take in the bank.

KROGSTAD: I believe you, if you say so. But now that you know it, are you not going to give it up to me?

MRS. LINDE: No, because that would not benefit you in the least.

KROGSTAD: Oh, benefit, benefit—I would have done it whether or no.

MRS. LINDE: I have learnt to act prudently. Life, and hard, bitter necessity have taught me that.

KROGSTAD: And life has taught me not to believe in fine speeches.

MRS. LINDE: Then life has taught you something very reasonable. But deeds you must believe in?

KROGSTAD: What do you mean by that?

MRS. LINDE: You said you were like a shipwrecked man clinging to some wreckage.

KROGSTAD: I had good reason to say so.

MRS. LINDE: Well, I am like a shipwrecked woman clinging to some wreckage—no one to mourn for, no one to care for.

KROGSTAD: It was your own choice.

MRS. LINDE: There was no other choice—then.

KROGSTAD: Well, what now?

MRS. LINDE: Nils, how would it be if we two shipwrecked people could join forces?

KROGSTAD: What are you saying?

MRS. LINDE: Two on the same piece of wreckage would stand a better chance than each on their own.

KROGSTAD: Christine!

MRS. LINDE: What do you suppose brought me to town?

KROGSTAD: Do you mean that you gave me a thought?

MRS. LINDE: I could not endure life without work. All my life, as long as I can remember, I have worked, and it has been my greatest and only pleasure. But now I am quite alone in the world—my life is so dreadfully empty and I feel so forsaken. There is not the least pleasure in working for one's self. Nils, give me someone and something to work for.

KROGSTAD: I don't trust that. It is nothing but a woman's overstrained sense of generosity that prompts you to make such an offer of yourself.

MRS. LINDE: Have you ever noticed anything of the sort in me?

KROGSTAD: Could you really do it? Tell me—do you know all about my past life?

MRS. LINDE: Yes.

KROGSTAD: And do you know what they think of me here?

MRS. LINDE: You seemed to me to imply that with me you might have been quite another man.

KROGSTAD: I am certain of it.

MRS. LINDE: Is it too late now?

KROGSTAD: Christine, are you saying this deliberately? Yes, I am sure you are. I see it in your face. Have you really the courage, then—?

MRS. LINDE: I want to be a mother to someone, and your children need a mother. We two need each other. Nils, I have faith in your real character—I can dare anything together with you.

KROGSTAD: (*Grasps her hands*) Thanks, thanks, Christine! Now I shall find a way to clear myself in the eyes of the world. Ah, but I forgot—

MRS. LINDE: (*Listening*) Hush! The Tarantella! Go, go!

KROGSTAD: Why? What is it?

MRS. LINDE: Do you hear them up there? When that is over, we may expect them back.

KROGSTAD: Yes, yes—I will go. But it is all no use. Of course you are not aware what steps I have taken in the matter of the Helmers.

MRS. LINDE: Yes, I know all about that.

KROGSTAD: And in spite of that have you the courage to—?

MRS. LINDE: I understand very well to what lengths a man like you might be driven by despair.

KROGSTAD: If I could only undo what I have done!

MRS. LINDE: You cannot. Your letter is lying in the letter-box now.

KROGSTAD: Are you sure of that?

MRS. LINDE: Quite sure, but—

KROGSTAD: (*With a searching look at her*) Is that what it all means?—that you want to save your friend at any cost? Tell me frankly. Is that it?

MRS. LINDE: Nils, a woman who has once sold herself for another's sake, doesn't do it a second time.

KROGSTAD: I will ask for my letter back.

MRS. LINDE: No, no.

KROGSTAD: Yes, of course I will. I will wait here till Helmer comes; I will tell him he must give me my letter back—that it only concerns my dismissal—that he is not to read it—

MRS. LINDE: No, Nils, you must not recall your letter.

KROGSTAD: But, tell me, wasn't it for that very purpose that you asked me to meet you here?

MRS. LINDE: In my first moment of fright, it was. But twenty-four hours have elapsed since then, and in that time I have witnessed incredible things in this house. Helmer must know all about it. This unhappy secret must be disclosed; they must have a complete understanding between them, which is impossible with all this concealment and falsehood going on.

KROGSTAD: Very well, if you will take the responsibility. But there is one thing I can do in any case, and I shall do it at once.

MRS. LINDE: *(Listening)* You must be quick and go! The dance is over; we are not safe a moment longer.

KROGSTAD: I will wait for you below.

MRS. LINDE: Yes, do. You must see me back to my door.

KROGSTAD: I have never had such an amazing piece of good fortune in my life! *(Goes out through the outer door. The door between the room and the hall remains open.)*

MRS. LINDE: *(Tidying up the room and laying her hat and cloak ready)* What a difference! what a difference! Someone to work for and live for—a home to bring comfort into. That I will do, indeed. I wish they would be quick and come— *(Listens)* Ah, there they are now. I must put on my things. *(Takes up her hat and cloak.* HELMER'S *and* NORA'S *voices are heard outside; a key is turned, and* HELMER *brings* NORA *almost by force into the hall. She is in an Italian costume with a large black shawl around her; he is in evening dress, and a black domino which is flying open.)*

NORA: *(Hanging back in the doorway, and struggling with him)* No, no, no!—don't take me in. I want to go upstairs again; I don't want to leave so early.

HELMER: But, my dearest Nora—

NORA: Please, Torvald dear—please, *please*—only an hour more.

HELMER: Not a single minute, my sweet Nora. You know that was our agreement. Come along into the room; you are catching cold standing there. *(He brings her gently into the room, in spite of her resistance.)*

MRS. LINDE: Good-evening.

NORA: Christine!

HELMER: You here, so late, Mrs. Linde?

MRS. LINDE: Yes, you must excuse me; I was so anxious to see Nora in her dress.

NORA: Have you been sitting here waiting for me?

MRS. LINDE: Yes, unfortunately I came too late, you had already gone upstairs; and I thought I couldn't go away again without having seen you.

HELMER: *(Taking off* NORA'S *shawl)* Yes, take a good look at her. I think she is worth looking at. Isn't she charming, Mrs. Linde?

MRS. LINDE: Yes, indeed she is.

HELMER: Doesn't she look remarkably pretty? Everyone thought so at the dance. But she is terribly self-willed, this sweet little person. What are we to do with her? You will hardly believe that I had almost to bring her away by force.

NORA: Torvald, you will repent not having let me stay, even if it were only for half an hour.

HELMER: Listen to her, Mrs. Linde! She had danced her Tarantella, and it had been a tremendous success, as it deserved—although possibly the performance was a trifle too realistic—a little more so, I mean, than was strictly compatible with the limitations of art. But never mind about that! The chief thing is, she had made a success—she had made a tremendous success. Do you think I was going to let her remain there after that, and spoil the effect? No indeed! I took my charming little Capri maiden—my capricious little Capri maiden, I should say—on my arm; took one quick turn around the room; a curtsey on either side, and, as they say in novels, the beautiful apparition disappeared. An exit ought always to be effective, Mrs. Linde; but that is what I cannot make Nora understand. Pooh! this room is hot. *(Throws his domino on a chair, and opens the door of his room)* Hullo! it's all dark in here. Oh, of course—excuse me—. *(He goes in, and lights some candles)*

NORA: *(In a hurried and breathless whisper)* Well?

MRS. LINDE: *(In a low voice)* I have had a talk with him.

NORA: Yes, and—

MRS. LINDE: Nora, you must tell your husband all about it.

NORA: *(In an expressionless voice)* I knew it.

MRS. LINDE: You have nothing to be afraid of as far as Krogstad is concerned; but you must tell him.

NORA: I won't tell him.

MRS. LINDE: Then the letter will.

NORA: Thank you, Christine. Now I know what I must do. Hush—!

HELMER: *(Coming in again)* Well, Mrs. Linde, have you admired her?

MRS. LINDE: Yes, and now I will say goodnight.

HELMER: What, already? Is this yours, this knitting?

MRS. LINDE: *(Taking it)* Yes, thank you, I had very nearly forgotten it.

HELMER: So you knit?

MRS. LINDE: Of course.

HELMER: Do you know, you ought to embroider.

MRS. LINDE: Really? Why?

HELMER: Yes, it's far more becoming. Let me show you. You hold the embroidery thus in your left hand, and use the needle with the right—like this—with a long, easy sweep. Do you see?

MRS. LINDE: Yes, perhaps—

HELMER: But in the case of knitting—that can never be anything but ungraceful; look here— the arms close together, the knitting-needles going up and down—it has a sort of Chinese effect—. That was really excellent champagne they gave us.

MRS. LINDE: Well,—good-night, Nora, and don't be self-willed any more.

HELMER: That's right, Mrs. Linde.

MRS. LINDE: Good-night, Mr. Helmer.

HELMER: *(Accompanying her to the door)* Good-night, good-night. I hope you will get home all right. I should be very happy to—but you haven't any great distance to go. Good-night, good-night. *(She goes out; he shuts the door after her, and comes in again.)* Ah!—at last we have got rid of her. She is a frightful bore, that woman.

NORA: Aren't you very tired, Torvald?

HELMER: No, not in the least.

NORA: Nor sleepy?

HELMER: Not a bit. On the contrary, I feel extraordinarily lively. And you?—you really look both tired and sleepy.

NORA: Yes, I am very tired. I want to go to sleep at once.

HELMER: There, you see it was quite right of me not to let you stay there any longer.

NORA: Everything you do is quite right, Torvald.

HELMER: *(Kissing her on the forehead)* Now my little skylark is speaking reasonably. Did you notice what good spirits Rank was in this evening?

NORA: Really? Was he? I didn't speak to him at all.

HELMER: And I very little, but I have not for a long time seen him in such good form. *(Looks for a while at her and then goes nearer to her.)* It is delightful to be at home by ourselves again, to be all alone with you—you fascinating, charming little darling!

NORA: Don't look at me like that, Torvald.

HELMER: Why shouldn't I not look at my dearest treasure?—at all the beauty that is mine, all my very own?

NORA: *(Going to the other side of the table).* You mustn't say things like that to me to-night.

HELMER: *(Following her)* You have still got the Tarantella in your blood, I see. And it makes you more captivating than ever. Listen—the guests are beginning to go now. *(In a lower voice)* Nora— soon the whole house will be quiet.

NORA: Yes, I hope so.

HELMER: Yes, my own darling Nora. Do you know, when I am out at a party with you like this, why I speak so little to you, keep away from you, and only send a stolen glance in your direction now and then?—do you know why I do that? It is because I make believe to myself that we are secretly in love, and you are my secretly promised bride, and that no one suspects there is anything between us.

NORA: Yes, yes—I know very well your thoughts are with me all the time.

HELMER: And when we are leaving, and I am putting the shawl over your beautiful young shoulders—on your lovely neck—then I imagine that you are my young bride and that we have just come from the wedding, and I am bringing you for the first time into our home—to be alone with you for the first time—quite alone with my shy little darling! All this evening I have longed for nothing but you. When I watched the seductive figures of the Tarantella, my blood was on fire; I could endure it no longer, and that was why I brought you down so early —

NORA: Go away, Torvald! You must let me go. I won't —

HELMER: What's that? You're joking, my little Nora! You won't — you won't? Am I not your husband —? *(A knock is heard at the outer door.)*

NORA: *(Starting)* Did you hear —?

HELMER: *(Going into the hall)* Who is it?

RANK: *(Outside)* It is I. May I come in for a moment?

HELMER: *(In a fretful whisper)*. Oh, what does he want now? *(Aloud)* Wait a minute? *(Unlocks the door)* Come, that's kind of you not to pass by our door.

RANK: I thought I heard your voice, and felt as if I should like to look in. *(With a swift glance round)* Ah, yes! — these dear familiar rooms. You are very happy and cosy in here, you two.

HELMER: It seems to me that you looked after yourself pretty well upstairs too.

RANK: Excellently. Why shouldn't I? Why shouldn't one enjoy everything in this world? — at any rate as much as one can, and as long as one can. The wine was capital —

HELMER: Especially the champagne.

RANK: So you noticed that too? It is almost incredible how much I managed to put away!

NORA: Torvald drank a great deal of champagne to-night, too.

RANK: Did he?

NORA: Yes, and he is always in such good spirits afterwards.

RANK: Well, why should one not enjoy a merry evening after a well-spent day?

HELMER: Well spent? I am afraid I can't take credit for that.

RANK: *(Clapping him on the back)*. But I can, you know!

NORA: Doctor Rank, you must have been occupied with some scientific investigation to-day.

RANK: Exactly.

HELMER: Just listen! — little Nora talking about scientific investigations!

NORA: And may I congratulate you on the result?

RANK: Indeed you may.

NORA: Was it favourable, then?

RANK: The best possible, for both doctor and patient — certainty.

NORA: *(Quickly and searchingly)*. Certainty?

RANK: Absolute certainty. So wasn't I entitled to make a merry evening of it after that?

NORA: Yes, you certainly were, Doctor Rank.

HELMER: I think so too, so long as you don't have to pay for it in the morning.

RANK: Oh well, one can't have anything in this life without paying for it.

NORA: Doctor Rank — are you fond of fancy-dress balls?

RANK: Yes, if there is a fine lot of pretty costumes.

NORA: Tell me — what shall we two wear at the next?

HELMER: Little featherbrain! — are you thinking of the next already?

RANK: We two? Yes, I can tell you. You shall go as a good fairy —

HELMER: Yes, but what do you suggest as an appropriate costume for that?

RANK: Let your wife go dressed just as she is in everyday life.

HELMER: That was really very prettily turned. But can't you tell us what you will be?

RANK: Yes, my dear friend, I have quite made up my mind about that.

HELMER: Well?

RANK: At the next fancy-dress ball I shall be invisible.

HELMER: That's a good joke!

RANK: There is a big black hat — have you never heard of hats that make you invisible? If you put one on, no one can see you.

HELMER: *(Suppressing a smile)* Yes, you are quite right.

RANK: But I am clean forgetting what I came for. Helmer, give me a cigar — one of the dark Havanas.

HELMER: With the greatest pleasure. *(Offers him his case.)*

RANK: *(Takes a cigar and cuts off the end)* Thanks.

NORA: *(Striking a match)* Let me give you a light.

RANK: Thank you. *(She holds the match for him to light his cigar.)* And now good-bye!

HELMER: Good-bye, good-bye, dear old man!

NORA: Sleep well, Doctor Rank.

RANK: Thank you for that wish.

NORA: Wish me the same.

RANK: You? Well, if you want me to sleep well! And thanks for the light. *(He nods to them both and goes out.)*

HELMER: *(In a subdued voice)* He has drunk more than he ought.

NORA: *(Absently)* Maybe. (HELMER *takes a bunch of keys out his pocket and goes into the hall.)* Torvald! what are you going to do there?

HELMER: Empty the letter-box; it is quite full; there will be no room to put the newspaper in to-morrow morning.

NORA: Are you going to work to-night?

HELMER: You know quite well I'm not. What is this? Some one has been at the lock.

NORA: At the lock—?

HELMER: Yes, someone has. What can it mean? I should never have thought the maid— Here is a broken hairpin. Nora, it is one of yours.

NORA: *(Quickly)* Then it must have been the children—

HELMER: Then you must get them out of those ways. There, at last I have got it open. *(Takes out the contents of the letter-box, and calls to the kitchen.)* Helen!—Helen, put out the light over the front door. *(Goes back into the room and shuts the door into the hall. He holds out his hand full of letters.)* Look at that—look what a heap of them there are. *(Turning them over)* What on earth is that?

NORA: *(At the window)* The letter—No! Torvald, no!

HELMER: Two cards—of Rank's.

NORA: Of Doctor Rank's?

HELMER: *(Looking at them)* Doctor Rank. They were on the top. He must have put them in when he went out.

NORA: Is there anything written on them?

HELMER: There is a black cross over the name. Look there—what an uncomfortable idea! It looks as if he were announcing his own death.

NORA: It is just what he is doing.

HELMER: What? Do you know anything about it? Has he said anything to you?

NORA: Yes. He told me that when the cards came it would be his leave-taking from us. He means to shut himself up and die.

HELMER: My poor old friend. Certainly I knew we should not have him very long with us. But so soon! And so he hides himself away like a wounded animal.

NORA: If it has to happen, it is best it should be without a word—don't you think so, Torvald?

HELMER: *(Walking up and down)* He had so grown into our lives. I can't think of him as having gone out of them. He, with his sufferings and his loneliness, was like a cloudy background to our sunlit happiness. Well, perhaps it is best so. For him, anyway. *(Standing still.)* And perhaps for us too, Nora. We two are thrown quite upon each other now. *(Puts his arms round her.)* My darling wife, I don't feel as if I could hold you tight enough. Do you know, Nora, I have often wished that you might be threatened by some great danger, so that I might risk my life's blood, and everything, for your sake.

NORA: *(Disengages herself, and says firmly and decidedly)* Now you must read your letters, Torvald.

HELMER: No, no; not to-night. I want to be with you, my darling wife.

NORA: With the thought of your friend's death—

HELMER: You are right, it has affected us both. Something ugly has come between us—the thought of the horrors of death. We must try and rid our minds of that. Until then—we will each go to our own room.

NORA: *(Hanging on his neck)* Good-night, Torvald—Good-night!

HELMER: *(Kissing her on the forehead)* Good-night, my little singing-bird. Sleep sound, Nora. Now I will read my letters through. *(He takes his letters and goes into his room, shutting the door after him.)*

NORA: *(Gropes distractedly about, seizes* HELMER'S *domino, throws it round her, while she says in quick, hoarse, spasmodic whispers).* Never to see him again. Never! Never! *(Puts her shawl over her head.)* Never to see my children again either— never again. Never! Never!—Ah! the icy, black water—the unfathomable depths—If only it were over! He has got it now—now he is reading it. Good-bye, Torvald and my children! *(She is about to rush out through the hall, when* HELMER *opens his door hurriedly and stands with an open letter in his hand.)*

HELMER: Nora!

NORA: Ah!—

HELMER: What is this? Do you know what is in this letter?

NORA: Yes, I know. Let me go! Let me get out!

HELMER: *(Holding her back)* Where are you going?

NORA: *(Trying to get free)* You shan't save me, Torvald!

HELMER: *(Reeling)* True? Is this true, that I read here? Horrible! No, no—it is impossible that it can be true.

NORA: It is true. I have loved you above everything else in the world.

HELMER: Oh, don't let us have any silly excuses.

NORA: *(Taking a step towards him)* Torvald—!

HELMER: Miserable creature—what have you done?

NORA: Let me go. You shall not suffer for my sake. You shall not take it upon yourself.

HELMER: No tragedy airs, please. *(Locks the hall door)* Here you shall stay and give me an explanation. Do you understand what you have done? Answer me? Do you understand what you have done?

NORA: *(Looks steadily at him and says with a growing look of coldness in her face)* Yes, now I am beginning to understand thoroughly.

HELMER: *(Walking about the room)* What a horrible awakening! All these eight years—she who was my joy and pride—a hypocrite, a liar—worse, worse—a criminal! The unutterable ugliness of it all!—For shame! For shame! *(NORA is silent and looks steadily at him. He stops in front of her.)* I ought to have suspected that something of the sort would happen. I ought to have foreseen it. All your father's want of principle—be silent!—all your father's want of principle has come out in you. No religion, no morality, no sense of duty—. How I am punished for having winked at what he did! I did it for your sake, and this is how you repay me.

NORA: Yes, that's just it.

HELMER: Now you have destroyed all my happiness. You have ruined all my future. It is horrible to think of! I am in the power of an unscrupulous man; he can do what he likes with me, ask anything he likes of me, give me any orders he pleases—I dare not refuse. And I must sink to such miserable depths because of a thoughtless woman!

NORA: When I am out of the way, you will be free.

HELMER: No fine speeches, please. Your father had always plenty of those ready, too. What good would it be to me if you were out of the way, as you say? Not the slightest. He can make the affair known everywhere; and if he does, I may be falsely suspected of having been a party to your criminal action. Very likely people will think I was behind it all—that it was I who prompted you! And I have to thank you for all this—you whom I have cherished during the whole of our married life. Do you understand now what it is you have done for me?

NORA: *(Coldly and quietly)* Yes.

HELMER: It is so incredible that I can't take it in. But we must come to some understanding. Take off that shawl. Take it off, I tell you. I must try and appease him some way or another. The matter must be hushed up at any cost. And as for you and me, it must appear as if everything between us were just as before—but naturally only in the eyes of the world. You will still remain in my house, that is a matter of course. But I shall not allow you to bring up the children; I dare not trust them to you. To think that I should be obliged to say so to one whom I have loved so dearly, and whom I still—. No, that is all over. From this moment happiness is not the question; all that concerns us is to save the remains, the fragments, the appearance—

(A ring is heard at the front-door bell.)

HELMER: *(With a start)*. What is that? So late! Can the worst—? Can he—? Hide yourself, Nora. Say you are ill.

(NORA stands motionless. HELMER goes and unlocks the hall door.)

MAID: *(Half-dressed, comes to the door)* A letter for the mistress.

HELMER: Give it to me. *(Takes the letter, and shuts the door)* Yes, it is from him. You shall not have it; I will read it myself.

NORA: Yes, read it.

HELMER: *(Standing by the lamp)* I scarcely have the courage to do it. It may mean ruin for both of us. No, I must know. *(Tears open the letter, runs his eye over a few lines, looks at a paper enclosed, and gives a shout of joy.)* Nora! *(She looks at him questioningly.)* Nora!—No, I must read it once again—. Yes, it is true! I am saved! Nora, I am saved!

NORA: And I?

HELMER: You too, of course; we are both saved, both you and I. Look, he sends you your bond back. He says he regrets and repents—that a happy change in his life—never mind what he says! We are saved, Nora! No one can do anything to you. Oh, Nora, Nora!—no, first I must destroy these hateful things. Let me see—. *(Takes a look at the bond.)* No, no, I won't look at it. The whole thing shall be nothing but a bad dream to me. *(Tears up the bond and both letters, throws them all into the stove, and watches them burn.)* There—now it doesn't exist any longer. He says that since Christmas Eve you—. These must have been three dreadful days for you, Nora.

NORA: I have fought a hard fight these three days.

HELMER: And suffered agonies, and seen no way out but—. No, we won't call any of the horrors to mind. We will only shout with joy, and keep saying, "It's all over! It's all over!" Listen to me, Nora. You don't seem to realise that it is all over. What is this?—such a cold, set face! My poor little Nora, I quite understand; you don't feel as if you could believe that I have forgiven you. But it is true, Nora, I swear it; I have forgiven you everything. I know that what you did, you did out of love for me.

NORA: That is true.

HELMER: You have loved me as a wife ought to love her husband. Only you had not sufficient knowledge to judge of the means you used. But do you suppose you are any the less dear to me, because you don't understand how to act on your own responsibility? No, no; only lean on me; I will advise you and direct you. I should not be a man if this womanly helplessness did not just give you a double attractiveness in my eyes. You must not think any more about the hard things I said in my first moment of consternation, when I thought everything was going to overwhelm me. I have forgiven you, Nora; I swear to you I have forgiven you.

NORA: Thank you for your forgiveness. *(She goes out through the door to the right.)*

HELMER: No, don't go— *(Looks in)* What are you doing in there?

NORA: *(From within)* Taking off my fancy dress.

HELMER: *(Standing at the open door)* Yes, do. Try and calm yourself, and make your mind easy again, my frightened little singing-bird. Be at rest, and feel secure; I have broad wings to shelter you under. *(Walks up and down by the door)* How warm and cosy our home is, Nora. Here is shelter for you; here I will protect you like a hunted dove that I have saved from a hawk's claws; I will bring peace to your poor beating heart. It will come, little by little, Nora, believe me. To-morrow morning you will look upon it all quite differently; soon everything will be just as it was before. Very soon you won't need me to assure you that I have forgiven you; you will yourself feel the certainty that I have done so. Can you suppose I should ever think of such a thing as repudiating you, or even reproaching you? You have no idea what a true man's heart is like, Nora. There is something so indescribably sweet and satisfying, to a man, in the knowledge that he has forgiven his wife—forgiven her freely, and with all his heart. It seems as if that had made her, as it were, doubly his own; he has given her a new life, so to speak; and she has in a way become both wife and child to him. So you shall be for me after this, my little scared, helpless darling. Have no anxiety about anything, Nora; only be frank and open with me, and I will serve as will and conscience both to you—. What is this? Not gone to bed? Have you changed your things?

NORA: *(In everyday dress)* Yes, Torvald, I have changed my things now.

HELMER: But what for?—so late as this.

NORA: I shall not sleep to-night.

HELMER: But, my dear Nora—

NORA: *(Looking at her watch)* It is not so very late. Sit down here, Torvald. You and I have much to say to one another. *(She sits down at one side of the table.)*

HELMER: Nora—what is this?—this cold, set face?

NORA: Sit down. It will take some time; I have a lot to talk over with you.

HELMER: *(Sits down at the opposite side of the table)* You alarm me, Nora!—and I don't understand you.

NORA: No, that is just it. You don't understand me, and I have never understood you either—before to-night. No, you mustn't interrupt me. You must simply listen to what I say. Torvald, this is a settling of accounts.

HELMER: What do you mean by that?

NORA: *(After a short silence)* Isn't there one thing that strikes you as strange in our sitting here like this?

HELMER: What is that?

NORA: We have been married now eight

years. Does it not occur to you that this is the first time we two, you and I, husband and wife, have had a serious conversation?

HELMER: What do you mean by serious?

NORA: In all these eight years — longer than that — from the very beginning of our acquaintance, we have never exchanged a word on any serious subject.

HELMER: Was it likely that I would be continually and for ever telling you about worries that you could not help me to bear?

NORA: I am not speaking about business matters. I say that we have never sat down in earnest together to try and get at the bottom of anything.

HELMER: But, dearest Nora, would it have been any good to you?

NORA: That is just it; you have never understood me. I have been greatly wronged, Torvald — first by papa and then by you.

HELMER: What! By us two — by us two, who have loved you better than anyone else in the world?

NORA: *(Shaking her head)* You have never loved me. You have only thought it pleasant to be in love with me.

HELMER: Nora, what do I hear you saying?

NORA: It is perfectly true, Torvald. When I was at home with papa, he told me his opinion about everything, and so I had the same opinions; and if I differed from him I concealed the fact, because he would not have liked it. He called me his doll-child, and he played with me just as I used to play with my dolls. And when I came to live with you —

HELMER: What sort of an expression is that to use about our marriage?

NORA: *(Undisturbed)* I mean that I was simply transferred from papa's hands into yours. You arranged everything according to your own taste, and so I got the same tastes as you — or else I pretended to, I am really not quite sure which — I think sometimes the one and sometimes the other. When I look back on it, it seems to me as if I had been living here like a poor woman — just from hand to mouth. I have existed merely to perform tricks for you, Torvald. But you would have it so. You and papa have committed a great sin against me. It is your fault that I have made nothing of my life.

HELMER: How unreasonable and how ungrateful you are, Nora! Have you not been happy here?

NORA: No, I have never been happy. I thought I was, but it has never really been so.

HELMER: Not — not happy!

NORA: No, only merry. And you have always been so kind to me. But our home has been nothing but a playroom. I have been your doll-wife, just as at home I was papa's doll-child; and here the children have been my dolls. I thought it great fun when you played with me, just as they thought it great fun when I played with them. That is what our marriage has been, Torvald.

HELMER: There is some truth in what you say — exaggerated and strained as your view of it is. But for the future it shall be different. Playtime shall be over, and lesson-time shall begin.

NORA: Whose lessons? Mine, or the children's?

HELMER: Both yours and the children's, my darling Nora.

NORA: Alas, Torvald, you are not the man to educate me into being a proper wife for you.

HELMER: And you can say that!

NORA: And I — how am I fitted to bring up the children?

HELMER: Nora!

NORA: Didn't you say so yourself a little while ago — that you dare not trust me to bring them up?

HELMER: In a moment of anger! Why do you pay any heed to that?

NORA: Indeed, you were perfectly right. I am not fit for the task. There is another task I must undertake first. I must try and educate myself — you are not the man to help me in that. I must do that for myself. And that is why I am going to leave you now.

HELMER: *(Springing up)* What do you say?

NORA: I must stand quite alone, if I am to understand myself and everything about me. It is for that reason that I cannot remain with you any longer.

HELMER: Now, Nora!

NORA: I am going away from here now, at once. I am sure Christine will take me in for the night —

HELMER: You are out of your mind! I won't allow it! I forbid you!

NORA: It is no use forbidding me anything any longer. I will take with me what belongs to myself. I will take nothing from you, either now or later.

HELMER: What sort of madness is this!

NORA: To-morrow I shall go home—I mean, to my old home. It will be easiest for me to find something to do there.

HELMER: You blind, foolish woman!

NORA: I must try and get some sense, Torvald.

HELMER: To desert your home, your husband and your children! And you don't consider what people will say!

NORA: I cannot consider that at all. I only know that it is necessary for me.

HELMER: It's shocking. This is how you would neglect your most sacred duties.

NORA: What do you consider my most sacred duties?

HELMER: Do I need to tell you that? Are they not your duties to your husband and your children?

NORA: I have other duties just as sacred.

HELMER: That you have not. What duties could those be?

NORA: Duties to myself.

HELMER: Before all else, you are a wife and a mother.

NORA: I don't believe that any longer. I believe that before all else I am a reasonable human being, just as you are—or, at all events, that I must try and become one. I know quite well, Torvald, that most people would think you right, and that views of that kind are to be found in books; but I can no longer content myself with what most people say, or with what is found in books. I must think over things for myself and get to understand them.

HELMER: Can you not understand your place in your own home? Have you not a reliable guide in such matters as that?—have you no religion?

NORA: I am afraid, Torvald, I do not exactly know what religion is.

HELMER: What are you saying?

NORA: I know nothing but what the clergyman said, when I went to be confirmed. He told us that religion was this, and that, and the other. When I am away from all this, and am alone, I will look into that matter too. I will see if what the clergyman said is true, or at all events if it is true for me.

HELMER: This is unheard of in a girl of your age! But if religion cannot lead you aright, let me try and awaken your conscience. I suppose you have some moral sense? Or—answer me—am I to think you have none?

NORA: I assure you, Torvald, that is not an easy question to answer. I really don't know. The thing perplexes me altogether. I only know that you and I look at it in quite a different light. I am learning, too, that the law is quite another thing from what I supposed; but I find it impossible to convince myself that the law is right. According to it a woman has no right to spare her old dying father, or to save her husband's life. I can't believe that.

HELMER: You talk like a child. You don't understand the conditions of the world in which you live.

NORA: No, I don't. But now I am going to try. I am going to see if I can make out who is right, the world or I.

HELMER: You are ill, Nora; you are delirious; I almost think you are out of your mind.

NORA: I have never felt my mind so clear and certain as to-night.

HELMER: And is it with a clear and certain mind that you forsake your husband and your children?

NORA: Yes, it is.

HELMER: Then there is only one possible explanation.

NORA: What is that?

HELMER: You do not love me any more.

NORA: No, that is just it.

HELMER: Nora!—and you can say that?

NORA: It gives me great pain, Torvald, for you have always been so kind to me, but I cannot help it. I do not love you any more.

HELMER: (Regaining his composure) Is that a clear and certain conviction too?

NORA: Yes, absolutely clear and certain. That is the reason why I will not stay here any longer.

HELMER: And can you tell me what I have done to forfeit your love?

NORA: Yes, indeed I can. It was to-night, when the wonderful thing did not happen; then I saw you were not the man I had thought you.

HELMER: Explain yourself better—I don't understand you.

NORA: I have waited so patiently for eight years; for, goodness knows, I knew very well that wonderful things don't happen every day. Then this horrible misfortune came upon me; and then I felt quite certain that the wonderful thing was going to happen at last. When Krogstad's letter was lying out there, never for a moment did I imagine that you would consent to accept this man's conditions. I was so absolutely certain that you would say to him: Publish the thing to the whole world. And when that was done —

HELMER: Yes, what then? — when I had exposed my wife to shame and disgrace?

NORA: When that was done, I was so absolutely certain, you would come forward and take everything upon yourself, and say: I am the guilty one.

HELMER: Nora — !

NORA: You mean that I would never have accepted such a sacrifice on your part? No, of course not. But what would my assurances have been worth against yours? That was the wonderful thing which I hoped for and feared; and it was to prevent that, that I wanted to kill myself.

HELMER: I would gladly work night and day for you, Nora — bear sorrow and want for your sake. But no man would sacrifice his honour for the one he loves.

NORA: It is a thing hundreds of thousands of women have done.

HELMER: Oh, you think and talk like a heedless child.

NORA: Maybe. But you neither think nor talk like the man I could bind myself to. As soon as your fear was over — and it was not fear for what threatened me, but for what might happen to you — when the whole thing was past, as far as you were concerned it was exactly as if nothing at all had happened. Exactly as before, I was your little skylark, your doll, which you would in future treat with doubly gentle care, because it was so brittle and fragile. *(Getting up)* Torvald — it was then it dawned upon me that for eight years I had been living here with a strange man, and had borne him three children —. Oh, I can't bear to think of it! I could tear myself into little bits!

HELMER: *(Sadly)* I see, I see. An abyss has opened between us — there is no denying it. But, Nora, would it not be possible to fill it up?

NORA: As I am now, I am no wife for you.

HELMER: I have it in me to become a different man.

NORA: Perhaps — if your doll is taken away from you.

HELMER: But to part! — to part from you! No, no. Nora, I can't understand that idea.

NORA: *(Going out to the right)* That makes it all the more certain that it must be done. *(She comes back with her cloak and hat and a small bag which she puts on a chair by the table.)*

HELMER: Nora, Nora, not now! Wait till to-morrow.

NORA: *(Putting on her cloak)* I cannot spend the night in a strange man's room.

HELMER: But can't we live here like brother and sister — ?

NORA: *(Putting on her hat)* You know very well that would not last long. *(Puts the shawl round her.)* Good-bye, Torvald. I won't see the little ones. I know they are in better hands than mine. As I am now, I can be of no use to them.

HELMER: But some day, Nora — some day?

NORA: How can I tell? I have no idea what is going to become of me.

HELMER: But you are my wife, whatever becomes of you.

NORA: Listen, Torvald. I have heard that when a wife deserts her husband's house, as I am doing now, he is legally freed from all obligations towards her. In any case I set you free from all your obligations. You are not to feel yourself bound in the slightest way, any more than I shall. There must be perfect freedom on both sides. See here is your ring back. Give me mine.

HELMER: That too?

NORA: That too.

HELMER: Here it is.

NORA: That's right. Now it is all over. I have put the keys here. The maids know all about everything in the house — better than I do. To-morrow, after I have left her, Christine will come here and pack up my own things that I brought with me from home. I will have them sent after me.

HELMER: All over! all over! — Nora, shall you never think of me again?

NORA: I know I shall often think of you and the children and this house.

HELMER: May I write to you, Nora?

NORA: No — never. You must not do that.

HELMER: But at least let me send you —

NORA: Nothing — nothing —

HELMER: Let me help you if you are in want.

NORA: No. I can receive nothing from a stranger.

HELMER: Nora — can I never be anything more than a stranger to you?

NORA: *(Taking her bag)* Ah, Torvald, the most wonderful thing of all would have to happen.

HELMER: Tell me what that would be!

NORA: Both you and I would have to be so changed that—. Oh, Torvald, I don't believe any longer in wonderful things happening.

HELMER: But I will believe in it. Tell me? So changed that—?

NORA: That our life together would be a real wedlock. Good-bye. *(She goes out through the hall.)*

HELMER: *(Sinks down on a chair at the door and buries his face in his hands)* Nora! Nora! *(Looks round, and rises)* Empty. She is gone. *(A hope flashes across his mind.)* The most wonderful thing of all—?

(The sound of a door shutting is heard from below.)

From today's perspective, *A Doll's House* is clearly about the status of women in the late nineteenth century. Both Nora's father and her husband have treated her as a plaything—or, as the play's title suggests, a doll—neither expecting nor wishing her to be sufficiently aware of social and legal matters to make judgments for herself and to take responsible action. It pleases Torvald to think of Nora as incapable of making decisions, even about what she should wear to a party. Quite apart from personal relationships, women are shown to be, by law, inferior to men. On the surface, then, Ibsen seems to have taken a fairly strong stand against the inequitable treatment of women in the 1870s.

It is likely, however, that Ibsen's views on this subject were more complex than they seem. In 1898 in an address to the Norwegian Women's Rights League, he said: "I thank you for your good wishes, but I must decline the honor of being said to have worked for the Women's Rights movement. I am not even very sure what Women's Rights actually are. For me it has been an affair of humanity." This passage is ambiguous, on the one hand denying any particular interest in the feminist cause, but on the other hand claiming a concern for all human beings. Did Ibsen mean that he thought all human beings should have the same rights? Perhaps, but the notes he made prior to writing *A Doll's House* contain these passages: "There are two kinds of moral law, two kinds of conscience, one in man and a completely different one in woman. They do not understand each other; but in matters of practical living the woman is judged by man's law, as if she were not a woman but a man. . . . A woman cannot be herself in contemporary society, it is an exclusively male society with laws drafted by men, and with lawyers and judges who judge feminine conduct from the male point of view." This implies that before society can be fair to both men and women there will have to be two versions of the law, one for men, another for women.

At the end of *A Doll's House*, Nora's alienation is not only from her husband but also from society in general. She chooses to leave her children because, finding herself in disagreement with both law and public opinion and not yet certain of her own convictions, she does not believe herself ready to meet her responsibilities as a mother. She leaves so she may consider objectively (that is, freed from the emotional blackmail of home and children) what it means to be a woman in her particular society and how she should respond to it. Here, as in his other plays, Ibsen addressed the problem of reconciling individual freedom with the demands of feeling, custom, and law. It is significant that Ibsen's best-known plays — *A Doll's House, Ghosts,* and *Hedda Gabler* — have women as protagonists, since in a male-dominated society the obstacles to freedom are greatest for women.

Mrs. Linde serves as a contrast to Nora and thereby further clarifies Ibsen's ideas about women. Mrs. Linde appears to have a realistic view of her status in society and to have accepted it; but she misses what Nora (on the surface) has — somebody and something to work for. It seems likely that Ibsen thought the two women between them possessed what was needed for fulfillment — that woman's natural role is that of wife and mother, but that its full realization comes only through knowledge of the world and through mutual respect between husband and wife. Evidence for this view is found in Ibsen's speech to the Norwegian Women's Rights League: "It rests with the *mothers* by means of strenuous and protracted exertions to rouse a conscious sense of *culture* and *discipline.* These must be created in human beings before the people can be raised higher. It is the women who shall solve the problems of humanity. As mothers they are to do it. And only *so* can they do it." But, if this is Ibsen's position, he does not satisfactorily articulate it in *A Doll's House.* Nor can it justify the inequities that reduce a woman legally to the status of a child (or a doll) by requiring her to have her husband's consent in almost all matters, whereas her husband can act wholly independently, even dispose of property that originally belonged to her, without her consent or knowledge.

Krogstad's story elaborates on the contrast in treatment of men and women. The mistake for which he has paid so dearly is the same one made by Nora, but as a woman she will be treated much more leniently than Krogstad has been and much of the blame will be laid to her husband's failure to control her. Both Krogstad and Mrs. Linde have learned about the world through harsh experience, but despite their suffering (or perhaps because of it) they appear at the play's end much more likely than Nora and Torvald to achieve a satisfying relationship. It is Mrs. Linde, out of the maturity she has gained through experience, who insists that Krogstad not retrieve his letter before it reveals to Torvald Nora's crime, for she believes it essential that Nora and Torvald cease their childlike games and build a mature relationship based on truth.

Dr. Rank serves as a contrast to Torvald. Nora can talk with Rank freely and share confidences with him; he probably would have been an excellent husband (a role he obviously covets) were it not for the congenital disease (probably syphilis) he has inherited from his father. Because of Rank, we also know that Nora is instinctively moral since she turned to Krogstad for money when she might easily and safely have gotten it from Rank, but to have done so would have compromised her in her own eyes, sensing as she does Rank's love for her.

Torvald embodies the attitudes and standards of his society. His condescension toward women, his smug conviction of his own moral superiority, his concern for public opinion and appearance, his fear of scandal — it is against these qualities that Nora's attitudes and actions are measured. The play's major reversal occurs when Nora realizes that rather than being transfigured by the discovery of the risks she has taken for him, Torvald is instead horrified at the threat to his own reputation. At this point Nora sees how thoroughly out of step she is with her society and how necessary it is for her to understand her world so she may assess whether it is she or society that is wrong and what she must do about it.

A great many critics and readers of the late nineteenth century took exception to the way *A Doll's House* ends, finding it impossible to accept that a woman would leave her children for the reasons Nora states; some considered Ibsen merely perverse and believed that he deliberately avoided an ending that upheld the sanctity of marriage and home out of a desire to be controversial. Others objected to the ending on the grounds that Nora's sophisticated arguments about women's rights in the final act seem out of keeping with the naive opinions of the doll-woman seen in the first two acts. Whatever the critical response, *A Doll's House* aroused heated debate wherever it was seen or read in the late nineteenth century.

Undergirding the characters and action of *A Doll's House* is a basic assumption of Realism — that character and action are determined by hereditary and environmental forces. What each character is and does in Ibsen's play is explained by information about parental background, upbringing, and experience. Throughout the play, Krogstad, Mrs. Linde, and Dr. Rank appear to be victims of heredity and environment, whereas originally Torvald and Nora seem to have been favored by circumstance. By the end of the play, the former three have come to terms with the forces that have shaped their lives, but Torvald and Nora are only beginning to face the consequences of the past. During the course of the action, we learn enough about all the characters to understand how they have arrived at where they are.

A Doll's House could serve as a model of dramatic construction. The first act sets up masterfully and with seeming naturalness all of the conditions out of which the subsequent action grows logically and inexorably, although not necessarily predictably. Ibsen could have made his play melodramatic by depicting Krogstad as villain and Nora as heroine. Instead, all of the characters strive for what they consider right; the complications arise from their differing conceptions of proper goals and means for attaining them. Thus, they appear to be complex, fallible human beings.

The issues raised by *A Doll's House* are near the surface at all times during the play. They concern differences in societal perceptions of men and women — their proper roles, their rights and responsibilities, their hierarchy of values. If not the same, these issues closely resemble those raised today by the feminist movement and a proposed Equal Rights Amendment to the Constitution.

Major Barbara

by George Bernard Shaw

George Bernard Shaw (1856–1950) was a great admirer of Ibsen and through his own controversial plays did more than anyone else to create modern British drama. Born in Ireland, Shaw moved to London in 1876 and began his literary career with five unsuccessful novels written between 1879 and 1883. In the 1880s and 1890s, he was also one of London's most admired critics of art, music, and drama. After studying the works of Karl Marx, Shaw became a firm believer in socialism, and in 1884 he was a founding member of the Fabian Society, which rejected Marx's call for a proletarian revolution in favor of gradual social and political reform. The Fabian ideal was to be a significant element in many of Shaw's plays.

Another important element in Shaw's drama is a set of interrelated concepts: the life force, creative evolution, and the superman. To Shaw, there is in the human race an instinctive and ongoing urge (the *life force*) that is manifested primarily in a few superior persons in each generation; this life force is seeking, through the process of *creative evolution* (the gradual improvement of the human capacity for rational thought and action), to create a society of supermen through which human potential can be fully realized.

Since both Fabianism and creative evolution involve gradual improvement, Shaw blended the two in his thought. The Fabians believed that the superior individual must lead lesser ones, and they rejected the idea that the opinion of the majority should serve as a basis for action. To Shaw, leadership should be based on intelligence and common sense rather than on birth, wealth, social position, class, or popularity. He foresaw gradual solutions to human problems, which would be eliminated only when the race of supermen fully evolved. For the time being, Shaw aimed at limited progress — better education and living conditions that can free human beings from immediate concern for survival and allow them to progress toward that time when humanity, fully using its rational power, has achieved its maximum potential. Thus, correcting wrongheaded notions, shaking prejudices, and arousing skepticism about conventional attitudes and customs were weapons Shaw adopted to assist in progress toward the ultimate goals. Fortunately, he had as keen an eye for what is entertaining as he did for what is intellectually striking. He was steeped in the popular drama of the nineteenth century, and he borrowed many of its techniques even though he often denounced popular playwrights for failing to use drama as a medium for ideas.

Shaw did not begin to write plays until 1892, when he was 36 years old. He wrote 47 full-length plays, plus a number of short ones. Unlike most playwrights concerned with social change, Shaw chose comedy as his medium for exposing the inconsistencies and mistaken premises of conventional morality, social customs, politics, medicine, economics, religion, and drama. Among his many plays, some of the best known are *Arms and the Man* (1894), *Candida* (1895), *The Devil's Disciple* (1897), *Man and Superman* (1903), *Major Barbara* (1905), *Pygmalion* (1913), *Heartbreak House* (1919), and *Saint Joan* (1923).

Few dramatists have believed as firmly as Shaw did in the power of dialectic to bring about progress. Perhaps because of his commitment to the idea of progress, Shaw seldom dwelt on the darker side of life, and he glossed over obstacles to progress. Thus, it is probably fortunate that he chose comedy as his medium, since his ready solutions to complex problems (which comedy, with its expected happy endings, makes acceptable) would probably have seemed shallow in serious dramas. Because Shaw believed that the key to progress lies in exposing ignorance, his dramatic actions usually follow this pattern: in the opening section, the commonly accepted attitudes about the subject of the play are established and are usually treated sympathetically; once these attitudes are established and made to appear logical and entrenched, they are gradually undermined and eventually shown to be false by the introduction of arguments that show them to be based on prejudice or lack of information; once new perceptions have removed the bases for conflict, the action is resolved harmoniously.

Although Shaw saw himself as a Realist, that estimate must be qualified, for though he wrote for the proscenium-arch stage and realistic settings, he had no patience with attempts to transfer nature directly to the stage or to recreate milieus in all their details. His statement about Charles Dickens might also be applied to himself: Shaw declared that Dickens combined a "mirror-like exactness of character-drawing with the wildest extravagance of humorous expression and grotesque situation." In writing dialogue, Shaw was never restrained by the notion that it must approximate real conversation. Although his characters are clearly distinguishable in peculiarities of speech and dialect, all are articulate and most are masters of the witty, well-turned phrase. Thus, Shaw's is a superrealism in which the essence of a situation is captured by sharpening and exaggerating carefully chosen elements.

In the beginning, Shaw's drama was sufficiently unusual that to most audiences it seemed either puzzling or outrageous. Not until around 1905 did his plays begin to be accepted by commercial producers. By 1915 Shaw's fame was assured, and today he is recognized as one of the dominant figures in the history of British drama.

CAST OF CHARACTERS

ANDREW UNDERSHAFT *a munitions manufacturer*

LADY BRITOMART UNDERSHAFT *his estranged wife*

STEPHEN UNDERSHAFT *their son*

SARAH UNDERSHAFT *their daughter*

BARBARA UNDERSHAFT *their daughter, a major in the Salvation Army*

CHARLES LOMAX *engaged to Sarah*

ADOLPHUS CUSINS *professor of Greek, engaged to Barbara*

MORRISON *butler to Lady Britomart*

JENNY HILL *Salvation Army girl*

MRS. BAINES *a Salvation Army commissioner*

SNOBBY PRICE *man at Salvation Army shelter*

RUMMY MITCHENS *woman at Salvation Army shelter*

PETER SHIRLEY *unemployed worker at Salvation Army shelter*

BILL WALKER *troublemaker at Salvation Army shelter*

BILTON *worker at munitions factory*

PERIOD

Three successive days in January 1906

ACT I

The library in Lady Britomart Undershaft's house in Wilton Crescent, London

ACT II

The West Ham Shelter of the Salvation Army

ACT III, SCENE 1

The library at Wilton Crescent

SCENE 2

Among the high-explosive sheds at the arsenal of Messrs. Undershaft and Lazarus, near the model town of Perivale St. Andrews

ACT I

It is after dinner in January 1906, in the library in Lady Britomart Undershaft's house in Wilton Crescent. A large and comfortable settee is in the middle of the room, upholstered in dark leather. A person sitting on it (it is vacant at present) would have, on his right, Lady Britomart's writing table, with the lady herself busy at it; a smaller writing table behind him on his left; the door behind him on LADY BRITOMART'S *side;*

and a window with a window seat directly on his left. Near the window is an armchair.

LADY BRITOMART *is a woman of fifty or thereabouts, well dressed and yet careless of her dress, well bred and quite reckless of her breeding, well mannered and yet appallingly outspoken and indifferent to the opinion of her interlocutors, amiable and yet peremptory, arbitrary, and high-tempered to the last bearable degree, and withal a very typical managing matron of the upper class, treated as a naughty child until she grew into a scolding mother, and finally settling down with plenty of practical ability and worldly experience, limited in the oddest way with domestic and class limitations, conceiving the universe exactly as if it were a large house in Wilton Crescent, though handling her corner of it very effectively on that assumption, and being quite enlightened and liberal as to the books in the library, the pictures on the walls, the music in the portfolios, and the articles in the papers.*

Her son, Stephen, comes in. He is a gravely correct young man under 25, taking himself very seriously, but still in some awe of his mother, from childish habit and bachelor shyness rather than from any weakness of character.

STEPHEN: What's the matter?

LADY BRITOMART: Presently, Stephen.

(STEPHEN *submissively walks to the settee and sits down. He takes up a Liberal weekly called The Speaker.*)

LADY BRITOMART: Dont begin to read, Stephen. I shall require all your attention.

STEPHEN: It was only while I was waiting—

LADY BRITOMART: Dont make excuses, Stephen. (*He puts down The Speaker.*) Now! (*She finishes her writing; rises; comes to the settee.*) I have not kept you waiting very long, I think.

STEPHEN: Not at all, mother.

LADY BRITOMART: Bring me my cushion. (*He takes the cushion from the chair at the desk and arranges it for her as she sits down on the settee.*) Sit down. (*He sits down and fingers his tie nervously.*) Dont fiddle with your tie, Stephen: there is nothing the matter with it.

STEPHEN: I beg your pardon. (*He fiddles with his watch chain instead.*)

LADY BRITOMART: Now are you attending to me, Stephen?

STEPHEN: Of course, mother.

LADY BRITOMART: No: it's not of course. I want something much more than your everyday matter-of-course attention. I am going to speak to you very seriously, Stephen. I wish you would let that chain alone.

STEPHEN: (*Hastily relinquishing the chain*) Have I done anything to annoy you, mother? If so, it was quite unintentional.

LADY BRITOMART: (*Astonished*) Nonsense! (*With some remorse*) My poor boy, did you think I was angry with you?

STEPHEN: What is it, then, mother? You are making me very uneasy.

LADY BRITOMART: (*Squaring herself at him rather aggressively*) Stephen: may I ask how soon you intend to realize that you are a grown-up man, and that I am only a woman?

STEPHEN: (*Amazed*) Only a—

LADY BRITOMART: Dont repeat my words, please: it is a most aggravating habit. You must learn to face life seriously, Stephen. I really cannot bear the whole burden of our family affairs any longer. You must advise me: you must assume the responsibility.

STEPHEN: I!

LADY BRITOMART: Yes, you, of course. You were 24 last June. Youve been at Harrow and Cambridge. Youve been to India and Japan. You must know a lot of things, now; unless you have wasted your time most scandalously. Well, advise me.

STEPHEN: (*Much perplexed*) You know I have never interfered in the household—

LADY BRITOMART: No: I should think not. I dont want you to order the dinner.

STEPHEN: I mean in our family affairs.

LADY BRITOMART: Well, you must interfere now; for they are getting quite beyond me.

STEPHEN: *(Troubled)* I have thought some-times that perhaps I ought; but really, mother, I know so little about them; and what I do know is so painful! it is so impossible to mention some things to you— *(He stops, ashamed.)*

LADY BRITOMART: I suppose you mean your father.

STEPHEN: *(Almost inaudibly)* Yes.

LADY BRITOMART: My dear: we cant go on all our lives not mentioning him. Of course you were quite right not to open the subject until I asked you to; but you are old enough now to be taken into my confidence, and to help me to deal with him about the girls.

STEPHEN: But the girls are all right. They are engaged.

LADY BRITOMART: *(Complacently)* Yes: I have made a very good match for Sarah. Charles Lomax will be a millionaire at 35. But that is ten years ahead; and in the meantime his trustees can-not under the terms of his father's will allow him more than £800 a year.

STEPHEN: But the will says also that if he increases his income by his own exertions, they may double the increase.

LADY BRITOMART: Charles Lomax's exer-tions are much more likely to decrease his income than to increase it. Sarah will have to find at least another £800 a year for the next ten years; and even then they will be as poor as church mice. And what about Barbara? I thought Barbara was going to make the most brilliant career of all of you. And what does she do? Joins the Salvation Army; discharges her maid; lives on a pound a week; and walks in one evening with a professor of Greek whom she has picked up in the street, and who pretends to be a Salvationist, and actually plays the big drum for her in public because he has fallen head over ears in love with her.

STEPHEN: I was certainly rather taken aback when I heard they were enaged. Cusins is a very nice fellow, certainly; nobody would ever guess that he was born in Australia; but—

LADY BRITOMART: Oh, Adolphus Cusins will make a very good husband. After all, nobody can say a word against Greek: it stamps a man at once as an educated gentleman. And my family, thank Heaven, is not a pig-headed Tory one. We are Whigs, and believe in liberty. Let snobbish people say what they please: Barbara shall marry, not the man they like, but the man I like.

STEPHEN: Of course I was thinking only of his income. However, he is not likely to be extravagant.

LADY BRITOMART: Dont be too sure of that, Stephen. I know your quiet, simple, refined, poetic people like Adolphus: quite content with the best of everything! They cost more than your extravagant people, who are always as mean as they are second rate. No: Barbara will need at least £2000 a year. You see it means two additional households. Besides, my dear, you must marry soon. I dont approve of the present fashion of philandering bach-elors and late marriages; and I am trying to arrange something for you.

STEPHEN: It's very good of you, mother; but perhaps I had better arrange that for myself.

LADY BRITOMART: Nonsense! you are much too young to begin matchmaking: you would be taken in by some pretty little nobody. Of course I dont mean that you are not to be consulted: you know that as well as I do. (STEPHEN *closes his lips and is silent)* Now dont sulk, Stephen.

STEPHEN: I am not sulking, mother. What has all this got to do with—with—with my father?

LADY BRITOMART: My dear Stephen: where is the money to come from? It is easy enough for you and the other children to live on my income as long as we are in the same house; but I cant keep four families in four separate houses. You know how poor my father is; he has barely seven thou-sand a year now; and really, if he were not the Earl of Stevenage, he would have to give up society. He can do nothing for us. He says, naturally enough, that it is absurd that he should be asked to provide for the children of a man who is rolling in money. You see, Stephen, your father must be fabulously wealthy, because there is always a war going on somewhere.

STEPHEN: You need not remind me of that, mother. I have hardly ever opened a newspaper in my life without seeing our name in it. The Under-shaft torpedo! The Undershaft quick firers! The Undershaft ten inch! the Undershaft disappearing rampart gun! the Undershaft submarine! and now the Undershaft aerial battleship! At Harrow they called me the Woolwich Infant. At Cambridge it was the same. A little brute at King's who was always trying to get up revivals, spoilt my Bible— your first birthday present to me—by writing under my name, ''Son and heir to Undershaft and Lazarus, Death and Destruction Dealers: address, Christendom and Judea.'' But that was not so bad as the way I was kowtowed to everywhere because my father was making millions by selling cannons.

LADY BRITOMART: It is not only the cannons, but the war loans that Lazarus arranges under cover of giving credit for the cannons. You know, Stephen, it's perfectly scandalous. Those two men, Andrew Undershaft and Lazarus, positively have Europe under their thumbs. That is why your father is able to behave as he does. He is above the law. Do you think Bismarck or Gladstone or Disraeli could have openly defied every social and moral obligation all their lives as your father has? They simply wouldnt have dared. I asked Gladstone to take it up. I asked The Times to take it up. I asked the Lord Chamberlain to take it up. But it was just like asking them to declare war on the Sultan. They wouldnt. They said they couldnt touch him. I believe they were afraid.

STEPHEN: What could they do? He does not actually break the law.

LADY BRITOMART: Not break the law! He is always breaking the law. He broke the law when he was born: his parents were not married.

STEPHEN: Mother! Is that true?

LADY BRITOMART: Of course it's true: that was why we separated.

STEPHEN: He married without letting you know this!

LADY BRITOMART: (Rather taken aback by this inference) Oh no. To do Andrew justice, that was not the sort of thing he did. Besides, you know the Undershaft motto: Unashamed. Everybody knew.

STEPHEN: But you said that was why you separated.

LADY BRITOMART: Yes, because he was not content with being a foundling himself: he wanted to disinherit you for another foundling. That was what I couldnt stand.

STEPHEN: (Ashamed) Do you mean for—for—for—

LADY BRITOMART: Dont stammer, Stephen. Speak distinctly.

STEPHEN: But this is so frightful to me, mother. To have to speak to you about such things!

LADY BRITOMART: It's not pleasant for me, either, especially if you are still so childish that you must make it worse by a display of embarrassment. It is only in the middle classes, Stephen, that people get into a state of dumb helpless horror when they find that there are wicked people in the world. In our class, we have to decide what is to be done with wicked people; and nothing should disturb our self-possession. Now ask your question properly.

STEPHEN: Mother: have you no consideration for me? For Heaven's sake either treat me as a child, as you always do, and tell me nothing at all; or tell me everything and let me take it as best I can.

LADY BRITOMART: Treat you as a child! What do you mean? It is most unkind and ungrateful of you to say such a thing. You know I have never treated any of you as children. I have always made you my companions and friends, and allowed you perfect freedom to do and say whatever you liked, so long as you liked what I could approve of.

STEPHEN: (Desperately) I daresay we have been the very imperfect children of a very perfect mother; but I do beg you to let me alone for once, and tell me about this horrible business of my father wanting to set me aside for another son.

LADY BRITOMART: (Amazed) Another son! I never said anything of the kind. I never dreamt of such a thing. This is what comes of interrupting me.

STEPHEN: But you said—

LADY BRITOMART: (Cutting him short) Now be a good boy, Stephen, and listen to me patiently. The Undershafts are descended from a foundling in the parish of St Andrew Undershaft in the city. That was long ago, in the reign of James the First. Well, this foundling was adopted by an armorer and gun-maker. In the course of time the foundling succeeded to the business; and from some notion of gratitude, or some vow or something, he adopted another foundling, and left the business to him. And that foundling did the same. Ever since that, the cannon business has always been left to an adopted foundling named Andrew Undershaft.

STEPHEN: But did they never marry? Were there no legitimate sons?

LADY BRITOMART: Oh yes: they married just as your father did; and they were rich enough to buy land for their own children and leave them well provided for. But they always adopted and trained some foundling to succeed them in the business; and of course they always quarrelled with their wives furiously over it. Your father was adopted in that way; and he pretends to consider himself bound to keep up the tradition and adopt somebody to leave the business to. Of course I was not going to stand that. There may have been some

408 / GEORGE BERNARD SHAW

reason for it when the Undershafts could only marry women in their own class, whose sons were not fit to govern great estates. But there could be no excuse for passing over my son.

STEPHEN: *(Dubiously)* I am afraid I should make a poor hand of managing a cannon foundry.

LADY BRITOMART: Nonsense! you could easily get a manager and pay him a salary.

STEPHEN: My father evidently had no great opinion of my capacity.

LADY BRITOMART: Stuff, child! you were only a baby: it had nothing to do with your capacity. Andrew did it on principle, just as he did every perverse and wicked thing on principle. When my father remonstrated, Andrew actually told him to his face that history tells us of only two successful institutions: one the Undershaft firm, and the other the Roman Empire under the Antonines. That was because the Antonine emperors all adopted their successors. Such rubbish! The Stevenages are as good as the Antonines, I hope; and you are a Stevenage. But that was Andrew all over. There you have the man! Always clever and unanswerable when he was defending nonsense and wickedness: always awkward and sullen when he had to behave sensibly and decently!

STEPHEN: Then it was on my account that your home life was broken up, mother. I am sorry.

LADY BRITOMART: Well, dear, there were other differences. I really cannot bear an immoral man. I am not a Pharisee, I hope; and I should not have minded his merely doing wrong things: we are none of us perfect. But your father didnt exactly do wrong things: he said them and thought them: that was what was so dreadful. He really had a sort of religion of wrongness. Just as one doesn't mind men practising immorality so long as they own that they are in the wrong by preaching morality; so I couldn't forgive Andrew for preaching immorality while he practised morality. You would all have grown up without principles, without any knowledge of right and wrong, if he had been in the house. You know, my dear, your father was a very attractive man in some ways. Children did not dislike him; and he took advantage of it to put the wickedest ideas into their heads, and make them quite unmanageable. I did not dislike him myself: very far from it; but nothing can bridge over moral disagreement.

STEPHEN: All this simply bewilders me, mother. People may differ about matters of opinion, or even about religion; but how can they differ about right and wrong? Right is right; and wrong is wrong; and if a man cannot distinguish them properly, he is either a fool or a rascal: thats all.

LADY BRITOMART: *(Touched)* Thats my own boy *(she pats his cheek)*! Your father never could answer that: he used to laugh and get out of it under cover of some affectionate nonsense. And now that you understand the situation, what do you advise me to do?

STEPHEN: Well, what can you do?

LADY BRITOMART: I must get the money somehow.

STEPHEN: We cannot take money from him. I had rather go and live in some cheap place like Bedford Square or even Hampstead than take a farthing of his money.

LADY BRITOMART: But after all, Stephen, our present income comes from Andrew.

STEPHEN: *(Shocked)* I never knew that.

LADY BRITOMART: Well, you surely didnt suppose your grandfather had anything to give me. The Stevenages could not do everything for you. We gave you social position. Andrew had to contribute something. He had a very good bargain, I think.

STEPHEN: *(Bitterly)* We are utterly dependent on him and his cannons, then?

LADY BRITOMART: Certainly not: the money is settled. But he provided it. So you see it is not a question of taking money from him or not: it is simply a question of how much. I dont want any more for myself.

STEPHEN: Nor do I.

LADY BRITOMART: But Sarah does; and Barbara does. That is, Charles Lomax and Adolphus Cusins will cost them more. So I must put my pride in my pocket and ask for it, I suppose. That is your advice, Stephen, is it not?

STEPHEN: No.

LADY BRITOMART: *(Sharply)* Stephen!

STEPHEN: Of course if you are determined—

LADY BRITOMART: I am not determined: I ask your advice; and I am waiting for it. I will not have all the responsibility thrown on my shoulders.

STEPHEN: *(Obstinately)* I would die sooner than ask him for another penny.

LADY BRITOMART: *(Resignedly)* You mean that *I* must ask him. Very well, Stephen: it shall be as you wish. You will be glad to know that your grandfather concurs. But he thinks I ought to ask Andrew to come here and see the girls. After all, he must have some natural affection for them.

STEPHEN: Ask him here!!!

LADY BRITOMART: Do not repeat my words, Stephen. Where else can I ask him?

STEPHEN: I never expected you to ask him at all.

LADY BRITOMART: Now dont tease, Stephen. Come! you see that it is necessary that he should pay us a visit, dont you?

STEPHEN: *(Reluctantly)* I suppose so, if the girls cannot do without his money.

LADY BRITOMART: Thank you, Stephen: I knew you would give me the right advice when it was properly explained to you. I have asked your father to come this evening. *(STEPHEN bounds from his seat)* Dont jump, Stephen: it fidgets me.

STEPHEN: *(In utter consternation)* Do you mean to say that my father is coming here tonight—that he may be here at any moment?

LADY BRITOMART: *(Looking at her watch)* I said nine. *(He gasps. She rises)*. Ring the bell, please. *(STEPHEN goes to the smaller writing table; presses a button on it; and sits at it with his elbows on the table and his head in his hands, outwitted and overwhelmed.)* It is ten minutes to nine yet: and I have to prepare the girls. I asked Charles Lomax and Adolphus to dinner on purpose that they might be here. Andrew had better see them in case he should cherish any delusions as to their being capable of supporting their wives. *(The butler enters: LADY BRITOMART goes behind the settee to speak to him.)* Morrison: go up to the drawing room and tell everybody to come down here at once. *(MORRISON withdraws, LADY BRITOMART turns to STEPHEN.)* Now remember, Stephen: I shall need all your countenance and authority. *(He rises and tries to recover some vestige of these attributes.)* Give me a chair, dear. *(He pushes a chair forward from the wall to where she stands, near the smaller writing table. She sits down; and he goes to the armchair, into which he throws himself.)* I dont know how Barbara will take it. Ever since they made her a major in the Salvation Army she has developed a propensity to have her own way and order people about which quite cows me sometimes. It's not lady-like: I'm sure I dont know where she picked it up. Anyhow, Barbara shant bully me; but still it's just

as well that your father should be here before she has time to refuse to meet him or make a fuss. Dont look nervous, Stephen: it will only encourage Barbara to make difficulties. *I* am nervous enough, goodness knows: but I dont shew it.

(SARAH and BARBARA come in with their respective young men, CHARLES LOMAX and ADOLPHUS CUSINS. SARAH is slender, bored, and mundane. BARBARA is robuster, jollier, much more energetic. SARAH is fashionably dressed: BARBARA is in Salvation Army uniform. LOMAX, a young man about town, is like many other young men about town. He is afflicted with a frivolous sense of humor which plunges him at the most inopportune moments into paroxysms of imperfectly suppressed laughter. CUSINS is a spectacled student, slight, thin haired, and sweet voiced, with a more complex form of LOMAX's complaint. His sense of humor is intellectual and subtle, and is complicated by an appalling temper. The lifelong struggle of a benevolent temperament and a high conscience against impulses of inhuman ridicule and fierce impatience has set up a chronic strain which has visibly wrecked his constitution. He is a most implacable, determined, tenacious, intolerant person who by mere force of character presents himself as—and indeed actually is—considerate, gentle, explanatory, even mild and apologetic, capable possibly of murder, but not of cruelty or coarseness. By the operation of some instinct which is not merciful enough to blind him with the illusions of love, he is obstinately bent on marrying BARBARA. LOMAX likes SARAH and thinks it will be rather a lark to marry her. Consequently he has not attempted to resist LADY BRITOMART's arrangements to that end.

All four look as if they had been having a good deal of fun in the drawing room. The girls enter first, leaving the swains outside. SARAH comes to the settee. BARBARA comes in after her and stops at the door.)

BARBARA: Are Cholly and Dolly to come in?

LADY BRITOMART: *(Forcibly)* Barbara: I will not have Charles called Cholly: the vulgarity of it positively makes me ill.

BARBARA: It's all right, mother: Cholly is quite correct nowadays. Are they to come in?

LADY BRITOMART: Yes, if they will behave themselves.

BARBARA: *(Through the door)* Come in, Dolly; and behave yourself.

*(*BARBARA *comes to her mother's writing table.* CUSINS *enters smiling, and wanders towards* LADY BRITOMART.)*

SARAH: *(Calling)* Come in, Cholly. *(*LOMAX *enters, controlling his features very imperfectly, and places himself vaguely between* SARAH *and* BARBARA.)*

LADY BRITOMART: *(Peremptorily)* Sit down, all of you. *(They sit.* CUSINS *crosses to the window and seats himself there.* LOMAX *takes a chair.* BARBARA *sits at the writing table and* SARAH *on the settee.)* I dont in the least know what you are laughing at, Adolphus. I am surprised at you, though I expected nothing better from Charles Lomax.

CUSINS: *(In a remarkably gentle voice)* Barbara has been trying to teach me the West Ham Salvation March.

LADY BRITOMART: I see nothing to laugh at in that; nor should you if you are really converted.

CUSINS: *(Sweetly)* You were not present. It was really funny, I believe.

LOMAX: Ripping.

LADY BRITOMART: Be quiet, Charles. Now listen to me, children. Your father is coming here this evening.

(General stupefaction. LOMAX, SARAH, *and* BARBARA *rise;* SARAH *scared, and* BARBARA *amused and expectant.)*

LOMAX: *(Remonstrating)* Oh I say!

LADY BRITOMART: You are not called on to say anything, Charles.

SARAH: Are you serious, mother?

LADY BRITOMART: Of course I am serious. It is on your accout, Sarah, and also on Charles's. *(Silence.* SARAH *sits, with a shrug.* CHARLES *looks painfully unworthy.)* I hope you are not going to object, Barbara.

BARBARA: I! why should I? My father has a soul to be saved like anybody else. He's quite welcome as far as I am concerned. *(She sits on the table, and softly whistles 'Onward Christian Soldiers.')*

LOMAX: *(Still remonstrant)* But really, dont you know! Oh I say!

LADY BRITOMART: *(Frigidly)* What do you wish to convey, Charles?

LOMAX: Well, you must admit that this is a bit thick.

LADY BRITOMART: *(Turning with ominous suavity to* CUSINS) Adolphus: you are a professor of Greek. Can you translate Charles Lomax's remarks into reputable English for us?

CUSINS: *(Cautiously)* If I may say so, Lady Brit, I think Charles has rather happily expressed what we all feel. Homer, speaking of Autolycus, uses the same phrase. πυκινὸν δόμον ἐλθὼν means a bit thick.

LOMAX: *(Handsomely)* Not that I mind, you know, if Sarah dont. *(He sits.)*

LADY BRITOMART: *(Crushingly)* Thank you. Have I your permission, Adolphus, to invite my own husband to my own house?

CUSINS: *(Gallantly)* You have my unhesitating support in everything you do.

LADY BRITOMART: Tush! Sarah: have you nothing to say?

SARAH: Do you mean that he is coming regularly to live here?

LADY BRITOMART: Certainly not. The spare room is ready for him if he likes to stay for a day or two and see a little more of you; but there are limits.

SARAH: Well, he cant eat us, I suppose. *I* dont mind.

LOMAX: *(Chuckling)* I wonder how the old man will take it.

LADY BRITOMART: Much as the old woman will, no doubt, Charles.

LOMAX: *(Abashed)* I didnt mean—at least—

LADY BRITOMART: You didnt think, Charles. You never do; and the result is, you never mean anything. And now please attend to me, children. Your father will be quite a stranger to us.

LOMAX: I suppose he hasnt seen Sarah since she was a little kid.

LADY BRITOMART: Not since she was a little kid, Charles, as you express it with that elegance of diction and refinement of thought that seem never to desert you. Accordingly—er—*(Impatiently)* Now I have forgotten what I was going to say. That comes of your provoking me to be sarcastic, Charles. Adolphus: you will kindly tell me where I was.

CUSINS: *(Sweetly)* You were saying that as Mr Undershaft has not seen his children since they were babies, he will form his opinion of the way you have brought them up from their behavior tonight, and that therefore you wish us all to be particularly careful to conduct ourselves well, especially Charles.

LADY BRITOMART: *(With emphatic approval)* Precisely.

LOMAX: Look here, Dolly: Lady Brit didnt say that.

LADY BRITOMART: *(Vehemently)* I did, Charles. Adolphus's recollection is perfectly correct. It is most important that you should be good; and I do beg you for once not to pair off into opposite corners and giggle and whisper while I am speaking to your father.

BARBARA: All right, mother. We'll do you credit. *(She comes off the table, and sits in her chair with ladylike elegance.)*

LADY BRITOMART: Remember, Charles, that Sarah will want to feel proud of you instead of ashamed of you.

LOMAX: Oh I say! theres nothing to be exactly proud of, dont you know.

LADY BRITOMART: Well, try and look as if there was.

(MORRISON, pale and dismayed, breaks into the room in unconcealed disorder.)

MORRISON: Might I speak a word to you, my lady?

LADY BRITOMART: Nonsense! Shew him up.

MORRISON: Yes, my lady. *(He goes)*

LOMAX: Does Morrison know who it is?

LADY BRITOMART: Of course. Morrison has always been with us.

LOMAX: It must be a regular corker for him, dont you know.

LADY BRITOMART: Is this a moment to get on my nerves, Charles, with your outrageous expressions?

LOMAX: But this is something out of the ordinary, really —

MORRISON: *(At the door)* The — er — Mr Undershaft. *(He retreats in confusion.)*

(ANDREW UNDERSHAFT comes in. All rise. LADY BRITOMART meets him in the middle of the room behind the settee.

ANDREW *is, on the surface, a stoutish, easygoing elderly man, with kindly patient manners, and an engaging simplicity of character. But he has a watchful, deliberate, waiting, listening face, and formidable reserves of power, both bodily and mental, in his capacious chest and long head. His gentleness is partly that of a strong man who has learnt by experience that his natural grip hurts ordinary people unless he handles them very carefully, and partly the mellowness of age and success. He is also a little shy in his present very delicate situation.)*

LADY BRITOMART: Good evening, Andrew.

UNDERSHAFT: How d'ye do, my dear.

LADY BRITOMART: You look a good deal older.

UNDERSHAFT: *(Apologetically)* I am somewhat older. *(Taking her hand with a touch of courtship.)* Time has stood still with you.

LADY BRITOMART: *(Throwing away his hand)* Rubbish! This is your family.

UNDERSHAFT: *(Surprised)* Is it so large? I am sorry to say my memory is failing very badly in some things. *(He offers his hand with paternal kindness to LOMAX.)*

LOMAX: *(Jerkily shaking his hand)* Ahdedoo.

UNDERSHAFT: I can see you are my eldest. I am very glad to meet you again, my boy.

LOMAX: *(Remonstrating)* No, but look here dont you know — *(Overcome)* Oh I say!

LADY BRITOMART: *(Recovering from momentary speechlessness)* Andrew: do you mean to say that you dont remember how many children you have?

UNDERSHAFT: Well, I am afraid I —. They have grown so much — er. Am I making any ridiculous mistake? I may as well confess: I recollect only one son. But so many things have happened since, of course — er —

LADY BRITOMART: *(Decisively)* Andrew: you are talking nonsense. Of course you have only one son.

UNDERSHAFT: Perhaps you will be good enough to introduce me, my dear.

LADY BRITOMART: That is Charles Lomax, who is engaged to Sarah.

UNDERSHAFT: My dear sir, I beg your pardon.

LOMAX: Notatall. Delighted, I assure you.

LADY BRITOMART: This is Stephen.

UNDERSHAFT: *(Bowing)* Happy to make your acquaintance, Mr Stephen. Then *(Going to*

CUSINS) you must be my son. (Taking CUSINS' hands in his) How are you, my young friend? (To LADY BRITOMART) He is very like you, my love.

CUSINS: You flatter me, Mr Undershaft. My name is Cusins: engaged to Barbara. (Very explicitly) That is Major Barbara Undershaft, of the Salvation Army. That is Sarah, your second daughter. This is Stephen Undershaft, your son.

UNDERSHAFT: My dear Stephen, I beg your pardon.

STEPHEN: Not at all.

UNDERSHAFT: Mr Cusins: I am much indebted to you for explaining so precisely. (Turning to SARAH) Barbara, my dear—

SARAH: (Prompting him) Sarah.

UNDERSHAFT: Sarah, of course. (They shake hands. He goes over to BARBARA.) Barbara—I am right this time, I hope?

BARBARA: Quite right. (They shake hands.)

LADY BRITOMART: (Resuming command.) Sit down, all of you. Sit down, Andrew.

(She comes forward and sits on the settee. CUSINS also brings his chair forward on her left. BARBARA and STEPHEN resume their seats. LOMAX gives his chair to SARAH and goes for another.)

UNDERSHAFT: Thank you, my love.

LOMAX: (Conversationally, as he brings a chair forward between the writing table and the settee, and offers it to UNDERSHAFT) Takes you some time to find out exactly where you are, dont it?

UNDERSHAFT: (Accepting the chair, but remaining standing) That is not what embarrasses me, Mr Lomax. My difficulty is that if I play the part of a father, I shall produce the effect of an intrusive stranger; and if I play the part of a discreet stranger, I may appear a callous father.

LADY BRITOMART: There is no need for you to play any part at all, Andrew. You had much better be sincere and natural.

UNDERSHAFT: (Submissively) Yes, my dear: I daresay that will be best. (He sits down comfortably.) Well, here I am. Now what can I do for you all?

LADY BRITOMART: You need not do anything, Andrew. You are one of the family. You can sit with us and enjoy yourself.

(A painfully conscious pause. BARBARA makes a face at LOMAX, whose too long suppressed mirth immediately explodes in agonized neighings.)

LADY BRITOMART: (Outraged) Charles Lomax: if you can behave yourself, behave yourself. If not, leave the room.

LOMAX: I'm awfully sorry, Lady Brit; but really you know, upon my soul! (He sits on the settee between LADY BRITOMART and UNDERSHAFT, quite overcome.)

BARBARA: Why dont you laugh if you want to, Cholly? It's good for your inside.

LADY BRITOMART: Barbara: you have had the education of a lady. Please let your father see that; and dont talk like a street girl.

UNDERSHAFT: Never mind me, my dear. As you know, I am not a gentleman; and I was never educated.

LOMAX: (Encouragingly) Nobody'd know it, I assure you. You look all right, you know.

CUSINS: Let me advise you to study Greek, Mr Undershaft. Greek scholars are privileged men. Few of them know Greek; and none of them know anything else; but their position is unchallengeable. Other languages are the qualifications of waiters and commercial travellers: Greek is to a man of position what the hallmark is to silver.

BARBARA: Dolly: dont be insincere. Cholly: fetch your concertina and play something for us.

LOMAX: (Jumps up eagerly, but checks himself to remark doubtfully to UNDERSHAFT) Perhaps that sort of thing isnt in your line, eh?

UNDERSHAFT: I am particularly fond of music.

LOMAX: (Delighted) Are you? Then I'll get it. (He goes upstairs for the instrument.)

UNDERSHAFT: Do you play, Barbara?

BARBARA: Only the tambourine. But Cholly's teaching me the concertina.

UNDERSHAFT: Is Cholly also a member of the Salvation Army?

BARBARA: No: he says it's bad form to be a dissenter. But I dont despair of Cholly. I made him come yesterday to a meeting at the dock gates, and take the collection in his hat.

UNDERSHAFT: (Looks whimsically at his wife!!)

LADY BRITOMART: It is not my doing, Andrew. Barbara is old enough to take her own way. She has no father to advise her.

BARBARA: Oh yes she has. There are no orphans in the Salvation Army.

UNDERSHAFT: Your father there has a great many children and plenty of experience, eh?

BARBARA: *(Looking at him with quick interest and nodding)* Just so. How did you come to understand that? *(LOMAX is heard at the door trying the concertina.)*

LADY BRITOMART: Come in, Charles. Play us something at once.

LOMAX: Righto! *(He sits down in his former place, and preludes.)*

UNDERSHAFT: One moment, Mr. Lomax. I am rather interested in the Salvation Army. Its motto might be my own: Blood and Fire.

LOMAX: *(Shocked)* But not your sort of blood and fire, you know.

UNDERSHAFT: My sort of blood cleanses: my sort of fire purifies.

BARBARA: So do ours. Come down tomorrow to my shelter—the West Ham shelter—and see what we're doing. We're going to march to a great meeting in the Assembly Hall at Mile End. Come and see the shelter and then march with us: it will do you a lot of good. Can you play anything?

UNDERSHAFT: In my youth I earned pennies, and even shillings occasionally, in the streets and in public parlors by my natural talent for stepdancing. Later on, I became a member of the Undershaft orchestral society, and performed passably on the tenor trombone.

LOMAX: *(Scandalized—putting down the concertina)* Oh I say!

BARBARA: Many a sinner has played himself into heaven on the trombone, thanks to the Army.

LOMAX: *(To BARBARA, still rather shocked)* Yes; but what about the cannon business, dont you know? *(To UNDERSHAFT)* Getting into heaven is not exactly in your line, is it?

LADY BRITOMART: Charles!!!

LOMAX: Well; but it stands to reason, dont it? The cannon business may be necessary and all that: we cant get on without cannons; but it isnt right, you know. On the other hand, there may be a certain amount of tosh about the Salvation Army—I belong to the Established Church myself—but still you cant deny that it's religion; and you cant go against religion, can you? At least unless youre downright immoral, dont you know.

UNDERSHAFT: You hardly appreciate my position, Mr Lomax—

LOMAX: *(Hastily)* I'm not saying anything against you personally—

UNDERSHAFT: Quite so, quite so. But consider for a moment. Here I am, a profiteer in mutilation and murder. I find myself in a specially amiable humor just now because, this morning, down at the foundry, we blew twenty-seven dummy soldiers into fragments with a gun which formerly destroyed only thirteen.

LOMAX: *(Leniently)* Well, the more destructive war becomes, the sooner it will be abolished, eh?

UNDERSHAFT: Not at all. The more destructive war becomes the more fascinating we find it. No, Mr Lomax: I am obliged to you for making the usual excuse for my trade; but I am not ashamed of it. I am not one of those men who keep their morals and their business in water-tight compartments. All the spare money my trade rivals spend on hospitals, cathedrals, and other receptacles for conscience money, I devote to experiments and researches in improved methods of destroying life and property. I have always done so; and I always shall. Therefore your Christmas card moralities of peace on earth and goodwill among men are of no use to me. Your Christianity, which enjoins you to resist not evil, and to turn the other cheek, would make me a bankrupt. My morality—my religion—must have a place for cannons and torpedoes in it.

STEPHEN: *(Coldly—almost sullenly)* You speak as if there were half a dozen moralities and religions to choose from, instead of one true morality and one true religion.

UNDERSHAFT: For me there is only one true morality; but it might not fit you, as you do not manufacture aerial battleships. There is only one true morality for every man; but every man has not the same true morality.

LOMAX: *(Overtaxed)* Would you mind saying that again? I didnt quite follow it.

CUSINS: It's quite simple. As Euripides says, one man's meat is another man's poison morally as well as physically.

UNDERSHAFT: Precisely.

LOMAX: Oh, that! Yes, yes, yes. True. True.

STEPHEN: In other words, some men are honest and some are scoundrels.

BARBARA: Bosh! There are no scoundrels.

UNDERSHAFT: Indeed? Are there any good men?

BARBARA: No. Not one. There are neither good men nor scoundrels: there are just children of one Father; and the sooner they stop calling one another names the better. You neednt talk to me: I know them. I've had scores of them through my hands: scoundrels, criminals, infidels, philanthropists, missionaries, county councillors, all sorts. Theyre all just the same sort of sinner; and theres the same salvation ready for them all.

UNDERSHAFT: May I ask have you ever saved a maker of cannons?

BARBARA: No. Will you let me try?

UNDERSHAFT: Well, I will make a bargain with you. If I go to see you tomorrow in your Salvation Shelter, will you come the day after to see me in my cannon works?

BARBARA: Take care. It may end in your giving up the cannons for the sake of the Salvation Army.

UNDERSHAFT: Are you sure it will not end in your giving up the Salvation Army for the sake of the cannons?

BARBARA: I will take my chance of that.

UNDERSHAFT: And I will take my chance of the other. *(They shake hands on it.)* Where is your shelter?

BARBARA: In West Ham. At the sign of the cross. Ask anybody in Canning Town. Where are your works?

UNDERSHAFT: In Perivale St Andrews. At the sign of the sword. Ask anybody in Europe.

LOMAX: Hadnt I better play something?

BARBARA: Yes. Give us Onward, Christian Soldiers.

LOMAX: Well, thats rather a strong order to begin with, dont you know. Suppose I sing Thourt passing hence, my brother. It's much the same tune.

BARBARA: It's too melancholy. You get saved, Cholly; and youll pass hence, my brother, without making such a fuss about it.

LADY BRITOMART: Really, Barbara, you go on as if religion were a pleasant subject. Do have some sense of propriety.

UNDERSHAFT: I do not find it an unpleasant subject, my dear. It is the only one that capable people really care for.

LADY BRITOMART: *(Looking at her watch)* Well, if you are determined to have it, I insist on having it in a proper and respectable way. Charles: ring for prayers.

(General amazement. STEPHEN *rises in dismay.)*

LOMAX: *(Rising)* Oh I say!

UNDERSHAFT: *(Rising)* I am afraid I must be going.

LADY BRITOMART: You cannot go now, Andrew: it would be most improper. Sit down. What will the servants think?

UNDERSHAFT: My dear: I have conscientious scruples. May I suggest a compromise? If Barbara will conduct a little service in the drawing room, with Mr Lomax as organist, I will attend it willingly. I will even take part, if a trombone can be procured.

LADY BRITOMART: Dont mock, Andrew.

UNDERSHAFT: *(Shocked—to* BARBARA*)* You dont think I am mocking, my love, I hope.

BARBARA: No, of course not; and it wouldnt matter if you were: half the Army came to their first meeting for a lark. *(Rising)* Come along. *(She throws her arm round her father and sweeps him out, calling to the others from the threshold.)* Come, Dolly. Come, Cholly.

*(*CUSINS *rises.)*

LADY BRITOMART: I will not be disobeyed by everybody. Adolphus: sit down. *(He does not)* Charles: you may go. You are not fit for prayers: you cannot keep your countenance.

LOMAX: Oh I say! *(He goes out.)*

LADY BRITOMART: *(Continuing)* But you, Adolphus, can behave yourself if you choose to. I insist on your staying.

CUSINS: My dear Lady Brit: there are things in the family prayer book that I couldnt bear to hear you say.

LADY BRITOMART: What things, pray?

CUSINS: Well, you would have to say before all the servants that we have done things we ought not to have done, and left undone things we ought to have done, and that there is no health in us. I cannot bear to hear you doing yourself such an injustice, and Barbara such an injustice. As for myself, I flatly deny it: I have done my best. I shouldnt dare to marry Barbara—I couldnt look you in the face—if it were true. So I must go to the drawing room.

LADY BRITOMART: *(Offended)* Well, go. *(He starts for the door.)* And remember this, Adolphus *(He turns to listen)*: I have a very strong suspicion that you went to the Salvation Army to worship Barbara and nothing else. And I quite appreciate the very clever way in which you systematically humbug me. I have found you out. Take care Barbara doesnt. Thats all.

CUSINS: *(With unruffled sweetness)* Dont tell on me. *(He steals out.)*

LADY BRITOMART: Sarah: if you want to go, go. Anything's better than to sit there as if you wished you were a thousand miles away.

SARAH: *(Languidly)* Very well, mamma. *(She goes.)*

(LADY BRITOMART, with a sudden flounce, gives way to a little gust of tears.)

STEPHEN: *(Going to her)* Mother: whats the matter?

LADY BRITOMART: *(Swishing away her tears with her handkerchief.)* Nothing! Foolishness. You can go with him, too, if you like, and leave me with the servants.

STEPHEN: Oh, you mustnt think that, mother. I—I dont like him.

LADY BRITOMART: The others do. That is the injustice of a woman's lot. A woman has to bring up her children; and that means to restrain them, to deny them things they want, to set them tasks, to punish them when they do wrong, to do all the unpleasant things. And the father, who has nothing to do but pet them and spoil them, comes in when all her work is done and steals their affection from her.

STEPHEN: He has not stolen our affection from you. It is only curiosity.

LADY BRITOMART: *(Violently)* I wont be consoled, Stephen. There is nothing the matter with me. *(She rises and goes towards the door.)*

STEPHEN: Where are you going, mother?

LADY BRITOMART: To the drawing room, of course. *(She goes out. Onward, Christian Soldiers, on the concertina, with tambourine accompaniment, is heard when the door opens.)* Are you coming, Stephen?

STEPHEN: No. Certainly not. *(She goes. He sits down on the settee, with compressed lips and an expression of strong dislike.)*

ACT II

The yard of the West Ham shelter of the Salvation Army is a cold place on a January morning. The building itself, an old warehouse, is newly whitewashed. Its gabled end projects into the yard in the middle, with a door on the ground floor, and another in the loft above it without any balcony or ladder, but with a pulley rigged over it for hoisting sacks. Those who come from this central gable end into the yard have the gateway leading to the street on their left, with a stone horse-trough just beyond it, and, on the right, a penthouse shielding a table from the weather. There are forms at the table; and on them are seated a man and a woman, both much down on their luck, finishing a meal of bread (one thick slice each, with margarine and golden syrup) and diluted milk.

The man, a workman out of employment, is young, agile, a talker, a poser, sharp enough to be capable of anything in reason except honesty or altruistic consideration of any kind. The woman is a commonplace old bundle of poverty and hard-worn humanity. She looks sixty and is probably forty-five. If they were rich people, gloved and muffed and well wrapped up in furs and overcoats, they would be numbed and miserable; for it is a grindingly cold raw January day; and a glance at the background of grimy warehouses and leaden sky visible over the whitewashed walls of the yard would drive any idle rich person straight to the Mediterranean. But these two, being no more troubled with visions of the Mediterranean than of the moon, and being compelled to keep more of their clothes in the pawnshop, and less on their persons, in winter than in summer, are not depressed by the cold: rather are they stung into vivacity, to which their meal has just now given an almost jolly turn. The man takes a pull at his mug, and then gets up and moves about the yard with his hands deep in his pockets, occasionally breaking into a stepdance.

THE WOMAN: Feel better arter your meal, sir?

THE MAN: No. Call that a meal! Good enough for you, praps; but wot is it to me, an intelligent workin man.

THE WOMAN: Workin man! Wot are you?

THE MAN: Painter.

THE WOMAN: (Sceptically) Yus, I dessay.

THE MAN: Yus, you dessay! I know. Every loafer that cant do nothink calls isself a painter. Well, I'm a real painter: grainer, finisher, thirty-eight bob a week when I can get it.

THE WOMAN: Then why dont you go and get it?

THE MAN: I'll tell you why. Fust: I'm intelligent — fffff! it's rotten cold here (He dances a step or two) — yes: intelligent beyond the station o life into which it has pleased the capitalists to call me; and they dont like a man that sees through em. Second, an intelligent bein needs a doo share of appiness; so I drink something cruel when I get the chawnce. Third, I stand by my class and do as little as I can so's to leave arf the job for me fellow workers. Fourth, I'm fly enough to know wots inside the law and wots outside it; and inside it I do as the capitalists do: pinch wot I can lay me hands on. In a proper state of society I am sober, industrious and honest: in Rome, so to speak, I do as the Romans do. Wots the consequence? When trade is bad — and it's rotten bad just now — and the employers az to sack arf their men, they generally start on me.

THE WOMAN: Whats your name?

THE MAN: Price. Bronterre O'Brien Price. Usually called Snobby Price, for short.

THE WOMAN: Snobby's a carpenter, aint it? You said you was a painter.

PRICE: Not that kind of snob, but the genteel sort. I'm too uppish, owing to my intelligence, and my father being a Chartist and a reading, thinking man: a stationer, too. I'm none of your common hewers of wood and drawers of water; and dont you forget it. (He returns to his seat at the table, and takes up his mug.) Wots your name?

THE WOMAN: Rummy Mitchens, sir.

PRICE: (Quaffing the remains of his milk to her) Your elth, Miss Mitchens.

RUMMY: (Correcting him) Missis Mitchens.

PRICE: Wot! Oh Rummy, Rummy! Respectable married woman, Rummy, gittin rescued by the Salvation Army by pretendin to be a bad un. Same old game!

RUMMY: What am I to do? I cant starve. Them Salvation lasses is dear good girls: but the better you are, the worse they likes to think you were before they rescued you. Why shouldnt they av a bit o credit, poor loves? theyre worn to rags by their work. And where would they get the money to rescue us if we was to let on we're no worse than other people? You know what ladies and gentlemen are.

PRICE: Thievin swine! Wish I ad their job, Rummy, all the same. Wot does Rummy stand for? Pet name praps?

RUMMY: Short for Romola.

PRICE: For wot!?

RUMMY: Romola. It was out of a new book. Somebody me mother wanted me to grow up like.

PRICE: We're companions in misfortune, Rummy. Both on us got names that nobody cawnt pronounce. Consequently I'm Snobby and youre Rummy because Bill and Sally wasnt good enough for our parents. Such is life!

RUMMY: Who saved you, Mr Price? Was it Major Barbara?

PRICE: No: I come here on my own. I'm going to be Bronterre O'Brien Price, the converted painter. I know wot they like. I'll tell em how I blasphemed and gambled and wopped my poor old mother —

RUMMY: (Shocked) Used you to beat your mother?

PRICE: Not likely. She used to beat me. No matter: you come and listen to the converted painter, and youll hear how she was a pious woman that taught me me prayers at er knee, an how I used to come home drunk and drag her out o bed be er snow white airs, an lam into er with the poker.

RUMMY: Thats whats so unfair to us women. Your confessions is just as big lies as ours: you dont tell what you really done no more than us; but you men can tell your lies right out at the meetins and be made much of for it; while the sort o confessions we az to make az to be whispered to one lady at a time. It aint right, spite of all their piety.

PRICE: Right! Do you spose the Army'd be allowed if it went and did right? Not much. It combs our air and makes us good little blokes to be robbed and put upon. But I'll play the game as good as any of em. I'll see somebody struck by lightnin, or hear a voice sayin "Snobby Price: where will you spend eternity?" I'll av a time of it, I tell you.

RUMMY: You wont be let drink, though.

PRICE: I'll take it out in gorspellin, then. I dont want to drink if I can get fun enough any other way.

(JENNY HILL, *a pale, overwrought, pretty Salvation lass of 18, comes in through the yard gate, leading* PETER SHIRLEY, *a half hardened, half worn-out elderly man, weak with hunger.*)

JENNY: (*Supporting him*) Come! pluck up. I'll get you something to eat. Youll be all right then.

PRICE: (*Rising and hurrying officiously to take the old man off* JENNY's *hands*) Poor old man! Cheer up, brother: youll find rest and peace and appiness ere. Hurry up with the food, miss: e's fair done. (JENNY *hurries into the shelter.*) Ere, buck up, daddy! she's fetchin y'a thick slice o breadn treacle, an a mug o sky-blue. (*He seats him at the corner of the table.*)

RUMMY: (*Gaily*) Keep up your old art! Never say die!

SHIRLEY: I'm not an old man. I'm only 46. I'm as good as ever I was. The grey patch come in my hair before I was thirty. All it wants is three pennorth o hair dye: am I to be turned on the streets to starve for it? Holy God! Ive worked ten to twelve hours a day since I was thirteen, and paid my way all through; and now am I to be thrown into the gutter and my job given to a young man that can do it no better than me because Ive black hair that goes white at the first change?

PRICE: (*Cheerfully*) No good jawrin about it. Youre only a jumped-up, jerked-off, orspittle-turned-out incurable of an ole workin man: who cares about you? Eh? Make the thievin swine give you a meal: theyve stole many a one from you. Get a bit o your own back. (JENNY *returns with the usual meal.*) There you are, brother. Awsk a blessin an tuck that into you.

SHIRLEY: (*Looking at it ravenously but not touching it, and crying like a child*) I never took anything before.

JENNY: (*Petting him*) Come, come! the Lord sends it to you: he wasnt above taking bread from his friends; and why should you be? Besides, when we find you a job you can pay us for it if you like.

SHIRLEY: (*Eagerly*) Yes, yes: that's true. I can pay you back: it's only a loan. (*Shivering*) Oh Lord! oh Lord! (*He turns to the table and attacks the meal ravenously.*)

JENNY: Well, Rummy, are you more comfortable now?

RUMMY: God bless you, lovey! youve fed my body and saved my soul, havnt you? (JENNY, *touched, kisses her.*) Sit down and rest a bit: you must be ready to drop.

JENNY: Ive been going hard since morning. But theres more work than we can do. I mustnt stop.

RUMMY: Try a prayer for just two minutes. Youll work all the better after.

JENNY: (*Her eyes lighting up*) Oh isnt it wonderful how a few minutes prayer revives you! I was quite light-headed at twelve o'clock, I was so tired; but Major Barbara just sent me to pray for five minutes; and I was able to go on as if I had only just begun. (*To* PRICE) Did you have a piece of bread?

PRICE: (*With unction*) Yes, miss; but Ive got the piece that I value more; and thats the peace that passeth hall hannerstennin.

RUMMY: (*Fervently*) Glory Hallelujah!

(BILL WALKER, *a rough customer of about 25, appears at the yard gate and looks malevolently at* JENNY.)

JENNY: That makes me so happy. When you say that, I feel wicked for loitering here. I must get to work again.

(*She is hurrying to the shelter, when the newcomer moves quickly up to the door and intercepts her. His manner is so threatening that she retreats as he comes at her truculently, driving her down the yard.*)

BILL: Aw knaow you. Youre the one that took awy maw girl. Youre the one that set er agen me. Well, I'm gowin to ev er aht. Not that Aw care a carse for er or you: see? Bat Aw'll let er knaow; and Aw'll let you knaow. Aw'm going to give her a doin thatll teach er to cat awy from me. Nah in wiv you and tell er to came aht afore Aw cam in and kick er aht. Tell er Bill Walker wants er. She'll knaow wot thet means; and if she keeps me witin it'll be worse. You stop to jawr beck at me; and Aw'll stawt on you: d'ye eah? Theres your wy. In you gow. (*He takes her by the arm and slings her towards the door of the shelter. She falls on her hand and knee.* RUMMY *helps her up again.)*

PRICE: *(Rising, and venturing irresolutely towards* BILL) Easy there, mate. She aint doin you no arm.

BILL: Oo are you callin mite? *(Standing over him threateningly)* Youre gowin to stend ap for er, aw yer? Put ap your ends.

RUMMY: *(Running indignantly to scold him)* Oh, you great brute — *(He instantly swings his left hand back against her face. She screams and reels back to the trough, where she sits down, covering her bruised face with her hands and rocking herself and moaning with pain.)*

JENNY: *(Going to her)* Oh, God forgive you! How could you strike an old woman like that?

BILL: *(Seizing her by the hair so violently that she also screams, and tearing her away from the old woman)* You Gawd forgimme again an Aw'll Gawd forgive you one on the jawr thetll stop you pryin for a week. *(Holding her and turning fiercely on* PRICE) Ev you ennything to sy agen it?

PRICE: *(Intimidated)* No, matey: she aint anything to do with me.

BILL: Good job for you! Aw'd pat two meals into you and fawt you with one finger arter, you stawved cur. *(To* JENNY) Nah are you gowin to fetch aht Mog Ebbijem; or em Aw to knock your fice off you and fetch her meself?

JENNY: *(Writhing in his grasp)* Oh please someone go in and tell Major Barbara — *(She screams again as he wrenches her head down; and* PRICE *and* RUMMY *flee into the shelter.)*

BILL: You want to gow in and tell your Mijor of me, do you?

JENNY: Oh please dont drag my hair. Let me go.

BILL: Do you or downt you? *(She stifles a scream.)* Yus or nao?

JENNY: God give me strength —

BILL: *(Striking her with his fist in the face)* Gow an shaow her thet, and tell her if she wants one lawk it to cam and interfere with me. (JENNY, *crying with pain, goes into the shed. He goes to the form and addresses the old man.)* Eah: finish your mess; an git aht o maw wy.

SHIRLEY: *(Springing up and facing him fiercely, with the mug in his hand)* You take a liberty with me, and I'll smash you over the face with the mug and cut your eye out. Aint you satisfied —

young whelps like you — with takin the bread out o the mouths of your elders that have brought you up and slaved for you, but you must come shovin and cheekin and bullyin in here, where the bread of charity is sickenin in our stummicks?

BILL: *(Contemptuously, but backing a little)* Wot good are you, you aold palsy mag? Wot good are you?

SHIRLEY: As good as you and better. I'll do a day's work agen you or any fat young soaker of your age. Go and take my job at Horrockses, where I worked for ten year. They want young men there: they cant afford to keep men over forty-five. Theyre very sorry — give you a character and happy to help you to get anything suited to your years — sure a steady man wont be long out of a job. Well, let em try you. Theyll find the differ. What do you know? Not as much as how to beeyave yourself — layin your dirty fist across the mouth of a respectable woman!

BILL: Downt provowk me to ly it acrost yours: d'ye eah?

SHIRLEY: *(With blighting contempt)* Yes: you like an old man to hit, dont you, when youve finished with the women. I aint seen you hit a young one yet.

BILL: *(Stung)* You loy, you aold soupkitchener, you. There was a yang menn eah. Did Aw offer to itt him or did Aw not?

SHIRLEY: Was he starvin or was he not? Was he a man or only a crosseyed thief an a loafer? Would you hit my son-in-law's brother?

BILL: Oo's ee?

SHIRLEY: Todger Fairmile o Balls Pond. Him that won £20 off the Japanese wrastler at the music hall by standin out 17 minutes 4 seconds agen him.

BILL: *(Sullenly)* Aw'm nao music awl wrastler. Ken he box?

SHIRLEY: Yes: an you cant.

BILL: Wot! Aw cawnt, cawnt Aw? Wots thet you sy *(Threatening him)?*

SHIRLEY: *(Not budging an inch)* Will you box Todger Fairmile if I put him on to you? Say the word.

BILL: *(Subsiding with a slouch)* Aw'll stend ap to enny menn alawv, if he was ten Todger Fairmawls. But Aw dont set ap to be a perfeshnal.

SHIRLEY: *(Looking down on him with unfathomable disdain)* You box? Slap an old woman with the back o your hand! You hadnt even the sense to hit her where a magistrate couldnt see the mark of it, you silly young lump of conceit and ignorance. Hit a girl in the jaw and only make her cry! If Todger Fairmile'd done it, she wouldnt a got up inside o ten minutes, no more than you would if he got on to you. Yah! I'd set about you myself if I had a week's feedin in me instead o two months' starvation. *(He turns his back on him and sits down moodily at the table.)*

BILL: *(Following him and stooping over him to drive the taunt in)* You loy! youve the bread and treacle in you that you cam eah to beg.

SHIRLEY: *(Bursting into tears)* Oh God! it's true: I'm only an old pauper on the scrap heap. *(Furiously)* But youll come to it yourself; and then youll know. Youll come to it sooner than a teetotaller like me, fillin yourself with gin at this hour o the mornin!

BILL: Aw'm nao gin drinker, you oald lawr; bat wen Aw want to give my girl a bloomin good awdin Aw lawk to ev a bit o devil in me: see? An eah Aw emm, talkin to a rotten aold blawter like you sted o given her wot for. *(Working himself into a rage)* Aw'm gowin in there to fetch her aht. *(He makes vengefully for the shelter door.)*

SHIRLEY: Youre goin to the station on a stretcher, more likely; and theyll take the gin and the devil out of you there when they get you inside. You mind what youre about: the major here is the Earl o Stevenage's granddaughter.

BILL: *(Checked)* Garn!

SHIRLEY: You'll see.

BILL: *(His resolution oozing)* Well, Aw aint dan nathin to er.

SHIRLEY: Spose she said you did! who'd believe you?

BILL: *(Very uneasy, skulking back to the corner of the penthouse)* Gawd! there's no jastice in this cantry. To think wot them people can do! Aw'm as good as er.

SHIRLEY: Tell her so. It's just what a fool like you would do.

(BARBARA, brisk and businesslike, comes from the shelter with a note book, and addresses herself to SHIRLEY. BILL, cowed, sits down in the corner on a form, and turns his back on them.)

BARBARA: Good morning.

SHIRLEY: *(Standing up and taking off his hat)* Good morning, miss.

BARBARA: Sit down: make yourself at home. *(He hesitates; but she puts a friendly hand on his shoulder and makes him obey.)* Now then! since youve made friends with us, we want to know all about you. Names and addresses and trades.

SHIRLEY: Peter Shirley. Fitter. Chucked out two months ago because I was too old.

BARBARA: *(Not at all surprised)* Youd pass still. Why didnt you dye your hair?

SHIRLEY: I did. Me age come out at a coroner's inquest on me daughter.

BARBARA: Steady?

SHIRLEY: Teetotaller. Never out of a job before. Good worker. And sent to the knackers like an old horse!

BARBARA: No matter: if you did your part God will do his.

SHIRLEY: *(Suddenly stubborn)* My religion's no concern of anybody but myself.

BARBARA: *(Guessing)* I know. Secularist?

SHIRLEY: *(Hotly)* Did I offer to deny it?

BARBARA: Why should you? My own father's a Secularist, I think. Our Father—yours and mine—fulfils himself in many ways; and I daresay he knew what he was about when he made a Secularist of you. So buck up, Peter! we can always find a job for a steady man like you. (SHIRLEY, *disarmed and a little bewildered, touches his hat. She turns from him to* BILL.) Whats your name?

BILL: *(Insolently)* Wots thet to you?

BARBARA: *(Calmly making a note)* Afraid to give his name. Any trade?

BILL: Oo's afride to give is nime? *(Doggedly, with a sense of heroically defying the House of Lords in the person of Lord Stevenage)* If you want to bring a chawge agen me, bring it. *(She waits, unruffled.)* Moy nime's Bill Walker.

BARBARA: *(As if the name were familiar: trying to remember how)* Bill Walker? *(Recollecting)* Oh, I know: youre the man that Jenny Hill was praying for inside just now. *(She enters his name in her note book.)*

BILL: Oo's Jenny Ill? And wot call as she to pry for me?

BARBARA: I don't know. Perhaps it was you that cut her lip.

BILL: *(Defiantly)* Yus, it was me that cat her lip. Aw aint afride o you.

BARBARA: How could you be, since youre not afraid of God? Youre a brave man, Mr. Walker. It takes some pluck to do our work here; but none of us dare lift our hand against a girl like that, for fear of her father in heaven.

BILL: (Sullenly) I want nan o your kentin jawr. I spowse you think Aw cam eah to beg from you, like this demmiged lot eah. Not me. Aw downt want your bread and scripe and keplep. Aw dont blieve in your Gawd, no more than you do yourself.

BARBARA: (Sunnily apologetic and ladylike, as on a new footing with him) Oh, I beg your pardon for putting your name down, Mr Walker. I didnt understand. I'll strike it out.

BILL: (Taking this as a slight, and deeply wounded by it) Eah! you let maw nime alown. Aint it good enaff to be in your book?

BARBARA: (Considering) Well, you see, theres no use putting down your name unless I can do something for you, is there? Whats your trade?

BILL: (Still smarting) Thets nao concern o yours.

BARBARA: Just so. (Very businesslike) I'll put you down as (Writing) the man who—struck—poor little Jenny Hill—in the mouth.

BILL: (Rising threateningly) See eah. Awve ed enaff o this.

BARBARA: (Quite sunny and fearless) What did you come to us for?

BILL: Aw cam for maw gel, see? Aw cam to tike her aht o this and to brike er jawr for er.

BARBARA: (Complacently) You see I was right about your trade. (BILL, on the point of retorting furiously, finds himself, to his great shame and terror, in danger of crying instead. He sits down again suddenly.) Whats her name?

BILL: (Dogged) Er nime's Mog Ebbijem: thets wot her nime is.

BARBARA: Mog Habbijam! Oh, she's gone to Canning Town, to our barracks there.

BILL: (Fortified by his resentment of Mog's perfidy) Is she? (Vindictively) Then Aw'm gowin to Kennintahn arter her. (He crosses to the gate; hesitates; finally comes back at BARBARA.) Are you loyin to me to git shat o me?

BARBARA: I dont want to get shut of you. I want to keep you here and save your soul. Youd better stay: youre going to have a bad time today, Bill.

BILL: Oo's gowin to give it to me? You, preps?

BARBARA: Someone you dont believe in. But youll be glad afterwards.

BILL: (Slinking off) Aw'll gow to Kennintahn

to be aht o reach o your tangue. (Suddenly turning on her with intense malice) And if Aw downt fawnd Mog there, Aw'll cam beck and do two years for you, selp me Gawd if Aw downt!

BARBARA: (A shade kindlier, if possible) It's no use, Bill. She's got another bloke.

BILL: Wot!

BARBARA: One of her own converts. He fell in love with her when he saw her with her soul saved, and her face clean, and her hair washed.

BILL: (Surprised) Wottud she wash it for, the carroty slat? It's red.

BARBARA: It's quite lovely now, because she wears a new look in her eyes with it. It's a pity youre too late. The new bloke has put your nose out of joint, Bill.

BILL: Aw'll put his nowse aht o joint for him. Not that Aw care a carse for er, mawnd thet. But Aw'll teach her to drop me as if Aw was dirt. And Aw'll teach him to meddle with maw judy. Wots iz bleedin nime?

BARBARA: Sergeant Todger Fairmile.

SHIRLEY: (Rising with grim joy) I'll go with him, miss. I want to see them two meet. I'll take him to the infirmary when it's over.

BILL: (To SHIRLEY, with undissembled misgiving) Is thet im you was speakin on?

SHIRLEY: Thats him.

BILL: Im that wrastled in the music awl?

SHIRLEY: The competitions at the National Sportin Club was worth nigh a hundred a year to him. He's gev em up now for religion; so he's a bit fresh for want of the exercise he was accustomed to. He'll be glad to see you. Come along.

BILL: Wots is wight?

SHIRLEY: Thirteen four. (BILL's last hope expires.)

BARBARA: Go and talk to him, Bill. He'll convert you.

SHIRLEY: He'll convert your head into a mashed potato.

BILL: (Sullenly) Aw aint afride of im. Aw aint afride of ennybody Bat e can lick me. She's dan me. (He sits down moodily on the edge of the horse trough.)

SHIRLEY: You aint goin. I thought not. (He resumes his seat.)

BARBARA: (Calling) Jenny!

JENNY: (Appearing at the shelter door with a plaster on the corner of her mouth) Yes, Major.

BARBARA: Send Rummy Mitchens out to clear away here.

JENNY: I think she's afraid.

BARBARA: (Her resemblance to her mother flashing out for a moment) Nonsense! she must do as she's told.

JENNY: (Calling into the shelter) Rummy: the Major says you must come.

(JENNY comes to BARBARA, purposely keeping on the side next BILL, lest he should suppose that she shrank from him or bore malice.)

BARBARA: Poor little Jenny! Are you tired? (Looking at the wounded cheek) Does it hurt?

JENNY: No: it's all right now. It was nothing.

BARBARA: (Critically) It was as hard as he could hit, I expect. Poor Bill! You dont feel angry with him, do you?

JENNY: Oh no, no, no: indeed I dont, Major, bless his poor heart!

(BARBARA kisses her; and she runs away merrily into the shelter. BILL writhes with an agonizing return of his new and alarming symptoms, but says nothing. RUMMY MITCHENS comes from the shelter.)

BARBARA: (Going to meet RUMMY) Now Rummy, bustle. Take in those mugs and plates to be washed; and throw the crumbs about for the birds.

(RUMMY takes the three plates and mugs; but SHIRLEY takes back his mug from her, as there is still some milk left in it.)

RUMMY: There aint any crumbs. This aint a time to waste good bread on birds.

PRICE: (Appearing at the shelter door) Gentleman come to see the shelter, Major. Says he's your father.

BARBARA: All right. Coming (SNOBBY goes back into the shelter, followed by BARBARA.)

RUMMY: (Stealing across to BILL and addressing him in a subdued voice, but with intense conviction) I'd av the lor of you, you flat eared pignosed potwalloper, if she'd let me. Youre no gentleman, to hit a lady in the face.

(BILL, with greater things moving in him, takes no notice.)

SHIRLEY: (Following her) Here! in with you and dont get yourself into more trouble by talking.

RUMMY: (With hauteur) I aint ad the pleasure o being hintroduced to you, as I can remember. (She goes into the shelter with the plates.)

SHIRLEY: Thats the —

BILL: (Savagely) Downt you talk to me, d'ye eah? You lea me alown, or Aw'll do you a mischief. Aw'm not dirt under your feet, ennywy.

SHIRLEY: (Calmly) Dont you be afeerd. You aint such prime company that you need expect to be sought after.

(He is about to go into the shelter when BARBARA comes out, with UNDERSHAFT on her right.)

BARBARA: Oh, there you are, Mr Shirley! (Between them) This is my father: I told you he was a Secularist, didnt I? Perhaps youll be able to comfort one another.

UNDERSHAFT: (Startled) A Secularist! Not the least in the world: on the contrary, a confirmed mystic.

BARBARA: Sorry, I'm sure. By the way, papa, what is your religion? in case I have to introduce you again.

UNDERSHAFT: My religion? Well, my dear, I am a Millionaire. That is my religion.

BARBARA: Then I'm afraid you and Mr Shirley wont be able to comfort one another after all. Youre not a Millionaire, are you, Peter?

SHIRLEY: No; and proud of it.

UNDERSHAFT: (Gravely) Poverty, my friend, is not a thing to be proud of.

SHIRLEY: (Angrily) Who made your millions for you? Me and my like. Whats kep us poor? Keepin you rich. I wouldnt have your conscience, not for all your income.

UNDERSHAFT: I wouldnt have your income, not for all your conscience, Mr Shirley. (He goes to the penthouse and sits down on a form.)

BARBARA: (Stopping SHIRLEY adroitly as he is about to retort) You wouldnt think he was my father, would you, Peter? Will you go into the shelter and lend the lasses a hand for a while: we're worked off our feet.

SHIRLEY: (Bitterly) Yes: I'm in their debt for a meal, aint I?

BARBARA: Oh, not because youre in their debt, but for love of them, Peter, for love of them. (He cannot understand, and is rather scandalized.)

There! dont stare at me. In with you; and give that conscience of yours a holiday. (*Bustling him into the shelter*)

SHIRLEY: (*As he goes in*) Ah! it's a pity you never was trained to use your reason, miss. Youd have been a very taking lecturer on Secularism.

(BARBARA *turns to her father.*)

UNDERSHAFT: Never mind me, my dear. Go about your work; and let me watch it for a while.

BARBARA: All right.

UNDERSHAFT: For instance, whats the matter with that outpatient over there?

BARBARA: (*Looking at* BILL, *whose attitude has never changed, and whose expression of brooding wrath has deepened*) Oh, we shall cure him in no time. Just watch (*She goes over to* BILL *and waits. He glances up at her and casts his eyes down again, uneasy, but grimmer than ever.*) It would be nice to just stamp on Mog Habbijam's face, wouldnt it, Bill?

BILL: (*Starting up from the trough in consternation*) It's a loy. Aw never said so. (*She shakes her head.*) Oo taold you wot was in moy mawnd?

BARBARA: Only your new friend.

BILL: Wot new friend?

BARBARA: The devil, Bill. When he gets round people they get miserable, just like you.

BILL: (*With a heartbreaking attempt at devil-may-care cheerfulness*) Aw aint miserable. (*He sits down again, and stretches his legs in an attempt to seem indifferent.*)

BARBARA: Well, if youre happy, why dont you look happy, as we do?

BILL: (*His legs curling back in spite of him*) Aw'm eppy enaff, Aw tell you. Woy cawnt you lea me alown? Wot ev I dan to you? Aw aint smashed your fice, ev Aw?

BARBARA: (*Softly: wooing his soul*) It's not me thats getting at you, Bill.

BILL: Oo else is it?

BARBARA: Somebody that doesnt intend you to smash women's faces, I suppose. Somebody or something that wants to make a man of you.

BILL: (*Blustering*) Mike a menn o me. Aint Aw a menn? eh? Oo sez Aw'm not a menn?

BARBARA: Theres a man in you somewhere, I suppose. But why did he let you hit poor little Jenny Hill? That wasnt very manly of him, was it?

BILL: (*Tormented*) Ev dan wiv it, Aw tell you.

Chack it. Aw'm sick o your Jenny Ill and er silly little fice.

BARBARA: Then why do you keep thinking about it? Why does it keep coming up against you in your mind? Youre not getting converted, are you?

BILL: (*With conviction*) Not ME. Not lawkly.

BARBARA: Thats right, Bill. Hold out against it. Put out your strength. Dont lets get you cheap. Todger Fairmile said he wrestled for three nights against his salvation harder than he ever wrestled with the Jap at the music hall. He gave in to the Jap when his arm was going to break. But he didnt give in to his salvation until his heart was going to break. Perhaps youll escape that. You havnt any heart, have you?

BILL: Wot d'ye mean? Woy aint Aw got a awt the sime as ennybody else?

BARBARA: A man with a heart wouldnt have bashed poor little Jenny's face, would he?

BILL: (*Almost crying*) Ow, will you lea me alown? Ev Aw ever offered to meddle with you, that you cam neggin and provowkin me lawk this? (*He writhes convulsively from his eyes to his toes.*)

BARBARA: (*With a steady soothing hand on his arm and a gentle voice that never lets him go*) It's your soul thats hurting you, Bill, and not me. Weve been through it all ourselves. Come with us, Bill. (*He looks wildly round.*) To brave manhood on earth and eternal glory in heaven. (*He is on the point of breaking down.*) Come.

(*A drum is heard in the shelter; and* BILL, *with a gasp, escapes from the spell as* BARBARA *turns quickly. Adolphus enters from the shelter with a big drum.*)

Oh! there you are, Dolly. Let me introduce a new friend of mine, Mr Bill Walker. This is my bloke, Bill: Mr Cusins. (CUSINS *salutes with his drumstick.*)

BILL: Gowin to merry im?

BARBARA: Yes.

BILL: (*Fervently*) Gawd elp im! Gaw-aw-aw-awd elp im!

BARBARA: Why? Do you think he wont be happy with me?

BILL: Awve aony ed to stend it for a mawnin: e'll ev to stend it for a lawftawm.

CUSINS: That is a frightful reflection, Mr Walker. But I cant tear myself away from her.

BILL: Well, Aw ken. (*To* BARBARA) Eah! do you

knaow where Aw'm gowin to, and wot Aw'm gowin to do?

BARBARA: Yes: youre going to heaven; and youre coming back here before the week's out to tell me so.

BILL: You loy. Aw'm gowin to Kennintahn, to spit in Todger Fairmawl's eye. Aw beshed Jenny Ill's fice; and nar Aw'll git me aown fice beshed and cam beck and shaow it to er. Ee'll itt me ardern Aw itt er. Thatll mike us square. (To ADOLPHUS) Is thet fair or is it not? Youre a genlmn: you oughter knaow.

BARBARA: Two black eyes wont make one white one, Bill.

BILL: Aw didnt awst you. Cawnt you never keep your mahth shat? Oy awst the genlmn.

CUSINS: (Reflectively) Yes: I think youre right, Mr Walker. Yes: I should do it. It's curious: it's exactly what an ancient Greek would have done.

BARBARA: But what good will it do?

CUSINS: Well, it will give Mr Fairmile some exercise; and it will satisfy Mr Walker's soul.

BILL: Rot! there aint nao sach a thing as a saoul. Ah kin you tell wevver Awve a saoul or not? You never seen it.

BARBARA: Ive seen it hurting you when you went against it.

BILL: (With compressed aggravation) If you was maw gel and took the word aht o me mahth lawk thet, Aw'd give you sathink youd feel urtin, Aw would. (To ADOLPHUS) You tike maw tip, mite. Stop er jawr; or youll doy afoah your tawm (With intense expression) Wore aht: thets wot youll be: wore aht. (He goes away through the gate.)

CUSINS: (Looking after him) I wonder!

BARBARA: Dolly! (Indignant, in her mother's manner.)

CUSINS: Yes, my dear, it's very wearing to be in love with you. If it lasts, I quite think I shall die young.

BARBARA: Should you mind?

CUSINS: Not at all. (He is suddenly softened, and kisses her over the drum, evidently not for the first time, as people cannot kiss over a big drum without practice. UNDERSHAFT coughs.)

BARBARA: It's all right, papa, weve not forgotten you. Dolly: explain the place to papa: I havnt time. (She goes busily into the shelter.)

(UNDERSHAFT and ADOLPHUS now have the yard to themselves. UNDERSHAFT, seated on a form, and still keenly attentive, looks hard at ADOLPHUS. ADOLPHUS looks hard at him.)

UNDERSHAFT: I fancy you guess something of what is in my mind, Mr Cusins. (CUSINS flourishes his drumsticks as if in the act of beating a lively rataplan, but makes no sound.) Exactly so. But suppose Barbara finds you out!

CUSINS: You know, I do not admit that I am imposing on Barbara. I am quite genuinely interested in the views of the Salvation Army. The fact is, I am a sort of collector of religions; and the curious thing is that I find I can believe them all. By the way, have you any religion?

UNDERSHAFT: Yes.

CUSINS: Anything out of the common?

UNDERSHAFT: Only that there are two things necessary to Salvation.

CUSINS: (Disappointed, but polite) Ah, the Church Catechism. Charles Lomax also belongs to the Established Church.

UNDERSHAFT: The two things are—

CUSINS: Baptism and—

UNDERSHAFT: No. Money and gunpowder.

CUSINS: (Surprised, but interested) That is the general opinion of our governing classes. The novelty is in hearing any man confess it.

UNDERSHAFT: Just so.

CUSINS: Excuse me: is there any place in your religion for honor, justice, truth, love, mercy and so forth?

UNDERSHAFT: Yes: they are the graces and luxuries of a rich, strong, and safe life.

CUSINS: Suppose one is forced to choose between them and money or gunpowder?

UNDERSHAFT: Choose money and gunpowder; for without enough of both you cannot afford the others.

CUSINS: That is your religion?

UNDERSHAFT: Yes.

(The cadence of this reply makes a full close in the conversation. CUSINS twists his face dubiously and contemplates UNDERSHAFT. UNDERSHAFT contemplates him.)

CUSINS: Barbara wont stand that. You will have to choose between your religion and Barbara.

UNDERSHAFT: So will you, my friend. She will find out that that drum of yours is hollow.

CUSINS: Father Undershaft: you are mistaken: I am a sincere Salvationist. You do not understand the Salvation Army. It is the army of joy, of love, of courage: it has banished the fear and remorse and despair of the old hell-ridden evangelical sects: it marches to fight the devil with trumpet and drum, with music and dancing, with banner and palm, as becomes a sally from heaven by its happy garrison. It picks the waster out of the public house and makes a man of him: it finds a worm wriggling in a back kitchen, and lo! a woman! Men and women of rank too, sons and daughters of the Highest. It takes the poor professor of Greek, the most artificial and self-suppressed of human creatures, from his meal of roots, and lets loose the rhapsodist in him; reveals the true worship of Dionysos to him; sends him down the public street drumming dithyrambs. *(He plays a thundering flourish on the drum.)*

UNDERSHAFT: You will alarm the shelter.

CUSINS: Oh, they are accustomed to these sudden ecstasies. However, if the drum worries you— *(He pockets the drumsticks; unhooks the drum; and stands it on the ground opposite the gateway.)*

UNDERSHAFT: Thank you.

CUSINS: You remember what Euripides says about your money and gunpowder?

UNDERSHAFT: No.

CUSINS: *(Declaiming)*

> One and another
> In money and guns may outpass his
>   brother;
> And men in their millions float and flow
> And seethe with a million hopes as leaven;
> And they win their will; or they miss
>   their will;
> And their hopes are dead or are pined for
>   still;
>   But who'er can know
>   As the long days go
> That to live is happy, has found his
>   heaven.[1]

My translation: what do you think of it?

UNDERSHAFT: I think, my friend, that if you wish to know, as the long days go, that to live

is happy, you must first acquire money enough for a decent life, and power enough to be your own master.

CUSINS: You are damnably discouraging. *(He resumes his declamation.)*

> Is it so hard a thing to see
> That the spirit of God—whate'er it be—
> The law that abides and changes not, ages
>   long,
> The Eternal and Nature-born: these things
>   be strong?
> What else is Wisdom? What of Man's
>   endeavor,
> Or God's high grace so lovely and so great?
> To stand from fear set free? to breathe and
>   wait?
> To hold a hand uplifted over Fate?
> And shall not Barbara be loved for ever?

UNDERSHAFT: Euripides mentions Barbara, does he?

CUSINS: It is a fair translation. The word means Loveliness.

UNDERSHAFT: May I ask—as Barbara's father—how much a year she is to be loved for ever on?

CUSINS: As Barbara's father, that is more your affair than mine. I can feed her by teaching Greek: that is about all.

UNDERSHAFT: Do you consider it a good match for her?

CUSINS: *(With polite obstinacy)* Mr Undershaft: I am in many ways a weak, timid, ineffectual person; and my health is far from satisfactory. But whenever I feel that I must have anything, I get it, sooner or later. I feel that way about Barbara. I dont like marriage: I feel intensely afraid of it; and I dont know what I shall do with Barbara or what she will do with me. But I feel that I and nobody else must marry her. Please regard that as settled.—Not that I wish to be arbitrary; but why should I waste your time in discussing what is inevitable?

UNDERSHAFT: You mean that you will stick at nothing: not even the conversion of the Salvation Army to the worship of Dionysos.

CUSINS: The business of the Salvation Army is to save, not to wrangle about the name of the pathfinder. Dionysos or another: what does it matter?

UNDERSHAFT: *(Rising and approaching*

---

[1]Shaw gives credit for the Greek translations in this act to Gilbert Murray.

him) Professor Cusins: you are a young man after my own heart.

CUSINS: Mr Undershaft: you are, as far as I am able to gather, a most infernal old rascal; but you appeal very strongly to my sense of ironic humor. *(*UNDERSHAFT *mutely offers his hand. They shake.)*

UNDERSHAFT: *(Suddenly concentrating himself)* And now to business.

CUSINS: Pardon me. We are discussing religion. Why go back to such an uninteresting and unimportant subject as business?

UNDERSHAFT: Religion is our business at present, because it is through religion alone that we can win Barbara.

CUSINS: Have you, too, fallen in love with Barbara?

UNDERSHAFT: Yes, with a father's love.

CUSINS: A father's love for a grown-up daughter is the most dangerous of all infatuations. I apologize for mentioning my own pale, coy, mistrustful fancy in the same breath with it.

UNDERSHAFT: Keep to the point. We have to win her; and we are neither of us Methodists.

CUSINS: That doesnt matter. The power Barbara wields here—the power that wields Barbara herself—is not Calvinism, not Presbyterianism, not Methodism—

UNDERSHAFT: Not Greek Paganism either, eh?

CUSINS: I admit that. Barbara is quite original in her religion.

UNDERSHAFT: *(Triumphantly)* Aha! Barbara Undershaft would be. Her inspiration comes from within herself.

CUSINS: How do you suppose it got there?

UNDERSHAFT: *(In towering excitement)* It is the Undershaft inheritance. I shall hand on my torch to my daughter. She shall make my converts and preach my gospel—

CUSINS: What! Money and gunpowder?

UNDERSHAFT: Yes, money and gunpowder. Freedom and power. Command of life and command of death.

CUSINS: *(Urbanely: trying to bring him down to earth)* This is extremely interesting, Mr Undershaft. Of course you know that you are mad.

UNDERSHAFT: *(With redoubled force)* And you?

CUSINS: Oh, mad as a hatter. You are wel-come to my secret since I have discovered yours. But I am astonished. Can a madman make cannons?

UNDERSHAFT: Would anyone else than a madman make them? And now *(With surging energy)* question for question. Can a sane man translate Euripides?

CUSINS: No.

UNDERSHAFT: *(Seizing him by the shoulder)* Can a sane woman make a man of a waster or a woman of a worm?

CUSINS: *(Reeling before the storm)* Father Colossus—Mammoth Millionaire—

UNDERSHAFT: *(Pressing him)* Are there two mad people or three in this Salvation shelter today?

CUSINS: You mean Barbara is as mad as we are?

UNDERSHAFT: *(Pushing him lightly off and resuming his equanimity suddenly and completely)* Pooh, Professor! let us call things by their proper names. I am a millionaire; you are a poet; Barbara is a savior of souls. What have we three to do with the commom mob of slaves and idolaters? *(He sits down again with a shrug of contempt for the mob.)*

CUSINS: Take care! Barbara is in love with the common people. So am I. Have you never felt the romance of that love?

UNDERSHAFT: *(Cold and sardonic)* Have you ever been in love with Poverty, like St Francis? Have you ever been in love with Dirt, like St Simeon! Have you ever been in love with disease and suffering, like our nurses and philanthropists? Such passions are not virtues, but the most unnatural of all the vices. This love of the common people may please an earl's granddaughter and a university professor; but I have been a common man and a poor man; and it has no romance for me. Leave it to the poor to pretend that poverty is a blessing: leave it to the coward to make a religion of his cowardice by preaching humility: we know better than that. We three must stand together above the common people: how else can we help their children to climb up beside us? Barbara must belong to us, not to the Salvation Army.

CUSINS: Well, I can only say that if you think you will get her away from the Salvation Army by talking to her as you have been talking to me, you dont know Barbara.

UNDERSHAFT: My friend: I never ask for what I can buy.

CUSINS: (In a white fury) Do I understand you to imply that you can buy Barbara?

UNDERSHAFT: No; but I can buy the Salvation Army.

CUSINS: Quite impossible.

UNDERSHAFT: You shall see. All religious organizations exist by selling themselves to the rich.

CUSINS: Not the Army. That is the Church of the poor.

UNDERSHAFT: All the more reason for buying it.

CUSINS: I dont think you quite know what the Army does for the poor.

UNDERSHAFT: Oh yes I do. It draws their teeth: that is enough for me as a man of business.

CUSINS: Nonsense! It makes them sober—

UNDERSHAFT: I prefer sober workmen. The profits are larger.

CUSINS: —honest—

UNDERSHAFT: Honest workmen are the most economical.

CUSINS: —attached to their homes—

UNDERSHAFT: So much the better: they will put up with anything sooner than change their shop.

CUSINS: —happy—

UNDERSHAFT: An invaluable safeguard against revolution.

CUSINS: —unselfish—

UNDERSHAFT: Indifferent to their own interests, which suits me exactly.

CUSINS: —with their thoughts on heavenly things—

UNDERSHAFT: (Rising) And not on Trade Unionism nor Socialism. Excellent.

CUSINS: (Revolted) You really are an infernal old rascal.

UNDERSHAFT: (Indicating PETER SHIRLEY, who has just come from the shelter and strolled dejectedly down the yard between them) And this is an honest man!

SHIRLEY: Yes; and what av I got by it? (He passes on bitterly and sits on the form, in the corner of the penthouse.)

(SNOBBY PRICE, beaming sanctimoniously, and JENNY HILL, with a tambourine full of coppers, come from the shelter and go to the drum, on which JENNY begins to count the money.)

UNDERSHAFT: (Replying to SHIRLEY) Oh, your employers must have got a good deal by it from first to last.

(He sits on the table, with one foot on the side form. CUSINS, overwhelmed, sits down on the same form nearer the shelter. BARBARA comes from the shelter to the middle of the yard. She is excited and a little overwrought.)

BARBARA: Weve just had a splendid experience meeting at the other gate in Cripps's lane. Ive hardly ever seen them so much moved as they were by your confession, Mr Price.

PRICE: I could almost be glad of my past wickedness if I could believe that it would elp to keep hathers stright.

BARBARA: So it will, Snobby. How much, Jenny?

JENNY: Four and tenpence, Major.

BARBARA: Oh Snobby, if you had given your poor mother just one more kick, we should have got the whole five shillings!

PRICE: If she heard you say that, miss, she'd be sorry I didnt. But I'm glad. Oh what a joy it will be to her when she hears I'm saved!

UNDERSHAFT: Shall I contribute the odd twopence, Barbara? The millionaire's mite, eh? (He takes a couple of pennies from his pocket.)

BARBARA: How did you make that twopence?

UNDERSHAFT: As usual. By selling cannons, torpedos, submarines, and my new patent Grand Duke hand grenade.

BARBARA: Put it back in your pocket. You cant buy your salvation here for twopence: you must work it out.

UNDERSHAFT: Is twopence not enough? I can afford little more, if you press me.

BARBARA: Two million millions would not be enough. There is bad blood on your hands; and nothing but good blood can cleanse them. Money is no use. Take it away. (She turns to CUSINS.) Dolly: you must write another letter for me to the papers. (He makes a wry face.) Yes: I know you dont like it; but it must be done. The starvation this winter is beating us: everybody is unemployed. The General says we must close this shelter if we cant get more money. I force the collections at the meetings until I am ashamed: dont I, Snobby?

PRICE: It's a fair treat to see you work it, miss.

The way you got them up from three-and-six to four-and-ten with that hymn, penny by penny and verse by verse, was a caution. Not a Cheap Jack on Mile End Waste could touch you at it.

BARBARA: Yes; but I wish we could do without it. I am getting at last to think more of the collection than of the people's souls. And what are those hatfuls of pence and halfpence? We want thousands! tens of thousands! hundreds of thousands! I want to convert people, not to be always begging for the Army in a way I'd die sooner than beg for myself.

UNDERSHAFT: (In profound irony) Genuine unselfishness is capable of anything, my dear.

BARBARA: (Unsuspectingly, as she turns away to take the money from the drum and put it in a cashbag she carries) Yes, isnt it? (UNDERSHAFT looks sardonically at CUSINS.)

CUSINS: (Aside to UNDERSHAFT) Mephistopheles! Machiavelli!

BARBARA: (Tears coming into her eyes as she ties the bag and pockets it) How are we to feed them? I cant talk religion to a man with bodily hunger in his eyes. (Almost breaking down) It's frightful.

JENNY: (Running to her) Major, dear—

BARBARA: (Rebounding) No: dont comfort me. It will be all right. We shall get the money.

UNDERSHAFT: How?

JENNY: By praying for it, of course. Mrs Baines says she prayed for it last night; and she has never prayed for it in vain; never once. (She goes to the gate and looks out into the street.)

BARBARA: (Who has dried her eyes and regained her composure) By the way, dad, Mrs Baines has come to march with us to our big meeting this afternoon; and she is very anxious to meet you, for some reason or other. Perhaps she'll convert you.

UNDERSHAFT: I shall be delighted, my dear.

JENNY: (At the gate: excitedly) Major! Major! heres that man back again.

BARBARA: What man?

JENNY: The man that hit me. Oh, I hope he's coming back to join us.

(BILL WALKER, with frost on his jacket, comes through the gate, his hands deep in his pockets and his chin sunk between his shoulders, like a cleaned-out gambler. He halts between BARBARA and the drum.)

BARBARA: Hullo, Bill! Back already!

BILL: (Nagging at her) Bin talkin ever sence, ev you?

BARBARA: Pretty nearly. Well, has Todger paid you out for poor Jenny's jaw?

BILL: Nao e aint.

BARBARA: I thought your jacket looked a bit snowy.

BILL: Sao it is snaowy. You want to knaow where the snaow cam from, downt you?

BARBARA: Yes.

BILL: Well, it cam from orf the grahnd in Pawkinses Corner in Kennintahn. It got rabbed orf be maw shaoulders: see?

BARBARA: Pity you didnt rub some off with your knees, Bill! That would have done you a lot of good.

BILL: (With sour mirthless humor) Aw was sivin anather menn's knees at the tawm. E was kneelin on moy ed e was.

JENNY: Who was kneeling on your head?

BILL: Todger was. E was pryin for me: pryin camfortable wiv me as a cawpet. Sow was Mog. Sao was the aol bloomin meetin. Mog she sez "Ow Lawd brike is stabborn sperrit: bat downt urt is dear art." Thet was wot she said. "Downt urt is dear art"! An er blowk—thirteen stun four!—kneelin wiv all is wight on me. Fanny, aint it?

JENNY: Oh no. We're so sorry, Mr Walker.

BARBARA: (Enjoying it frankly) Nonsense! of course it's funny. Served you right, Bill! You must have done something to him first.

BILL: (Doggedly) Aw did wot Aw said Aw'd do. Aw spit in is eye. E looks ap at the skoy and sez, "Ow that Aw should be fahnd worthy to be spit upon for the gospel's sike!" e sez; an Mog sez "Glaory Alleiloolier!"; and then e called me Braddher, and dahned me as if Aw was a kid and e was me mather worshin me a Setterda nawt. Aw ednt jast nao shaow wiv im at all. Arf the street pryed; an the tather arf larfed fit to split theirselves. (To BARBARA) There! are you settisfawd nah?

BARBARA: (Her eyes dancing) Wish I'd been there, Bill.

BILL: Yus: youd a got in a hextra bit o talk on me, wouldnt you?

JENNY: I'm so sorry, Mr Walker.

BILL: (Fiercely) Downt you gow bein sorry for me: youve no call. Listen eah. Aw browk your jawr.

JENNY: No, it didnt hurt me: indeed it didnt, except for a moment. It was only that I was frightened.

BILL: Aw downt want to be forgive be you, or be ennybody. Wot Aw did Aw'll py for. Aw trawd to gat me aown jawr browk to settisfaw you—

JENNY: (Distressed) Oh no—

BILL: (Impatiently) Tell y' Aw did; cawnt you listen to wots bein taold you? All Aw got be it was bein mide a sawt of in the pablic street for me pines. Well, if Aw cawnt settisfaw you one wy, Aw ken anather. Listen eah! Aw ed two quid sived agen the frost; an Awve a pahnd of it left. A mite o mawn last week ed words with the judy e's gowin to merry. E give er wot-for; an e's bin fawnd fifteen bob. E ed a rawt to itt er cause they was gowin to be merrid; but Aw ednt nao rawt to itt you; sao put another fawv bob on an call it a pahnd's worth. (He produces a sovereign.) Eahs the manney. Tike it; and lets ev no more o your forgivin an pryin and your Mijor jawrin me. Let wot Aw dan be dan an pide for; and let there be a end of it.

JENNY: Oh, I couldnt take it, Mr Walker. But if you would give a shilling or two to poor Rummy Mitchens! you really did hurt her; and she's old.

BILL: (Contemptuously) Not lawkly. Aw'd give her anather as soon as look at er. Let her ev the lawr o me as she threatened! She aint forgiven me: not mach. Wot Aw dan to er is not on me mawnd—wot she (Indicating BARBARA) mawt call on me conscience—no more than stickin a pig. It's this Christian gime o yours that Aw wownt ev plyed agen me: this bloomin forgivin an neggin an jawrin that mikes a menn thet sore that iz lawf's a burdn to im. Aw wownt ev it, Aw tell you; sao tike your manney and stop thraowin your silly beshed fice hap agen me.

JENNY: Major: may I take a little of it for the Army?

BARBARA: No: the Army is not to be bought. We want your soul, Bill; and we'll take nothing less.

BILL: (Bitterly) Aw knaow. Me an maw few shillins is not good enaff for you. Youre a earl's grendorter, you are. Nathink less than a anderd pahnd for you.

UNDERSHAFT: Come, Barbara! you could do a great deal of good with a hundred pounds. If you will set this gentleman's mind at ease by taking his pound, I will give the other ninety-nine.

(BILL, *dazed by such opulence, instinctively touches his cap.*)

BARBARA: Oh, youre too extravagant, papa. Bill offers twenty pieces of silver. All you need offer is the other ten. That will make the standard price to buy anybody who's for sale. I'm not; and the Army's not. (To BILL) Youll never have another quiet moment, Bill, until you come round to us. You cant stand out against your salvation.

BILL: (Sullenly) Aw cawnt stend aht agen music awl wrastlers and awtful tangued women. Awve offered to py. Aw can do no more. Tike it or leave it. There it is. (He throws the sovereign on the drum, and sits down on the horse-trough. The coin fascinates SNOBBY PRICE, who takes an early opportunity of dropping his cap on it.)

(MRS BAINES *comes from the shelter. She is dressed as a Salvation Army Commissioner. She is an earnest looking woman of about 40, with a caressing, urgent voice, and an appealing manner.*)

BARBARA: This is my father, Mrs Baines. (UNDERSHAFT *comes from the table, taking off his hat with marked civility.*) Try what you can do with him. He wont listen to me, because he remembers what a fool I was when I was a baby. (She leaves them together and chats with JENNY.)

MRS BAINES: Have you been shewn over the shelter, Mr Undershaft? You know the work we're doing, of course.

UNDERSHAFT: (Very civilly) The whole nation knows it, Mrs Baines.

MRS BAINES: No, sir: the whole nation does not know it, or we should not be crippled as we are for want of money to carry our work through the length and breadth of the land. Let me tell you that there would have been rioting this winter in London but for us.

UNDERSHAFT: You really think so?

MRS BAINES: I know it. I remember 1886, when you rich gentlemen hardened your hearts against the cry of the poor. They broke the windows of your clubs in Pall Mall.

UNDERSHAFT: (Gleaming with approval of their method) And the Mansion House Fund went up next day from thirty thousand pounds to seventy-nine thousand! I remember quite well.

MRS BAINES: Well, wont you help me to get at the people? They wont break windows then. Come here, Price. Let me shew you to this gentleman (PRICE *comes to be inspected.)* Do you remember the window breaking?

PRICE: My ole father thought it was the revolution, maam.

MRS BAINES: Would you break windows now?

PRICE: Oh no, maam. The windows of eaven av bin opened to me. I know now that the rich man is a sinner like myself.

RUMMY: *(Appearing above at the loft door)* Snobby Price!

SNOBBY: Wot is it?

RUMMY: Your mother's askin for you at the other gate in Cripps's Lane. She's heard about your confession *(PRICE turns pale.)*

MRS BAINES: Go, Mr Price; and pray with her.

JENNY: You can go through the shelter, Snobby.

PRICE: *(To MRS BAINES)* I couldnt face her now, maam, with all the weight of my sins fresh on me. Tell her she'll find her son at ome, waitin for her in prayer. *(He skulks off through the gate, incidentally stealing the sovereign on his way by picking up his cap from the drum.)*

MRS BAINES: *(With swimming eyes)* You see how we take the anger and the bitterness against you out of their hearts, Mr Undershaft.

UNDERSHAFT: It is certainly most convenient and gratifying to all large employers of labor, Mrs Baines.

MRS BAINES: Barbara: Jenny: I have good news: most wonderful news. (JENNY *runs to her.)* My prayers have been answered. I told you they would, Jenny, didnt I?

JENNY: Yes, yes.

BARBARA: *(Moving nearer to the drum)* Have we got money enough to keep the shelter open?

MRS BAINES: I hope we shall have enough to keep all the shelters open. Lord Saxmundham has promised us five thousand pounds—

BARBARA: Hooray!

JENNY: Glory!

MRS BAINES: —if—

BARBARA: "If!" If what?

MRS. BAINES: —if five other gentlemen will give a thousand each to make it up to ten thousand.

BARBARA: Who is Lord Saxmundham? I never heard of him.

UNDERSHAFT: *(Who has pricked up his ears at the peer's name, and is now watching* BARBARA *curiously)* A new creation, my dear. You have heard of Sir Horace Bodger?

BARBARA: Bodger! Do you mean the distiller? Bodger's whisky!

UNDERSHAFT: That is the man. He is one of the greatest of our public benefactors. He restored the cathedral at Hakington. They made him a baronet for that. He gave half a million to the funds of his party: they made him a baron for that.

SHIRLEY: What will they give him for the five thousand?

UNDERSHAFT: There is nothing left to give him. So the five thousand, I should think is to save his soul.

MRS BAINES: Heaven grant it may! Oh Mr Undershaft, you have some very rich friends. Cant you help us towards the other five thousand? We are going to hold a great meeting this afternoon at the Assembly Hall in the Mile End Road. If I could only announce that one gentleman had come forward to support Lord Saxmundham, others would follow. Dont you know somebody? couldnt you? wouldnt you? *(Her eyes fill with tears)* oh, think of those poor people, Mr Undershaft: think of how much it means to them, and how little to a great man like you.

UNDERSHAFT: *(Sardonically gallant)* Mrs Baines: you are irresistible. I cant disappoint you; and I cant deny myself the satisfaction of making Bodger pay up. You shall have your five thousand pounds.

MRS BAINES: Thank God!

UNDERSHAFT: You dont thank me?

MRS BAINES: Oh sir, dont try to be cynical: dont be ashamed of being a good man. The Lord will bless you abundantly; and our prayers will be like a strong fortification round you all the days of your life. *(With a touch of caution)* You will let me have the cheque to shew at the meeting, wont you? Jenny: go in and fetch a pen and ink. (JENNY *runs to the shelter door.)*

UNDERSHAFT: Do not disturb Miss Hill: I have a fountain pen (JENNY *halts. He sits at the table and writes the cheque.* CUSINS *rises to make room for him. They all watch him silently.*)

BILL: (*Cynically, aside to* BARBARA, *his voice and accent horribly debased*) Wot prawce selvytion nah?

BARBARA: Stop. (UNDERSHAFT *stops writing: they all turn to her in surprise.*) Mrs Baines: are you really going to take this money?

MRS BAINES: (*Astonished*) Why not, dear?

BARBARA: Why not! Do you know what my father is? Have you forgotten that Lord Saxmundham is Bodger the whisky man? Do you remember how we implored the County Council to stop him from writing Bodger's Whisky in letters of fire against the sky; so that the poor drink-ruined creatures on the Embankment could not wake up from their snatches of sleep without being reminded of their deadly thirst by that wicked sky sign? Do you know that the worst thing I have had to fight here is not the devil, but Bodger, Bodger, Bodger, with his whisky, his distilleries, and his tied houses? Are you going to make our shelter another tied house for him, and ask me to keep it?

BILL: Rotten dranken whisky it is too.

MRS BAINES: Dear Barbara: Lord Saxmundham has a soul to be saved like any of us. If heaven has found the way to make a good use of his money, are we to set ourselves up against the answer to our prayers?

BARBARA: I know he has a soul to be saved. Let him come down here; and I'll do my best to help him to his salvation. But he wants to send his cheque down to buy us, and go on being as wicked as ever.

UNDERSHAFT: (*With a reasonableness which* CUSINS *alone perceives to be ironical*) My dear Barbara: alcohol is a very necessary article. It heals the sick—

BARBARA: It does nothing of the sort.

UNDERSHAFT: Well, it assists the doctor: that is perhaps a less questionable way of putting it. It makes life bearable to millions of people who could not endure their existence if they were quite sober. It enables Parliament to do things at eleven at night that no sane person would do at eleven in the morning. Is it Bodger's fault that this inestimable gift is deplorably abused by less than one per cent

of the poor? (*He turns again to the table; signs the cheque; and crosses it.*)

MRS BAINES: Barbara: will there be less drinking or more if all those poor souls we are saving come tomorrow and find the doors of our shelters shut in their faces? Lord Saxmundham gives us the money to stop drinking—to take his own business from him.

CUSINS: (*Impishly*) Pure self-sacrifice on Bodger's part, clearly! Bless dear Bodger! (BARBARA *almost breaks down as* ADOLPHUS, *too, fails her.*)

UNDERSHAFT: (*Tearing out the cheque and pocketing the book as he rises and goes past* CUSINS *to* MRS BAINES) I also, Mrs Baines, may claim a little disinterestedness. Think of my business! think of the widows and orphans! the men and lads torn to pieces with shrapnel and poisoned with lyddite! (MRS BAINES *shrinks; but he goes on remorselessly.*) The oceans of blood, not one drop of which is shed in a really just cause! the ravaged crops! the peaceful peasants forced, women and men, to till their fields under the fire of opposing armies on pain of starvation! the bad blood of the fierce little cowards at home who egg on others to fight for the gratification of their national vanity! All this makes money for me: I am never richer, never busier than when the papers are full of it. Well, it is your work to preach peace on earth and goodwill to men. (MRS BAINES'S *face lights up again.*) Every convert you make is a vote against war. (*Her lips move in prayer.*) Yet I give you this money to help you to hasten my own commercial ruin. (*He gives her the cheque.*)

CUSINS: (*Mounting the form in an ectasy of mischief*) The millennium will be inaugurated by the unselfishness of Undershaft and Bodger. Oh be joyful! (*He takes the drum-sticks from his pocket and flourishes them.*)

MRS BAINES: (*Taking the cheque*) The longer I live the more proof I see that there is an Infinite Goodness that turns everything to the work of salvation sooner or later. Who would have thought that any good could have come out of war and drink? And yet their profits are brought today to the feet of salvation to do its blessed work. (*She is affected to tears.*)

JENNY: (*Running to* MRS BAINES *and throwing her arms around her*) Oh dear! how blessed, how glorious it all is!

CUSINS: (In a convulsion of irony) Let us seize this unspeakable moment. Let us march to the great meeting at once. Excuse me just an instant. (He rushes into the shelter. JENNY takes her tambourine from the drum head.)

MRS BAINES: Mr Undershaft: have you ever seen a thousand people fall on their knees with one impulse and pray? Come with us to the meeting. Barbara shall tell them that the Army is saved, and saved through you.

CUSINS: (Returning impetuously from the shelter with a flag and a trombone, and coming between MRS BAINES and UNDERSHAFT) You shall carry the flag down the first street, Mrs Baines (He gives her the flag.) Mr Undershaft is a gifted trombonist: he shall intone an Olympian diapason to the West Ham Salvation March. (Aside to UNDERSHAFT, as he forces the trombone on him) Blow, Machiavelli, blow.

UNDERSHAFT: (Aside to him, as he takes the trombone) The trumpet in Zion! (CUSINS rushes to the drum, which he takes up and puts on. UNDERSHAFT continues, aloud) I will do my best. I could vamp a bass if I knew the tune.

CUSINS: It is a wedding chorus from one of Donizetti's operas; but we have converted it. We convert everything to good here, including Bodger. You remember the chorus. "For thee immense rejoicing—immenso giubilo—immenso giubilo." (With drum obbligato) Rum tum ti tum tum, tum tum ti ta—

BARBARA: Dolly: you are breaking my heart.

CUSINS: What is a broken heart more or less here? Dionysos Undershaft has descended. I am possessed.

MRS BAINES: Come, Barbara: I must have my dear Major to carry the flag with me.

JENNY: Yes, yes, Major darling.

CUSINS: (Snatches the tambourine out of JENNY's hand and mutely offers it to BARBARA.)

BARBARA: (Coming forward a little as she puts the offer behind her with a shudder, whilst CUSINS recklessly tosses the tambourine back to JENNY and goes to the gate.) I cant come.

JENNY: Not come!

MRS BAINES: (With tears in her eyes) Barbara: do you think I am wrong to take the money?

BARBARA: (Impulsively going to her and kissing her) No, no: God help you, dear, you must;

you are saving the Army. Go; and may you have a great meeting!

JENNY: But arnt you coming?

BARBARA: No. (She begins taking off the silver S brooch from her collar.)

MRS BAINES: Barbara: what are you doing?

JENNY: Why are you taking your badge off? You cant be going to leave us, Major.

BARBARA: (Quietly) Father: come here.

UNDERSHAFT: (Coming to her) My dear! (Seeing that she is going to pin the badge on his collar, he retreats to the penthouse in some alarm.)

BARBARA: (Following him) Don't be frightened. (She pins the badge on and steps back towards the table, shewing him to the others.) There! It's not much for £5000, is it?

MRS BAINES: Barbara: if you wont come and pray with us, promise me you will pray for us.

BARBARA: I cant pray now. Perhaps I shall never pray again.

MRS BAINES: Barbara!

JENNY: Major!

BARBARA: (Almost delirious) I cant bear any more. Quick march!

CUSINS: (Calling to the procession in the street outside.) Off we go. Play up, there! Immenso giubilo. (He gives the time with his drum; and the band strikes up the march, which rapidly becomes more distant as the procession moves briskly away.)

MRS BAINES: I must go, dear. Youre overworked: you will be all right tomorrow. We'll never lose you. Now Jenny: step out with the old flag. Blood and Fire! (She marches out through the gate with her flag.)

JENNY: Glory Hallelujah! (Flourishing her tambourine and marching.)

UNDERSHAFT: (To CUSINS, as he marches out past him easing the slide of his trombone) "My ducats and my daughter"!

CUSINS: (Following him out) Money and gunpowder!

BARBARA: Drunkenness and Murder! My God: why hast thou forsaken me?

(She sinks on the form with her face buried in her hands. The march passes away into silence. BILL WALKER steals across to her.)

BILL: (Taunting) Wot prawce selvytion nah?

SHIRLEY: Dont you hit her when she's down.

BILL: She itt me wen aw wiz dahn. Waw shouldnt Aw git a bit o me aown beck?

BARBARA: (Raising her head) I didnt take your money, Bill. (She crosses the yard to the gate and turns her back on the two men to hide her face from them.)

BILL: (Sneering after her) Naow, it warnt enaff for you. (Turning to the drum, he misses the money.) Ellow! If you aint took it sammun else ez. Weres it gorn? Bly me if Jenny Ill didnt tike it arter all!

RUMMY: (Screaming at him from the loft) You lie, you dirty blackguard! Snobby Price pinched it off the drum when he took up his cap. I was up here all the time an see im do it.

BILL: Wot! Stowl maw manney? Waw didnt you call thief on him, you silly aold macker you?

RUMMY: To serve you aht for ittin me acrost the fice. It's cost y'pahnd, that az. (Raising a pæan of squalid triumph) I done you. I'm even with you. Ive ad it aht o y— (BILL snatches up SHIRLEY's mug and hurls it at her. She slams the loft door and vanishes. The mug smashes against the door and falls in fragments.)

BILL: (Beginning to chuckle) Tell us, aol menn, wot o'clock this mawnin was it wen im as they call Snobby Prawce was sived?

BARBARA: (Turning to him more composedly, and with unspoiled sweetness) About half past twelve, Bill. And he pinched your pound at a quarter to two. I know. Well, you cant afford to lose it. I'll send it to you.

BILL: (His voice and accent suddenly improving) Not if Aw wiz to stawve for it. Aw aint to be bought.

SHIRLEY: Aint you? Youd sell yourself to the devil for a pint o beer; ony there aint no devil to make the offer.

BILL: (Unshamed) Sao Aw would, mite, and often ev, cheerful. But she cawnt baw me. (Approaching BARBARA) You wanted maw saoul, did you? Well, you aint got it.

BARBARA: I nearly got it, Bill. But weve sold it back to you for ten thousand pounds.

SHIRLEY: And dear at the money!

BARBARA: No, Peter: it was worth more than money.

BILL: (Salvationproof) It's nao good: you cawnt get rahnd me nah. Aw downt blieve in it; and Awve seen tody that Aw was rawt. (Going) Sao long, aol soup-kitchener! Ta ta, Mijor Earl's Grendorter! (Turning at the gate) Wot prawce selvytion nah? Snobby Prawce! Ha! ha!

BARBARA: (Offering her hand) Goodbye, Bill.

BILL: (Taken aback, half plucks his cap off; then shoves it on again defiantly) Git aht. (BARBARA drops her hand, discouraged. He has a twinge of remorse.) But thets aw rawt, you knaow. Nathink pasnl. Naow mellice. Sao long, Judy. (He goes.)

BARBARA: No malice. So long, Bill.

SHIRLEY: (Shaking his head) You make too much of him, miss, in your innocence.

BARBARA: (Going to him) Peter: I'm like you now. Cleaned out, and lost my job.

SHIRLEY: Youve youth an hope. Thats two better than me.

BARBARA: I'll get you a job, Peter. Thats hope for you: the youth will have to be enough for me. (She counts her money.) I have just enough left for two teas at Lockharts, a Rowton doss for you, and my tram and bus home. (He frowns and rises with offended pride. She takes his arm.) Don't be proud, Peter: it's sharing between friends. And promise me youll talk to me and not let me cry. (She draws him towards the gate.)

SHIRLEY: Well, I'm not accustomed to talk to the like of you—

BARBARA: (Urgently) Yes, yes: you must talk to me. Tell me about Tom Paine's books and Bradlaugh's lectures. Come along.

SHIRLEY: Ah, if you would only read Tom Paine in the proper spirit, miss! (They go out through the gate together.)

ACT III

Next day after lunch Lady Britomart is writing in the library in Wilton Crescent. SARAH is reading in the armchair near the window. Barbara, in ordinary fashionable dress, pale and brooding, is on the settee. Charles Lomax enters. He starts on seeing BARBARA *fashionably attired and in low spirits.*

LOMAX: You've left off your uniform!

(BARBARA *says nothing; but an expression of pain passes over her face.*)

LADY BRITOMART: *(Warning him in low tones to be careful)* Charles!

LOMAX: *(Much concerned, coming behind the settee and bending sympathetically over* BARBARA*)* I'm awfully sorry, Barbara. You know I helped you all I could with the concertina and so forth. *(Momentously)* Still, I have never shut my eyes to the fact that there is a certain amount of tosh about the Salvation Army. Now the claims of the Church of England—

LADY BRITOMART: That's enough, Charles. Speak of something suited to your mental capacity.

LOMAX: But surely the Church of England is suited to all our capacities.

BARBARA: *(Pressing his hand)* Thank you for your sympathy, Cholly. Now go and spoon with Sarah.

LOMAX: *(Dragging a chair from the writing table and seating himself affectionately by* SARAH'*s side)* How is my ownest today?

SARAH: I wish you wouldn't tell Cholly to do things, Barbara. He always comes straight and does them. Cholly: we're going to the works this afternoon.

LOMAX: What works?

SARAH: The cannon works.

LOMAX: What! your governor's shop!

SARAH: Yes.

LOMAX: Oh I say!

(CUSINS *enters in poor condition. He also starts visibly when he sees* BARBARA *without her uniform.*)

BARBARA: I expected you this morning, Dolly. Didn't you guess that?

CUSINS: *(Sitting down beside her)* I'm sorry. I have only just breakfasted.

SARAH: But we've just finished lunch.

BARBARA: Have you had one of your bad nights?

CUSINS: No: I had rather a good night: in fact, one of the most remarkable nights I have ever passed.

BARBARA: The meeting?

CUSINS: No: after the meeting.

LADY BRITOMART: You should have gone to bed after the meeting. What were you doing?

CUSINS: Drinking.

LADY BRITOMART: ⎫ ⎧ Adolphus!
SARAH: ⎪ ⎪ Dolly!
BARBARA: ⎬ ⎨ Dolly!
LOMAX: ⎭ ⎩ Oh I say!

LADY BRITOMART: What were you drinking, may I ask?

CUSINS: A most devilish kind of Spanish burgundy, warranted free from added alcohol: a Temperance burgundy in fact. Its richness in natural alcohol made any addition superfluous.

BARBARA: Are you joking, Dolly?

CUSINS: *(Patiently)* No. I have been making a night of it with the nominal head of this household: that is all.

LADY BRITOMART: Andrew made you drunk!

CUSINS: No: he only provided the wine. I think it was Dionysos who made me drunk. *(To* BARBARA*)* I told you I was possessed.

LADY BRITOMART: You're not sober yet. Go home to bed at once.

CUSINS: I have never before ventured to reproach you, Lady Brit; but how could you marry the Prince of Darkness?

LADY BRITOMART: It was much more excusable to marry him than to get drunk with him. That is a new accomplishment of Andrew's, by the way. He usent to drink.

CUSINS: He doesnt now. He only sat there and completed the wreck of my moral basis, the rout of my convictions, the purchase of my soul. He cares for you, Barbara. That is what makes him so dangerous to me.

BARBARA: That has nothing to do with it, Dolly. There are larger loves and diviner dreams than the fireside ones. You know that, dont you?

CUSINS: Yes: that is our understanding. I know it. I hold to it. Unless he can win me on that holier ground he may amuse me for a while; but he can get no deeper hold, strong as he is.

BARBARA: Keep to that; and the end will be right. Now tell me what happened at the meeting?

CUSINS: It was an amazing meeting. Mrs Baines almost died of emotion. Jenny Hill simply gibbered with hysteria. The Prince of Darkness played his trombone like a madman: its brazen roarings were like the laughter of the damned. 117 conversions took place then and there. They prayed with the most touching sincerity and gratitude for Bodger, and for the anonymous donor of the £5000. Your father would not let his name be given.

LOMAX: That was rather fine of the old man, you know. Most chaps would have wanted the advertisement.

CUSINS: He said all the charitable institutions would be down on him like kites on a battle-field if he gave his name.

LADY BRITOMART: That's Andrew all over. He never does a proper thing without giving an improper reason for it.

CUSINS: He convinced me that I have all my life been doing improper things for proper reasons.

LADY BRITOMART: Adolphus: now that Barbara has left the Salvation Army, you had better leave it too. I will not have you playing that drum in the streets.

CUSINS: Your orders are already obeyed, Lady Brit.

BARBARA: Dolly: were you ever really in earnest about it? Would you have joined if you had never seen me?

CUSINS: (Disingenuously) Well—er—well, possibly, as a collector of religions—

LOMAX: (Cunningly) Not as a drummer, though, you know. You are a very clearheaded brainy chap, Dolly; and it must have been apparent to you that there is a certain amount of tosh about—

LADY BRITOMART: Charles: if you must drivel, drivel like a grown-up man and not like a schoolboy.

LOMAX: (Out of countenance) Well, drivel is drivel, dont you know, whatever a man's age.

LADY BRITOMART: In good society in England, Charles, men drivel at all ages by repeating silly formulas with an air of wisdom. Schoolboys make their own formulas out of slang, like you. When they reach your age, and get political private secretaryships and things of that sort, they drop slang and get their formulas out of The Spectator or The Times. You had better confine yourself to The Times. You will find that there is a certain amount of tosh about The Times; but at least its language is reputable.

LOMAX: (Overwhelmed) You are so awfully strongminded, Lady Brit—

LADY BRITOMART: Rubbish! (MORRISON comes in.) What is it?

MORRISON: If you please, my lady. Mr Undershaft has just drove up to the door.

LADY BRITOMART: Well, let him in. (MORRISON hesitates.) Whats the matter with you?

MORRISON: Shall I announce him, my lady; or is he at home here, so to speak, my lady?

LADY BRITOMART: Announce him.

MORRISON: Thank you, my lady. You wont mind my asking, I hope. The occasion is in a manner of speaking new to me.

LADY BRITOMART: Quite right. Go and let him in.

MORRISON: Thank you, my lady. (He withdraws.)

LADY BRITOMART: Children: go and get ready. (SARAH and BARBARA go upstairs for their out-of-door wraps.) Charles: go and tell Stephen to come down here in five minutes: you will find him in the drawing room. (CHARLES goes.) Adolphus: tell them to send round the carriage in about fifteen minutes. (ADOLPHUS goes.)

MORRISON: (At the door) Mr Undershaft.

(UNDERSHAFT comes in. MORRISON goes out.)

UNDERSHAFT: Alone! How fortunate!

LADY BRITOMART: Rising Don't be sentimental, Andrew. Sit down. (She sits on the settee: he sits beside her, on her left. She comes to the point before he has time to breathe.) Sarah must have £800 a year until Charles Lomax comes into his property. Barbara will need more, and need it permanently, because Adolphus hasnt any property.

UNDERSHAFT: (Resignedly) Yes, my dear: I will see to it. Anything else? for yourself, for instance?

LADY BRITOMART: I want to talk to you about Stephen.

UNDERSHAFT: (*Rather wearily*) Dont, my dear. Stephen doesnt interest me.

LADY BRITOMART: He does interest me. He is our son.

UNDERSHAFT: Do you really think so? He has induced us to bring him into the world; but he chose his parents very incongruously, I think. I see nothing of myself in him, and less of you.

LADY BRITOMART: Andrew: Stephen is an excellent son, and a most steady, capable, high-minded young man. You are simply trying to find an excuse for disinheriting him.

UNDERSHAFT: My dear Biddy: the Undershaft tradition disinherits him. It would be dishonest of me to leave the cannon foundry to my son.

LADY BRITOMART: It would be most unnatural and improper of you to leave it to anyone else, Andrew. Do you suppose this wicked and immoral tradition can be kept up for ever? Do you pretend that Stephen could not carry on the foundry just as well as all the other sons of the big business houses?

UNDERSHAFT: Yes: he could learn the office routine without understanding the business, like all the other sons; and the firm would go on by its own momentum until the real Undershaft—probably an Italian or a German—would invent a new method and cut him out.

LADY BRITOMART: There is nothing that any Italian or German could do that Stephen could not do. And Stephen at least has breeding.

UNDERSHAFT: The son of a foundling! Nonsense!

LADY BRITOMART: My son, Andrew! And even you may have good blood in your veins for all you know.

UNDERSHAFT: True. Probably I have. That is another argument in favor of a foundling.

LADY BRITOMART: Andrew: dont be aggravating. And dont be wicked. At present you are both.

UNDERSHAFT: This conversation is part of the Undershaft tradition, Biddy. Every Undershaft's wife has treated him to it ever since the house was founded. It is mere waste of breath. If the tradition be ever broken it will be for an abler man than Stephen.

LADY BRITOMART: (*Pouting*) Then go away.

UNDERSHAFT: (*Deprecatory*) Go away!

LADY BRITOMART: Yes: go away. If you will do nothing for Stephen, you are not wanted here. Go to your foundling, whoever he is; and look after him.

UNDERSHAFT: The fact is, Biddy—

LADY BRITOMART: Don't call me Biddy. I don't call you Andy.

UNDERSHAFT: I will not call my wife Britomart: it is not good sense. Seriously, my love, the Undershaft tradition has landed me in a difficulty. I am getting on in years; and my partner Lazarus has at last made a stand and insisted that the succession must be settled one way or the other; and of course he is quite right. You see, I havnt found a fit successor yet.

LADY BRITOMART: (*Obstinately*) There is Stephen.

UNDERSHAFT: Thats just it: all the foundlings I can find are exactly like Stephen.

LADY BRITOMART: Andrew!!

UNDERSHAFT: I want a man with no relations and no schooling: that is, a man who would be out of the running altogether if he were not a strong man. And I cant find him. Every blessed foundling nowadays is snapped up in his infancy by Barnardo homes, or School Board Officers, or Boards of Guardians; and if he shews the least ability he is fastened on by schoolmasters; trained to win scholarships like a racehorse; crammed with secondhand ideas; drilled and disciplined in docility and what they call good taste; and lamed for life so that he is fit for nothing but teaching. If you want to keep the foundry in the family, you had better find an eligible foundling and marry him to Barbara.

LADY BRITOMART: Ah! Barbara! Your pet! You would sacrifice Stephen to Barbara.

UNDERSHAFT: Cheerfully. And you, my dear, would boil Barbara to make soup for Stephen.

LADY BRITOMART: Andrew: this is not a question of our likings and dislikings: it is a question of duty. It is your duty to make Stephen your successor.

UNDERSHAFT: Just as much as it is your duty to submit to your husband. Come, Biddy! these tricks of the governing class are of no use with me. I am one of the governing class myself; and it is waste of time giving tracts to a missionary. I have the power in this matter; and I am not to be humbugged into using it for your purposes.

LADY BRITOMART: Andrew: you can talk my head off; but you cant change wrong into right. And your tie is all on one side. Put it straight.

UNDERSHAFT: *(Disconcerted)* It wont stay unless it's pinned *(He fumbles at it with childish grimaces)* —

(STEPHEN comes in.)

STEPHEN: *(At the door)* I beg your pardon *(About to retire.)*

LADY BRITOMART: No: come in, Stephen. *(STEPHEN comes forward to his mother's writing table.)*

UNDERSHAFT: *(Not very cordially)* Good afternoon.

STEPHEN: *(Coldly)* Good afternoon.

UNDERSHAFT: *(To LADY BRITOMART)* He knows all about the tradition, I suppose?

LADY BRITOMART: Yes. *(To STEPHEN)* It is what I told you last night, Stephen.

UNDERSHAFT: *(Sulkily)* I understand you want to come into the cannon business.

STEPHEN: I go into trade! Certainly not.

UNDERSHAFT: *(Opening his eyes, greatly eased in mind and manner)* Oh! in that case —

LADY BRITOMART: Cannons are not trade, Stephen. They are enterprise.

STEPHEN: I have no intention of becoming a man of business in any sense. I have no capacity for business and no taste for it. I intend to devote myself to politics.

UNDERSHAFT: *(Rising)* My dear boy: this is an immense relief to me. And I trust it may prove an equally good thing for the country. I was afraid you would consider yourself disparaged and slighted. *(He moves towards STEPHEN as if to shake hands with him.)*

LADY BRITOMART: *Rising and interposing)* Stephen: I cannot allow you to throw away an enormous property like this.

STEPHEN: *(Stiffly)* Mother: there must be an end of treating me as a child, if you please. *(LADY BRITOMART recoils, deeply wounded by his tone.)* Until last night I did not take your attitude seriously, because I did not think you meant it seriously. But I find now that you left me in the dark as to matters which you should have explained to me years ago. I am extremely hurt and offended. Any further discussion of my intentions had better

take place with my father, as between one man and another.

LADY BRITOMART: Stephen! *(She sits down again, her eyes filling with tears.)*

UNDERSHAFT: *(With grave compassion)* You see, my dear, it is only the big men who can be treated as children.

STEPHEN: I am sorry, mother, that you have forced me —

UNDERSHAFT: *(Stopping him)* Yes, yes, yes, yes: thats all right, Stephen. She wont interfere with you any more: your independence is achieved: you have won your latchkey. Dont rub it in; and above all, dont apologize. *(He resumes his seat.)* Now what about your future, as between one man and another — I beg your pardon, Biddy: as between two men and a woman.

LADY BRITOMART: *(Who has pulled herself together strongly)* I quite understand, Stephen. By all means go your own way if you feel strong enough. *(STEPHEN sits down magisterially in the chair at the writing table with an air of affirming his majority.)*

UNDERSHAFT: It is settled that you do not ask for the succession to the cannon business.

STEPHEN: I hope it is settled that I repudiate the cannon business.

UNDERSHAFT: Come, come! dont be so devilishly sulky: it's boyish. Freedom should be generous. Besides, I owe you a fair start in life in exchange for disinheriting you. You cant become prime minister all at once. Havnt you a turn for something? What about literature, art, and so forth?

STEPHEN: I have nothing of the artist about me, either in faculty or character, thank Heaven.

UNDERSHAFT: A philosopher, perhaps? Eh?

STEPHEN: I make no such ridiculous pretension.

UNDERSHAFT: Just so. Well, there is the army, the navy, the Church, the Bar. The Bar requires some ability. What about the Bar?

STEPHEN: I have not studied law. And I am afraid I have not the necessary push — I believe that is the name barristers give to their vulgarity — for success in pleading.

UNDERSHAFT: Rather a difficult case, Stephen. Hardly anything left but the stage, is there? *(STEPHEN makes an impatient movement.)* Well, come! is there anything you know or care for?

STEPHEN: (Rising and looking at him steadily) I know the difference between right and wrong.

UNDERSHAFT: (Hugely tickled) You dont say so! What! no capacity for business, no knowledge of law, no sympathy with art, no pretension to philosophy; only a simple knowledge of the secret that has puzzled all the philosophers, baffled all the lawyers, muddled all the men of business, and ruined most of the artists: the secret of right and wrong. Why, man, youre a genius, a master of masters, a god! At twentyfour, too!

STEPHEN: (Keeping his temper with difficulty) You are pleased to be facetious. I pretend to nothing more than any honourable English gentleman claims as his birthright (He sits down angrily.)

UNDERSHAFT: Oh, thats everybody's birthright. Look at poor little Jenny Hill, the Salvation lassie! she would think you were laughing at her if you asked her to stand up in the street and teach grammar or geography or mathematics or even drawing room dancing; but it never occurs to her to doubt that she can teach morals and religion. You are all alike, you respectable people. You cant tell me the bursting strain of a ten-inch gun, which is a very simple matter; but you all think you can tell me the bursting strain of a man under temptation. You darent handle high explosives; but youre all ready to handle honesty and truth and justice and the whole duty of man, and kill one another at that game. What a country! What a world!

LADY BRITOMART: (Uneasily) What do you think he had better do, Andrew?

UNDERSHAFT: Oh, just what he wants to do. He knows nothing and he thinks he knows everything. That points clearly to a political career. Get him a private secretaryship to someone who can get him an Under Secretaryship; and then leave him alone. He will find his natural and proper place in the end on the Treasury Bench.

STEPHEN: (Springing up again) I am sorry, sir, that you force me to forget the respect due to you as my father. I am an Englishman and I will not hear the Government of my country insulted. (He thrusts his hands in his pockets, and walks angrily across to the window.)

UNDERSHAFT: (With a touch of brutality) The government of your country! I am the government of your country: I, and Lazarus. Do you suppose that you and half a dozen amateurs like you,

sitting in a row in that foolish gabble shop, can govern Undershaft and Lazarus? No, my friend: you will do what pays us. You will make war when it suits us, and keep peace when it doesnt. You will find out that trade requires certain measures when we have decided on those measures. When I want anything to keep my dividends up, you will discover that my want is a national need. When other people want something to keep my dividends down, you will call out the police and military. And in return you shall have the support and applause of my newspapers, and the delight of imagining that you are a great statesman. Government of your country! Be off with you, my boy, and play with your caucuses and leading articles and historic parties and great leaders and burning questions and the rest of your toys. I am going back to my counting-house to pay the piper and call the tune.

STEPHEN: (Actually smiling, and putting his hand on his father's shoulder with indulgent patronage) Really, my dear father, it is impossible to be angry with you. You dont know how absurd all this sounds to me. You are properly proud of having been industrious enough to make money; and it is greatly to your credit that you have made so much of it. But it has kept you in circles where you are valued for your money and deferred to for it, instead of in the doubtless very old-fashioned and behind-the-times public school and university where I formed my habits of mind. It is natural for you to think that money governs England; but you must allow me to think I know better.

UNDERSHAFT: And what does govern England, pray?

STEPHEN: Character, father, character.

UNDERSHAFT: Whose character? Yours or mine?

STEPHEN: Neither yours nor mine, father, but the best elements in the English national character.

UNDERSHAFT: Stephen: Ive found your profession for you. Youre a born journalist. I'll start you with a high-toned weekly review. There!

(Before STEPHEN can reply SARAH, BARBARA, LOMAX, and CUSINS come in ready for walking. BARBARA crosses the room to the window and looks out. CUSINS drifts amiably to the armchair. LOMAX *remains near the door, whilst* SARA *comes to her mother.*

STEPHEN *goes to the smaller writing table and busies himself with his letters.)*

SARAH: Go and get ready, mamma: the carriage is waiting. (LADY BITOMART *leaves the room.)*

UNDERSHAFT: *(TO SARAH)* Good day, my dear. Good afternoon, Mr. Lomax.

LOMAX: *(Vaguely)* Ahdedoo.

UNDERSHAFT *(To* CUSINS*)* Quite well after last night, Euripides, eh?

CUSINS: As well as can be expected.

UNDERSHAFT: Thats right. *(To* BARBARA*)* So you are coming to see my death and devastation factory, Barbara?

BARBARA: *(At the window)* You came yesterday to see my salvation factory. I promised you a return visit.

LOMAX: *(Coming forward between* SARAH *and* UNDERSHAFT*)* Youll find it awfully interesting. Ive been through the Woolwich Arsenal; and it gives you a ripping feeling of security, you know, to think of the lot of beggars we could kill if it came to fighting. *(To* UNDERSHAFT*, with sudden solemnity)* Still, it must be rather an awful reflection for you, from the religious point of view as it were. Youre getting on, you know, and all that.

SARAH: You dont mind Cholly's imbecility, papa, do you?

LOMAX: *(Much taken aback)* Oh I say!

UNDERSHAFT: Mr Lomax looks at the matter in a very proper spirit, my dear.

LOMAX: Just so. Thats all I meant, I assure you.

SARAH: Are you coming, Stephen?

STEPHEN: Well, I am rather busy — er — *(Magnanimously)* Oh well, yes: I'll come. That is, if there is room for me.

UNDERSHAFT: I can take two with me in a little motor I am experimenting with for field use. You wont mind its being rather unfashionable. It's not painted yet; but it's bullet proof.

LOMAX: *(Appalled at the prospect of confronting Wilton Crescent in an unpainted motor)* Oh I say!

SARAH: The carriage for me, thank you. Barbara doesnt mind what she's seen in.

LOMAX: I say, Dolly, old chap: do you really mind the car being a guy? Because of course if you do I'll go in it. Still —

CUSINS: I prefer it.

LOMAX: Thanks awfully, old man. Come, my ownest. *(He hurries out to secure his seat in the carriage. Sarah follows him.)*

CUSINS: *(Moodily walking across to* LADY BRITOMART's *writing table)* Why are we two coming to this Works Department of Hell? that is what I ask myself.

BARBARA: I have always thought of it as a sort of pit where lost creatures with blackened faces stirred up smoky fires and were driven and tormented by my father? Is it like that, dad?

UNDERSHAFT: *(Scandalized)* My dear! It is a spotlessly clean and beautiful hillside town.

CUSINS: With a Methodist chapel? Oh do say theres a Methodist chapel.

UNDERSHAFT: There are two: a Primitive one and a sophisticated one. There is even an Ethical Society; but it is not much patronized, as my men are all strongly religious. In the High Explosives Sheds they object to the presence of Agnostics as unsafe.

CUSINS: And yet they dont object to you!

BARBARA: Do they obey all your orders?

UNDERSHAFT: I never give them any orders. When I speak to one of them it is "Well, Jones, is baby doing well? and has Mrs Jones made a good recovery?" "Nicely, thank you, sir." And thats all.

CUSINS: But Jones has to be kept in order. How do you maintain discipline among your men?

UNDERSHAFT: I dont. They do. You see, the one thing Jones wont stand is any rebellion from the man under him, or any assertion of social equality between the wife of the man with 4 shillings a week less than himself, and Mrs Jones! Of course they all rebel against me, theoretically. Practically, every man of them keeps the man just below him in his place. I never meddle with them. I never bully them. I dont even bully Lazarus. I say that certain things are to be done; but I dont order anybody to do them. I dont say, mind you, that there is no ordering about and snubbing and even bullying. The men snub the boys and order them about; the carmen snub the sweepers; the artisans snub the unskilled laborers; the foremen drive and bully both the laborers and artisans; the assistant engineers find fault with the foremen; the chief engineers drop on the assistants; the departmental managers worry the chiefs; and the clerks have tall hats and hymnbooks and keep up the social tone by refusing to associate on equal terms with anybody. The result is a colossal profit, which comes to me.

CUSINS: *(Revolted)* You really are a—well, what I was saying yesterday.

BARBARA: What was he saying yesterday?

UNDERSHAFT: Never mind, my dear. He thinks I have made you unhappy. Have I?

BARBARA: Do you think I can be happy in this vulgar silly dress? I! who have worn the uniform. Do you understand what you have done to me? Yesterday I had a man's soul in my hand. I set him in the way of life with his face to salvation. But when we took your money he turned back to drunkenness and derision. *(With intense conviction)* I will never forgive you that. If I had a child, and you destroyed its body with your explosives— if you murdered Dolly with your horrible guns—I could forgive you if my forgiveness would open the gates of heaven to you. But to take a human soul from me, and turn it into the soul of a wolf! that is worse than any murder.

UNDERSHAFT: Does my daughter despair so easily? Can you strike a man to the heart and leave no mark on him?

BARBARA: *(Her face lighting up)* Oh, you are right: he can never be lost now; where was my faith?

CUSINS: Oh, clever clever devil!

BARBARA: You may be a devil; but God speaks through you sometimes. *(She takes her father's hands and kisses them.)* You have given me back my happiness: I feel it deep down now, though my spirit is troubled.

UNDERSHAFT: You have learnt something. That always feels at first as if you had lost something.

BARBARA: Well, take me to the factory of death; and let me learn something more. There must be some truth or other behind all this frightful irony. Come, Dolly. *(She goes out.)*

CUSINS: My guardian angel! *(To UNDERSHAFT)* Avaunt! *(He follows BARBARA.)*

STEPHEN: *(Quietly, at the writing table)* You must not mind Cusins, father. He is a very amiable good fellow; but he is a Greek scholar and naturally a little eccentric.

UNDERSHAFT: Ah, quite so. Thank you, Stephen. Thank you. *(He goes out.)*

(STEPHEN smiles patronizingly; buttons his coat responsibly; and crosses the room to the door. LADY BRITOMART, dressed for out-of-doors, opens it before he reaches it. She looks round for the others; looks at STEPHEN; and turns to go without a word.)

STEPHEN: *(Embarrassed)* Mother—

LADY BRITOMART: Dont be apologetic, Stephen, And dont forget that you have outgrown your mother. *(She goes out.)*

(Perivale St Andrews lies between two Middlesex hills, half climbing the northern one. It is an almost smokeless town of white walls, roofs of narrow green slates or red tiles, tall trees, domes, campaniles, and slender chimney shafts, beautifully situated and beautiful in itself. The best view of it is obtained from the crest of a slope about half a mile to the east, where the high explosives are dealt with. The foundry lies hidden in the depths between, the tops of its chimneys sprouting like huge skittles into the middle distance. Across the crest runs an emplacement of concrete, with a firestep, and a parapet which suggests a fortification, because there is a huge cannon of the obsolete Woolwich Infant pattern peering across it at the town. The cannon is mounted on an experimental gun carriage: possibly the original model of the Undershaft disappearing rampart gun alluded to by STEPHEN. The firestep, being a convenient place to sit, is furnished here and there with straw disc cushions; and at one place there is the additional luxury of a fur rug.

BARBARA is standing on the firestep, looking over the parapet towards the town. On her right is the cannon; on her left the end of a shed raised on piles, with a ladder of three or four steps up to the door, which opens outwards and has a little wooden landing at the threshold, with a fire bucket in the corner of the landing. Several dummy soldiers more or less mutilated, with straw protruding from their gashes, have been shoved out of the way under the landing. A few others are nearly upright against the shed; and one has fallen forward and lies, like a grotesque corpse, on the emplacement. The parapet stops short of the shed, leaving a gap which is the beginning of the path down the hill through the foundry to the town. The rug is on the firestep near this gap. Down on the emplacement behind the cannon is a trolley carrying a huge conical bombshell with a red band painted on it. Further to the right is the door of an office, which, like the sheds, is of the lightest possible construction. CUSINS *arrives by the path from the town.)*

BARBARA: Well?

CUSINS: Not a ray of hope. Everything perfect! wonderful! real! It only needs a cathedral to be a heavenly city instead of a hellish one.

BARBARA: Have you found out whether they have done anything for old Peter Shirley?

CUSINS: They have found him a job as gate-keeper and timekeeper. He's frightfully miserable. He calls the time-keeping brainwork, and says he isnt used to it; and his gate lodge is so splendid that he's ashamed to use the rooms, and skulks in the scullery.

BARBARA: Poor Peter!

*(*STEPHEN *arrives from the town. He carries a fieldglass.)*

STEPHEN: *(Enthusiastically)* Have you two seen the place? Why did you leave us?

CUSINS: I wanted to see everything I was not intended to see; and Barbara wanted to make the men talk.

STEPHEN: Have you found anything discreditable?

CUSINS: No. They call him Dandy Andy and are proud of his being a cunning old rascal; but it's all horribly, frightfully, immorally, unanswerably perfect.

*(*SARAH *arrives.)*

SARAH: Heavens! what a place! *(She crosses to the trolley.)* Did you see the nursing home!? *(She sits down on the shell.)*

STEPHEN: Did you see the libraries and schools!?

SARAH: Did you see the ball room and the banqueting chamber in the Town Hall!?

STEPHEN: Have you gone into the insurance fund, the pension fund, the building society, the various applications of co-operation!?

*(*UNDERSHAFT *comes from the office, with a sheaf of telegrams in his hand.)*

UNDERSHAFT: Well, have you seen everything! I'm sorry I was called away. *(Indicating the telegrams)* Good news from Manchuria.

STEPHEN: Another Japanese victory?

UNDERSHAFT: Oh, I dont know. Which side wins does not concern us here. No: the good news is that the aerial battleship is a tremendous success. At the first trial it has wiped out a fort with three hundred soldiers in it.

CUSINS: *(From the platform)* Dummy soldiers?

UNDERSHAFT: *(Striding across to* STEPHEN *and kicking the prostrate dummy brutally out of his way)* No: the real thing.

*(*CUSINS *and* BARBARA *exchange glances. Then* CUSINS *sits on the step and buries his face in his hands.* BARBARA *gravely lays her hand on his shoulder. He looks up at her in whimsical desperation.)*

UNDERSHAFT: Well, Stephen, what do you think of the place?

STEPHEN: Oh, magnificent. A perfect triumph of modern industry. Frankly, my dear father, I have been a fool: I had no idea of what it all meant: of the wonderful forethought, the power of organization, the administrative capacity, the financial genius, the colossal capital it represents. I have been repeating to myself as I came through your streets "Peace hath her victories no less renowned than War." I have only one misgiving about it all.

UNDERSHAFT. Out with it.

STEPHEN: Well, I cannot help thinking that all this provision for every want of your workmen may sap their independence and weaken their sense of responsibility. And greatly as we enjoyed our tea at that splendid restaurant—how they gave us all that luxury and cake and jam and cream for three-pence I really cannot imagine!—still you must remember that restaurants break up home life. Look at the continent, for instance! Are you sure so much pampering is really good for the men's characters?

UNDERSHAFT: Well you see, my dear boy,

when you are organizing civilization you have to make up your mind whether trouble and anxiety are good things or not. If you decide that they are, then, I take it, you simply dont organize civilization; and there you are, with trouble and anxiety enough to make us all angels! But if you decide the other way, you may as well go through with it. However, Stephen, our characters are safe here. A sufficient dose of anxiety is always provided by the fact that we may be blown to smithereens at any moment.

SARAH: By the way, papa, where do you make the explosives?

UNDERSHAFT: In separate little sheds, like that one. When one of them blows up, it costs very little; and only the people quite close to it are killed.

(STEPHEN, *who is quite close to it, looks at it rather scaredly, and moves away quickly to the cannon. At the same moment the door of the shed is thrown abruptly open; and a foreman in overalls and list slippers comes out on the little landing and holds the door for* LOMAX, *who appears in the doorway.*)

LOMAX: (*With studied coolness*) My good fellow: you neednt get into a state of nerves. Nothing's going to happen to you; and I suppose it wouldnt be the end of the world if anything did. A little bit of British pluck is what you want, old chap. (*He descends and strolls across to Sarah.*)

UNDERSHAFT: (*To the foreman*) Anything wrong, Bilton?

BILTON: (*With ironic calm*) Gentleman walked into the high explosives shed and lit a cigaret, sir; thats all.

UNDERSHAFT: Ah, quite so. (*Going over to* LOMAX) Do you happen to remember what you did with the match?

LOMAX: Oh come! I'm not a fool. I took jolly good care to blow it out before I chucked it away.

BILTON: The top of it was red hot inside, sir.

LOMAX: Well, suppose it was! I didn't chuck it into any of your messes.

UNDERSHAFT: Think no more of it, Mr. Lomax. By the way, would you mind lending me your matches.

LOMAX: (*Offering his box*) Certainly.

UNDERSHAFT: Thanks. (*He pockets the matches.*)

LOMAX: (*Lecturing to the company generally*) You know, these high explosives dont go off like gunpowder, except when theyre in a gun. When theyre spread loose, you can put a match to them without the least risk; they just burn quietly like a bit of paper. (*Warming to the scientific interest of the subject*) Did you know that, Undershaft? Have you ever tried?

UNDERSHAFT: Not on a large scale, Mr. Lomax. Bilton will give you a sample of gun cotton when you are leaving if you ask him. You can experiment with it at home (BILTON *looks puzzled.*)

SARAH: Bilton will do nothing of the sort, papa. I suppose it's your business to blow up the Russians and Japs; but you might really stop short of blowing up poor Cholly. (BILTON *gives it up and retires into the shed.*)

LOMAX: My ownest, there is no danger. (*He sits beside her on the shell.*)

(LADY BRITOMART *arrives from the town with a bouquet.*)

LADY BRITOMART: (*Impetuously*) Andrew: you shouldnt have let me see this place.

UNDERSHAFT: Why, my dear?

LADY BRITOMART: Never mind why: you shouldnt have: thats all. To think of all that (*Indicating the town*) being yours! and that you have kept it to yourself all these years!

UNDERSHAFT: It does not belong to me. I belong to it. It is the Undershaft inheritance.

LADY BRITOMART: It is not. Your ridiculous cannons and that noisy banging foundry may be the Undershaft inheritance; but all that plate and linen, all that furniture and those houses and orchards and gardens belong to us. They belong to me: they are not a man's business. I wont give them up. You must be out of your senses to throw them all away; and if you persist in such folly, I will call in a doctor.

UNDERSHAFT: (*Stooping to smell the bouquet*) Where did you get the flowers, my dear?

LADY BRITOMART: Your men presented them to me in your William Morris Labor Church.

CUSINS: Oh! It needed only that. A Labor Church! (*He mounts the firestep distractedly, and leans with his elbows on the parapet, turning his back to them.*)

LADY BRITOMART: Yes, with Morris's

words in mosaic letters ten feet high round the dome. NO MAN IS GOOD ENOUGH TO BE ANOTHER MAN'S MASTER. The cynicism of it!

UNDERSHAFT: It shocked the men at first, I am afraid. But now they take no more notice of it than of the ten commandments in church.

LADY BRITOMART: Andrew: you are trying to put me off the subject of the inheritance by profane jokes. Well, you shant. I dont ask it any longer for Stephen: he has inherited far too much of your perversity to be fit for it. But Barbara has rights as well as Stephen. Why should not Adolphus succeed to the inheritance? I could manage the town for him; and he can look after the cannons, if they are really necessary.

UNDERSHAFT: I should ask nothing better if Adolphus were a foundling. He is exactly the sort of new blood that is wanted in English business. But he's not a foundling; and theres an end of it. (He makes for the office door.)

CUSINS: (Turning to them) Not quite. (They all turn and stare at him.) I think—Mind! I am not committing myself in any way as to my future course—but I think the foundling difficulty can be got over. (He jumps down to the emplacement.)

UNDERSHAFT: (Coming back to him) What do you mean?

CUSINS: Well, I have something to say which is in the nature of a confession.

SARAH:
LADY BRITOMART:
BARBARA: } Confession!
STEPHEN:
LOMAX: Oh I say!

CUSINS: Yes, a confession. Listen, all. Until I met Barbara I thought myself in the main an honorable, truthful man, because I wanted the approval of my conscience more than I wanted anything else. But the moment I saw Barbara, I wanted her far more than the approval of my conscience.

LADY BRITOMART: Adolphus!

CUSINS: It is true. You accused me yourself, Lady Brit, of joining the Army to worship Barbara; and so I did. She bought my soul like a flower at a street corner; but she bought it for herself.

UNDERSHAFT: What! Not for Dionysos or another?

CUSINS: Dionysos and all the others are in herself. I adored what was divine in her, and was therefore a true worshipper. But I was romantic about her too. I thought she was a woman of the people, and that a marriage with a professor of Greek would be far beyond the wildest social ambitions of her rank.

LADY BRITOMART: Adolphus!!

LOMAX: Oh I say!!!

CUSINS: When I learnt the horrible truth—

LADY BRITOMART: What do you mean by the horrible truth, pray?

CUSINS: That she was enormously rich; that her grandfather was an earl; that her father was the Prince of Darkness—

UNDERSHAFT: Chut!

CUSINS:—And that I was only an adventurer trying to catch a rich wife, then I stooped to deceive her about my birth.

BARBARA: (Rising) Dolly!

LADY BRITOMART: Your birth! Now Adolphus, dont dare to make up a wicked story for the sake of these wretched cannons. Remember: I have seen photographs of your parents; and the Agent General for South Western Australia knows them personally and has assured me that they are most respectable married people.

CUSINS: So they are in Australia; but here they are outcasts. Their marriage is legal in Australia, but not in England. My mother is my father's deceased wife's sister; and in this island I am consequently a foundling. (Sensation)

BARBARA: Silly! (She climbs to the cannon, and leans, listening, in the angle it makes with the parapet.)

CUSINS: Is the subterfuge good enough, Machiavelli?

UNDERSHAFT: (Thoughtfully) Biddy: this may be a way out of the difficulty.

LADY BRITOMART: Stuff! A man cant make cannons any the better for being his own cousin instead of his proper self (She sits down on the rug with a bounce that expresses her downright contempt for their casuistry.)

UNDERSHAFT: (To CUSINS) You are an educated man. That is against the tradition.

CUSINS: Once in ten thousand times it happens that the schoolboy is a born master of what they try to teach him. Greek has not destroyed my mind: it has nourished it. Besides, I did not learn it at an English public school.

UNDERSHAFT: Hm! Well, I cannot afforD to be too particular: you have cornered the foundling market. Let it pass. You are eligible, Euripides: you are eligible.

BARBARA: Dolly: yesterday morning, when Stephen told us all about the tradition, you became very silent; and you have been strange and excited ever since. Were you thinking of your birth then?

CUSINS: When the finger of Destiny suddenly points at a man in the middle of his breakfast, it makes him thoughtful.

UNDERSHAFT: Aha! You have had your eye on the business, my young friend, have you?

CUSINS: Take care! There is an abyss of moral horror between me and your accursed aerial battleships.

UNDERSHAFT: Never mind the abyss for the present. Let us settle the practical details and leave your final decision open. You know that you will have to change your name. Do you object to that?

CUSINS: Would any man named Adolphus— any man called Dolly!—object to be called something else?

UNDERSHAFT: Good. Now, as to money! I propose to treat you handsomely from the beginning. You shall start at a thousand a year.

CUSINS: *(With sudden heat, his spectacles twinkling with mischief)* A thousand! You dare offer a miserable thousand to the son-in-law of a millionaire! No, by Heavens, Machiavelli! you shall not cheat me. You cannot do without me; and I can do without you. I must have two thousand five hundred a year for two years. At the end of that time, if I am a failure, I go. But if I am a success, and stay on, you must give me the other five thousand.

UNDERSHAFT: What other five thousand?

CUSINS: To make the two years up to five thousand a year. The two thousand five hundred is only half pay in case I should turn out a failure. The third year I must have ten per cent on the profits.

UNDERSHAFT: *(Taken aback)* Ten per cent! Why, man, do you know what my profits are?

CUSINS: Enormous, I hope: otherwise I shall require twentyfive per cent.

UNDERSHAFT: But, Mr Cusins, this is a serious matter of business. You are not bringing any capital into the concern.

CUSINS: What! no capital! Is my mastery of Greek no capital? Is my access to the subtlest thought, the loftiest poetry yet attained by humanity, no capital? My character! my intellect! my life!

my career! what Barbara calls my soul! are these no capital? Say another word; and I double my salary.

UNDERSHAFT: Be reasonable—

CUSINS: *(Peremptorily)* Mr Undershaft: you have my terms. Take them or leave them.

UNDERSHAFT: *(Recovering himself)* Very well, I note your terms; and I offer you half.

CUSINS: *(Disgusted)* Half!

UNDERSHAFT: *(Firmly)* Half.

CUSINS: You call yourself a gentleman; and you offer me half!

UNDERSHAFT: I do not call myself a gentleman; but I offer you half.

CUSINS: This to your future partner! your successor! your son-in-law!

BARBARA: You are selling your own soul, Dolly, not mine. Leave me out of the bargain, please.

UNDERSHAFT: Come! I will go a step further for Barbara's sake. I will give you three fifths; but that is my last word.

CUSINS: Done!

LOMAX: Done in the eye! Why, *I* get only eight hundred, you know.

CUSINS: By the way, Mac, I am a classical scholar, not an arithmetical one. Is three fifths more than half or less?

UNDERSHAFT: More, of course.

CUSINS: I would have taken two hundred and fifty. How you can succeed in business when you are willing to pay all that money to a University don who is obviously not worth a junior clerk's wages!—well! What will Lazarus say?

UNDERSHAFT: Lazarus is a gentle romantic Jew who cares for nothing but string quartets and stalls at fashionable theatres. He will be blamed for your rapacity in money matters, poor fellow! as he has hitherto been blamed for mine. You are a shark of the first order, Euripides. So much the better for the firm!

BARBARA: Is the bargain closed, Dolly? Does your soul belong to him now?

CUSINS: No: the price is settled: that is all. The real tug of was is still to come. What about the moral question?

LADY BRITOMART: There is no moral question in the matter at all, Adolphus. You must simply sell cannons and weapons to people whose cause is right and just, and refuse them to foreigners and criminals.

UNDERSHAFT: *(Determinedly)* No: none of that. You must keep the true faith of an Armorer, or you dont come in here.

CUSINS: What on earth is the true faith of an Armorer?

UNDERSHAFT: To give arms to all men who offer an honest price for them, without respect of persons or principles: to aristocrat and republican, to Nihilist and Tsar, to Capitalist and Socialist, to Protestant and Catholic, to burglar and policeman, to black man, white man and yellow man, to all sorts and conditions, all nationalities, all faiths, all follies, all causes and all crimes. The first Undershaft wrote up in his shop IF GOD GAVE THE HAND, LET NOT MAN WITHHOLD THE SWORD. The second wrote up ALL HAVE THE RIGHT TO FIGHT: NONE HAVE THE RIGHT TO JUDGE. The third wrote up TO MAN THE WEAPON: TO HEAVEN THE VICTORY. The fourth had no literary turn; so he did not write up anything; but he sold cannons to Napoleon under the nose of George the Third. The fifth wrote up PEACE SHALL NOT PREVAIL SAVE WITH A SWORD IN HER HAND. The sixth, my master, was the best of all. He wrote up NOTHING IS EVER DONE IN THIS WORLD UNTIL MEN ARE PREPARED TO KILL ONE ANOTHER IF IT IS NOT DONE. After that, there was nothing left for the seventh to say. So he wrote up, simply, UNASHAMED.

CUSINS: My good Machiavelli, I shall certainly write something up on the wall; only, as I shall write it in Greek, you wont be able to read it. But as to your Armorer's faith, if I take my neck out of the noose of my own morality I am not going to put it into the noose of yours. I shall sell cannons to whom I please and refuse them to whom I please. So there!

UNDERSHAFT: From the moment when you become Andrew Undershaft, you will never do as you please again. Dont come here lusting for power, young man.

CUSINS: If power were my aim I should not come here for it. You have no power.

UNDERSHAFT: None of my own certainly.

CUSINS: I have more power than you, more will. You do not drive this place: it drives you. And what drives the place?

UNDERSHAFT: *(Enigmatically)* A will of which I am a part.

BARBARA: *(Startled)* Father! Do you know what you are saying; or are you laying a snare for my soul?

CUSINS: Dont listen to his metaphysics, Barbara. The place is driven by the most rascally part of society, the money hunters, the pleasure hunters, the military promotion hunters; and he is their slave.

UNDERSHAFT: Not necessarily. Remember the Armorer's Faith. I will take an order from a good man as cheerfully as from a bad one. If you good people perfer preaching and shirking to buying my weapons and fighting the rascals, dont blame me. I can make cannons: I cannot make courage and conviction. Bah! you tire me, Euripides, with your morality mongering. Ask Barbara: she understands. *(He suddenly reaches up and takes* BARBARA's *hands, looking powerfully into her eyes.)* Tell him, my love, what power really means.

BARBARA: *(Hypnotized)* Before I joined the Salvation Army, I was in my own power; and the consequence was that I never knew what to do with myself. When I joined it, I had not time enough for all the things I had to do.

UNDERSHAFT: *(Approvingly)* Just so. And why was that, do you suppose?

BARBARA: Yesterday I should have said, because I was in the power of God. *(She resumes her self-possession, withdrawing her hands from his with a power equal to his own.)* But you came and shewed me that I was in the power of Bodger and Undershaft. Today I feel—oh! how can I put it into words? Sarah: do you remember the earthquake at Cannes, when we were little children?—how little the surprise of the first shock mattered compared to the dread and horror of waiting for the second? That is how I feel in this place today. I stood on the rock I thought eternal: and without a word of warning it reeled and crumbled under me. I was safe with an infinite wisdom watching me, an army marching to Salvation with me; and in a moment, at a stroke of your pen in a cheque book, I stood alone; and the heavens were empty. That was the first shock of the earthquake: I am waiting for the second.

UNDERSHAFT: Come, come, my daughter! dont make too much of your little tinpot tragedy. What do we do here when we spend years of work and thought and thousands of pounds of solid cash on a new gun or an aerial battleship that turns out just a hairsbreadth wrong after all? Scrap it. Scrap it without wasting another hour or another pound on it. Well, you have made for yourself something that you call a morality or a religion or what not. It doesnt fit the facts. Well, scrap it. Scrap it and get one that does fit. That is what is wrong with the world at present. It scraps its obsolete steam engines and dynamos; but it wont scrap its old prejudices and its old moralities and its old religions and its old political constitutions. Whats the result? In machinery it does very well; but in morals and religion and politics it is working at a loss that brings it nearer bankruptcy every year. Dont persist in that folly. If your old religion broke down yesterday, get a newer and better one for tomorrow.

BARBARA: Oh how gladly I would take a better one to my soul! But you offer me a worse one. *(Turning on him with sudden vehemence.)* Justify yourself: shew me some light through the darkness of this dreadful place, with its beautifully clean workshops, and respectable workmen, and model homes.

UNDERSHAFT: Cleanliness and respectability do not need justification, Barbara: they justify themselves. I see no darkness here, no dreadfulness. In your Salvation shelter I saw poverty, misery, cold and hunger. You gave them bread and treacle and dreams of heaven. I give from thirty shillings a week to twelve thousand a year. They find their own dreams; but I look after the drainage.

BARBARA: And their souls?

UNDERSHAFT: I save their souls just as I saved yours.

BARBARA: *(Revolted)* You saved my soul! What do you mean?

UNDERSHAFT: I fed you and clothed you and housed you. I took care that you should have money enough to live handsomely — more than enough; so that you could be wasteful, careless, generous. That saved your soul from the seven deadly sins.

BARBARA: *(Bewildered)* The seven deadly sins!

UNDERSHAFT: Yes, the deadly seven. *(Counting on his fingers)* Food, clothing, firing, rent, taxes, respectability and children. Nothing can lift those seven millstones from Man's neck but money; and the spirit cannot soar until the millstones are lifted. I lifted them from your spirit. I enabled Barbara to become Major Barbara; and I saved her from the crime of poverty.

CUSINS: Do you call poverty a crime?

UNDERSHAFT: The worst of crimes. All the other crimes are virtues beside it: all the other dishonors are chivalry itself by comparison. Poverty blights whole cities; spreads horrible pestilences; strikes dead the very souls of all who come within sight, sound, or smell of it. What you call crime is nothing: a murder here and a theft there, a blow now and a curse then: what do they matter? they are only the accidents and illnesses of life: there are not fifty genuine professional criminals in London. But there are millions of poor people, abject people, dirty people, ill fed, ill clothed people. They poison us morally and physically: they kill the happiness of society: they force us to do away with our own liberties and to organize unnatural cruelties for fear they should rise against us and drag us down into their abyss. Only fools fear crime: we all fear poverty. Pah! *(Turning on* BARBARA*)* you talk of your half-saved ruffian in West Ham: you accuse me of dragging his soul back to perdition. Well, bring him to me here; and I will drag his soul back again to salvation for you. Not by words and dreams; but by thirty-eight shillings a week, a sound house in a handsome street, and a permanent job. In three weeks he will have a fancy waistcoat; in three months a tall hat and a chapel sitting; before the end of the year he will shake hands with a duchess at a Primrose League meeting, and join the Conservative Party.

BARBARA: And will he be the better for that?

UNDERSHAFT: You know he will. Dont be a hypocrite, Barbara. He will be better fed, better housed, better clothed, better behaved; and his children will be pounds heavier and bigger. That will be better than an American cloth mattress in a shelter, chopping firewood, eating bread and treacle, and being forced to kneel down from time to time to thank heaven for it: knee drill, I think you call it. It is cheap work converting starving men with a Bible in one hand and a slice of bread in the other. I will undertake to convert West Ham to Mahometanism on the same terms. Try your hand on my men: their souls are hungry because their bodies are full.

BARBARA: And leave the east end to starve?

UNDERSHAFT: *(His energetic tone dropping into one of bitter and brooding remembrance.)* I was an east ender. I moralized and starved until one day I swore that I would be a full-fed free man at all costs; that nothing should stop me except a bullet, neither reason nor morals nor the lives of other men. I said "Thou shalt starve ere I starve"; and with that word I became free and great. I was a dangerous man until I had my will; now I am a useful, beneficent, kindly person. That is the history of most self-made millionaires, I fancy. When it is the history of every Englishman we shall have an England worth living in.

LADY BRITOMART: Stop making speeches, Andrew. This is not the place for them.

UNDERSHAFT: *(Punctured)* My dear: I have no other means of conveying my ideas.

LADY BRITOMART: Your ideas are nonsense. You got on because you were selfish and unscrupulous.

UNDERSHAFT: Not at all. I had the strongest scruples about poverty and starvation. Your moralists are quite unscrupulous about both: they make virtues of them. I had rather be a thief than a pauper. I had rather be a murderer than a slave. I dont want to be either; but if you force the alternative on me, then, by Heaven, I'll choose the braver and more moral one. I hate poverty and slavery worse than any other crimes whatsoever. And let me tell you this. Poverty and slavery have stood up for centuries to your sermons and leading articles: they will not stand up to my machine guns. Dont preach at them: dont reason with them. Kill them.

BARBARA: Killing. Is that your remedy for everything?

UNDERSHAFT: It is the final test of conviction, the only lever strong enough to overturn a social system, the only way of saying Must. Let six hundred and seventy fools loose in the streets; and three policemen can scatter them. But huddle them together in a certain house in Westminster; and let them go through certain ceremonies and call themselves certain names until at last they get the courage to kill; and your six hundred and seventy fools become a government. Your pious mob fills up ballot papers and imagines it is governing its masters; but the ballot paper that really governs is the paper that has a bullet wrapped up in it.

CUSINS: That is perhaps why, like most intelligent people, I never vote.

UNDERSHAFT: Vote! Bah! When you vote, you only change the names of the cabinet. When you shoot, you pull down governments, inaugurate new epochs, abolish old orders and set up new. Is that historically true, Mr Learned Man, or is it not?

CUSINS: It is historically true. I loathe having to admit it. I repudiate your sentiments. I abhor your nature. I defy you in every possible way. Still, it is true. But it ought not to be true.

UNDERSHAFT: Ought! ought! ought! ought! ought! Are you going to spend your life saying ought, like the rest of our moralists? Turn your oughts into shalls, man. Come and make explosives with me. Whatever can blow men up can blow society up. The history of the world is the history of those who had courage enough to embrace this truth. Have you the courage to embrace it, Barbara?

LADY BRITOMART: Barbara: I positively forbid you to listen to your father's abominable wickedness. And you, Adolphus, ought to know better than to go about saying that wrong things are true. What does it matter whether they are true if they are wrong?

UNDERSHAFT: What does it matter whether they are wrong if they are true?

LADY BRITOMART: *(Rising)* Children: come home instantly. Andrew: I am exceedingly sorry I allowed you to call on us. You are wickeder than ever. Come at once.

BARBARA: *(Shaking her head)* It's no use running away from wicked people, mamma.

LADY BRITOMART: It is every use. It shews your disapprobation of them.

BARBARA: It does not save them.

LADY BRITOMART: I can see that you are going to disobey me. Sarah: are you coming home or are you not?

SARAH: I daresay it's very wicked of papa to make cannons; but I dont think I shall cut him on that account.

LOMAX: *(Pouring oil on the troubled waters)* The fact is, you know, there is a certain amount of tosh about this notion of wickedness. It doesnt work. You must look at facts. Not that I would say a word in favor of anything wrong; but then, you see, all sorts of chaps are always doing all sorts of things; and we have to fit them in somehow, dont you know. What I mean is that you cant go cutting everybody; and thats about what it comes to. *(Their rapt attention to his eloquence makes him nervous.)* Perhaps I dont make myself clear.

LADY BRITOMART: You are lucidity itself, Charles. Because Andrew is successful and has plenty of money to give to Sarah, you will flatter him and encourage him in his wickedness.

LOMAX: *(Unruffled)* Well, where the carcase is, there will the eagles be gathered, dont you know. *(To* UNDERSHAFT*)* Eh? What?

UNDERSHAFT: Precisely. By the way, may I call you Charles?

LOMAX: Delighted. Cholly is the usual ticket.

UNDERSHAFT: *(To* LADY BRITOMART*)* Biddy—

LADY BRITOMART: *(Violently)* Dont dare call me Biddy. Charles Lomax: you are a fool. Adolphus Cusins: you are a Jesuit. Stephen: you are a prig. Barbara: you are a lunatic. Andrew: you are a vulgar tradesman. Now you all know my opinion; and my conscience is clear, at all events *(She sits down with a vehemence that the rug fortunately softens.)*

UNDERSHAFT: My dear: you are the incarnation of morality. *(She snorts)* Your conscience is clear and your duty done when you have called everybody names. Come, Euripides! it is getting late; and we all want to go home. Make up your mind.

CUSINS: Understand this, you old demon—

LADY BRITOMART: Adolphus!

UNDERSHAFT: Let him alone, Biddy. Proceed, Euripides.

CUSINS: You have me in a horrible dilemma. I want Barbara.

UNDERSHAFT: Like all young men, you greatly exaggerate the difference between one young woman and another.

BARBARA: Quite true, Dolly.

CUSINS: I also want to avoid being a rascal.

UNDERSHAFT: *(With biting contempt)* You lust for personal righteousness, for self-approval, for what you call a good conscience, for what Barbara calls salvation, for what I call patronizing people who are not so lucky as yourself.

CUSINS: I do not: all the poet in me recoils from being a good man. But there are things in me that I must reckon with. Pity—

UNDERSHAFT: Pity! The scavenger of misery.

CUSINS: Well, love.

UNDERSHAFT: I know. You love the needy and the outcast: you love the oppressed races, the negro, the Indian ryot, the underdog everywhere. Do you love the Japanese? Do you love the French? Do you love the English?

CUSINS: No. Every true Englishman detests the English. We are the wickedest nation on earth; and our success is a moral horror.

UNDERSHAFT: That is what comes of your gospel of love, is it?

CUSINS: May I not love even my father-in-law?

UNDERSHAFT: Who wants your love, man?

By what right do you take the liberty of offering it to me? I will have your due heed and respect, or I will kill you. But your love! Damn your impertinence!

CUSINS: *(Grinning)* I may not be able to control my affections, Mac.

UNDERSHAFT: You are fencing, Euripides. You are weakening: your grip is slipping. Come! try your last weapon. Pity and love have broken in your hand: forgiveness is still left.

CUSINS: No: forgiveness is a beggar's refuge. I am with you there: we must pay our debts.

UNDERSHAFT: Well said. Come! you will suit me. Remember the words of Plato.

CUSINS: *(Starting)* Plato! You dare quote Plato to me!

UNDERSHAFT: Plato says, my friend, that society cannot be saved until either the Professors of Greek take to making gunpowder, or else the makers of gunpowder become Professors of Greek.

CUSINS: Oh, tempter, cunning tempter!

UNDERSHAFT: Come! choose, man, choose.

CUSINS: But perhaps Barbara will not marry me if I make the wrong choice.

BARBARA: Perhaps not.

CUSINS: *(Desperately perplexed)* You hear!

BARBARA: Father: do you love nobody?

UNDERSHAFT: I love my best friend.

LADY BRITOMART: And who is that, pray?

UNDERSHAFT: My bravest enemy. That is the man who keeps me up to the mark.

CUSINS: You know, the creature is really a sort of poet in his way. Suppose he is a great man, after all!

UNDERSHAFT: Suppose you stop talking and make up your mind, my young friend.

CUSINS: But you are driving me against my nature. I hate war.

UNDERSHAFT: Hatred is the coward's revenge for being intimidated. Dare you make war on war? Here are the means: my friend Mr Lomax is sitting on them.

LOMAX: *(Springing up)* Oh I say! You dont mean that this thing is loaded, do you? My ownest: come off it.

SARAH: *(Sitting placidly on the shell)* If I am to be blown up, the more thoroughly it is done the better. Dont fuss. Cholly.

LOMAX: *(To* UNDERSHAFT, *strongly remonstrant)* Your own daughter, you know!

UNDERSHAFT: So I see. *(To* CUSINS*)* Well,

my friend, may we expect you here at six tomorrow morning?

CUSINS: *(Firmly)* Not on any account. I will see the whole establishment blown up with its own dynamite before I will get up at five. My hours are healthy, rational hours: eleven to five.

UNDERSHAFT: Come when you please: before a week you will come at six and stay until I turn you out for the sake of your health. *(Calling)* Bilton! *(He turns to* LADY BRITOMART, *who rises.)* My dear: let us leave these two young people to themselves for a moment. *(*BILTON *comes from the shed.)* I am going to take you through the gun cotton shed.

BILTON: *(Barring the way)* You cant take anything explosive in here, sir.

LADY BRITOMART: What do you mean? Are you alluding to me?

BILTON: *(Unmoved)* No, maam. Mr Undershaft has the other gentleman's matches in his pocket.

LADY BRITOMART: *(Abruptly)* Oh! I beg your pardon. *(She goes into the shed.)*

UNDERSHAFT: Quite right, Bilton, quite right: here you are. *(He gives* BILTON *the box of matches.)* Come, Stephen. Come, Charles, Bring Sarah. *(He passes into the shed.)*

*(*BILTON *opens the box and deliberately drops the matches into the fire-bucket.)*

LOMAX: Oh! I say *(*BILTON *hands him the empty box.)* Infernal nonsense! Pure scientific ignorance! *(He goes in.)*

SARAH: Am I all right, Bilton?

BILTON: Youll have to put on list slippers, miss: thats all Weve got em inside. *(She goes in.)*

STEPHEN: *(Very seriously to* CUSINS*)* Dolly, old fellow, think. Think before you decide. Do you feel that you are a sufficiently practical man? It is a huge undertaking, an enormous responsibility. All this mass of business will be Greek to you.

CUSINS: Oh, I think it will be much less difficult than Greek.

STEPHEN: Well, I just want to say this before I leave you to yourselves. Dont let anything I have said about right and wrong prejudice you against this great chance in life. I have satisfied myself that the business is one of the highest character and a credit to our country. *(Emotionally)* I am very proud of my father. I—*(Unable to proceed, he*

presses CUSINS' *hand and goes hastily into the shed, followed by* BILTON.*)*

*(*BARBARA *and* CUSINS, *left along together, look at one another silently.)*

CUSINS: Barbara: I am going to accept this offer.

BARBARA: I thought you would.

CUSINS: You understand, dont you, that I had to decide without consulting you. If I had thrown the burden of the choice on you, you would sooner or later have despised me for it.

BARBARA: Yes: I did not want you to sell your soul for me any more than for this inheritance.

CUSINS: It is not the sale of my soul that troubles me: I have sold it too often to care about that. I have sold it for a professorship. I have sold it for an income. I have sold it to escape being imprisoned for refusing to pay taxes for hangmen's ropes and unjust wars and things that I abhor. What is all human conduct but the daily and hourly sale of our souls for trifles? What I am now selling it for is neither money nor position nor comfort, but for reality and for power.

BARBARA: You know that you will have no power, and that he has none.

CUSINS: I know. It is not for myself alone. I want to make power for the world.

BARBARA: I want to make power for the world too; but it must be spiritual power.

CUSINS: I think all power is spiritual: these cannons will not go off by themselves. I have tried to make spiritual power by teaching Greek. But the world can never be really touched by a dead language and a dead civilization. The people must have power; and the people cannot have Greek. Now the power that is made here can be wielded by all men.

BARBARA: Power to burn women's houses down and kill their sons and tear their husbands to pieces.

CUSINS: You cannot have power for good without having power for evil too. Even mother's milk nourishes murderers as well as heroes. This power which only tears men's bodies to pieces has never been so horribly abused as the intellectual power, the imaginative power, the poetic, religious power that can enslave men's souls. As a teacher of Greek I gave the intellectual man weapons against the common man. I now want to give the common man weapons against the intellectual man. I love the common people. I want to arm them against the lawyers, the doctors, the priests, the literary men, the professors, the artists, and the politicians, who, once in authority, are more disastrous and tyrannical than all the fools, rascals, and imposters. I want a power simple enough for common men to use, yet strong enough to force the intellectual oligarchy to use its genius for the general good.

BARBARA: Is there no higher power than that? *(Pointing to the shell)*

CUSINS: Yes: but that power can destroy the higher powers just as a tiger can destroy a man: there Man must master that power first. I admitted this when the Turks and Greeks were last at war. My best pupil went out to fight for Hellas. My parting gift to him was not a copy of Plato's Republic, but a revolver and a hundred Undershaft cartridges. The blood of every Turk he shot—if he shot any— is on my head as well as on Undershaft's. That act committed me to this place for ever. Your father's challenge has beaten me. Dare I make war on war? I dare. I must. I will. And now, is it all over between us?

BARBARA: *(Touched by his evident dread of her answer)* Silly baby Dolly! How could it be!

CUSINS: *(Overjoyed)* Then you—you— you—Oh for my drum! *(He flourishes imaginary drumsticks.)*

BARBARA: *(Angered by his levity)* Take care, Dolly, take care. Oh, if only I could get away from you and from father and from it all! if I could have the wings of a dove and fly away to heaven!

CUSINS: And leave me!

BARBARA: Yes, you, and all the other naughty mischievous children of men. But I cant. I was happy in the Salvation Army for a moment. I escaped from the world into a paradise of enthusiasm and prayer and soul saving; but the moment our money ran short, it all came back to Bodger: it was he who saved our people: he, and the Prince of Darkness, my papa. Undershaft and Bodger: their hands stretch everywhere: when we feed a starving fellow creature, it is with their bread, because there is no other bread; when we tend the sick, it is in the hospitals they endow; if we turn from the churches they build, we must kneel on the stones of the streets they pave. As long as that lasts, there is no getting away from them. Turning our backs on Bodger and Undershaft is turning our backs on life.

CUSINS: I thought you were determined to turn your back on the wicked side of life.

BARBARA: There is no wicked side: life is all one. And I never wanted to shirk my share in whatever evil must be endured, whether it be sin or suffering. I wish I could cure you of middle-class ideas, Dolly.

CUSINS: *(gasping)* Middle cl—! A snub! A social snub to me! from the daughter of a foundling!

BARBARA: That is why I have no class, Dolly: I come straight out of the heart of the whole people. If I were middle-class I should turn my back on my father's business; and we should both live in an artistic drawing room, with you reading the reviews in one corner, and I in the other at the piano, playing Schumann: both very superior persons, and neither of us a bit of use. Sooner than that, I would sweep out the guncotton shed, or be one of Bodger's barmaids. Do you know what would have happened if you had refused papa's offer?

CUSINS: I wonder!

BARBARA: I should have given you up and married the man who accepted it. After all, my dear old mother has more sense than any of you. I felt like her when I saw this place—felt that I must have it—that never, never, never could I let it go; only she thought it was the houses and the kitchen ranges and the linen and china, when it was really all the human souls to be saved: not weak souls in starved bodies, sobbing with gratitude for a scrap of bread and treacle, but fulfilled, quarrelsome, snobbish, uppish creatures, all standing on their little rights and dignities, and thinking that my father ought to be greatly obliged to them for making so much money for him—and so he ought. That is where salvation is really wanted. My father shall never throw it in my teeth again that my converts were bribed with bread. *(She is transfigured.)* I have got rid of the bribe of bread. I have got rid of the bribe of heaven. Let God's work be done for its own sake: the work he had to create us to do because it cannot be done except by living men and women. When I die, let him be in my debt, not I in his; and let me forgive him as becomes a woman of my rank.

CUSINS: Then the way of life lies through the factory of death?

BARBARA: Yes, through the raising of hell to heaven and of man to God, through the unveiling of an eternal light in the Valley of The Shadow. *(Seizing him with both hands)* Oh, did you think my courage would never come back? did you believe that I was a deserter? that I, who have stood in the streets, and taken my people to my heart, and talked of the holiest and greatest things with them, could ever turn back and chatter foolishly to fashionable people about nothing in a drawing room? Never, never, never, never: Major Barbara will die with the colors. Oh! and I have my dear little Dolly boy still; and he has found me my place and my work. Glory Hallelujah! *(She kisses him.)*

CUSINS: My dearest: consider my delicate health. I cannot stand as much happiness as you can.

BARBARA: Yes: it is not easy work being in love with me, is it? But it's good for you. *(She runs to the shed, and calls, childlike.)* Mamma! Mamma! (BILTON *comes out of the shed, followed by* UNDERSHAFT.*)* I want Mamma.

UNDERSHAFT: She is taking off her list slippers, dear. *(He passes on to* CUSINS.*)* Well? What does she say?

CUSINS: She has gone right up into the skies.

LADY BRITOMART: *(Coming from the shed and stopping on the steps, obstructing* SARAH, *who follows with* LOMAX. BARBARA *clutches like a baby at her mother's skirt.)* Barbara: when will you learn to be independent and to act and think for yourself? I know as well as possible what that cry of "Mamma, Mamma," means. Always running to me!

SARAH: *(Touching* LADY BRITOMART's *ribs with her finger tips and imitating a bicycle horn)* Pip! pip!

LADY BRITOMART: *(Highly indignant)* How dare you say Pip! pip! to me, Sarah? You are both very naughty children. What do you want, Barbara?

BARBARA: I want a house in the village to live in with Dolly. *(Dragging at the skirt)* Come and tell me which one to take.

UNDERSHAFT: *(To* CUSINS*)* Six o'clock tomorrow morning, Euripides.

In *Major Barbara*, Shaw presents the paradoxical argument that the Undershaft firm (a manufacturer of munitions) provides a sounder basis for human progress than does the Salvation Army. In presenting this argument, Shaw uses a method typical of his plays. In the first act, his characters react conventionally to munitions manufacture — as something shameful and antihumanitarian, although perhaps necessary. They accept the Salvation Army as an organization that ministers charitably and humanely to the poor (although Barbara, as a member of a privileged class is considered eccentric for having joined it). Barbara, upon meeting her father (head of the munitions firm) for the first time since her childhood, believes that he would give up his bloody trade if she could convert him; and he, upon perceiving this, makes a bargain with her — that he will visit the Salvation Army shelter if she will visit his factory, after which they will decide which is the more desirable organization. Thus, the challenge is posed and accepted, although at this point no one except Undershaft takes seriously the possibility that he might best the Salvation Army.

Act II is set in a Salvation Army shelter in one of London's worst slums. We see representative poor people being fed and hear them discuss how they invent lurid sins, from which they claim to have been redeemed by the Salvation Army. We also see the shame that some feel for having to accept a handout, and in Bill Walker's case how someone can be manipulated into feeling guilt and the need to atone in some way. The shelter, under threat of closure for lack of funds, receives and enthusiastically accepts a gift of 5,000 pounds from Bodger's whiskey firm, upon which Undershaft offers a like amount. Major Barbara objects that these manufacturers are merely trying to buy salvation with tainted money and that to accept would be to undermine everything the Salvation Army stands for. When she is told that the Army will accept money from any source and turn it from bad to good use, she decides that she must resign.

In Act III, all the characters visit Undershaft's factory and the town where his employees live. They discover that the excellent wages Undershaft pays and the money he expends to create good living conditions for his workers have produced an ideal community in which the residents, no longer preoccupied with mere survival, can turn their thoughts to fulfilling their dreams. As Undershaft puts it: "Their souls are hungry because their bodies are full." Barbara sees the logic of Undershaft's arguments and determines to accept the challenge of converting these people, since they no longer need to pretend conversion for the sake of being fed. Thus, during the course of the action, Shaw upends conventional ideas and reverses expectations.

As for many others of his plays, for *Major Barbara* Shaw wrote a lengthy preface in which he sought to clarify his basic ideas.[2] In the preface to *Major Barbara*, he writes: "the greatest of our evils, and the worst of our crimes is poverty. . . . money is the counter that enables life to be distributed socially." Shaw's Undershaft accepts this and makes certain that those who work for him are well paid and can develop their human potential beyond the concern for survival.

Undershaft's approach contrasts markedly with that of the Salvation Army, which merely tries to alleviate the effects of poverty rather than working to eliminate the social conditions that cause poverty. According to Shaw's preface: "religious bodies, as the almoners of the rich, become a sort of auxiliary police, taking off the insurrectionary edge of poverty with coals and blankets, bread and treacle, and soothing and cheering the victims with hopes of immense and inexpensive happiness in another world when the process of working them to premature death in the service of the rich is complete in this." Thus, Shaw sees the Salvation Army as being used to reconcile humanity to the injustices of the world, thereby avoiding the social reform needed to rectify injustice. He sees this as doubly harmful because organizations such as the Salvation Army are supported in large part by those who are sufficiently ruthless to become rich and who then seek respectability through monetary gifts to churches, hospitals, and similar institutions; thus, they win a kind of absolution for their sins by giving to those very institutions that help to maintain the status quo upon which their prosperity depends. Shaw considers Major Barbara very naive in wanting to refuse the gift from Bodger, whose whiskey has created much of the misery that the Salvation Army must deal with. According to Shaw, almost all money is tainted. "Practically all the spare money in the country consists of a mass of rent, interest, and profit, every penny of which is bound up with crime, drink, prostitution, disease, and all the evil fruits of poverty, as inextricably as with enterprise, wealth, commercial probity, and national prosperity. The notion that you can earmark certain coins as tainted is an unpractical individualist superstition." The remedy, accord-

---

[2] Shaw's preface to *Major Barbara* appears at the end of this book.

ing to Shaw, lies not in seeking untainted money but in accepting that everyone shares in the guilt and in the necessity to change those conditions that produce tainted money. "He [a clergyman] must either share the world's guilt or go to another planet. He must save the world's honor if he is to save his own. . . . Her [Major Barbara's] discovery that she is her father's accomplice; that the Salvation Army is the accomplice of the distiller and the dynamite maker; that they can no more escape one another than they can escape the air they breathe; that there is no salvation for them through personal righteousness, but only through the redemption of the whole nation from its vicious, lazy, competitive anarchy: this discovery has been made by everyone except the Pharisees. . . ." Thus, Shaw's message is that everyone must accept responsibility for social and economic change but that, until ideal conditions are achieved, those (like Undershaft) who raise workers above the poverty level are more constructive than institutions (like the Salvation Army) that merely maintain the status quo.

Interwoven into the action of *Major Barbara* is the theme of creative evolution. Shaw says in his preface that Undershaft is "only the instrument of a Will or Life Force which uses him for purposes wider than his own." During the course of the play, Undershaft recognizes in Barbara's fiancé, the Greek professor Adolphus Cusins, a similar spirit and decides to make him heir to his firm. Cusins has felt a compulsion greater than love to marry Barbara. Shaw implies that through this union between Barbara and Cusins the life force will work toward the creation of the superman.

In many ways *Major Barbara* sums up Shaw's favorite themes: the unpleasant truths that lurk behind the facade of conventional ideas; the need to transform society gradually by dispelling false notions and improving working conditions; the necessity to free people from proverty before you can expect them to be concerned about higher things; the need for those of superior intellect to assume leadership; and the gradual evolution of mankind through the instinctive workings of the life force.

As the author of *Major Barbara*, Shaw could easily construct his play so as to make his arguments prevail. But his arguments rest on premises not universally acceptable: that human beings are fundamentally good; that it will be possible eventually to create a socioeconomic–political system under which poverty will be eliminated, in which class structure does not exist, in which laws are so equitable that there is no incentive for criminal behavior, and in which every person can fulfill his potential. Such premises are further grounded in the conviction that human beings can and will act rationally for the good of the entire human race. One cannot prove or disprove such basic assumptions; one can only accept them or propose alternative views (along with arguments to support them). While many people today probably find Shaw's ideal attractive, it is questionable how many consider it attainable. Arguments about ideal systems are important, nevertheless, for they are implied (thought not always stated) in the ongoing conflict about the relative merits of such socioeconomic–political systems as capitalism, socialism, and communism. Furthermore, assumptions about the ideal system undergird political convictions, legislative action, and governmental policy. Thus, they affect our daily lives not only through what goes on within our own country but also because of the recurrent international conflicts among systems for which countless people have fought and died. Therefore, though Shaw's play is a light-hearted treatment of ideas as they affect a small group, ultimately it advocates views Shaw would like to see universally applied.

The Little Foxes

by Lillian Hellman

As in many other professions, in the theatre women have been denied a significant role through much of history. They were not permitted to appear as actresses in regular tragedy and comedy in Greece or Rome, although they did perform in minor theatrical entertainments, especially mime, noted for their licentiousness. Women who appeared in such performances were usually ranked with prostitutes. During the Middle Ages, women occasionally appeared in religious spectacles, especially in the role of the Virgin Mary, but these productions were community projects, not the work of professional actors. Women seem first to have gained a foothold in the theatre in Spain in the 1500s, but regulations required that no woman be admitted to a company unless it included her husband or a close male relative. Actresses were not accepted on the English stage until 1661. Since then they have been an integral part of the western theatrical tradition.

It was easier for women to gain acceptance as actresses than as managers, although they occasionally filled this function. Following Molière's death in 1673, his wife served as joint manager of the company for a time; around 1730 Carolina Neuber's company set new standards for the German stage; and in England a century later Mme. Vestris's theatre introduced several significant innovations. Other examples could be cited but they would serve primarily to illustrate how rare it was for women to assume managerial positions. Except for actresses, the theatre was essentially a male institution; and even in acting, men dominated, as the cast of characters of almost any play will show, for with few exceptions male roles outnumber female roles two or more to one. Women's status in the theatre, however, was merely a reflection of their status in society, where they had few rights and seldom were considered capable or given the opportunity to assume positions of authority.

In playwriting, the situation was much the same. Hrosvitha, a German nun of the tenth century, wrote six religious plays, perhaps not intended for performance. The first woman in England to write professionally for the stage was Aphra Behn (1640–1689), author of many witty, salacious, and theatrically effective plays that reflected the tastes of the Restoration. In America, Anna Cora

Mowatt (1819–1870), a socialite turned actress, wrote one of the best-known plays of the nineteenth century, *Fashion* (1845), a comedy of manners set in New York. Although prior to the twentieth century a number of women wrote plays, they were relatively rare, and few, if any, ever appear on lists of the world's great playwrights — perhaps because men have also dominated dramatic criticism and have made the lists of great plays.

In the twentieth century, as women have won previously denied rights, their involvement in theatre has also increased. Women now work in every aspect of theatre, although relatively few are found in positions of major authority. Like blacks and other minorities, since around 1960 women have been increasingly concerned with winning full equality. Out of these concerns have come a number of women's theatres, coalitions of women playwrights, and committees that monitor and urge more equitable employment practices in theatrical organizations. This increased activity has also greatly enlarged the number of women playwrights, among the most prominent of whom have been Megan Terry, Maria Irene Fornes, Alice Childress, Wendy Wasserstein, and Beth Henley (whose *Crimes of the Heart* won the Pulitzer Prize in 1980).

Of American women playwrights of the twentieth century, perhaps the most honored has been Lillian Hellman (1905–   ); certainly she is one of those who most resents being labeled a woman playwright, since this implies that her worth might be questioned were she called merely a playwright. She first won recognition in 1934 with *The Children's Hour*, concerning a girls' school that is torn apart when a student accuses two teachers of having a lesbian relationship. Hellman went on to write *Days to Come* (1936), *The Little Foxes* (1939), *Watch on the Rhine* (1941), *The Searching Wind* (1944), and *Another Part of the Forest* (1951). In the 1950s, because of her past association with a number of liberal causes, she became a target for Senator Joseph McCarthy, who, playing on the fears engendered by the Cold War with Russia, used undocumented accusations and innuendo to destroy the reputations of those he considered dangerous. Many writers and actors were blacklisted and unable thereafter to obtain employment. As one of these, Hellman worked for a time as a clerk in a department store. When tensions eased, she made a forceful comeback as a dramatist in 1960 with *Toys in the Attic*. Since that time she has restricted her writing primarily to fiction, essays, and autobiography.

Hellman's best-known play is *The Little Foxes*, which, with its powerful story and characters, has retained its popularity, and most recently was revived with Elizabeth Taylor in the role of Regina. Hellman has also used many of the same characters in *Another Part of the Forest* (set in 1880, 20 years earlier than the time of *The Little Foxes*). In it, she explores the background that shaped her most memorable characters, the Hubbard family.

Take us the foxes, the little foxes,
that spoil the vines; for our vines
have tender grapes.

CAST OF CHARACTERS

ADDIE *Negro woman, aged 55, servant in the Giddens household*

CAL *middle-aged Negro man, servant in the Giddens household*

BIRDIE HUBBARD *wife to Oscar and mother of Leo, about 40*

LEO HUBBARD *her son, 20 years old*

OSCAR HUBBARD *her husband, in his late forties*

BEN HUBBARD *brother to Oscar and Regina, aged 55*

WILLIAM MARSHALL *businessman from Chicago, aged 45*

REGINA GIDDENS *sister to Oscar and Ben, wife of Horace and mother of Alexandra, aged 40*

ALEXANDRA GIDDENS *daughter of Regina and Horace, aged 17*

HORACE GIDDENS *banker, husband to Regina, father of Alexandra, aged 45*

SCENE

The scene of the play is the living room of the Giddens house, in a small town in the South.

ACT ONE

The Spring of 1900, evening.

ACT TWO

A week later, early morning.

ACT THREE

Two weeks later, late afternoon.

There has been no attempt to write Southern dialect. It is to be understood that the accents are Southern.

ACT ONE

SCENE:

The living room of the Giddens home, in a small town in the deep South, the spring of 1900. Upstage is a staircase leading to the second story. Upstage, right, are double doors to the dining room. When these doors are open we see a section of the dining room and the furniture. Upstage, left, is an entrance hall with a coatrack and umbrella stand. There are large lace-curtained windows on the left wall. The room is lit by a center gas chandelier and painted china oil lamps on the tables. Against the wall is a large piano. Downstage, right, are a high couch, a large table, several chairs. Against the left back wall are a table and several chairs. Near the window there are a smaller couch and tables. The room is good looking, the furniture expensive; but it reflects no particular taste. Everything is of the best and that is all.

(At Rise: ADDIE, *a tall, nice-looking Negro woman of about fifty-five, is closing the windows. From behind the closed dining-room doors there is the sound of voices. After a second,* CAL, *a middle-aged Negro, comes in from the entrance hall carrying a tray with glasses and a bottle of port.* ADDIE *crosses, takes the tray from him, puts it on table, begins to arrange it.)*

ADDIE: *(Pointing to the bottle)* You gone stark out of your head?

CAL: No, smart lady, I ain't. Miss Regina told me to get out that bottle. *(Points to bottle)* That very bottle for the mighty honored guest. When Miss Regina changes orders like that you can bet your dime she got her reason.

ADDIE: *(Points to dining room)* Go on. You'll be needed.

CAL: Miss Zan she had two helpings frozen fruit cream and she tell that honored guest, she tell him that you make the best frozen fruit cream in all the South.

ADDIE: *(Smiles, pleased)* Did she? Well, see that Belle saves a little for her. She like it right before she go to bed. Save a few little cakes, too, she like—

(The dining room doors are opened and quickly closed again by BIRDIE HUBBARD. BIRDIE *is a woman of about forty, with a pretty, well-bred, faded face. Her movements are usually nervous and timid, but now, as she comes running into the room, she is gay and excited.* CAL *turns to* BIRDIE.*)*

BIRDIE: Oh, Cal. *(Closes door)* I want you to get one of the kitchen boys to run home for me. He's to look in my desk drawer and—*(To* ADDIE*)* My, Addie. What a good supper! Just as good as good can be.

ADDIE: You look pretty this evening, Miss Birdie, and young.

BIRDIE: *(Laughing)* Me, young? *(Turns back to* CAL*)* Maybe you better find Simon and tell him to do it himself. He's to look in my desk, the left drawer, and bring my music album right away. Mr. Marshall is very anxious to see it because of his father and the opera in Chicago. *(To* ADDIE*)* Mr. Marshall is such a polite man with his manners and very educated and cultured and I've told him all about how my mama and papa used to go Europe for the music— *(Laughs. To* ADDIE*)* Imagine going

all the way to Europe just to listen to music. Wouldn't that be nice, Addie? Just to sit there and listen and— *(Turns and steps to* CAL*)* Left drawer, Cal. Tell him that twice because he forgets. And tell him not to let any of the things drop out of the album and to bring it right in here when he comes back.

(The dining-room doors are opened and quickly closed by OSCAR HUBBARD. *He is a man in his late forties.)*

CAL: Yes'm. But Simon he won't get it right. But I'll tell him.

BIRDIE: Left drawer, Cal, and tell him to bring the blue book and—

OSCAR: *(Sharply)* Birdie.

BIRDIE: *(Turning nervously)* Oh, Oscar. I was just sending Simon for my music album.

OSCAR: *(To* CAL*)* Never mind about the album. Miss Birdie has changed her mind.

BIRDIE: But, really, Oscar. Really I promised Mr. Marshall. I—

*(*CAL *looks at them, exits.)*

OSCAR: Why do you leave the dinner table and go running about like a child?

BIRDIE: *(Trying to be gay)* But, Oscar, Mr. Marshall said most specially he *wanted* to see my album. I told him about the time Mama met Wagner, and Mrs. Wagner gave her the signed program and the big picture. Mr. Marshall wants to see that. Very, very much. We had such a nice talk and—

OSCAR: *(Taking a step to her)* You have been chattering to him like a magpie. You haven't let him be for a second. I can't think he came South to be bored with you.

BIRDIE: *(Quickly, hurt)* He wasn't bored. I don't believe he was bored. He's a very educated, cultured gentleman. *(Her voice rises)* I just don't believe it. You always talk like that when I'm having a nice time.

OSCAR: *(Turning to her, sharply)* You have had too much wine. Get yourself in hand now.

BIRDIE: *(Drawing back, about to cry, shrilly)* What am I doing? I am not doing anything. What am I doing?

OSCAR: *(Taking a step to her, tensely)* I said get yourself in hand. Stop acting like a fool.

BIRDIE: *(Turns to him, quietly)* I don't believe he was bored. I just don't believe it. Some people like music and like to talk about it. That's all I was doing.

(LEO HUBBARD *comes hurrying through the dining-room door. He is a young man of twenty, with a weak kind of good looks.*)

LEO: Mama! Papa! They are coming in now.

OSCAR: (*Softly*) Sit down, Birdie. Sit down now. (BIRDIE *sits down, bows her head as if to hide her face.*)

(*The dining-room doors are opened by* CAL. *We see people beginning to rise from the table.* REGINA GIDDENS *comes in with* WILLIAM MARSHALL. REGINA *is a handsome woman of forty.* MARSHALL *is forty-five, pleasant-looking, self-possessed. Behind them comes* ALEXANDRA GIDDENS, *a very pretty, rather delicate-looking girl of seventeen. She is followed by* BENJAMIN HUBBARD, *fifty-five, with a large jovial face and the light graceful movements that one often finds in large men.*)

REGINA: Mr. Marshall, I think you're trying to console me. Chicago may be the noisiest, dirtiest city in the world but I should still prefer it to the sound of our horses and the smell of our azaleas. I should like crowds of people, and theaters, and lovely women — *Very* lovely women, Mr. Marshall?

MARSHALL: (*Crossing to sofa*) In Chicago? Oh, I suppose so. But I can tell you this: I've never dined there with *three* such lovely ladies.

(ADDIE *begins to pass the port.*)

BEN: Our Southern women are well favored.

LEO: (*Laughs*) But one must go to Mobile for the ladies, sir. Very elegant worldly ladies, too.

BEN: (*Looks at him very deliberately*) Worldly, eh? *Worldly*, did you say?

OSCAR: (*Hastily, to* LEO) Your uncle Ben means that worldliness is not a mark of beauty in any woman.

LEO: (*Quickly*) Of course, Uncle Ben. I didn't mean —

MARSHALL: Your port is excellent, Mrs. Giddens.

REGINA: Thank you, Mr. Marshall. We had been saving that bottle, hoping we could open it just for you.

ALEXANDRA: (*As* ADDIE *comes to her with the tray*) Oh, May I *really*, Addie?

ADDIE: Better ask Mama.

ALEXANDRA: May I, Mama?

REGINA: (*Nods, smiles*) In Mr. Marshall's honor.

ALEXANDRA: (*Smiles*) Mr. Marshall, this will be the first taste of port I've ever had.

(ADDIE *serves* LEO.)

MARSHALL: No one ever had their first taste of a better port. (*He lifts his glass in a toast; she lifts hers; they both drink*) Well, I suppose it is all true, Mrs. Giddens.

REGINA: What is true?

MARSHALL: That you Southerners occupy a unique position in America. You live better than the rest of us, you eat better, you drink better. I wonder you find time, or want to find time, to do business.

BEN: A great many Southerners don't.

MARSHALL: Do all of you live here together?

REGINA: Here with me? (*Laughs*) Oh, no. My brother Ben lives next door. My brother Oscar and his family live in the next square.

BEN: But we are a very close family. We've always wanted it that way.

MARSHALL: That is very pleasant. Keeping your family together to share each other's lives. My family moves around too much. My children seem never to come home. Away at school in the winter; in the summer, Europe with their mother —

REGINA: (*Eagerly*) Oh, yes. Even down here we read about Mrs. Marshall in the society pages.

MARSHALL: I dare say. She moves about a great deal. And all of you are part of the same business? Hubbard Sons?

BEN: (*Motions to* OSCAR) Oscar and me. (*Motions to* REGINA) My sister's good husband is a banker.

MARSHALL: (*Looks at* REGINA, *surprised*) Oh.

REGINA: I am so sorry that my husband isn't here to meet you. He's been very ill. He is at Johns Hopkins. But he will be home soon. We think he is getting better now.

LEO: I work for Uncle Horace. (REGINA *looks at him*) I mean I work for Uncle Horace at his bank. I keep an eye on things while he's away.

REGINA: (*Smiles*) Really, Leo?

BEN: (*Looks at* LEO, *then to* MARSHALL) Modesty in the young is as excellent as it is rare. (*Looks at* LEO *again.*)

OSCAR: (*To* LEO) Your uncle means that a young man should speak more modestly.

LEO: *(Hastily, taking a step to* BEN*)* Oh, I didn't mean, sir—

MARSHALL: Oh, Mrs. Hubbard. Where's that Wagner autograph you promised to let me see? My train will be leaving soon and—

BIRDIE: The autograph? Oh. Well. Really, Mr. Marshall, I didn't mean to chatter so about it. Really I— *(Nervously, looking at* OSCAR*)* You must excuse me. I didn't get it because, well, because I had—I— I had a little headache and—

OSCAR: My wife is a miserable victim of headaches.

REGINA: *(Quickly)* Mr. Marshall said at supper that he would like you to play for him, Alexandra.

ALEXANDRA: *(Who has been looking at* BIRDIE*)* It's not I who play well, sir. It's my aunt. She plays just wonderfully. She's my teacher. *(Rises. Eagerly)* May we play a duet? May we, Mama?

BIRDIE: *(Taking* ALEXANDRA*'s hand)* Thank you, dear. But I have my headache now. I—

OSCAR: *(Sharply)* Don't be stubborn, Birdie. Mr. Marshall wants you to play.

MARSHALL: Indeed I do. If your headache isn't—

BIRDIE: *(Hesitates, then gets up, pleased)* But I'd like to, sir. Very much. *(She and* ALEXANDRA *go to the piano.)*

MARSHALL: It's very remarkable how you Southern aristocrats have kept together. Kept together and kept what belonged to you.

BEN: You misunderstand, sir. Southern aristocrats have *not* kept together and have *not* kept what belonged to them.

MARSHALL: *(Laughs, indicates room)* You don't call this keeping what belongs to you?

BEN: But we are not aristocrats. *(Points to* BIRDIE *at the piano)* Our brother's wife is the only one of us who belongs to the Southern aristocracy.

*(*BIRDIE *looks toward* BEN*.)*

MARSHALL: *(Smiles)* My information is that you people have been here, and solidly here, for a long time.

OSCAR: And so we have. Since our great-grandfather.

BEN: *(Smiles)* Who was *not* an aristocrat, like Birdie's.

MARSHALL: *(A little sharply)* You make great distinctions.

BEN: Oh, they have been made for us. And maybe they are important distinctions. *(Leans forward, intimately)* Now you take Birdie's family. When my great-grandfather came here they were the highest-tone plantation owners in this state.

LEO: *(Steps to* MARSHALL. *Proudly)* My mother's grandfather was *governor* of the state before the war.

OSCAR: They owned the plantation, Lionnet. You may have heard of it, sir?

MARSHALL: *(Laughs)* No, I've never heard of anything but brick houses on a lake, and cotton mills.

BEN: Lionnet in its day was the best cotton land in the South. It still brings us in a fair crop. *(Sits back)* Ah, they were great days for those people—even when I can remember. They had the best of everything. *(*BIRDIE *turns to them)* Cloth from Paris, trips to Europe, horses you can't raise any more, niggers to lift their fingers—

BIRDIE: *(Suddenly)* We were good to our people. Everybody knew that. We were better to them than—

*(*MARSHALL *looks up at* BIRDIE*.)*

REGINA: Why, Birdie. You aren't playing.

BEN: But when the war comes these fine gentlemen ride off and leave the cotton, *and* the women, to rot.

BIRDIE: My father was killed in the war. He was a fine soldier, Mr. Marshall. A fine man.

REGINA: Oh, certainly, Birdie. A famous soldier.

BEN: *(To* BIRDIE*)* But that isn't the tale I am telling Mr. Marshall. *(To* MARSHALL*)* Well, sir, the war ends. *(*BIRDIE *goes back to piano)* Lionnet is almost ruined, and the sons finish ruining it. And there were thousands like them. Why? *(Leans forward)* Because the Southern aristocrat can adapt himself to nothing. Too high-tone to try.

MARSHALL: Sometimes it is difficult to learn new ways. *(*BIRDIE *and* ALEXANDRA *begin to play.* MARSHALL *leans forward, listening.)*

BEN: Perhaps, perhaps. *(He sees that* MARSHALL *is listening to the music. Irritated, he turns to* BIRDIE *and* ALEXANDRA *at the piano, then back to* MARSHALL*.)* You're right, Mr. Marshall. It is difficult to learn new ways. But maybe that's why it's profitable. *Our* grandfather and *our* father learned the new ways and learned how to make them pay. *(Smiles nastily)* *They* were in trade. Hubbard Sons, Merchandise. Others, Birdie's family, for example, looked down on them. *(Settles back in chair)* To make a long story short, Lionnet now belongs to *us*. (BIRDIE *stops playing)* Twenty years ago we took over their land, their cotton, and their daughter.

(BIRDIE rises and stands stiffly by the piano. MARSHALL, who has been watching her, rises.)

MARSHALL: May I bring you a glass of port, Mrs. Hubbard?

BIRDIE: *(Softly)* No, thank you, sir. You are most polite.

REGINA: *(Sharply, to BEN)* You are boring Mr. Marshall with these ancient family tales.

BEN: I hope not. I hope not. I am trying to make an important point— *(Bows to MARSHALL)* for our future business partner.

OSCAR: *(To MARSHALL)* My brother always says that it's folks like us who have struggled and fought to bring to our land some of the prosperity of your land.

BEN: Some people call that patriotism.

REGINA: *(Laughs gaily)* I hope you don't find my brothers too obvious, Mr. Marshall. I'm afraid they mean that this is the time for the ladies to leave the gentlemen to talk business.

MARSHALL: *(Hastily)* Not at all. We settled everything this afternoon. (MARSHALL *looks at his watch)* I have only a few minutes before I must leave for the train. *(Smiles at her)* And I insist they be spent with you.

REGINA: *And* with another glass of port.

MARSHALL: Thank you.

BEN: *(To REGINA)* My sister is right. *(To MARSHALL)* I am a plain man and I am trying to say a plain thing. A man ain't only in business for what he can get out of it. It's got to give him something here. *(Puts hand to his breast)* That's every bit as true for the nigger picking cotton for a silver quarter, as it is for you and me. (REGINA *gives* MARSHALL *a glass of port)* If it don't give him something here, then he don't pick the cotton right. Money isn't all. Not by three shots.

MARSHALL: Really? Well, I always thought it was a great deal.

REGINA: And so did I, Mr. Marshall.

MARSHALL: *(Leans forward. Pleasantly, but with meaning)* Now you don't have to convince me that you are the right people for the deal. I wouldn't be here if you hadn't convinced me six months ago.

You want the mill here, and I want it here. It isn't my business to find out why you want it.

BEN: To bring the machine to the cotton, and not the cotton to the machine.

MARSHALL: *(Amused)* You have a turn for neat phrases, Hubbard. Well, however grand your reasons are, mine are simple: I want to make money and I believe I'll make it on you. *(As BEN starts to speak, he smiles)* Mind you, I have no objections to more high-minded reasons. They are mighty valuable in business. It's fine to have partners who so closely follow the teachings of Christ. *(Gets up)* And now I must leave for my train.

REGINA: I'm sorry you won't stay over with us, Mr. Marshall, but you'll come again. Any time you like.

BEN: *(Motions to LEO, indicating the bottle)* Fill them up, boy, fill them up. (LEO *moves around filling the glasses as BEN speaks)* Down here, sir, we have a strange custom. We drink the *last* drink for a toast. That's to prove that the Southerner is always still on his feet for the last drink. *(Picks up his glass)* It was Henry Frick, your Mr. Henry Frick, who said, "Railroads are the Rembrandts of investments." Well, *I* say, "Southern cotton mills *will be* the Rembrandts of investment." So I give you the firm of Hubbard Sons and Marshall, Cotton Mills, and to it a long and prosperous life.

(They all pick up their glasses. MARSHALL looks at them, amused. Then he, too, lifts his glass, smiles.)

OSCAR: The children will drive you to the depot. Leo! Alexandra! You will drive Mr. Marshall down.

LEO: *(Eagerly, looks at BEN who nods)* Yes, sir. *(To MARSHALL)* Not often Uncle Ben lets *me* drive the horses. And a beautiful pair they are. *(Starts for hall)* Come on, Zan.

ALEXANDRA: May I drive tonight, Uncle Ben, please? I'd like to and—

BEN: *(Shakes his head, laughs)* In your evening clothes? Oh, no, my dear.

ALEXANDRA: But Leo always—*(Stops, exits quickly.)*

REGINA: I don't like to say good-bye to you, Mr. Marshall.

MARSHALL: Then we won't say good-bye. You have promised that you would come and let me show you Chicago. Do I have to make you promise again?

REGINA: (Looks at him as he presses her hand) I promise again.

MARSHALL: (Touches her hand again, then moves to BIRDIE) Good-bye, Mrs. Hubbard.

BIRDIE: (Shyly, with sweetness and dignity) Good-bye, sir.

MARSHALL: (As he passes REGINA) Remember.

REGINA: I will.

OSCAR: We'll see you to the carriage. (MARSHALL exits, followed by BEN and OSCAR. For a second REGINA and BIRDIE stand looking after them. Then REGINA throws up her arms, laughs happily.)

REGINA: And there, Birdie, goes the man who has opened the door to our future.

BIRDIE: (Surprised at the unaccustomed friendliness) What?

REGINA: (Turning to her) Our future. Yours and mine, Ben's and Oscar's, the children— (Looks at BIRDIE's puzzled face, laughs) Our future! (Gaily) You were charming at supper, Birdie. Mr. Marshall certainly thought so.

BIRDIE: (Pleased) Why, Regina! Do you think he did?

REGINA: Can't you tell when you're being admired?

BIRDIE: Oscar said I bored Mr. Marshall. (Then quietly) But he admired you. He told me so.

REGINA: What did he say?

BIRDIE: He said to me, "I hope your sister-in-law will come to Chicago. Chicago will be at her feet." He said the ladies would bow to your manners and the gentlemen to your looks.

REGINA: Did he? He seems a lonely man. Imagine being lonely with all that money. I don't think he likes his wife.

BIRDIE: Not like his wife? What a thing to say.

REGINA: She's away a great deal. He said that several times. And once he made fun of her being so social and high-tone. But that fits in all right. (Sits back, arms on back of sofa, stretches) Her being social, I mean. She can introduce me. It won't take long with an introduction from her.

BIRDIE: (Bewildered) Introduce you? In Chicago? You mean you really might go? Oh, Regina, you can't leave here. What about Horace?

REGINA: Don't look so scared about everything, Birdie. I'm going to live in Chicago. I've always wanted to. And now there'll be plenty of money to go with.

BIRDIE: But Horace won't be able to move around. You know what the doctor wrote.

REGINA: There'll be millions, Birdie, millions. You know what I've always said when people told me we were rich? I said I think you should either be a nigger or a millionaire. In between, like us, what for? (Laughs. Looks at BIRDIE) But I'm not going away tomorrow, Birdie. There's plenty of time to worry about Horace when he comes home. If he ever decides to come home.

BIRDIE: Will we be going to Chicago? I mean, Oscar and Leo and me?

REGINA: You? I shouldn't think so. (Laughs) Well, we must remember tonight. It's a very important night and we mustn't forget it. We shall plan all the things we'd like to have and then we'll really have them. Make a wish, Birdie, any wish. It's bound to come true now. (BEN and OSCAR enter.)

BIRDIE: (Laughs) Well. Well, I don't know. Maybe. (REGINA turns to look at BEN) Well, I guess I'd know right off what I wanted. (OSCAR stands by the upper window, waves to the departing carriage.)

REGINA: (Looks up at BEN, smiles. He smiles back at her) Well, you did it.

BEN: Looks like it might be we did.

REGINA: (Springs up, laughs) Looks like it! Don't pretend. You're like a cat who's been licking the cream. (Crosses to wine bottle) Now we must all have a drink to celebrate.

OSCAR: The children, Alexandra and Leo, make a very handsome couple, Regina. Marshall remarked himself what fine young folks they were. How well they looked together!

REGINA: (Sharply) Yes. You said that before, Oscar.

BEN: Yes, sir. It's beginning to look as if the deal's all set. I may not be a subtle man—but— (Turns to them. After a second) Now somebody ask me how I know the deal is set.

OSCAR: What do you mean, Ben?

BEN: You remember I told him that down here we drink the last drink for a toast?

OSCAR: (Thoughtfully) Yes. I never heard that before.

BEN: Nobody's ever heard it before. God forgives those who invent what they need. I already had his signature. But we've all done business with men whose word over a glass is better than a bond. Anyway it don't hurt to have both.

OSCAR: *(Turns to* REGINA*)* You understand what Ben means?

REGINA: *(Smiles)* Yes, Oscar. I understand. I understood immediately.

BEN: *(Looks at her admiringly)* Did you, Regina? Well, when he lifted his glass to drink, I closed my eyes and saw the bricks going into place.

REGINA: And *I* saw a lot more than that.

BEN: Slowly, slowly. As yet we have only our hopes.

REGINA: Birdie and I have just been planning what we want. I know what I want. What will you want, Ben?

BEN: Caution. Don't count the chickens. *(Leans back, laughs)* Well, God would allow us a little daydreaming. Good for the soul when you've worked hard enough to deserve it. *(Pauses)* I think I'll have a stable. For a long time I've had my good eyes on Carter's in Savannah. A rich man's pleasure, the sport of kings, why not the sport of Hubbards? Why not?

REGINA: *(Smiles)* Why not? What will you have, Oscar?

OSCAR: I don't know. *(Thoughtfully)* The pleasure of seeing the bricks grow will be enough for me.

BEN: Oh, of course. Our greatest pleasure will be to see the bricks grow. But we are all entitled to a little side indulgence.

OSCAR: Yes, I suppose so. Well, then, I think we might take a few trips here and there, eh, Birdie?

BIRDIE: *(Surprised at being consulted)* Yes, Oscar. I'd like that.

OSCAR: We might even make a regular trip to Jekyll Island. I've heard the Cornelly place is for sale. We might think about buying it. Make a nice change. Do you good, Birdie, a change of climate. Fine shooting on Jekyll, the best.

BIRDIE: I'd like —

OSCAR: *(Indulgently)* What would you like?

BIRDIE: Two things. Two things I'd like most.

REGINA: Two! I should like a thousand. You are modest, Birdie.

BIRDIE: *(Warmly, delighted with the unexpected interest)* I should like to have Lionnet back. I know you own it now, but I'd like to see it fixed up again, the way Mama and Papa had it. Every year it used to get a nice coat of paint — Papa was very particular about the paint — and the lawn was so smooth all the way down to the river, with the trims of zinnias and red-feather plush. And the figs and blue little plums and the scuppernongs — *(Smiles. Turns to* REGINA*)* The organ is still there and it wouldn't cost much to fix. We could have parties for Zan, the way Mama used to have for me.

BEN: That's a pretty picture, Birdie. Might be a most pleasant way to live. *(Dismissing* BIRDIE*)* What do you want, Regina?

BIRDIE: *(Very happily, not noticing that they are no longer listening to her)* I could have a cutting garden. Just where Mama's used to be. Oh, I do think we could be happier there. Papa used to say that *nobody* had ever lost their temper at Lionnet, and *nobody* ever would. Papa would never let anybody be nasty-spoken or mean. No, sir. He just didn't like it.

BEN: What do you want, Regina?

REGINA: I'm going to Chicago. And when I'm settled there and know the right people and the right things to buy — because I certainly don't now — I shall go to Paris and buy them. *(Laughs)* I'm going to leave you and Oscar to count the bricks.

BIRDIE: Oscar. Please let me have Lionnet back.

OSCAR: *(To* REGINA*)* You are serious about moving to Chicago?

BEN: She is going to see the great world and leave us in the little one. Well, we'll come and visit you and meet all the great and be proud you are our sister.

REGINA: *(Gaily)* Certainly. And you won't even have to learn to be subtle, Ben. Stay as you are. You will be rich and the rich don't have to be subtle.

OSCAR: But what about Alexandra? She's seventeen. Old enough to be thinking about marrying.

BIRDIE: And Oscar, I have one more wish. Just one more wish.

OSCAR: *(Turns)* What is it, Birdie? What are you saying?

BIRDIE: I want you to stop shooting. I mean, so much. I don't like to see animals and birds killed just for the killing. You only throw them away —

BEN: *(To* REGINA*)* It'll take a great deal of money to live as you're planning, Regina.

REGINA: Certainly. But there'll be plenty of money. You have estimated the profits very high.

BEN: I have—

BIRDIE: (OSCAR *is looking at her furiously*) And you never let anybody else shoot, and the niggers need it so much to keep from starving. It's wicked to shoot food just because you like to shoot, when poor people need it so—

BEN: (*Laughs*) I have estimated the profits very high—for myself.

REGINA: What did you say?

BIRDIE: I've always wanted to speak about it, Oscar.

OSCAR: (*Slowly, carefully*) What are you chattering about?

BIRDIE: (*Nervously*) I was talking about Lionnet and—and about your shooting—

OSCAR: You are exciting yourself.

REGINA: (*To* BEN) I didn't hear you. There was so much talking.

OSCAR: (*To* BIRDIE) You have been acting very childish, very excited, all evening.

BIRDIE: Regina asked me what I'd like.

REGINA: What did you say, Ben?

BIRDIE: Now that we'll be so rich everybody was saying what they would like, so *I* said what *I* would like, too.

BEN: I said— (*He is interrupted by* OSCAR.)

OSCAR: (*To* BIRDIE) Very well. We've all heard you. That's enough now.

BEN: I am waiting. (*They stop*) I am waiting for you to finish. You and Birdie. Four conversations are three too many. (BIRDIE *slowly sits down.* BEN *smiles, to* REGINA) I said that I had, and I do, estimate the profits very high—for myself, and Oscar, of course.

REGINA: (*Slowly*) And what does that mean? (BEN *shrugs, looks toward* OSCAR)

OSCAR: (*Looks at* BEN, *clears throat*) Well, Regina, it's like this. For forty-nine per cent Marshall will put up four hundred thousand dollars. For fifty-one per cent— (*Smiles archly*) a controlling interest, mind you, we will put up two hundred and twenty-five thousand dollars besides offering him certain benefits that our (*Looks at* BEN) local position allows us to manage. Ben means that two hundred and twenty-five thousand dollars is a lot of money.

REGINA: I know the terms and I know it's a lot of money.

BEN: (*Nodding*) It is.

OSCAR: Ben means that we are ready with our two-thirds of the money. Your third, Horace's I mean, doesn't seem to be ready. (*Raises his hand as* REGINA *starts to speak*) Ben has written to Horace, I have written, and you have written. He answers. But he never mentions this business. Yet we have explained it to him in great detail, and told him the urgency. Still he never mentions it. Ben has been very patient, Regina. Naturally, you are our sister and we want you to benefit from anything we do.

REGINA: And in addition to your concern for me, you do not want control to go out of the family. (*To* BEN) That right, Ben?

BEN: That's cynical. (*Smiles*) Cynicism is an unpleasant way of saying the truth.

OSCAR: No need to be cynical. We'd have no trouble raising the third share, the share that you want to take.

REGINA: I am sure you could get the third share, the share you were saving for me. But that would give you a strange partner. And strange partners sometimes want a great deal. (*Smiles unpleasantly*) But perhaps it would be wise for you to find him.

OSCAR: Now, now. Nobody says we *want* to do that. We would like to have you in and you would like to come in.

REGINA: Yes. I certainly would.

BEN: (*Laughs, puts up his hand*) But we haven't heard from Horace.

REGINA: I've given my word that Horace will put up the money. That should be enough.

BEN: Oh, it was enough. I took your word. But I've got to have more than your word now. The contracts will be signed this week, and Marshall will want to see our money soon after. Regina, Horace has been in Baltimore for five months. I know that you've written him to come home, and that he hasn't come.

OSCAR: It's beginning to look as if he doesn't want to come home.

REGINA: Of course he wants to come home. You can't move around with heart trouble at any moment you choose. You know what doctors are like once they get their hands on a case like this—

OSCAR: They can't very well keep him from answering letters, can they? (REGINA *turns to* BEN) They couldn't keep him from arranging for the money if he wanted to—

REGINA: Has it occurred to you that Horace is also a good businessman?

BEN: Certainly. He is a shrewd trader. Always has been. The bank is proof of that.

REGINA: Then, possibly, he may be keeping silent because he doesn't think he is getting enough for his money. *(Looks at* OSCAR*)* Seventy-five thousand he has to put up. That's a lot of money, too.

OSCAR: Nonsense. He knows a good thing when he hears it. He knows that we can make *twice* the profit on cotton goods manufactured here than can be made in the North.

BEN: That isn't what Regina means. *(Smiles)* May I interpret you, Regina? *(To* OSCAR*)* Regina is saying that Horace wants *more* than a third of our share.

OSCAR: But he's only putting up a third of the money. You put up a third and you get a third. What else could he expect?

REGINA: Well, *I* don't know. I don't know about these things. It would seem that if you put up a third you should only get a third. But then again, there's no law about it, is there? I should think that if you knew your money was very badly needed, well, you just might say, I want more, I want a bigger share. You boys have done that. I've heard you say so.

BEN: *(After a pause, laughs)* So you believe he has deliberately held out? For a larger share? *(Leaning forward)* Well, I don't believe it. But I do believe that's what *you* want. Am I right, Regina?

REGINA: Oh, I shouldn't like to be too definite. But I could say that I wouldn't like to persuade Horace unless he did get a larger share. I must look after his interests. It seems only natural —

OSCAR: And where would the larger share come from?

REGINA: I don't know. That's not my business. *(Giggles)* But perhaps it could come off your share, Oscar. *(*REGINA *and* BEN *laugh.)*

OSCAR: *(Rises and wheels furiously on both of them as they laugh)* What kind of talk is this?

BEN: I haven't said a thing.

OSCAR: *(To* REGINA*) You* are talking very big tonight.

REGINA: *(Stops laughing)* Am I? Well, you should know me well enough to know that I wouldn't be asking for things I didn't think I could get.

OSCAR: Listen. I don't believe you can even get Horace to come home, much less get money from him or talk quite so big about what you want.

REGINA: Oh, I can get him home.

OSCAR: Then why haven't you?

REGINA: I thought I should fight his battles for him, before he came home. Horace is a very sick man. And even if *you* don't care how sick he is, I do.

BEN: Stop this foolish squabbling. How can you get him home?

REGINA: I will send Alexandra to Baltimore. She will ask him to come home. She will say that she wants him to come home, and that *I* want him to come home.

BIRDIE: *(Suddenly)* Well, of course she wants him here, but he's sick and maybe he's happy where he is.

REGINA: *(Ignores* BIRDIE, *to* BEN*)* You agree that he will come home if she asks him to, if she says that I miss him and want him —

BEN: *(Looks at her, smiles)* I admire you, Regina. And I agree. That's settled now and — *(Starts to rise.)*

REGINA: *(Quickly)* But before she brings him home, I want to know what he's going to get.

BEN: What do you want?

REGINA: Twice what you offered.

BEN: Well, you won't get it.

OSCAR: *(To* REGINA*)* I think you've gone crazy.

REGINA: I don't want to fight, Ben —

BEN: I don't either. You won't get it. There isn't any chance of that. *(Roguishly)* You're holding us up, and that's not pretty, Regina, not pretty. *(Holds up his hand as he sees she is about to speak)* But we need you, and I don't want to fight. Here's what I'll do: I'll give Horace forty per cent, instead of the thirty-three and a third he really should get. I'll do that, provided he is home and his money is up within two weeks. How's that?

REGINA: All right.

OSCAR: I've asked before: where is this extra share coming from?

BEN: *(Pleasantly)* From you. From your share.

OSCAR: *(Furiously)* From me, is it? That's just fine and dandy. That's my reward. For thirty-five years I've worked my hands to the bone for you. For thirty-five years I've done all the things you didn't want to do. And this is what I —

BEN: *(Turns slowly to look at* OSCAR. OSCAR *breaks off)* My, my. I am being attacked tonight on all sides. First by my sister, then by my brother. And I ain't a man who likes being attacked. I can't believe that God wants the strong to parade their strength, but I don't mind doing it if it's got to be done. *(Leans back in his chair)* You ought to take these things better, Oscar. I've made you money in the past. I'm going to make you more money now. You'll be a very rich man. What's the difference to any of us if a little more goes here, a little less goes there—it's all in the family. And it will stay in the family. I'll never marry. *(ADDIE enters, begins to gather the glasses from the table. OSCAR turns to BEN)* So my money will go to Alexandra and Leo. They may even marry some day and— *(ADDIE looks at BEN.)*

BIRDIE: *(Rising)* Marry—Zan and Leo—

OSCAR: *(Carefully)* That would make a great difference in my feelings. If they married.

BEN: Yes, that's what I mean. Of course it would make a difference.

OSCAR: *(Carefully)* Is that what *you* mean, Regina?

REGINA: Oh, it's too far away. We'll talk about it in a few years.

OSCAR: I want to talk about it now.

BEN: *(Nods)* Naturally.

REGINA: There's a lot of things to consider. They are first cousins, and—

OSCAR: That isn't unusual. Our grandmother and grandfather were first cousins.

REGINA: *(Giggles)* And look at us. *(BEN giggles.)*

OSCAR: *(Angrily)* You're both being very gay with my money.

BEN: *(Sighs)* These quarrels. I dislike them so. *(Leans forward to REGINA)* A marriage might be a very wise arrangement, for several reasons. And then, Oscar has given up something for you. You should try to manage something for him.

REGINA: I haven't said I was opposed to it. But Leo is a wild boy. There were those times when he took a little money from the bank and—

OSCAR: That's all past history—

REGINA: Oh, I know. And I know all young men are wild. I'm only mentioning it to show you that there are considerations—

BEN: *(Irritated because she does not understand that he is trying to keep OSCAR quiet)* All right, so there are. But please assure Oscar that you will think about it very seriously.

REGINA: *(Smiles, nods)* Very well. I assure Oscar that I will think about it seriously.

OSCAR: *(Sharply)* That is not an answer.

REGINA: *(Rises)* My, you're in a bad humor and you shall put me in one. I have said all that I am willing to say now. After all, Horace has to give his consent, too.

OSCAR: Horace will do what you tell him to.

REGINA: Yes, I think he will.

OSCAR: And I have your word that you will try to—

REGINA: *(Patiently)* Yes, Oscar. You have my word that I will think about it. Now do leave me alone. *(There is the sound of the front door being closed.)*

BIRDIE: I—Alexandra is only seventeen. She—

REGINA: *(Calling)* Alexandra? Are you back?

ALEXANDRA: Yes, Mama.

LEO: *(Comes into the room)* Mr. Marshall got off safe and sound. Weren't those fine clothes he had? You can always spot clothes made in a good place. Looks like maybe they were done in England. Lots of men in the North send all the way to England for their stuff.

BEN: *(To LEO)* Were you careful driving the horses?

LEO: Oh, yes, sir. I was. *(ALEXANDRA has come in on BEN's question, hears the answer, looks angrily at LEO.)*

ALEXANDRA: It's a lovely night. You should have come, Aunt Birdie.

REGINA: Were you gracious to Mr. Marshall?

ALEXANDRA: I think so, Mama. I liked him.

REGINA: Good. And now I have great news for you. You are going to Baltimore in the morning to bring your father home.

ALEXANDRA: *(Gasps, then delighted)* Me? Papa said I should come? That must mean— *(Turns to ADDIE)* Addie, he must be well. Think of it, he'll be back home again. We'll bring him home.

REGINA: You are going alone, Alexandra.

ADDIE: *(ALEXANDRA has turned in surprise)* Going alone? Going by herself? A child that age! Mr. Horace ain't going to like Zan traipsing up there by herself.

REGINA: *(Sharply)* Go upstairs and lay out Alexandra's things.

ADDIE: He'd expect me to be along—

REGINA: I'll be up in a few minutes to tell you what to pack. *(ADDIE slowly begins to climb the steps. To ALEXANDRA)* I should think you'd like going alone. At your age it certainly would have delighted me. You're a strange girl, Alexandra. Addie has babied you so much.

ALEXANDRA: I only thought it would be more fun if Addie and I went together.

BIRDIE: *(Timidly)* Maybe I could go with her, Regina. I'd really like to.

REGINA: She is going alone. She is getting old enough to take some responsibilities.

OSCAR: She'd better learn now. She's almost old enough to get married. *(Jovially, to* LEO, *slapping him on shoulder)* Eh, son?

LEO: Huh?

OSCAR: *(Annoyed with* LEO *for not understanding)* Old enough to get married, you're thinking, eh?

LEO: Oh, yes, sir. *(Feebly)* Lots of girls get married at Zan's age. Look at Mary Prester and Johanna and —

REGINA: Well, she's not getting married tomorrow. But she is going to Baltimore tomorrow, so let's talk about that. *(To* ALEXANDRA*)* You'll be glad to have Papa home again.

ALEXANDRA: I wanted to go before, Mama. You remember that. But you said *you* couldn't go, and that *I* couldn't go alone.

REGINA: I've changed my mind. *(Too casually)* You're to tell Papa how much you missed him, and that he must come home now — for your sake. Tell him that you *need* him home.

ALEXANDRA: Need him home? I don't understand.

REGINA: There is nothing for you to understand. You are simply to say what I have told you.

BIRDIE: *(Rises)* He may be too sick. She couldn't do that —

ALEXANDRA: Yes. He may be too sick to travel. I couldn't make him think he had to come home for me, if he is too sick to —

REGINA: *(Looks at her, sharply, challengingly)* You *couldn't* do what I tell you to do, Alexandra?

ALEXANDRA: *(Quietly)* No. I couldn't. If I thought it would hurt him.

REGINA: *(After a second's silence, smiles pleasantly)* But you are doing this for Papa's own good. *(Takes* ALEXANDRA*'s hand)* You must let me be the judge of his condition. It's the best possible cure for him to come home and be taken care of here. He mustn't stay there any longer and listen to those alarmist doctors. You are doing this entirely for his sake. Tell your papa that I want him to come home, that I miss him very much.

ALEXANDRA: *(Slowly)* Yes, Mama.

REGINA: *(To the others. Rises)* I must go and start getting Alexandra ready now. Why don't you all go home?

BEN: *(Rises)* I'll attend to the railroad ticket. One of the boys will bring it over. Good night, everybody. Have a nice trip, Alexandra. The food on the train is very good. The celery is so crisp. Have a good time and act like a little lady. *(Exits)*

REGINA: Good night, Ben. Good night, Oscar — *(Playfully)* Don't be so glum, Oscar. It makes you look as if you had chronic indigestion.

BIRDIE: Good night, Regina.

REGINA: Good night, Birdie. *(Exits upstairs.)*

OSCAR: *(Starts for hall)* Come along.

LEO: *(To* ALEXANDRA*)* Imagine your not wanting to go! What a little fool you are. Wish it were me. What I could do in a place like Baltimore!

ALEXANDRA: *(Angrily, looking away from him)* Mind your business. I can guess the kind of things *you* could do.

LEO: *(Laughs)* Oh, no, you couldn't. *(He exits.)*

REGINA: *(Calling from the top of the stairs)* Come on, Alexandra.

BIRDIE: *(Quickly, softly)* Zan.

ALEXANDRA: I don't understand about my going, Aunt Birdie. *(Shrugs)* But anyway, Papa will be home again. *(Pats* BIRDIE*'s arm)* Don't worry about me. I can take care of myself. Really I can.

BIRDIE: *(Shakes her head, softly)* That's not what I'm worried about. Zan —

ALEXANDRA: *(Comes close to her)* What's the matter?

BIRDIE: It's about Leo —

ALEXANDRA: *(Whispering)* He beat the horses. That's why we were late getting back. We had to wait until they cooled off. He always beats the horses as if —

BIRDIE: *(Whispering frantically, holding* ALEXANDRA*'s hands)* He's my son. My own son. But you are more to me — more to me than my own child. I love you more than anybody else —

ALEXANDRA: Don't worry about the horses. I'm sorry I told you.

BIRDIE: *(Her voice rising)* I am not worrying about the horses. I am worrying about *you*. You are *not* going to marry Leo. I am not going to let them do that to you —

ALEXANDRA: Marry? To Leo? *(Laughs)* I wouldn't marry, Aunt Birdie. I've never even thought about it —

BIRDIE: But they have thought about it.

(Wildly) Zan, I couldn't stand to think about such a thing. You and— *(OSCAR has come into the doorway on ALEXANDRA's speech. He is standing quietly, listening.)*

ALEXANDRA: *(Laughs)* But I'm not going to marry. And I'm certainly not going to marry Leo.

BIRDIE: Don't you understand? They'll make you. They'll make you—

ALEXANDRA: *(Takes BIRDIE's hands, quietly, firmly)* That's foolish, Aunt Birdie. I'm grown now. Nobody can make me do anything.

BIRDIE: I just couldn't stand—

OSCAR: *(Sharply)* Birdie. *(BIRDIE looks up, draws quickly away from ALEXANDRA. She stands rigid, frightened. Quietly)* Birdie, get your hat and coat.

ADDIE: *(Calls from upstairs)* Come on, baby. Your mama's waiting for you, and she ain't nobody to keep waiting.

ALEXANDRA: All right. *(Then softly, embracing BIRDIE)* Good night, Aunt Birdie. *(As she passes OSCAR)* Good night, Uncle Oscar. *(BIRDIE begins to move slowly toward the door as ALEXANDRA climbs the stairs. ALEXANDRA is almost out of view when BIRDIE reaches OSCAR in the doorway. As BIRDIE quickly attempts to pass him, he slaps her hard, across the face. BIRDIE cries out, puts her hand to her face. On the cry, ALEXANDRA turns, begins to run down the stairs)* Aunt Birdie! What happened? What happened? I—

BIRDIE: *(Softly, without turning)* Nothing, darling. Nothing happened. *(Quickly, as if anxious to keep ALEXANDRA from coming close)* Now go to bed. *(OSCAR exits)* Nothing happened. I only—I only twisted my ankle. *(She goes out. ALEXANDRA stands on the stairs looking after her as if she were puzzled and frightened.)*

CURTAIN

ACT TWO

SCENE:

Same as Act One. A week later, morning.

(At Rise: The light comes from the open shutter of the right window; the other shutters are tightly closed. ADDIE is standing at the window, looking out. Near the dining room doors are brooms, mops, rags, etc. After a second, OSCAR comes into the entrance hall, looks in the room, shivers, decides not to take his hat and coat off, comes into the room. At the sound of the door, ADDIE turns.)

ADDIE: *(Without interest)* Oh, it's you, Mr. Oscar.

OSCAR: What is this? It's not night. What's the matter here? *(Shivers)* Fine thing at this time of the morning. Blinds all closed. *(ADDIE begins to open shutters)* Where's Miss Regina? It's cold in here.

ADDIE: Miss Regina ain't down yet.

OSCAR: She had any word?

ADDIE: *(Wearily)* No, sir.

OSCAR: Wouldn't you think a girl that age could get on a train at one place and have sense enough to get off at another?

ADDIE: Something must have happened. If Zan say she was coming last night, she's coming last night. Unless something happened. Sure fire disgrace to let a baby like that go all that way alone to bring home a sick man without—

OSCAR: You do a lot of judging around here, Addie, eh? Judging of your white folks, I mean.

ADDIE: *(Looks at him, sighs)* I'm tired. I been up all night watching for them.

REGINA: *(Speaking from the upstairs hall)* Who's downstairs, Addie? *(She appears in a dressing gown, peers down from the landing. ADDIE picks up broom, dustpan and brush and exits.)* Oh, it's you, Oscar. What are you doing here so early? I haven't been down yet. I'm not finished dressing.

OSCAR: *(Speaking up to her)* You had any word from them?

REGINA: No.

OSCAR: Then something certainly has happened. People don't just say they are arriving on Thursday night, and they haven't come by Friday morning.

REGINA: Oh, nothing has happened. Alexandra just hasn't got sense enough to send a message.

OSCAR: If nothing's happened, then why aren't they here?

REGINA: You asked me that ten times last night. My, you do fret so, Oscar. Anything might have happened. They may have missed connections in Atlanta, the train may have been delayed—oh, a hundred things could have kept them.

OSCAR: Where's Ben?

REGINA: *(As she disappears upstairs)* Where should he be? At home, probably. Really, Oscar, I don't tuck him in his bed and I don't take him out of it. Have some coffee and don't worry so much.

OSCAR: Have some coffee? There isn't any coffee. *(Looks at his watch, shakes his head. After a second* CAL *enters with a large silver tray, coffee urn, small cups, newspaper.)* Oh, there you are. Is everything in this fancy house always late?

CAL: *(Looks at him surprised)* You ain't out shooting this morning, Mr. Oscar?

OSCAR: First day I missed since I had my head cold. First day I missed in eight years.

CAL: Yes, sir. I bet you. Simon he say you had a mighty good day yesterday morning. That's what Simon say. *(Brings* OSCAR *coffee and newspaper.)*

OSCAR: Pretty good, pretty good.

CAL: *(Laughs, slyly)* Bet you got enough bob-white and squirrel to give every nigger in town a Jesus-party. Most of 'em ain't had no meat since the cotton picking was over. Bet they'd give anything for a little piece of that meat—

OSCAR: *(Turns his head to look at* CAL*)* Cal, if I catch a nigger in this town going shooting, you know what's going to happen. *(*LEO *enters.)*

CAL: *(Hastily)* Yes, sir, Mr. Oscar. I didn't say nothing about nothing. It was Simon who told me and— Morning, Mr. Leo. You gentlemen having your breakfast with us here?

LEO: The boys in the bank don't know a thing. They haven't had any message.

*(*CAL *waits for an answer, gets none, shrugs, moves to door, exits.)*

OSCAR: *(Peers at* LEO*)* What you doing here, son?

LEO: You told me to find out if the boys at the bank had any message from Uncle Horace or Zan—

OSCAR: I told you if they had a message to bring it here. I told you that if they didn't have a message to stay at the bank and do your work.

LEO: Oh, I guess I misunderstood.

OSCAR: You didn't misunderstand. You just were looking for any excuse to take an hour off. *(*LEO *pours a cup of coffee)* You got to stop that kind of thing. You got to start settling down. You going to be a married man one of these days.

LEO: Yes, sir.

OSCAR: You also got to stop with that woman in Mobile. *(As* LEO *is about to speak)* You're young and I haven't got no objections to outside women. That is, I haven't got no objections so long as they don't interfere with serious things. Outside women are all right in their place, but *now* isn't their place. You got to realize that.

LEO: *(Nods)* Yes, sir. I'll tell her. She'll act all right about it.

OSCAR: Also, you got to start working harder at the bank. You got to convince your Uncle Horace you going to make a fit husband for Alexandra.

LEO: What do you think has happened to them? Supposed to be here last night— *(Laughs)* Bet you Uncle Ben's mighty worried. Seventy-five thousand dollars worried.

OSCAR: *(Smiles happily)* Ought to be worried. Damn well ought to be. First he don't answer the letters, then he don't come home— *(Giggles.)*

LEO: What will happen if Uncle Horace don't come home or don't—

OSCAR: Or don't put up the money? Oh, we'll get it from outside. Easy enough.

LEO: *(Surprised)* But *you* don't want outsiders.

OSCAR: What do I care who gets my share? I been shaved already. Serve Ben right if he had to give away some of his.

LEO: Damn shame what they did to you.

OSCAR: *(Looking up the stairs)* Don't talk so loud. Don't you worry. When I die, you'll have as much as the rest. You might have yours *and* Alexandra's. I'm not so easily licked.

LEO: I wasn't thinking of myself, Papa—

OSCAR: Well, you should be, you should be. It's every man's duty to think of himself.

LEO: You think Uncle Horace don't want to go in on this?

OSCAR: *(Giggles)* That's my hunch. He hasn't showed any signs of loving it yet.

LEO: *(Laughs)* But he hasn't listened to Aunt Regina yet, either. Oh, he'll go along. It's too good a thing. Why wouldn't he want to? He's got plenty and plenty to invest with. He don't even have to sell anything. Eighty-eight thousand worth of Union Pacific bonds sitting right in his safe deposit box. All he's got to do is open the box.

OSCAR: *(After a pause. Looks at his watch)* Mighty late breakfast in this fancy house. Yes, he's had those bonds for fifteen years. Bought them when they were low and just locked them up.

LEO: Yeah. Just has to open the box and take them out. That's all. Easy as easy can be. *(Laughs)* The things in that box! There's all those bonds, looking mighty fine. *(OSCAR slowly puts down his newspaper and turns to LEO)* Then right next to them is a baby shoe of Zan's and a cheap old cameo on a string, and, *and*—nobody'd believe this—a piece of an old violin. Not even a whole violin. Just a piece of an old thing, a piece of a violin.

OSCAR: *(Very softly, as if he were trying to control his voice)* A piece of a violin! What do you think of that!

LEO: Yes, sirree. A lot of other crazy things, too. A poem, I guess it is, signed with his mother's name, and two old schoolbooks with notes and— *(LEO catches OSCAR's look. His voice trails off. He turns his head away.)*

OSCAR: *(Very softly)* How do you know what's in the box, son?

LEO: *(Stops, draws back, frightened, realizing what he has said)* Oh, well. Well, er. Well, one of the boys, sir. It was one of the boys at the bank. He took old Manders' keys. It was Joe Horns. He just up and took Manders' keys and, and—well, took the box out. *(Quickly)* Then they all asked me if I wanted to see, too. So I looked a little, I guess, but then I made them close up the box quick and I told them never—

OSCAR: *(Looks at him)* Joe Horns, you say? He opened it?

LEO: Yes, sir, yes, he did. My word of honor. *(Very nervously looking away)* I suppose that don't excuse *me* for looking— *(Looking at OSCAR)* but I did make him close it up and put the keys back in Manders' drawer—

OSCAR: *(Leans forward, very softly)* Tell me the truth, Leo. I am not going to be angry with you. Did you open the box yourself?

LEO: *No, sir, I didn't.* I told you I didn't. No, I—

OSCAR: *(Irritated, patient)* I am *not* going to be angry with you. *(Watching LEO carefully)* Some-

times a young fellow deserves credit for looking round him to see what's going on. Sometimes that's a good sign in a fellow your age. *(OSCAR rises)* Many great men have made their fortune with their eyes. Did you open the box?

LEO: *(Very puzzled)* No. I—

OSCAR: *(Moves to LEO)* Did you open the box? It may have been—well, it may have been a good thing if you had.

LEO: *(After a long pause)* I opened it.

OSCAR: *(Quickly)* Is that the truth? *(LEO nods)* Does anybody else know that you opened it? Come, Leo, don't be afraid of speaking the truth to me.

LEO: No. Nobody knew. Nobody was in the bank when I did it. But—

OSCAR: Did your Uncle Horace ever know you opened it?

LEO: *(Shakes his head)* He only looks in it once every six months when he cuts the coupons, and sometimes Manders even does that for him. Uncle Horace don't even have the keys. Manders keeps them for him. Imagine not looking at all that. You can bet if I had the bonds, I'd watch 'em like—

OSCAR: If you had them. *(LEO watches him)* If you had them. Then you could have a share in the mill, you and me. A fine, big share, too. *(Pauses, shrugs)* Well, a man can't be shot for wanting to see his son get on in the world, can he, boy?

LEO: *(Looks up, begins to understand)* No, he can't. Natural enough. *(Laughs)* But I haven't got the bonds and Uncle Horace has. And now he can just sit back and wait to be a millionaire.

OSCAR: *(Innocently)* You think your Uncle Horace likes you well enough to lend you the bonds if he decides not to use them himself?

LEO: Papa, it must be that you haven't had your breakfast! *(Laughs loudly)* Lend me the bonds! My God—

OSCAR: *(Disappointed)* No, I suppose not. Just a fancy of mine. A loan for three months, maybe four, easy enough for us to pay it back then. Anyway, this is only April— *(Slowly counting the months on his fingers)* and if he doesn't look at them until Fall, he wouldn't even miss them out of the box.

LEO: That's it. He wouldn't even miss them. Ah, well—

OSCAR: No, sir. Wouldn't even miss them. How could he miss them if he never looks at them? *(Sighs as LEO stares at him)* Well, here we are sitting around waiting for him to come home and invest his money in something he hasn't lifted his hand to get. But I can't help thinking he's acting strange. You laugh when I say he could lend you the bonds if he's not going to use them himself. But would it hurt him?

LEO: *(Slowly looking at* OSCAR*)* No. No, it wouldn't.

OSCAR: People ought to help other people. But that's not always the way it happens. *(*BEN *enters, hangs his coat and hat in hall. Very carefully)* And so sometimes you got to think of yourself. *(As* LEO *stares at him,* BEN *appears in the doorway)* Morning, Ben.

BEN: *(Coming in, carrying his newspaper)* Fine sunny morning. Any news from the runaways?

REGINA: *(On the staircase)* There's no news or you would have heard it. Quite a convention so early in the morning, aren't you all? *(Goes to coffee urn.)*

OSCAR: You rising mighty late these days. Is that the way they do things in Chicago society?

BEN: *(Looking at his paper)* Old Carter died up in Senateville. Eighty-one is a good time for us all, eh? What do you think has really happened to Horace, Regina?

REGINA: Nothing.

BEN: *(Too casually)* You don't think maybe he never started from Baltimore and never intends to start?

REGINA: *(Irritated)* Of course they've started. Didn't I have a letter from Alexandra? What is so strange about people arriving late? He has that cousin in Savannah he's so fond of. He may have stopped to see him. They'll be along today some time, very flattered that you and Oscar are so worried about them.

BEN: I'm a natural worrier. Especially when I am getting ready to close a business deal and one of my partners remains silent *and* invisible.

REGINA: *(Laughs)* Oh, is that it? I thought you were worried about Horace's health.

OSCAR: Oh, that too. Who could help but worry? I'm worried. This is the first day I haven't shot since my head cold.

REGINA: *(Starts toward dining room)* Then you haven't had your breakfast. Come along. *(*OSCAR *and* LEO *follow her.)*

BEN: Regina. *(She turns at dining-room door)* That cousin of Horace's has been dead for years and, in any case, the train does not go through Savannah.

REGINA: *(Laughs, continues into dining room, seats herself)* Did he die? You're always remembering about people dying. *(*BEN *rises)* Now I intend to eat my breakfast in peace, and read my newspaper.

BEN: *(Goes toward dining room as he talks)* This is second breakfast for me. My first was bad. Celia ain't the cook she used to be. Too old to have taste any more. If she hadn't belonged to Mama, I'd send her off to the country.

*(*OSCAR *and* LEO *start to eat.* BEN *seats himself.)*

LEO: Uncle Horace will have some tales to tell, I bet. Baltimore is a lively town.

REGINA: *(To* CAL*)* The grits isn't hot enough. Take it back.

CAL: Oh, yes'm. *(Calling into the kitchen as he exits)* Grits didn't hold the heat. Grits didn't hold the heat.

LEO: When I was at school three of the boys and myself took a train once and went over to Baltimore. It was so big we thought we were in Europe. I was just a kid then—

REGINA: I find it very pleasant *(*ADDIE *enters)* to have breakfast alone. I hate chattering before I've had something hot. *(*CAL *closes the dining-room doors)* Do be still, Leo.

*(*ADDIE *comes into the room, begins gathering up the cups, carries them to the large tray. Outside there are the sounds of voices. Quickly* ADDIE *runs into the hall. A few seconds later she appears again in the doorway, her arm around the shoulders of* HORACE GIDDENS, *supporting him.* HORACE *is a tall man of about forty-five. He has been good looking, but now his face is tired and ill. He walks stiffly, as if it were an enormous effort, and carefully, as if he were unsure of his balance.* ADDIE *takes off his overcoat and hangs it on the hall tree. She then helps him to a chair.)*

HORACE: How are you, Addie? How have you been?

ADDIE: I'm all right, Mr. Horace. I've just been worried about you.

*(*ALEXANDRA *enters. She is flushed and excited, her hat awry, her face dirty. Her arms are full of packages, but she comes quickly to* ADDIE.*)*

ALEXANDRA: Don't tell me how worried you were. We couldn't help it and there was no way to send a message.

ADDIE: (*Begins to take packages from* ALEX-ANDRA) Yes, sir, I was mighty worried.

ALEXANDRA: We had to stop in Mobile over night. Papa— (*Looks at him*) Papa didn't feel well. The trip was too much for him, and I made him stop and rest— (*As* ADDIE *takes the last package*) No, don't take that. That's father's medicine. I'll hold it. It mustn't break. Now, about the stuff outside. Papa must have his wheel chair. I'll get that and the valises—

ADDIE: (*Very happy, holding* ALEXANDRA's *arms*) Since when you got to carry your own valises? Since when I ain't old enough to hold a bottle of medicine? (HORACE *coughs*) You feel all right, Mr. Horace?

HORACE: (*Nods*) Glad to be sitting down.

ALEXANDRA: (*Opening package of medicine*) He doesn't feel all right. (ADDIE *looks at her, then at* HORACE) He just says that. The trip was very hard on him, and now he must go right to bed.

ADDIE: (*Looking at him carefully*) Them fancy doctors, they give you help?

HORACE: They did their best.

ALEXANDRA: (*Has become conscious of the voices in the dining room*) I bet Mama was worried. I better tell her we're here now. (*She starts for door.*)

HORACE: Zan. (*She stops*) Not for a minute, dear.

ALEXANDRA: Oh, Papa, you feel bad again. I knew you did. Do you want your medicine?

HORACE: No, I don't feel that way. I'm just tired, darling. Let me rest a little.

ALEXANDRA: Yes, but Mama will be mad if I don't tell her we're here.

ADDIE: They're all in there eating breakfast.

ALEXANDRA: Oh, are they all here? Why do they *always* have to be here? I was hoping Papa wouldn't have to see anybody, that it would be nice for him and quiet.

ADDIE: Then let your papa rest for a minute.

HORACE: Addie, I bet your coffee's as good as ever. They don't have such good coffee up north. (*Looks at the urn*) Is it as good, Addie? (ADDIE *starts for coffee urn.*)

ALEXANDRA: No. Dr. Reeves said not much coffee. Just now and then. I'm the nurse now, Addie.

ADDIE: You'd be a better one if you didn't look so dirty. Now go and take a bath. Change your linens, get out a fresh dress and give your hair a good brushing—go on—

ALEXANDRA: Will you be all right, Papa?

ADDIE: Go on.

ALEXANDRA: (*On stairs, talks as she goes up*) The pills Papa must take once every four hours. And the bottle only when—only if he feels very bad. Now don't move until I come back and don't talk much and remember about his medicine, Addie—

ADDIE: Ring for Belle and have her help you and then I'll make you a fresh breakfast.

ALEXANDRA: (*As she disappears*) How's Aunt Birdie? Is she here?

ADDIE: It ain't right for you to have coffee? It will hurt you?

HORACE: (*Slowly*) Nothing can make much difference now. Get me a cup, Addie. (*She looks at him, crosses to urn, pours a cup*) Funny. They can't make coffee up north. (ADDIE *brings him a cup*) They don't like red pepper, either. (*He takes the cup and gulps it greedily*) God, that's good. You remember how I used to drink it? Ten, twelve cups a day. So strong it had to stain the cup. (*Then slowly*) Addie, before I see anybody else, I want to know why Zan came to fetch me home. She's tried to tell me, but she doesn't seem to know herself.

ADDIE: (*Turns away*) I don't know. All I know is big things are going on. Everybody going to be high-tone rich. Big rich. You too. All because smoke's going to start out of a building that ain't even up yet.

HORACE: I've heard about it.

ADDIE: And, er— (*Hesitates—steps to him*) And—well, Zan, she going to marry Mr. Leo in a little while.

HORACE: (*Looks at her, then very slowly*). What are you talking about?

ADDIE: That's right. That's the talk, God help us.

HORACE: (*Angrily*) What's the talk?

ADDIE: I'm telling you. There's going to be a wedding— (*Angrily turns away*) Over my dead body there is.

HORACE: (*After a second, quietly*) Go and tell them I'm home.

ADDIE: (*Hesitates*) Now you ain't to get excited. You're to be in your bed—

HORACE: Go on, Addie. Go and say I'm back. (ADDIE *opens dining-room doors. He rises with dif-*

ficulty, stands stiff, as if he were in pain, facing the dining room.)

ADDIE: Miss Regina. They're home. They got here —

REGINA: Horace! (REGINA *quickly, rises, runs into the room. Warmly)* Horace! You've finally arrived. *(As she kisses him, the others come forward, all talking together.)*

BEN: *(In doorway, carrying a napkin)* Well, sir, you had us all mighty worried. *(He steps forward. They shake hands.* ADDIE *exits.)*

OSCAR: You're a sight for sore eyes.

HORACE: Hello, Ben.

*(*LEO *enters, eating a biscuit.)*

OSCAR: And how you feel? Tip-top, I bet, because that's the way you're looking.

HORACE: *(Coldly, irritated with* OSCAR's *lie)* Hello, Oscar. Hello, Leo, how are you?

LEO: *(Shaking hands)* I'm fine, sir. But a lot better now that you're back.

REGINA: Now sit down. What did happen to you and where's Alexandra? I am so excited about seeing you that I almost forgot about her.

HORACE: I didn't feel good, a little weak, I guess, and we stopped over night to rest. Zan's upstairs washing off the train dirt.

REGINA: Oh, I am so sorry the trip was hard on you. I didn't think that —

HORACE: Well, it's just as if I had never been away. All of you here —

BEN: Waiting to welcome you home.

*(*BIRDIE *bursts in. She is wearing a flannel kimono and her face is flushed and excited.)*

BIRDIE: *(Runs to him, kisses him)* Horace!

HORACE: *(Warmly pressing her arm).* I was just wondering where you were, Birdie.

BIRDIE: *(Excited)* Oh, I would have been here. I didn't know you were back until Simon said he saw the buggy. *(She draws back to look at him. Her face sobers)* Oh, you don't look well, Horace. No, you don't.

REGINA: *(Laughs)* Birdie, what a thing to say —

HORACE: *(Looking at* OSCAR*)* Oscar thinks I look very well.

OSCAR: *(Annoyed. Turns on* LEO*)* Don't stand there holding that biscuit in your hand.

LEO: Oh, well. I'll just finish my breakfast, Uncle Horace, and then I'll give you all the news about the bank — *(He exits into the dining room.)*

OSCAR: And what is that costume you have on?

BIRDIE: *(Looking at* HORACE*)* Now that you're home, you'll feel better. Plenty of good rest and we'll take such fine care of you. *(Stops)* But where is Zan? I missed her so much.

OSCAR: I asked you what is that strange costume you're parading around in?

BIRDIE: *(Nervously, backing toward stairs)* Me? Oh! It's my wrapper. I was so excited about Horace I just rushed out of the house —

OSCAR: Did you come across the square dressed that way? My dear Birdie, I —

HORACE: *(To* REGINA *wearily)* Yes, it's just like old times.

REGINA: *(Quickly to* OSCAR*)* Now, no fights. This is a holiday.

BIRDIE: *(Runs quickly up the stairs)* Zan! Zannie!

OSCAR: Birdie! *(She stops.)*

BIRDIE: Oh. Tell Zan I'll be back in a little while. *(Whispers)* Sorry, Oscar. *(Exits.)*

REGINA: *(To* OSCAR *and* BEN*)* Why don't you go finish your breakfast and let Horace rest for a minute?

BEN: *(Crossing to dining room with* OSCAR*)* Never leave a meal unfinished. There are too many poor people who need the food. Mighty glad to see you home, Horace. Fine to have you back. Fine to have you back.

OSCAR: *(To* LEO *as* BEN *closes dining-room doors)* Your mother has gone crazy. Running around the streets like a woman —

(The moment REGINA *and* HORACE *are alone, they become awkward and self-conscious.)*

REGINA: *(Laughs awkwardly)* Well. Here we are. It's been a long time. (HORACE *smiles)* Five months. You know, Horace, I wanted to come and be with you in the hospital, but I didn't know where my duty was. Here, or with you. But you know how much I *wanted* to come.

HORACE: That's kind of you, Regina. There was no need to come.

REGINA: Oh, but there was. Five months lying there all by yourself, no kinfolks, no friends. Don't try to tell me you didn't have a bad time of it.

HORACE: I didn't have a bad time. *(As she shakes her head, he becomes insistent)* No, I didn't, Regina. Oh, at first when I — when I heard the news about myself — but after I got used to that, I liked it there.

REGINA: You *liked* it? *(Coldly)* Isn't that strange. You liked it so well you didn't want to come home?

HORACE: That's not the way to put it. *(Then, kindly, as he sees her turn her head away)* But there I was and I got kind of used to it, kind of to like lying there and thinking. *(Smiles)* I never had much time to think before. And time's become valuable to me.

REGINA: It sounds almost like a holiday.

HORACE: *(Laughs)* It was, sort of. The first holiday I've had since I was a little kid.

REGINA: And here I was thinking you were in pain and —

HORACE: *(Quietly)* I was in pain.

REGINA: And instead you were having a holiday! A holiday of thinking. Couldn't you have done that here?

HORACE: I wanted to do it before I came here. I was thinking about us.

REGINA: About us? About you and me? Thinking about you and me after all these years. *(Unpleasantly)* You shall tell me everything you thought — some day.

HORACE: *(There is silence for a minute)* Regina. *(She turns to him)* Why did you send Zan to Baltimore?

REGINA: Why? Because I wanted you home. You can't make anything suspicious out of that, can you?

HORACE: I didn't mean to make anything suspicious about it. *(Hesitantly, taking her hand)* Zan said you wanted me to come home. I was so pleased at that and touched, it made me feel good.

REGINA: *(Taking away her hand, turns)* Touched that I should want you home?

HORACE: *(Sighs)* I'm saying all the wrong things as usual. Let's try to get along better. There isn't so much more time. Regina, what's all this crazy talk I've been hearing about Zan and Leo? Zan and Leo marrying?

REGINA: *(Turning to him, sharply)* Who gossips so much around here?

HORACE: *(Shocked)* Regina!

REGINA: *(Annoyed, anxious to quiet him)*

It's some foolishness that Oscar thought up. I'll explain later. I have no intention of allowing any such arrangement. It was simply a way of keeping Oscar quiet in all this business I've been writing you about —

HORACE: *(Carefully)* What has Zan to do with any business of Oscar's? Whatever it is, you had better put it out of Oscar's head immediately. You know what I think of Leo.

REGINA: But there's no need to talk about it now.

HORACE: There is no need to talk about it ever. Not as long as I live. *(HORACE stops, slowly turns to look at her)* As long as I live. I've been in a hospital for five months. Yet since I've been here you have not once asked me about — about my health. *(Then gently)* Well, I suppose they've written you. I can't live very long.

REGINA: *(Coldly)* I've never understood why people have to talk about this kind of thing.

HORACE: *(There is a silence. Then he looks up at her, his face cold)* You misunderstand. I don't intend to gossip about my sickness. I thought it was only fair to tell you. I was not asking for your sympathy.

REGINA: *(Sharply, turns to him)* What do the doctors think caused your bad heart?

HORACE: What do you mean?

REGINA: They didn't think it possible, did they, that your fancy women may have —

HORACE: *(Smiles unpleasantly)* Caused my heart to be bad? I don't think that's the best scientific theory. You don't catch heart trouble in bed.

REGINA: *(Angrily)* I didn't think you did. I only thought you might catch a bad conscience — in bed, as you say.

HORACE: I didn't tell them about my bad conscience. Or about my fancy women. Nor did I tell them that my wife has not wanted me in bed with her for — *(Sharply)* How long is it, Regina? (REGINA *turns to him*) Ten years? Did you bring me home for this, to make me feel guilty again? That means you want something. But you'll not make me feel guilty any more. My "thinking" has made a difference.

REGINA: I see that it has. *(She looks toward dining-room door. Then comes to him, her manner warm and friendly)* It's foolish for us to fight this way. I didn't mean to be unpleasant. I was stupid.

HORACE: *(Wearily)* God knows I didn't

either. I came home wanting so much not to fight, and then all of a sudden there we were. I got hurt and—

REGINA: *(Hastily)* It's all my fault. I didn't ask about—about your illness because I didn't want to remind you of it. Anyway, I never believe doctors when they talk about— *(Brightly)* when they talk like that.

HORACE: *(Not looking at her)* Well, we'll try our best with each other. *(He rises.)*

REGINA: *(Quickly)* I'll try. Honestly, I will. Horace, Horace, I know you're tired but, but— couldn't you stay down here a few minutes longer? I want Ben to tell you something.

HORACE: Tomorrow.

REGINA: I'd like to now. It's very important to me. It's very important to all of us. *(Gaily, as she moves toward dining room)* Important to your beloved daughter. She'll be a very great heiress—

HORACE: Will she? That's nice.

REGINA: *(Opens doors)* Ben, are you finished breakfast?

HORACE: Is this the mill business I've had so many letters about?

REGINA: *(To* BEN *)* Horace would like to talk to you now.

HORACE: Horace would not like to talk to you now. I am very tired, Regina—

REGINA: *(Comes to him)* Please. You've said we'll try our best with each other. I'll try. Really, I will. Please do this for me now. You will see what I've done while you've been away. How I watched your interests. *(Laughs gaily)* And I've done very well too. But things can't be delayed any longer. Everything must be settled this week— *(*HORACE *sits down.* BEN *enters.* OSCAR *has stayed in the dining room, his head turned to watch them.* LEO *is pretending to read the newspaper)* Now you must tell Horace all about it. Only be quick because he is very tired and must go to bed. *(*HORACE *is looking up at her. His face hardens as she speaks)* But I think your news will be better for him than all the medicine in the world.

BEN: *(Looking at* HORACE*)* It could wait. Horace may not feel like talking today.

REGINA: What an old faker you are! You know it can't wait. You know it must be finished this week. You've been just as anxious for Horace to get here as I've been.

BEN: *(Very jovial)* I suppose I have been. And

why not? Horace has done Hubbard Sons many a good turn. Why shouldn't I be anxious to help him now?

REGINA: *(Laughs)* Help him! Help him when you need him, that's what you mean.

BEN: What a woman you married, Horace. *(Laughs awkwardly when* HORACE *does not answer)* Well, then I'll make it quick. You know what I've been telling you for years. How I've always said that every one of us little Southern businessmen had great things— *(Extends his arm)*—right beyond our finger tips. It's been my dream: my dream to make those fingers grow longer. I'm a lucky man, Horace, a lucky man. To dream and to live to get what you've dreamed of. That's *my* idea of a lucky man. *(Looks at his fingers as his arm drops slowly)* For thirty years I've cried bring the cotton mills to the cotton. *(*HORACE *opens medicine bottle)* Well, finally I got up nerve to go to Marshall Company in Chicago.

HORACE: I know all this.

(He takes the medicine. REGINA *rises, steps to him.)*

BEN: Can I get you something?

HORACE: Some water, please.

REGINA: *(Turns quickly)* Oh, I'm sorry. Let me. *(Brings him a glass of water. He drinks as they wait in silence)* You feel all right now?

HORACE: Yes. You wrote me. I know all that.

*(*OSCAR *enters from dining room.)*

REGINA: *(Triumphantly)* But you don't know that in the last few days Ben has agreed to give us—you, I mean—a much larger share.

HORACE: Really? That's very generous of him.

BEN: *(Laughs)* It wasn't so generous of me. It was smart of Regina.

REGINA: *(As if she were signaling* HORACE*)* I explained to Ben that perhaps you hadn't answered his letters because you didn't think he was offering you enough, and that the time was getting short and you could guess how much he needed you—

HORACE: *(Smiles at her, nods)* And I could guess that he wants to keep control in the family.

REGINA: *(To* BEN, *triumphantly)* Exactly. *(To* HORACE*)* So I did a little bargaining for you and convinced my brothers they weren't the only Hubbards who had a business sense.

HORACE: Did you have to convince them of that? How little people know about each other! *(Laughs)* But you'll know better about Regina next time, eh, Ben? (BEN, REGINA, HORACE *laugh together.* OSCAR's *face is angry)* Now let's see. We're getting a bigger share. *(Looking at* OSCAR*)* Who's getting less?

BEN: Oscar.

HORACE: Well, Oscar, you've grown very unselfish. What's happened to you?

*(*LEO *enters from dining room.)*

BEN: *(Quickly, before* OSCAR *can answer)* Oscar doesn't mind. Not worth fighting about now, eh, Oscar?

OSCAR: *(Angrily)* I'll get mine in the end. You can be sure of that. I've got my son's future to think about.

HORACE: *(Sharply)* Leo? Oh, I see. *(Puts his head back, laughs.* REGINA *looks at him nervously)* I am beginning to see. Everybody will get theirs.

BEN: I knew you'd see it. Seventy-five thousand, and that seventy-five thousand will make you a million.

REGINA: *(Steps to table, leaning forward)* It will, Horace, it will.

HORACE: I believe you. *(After a second)* Now I can understand Oscar's self-sacrifice, but what did you have to promise Marshall Company besides the money you're putting up?

BEN: They wouldn't take promises. They wanted guarantees.

HORACE: Of what?

BEN: *(Nods)* Water power. Free and plenty of it.

HORACE: You got them that, of course.

BEN: Cheap. You'd think the Governor of a great state would make his price a little higher. From pride, you know. (HORACE *smiles.* BEN *smiles)* Cheap wages. "What do you mean by cheap wages?" I say to Marshall. "Less than Massachusetts," he says to me, "and that averages eight a week." "Eight a week! By God," I tell him, "I'd work for eight a week myself." Why, there ain't a mountain white or a town nigger but wouldn't give his right arm for three silver dollars every week, eh, Horace?

HORACE: Sure. And they'll take less than that when you get around to playing them off against each other. You can save a little money that way,

Ben. *(Angrily)* And make them hate each other just a little more than they do now.

REGINA: What's all this about?

BEN: *(Laughs)* There'll be no trouble from anybody, white or black. Marshall said that to me. "What about strikes? That's all we've had in Massachusetts for the last three years." I say to him. "What's a strike? I never heard of one. Come South, Marshall. We got good folks and we don't stand for any fancy fooling."

HORACE: You're right. *(Slowly)* Well, it looks like you made a good deal for yourselves, and for Marshall, too. *(To* BEN*)* Your father used to say he made the thousands and you boys would make the millions. I think he was right. *(Rises.)*

REGINA: *(They are all looking at* HORACE. *She laughs nervously)* Millions for us, too.

HORACE: Us? You and me? I don't think so. We've got enough money, Regina. We'll just sit by and watch the boys grow rich. *(They watch* HORACE *tensely as he begins to move toward the staircase. He passes* LEO, *looks at him for a second)* How's everything at the bank, Leo?

LEO: Fine, sir. Everything is fine.

HORACE: How are all the ladies in Mobile? (HORACE *turns to* REGINA, *sharply)* Whatever made you think I'd let Zan marry —

REGINA: Do you mean that you are turning this down? Is it possible that's what you mean?

BEN: No, that's not what he means. Turning down a fortune. Horace is tired. He'd rather talk about it tomorrow —

REGINA: We can't keep putting it off this way. Oscar must be in Chicago by the end of the week with the money and contracts.

OSCAR: *(Giggles, pleased)* Yes, sir. Got to be there end of the week. No sense going without the money.

REGINA: *(Tensely)* I've waited long enough for your answer. I'm not going to wait any longer.

HORACE: *(Very deliberately)* I'm very tired now, Regina.

BEN: *(Hastily)* Now, Horace probably has his reasons. Things he'd like explained. Tomorrow will do. I can —

REGINA: *(Turns to* BEN, *sharply)* I want to know his reasons now! *(Turns back to* HORACE.*)*

HORACE: *(As he climbs the steps)* I don't know them all myself. Let's leave it at that.

REGINA: We shall not leave it at that! We

have waited for you here like children. Waited for you to come home.

HORACE: So that you could invest my money. So that is why you wanted me home? Well, I had hoped— *(Quietly)* If you are disappointed, Regina, I'm sorry. But I must do what I think best. We'll talk about it another day.

REGINA: We'll talk about it now. Just you and me.

HORACE: *(Looks down at her. His voice is tense)* Please, Regina, it's been a hard trip. I don't feel well. Please leave me alone now.

REGINA: *(Quietly)* I want to talk to you, Horace. I'm coming up. *(He looks at her for a minute, then moves on again out of sight. She begins to climb the stairs.)*

BEN: *(Softly.* REGINA *turns to him as he speaks)* Sometimes it is better to wait for the sun to rise again. *(She does not answer)* And sometimes, as our mother used to tell you, *(*REGINA *starts up stairs)* it's unwise for a good-looking woman to frown. *(*BEN *rises, moves toward stairs)* Softness and a smile do more to the heart of men—

(She disappears. BEN *stands looking up the stairs. There is a long silence. Then, suddenly,* OSCAR *giggles.)*

OSCAR: Let us hope she'll change his mind. Let us hope.

(After a second BEN *crosses to table, picks up his newspaper.* OSCAR *looks at* BEN. *The silence makes* LEO *uncomfortable.)*

LEO: The paper says twenty-seven cases of yellow fever in New Orleans. Guess the flood-waters caused it. *(Nobody pays attention)* Thought they were building the levees high enough. Like the niggers always say: a man born of woman can't build nothing high enough for the Mississippi. *(Gets no answer. Gives an embarrassed laugh.)*

(Upstairs there is the sound of voices. The voices are not loud, but BEN, OSCAR, LEO *become conscious of them.* LEO *crosses to landing, looks up, listens.)*

OSCAR: *(Pointing up)* Now just suppose she don't change his mind? Just suppose he keeps on refusing?

BEN: *(Without conviction)* He's tired. It was a mistake to talk to him today. He's a sick man, but he isn't a crazy one.

OSCAR: *(Giggles)* But just suppose he is crazy. What then?

BEN: *(Puts down his paper, peers at* OSCAR*)* Then we'll go outside for the money. There's plenty who would give it.

OSCAR: And plenty who will want a lot for what they give. The ones who are rich enough to give will be smart enough to want. That means we'd be working for them, don't it, Ben?

BEN: You don't have to tell me the things I told you six months ago.

OSCAR: Oh, you're right not to worry. She'll change his mind. She always has. *(There is a silence. Suddenly* REGINA'S *voice becomes louder and sharper. All of them begin to listen now. Slowly* BEN *rises, goes to listen by the staircase.* OSCAR, *watching him, smiles. As they listen* REGINA'S *voice becomes very loud.* HORACE'S *voice is no longer heard)* Maybe. But I don't believe it. I never did believe he was going in with us.

BEN: *(Turning on him)* What the hell do you expect me to do?

OSCAR: *(Mildly)* Nothing. You done your almighty best. Nobody could blame you if the whole thing just dripped away right through our fingers. You can't do a thing. But there may be something I could do for us. *(*OSCAR *rises)* Or, I might better say, Leo could do for us. *(*BEN *stops, turns, looks at* OSCAR. LEO *is staring at* OSCAR*)* Ain't that true, son? Ain't it true you might be able to help your own kinfolks?

LEO: *(Nervously taking a step to him)* Papa, I—

BEN: *(Slowly)* How would he help us, Oscar?

OSCAR: Leo's got a friend. Leo's friend owns eighty-eight thousand dollars in Union Pacific bonds. *(*BEN *turns to look at* LEO*)* Leo's friend don't look at the bonds much—not for five or six months at a time.

BEN: *(After a pause)* Union Pacific. Uh, huh. Let me understand. Leo's friend would—would lend him these bonds and he—

OSCAR: *(Nods)* Would be kind enough to lend them to us.

BEN: Leo.

LEO: *(Excited, comes to him)* Yes, sir?

BEN: When would your friend be wanting the bonds back?

LEO: *(Very nervous)* I don't know. I—well, I—

OSCAR: *(Sharply. Steps to him)* You told me he won't look at them until Fall—

LEO: Oh, that's right. But I—not till Fall. Uncle Horace never—

BEN: *(Sharply)* Be still.

OSCAR: *(Smiles at LEO)* Your uncle doesn't wish to know your friend's name.

LEO: *(Starts to laugh)* That's a good one. Not know his name—

OSCAR: Shut up, Leo! *(LEO turns away slowly, moves to table. BEN turns to OSCAR)* He won't look at them again until September. That gives us five months. Leo will return the bonds in three months. And we'll have no trouble raising the money once the mills are going up. Will Marshall accept bonds?

(BEN stops to listen to sudden sharp voices from above. The voices are now very angry and very loud.)

BEN: *(Smiling)* Why not? Why not? *(Laughs)* Good. We are lucky. We'll take the loan from Leo's friend—I think he will make a safer partner than our sister. *(Nods toward stairs. Turns to LEO)* How soon can you get them?

LEO: Today. Right now. They're in the safe-deposit box and—

BEN: *(Sharply)* I don't want to know where they are.

OSCAR: *(Laughs)* We will keep it secret from you. *(Pats BEN's arm.)*

BEN: *(Smiles)* Good. Draw a check for our part. You can take the night train for Chicago. Well, Oscar *(Holds out his hand)* good luck to us.

OSCAR: Leo will be taken care of?

LEO: I'm entitled to Uncle Horace's share. I'd enjoy being a partner—

BEN: *(Turns to stare at him)* You would? You can go to hell, you little— *(Starts toward LEO.)*

OSCAR: *(Nervously)* Now, now. He didn't mean that. I only want to be sure he'll get something out of all this.

BEN: Of course. We'll take care of him. We won't have any trouble about that. I'll see you at the store.

OSCAR: *(Nods)* That's settled then. Come on, son. *(Starts for door.)*

LEO: *(Puts out his hand)* I was only going to say what a great day this was for me and— *(BEN ignores his hand.)*

BEN: Go on.

(LEO looks at him, turns, follows OSCAR out. BEN stands where he is, thinking. Again the voices upstairs can be heard. REGINA's voice is high and furious. BEN looks up, smiles, winces at the noise.)

ALEXANDRA: *(Upstairs)* Mama—Mama—don't . . . *(The noise of running footsteps is heard and ALEXANDRA comes running down the steps, speaking as she comes)* Uncle Ben! Uncle Ben! Please go up. Please make Mama stop. Uncle Ben, he's sick, he's so sick. How can Mama talk to him like that—please, make her stop. She'll—

BEN: Alexandra, you have a tender heart.

ALEXANDRA: *(Crying)* Go on up, Uncle Ben, please—

(Suddenly the voices stop. A second later there is the sound of a door being slammed.)

BEN: Now you see. Everything is over. Don't worry. *(He starts for the door)* Alexandra, I want you to tell your mother how sorry I am that I had to leave. And don't worry so, my dear. Married folk frequently raise their voices, unfortunately. *(He starts to put on his hat and coat as REGINA appears on the stairs.)*

ALEXANDRA: *(Furiously)* How can you treat Papa like this? He's sick. He's very sick. Don't you know that? I won't let you.

REGINA: Mind your business, Alexandra. *(To BEN. Her voice is cold and calm)* How much longer can you wait for the money?

BEN: *(Putting on his coat)* He has refused? My, that's too bad.

REGINA: He will change his mind. I'll find a way to make him. What's the longest you can wait now?

BEN: I could wait until next week. But I can't wait until next week. *(He giggles, pleased at the joke)* I could but I can't. Could and can't. Well, I must go now. I'm very late—

REGINA: *(Coming downstairs toward him)* You're not going. I want to talk to you.

BEN: I was about to give Alexandra a message for you. I wanted to tell you that Oscar is going to Chicago tonight, so we can't be here for our usual Friday supper.

REGINA: *(Tensely)*. Oscar is going to Chi— *(Softly)* What do you mean?

BEN: Just that. Everything is settled. He's going on to deliver to Marshall—

REGINA: *(Taking a step to him)* I demand to know what— You are lying. You are trying to scare me. *You haven't got the money.* How could you have it? You can't have— *(BEN laughs)* You will wait until I—

(HORACE comes into view on the landing.)

BEN: You are getting out of hand. Since when do I take orders from you?

REGINA: Wait, you— *(BEN stops)* How *can* he go to Chicago? Did a ghost arrive with the money? *(BEN starts for the hall)* I don't believe you. Come back here. *(REGINA starts after him)* Come back here, you—

(The door slams. She stops in the doorway, staring, her fists clenched. After a pause she turns slowly.)

HORACE: *(Very quietly)* It's a great day when you and Ben cross swords. I've been waiting for it for years.

ALEXANDRA: Papa, Papa, please go back! You will—

HORACE: And so they don't need you, and so you will not have your millions, after all.

REGINA: *(Turns slowly)* You hate to see any-body live now, don't you? You hate to think that I'm going to be alive and have what I want.

HORACE: I should have known you'd think that was the reason.

REGINA: Because you're going to die and you know you're going to die.

ALEXANDRA: *(Shrilly)* Mama! Don't— Don't listen, Papa. Just don't listen. Go away—

HORACE: Not to keep you from getting what you want. Not even partly that. *(Holding to the rail)* I'm sick of you, sick of this house, sick of my life here. I'm sick of your brothers and their dirty tricks to make a dime. There must be better ways of getting rich than cheating niggers on a pound of bacon. Why should I give you the money? *(Very angrily)* To pound the bones of this town to make dividends for you to spend? You wreck the town, you and your brothers, *you* wreck the town and live on it. Not me. Maybe it's easy for the dying to be honest. But it's not my fault I'm dying. *(ADDIE enters, stands at door quietly)* I'll do no more harm now. I've done enough. I'll die my own way. And I'll do it without making the world any worse. I leave that to you.

REGINA: *(Looks up at him slowly, calmly)* I hope you die. I hope you die soon. *(Smiles)* I'll be waiting for you to die.

ALEXANDRA: *(Shrieking)* Papa! Don't— Don't listen— Don't—

ADDIE: Come here, Zan. Come out of this room.

(ALEXANDRA runs quickly to ADDIE, who holds her. HORACE turns slowly and starts upstairs.)

CURTAIN

ACT THREE

SCENE:

Same as Act One. Two weeks later. It is late afternoon and it is raining.

(At Rise: HORACE is sitting near the window in a wheel chair. On the table next to him is a safe-deposit box, and a small bottle of medicine. BIRDIE and ALEXANDRA are playing the piano. On a chair is a large sewing basket.)

BIRDIE: *(Counting for ALEXANDRA)* One and two and three and four. One and two and three and four. *(Nods—turns to HORACE)* We once played together, Horace. Remember?

HORACE: *(Has been looking out of the window)* What, Birdie?

BIRDIE: We played together. You and me.

ALEXANDRA: *Papa* used to play?

BIRDIE: Indeed he did. *(ADDIE appears at the door in a large kitchen apron. She is wiping her hands on a towel)* He played the fiddle and very well, too.

ALEXANDRA: *(Turns to smile at HORACE)* I never knew—

ADDIE: Where's your mama?

ALEXANDRA: Gone to Miss Safronia's to fit her dresses.

(ADDIE *nods, starts to exit.*)

HORACE: Addie.

ADDIE: Yes, Mr. Horace.

HORACE: *(Speaks as if he had made a sudden decision)* Tell Cal to get on his things. I want him to go an errand.

(ADDIE *nods, exits.* HORACE *moves nervously in his chair, looks out of the window.*)

ALEXANDRA: *(Who has been watching him)* It's too bad it's been raining all day, Papa. But you can go out in the yard tomorrow. Don't be restless.

HORACE: I'm not restless, darling.

BIRDIE: I remember so well the time we played together, your papa and me. It was the first time Oscar brought me here to supper. I had never seen all the Hubbards together before, and you know what a ninny I am and how shy. *(Turns to look at* HORACE*)* You said you could play the fiddle and you'd be much obliged if I'd play with you. *I* was obliged to *you*, all right, all right. *(Laughs when he does not answer her)* Horace, you haven't heard a word I've said.

HORACE: Birdie, when did Oscar get back from Chicago?

BIRDIE: Yesterday. Hasn't he been here yet?

ALEXANDRA: *(Stops playing)* No. Neither has Uncle Ben since — since that day.

BIRDIE: Oh, I didn't know it was *that* bad. Oscar never tells me anything —

HORACE: *(Smiles, nods)* The Hubbards have had their great quarrel. I knew it would come some day. *(Laughs)* It came.

ALEXANDRA: It came. It certainly came all right.

BIRDIE: *(Amazed)* But Oscar was in such a good humor when he got home, I didn't —

HORACE: Yes, I can understand that.

(ADDIE *enters carrying a large tray with glasses, a carafe of elderberry wine and a plate of cookies, which she puts on the table.*)

ALEXANDRA: Addie! A party! What for?

ADDIE: Nothing for. I had the fresh butter, so I made the cakes, and a little elderberry does the stomach good in the rain.

BIRDIE: Isn't this nice! A party just for us. Let's play party music, Zan.

(ALEXANDRA *begins to play a gay piece.*)

ADDIE: *(To* HORACE, *wheeling his chair to center)* Come over here, Mr. Horace, and don't be thinking so much. A glass of elderberry will do more good.

(ALEXANDRA *reaches for a cake.* BIRDIE *pours herself a glass of wine.*)

ALEXANDRA: Good cakes, Addie. It's nice here. Just us. Be nice if it could always be this way.

BIRDIE: *(Nods happily)* Quiet and restful.

ADDIE: Well, it won't be that way long. Little while now, even sitting here, you'll hear the red bricks going into place. The next day the smoke'll be pushing out the chimneys and by church time that Sunday every human born of woman will be living on chicken. That's how Mr. Ben's been telling the story.

HORACE: *(Looks at her)* They believe it that way?

ADDIE: Believe it? They use to believing what Mr. Ben orders. There ain't been so much talk around here since Sherman's army didn't come near.

HORACE: *(Softly)* They are fools.

ADDIE: *(Nods, sits down with the sewing basket)* You ain't born in the South unless you're a fool.

BIRDIE: *(Has drunk another glass of wine)* But we didn't play together after that night. Oscar said he didn't like me to play on the piano. *(Turns to* ALEXANDRA*)* You know what he said that night?

ALEXANDRA: Who?

BIRDIE: Oscar. He said that music made him nervous. He said he just sat and waited for the next note. (ALEXANDRA *laughs)* He wasn't poking fun. He meant it. Ah, well — *(She finishes her glass, shakes her head.* HORACE *looks at her, smiles)* Your papa don't like to admit it, but he's been mighty kind to me all these years. *(Running the back of her hand along his sleeve)* Often he'd step in when somebody said something and once — *(She stops, turns away, her face still)* Once he stopped Oscar from — *(She stops, turns. Quickly)* I'm sorry I said that. Why, here I am so happy and yet I think about bad things. *(Laughs nervously)* That's not right, now, is it?

(She pours a drink. CAL *appears in the door. He has on an old coat and is carrying a torn umbrella.)*

ALEXANDRA: Have a cake, Cal.

CAL: *(Comes in, takes a cake)* Yes'm. You want me, Mr. Horace?

HORACE: What time is it, Cal?

CAL: 'Bout ten minutes before it's five.

HORACE: All right. Now you walk yourself down to the bank.

CAL: It'll be closed. Nobody'll be there but Mr. Manders, Mr. Joe Horns, Mr. Leo—

HORACE: Go in the back way. They'll be at the table, going over the day's business. *(Points to the deposit box)* See that box?

CAL: *(Nods)* Yes, sir.

HORACE: You tell Mr. Manders that Mr. Horace says he's much obliged to him for bringing the box, it arrived all right.

CAL: *(Bewildered)* He know you got the box. He bring it himself Wednesday. I opened the door to him and he say, "Hello, Cal, coming on to summer weather."

HORACE: You say just what I tell you. Understand?

*(*BIRDIE *pours another drink, stands at table.)*

CAL: No, sir. I ain't going to say I understand. I'm going down and tell a man he give you something he already know he give you, and you say "understand."

HORACE: Now, Cal.

CAL: Yes, sir. I just going to say you obliged for the box coming all right. I ain't going to understand it, but I'm going to say it.

HORACE: And tell him I want him to come over here after supper, and to bring Mr. Sol Fowler with him.

CAL: *(Nods)* He's to come after supper and bring Mr. Sol Fowler, your attorney-*at*-law, with him.

HORACE: *(Smiles)* That's right. Just walk right in the back room and say your piece. *(Slowly)* In front of everybody.

CAL: Yes, sir. *(Mumbles to himself as he exits.)*

ALEXANDRA: *(Who has been watching* HORACE*)* Is anything the matter, Papa?

HORACE: Oh, no. Nothing.

ADDIE: Miss Birdie, that elderberry going to give you a headache spell.

BIRDIE: *(Beginning to be drunk. Gaily)* Oh, I don't think so. I don't think it will.

ALEXANDRA: *(As* HORACE *puts his hand to his throat)* Do you want your medicine, Papa?

HORACE: No, no. I'm all right, darling.

BIRDIE: Mama used to give me elderberry wine when I was a little girl. For hiccoughs. *(Laughs)* You know, I don't think people get hiccoughs any more. Isn't that funny? *(*BIRDIE *laughs.* HORACE *and* ALEXANDRA *laugh)* I used to get hiccoughs just when I shouldn't have.

ADDIE: *(Nods)* And nobody gets growing pains no more. That is funny. Just as if there was some style in what you get. One year an ailment's stylish and the next year it ain't.

BIRDIE: *(Turns)* I remember. It was my first big party, at Lionnet I mean, and I was so excited, and there I was with hiccoughs and Mama laughing. *(Softly. Looking at carafe)* Mama always laughed. *(Picks up carafe)* A big party, a lovely dress from Mr. Worth in Paris, France, and hiccoughs. *(Pours drink)* My brother pounding me on the back and Mama with the elderberry bottle, laughing at me. Everybody was on their way to come, and I was such a ninny, hiccoughing away. *(Drinks)* You know, that was the first day I ever saw Oscar Hubbard. The Ballongs were selling their horses and he was going there to buy. He passed and lifted his hat—we could see him from the window—and my brother, to tease Mama, said maybe we should have invited the Hubbards to the party. He said Mama didn't like them because they kept a store, and he said that was old-fashioned of her. *(Her face lights up)* And then, and *then*, I saw Mama angry for the first time in my life. She said that wasn't the reason. She said she was old-fashioned, but not that way. She said she was old-fashioned enough not to like people who killed animals they couldn't use, and who made their money charging awful interest to poor, ignorant niggers and cheating them on what they bought. She was very angry, Mama was. I had never seen her face like that. And then suddenly she laughed and said, "Look, I've frightened Birdie out of the hiccoughs." *(Her head drops. Then softly)* And so she had. They were all gone. *(Moves to sofa, sits.)*

ADDIE: Yeah, they got mighty well off cheating niggers. Well, there are people who eat the earth and eat all the people on it like in the Bible with the locusts. Then there are people who stand around and watch them eat it. *(Softly)* Sometimes I think it ain't right to stand and watch them do it.

BIRDIE: *(Thoughtfully)* Like I say, if we could only go back to Lionnet. Everybody'd be better there. They'd be good and kind. I like people to be kind. *(Pours drink)* Don't you, Horace; don't you like people to be kind?

HORACE: Yes, Birdie.

BIRDIE: *(Very drunk now)* Yes, that was the first day I ever saw Oscar. Who would have thought— *(Quickly)* You all want to know something? Well, I don't like Leo. My very own son, and I don't like him. *(Laughs, gaily)* My, I guess I even like Oscar more.

ALEXANDRA: Why did you marry Uncle Oscar?

ADDIE: *(Sharply)* That's no question for you to be asking.

HORACE: *(Sharply)* Why not? She's heard enough around here to ask anything.

ALEXANDRA: Aunt Birdie, why did you marry Uncle Oscar?

BIRDIE: I don't know. I thought I liked him. He was kind to me and I thought it was because he liked me too. But that wasn't the reason— *(Wheels on* ALEXANDRA*)* Ask why *he* married *me.* I can tell you that: he's told it to me often enough.

ADDIE: *(Leaning forward)* Miss Birdie, don't—

BIRDIE: *(Speaking very rapidly, tensely)* My family was good and the cotton on Lionnet's fields was better. Ben Hubbard wanted the cotton and *(Rises)* Oscar Hubbard married it for him. He was kind to me, then. He used to smile at me. He hasn't smiled at me since. Everybody knew that's what he married me for. *(*ADDIE *rises)* Everybody but me. Stupid, stupid me.

ALEXANDRA: *(To* HORACE, *holding his hand, softly)* I see. *(Hesitates)* Papa, I mean—when you feel better couldn't we go away? I mean, by ourselves. Couldn't we find a way to go—

HORACE: Yes, I know what you mean. We'll try to find a way. I promise you, darling.

ADDIE: *(Moves to* BIRDIE*)* Rest a bit, Miss Birdie. You get talking like this you'll get a headache and—

BIRDIE: *(Sharply, turning to her)* I've never had a headache in my life. *(Begins to cry hysterically)* You know it as well as I do. *(Turns to* ALEXANDRA*)* I never had a headache, Zan. That's a lie they tell for me. I drink. All by myself, in my own room, by myself, I drink. Then, when they want to hide it, they say, "Birdie's got a headache again"—

ALEXANDRA: *(Comes to her quickly)* Aunt Birdie.

BIRDIE: *(Turning away)* Even you won't like me now. You won't like me any more.

ALEXANDRA: I love you. I'll always love you.

BIRDIE: *(Furiously)* Well, don't. Don't love me. Because in twenty years you'll just be like me. They'll do all the same things to you. *(Begins to laugh hysterically)* You know what? In twenty-two years I haven't had a whole day of happiness. Oh, a little, like today with you all. But never a single, whole day. I say to myself, if only I had one more *whole* day, then— *(The laugh stops)* And that's the way you'll be. And you'll trail after them, just like me, hoping they won't be so mean that day or say something to make you feel so bad—only you'll be worse off because you haven't got my Mama to remember— *(Turns away, her head drops. She stands quietly, swaying a little, holding to the sofa.* ALEXANDRA *leans down, puts her cheek on* BIRDIE's *arm.)*

ALEXANDRA: *(To* BIRDIE*)* I guess we were all trying to make a happy day. You know, we sit around and try to pretend nothing's happened. We try to pretend we are not here. We make believe we are just by ourselves, some place else, and it doesn't seem to work. *(Kisses* BIRDIE's *hand)* Come now, Aunt Birdie, I'll walk you home. You and me. *(She takes* BIRDIE's *arm. They move slowly out.)*

BIRDIE: *(Softly as they exit)* You and me.

ADDIE: *(After a minute)* Well. First time I ever heard Miss Birdie say a word. (HORACE *looks at her)* Maybe it's good for her. I'm just sorry Zan had to hear it. (HORACE *moves his head as if he were uncomfortable)* You feel bad, don't you? *(He shrugs.)*

HORACE: So you didn't want Zan to hear? It would be nice to let her stay innocent, like Birdie at her age. Let her listen now. Let her see everything.

How else is she going to know that she's got to get away? I'm trying to show her that. I'm trying, but I've only got a little time left. She can even hate me when I'm dead, if she'll only learn to hate and fear this.

ADDIE: Mr. Horace —

HORACE: Pretty soon there'll be nobody to help her but you.

ADDIE: *(Crossing to him)* What can I do?

HORACE: Take her away.

ADDIE: How can I do that? Do you think they'd let me just go away with her?

HORACE: I'll fix it so they can't stop you when you're ready to go. You'll go, Addie?

ADDIE: *(After a second, softly)* Yes, sir. I promise. *(He touches her arm, nods.)*

HORACE: *(Quietly)* I'm going to have Sol Fowler make me a new will. They'll make trouble, but you make Zan stand firm and Fowler'll do the rest. Addie, I'd like to leave you something for yourself. I always wanted to.

ADDIE: *(Laughs)* Don't you do that, Mr. Horace. A nigger woman in a white man's will! I'd never get it nohow.

HORACE: I know. But upstairs in the armoire drawer there's seventeen hundred dollar bills. It's money left from my trip. It's in an envelope with your name. It's for you.

ADDIE: Seventeen hundred dollar bills! My God, Mr. Horace. I won't know how to count up that high. *(Shyly)* It's mighty kind and good of you. I don't know what to say for thanks —

CAL: *(Appears in doorway)* I'm back. *(No answer)* I'm back.

ADDIE: So we see.

HORACE: Well?

CAL: Nothing. I just went down and spoke my piece. Just like you told me. I say, "Mr. Horace he thank you mightily for the safe box arriving in good shape and he say you come right after supper to his house and bring Mr. Attorney-at-law Sol Fowler with you." Then I wipe my hands on my coat. Every time I ever told a lie in my whole life, I wipe my hands right after. Can't help doing it. Well, while I'm wiping my hands, Mr. Leo jump up and say to me, "What box? What you talking about?"

HORACE: *(Smiles)* Did he?

CAL: And Mr. Leo say he got to leave a little early cause he got something to do. And then Mr.

Manders say Mr. Leo should sit right down and finish up his work and stop acting like somebody made him Mr. President. So he sit down. Now, just like I told you, Mr. Manders was mighty surprised with the message because he knows right well he brought the box — *(Points to box, sighs)* But he took it all right. Some men take everything easy and some do not.

HORACE: *(Puts his head back, laughs)* Mr. Leo was telling the truth; he *has* got something to do. I hope Manders don't keep him too long. *(Outside there is the sound of voices.* CAL *exits.* ADDIE *crosses quickly to* HORACE, *puts basket on table, begins to wheel his chair toward the stairs. Sharply)* No. Leave me where I am.

ADDIE: But that's Miss Regina coming back.

HORACE: *(Nods, looking at door)* Go away, Addie.

ADDIE: *(Hesitates)* Mr. Horace. Don't talk no more today. You don't feel well and it won't do no good —

HORACE: *(As he hears footsteps in the hall)* Go on.

(She looks at him for a second, then picks up her sewing from table and exits as REGINA *comes in from hall.* HORACE's *chair is now so placed that he is in front of the table with the medicine.* REGINA *stands in the hall, shakes umbrella, stands it in the corner, takes off her cloak and throws it over the banister. She stares at* HORACE.*)*

REGINA: *(As she takes off her gloves)* We had agreed that you were to stay in your part of this house and I in mine. This room is *my* part of the house. Please don't come down here again.

HORACE: I won't.

REGINA: *(Crosses toward bell-cord)* I'll get Cal to take you upstairs.

HORACE: *(Smiles)* Before you do I want to tell you that after all, we have invested our money in Hubbard Sons and Marshall, Cotton Manufacturers.

REGINA: *(Stops, turns, stares at him)* What are you talking about? You haven't seen Ben — When did you change your mind?

HORACE: I didn't change my mind. *I* didn't invest the money. *(Smiles)* It was invested for me.

REGINA: *(Angrily)* What —?

HORACE: I had eighty-eight thousand dollars' worth of Union Pacific bonds in that safe-deposit box. They are not there now. Go and look. *(As she stares at him, he points to the box)* Go and look, Regina. *(She crosses quickly to the box, opens it)* Those bonds are as negotiable as money.

REGINA: *(Turns back to him)* What kind of joke are you playing now? Is this for my benefit?

HORACE: I don't look in that box very often, but three days ago, on Wednesday it was, because I had made a decision —

REGINA: I want to know what you are talking about.

HORACE: *(Sharply)* Don't interrupt me again. Because I had made a decision, I sent for the box. The bonds were gone. Eighty-eight thousand dollars gone. *(He smiles at her.)*

REGINA: *(After a moment's silence, quietly)* Do you think I'm crazy enough to believe what you're saying?

HORACE: *(Shrugs)* Believe anything you like.

REGINA: *(Stares at him, slowly)* Where did they go to?

HORACE: They are in Chicago. With Mr. Marshall, I should guess.

REGINA: What did they do? Walk to Chicago? Have you really gone crazy?

HORACE: Leo took the bonds.

REGINA: *(Turns sharply then speaks softly, without conviction)* I don't believe it.

HORACE: *(Leans forward)* I wasn't there but I can guess what happened. This fine gentleman, to whom you were willing to marry your daughter, took the keys and opened the box. You remember that the day of the fight Oscar went to Chicago? Well, he went with my bonds that his son Leo had stolen for him. *(Pleasantly)* And for Ben, of course, too.

REGINA: *(Slowly, nods)* When did you find out the bonds were gone?

HORACE: Wednesday night.

REGINA: I thought that's what you said. Why have you waited three days to do anything? *(Suddenly laughs)* This *will* make a fine story.

HORACE: *(Nods)* Couldn't it?

REGINA: *(Still laughing)* A fine story to hold over their heads. How could they be such fools? *(Turns to him)*

HORACE: But I'm not going to hold it over their heads.

REGINA: *(The laugh stops)* What?

HORACE: *(Turns his chair to face her)* I'm going to let them keep the bonds — as a loan from you. An eighty-eight-thousand-dollar loan; they should be grateful to you. They will be, I think.

REGINA: *(Slowly, smiles)* I see. You are punishing me. But I won't let you punish me. If you won't do anything, I will. Now. *(She starts for door.)*

HORACE: You won't do anything. Because you can't. *(REGINA stops)* It won't do you any good to make trouble because I shall simply say that I lent them the bonds.

REGINA: *(Slowly)* You would do that?

HORACE: Yes. For once in your life I am tying your hands. There is nothing for you to do. *(There is silence. Then she sits down.)*

REGINA: I see. You are going to lend them the bonds and let them keep all the profit they make on them, and there is nothing I can do about it. Is that right?

HORACE: Yes.

REGINA: *(Softly)* Why did you say that I was making this gift?

HORACE: I was coming to that. I am going to make a new will, Regina, leaving you eighty-eight thousand dollars in Union Pacific bonds. The rest will go to Zan. It's true that your brothers have borrowed your share for a little while. After my death I advise you to talk to Ben and Oscar. They won't admit anything and Ben, I think, will be smart enough to see that he's safe. Because I knew about the theft and said nothing. Nor will I say anything as long as I live. Is that clear to you?

REGINA: *(Nods, softly, without looking at him)* You will not say anything as long as you live.

HORACE: That's right. And by that time they will probably have replaced your bonds, and then they'll belong to you and nobody but us will ever know what happened. *(Stops, smiles)* They'll be around any minute to see what I am going to do. I took good care to see that word reached Leo. They'll be mighty relieved to know I'm going to do nothing and Ben will think it all a capital joke on you. And that will be the end of that. There's nothing you can do to them, nothing you can do to me.

REGINA: You hate me very much.

HORACE: No.

REGINA: Oh, I think you do. *(Puts her head back, sighs)* Well, we haven't been very good together. Anyway, I don't hate you either. I have only contempt for you. I've always had.

HORACE: From the very first?

REGINA: I think so.

HORACE: I was in love with *you*. But why did *you* marry *me*?

REGINA: I was lonely when I was young.

HORACE: *You* were lonely?

REGINA: Not the way people usually mean. Lonely for all the things I wasn't going to get. Everybody in this house was so busy and there was so little place for what I wanted. I wanted the world. Then, and then— *(Smiles)* Papa died and left the money to Ben and Oscar.

HORACE: And you married me?

REGINA: Yes, I thought— But I was wrong. You were a small-town clerk then. You haven't changed.

HORACE: *(Nods, smiles)* And that wasn't what you wanted.

REGINA: No. No, it wasn't what I wanted. *(Pauses, leans back, pleasantly)* It took me a little while to find out I had made a mistake. As for you—I don't know. It was almost as if I couldn't stand the kind of man you were— *(Smiles, softly)* I used to lie there at night, praying you wouldn't come near—

HORACE: Really? It was as bad as that?

REGINA: *(Nods)* Remember when I went to Doctor Sloan and I told you he said there was something the matter with me and that you shouldn't touch me any more?

HORACE: I remember.

REGINA: But you believed it. I couldn't understand that. I couldn't understand that anybody could be such a soft fool. That was when I began to despise you.

HORACE: *(Puts his hand to his throat, looks at the bottle of medicine on table)* Why didn't you leave me?

REGINA: I told you I married you for something. It turned out it was only for this. *(Carefully)* This wasn't what I wanted, but it was something. I never thought about it much but if I had *(HORACE puts his hand to his throat)* I'd have known that you would die before I would. But I couldn't have known that you would get heart trouble so early and so bad. I'm lucky, Horace. I've always been

lucky. *(HORACE turns slowly to the medicine)* I'll be lucky again.

(HORACE looks at her. Then he puts his hand to his throat. Because he cannot reach the bottle he moves the chair closer. He reaches for the medicine, takes out the cork, picks up the spoon. The bottle slips and smashes on the table. He draws in his breath, gasps.)

HORACE: Please. Tell Addie— The other bottle is upstairs. *(REGINA has not moved. She does not move now. He stares at her. Then, suddenly as if he understood, he raises his voice. It is a panic-stricken whisper, too small to be heard outside the room)* Addie! Addie! Come—

(Stops as he hears the softness of his voice. He makes a sudden, furious spring from the chair to the stairs, taking the first few steps as if he were a desperate runner. On the fourth step he slips, gasps, grasps the rail, makes a great effort to reach the landing. When he reaches the landing, he is on his knees. His knees give way, he falls on the landing, out of view. REGINA has not turned during his climb up the stairs. Now she waits a second. Then she goes below the landing, speaks up.)

REGINA: Horace. Horace. *(When there is no answer, she turns, calls)* Addie! Cal! Come in here. *(She starts up the steps. ADDIE and CAL appear. Both run toward the stairs)* He's had an attack. Come up here. *(They run up the steps quickly.)*

CAL: My God. Mr. Horace—

(They cannot be seen now.)

REGINA: *(Her voice comes from the head of the stairs)* Be still, Cal. Bring him in here.

(Before the footsteps and the voices have completely died away, ALEXANDRA appears in the hall door, in her raincloak and hood. She comes into the room, begins to unfasten the cloak, suddenly looks around, sees the empty wheel chair, stares, begins to move swiftly as if to look in the dining room. At the same moment ADDIE runs down the stairs. ALEXANDRA turns and stares up at ADDIE.)

ALEXANDRA: Addie! What?

ADDIE: *(Takes* ALEXANDRA *by the shoulders)* I'm going for the doctor. Go upstairs.

*(*ALEXANDRA *looks at her, then quickly breaks away and runs up the steps.* ADDIE *exits. The stage is empty for a minute. Then the front door bell begins to ring. When there is no answer, it rings again. A second later* LEO *appears in the hall, talking as he comes in.)*

LEO: *(Very nervous)* Hello. *(Irritably)* Never saw any use ringing a bell when a door was open. If you are going to ring a bell, then somebody should answer it. *(Gets in the room, looks around, puzzled, listens, hears no sound)* Aunt Regina. *(He moves around restlessly)* Addie. *(Waits)* Where the hell— *(Crosses to the bell cord, rings it impatiently, waits, gets no answer, calls)* Cal! Cal! *(*CAL *appears on the stair landing.)*

CAL: *(His voice is soft, shaken.)* Mr. Leo. Miss Regina says you stop that screaming noise.

LEO: *(Angrily)* Where is everybody?

CAL: Mr. Horace he got an attack. He's bad. Miss Regina says you stop that noise.

LEO: Uncle Horace— What— What happened? *(*CAL *starts down the stairs, shakes his head, begins to move swiftly off.* LEO *looks around wildly)* But when— You seen Mr. Oscar or Mr. Ben? *(*CAL *shakes his head. Moves on.* LEO *grabs him by the arm)* Answer me, will you?

CAL: No, I ain't seen 'em. I ain't got time to answer you. I got to get things. *(*CAL *runs off.)*

LEO: But what's the matter with him? When did this happen— *(Calling after* CAL*)* You'd think Papa'd be some place where you could find him. I been chasing him all afternoon.

*(*OSCAR *and* BEN *come quickly into the room.)*

LEO: Papa, I've been looking all over town for you and Uncle Ben—

BEN: Where is he?

OSCAR: Addie just told us it was a sudden attack, and—

BEN: *(To* LEO*)* Where is he? When did it happen?

LEO: Upstairs. Will you listen to me, please? I been looking for you for—

OSCAR: *(To* BEN*)* You think we should go up? *(*BEN, *looking up the steps, shakes his head.)*

BEN: I don't know. I don't know.

OSCAR: *(Shakes his head)* But he was all right—

LEO: *(Yelling)* Will you listen to me?

OSCAR: *(Sharply)* What is the matter with you?

LEO: I been trying to tell you. I been trying to find you for an hour—

OSCAR: Tell me what?

LEO: Uncle Horace knows about the bonds. He knows about them. He's had the box since Wednesday—

BEN: *(Sharply)* Stop shouting! What the hell are you talking about?

LEO *(Furiously)* I'm telling you he knows about the bonds. Ain't that clear enough—

OSCAR: *(Grabbing* LEO*'s arm)* You God-damn fool! Stop screaming!

BEN: Now what happened? Talk quietly.

LEO: You heard me. Uncle Horace knows about the bonds. He's known since Wednesday.

BEN: *(After a second)* How do you know that?

LEO: Because Cal comes down to Manders and says the box came O.K. and—

OSCAR: *(Trembling)* That might not mean a thing—

LEO: *(Angrily)* No? It might not, huh? Then he says Manders should come here tonight and bring Sol Fowler with him. I guess that don't mean a thing either.

OSCAR: *(To* BEN*)* Ben— What— Do you think he's seen the—

BEN: *(Motions to the box)* There's the box. *(Both* OSCAR *and* LEO *turn sharply.* LEO *makes a leap to the box)* You ass. Put it down. What are you going to do with it, eat it?

LEO: I'm going to— *(Starts.)*

BEN: *(Furiously)* Put it down. Don't touch it again. Now sit down and shut up for a minute.

OSCAR: Since Wednesday. *(To* LEO*)* You said he had it since Wednesday. Why didn't he say something— *(To* BEN*)* I don't understand—

LEO: *(Taking a step)* I can put it back. I can put it back before anybody knows.

BEN: *(Who is standing at the table, softly)* He's had it since Wednesday. Yet he hasn't said a word to us.

OSCAR: *Why? Why?*

LEO: What's the difference why? He was getting ready to say plenty. He was going to say it to Fowler tonight—

OSCAR: *(Angrily)* Be still. *(Turns to* BEN, *looks at him, waits.)*

BEN: *(After a minute)* I don't believe that.

LEO: *(Wildly)* You don't believe it? What do I care what *you* believe? I do the dirty work and then—

BEN: *(Turning his head sharply to* LEO*)* I'm remembering that. I'm remembering that, Leo.

OSCAR: What do you mean?

LEO: You—

BEN: *(To* OSCAR*)* If you don't shut that little fool up, I'll show you what I mean. For some reason he knows, but he don't say a word.

OSCAR: Maybe he didn't know that *we*—

BEN: *(Quickly)* That *Leo*— He's no fool. Does Manders know the bonds are missing?

LEO: How could I tell? I was half crazy. I don't think so. Because Manders seemed kind of puzzled and—

OSCAR: But we got to find out— *(He breaks off as* CAL *comes into the room carrying a kettle of hot water.)*

BEN: How is he, Cal?

CAL: I don't know, Mr. Ben. He was bad. *(Going toward stairs.)*

OSCAR: But when did it happen?

CAL: *(Shrugs)* He wasn't feeling bad early. *(*ADDIE *comes in quickly from the hall)* Then there he is next thing on the landing, fallen over, his eyes tight—

ADDIE: *(To* CAL*)* Dr. Sloan's over at the Ballongs. Hitch the buggy and go get him. *(She takes the kettle and cloths from him, pushes him, runs up the stairs)* Go on. *(She disappears.* CAL *exits.)*

BEN: Never seen Sloan anywhere when you need him.

OSCAR: *(Softly)* Sounds bad.

LEO: He would have told *her* about it. Aunt Regina. He would have told his own wife—

BEN: *(Turning to* LEO*)* Yes, he might have told her. But they weren't on such pretty terms and maybe he didn't. Maybe he didn't. *(Goes quickly to* LEO*)* Now, listen to me. If she doesn't know, it may work out all right. If she does know, you're to say he lent you the bonds.

LEO: Lent them to me! Who's going to believe that?

BEN: Nobody.

OSCAR: *(To* LEO*)* Don't you understand? It can't do no harm to say it—

LEO: Why should I say he lent them to me? Why not to you? *(Carefully)* Why not to Uncle Ben?

BEN: *(Smiles)* Just because he didn't lend them to me. Remember that.

LEO: But all he has to do is say he didn't lend them to me—

BEN: *(Furiously)* But for some reason, he doesn't seem to be talking, does he?

(There are footsteps above. They all stand looking at the stairs. REGINA *begins to come slowly down.)*

BEN: What happened?

REGINA: He's had a bad attack.

OSCAR: Too bad. I'm sorry we weren't here when—when Horace needed us.

BEN: When *you* needed us.

REGINA: *(Looks at him)* Yes.

BEN: How is he? Can we—can we go up?

REGINA: *(Shakes her head)* He's not conscious.

OSCAR: *(Pacing around)* It's that—it's that bad? Wouldn't you think Sloan could be found quickly, just once, just once?

REGINA: I don't think there is much for him to do.

BEN: Oh, don't talk like that. He's come through attacks before. He will now.

*(*REGINA *sits down. After a second she speaks softly.)*

REGINA: Well. We haven't seen each other since the day of our fight.

BEN: *(Tenderly)* That was nothing. Why, you and Oscar and I used to fight when we were kids.

OSCAR: *(Hurriedly)* Don't you think we should go up? Is there anything we can do for Horace—

BEN: You don't feel well. Ah—

REGINA: *(Without looking at them.)* No, I don't. *(Slight pause)* Horace told me about the bonds this afternoon. *(There is an immediate shocked silence.)*

LEO: The bonds. What do you mean? What bonds? What—

BEN: *(Looks at him furiously. Then to*

REGINA) The Union Pacific bonds? *Horace's* Union Pacific bonds?

REGINA: Yes.

OSCAR: *(Steps to her, very nervously)* Well. Well what—what about them? What—what could he say?

REGINA: He said that Leo had stolen the bonds and given them to you.

OSCAR: *(Aghast, very loudly)* That's ridiculous, Regina, absolutely—

LEO: I don't know what you're talking about. What would I— Why—

REGINA: *(Wearily to* BEN) Isn't it enough that he stole them from me? Do I have to listen to this in the bargain?

OSCAR: You are talking—

LEO: I didn't steal anything. I don't know why—

REGINA: *(To* BEN) Would you ask them to stop that, please?

(There is silence for a minute. BEN *glowers at* OSCAR *and* LEO.)

BEN: Aren't we starting at the wrong end, Regina? What did Horace tell you?

REGINA: *(Smiles at him)* He told me that Leo had stolen the bonds.

LEO: I didn't steal—

REGINA: Please. Let me finish. Then he told me that he was going to pretend that he had lent them to you (LEO *turns sharply to* REGINA, *then looks at* OSCAR, *then looks back at* REGINA) as a present from me—to my brothers. He said there was nothing I could do about it. He said the rest of his money would go to Alexandra. That is all.

(There is a silence. OSCAR *coughs,* LEO *smiles slyly.)*

LEO: *(Taking a step to her)* I told you he had lent them—I could have told you—

REGINA: *(Ignores him, smiles sadly at* BEN) So I'm very badly off, you see. *(Carefully)* But Horace said there was nothing I could do about it as long as he was alive to say he had lent you the bonds.

BEN: You shouldn't feel that way. It can all be explained, all be adjusted. It isn't as bad—

REGINA: So you, at least, are willing to admit that the bonds were stolen?

BEN: (OSCAR *laughs nervously)* I admit no such thing. It's possible that Horace made up that part of

the story to tease you— *(Looks at her)* Or perhaps to punish you. Punish you.

REGINA: *(Sadly)* It's not a pleasant story. I feel bad, Ben, naturally. I hadn't thought—

BEN: Now you shall have the bonds safely back. That was the understanding, wasn't it, Oscar?

OSCAR: Yes.

REGINA: I'm glad to know that *(Smiles)* Ah, I had greater hopes—

BEN: Don't talk that way. That's foolish. *(Looks at his watch)* I think we ought to drive out for Sloan ourselves. If we can't find him we'll go over to Senateville for Doctor Morris. And don't think I'm dismissing this other business. I'm not. We'll have it all out on a more appropriate day.

REGINA: *(Looks up, quietly)* I don't think you had better go yet. I think you had better stay and sit down.

BEN: We'll be back with Sloan.

REGINA: Cal has gone for him. I don't want you to go.

BEN: Now don't worry and—

REGINA: You will come back in this room and sit down. I have something more to say.

BEN: *(Turns, comes toward her)* Since when do I take orders from you?

REGINA: *(Smiles)* You don't—yet. *(Sharply)* Come back, Oscar. You too, Leo.

OSCAR: *(Sure of himself, laughs)* My dear Regina—

BEN: *(Softly, pats her hand)* Horace has already clipped your wings and very wittily. Do I have to clip them, too? *(Smiles at her)* You'd get farther with a smile, Regina. I'm a soft man for a woman's smile.

REGINA: I'm smiling, Ben. I'm smiling because you are quite safe while Horace lives. But I don't think Horace will live. And if he doesn't live I shall want seventy-five per cent in exchange for the bonds.

BEN: *(Steps back, whistles, laughs)* Greedy! What a greedy girl you are! You want so much of everything.

REGINA: Yes. And if I don't get what I want I am going to put all three of you in jail.

OSCAR: *(Furiously)* You're mighty crazy. Having just admitted—

BEN: And on what evidence would you put Oscar and Leo in jail?

REGINA: (Laughs, gaily) Oscar, listen to him. He's getting ready to swear that it was you and Leo! What do you say to that? (OSCAR turns furiously toward BEN) Oh, don't be angry, Oscar. I'm going to see that he goes in with you.

BEN: Try anything you like, Regina. (Sharply) And now we can stop all this and say good-bye to you. (ALEXANDRA comes slowly down the steps) It's his money and he's obviously willing to let us borrow it. (More pleasantly) Learn to make threats when you can carry them through. For how many years have I told you a good-looking woman gets more by being soft and appealing? Mama used to tell you that. (Looks at his watch) Where the hell is Sloan? (To OSCAR) Take the buggy and—

(As BEN turns to OSCAR, he sees ALEXANDRA. She walks stiffly. She goes slowly to the lower window, her head bent. They all turn to look at her.)

OSCAR: (After a second, moving toward her) What? Alexandra—

(She does not answer. After a second, ADDIE comes slowly down the stairs, moving as if she were very tired. At foot of steps, she looks at ALEXANDRA, then turns and slowly crosses to door and exits. REGINA rises. BEN looks nervously at ALEXANDRA, at REGINA.)

OSCAR: (As ADDIE passes him, irritably to ALEXANDRA) Well, what is— (Turns into room— sees ADDIE at foot of steps) —what's? (BEN puts up a hand, shakes his head) My God, I didn't know— who could have known—I didn't know he was that sick. Well, well—I— (REGINA stands quietly, her back to them.)

BEN: (Softly, sincerely) Seems like yesterday when he first came here.

OSCAR: (Sincerely, nervously) Yes, that's true. (Turns to BEN) The whole town loved him and respected him.

ALEXANDRA: (Turns) Did you love him, Uncle Oscar?

OSCAR: Certainly, I— What a strange thing to ask! I—

ALEXANDRA: Did you love him, Uncle Ben?

BEN: (Simply) He had—

ALEXANDRA: (Suddenly starts to laugh very loudly) And you, Mama, did you love him, too?

REGINA: I know what you feel, Alexandra, but please try to control yourself.

ALEXANDRA: (Still laughing) I'm trying, Mama. I'm trying very hard.

BEN: Grief makes some people laugh and some people cry. It's better to cry, Alexandra.

ALEXANDRA: (The laugh has stopped. Tensely moves toward REGINA) What was Papa doing on the staircase?

(BEN turns to look at ALEXANDRA.)

REGINA: Please go and lie down, my dear. We all need time to get over shocks like this. (ALEXANDRA does not move. REGINA'S voice becomes softer, more insistent) Please go, Alexandra.

ALEXANDRA: No, Mama. I'll wait. I've got to talk to you.

REGINA: Later. Go and rest now.

ALEXANDRA: (Quietly) I'll wait, Mama. I've plenty of time.

REGINA: (Hesitates, stares, makes a half shrug, turns back to BEN) As I was saying. Tomorrow morning I am going up to Judge Simmes. I shall tell him about Leo.

BEN: (Motioning toward ALEXANDRA) Not in front of the child, Regina. I—

REGINA: (Turns to him. Sharply) I didn't ask her to stay. Tomorrow morning I go to Judge Simmes—

OSCAR: And what proof? What proof of all this—

REGINA: (Turns sharply) None. I won't need any. The bonds are missing and they are with Marshall. That will be enough. If it isn't, I'll add what's necessary.

BEN: I'm sure of that.

REGINA: (Turns to BEN) You can be quite sure.

OSCAR: We'll deny—

REGINA: Deny your heads off. You couldn't find a jury that wouldn't weep for a woman whose brothers steal from her. And you couldn't find twelve men in this state you haven't cheated and who hate you for it.

OSCAR: What kind of talk is this? You couldn't do anything like that! We're your own brothers. (Points upstairs) How can you talk that way when upstairs not five minutes ago—

REGINA: (Slowly) There are people who can't go back, who must finish what they start. I am one of those people, Oscar. *(After a slight pause)* Where was I? *(Smiles at* BEN*)* Well, they'll convict you. But I won't care much if they don't. *(Leans forward, pleasantly)* Because by that time you'll be ruined. I shall also tell my story to Mr. Marshall, who likes me, I think, and who will not want to be involved in your scandal. A respectable firm like Marshall and Company. The deal would be off in an hour. *(Turns to them angrily)* And you know it. Now I don't want to hear any more from any of you. *You'll do no more bargaining in this house.* I'll take my seventy-five per cent and we'll forget the story forever. That's one way of doing it, and the way I prefer. You know me well enough to know that I don't mind taking the other way.

BEN: *(After a second, slowly)* None of us has ever known you well enough, Regina.

REGINA: You're getting old, Ben. Your tricks aren't as smart as they used to be. *(There is no answer. She waits, then smiles)* All right. I take it that's settled and I get what I asked for.

OSCAR: *(Furiously to* BEN*)* Are you going to let her do this—

BEN: *(Turns to look at him, slowly)* You have a suggestion?

REGINA: *(Puts her arms above her head, stretches, laughs)* No, he hasn't. All right. Now, Leo, I have forgotten that you ever saw the bonds. *(Archly, to* BEN *and* OSCAR*)* And as long as you boys both behave yourselves, I've forgotten that we ever talked about them. You can draw up the necessary papers tomorrow.

*(*BEN *laughs.* LEO *stares at him, starts for door. Exits.* OSCAR *moves toward door angrily.* REGINA *looks at* BEN, *nods, laughs with him. For a second,* OSCAR *stands in the door, looking back at them. Then he exits.)*

REGINA: You're a good loser, Ben. I like that.

BEN: *(He picks up his coat, then turns to her)* Well, I say to myself, what's the good? You and I aren't like Oscar. We're not sour people. I think that comes from a good digestion. Then, too, one loses today and wins tomorrow. I say to myself, years of planning and I get what I want. Then I don't get it. But I'm not discouraged. The century's turning, the world is open. Open for people like you and me. Ready for us, waiting for us. After all this is just the beginning. There are hundreds of Hubbards sitting in rooms like this throughout the country. All their

names aren't Hubbard, but they are all Hubbards and they will own this country some day. We'll get along.

REGINA: *(Smiles)* I think so.

BEN: Then, too, I say to myself, things may change. *(Looks at* ALEXANDRA*)* I agree with Alexandra. What is a man in a wheel chair doing on a staircase? I ask myself that.

REGINA: *(Looks up at him)* And what do you answer?

BEN: I have no answer. But maybe some day I will. Maybe never, but maybe some day. *(Smiles. Pats her arm)* When I do, I'll let you know. *(Goes toward hall.)*

REGINA: When you do, write me. I will be in Chicago. *(Gaily)* Ah, Ben, if Papa had only left me his money.

BEN: I'll see you tomorrow.

REGINA: Oh, yes. Certainly. You'll be sort of working for me now.

BEN: *(As he passes* ALEXANDRA, *smiles)* Alexandra, you're turning out to be a right interesting girl. *(Looks at* REGINA*)* Well, good night all. *(He exits.)*

REGINA: *(Sits quietly for a second, stretches, turns to look at* ALEXANDRA*)* What do you want to talk to me about, Alexandra?

ALEXANDRA: *(Slowly)* I've changed my mind. I don't want to talk. There's nothing to talk about now.

REGINA: You're acting very strange. Not like yourself. You've had a bad shock today. I know that. And you loved Papa, but you must have expected this to come some day. You knew how sick he was.

ALEXANDRA: I knew. We all knew.

REGINA: It will be good for you to get away from here. Good for me, too. Time heals most wounds, Alexandra. You're young, you shall have all the things I wanted. I'll make the world for you the way I wanted it to be for me. *(Uncomfortably)* Don't sit there staring. You've been around Birdie so much you're getting just like her.

ALEXANDRA: *(Nods)* Funny. That's what Aunt Birdie said today.

REGINA: *(Nods)* Be good for you to get away from all this. *(*ADDIE *enters.)*

ADDIE: Cal is back, Miss Regina. He says Dr. Sloan will be coming in a few minutes.

REGINA: We'll go in a few weeks. A few weeks! That means two or three Saturdays, two or three Sundays. *(Sighs)* Well, I'm very tired. I shall go to bed. I don't want any supper. Put the lights out and lock up. (ADDIE *moves to the piano lamp, turns it out)* You go to your room, Alexandra. Addie will bring you something hot. You look very tired. *(Rises. To* ADDIE*)* Call me when Dr. Sloan gets here. I don't want to see anybody else. I don't want any condolence calls tonight. The whole town will be over.

ALEXANDRA: Mama, I'm not coming with you. I'm not going to Chicago.

REGINA: *(Turns to her)* You're very upset, Alexandra.

ALEXANDRA: *(Quietly)* I mean what I say. With all my heart.

REGINA: We'll talk about it tomorrow. The morning will make a difference.

ALEXANDRA: It won't make any difference. And there isn't anything to talk about. I am going away from you. Because I want to. Because I know Papa would want me to.

REGINA: *(Puzzled, careful, polite)* You *know* your papa wanted you to go away from me?

ALEXANDRA: Yes.

REGINA: *(Softly)* And if I say no?

ALEXANDRA: *(Looks at her)* Say it Mama, say it. And see what happens.

REGINA: *(Softly, after a pause)* And if I make you stay?

ALEXANDRA: That would be foolish. It wouldn't work in the end.

REGINA: You're very serious about it, aren't you? *(Crosses to stairs)* Well, you'll change your mind in a few days.

ALEXANDRA: You only change your mind when you want to. And I won't want to.

REGINA: *(Going up the steps)* Alexandra, I've come to the end of my rope. Somewhere there has to be what I want, too. Life goes too fast. Do what you want; think what you want; go where you want. I'd like to keep you with me, but I won't make you stay. Too many people used to make me do too many things. No, I won't make you stay.

ALEXANDRA: You couldn't, Mama, because I want to leave here. As I've never wanted anything in my life before. Because now I understand what Papa was trying to tell me. *(Pause)* All in one day: Addie said there were people who ate the earth and other people who stood around and watched them do it. And just now Uncle Ben said the same thing. Really, he said the same thing. *(Tensely)* Well, tell him for me, Mama, I'm not going to stand around and watch you do it. Tell him I'll be fighting as hard as he'll be fighting *(Rises)* some place where people don't just stand around and watch.

REGINA: Well, you have spirit, after all. I used to think you were all sugar water. We don't have to be bad friends. I don't want us to be bad friends, Alexandra. *(Starts, stops, turns to* ALEXAN-DRA*)* Would you like to come and talk to me, Alexandra? Would you — would you like to sleep in my room tonight?

ALEXANDRA: *(Takes a step toward her)* Are you afraid, Mama?

(REGINA *does not answer. She moves slowly out of sight.* ADDIE *comes to* ALEXANDRA, *presses her arm.)*

THE CURTAIN FALLS

The Little Foxes, with its suspenseful story and sharply etched characters, is a powerful theatrical piece readily accessible to almost any audience. Its structure is so carefully wrought that each part seems both essential and natural. It is an excellent example of what is sometimes called the well-made play — that is, one in which the cause-to-effect arrangement builds logically and convincingly to the outcome.

Despite the play's undeniable strengths, critical response to it has been luke-warm, perhaps because, falling somewhere between melodrama and thesis play, its intention remains uncertain. As in melodrama, the characters are rather clearly divided between good and evil. The evil Hubbards—Regina, Ben, Oscar, and Leo—are concerned only with power and wealth. In addition, Ben and Regina cleverly and ruthlessly manipulate others to achieve their own ends. Oscar and Leo would be equally ruthless had they the necessary cunning. None of the four exhibits more than passing concern for anyone else, and none is willing to forgo personal advantage for the sake of another. They are the foxes of the title (predators and despoilers), preying on those too naive or too innocent to see the truth or too powerless to defend themselves. They are set off through contrast with the good but ineffectual characters—Horace, Alexandra, Birdie, Addie, and Cal.

The story also progresses through typical melodramatic devices—the devious plans of the villains, fortuitous entrances and exits that make it possible for someone to overhear an important statement or to get characters out of the way so they won't witness key events, the stolen bonds, the heart attack (and the broken medicine bottle) at just the right moment, and the numerous powerful reversals. These devices also keep suspense at a high pitch.

Much in *The Little Foxes*, however, deviates from melodrama. The denouement, especially, avoids the typical happy ending of melodrama in which the good are rewarded and the evil punished. We are led instead to believe that the Hubbards will achieve what they have set out to do, and that, while Regina would prefer that Alexandra go along with her plans, she will not let her daughter's opposition stop her. The only note of triumph for good is Alexandra's perception of the truth and her determination to disassociate herself from it.

Perhaps the play differs most from typical melodrama in seeking to uphold a thesis. One aspect of this thesis is found in the epigraph which precedes the script: "Take us the foxes, the little foxes, that spoil the vines; for our vines have tender grapes" (Song of Solomon, II, 15). A more specific summation is found in one of Addie's speeches in Act III: " . . . there are people who eat the earth and eat all the people on it like in the Bible with the locusts. Then there are people who stand around and watch them eat it. Sometimes I think it ain't right to stand and watch them do it." The Hubbards are the little foxes who spoil the vines *and* those who eat the earth. Many critics have thought Hellman meant the Hubbards to represent the capitalist system and thereby to denounce it. Perhaps she did. The action is set in 1900, the era of robber barons who made enormous fortunes at the expense of the general public; it was as well the time when the South was accepting industrialization. Thus, there was a factual basis for Hellman's characterization of the Hubbards. Furthermore, when the play was written in 1939 the world had been undergoing a terrible economic depression for about ten years, and during that time many people questioned whether capitalism would or should survive. It is also true that during this period Hellman supported many leftist causes. In *The Little Foxes*, the author depicts the worst aspects of capitalism and to that degree implies criticism of it. But she does not argue that some alternative system should be adopted.

It seems likely that, rather than offering an economic critique, Hellman was making a moral statement. Much of her writing exhibits a strong concern for justice and expresses moral outrage at the exploitation of the weak by the strong.

It is the moral bankruptcy of the exploiters that seems to interest her most in *The Little Foxes*. But this makes for a rather one-sided play, for the exploited are scarcely represented. We are told that the Hubbards have made their money by cheating uneducated blacks and that the proposed factory is expected to make a fortune because the workers will be grossly underpaid, but we do not see any one being exploited. Furthermore, Addie's statement about the guilt of those who "stand around and watch" others eat the earth implies that someone should oppose the Hubbards, although we are shown no likely candidates. Horace intends to oppose them, but he is too ill to follow through; Birdie, Alexandra, and Addie are unlikely victors. Thus, although Addie's position commands moral acquiescence, the play shows it to be ineffectual and impractical. Consequently, we cannot be surprised when the play ends with the exploiters triumphant. It is perhaps this imbalance in opposing forces that makes the play's ideas seem secondary and its melodramatic action primary; it probably also explains why critics have not been entirely certain where Hellman intended to place major emphasis. Despite all critical reservations, the play remains one of the most theatrically effective works of its time.

The implications of *The Little Foxes* are primarily those that grow out of Hellman's thesis that those who do not actively oppose evil are as guilty as those who commit evil. But, how is one to fight evil? Horace could have brought criminal charges against Leo and thereby publicly embarrass the Hubbards, but he settles for trying to thwart Regina. At the end, Alexandra plans to fight elsewhere. Nevertheless, *The Little Foxes* urges the need to oppose evil, even if it is not specific about the means for doing so. Does Hellman mean her thesis to apply only in situations where we know the exploiters? Would she extend it to cover the full range of social and economic systems under which we live? If so, this would argue the need for everyone to take an active role in the myriad activities that affect society. Must we accept a share in official corruption if we have done nothing to keep informed or have done nothing to oppose the corruption? If we merely shake our heads and express amazement at the world's depravity without actively seeking to end the corruption, are we mere hypocrites? How is it possible in a complex society to be fully informed and how can one person among so many make his or her views heard?

Another set of implications is indicated by Hellman's depiction of capitalism. Is the kind of exploitation seen in *The Little Foxes* typical only of capitalism? Is it the economic system that is to blame or the individuals who manipulate the system? Can any economic system be used to exploit the weak by those determined to do so?

Clearly we cannot live in today's world without being aware of both exploiters and the exploited. What is our responsibility when we become aware of exploitation? Can we excuse ourselves by insisting that we are mere spectators? Hellman's thesis is that we cannot.

Life of Galileo

by Bertolt Brecht / Translated by Wolfgang Sauerlander and Ralph Manheim

Bertolt Brecht (1891–1956) was the primary exponent of a type of drama and performance—epic theatre—that emerged in Germany in the 1920s. Brecht began his playwriting career in 1918 with *Baal*, a nihilistic work that questions all of society's restraints, and not until 1926 with *Man Is Man* did he display the social consciousness and didacticism that would characterize his subsequent work. It was also around 1926 that Brecht embraced Marxism, which was to influence all his later plays. Brecht's reputation as a dramatist was first fully established with *The Threepenny Opera* (1928), but most of his major plays were written after 1933 when he fled Germany to escape the Nazis. The plays written in exile include *The Private Life of the Master Race* (1935–1938), *Mother Courage and Her Children* (1938), *Life of Galileo* (1938–1939), *The Good Woman of Setzuan* (1938–1939), and *The Caucasian Chalk Circle* (1944–1945). In 1947 Brecht returned to Germany, and from 1949 until his death in 1956 he worked with his own company, the Berliner Ensemble, seeking to stage his plays in the manner he thought most appropriate to them. The company, located in East Berlin, is still considered to be one of the major theatres of the world, and its repertory is still devoted primarily to the works of Brecht.

Brecht's theory of theatre and drama has become almost as well-known as his plays. Developed over a long period, his theoretical ideas are summed up in "Little Organon for the Theatre" (1948). To distinguish his approach from the dramatic or Aristotelean theatre, Brecht adopted the term *epic*. He declared that the dramatic theatre has outlived its usefulness because it has reduced its spectators to complete passivity; in it, events are presented as fixed and unchangeable, for even when historical subjects are treated, they are couched in modern terms and thus give the impression that things have always been as they now are. Furthermore, illusionistic staging gives everything such an air of stability that traditional values and modes of behavior seem permanently entrenched. Since everything seems fixed, the spectator can only watch passively.

In place of this approach, Brecht envisioned one in which the audience would play an active role. He wanted the spectator to watch a performance critically and to apply what he saw to conditions outside the theatre. But if the spectator were to watch productively, he had to be assisted. Perhaps the most important term in Brecht's theoretical writings is *alienation—Verfremdung*—the process of making events and characters strange, of sufficiently distancing the spectator from the play that he can watch critically. Brecht sought to short-circuit empathy by breaking the illusion and reminding the audience that it is in a theatre watching a reflection of reality, not reality itself. In addition to alienation, Brecht at times wrote of *historification*, a process through which the "pastness" of events is emphasized so that the audience not only can judge them but also can be led to recognize that, since things have changed, present conditions can also be altered. Regardless of the label he used, Brecht manipulated esthetic distance so as to involve spectators emotionally and then to jar them out of their empathic response so they might judge what they have experienced.

Structurally, Brecht's plays are divided into carefully separated episodes. As he wrote: "Individual events must be tied together in such a way that the knots are strikingly noticeable . . . one must be able to pass judgment in the midst of them." Therefore, he separated his episodes with songs, brief speeches, or visual devices. He was little concerned with the individual psychology of characters and sought instead to portray their responses to social and economic forces. His plays are unified primarily by thought; nevertheless, they seldom end with a neat solution; instead, they suggest the need to find an answer outside the theatre.

In production, Brecht used various means to distance the audience. He mounted lighting instruments where they would be seen, placed musicians on stage, and changed scenery in full view of the audience. Instead of full-stage, realistic settings, he used fragments or projections. Scenery was never allowed to give the illusion of a place in its entirety but rather created a sense of impermanence and changeability. He sometimes advised actors not to impersonate a character so much as to present the behavior of a kind of person in a type of situation — to think of their roles in the third person. He wanted each element of production to comment on the action, but each in a different way. In a satirical song, for example, the music need not be satirical, but rather might contrast with the words so as to create conflict in the minds of spectators and force them to reconcile the two elements. Through such means, Brecht sought to stir up thought and motivate social action.

Critics are fond of pointing out that Brecht did not always follow his own theory, that the dramatist overcame the dialectician and the humanitarian the Marxist. For example, Brecht has written that he intended *Galileo* to show the scientist as a traitor to his profession, but audiences have usually seen Galileo as a genius victimized by prejudice.

Today, Brecht's plays do not always arouse the response he envisioned because his dramatic techniques have been so thoroughly assimilated. Since the

1950s theatrical productions, whether of epic drama or other types, have increasingly used Brechtian devices: the front curtain has virtually been abandoned so that the stage and all its mechanisms are visible at all times; full-stage settings have been replaced by set pieces that suggest place, or by projections that serve to associate the onstage action with other similar events or arguments; lighting instruments and musicians are almost always in full view. These and other devices now continually remind audiences that they are in a theatre watching a play. Since these staging methods are used even for the most traditional Aristotelean plays, the distinctions that Brecht drew between his and traditional theatre have been blurred or lost. As a result, audiences now tend to watch Brecht's plays in much the same way they do other plays rather than in the critical, analytical way he envisioned and without feeling the need to resolve the conflict in the world outside the theatre. Today's theatrical practices, then, demonstrate Brecht's enormous influence, but they also indicate that, while his techniques have been accepted, his ultimate goals quite frequently are ignored.

CHARACTERS

GALILEO GALILEI

ANDREA SARTI

MRS. SARTI *Galileo's housekeeper, Andrea's mother*

LUDOVICO MARSILI *a rich young man*

MR. PRIULI *procurator of the University of Padua*

SAGREDO *Galileo's friend*

VIRGINIA *Galileo's daughter*

FEDERZONI *a lens grinder, Galileo's collaborator*

THE DOGE

SENATORS

COSMO DE' MEDICI *Grand Duke of Florence*

THE LORD CHAMBERLAIN

THE THEOLOGIAN

THE PHILOSOPHER

THE MATHEMATICIAN

THE OLDER LADY-IN-WAITING

THE YOUNGER LADY-IN-WAITING

A LACKEY at the Grand Duke's court

TWO NUNS

TWO SOLDIERS

THE OLD WOMAN

A FAT PRELATE

TWO SCHOLARS

TWO MONKS

TWO ASTRONOMERS

A VERY THIN MONK

THE VERY OLD CARDINAL

FATHER CHRISTOPHER CLAVIUS *an astronomer*

THE LITTLE MONK

THE CARDINAL INQUISITOR

CARDINAL BARBERINI *later Pope Urban VIII*

CARDINAL BELLARMINE

TWO ECCLESIASTICAL SECRETARIES

TWO YOUNG LADIES

FILIPPO MUCIUS *a scholar*

MR. GAFFONE *rector of the University of Pisa*

THE BALLAD SINGER

HIS WIFE

VANNI *an iron founder*

AN ATTENDANT

A HIGH OFFICIAL

A SHADY INDIVIDUAL

A MONK

A PEASANT

A BORDER GUARD

A CLERK

MEN, WOMEN, CHILDREN

SCENE I

GALILEO GALILEI *teacher of mathematics in Padua, sets out to demonstrate the new Copernican system.*

In the year sixteen hundred and nine
Science's light began to shine.
At Padua city, in a modest house
Galileo Galilei set out to prove
The sun is still, the earth is on the move.

---

*(*GALILEO*'s modest study in Padua. It is morning. A boy,* ANDREA, *the housekeeper's son, brings in a glass of milk and a roll.)*

GALILEO: *(Washing his torso, puffing and happy)* Put the milk on the table, but don't shut any books.

ANDREA: Mother says we've got to pay the milkman. Or he'll make a circle around our house, Mr. Galilei.

GALILEO: You must say, "describe a circle," Andrea.

ANDREA: Of course. If we don't pay he'll describe a circle around us, Mr. Galilei.

GALILEO: And Mr. Cambione, the bailiff, will head for us in a straight line, covering what sort of distance between two points?

ANDREA: *(Grinning)* The shortest.

GALILEO: Good. I've got something for you. Look behind the star charts.

*(*ANDREA *fishes a large wooden model of the Ptolemaic system from behind the star charts.)*

ANDREA: What is it?

GALILEO: An armillary sphere. It shows how the stars move around the earth, in the opinion of the ancients.

ANDREA: How?

GALILEO: Let's examine it. First of all: description.

ANDREA: There's a little stone in the middle.

GALILEO: That's the earth.

ANDREA: There are rings around it, one inside another.

GALILEO: How many?

ANDREA: Eight.

GALILEO: Those are the crystal spheres.

ANDREA: There are balls fastened to the rings . . .

GALILEO: The stars.

ANDREA: There are tags with words painted on them.

GALILEO: What kind of words?

ANDREA: Names of stars.

GALILEO: Such as?

ANDREA: The bottommost ball is the moon, it says. The one above it is the sun.

GALILEO: Now spin the sun around.

ANDREA: *(Sets the rings in motion)* That's pretty. But we're so shut in.

GALILEO: *(Drying himself)* Yes, that's just what I felt when I saw the thing for the first time. Some people feel that way. *(Throws* ANDREA *the towel, meaning that he should rub his back)* Walls and rings and immobility. For two thousand years men believed that the sun and all the stars of heaven were circling around them. The pope, the cardinals, princes and scholars, the captains, merchants, fishwives and schoolchildren, all thought they were sitting motionless inside this crystal sphere. But now we'll get out of it, Andrea, we're in full sail. Because the old times are gone, and this is a new age. For the last hundred years mankind has seemed to be expecting something.

Cities are narrow, and so are minds. Superstition and plague. But now we say: Since things are thus and so, they will not remain thus and so. Because, my friend, everything is in motion.

I like to think that it all started with ships. From time immemorial ships had hugged the shores, but suddenly they abandoned the shores, and sailed out upon the oceans.

A rumor has sprung up on our old continent — that there are new continents. And now that our ships have been going there, people on all the laughing continents are saying that the big dreaded ocean is nothing but a small lake. And a great desire has arisen to find the causes of all things: Why a stone falls when it's released and how it goes up when it's thrown into the air. Every day something new is being discovered. Even men a hundred years old let youngsters shout in their ears to tell them about the latest discoveries.

A great deal has been discovered, but there's much more to be discovered. Plenty of work for future generations.

When I was a young man in Siena I saw some masons, after arguing for five minutes, discard an age-old method of moving granite blocks in favor of a new and more practical arrangement of the ropes. Then and there I realized that the old times are over and that this is a new day. Some men will know all about their habitat, this heavenly body they live on. They're no longer satisfied with what it says in the ancient books.

Because where faith had ruled for a thousand years, doubt has now set in. Today everybody is saying: Yes, that's what the books tell us, but we want to see for ourselves. The most sacred truths are being looked into. Things that were never held in doubt are being doubted now.

All this has stirred up a breeze that lifts even the gold-braided coats of princes and prelates, revealing stout or spindly legs, legs just the same as ours. The heavens, we know now, are empty. And that has given rise to joyous laughter.

The waters of the earth supply power to the new spinning wheels, and in shipyards and the workshops of ropers and sailmakers new methods enable five hundred hands to work together.

I foresee that in our lifetime people will talk astronomy in the market place. Even the sons of fishwives will go to school. The people of our cities are always eager for novelty, they will be glad to hear that in our new astronomy the earth moves too. It has always been taught that the stars are pinned to a crystal vault, which prevents them from falling down. Now we've mustered the courage to let them float free, with nothing to hold them; they're in full sail, just as our ships are in full sail.

And the earth rolls merrily around the sun, and all the fishwives, merchants, princes and cardinals, and even the pope, roll with it.

Overnight, the universe has lost its center and now in the morning it has any number of centers. Now any point in the universe may be taken as a center. Because, suddenly, there's plenty of room.

Our ships sail far out into the ocean, our planets revolve far out in space, and even in chess nowadays the rooks range over many fields.

What does the poet say? "Oh, early morning . . ."

ANDREA:
"Oh, early morning of beginning!
Oh, breath of wind that
Comes from new-found shores!"
And you'd better drink your milk.
There'll be people coming in a minute.

GALILEO: Did you figure out what I told you yesterday?

ANDREA: What? You mean Kippernick and all that turning business?

GALILEO: Yes.

ANDREA: No. Why do you want me to figure it out? It's too hard for me, I'll only be eleven in October.

GALILEO: I want you to understand it, you in particular. To make everybody understand, that's why I work and buy expensive books instead of paying the milkman.

ANDREA: But I can see that the sun's not in the same place in the evening and morning. So it can't stand still. It just can't.

GALILEO: You "see"! What do you see? You see nothing at all. You're just gaping. Gaping isn't seeing. (He places the iron washstand in the center of the room) Now, that's the sun. Sit down. (ANDREA sits down in the only chair. GALILEO stands behind him) Where is the sun, right or left?

ANDREA: Left.

GALILEO: And how does it get to the right?

ANDREA: When you carry it over to the right. Naturally.

GALILEO: Only then? (He picks up the chair with him in it and turns it halfway around) Where's the sun now?

ANDREA: On the right.

GALILEO: Has it moved?

ANDREA: I guess it hasn't.

GALILEO: What moved?

ANDREA: Me.

GALILEO: (Roars) Wrong! Stupid! the chair!

ANDREA: But me with it!

GALILEO: Obviously. The chair is the earth. You're sitting on it.

MRS. SARTI: (Has come in to make the bed. She has watched the scene) Mr. Galilei, what on earth are you doing with my boy?

GALILELO: I'm teaching him how to see, Mrs. Sarti.

MRS. SARTI: By carrying him around the room?

ANDREA: Never mind, mother. You don't understand.

MRS. SARTI: Is that so? But of course you understand. A young gentleman is here, he wants to take lessons. Very well dressed, and he has a letter of recommendation. *(Hands over the letter)* When you get through with my Andrea, he'll be saying that two times two make five. You've got him all mixed up. Last night he tried to prove to me that the earth moves around the sun. He says some fellow by the name of Kippernick figured it out.

ANDREA: Didn't that Kippernick figure it out, Mr. Galilei? You tell her.

MRS. SARTI: Do you really tell him such nonsense? He blabs it out in school and the priests come running to me because of all the sinful stuff he says. You should be ashamed of yourself, Mr. Galilei.

GALILEO: *(Eating his breakfast)* Mrs. Sarti, as a result of our investigations, and after heated arguments, Andrea and I have made discoveries which we can no longer keep secret from the world. A new age has dawned, a great age, and it's a joy to be alive.

MRS. SARTI: I see. I hope we'll be able to pay the milkman in the new age, Mr. Galilei. *(Pointing at the letter)* Just do me a favor and don't turn this one away. I'm thinking of the milk bill. *(Out)*

GALILEO: *(Laughing)* Just give me time to finish my milk! — *(To* ANDREA*)* Well, you seem to have understood something yesterday after all.

ANDREA: I only told her to get a rise out of her. But it's not true. You only turned the chair with me in it around sideways, but not like this. *(He moves his arm in a circle to the front)* Because I'd have fallen off the chair, and that's a fact. Why didn't you turn the chair over? Because that would prove I'd fall off the earth if it moved that way. There.

GALILEO: But I proved to you . . .

ANDREA: But last night I figured out that if the earth turned that way I'd hang down head first at night, and that's a fact.

GALILEO: *(Takes an apple from the table)* Look here. This is the earth.

ANDREA: Don't always use that kind of example, Mr. Galilei. That way you can prove anything.

GALILEO: *(Putting the apple back)* Very well.

ANDREA: You can do anything with examples if you're clever. But I can't carry my mother around in a chair like that. So you see, it was a bad example. And what would happen if the apple were the earth? Nothing would happen.

GALILEO: *(Laughs)* I thought you weren't interested.

ANDREA: All right, take the apple. What would keep me from hanging head down at night?

GALILEO: Well, here's the earth, and you're standing here. *(He sticks a splinter from a log into the apple)* And now the earth turns.

ANDREA: And now I'm hanging head down.

GALILEO: What do you mean? Look closely! Where's the head?

ANDREA: *(Shows on the apple)* There. Below.

GALILEO: Sure? *(Turns the apple back)* Isn't the head still in the same place? Aren't the feet still below it? When I turn it, do you stand like this? *(He takes the splinter out and turns it upside down)*

ANDREA: No. Then, why don't I notice the turning?

GALILEO: Because you're turning too. You and the air above you and everything else on the globe.

ANDREA: But why does it look as if the sun were moving?

GALILEO: *(Again turns the apple with the splinter)* Look, you see the earth underneath, it stays that way, it's always underneath and as far as you're concerned it doesn't move. Now look up. The lamp is over your head. But now that I've turned it, what's over your head, in other words, above?

ANDREA: *(Making the same turn)* The stove.

GALILEO: And where's the lamp?

ANDREA: Below.

GALILEO: Aha!

ANDREA: That's great. That'll get a rise out of her.

*(*LUDOVICO MARSILI, *a rich young man, enters)*

GALILEO: This place is as busy as a pigeon house.

LUDOVICO: Good morning, sir. My name is Ludovico Marsili.

GALILEO: *(Examining his letter of recommendation)* You've been in Holland?

LUDOVICO: Where I heard a great deal about you, Mr. Galilei.

GALILEO: Your family owns property in the Campagna?

LUDOVICO: My mother wanted me to look around and see what's going on in the world. That kind of thing.

GALILEO: And in Holland they told you that in Italy, for instance, I was going on?

LUDOVICO: And since mother also wanted me to take a look at the sciences . . .

GALILEO: Private lessons: Ten scudi a month.

LUDOVICO: Very well, sir.

GALILEO: What are your interests?

LUDOVICO: Horses.

GALILEO: I see.

LUDOVICO: I have no head for science, Mr. Galilei.

GALILEO: I see. In that case it'll be fifteen scudi a month.

LUDIVICO: Very well, Mr. Galilei.

GALILEO: I'll have to take you first thing in the morning. You'll be the loser, Andrea. Naturally I'll have to drop you. You understand, you don't pay.

ANDREA: All right, I'm going. Can I take the apple?

GALILEO: Yes.

(ANDREA leaves)

LUDOVICO: You'll have to be patient with me. Mostly because in science everything's the opposite of common sense. Take that crazy tube they're selling in Amsterdam. I've examined it carefully. A green leather casing and two lenses, one like this *(He indicates a concave lens)* and one like this *(Indicates a convex lens)*. As far as I know, one magnifies and the other reduces. Any sensible person would expect them to cancel each other out. But they don't. When you look through the thing everything's five times as big. That's science for you.

GALILEO: What do you see five times as big?

LUDOVICO: Steeples, pigeons, anything far away.

GALILEO: Have you seen these magnified steeples?

LUDOVICO: Certainly, sir.

GALILEO: You say the tube has two lenses?

(He makes a sketch on a sheet of paper) Like this? *(LUDOVICO nods)* How old is this invention?

LUDOVICO: I believe it wasn't much more than a few days old when I left Holland, at least it hadn't been on the market any longer than that.

GALILEO: *(Almost friendly)* Why do you insist on physics? Why not horse breeding?

(Enter MRS. SARTI, unnoticed by GALILEO)

LUDOVICO: Mother thinks a little science won't hurt me. Everybody's eating and drinking science nowadays, you know.

GALILEO: Why not try a dead language or theology? They're easier. *(Sees MRS. SARTI)* All right, come Tuesday morning.

(LUDOVICO leaves)

GALILEO: Don't look at me like that. I've accepted him.

MRS. SARTI: Because you saw me in the nick of time. The procurator of the university is here.

GALILEO: Bring him in. He's important. It might mean five hundred scudi. Then I wouldn't have to take pupils.

(MRS. SARTI shows the procurator in. GALILEO has completed dressing while scribbling figures on a slip of paper)

GALILEO: Good morning, lend me half a scudo. *(Gives the coin the procurator has fished out of his purse to MRS. SARTI)* Sarti, would you send Andrea to the spectacle maker for some lenses? Here are the measurements.

(MRS. SARTI goes out with the slip of paper)

THE PROCURATOR: I've come in regard to your request for a raise of salary. You have asked for a thousand scudi. Unfortunately I cannot recommend such an increase to the university. You are aware, I am sure, that courses in mathematics don't attract students to the university. Mathematics doesn't pay. Not that the republic doesn't value it highly. It may not be as important as philosophy or as useful as theology; still, it gives endless pleasure to the connoisseur.

GALILEO: *(Immersed in his papers)* My dear man, I can't get along on five-hundred scudi.

THE PROCURATOR: But, Mr. Galilei, all you

do is give a two-hour lecture twice a week. Surely your extraordinary reputation must attract any number of students who can afford private lessons. Haven't you got private pupils?

GALILEO: Sir, I have too many! I'm teaching all the time. When am I to learn? Good God, man, I'm not as clever as the gentlemen of the philosophical faculty. I'm stupid. I don't understand a thing. I've got to plug the holes in my knowledge. And where am I to find time for that? When am I to study and experiment? My knowledge, sir, is thirsty for more knowledge. In all the biggest problems we still have nothing but hypotheses to go by. What we need is proofs. How can I get anywhere if, to keep my household going, I have to drum it into the head of every idiot who can pay that parallel lines meet in infinity?

THE PROCURATOR: The republic may not pay as much as certain princes, but don't forget, it guarantees freedom of inquiry. We in Padua even admit Protestants as students. And we grant them doctor's degrees. Did we hand Mr. Cremonini over to the Inquisition when we had proof—proof, Mr. Galilei!—that he had made sacrilegious statements? No, we even granted him an increase in salary. As far away as Holland Venice is known as the republic where the Inquisition has nothing to say. That ought to be worth something to an astronomer like you, working in a field where the doctrines of the church have not been held in due respect of late.

GALILEO: You handed Giordano Bruno over to Rome. Because he professed the teachings of Copernicus.

THE PROCURATOR: Not because he professed the teachings of Mr. Copernicus which, incidentally, are wrong, but because he was not a citizen of Venice and was not employed here. You can leave him out of it, even if they did burn him. And by the by, for all our liberties I shouldn't advise you to make too free with a name that has been expressly anathematized by the church, not even here, no, not even here.

GALILEO: Your protection of freedom of thought is rather good business, isn't it? You get good teachers for low pay by pointing out that other towns are run by the Inquisition, which burns people. In return for protection from the Inquisition, your professors work for next to nothing.

THE PROCURATOR: You're being unfair. What good would it do you to have all the time you want for research if any witless monk of the Inquisition could simply suppress your ideas? No rose without thorns, Mr. Galilei, no prince without monks!

GALILEO: And what's the use of free investigation without free time to investigate? What happens to the results? Why don't you submit my work on the laws of falling bodies (He points at a sheaf of manuscript) to the gentlemen of the signoria and ask them if it's not worth a few scudi more.

THE PROCURATOR: It's worth infinitely more, Mr. Galilei.

GALILEO: Not infinitely more, sir, but five hundred scudi more.

THE PROCURATOR: Only what brings in scudi is worth scudi. If you want money, you'll have to come up with something different. If you have knowledge to sell, you can ask only as much as it earns the purchaser. For instance, the philosophy Mr. Colombe is selling in Florence brings the prince at least ten thousand scudi a year. Granted, your laws of falling bodies raised some dust. They're applauding you in Paris and Prague. But the gentlemen who applaud don't pay the university of Padua what you cost it. Your misfortune, Mr. Galilei, is your field.

GALILEO: I get it: free trade, free research. Free trade in research, is that it?

THE PROCURATOR: But Mr. Galilei! How can you say such a thing? Permit me to observe that I don't fully appreciate your witticism. The flourishing trade of the republic is hardly to be sneered at. Much less can I, as long-time procurator of the university, countenance the, I must say, frivolous tone in which you speak of research. (While GALILEO sends longing glances toward his worktable) Think of the world around us! The whip of slavery under which science is groaning at certain universities—where old leather-bound tomes have been cut into whips. Where no one cares how the pebble falls, but only what Aristotle writes about it. The eyes have only one purpose: reading. What use are the new laws of gravity when the law of suavity is all that matters? And then think of the immense joy with which our republic accepts your ideas. Here you can do research! Here you can work! Nobody spies on you, nobody oppresses you. Our merchants, who know the importance of better linen in their competition with Florence, listen with interest to your cry for "Better physics!" And don't forget how much physics owes to the campaign for better looms! Our most eminent citizens—men for whom time is money—take an interest in your work, they come to see you and watch demonstrations of your discoveries. Don't despise trade, Mr. Galilei! None of us here would ever allow your work to be interfered with or permit outsiders to create difficulties for you. You've got to admit, Mr. Galilei, that this is the ideal place for your work!

GALILEO: *(In despair)* Yes.

THE PROCURATOR: Then the financial aspect. All you have to do is come up with another invention as clever as that splendid proportional compass of yours which a person ignorant of mathematics can use to *(He counts on his fingers)* trace a line, compute compound interest, reproduce a land survey in enlarged or reduced scale, and determine the weight of cannon balls.

GALILEO: Flimflam.

THE PROCURATOR: An invention that delighted and amazed our leading citizens and brought in money—you call that flimflam. I'm told that even General Stefano Gritti can do square roots with it.

GALILEO: Quite a gadget—all the same, Priuli, you've given me an idea. Priuli, I may have something along those lines for you. *(He picks up the sheet with his sketch)*

THE PROCURATOR: Really? That would be the solution. *(Gets up)* Mr. Galilei, we know you are a great man. A great but dissatisfied man, if I may say so.

GALILEO: Yes, I am dissatisfied and that's what you should be paying me for if you had any sense. Because I'm dissatisfied with myself. But you do everything to make me dissatisfied with you. I admit it amuses me to do my bit for my Venetian friends, working in your great arsenal with its shipyards and armories. But you leave me no time to follow up the speculations which result from this work. You muzzle the ox that does your threshing. I'm forty-six years old and I've accomplished nothing that satisfies me.

THE PROCURATOR: In that case I won't disturb you any longer.

GALILEO: Thank you.

(THE PROCURATOR leaves. GALILEO remains alone for a few moments and begins to work. Then ANDREA comes running in)

GALILEO: *(At work)* Why didn't you eat the apple?

ANDREA: I need it to show her that the earth turns.

GALILEO: I must tell you something, Andrea. Don't mention our ideas to other people.

ANDREA: Why not?

GALILEO: Our rulers have forbidden it.

ANDREA: But it's the truth.

GALILEO: Even so, they forbid it.—And there's another reason. We still have no proofs for what we know to be right. Even the doctrine of the great Copernicus is not yet proven. It's only a hypothesis. Give me the lenses.

ANDREA: Half a scudo wasn't enough. I had to leave him my jacket. As a pledge.

GALILEO: How will you get through the winter without a jacket?

(Pause. GALILEO arranges the lenses on the sheet with the sketch)

ANDREA: What's a hypothesis?

GALILEO: It's when we consider something probable but have no facts. We assume that Felice, nursing her baby down there outside the basket weaver's shop, is giving milk to the baby and not getting milk from it. That's a hypothesis as long as we can't go and see for ourselves and prove it. In the face of the heavenly bodies we're like worms with dim eyes that see very little. The ancient doctrines that have been accepted for a thousand years are rickety. There's less solid timber in those immense edifices than in the props needed to keep them from collapsing. Too many laws that explain too little, whereas our new hypothesis has few laws that explain a great deal.

ANDREA: But you've proved it all to me.

GALILEO: Only that it's possible. You see, the hypothesis is a very elegant one and there's no evidence to the contrary.

ANDREA: I want to be a physicist too, Mr. Galilei.

GALILEO: Very sensible in view of all the problems remaining to be solved in our field. *(He has gone to the window and looked through the lenses. Mildly interested)* Take a look, Andrea.

ANDREA: Holy Mary! Everything comes close. The bells of the campanile are right here. I can even read the copper letters: GRACIA DEI.

GALILEO: It'll get us five hundred scudi.

SCENE II

GALILEO *presents a new invention to the republic of Venice.*

No one's virtue is complete:
Great Galileo liked to eat.
You will not resent, we hope
The truth about his telescope.

The great arsenal of Venice near the harbor. SENATORS, *headed by the* DOGE. *On one side* GALILEO's *friend* SAGREDO *and* VIRGINIA GALILEI, *fifteen; she is holding a velvet cushion on which lies a telescope about two feet long, encased in red leather.* GALILEO *is standing on a dais. Behind him the tripod for the telescope; the lens grinder* FEDER-ZONI *is in charge of it.*

GALILEO: Your Excellency, august signoria! As professor of mathematics at your university in Padua and director of the great arsenal here in Venice, I have always felt it incumbent upon me not only to fulfill my duties as a teacher but also to procure special advantages to the republic of Venice by means of useful inventions. With great satisfaction and in all due humility, I shall demonstrate and present to you today an entirely new instrument, my spyglass or telescope, manufactured in your world-famous great arsenal in accordance with the highest scientific and Christian principles, the fruit of seventeen years of your obedient servant's patient labors.

(GALILEO *leaves the dais and stands next to* SAGREDO)
(*Applause,* GALILEO *takes a bow*)

GALILEO (*Softly to* SAGREDO) What a waste of time!

SAGREDO (*Softly*) You'll be able to pay the butcher, old friend.

GALILEO: Yes, they'll make money on it. (*Makes another bow*)

THE PROCURATOR: (*Steps up on the dais*) Your Excellency, august signoria! Once again a glorious page in the great book of human accomplishments is being written in Venetian characters. (*Polite applause*) A scholar of world renown is presenting to you, and to you alone, a highly salable tube for you to manufacture and market at your pleasure. (*Stronger applause*) Has it occurred to you that in the event of war this instrument will enable us to recognize the nature and number of the enemy's ships at least two hours before they have a clear view of ours and, in full cognizance of his strength, decide whether to pursue, engage or withdraw? (*Loud applause*) And now, Your Excellency, august signoria, Mr. Galilei bids you accept this instrument of his invention, this evidence of his genius, from the hands of his charming daughter.

(*Music.* VIRGINIA *steps forward, bows, hands the telescope to the* PROCURATOR *who passes it on to* FEDERZONI. FEDERZONI *places it on the tripod and adjusts it. The* DOGE *and the* SENATORS *mount the dais and look through the tube*)

GALILEO: (*Softly*) I can't promise to go through with this farce. They think they're getting a profitable gadget, but it's much more than that. Last night I turned the tube on the moon.

SAGREDO: What did you see?

GALILEO: It has no light of its own.

SAGREDO: What?

SENATORS: Mr. Galilei, I can see the fortifications of Santa Rosita.—Over there on that boat they're having lunch. Fried fish. I'm getting hungry.

GALILEO: I tell you, astronomy has been marking time for a thousand years for a lack of a telescope.

SENATOR: Mr. Galilei!

SAGREDO: You're wanted.

SENATOR: One sees too well with that thing. I'll have to warn my ladies to stop bathing on the roof.

GALILEO: Do you know what the Milky Way consists of?

SAGREDO: No.

GALILEO: I do.

SENATOR: A thing like that is worth its ten scudi, Mr. Galilei.

(GALILEO bows)

VIRGINIA: (Takes LUDOVICO to her father) Ludovico wants to congratulate you, father.

LUDOVICO: (Embarrassed) Congratulations, sir.

GALILEO: I've improved on it.

LUDOVICO: So I see, sir. You made the casing red. In Holland it was green.

GALILEO: (Turns to SAGREDO) I wonder if I couldn't prove a certain doctrine with that thing.

SAGREDO: Watch your step!

THE PROCURATOR: Your five hundred scudi are in the bag, Mr. Galilei.

GALILEO: (Paying no attention to him) Of course, I'm always wary of rash conclusions.

(The DOGE, a fat, modest man, has approached GALILEO and is attempting, with clumsy dignity, to address him)

THE PROCURATOR: Mr. Galilei, His Excellency the doge.

(The DOGE shakes GALILEO's hand)

GALILEO: Oh yes, the five hundred! Are you satisfied, Your Excellency?

DOGE: Unfortunately our city fathers always need some sort of pretext before they can do anything for our scholars.

THE PROCURATOR: Otherwise, where would the incentive be, Mr. Galilei?

DOGE: (Smiling) This is our pretext.

(The DOGE and the PROCURATOR lead GALILEO to the SENATORS, who surround him. VIRGINIA and LUDOVICO slowly go away)

VIRGINIA: Did I do it all right?

LUDOVICO: It seemed all right to me.

VIRGINIA: What's the matter?

LUDOVICO: Oh, nothing. A green casing might have done just as well.

VIRGINIA: I think they're all very pleased with father.

LUDOVICO: And I think I'm beginning to understand something about science.

SCENE III

January 10, 1610: By means of the telescope GALILEO *discovers celestial phenomena which prove the Copernican system. Warned by his friend of the possible consequences of his investigations,* GALILEO *affirms his faith in reason.*

January ten, sixteen ten:
Galileo Galilei abolishes heaven.

(GALILEO's *study in Padua. Night.* GALILEO *and* SAGREDO, *both in heavy overcoats, at the telescope.*)

SAGREDO: (Looking through the telescope, in an undertone) The edge of the crescent is quite irregular, rough and serrated. In the dark part near the luminous edge there are luminous points. They are emerging, one after another. From these points the light spreads out over wider and wider areas and finally merges with the larger luminous part.

GALILEO: How do you account for those luminous points?

SAGREDO: It can't be.

GALILEO: But it is. They're mountains.

SAGREDO: On a star?

GALILEO: Gigantic mountains. Their peaks are gilded by the rising sun while the surrounding slopes are still deep in darkness. You can see the light descending from the highest peaks into the valleys.

SAGREDO: But that contradicts all the astronomy of two thousand years.

GALILEO: True. No mortal has ever seen what you are seeing, except me. You're the second.

SAGREDO: But the moon can't be another earth with mountains and valleys, any more than the earth can be a planet.

GALILEO: The moon can be an earth with mountains and valleys, and the earth can be a planet. Simply another heavenly body, one among thousands. Take another look. Is the dark part of the moon entirely dark?

SAGREDO: No. When I look closely, I see a feeble gray light on it.

GALILEO: What can that light be?

SACREDO: ?

GALILEO: It's from the earth.

SAGREDO: Nonsense. How can the earth with its mountains and forests and oceans—a cold body—give light?

GALILEO: The same way the moon sheds light. Because both bodies are illuminated by the sun, that's why they shed light. What the moon is to us we are to the moon. The moon sees us by turns as a crescent, as a half-circle, as full, and then not at all.

SAGREDO: Then there's no difference between moon and earth?

GALILEO: Apparently not.

SAGREDO: Less than ten years ago a man was burned in Rome. His name was Giordano Bruno and he had said the same thing.

GALILEO: I know. But we can see it. Keep your eyes to the tube. What you see is that there's no difference between heaven and earth. This is the tenth of January, 1610. Humanity notes in its diary: Heaven abolished.

SAGREDO: It's terrifying.

GALILEO: I've discovered something else. Perhaps something even more amazing.

MRS. SARTI: (Comes in) The procurator.

(The PROCURATOR *rushes in)*

THE PROCURATOR: I apologize for the late hour. I'd be much obliged if we could talk privately.

GALILEO: Mr. Sagredo can hear anything I can hear, Mr. Priuli.

THE PROCURATOR: It might embarrass you to have the gentleman hear what has happened. Unfortunately, it's something quite incredible.

GALILEO: Mr. Sagredo is used to hearing incredible things in my presence.

THE PROCURATOR: I wonder. *(Pointing at the telescope)* There it is, your splendid gadget. You might as well throw it away. It's worthless, absolutely worthless.

SAGREDO: *(Who has been restlessly pacing the floor)* What do you mean?

THE PROCURATOR: Do you realize that his invention of yours, "the fruit of seventeen years of patient labor," is for sale on every street corner in Italy for a couple of scudi? Made in Holland, I might add. At this very moment a Dutch freighter is unloading five hundred telescopes in the harbor?

GALILEO: You don't say.

THE PROCURATOR: Your equanimity, sir, is beyond me.

SAGREDO: I fail to see what's troubling you. Let me tell you that just in these last few days Mr. Galilei—with this very instrument—has made the most revolutionary discoveries concerning heavenly bodies.

GALILEO: *(Laughing)* Have a look for yourself, Priuli.

THE PROCURATOR: Let me tell you that after having Mr. Galilei's salary doubled on the strength of this worthless gadget I'm quite satisfied with the discovery I've already made. It's sheer accident that when the gentlemen of the signoria first looked through your tube, confident of having acquired something for the republic that could be manufactured only here, they failed to see—seven times magnified—a common peddler on the next corner hawking that same tube for a song.

*(*GALILEO *roars with laughter.)*

SAGREDO: Dear Mr. Priuli, I may not be able to judge the instrument's value to the economy, but its value to philosophy is so enormous that . . .

THE PROCURATOR: To philosophy! What business has Mr. Galilei, a mathematician, meddling with philosophy? Mr. Galilei, you once invented a very respectable pump for the city; your irrigation system functions. The weavers, too, are very pleased with your machine. How on earth could I have anticipated anything like this?

GALILEO: Not so fast, Priuli. Sea routes are still long, unsafe and expensive. We lack a dependable clock in the sky. A guide to navigation. I have reason to believe that with the telescope we can very clearly perceive certain stars with very regular motions. New star charts, Mr. Priuli, could save the shipping interests millions of scudi.

THE PROCURATOR: Forget it. I've heard more than enough. In return for my kindness you've made me the laughingstock of the city. I'll be remembered as the procurator who fell for a worthless telescope. You have every reason to laugh. You've got your five hundred scudi. But I'm telling you, and I speak as an honest man: This world makes me sick! *(He leaves, banging the door behind him)*

GALILEO: He's rather likable when he gets angry. Did you hear what he said: A world where you can't do business makes him sick.

SAGREDO: Did you know about the Dutch instruments?

GALILEO: Of course. From hearsay. But the one I made for those skinflints in the signoria is twice as good. How can I do my work with the bailiff at the door? And Virginia will need her trousseau soon, she's not bright. Besides, I like to buy books, and not only about physics, and I like to eat well. I get my best ideas over a good meal. A rotten time to live in! They weren't paying me as much as the teamster who carts their wine barrels. Four cords of firewood for two courses in mathematics. I've wormed five hundred scudi out of them, but I've got debts, some of them twenty years old. Give me five years of leisure and I'll prove everything. Let me show you something else.

SAGREDO: *(Hesitates to go to the telescope)* I almost think I'm afraid, Galileo.

GALILEO: I want to show you a milky-white patch of luminous mist in the galaxy. Tell me what it's made of.

SAGREDO: Why, stars, countless stars.

GALILEO: In the constellation of Orion alone there are five hundred fixed stars. Those are the many worlds, the countless other worlds, the stars beyond stars that the man they burned talked about. He didn't see them, but he knew they would be there.

SAGREDO: Even if our earth is a star, it's still a long way to Copernicus' contention that the earth revolves around the sun. There isn't any star in the heavens with another revolving around it. And the earth, you'll have to admit, has the moon revolving around it.

GALILEO: Sagredo, I wonder. I've been wondering for two days. There's Jupiter. *(He adjusts the telescope)* Now, near it there are four smaller stars that you can only make out through the tube. I saw them on Monday but I didn't pay too much attention to their positions. Yesterday I looked again. I could have sworn that all four had moved. I

recorded their positions. Now they're different again. What's that now? There were four of them. *(Getting excited)* You look!

SAGREDO: I see three.

GALILEO: Where's the fourth? Here are the tables. We must compute the movements they can have made.

(Agitated, they sit down to work. The stage turns dark, but on a cyclorama Jupiter and its satellites remain visible. When it grows light again, they are still sitting there in their winter coats.)

GALILEO: Now we have proof. The fourth must have moved behind Jupiter where we can't see it. There you have a star with another revolving around it.

SAGREDO: But the crystal sphere that Jupiter is fastened to?

GALILEO: Where is it indeed? How can Jupiter be fastened to anything if other stars revolve around it? There is no scaffolding in the sky, there's nothing holding the universe up! There you have another sun!

SAGREDO: Calm down. You're thinking too fast.

GALILEO: Fast, hell! Man, get excited! You're seeing something that nobody ever saw before. They were right!

SAGREDO: Who? The Copernicans?

GALILEO: Yes, and you know who. The whole world was against them, and yet they were right. That's something for Andrea! *(Beside himself, he runs to the door and shouts)* Mrs. Sarti! Mrs. Sarti!

SAGREDO: Galileo, please calm yourself!

GALILEO: Sagredo, please get excited! Mrs. Sarti!

SAGREDO: *(Turning the telescope aside)* Will you stop yelling like a fool?

GALILEO: Will you stop standing there like a stockfish when we've discovered the truth?

SAGREDO: I'm not standing here like a stockfish, I'm trembling for fear it's the truth.

GALILEO: What?

SAGREDO: Have you taken leave of your senses? Don't you realize what you're getting into if what you see is really true? And if you go shouting all over town that the earth is a planet and not the center of the universe?

GALILEO: Yes, and that the whole enormous cosmos with all its stars doesn't revolve around our tiny earth, as anyone could have guessed anyway.

SAGREDO: So that there's nothing but stars! — But where does that put God?

GALILEO: What do you mean?

SAGREDO: God! Where's God?

GALILEO: (Furious) Not out there! Any more than He'd be on earth if somebody out there started looking for Him here.

SAGREDO: Where is God then?

GALILEO: Am I a theologian? I'm a mathematician.

SAGREDO: First of all you're a human being. And I ask you: Where is God in your whole system?

GALILEO: Inside us or nowhere!

SAGREDO: (Shouting) As the man who was burned said?

GALILEO: As the man who was burned said!

SAGREDO: That's why he was burned! Less than ten years ago!

GALILEO: Because he couldn't prove it! Because all he could do was say so! Mrs. Sarti!

SAGREDO: Galileo, I know you're a clever man. For three years in Pisa and seventeen here in Padua you've patiently instructed hundreds of students in the Ptolemaic system as advocated by the church and confirmed by the scriptures on which the church is grounded. Like Copernicus you thought it was wrong, but you taught it.

GALILEO: Because I couldn't prove anything.

SAGREDO: (Incredulous) You think that makes a difference?

GALILEO: All the difference in the world! Look here, Sagredo! I believe in man and that means I believe in reason. Without that belief I wouldn't have the strength to get out of bed in the morning.

SAGREDO: Then let me tell you this: I don't believe in reason. Forty years' experience has taught me that human beings are not accessible to reason. Show them a comet with a red tail, put dark fear into them, and they'll rush out of their houses and break their legs. But make a reasonable statement, prove it with seven good reasons, and they'll just laugh at you.

GALILEO: That's all wrong and it's slander. I don't see how you can love science if you believe that. Only the dead are impervious to argument.

SAGREDO: How can you mistake their contemptible cunning for reason?

GALILEO: I'm not talking about their cunning. I know they call a donkey a horse when they're selling and a horse a donkey when they're buying. That's their cunning. But the old woman with calloused hands who gives her mule an extra bunch of hay the night before setting out on a trip; the sea captain who allows for storms and doldrums when he lays in his stores; the child who puts on his cap when he realizes that it may rain—these people are my hope, they accept the law of cause and effect. Yes, I believe in the gentle force of reason, in the long run no one can resist it. Nobody can watch me drop (He lets a pebble fall from his hand to the floor) a pebble and say: It doesn't fall. Nobody can do that. The seduction of proof is too strong. Most people will succumb to it and in time they all will. Thinking is one of the greatest pleasures of the human race.

MRS. SARTI: (Comes in) Did you want something, Mr. Galilei?

GALILEO: (Back at the telescope, scribbling notes, very kindly) Yes, I want Andrea.

MRS. SARTI: Andrea? But he's in bed, he's sound asleep.

GALILEO: Can't you wake him?

MRS. SARTI: What do you want him for, may I ask?

GALILEO: I want to show him something that'll please him. He's going to see something that no one but us has ever seen since the earth began.

MRS. SARTI: Something through your tube?

GALILEO: Something through my tube, Mrs. Sarti.

MRS. SARTI: And for that you want me to wake him in the middle of the night? Are you out of your mind? He needs his sleep. I wouldn't think of waking him.

GALILEO: Not a chance?

MRS. SARTI: Not a chance.

GALILEO: Mrs. Sarti, in that case maybe you can help me. You see, a question has come up that we can't agree on, perhaps because we've read too many books. It's a question about the sky, involving the stars. Here it is: Which seems more likely, that large bodies turn around small bodies or small bodies around large ones?

MRS. SARTI: (Suspiciously) I never know what you're up to, Mr. Galilei. Is this a serious question or are you pulling my leg again?

GALILEO: A serious question.

MRS. SARTI: Then I can give you a quick answer. Do I serve your dinner or do you serve mine?

GALILEO: You serve mine. Yesterday it was burned.

MRS. SARTI: And why was it burned? Because you made me get your shoes while I was cooking it. Didn't I bring you your shoes?

GALILEO: I presume you did.

MRS. SARTI: Because it's you who went to school and can pay.

GALILEO: I see. I see there's no difficulty. Good morning, Mrs. Sarti.

(MRS. SARTI, *amused, goes out*)

GALILEO: And such people are supposed not to be able to grasp the truth? They snatch at it.

(The matins bell has begun to peal. In comes VIRGINIA *in a cloak, carrying a shaded candle)*

VIRGINIA: Good morning, father.

GALILEO: Up so early.

VIRGINIA: I'm going to matins with Mrs. Sarti. Ludovico will be there too. How was the night, father?

GALILEO: Clear.

VIRGINIA: May I look through it?

GALILEO: What for? (VIRGINIA *has no answer)* It's not a toy.

VIRGINIA: I know, father.

GALILEO: By the way, the tube's a big flop. You'll hear all about it soon. It's being sold on the street for three scudi, it was invented in Holland.

VIRGINIA: Didn't you find anything new in the sky with it?

GALILEO: Nothing for you. Only a few dim specks on the left side of a big star, I'll have to find a way of calling attention to them. *(Speaking to* SAGREDO *over his daughter's head)* Maybe I'll call them the "Medicean Stars" to please the grand duke of Florence. *(Again to* VIRGINIA*)* It may interest you, Virginia, to know that we'll probably move to Florence. I've written to ask if the grand duke can use me as court mathematician.

VIRGINIA: *(Radiant)* At court?

SAGREDO: Galileo!

GALILEO: I need leisure, old friend. I need proofs. And I want the fleshpots. With a position like that I won't have to ram the Ptolemaic system down the throats of private students, I'll have time—time, time, time, time!—to work out my proofs. What I've got now isn't enough. It's nothing, it's just bits and pieces. I can't stand up to the whole world with that. There's still no proof that any heavenly body revolves around the sun. But I'm going to find the proofs, proofs for everybody from Mrs. Sarti to the pope. The only thing that worries me is that the court may not want me.

VIRGINIA: Oh, I'm sure they'll take you, father, with your new stars and all.

GALILEO: Go to your mass.

*(*VIRGINIA *leaves)*

GALILEO: I'm not used to writing letters to important people. *(He hands* SAGREDO *a letter)* Do you think this will do?

SAGREDO: *(Reading aloud the end of the letter which* GALILEO *has handed him)* "Withal I am yearning for nothing so much as to be nearer to Your Highness, the rising sun which will illuminate this age." The grand duke of Florence is nine years old.

GALILEO: I know. I see, you think my letter is too servile. I wonder if it's servile enough, not too formal, as if I were lacking in genuine devotion. A more restrained letter might be all right for someone with the distinction of having proved the truth of Aristotle; not for me. A man like me can only get a halfway decent position by crawling on his belly. And you know I despise men whose brains are incapable of filling their stomachs.

*(*MRS. SARTI *and* VIRGINIA *walk past the two men on their way to mass.)*

SAGREDO: Don't go to Florence, Galileo.

GALILEO: Why not?

SAGREDO: Because it's ruled by monks.

GALILEO: There are distinguished scholars at the Florentine court.

SAGREDO: Toadies.

GALILEO: I'll take them by the scruff of their necks and drag them to my tube. Even monks are human beings, Sagredo. Even monks can be seduced by proofs. Copernicus—don't forget that—wanted them to trust his figures, I'm only asking them to trust the evidence of their eyes. When truth is too weak to defend itself, it has to attack. I'll take them by the scruff of their necks and make them look through the tube.

SAGREDO: Galileo, you're on a dangerous path. It's bad luck when a man sees the truth. And delusion when he believes in the rationality of the human race. Who do we say walks with open eyes? The man who's headed for perdition. How can the mighty leave a man at large who knows the truth, even if it's only about the remotest stars? Do you think the pope will hear your truth when you tell him he's wrong? No, he'll hear only one thing, that you've said he's wrong. Do you think he will calmly write in his diary: January 10, 1610, Heaven abolished? How can you want to leave the republic with the truth in your pocket and walk straight into the trap of the monks and princes with your tube in your hands? You may be very skeptical in your science, but you're as gullible as a child about anything that looks like a help in pursuing it. You may not believe in Aristotle, but you believe in the grand duke of Florence. A moment ago when I saw you at your tube looking at the new stars I thought I saw you on a flaming pyre and when you said you believed in proofs I smelled burnt flesh. I love science, but I love you more, my friend. Galileo, don't go to Florence!

GALILEO: If they'll have me I'll go.

(On a curtain appears the last page of the letter)

In assigning the sublime name of the Medicean line to these stars newly discovered by me I am fully aware that when gods and heroes were elevated to the starry skies they were thereby glorified, but that in the present case it is the stars that will be glorified by receiving the name of the Medici. With this I recommend myself as one among the number of your most faithful and obedient servants, who holds it the highest honor to have been born your subject.

Withal I yearn for nothing so much as to be nearer to Your Highness, the rising sun which will illuminate this age.

Galileo Galilei

SCENE IV

GALILEO *has exchanged the Venetian republic for the court of Florence. The discoveries he has made with the help of the telescope are met with disbelief by the court scholars.*

The old says: What I've always done I'll
always do.
The new says: If you're useless you must go.

(GALILEO's house in Florence. MRS. SARTI is getting GALILEO's study ready to receive guests. Her son ANDREA is seated, putting celestial charts away.)

MRS. SARTI: Ever since we arrived in this marvelous Florence I've seen nothing but bowing and scraping. The whole town files past this tube and I can scrub the floor afterwards. But it won't do us a bit of good. If these discoveries amounted to anything, the reverend fathers would know it, wouldn't they? For four years I was in service with Monsignor Filippo, I never managed to dust the whole of his library. Leather-bound volumes up to the ceiling and no love poems either. And the good monsignor had two pounds of boils on his behind from poring over all that learning. Wouldn't a man like that know what's what? The big demonstration today will be another flop and tomorrow I won't be able to look the milkman in the face. I knew what I was saying when I told him to give the gentlemen a good dinner first, a nice piece of lamb, before they start in on his tube. Oh no! *(She imitates GALILEO)* "I've got something better for them."

(Knocking downstairs.)

MRS. SARTI: *(Looks in the window-mirror)* Goodness, there's the grand duke already. And Galileo still at the university!

(She runs downstairs and admits COSMO DE' MEDICI, grand duke of Tuscany, accompanied by THE LORD CHAMBERLAIN and two LADIES-IN-WAITING.)

COSMO: I want to see the tube.

THE LORD CHAMBERLAIN: Perhaps Your

Highness would prefer to wait until Mr. Galilei and the other gentlemen have returned from the university. *(To* MRS. SARTI*)* Mr. Galilei wanted the professors of astronomy to examine the newly discovered stars which he calls the Medicean stars.

COSMO: They don't believe in the tube, far from it. Where is it?

MRS. SARTI: Upstairs, in his workroom.

(The boy nods, points to the staircase, and upon a nod from MRS. SARTI *dashes up the stairs)*

THE LORD CHAMBERLAIN: *(A very old man)* Your Highness! *(To* MRS. SARTI*) Must* we go up there? I only came because the tutor is ill.

MRS. SARTI: Nothing can happen to the young gentleman. My boy's upstairs.

COSMO: *(Entering above)* Good evening.

(The two boys ceremoniously bow to each other. Pause. Then ANDREA *goes back to his work.)*

ANDREA: *(Much like his teacher)* This place is as busy as a pigeon house.

COSMO: Lots of visitors?

ANDREA: Stumble about and gape and don't know beans.

COSMO: I see. Is that . . .? *(Points at the tube)*

ANDREA: Yes, that's it. But don't touch it. It's not allowed.

COSMO: And what's that? *(He indicates the wooden model of the Ptolemaic system)*

ANDREA: That's the Ptolemaic system.

COSMO: It shows how the sun moves, doesn't it?

ANDREA: Yes, so they say.

COSMO: *(Sitting down in a chair, he takes the model on his knees)* My tutor has a cold. So I was able to get away early. It's nice here.

ANDREA: *(Is restless, ambles about irresolutely, throwing suspicious glances at the strange boy, and at last, unable to resist the temptation any longer, takes from behind the star charts another wooden model representing the Copernican system)* But of course it's really like this.

COSMO: What's like this?

ANDREA: *(Pointing at the model on* COSMO's *knees)* That's the way people think it is and that's *(Pointing at his model)* the way it really is. The earth turns around the sun. See?

COSMO: You really think so?

ANDREA: Of course. It's been proven.

COSMO: You don't say!—I wish I knew why they didn't let me go in to see the old man. Last night he was at dinner as usual.

ANDREA: You don't seem to believe it, or do you?

COSMO: Why certainly, I do.

ANDREA: *(Pointing at the model on* COSMO's *knees)* Give it back, you don't understand that one!

COSMO: But you don't need two.

ANDREA: Give it back this minute. It's not a toy for little boys.

COSMO: I don't mind giving it back but you ought to be a little more polite, you know.

ANDREA: You're stupid and I don't care about being polite. Give it back or you'll see.

COSMO: Hands off, do you hear.

(They start fighting and are soon rolling on the floor.)

ANDREA: I'll show you how to treat a model. Give up!

COSMO: You've broken it. You're twisting my hand.

ANDREA: We'll see who's right and who isn't. Say it turns or I'll box your ears.

COSMO: I won't. Ouch, you redhead. I'll teach you good manners.

ANDREA: Redhead? Am I a redhead?

(They continue to fight in silence. Below, GALILEO *and several university professors enter. Behind them* FEDERZONI.*)*

THE LORD CHAMBERLAIN: Gentlemen, a slight illness has prevented Mr. Suri, His Highness' tutor, from accompanying His Highness.

THE THEOLOGIAN: Nothing serious, I hope.

THE LORD CHAMBERLAIN: No, no, by no means.

GALILEO: *(Disappointed)* Isn't His Highness here?

THE LORD CHAMBERLAIN: His Highness is upstairs. May I ask you gentlemen to proceed. The court is so very anxious to hear the opinion of our illustrious university about Mr. Galilei's extraordinary instrument and those marvelous new stars.

(They go upstairs.)
(The boys lie still. They have heard sounds downstairs.)

COSMO: Here they come. Let me up.

(They quickly get up.)

THE GENTLEMEN: *(As they file upstairs)* No. No, there's nothing to worry about. — The faculty of medicine has declared that the cases in the inner city can't possibly be plague. The miasma would freeze at the present temperature. — The worst danger in these situations is panic. — We can always expect an epidemic of colds at this time of year. — No ground for suspicion. — Nothing to worry about.

(Salutations upstairs.)

GALILEO: Your Highness, I am extremely pleased that you should be present while I communicate our new discoveries to the gentlemen of your university.

(COSMO makes formal bows to all, including ANDREA.)

THE THEOLOGIAN: *(Seeing the broken Ptolemaic model on the floor)* There seems to have been some breakage here.

(COSMO stoops quickly and hands the model politely to ANDREA. At the same time GALILEO slyly puts away the other model.)

GALILEO: *(At the telescope)* As Your Highness no doubt knows, we astonomers have for some time been encountering great difficulties in our calculations. We are using a very old system which seems to be in agreement with philosophy but unfortunately not with the facts. According to this old system, the Ptolemaic system, the movements of the planets are extremely complicated. Venus, for instance, is supposed to move something like this. *(He sketches on a blackboard the epicyclic course of Venus according to Ptolemy)* But if we predicate these complicated movements, we are unable to calculate the position of any star accurately in advance. We do not find it in the place where it should be. Furthermore there are stellar motions for which the Ptolemaic system has no explanation at all. According to my observations, certain small stars I have discovered describe motions of this kind around the planet Jupiter. If you gentlemen are agreeable, we shall begin with the inspection of the satellites of Jupiter, the Medicean stars.

ANDREA: *(Pointing to the stool in front of the telescope)* Kindly sit here.

THE PHILOSOPHER: Thank you, my child.

I'm afraid it will not be so simple. Mr. Galilei, before we apply ourselves to your famous tube, we should like to request the pleasure of a disputation: Can such planets exist?

THE MATHEMATICIAN: A formal disputation.

GALILEO: I thought you'd just look through the telescope and see for yourselves.

ANDREA: Here, if you please.

THE MATHEMATICIAN: Yes, yes. — You are aware, of course, that in the view of the ancients no star can revolve around any center other than the earth and that there can be no stars without firm support in the sky.

GALILEO: Yes.

THE PHILOSOPHER: And, regardless of whether such stars are possible, a proposition which the mathematician *(He bows to the mathematician)* seems to doubt, I as a philsopher should like with all due modesty to raise this question: Are such stars necessary? Aristotelis divini universum . . .

GALILEO: Oughtn't we to continue in the vernacular? My colleague, Mr. Federzoni, doesn't understand Latin.

THE PHILOSOPHER: Does it matter whether he understands us?

GALILEO: Yes.

THE PHILOSOPHER: I beg your pardon. I thought he was your lens grinder.

ANDREA: Mr. Federzoni is a lens grinder and a scholar.

THE PHILOSOPHER: Thank you, my child. If Mr. Federzoni insists . . .

GALILEO: I insist.

THE PHILOSOPHER: The debate will lose in brilliance, but this is your house. — The cosmos of the divine Aristotle with its spheres and their mystical music, with its crystal vaults and the circular courses of its heavenly bodies, with the oblique angle of the sun's course and the mysteries of its tables of satellites and the wealth of stars in the catalog of the southern hemisphere and the inspired construction of the celestial globe is an edifice of such order and beauty that we shall be well advised not to disturb its harmony.

GALILEO: Your Highness, would you care to observe those impossible and unnecessary stars through the telescope?

THE MATHEMATICIAN: One might be

tempted to reply that if your tube shows something that cannot exist it must be a rather unreliable tube.

GALILEO: What do you mean by that?

THE MATHEMATICIAN: It certainly would be much more to the point, Mr. Galilei, if you were to tell us your reasons for supposing that there can be free-floating stars moving about in the highest sphere of the immutable heavens.

THE PHILOSOPHER: Reasons, Mr. Galilei, reasons!

GALILEO: My reasons? When a look at these stars and my calculations demonstrate the phenomenon? This debate is getting absurd, sir.

THE MATHEMATICIAN: If it were not to be feared that you would get even more excited than you are, one might suggest that what is in your tube and what is in the sky might be two different things.

THE PHILOSOPHER: It would be difficult to put it more politely.

FEDERZONI: They think we painted the Medicean stars on the lens!

GALILEO: You accuse me of fraud?

THE PHILOSOPHER: We wouldn't dream of it! In the presence of His Highness!

THE MATHEMATICIAN: Your instrument, whether we call it your own or your adoptive child, has doubtless been very cleverly constructed.

THE PHILOSOPHER: And we are convinced, Mr. Galilei, that neither you nor anyone else would ever dare to grace stars with the illustrious name of the ruling house if there were the slightest doubt of their existence.

(All bow deeply to the grand duke)

COSMO: *(Turning to the* LADIES-IN-WAITING*)* Is there something wrong with my stars?

THE OLDER LADY-IN-WAITING: *(To the* GRAND DUKE*)* Your Highness' stars are fine. The gentlemen are only wondering whether they really and truly exist.

(Pause.)

THE YOUNGER LADY-IN-WAITING: They say you can see the scales of the Dragon with this instrument.

FEDERZONI: Yes, and you can see all sorts of things on the Bull.

GALILEO: Are you gentlemen going to look through it, or not?

THE PHILOSOPHER: Certainly, certainly.

THE MATHEMATICIAN: Certainly.

(Pause. Suddenly ANDREA *turns around and walks stiffly out through the length of the room. His mother intercepts him.)*

MRS. SARTI: What's got into you?

ANDREA: They're stupid. *(Tears himself loose and runs away)*

THE PHILOSOPHER: A deplorable child.

THE LORD CHAMBERLAIN: Your Highness, gentlemen, may I remind you that the state ball is due to start in forty-five minutes?

THE MATHEMATICIAN: Why beat about the bush? Sooner or later Mr. Galilei will have to face up to the facts. His moons of Jupiter would pierce the crystal sphere. That's all there is to it.

FEDERZONI: You'll be surprised, but there is no crystal sphere.

THE PHILOSOPHER: Any textbook will tell you there is, my good man.

FEDERZONI: Then we need new textbooks.

THE PHILOSPHER: Your Highness, my esteemed colleague and I are supported by no less an authority than the divine Aristotle.

GALILEO: *(Almost abjectly)* Gentlemen, belief in the authority of Aristotle is one thing, observable facts are another. You say that according to Aristotle there are crystal spheres up there and that certain motions are impossible because the stars would have to pierce the spheres. But what if you observed these motions? Wouldn't that suggest to you that the spheres do not exist? Gentlemen, I humbly beseech you to trust your own eyes.

THE MATHEMATICIAN: My dear Galilei, though it may seem dreadfully old-fashioned to you, I'm in the habit of reading Aristotle now and then, and I can assure you that when I read Aristotle I do trust my eyes.

GALILEO: I'm used to seeing the gentlemen of all faculties close their eyes to all facts and act as if nothing had happened. I show them my calculations, and they smile; I make my telescope available to help them see for themselves, and they quote Aristotle.

FEDERZONI: The man had no telescope!

THE MATHEMATICIAN: Exactly!

THE PHILOSOPHER: *(Grandly)* If Aristotle, an authority acknowledged not only by all the scientists of antiquity but by the church fathers themselves, is to be dragged through the mire, a continuation of this discussion seems superfluous, at least to me. I refuse to take part in irrelevant arguments. Basta.

GALILEO: Truth is the child of time, not of authority. Our ignorance is infinite, let's whittle away just one cubic millimeter. Why should we still want to be so clever when at long last we have a chance of being a little less stupid? I've had the good fortune to lay hands on a new instrument with which we can observe a tiny corner of the universe a little more closely, not much though. Make use of it.

THE PHILOSOPHER: Your Highness, ladies and gentlemen, I can only wonder what all this will lead to.

GALILEO: I submit that as scientists we have no business asking what the truth may lead to.

THE PHILOSOPHER: (In wild alarm) Mr. Galilei, the truth can lead to all sorts of things!

GALILEO: Your Highness. In these nights telescopes are being directed at the sky all over Italy. The moons of Jupiter don't lower the price of milk. But they have never been seen before, and yet they exist. The man in the street will conclude that a good many things may exist if only he opens his eyes. And you ought to back him up. It's not the motions of some remote stars that make Italy sit up and take notice, but the news that doctrines believed to be unshakeable are beginning to totter, and we all know that of these there are far too many. Gentlemen, we oughtn't to be defending shaky doctrines!

FEDERZONI: You are teachers, you ought to be doing the shaking.

THE PHILOSOPHER: I wish your man there would keep out of a scientific debate.

GALILEO: Your Highness! My work in the great arsenal of Venice brought me into daily contact with draftsmen, architects and instrument makers. Those people taught me many new ways of doing things. They don't read books but they trust the testimony of their five senses, most of them without fear as to where it will lead them . . .

THE PHILOSOPHER: Fancy that!

GALILEO: Very much like our seamen who left our shores a hundred years ago, without the slightest idea of what other shores, if any, they might reach. It looks as if we had to go to the shipyards nowadays to find the high curiosity that was the glory of ancient Greece.

THE PHILOSOPHER: After what we have heard here today, I have no doubt that Mr. Galilei will find admirers in the shipyards.

THE LORD CHAMBERLAIN: Your Highness, I note to my great dismay that this exceedingly instructive conversation has taken a little longer than foreseen. Your Highness must rest a while before the court ball.

(At a signal, the grand duke bows to GALILEO. The court quickly prepares to leave)

MRS. SARTI: (Stepping in the way of the grand duke and offering him a plate of pastry) A bun, Your Highness!

(The OLDER LADY-IN-WAITING leads the grand duke away.)

GALILEO: (Running after them) But all you gentlemen need do is look through the instrument.

THE LORD CHAMBERLAIN: His Highness will not fail to obtain an expert opinion on your statements by consulting our greatest living astronomer, Father Christopher Clavius, astronomer-in-chief at the papal college in Rome.

SCENE V

Undaunted even by the plague, GALILEO *continues his investigations.*

(a)

(*Early morning.* GALILEO *bending over his notes at the telescope.* VIRGINIA *comes in with a traveling bag.*)

GALILEO: Virginia! Is anything wrong?

VIRGINIA: The convent is closed. They sent us home. There are five cases of plague in Arcetri.

GALILEO: (Calls out) Sarti!

VIRGINIA: And last night our market was

roped off. They say two people have died in the old city, and there are three more dying in the hospital.

GALILEO: As usual, they've hushed it up until the last minute.

MRS. SARTI: *(Comes in)* What are you doing here?

VIRGINIA: The plague.

MRS. SARTI: My God! I'd better pack. *(Sits down)*

GALILEO: No need to pack. Take Virginia and Andrea. I'll go get my notes.

(He hurries back to the table and gathers his papers in great haste. MRS. SARTI puts a coat on ANDREA as he runs in, and goes to get some food and bedding. One of the grand duke's LACKEYS enters.)

LACKEY: His Highness has left the city for Bologna because of the raging disease. Before leaving he insisted that Mr. Galilei should be given an opportunity to escape. The coach will be here in two minutes.

MRS. SARTI: *(To VIRGINIA and ANDREA)* Go right outside, you two. Here, take this.

ANDREA: Why? If you don't tell me why, I won't go.

MRS. SARTI: It's the plague, my child.

VIRGINIA: We'll wait for father.

MRS. SARTI: Mr. Galilei, are you ready?

GALILEO: *(Wrapping the telescope in a table-cloth)* Put Virginia and Andrea in the coach. I'll join you in a minute.

VIRGINIA: No, we won't leave without you. You'll never be ready if you start packing your books.

MRS. SARTI: The carriage is here.

GALILEO: Be reasonable, Virginia. If no one gets in, the coachman will just drive away. The plague is no joke.

VIRGINIA: *(Protesting as MRS. SARTI leads her and Andrea out)* Help him with his books or he won't come.

MRS. SARTI: *(Calls out from the house door)* Mr. Galilei! The coachman says he won't wait.

GALILEO: Mrs. Sarti, I don't think I should leave. Everything is in such a muddle here, you know, all my notes of the last three months, I might as well throw them away if I don't go on with them for a night or two. And anyway the plague is everywhere.

MRS. SARTI: Mr. Galilei! Come this minute! You're out of your mind.

GALILEO: You go with Virginia and Andrea. I'll come later.

MRS. SARTI: In another hour they won't let anyone leave the city. You must come! *(Listens)* He's driving off! I've got to stop him. *(Out)*

(GALILEO walks back and forth. MRS. SARTI returns, very pale, without her bundle.)

GALILEO: Don't stand around like that! The coach with the children will leave without you.

MRS. SARTI: They've left. They had to hold Virginia down. The children will be taken care of in Bologna. But who'd get you your meals?

GALILEO: You're crazy. Staying in the city to cook! ... *(Takes up his papers)* You mustn't take me for a fool, Mrs. Sarti. I can't interrupt my observations. I have powerful enemies, I've got to supply proofs for certain propositions.

MRS. SARTI: You needn't apologize. But it's not reasonable.

(b)

(Outside GALILEO's house in Florence. GALILEO comes out of the door and looks down the street. TWO NUNS are passing by.)

GALILEO: *(Addresses them)* Sisters, could you tell me where I can buy milk? This morning the milk woman didn't come, and my housekeeper is away.

THE FIRST NUN: Only the shops in the lower city are open.

THE OTHER NUN: Did you come out of this house? *(GALILEO nods)* This is the street!

(The TWO NUNS cross themselves, mumble an Ave Maria and run. A man passes.)

GALILEO: *(Addresses him)* Aren't you the baker who brings us our bread? *(The man nods)* Have you seen my housekeeper? She must have gone out last night. She hasn't been here all morning.

(The man shakes his head. A window across the street is opened and a woman looks out.)

THE WOMAN: *(Screams)* Run! Quick! They've got the plague!

(Frightened, the man runs away.)

GALILEO: Do you know anything about my housekeeper?

THE WOMAN: Your housekeeper collapsed in the street. Up there. She must have known. That's why she left you. How can people be so inconsiderate? *(She bangs the window shut)*

(Children come down the street. When they see GALILEO *they run away screaming. As* GALILEO *turns around,* TWO SOLDIERS *in full armor come rushing in)*

THE SOLDIERS: Get back in that house!

(With their long lances they push GALILEO *back into his house. They bolt the door behind him.)*

GALILEO: *(At a window)* Can you tell me what's happened to the woman?

THE SOLDIERS: They take 'em to potter's field.

THE WOMAN: *(Appears at her window again)* The whole street back there's infected. Why don't you close it off?

(The SOLDIERS *stretch a rope across the street.)*

THE WOMAN: But now nobody can get into our house! Don't put your rope there. We're all well here. Stop! Stop! Can't you hear? My husband's gone to the city, he won't be able to get back. You beasts! You beasts!

(Her sobbing and screaming are heard from inside. The SOLDIERS *leave. An* OLD WOMAN *appears at another window.)*

GALILEO: There seems to be a fire back there.

THE OLD WOMAN: The firemen won't touch it if there's any suspicion of plague. All they can think about is the plague.

GALILEO: Just like them! Their whole system of government is like that. They cut us off like a withered fig branch that's stopped bearing fruit.

THE OLD WOMAN: You mustn't say that. They're helpless, that's all.

GALILEO: Are you alone in your house?

THE OLD WOMAN: Yes. My son sent me a note. Thank God he heard last night that someone had died around here, so he didn't come home. There've been eleven cases in the neighborhood during the night.

GALILEO: I can't forgive myself for not sending my housekeeper away in time. I had urgent work to finish, but she had no reason to stay.

THE OLD WOMAN: We can't go away either. Who would take us in? You mustn't reproach yourself. I saw her. She left this morning, at about seven o'clock. She was sick, because when she saw me step out to bring in the bread she circled around me. I suppose she didn't want your house to be sealed off. But they get wise to everything.

(A rattling sound is heard.)

GALILEO: What's that?

THE OLD WOMAN: They're making noise to drive away the clouds that carry the seeds of the plague.

(GALILEO roars with laughter.)

THE OLD WOMAN: How can you laugh?

(A man comes down the street and finds it roped off.)

GALILEO: Hey, you! The street's closed and there's nothing to eat in the house.

(The man has already run away.)

GALILEO: You can't just let us starve here! Hey! Hey!

THE OLD WOMAN: Maybe they'll bring us something. If they don't, I can put a pitcher of milk on your doorstep, if you're not afraid, but not until after dark.

GALILEO: Hey! Hey! Somebody ought to hear us.

(Suddenly ANDREA *stands at the rope. His face is stained with tears.)*

GALILEO: Andrea! How did you get here?

ANDREA: I was here this morning. I knocked, but you didn't open. People told me . . .

GALILEO: Didn't you go away?

ANDREA: I did. But I managed to jump out. Virginia went on. Can I come in?

THE OLD WOMAN: No, you can not. You must go the the Ursulines. Maybe your mother is there too.

ANDREA: I've been there. But they wouldn't let me see her. She's too sick.

GALILEO: Did you walk the whole way back? You've been gone for three days.

ANDREA: That's how long it took, don't be angry. And once they caught me.

GALILEO: *(Helplessly)* Don't cry, Andrea. You know, I've found out a few things in the meantime. Shall I tell you? *(ANDREA nods, sobbing)* But listen carefully, or you won't understand. Remember when I showed you the planet Venus? Don't listen to that noise, it's nothing. Remember? You know what I saw? It's like the moon. I saw it as a half-circle and I saw it as a crescent. What do you think of that? I can show you the whole thing with a little ball and a lamp. It proves that Venus has no light of its own either. And it describes a simple circle around the sun, isn't that marvelous?

ANDREA: *(Sobbing)* Yes, and that's a fact.

GALILEO: *(Softly)* I didn't stop her from leaving.

(ANDREA is silent.)

GALILEO: But of course if I hadn't stayed it wouldn't have happened.

ANDREA: Will they have to believe you now?

GALILEO: I've got all the proofs I need. You know what? When all this is over, I'll go to Rome and show them.

(Two MUFFLED MEN men with long poles and buckets come down the street. With the poles they hold out bread to GALILEO and the old woman in their windows.)

THE OLD WOMAN: There's a woman with three children over there. Give her some too.

GALILEO: I've nothing to drink. There's no water in the house. *(The two shrug their shoulders)* Will you be back tomorrow?

THE MAN: *(With muffled voice, his mouth covered by a cloth)* Who knows what tomorrow will bring?

GALILEO: If you do come, could you reach up to me a little book that I need for my work?

THE MAN: *(With a muffled laugh)* A book won't do you any good now. Lucky if you get bread.

GALILEO: This boy, my pupil, will be here to give it to you. It's a table showing the period of Mercury, Andrea. I've mislaid mine. Will you find me one at school?

(The men have already moved on.)

ANDREA: Sure. I'll get it for you, Mr. Galilei. *(Out)*

(GALILEO retires. THE OLD WOMAN steps out of the house opposite and places a pitcher at GALILEO's door.)

SCENE VI

1616: The Collegium Romanum, the research institute of the Vatican, confirms Galileo's discoveries.

> Things take indeed a wondrous turn
> When learned men do stoop to learn.
> Clavius, we are pleased to say
> Upheld Galileo Galilei.

(Large ball in the Collegium Romanum, Rome. It is night. High ecclesiastics, monks, scholars, in groups. GALILEO on one side, alone. Great merriment. Before the scene opens, boisterous laughter is heard.)

A FAT PRELATE: *(Holds his belly for laughter)* Oh stupidy! Oh stupidity! Can anyone tell me of a proposition that has *not* been believed?

A SCHOLAR: What about the proposition that you have an inconquerable aversion to food, monsignor!

THE FAT PRELATE: Will be believed, never fear. Only reasonable statements are not believed. The existence of the devil is being doubted. But that the earth spins around like a marble in a gutter, that's being believed. Sancta simplicitas!

A MONK: *(Acting out a comedy)* I'm dizzy. The earth is turning too fast. Permit me to hold on to you, professor. *(He pretends to stagger and holds on to a scholar)*

THE SCHOLAR: *(Joining in the fun)* Yes, she's dead drunk again, the old hag.

THE MONK: Stop, stop! We're sliding off! Stop, I say!

ANOTHER SCHOLAR: Venus is listing badly. I can only see half of her behind. Help!

(A cluster of MONKS *is forming who with much laughter pretend to be on a storm-tossed ship, struggling to avoid being thrown overboard.)*

ANOTHER MONK: If only we don't get thrown on the moon. Brothers, they say it bristles with sharp mountain peaks!

THE FIRST SCHOLAR: Plant your foot against it.

THE FIRST MONK: And don't look down. I feel as sick as a monkey.

THE FAT PRELATE: *(Pointedly loud in* GALILEO'S *direction)* What! Monkey business in the Collegium Romanum?

(Loud laughter. TWO ASTRONOMERS *of the Collegium come out of a door. Quiet sets in.)*

A MONK: Still investigating? That's a scandal!

THE FIRST ASTRONOMER: *(Angrily)* Not us!

THE SECOND ASTRONOMER: Where's this going to end? I can't understand Clavius . . . Are all the claims made in the last fifty years to be taken at face value? In 1572 a new star appeared in the highest sphere, the eighth, the sphere of the fixed stars. It was rather larger and brighter than its neighbors and a year and a half later it was gone, overtaken by perdition. Is that any reason to question the eternal immutability of the heavens?

THE PHILOSOPHER: If we let them, they'd smash up the whole universe.

THE FIRST ASTRONOMER: Yes, what's the world coming to! Five years later, Tycho Brahe, a Dane, determined the trajectory of a comet. It started above the moon and broke through all the spheres, the material carriers of all movable celestial bodies. It met with no resistance, its light was not deflected. Is that any reason to doubt the existence of the spheres?

THE PHILOSOPHER: Out of the question! How can Christopher Clavius, the greatest astronomer of Italy and of the church, lower himself to investigating such stuff!

THE FAT PRELATE: Scandalous!

THE FIRST ASTRONOMER: But there he is, investigating. There he sits, gaping through that devil's tube.

THE SECOND ASTRONOMER: Principiis

obsta! The whole trouble began years ago when we started using the tables of Copernicus—a heretic—for calculating such things as the length of the solar year, the dates of solar and lunar eclipses, the positions of the celestial bodies.

A MONK: I ask you: What is better, to get a lunar eclipse three days behind schedule or to miss out on eternal salvation altogether?

A VERY THIN MONK: *(Steps forward with an open Bible, fanatically stabbing his finger at a passage)* What does the Book say? "Sun, stand thou still upon Gibeon; and thou, moon, in the valley of Ajalon." How can the sun stand still if it never moves as these heretics claim? Does the Book lie?

THE FIRST ASTRONOMER: No, and that's why we're leaving.

THE SECOND ASTROMONER: Yes, there *are* phenomena that preplex us astronomers, but must man understand everything? *(Both go out)*

THE VERY THIN MONK: They degrade the home of mankind, a planet they call it. They load man, animal, plant and soil on a cart and chase it in circles through the empty sky. Heaven and earth, they claim, have ceased to exist. The earth because it's a star in the sky, and the sky because it consists of many earths. There's no longer any difference between above and below, between eternal and transient. That we are transient, that we know. But now they tell us that heaven itself is transient. There are sun, moon and stars, but we live on this earth, that's what we've learned and what the Book says; but now, according to them, the earth is just another star. One day they'll be saying there's no difference between man and beast, that man himself is an animal and only animals exist.

THE FIRST SCHOLAR: *(To* GALILEO*)* Mr. Galilei, you've dropped something.

GALILEO: *(Who had taken his pebble out of his pocket during the preceding speech and dropped it on the floor, as he stoops to pick it up)* It didn't drop, monsignor, it rose.

THE FAT PRELATE: *(Turns his back on him)* The insolence of the man!

(A VERY OLD CARDINAL *comes in, supported by a* MONK. *The others reverentially make room for him.)*

THE VERY OLD CARDINAL: Are they still in there? Can't they get this foolishness over with? Surely Clavius knows his astronomy. I hear this Mr.

Galilei has moved man from the center of the universe to somewhere on the edge. Obviously he's an enemy of mankind. And ought to be treated as such. Man is the crown of creation, every child knows that, he's God's highest and most beloved creature. Would God have put his most marvelous work, his supreme effort on a little far-away star that's constantly on the move? Would he have sent His Son to such a place? How can there be men so perverse as to believe these slaves of their mathematical tables? How can one of God's creatures put up with such a thing?

THE FAT PRELATE: *(In an undertone)* The gentleman is present.

THE VERY OLD CARDINAL: *(To* GALILEO*)* Oh, you're the man? You know, I don't see too well any more, but I can see that you look remarkably like the man—what was his name again?—whom we burned a few years ago.

THE MONK: Your Eminence, you mustn't excite yourself. The doctor . . .

THE VERY OLD CARDINAL: *(Brushing him off, to* GALILEO*)* You want to degrade our earth, though you live on it and receive everything from it. You're fouling your own nest! But I for one will not stand for it. *(He pushes the* MONK *out of the way and struts proudly back and forth)* I'm not some nondescript being on some little star that briefly circles around somewhere. I walk with assurance on a firm earth, it stands still, it is the center of the universe, I am in the center, and the Creator's eye rests on me, on me alone. Around me, fixed to eight crystal spheres, revolve the fixed stars and the mighty sun, which was created to illumine my surroundings. And myself as well, in order that God may see me. Hence obviously and irrefutably, everything depends on me, man, the supreme work of God, the creature in the center, the image of God, imperishable and . . . *(He collapses)*

THE MONK: Your Eminence, you have overtaxed yourself!

(At this moment the door in the rear is opened and the great CLAVIUS *comes in at the head of his astronomers. Quickly, without a word or a glance aside, he traverses the hall and, near the exit, says to a* MONK*.)*

CLAVIUS: He's right.

(He goes out, followed by the astronomers. The door in the rear remains open. Deadly silence. THE VERY OLD CARDINAL *revives.)*

THE VERY OLD CARDINAL: What happened? Has there been a decision?

(No one dares to tell him.)

THE MONK: Your Eminence, you must let them take you home.

(The old man is helped out. All leave the hall, perturbed. A LITTLE MONK, *a member of* CLAVIUS' *investigating commission, stops at* GALILEO's *side.)*

THE LITTLE MONK: *(Furtively)* Mr. Galilei, before he left Father Clavius said: Now the theologians can see about setting the heavenly spheres right again. You have prevailed. *(Out)*

GALILEO: *(Trying to hold him back)* It has prevailed. Not I, reason has prevailed!

(The LITTLE MONK *has gone.* GALILEO *is leaving too. In the doorway he meets a tall* CLERIC, *the* CARDINAL INQUISITOR, *accompanied by an* ASTRONOMER. GALILEO *bows. Before going out, he whispers a question to a* DOORKEEPER.*)*

DOORKEEPER: *(Whispering back)* His Eminence the cardinal inquisitor.

(The ASTRONOMER *leads the* CARDINAL INQUISITOR *to the telescope.)*

SCENE VII

But the Inquisition places the Copernican doctrine on the Index (March 5, 1616).

When Galileo was in Rome
A Cardinal asked him to his home.
He wined and dined him as his guest
And only made one small request.

(The house of CARDINAL BELLARMINE *in Rome. A ball is in progress. In the vestibule, where two ecclesiastical* SECRETARIES *are playing chess and exchanging observations about the guests,* GALILEO *is received by an applauding group of masked ladies and gentlemen. He is accompanied by his daughter* VIRGINIA *and her fiancé* LUDOVICO MARSILI.)*

VIRGINIA: I won't dance with anyone else, Ludovico.

LUDOVICO: Your shoulder clasp is loose.

GALILEO:
"Your tucker, Thaïs, is askew. Don't
Set it straight, for preciously it shows me
And others too some deeper disorder.
In the candlelight of the swirling ballroom
It makes them dream of
Darker coigns in the expectant park."

VIRGINIA: Feel my heart.

GALILEO: *(Places his hand on her heart)* It's beating.

VIRGINIA: I want to look beautiful.

GALILEO: You'd better, or else they'll start doubting again that the earth revolves.

LUDOVICO: It doesn't revolve at all. *(GALILEO laughs)* All Rome is talking of nothing but you, sir. After tonight Rome will be talking about your daughter.

GALILEO: Everybody agrees that it's easy to look beautiful in the Roman spring. I myself probably look like a paunchy Adonis. *(To the* SECRETARIES*)* I'm to wait here for the cardinal. *(To the couple)* Run along and enjoy yourselves!

(Before they reach the ballroom in the rear VIRGINIA *skips back once more.)*

VIRGINIA: Father, the hairdresser on Via del Trionfo took me first and made four ladies wait. He knew your name right away. *(Out)*

GALILEO: *(To the* SECRETARIES *playing chess)* How can you go on playing chess the old way? Too confined. As it's played now, the larger pieces can range over many fields. The rook goes like this *(He demonstrates it)* and the bishop like this, and the queen like this and this. That gives you plenty of room and you can plan ahead.

THE FIRST SECRETARY: It doesn't fit in with our small salaries. We can only afford to move like this. *(He makes a short move)*

GALILEO: It's the other way round, my friend.

If you live grandly, you can get away with anything. You must go with the times, gentlemen. You mustn't keep hugging the shore, one fine day you must venture out on the high seas.

(The VERY OLD CARDINAL *of the previous scene crosses the stage, steered by his* MONK. *He notices* GALILEO, *passes him by, then turns uncertainly and greets him.* GALILEO *sits down. The beginning of Lorenzo de' Medici's famous poem about the transience of the world is heard from the ballroom, sung by boys.)*

"I who have seen the summer's roses die
And all their petals pale and shriveled lie
Upon the chilly ground, I know the truth:
How evanescent is the flower of youth."

GALILEO: Rome. — Big party?

THE FIRST SECRETARY: The first carnival after the years of plague. All the great families of Italy are represented here tonight. The Orsinis, the Villanis, the Nuccolis, the Soldanieris, the Canes, the Lecchis, the Estensis, the Colombinis . . .

THE SECOND SECRETARY: *(Interrupts)* Their Eminences, Cardinals Bellarmine and Barberini.

(Enter CARDINAL BELLARMINE *and* CARDINAL BARBERINI. *They hold, respectively, a lamb's and a dove's mask mounted on sticks before their faces.)*

BARBERINI: *(Pointing his index finger at* GALILEO*)* "The sun also ariseth, and the sun goeth down, and hasteth to his place where he arose." So says Solomon, and what does Galileo say?

GALILEO: When I was this big *(He shows with his hand)*, Your Eminence, I was on a ship, and I cried out: The shore's moving away. — Today I know that the shore stood still and the ship was moving.

BARBERINI: Clever, clever. What we see, Bellarmine, to wit, that the stars in heaven are turning, need not be so, witness ship and shore. And what is true, to wit, that the earth turns, cannot be observed! Very clever. On the other hand, his satellites of Jupiter are hard nuts for our astronomers. Unfortunately, I too once read a little astronomy, Bellarmine. It clings to you like the itch.

BELLARMINE: We must go with the times, Barberini. If star charts based on a new hypothesis make navigation easier for our seamen, let's use them. We disapprove only of doctrines that put scripture in the wrong. *(He waves a greeting to the ballroom)*

GALILEO: Scripture. — "He that withholdeth corn, the people shall curse him." Proverbs of Solomon.

BARBERINI: "A prudent man concealeth knowledge." Proverbs of Solomon.

GALILEO: "Where no oxen are, the crib is clean: but much increase is by the strength of the ox."

BARBERINI: "He that ruleth his spirit is better than he that taketh a city."

GALILEO: "But a broken spirit drieth the bones." *(Pause)* "Doth not wisdom cry?"

BARBERINI: "Can one go upon hot coals, and his feet not be burned?" — Welcome to Rome, my dear Galileo. You remember the founding of Rome? Two little boys, the story goes, received milk and shelter from a she-wolf. Ever since then all the she-wolf's children have had to pay for their milk. In return, the she-wolf provides all manner of pleasures spiritual and worldly, from conversations with my learned friend Bellarmine to three or four ladies of international repute, would you like to see them? *(He leads* GALILEO *toward the rear to show him the ballroom.* GALILEO *follows reluctantly)* No? He prefers a serious discussion. Very well, Are you sure, friend Galilei, that you astronomers aren't just trying to make astronomy a little easier for yourselves? *(He leads him back to the front)* You like to think in circles or ellipses and in uniform velocities, in simple motions commensurate with your minds. But what if God has been pleased to make His stars move like this? *(He moves his finger through the air in a very complicated course with varying velocity in the air)* What would become of your calculations?

GALILEO: Your Eminence, if God had created the world like this *(He retraces* BARBERINI'S *course)* He would have constructed our minds like this too *(He repeats the same course)* to enable them to recognize these courses as the simplest. I believe in reason.

BARBERINI: I consider reason inadequate. No answer. He's too polite to say he considers mine inadequate. *(Laughs and returns to the balustrade)*

BELLARMINE: Reason, my friend, doesn't go very far. All around us we see nothing but falsehood, crime and weakness. Where is the truth?

GALILEO: *(Angrily)* I belive in reason.

BARBERINI: *(To the* SECRETARIES*)* Don't take

anything down. This is a scientific discussion among friends.

BELLARMINE: Consider for a moment the intellectual effort it cost the church fathers and many after them to make some sense out of this world (abominable, isn't it?). Consider the cruelty of those who have their peasants whipped half-naked around their estates in the Campagna and the stupidity of the wretches who kiss their feet in return.

GALILEO: Shameful! On my way here I saw . . .

BELLARMINE: We've transferred the responsibility for such conditions (the very stuff of life) which we cannot understand to a higher being, we say that certain purposes are served thereby, that a master plan is being followed. Not that our minds are set entirely at ease. But now you come along and accuse this supreme being of not knowing how the planets move, when it's perfectly clear to you. Is that wise?

GALILEO: *(Launching into an explanation)* I'm a faithful son of the church . . .

BARBERINI: He's really dreadful. In all innocence he accuses God of the juiciest boners in astronomy! I suppose God didn't work hard enough at His astronomy before He wrote Holy Scripture? My *dear* friend!

BELLARMINE: Don't you think it likely that the Creator knows more about His creation than any of His creatures?

GALILEO: But, gentlemen, after all we can misinterpret not only the movement of the heavenly bodies, but the Bible as well.

BELLARMINE: But wouldn't you say that after all the interpretation of the Bible is the business of the Holy Church? *(Galileo is silent)*

BELLARMINE: You see, you don't answer. *(He makes a sign to the* SECRETARIES*)* Mr. Galilei, the Holy Office has decided tonight that the doctrine of Copernicus, according to which the sun is the center of the cosmos and motionless, whereas the earth moves and is not the center of the cosmos, is inane, asburd, and heretical. I have been charged to admonish you to relinquish this opinion. *(To the first* SECRETARY*)* Please repeat.

FIRST SECRETARY: His Eminence, Cardinal Bellarmine, to the aforementioned Galileo Galilei: The Holy Office has decided that the doctrine of Copernicus, according to which the sun is the center of the cosmos and motionless, whereas the earth moves and is not the center of the cosmos, is inane, absurd, and heretical. I have been charged to admonish you to relinquish this opinion.

GALILEO: What does this mean?

(From the ballroom another verse of the poem is heard, sung by boys.)

"I said, the seasons do not stay
  Pluck the roses while it's May."

(BARBERINI motions GALILEO to keep quiet while the singing continues. They all listen.)

GALILEO: What about the facts? I understand that the astronomers of the Collegium Romanum have confirmed my observations.

BELLARMINE: And expressed their profound satisfaction, in a manner most complimentary to you.

GALILEO: But the satellites of Jupiter, the phases of Venus . . .

BELLARMINE: The Holy Congregation has arrived at its decision without taking these particulars into account.

GALILEO: In other words, all further scientific research . . .

BELLARMINE: Is guaranteed, Mr. Galilei. In keeping with the church tenet that we cannot know but may investigate. *(Again he salutes a guest in the ballroom)* You are at liberty to deal with this doctrine as a mathematical hypothesis. Science is the legitimate and most beloved daughter of the church, Mr. Galilei. None of us seriously believes that you wish to undermine man's trust in the church.

GALILEO: *(Angrily)* To invoke trust is to exhaust it.

BARBERINI: Really? *(Laughing heartily, he slaps his shoulder. Then with a sharp look he says, not unkindly)* Don't throw the baby out with the bath water, my friend. Nor shall we. We need you more than you need us.

BELLARMINE: I can't wait to introduce Italy's greatest mathematician to the commissioner of the Holy Office who has the highest regard for you.

BARBERINI: *(Taking GALILEO's other arm)* Whereupon he changes back into a lamb. You too, my friend, should have come here in disguise — as a respectable doctor of scholastic philosophy. It's my mask that allows me a little freedom tonight. When I wear it, you may even hear me murmuring: If God did not exist, we should have to invent Him. Well,

let's put our masks on again. Poor Galilei hasn't got one.

(They take GALILEO between them and lead him into the ballroom.)

FIRST SECRETARY: Have you got the last sentence?

SECOND SECRETARY: Putting it down. *(They write eagerly)* What was that about his believing in reason?

(Enter the CARDINAL INQUISITOR.)

THE INQUISITOR: Has the interview taken place?

FIRST SECRETARY: *(Mechanically)* First Mr. Galilei arrived with his daughter. She was betrothed today to Mr. . . . *(The INQUISITOR motions him to skip it)* Mr. Galilei went on to tell us about the new method of playing chess in which, contrary to the rules, the pieces are moved over many squares.

THE INQUISITOR: *(Again beckons "no")* The minutes.

(A SECRETARY hands him the minutes and the CARDINAL sits down to skim through them. TWO YOUNG LADIES in masks cross the stage and curtsy to the CARDINAL.)

THE FIRST LADY: Who's that?

THE SECOND LADY: The cardinal inquisitor.

(They giggle and leave. Enter VIRGINIA, looking around for someone.)

THE INQUISITOR: *(From his corner)* Well, my daughter?

VIRGINIA: *(With a little start as she has not seen him)* Oh, Your Eminence!

(The INQUISITOR, without looking up, tenders his right hand. She approaches, kneels down, and kisses his ring.)

THE INQUISITOR: Glorious night! Allow me to congratulate you on your engagement. Your fiancé comes of a distinguished family. Will you stay in Rome?

VIRGINIA: Not for the present, Your Eminence. There's so much to be done for a wedding.

THE INQUISITOR: Then you'll go back to Florence with your father. I'm glad to hear it. I imagine your father needs you. Mathematics is a cold housewife, I should say. A woman of flesh and blood in such surroundings makes all the difference. It's so easy to lose oneself in the universe which is so very immense if one happens to be a great man.

VIRGINIA: *(breathless)* You're very kind, Your Eminence. I really know practically nothing about these things.

THE INQUISITOR: Indeed? *(He laughs)* Well, I suppose they don't eat fish in the fisherman's house. It will amuse your father to hear that, come right down to it, you learned what you know about the heavenly bodies from me. *(Leafing through the minutes)* I read here that our innovators, whose acknowledged leader is your father—a great man, one of the greatest—regard our present ideas about the importance of our good earth as somewhat exaggerated. Well then, from the age of Ptolemy, a sage of antiquity, to the present day, the whole of creation, that is, the entire crystal globe with the earth at its center, has been computed to measure approximately two thousand earth diameters. Quite a lot of space, but not enough, not nearly enough, for the innovators. They maintain, so I hear, that the universe extends further than we can imagine, that the distance between earth and sun—a rather considerable distance, we always thought—is so negligibly small when compared with the distance between our poor earth and the fixed stars on the outermost crystal sphere, that there is no need whatever to consider it in our calculations. Yes, our innovators live on a very grand scale.

*(*VIRGINIA *laughs. The* INQUISITOR, *too, laughs.)*

THE INQUISITOR: And indeed, certain gentlemen of the Holy Office, not so long ago, came very close to taking offence at such a picture of the world, compared to which our old picture is a mere miniature that might well be hanging from the charming neck of a certain young lady. The gentlemen of the Holy Office are worried that a prelate or even a cardinal might get lost in such enormous spaces. The Almighty might even lose sight of the pope himself. Yes, it's all very amusing. But even so, my dear child, I'm glad that you'll be staying with your eminent father, whom we all hold in the highest esteem. I wonder if I know your father confessor . . .

VIRGINIA: Father Christopher of St. Ursula.

THE INQUISITOR: Well then, I'm glad you'll be going with your father. He will need you, perhaps you can't conceive of such a thing, but the time will come. You're very young and very much alive and greatness is not always an easy thing to bear for those to whom God has given it, no, not always. No mortal is too great to be included in a prayer. But I'm keeping you, dear child, and I'm making your fiancé jealous and perhaps your father too by telling you something about the heavenly bodies—which may, to be sure, be quite obsolete. Hurry back to the ball, but don't forget to give Father Christopher my regards.

*(*VIRGINIA, *after a deep curtsy, leaves quickly.)*

SCENE VIII

A Conversation

Galileo, feeling grim
A young monk came to visit him.
The monk was born of common folk.
It was of science that they spoke.

(In the palace of the Florentine ambassador to Rome, GALILEO *listens to the* LITTLE MONK, *who after the session of the Collegium Romanum repeated* FATHER CLAVIUS' *remark to him in a whisper.)*

GALILEO: Speak up, speak up! The cloth you wear entitles you to say what you please.

THE LITTLE MONK: I've studied mathematics, Mr. Galilei.

GALILEO: That might be a good thing if it led you to admit that two times two is sometimes four.

THE LITTLE MONK: For three nights I haven't been able to sleep, Mr. Galilei. I can't figure out how to reconcile the decree which I've read with the satellites of Jupiter which I've seen. So I decided to read mass this morning and come and see you.

GALILEO: To tell me that Jupiter has no satellites?

THE LITTLE MONK: No. I recognized the wisdom of the decree. It showed me how dangerous unrestricted inquiry can be to mankind, and I've decided to give up astronomy. Still, I felt I had to acquaint you with the motives which compel me, even though I'm an astronomer, to desist from pursuing a certain doctrine.

GALILEO: I can assure you that such motives are well known to me.

THE LITTLE MONK: I understand your bitterness. You're thinking of certain exceptional means of pressure exerted by the church.

GALILEO: Don't beat about the bush: instruments of torture.

THE LITTLE MONK: Yes, but I'd like to speak of other motives. Forgive me if I talk about myself. I grew up in the Campagna. My parents are peasants, simple folk. They know all about olive trees, but very little else. As I observe the phases of Venus, I can see my parents sitting by the stove with my sister, eating lasagna. I see the beams over their heads, blackened by the smoke of centuries, I see distinctly their workworn old hands and the little spoons they hold in them. They're very poor, but even in their misery there is a certain order. There are cyclic rhythms, scrubbing the floor, tending the olive trees in their seasons, paying taxes. There's a regularity in the calamities that descend on them. My father's back wasn't bowed all at once, no, a little more with every spring in the olive grove, just as the child-bearing that has made my mother more and more sexless occurred at regular intervals. What gives them the strength to sweat their way up stony paths with heavy baskets, to bear children, even to eat, is the feeling of stability and necessity they get from the sight of the soil, of the trees turning green every year, of their little church standing there, and from hearing Bible verses read every Sunday. They have been assured that the eye of God is upon them, searching and almost anxious, that the whole world-wide stage is built around them in order that they, the players, may prove themselves in their great or small roles. What would my people say if I were to tell them they were living on a small chunk of stone that moves around another star, turning incessantly in empty space, one among many and more or less significant? What would be the good or necessity of their patience, of their acquiescence in their misery? What would be the good of the Holy Scripture which explains everything and demonstrates the necessity of all their sweat, patience, hunger and submission, if it turns out to be full of errors? No, I can see their eyes waver, I can see them rest their spoons on the table, I can see how cheated and betrayed they feel. In that case, they will say, no one is watching over us. Must we, untaught, old and exhausted as we are, look out for ourselves? No one has given us a part to play, only this wretched role on a tiny star which is wholly dependent, around which nothing turns? There is no sense in our misery, hunger means no more than going without food, it is no longer a test of strength; effort means no more than bending and carrying, there is no virtue in it. Can you understand now that in the decree of the Holy Congregation I discern a noble motherly compassion, a great goodness of soul?

GALILEO: Goodness of soul! Don't you simply mean that there's nothing left, the wine's been drunk, their lips are parched, so let them kiss the cassock. But why is nothing left? Why is there no order in this country but the order in an empty drawer, and no necessity but the necessity of working oneself to death? Amid overflowing vineyards and wheat fields? Your peasants in the Campagna are paying for the wars which the vicar of gentle Jesus is waging in Spain and Germany. Why does he put the earth at the center of the universe? Because he wants the See of St. Peter to be in the center of the world! That's the crux of the matter. You're right; the question is not the planets, but the peasants of the Campagna. And don't talk to me about the beauty of phenomena in the golden glow of old age. Do you know how the Margaritifera oyster produces pearls? By contracting a near-fatal disease, by enveloping an unassimilable foreign body, a grain of sand, for instance, in a ball of mucus. It almost dies in the process. To hell with the pearl, give me the healthy oyster. Virtue is not bound up with misery, my friend. If your people were prosperous and happy, they could develop the virtues of prosperity and happiness. But today the virtues of exhausted people derive from exhausted fields, and I reject those virtues. Yes, sir, my new water pumps can work more miracles than your preposterous superhuman toil.—"Be fruitful and multiply," because your fields are barren and you are decimated by wars. You want me to lie to your people?

THE LITTLE MONK: *(In great agitation)* The very highest motives bid us keep silent: the peace of mind of the wretched and lowly!

GALILEO: Would you care to see a Cellini clock that Cardinal Bellarmine's coachman left here this morning? You see, my friend, as a reward for my letting your good parents have their peace of mind, the government offers me the wine which they press in the sweat of their countenance, which as you know was fashioned in the image of God. If I agreed to keep silent, my motives would undoubtedly be rather sordid: an easy life, no persecution, and so on.

THE LITTLE MONK: Mr. Galilei, I'm a priest.

GALILEO: You're also a physicist. And you can see that Venus has phases. Look out there. *(He points out the window)* Can you see the little Priapus by the laurel tree at the well? The god of gardens, birds, and thieves, rustic, obscene, two thousand years old. He wasn't so much of a liar. All right, we'll skip that, I too am a son of the church. But do you know the *Eighth Satire* of Horace? I've been rereading him lately, he gives me a certain balance. *(He reaches for a small book)* He puts words in the mouth of this same Priapus, a little statue that used to stand in the Esquiline Gardens. Here's how it starts:

> "I was a figtree stump, wood of little use
> When once a carpenter, pondering
> whether
> To fashion a Priapus or a footstool
> Decided on the god . . ."

Do you think Horace would have let anyone forbid him the footstool and put a table in the poem instead? Sir, a cosmology in which Venus has no phases violates my esthetic sense! We can't invent machines for pumping river water if we're forbidden to study the greatest machine before our eyes, the mechanism of the heavenly bodies. The sum total of the angles in a triangle can't be changed to suit the requirements of the curia. Nor can I calculate the courses of flying bodies in such a way as to account for witches riding on broomsticks.

THE LITTLE MONK: Don't you think the truth will prevail, even without us, if it is the truth?

GALILEO: No, no, no. Truth prevails only when we make it prevail. The triumph of reason can only be the triumph of reasoning men. You describe your peasants in the Campagna as if they were moss on their huts. How can anyone imagine that the sum of the angles of a triangle runs counter to *their* needs! But if they don't rouse themselves and learn how to think, the best irrigation systems in the world won't do them any good. Damn it, I see the divine patience of your people, but where is their divine wrath?

THE LITTLE MONK: They're tired.

GALILEO: *(Throws a bundle of manuscripts in front of him)* Are you a physicist, my son? Here you'll find the reasons for the ocean's tides. But don't read it, do you hear. Ah, reading already? I see you're a physicist.

(The LITTLE MONK *has immersed himself in the papers)*

GALILEO: An apple from the tree of knowledge. He gobbles it up. He'll be damned for all eternity, but he's got to bolt it down, the hapless glutton. Sometimes I think I'd gladly be locked up in a dungeon ten fathoms below ground, if in return I could find out one thing: What is light? And the worst of it is: What I know I must tell others. Like a lover, a drunkard, a traitor. It's a vice, I know, and leads to ruin. But how long can I go on shouting into empty air — that is, the question.

THE LITTLE MONK: *(Points at a passage in the papers)* I don't understand this sentence.

GALILEO: I'll explain it to you, I'll explain it to you.

SCENE IX

After a silence of eight years GALILEO *feels encouraged by the enthronement of a new pope, himself a scientist, to resume his research in the forbidden field. The sunspots.*

> *Eight long years with tongue in cheek*
> *Of what he knew he did not speak*
> *The temptations grew too great*
> *And Galileo challenged fate.*

(GALILEO's house in Florence. GALILEO's pupils, FEDERZONI, THE LITTLE MONK and ANDREA SARTI, now a young man, are gathered for an experiment. GALILEO, standing, is reading a book.—VIRGINIA and MRS. SARTI are sewing bridal linen.)

VIRGINIA: Sewing a trousseau is fun. This is for the long dining table, Ludovico loves to have company. But it has got to be right, his mother notices every stitch. She isn't happy about father's books. Any more than Father Christopher.

MRS. SARTI: He hasn't written a book in years.

VIRGINIA: I think he saw he was mistaken. In Rome, a very high ecclesiastic told me a lot of things about astronomy. The distances are too great.

ANDREA: *(Writes the program for the day on a blackboard and reads aloud)* "Thursday afternoon: Floating bodies."—That means ice again; bucket of water; scales; iron needle; Aristotle. *(He fetches the objects)*

(The others are looking up things in books. Enter FILIPPO MUCIUS, a scholar in his middle years. He appears to be upset.)

MUCIUS: Would you tell Mr. Galilei he must see me? He has condemned me without a hearing.

MRS. SARTI: I've told you he doesn't wish to see you.

MUCIUS: God will reward you if you ask him again. I must speak to him.

VIRGINIA: *(Goes to the staircase)* Father!

GALILEO: What is it?

VIRGINIA: Mr. Mucius!

GALILEO: *(Looks up brusquely, goes to the head of the stairs, his pupils trailing behind him)* What do you want?

MUCIUS: Mr. Galilei, I request permission to explain the passages in my book which seem to indicate a condemnation of the Copernican doctrine that the earth revolves. I've . . .

GALILEO: What is there to explain? You are in full agreement with the Holy Congregation's decree of 1616. You are perfectly within your rights. It's true, you studied mathematics with us, but we have no authority to make you say that two times two is four. You have every right to say that this stone *(He takes the pebble from his pocket and throws it down to the ground floor)* has just flown up to the ceiling.

MUCIUS: Mr. Galilei, I . . .

GALILEO: Don't talk about difficulties! The plague didn't prevent me from going on with my observations.

MUCIUS: Mr. Galilei, the plague is not the worst.

GALILEO: Let me tell you this: Not to know the truth is just stupid. To know the truth and call it a lie is criminal! Leave my house at once!

MUCIUS: *(Tonelessly)* You are right. *(He goes out)*

(GALILEO returns to his study.)

FEDERZONI: That's how it is, I'm afraid. He doesn't amount to much and no one could pay any attention to him if he hadn't been your pupil. But now of course they all say: He's heard everything Galileo had to say and is forced to admit that it's all wrong.

MRS. SARTI: I feel sorry for the gentleman.

VIRGINIA: Father was very fond of him.

MRS. SARTI: I wanted to talk to you about your marriage, Virginia. You're such a young thing, and you have no mother, and your father just puts little pieces of ice in water. Anyway, I wouldn't ask him questions about your marriage if I were you. He would say the most dreadful things for a week, naturally at meals when the young people are there, because he hasn't half a scudo's worth of shame in him, never did have. That's not what I had in mind, I'm thinking of what the future has in store. Not that I know anything, I'm only an ignorant woman. But this is a very serious thing, you mustn't go into it blindly. I do think you should go to a real astronomer at the university and consult him about your horoscope. Then you'll know what to expect. Why are you laughing?

VIRGINIA: Because I've been.

MRS. SARTI: *(Very curious)* What did he say?

VIRGINIA: For three months I must be careful because the sun will be in Aries, but then I get a very good ascendant and the clouds will part. As long as I don't lose sight of Jupiter, I can go on any journey I please, because I'm an Aries.

MRS. SARTI: And Ludovico?

VIRGINIA: He's a Leo. *(After a little pause)* That means sensual, I think.

(Pause.)

VIRGINIA: I know that step. It's Mr. Gaffone, the rector.

(Enter MR. GAFFONE, *the rector of the university.)*

GAFFONE: Just thought I'd bring you a book that might be of interest to your father. For heaven's sake don't disturb Mr. Galilei. I can't help feeling that every minute taken from that great man is a minute taken from Italy. I'll just put the book in your little hands, and disappear, on tiptoe.

(He goes out. VIRGINIA *hands the book to* FEDERZONI.*)*

GALILEO: What's it about?
FEDERZONI: I don't know. *(Spelling it out)* "De maculis in sole."
ANDREA: On the sunspots. Another one!

*(*FEDERZONI *angrily hands it to him.)*

ANDREA: Listen to this dedication! "To the greatest living authority on physics. Galileo Galiei."

*(*GALILEO *has immersed himself once more in his book.)*

ANDREA: I've read the treatise by Fabricius in Holland. He believes the spots are clusters of stars passing between the earth and the sun.
THE LITTLE MONK: Isn't that doubtful, Mr. Galilei?

*(*GALILEO *does not answer.)*

ANDREA: In Paris and Prague they think they're vapors from the sun.
FEDERZONI: Hm.
ANDREA: Federzoni has his doubts.
FEDERZONI: Kindly leave me out of it. I said "Hm," that's all. I'm the lens grinder, I grind lenses, you people look through them and observe the sky, and what you see is not spots, but "maculis." How can I doubt anything? How many times do I have to tell you I can't read these books, they're in Latin.

(In his anger he gesticulates with the scales. A pan falls to the floor. GALILEO *walks over and silently picks it up.)*

THE LITTLE MONK: It's blissful to doubt; I wonder why.
ANDREA: Every sunny day in the last two weeks I've climbed up to the attic, right under the roof. A thin beam of light comes down through a tiny crack in the tiles. With that beam you can catch the reverse image of the sun on a sheet of paper. I saw a spot as big as a fly and blurred like a small cloud. It moved. Why don't we investigate those spots, Mr. Galilei?
GALILEO: Because we're working on floating bodies.
ANDREA: Mother has whole baskets full of letters. All Europe wants your opinion. With the reputation you've built up, you can't be silent.
GALILEO: Rome has allowed me to build up a reputation because I've kept silent.
FEDERZONI: But you can't afford to be silent any more.
GALILEO: Nor can I afford to be roasted over a wood fire like a ham.
ANDREA: Do you think the spots come into it?

*(*GALILEO *does not answer.)*

ANDREA: All right, let's stick to our little pieces of ice. They can't hurt you.
GALILEO: Exactly.—Our proposition, Andrea!
ANDREA: We assume that whether a body floats or not depends essentially not on its shape, but on whether it is lighter or heavier than water.
GALILEO: What does Aristotle say?
THE LITTLE MONK: "Discus latus platique . . ."
GALILEO: Translate, translate!
THE LITTLE MONK: "A broad, flat disk of ice floats in water, whereas an iron needle sinks."
GALILEO: Why then, according to Aristotle, doesn't ice sink?
THE LITTLE MONK: Because, being broad and flat, it cannot divide the water.
GALILEO: Very well. *(A piece of ice is handed to him and he puts it into the bucket)* Now I press the ice firmly down to the bottom of the bucket. I remove the pressure of my hands. What happens?
THE LITTLE MONK: It rises to the surface.
GALILEO: Correct. In rising it seems to be able to divide the water. Fulganzio!
THE LITTLE MONK: But why then does it float at all? Ice is heavier than water, because it is condensed water.
GALILEO: What if it were diluted water?
ANDREA: It must be lighter than water, or it wouldn't float.
GALILEO: Aha!
ANDREA: Just as an iron needle can't float. Everything lighter than water floats, everything heavier sinks. Which was to be proved.

GALILEO: Andrea, you must learn to think carefully. Give me the iron needle. A sheet of paper. Is iron heavier than water?

ANDREA: Yes.

(GALILEO *places the needle on a sheet of paper and floats it in the water. Pause.*)

GALILEO: What happens?

FEDERZONI: The needle floats! Holy Aristotle, they never checked up on him!

(*They laugh*)

GALILEO: One of the main reasons for the poverty of science is that it is supposed to be so rich. The aim of science is not to open the door to everlasting wisdom, but to set a limit to everlasting error. Take that down.

VIRGINIA: What's the matter?

MRS. SARTI: Every time they laugh, a fright comes over me. I wonder what they're laughing about.

VIRGINIA: Father says theologians have their church bells and physicists have their laughter.

MRS. SARTI: At least I'm glad he doesn't look through his tube so much any more. That was much worse.

VIRGINIA: No, he only puts pieces of ice in water. No harm can come of that.

MRS. SARTI: Who knows?

(*Enter* LUDOVICO MARSILI *in traveling garb, followed by a manservant with luggage.* VIRGINIA *runs toward him and embraces him.*)

VIRGINIA: Why didn't you let us know you were coming?

LUDOVICO: I was near here inspecting our vineyards, and I just couldn't stay away.

GALILEO: (*As though nearsighted*) Who's that?

VIRGINIA: Ludovico.

THE LITTLE MONK: Can't you see him?

GALILEO: Oh, yes, Ludovico. (*Goes toward him*) How are the horses?

LUDOVICO: They're fine, sir.

GALILEO: Sarti, let's celebrate. Bring us a jug of that old Sicilian wine!

(MRS. SARTI *goes out with* ANDREA.)

LUDOVICO: (*To* VIRGINIA) You look pale.

Country life will do you good. Mother is expecting you in September.

VIRGINIA: Wait, I want to show you my wedding dress. (*Runs out*)

GALILEO: Sit down.

LUDOVICO: I hear you have more than a thousand students in your lectures at the university, sir. What are you working on at the moment?

GALILEO: Routine stuff. Did you come through Rome?

LUDOVICO: Yes. — Before I forget, mother congratulates you on your admirable tact in connection with all that fuss over the sunspots in Holland.

GALILEO: (*Dryly*) That's kind of her.

(MRS. SARTI *and* ANDREA *bring wine and glasses. All gather around the table.*)

LUDOVICO: Rome has found a topic of conversation for February. Christopher Clavius said he was afraid the whole earth-around-the-sun circus would flare up again because of those sunspots.

ANDREA: Don't let it worry you.

GALILEO: Any other news from the Holy City, apart from hopes for new sins on my part?

LUDOVICO: You heard, of course, that the Holy Father is dying?

THE LITTLE MONK: Oh.

GALILEO: Who's mentioned as successor?

LUDOVICO: Mostly Barberini.

GALILEO: Barberini.

ANDREA: Mr. Galilei knows Barberini personally.

THE LITTLE MONK: Cardinal Barberini is a mathematician.

FEDERZONI: A scientist in the chair of St. Peter! (*Pause*)

GALILEO: I see, now they need men like Barberini who've read a little mathematics. Things will start moving, Federzoni, we may live to see the day when we won't have to glance over our shoulders like criminals every time we say that two times two is four. (*To* LUDOVICO) I like this wine, Ludovico. What do you think of it?

LUDOVICO: It's good.

GALILEO: I know the vineyard. The slope is steep and stony, the grapes are almost blue. I love this wine.

LUDOVICO: Yes, sir.

GALILEO: There are little shadows in it. And

it's almost sweet, but stops at the "almost." — Andrea, put the stuff away, the ice and bucket and needle. — I value the consolations of the flesh. I have no patience with cowardly souls who speak of weakness. I say: To enjoy yourself is an achievement.

THE LITTLE MONK: What are you taking up next?

FEDERZONI: We're starting in again on the earth-around-the-sun circus.

ANDREA: *(Singing in an undertone)*
The Book says it stands still. And so
Each learned doctor proves.
The Holy Father takes it by the ears
And holds it fast. And yet it moves.

(ANDREA, FEDERZONI and THE LITTLE MONK *hurry to the workbench and clear it.)*

ANDREA: We might even find out that the sun revolves too. How would you like that, Marsili?

LUDOVICO: What's the excitement about?

MRS. SARTI: You're not going back to those abominations, Mr. Galilei?

GALILEO: Now I know why your mother sent you here. Barberini is on the rise. Knowledge will be a passion and research a delight. Clavius is right, these sunspots do interest me. You like my wine, Ludovico?

LUDOVICO: I said I did, sir.

GALILEO: You really like it?

LUDOVICO: *(Stiffly)* I like it.

GALILEO: Would you go so far as to accept a man's wine or his daughter without asking him to give up his profession? What has my astronomy got to do with my daughter? The phases of Venus don't affect my daughter's rear end.

MRS. SARTI: Don't be vulgar. I'll go get Virginia.

LUDOVICO: *(Holds her back)* In families like mine marriages are not decided by sexual considerations alone.

GALILEO: Did they prevent you from marrying my daughter for the last eight years because I was on probation?

LUDOVICO: My wife will also have to cut a figure in our village church.

GALILEO: You mean, your peasants won't pay their rent if the lady of the manor is insufficiently saintly?

LUDOVICO: In a way.

GALILEO: Andrea, Fulganzio, get the brass mirror and the screen! We'll project the sun's image on it to protect our eyes. That's your method, Andrea.

(ANDREA and THE LITTLE MONK *get mirror and screen.)*

LUDOVICO: Years ago in Rome, sir, you signed a pledge to stay away from this earth-around-the-sun business.

GALILEO: Oh well. We had a reactionary pope in those days.

MRS. SARTI: Had! His Holiness isn't even dead yet!

GALILEO: Pretty near, pretty near! — Put a grid over the screen. We'll proceed methodically. And we'll be able to answer all those letters, won't we, Andrea?

MRS. SARTI: "Pretty near!" Fifty times that man weighs his pieces of ice, but when something happens that suits his purposes he belives it blindly!

(The screen is put up.)

LUDOVICO: Mr. Galilei, if His Holiness should die, the next pope — no matter who he is or how much he loves science — will have to take account of how much the country's leading families love him.

THE LITTLE MONK: God made the physical world, Ludovico; God made the human brain; God will allow physics.

MRS. SARTI: Galileo, let me tell you something. I've watched my son fall into sin for the sake of these "experiments" and "theories" and "observations," and I haven't been able to do anything about it. You set yourself against the authorities and they gave you a warning. The greatest cardinals spoke to you the way you'd speak to a sick horse. It worked for a while, but two months ago, right after the Immaculate Conception, I caught you sneaking back to your "observations." In the attic! I didn't say anything, but I knew. I ran out and lit a candle for St. Joseph. It's more than I can bear. When we're alone you show some sense, you say you've got to behave because it's dangerous, but two days of "experiments" and you're as bad as ever. If I lose my eternal salvation because I stand by a heretic, that's my business, but you have no right to trample your daughter's happiness with your big feet!

GALILEO: *(Gruffly)* Get the telescope!

LUDOVICO: Giuseppe, put the luggage back in the coach.

(The manservant goes out.)

MRS. SARTI: She'll never get over this. You can tell her yourself.

(She runs out, still holding the pitcher.)

LUDOVICO: I see you've made up your mind. Mr. Galilei, three quarters of the year mother and I live on our estate in the Campagna and I can assure you that our peasants lose no sleep over your treatises on the moons of Jupiter. They work too hard in the fields. It might upset them, though, if they heard that attacks on the holy doctrine of the church were going unpunished. Don't forget that those poor brutalized wretches get everything mixed up. They really are brutes, you have no idea. A rumor that somebody's seen a pear growing on an apple tree makes them run away from their work to gab about it.

GALILEO: *(With interest)* Really?

LUDOVICO: Animals. When they come to the manor with a trifling complaint, mother has to have a dog whipped in front of them to remind them of discipline and order and good manners. You, Mr. Galilei, you may occasionally see flowering corn fields from your traveling coach, or absent-mindedly eat our olives and our cheese, but you have no idea how much effort it takes to raise all these things — all the supervision!

GALILEO: Young man, I never eat my olives absent-mindedly. *(Rudely)* You're wasting my time. *(Calls toward outside)* Is the screen ready?

ANDREA: Yes. Are you coming?

GALILEO: You whip more than dogs to keep discipline, don't you, Marsili?

LUDOVICO: Mr. Galilei, you have a marvelous brain. Too bad.

THE LITTLE MONK: *(Amazed)* He's threatening you.

GALILEO: Yes, I might stir up his peasants to think new thoughts. And his servants and his overseers.

FEDERZONI: How? They don't know Latin.

GALILEO: I could write in the vernacular for the many instead of in Latin for the few. For our new ideas we need people who work with their hands. Who else wants to know the causes of everything? People who never see bread except on their tables have no desire to know how it's baked; those bastards would rather thank God than the baker. But the men who make the bread will understand that nothing can move unless something moves it. Fulganzio, your sister at the olive press won't be much surprised — she'll probably laugh — when she hears that the sun is not a gold escutcheon, but a lever: The earth moves because the sun moves it.

LUDOVICO: You'll always be a slave to your passions. Convey my apologies to Virginia. It's better, I think, if I don't see her now.

GALILEO: The dowry is at your disposal. At any time.

LUDOVICO: Good day. *(He goes)*

ANDREA: Our regards to all the Marsilis!

FEDERZONI: Who tell the earth to stand still so their castles won't fall off.

ANDREA: And to the Cencis and Villanis!

FEDERZONI: The Cervillis!

ANDREA: The Lecchis!

FEDERZONI: The Pierleonis!

ANDREA: Who'll only kiss the pope's foot as long as he tramples the people with it.

THE LITTLE MONK: *(Also at the instruments)* The new pope will be an enlightened man.

GALILEO: And now let's start observing these spots in the sun which interest us — at our own risk, not counting too much on the protection of a new pope . . .

ANDREA: *(Interrupting)* But fully confident of dispelling Mr. Fabricius' star shadows and the solar vapors of Prague and Paris, and proving that the sun rotates.

GALILEO: Reasonably confident that the sun rotates. My aim is not to prove that I've been right, but to find out whether or not I have been. I say: Abandon hope, all ye who enter upon observation. Maybe it's vapors, maybe it's spots, but before we assume that they're spots, though it would suit us if they were, we'd do better to assume they're fish-tails. Yes, we shall start all over again from scratch. And we won't rush ahead with seven-league boots, but crawl at a snail's pace. And what we find today we'll wipe from the blackboard tomorrow, and not write it down again until we find it a second time. And if there's something we hope to find, we'll regard it with particular distrust when we do find it. Accordingly let us approach our observation of the sun with the inexorable resolve to prove that the earth *stands still!* Only after we have failed, after we have been totally and hopelessly defeated and are licking our wounds in utter dejection, only then shall we begin to ask whether the earth does not indeed move! *(With a twinkle)* But then, when every other hypothesis has gone up in smoke, then no mercy for those who have never observed any-thing, yet go on talking. Take the cloth off the tube and focus it on the sun! *(He adjusts the brass mirror)*

THE LITTLE MONK: I knew you had taken up your work again. I knew it when you didn't recognize Mr. Marsili.

(In silence they begin their examinations. When the flaming image of the sun appears on the screen VIRGINIA *in her bridal gown runs in.)*

VIRGINIA: You've sent him away! *(She faints.* ANDREA *and* THE LITTLE MONK *rush to her aid)*

GALILEO: I've got to know.

SCENE X

In the course of the next ten years GALILEO's *doctrine is disseminated among the common people. Pamphleteers and ballad singers everywhere seize upon the new ideas. In the carnival of 1632 the guilds in many Italian cities take astronomy as the theme for their carnival processions.*

(A half-starved couple of show people with a five-year-old girl and an infant enter a market place where many people, some with masks, are awaiting the carnival procession. They carry bundles, a drum and other props.)

THE BALLAD SINGER: *(Drumming)* Citizens, ladies and gentlemen! Before the great carnival procession of the guilds arrives we bring you the latest Florentine song which is being sung all over northern Italy. We've imported it at great expense. The title is: The horrendous doctrine and teaching of Mr. Galileo Galilei, court physicist, or, A Foretaste of the Future. *(He sings)*

When the Almighty made the universe
He made the earth and then he made the sun.
Then round the earth he bade the sun to turn —
That's in the Bible, Genesis, Chapter One.
And from that time all beings here below
Were in obedient circles meant to go.

They all began to turn around
The little fellows round the big shots
And the hindmost round the foremost
On earth as it is in heaven.

Around the popes the cardinals
Around the cardinals the bishops
Around the bishops the secretaries
Around the secretaries the aldermen
Around the aldermen the craftsmen
Around the craftsmen the servants
Around the servants the dogs, the chickens and
    the beggars.

That, my friends, is the great order, ordo ordinum, as the theologians call it, regula aeternis, the rule of rules. And then, my friends, what happened then? *(He sings)*

Up stood the learned Galileo
(Chucked the Bible, pulled out his telescope,
    and took a look at the universe)
And told the sun: Stand stlll!
From this time on, the wheels
Shall turn the other way.
Henceforth the mistress, ho!
Shall turn around the maid.
Now that was rash, my friends, it is no matter
    small:
For heresy will spread today like foul diseases.
Change Holy Writ, forsooth? What will be left at
    all?

Why: each of us would say and do just what he
    pleases!

Esteemed citizens, such doctrines are utterly impossible. *(He sings)*

    Good people, what will come to pass
    If Galileo's teachings spread?
    The server will not serve at mass
    No servant girl will make the bed.
Now that is grave, my friends, it is no matter
    small:
For independent spirit spreads like foul diseases!
Yet life is sweet and man is weak and after all—
How nice it is, for once, to do just as one pleases!

Now, my good friends, here, look to the future and
see what the most learned doctor Galileo Galilei
predicts. *(He sings)*

    Two ladies at a fishwife's stall
    Are in for quite a shock
    The fishwife takes a loaf of bread
    And gobbles up all her stock.
    The carpenters take wood and build
    Houses for themselves, not pews
    And members of the cobblers' guild
    Now walk around in shoes!
Is this permitted? No, it is no matter small:
For independent spirit spreads like foul diseases!
Yet life is sweet and man is weak and after all—
How nice it is, for once, to do just as one pleases!

    The tenant kicks his noble master
    Smack in the ass like that
    The tenant's wife now gives her children
    Milk that made the parson fat.
No, no my friends, for the Bible is no matter
    small:
For independent spirit spreads like foul diseases!
Yet life is sweet and man is weak and after all—
How nice it is for once to do just as one pleases!

THE SINGER'S WIFE:

    The other day I tried it too
    And did my husband frankly tell
    Let's see now if what you can do
    Other stars can do as well.

No, no, no, no, no, no, stop, Galileo, stop!
For independent spirit spreads like foul diseases.
People must keep their place, some down and
    some on top!
Though it is nice for once to do just as one pleases.

    BOTH:

Good people who have trouble here below
In serving cruel lords and gentle Jesus
Who bids you turn the other cheek just so
While they prepare to strike the second blow:
Obedience will never cure your woe
So each of you wake up and do just as he pleases!

THE BALLAD SINGER: Esteemed citizens,
behold Galileo Galilei's phenomenal discovery. The
earth revolving around the sun!

*(He belabors the drum violently. His wife and
child step forward. The wife holds a crude replica
of the sun, and the child, holding a gourd, image
of the earth, over her head, circles around the
woman.* THE SINGER *excitedly points at the little
girl as if she were performing a dangerous
acrobatic feat in jerkily taking step after step in
rhythm with the drumbeats. Then drumming
from the rear.)*

A DEEP VOICE: *(Calls out)* The procession!

*(Enter two men in rags drawing a little cart. The
"Grand Duke of Florence," a figure in sackcloth
with a cardboard crown, sits on a ridiculous
throne and peers through a telescope. Over the
throne a painted sign "Looking for trouble." Next,
four masked men march in carrying a huge
tarpaulin. They stop and bounce a large doll
representing a cardinal. A dwarf has posted
himself to one side with a sign "The New Age."
Among the crowd a beggar raises himself by his
crutches and stomps the ground in a dance until
he collapses. Enter a stuffed figure, more than life-
size,* GALILEO GALILEI, *which bows to the audience.
In front of it a child displays a giant open Bible
with crossed-out pages.)*

THE BALLAD SINGER: Galileo Galilei, the
Bible-smasher!

(An outburst of laughter among the crowd.)

SCENE XI

1633. The inquisition summons the world-famous scholar to Rome.

The depths are hot, the heights are chill
The streets are loud, the court is still.

(Antechamber and staircase of the Medici Palace, Florence. GALILEO *and his daughter are waiting to be admitted to the grand duke.)*

VIRGINIA: It's been a long wait.

GALILEO: Yes.

VIRGINIA: There's that man again who's been following us. *(She points at a shady individual who passes by without paying attention to them)*

GALILEO: *(Whose eyesight is impaired)* I don't know him.

VIRGINIA: I've seen him several times lately. He gives me the shivers.

GALILEO: Nonsense. We're in Florence, not among Corsican robbers.

VIRGINA: There's Rector Gaffone.

GALILEO: *He* frightens *me.* The blockhead will draw me into another interminable conversation.

(MR. GAFFONE, the rector of the university, descends the stairs. He is visibly startled when he sees GALILEO *and walks stiffly past the two, with rigidly averted head and barely nodding.)*

GALILEO: What's got into him? My eyes are bad again. Did he greet us at all?

VIRGINIA: Just barely.—What have you said in your book? Can they think it's heretical?

GALILEO: You hang around church too much. Getting up before dawn and running to mass is ruining your complexion. You pray for me, don't you?

VIRGINIA: There's Mr. Vanni, the iron founder. The one you designed the smelting furnace for. Don't forget to thank him for the quails.

(A man has come down the stairs.)

VANNI: How did you like the quails I sent you, Mr. Galileo?

GALILEO: Maestro Vanni, the quails were excellent. Again many thanks.

VANNI: They're talking about you upstairs. They claim you're responsible for those pamphlets against the Bible that are being sold all over.

GALILEO: I know nothing about pamphlets. My favorite books are the Bible and Homer.

VANNI: Even if that were not the case: Let me take this opportunity of assuring you that we manufacturers are on your side. I don't know much about the movement of stars, but the way I look at it, you're the man who is fighting for the freedom to teach new knowledge. Just take that mechanical cultivator from Germany that you described to me. Last year alone five works on agriculture were published in London. Here we'd be grateful for one book about the Dutch canals. It's the same people who are making trouble for you and preventing the physicians in Bologna from dissecting corpses for research.

GALILEO: Your vote counts, Vanni.

VANNI: I hope so. Do you know that in Amsterdam and London they have money markets? And trade schools too. And newspapers that appear regularly. Here we're not even free to make money. They're against iron foundries because they claim too many workers in one place promote immorality. I swim or sink with men like you, Mr. Galileo! If ever they try to harm you, please remember that you have friends in every branch of industry. The cities of northern Italy are behind you, sir.

GALILEO: As far as I know no one has any intention of harming me.

VANNI: Really?

GALILEO: Really.

VANNI: I believe you'd be better off in Venice. Not so many cassocks. You'd be free to carry on the fight: I have a coach and horses, Mr. Galileo.

GALILEO: I can't see myself as a refugee. I love comfort.

VANNI: I understand. But to judge by what I heard up there, there's no time to be lost. I got the impression that right now they'd prefer not to have you in Florence.

GALILEO: Nonsense. The grand duke is a pupil of mine, not to mention the fact that if anyone tries to trip me up the pope himself will tell him where to get off.

VANNI: You don't seem able to distinguish your friends from your enemies, Mr. Galilei.

GALILEO: I'm able to distinguish power from lack of power. *(He brusquely steps away)*

VANNI: Well, I wish you luck. *(Goes out)*

GALILEO: *(Back at* VIRGINIA'S *side)* Every Tom, Dick and Harry with a grievance picks me as his spokesman, especially in places where it doesn't exactly help me. I've written a book on the mechanism of the universe, that's all. What people make or don't make of it is no concern of mine.

VIRGINIA: *(In a loud voice)* If people only knew how you condemned the goings-on at last year's carnival.

GALILEO: Yes. Give a bear honey if it's hungry and you'll lose your arm.

VIRGINIA: *(In an undertone)* Did the grand duke send for you today?

GALILEO: No, but I've sent in my name. He wants the book, he's paid for it. Ask somebody, complain about the long wait.

VIRGINIA: *(Goes to talk to an attendant, followed by the individual)* Mr. Mincio, has His Highness been informed that my father wishes to speak to him?

THE ATTENDANT: How should I know?

VIRGINIA: That's no answer.

THE ATTENDANT: Really?

VIRGINIA: You ought to be polite.

(The attendant half turns his back on her and yawns while looking at the shady individual)

VIRGINIA: *(Has come back)* He says the grand duke is still busy.

GALILEO: I heard you say something about "polite." What was it?

VIRGINIA: I thanked him for his polite answer, that's all. Can't you just leave the book for him? You're wasting your time.

GALILEO: I'm beginning to wonder what my time is worth. Maybe I should accept Sagredo's invitation to go to Padua for a few weeks. My health hasn't been up to snuff.

VIRGINIA: You couldn't live without your books.

GALILEO: We could take some of the Sicilian wine, one, two cases.

VIRGINIA: You always say it doesn't travel. And the court owes you three months' salary. They won't forward it.

GALILEO: That's true.

VIRGINIA: *(Whispers)* The cardinal inquisitor!

(The cardinal inquisitor descends the stairs. Passing them, he bows low to GALILEO.*)*

VIRGINIA: What's the cardinal inquisitor doing in Florence, father?

GALILEO: I don't know. His attitude was respectful, I think. I knew what I was doing when I came to Florence and held my peace all these years. Their praises have raised me so high that they have to take me as I am.

THE ATTENDANT: *(Announces)* His Highness, the grand duke!

*(*COSMO DE'MEDICI *comes down the stairs.* GALILEO *approaches him.* COSMO, *slightly embarrassed, stops.)*

GALILEO: May I present Your Highness with my *Dialogues on the Two Chief Syst* . . .

COSMO: I see, I see. How are your eyes?

GALILEO: Not too good, Your Highness. With Your Highness' permission, I should like to present my . . .

COSMO: The state of your eyes alarms me. Yes, it alarms me a good deal. Haven't you been using your splendid tube a little too much? *(He walks off without accepting the book)*

GALILEO: He didn't take the book, did he?

VIRGINIA: Father, I'm afraid.

GALILEO: *(Subdued, but firmly)* Don't show your feelings. We are not going home, but to Volpi, the glass cutter's. I've arranged with him to have a cart with empty wine casks ready in the tavern yard next door, to take me away at any time.

VIRGINIA: Then you knew . . .

GALILEO: Don't look back.

(They start to leave.)

A HIGH OFFICIAL: *(Descending the stairs)* Mr. Galilei, I have orders to inform you that the court of Florence is no longer in a position to oppose the request of the Holy Inquisition for your interrogation in Rome. Mr. Galilei, the coach of the Holy Inquisition is waiting for you.

SCENE XII
The pope.

(A room in the Vatican. POPE URBAN VIII *(formerly* CARDINAL BARBERINI*) has received the* CARDINAL INQUISITOR. *During the audience* THE POPE *is being dressed. From outside the shuffling of many feet is heard.)*

THE POPE: *(Very loud)* No! No! No!

THE INQUISITOR: Then Your Holiness really means to tell the doctors of all the faculties, the representatives of all the religious orders and of the entire clergy, who have come here guided by their childlike faith in the word of God as recorded in scripture to hear Your Holiness confirm them in their faith — you mean to inform them that scripture can no longer be considered true?

THE POPE: I won't permit the multiplication tables to be broken. No!

THE INQUISITOR: Yes, these people say it is only a matter of the multiplication tables, not of the spirit of rebellion and doubt. But it is not the multiplication tables. It is an alarming unrest that has come over the world. It is the unrest of their own minds, which they transfer to the immovable earth. They cry out: The figures force our hands! But where do these figures come from? Everyone knows they come from doubt. These people doubt everything. Is our human community to be built on doubt and no longer on faith? "You are my master, but I doubt whether that is a good arrangement." "This is your house and your wife, but I doubt whether they should not be mine." On the other hand, as we can read on the house walls of Rome, disgraceful interpretations are being put on Your Holiness' great love for art, to which we owe such marvelous collections: "The Barberinis are stripping Rome of what the barbarians failed to take." And abroad? It has pleased God to visit heavy tribulation upon the Holy See. Your Holiness' policy in Spain is misunderstood by persons lacking in insight, your rift with the emperor is deplored. For fifteen years Germany has been a shambles, people have been slaughtering one another with Bible quotations on their lips. And at a time when under the onslaught of plague, war and reformation, Christianity is being reduced to a few disorganized bands, a rumor is spreading through Europe that you are in secret league with Lutheran Sweden to weaken the Catholic emperor. This is the moment these mathematicians, these worms, choose to turn their tubes to the sky and inform the world that even here, the one place where your authority is not yet contested, Your Holiness is on shaky ground. Why, one is tempted to ask, this sudden interest in so recondite a science as astronomy? Does it make any difference how these bodies move? Yet, thanks to the bad example of that Florentine, all Italy, down to the last stableboy, is prattling about the phases of Venus and thinking at the same time of many irksome things which are held in our schools and elsewhere to be immutable. Where will it end, if all these people, weak in the flesh and inclined to excess, come to rely exclusively on their own reason, which this madman declares to be the ultimate authority? They begin by doubting whether the sun stood still at Gibeon and end up directing their unclean doubts at the church collections. Since they began sailing the high seas — to which I have no objection — they have been putting their trust in a brass sphere that they call a compass, and no longer in God. Even as a young man this Galileo wrote about machines. With machines they expect to work miracles. What kind of miracles? Of course they have no more use for God, but what is to be the nature of these miracles? For one thing, they expect to do away with Above and Below. They don't need it any more. Aristotle, whom in other respects they regard as a dead dog, said — and this they quote — : If the shuttle were to weave by itself and the plectron to pluck by itself, masters would no longer need apprentices nor lords servants. They believe that this time has come. This evil man knows what he is doing when he writes his astronomical works not in Latin but in the idiom of fishwives and wool merchants.

THE POPE: It's certainly in bad taste. I'll tell him.

THE INQUISITOR: Some he incites, others he bribes. The north Italian ship owners keep clamoring for Mr. Galilei's star charts. We shall have to yield to them, since material interests are involved.

THE POPE: But these star charts are based on

his heretical statements, on the movements of certain heavenly bodies which become impossible if his doctrine is rejected. You can't reject the doctrine and accept the star charts.

THE INQUISITOR: Why not? It's the only solution.

THE POPE: This shuffling makes me nervous. Forgive me if I seem distracted.

THE INQUISITOR: Perhaps it speaks to you more clearly than I can, Your Holiness. Are all these people to go home with doubts in their hearts?

THE POPE: After all the man is the greatest physicist of our time, a beacon for Italy, and not some good-for-nothing crank. He has friends. There's Versailles. There's the court in Vienna. They will call the church a cesspool of rotten prejudices. Hands off!

THE INQUISITOR: Actually, we wouldn't have to go very far in his case. He is a man of the flesh. He would cave in very quickly.

THE POPE: He gets pleasure out of more things than any man I ever met. Even his thinking is sensual. He can never say no to an old wine or a new idea. I will not stand for any condemning of physical facts, any battle cry of "church" against "reason." I gave him leave to write his book provided it ended with a statement that the last word is not with science but with faith. He has complied.

THE INQUISITOR: But how did he comply? His book is an argument between a simpleton who—naturally—propounds the opinions of Aristotle, and an intelligent man, just as naturally voicing Mr. Galilei's opinions; and the concluding remark, Your Holiness, is made by whom?

THE POPE: What was that again? Who states our opinion?

THE INQUISITOR: Not the intelligent one.

THE POPE: That is impudence. This stamping in the halls is insufferable. Is the whole world coming here?

THE INQUISITOR: Not the whole world, but the best part of it.

(Pause. THE POPE is now fully robed.)

THE POPE: At the very most the instruments may be shown to him.

THE INQUISITOR: That will suffice, Your Holiness. Mr. Galilei is well versed in instruments.

SCENE XIII

On June 22, 1633, GALILEO GALILEI abjures his doctrine of the motion of the earth before the Inquisition.

> *June twenty-second, sixteen thirty-three*
> *A momentous day for you and me.*
> *Of all the days that was the one*
> *An age of reason could have begun.*

(Palace of the Florentine ambassador in Rome. GALILEO's pupils are waiting for news. THE LITTLE MONK and FEDERZONI are playing the new chess with its sweeping movements. VIRGINIA kneels in a corner saying an Ave Maria.)

THE LITTLE MONK: The pope refused to see him. No more scientific debates.

FEDERZONI: The pope was his last hope. I guess Cardinal Barberini was right when he said to him years ago: We need you. Now they've got him.

ANDREA: They'll kill him. The *Discorsi* will never be finished.

FEDERZONI: *(With a furtive glance at him)* You think so?

ANDREA: Because he'll never recant.

(Pause.)

THE LITTLE MONK: When you lie awake at night you chew on the most useless ideas. Last night I couldn't get rid of the thought that he should never have left the republic of Venice.

ANDREA: He couldn't write his book there.

FEDERZONI: And in Florence he couldn't publish it.

(Pause)

THE LITTLE MONK: I also kept wondering whether they'd let him keep the stone he always carries in his pocket. His touchstone.

FEDERZONI: Where they're taking him people don't wear pockets.

ANDREA: (Screaming) They won't dare! And even if they do, he'll never recant. "Not to know the truth is just stupid. To know the truth and call it a lie is criminal."

FEDERZONI: I don't think so either, and I wouldn't want to go on living if he did, but they have the power.

ANDREA: Power isn't everything.

FEDERZONI: Maybe not.

THE LITTLE MONK: (Softly) He's been in prison for twenty-three days. Yesterday was the great interrogation. Today the judges are in session. (As ANDREA is listening, he raises his voice) When I came to see him here two days after the decree, we were sitting over there; he showed me the little Priapus by the sundial in the garden—you can see it from here—and compared his own work with a poem by Horace, in which it is also impossible to change anything. He spoke of his esthetic sense, which compels him to look for the truth. And he told me his motto: Hieme et aestate, et prope et procul, usque dum vivam et ultra. He was referring to the truth.

ANDREA: (To THE LITTLE MONK) Did you tell him what he did in the Collegium Romanum while they were examining his tube? Tell him! (THE LITTLE MONK shakes his head) He acted the same as always. He put his hands on his hams, stuck out his belly and said: Gentlemen, I beg for reason! (Laughingly he imitates GALILEO)

(Pause.)

ANDREA: (Referring to VIRGINIA) She's praying for him to recant.

FEDERZONI: Let her pray. She's all mixed up since they talked to her. They brought her confessor down from Florence.

(Enter THE SHADY INDIVIDUAL from the grand ducal palace in Florence.)

THE SHADY INDIVIDUAL: Mr. Galilei will be here soon. He may want a bed.

FEDERZONI: Has he been released?

THE SHADY INDIVIDUAL: Mr. Galilei is expected to recant at five o'clock before the plenary session of the Inquisition. The big bell of St. Mark's will be rung and the wording of the abjuration will be proclaimed publicly.

ANDREA: I don't believe it.

THE SHADY INDIVIDUAL: Because of the crowds in the streets, Mr. Galilei will be conducted to the postern on this side of the palace. (Out)

ANDREA: (Suddenly in a loud voice) The moon is an earth and has no light of its own. And Venus has no light of its own either and is like the earth and moves around the sun. And four moons revolve around the planet Jupiter which is as far away as the fixed stars and not fastened to any sphere. And the sun is the center of the universe and immovable in its place, and the earth is not the center and not immovable. And he was the man who proved it.

THE LITTLE MONK: No force can make what has been seen unseen.

(Silence.)

FEDERZONI: (Looks at the sundial in the garden) Five o'clock.

(VIRGINIA prays louder.)

ANDREA: I can't stand it! They're beheading the truth!

(He holds his hands to his ears, so does THE LITTLE MONK. The bell is not rung. After a pause filled with VIRGINIA's murmured prayers FEDERZONI shakes his head in the negative. The others drop their hands.)

FEDERZONI: (Hoarsely) Nothing. It's three minutes past five.

ANDREA: He's resisting.

THE LITTLE MONK: He hasn't recanted!

FEDERZONI: No. Oh, my friends!

(They embrace. They are wildly happy.)

ANDREA: You see: They can't do it with force! Force isn't everything! Hence: Stupidity is defeated, it's not invulnerable! Hence: Man is not afraid of death!

FEDERZONI: Now the age of knowledge will begin in earnest. This is the hour of its birth. Just think! If he had recanted!

THE LITTLE MONK: I didn't say anything but I was very worried. I was faint of heart.

ANDREA: I knew it.

FEDERZONI: It would have been as if morning had turned back to night.

ANDREA: As if the mountain said: I'm water.

THE LITTLE MONK: *(Kneels down in tears)* Lord, I thank Thee.

ANDREA: But now everything has changed. Man is lifting his head, tormented man, and saying: I can live. All this is accomplished when one man gets up and says No!

(At this moment the big bell of St. Mark's begins to boom. All stand transfixed.)

VIRGINIA: *(Getting up)* The bell of St. Mark's. He hasn't been condemned!

(From the street the announcer is heard reciting GALILEO'S *recantation.)*

ANNOUNCER'S VOICE: "I, Galileo Galilei, professor of mathematics and physics in Florence, hereby abjure what I have taught, to wit, that the sun is the center of the world and motionless in its place, and the earth is not the center and not motionless. Out of a sincere heart and unfeigned faith, I abjure, condemn and execrate all these errors and heresies as I do all other errors and all other opinions in opposition to the Holy Church."

(Darkness)

(When it grows light again, the bell is still booming, then it stops. VIRGINIA *has left.* GALILEO'S *pupils are still there.)*

FEDERZONI: He never paid you properly for your work. You couldn't buy a pair of pants or publish anything. You had to put up with all that because you were "working for science"!

ANDREA: *(Loudly)* Unhappy the land that has no heroes!

*(*GALILEO *has come in, completely, almost unrecognizably, changed by the trial. He has heard* ANDREA'S *exclamation. For a few moments he hesitates at the door, expecting a greeting. As none is forthcoming and his pupils shrink back from him, he goes slowly and because of his bad eyesight uncertainly to the front where he finds a footstool and sits down.)*

ANDREA: I can't look at him. I wish he'd go away.

FEDERZONI: Calm yourself.

ANDREA: *(Screams at* GALILEO*)* Wine barrel! Snail eater! Have you saved your precious skin? *(Sits down)* I feel sick.

GALILEO: *(Calmly)* Get him a glass of water.

*(*THE LITTLE MONK *goes out to get* ANDREA *a glass of water. The others pay no attention to* GALILEO *who sits on his footstool, listening. From far off the announcer's voice is heard again.)*

ANDREA: I can walk now if you'll help me.

(They lead him to the door. Whey they reach it, GALILEO *begins to speak.)*

GALILEO: No. Unhappy the land that needs a hero.

(A reading in front of the curtain.)

Is it not obvious that a horse falling from a height of three or four ells will break its legs, whereas a dog would not suffer any damage, nor would a cat from a height of eight or nine ells, or a cricket from a tower, or an ant even if it were to fall from the moon? And just as smaller animals are comparatively stronger than larger ones, so small plants too stand up better: an oak tree two hundred ells high cannot sustain its branches in the same proportion as a small oak tree, nor can nature let a horse grow as large as twenty horses or produce a giant ten times the size of man unless it changes all the proportions of the limbs and especially of the bones, which would have to be strengthened far beyond the size demanded by mere proportion.—The common assumption that large and small machines are equally durable is apparently erroneous.

Galileo, *Discorsi*

SCENE XIV

1633–1642. GALILEO GALILEI *spends the rest of his life in a villa near Florence, as a prisoner of the Inquisition. The* Discorsi.

> Sixteen hundred thirty-three to
> sixteen hundred forty-two
> Galileo Galilei remains a prisoner
> of the church until his death.

(A large room with a table, a leather chair and a globe. GALILEO, *now old and almost blind, is experimenting carefully with a small wooden ball rolling on a curved wooden rail. In the anteroom a monk is sitting on guard. A knock at the door.* THE MONK *opens and a* PEASANT *comes in carrying two plucked geese.* VIRGINIA *emerges from the kitchen. She is now about forty years old.)*

THE PEASANT: I'm supposed to deliver these.

VIRGINIA: Who from? I didn't order any geese.

THE PEASANT: I was told to say from someone that's passing through. *(Out)*

*(*VIRGINIA *looks at the geese in astonishment.* THE MONK *takes them from her and examines them suspiciously. Satisfied, he gives them back and she carries them by the necks to* GALILEO *in the large room.)*

VIRGINIA: A present, dropped off by someone, who's passing through.

GALILEO: What is it?

VIRGINIA: Can't you see?

GALILEO: No. *(He goes closer)* Geese. Was there any name?

VIRGINIA: No.

GALILEO: *(Taking one goose from her.)* Heavy. Maybe I'll have some.

VIRGINIA: You can't be hungry again. You just finished dinner. And what's wrong with your eyes today? You ought to be able to see them from where you are.

GALILEO: You're standing in the shadow.

VIRGINIA: I'm not in the shadow. *(She carries the geese out)*

GALILEO: Put in thyme and apples.

VIRGINIA: *(To* THE MONK*)* We must send for the eye doctor. Father couldn't see the geese.

THE MONK: I'll need permission from Monsignor Carpula. — Has he been writing again?

VIRGINIA: No. He's dictating his book to me, you know that. You have pages 131 and 132, they were the last.

THE MONK: He's an old fox.

VIRGINIA: He doesn't do anything against the rules. His repentance is real. I keep an eye on him. *(She gives him the geese)* Tell them in the kitchen to fry the liver with an apple and an onion. *(She comes back into the larger room)* And now we're going to think of our eyes and stop playing with that ball and dictate a little more of our weekly letter to the archbishop.

GALILEO: I don't feel up to it. Read me some Horace.

VIRGINIA: Only last week Monsignor Carpula, to whom we owe so much — those vegetables the other day — told me the archbishop keeps asking him what you think of the questions and quotations he's been sending you. *(She has sat down ready for dictation)*

GALILEO: Where was I?

VIRGINIA: Section four: Concerning the reaction of the church to the unrest in the arsenal in Venice, I agree with Cardinal Spoletti's attitude concerning the rebellious rope makers . . .

GALILEO: Yes. *(Dictates)* . . . agree with Cardinal Spoletti's attitude concerning the rebellious rope makers, to wit, that it is better to dispense soup to them in the name of Christian charity than to pay them more for their ship's cables and bell ropes. All the more so, since it seems wiser to strengthen their faith than their greed. The Apostle Paul says: Charity never faileth. — How does that sound?

VIRGINIA: It's wonderful, father.

GALILEO: You don't think it could be mistaken for irony?

VIRGINIA: No, the archbishop will be very pleased. He's a practical man.

GALILEO: I rely on your judgment. What's the next point?

VIRGINIA: A very beautiful saying: "When I am weak then I am strong."

GALILEO: No comment.

VIRGINIA: Why not?

GALILEO: What's next?

VIRGINIA: "And to know the love of Christ, which passeth knowledge." Paul to the Ephesians three nineteen.

GALILEO: I must especially thank Your Eminence for the magnificent quotation from the epistle to the Ephesians. Inspired by it, I found the following in our incomparable "Imitation": *(He quotes from memory)* "He to whom speaketh the eternal word is free from much questioning." May I seize this opportunity to say something on my own behalf? To this day I am being reproached for once having written a book on celestial bodies in the language of the market place. In so doing, I did not mean to suggest, or to express my approval of the writing of books on such important subjects as theology in the jargon of spaghetti vendors. The argument in favor of the service in Latin—that the universality of this language enables all nations to hear mass in exactly the same way—seems less than fortunate since the scoffers, who are never at a loss, may well argue that the use of this language prevents all nations from understanding the text. I for my part prefer to forego the cheap intelligibility of things holy. The Latin tongue, which protects the eternal verities of the church from the prying of the ignorant, inspires confidence when recited by priests, sons of the lower classes, in the pronunciation of their local dialects.—No, strike that out.

VIRGINIA: The whole thing?

GALILEO: Everything after the spaghetti vendors.

(A knocking at the door. VIRGINIA *goes into the anteroom.* THE MONK *opens the door.* ANDREA SARTI *appears. He is a man in his middle years.)*

ANDREA: Good evening. I am leaving Italy. To do scientific work in Holland. I was asked to see him on my way through and bring the latest news of him.

VIRGINIA: I don't know if he'll want to see you. You never came to visit us.

ANDREA: Ask him.

*(*GALILEO *has recognized the voice. He sits motionless.* VIRGINIA *goes in to him.)*

GALILEO: Is it Andrea?

VIRGINIA: Yes. Should I send him away?

GALILEO: *(After a pause)* Bring him in.

*(*VIRGINIA *leads* ANDREA *inside.)*

VIRGINIA: *(To* THE MONK*)* He's harmless. He was his pupil. So now he's his enemy.

GALILEO: Leave us alone, Virginia.

VIRGINIA: I want to hear what he says. *(She sits down)*

ANDREA: *(Cool)* How are you?

GALILEO: Come closer. What are you doing? Tell me about your work. I hear you're on hydraulics.

ANDREA: Fabricius in Amsterdam has asked me to inquire about your health.

(Pause.)

GALILEO: I'm well. I receive every attention.

ANDREA: I shall be glad to report that you are well.

GALILEO: Fabricius will be glad to hear it. And you may add that I am living in reasonable comfort. The depth of my repentance has moved my superiors to allow me limited scientific pursuits under clerical control.

ANDREA: Oh yes. We too have heard that the church is pleased with you. Your total submission has borne fruit. The authorities, I am told, are most gratified to note that since your submission no work containing any new hypothesis has been published in Italy.

GALILEO: *(Listening in the direction of the anteroom.)* Unfortunately there are countries which elude the protection of the church. I fear the condemned doctrines are being perpetuated in those countries.

ANDREA: There too your recantation has resulted in a setback most gratifying to the church.

GALILEO: You don't say. *(Pause)* Nothing from Descartes? No news from Paris?

ANDREA: Oh yes. When he heard you had recanted he stuffed his treatise on the nature of light in his desk drawer.

(Long pause.)

GALILEO: I keep worrying about some of my scientific friends whom I led down the path of error. Has my recantation helped them to mend their ways?

ANDREA: I am going to Holland to carry on my work. The ox is not allowed to do what Jupiter denies himself.

GALILEO: I understand.

ANDREA: Federzoni is back at his lens grinding, in some shop in Milan.

GALILEO: *(Laughs)* He doesn't know Latin.

(Pause.)

ANDREA: Fulganzio, our little monk, has given up science and returned to the fold.

GALILEO: Yes. *(Pause)* My superiors are looking forward to my complete spiritual recovery. I'm making better progress than expected.

ANDREA: I see.

VIRGINIA: The Lord be praised.

GALILEO: *(Gruffly)* Attend to the geese, Virginia.

*(*VIRGINIA *leaves angrily. In passing she is addressed by* THE MONK.*)*

THE MONK: I don't like that man.

VIRGINIA: He's harmless. You heard what he said. *(On her way out)* We've got fresh goat cheese.

(THE MONK follows her out)

ANDREA: I'm going to travel through the night so as to cross the border by morning. May I go now?

GALILEO: I can't see why you've come, Sarti. To stir me up? I've been living prudently and thinking prudently since I came here. I have my relapses even so.

ANDREA: I have no desire to upset you, Mr. Galilei.

GALILEO: Barberini called it the itch. He wasn't entirely free from it himself. I've been writing again.

ANDREA: You have?

GALILEO: I've finished the *Discorsi.*

ANDREA: What? The *Discourses Concerning Two New Sciences: Mechanics and Local Motion?* Here?

GALILEO: Oh, they let me have paper and pen. My superiors aren't stupid. They know that ingrained vices can't be uprooted overnight. They protect me from unpleasant consequences by locking up page after page.

ANDREA: Oh God!

GALILEO: Did you say something?

ANDREA: They let you plow water! They give you pen and paper to quiet you! How could you ever write under such conditions?

GALILEO: Oh, I'm a slave of habit.

ANDREA: The *Discorsi* in the hands of monks! When Amsterdam and London and Prague are clamoring for them!

GALILEO: I can just hear Fabricius wailing, demanding his pound of flesh, while he himself sits safely in Amsterdam.

ANDREA: Two new branches of science as good as lost!

GALILEO: No doubt he and some others will feel uplifted when they hear that I jeopardized the last pitiful remnants of my comfort to make a copy, behind my own back so to speak, for six months using up the last ounces of light on the clearer nights.

ANDREA: You have a copy?

GALILEO: So far my vanity has prevented me from destroying it.

ANDREA: Where is it?

GALILEO: "If thine eye offend thee, pluck it out." Whoever wrote that knew more about comfort than I do. I'm sure it's the height of folly to let it out of my hands. But since I've been unable to leave science alone, you may just as well have it. The copy is in the globe. Should you consider taking it to Holland, you would of course have to bear full responsibility. You'd say you bought it from someone with access to the Holy Office.

(ANDREA has gone to the globe. He takes out the copy.)

ANDREA: The *Discorsi! (He leafs through the manuscript. He reads)* "It is my purpose to establish an entirely new science in regard to a very old problem, namely, motion. By means of experiments I have discovered some of its properties, which are worth knowing."

GALILEO: I had to do something with my time.

ANDREA: This will be the foundation of a new physics.

GALILEO: Put it under your coat.

ANDREA: And we thought you had deserted us! My voice was the loudest against you!

GALILEO: You were absolutely right. I taught you science and I denied the truth.

ANDREA: That changes everything. Everything.

GALILEO: You think so?

ANDREA: You were hiding the truth. From the enemy. Even in ethics you were centuries ahead of us.

GALILEO: Explain that to me, Andrea.

ANDREA: With the man on the street we said: He'll die, but he'll never recant. — You came back and said: I've recanted but I shall live. — Your hands are stained, we said. — You said: Better stained than empty.

GALILEO: Better stained than empty. Sounds realistic. Sounds like me. A new science, a new ethics.

ANDREA: I should have known — better than anyone else. I was eleven when you sold another man's telescope to the senate in Venice. And I watched you make immortal use of that instrument. Your friends shook their heads when you humbled yourself to that child in Florence: But science found an audience. You've always laughed at heroes. "People who suffer bore me," you said. "Bad luck comes from faulty calculations," and "If there are obstacles the shortest line between two points may well be a crooked line."

GALILEO: I remember.

ANDREA: And in thirty-three when you decided to abjure a popular item of your doctrine, I should have known that you were merely withdrawing from a hopeless political brawl in order to further the true interests of science.

GALILEO: Which consist in . . .

ANDREA: . . . the study of the properties of motion, the mother of machines, which alone will make the earth so good to live on that we shall be able to do without heaven.

GALILEO: Hm.

ANDREA: You won the leisure to write a scientific work which you alone could write. Had you perished in the fiery halo of the stake, the others would have been the victors.

GALILEO: They are the victors. Besides, there is no scientific work that one man alone can write.

ANDREA: Then why did you recant?

GALILEO: I recanted because I was afraid of physical pain.

ANDREA: No!

GALILEO: They showed me the instruments.

ANDREA: Then it was not premeditated?

GALILEO: It was not.

(Pause.)

ANDREA: *(Loud)* In science only one thing counts: contribution to knowledge.

GALILEO: And that I have supplied. Welcome to the gutter, brother in science and cousin in treason! You like fish? I have fish. What stinks is not my fish, it's me. I'm selling out, you are the buyer. Oh, irresistible sight of a book, that hallowed commodity. The mouth waters, the curses are drowned. The great Babylonian whore, the murderous beast, the scarlet woman, opens her thighs, and everything is different! Hallowed be our haggling, whitewashing, death-shunning community!

ANDREA: To shun death is human. Human weaknesses are no concern of science.

GALILEO: No?!— My dear Sarti, even in my present condition I believe I can give you a few hints about the science you are devoting yourself to.

(A short pause.)

GALILEO: *(In lecture style, hands folded over his paunch)* In my free time, and I've got plenty of that, I have reviewed my case and asked myself how the world of science, of which I no longer consider myself a member, will judge it. Even a wool merchant, in addition to buying cheap and selling dear, has to worry about the obstacles that may be put in the way of the wool trade itself. In this sense, the pursuit of science seems to call for special courage. Science trades in knowledge distilled from doubt. Providing everybody with knowledge of everything, science aims at making doubters of everybody. But princes, landlords and priests keep the majority of the people in a pearly haze of superstition and outworn words to cover up their own machinations. The misery of the many is as old as the hills and is proclaimed in church and lecture hall to be as indestructible as the hills. Our new art of doubting delighted the common people. They grabbed the telescope out of our hands and focused it on their tormentors—princes, landlords, priests. Those self-seeking violent men greedily exploited the fruits of science for their own ends but at the same time they felt the cold stare of science focused upon the millennial, yet artificial miseries which mankind could obviously get rid of by getting rid of them. They showered us with threats and bribes, which weak souls cannot resist. But can we turn our backs on the people and still remain scientists? The movements of the heavenly bodies have become more comprehensible; but the movements of their rulers remain unpredictable to the people. The battle to measure the sky was won by doubt; but credulity still prevents the Roman housewife from winning her battle for milk. Science, Sarti, is involved in both battles. If mankind goes on stumbling in a pearly haze of superstition and outworn words and remains too ignorant to make full use of its own strength, it will never be able to use the forces of nature which science has discovered. What end are you scientists working for? To my mind, the only purpose of science is to lighten the toil of human existence. If scientists, browbeaten by selfish rulers, confine themselves to the accumulation of knowledge for the sake of knowledge, science will be crippled and your new machines will only mean new hardships. Given time, you may well discover everything there is to discover, but your progress will be a progression away from humanity. The gulf between you and humanity may one day be so wide that the response to your exultation about some new achievement will be a universal outcry

LIFE OF GALILEO / 541

of horror. — As a scientist, I had a unique opportunity. In my time astronomy reached the market place. Under these very special circumstances, one man's steadfastness might have had tremendous repercussions. If I had held out, scientists might have developed something like the physicians' Hippocratic oath, the vow to use their knowledge only for the good of mankind. As things stand now, the best we can hope for is a generation of inventive dwarfs who can be hired for any purpose. Furthermore, I have come to the conclusion, Sarti, that I was never in any real danger. For a few years I was as strong as the authorities. And yet I handed the powerful my knowledge to use, or not to use, or to misuse as served their purposes.

(VIRGINIA *has come in with a dish and stops now.*)

I have betrayed my calling. A man who does what I have done, cannot be tolerated in the ranks of science.

VIRGINIA: You have been received in the ranks of the faithful.

(*She walks on and sets the dish on the table.*)

GALILEO: Yes. — I must eat now.

SCENE XV

1637. GALILEO's book Discorsi *crosses the Italian border.*

> The great book o'er the border went
> And, good folk, that was the end.
> But we hope you'll keep in mind
> You and I were left behind.
> May you now guard science' light
> Keep it up and use it right
> Lest it be a flame to fall
> One day to consume us all.

(ANDREA *offers him his hand.* GALILEO *sees it but does not take it.*)

GALILEO: You are teaching now yourself. Can you afford to shake a hand such as mine? (*He goes to the table*) Somebody on the way through has sent me two geese. I still like to eat.

ANDREA: Then you no longer believe that a new era has dawned?

GALILEO: I do. — Take good care of yourself when you pass through Germany with the truth under your coat.

ANDREA: (*Unable to leave*) Regarding your opinion of the author we discussed I cannot answer you. But I refuse to believe that your devastating analysis can be the last word.

GALILEO: Thank you, sir. (*He begins to eat*)

VIRGINIA: (*Seeing* ANDREA *out*) We don't like visitors from the past. They upset him.

(ANDREA *leaves.* VIRGINIA *comes back*)

GALILEO: Any idea who could have sent the geese?

VIRGINIA: Not Andrea.

GALILEO: Maybe not. How is the night?

VIRGINIA: (*At the window*) Clear.

(*A small Italian border town. Early morning.* CHILDREN *are playing by the turnpike near the guard house.* ANDREA, *beside a coachman, is waiting for his papers to be examined by the guards. He is sitting on a small box reading in* GALILEO'S *manuscript. The coach is on the far side of the turnpike.*)

THE CHILDREN: (*Sing*)

Mary sat upon a stone
Had a pink shift of her own
The shift was full of shit.
But when cold weather came along
Mary put her shift back on
Shitty is better than split.

THE BORDER GUARD: Why are you leaving Italy?

ANDREA: I'm a scholar.

THE BORDER GUARD: (*To the clerk*) Write under "Reason for Leaving": Scholar.

(*The clerk does so.*)

THE FIRST BOY: *(To* ANDREA*)* Don't sit there. *(He points at the hut in front of which* ANDREA *is sitting.)* A witch lives there.

THE SECOND BOY: Old Marina isn't a witch.

THE FIRST BOY: Want me to twist your arm?

THE THIRD BOY: She is too. She flies through the air at night.

THE FIRST BOY: If she's not a witch, why can't she get any milk anywhere in town?

THE SECOND BOY: How can she fly through the air? Nobody can do that. *(To* ANDREA*)* Or can they?

THE FIRST BOY: *(Referring to* THE SECOND BOY*)* That's Giuseppe. He doesn't know anything, because he doesn't go to school, because his pants are torn.

THE BORDER GUARD: What's that book?

ANDREA: *(Without looking up)* It's by Aristotle, the great philosopher.

THE BORDER GUARD: *(Suspiciously)* What's he up to?

ANDREA: He's dead.

(To tease ANDREA, *the boys walk around him in a way indicating that they too are reading books.)*

THE BORDER GUARD: *(To* THE CLERK*)* See if there's anything about religion in it.

THE CLERK: *(Turning leaves)* Can't see anything.

THE BORDER GUARD: Anyway there's no point in looking. Nobody'd be so open about anything he wanted to hide. *(To* ANDREA*)* You'll have to sign a paper saying we examined everything.

*(*ANDREA *hesitantly gets up and reading all the time goes into the house with the guards.)*

THE THIRD BOY: *(To* THE CLERK, *pointing at the box)* Look, there's something else.

THE CLERK: Wasn't it here before?

THE THIRD BOY: The devil's put it there. It's a box.

THE SECOND BOY: No, it belongs to the traveler.

THE THIRD BOY: I wouldn't go near it. She's bewitched Passi the coachman's horses. I looked through the hole in the roof that the snowstorm made, and I heard them coughing.

THE CLERK: *(Almost at the box hesitates and goes back)* Witchery, ha? Well, we can't examine everything. We'd never get through.

*(*ANDREA *returns with a pitcher of milk. He sits down on the box again and continues to read.)*

THE BORDER GUARD: *(Following him with papers)* Close the boxes. Is that all?

THE CLERK: Yes.

THE SECOND BOY: *(To* ANDREA*)* You say you're a scholar. Then tell me: Can people fly through the air?

ANDREA: Just a moment.

THE BORDER GUARD: You may proceed.

(The luggage has been picked up by the coachman. ANDREA *takes his box and prepares to go.)*

THE BORDER GUARD: Wait! What's in that box?

ANDREA: *(Taking up his book again)* Books.

THE FIRST BOY: It's the witch's box.

THE BORDER GUARD: Nonsense. How could she hex a box?

THE THIRD BOY: If the devil's helping her!

THE BORDER GUARD: *(Laughs)* Not in our rule book. *(To* THE CLERK*)* Open it.

(The box is opened.)

THE BORDER GUARD: *(Listlessly)* How many?

ANDREA: Thirty-four.

THE BORDER GUARD: *(To* THE CLERK*)* How long will it take you?

THE CLERK: *(Who has started rummaging superficially through the box)* All printed stuff. You'd have no time for breakfast, and when do you expect me to collect the overdue toll from Passi the coachman when his house is auctioned off, if I go through all these books?

THE BORDER GUARD: You're right, we've got to get that money. *(He kicks at the books)* What could be in them anyway? *(To the coachman)* Pfftt!

*(*ANDREA *and the coachman who carries the box cross the border. Beyond it* ANDREA *puts* GALILEO'S *manuscript in his bag.)*

THE THIRD BOY: *(Points at the pitcher which* ANDREA *had left behind)* Look!

THE FIRST BOY: And the box is gone! Now do you see it was the devil?

ANDREA: *(Turning around)* No, it was me. You must learn to use your eyes. The milk and the pitcher are paid for. Give them to the old woman. Oh yes, Giuseppe, I haven't answered your question. No one can fly through the air on a stick. Unless it has some sort of machine attached to it. Such machines don't exist yet. Maybe they never will because man is too heavy. But of course, we don't know. We don't know nearly enough, Giuseppe. We've hardly begun.

Life of Galileo is the play most thoroughly reworked by Brecht. He completed the first version in 1939, the second (in collaboration with Charles Laughton) in 1947, and the third in 1955. It is this third version that is reprinted here. *Life of Galileo* may have given Brecht so much trouble because it is the only one of his plays based on a well-known historical personage.

Brecht's major concern in *Life of Galileo* is the conflict between truth (scientific knowledge) and established authority. In a number of statements about the play, Brecht insisted that in it he was not attacking the church as such but as the supreme power in Italy, both religious and secular, in Galileo's time. His overall argument is that science should be freed from restraints and placed in the service of the common man rather than under the control of some authority that can use whatever part of truth serves its purpose and suppress whatever part challenges its power. Thus, Brecht sees Galileo's experience as crucial to the subsequent history of European thought; he wishes the audience to see Galileo's capitulation to the Inquisition as a betrayal not only of freedom of inquiry but as an act that, by affirming the prevailing version of the universe, gave the church time in which to adjust its dogma before the truth was acknowledged, thereby perpetuating the existing class structure and socioeconomic system.

In the opening scene, Galileo declares that his is a new age, that for almost a century there has been a sense of growing expectation; in subsequent scenes we see how Galileo's use of the telescope to observe the movement of the planets establishes the bases for the new age. For centuries the church had accepted as authoritative the description of the universe's structure set forth by Claudius Ptolemy around 150 A.D. In the opening scene, Galileo shows Andrea a model of the Ptolemaic system and then explains it with great exactness. The Ptolemaic system embodied the belief that God's primary concern is man and that in creating the universe He had placed the earth at its center and made everything else revolve around it as the home of mankind. Furthermore, the biblical account of creation was invoked as proof of Ptolemy's accuracy.

A class-structured society was also justified through an extension of these ideas. The concept of a "great chain of being" was used to account for the hierarchy of classes and authority. According to this concept, all things that exist are like the links in a chain, with God at the apex and below him the angels, the pope (as Christ's vicar on earth), secular rulers, the clergy, noblemen, merchants, artisans, and peasants; then came the animals and lower forms of life. This chain was considered to have been ordained by God and therefore any attempt to alter it was viewed as rebellion not merely against earthly authority but against God himself. The church sought to instill unquestioning acceptance of the existing order and saw any challenge to any part of it as an attack on church authority.

The first serious challenge to the Ptolemaic system came in 1543 in a treatise by Nicolaus Copernicus, but Copernicus did not have any means (such as the telescope) for making the detailed observations needed to verify his theory. The significance of Galileo's work lies in his accumulation of evidence to support Copernicus's claims. Thus, in Brecht's play Galileo poses an enormous challenge to the church, for if his views are accepted as true, the church must admit its own fallibility; if it admits that it is wrong about the structure of the universe, on what other points may it also be mistaken? Furthermore, Galileo's version of the universe appears to contradict the biblical account. If the Bible is incorrect on this point, why should it be believed on others? Faced with this problem, the church takes up contradictory positions—denying the truth of Galileo's findings, but permitting their application wherever they serve the needs of commerce. (For example, while denying the correctness of Galileo's version of the universe's structure, the church permits star charts based on his calculations to be used in ship navigation.)

The aspect of the confrontation between Galileo and the church that most interested Brecht is its implications for social and economic change. Galileo's system places man not at the fixed center of the universe but on the periphery of the solar system. Challenging the fixity of the earth also implies a challenge to the fixity of the social order. In Scene X, Brecht shows the excitement created in the working classes by Galileo's ideas, how those ideas were causing people to question authority, and how workers were applying new knowledge to solve old problems. Thus, a potential union between the scientist and the workers is established. In Scene XII, the opposition of the church to this new spirit is shown. (The theatricality of this scene may not be evident from a reading of the script.) When the scene begins, the pope is dressed only in simple undergarments—in other words, he is seen as an ordinary man—and he protests the Inquisition's desire to silence Galileo. But as the scene progresses, layer after layer of clothing is put on the pope until at the end he is in full papal attire; through this process a man is transformed into a symbol of authority and his protests transformed into acquiescence. Galileo's recantation in Scene XIII is crucial, for he thereby betrays humanity by delivering truth into the hands of established authority, thus permitting truth to be manipulated in the cause of the status quo. The potential alliance between the scientist and the worker is destroyed.

As in his other plays, Brecht wants his audience to apply to the present situation what it has learned from *Life of Galileo*. He rewrote the play three times in part because of the changing world situation. Originally, he was concerned about the parallels between the role of science in Italy in the seventeenth century and its role in Nazi Germany of the 1930s. By the time the second version was completed, the atomic bomb had created new problems and various governments were seeking to suppress information about atomic fusion. When the third version was written, the Cold War between America and Russia was at its height and Brecht saw the human race endangered by the manipulation of scientific information by governments seeking to maintain themselves while suppressing whatever might threaten them. He saw a parallel between Galileo and those modern scientists who cooperate with the authorities. By implication Brecht asks: Should we go on repeating the mistakes of the seventeenth century or should we insist that truth be freed and used for the good of all mankind rather than channeled to maintain the power of vested authority? In Scene XIV, Andrea tries to make excuses for Galileo's recantation, but Galileo refuses to permit this and insists that he has betrayed humanity. "As things stand now, the best we can hope for is a generation of inventive dwarfs who can be hired for any purpose." He also predicts that, if science permits itself to be divorced from service to humanity, the gulf between scientists and ordinary people will become so great "that the response to your exultation about some new achievement will be a universal outcry of horror." It seems likely that Brecht wanted these statements to bring to mind those scientists who served Hitler and those who developed the atomic bomb and other forms of destruction.

While undoubtedly Brecht was drawn to Galileo's story because of its didactic potential, he was also led by his instincts as a dramatist to create a complex protagonist. His Galileo is a sensualist who relishes food, wine, and all the material comforts, and for whom the pursuit of knowledge is such a passion that he can no more abandon his inquiries than he can give up food and drink. So consuming is his work that he cannot be seriously concerned about anyone who is not committed to it; thus, he sacrifices his daughter to his work and deceives the senators of Venice in order to get funds for his studies. To Brecht, it is this passion for truth that makes Galileo's denial of it so shocking.

Many of the theatrical devices associated with Brecht are not readily evident in the script of *Life of Galileo*. For the most part, this play can be read much like any other, but some typical Brechtian devices are obvious. Each scene has a title, which Brecht assumed would be announced or projected onto a screen, along with the brief poems that precede the scenes. There are a few songs, and in performance production elements such as lighting instruments and musicians would be visible. Scene X (the carnival) incorporates the greatest number of typical Brechtian devices.

The issues raised by *Life of Galileo* are made fairly clear in the play. They are related to numerous concerns about scientific inquiry today. Among these are: Should scientists refuse to assist governments in developing lethal weapons or substances? Are governments justified in classifying some scientific knowledge as secret? Do government grants endanger freedom of inquiry and dissemination of knowledge? Religious issues similar to those raised by Brecht are also still with us, as, for example, in arguments over the merits of teaching creationism as an alternative to evolution. Thus, though Galileo's version of the universe's structure may have prevailed eventually, the basic conflict with which he had to cope continues and is likely to do so hereafter.

Brecht also avoids some important issues. Is it possible, as he implies, for scientific inquiry to be wholly free from outside pressure or restraint? Since financial support for science must come from some source, doesn't the ability to grant or withhold support constitute a threat to freedom? Is there any reason to assume that an alliance between scientists and workers would be more productive or freer from restraint than one between scientists and governments or other power groups, or would the focus of inquiry merely change? Brecht, an avowed supporter of communism, also avoids the paradox that workers' states (as Russia and most East European countries call themselves) seem to be more repressive of scientific inquiry than are most of the capitalist states they oppose.

Krapp's Last Tape

by Samuel Beckett

Following World War II, the most distinctive drama came from a group of writers later to be called Absurdists. The horrors of the Nazi concentration camps, the destructive power of the atomic bomb, and the threat of a nuclear holocaust during the Cold War of the 1950s were among the conditions that raised doubt not only about the human ability to act rationally but also about the validity of reason itself. Out of the anxiety and doubt the Absurdist movement emerged.

The label *absurd* was derived from Albert Camus's essay, "The Myth of Sisyphus" (1943). In it, Camus states: "A world that can be explained even with bad reasons is a familiar world. But, on the other hand, in a universe suddenly divested of illusions and lights, man feels an alien, a stranger. His exile is without remedy since he is deprived of the memory of a lost home or the hope of a promised land. This divorce between man and his life . . . is properly the feeling of absurdity." Not until 1961 (in Martin Esslin's *The Theatre of the Absurd*) was Absurdist suggested as an appropriate label for a group of plays that embodied Camus's concept. Esslin wrote: "The hallmark [of the Theatre of the Absurd] is its sense that the certitudes and unshakable basic assumptions of former ages have been swept away, that they have been tested and found wanting, that they have been discredited as cheap and somewhat childish illusions. . . . This sense of metaphysical anguish at the absurdity of the human condition is, broadly speaking, the theme [of Absurdist drama]." Eugène Ionesco, one of the major Absurdist playwrights, has put it this way: "Cut off from his religious, metaphysical, and transcendental roots, man is lost; all his actions become senseless, absurd, useless." It is man's plight in this world of uncertainty that the plays dramatize.

The Absurdist vision not only influenced subject matter but also dramatic structure. The Absurdist writers abandoned traditional patterns of cause-to-effect arrangement of incidents; rather than developing an action linearly, they show its circularity (the tendency for experience to repeat itself); they explore the texture of a condition rather than tell a connected story. In these plays, situations are seldom resolved; most often place is generalized, a near-void cut off from the concrete world; time is flexible as in dreams. Traditional distinctions between dramatic forms disappear. The serious often becomes grotesque and the comic ominous or near-tragic. The plays are unified above all by theme or idea: human entrapment in an illogical, impersonal, and indifferent existence.

Each of the major Absurdist playwrights conceives this subject somewhat differently, although all ultimately agree that the world is irrational and the truth unknowable. While a number of playwrights have been called Absurdists, the two that appear most basic to the movement are Eugène Ionesco (1912–   ) and Samuel Beckett (1906–   ). Ionesco began his playwriting career in 1950 with *The Bald Soprano* and continued with *The Chairs, Exit the King, Rhinoceros,* and many other plays. Ionesco has tended to explore the absurdity of typical social situations. His plays discredit clichés, ideologies, and materialism; his characters are products of conformity—unthinking automatons oblivious of their own mechanical behavior and speech. Ionesco also tends to use spectacle surrealistically. Objects proliferate, dead bodies grow, things usurp the space in which human beings should live.

Beckett, Irish by birth, has lived in France since the 1930s and since 1945 has written many of his works in French. For a time he was associated with James Joyce, to whom his early essays, poems, and novels are indebted. His first play, *Waiting for Godot* (produced in 1953), brought the emerging Absurdist drama worldwide attention. It is now one of the best known of contemporary plays, perhaps because it captures most fully the Absurdist view. Beckett's subsequent plays include *Endgame* (1957), *Krapp's Last Tape* (1958), *Happy Days* (1961), and many others, as well as novels and short stories.

Beckett is concerned with humanity's metaphysical plight—our place in the scheme of existence. His characters are usually isolated in space, cut off from the world, seeking to survive even though life has lost its savor. They derive pleasure from momentary activity, memories, routine, and language (although in a senseless universe language too loses its sense and serves to emphasize the betrayal of hope and youthful ambition). Beckett's later works have become increasingly "minimalist," progressively reducing the number of characters, scope of action, and demands on production elements. In them, everything not absolutely essential has been eliminated. Even in his earlier plays, his characters pay little attention to each other and seldom understand each other when they do; they seem unable to make meaningful contact. They ruminate on experience, search for meaning or comfort, sorrow over losses, but go on gamely in the face of increasing loss, relinquishing almost everything except the will to continue. Today, Beckett is one of the world's most respected writers. In 1969 he was awarded the Nobel Prize for Literature.

A late evening in the future.
KRAPP's *den.*
Front centre a small table, the two drawers of which open towards the audience.
Sitting at the table, facing front, i.e. across from the drawers, a wearish old man: KRAPP.
Rusty black narrow trousers too short for him. Rusty black sleeveless waistcoat, four

capacious pockets. Heavy silver watch and chain. Grimy white shirt open at neck, no collar. Surprising pair of dirty white boots, size ten at least, very narrow and pointed. White face. Purple nose. Disordered grey hair. Unshaven.
Very near-sighted (but unspectacled). Hard of hearing.
Cracked voice. Distinctive intonation.
Laborious walk.
On the table a tape-recorder with microphone and a number of cardboard boxes containing reels of recorded tapes.
Table and immediately adjacent area in strong white light. Rest of stage in darkness.
KRAPP *remains a moment motionless, heaves a great sigh, looks at his watch, fumbles in his pockets, takes out an envelope, puts it back, fumbles, takes out a small bunch of keys, raises it to his eyes, chooses a key, gets up and moves to front of table. He stoops, unlocks first drawer, peers into it, feels about inside it, takes out a reel of tape, peers at it, puts it back, locks drawer, unlocks second drawer, peers into it, feels about inside it, takes out a large banana, peers at it, locks drawer, puts keys back in his pocket. He turns, advances to edge of stage, halts, strokes banana, peels it, drops skin at his feet, puts end of banana in his mouth and remains motionless, staring vacuously before him. Finally, he bites off the end, turns aside and begins pacing to and fro at edge of stage, in the light, i.e. not more than four or five paces either way, meditatively eating banana. He treads on skin, slips, nearly falls, recovers himself, stoops and peers at skin and finally pushes it, still stooping, with his foot over edge of stage into pit. He resumes his pacing, finishes banana, returns to table, sits down, remains a moment motionless, heaves a great sigh, takes keys from his pockets, raises them to his eyes, chooses key, gets up and moves to front of table, unlocks second drawer, takes out a second large banana, peers at it, locks drawer, puts back keys in his pocket, turns, advances to edge of stage, halts, strokes banana, peels it, tosses skin into pit, puts end of banana in his mouth and remains motionless, staring vacuously before him. Finally he has an idea, puts banana in his waistcoat pocket, the end emerging, and goes with all the speed he can muster backstage into darkness. Ten seconds. Loud pop of cork. Fifteen seconds. He comes back into light carrying an old ledger and sits down at table. He lays ledger on table, wipes his mouth, wipes his hands on the front of his waistcoat, brings them smartly together and rubs them.*

KRAPP: *(Briskly)* Ah! *(He bends over ledger, turns the pages, finds the entry he wants, reads.)* Box . . . thrree . . . spool . . . five. *(He raises his head and stares front. With relish.)* Spool! *(Pause.)* Spooool! *(Happy smile. Pause. He bends over table, starts peering and poking at the boxes.)* Box . . . thrree . . . thrree . . . four . . . two . . . *(with surprise)* nine! good God! . . . seven . . . ah! the little rascal! *(He takes up box, peers at it.)* Box thrree. *(He lays it on table, opens it and peers at spools inside.)* Spool . . . *(He peers at ledger)* . . . five *(He peers at spools)* . . . five . . . five . . . ah! the little scoundrel! *(He takes out a spool, peers at it.)* Spool five. *(He lays it on table, closes box three, puts it back with the others, takes up the spool.)* Box three, spool five.

(He bends over the machine, looks up. With relish.) Spooool! *(Happy smile. He bends, loads spool on machine, rubs his hands.)* Ah! *(He peers at ledger, reads entry at foot of page.)* Mother at rest at last. . . . Hm. . . . The black ball. . . . *(He raises his head, stares blankly front. Puzzled.)* Black ball? . . . *(He peers again at ledger, reads.)* The dark nurse. . . . *(He raises his head, broods, peers again at ledger, reads.)* Slight improvement in bowel condition. . . . Hm. . . . Memorable . . . what? *(He peers closer.)* Equinox, memorable equinox. *(He raises his head, stares blankly front. Puzzled.)* Memorable equinox? . . . *(Pause. He shrugs his shoulders, peers again at ledger, reads.)* Farewell to—*(He turns page)*—love.

(He raises his head, broods, bends over machine, switches on and assumes listening posture, i.e. leaning forward, elbows on table, hand cupping ear towards machine, face front.)

TAPE: *(Strong voice, rather pompous, clearly* KRAPP'S *at a much earlier time)* Thrity-nine today, sound as a — *(Settling himself more comfortably he knocks one of the boxes off the table, curses, switches off, sweeps boxes and ledger violently to the ground, winds tape back to beginning, switches on, resumes posture.)* Thirty-nine today, sound as a bell, apart from my old weakness, and intellectually I have now every reason to suspect at the . . . *(Hesitates)* . . . crest of the wave — or thereabouts. Celebrated the awful occasion, as in recent years, quietly at the Winehouse. Not a soul. Sat before the fire with closed eyes, separating the grain from the husks. Jotted down a few notes, on the back of an envelope. Good to be back in my den, in my old rags. Have just eaten I regret to say three bananas and only with difficulty refrained from a fourth. Fatal things for a man with my condition. *(Vehemently.)* Cut 'em out! *(Pause.)* The new light above my table is a great improvement. With all this darkness round me I feel less alone. *(Pause.)* In a way. *(Pause.)* I love to get up and move about in it, then back here to . . . *(Hesitates)* . . . me. *(Pause.)* Krapp.

(Pause.)

The grain, now what I wonder do I mean by that, I mean . . . *(Hesitates)* . . . I suppose I mean those things worth having when all the dust has — when all *my* dust has settled. I close my eyes and try and imagine them.

(Pause. KRAPP *closes his eyes briefly.)*

Extraordinary silence this evening, I strain my ears and do not hear a sound. Old Miss McGlome always sings at this hour. But not tonight. Songs of her girlhood, she says. Hard to think of her as a girl. Wonderful woman though. Connaught, I fancy. *(Pause.)* Shall I sing when I am her age, if I ever am? No. *(Pause.)* Did I sing as a boy? No. *(Pause.)* Did I ever sing? No.

(Pause.)

Just been listening to an old year, passages at random. I did not check in the book, but it must be at least ten or twelve years ago. At that time I think I was still living on and off with Bianca in Kedar

Street. Well out of that, Jesus yes! Hopeless business. *(Pause.)* Not much about her, apart from a tribute to her eyes. Very warm. I suddenly saw them again. *(Pause.)* Incomparable! *(Pause.)* Ah well. . . . *(Pause.)* These old P.M.s are gruesome, but I often find them — *(*KRAPP *switches off, broods, switches on)* — a help before embarking on a new . . . *(Hesitates)* . . . retrospect. Hard to believe I was ever that young whelp. The voice! Jesus! And the aspirations! *(Brief laugh in which* KRAPP *joins.)* And the resolutions! *(Brief laugh in which* KRAPP *joins.)* To drink less, in particular. *(Brief laugh of* KRAPP *alone.)* Statistics. Seventeen hundred hours, out of the preceding eight thousand odd, consumed on licensed premises alone. More than 20 per cent, say 40 per cent of his waking life. *(Pause.)* Plans for a less . . . *(Hesitates)* . . . engrossing sexual life. Last illness of his father. Flagging pursuit of happiness. Unattainable laxation. Sneers at what he calls his youth and thanks to God that it's over. *(Pause.)* False ring there. *(Pause.)* Shadows of the opus . . . magnum. Closing with a — *(Brief laugh)* — yelp to Providence. *(Prolonged laugh in which* KRAPP *joins.)* What remains of all that misery? A girl in a shabby green coat, on a railway-station platform? No?

(Pause.)

When I look —

*(*KRAPP *switches off, broods, looks at his watch, gets up, goes backstage into darkness. Ten seconds. Pop of cork. Ten seconds. Second cork. Ten seconds. Third cork. Ten seconds. Brief burst of quavering song.)*

KRAPP: *(Sings)*
Now the day is over,
Night is drawing nigh-igh,
Shadows —

(Fit of coughing. He comes back into light, sits down, wipes his mouth, switches on, resumes his listening posture.)

TAPE: — back on the year that is gone, with what I hope is perhaps a glint of the old eye to come, there is of course, the house on the canal where mother lay a-dying, in the late autumn, after her long viduity *(*KRAPP *gives a start)*, and the — *(*KRAPP *switches off, winds back tape a little, bends his ear closer to machine, switches on)* — a-dying, after her long viduity, and the —

(KRAPP switches off, raises his head, stares blankly before him. His lips move in the syllables of 'viduity.' No sound. He gets up, goes backstage into darkness, comes back with an enormous dictionary, lays it on table, sits down and looks up the word.)

KRAPP: *(Reading from dictionary)* State — or condition — of being — or remaining — a widow — or widower. *(Looks up. Puzzled.)* Being — or remaining? . . . *(Pause. He peers again at dictionary. Reading.)* 'Deep weeds of viduity.' . . . Also of an animal, especially a bird . . . the vidua or weaver-bird. . . . Black plumage of male. . . . *(He looks up. With relish.)* The vidua-bird!

(Pause. He closes dictionary, switches on, resumes listening posture.)

TAPE: — bench by the weir from where I could see her window. There I sat, in the biting wind, wishing she were gone. *(Pause.)* Hardly a soul, just a few regulars, nursemaids, infants, old men, dogs, I got to know them quite well — oh by appearance of course I mean! One dark young beauty I recollect particularly, all white and starch, incomparable bosom, with a big black hooded perambulator, most funereal thing. Whenever I looked in her direction she had her eyes on me. And yet when I was bold enough to speak to her — not having been introduced — she threatened to call a policeman. As if I had designs on her virtue! *(Laugh. Pause.)* The face she had! The eyes! Like . . . *(Hesitates)* . . . chrysolite! *(Pause.)* Ah well. . . . *(Pause.)* I was there when — *(KRAPP switches off, broods, switches on again)* — the blind went down, one of those dirty brown roller affairs, throwing a ball for a little white dog as chance would have it. I happened to look up and there it was. All over and done with, at last. I sat on for a few moments with the ball in my hand and the dog yelping and pawing at me. *(Pause.)* Moments. Her moments, my moments. *(Pause.)* The dog's moments. *(Pause.)* In the end I held it out to him and he took it in his mouth, gently, gently. A small, old, black, hard, solid rubber ball. *(Pause.)* I shall feel it, in my hand, until my dying day. *(Pause.)* I might have kept it. *(Pause.)* But I gave it to the dog.

(Pause.)

Ah well. . . .

(Pause.)

Spiritually a year of profound gloom and indigence until that memorable night in March, at the end of the jetty, in the howling wind, never to be forgotten, when suddenly I saw the whole thing. The vision at last. This I fancy is what I have chiefly to record this evening, against the day when my work will be done and perhaps no place left in my memory, warm or cold, for the miracle that . . . *(Hesitates)* . . . for the fire that set it alight. What I suddenly saw then was this, that the belief I had been going on all my life, namely — *(KRAPP switches off impatiently, winds tape forward, switches on again)* — great granite rocks the foam flying up in the light of the lighthouse and the wind-gauge spinning like a propeller, clear to me at last that the dark I have always struggled to keep under is in reality my most — *(KRAPP curses, switches off, winds tape forward, switches on again)* — unshatterable association until my dissolution of storm and night with the light of the understanding and the fire — *(KRAPP curses louder, switches off, winds tape forward, switches on again)* — my face in her breast and my hand on her. We lay there without moving. But under us all moved, and moved us, gently, up and down, and from side to side.

(Pause.)

Past midnight. Never knew such silence. The earth might be uninhabited.

(Pause.)

Here I end —

(KRAPP switches off, winds tape back, switches on again.) — upper lake, with the punt, bathed off the bank, then pushed out into the stream and drifted. She lay stretched out on the floorboards with her hands under her head and her eyes closed. Sun blazing down, bit of a breeze, water nice and lively. I noticed a scratch on her thigh and asked her how she came by it. Picking gooseberries, she said. I said again I thought it was hopeless and no good going on and she agreed, without opening her eyes. *(Pause.)* I asked her to look at me and after a few moments — *(Pause)* — after a few moments she did, but the eyes just slits, because of the glare. I bent over her to get them in the shadow and they opened. *(Pause. Low.)* Let me in. *(Pause.)* We drifted in among the flags and stuck. The way they went down, sighing, before the stem! *(Pause.)* I lay

down across her with my face in her breasts and my hand on her. We lay there without moving. But under us all moved, and moved us, gently, up and down, and from side to side.

(Pause.)

Past midnight. Never knew —

(KRAPP *switches off, broods. Finally he fumbles in his pockets, encounters the banana, takes it out, peers at it, puts it back, fumbles, brings out envelope, fumbles, puts back envelope, looks at his watch, gets up and goes backstage into darkness. Ten seconds. Sound of bottle against glass, then brief siphon. Ten seconds. Bottle against glass alone. Ten seconds. He comes back a little unsteadily into light, goes to front of table, takes out keys, raises them to his eyes, chooses key, unlocks first drawer, peers into it, feels about inside, takes out reel, peers at it, locks drawer, puts keys back in his pocket, goes and sits down, takes reel off machine, lays it on dictionary, loads virgin reel on machine, takes envelope from his pocket, consults back of it, lays it on table, switches on, clears his throat and begins to record.*)

KRAPP: Just been listening to that stupid bastard I took myself for thirty years ago, hard to believe I was ever as bad as that. Thank God that's all done with anyway. *(Pause.)* The eyes she had! *(Broods, realizes he is recording silence, switches off, broods. Finally.)* Everything there, everything, all the — *(Realizes this is not being recorded, switches on.)* Everything there, everything on this old muckball, all the light and dark and famine and feasting of . . . *(Hesitates)* . . . the ages! *(In a shout.)* Yes! *(Pause.)* Let that go! Jesus! Take his mind off his homework! Jesus! *(Pause. Weary.)* Ah well, maybe he was right. *(Pause.)* Maybe he was right. *(Broods. Realizes. Switches off. Consults envelope.)* Pah! *(Crumples it and throws it away. Broods. Switches on.)* Nothing to say, not a squeak. What's a year now? The sour cud and the iron stool. *(Pause.)* Revelled in the word spool *(With relish.)* Spoool! Happiest moment of the past half million. *(Pause.)* Seventeen copies sold, of which eleven at trade price to free circulating libraries beyond the seas. Getting known. *(Pause.)* One pound six and something, eight I have little doubt. *(Pause.)* Crawled out once or twice, before the summer was

cold. Sat shivering in the park, drowned in dreams and burning to be gone. Not a soul. *(Pause.)* Last fancies. *(Vehemently.)* Keep 'em under! *(Pause.)* Scalded the eyes out of me reading *Effie* again, a page a day, with tears again. Effie. . . . *(Pause.)* Could have been happy with her, up there on the Baltic, and the pines, and the dunes. *(Pause.)* Could I? *(Pause.)* And she? *(Pause.)* Pah! *(Pause.)* Fanny came in a couple of times. Bony old ghost of a whore. Couldn't do much, but I suppose better than a kick in the crutch. The last time wasn't so bad. How do you manage it, she said, at your age? I told her I'd been saving up for her all my life. *(Pause.)* Went to Vespers once, like when I was in short trousers. *(Pause. Sings.)*

Now the day is over,
Night is drawing nigh-igh,
Shadows — *(coughing, then almost inaudible)* —
    of the evening
Steal across the sky.

(Gasping.) Went to sleep and fell off the pew. *(Pause.)* Sometimes wondered in the night if a last effort mightn't — *(Pause.)* Ah finish your booze now and get to your bed. Go on with this drivel in the morning. Or leave it at that. *(Pause.)* Leave it at that. *(Pause.)* Lie propped up in the dark — and wander. Be again in the dingle on a Christmas Eve, gathering holly, the red-berried. *(Pause.)* Be again on Croghan on a Sunday morning, in the haze, with the bitch, stop and listen to the bells. *(Pause.)* And so on. *(Pause.)* Be again, be again. *(Pause.)* All that old misery. *(Pause.)* Once wasn't enough for you. *(Pause.)* Lie down across her.

(Long pause. He suddenly bends over machine, switches off, wrenches off tape, throws it away, puts on the other, winds it forward to the passage he wants, switches on, listens staring front.)

TAPE: — gooseberries, she said. I said again I thought it was hopeless and no good going on and she agreed, without opening her eyes. *(Pause.)* I asked her to look at me and after a few moments — *(Pause)* — after a few moments she did, but the eyes just slits, because of the glare. I bent over her to get them in the shadow and they opened. *(Pause. Low.)* Let me in. *(Pause.)* We drifted in among the flags and stuck. The way they went down, sighing, before the stem! *(Pause.)* I lay down across her with my face in her breasts and my hand on her. We lay there without moving. But under us all moved, and moved us, gently, up and down, and from side to side.

(Pause, KRAPP'S *lips move. No sound.)*

Past midnight. Never knew such silence. The earth might be uninhabited.

(Pause.)

Here I end this reel. Box — *(Pause)* — three, spool — *(Pause)* — five. *(Pause.)* Perhaps my best years are gone. When there was a chance of happiness. But I wouldn't want them back. Not with the fire in me now. No, I wouldn't want them back.

*(*KRAPP *motionless staring before him. The tape runs on in silence.)*

CURTAIN

One of Beckett's favorite devices is the monologue. His novels are essentially extended monologues, and several of his plays have only one speaking character. In *Krapp's Last Tape*, Beckett gives the protagonist's monologue considerable variety through the use of the tape recorder; at the same time, he shows, through tapes made by Krapp at various times in his life, the impermanence of memory and even of self.

For decades, Krapp has made a taped recording annually on his birthday, summing up the major events and significant perceptions of the year. The tapes are carefully catalogued and indexed topically for ready reference. Thus, Krapp can look back over his life, pick out specific times and events, and listen to his own voice commenting on the occurrences, ideas, and plans that then seemed significant. It quickly becomes clear that, without the tapes, Krapp's past would virtually have vanished, for he no longer remembers most of the things the tapes have recorded; in one instance, he must resort to a dictionary before he can understand one of his own comments.

As Krapp plays portions of tapes from the past, on each we hear him comment on the foolishness of his ideas and dreams of earlier times and congratulate himself on having passed beyond such delusions. So contemptuous is he of his many former perceptions that he can no longer listen to them. Through Krapp's reactions, the audience is expected to perceive the lack of any foundation for even the most treasured beliefs, for as time passes the hopes and ideas of the past come to seem mere drivel; seemingly solid hopes, dreams, and ideas are inexorably swallowed up in the quicksands of experience and doubt. But one condition does remain constant: the difficulty of establishing contact with others. Even in the midst of activity, Krapp has remained isolated. His world also has steadily shrunk, until now nothing remains except a few creature comforts: his passion for bananas and drink, and an occasional need for sex. He has progressively confined himself to his own small space, seldom venturing outside it. For his last tape (being made on his sixty-ninth birthday), the only pleasure he can recall from the preceeding year is the sound of the word *spool*. His dreams and hopes are gone; he considers almost everything in his past to have been a mistake. His dream of being an important writer is summed up in his report that during the past year only 17 copies of his book have been sold.

The one memory to which Krapp seems to cling and to which he returns several times is a moment from 30 years ago, indexed in his ledger as "Farewell to Love": "Be again on Croghan on a Sunday morning, in the haze, with the bitch, stop and listen to the bells. *(Pause)* And so on. *(Pause)* Be again, be again. *(Pause)* All that old misery. *(Pause)* Once wasn't enough for you. *(Pause)* Lie down across her." At the end of the play, the tape from 30 years ago recalls: "Perhaps my best years are gone. When there was a chance of happiness. But I wouldn't want them back. Not with the fire in me now. No, I wouldn't want them back." And the play ends with Krapp staring into nothingness as the tape runs on silently. We recognize that, though Krapp might now want those times back, they have disappeared as irrevocably as the years of his life, which have been reduced to a mechanically recorded voice.

On the tape from 30 years ago, we also hear Krapp say: "The new light above my table is a great improvement. With all this darkness round me I feel less alone. *(Pause)* In a way. *(Pause)* I love to get up and move about in it, then back here to . . . *(hesitates)* . . . me. *(Pause)* Krapp." This sums up Krapp's situation as it still exists 30 years later—isolated, trying to remember the past, finding the person he used to be as alien as everything else in his world. Through Krapp, Beckett projects a vision of the human experience.

A comparison of *Krapp's Last Tape* with *Everyman* is revealing. In both we see a protagonist at the end of his life seeking to come to terms with both past and future. Both come to see their past activities and values as frivolous and mistaken. Both find themselves having to face the void alone. Both raise questions about the nature and value of human experience.

Despite these similarities, the differences between the two plays are great. Not only does *Everyman* include a large number of characters who personify traits or qualities, it is unabashedly didactic. *Krapp's Last Tape*, with only one character, implies much but only indirectly. The most fundamental difference between the two plays, however, is in their vision of the human condition. Everyman's acknowledgment of mistakes is accompanied by renewed awareness of God's love and the necessity to prepare for the life to come; Krapp's rejection of his past is a progression toward nothingness. Everyman's universe is dominated by religious faith. In Krapp's universe, religion plays no part; as time has passed, beliefs have been abandoned and new ones have taken their place, but ultimately all beliefs have become equally absurd. Everyman's world promises eternal bliss through adherence to God's commands; Krapp's world is devoid of promise. In *Everyman*, humanity finds its fulfillment in God and conformity to His commandments; in *Krapp's Last Tape*, humanity's greatest achievement is stoical acceptance that existence is meaningless.

It is impossible to *prove* either of these views correct. Each is characteristic of its time. They do remind us that beliefs, regardless of validity, are the foundations of behavior. It seems likely that the majority of people today subscribe fully neither to Everyman's nor to Krapp's views. Nevertheless, some conception, whether vague or clearly defined, underlies each person's behavioral patterns and ethical standards. Defining and assessing our own beliefs may be the most important task that faces us as human beings trying to find our way in a world where the great diversity of convictions has encouraged divisiveness and instability.

The Strong Breed

by Wole Soyinka

In the 1950s black Africa began to gain its freedom after a century of European colonization. As new African states emerged and were admitted to the United Nations and other international bodies, they attracted attention to a continent that had long been neglected. Much of the concern took the form of competition for economic and political alliances with the new nations, but some focused on the arts of Africa. The visual arts, especially sculpture, had commanded attention since around 1900 and had already exerted considerable influence on twentieth-century western art. Drama, however, remained unknown and was usually thought virtually nonexistent. If one judges African drama by European standards, this view was perhaps defensible, but from another perspective, Africa had a dramatic tradition that reached back into prehistory.

The theory most widely accepted today about how drama originated traces its evolution to rituals, with which Africa has always been particularly blessed. We do not know when or where rituals first appeared, but since scientific research increasingly points to Africa as the place where mankind as a distinct species first emerged, it seems likely that it was there that ritual also first appeared. It is impossible to document the development of ritual in Africa because the necessary evidence does not exist. As far back as our knowledge extends, however, we find ritual playing a significant role in African tribal life. But if ritual is the activity out of which drama emerged, it is not itself drama.

Reliable accounts of African dramatic activity are so scarce that prior to recent times it is impossible to determine its extent, for most surviving accounts were written by Europeans who did not or could not distinguish between religious ritual and dramatic presentation. (It all looked alike to the white observer.) Recent information suggests, however, that Africa has long had numerous dramatic ceremonies and entertainments, although the texts were not written down and did not adhere to European structural principles. We know that there were satirical comedy, entertainment with clowns and acrobats, dramatic storytelling, reenactment of historical and mythic events, and recreation of hunts. Most of these performances were given at local festivals (as in ancient Greece and Rome), and were created by a community for the community. The same dramas might be repeated from year to year, but changes were introduced often to increase effectiveness. The performances took place out of doors in playing spaces sufficiently flexible to permit both performers and spectators to move about freely; most (but not all) made use of masks, music, and dance. The characteristic features of traditional entertainments were to remain important even after western dramatic forms became familiar during the colonial period.

Although Europeans had had trading stations and had trafficked in slaves since the seventeenth century, they did not begin to colonize Africa extensively until around 1880. Under colonialism, government officials and missionaries sought to impose new social patterns and beliefs. Village life and tradition altered as young men sought work in towns and as children were sent to European-style schools. To aid in the acculturation process, missions, state-run schools, and cultural centers sponsored productions of European plays, and plays in the western manner began to be written by native Africans. But no play by a black African was published prior to 1933, and by 1957, when the first black African state gained independence, only seven full-length and thirty short plays had been printed.

With independence, writers were freed from the pressure to please both colonial authorities and native audiences, but they were faced with other pressures from those who wished to return to the traditions of precolonial times and those who sought to modernize Africa. These pressures have influenced most contemporary black African drama. Most of the new African nations gave official support to theatre or dance companies that performed traditional forms (although these often became tourist attractions rather than expressions of native needs). Spaces for performances also were built by the new states but a large proportion of them had proscenium-arch stages not well suited to indigenous forms; fortunately, in recent years the need for more flexible spaces has been recognized. African universities played a large role in shaping the emerging theatre, since they trained personnel, produced plays, and sponsored many of the best companies.

Contemporary African dramatic entertainments have taken many forms. Among the most distinctive are Concert Parties and Yoruba Opera, didactic musical plays. In Yoruba Opera, plot and moral are outlined in an opening musical section; the dialogue draws heavily on proverbial sayings and familiar oral literature; the dialogue is sometimes improvised and sometimes sung in its entirety; the setting is urban and the play warns of the perils of urban life. The great attraction lies in the singing and dancing.

Writers of spoken drama often use music and dance but most blend traditional materials and themes with European dramatic forms. Among major African playwrights are J. P. Clark, Wole Soyinka, and Ola Rotimi in Nigeria; Efua Sutherland, Joe de Graft, and Ama Ata Aidoo in Ghana; R. Sarif Easmon in Sierra Leone; James Ngugi and Kenneth Watene in Kenya; and John Ruganda and Robert Serumaga in Uganda.

Perhaps the best known and most influential of black African playwrights is Wole Soyinka (1934–   ). Born in Nigeria and educated at the universities of Ibadan (Nigeria) and Leeds (England), he worked at the Royal Court Theatre in London before organizing his own company in Nigeria in 1960. In 1967 he was named director of the Drama School at Ibadan University, where he had taught English. During the Nigerian civil war (1967–1969), Soyinka was imprisoned and upon release left the country. His plays include *The Swamp Dwellers* (1957), *The Lion and the Jewel* (1963), *A Dance of the Forests* (1963), *The Trials of Brother Jero* (1964), *The Strong Breed* (1964), *The Road* (1965), *Kongi's Harvest* (1967), and *Madmen and Specialists* (1970). Soyinka draws his material from native sources but reinterprets it, often showing the conflict between traditional customs and modern consciousness. He has sought a balance between appreciation for the culture of the past and the need to alter conditions to achieve a just society. Many critics consider him to be the major force in the development of contemporary black African drama.

CHARACTERS

EMAN *a stranger*
SUNMA *Jaguna's daughter*
IFADA *an idiot*
A GIRL
JAGUNA
OROGE
ATTENDANT STALWARTS *the villagers from Eman's past—*

OLD MAN *his father*
OMAE *his betrothed*
TUTOR
PRIEST
ATTENDANTS *the villagers*

The scenes are described briefly, but very often a darkened stage with lit area will not only suffice but is necessary. Except for the one indicated place, there can be no break in the action. A distracting scene-change would be ruinous. A mud house, with space in front of it. EMAN, in light buba and trousers stands at the window, looking out. Inside, SUNMA is clearing the table of what looks like a modest clinic, putting the things away in a cupboard. Another rough table in the room is piled with exercise books, two or three worn textbooks, etc. SUNMA appears agitated. Outside, just below the window crouches IFADA. He looks up with a shy smile from time to time, waiting for EMAN to notice him.

SUNMA: *(Hesitant)* You will have to make up your mind soon, Eman. The lorry leaves very shortly.

(As EMAN does not answer, SUNMA continues her work, more nervously. Two villagers, obvious travellers, pass hurriedly in front of the house, the man has a small raffia sack, the woman a cloth-covered basket, the man enters first, turns and urges the woman who is just emerging to hurry.)

SUNMA: *(Seeing them, her tone is more intense)* Eman, are we going or aren't we? You will leave it till too late.

EMAN: *(Quietly)* There is still time—if you want to go.

SUNMA: If I want to go . . . and you?

(EMAN makes no reply.)

SUNMA: *(Bitterly)* You don't really want to leave here. You never want to go away—even for a minute.

(IFADA continues his antics. EMAN eventually pats him on the head and the boy grins happily. Leaps up suddenly and returns with a basket of oranges which he offers EMAN.)

EMAN: My gift for today's festival enh?

(IFADA *nods, grinning.*)

EMAN: They look ripe — that's a change.

SUNMA: *(She has gone inside the room. Looks round the door)* Did you call me?

EMAN: No. *(She goes back)* And what will you do tonight, Ifada? Will you take part in the dancing? Or perhaps you will mount your own masquerade?

(IFADA *shakes his head, regretfully.*)

EMAN: You won't? So you haven't any? But you would like to own one.

(IFADA *nods eagerly.*)

EMAN: Then why don't you make your own?

(IFADA *stares, puzzled by this idea.*)

EMAN: Sunma will let you have some cloth you know. And bits of wool . . .

SUNMA: *(Coming out)* Who are you talking to, Eman?

EMAN: Ifada. I am trying to persuade him to join the young maskers.

SUNMA: *(Losing control)* What does he want here? Why is he hanging round us?

EMAN: *(Amazed)* What . . . ? I said Ifada, Ifada.

SUNMA: Just tell him to go away. Let him go and play somewhere else!

EMAN: What is this? Hasn't he always played here?

SUNMA: I don't want him here. *(Rushes to the window.)* Get away, idiot. Don't bring your foolish face here any more, do you hear? Go on, go away from here . . .

EMAN: *(restraining her)* Control yourself, Sunma. What on earth has got into you?

(IFADA, *hurt and bewildered, backs slowly away.*)

SUNMA: He comes crawling round here like some horrible insect. I never want to lay my eyes on him again.

EMAN: I don't understand. It *is* Ifada you know, Ifada! The unfortunate one who runs errands for you and doesn't hurt a soul.

SUNMA: I cannot bear the sight of him.

EMAN: You can't do what? It can't be two days since he last fetched water for you.

SUNMA: What else can he do except that? He is useless. Just because we have been kind to him . . . Others would have put him in an asylum.

EMAN: You are not making sense. He is not a madman, he is just a little more unlucky than other children. *(Looks keenly at her.)* But what is the matter?

SUNMA: It's nothing. I only wish we had sent him off to one of those places for creatures like him.

EMAN: He is quite happy here. He doesn't bother anyone and he makes himself useful.

SUNMA: Useful! Is that one of any use to anybody? Boys of his age are already earning a living but all he can do is hang around and drool at the mouth.

EMAN: But he does work. You know he does a lot for you.

SUNMA: Does he? And what about the farm you started for him! Does he ever work on it? Or have you forgotten that it was really for Ifada you cleared that brush. Now you have to go and work it yourself. You spend all your time on it and you have no room for anything else.

EMAN: That wasn't his fault. I should first have asked him if he was fond of farming.

SUNMA: Oh, so he can choose? As if he shouldn't be thankful for being allowed to live.

EMAN: Sunma!

SUNMA: He does not like farming but he knows how to feast his dumb mouth on the fruits.

EMAN: But I want him to. I encourage him.

SUNMA: Well keep him. I don't want to see him any more.

EMAN: *(After some moments)* But why? You cannot be telling all the truth. What has he done?

SUNMA: The sight of him fills me with revulsion.

EMAN: *(Goes to her and holds her)* What really is it? *(Sunma avoids his eyes.)* It is almost as if you are forcing yourself to hate him. Why?

SUNMA: That is not true. Why should I?

EMAN: Then what is the secret? You've even played with him before.

SUNMA: I have always merely tolerated him. But I cannot any more. Suddenly my disgust won't take him any more. Perhaps . . . perhaps it is the new year. Yes, yes, it must be the new year.

EMAN: I don't believe that.

SUNMA: It must be. I am a woman, and these things matter. I don't want a mis-shape near me.

Surely for one day in the year, I may demand some wholesomeness.

EMAN: I do not understand you.

(SUNMA *is silent.*)

It was cruel of you. And to Ifada who is so help-less and alone. We are the only friends he has.

SUNMA: No, just you. I have told you, with me it has always been only an act of kindness. And now I haven't any pity left for him.

EMAN: No. He is not a wholesome being.

(*He turns back to looking through the window.*)

SUNMA: (*half-pleading*) Ifada can rouse your pity. And yet if anything, I need more kindness from you. Every time my weakness betrays me, you close your mind against me . . . Eman . . . Eman . . .

(A GIRL *comes in view, dragging an effigy by a rope attached to one of its legs. She stands for a while gazing at* EMAN. IFADA, *who has crept back shyly to his accustomed position, becomes somewhat excited when he sees the effigy. The girl is unsmiling. She possesses in fact, a kind of inscrutability which does not make her hard but is unsettling.*)

GIRL: Is the teacher in?
EMAN: (*Smiling*) No.
GIRL: Where is he gone?
EMAN: I don't really know. Shall I ask?
GIRL: Yes, do.
EMAN: (*Turning slightly*) Sunma, a girl out-side wants to know . . .

(SUNMA *turns away, goes into the inside room.*)

EMAN: Oh. (*Returns to the girl, but his slight gaiety is lost.*) There is no one at home who can tell me.

GIRL: Why are you not in?
EMAN: I don't really know. Maybe I went somewhere.
GIRL: All right. I will wait until you get back.

(*She pulls the effigy to her, sits down.*)

EMAN: (*Slowly regaining his amusement*) So you are all ready for the new year.

GIRL: (*Without turning round*) I am not going to the festival.
EMAN: Then why have you got that?
GIRL: Do you mean my carrier? I am unwell

you know. My mother says it will take away my sickness with the old year.

EMAN: Won't you share the carrier with your playmates?

GIRL: Oh, no. Don't you know I play alone? The other children won't come near me. Their mothers would beat them.

EMAN: But I have never seen you here. Why don't you come to the clinic?

GIRL: My mother said No.

(*Gets up, begins to move off.*)

EMAN: You are not going away?
GIRL: I must not stay talking to you. If my mother caught me . . .
EMAN: All right, tell me what you want before you go.
GIRL: (*Stops. For some moments she remains silent*) I must have some clothes for my carrier.
EMAN: Is that all? You wait a moment.

(SUNMA *comes out as he takes down a buba from the wall. She goes to the window and glares almost with hatred at the girl. The girl retreats hastily, still impassive.*)

By the way Sunma, do you know who that girl is?

SUNMA: I hope you don't really mean to give her that.
EMAN: Why not? I hardly ever use it.
SUNMA: Just the same don't give it to her. She is not a child. She is as evil as the rest of them.
EMAN: What has got into you today?
SUNMA: All right, all right. Do what you wish.

(*She withdraws. Baffled,* EMAN *returns to the window.*)

EMAN: Here . . . will this do? Come and look at it.
GIRL: Throw it.
EMAN: What is the matter? I am not going to eat you.
GIRL: No one lets me come near them.
EMAN: But I am not afraid of catching your disease.
GIRL: Throw it.

(EMAN *shrugs and tosses the buba. She takes it without a word and slips it on the effigy, completely absorbed in the task.* EMAN *watches for a while, then joins* SUNMA *in the inner room.)*

GIRL: *(After a long, cool survey of* IFADA*)* You have a head like a spider's egg, and your mouth dribbles like a roof. But there is no one else. Would you like to play?

*(*IFADA *nods eagerly, quite excited.)*

GIRL: You will have to get a stick.

*(*IFADA *rushes around, finds a big stick and whirls it aloft, bearing down on the carrier.)*

GIRL: Wait. I don't want you to spoil it. If it gets torn I shall drive you away. Now, let me see how you are going to beat it.

*(*IFADA *hits it gently.)*

GIRL: You may hit harder than that. As long as there is something left to hang at the end.

(She appraises him up and down.)

You are not very tall ... will you be able to hang if from a tree?

*(*IFADA *nods, grinning happily.)*

GIRL: You will hang it up and I will set fire to it. *(Then, with surprising venom.)* But just because you are helping me, don't think it is going to cure you. I am the one who will get well at midnight, do you understand? It is my carrier and it is for me alone.

(She pulls at the rope to make sure that it is well attached to the leg.)

Well don't stand there drooling. Let's go.

(She begins to walk off, dragging the effigy in the dust. IFADA *remains where he is for some moments, seemingly puzzled. Then his face breaks into a large grin and he leaps after the procession, belabouring the effigy with all his strength. The stage remains empty for some moments. Then the horn of a lorry is sounded and* SUNMA *rushes out. The hooting continues for some time with a rhythmic pattern.* EMAN *comes out.)*

EMAN: I am going to the village ... I shan't be back before nightfall.

SUNMA: *(Blankly)* Yes.

EMAN: *(Hesitates)* Well what do you want me to do?

SUNMA: The lorry was hooting just now.

EMAN: I didn't hear it.

SUNMA: It will leave in a few minutes. And you did promise we could go away.

EMAN: I promised nothing. Will you go home by yourself or shall I come back for you?

SUNMA: You don't even want me here?

EMAN: But you have to go home haven't you?

SUNMA: I had hoped we would watch the new year together—in some other place.

EMAN: Why do you continue to distress yourself?

SUNMA: Because you will not listen to me. Why do you continue to stay where nobody wants you?

EMAN: That is not true.

SUNMA: It is. You are wasting your life on people who really want you out of their way.

EMAN: You don't know what you are saying.

SUNMA: You think they love you? Do you think they care at all for what you—or I—do for them?

EMAN: *Them?* These are your own people. Sometimes you talk as if you were a stranger too.

SUNMA: I wonder if I really sprang from here. I know they are evil and I am not. From the oldest to the smallest child, they are nourished in evil and unwholesomeness in which I have no part.

EMAN: You knew this when you returned?

SUNMA: You reproach me then for trying at all?

EMAN: I reproach you with nothing? But you must leave me out of your plans. I can have no part in them.

SUNMA *(Nearly pleading)* Once I could have run away. I would have gone and never looked back.

EMAN: I cannot listen when you talk like that.

SUNMA: I swear to you, I do not mind what happens afterwards. But you must help me tear myself away from here. I can no longer do it by myself ... It is only a little thing. And we have worked so hard this past year ... surely we can go away for a week ... even a few days would be enough.

EMAN: I have told you Sunma ...

SUNMA: *(Desperately)* Two days, Eman. Only two days.

EMAN: *(Distressed)* But I tell you I have no wish to go.

SUNMA: *(Suddenly angry)* Are you so afraid then?

EMAN: Me? Afraid of what?

SUNMA: You think you will not want to come back.

EMAN: *(Pitying)* You cannot dare me that way.

SUNMA: Then why won't you leave here, even for an hour? If you are so sure that your life is settled here, why are you afraid to do this thing for me? What is so wrong that you will not go into the next town for a day or two?

EMAN: I don't want to. I do not have to persuade you, or myself about anything. I simply have no desire to go away.

SUNMA: *(His quiet confidence appears to incense her)* You are afraid. You accuse me of losing my sense of mission, but you are afraid to put yours to the test.

EMAN: You are wrong, Sunma. I have no sense of mission. But I have found peace here and I am content with that.

SUNMA: I haven't. For a while I thought that too, but I found there could be no peace in the midst of so much cruelty. Eman, tonight at least, the last night of the old year . . .

EMAN: No, Sunma. I find this too distressing; you should go home now.

SUNMA: It is the time for making changes in one's life, Eman. Let's breathe in the new year away from here.

EMAN: You are hurting yourself.

SUNMA: Tonight. Only tonight. We will come back tomorrow, as early as you like. But let us go away for this one night. Don't let another year break on me in this place . . . you don't know how important it is to me, but I will tell you, I will tell you on the way . . . but we must not be here today, Eman, do this one thing for me.

EMAN: *(Sadly)* I cannot.

SUNMA: *(Suddenly calm)* I was a fool to think it would be otherwise. The whole village may use you as they will but for me there is nothing. Sometimes I think you believe that doing anything for me makes you unfaithful to some part of your life. If it was a woman then I pity her for what she must have suffered.

(EMAN winces and hardens slowly. SUNMA notices nothing.)

Keeping faith with so much is slowly making you inhuman.

(Seeing the change in EMAN)

Eman. Eman. What is it?

(As she goes towards him, EMAN goes into the house.)

SUNMA: *(Apprehensive, follows him)* What did I say? Eman, forgive me, forgive me please.

(EMAN remains facing into the slow darkness of the room. SUNMA, distressed, cannot decide what to do.)

I swear I didn't know . . . I would not have said it for all the world.

(A lorry is heard taking off somewhere nearby. The sound comes up and slowly fades away into the distance. SUNMA starts visibly, goes slowly to the window.)

SUNMA: *(As the sound dies off, to herself)* What happens now?

EMAN: *(Joining her at the window)* What did you say?

SUNMA: Nothing.

EMAN: Was that not the lorry going off?

SUNMA: It was.

EMAN: I am sorry I couldn't help you.

(SUNMA, about to speak, changes her mind.)

EMAN: I think you ought to go home now.

SUNMA: No, don't send me away. It's the least you can do for me. Let me stay here until all the noise is over.

EMAN: But are you not needed at home? You have a part in the festival.

SUMNA: I have renounced it; I am Jaguna's eldest daughter only in name.

EMAN: Renouncing one's self is not so easy — surely you know that.

SUNMA: I don't want to talk about it. Will you at least let us be together tonight?

EMAN: But . . .

SUNMA: Unless you are afraid my father will accuse you of harbouring me.

EMAN: All right, we will go out together.

SUNMA: Go out? I want us to stay here.

EMAN: When there is so much going on outside?

SUNMA: Some day you will wish that you went away when I tried to make you.

EMAN: Are we going back to that?

SUNMA: No. I promise you I will not recall it again. But you must know that it was also for your sake that I tried to get us away.

EMAN: For me? How?

SUNMA: By yourself you can do nothing here. Have you not noticed how tightly we shut out strangers? Even if you lived here for a lifetime, you would remain a stranger.

EMAN: Perhaps that is what I like. There is peace in being a stranger.

SUNMA: For a while perhaps. But they would reject you in the end. I tell you it is only I who stand between you and contempt. And because of this you have earned their hatred. I don't know why I say this now, except that somehow, I feel that it no longer matters. It is only I who have stood between you and much humiliation.

EMAN: Think carefully before you say any more. I am incapable of feeling indebted to you. This will make no difference at all.

SUNMA: I ask for nothing. But you must know it all the same. It is true I hadn't the strength to go by myself. And I must confess this now, if you had come with me, I would have done everything to keep you from returning.

EMAN: I know that.

SUNMA: You see, I bare myself to you. For days I had thought it over, this was to be a new beginning for us. And I placed my fate wholly in your hands. Now the thought will not leave me, I have a feeling which will not be shaken off, that in some way, you have tonight totally destroyed my life.

EMAN: You are depressed, you don't know what you are saying.

SUNMA: Don't think I am accusing you. I say all this only because I cannot help it.

EMAN: We must not remain shut up here. Let us go and be part of the living.

SUNMA: No. Leave them alone.

EMAN: Surely you don't want to stay indoors when the whole town is alive with rejoicing.

SUNMA: Rejoicing! Is that what it seems to you? No, let us remain here. Whatever happens I must not go out until all this is over.

(There is silence. It has grown much darker.)

EMAN: I shall light the lamp.

SUNMA: *(Eager to do something)* No, let me do it.

*(She goes into the inner room.
EMAN paces the room, stops by a shelf and toys with the seeds in an 'ayo' board, takes down the whole board and places it on a table, playing by himself.
The GIRL is now seen coming back, still dragging her 'carrier.' IFADA brings up the rear as before. As he comes round the corner of the house two men emerge from the shadows. A sack is thrown over IFADA's head, the rope is pulled tight rendering him instantly helpless. The GIRL has reached the front of the house before she turns round at the sound of scuffle. She is in time to see IFADA thrown over the shoulders and borne away. Her face betraying no emotion at all, the girl backs slowly away, turns and flees, leaving the 'carrier' behind. SUMNA enters, carrying two kerosene lamps. She hangs one up from the wall.)*

EMAN: One is enough.

SUNMA: I want to leave one outside.

(She goes out, hangs the lamp from a nail just above the door. As she turns she sees the effigy and gasps. EMAN rushes out.)

EMAN: What is it? Oh, is that what frightened you?

SUNMA: I thought . . . I didn't really see it properly.

(EMAN goes towards the object, stoops to pick it up.)

EMAN: It must belong to that sick girl.

SUNMA: Don't touch it.

EMAN: Let's keep it for her.

SUNMA: Leave it alone. Don't touch it, Eman.

EMAN: *(Shrugs and goes back)* You are very nervous.

SUNMA: Lets go in.

EMAN: Wait. *(He detains her by the door, under the lamp.)* I know there is something more than you've told me. What are you afraid of tonight?

SUNMA: I was only scared by that thing. There is nothing else.

EMAN: I am not blind, Sunma. It is true I would not run away when you wanted me to, but that doesn't mean I do not feel things. What does tonight really mean that it makes you so helpless?

SUNMA: It is only a mood. And your indifference to me . . . let's go in.

(EMAN *moves aside and she enters; he remains there for a moment and then follows.*
She fiddles with the lamp, looks vaguely round the room, then goes and shuts the door, bolting it. When she turns, it is to meet EMAN'S *eyes, questioning.)*

SUNMA: There is a cold wind coming in.

(EMAN *keeps his gaze on her.)*

SUNMA: It *was* getting cold.

(*She moves guiltily to the table and stands by the 'ayo' board, rearranging the seeds.* EMAN *remains where he is a few moments, then brings a stool and sits opposite her. She sits down also and they begin to play in silence.)*

SUNMA: What brought you here at all, Eman? And what makes you stay?

(*There is another silence.)*

SUNMA: I am not trying to share your life. I know you too well by now. But at least we have worked together since you came. Is there nothing at all I deserve to know?

EMAN: Let me continue a stranger—especially to you. Those who have much to give fulfil themselves only in total loneliness.

SUNMA: Then there is no love in what you do.

EMAN: There is. Love comes to me more easily with strangers.

SUNMA: That is unnatural.

EMAN: Not for me. I know I find consummation only when I have spent myself for a total stranger.

SUNMA: It seems unnatural to me. But then I am a woman. I have a woman's longings and weaknesses. And the ties of blood are very strong in me.

EMAN: (*smiling.)* You think I have cut loose from all these—ties of blood.

SUNMA: Sometimes you are so inhuman.

EMAN: I don't know what that means. But I am very much my father's son.

(*They play in silence. Suddenly* EMAN *pauses listening.)*

EMAN: Did you hear that?

SUNMA: (*Quickly)* I heard nothing . . . it's your turn.

EMAN: Perhaps some of the mummers are coming this way.

(EMAN *about to play, leaps up suddenly.)*

SUNMA: What is it? Don't you want to play any more?

(EMAN *moves to the door.)*

SUNMA: No. Don't go out, Eman.

EMAN: If it's the dancers I want to ask them to stay. At least we won't have to miss everything.

SUNMA: No, no. Don't open the door. Let us keep out everyone tonight.

(*A terrified and disordered figure bursts suddenly round the corner, past the window and begins hammering at the door. It is* IFADA. *Desperate with terror, he pounds madly at the door, dumb-moaning all the while.)*

EMAN: Isn't that Ifada?

SUNMA: They are only fooling about. Don't pay any attention.

EMAN: (*Looks round the window)* That is Ifada. (*Begins to unbolt the door.)*

SUNMA: (*Pulling at his hands)* It is only a trick they are playing on you. Don't take any notice, Eman.

EMAN: What are you saying? The boy is out of his senses with fear.

SUNMA: No, no. Don't interfere, Eman. For God's sake don't interfere.

EMAN: Do you know something of this then?

SUNMA: You are a stranger here, Eman. Just leave us alone and go your own way. There is nothing you can do.

EMAN: (*He tries to push her out of the way but she clings fiercely to him)* Have you gone mad? I tell you the boy must come in.

SUNMA: Why won't you listen to me, Eman? I tell you it's none of your business. For your own sake do as I say.

(EMAN *pushes her off, unbolts the door.* IFADA *rushes in, clasps* EMAN *round the knees, dumb-moaning against his legs.)*

EMAN: (*Manages to re-bolt the door)* What is it, Ifada? What is the matter?

(Shouts and voices are heard coming nearer the house.)

SUNMA: Before it's too late, let him go. For once, Eman, believe what I tell you. Don't harbour him or you will regret it all your life.

(EMAN tries to calm IFADA who becomes more and more abject as the outside voices get nearer.)

EMAN: What have they done to him? At least tell me that. What is going on, Sunma?

SUNMA: *(With sudden venom)* Monster! Could you not take yourself somewhere else?

EMAN: Stop talking like that.

SUNMA: He could have run into the bush couldn't he? Toad! Why must he follow us with his own disasters!

VOICES OUTSIDE: It's here. . . . Round the back . . . Spread, spread . . . this way . . . no, head him off . . . use the bush path and head him off . . . get some more lights . . .

(EMAN listens. Lifts IFADA bodily and carries him into the inner room. Returns at once, shutting the door behind him.)

SUNMA: *(Slumps into a chair, resigned)* You always follow your own way.

JAGUNA *(Comes round the corner followed by Oroge and three men, one bearing a torch)* I knew he would come here.

OROGE: I hope our friend won't make trouble.

JAGUNA: He had better not. You, recall all the men and tell them to surround the house.

OROGE: But he may not be in the house after all.

JAGUNA: I know he is here . . . *(To the men)* . . . go on, do as I say.

(He bangs on the door.)

Teacher, open your door . . . you two stay by the door. If I need you I will call you.

(EMAN opens the door.)

JAGUNA: *(Speaks as he enters)* We know he is here.

EMAN: Who?

JAGUNA: Don't let us waste time. We are grown men, teacher. You understand me and I understand you. But we must take back the boy.

EMAN: This is my house.

JAGUNA: Daughter, you'd better tell your friend. I don't think he quite knows our ways. Tell him why he must give up the boy.

SUNMA: Father, I . . .

JAGUNA: Are you going to tell him or aren't you?

SUNMA: Father, I beg you, leave us alone tonight . . .

JAGUNA: I thought you might be a hindrance. Go home then if you will not use your sense.

SUNMA: But there are other ways . . .

JAGUNA: *(Turning to the men)* See that she gets home. I no longer trust her. If she gives trouble carry her. And see that the women stay with her until all this is over.

(SUMNA departs, accompanied by one of the men.)

JAGUNA: Now, teacher . . .

OROGE: *(Restrains him)* You see, Mister Eman, it is like this. Right now, nobody knows that Ifada has taken refuge here. No one except us and our men—and they know how to keep their mouths shut. We don't want to have to burn down the house you see, but if the word gets around, we would have no choice.

JAGUNA: In fact, it may be too late already. A carrier should end up in the bush, not in a house. Anyone who doesn't guard his door when the carrier goes by has himself to blame. A contaminated house should be burnt down.

OROGE: But we are willing to let it pass. Only, you must bring him out quickly.

EMAN: All right. But at least you will let me ask you something.

JAGUNA: What is there to ask? Don't you understand what we have told you?

EMAN: Yes. But why did you pick on a helpless boy. Obviously he is not willing.

JAGUNA: What is the man talking about? Ifada is a godsend. Does he have to be willing?

EMAN: In my home, we believe that a man should be willing.

OROGE: Mister Eman, I don't think you quite understand. This is not a simple matter at all. I don't know what you do, but here, it is not a cheap task for anybody. No one in his senses would do such a job. Why do you think we give refuge to idiots like him? We don't know where he came from. One morning, he is simply there, just like that. From nowhere at all. You see, there is a purpose in that.

JAGUNA: We only waste time.

OROGE: Jaguna, be patient. After all, the man has been with us for some time now and deserves to know. The evil of the old year is no light thing to load on any man's head.

EMAN: I know something about that.

OROGE: You do? *(Turns to* JAGUNA *who snorts impatiently.)* You see I told you so didn't I? From the moment you came I saw you were one of the knowing ones.

JAGUNA: Then let him behave like a man and give back the boy.

EMAN: It is you who are not behaving like men.

JAGUNA: *(Advances aggressively)* That is a quick mouth you have . . .

OROGE: Patience, Jaguna . . . if you want the new year to cushion the land there must be no deeds of anger. What did you mean, my friend?

EMAN: It is a simple thing. A village which cannot produce its own carrier contains no men.

JAGUNA: Enough. Let there be no more talk or this business will be ruined by some rashness. You . . . come inside. Bring the boy out, he must be in the room there.

EMAN: Wait.

(The men hesitate.)

JAGUNA: *(Hitting the nearer one and propelling him forward)* Go on. Have you changed masters now that you listen to what he says?

OROGE: *(Sadly)* I am sorry you would not understand, Mister Eman. But you ought to know that no carrier may return to the village. If he does, the people will stone him to death. It has happened before. Surely it is too much to ask a man to give up his own soil.

EMAN: I know others who have done more.

(IFADA is brought out, abjectly dumb-moaning.)

EMAN: You can see him with your own eyes. Does it really have meaning to use one as unwilling as that.

OROGE: *(Smiling)* He shall be willing. Not only willing but actually joyous. I am the one who prepares them all, and I have seen worse. This one escaped before I began to prepare him for the event. But you will see him later tonight, the most joyous creature in the festival. Then perhaps you will understand.

EMAN: Then it is only a deceit. Do you believe the spirit of a new year is so easily fooled?

JAGUNA: Take him out. *(The men carry out* IFADA.) You see, it is so easy to talk. You say there are no men in this village because they cannot provide a willing carrier. And yet I heard Oroge tell you we only use strangers. There is only one other stranger in the village, but I have not heard him offer himself *(spits.)* It is so easy to talk is it not?

(He turns his back on him.
They go off, taking IFADA *with them, limp and*
silent. The only sign of life is that he strains his
neck to keep his eyes on EMAN *till the very*
moment that he disappears from sight. EMAN
remains where they left him, staring after the
group.)

(A black-out lasting no more than a minute. The
lights come up slowly and IFADA *is seen returning*
to the house. He stops at the window and looks
in. Seeing no one, he bangs on the sill. Appears
surprised that there is no response. He slithers
down on his favourite spot, then sees the effigy
still lying where the GIRL *had dropped it in her*
flight. After some hesitation, he goes towards it,
begins to strip it of the clothing. Just then the GIRL
comes in.)

GIRL: Hey, leave that alone. You know it's mine.

(IFADA pauses, then speeds up his action.)

GIRL: I said it is mine. Leave it where you found it.

(She rushes at him and begins to struggle for
possession of the carrier.)

GIRL: Thief! Thief! Let it go, it is mine. Let it go. You animal, just because I let you play with it. Idiot! Idiot!

(The struggle becomes quite violent. The GIRL *is*
hanging to the effigy and IFADA *lifts her with it,*
flinging her all about. The GIRL *hangs on grimly.)*

GIRL: You are spoiling it . . . why don't you get your own? Thief! Let it go you thief!

(SUNMA comes in walking very fast, throwing
apprehensive glances over her shoulder. Seeing the
two children, she becomes immediately angry.
Advances on them.)

SUNMA: So you've made this place your playground. Get away you untrained pigs. Get out of here.

(IFADA *flees at once, the girl retreats also, retaining possession of the 'carrier.'*
SUNMA *goes to the door. She has her hand on the door when the significance of* IFADA'S *presence strikes her for the first time. She stands rooted to the spot, then turns slowly round.*)

SUNMA: Ifada! What are you doing here?

(IFADA *is bewildered.* SUNMA *turns suddenly and rushes into the house, flying into the inner room and out again.*)

Eman! Eman! Eman!

(*She rushes outside.*)

Where did he go? Where did they take him?

(IFADA *distressed, points.* SUNMA *seizes him by the arm, drags him off.*)

Take me there at once. God help you if we are too late. You loathsome thing, if you have let him suffer . . .

(*Her voice fades into other shouts, running footsteps, banged tins, bells, dogs, etc., rising in volume.*)

(*It is a narrow passage-way between two mudhouses. At the far end one man after another is seen running across the entry, the noise dying off gradually.*
About half-way down the passage, EMAN *is crouching against the wall, tense with apprehension. As the noise dies off, he seems to relax, but the alert hunted look is still in his eyes which are ringed in a reddish colour. The rest of his body has been whitened with a floury substance. He is naked down to the waist, wears a baggy pair of trousers, calf-length, and around both feet are bangles.*)

EMAN: I will simply stay here till dawn. I have done enough.

(*A window is thrown open and a woman empties some slop from a pail. With a startled cry* EMAN *leaps aside to avoid it and the woman puts out her head.*)

WOMAN: Oh, my head. What have I done! Forgive me, neighbor . . . Eh, it's the carrier!

(*Very rapidly she clears her throat and spits on him, flings the pail at him and runs off, shouting.*)

He's here. The carrier is hiding in the passage. Quickly, I have found the carrier!

(*The cry is taken up and* EMAN *flees down the passage. Shortly afterwards his pursuers come pouring down the passage in full cry. After the last of them come* JAGUNA *and* OROGE.)

OROGE: Wait, wait. I cannot go so fast.
JAGUNA: We will rest a little then. We can do nothing anyway.
OROGE: If only he had let me prepare him.
JAGUNA: They are the ones who break first, these fools who think they were born to carry suffering like a hat. What are we to do now?
OROGE: When they catch him I must prepare him.
JAGUNA: He? It will be impossible now. There can be no joy left in that one.
OROGE: Still, it took him by surprise. He was not expecting what he met.
JAGUNA: Why then did he refuse to listen? Did he think he was coming to sit down to a feast. He had not even gone through one compound before he bolted. Did he think he was taken round the people to be blessed? A woman, that is all he is.
OROGE: No, no. He took the beating well enough. I think he is the kind who would let himself be beaten from night till dawn and not utter a sound. He would let himself be stoned until he dropped dead.
JAGUNA: Then what made him run like a coward?
OROGE: I don't know. I don't really know. It is a night of curses, Jaguna. It is not many unprepared minds will remain unhinged under the load.
JAGUNA: We must find him. It is a poor beginning for a year when our own curses remain hovering over our homes because the carrier refused to take them.

(*They go. The scene changes.* EMAN *is crouching beside some shrubs, torn and bleeding.*)

EMAN: They are even guarding my house . . . as if I would go there, but I need water . . . they could at least grant me that . . . I can be thirsty too . . . *(He pricks his ears)* . . . there must be a stream nearby . . . *(As he looks round him, his eyes widen at a scene he encounters.)*

(An OLD MAN, *short and vigorous looking is seated on a stool. He also is wearing calf-length baggy trousers, white. On his head, a white cap. An attendant is engaged in rubbing his body with oil. Round his eyes, two white rings have already been marked.)*

OLD MAN: Have they prepared the boat?

ATTENDANT: They are making the last sacrifice.

OLD MAN: Good. Did you send for my son?

ATTENDANT: He's on his way.

OLD MAN: I have never met the carrying of the boat with such a heavy heart. I hope nothing comes of it.

ATTENDANT: The gods will not desert us on that account.

OLD MAN: A man should be at his strongest when he takes the boat, my friend. To be weighed down inside and out is not a wise thing. I hope when the moment comes I shall have found my strength.

(Enter EMAN, *a wrapper round his waist and a danski¹ over it.)*

OLD MAN: I meant to wait until after my journey to the river, but my mind is so burdened with my own grief and yours I could not delay it. You know I must have all my strength. But I sit here, feeling it all eaten slowly away by my unspoken grief. It helps to say it out. It even helps to cry sometimes.

(He signals to the attendant to leave them.)

Come nearer . . . we will never meet again, son. Not on this side of the flesh. What I do not know is whether you will return to take my place.

EMAN: I will never come back.

OLD MAN: Do you know what you are saying? Ours is a strong breed, my son. It is only a strong breed that can take this boat to the river year after year and wax stronger on it. I have taken down each year's evils for over twenty years. I hoped you would follow me.

¹a short garment

EMAN: My life here died with Omae.

OLD MAN: Omae died giving birth to your child and you think the world is ended. Eman, my pain did not begin when Omae died. Since you sent her to stay with me son, I lived with the burden of knowing that this child would die bearing your son.

EMAN: Father . . .

OLD MAN: Don't you know it was the same with you? And me? No woman survives the bearing of the strong ones. Son, it is not the mouth of the boaster that says he belongs to the strong breed. It is the tongue that is red with pain and black with sorrow. Twelve years you were away, my son, and for those twelve years I knew the love of an old man for his daughter and the pain of a man helplessly awaiting his loss.

EMAN: I wish I had stayed away. I wish I never came back to meet her.

OLD MAN: It had to be. But you know now what slowly ate away my strength. I awaited your return with love and fear. Forgive me then if I say that your grief is light. It will pass. This grief may drive you now from home. But you must return.

EMAN: You do not understand. It is not grief alone.

OLD MAN: What is it then? Tell me, I can still learn.

EMAN: I was away twelve years. I changed much in that time.

OLD MAN: I am listening.

EMAN: I am unfitted for your work, father. I wish to say no more. But I am totally unfitted for your call.

OLD MAN: It is only time you need, son. Stay longer and you will answer the urge of your blood.

EMAN: That I stayed at all was because of Omae. I did not expect to find her waiting. I would have taken her away, but hard as you claim to be, it would have killed you. And I was a tired man. I needed peace. Because Omae was peace, I stayed. Now nothing holds me here.

OLD MAN: Other men would rot and die doing this task year after year. It is strong medicine which only we can take. Our blood is strong like no other. Anything you do in life must be less than this, son.

EMAN: That is not true, father.

OLD MAN: I tell you it is true. Your own blood will betray you son, because you cannot hold it back. If you make it do less than this, it will rush to your head and burst it open. I say what I know, my son.

EMAN: There are other tasks in life, father. This one is not for me. There are even greater things you know nothing of.

OLD MAN: I am very sad. You only go to give to others what rightly belongs to us. You will use your strength among thieves. They are thieves because they take what is ours, they have no claim of blood to it. They will even lack the knowledge to use it wisely. Truth is my companion at this moment, my son. I know everything I say will surely bring the sadness of truth.

EMAN: I am going, father.

OLD MAN: Call my attendant. And be with me in your strength for this last journey. A-ah, did you hear that? It came out without my knowing it; this is indeed my last journey. But I am not afraid.

(EMAN *goes out. A few moments later, the attendant enters.*)

ATTENDANT: The boat is ready.
OLD MAN: So am I.

(*He sits perfectly still for several moments. Drumming begins somewhere in the distance, and the* OLD MAN *sways his head almost imperceptibly. Two men come in bearing a miniature boat, containing an indefinable mound. They rush it in and set it briskly down near the* OLD MAN, *and stand well back. The* OLD MAN *gets up slowly, the attendant watching him keenly. He signs to the men, who lift the boat quickly onto the* OLD MAN's *head. As soon as it touches his head, he holds it down with both hands and runs off, the men give him a start, then follow at a trot. As the last man disappears* OROGE *limps in and comes face to face with* EMAN—*as carrier*—*who is now seen still standing beside the shrubs, staring into the scene he has just witnessed.* OROGE, *struck by the look on* EMAN's *face, looks anxiously behind him to see what has engaged* EMAN's *attention.* EMAN *notices him then, and the pair stare at each other.* JAGUNA *enters, sees him and shouts, 'Here he is,' rushes at* EMAN *who is whipped back to the immediate and flees,* JAGUNA *in pursuit. Three or four others enter and follow them.* OROGE *remains where he is, thoughtful.*)

JAGUNA: (*Re-enters*) They have closed in on him now, we'll get him this time.

OROGE: It is nearly midnight.

JAGUNA: You were standing there looking at him as if he was some strange spirit. Why didn't you shout?

OROGE: You shouted didn't you? Did that catch him?

JAGUNA: Don't worry. We have him now. But things have taken a bad turn. It is no longer enough to drive him past every house. There is too much contamination about already.

OROGE: (*Not listening*) He saw something. Why may I not know what it was?

JAGUNA: What are you talking about?

OROGE: Hm. What is it?

JAGUNA: I said there is too much harm done already. The year will demand more from this carrier than we thought.

OROGE: What do you mean?

JAGUNA: Do we have to talk with the full mouth?

OROGE: S-sh . . . look!

(JAGUNA *turns just in time to see* SUNMA *fly at him, clawing at his face like a crazed tigress.*)

SUNMA: Murderer! What are you doing to him. Murderer! Murderer!

(JAGUNA *finds himself struggling really hard to keep off his daughter, he succeeds in pushing her off and striking her so hard on the face that she falls to her knees. He moves on her to hit her again.*)

OROGE: (*Comes between*) Think what you are doing, Jaguna, she is your daughter.

JAGUNA: My daughter! Does this one look like my daughter? Let me cripple the harlot for life.

OROGE: That is a wicked thought, Jaguna.

JAGUNA: Don't come between me and her.

OROGE: Nothing in anger—do you forget what tonight is?

JAGUNA: Can you blame me for forgetting?

(*Draws his hand across his cheek—it is covered with blood.*)

OROGE: This is an unhappy night for us all. I fear what is to come of it.

JAGUNA: Let's go. I cannot restrain myself in this creature's presence. My own daughter . . . and for a stranger . . .

(They go off, IFADA, *who came in with* SUNMA *and had stood apart, horror-stricken, comes shyly forward. He helps* SUNMA *up. They go off, he holding* SUNMA *bent and sobbing.)*

(Enter EMAN—*as carrier. He is physically present in the bounds of this next scene, a side of a round thatched hut. A young girl, about fourteen runs in, stops beside the hut. She looks carefully to see that she is not observed, puts her mouth to a little hole in the wall.)*

OMAE: Eman . . . Eman . . .

*(*EMAN—*as carrier—responds, as he does throughout the scene, but they are unaware of him.)*

EMAN: *(From inside)* Who is it?
OMAE: It is me, Omae.
EMAN: How dare you come here!

(Two hands appear at the hole and pushing outwards, create a much larger hole through which EMAN *puts out his head. It is* EMAN *as a boy, the same age as the girl.)*

Go away at once. Are you trying to get me into trouble!
OMAE: What is the matter?
EMAN: You. Go away.
OMAE: But I came to see you.
EMAN: Are you deaf? I say I don't want to see you. Now go before my tutor catches you.
OMAE: All right. Come out.
EMAN: Do what!
OMAE: Come out.
EMAN: You must be mad.
OMAE: *(Sits on the ground)* All right, if you don't come out I shall simply stay here until your tutor arrives.
EMAN: *(About to explode, thinks better of it and the head disappears. A moment later he emerges from behind the hut.)* What sort of a devil has got into you?
OMAE: None. I just wanted to see you.
EMAN: *(His mimicry is nearly hysterical)*

'None. I just wanted to see you.' Do you think this place is the stream where you can go and molest innocent people?
OMAE: *(Coyly)* Aren't you glad to see me?
EMAN: I am not.
OMAE: Why?
EMAN: Why? Do you really ask me why? Because you are a woman and a most troublesome woman. Don't you know anything about this at all. We are not meant to see any woman. So go away before more harm is done.
OMAE: *(Flirtatious)* What is so secret about it anyway? What do they teach you.
EMAN: Nothing any woman can understand.
OMAE: Ha ha. You think we don't know eh? You've all come to be circumcised.
EMAN: Shut up. You don't know anything.
OMAE: Just think, all this time you haven't been circumcised, and you dared make eyes at us women.
EMAN: Thank you—woman. Now go.
OMAE: Do they give you enough to eat?
EMAN *(Testily)* No. We are so hungry that when silly girls like you turn up, we eat them.
OMAE: *(Feigning tears)* Oh, oh, oh, he's abusing me. He's abusing me.
EMAN: *(Alarmed)* Don't try that here. Go quickly if you are going to cry.
OMAE: All right, I won't cry.
EMAN: Cry or no cry, go away and leave me alone. What do you think will happen if my tutor turns up now.
OMAE: He won't.
EMAN: *(Mimicking)* 'He won't.' I suppose you are his wife and he tells you where he goes. In fact this is just the time he comes round to our huts. He could be at the next hut this very moment.
OMAE: Ha-ha. You're lying. I left him by the stream, pinching the girls' bottoms. Is that the sort of thing he teaches you?
EMAN: Don't say anything against him or I shall beat you. Isn't it you loose girls who tease him, wiggling your bottoms under his nose?
OMAE: *(Going tearful again)* A-ah, so I am one of the loose girls eh?
EMAN: Now don't start accusing me of things I didn't say.
OMAE: But you said it. You said it.
EMAN: I didn't. Look Omae, someone will

hear you and I'll be in disgrace. Why don't you go before anything happens.

OMAE: It's all right. My friends have promised to hold your old rascal tutor till I get back.

EMAN: Then you go back right now. I have work to do. *(Going in.)*

OMAE: *(Runs after and tries to hold him. EMAN leaps back, genuinely scared)* What is the matter? I was not going to bite you.

EMAN: Do you know what you nearly did? You almost touched me!

OMAE: Well?

EMAN: Well! Isn't it enough that you let me set my eyes on you? Must you now totally pollute me with your touch? Don't you understand anything?

OMAE: Oh, that.

EMAN: *(Nearly screaming.)* It is not 'oh that.' Do you think this is only a joke or a little visit like spending the night with your grandmother? This is an important period of my life. Look, these huts, we built them with our own hands. Every boy builds his own. We learn things, do you understand? And we spend much time just thinking. At least, I do. It is the first time I have had nothing to do except think. Don't you see, I am becoming a man. For the first time, I understand that I have a life to fulfil. Has that thought ever worried you?

OMAE: You are frightening me.

EMAN: There. That is all you can say. And what use will that be when a man finds himself alone—like that? *(Points to the hut.)* A man must go on his own, go where no one can help him, and test his strength. Because he may find himself one day sitting alone in a wall as round as that. In there, my mind could hold no other thought. I may never have such moments again to myself. Don't dare to come and steal any more of it.

OMAE: *(This time, genuinely tearful)* Oh, I know you hate me. You only want to drive me away.

EMAN: *(Impatiently)* Yes, yes, I know I hate you—but go.

OMAE: *(Going, all tears. Wipes her eyes, suddenly all mischief)* Eman.

EMAN: What now?

OMAE: I only want to ask one thing . . . do you promise to tell me?

EMAN: Well, what is it?

OMAE: *(Gleefully)* Does it hurt?

(She turns instantly and flees, landing straight into the arms of the returning tutor.)

TUTOR: Te-he-he . . . what have we here? What little mouse leaps straight into the beak of the wise old owl eh?

(OMAE struggles to free herself, flies to the opposite side, grimacing with distaste.)

TUTOR: I suppose you merely came to pick some fruits eh? You did not sneak here to see any of my children.

OMAE: Yes, I came to steal your fruits.

TUTOR: Te-he-he . . . I thought so. And that dutiful son of mine over there. He saw you and came to chase you off my fruit trees didn't he? Te-he-he . . . I'm sure he did, isn't that so, my young Eman?

EMAN: I was talking to her.

TUTOR: Indeed you were. Now be good enough to go into your hut until I decide your punishment. *(EMAN withdraws.)* Te-he-he . . . now now my little daughter, you need not be afraid of me.

OMAE: *(Spiritedly)* I am not.

TUTOR: Good. Very good. We ought to be friendly. *(His voice becomes leering.)* Now this is nothing to worry you, my daughter . . . a very small thing indeed. Although of course if I were to let it slip that your young Eman had broken a strong taboo, it might go hard on him you know. I am sure you would not like that to happen, would you?

OMAE: No.

TUTOR: Good. You are sensible, my girl. Can you wash clothes?

OMAE: Yes.

TUTOR: Good. If you will come with me now to my hut, I shall give you some clothes to wash, and then we will forget all about this matter eh? Well, come on.

OMAE: I shall wait here. You go and bring the clothes.

TUTOR: Eh? What is that? Now now, don't make me angry. You should know better than to talk back at your elders. Come now.

(He takes her by the arm, and tries to drag her off.)

OMAE: No no, I won't come to your hut. Leave me. Leave me alone you shameless old man.

TUTOR: If you don't come I shall disgrace the whole family of Eman, and yours too.

(EMAN *re-enters with a small bundle.*)

EMAN: Leave her alone. Let us go, Omae.

TUTOR: And where do you think you are going?

EMAN: Home.

TUTOR: Te-he-he . . . As easy as that eh? You think you can leave here any time you please? Get right back inside that hut!

(EMAN *takes* OMAE *by the arm and begins to walk off.*)

TUTOR: Come back at once.

(*He goes after him and raises his stick.* EMAN *catches it, wrenches it from him and throws it away.*)

OMAE: (*Hopping delightedly*) Kill him. Beat him to death.

TUTOR: Help! Help! He is killing me! Help!

(*Alarmed,* EMAN *clamps his hand over his mouth.*)

EMAN: Old tutor, I don't mean you any harm, but you mustn't try to harm me either. (*He removes his hand.*)

TUTOR: You think you can get away with your crime. My report shall reach the elders before you ever get into town.

EMAN: You are afraid of what I will say about you? Don't worry. Only if you try to shame me, then I will speak. I am not going back to the village anyway. Just tell them I have gone, no more. If you say one word more than that I shall hear of it the same day and I shall come back.

TUTOR: You are telling me what to do? But don't think to come back next year because I will drive you away. Don't think to come back here even ten years from now. And don't send your children.

(*Goes off with threatening gestures.*)

EMAN: I won't come back.

OMAE: Smoked vulture! But Eman, he says you cannot return next year. What will you do?

EMAN: It is a small thing one can do in the big towns.

OMAE: I thought you were going to beat him that time. Why didn't you crack his dirty hide?

EMAN: Listen carefully, Omae . . . I am going on a journey.

OMAE: Come on. Tell me about it on the way.

EMAN: No, I go that way. I cannot return to the village.

OMAE: Because of that wretched man? Anyway you will first talk to your father.

EMAN: Go and see him for me. Tell him I have gone away for some time. I think he will know.

OMAE: But, Eman . . .

EMAN: I haven't finished. You will go and live with him till I get back. I have spoken to him about you. Look after him!

OMAE: But what is this journey? When will you come back?

EMAN: I don't know. But this is a good moment to go. Nothing ties me down.

OMAE: But Eman, you want to leave me.

EMAN: Don't forget all I said. I don't know how long I will be. Stay in my father's house as long as you remember me. When you become tired of waiting, you must do as you please. You understand? You must do as you please.

OMAE: I cannot understand anything, Eman. I don't know where you are going or why. Suppose you never came back! Don't go, Eman. Don't leave me by myself.

EMAN: I must go. Now let me see you on your way.

OMAE: I shall come with you.

EMAN: Come with me! And who will look after you? Me? You will only be in my way, you know that! You will hold me back and I shall desert you in a strange place. Go home and do as I say. Take care of my father and let him take care of you. (*He starts going but* OMAE *clings to him.*)

OMAE: But Eman, stay the night at least. You will only lose your way. Your father, Eman, what will he say? I won't remember what you said . . . come back to the village . . . I cannot return alone, Eman . . . come with me as far as the crossroads.

(*His face set,* EMAN *strides off and* OMAE *loses balance as he increases his pace. Falling, she quickly wraps her arms around his ankle, but* EMAN *continues unchecked, dragging her along.*)

OMAE: Don't go, Eman . . . Eman, don't leave me, don't leave me . . . don't leave your Omae . . . don't go, Eman . . . don't leave your Omae . . .

(EMAN—*as carrier—makes a nervous move as if he intends to go after the vanished pair. He stops but continues to stare at the point where he last saw them. There is stillness for a while. Then the* GIRL *enters from the same place and remains looking at* EMAN. *Startled,* EMAN *looks apprehensively round him. The* GIRL *goes nearer but keeps beyond arm's length.)*

GIRL: Are you the carrier?

EMAN: Yes, I am Eman.

GIRL: Why are you hiding?

EMAN: I really came for a drink of water . . . er . . . is there anyone in front of the house?

GIRL: No.

EMAN: But there might be people in the house. Did you hear voices?

GIRL: There is no one here.

EMAN: Good. Thank you. *(He is about to go, stops suddenly.)* Er . . . would you . . . you will find a cup on the table. Could you bring me the water out here? The water-pot is in a corner.

(The GIRL *goes. She enters the house, then, watching* EMAN *carefully, slips out and runs off.)*

EMAN: *(Sitting)* Perhaps they have all gone home. It will be good to rest. *(He hears voices and listens hard.)* Too late. *(Moves cautiously nearer the house.)* Quickly girl, I can hear people coming. Hurry up. *(Looks through the window.)* Where are you? Where is she? *(The truth dawns on him suddenly and he moves off, sadly.)*

(Enter JAGUNA *and* OROGE, *led by the* GIRL.)

GIRL: *(Pointing)* He was there.

JAGUNA: Ay, he's gone now. He is a sly one is your friend. But it won't save him forever.

OROGE: What was he doing when you saw him?

GIRL: He asked me for a drink of water.

JAGUNA
OROGE } : Ah! *(They look at each other.)*

OROGE: We should have thought of that.

JAGUNA: He is surely finished now. If only we had thought of it earlier.

OROGE: It is not too late. There is still an hour before midnight.

JAGUNA: We must call back all the men. Now we need only wait for him—in the right place.

OROGE: Everyone must be told. We don't want anyone heading him off again.

JAGUNA: And it works so well. This is surely the help of the gods themselves, Oroge. Don't you know at once what is on the path to the stream?

OROGE: The sacred trees.

JAGUNA: I tell you it is the very hand of the gods. Let us go.

(An overgrown part of the village. EMAN *wanders in, aimlessly, seemingly uncaring of discovery. Beyond him, an area lights up, revealing a group of people clustered round a spot, all the heads are bowed. One figure stands away and separate from them. Even as* EMAN *looks, the group breaks up and the people disperse, coming down and past him. Only three people are left, a man (*EMAN*) whose back is turned, the village* PRIEST *and the isolated one. They stand on opposite sides of the grave, the man on the mound of earth. The* PRIEST *walks round to the man's side and lays a hand on his shoulder.)*

PRIEST: Come.

EMAN: I will. Give me a few moments here alone.

PRIEST: Be comforted.

(They fall silent.)

EMAN: I was gone twelve years but she waited. She whom I thought had too much of the laughing child in her. Twelve years I was a pilgrim, seeking the vain shrine of secret strength. And all the time, strange knowledge, this silent strength of my child-woman.

PRIEST: We all saw it. It was a lesson to us; we did not know that such goodness could be found among us.

EMAN: Then why? Why the wasted years if she had to perish giving birth to my child? *(They are both silent.)* I do not really know for what great meaning I searched. When I returned, I could not be certain I had found it. Until I reached my home and I found her a full-grown woman, still a child at heart. When I grew to believe it, I thought, this, after all, is what I sought. It was here all the time. And I threw away my new-gained knowledge. I buried the part of me that was formed in strange places. I made a home in my birthplace.

PRIEST: That was as it should be.

EMAN: Any truth of that was killed in the cruelty of her brief happiness.

PRIEST: (*Looks up and sees the figure standing away from them, the child in his arms. He is totally still.*) Your father—he is over there.

EMAN: I knew he would come. Has he my son with him?

PRIEST: Yes.

EMAN: He will let no one take the child. Go and comfort him, priest. He loved Omae like a daughter, and you all know how well she looked after him. You see how strong we really are. In his heart of hearts the old man's love really awaited a daughter. Go and comfort him. His grief is more than mine.

(*The PRIEST goes. The OLD MAN has stood well away from the burial group. His face is hard and his gaze unswerving from the grave. The PRIEST goes to him, pauses, but sees that he can make no dent in the man's grief. Bowed, he goes on his way.*)

(EMAN, *as carrier, walking towards the graveside, the other EMAN having gone. His feet sink into the mound and he breaks slowly on to his knees, scooping up the sand in his hands and pouring it on his head. The scene blacks out slowly.*)

(*Enter JAGUNA and OROGE.*)

OROGE: We have only a little time.

JAGUNA: He will come. All the wells are guarded. There is only the stream left him. The animal must come to drink.

OROGE: You are sure it will not fail—the trap I mean.

JAGUNA: When Jaguna sets the trap, even elephants pay homage—their trunks downwards and one leg up in the sky. When the carrier steps on the fallen twigs, it is up in the sacred trees with him.

OROGE: I shall breathe again when this long night is over.

(*They go out.*)

(*Enter EMAN—as carrier—from the same direction as the last two entered. In front of him is a still figure, the old man as he was, carrying the dwarf boat.*)

EMAN: (*Joyfully*) Father.

(*The figure does not turn round.*)

EMAN: It is your son. Eman. (*He moves nearer.*) Don't you want to look at me? It is I, Eman. (*He moves nearer still.*)

OLD MAN: You are coming too close. Don't you know what I carry on my head?

EMAN: But Father, I am your son.

OLD MAN: Then go back. We cannot give the two of us.

EMAN: Tell me first where you are going.

OLD MAN: Do you ask that? Where else but to the river?

EMAN: (*Visibly relieved*) I only wanted to be sure. My throat is burning. I have been looking for the stream all night.

OLD MAN: It is the other way.

EMAN: But you said . . .

OLD MAN: I take the longer way, you know how I must do this. It is quicker if you take the other way. Go now.

EMAN: No, I will only get lost again. I shall go with you.

OLD MAN: Go back, my son. Go back.

EMAN: Why? Won't you even look at me?

OLD MAN: Listen to your father. Go back.

EMAN: But, father!

(*He makes to hold him. Instantly the old man breaks into a rapid trot. EMAN hesitates, then follows, his strength nearly gone.*)

EMAN: Wait, father. I am coming with you . . . wait . . . wait for me, father . . .

(*There is a sound of twigs breaking, of a sudden trembling in the branches. Then silence.*)

(*The front of EMAN's house. The effigy is hanging from the sheaves. Enter SUNMA, still supported by IFADA, she stands transfixed as she sees the hanging figure. IFADA appears to go mad, rushes at the object and tears it down. SUNMA, her last bit of will gone, crumbles against the wall. Some distance away from them, partly hidden, stands the GIRL, impassively watching. IFADA hugs the effigy to him, stands above SUNMA. The GIRL remains where she is, observing.*

Almost at once, the villagers begin to return, subdued and guilty. They walk across the front, skirting the house as widely as they can. No word is exchanged. JAGUNA and OROGE eventually appear. JAGUNA, *who is leading, sees* SUNMA *as soon as he comes in view. He stops at once, retreating slightly.)*

OROGE: *(Almost whispering)* What is it?
JAGUNA: The viper.

*(*OROGE *looks cautiously at the woman.)*

OROGE: I don't think she will even see you.
JAGUNA: Are you sure? I am in no frame of mind for another meeting with her.
OROGE: Let's go home.
JAGUNA: I am sick to the heart of the cowardice I have seen tonight.
OROGE: That is the nature of men.
JAGUNA: Then it is a sorry world to live in. We did it for them. It was all for their own common good. What did it benefit me whether the man lived or died. But did you see them? One and all they looked up at the man and words died in their throats.
OROGE: It was no common sight.
JAGUNA: Women could not have behaved so shamefully. One by one they crept off like sick dogs. Not one could raise a curse.
OROGE: It was not only him they fled. Do you see how unattended we are?
JAGUNA: There are those who will pay for this night's work!
OROGE: Ay, let us go home.

(They go off. SUNMA, IFADA, *and the* GIRL *remain as they are, the light fading slowly on them.)*

THE END

In *The Strong Breed*, the dramatic action focuses on a ritual that in one form or another is found in various societies—the selection and expulsion of a scapegoat. Details of the ritual differ considerably from one place to another. (In our society, the death of Christ is the best-known variant.) Eman's mistake lies in thinking that the ritual is observed elsewhere as it is in his own community where someone willingly allows the troubles and cares of the village, loaded onto a symbolic vessel, to be placed on his head so he can carry it down the river and thereby cleanse the community and make way for happiness and prosperity in the new year. In Eman's village, the carrier is honored for his strength, courage, and wisdom, but in the village to which Eman has recently come the ritual is quite different. Here the carrier himself becomes the object of loathing and is driven from the village permanently. Consequently, only outsiders are chosen as carriers, and since they are not expected to accept the role willingly, they are drugged and hypnotized so they appear happy to receive the beatings, curses, and other forms of abuse heaped upon them. On this particular New Year's Eve, the community contains only two outsiders—Eman and the idiot Ifada—and as the play begins neither is aware that one of them must serve as carrier.

The opening section of *The Strong Breed* progresses somewhat leisurely, even though Sunma's obvious anxiety creates a sense of danger as she attempts to persuade Eman to go away with her for a few days. It is never made clear why Sunma will not tell Eman about the danger. There are a number of possibilities. She is the daughter of the chieftain Jaguna, and she may have been placed under an oath not to reveal village secrets to Eman. Or, despite her protestations of dislike for her native village, she may still be under the influence of its attitudes, for, though she loves Eman, she does not know where he comes from or anything about his prior life; thus, she may unconsciously share the villagers' fear that any outsider may be an evil force in disguise. In a society where tradition and belonging are all-important, Eman's unwillingness to reveal anything about himself can only arouse suspicion. Similarly, no one knows anything about Ifada, the idiot who has wandered into the village, and when Eman befriends him, suspicion of Eman increases. Knowing what she does about the ritual, Sunma berates Ifada and tries to drive him away from Eman's house, thus hoping to identify Ifada, rather than Eman, as the carrier.

The action begins a new phase with the entrance of the girl dragging an effigy. Sunma calls her evil, but it seems likely that she has been sent, for the ritual requires that the intended carrier be lured into the bush where he can be captured and prepared. The girl is successful in getting Ifada to follow her, but Eman also has been marked as potential carrier when he gives her one of his garments to put on her effigy and when, instead of shutting his doors and driving the girl and her effigy away, as other villagers would, he goes out to examine the effigy — a sign to the community of his own contamination.

When Ifada escapes from his captors and returns to Eman's hut, he is pursued by the villagers, represented primarily by Jaguna and Oroge. Eman argues that a carrier should be willing to take on the role. Jaguna explains why the carrier must be an outsider and taunts Eman, as the only other potential carrier, for not volunteering to take Ifada's place if he feels so deeply about it. This exchange is followed by a break in the action (indicated by a brief blackout).

Up to this point, Eman has been the detached, rational observer. He views the upcoming festival much as a tourist might — as an interesting spectacle. His calm logic contrasts sharply with the urgency projected by Sunma, Oroge, and Jaguna. He is, in effect, an outsider who has assumed the role of voluntary, altruistic helper while refusing to become involved in village life. His role and principles are called into question by Jaguna's taunt.

Following the blackout, the direction of the action changes. Eman has volunteered to take Ifada's place; thus, he has become a participant, not merely an observer. His is still serving the village but in a way he had not envisioned. His detached rationality has given way to near panic, provoking, through flashbacks, a reliving of the events that have led him to this moment. We learn that he is descended from a line of carriers; that he has rejected the traditions of his village out of disillusionment with his tutor; that he spent 12 years away from his home searching for some new truth; that he returned to his village and his childhood sweetheart, Omae; that his marriage to Omae brought him the fulfillment he had been seeking elsewhere; that this happiness was shattered when Omae died giving birth to his son (as Eman's mother had died giving birth to him); that he left home once more, rejecting his father's reminder that, as a descendant of carriers (the strong breed), his role is that of carrier. These scenes from the past are interspersed with scenes from the present in which Eman is pursued by the villagers who become increasingly desparate as midnight approaches and the carrier has not been prepared to carry away the year's burdens. These scenes also demonstrate the inescapable continuity of past, present, and future.

At the end of the play, Eman, unlike past carriers, has been killed and his death has filled the villagers with shame rather than joy. Jaguna complains: "One and all they looked up at the man and words died in their throats. . . . One by one they crept off like sick dogs. Not one could raise a curse." Oroge reminds Jaguna: "It was not only him they fled. Do you see how unattended we are?" Thus, Eman's sacrifice signifies the beginning of change. The villagers, ashamed of their own behavior and no longer willing to follow blindly their leaders (Jaguna and Oroge), may cease viewing all strangers as justified victims and may behave more thoughtfully and humanely.

The Strong Breed creates a sense of fate or inevitability. Eman has sought to escape his destiny as carrier; he has rejected his own people's traditions and has exiled himself to a strange village, which he hopes to serve unselfishly through rational means; but, as in Greek tragedy, Eman cannot escape his fate and inexorably he is forced to take on the role he has sought to avoid; rather than limited commitment (altruistic but impersonal service), he is driven to total involvement (sacrifice of life for the betterment of mankind).

The Strong Breed develops a number of themes common in Soyinka's plays: the conflict between the traditional and the modern; the ongoing need to save society from its tendency to follow custom and mistaken belief unquestioningly; the special individual, who through dedication and vision awakens the people and leads them toward better ways, even though he may become a victim of the society he seeks to benefit. It has been suggested that through Eman Soyinka expresses his view of the role of the artist in present-day Africa. (Soyinka has also been accused of having a messianic complex.) But, since Eman finds that society is not as simple as he first thought, Soyinka may also be suggesting that one cannot escape tradition and therefore must come to grips with it.

The Strange Breed should call to mind the excesses that can occur in any closed group in which distrust of outsiders often leads to brutality. Why are those who are different in some way (in religion, race, nationality, social class, occupation, intellectual capacity, physical attributes, behavior and dress, etc.) considered to be threats? Soyinka's play also raises another question: Why have societies since the beginning of time and all over the world singled out individuals onto whom they project collective guilt as a means of cleansing the group? (Complex societies, such as our own, still do this, though not necessarily consciously, as when frustration and anxiety lead them to make examples of political and social offenders.) Is guilt so easily gotten rid of? If so, does it not lead to evasion by projecting blame onto someone else? Soyinka's play should also remind us of how little we know of other cultures and how lack of knowledge can lead to attitudes not unlike those of the villagers.

Slave Ship: An Historical Pageant

by Imamu Amiri Baraka

During the 1960s black playwrights began to make considerable impact in the American theatre. Although blacks had been a part of American life since colonial times, they had had little part in the theatre. They had been depicted on stage as servants, slaves, or as song-and-dance performers, but in white companies these roles were played by white actors in blackface. In the 1820s, blacks founded their own theatre in New York, but it did not survive long, largely because of disturbances by white troublemakers. Out of this venture did come one great actor, Ira Aldridge (1807–1867), although because of conditions in America he had to pursue his career in Europe, where he was highly praised and much honored.

In the 1840s a new form of entertainment emerged — the minstrel show — in which the performers represented blacks who sang, danced, exchanged jokes, and did specialty acts. It was to retain its enormous popularity until the 1920s. Eventually there were minstrel companies made up entirely of blacks, but they were forced to imitate the white minstrels with their caricatured blackface makeup, wigs, and costumes, thereby becoming caricatures of caricatures.

In such a theatrical climate, there was little opportunity for the black dramatist. The oldest surviving play by a black author, *The Escape* (1858) by William Wells Brown (c.1816–1884), was not staged; instead, Brown had to content himself by reading his play to literary and abolitionist societies at the very time when *Uncle Tom's Cabin* was the rage of the day.

As blacks moved to New York after 1900, black artists in sizable numbers were brought together for the first time. The result was the Harlem Renaissance. Here the black musical flourished, and by the 1920s was being seen regularly on Broadway (those by Noble Sissle and Eubie Blake were especially popular). Non-musical plays also had some success. Around 1915 a repertory company was established in Harlem, and after World War I plays by and about blacks (among them Willis Richardson's *The Chipwoman's Fortune* and Langston Hughes's *Mulatto*) began to appear on Broadway. Black theatre received a major boost during the 1930s with the formation of the Federal Theatre Project (a part of the Works Progress Administration created by the United States government to reduce unemployment). Black units of the Federal Theatre presented 75 plays during the four years of its life and provided experience for a large number of black writers and actors. But even these units were segregated, and when the Federal Theatre was abolished in 1939, the demand for black writers and performers greatly diminished.

As the battle for civil rights accelerated in the 1950s and 1960s, plays by black dramatists about the black experience also increased. Among the new playwrights, Lorraine Hansberry (1930–1965) made the greatest initial impact with *A Raisin in the Sun* (1959), a compassionate drama about a black family struggling to realize its dreams. But the major impetus for black theatre came in 1963–1964, when the Free Southern Theatre was founded in New Orleans as an extension of the civil rights movement and when LeRoi Jones and others founded the Black Arts Repertoire Theatre School in New York. Other organizations soon followed, and by the late 1960s there were more than 40 similar organizations scattered throughout the country. The most influential of these organizations were the New Lafayette Theatre (located in Harlem) which, until it ceased operation in 1973, served as a clearinghouse for the movement, and the Negro Ensemble Company, which continues to be a major producer of plays by black playwrights in New York.

The proliferation of black theatres created a greatly increased demand for plays by black dramatists. Among these writers, one of the best and probably the most influential was LeRoi Jones (1934–   ). Born in Newark and educated at Rutgers, Howard, and Columbia Universities, Jones edited a literary magazine and wrote poetry and essays before he turned to drama. In 1964 four of his one-act plays were produced off-Broadway and one, *Dutchman*, won an award as the best play of the season. In 1965, Jones broke with his past, took the name Imamu Amiri Baraka (which can be translated as Priest Warrior Blessing), returned to Newark, founded Spirit House as the base for his revolutionary movement, and wrote a manifesto entitled "The Revolutionary Theatre" in which he demanded that theatre force change and "show up the insides of these humans, look into black skulls." He predicted, "White men will cower before this theatre because it hates them." All of his subsequent plays were informed by this manifesto and were militantly antiwhite. They include *Jello, Black Mass, Great Goodness of Life, Bloodrites,* and perhaps most importantly, *Slave Ship* (written in 1967 and produced in 1969).

A drama presented without intermission. The action takes place in the hold of a ship.

CAST

AFRICAN SLAVES *voices of African slaves*
1ST MAN *prayer—husband of* DADEMI
2ND MAN *curser*
3RD MAN *struggler*
1ST WOMAN *prayer*
2ND WOMAN *screamer—attacked*
3RD WOMAN *with child*
DANCERS
MUSICIANS

CHILDREN
Plus voices and bodies in the slave ship
OLD TOM SLAVE
NEW TOM *preacher*
WHITE MEN *voices of white men*
CAPTAIN
SAILOR
PLANTATION OWNER *"Eternal Oppressor"*

PROPS

Smell effects: incense, dirt/filth smells/bodies
Heavy chains
Drums (African bata drums, and bass and snare)
Rattles and tambourines
Banjo music for plantation atmosphere
Ship noises
Ship bells
Rocking and splashing of sea
Guns and cartridges
Whips/whip sounds

Slave Ship

Whole theatre in darkness. Dark. For a long time. Just dark. Occasional sound, like ship groaning, squeaking, rocking. Sea smells. In the dark. Keep the people in the dark, and gradually the odors of the sea, and the sounds of the ship, creep up. Burn incense, but make a significant almost stifling smell come up. Pee. Shit. Death. Life processes going on anyway. Eating. These smells, and cries, the slash and tear of the lash, in a total atmos-feeling, gotten some way.
African drums like the worship of some Orisha. Obatala. Mbwanga rattles of the priests. BamBamBamBamBoom BoomBoom BamBam. Rocking of the slave ship, in darkness, without sound. But smells. Then sound. Now slowly, out of blackness with smells and drums staccato the hideous screams. All the women together, scream: AAAAAIIIIEEEEEEEEEEE. Drums come up again, rocking rocking, black darkness of the slave ship. Smells. Drums go up high. Stop. Scream: AAAAAIIIIEEEEEEEE. Drums. Black darkness with smells.

Chains, the lash, the people moaning. Listen to the sounds come up out of the actors of Black People dragged and thrown down into the hold. AAAAIIIEEEEEEE. Of people, dropped down in the darkness, frightened, angry, mashed together in common terror. The bells of the ship. WHITE MEN'S VOICES, *on top, ready to set sail.*

VOICE 1: Okay, let's go! A good cargo of black gold. Let's go! We head West! We head West. *(Long laughter)* Black gold in the West. We got our full cargo.

V-2: Aye, aye, Cap'n. We're on our way. Riches to be ours, by God.

V-1: Aye, riches riches be ours. We're on our way. America!

(Laughter. There is just dim light at top of set, to indicate where voices are. African drums. With the swiftness of dance, but running into the heaviness the dark enforces. The drums slow. The beat beat of the darkness. "Where are we, God?"

The mumble murmur rattle below. The drone of terror. The voices begin to beat against the dark.)

W-1: Oooooooooo, Obatala!

W-2: Shango!

W-1: Ooooooooooo, Obatala. . . .

(Children's crying in the hold, and the women trying to comfort them. Trying to keep their sanity too.)

W-3: Moshake, chile, calm calm be you. Moshake, chile. O calm Orisha, save us!

W-2: AAAIIIIEEEEEEEEEEE.

M-1: Quiet woman! Quiet. Save your strength for your child.

W-2: AAAIIIIEEEEEEEEEEEE.

M-1: Quite, foolish woman! Be quiet!

W-3: Moshake, baby, chile, be calm, be calm, it give you, oooooo.

M-1: Shango, Obatala, make your lightning, beat the inside bright with paths for your people. Beat Beat Beat.

(Drums come up, but they are walls and floors being beaten. Chains rattled. Chains rattled. Drag the chains.

We get the feeling of many, many people jammed together, men, women, children, aching in the darkness. The chains, the whips, magnify the chains and whips. The dragging together. The pain. The terror.)

(Women begin to moan a chant-song: African sorrow song, with scraping of floor and chains to accompaniment.)

M-2: Fukwididila! Fukwididila! Fukwididila! Fuck you, Orisha! God! Where you be? Where you now, Black God? Help me. I be a strong warrior, and no woman. And I strain against these chains! But you must help me, Orisha. OBATALA!

M-3: Quiet, you fool, you frighten the women!

(Women still chanting, moaning. Children now crying. Mothers trying to comfort them. Feeling of people moving around, tumbling over each other. Screaming as they try to find "a place" in the bottom of the boat, and then the long stream of different wills, articulated as screams, grunts, cries, songs, etc.)

M-3: Pull, pull, break them. Pull.

W-1: Oh. Obatala!

W-3: Oh, chile . . . my chile, please please get away . . . you crush . . . !

M-3: Break . . . Break. . . .

ALL: Uhh, Uhhh, Uhhh, Uhhh, OOOOOOOOOOOOOOOOOO.

WOMEN: AAAAAIIIIIEEEEEEEEE.

ALL: Uhhh, Uhhh, Uhhh, Uhhh, OOOOOOOOOOOOO.

WOMEN: AAAIIIIEEEEEEE.

(Drums down low, like tapping, turns to beating floor, walls, rattling, dragging chains, percussive sounds people make in the hold of a ship. The moans and pushed-together agony. Children crying incessantly. The mothers trying to calm them. More than one child. Young girls afraid they may be violated. Men trying to break out. Or turning into frightened children. Families separated for the first time.)

W-2: Ifanami, Ifanami . . . where you? Where you?? Ifanami *(Cries)* Please, oh God.

M-1: Obata . . .

(Drums beat down, softer . . . humming starts . . . hummmmmm hummmm, like old colored women humming for three centuries in the slow misery of slavery . . . hummmmmmm hummmmmmmmmmmmmmmmmm. Lights flash up on the faces of white men in sailor suits, grinning . . . humming voices down, humming, "hummmmmmmmmm. . . . hummmm . . ." Lights flash on white men in sailor suits grinning their vices . . . voices down, hummmummin . . . hummmmmmmmmmmmmmmmmmmm mmmm. Lights to light white people are sudden, very bright and blinding. The white men begin to laugh and point, as if they were pointing at the filth, misery and degradation of the Black People. They laugh: "HHAAAAAAHAAAHAAHAAHAAHAAHHAA-HAHAHAHAHA." When they are outlined again they are rolling in merriment. Pointing, dancing, jumping up and down. HaHaHa Ha hahaha Haaaa.

Laughter is drowned in the drums. Then the chant-moan of the woman . . . then silence. Then the drums, softer, then the humming, on and on in a maddening, building death-patience, broken

*by the screams, and the babies and the farts, and
the babies crying for light, and young wives
crying for their men. Old people calling for God.
Warriors calling for freedom. Some crying out
against the white man.)*

M-3: Devils! Devils! Devils! White beasts! Shit
eaters! Beasts! *(They beat the walls, and try to tear
chains out of the walls)* White shit eaters.

W-3: Aiiiiieeeeeeeee.

M-1: God, she's killed herself, and the child.
Oh, God. Oh, God.

*(Moans. Moans. Soft drums, and the constant,
now almost maddening humming . . .
hummmmmmmmmmm, hummmmmmmmmmm,
hummmmmmmmmmmm . . . like mad old nigger
ladies humming forever, in deathly patience . . .
hummmmmm hummmmmm hmmm.)*

W-1: She strangled herself with the chain.
Choked the child! Oh, Shango! Help us Lord. Oh,
please.

W-2: Why you leave us, Lord?

M-1: Dademi, Dademi . . . she dead, she dead
. . . Dademi . . . *(Hear man wracked with death
cries, screams)* Dademi, Dademi!!!!

*(Hummmmmmmmmmm, Hummmmmmmmmmmm,
Hummmmmmmmmmmm, Hummmmmmmmm.
Drums low, and moans . . . the chains, and Black
People pushed against each other struggling for
breath and room to live. The Black Man weeps
for his woman. The Black Woman weeps for her
man together in the darkness, some calling for
God.)*

W-2: Oh, please, please don't touch me . . .
Please . . . *(Frantic)* Ifanami, where you? *(Screams
at someone's touch in the dark, grabbing her, trying
to drag her in the darkness, press her down against
the floor)* Akiyele . . . please . . . please . . . don't
don't touch me . . . please. Ifanami, where you?
Please help me. . . . Go . . .

M-1: What you doing? Get away from that
woman. That's not your woman. You turn into a
beast too.

*(Scuffle of two men turning in the darkness trying
to kill each other. Lights show white men
laughing silently, dangling their whips, in
pantomine, still pointing.)*

M-3: Devils. Devils. Cold walking shit.

*(All Mad Sounds Together.
Humming begins again. Bells of ship. Silence. And
moans. And humming. And movement in the
dark, of people. Sliding back and forth. Trying to
stay alive, and now, over it, the constant crazy
laughter of the sailors.)*

SAILORS: AHAHAHAHAHAHAHAHAHA-
HAHAHAAAAA HHHAHAHAHAHAHAHHA
HAHAH.

M-3: I kill you devils. I break these chains
(Sound of men struggling against heavy chains) I
tear your face off. Crush your throat. Devils. Devils.

W-1: Oh, oh, God, she dead . . . and the child.
(Silence. Sound of the sea . . . fades) (Humming)
HMMMMMMMMMMMMMM HMMMMMMM
HMMMMMMMMMMMMMM HMMMMMMMM
HMMMMMMMM HMMMMMMM.

*(Lights on suddenly show a shuffling "Negro."
Lights off . . . drums of ancient African warriors
come up . . . hero-warriors. Lights blink back on
show shuffling Black Man, hat in his hand,
scratching his head. Lights off. Drums again. Black
dancing in the dark, with bells, as if free, dancing
wild old dances. BamBoom Bam Booma Bimbam
Boomama boom beem bam. Dancing in the
darkness . . . Yoruba Dance: Lights flash on briefly,
spot on off the dance. Then off. Then on to show*
THE SLAVE *raggedy ass raggedy hat in hand
shuffling toward the audience, shuffling,
scratching his head and butt. Shaking his head up
and down, agreeing with massa, agreeing, and
agreeing, while the whips snap. Lights off, flash
on, and the sailors, with hats changed to show
them as plantation owners, are still laughing, no
sound, but laughing and pointing, holding their
sides, and they laugh and point.)*

SLAVE: *(In darkness)* Yassa, boss, yassa, massa
Tim, yassa, Boss. *(Lights up)* I'se happy as a brand-
new monkey ass, yassa boss, yassa, mass' Tim, Yass,
mass Booboo, I'se so happy I'se so happy I jus' don'
know what to do. Yass, mas' boa, youse so han'some
and good and youse hip too, yass, I'se so happy I jus'
stan' and scratch my ol nigger haid. *(Lights flash on
slave doing an old-new dance for the boss, when he
finishes he bows and scratches)*

(Lights out . . . the same hummmmmm rises up

. . . with low drums, but the hum grown louder drowns it out . . . hummmmmmhummmmmm hummmmmmhummmmmmmmmmmm. The laughter now drowns out the humming, the same cold, hideous laughter.)

W-3: *(Whispering after death)* Moshake . . . Moshake. . . . Moshake-chile, calm yourself, love *(Woman runs down into soft weep, with no other distracting sound, just her moaning sad cry, for her baby)*

(Chains. Chains. Dragging the chains. The humming. Hummmmmmmmmmmmmmmm.)

WOM: AIEEEEEEEEEEEEEEEEEEEEE.

ALL: Uhh, Uhhh, Uhhh, Uhhh, Oooooooooooooooooo.

*(Silence.
Soft at first, then rising. Banjos of the plantation.)*

SLAVE 1: Reverend, what we gon' do when mass come? *(He sounds afraid)*

SLAVE 2: We gon' cut his fuckin' throat!

(Banjos. Humming. . . . Hummmmmmmmmmm.)

S-1: Reverend, what we gon' do when the white man come?

S-2: We gon' cut his fuckin' throat.

S-3: Devil. Beast. Murderer of women and children. Soulless shit eater.

S-1: Reverend Turner, sir, what we gon' do when the mass come?

S-2: Cut his Godless throat.

(Lights flash up on same tomish slave, still scratching his head, but now apparently talking to a white man.)

SLAVE: Uhh, dass right, massa Time . . . dey gon' 'volt.

WH VO1: What? Vote? Are you crazy?

SLAVE: Nawsaw . . . I said 'volt . . . uhhhh . . . re-volt.

(Laughter now, rising behind the dialogue.)

WH V: When boy?

S: Ahhh, t'night, boss, t'night . . . they say they gon' . . . 'scuse de 'spression . . . cut you . . . uhhh fockin' . . . uhh throat . . .

V: *(Laughs)* And who's in charge of this "'volt"?

S: Uhh . . . Reverend Turner . . . suh . . .

V: What?

S: Uhh . . . das right . . . Reverend Turner . . . suh. . . . Now can I have dat extra chop you promised me??? *(Screams now, as soon as the lights go down)* AIEEEEEEIEIEIEIEIEI.

(Gunshots, combination of slave ship and breakup of the revolt. Voices of master and slaves in combat.)

WH VOICE: I kill you niggahs. You Black savages.

BL VOICE: White Beast. Devil, from hell. *(Voice, now, humming, humming, slow, deathly patient hum)* HUMMMMMMMMMM.

(Drums of Africa and the screams of Black and White in combat. Lights flash on Tom, cringing as if he is hiding from combat, gnawing on pork chop. Voice of white man laughing in triumph. Another chop comes sailing out of the darkness. Tom grabs it and scoffs it down, grinning, and doing the dead-ape shuffle, humming while he eats.)

W-3: *(Dead whispered voice)* Moshake, Moshake . . . chile . . . calm calm . . . We be all right, now . . . Moshake, be calm.

M: White beasts!

ALL: Uhh. Ohhh. Uhhh. Uhhh. Uhhh. *(As if pulling a tremendous weight)* Uhhh. Ohhh. Uhhh. Uhhh. Uhhh.

W: Ifanami. . . .

M-1: Dademi . . . Dademi.

W-2: Akiyele . . . Akiyele. Lord, husband, where you . . . help me.

M: Olabumi . . . Olabumi . . . Touch my hand . . . woman . . .

W: Ifanami!

W: Moshake!

(Now same voices as if transported in time to the slave farms . . . call names, English slave names.)

ALL: *(Alternating* MAN *and* WOMAN *losing mate in death, or thru slavesale, or the aura of constant fear of separation)* "Luke. Oh, my God."

M: Sarah.

W: John. Everett. My God, they killed him.

ALL: Mama, Mama. . . . Nana. Nana. Willie, Ohhh, Lord . . . They done. Uhh. Uhhh. Uhh. Obatala. Obatala. Save Us. Lord. Shango. Lord of forests. Give us back our strength.

(Chains. Chains. Dragging and grunting of people pushed against each other. The sound of a spiritual. "Oh, Lord Deliver Me. . . . Oh Lord" . . . and now cries of "JESUS LORD JESUS . . . HELP US JESUS.")

M-1: Ogun. Give me weapons. Give me iron. My spear. My bone and muscle make them tight with tension of combat. Ogun, give me fire and death to give these beasts. Sarava! Sarava! Ogun.

(Drums of fire and blood briefly loud and smashing against the dark, but now calming, dying down, till only the moans, and then the same patient humming . . . of women now, no men, only the women . . . strains of "The Old Rugged Cross" . . . and only the women and the humming . . . the time passing in the darkness, soft soft mournful weeping. "Jesus . . . Jesus . . . Jesus . . . Jesus . . . Jesus . . . Jesus . . . Jesus . . . Jesus . . . Jesus."
Now lights flash on, and PREACHER in modern business suit stands with hat in his hand. He is the same Tom as before. He stands at first talking to his congregation: "Jesus, Jesus, Jesus, Jesus, Jesus, Jesus," then with a big grin, speaking in the pseudo-intelligent patter he uses for the boss. He tries to be, in fact, assumes he is, dignified, trying to hold his shoulders straight, but only succeeds in giving his entire body an odd slant like a diseased coal shute.)*

PRE: Yasss, we under-stand . . . the problem. And personally I think some agreement can be reached! We will be nonviolenk . . . to the last . . . because we under-stand the dignity of pruty mcbonk and the greasy ghost. Of course diddy rip to bink, of vout juice. And penguins would do the same. I have a trauma, that the gold sewers won't integrate. Present fink. I have an enema . . . a trauma, on the coaster with your wife bird-shit.

W-3: *(Black woman's voice screaming for her child again)* Moshake! Moshake! Moshake . . . beeba . . . beeba . . . Wafwa Ko wafwa ko fukwididila

(Screams moans . . . drums . . . mournful deathtone. . . . The PREACHER looks head turned

just slightly, as if embarrassed, trying still to talk to the white man. Then, one of the Black Men, out of the darkness, comes and sits before the Tom, a wrapped-up bloody corpse of the dead burned baby, as if they had just taken the body from a blown-up church, sets corpse in front of PREACHER. PREACHER stops. Looks up at "person" he's tomming before, then, with his foot, tries to push baby's body behind him, grinning, and jeffing all the time, showing teeth, and being "dignified.")*

PR: Uhherr . . . as I was sayin' . . . Mas' un . . . Mister Tastyslop. . . . We Kneegrows are ready to integrate . . . the blippy rump of stomach bat has corrinked a lip to push the thimble. Yass Yass Yass.

(In the background while preacher is frozen in his "Jeff" position . . . high hard sound of saxophone, backed up by drums. New sound saxophone tearing up the darkness. At height of screaming saxophone, instruments and drums comes voices screaming.)

M: Beasts. Beasts. Beasts. Ogun. Give me spear and iron. Let me kill . . .

(Humming as before . . . long . . . incredible patience, as if it would go on forever, turns into OMMMMMMMMMMMMMMMMMMMMMMMM: all take it up, as the climax rise. Lights down. Ommmmm sound, mixed with sounds of slave ship, saxophone and drums. Sounds of people, thrown against each other, now as if trying all, to rise, pick up. Sounds of people picking up. Like dead people rising. And against that the same sounds of slave ship. White laughter over all of it. White laughter. Song begins to build with the saxophone and drums. First chanted.)

ALL:
Rise, Rise, Rise
  Cut these ties, Black Man, Rise
  We gon' be the thing we are . . .

(Now all sing "When We Gonna Rise" When We Gonna Rise)
When we gonna rise/ up
When we gonna rise/ up
When we gonna rise/ up
When we gonna rise
I mean when we gonna lift our heads and voices

When we gonna show the world who we really
    are
When we gonna rise up, brother
When we gonna rise above the sun
When we gonna take our own place, brother
Like the world had just begun
I mean when we gonna lift our heads and voices
Show the world who we really are
Warrior-Gods, and lovers, the first Men to walk
    this star
Yes, oh, yes, the First Men to walk this star
How far, How long will it be
When the world belongs to you and me
When we gonna rise up, brother
When we gonna rise above the sun
When we gonna take our own place, brother
Like the world had just begun.

*(Drum—new sax—voice arrangement. Bodies
dragging up, in darkness. Lights up on the
preacher in one part of the stage. He stands still
jabbering senselessly to the white man. And the
white man's laughter is heard trying to drown out
the music, but the music is rising.* PREACHER *turns
to look into the darkness at the people dragging
up behind him, embarrassed at first, then
beginning to get frightened. The laughter too
takes on a less arrogant tone.)*

W: Moshake. Moshake.
M: Ogun, give me steel.
ALL: Uhh. Uhh. Ohhh. Uhhh. Uhhh.

*(Humming rising too behind. Still singing "When
We Gonna Rise."* PREACHER *squirms, turns to see,
and suddenly his eyes begin to open very wide,
lights are coming up very slowly, almost
imperceptibly at first. Now singing is beginning to
be heard, mixed with old African drums, and
voices, cries, pushing screams, of the slave ship.*
PREACHER *begins to fidget, as if he does not want
to be where he is. He looks to boss for help. Voice
is breaking, as lights come up and we see all the
people in the slave ship in Miracles'/Temptations'
dancing line. Some doing African dance. Some
doing new Boogaloo, but all moving toward*
PREACHER, *and toward voice. It is a new-old
Boogalooyoruba line, women children all moving
popping fingers all singing, and drummers, beating*

*out old and new, and moving all moving. Finally
the* PREACHER *begins to cringe and plead for help
from the white voice.)*

PRE: Please, boss, these niggers goin' crazy,
please, boss, throw yo lightnin' at 'em, white Jesus
boss, white light god, they goin' crazy! Help!
VOICE: *(Coughing as if choking on something, trying to laugh because sight of* PREACHER *is
funny . . . still managing to laugh at* PREACHER*)* Fool.
Fool.
PR: Please, boss, please . . . I do anything for
you . . . you know that, boss . . . Please . . . please . . .

*(All group merge on him and kill him daid. Then
they turn in the direction of where the voice is
coming from. Dancing, singing, right on toward
the now pleading* VOICE.*)*

VOICE: HaaHaaHaaHaa *(Laugh gets stuck in
his throat)* Uhh . . . now what . . . you' haha can't
touch me . . . you scared of me, niggers. I'm god.
You cain't kill white Jesus God. I got long blonde
blow hair. I don't even need to wear a wig. You love
the way I look. You want to look like me. You love
me. You want me. Please. I'm good. I'm kind. I'll
give you anything you want. I'm white Jesus
saviour right God pay you money nigger me is good
God be please . . . please don't . . .

*(Lights begin to fade . . . drums and voices of old
slave ship come back.)*

ALL: Uhh. Ohh. Uhh. Ohh. Uhh. Ohh. Uhh.
Ohh. *(And then the terrible humming, turning to
the   OMMMMMMMMMMMMMmmmmmmm-
mmm sound, broken now by the finally awful
scream of the killed white voice)* AWHAWHAEHA-
HWAWHWHAHW.

*(All players fixed in half light, at the moment of
the act. Then lights go down. Black.
Lights come up abruptly, and people onstage begin
to dance, same hip Boogalyoruba, fingerpop, skate,
monkey, dog. Enter audience, get members of
audience to dance. To same music* RISE UP.
*Turns into an actual party. When the party
reaches some loose improvisation, etc., audience
relaxed, somebody throws the preachers head into
center of floor, i.e., after the dancing starts for
real. Then black.)*

As its subtitle, "an historical pageant," suggests, *Slave Ship* is not conceived as a play in the traditional sense but rather as a spectacle illustrating aspects of a social institution. It sketches American black-white relationships from the first slave trade to the present; it covers a wide sweep of time and uses generalized types of groups instead of individualized characters to tell its story.

The action is developed in four discernible steps. In the first, blacks are transported from Africa to America. In terms of the play's theme, this step is the most important one, since, as the title indicates, Baraka uses the slave ship as a symbol for the black American experience — physical entrapment, brutalization, violent and inhumane treatment. Baraka wishes the audience to feel the experience of slavery: the pitch-black hold of the ship with bodies crowded together and chained to the walls; the disbelief, rage, and despair; the separation of families, sexual violation, and death; the sounds, smells, and claustrophobia; and, above all, the sufferings of blacks at the hands of unfeeling, jeering whites. In this part, the African origin of blacks is emphasized in the characters' names and the gods they call upon.

Once the atmosphere and sensations of the slave ship have been established, the second phase of the action begins — black slavery in America. The African heritage now begins to fade as slaves are given new names, new living patterns, and a new religion. Nevertheless, the essential responses of those subjected to slavery do not change, although they may be disguised in the interest of survival. An important new element is the black who collaborates with whites and betrays his own people for the petty reward of a pork chop. (Baraka associates this type of black with Uncle Tom.)

The third step shows conditions after the slaves have been freed. Uncle Tom has now become a preacher, trying to keep his people calm and assuring whites that blacks are anxious to integrate. He accepts whites as appropriate models of behavior, parroting their language, which he does not fully understand, with the result that he speaks sacrilegious and obscene nonsense. When the blacks, no longer willing to remain subservient, seek to obtain their constitutionally guaranteed civil rights, their churches (with children inside) are burned by whites. The blacks place the charred body of a baby before the preacher to show him what is happening, but he merely kicks it away so whites will not have to look at it. Peaceful methods having failed, the blacks begin a destructive sweep, first killing the black preacher and then the whites who have considered themselves too powerful to be punished. Thus, retribution and justice assert themselves.

The fourth and final step is one of celebration combined with an attempt to unite the audience through acquiescence to the justness of the black cause and rejection of all that is white. It also implies, when the preacher's head is thrown onto the stage, that blacks who cooperate with whites should be destroyed.

The power of *Slave Ship* derives in large part from oversimplification. All whites are depicted as evil and as guilty of the sins associated with slavery; all blacks, insofar as they have remained faithful to their black heritage and have set themselves against whites, are good and heroic. The play implies that there is an irremediable enmity between black and white, and it demands punishment for the sins committed by whites against blacks.

Slave Ship also derives its power from production elements, especially the manipulation of sound to create the sense of confinement, suffering, and atrocity, and the human (black) and inhuman (white) response to the slave experience. In its use of theatrical means, *Slave Ship* exemplifies a type of play common during the 1960s (not only black plays but others about injustices or various social causes), one which used visual and aural devices to support a point of view and to urge action to overcome problems.

Slave Ship was written for black audiences (although many whites saw it). It sought to remind them forcefully of the injustices they had suffered and to promote unified support for black causes. It also sought to make blacks see whites as their natural enemies, a view that offended many whites who were working to correct inequities and who resented being grouped with die-hard segregationists and haters of blacks; to them the play's message appeared as racist as that of the white characters.

The play, then, raised significant issues about guilt and responsibility. To what extent should we be held responsible for the sins and mistakes of our parents and grandparents? Must all members of a ruling group accept responsibility for that group's treatment of other groups? Many of the laws and regulations of the 1960s and 1970s were intended to right past wrongs, to give minorities preference in certain situations in an attempt to let them make up for decades of lost opportunities. Inevitably, many whites felt that they had become victims of reverse discrimination. Thus, the attempts to right past wrongs became (and remain) issues heatedly debated. Is it possible to make amends for or to wipe out the injustices and inequities of the past? Do attempts to make amends create new inequities which in their turn will haunt future generations?

Clearly the inequities inherited from the past have not been fully corrected. Until we discover means to achieve harmony between blacks and whites, we must live with the serious problems created by slavery and its aftermath. *Slave Ship* suggests one solution to the problems, but undoubtedly there are other possibilities.

Buried Child

by Sam Shepard

Throughout most of the twentieth century, the hallmark of success for dramatists in America has been a long run on Broadway. But economic realities have never permitted Broadway producers to choose plays solely on the basis of excellence; high production costs have forced even the best of producers to restrict their choices to plays thought capable of attracting an audience sufficiently large to repay their investment. Broadway has also been relatively conservative in its choice of plays because the high price of tickets has tended to limit its audience to the relatively affluent, and the need to attract large numbers of spectators has made producers wary of controversial or difficult plays.

Around 1950 the limitations of Broadway motivated the establishment of what came to be called Off-Broadway. By playing in out-of-the-way theatres or improvised auditoriums, production costs could be cut considerably, and works that would not appeal to a large audience could be played for a more restricted group. The major upturn in the prestige of Off-Broadway came in 1952 when Tennessee Williams's *Summer and Smoke* (a failure on Broadway) was presented there to high critical acclaim. Soon Off-Broadway was viewed as a workable alternative to Broadway's commercialism. By 1955–1956, there were more than 90 Off-Broadway companies, and they, rather than Broadway, became the primary producers of works by Brecht, Beckett, Ionesco, and other new European and American playwrights.

Unfortunately, by the early 1960s the Off-Broadway theatre was feeling many of the same economic pressures that had affected Broadway as production costs soared and unions demanded new employment rules and higher wages for their members. Consequently, a new solution had to be found. The result was Off-Off-Broadway, which came into being as plays were presented in coffee houses, lofts, and other spaces never intended for theatrical performances. Budgets were infinitesimal since participants usually were not paid. By 1965 some 400 plays by more than 200 playwrights had been seen Off-Off-Broadway. Since that time, Off-Off-Broadway has undergone many changes as it has sought to evade the regulations and restrictions that govern more established companies. In the early 1980s there were about 150 Off-Off-Broadway groups of one sort or another and together they were producing about 50 plays per week. They varied enormously in their goals and in the quality of their work, but they greatly diversified the theatre. Perhaps most important, they created a demand for large numbers of plays.

Reprinted by permission of the author.

It is significant that the Off-Off-Broadway theatre came into existence just at the time when dissatisfaction over racial discrimination, the Vietnam war, and other social and political issues were creating antiestablishment coalitions and alternative life-styles. As accepted ideas, long-standing moral standards, and conservative conventions of behavior and dress were rejected, society became increasingly fragmented. Many young playwrights associated with Off-Off-Broadway were members of the counterculture that developed out of the new values. Their changed perspective led them to reject the long run on Broadway as a criterion of success. They also did much to shift American drama toward experimentation with form and toward disaffection from the behavioral standards of the past. Many abandoned the cause-to-effect arrangement of incidents (leading from exposition to complications, crisis, and resolution) in favor of organizational patterns more nearly musical (that is, the presentation of a theme and variations on it). Many of the plays were episodic and loosely organized, and most rejected earlier strictures on acceptable subject matter, behavior, and language. Among the notable changes were the introduction of nudity and obscenity, both of which made their first impact in 1968 in the musical, *Hair*. By the early 1970s, although the limits of permissibility were still somewhat vague, almost any subject, behavior, and language had become possible on the stage.

Freedom from strictures opened opportunities for many dramatists whose plays otherwise would not have been performed, but the rejection of established standards also meant that many young dramatists did not feel any need to perfect their work. Consequently, numerous playwrights failed to live up to their early promise and, despite the great number of dramatists whose works were produced, few achieved widespread recognition.

Of the writers who emerged from Off-Off-Broadway, one of the best has been Sam Shepard (1943–   ). Because his father was in the Army, Shepard was moved about frequently during his childhood — from Illinois to South Dakota, Utah, Florida, Guam, and, upon his father's retirement, to Southern California. His earliest literary influences came from the writers of the "beat generation" — Kerouac, Ferlinghetti, and Corso. In his late teens, Shepard worked his way across country by performing in a repertory company. Soon after arriving in New York he began writing plays and received his first production in 1964 (just prior to his twenty-first birthday) at Theatre Genesis, an Off-Off-Broadway theatre. He was extremely prolific, sometimes writing an entire play in a few hours. Many of these early plays have been lost.

When Shepard began writing he had read few plays and had no firm notion of what a play should be. He has said that he usually began with a visual image and merely wrote as things came to him. He also did little rewriting: "I used to be dead set against rewriting on any level. My attitude was that if the play had faults, those faults were part and parcel of the original process, and that any attempt to correct them was cheating."[1] These plays were characterized by their

---

[1] "Language, Visualization, and the Inner Library," *American Dreams: The Imagination of Sam Shepard*, ed. Bonnie Marranca (New York: Performing Arts Journal Publications, 1981), p. 218.

originality of form, vivid verbal and visual imagery, lengthy monologues, popular-culture myths, rapid shifts in action and mood, the absence of psychologically motivated transitions, and the intermingling of the realistic and nonrealistic. These traits often made interpretation of the plays difficult, although their dramatic intensity was always evident.

During a stay in England in the early 1970s, Shepard became aware of the need for greater discipline in his writing. Since that time he has placed greater emphasis on story line and overall cohesiveness. Shepard has remained wary of discussing the meaning of what he writes and insists that his plays should be approached intuitively rather than as conveyors of messages. Nevertheless, a number of themes and motifs recur in his plays, among the most common being depiction of the world as battered or broken and the family environment as a battle zone; characters who are alienated from society, whose expectations are few, and who are caught between empty dreams and insubstantial reality; the cowboy as the quintessential American; attempts to create protective environments as insulation against unpleasant truths; and attempts to escape or deny the past. Thus, although it is not possible to arrive at precise interpretations of Shepard's plays, it is possible to see in them a rather specific vision of the contemporary world.

Shepard's better-known plays include *Chicago, Icarus' Mother, La Turista, Operation Sidewinder, The Mad Dog Blues, The Unseen Hand, Seduced, Suicide in B-Flat, The Tooth of Crime, Geography of a Horse Dreamer, Angel City, Curse of the Starving Class, Buried Child,* and *True West.* Most of Shepard's early plays were produced Off-Off-Broadway, but in recent years he has worked closely with the Magic Theatre in San Francisco. He has directed a number of his own plays and has written for and acted in films.

Buried Child, chosen for inclusion here, was first performed in 1978 and was awarded the Pulitzer Prize in 1979.

While the rain of your fingertips falls, while the rain of your bones falls, and your laughter and marrow fall down, you come flying.
                    Pablo Neruda

CHARACTERS

DODGE *In his seventies*
HALIE *His wife. Mid-sixties*
TILDEN *Their oldest son*
BRADLEY *Their next oldest son, an amputee*

VINCE *Tilden's son*
SHELLY *Vince's girl friend*
FATHER DEWIS *A Protestant minister*

ACT I

SCENE

Day. Old wooden staircase down left with pale, frayed carpet laid down on the steps. The stairs lead off stage left up into the wings with no landing. Up right is an old, dark green sofa with the stuffing coming out in spots. Stage right of the sofa is an upright lamp with a faded yellow shade and a small night table with several small bottles of pills on it. Down right of the sofa, with the screen facing the sofa, is a large, old-fashioned brown T.V. A flickering blue light comes from the screen, but no image, no sound. In the dark, the light of the lamp and the T.V. slowly brighten in the black space. The space behind the sofa, upstage, is a large, screened-in porch with a board floor. A solid interior door to stage right of the sofa, leading into the room on stage; and another screen door up left, leading from the porch to the outside. Beyond that are the shapes of dark elm trees.

Gradually the form of DODGE *is made out, sitting on the couch, facing the T.V., the blue light flickering on his face. He wears a well-worn T-shirt, suspenders, khaki work pants and brown slippers. He's covered himself in an old brown blanket. He's very thin and sickly looking, in his late seventies. He just stares at the T.V. More light fills the stage softly. The sound of light rain.* DODGE *slowly tilts his head back and stares at the ceiling for a while, listening to the rain. He lowers his head again and stares at the T.V. He turns his head slowly to the left and stares at the cushion of the sofa next to the one he's sitting on. He pulls his left arm out from under the blanket, slides his hand under the cushion, and pulls out a bottle of whiskey. He looks down left toward the staircase, listens, then uncaps the bottle, takes a long swig and caps it again. He puts the bottle back under the cushion and stares at the T.V. He starts to cough slowly and softly. The coughing gradually builds. He holds one hand to his mouth and tries to stifle it. The coughing gets louder, then suddenly stops when he hears the sound of his wife's voice coming from the top of the staircase.*

HALIE'S VOICE: Dodge?

*(*DODGE *just stares at the T.V. Long pause. He stifles two short coughs.)*

HALIE'S VOICE: Dodge! You want a pill, Dodge?

(He doesn't answer. Takes the bottle out again and takes another long swig. Puts the bottle back, stares at T.V., pulls blanket up around his neck.)

HALIE'S VOICE: You know what it is, don't you? It's the rain! Weather. That's it. Every time. Every time you get like this, it's the rain. No sooner does the rain start then you start. (Pause) Dodge?

(He makes no reply. Pulls a pack of cigarettes out from his sweater and lights one. Stares at T.V. Pause)

HALIE'S VOICE: You should see it coming down up here. Just coming down in sheets. Blue sheets. The bridge is pretty near flooded. What's it like down there? Dodge?

DODGE *turns his head back over his left shoulder and takes a look out through the porch. He turns back to the T.V.*

DODGE: *(To himself)* Catastrophic.
HALIE'S VOICE: What? What'd you say, Dodge?
DODGE: *(Louder)* It looks like rain to me! Plain old rain!
HALIE'S VOICE: Rain? Of course it's rain! Are you having a seizure or something! Dodge? *(Pause)* I'm coming down there in about five minutes if you don't answer me!
DODGE: Don't come down.
HALIE'S VOICE: What!
DODGE: *(Louder)* Don't come down!

(He has another coughing attack. Stops.)

HALIE'S VOICE: You should take a pill for that! I don't see why you just don't take a pill. Be done with it once and for all. Put a stop to it.

(He takes bottle out again. Another swig. Returns bottle.)

HALIE'S VOICE: It's not Christian, but it works. It's not necessarily Christian, that is. We don't know. There's some things the ministers can't even answer. I, personally, can't see anything wrong with it. Pain is pain. Pure and simple. Suffering is a different matter. That's entirely different. A pill seems as good an answer as any. Dodge? *(Pause)* Dodge, are you watching baseball?

DODGE: No.

HALIE'S VOICE: What?

DODGE: *(Louder)* No!

HALIE'S VOICE: What're you watching? You shouldn't be watching anything that'll get you excited! No horse racing!

DODGE: They don't race on Sundays.

HALIE'S VOICE: What?

DODGE: *(Louder)* They don't race on Sundays!

HALIE'S VOICE: Well they shouldn't race on Sundays.

DODGE: Well they don't!

HALIE'S VOICE: Good. I'm amazed they still have that kind of legislation. That's amazing.

DODGE: Yeah, it's amazing.

HALIE'S VOICE: What?

DODGE: *(Louder)* It is amazing!

HALIE'S VOICE: It is. It truly is. I would've thought these days they'd be racing on Christmas even. A big flashing Christmas tree right down at the finish line.

DODGE: *(Shakes his head)* No.

HALIE'S VOICE: They used to race on New Year's! I remember that.

DODGE: They never raced on New Year's!

HALIE'S VOICE: Sometimes they did.

DODGE: They never did!

HALIE'S VOICE: Before we were married they did!

(DODGE waves his hand in disgust at the staircase. Leans back in sofa. Stares at T.V.)

HALIE'S VOICE: I went once. With a man.

DODGE: *(Mimicking her)* Oh, a "man."

HALIE'S VOICE: What?

DODGE: Nothing!

HALIE'S VOICE: A wonderful man. A breeder.

DODGE: A what?

HALIE'S VOICE: A breeder! A horse breeder! Thoroughbreds.

DODGE: Oh, Thoroughbreds. Wonderful.

HALIE'S VOICE: That's right. He knew everything there was to know.

DODGE: I bet he taught you a thing or two huh? Gave you a good turn around the old stable!

HALIE'S VOICE: Knew everything there was to know about horses. We won bookoos of money that day.

DODGE: What?

HALIE'S VOICE: Money! We won every race I think.

DODGE: Bookoos?

HALIE'S VOICE: Every single race.

DODGE: Bookoos of money?

HALIE'S VOICE: It was one of those kind of days.

DODGE: New Year's!

HALIE'S VOICE: Yes! It might've been Florida. Or California! One of those two.

DODGE: Can I take my pick?

HALIE'S VOICE: It was Florida!

DODGE: Aha!

HALIE'S VOICE: Wonderful! Absolutely wonderful! The sun was just gleaming. Flamingos. Bougainvilleas. Palm trees.

DODGE: *(To himself, mimicking her)* Bougainvilleas. Palm trees.

HALIE'S VOICE: Everything was dancing with life! There were all kinds of people from everywhere. Everyone was dressed to the nines. Not like today. Not like they dress today.

DODGE: When was this anyway?

HALIE'S VOICE: This was long before I knew you.

DODGE: Must've been.

HALIE'S VOICE: Long before. I was escorted.

DODGE: To Florida?

HALIE'S VOICE: Yes. Or it might've been California. I'm not sure which.

DODGE: All that way you were escorted?

HALIE'S VOICE: Yes.

DODGE: And he never laid a finger on you I suppose? *(Long silence)* Halie?

(No answer. Long pause.)

HALIE'S VOICE: Are you going out today?

DODGE: (Gesturing toward rain) In this?

HALIE'S VOICE: I'm just asking a simple question.

DODGE: I rarely go out in the bright sunshine, why would I go out in this?

HALIE'S VOICE: I'm just asking because I'm not doing any shopping today. And if you need anything you should ask Tilden.

DODGE: Tilden's not here!

HALIE'S VOICE: He's in the kitchen.

(DODGE looks toward stage left, then back toward T.V.)

DODGE: All right.

HALIE'S VOICE: What?

DODGE: (Louder) All right!

HALIE'S VOICE: Don't scream. It'll only get your coughing started.

DODGE: All right.

HALIE'S VOICE: Just tell Tilden what you want and he'll get it. (Pause) Bradley should be over later.

DODGE: Bradley?

HALIE'S VOICE: Yes. To cut your hair.

DODGE: My hair? I don't need my hair cut!

HALIE'S VOICE: It won't hurt!

DODGE: I don't need it!

HALIE'S VOICE: It's been more than two weeks Dodge.

DODGE: I don't need it!

HALIE'S VOICE: I have to meet Father Dewis for lunch.

DODGE: You tell Bradley that if he shows up here with those clippers, I'll kill him!

HALIE'S VOICE: I won't be very late. No later than four at the very latest.

DODGE: You tell him! Last time he left me almost bald! And I wasn't even awake! I was sleeping! I woke up and he'd already left!

HALIE'S VOICE: That's not my fault!

DODGE: You put him up to it!

HALIE'S VOICE: I never did!

DODGE: You did too! You had some fancy, stupid meeting planned! Time to dress up the corpse for company! Lower the ears a little! Put up a little front! Surprised you didn't tape a pipe to my mouth while you were at it! That woulda' looked nice! Huh? A pipe? Maybe a bowler hat! Maybe a copy of the Wall Street Journal casually placed on my lap!

HALIE'S VOICE: You always imagine the worst things of people!

DODGE: That's not the worst! That's the least of the worst!

HALIE'S VOICE: I don't need to hear it! All day long I hear things like that and I don't need to hear more.

DODGE: You better tell him!

HALIE'S VOICE: You tell him yourself! He's your own son. You should be able to talk to your own son.

DODGE: Not while I'm sleeping! He cut my hair while I was sleeping!

HALIE'S VOICE: Well he won't do it again.

DODGE: There's no guarantee.

HALIE'S VOICE: I promise he won't do it without your consent.

DODGE: (After pause) There's no reason for him to even come over here.

HALIE'S VOICE: He feels responsible.

DODGE: For my hair?

HALIE'S VOICE: For your appearance.

DODGE: My appearance is out of his domain! It's even out of mine! In fact, it's disappeared! I'm an invisible man!

HALIE'S VOICE: Don't be ridiculous.

DODGE: He better not try it. That's all I've got to say.

HALIE'S VOICE: Tilden will watch out for you.

DODGE: Tilden won't protect me from Bradley!

HALIE'S VOICE: Tilden's the oldest. He'll protect you.

DODGE: Tilden can't even protect himself!

HALIE'S VOICE: Not so loud! He'll hear you. He's right in the kitchen.

DODGE: (Yelling off left) Tilden!

HALIE'S VOICE: Dodge, what are you trying to do?

DODGE: (Yelling off left) Tilden, get in here!

HALIE'S VOICE: Why do you enjoy stirring things up?

DODGE: I don't enjoy anything!

HALIE'S VOICE: That's a terrible thing to say.

DODGE: Tilden!

HALIE'S VOICE: That's the kind of statement that leads people right to the end of their rope.

DODGE: Tilden!

HALIE'S VOICE: It's no wonder people turn to Christ!

DODGE: TILDEN!!

HALIE'S VOICE: It's no wonder the messengers of God's word are shouted down in public places!

DODGE: TILDEN!!!!

(DODGE *goes into a violent, spasmodic coughing attack as* TILDEN *enters from stage left, his arms loaded with fresh ears of corn.* TILDEN *is* DODGE'S *oldest son, late forties, wears heavy construction boots, covered with mud, dark green work pants, a plaid shirt and a faded brown windbreaker. He has a butch haircut, wet from the rain. Something about him is profoundly burned out and displaced. He stops center stage with the ears of corn in his arms and just stares at Dodge until he slowly finishes his coughing attack.* DODGE *looks up at him slowly. He stares at the corn. Long pause as they watch each other.*)

HALIE'S VOICE: Dodge, if you don't take that pill nobody's going to force you.

(*The two men ignore the voice.*)

DODGE: (*To* TILDEN) Where'd you get that?
TILDEN: Picked it.
DODGE: You picked all that?

(TILDEN *nods.*)

DODGE: You expecting company?
TILDEN: No.
DODGE: Where'd you pick it from?
TILDEN: Right out back.
DODGE: Out back where!
TILDEN: Right out in back.
DODGE: There's nothing out there!
TILDEN: There's corn.
DODGE: There hasn't been corn out there since about nineteen thirty five! That's the last time I planted corn out there!
TILDEN: It's out there now.
DODGE: (*Yelling at stairs*) Halie!
HALIE'S VOICE: Yes dear!
DODGE: Tilden's brought a whole bunch of corn in here! There's no corn out in back is there?
TILDEN: (*To himself*) There's tons of corn.
HALIE'S VOICE: Not that I know of!
DODGE: That's what I thought.
HALIE'S VOICE: Not since about nineteen thirty five!

DODGE: (*To* TILDEN) That's right. Nineteen thirty five.
TILDEN: It's out there now.
DODGE: You go and take that corn back to wherever you got it from!
TILDEN: (*After pause, staring at* DODGE) It's picked. I picked it all in the rain. Once it's picked you can't put it back.
DODGE: I haven't had trouble with neighbors here for fifty-seven years. I don't even know who the neighbors are! And I don't wanna know! Now go put that corn back where it came from!

(TILDEN *stares at* DODGE *then walks slowly over to him and dumps all the corn on* DODGE'S *lap and steps back.* DODGE *stares at the corn then back to* TILDEN. *Long pause.*)

DODGE: Are you having trouble here, Tilden? Are you in some kind of trouble?
TILDEN: I'm not in any trouble.
DODGE: You can tell me if you are. I'm still your father.
TILDEN: I know you're still my father.
DODGE: I know you had a little trouble back in New Mexico. That's why you came out here.
TILDEN: I never had any trouble.
DODGE: Tilden, your mother told me all about it.
TILDEN: What'd she tell you?

(TILDEN *pulls some chewing tobacco out of his jacket and bites off a plug.*)

DODGE: I don't have to repeat what she told me! She told me all about it!
TILDEN: Can I bring my chair in from the kitchen?
DODGE: What?
TILDEN: Can I bring in my chair from the kitchen?
DODGE: Sure. Bring your chair in.

(TILDEN *exits left.* DODGE *pushes all the corn off his lap onto the floor. He pulls the blanket off angrily and tosses it at one end of the sofa, pulls out the bottle and takes another swig.* TILDEN *enters again from left with a milking stool and a pail.* DODGE *hides the bottle quickly under the cushion before* TILDEN *sees it.* TILDEN *sets the stool down by the sofa, sits on it, puts the pail in front of him on the floor.* TILDEN *starts picking up the ears of corn one at a time and husking them. He throws the husks and silk in the center of the stage and drops the ears into the pail each time he cleans one. He repeats this process as they talk.)*

DODGE: *(After pause)* Sure is nice-looking corn.

TILDEN: It's the best.

DODGE: Hybrid?

TILDEN: What?

DODGE: Some kinda fancy hybrid?

TILDEN: You planted it. I don't know what it is.

DODGE: *(Pause)* Tilden, look, you can't stay here forever. You know that, don't you?

TILDEN: *(Spits in spittoon)* I'm not.

DODGE: I know you're not. I'm not worried about that. That's not the reason I brought it up.

TILDEN: What's the reason?

DODGE: The reason is I'm wondering what you're gonna do.

TILDEN: You're not worried about me, are you?

DODGE: I'm not worried about you.

TILDEN: You weren't worried about me when I wasn't here. When I was in New Mexico.

DODGE: No, I wasn't worried about you then either.

TILDEN: You shoulda worried about me then.

DODGE: Why's that? You didn't do anything down there, did you?

TILDEN: I didn't do anything.

DODGE: Then why should I have worried about you?

TILDEN: Because I was lonely.

DODGE: Because you were lonely?

TILDEN: Yeah. I was more lonely than I've ever been before.

DODGE: Why was that?

TILDEN: *(Pause)* Could I have some of that whiskey you've got?

DODGE: What whiskey? I haven't got any whiskey.

TILDEN: You've got some under the sofa.

DODGE: I haven't got anything under the sofa! Now mind your own damn business! Jesus God, you come into the house outa the middle of nowhere, haven't heard or seen you in twenty years and suddenly you're making accusations.

TILDEN: I'm not making accusations.

DODGE: You're accusing me of hoarding whiskey under the sofa!

TILDEN: I'm not accusing you.

DODGE: You just got through telling me I had whiskey under the sofa!

HALIE'S VOICE: Dodge?

DODGE: *(To TILDEN)* Now she knows about it!

TILDEN: She doesn't know about it.

HALIE'S VOICE: Dodge, are you talking to yourself down there?

DODGE: I'm talking to Tilden!

HALIE'S VOICE: Tilden's down there?

DODGE: He's right here!

HALIE'S VOICE: What?

DODGE: *(Louder)* He's right here!

HALIE'S VOICE: What's he doing?

DODGE: *(To TILDEN)* Don't answer her.

TILDEN: *(To DODGE)* I'm not doing anything wrong.

DODGE: I know you're not.

HALIE'S VOICE: What's he doing down there!

DODGE: *(To TILDEN)* Don't answer.

TILDEN: I'm not.

HALIE'S VOICE: Dodge!

(The men sit in silence. DODGE *lights a cigarette.* TILDEN *keeps husking corn, spits tobacco now and then in spittoon.)*

HALIE'S VOICE: Dodge! He's not drinking anything, is he? You see to it that he doesn't drink anything! You've gotta watch out for him. It's our responsibility. He can't look after himself anymore, so we have to do it. Nobody else will do it. We can't just send him away somewhere. If we had lots of money we could send him away. But we don't. We never will. That's why we have to stay healthy. You and me. Nobody's going to look after us. Bradley can't look after us. Bradley can hardly look after himself. I was always hoping that Tilden would look out for Bradley when they got older. After Bradley lost his leg. Tilden's the oldest. I always thought he'd be the one to take responsibility. I had no idea in the world that Tilden would be so much trouble. Who would've dreamed. Tilden was an All-American, don't forget. Don't forget that. Fullback. Or quarterback. I forget which.

TILDEN: *(To himself)* Fullback. *(Still husking)*

HALIE'S VOICE: Then when Tilden turned out to be so much trouble, I put all my hopes on

Ansel. Of course Ansel wasn't as handsome, but he was smart. He was the smartest probably. I think he probably was. Smarter than Bradley, that's for sure. Didn't go and chop his leg off with a chain saw. Smart enough not to go and do that. I think he was smarter than Tilden too. Especially after Tilden got in all that trouble. Doesn't take brains to go to jail. Anybody knows that. Course then when Ansel died that left us all alone. Same as being alone. No different. Same as if they'd all died. He was the smartest. He could've earned lots of money. Lots and lots of money.

(HALIE *enters slowly from the top of the staircase as she continues talking. Just her feet are seen at first as she makes her way down the stairs, a step at a time. She appears dressed completely in black, as though in mourning. Black handbag, hat with a veil, and pulling on elbow length black gloves. She is about sixty-five, with pure white hair. She remains absorbed in what she's saying as she descends the stairs and doesn't really notice the two men who continue sitting there as they were before she came down, smoking and husking.)*

HALIE: He would've took care of us, too. He would've seen to it that we were repaid. He was like that. He was a hero. Don't forget that. A genuine hero. Brave. Strong. And very intelligent. Ansel could've been a great man. One of the greatest. I only regret that he didn't die in action. It's not fitting for a man like that to die in a motel room. A soldier. He could've won a medal. He could've been decorated for valor. I've talked to Father Dewis about putting up a plaque for Ansel. He thinks it's a good idea. He agrees. He knew Ansel when he used to play basketball. Went to every game. Ansel was his favorite player. He even recommended to the City Council that they put up a statue of Ansel. A big, tall statue with a basketball in one hand and a rifle in the other. That's how much he thinks of Ansel.

(HALIE *reaches the stage and begins to wander around, still absorbed in pulling on her gloves, brushing lint off her dress and continuously talking to herself as the men just sit.)*

HALIE: Of course, he'd still be alive today if he hadn't married into the Catholics. The Mob. How in the world he never opened his eyes to that is beyond me. Just beyond me. Everyone around

him could see the truth. Even Tilden. Tilden told him time and again. Catholic women are the Devil incarnate. He wouldn't listen. He was blind with love. Blind. I knew. Everyone knew. The wedding was more like a funeral. You remember? All those Italians. All that horrible black, greasy hair. The smell of cheap cologne. I think even the priest was wearing a pistol. When he gave her the ring I knew he was a dead man. I knew it. As soon as he gave her the ring. But then it was the honeymoon that killed him. The honeymoon. I knew he'd never come back from the honeymoon. I kissed him and he felt like a corpse. All white. Cold. Icy blue lips. He never used to kiss like that. Never before. I knew then that she'd cursed him. Taken his soul. I saw it in her eyes. She smiled at me with that Catholic sneer of hers. She told me with her eyes that she'd murder him in his bed. Murder my son. She told me. And there was nothing I could do. Absolutely nothing. He was going with her, thinking he was free. Thinking it was love. What could I do? I couldn't tell him she was a witch. I couldn't tell him that. He'd have turned on me. Hated me. I couldn't stand him hating me and then dying before he ever saw me again. Hating me in his death bed. Hating me and loving her! How could I do that? I had to let him go. I had to. I watched him leave. I watched him throw gardenias as he helped her into the limousine. I watched his face disappear behind the glass.

(She stops abruptly and stares at the corn husks. She looks around the space as though just waking up. She turns and looks hard at TILDEN and DODGE who continue sitting calmly. She looks again at the corn husks.)

HALIE: *(Pointing to the husks)* What's this in my house! *(Kicks husks)* What's all this!

(TILDEN *stops husking and stares at her.)*

HALIE: *(To DODGE)* And you encourage him!

(DODGE *pulls blanket over him again.)*

DODGE: You're going out in the rain?
HALIE: It's not raining.

(TILDEN *starts husking again.)*

DODGE: Not in Florida it's not.
HALIE: We're not in Florida!
DODGE: It's not raining at the race track.

HALIE: Have you been taking those pills? Those pills always make you talk crazy. Tilden, has he been taking those pills?

TILDEN: He hasn't took anything.

HALIE: *(To DODGE)* What've you been taking?

DODGE: It's not raining in California or Florida or the race track. Only in Illinois. This is the only place it's raining. All over the rest of the world it's bright golden sunshine.

(HALIE goes to the night table next to the sofa and checks the bottle of pills.)

HALIE: Which ones did you take? Tilden, you must've seen him take something.

TILDEN: He never took a thing.

HALIE: Then why's he talking crazy?

TILDEN: I've been here the whole time.

HALIE: Then you've both been taking something!

TILDEN: I've just been husking the corn.

HALIE: Where'd you get that corn anyway? Why is the house suddenly full of corn?

DODGE: Bumper crop!

HALIE: *(Moving center)* We haven't had corn here for over thirty years.

TILDEN: The whole back lot's full of corn. Far as the eye can see.

DODGE: *(To HALIE)* Things keep happening while you're upstairs, ya know. The world doesn't stop just because you're upstairs. Corn keeps growing. Rain keeps raining.

HALIE: I'm not unaware of the world around me! Thank you very much. It so happens that I have an over-all view from the upstairs. The back yard's in plain view of my window. And there's no corn to speak of. Absolutely none!

DODGE: Tilden wouldn't lie. If he says there's corn, there's corn.

HALIE: What's the meaning of this corn Tilden!

TILDEN: It's a mystery to me. I was out in back there. And the rain was coming down. And I didn't feel like coming back inside. I didn't feel the cold so much. I didn't mind the wet. So I was just walking. I was muddy but I didn't mind the mud so much. And I looked up. And I saw this stand of corn. In fact I was standing in it. So, I was standing in it.

HALIE: There isn't any corn outside Tilden!

There's no corn! Now, you must've either stolen this corn or you bought it.

DODGE: He doesn't have any money.

HALIE: *(To TILDEN)* So you stole it!

TILDEN: I didn't steal it. I don't want to get kicked out of Illinois. I was kicked out of New Mexico and I don't want to get kicked out of Illinois.

HALIE: You're going to get kicked out of this house, Tilden, if you don't tell me where you got that corn!

(TILDEN starts crying softly to himself but keeps husking corn. Pause.)

DODGE: *(To HALIE)* Why'd you have to tell him that? Who cares where he got the corn? Why'd you have to go and tell him that?

HALIE: *(To DODGE)* It's your fault you know! You're the one that's behind all this! I suppose you thought it'd be funny! Some joke! Cover the house with corn husks. You better get this cleaned up before Bradley sees it.

DODGE: Bradley's not getting in the front door!

HALIE: *(Kicking husks, striding back and forth)* Bradley's going to be very upset when he sees this. He doesn't like to see the house in disarray. He can't stand it when one thing is out of place. The slightest thing. You know how he gets.

DODGE: Bradley doesn't even live here!

HALIE: It's his home as much as ours. He was born in this house!

DODGE: He was born in a hog wallow.

HALIE: Don't you say that! Don't you ever say that!

DODGE: He was born in a goddamn hog wallow! That's where he was born and that's where he belongs! He doesn't belong in this house!

HALIE: *(She stops)* I don't know what's come over you, Dodge. I don't know what in the world's come over you. You've become an evil man. You used to be a good man.

DODGE: Six of one, a half dozen of another.

HALIE: You sit here day and night, festering away! Decomposing! Smelling up the house with your putrid body! Hacking your head off til all hours of the morning! Thinking up mean, evil, stupid things to say about your own flesh and blood!

DODGE: He's not my flesh and blood! My flesh and blood's buried in the back yard!

(They freeze. Long pause. The men stare at her.)

HALIE: *(Quietly)* That's enough, Dodge. That's quite enough. I'm going out now. I'm going to have lunch with Father Dewis. I'm going to ask him about a monument. A statue. At least a plaque.

(She crosses to the door up right. She stops.)

HALIE: If you need anything, ask Tilden. He's the oldest. I've left some money on the kitchen table.

DODGE: I don't need anything.

HALIE: No, I suppose not. *(She opens the door and looks out through porch)* Still raining. I love the smell just after it stops. The ground. I won't be too late.

(She goes out door and closes it. She's still visible on the porch as she crosses toward stage left screen door. She stops in the middle of the porch, speaks to DODGE but doesn't turn to him.)

HALIE: Dodge, tell Tilden not to go out in the back lot anymore. I don't want him back there in the rain.

DODGE: You tell him. He's sitting right here.

HALIE: He never listens to me, Dodge. He's never listened to me in the past.

DODGE: I'll tell him.

HALIE: We have to watch him just like we used to now. Just like we always have. He's still a child.

DODGE: I'll watch him.

HALIE: Good.

(She crosses to screen door, left, takes an umbrella off a hook and goes out the door. The door slams behind her. Long pause. TILDEN husks corn, stares at pail. DODGE lights a cigarette, stares at T.V.)

TILDEN: *(Still husking)* You shouldn't a told her that.

DODGE: *(Staring at T.V.)* What?

TILDEN: What you told her. You know.

DODGE: What do you know about it?

TILDEN: I know. I know all about it. We all know.

DODGE: So what difference does it make? Everybody knows, everybody's forgot.

TILDEN: She hasn't forgot.

DODGE: She should've forgot.

TILDEN: It's different for a woman. She couldn't forget that. How could she forget that?

DODGE: I don't want to talk about it!

TILDEN: What do you want to talk about?

DODGE: I don't want to talk about anything! I don't want to talk about troubles or what happened fifty years ago or thirty years ago or the race track or Florida or the last time I seeded the corn! I don't want to talk!

TILDEN: You don't wanna die do you?

DODGE: No, I don't wanna die either.

TILDEN: Well, you gotta talk or you'll die.

DODGE: Who told you that?

TILDEN: That's what I know. I found that out in New Mexico. I thought I was dying but I just lost my voice.

DODGE: Were you with somebody?

TILDEN: I was alone. I thought I was dead.

DODGE: Might as well have been. What'd you come back here for?

TILDEN: I didn't know where to go.

DODGE: You're a grown man. You shouldn't be needing your parents at your age. It's un-natural. There's nothing we can do for you now anyway. Couldn't you make a living down there? Couldn't you find some way to make a living? Support yourself? What'd'ya come back here for? You expect us to feed you forever?

TILDEN: I didn't know where else to go.

DODGE: I never went back to my parents. Never. Never even had the urge. I was independent. Always independent. Always found a way.

TILDEN: I didn't know what to do. I couldn't figure anything out.

DODGE: There's nothing to figure out. You just forge ahead. What's there to figure out?

(TILDEN stands.)

TILDEN: I don't know.

DODGE: Where are you going?

TILDEN: Out back.

DODGE: You're not supposed to go out there. You heard what she said. Don't play deaf with me!

TILDEN: I like it out there.

DODGE: In the rain?

TILDEN: Especially in the rain. I like the feeling of it. Feels like it always did.

DODGE: You're supposed to watch out for me. Get me things when I need them.

TILDEN: What do you need?

DODGE: I don't need anything! But I might. I might need something any second. Any second now. I can't be left alone for a minute!

(DODGE *starts to cough.*)

TILDEN: I'll be right outside. You can just yell.

DODGE: *(Between coughs)* No! It's too far! You can't go out there! It's too far! You might not ever hear me!

TILDEN: *(Moving to pills)* Why don't you take a pill? You want a pill?

(DODGE *coughs more violently, throws himself back against sofa, clutches his throat.* TILDEN *stands by helplessly.*)

DODGE: Water! Get me some water!

(TILDEN *rushes off left.* DODGE *reaches out for the pills, knocking some bottles to the floor, coughing in spasms. He grabs a small bottle, takes out pills and swallows them.* TILDEN *rushes back on with a glass of water.* DODGE *takes it and drinks, his coughing subsides.*)

TILDEN: You all right now?

(DODGE *nods. Drinks more water.* TILDEN *moves in closer to him.* DODGE *sets glass of water on the night table. His coughing is almost gone.*)

TILDEN: Why don't you lay down for a while? Just rest a little.

(TILDEN *helps* DODGE *lay down on the sofa. Covers him with blanket.*)

DODGE: You're not going outside are you?

TILDEN: No.

DODGE: I don't want to wake up and find you not here.

TILDEN: I'll be here.

(TILDEN *tucks blanket around* DODGE.)

DODGE: You'll stay right here?

TILDEN: I'll stay in my chair.

DODGE: That's not a chair. That's my old milking stool.

TILDEN: I know.

DODGE: Don't call it a chair.

TILDEN: I won't.

(TILDEN *tries to take* DODGE'S *baseball cap off.*)

DODGE: What're you doing! Leave that on me! Don't take that offa me! That's my cap!

(TILDEN *leaves the cap on* DODGE.)

TILDEN: I know.

DODGE: Bradley'll shave my head if I don't have that on. That's my cap.

TILDEN: I know it is.

DODGE: Don't take my cap off.

TILDEN: I won't.

DODGE: You stay right here now.

TILDEN: *(Sits on stool)* I will.

DODGE: Don't go outside. There's nothing out there.

TILDEN: I won't.

DODGE: Everything's in here. Everything you need. Money's on the table. T.V. Is the T.V. on?

TILDEN: Yeah.

DODGE: Turn it off! Turn the damn thing off! What's it doing on?

TILDEN: *(Shuts off T.V., light goes out)* You left it on.

DODGE: Well turn it off.

TILDEN: *(Sits on stool again)* It's off.

DODGE: Leave it off.

TILDEN: I will.

DODGE: When I fall asleep you can turn it on.

TILDEN: Okay.

DODGE: You can watch the ball game. Red Sox. You like the Red Sox don't you?

TILDEN: Yeah.

DODGE: You can watch the Red Sox. Pee Wee Reese. Pee Wee Reese. You remember Pee Wee Reese?

TILDEN: No.

DODGE: Was he with the Red Sox?

TILDEN: I don't know.

DODGE: Pee Wee Reese. *(Falling asleep)* You can watch the Cardinals. You remember Stan Musial.

TILDEN: No.

DODGE: Stan Musial. *(Falling into sleep)* Bases loaded. Top a' the sixth. Bases loaded. Runner on first and third. Big fat knuckle ball. Floater. Big as a blimp. Cracko! Ball just took off like a rocket. Just pulverized. I marked it. Marked it with my eyes. Straight between the clock and the Burma

Shave ad. I was the first kid out there. First kid. I had to fight hard for that ball. I wouldn't give it up. They almost tore the ears right off me. But I wouldn't give it up.

(DODGE *falls into deep sleep.* TILDEN *just sits staring at him for a while. Slowly he leans toward the sofa, checking to see if* DODGE *is well asleep. He reaches slowly under the cushion and pulls out the bottle of booze.* DODGE *sleeps soundly.* TILDEN *stands quietly, staring at* DODGE *as he uncaps the bottle and takes a long drink. He caps the bottle and sticks it in his hip pocket. He looks around at the husks on the floor and then back to* DODGE. *He moves center stage and gathers an armload of corn husks then crosses back to the sofa. He stands holding the husks over* DODGE *and looking down at him he gently spreads the corn husks over the whole length of* DODGE'S *body. He stands back and looks at* DODGE. *Pulls out bottle, takes another drink, returns bottle to his hip pocket. He gathers more husks and repeats the procedure until the floor is clean of corn husks and* DODGE *is completely covered in them except for his head.* TILDEN *takes another long drink, stares at* DODGE *sleeping then quietly exits stage left. Long pause as the sound of rain continues.* DODGE *sleeps on. The figure of* BRADLEY *appears up left, outside the screen porch door. He holds a wet newspaper over his head as a protection from the rain. He seems to be struggling with the door then slips and almost falls to the ground.* DODGE *sleeps on, undisturbed.*)

BRADLEY: Sonuvabitch! Sonuvagoddamn-bitch!

(BRADLEY *recovers his footing and makes it through the screen door onto the porch. He throws the newspaper down, shakes the water out of his hair, and brushes the rain off of his shoulders. He is a big man dressed in a gray sweat shirt, black suspenders, baggy dark blue pants and black janitor's shoes. His left leg is wooden, having been amputated above the knee. He moves with an exaggerated, almost mechanical limp. The squeaking sounds of leather and metal accompany his walk coming from the harness and hinges of the false leg. His arms and shoulders are extremely powerful and muscular due to a lifetime dependency on the upper torso doing all the work for the legs. He is about five years younger than* TILDEN. *He moves laboriously to the stage right door and enters, closing the door behind him. He doesn't notice* DODGE *at first. He moves toward the staircase.*)

BRADLEY: (*Calling to upstairs*) Mom!

(*He stops and listens. Turns upstage and sees* DODGE *sleeping. Notices corn husks. He moves slowly toward sofa. Stops next to pail and looks into it. Looks at husks.* DODGE *stays asleep. Talks to himself.*)

BRADLEY: What in the hell is this?

(*He looks at* DODGE'S *sleeping face and shakes his head in disgust. He pulls out a pair of black electric hair clippers from his pocket. Unwinds the cord and crosses to the lamp. He jabs his wooden leg behind the knee, causing it to bend at the joint and awkwardly kneels to plug the cord into a floor outlet. He pulls himself to his feet again by using the sofa as leverage. He moves to* DODGE'S *head and again jabs his false leg. Goes down on one knee. He violently knocks away some of the corn husks then jerks off* DODGE'S *baseball cap and throws it down center stage.* DODGE *stays asleep.* BRADLEY *switches on the clippers. Lights start dimming.* BRADLEY *cuts* DODGE'S *hair while he sleeps. Lights dim slowly to black with the sound of clippers and rain.*)

ACT II

SCENE

Same set as Act I. Night. Sound of rain. DODGE *still asleep on sofa. His hair is cut extremely short and in places the scalp is cut and bleeding. His cap is still center stage. All the corn and husks, pail and milking stool have been cleared away. The lights come up to the sound of a young girl laughing off stage left.* DODGE *remains asleep.* SHELLY *and* VINCE *appear up left outside the screen porch door sharing the shelter of* VINCE'S *overcoat above their heads.* SHELLY *is about nineteen, black hair, very beautiful. She wears tight jeans, high heels, purple T-shirt and a short rabbit fur coat. Her makeup is exaggerated and her hair has been curled.* VINCE *is* TILDEN'S *son, about twenty-two, wears a plaid shirt, jeans, dark glasses, cowboy boots and carries a black saxophone case. They shake the rain off themselves as they enter the porch through the screen door.*

SHELLY: *(Laughing, gesturing to house)* This is it? I don't believe this is it!

VINCE: This is it.

SHELLY: This is the house?

VINCE: This is the house.

SHELLY: I don't believe it!

VINCE: How come?

SHELLY: It's like a Norman Rockwell cover or something.

VINCE: What's a' matter with that? It's American.

SHELLY: Where's the milkman and the little dog? What's the little dog's name? Spot. Spot and Jane. Dick and Jane and Spot.

VINCE: Knock it off.

SHELLY: Dick and Jane and Spot and Mom and Dad and Junior and Sissy!

(She laughs. Slaps her knee.)

VINCE: Come on! It's my heritage. What dya' expect?

(She laughs more hysterically, out of control.)

SHELLY: "And Tuffy and Toto and Dooda and Bonzo all went down one day to the corner grocery store to buy a big bag of licorice for Mr. Marshall's pussy cat!"

(She laughs so hard she falls to her knees holding her stomach. VINCE *stands there looking at her.)*

VINCE: Shelly will you get up!

(She keeps laughing. Staggers to her feet. Turning in circles holding her stomach.)

SHELLY: *(Continuing her story in kid's voice)* "Mr. Marshall was on vacation. He had no idea that the four little boys had taken such a liking to his little kitty cat."

VINCE: Have some respect would ya'!

SHELLY: *(Trying to control herself)* I'm sorry.

VINCE: Pull yourself together.

SHELLY: *(Salutes him)* Yes sir.

(She giggles.)

VINCE: Jesus Christ, Shelly.

SHELLY: *(Pause, smiling)* And Mr. Marshall—

VINCE: Cut it out.

(She stops. Stands there staring at him. Stifles a giggle.)

VINCE: *(After pause)* Are you finished?

SHELLY: Oh brother!

VINCE: I don't wanna go in there with you acting like an idiot.

SHELLY: Thanks.

VINCE: Well, I don't.

SHELLY: I won't embarrass you. Don't worry.

VINCE: I'm not worried.

SHELLY: You are too.

VINCE: Shelly look, I just don't wanna go in there with you giggling your head off. They might think something's wrong with you.

SHELLY: There is.

VINCE: There is not!

SHELLY: Something's definitely wrong with me.

VINCE: There is not!

SHELLY: There's something wrong with you too.

VINCE: There's nothing wrong with me either!

SHELLY: You wanna know what's wrong with you?

VINCE: What?

(SHELLY laughs.)

VINCE: *(Crosses back left toward screen door)* I'm leaving!

SHELLY: *(Stops laughing)* Wait! Stop. Stop! *(VINCE stops)* What's wrong with you is that you take the situation too seriously.

VINCE: I just don't want to have them think that I've suddenly arrived out of the middle of nowhere completely deranged.

SHELLY: What do you want them to think then?

VINCE: *(Pause)* Nothing. Let's go in.

(He crosses porch toward stage right interior door. SHELLY *follows him. The stage right door opens slowly.* VINCE *sticks his head in, doesn't notice* DODGE *sleeping. Calls out toward staircase.)*

VINCE: Grandma!

*(*SHELLY *breaks into laughter, unseen behind* VINCE. VINCE *pulls his head back outside and pulls door shut. We hear their voices again without seeing them.)*

SHELLY'S VOICE: *(Stops laughing)* I'm sorry. I'm sorry Vince. I really am. I really am sorry. I won't do it again. I couldn't help it.

VINCE'S VOICE: It's not all that funny.

SHELLY'S VOICE: I know it's not. I'm sorry.

VINCE'S VOICE: I mean this is a tense situation for me! I haven't seen them for over six years. I don't know what to expect.

SHELLY'S VOICE: I know. I won't do it again.

VINCE'S VOICE: Can't you bite your tongue or something?

SHELLY'S VOICE: Just don't say "Grandma," okay? *(She giggles, stops)* I mean if you say "Grandma" I don't know if I can stop myself.

VINCE'S VOICE: Well try!

SHELLY'S VOICE: Okay. Sorry.

(Door opens again. VINCE *sticks his head in then enters.* SHELLY *follows behind him.* VINCE *crosses to staircase, sets down saxophone case and overcoat, looks up staircase.* SHELLY *notices* DODGE'S *baseball cap. Crosses to it. Picks it up and puts it on her head.* VINCE *goes up the stairs and disappears at the top.* SHELLY *watches him then turns and sees* DODGE *on the sofa. She takes off the baseball cap.)*

VINCE'S VOICE: *(From above stairs)* Grandma!

*(*SHELLY *crosses over to* DODGE *slowly and stands next to him. She stands at his head, reaches out slowly and touches one of the cuts. The second she touches his head,* DODGE *jerks up to a sitting position on the sofa, eyes open.* SHELLY *gasps.)*

DODGE *looks at her, sees his cap in her hands, quickly puts his hand to his bare head. He glares at* SHELLY *then whips the cap out of her hands and puts it on.* SHELLY *backs away from him.* DODGE *stares at her.)*

SHELLY: I'm uh- with Vince.

*(*DODGE *just glares at her.)*

SHELLY: He's upstairs.

*(*DODGE *looks at the staircase then back to* SHELLY.*)*

SHELLY: *(Calling upstairs)* Vince!

VINCE'S VOICE: Just a second!

SHELLY: You better get down here!

VINCE'S VOICE: Just a minute! I'm looking at the pictures.

*(*DODGE *keeps staring at her.)*

SHELLY: *(To* DODGE*)* We just got here. Pouring rain on the freeway so we thought we'd stop by. I mean Vince was planning on stopping anyway. He wanted to see you. He said he hadn't seen you in a long time.

(Pause. DODGE *just keeps staring at her.)*

SHELLY: We were going all the way through to New Mexico. To see his father. I guess his father lives out there. We thought we'd stop by and see you on the way. Kill two birds with one stone, you know? *(She laughs,* DODGE *stares, she stops laughing)* I mean Vince has this thing about his family now. I guess it's a new thing with him. I kind of find it hard to relate to. But he feels it's important. You know. I mean he feels he wants to get to know you all again. After all this time.

(Pause. DODGE *just stares at her. She moves nervously to staircase and yells up to* VINCE.*)*

SHELLY: Vince will you come down here please!

*(*VINCE *comes half way down the stairs.)*

VINCE: I guess they went out for a while.

*(*SHELLY *points to sofa and* DODGE. VINCE *turns and sees* DODGE. *He comes all the way down staircase and crosses to* DODGE. SHELLY *stays behind near staircase, keeping her distance.)*

VINCE: Grandpa?

(DODGE looks up at him, not recognizing him.)

DODGE: Did you bring the whiskey?

(VINCE looks back at SHELLY then back to DODGE.)

VINCE: Grandpa, it's Vince. I'm Vince. Tilden's son. You remember?

(DODGE stares at him.)

DODGE: You didn't do what you told me. You didn't stay here with me.

VINCE: Grandpa, I haven't been here until just now. I just got here.

DODGE: You left. You went outside like we told you not to do. You went out there in back. In the rain.

(VINCE looks back at SHELLY. She moves slowly toward sofa.)

SHELLY: Is he okay?

VINCE: I don't know. *(Takes off his shades)* Look, Grandpa, don't you remember me? Vince. Your Grandson.

(DODGE stares at him then takes off his baseball cap.)

DODGE: *(Points to his head)* See what happens when you leave me alone? See that? That's what happens.

(VINCE looks at his head. VINCE reaches out to touch his head. DODGE slaps his hand away with the cap and puts it back on his head.)

VINCE: What's going on Grandpa? Where's Halie?

DODGE: Don't worry about her. She won't be back for days. She says she'll be back but she won't be. *(He starts laughing)* There's life in the old girl yet! *(Stops laughing)*

VINCE: How did you do that to your head?

DODGE: I didn't do it! Don't be ridiculous!

VINCE: Well who did then?

(Pause. DODGE stares at VINCE.)

DODGE: Who do you think did it? Who do you think?

(SHELLY moves toward VINCE.)

SHELLY: Vince, maybe we oughta' go. I don't like this. I mean this isn't my idea of a good time.

VINCE: *(To SHELLY)* Just a second. *(To DODGE)* Grandpa, look, I just got here. I just now got here. I haven't been here for six years. I don't know anything that's happened.

(Pause. DODGE stares at him.)

DODGE: You don't know anything?

VINCE: No.

DODGE: Well that's good. That's good. It's much better not to know anything. Much, much better.

VINCE: Isn't there anybody here with you?

(DODGE turns slowly and looks off to stage left.)

DODGE: Tilden's here.

VINCE: No, Grandpa, Tilden's in New Mexico. That's where I was going. I'm going out there to see him.

(DODGE turns slowly back to VINCE.)

DODGE: Tilden's here.

(VINCE backs away and joins SHELLY. DODGE stares at them.)

SHELLY: Vince, why don't we spend the night in a motel and come back in the morning? We could have breakfast. Maybe everything would be different.

VINCE: Don't be scared. There's nothing to be scared of. He's just old.

SHELLY: I'm not scared!

DODGE: You two are not my idea of the perfect couple!

SHELLY: *(After pause)* Oh really? Why's that?

VINCE: Shh! Don't aggravate him.

DODGE: There's something wrong between the two of you. Something not compatible.

VINCE: Grandpa, where did Halie go? Maybe we should call her.

DODGE: What are you talking about? Do you know what you're talking about? Are you just talking for the sake of talking? Lubricating the gums?

VINCE: I'm trying to figure out what's going on here!

DODGE: Is that it?

VINCE: Yes. I mean I expected everything to be different.

DODGE: Who are you to expect anything? Who are you supposed to be?

VINCE: I'm Vince! Your Grandson!

DODGE: Vince. My Grandson.

VINCE: Tilden's son.

DODGE: Tilden's son, Vince.

VINCE: You haven't seen me for a long time.

DODGE: When was the last time?

VINCE: I don't remember.

DODGE: You don't remember?

VINCE: No.

DODGE: You don't remember. How am I supposed to remember if you don't remember?

SHELLY: Vince, come on. This isn't going to work out.

VINCE: *(To* SHELLY*)* Just take it easy.

SHELLY: I'm taking it easy! He doesn't even know who you are!

VINCE: *(Crossing toward* DODGE*)* Grandpa, Look —

DODGE: Stay where you are! Keep your distance!

(VINCE stops. Looks back at SHELLY *then to* DODGE*.)*

SHELLY: Vince, this is really making me nervous. I mean he doesn't even want us here. He doesn't even like us.

DODGE: She's a beautiful girl.

VINCE: Thanks.

DODGE: Very Beautiful Girl.

SHELLY: Oh my God.

DODGE: *(To* SHELLY*)* What's your name?

SHELLY: Shelly.

DODGE: Shelly. That's a man's name isn't it?

SHELLY: Not in this case.

DODGE: *(To* VINCE*)* She's a smart-ass too.

SHELLY: Vince! Can we go?

DODGE: She wants to go. She just got here and she wants to go.

VINCE: This is kind of strange for her.

DODGE: She'll get used to it. *(To* SHELLY*)* What part of the country do you come from?

SHELLY: Originally?

DODGE: That's right. Originally. At the very start.

SHELLY: L.A.

DODGE: L.A. Stupid country.

SHELLY: I can't stand this Vince! This is really unbelievable!

DODGE: It's stupid! L.A. is stupid! So is Florida! All those Sunshine States. They're all stupid! Do you know why they're stupid?

SHELLY: Illuminate me.

DODGE: I'll tell you why. Because they're full of smart-asses! That's why.

(SHELLY turns her back to DODGE, crosses to staircase and sits on bottom step.)

DODGE: *(To* VINCE*)* Now she's insulted.

VINCE: Well you weren't very polite.

DODGE: She's insulted! Look at her! In my house she's insulted! She's over there sulking because I insulted her!

SHELLY: *(To* VINCE*)* This is really terrific. This is wonderful. And you were worried about me making the right first impression!

DODGE: *(To* VINCE*)* She's a fireball isn't she? Regular fireball. I had some a' them in my day. Temporary stuff. Never lasted more than a week.

VINCE: Grandpa —

DODGE: Stop calling me Grandpa will ya'! It's sickening. "Grandpa." I'm nobody's Grandpa!

(DODGE starts feeling around under the cushion for the bottle of whiskey. SHELLY gets up from the staircase.)

SHELLY: *(To* VINCE*)* Maybe you've got the wrong house. Did you ever think of that? Maybe this is the wrong address!

VINCE: It's not the wrong address! I recognize the yard.

SHELLY: Yeah but do you recognize the people? He says he's not your Grandfather.

DODGE: *(Digging for bottle)* Where's that bottle!

VINCE: He's just sick or something. I don't know what's happened to him.

DODGE: Where's my goddamn bottle!

(DODGE gets up from sofa and starts tearing the cushions off it and throwing them downstage, looking for the whiskey.)

SHELLY: Can't we just drive on to New Mexico? This is terrible, Vince! I don't want to stay here. In this house. I thought it was going to be turkey dinners and apple pie and all that kinda stuff.

VINCE: Well I hate to disappoint you!

SHELLY: I'm not disappointed! I'm fuckin' terrified! I wanna' go!

(DODGE yells toward stage left.)

DODGE: Tilden! Tilden!

(DODGE *keeps ripping away at the sofa looking for his bottle, he knocks over the night stand with the bottles.* VINCE *and* SHELLY *watch as he starts ripping the stuffing out of the sofa.*)

VINCE: *(To* SHELLY*)* He's lost his mind or something. I've got to try to help him.

SHELLY: You help him! I'm leaving!

(SHELLY *starts to leave.* VINCE *grabs her. They struggle as* DODGE *keeps ripping away at the sofa and yelling.*)

DODGE: Tilden! Tilden get your ass in here! Tilden!

SHELLY: Let go of me!

VINCE: You're not going anywhere! You're going to stay right here!

SHELLY: Let go of me you sonuvabitch! I'm not your property!

(*Suddenly* TILDEN *walks on from stage left just as he did before. This time his arms are full of carrots.* DODGE, VINCE *and* SHELLY *stop suddenly when they see him. They all stare at* TILDEN *as he crosses slowly center stage with the carrots and stops.* DODGE *sits on sofa, exhausted.*)

DODGE: *(Panting, to* TILDEN*)* Where in the hell have you been?

TILDEN: Out back.

DODGE: Where's my bottle?

TILDEN: Gone.

(TILDEN *and* VINCE *stare at each other.* SHELLY *backs away.*)

DODGE: *(To* TILDEN*)* You stole my bottle!

VINCE: *(To* TILDEN*)* Dad?

(TILDEN *just stares at* VINCE.)

DODGE: You had no right to steal my bottle! No right at all!

VINCE: *(To* TILDEN*)* It's Vince. I'm Vince.

(TILDEN *stares at* VINCE *then looks at* DODGE *then turns to* SHELLY.)

TILDEN: *(After pause)* I picked these carrots. If anybody wants any carrots, I picked 'em.

SHELLY: *(To* VINCE*)* This is your father?

VINCE: *(To* TILDEN*)* Dad, what're you doing here?

(TILDEN *just stares at* VINCE, *holding carrots,* DODGE *pulls the blanket back over himself.*)

DODGE: *(To* TILDEN*)* You're going to have to get me another bottle! You gotta get me a bottle before Halie comes back! There's money on the table. *(Points to stage left kitchen)*

TILDEN: *(Shaking his head)* I'm not going down there. Into town.

(SHELLY *crosses to* TILDEN. TILDEN *stares at her.*)

SHELLY: *(To* TILDEN*)* Are you Vince's father?

TILDEN: *(To* SHELLY*)* Vince?

SHELLY: *(Pointing to* VINCE*)* This is supposed to be your son! Is he your son? Do you recognize him? I'm just along for the ride here. I thought everybody knew each other!

(TILDEN *stares at* VINCE. DODGE *wraps himself up in the blanket and sits on sofa staring at the floor.*)

TILDEN: I had a son once but we buried him.

(DODGE *quickly looks at* TILDEN. SHELLY *looks to* VINCE.)

DODGE: You shut up about that! You don't know anything about that!

VINCE: Dad, I thought you were in New Mexico. We were going to drive down there and see you.

TILDEN: Long way to drive.

DODGE: *(To* TILDEN*)* You don't know anything about that! That happened before you were born! Long before!

VINCE: What's happened, Dad? What's going on here? I thought everything was all right. What's happened to Halie?

TILDEN: She left.

SHELLY: *(To* TILDEN*)* Do you want me to take those carrots for you?

(TILDEN *stares at her. She moves in close to him. Holds out her arms.* TILDEN *stares at her arms then slowly dumps the carrots into her arms.* SHELLY *stands there holding the carrots.*)

TILDEN: *(To* SHELLY*)* You like Carrots?

SHELLY: Sure. I like all kinds of vegetables.

DODGE: *(To* TILDEN*)* You gotta get me a bottle before Halie comes back!

(DODGE *hits sofa with his fist.* VINCE *crosses up to* DODGE *and tries to console him.* SHELLY *and* TILDEN *stay facing each other.*)

TILDEN: *(To* SHELLY*)* Back yard's full of carrots. Corn. Potatoes.

SHELLY: You're Vince's father, right?

TILDEN: All kinds of vegetables. You like vegetables?

SHELLY: *(Laughs)* Yeah, I love vegetables.

TILDEN: We could cook these carrots ya' know. You could cut 'em up and we could cook 'em.

SHELLY: All right.

TILDEN: I'll get you a pail and a knife.

SHELLY: Okay.

TILDEN: I'll be right back. Don't go.

(TILDEN exits off stage left. SHELLY stands center, arms full of carrots. VINCE stands next to DODGE. SHELLY looks toward VINCE then down at the carrots.)

DODGE: *(To VINCE)* You could get me a bottle. *(Pointing off left)* There's money on the table.

VINCE: Grandpa why don't you lay down for a while?

DODGE: I don't wanna lay down for a while! Every time I lay down something happens! *(Whips off his cap, points at his head)* Look what happens! That's what happens! *(Pulls his cap back on)* You go lie down and see what happens to you! See how you like it! They'll steal your bottle! They'll cut your hair! They'll murder your children! That's what'll happen.

VINCE: Just relax for a while.

DODGE: *(Pause)* You could get me a bottle ya' know. There's nothing stopping you from getting me a bottle.

SHELLY: Why don't you get him a bottle Vince? Maybe it would help everybody identify each other.

DODGE: *(Pointing to SHELLY)* There, see? She thinks you should get me a bottle.

(VINCE crosses to SHELLY.)

VINCE: What're you doing with those carrots.

SHELLY: I'm waiting for your father.

DODGE: She thinks you should get me a bottle!

VINCE: Shelly put the carrots down will ya'! We gotta deal with the situation here! I'm gonna need your help.

SHELLY: I'm helping.

VINCE: You're only adding to the problem! You're making things worse! Put the carrots down!

(VINCE tries to knock the carrots out of her arms. She turns away from him, protecting the carrots.)

SHELLY: Get away from me! Stop it!

(VINCE stands back from her. She turns to him still holding the carrots.)

VINCE: *(To SHELLY)* Why are you doing this! Are you trying to make fun of me? This is my family you know!

SHELLY: You coulda' fooled me! I'd just as soon not be here myself. I'd just as soon be a thousand miles from here. I'd rather be anywhere but here. You're the one who wants to stay. So I'll stay. I'll stay and I'll cut the carrots. And I'll cook the carrots. And I'll do whatever I have to do to survive. Just to make it through this.

VINCE: Put the carrots down Shelly.

(TILDEN enters from left with pail, milking stool and a knife. He sets the stool and pail center stage for SHELLY. SHELLY looks at VINCE then sits down on stool, sets the carrots on the floor and takes the knife from TILDEN. She looks at VINCE again then picks up a carrot, cuts the ends off, scrapes it and drops it in pail. She repeats this. VINCE glares at her. She smiles.)

DODGE: She could get me a bottle. She's the type a' girl that could get me a bottle. Easy. She'd go down there. Slink up to the counter. They'd probably give her two bottles for the price of one. She could do that.

(SHELLY laughs. Keeps cutting carrots. VINCE crosses up to DODGE, looks at him. TILDEN watches SHELLY's hands. Long pause.)

VINCE: *(To DODGE)* I haven't changed that much. I mean physically. Physically I'm just about the same. Same size. Same weight. Everything's the same.

(DODGE keeps staring at SHELLY while VINCE talks to him.)

DODGE: She's a beautiful girl. Exceptional.

(VINCE moves in front of DODGE to block his view of SHELLY. DODGE keeps craning his head around to see her as VINCE demonstrates tricks from his past.)

VINCE: Look. Look at this. Do you remember this? I used to bend my thumb behind my knuckles. You remember? I used to do it at the dinner table.

(VINCE *bends a thumb behind his knuckles for* DODGE *and holds it out to him.* DODGE *takes a short glance then looks back at* SHELLY. VINCE *shifts position and shows him something else.*)

VINCE: What about this?

(VINCE *curls his lips back and starts drumming on his teeth with his fingernails making little tapping sounds.* DODGE *watches a while.* TILDEN *turns toward the sound.* VINCE *keeps it up. He sees* TILDEN *taking notice and crosses to* TILDEN *as he drums on his teeth.* DODGE *turns T.V. on. Watches it.*)

VINCE: You remember this Dad?

(VINCE *keeps on drumming for* TILDEN. TILDEN *watches a while, fascinated, then turns back to* SHELLY. VINCE *keeps up the drumming on his teeth, crosses back to* DODGE *doing it.* SHELLY *keeps working on carrots, talking to* TILDEN.)

SHELLY: (*To* TILDEN) He drives me crazy with that sometimes.
VINCE: (*To* DODGE) I Know! Here's one you'll remember. You used to kick me out of the house for this one.

(VINCE *pulls his shirt out of his belt and holds it tucked under his chin with his stomach exposed. He grabs the flesh on either side of his belly button and pushes it in and out to make it look like a mouth talking. He watches his belly button and makes a deep sounding cartoon voice to synchronize with the movement. He demonstrates it to* DODGE *then crosses down to* TILDEN *doing it. Both* DODGE *and* TILDEN *take short, uninterested glances then ignore him.*)

VINCE: (*Deep cartoon voice*) "Hello. How are you? I'm fine. Thank you very much. It's so good to see you looking well this fine Sunday morning. I was going down to the hardware store to fetch a pail of water."
SHELLY: Vince, don't be pathetic will ya'!

(VINCE *stops. Tucks his shirt back in.*)

SHELLY: Jesus Christ. They're not gonna play. Can't you see that?

(SHELLY *keeps cutting carrots.* VINCE *slowly moves toward* TILDEN. TILDEN *keeps watching* SHELLY. DODGE *watches T.V.*)

VINCE: (*To* SHELLY) I don't get it. I really don't get it. Maybe it's me. Maybe I forgot something.
DODGE: (*From sofa*) You forgot to get me a bottle! That's what you forgot. Anybody in this house could get me a bottle. Anybody! But nobody will. Nobody understands the urgency! Peelin carrots is more important. Playin piano on your teeth! Well I hope you all remember this when you get up in years. When you find yourself immobilized. Dependent on the whims of others.

(VINCE *moves up toward* DODGE. *Pause as he looks at him.*)

VINCE: I'll get you a bottle.
DODGE: You will?
VINCE: Sure.

(SHELLY *stands holding knife and carrot.*)

SHELLY: You're not going to leave me here are you?
VINCE: (*Moving to her*) You suggested it! You said, "why don't I go get him a bottle." So I'll go get him a bottle!
SHELLY: But I can't stay here.
VINCE: What is going on! A minute ago you were ready to cut carrots all night!
SHELLY: That was only if you stayed. Something to keep me busy, so I wouldn't be so nervous. I don't want to stay here alone.
DODGE: Don't let her talk you out of it! She's a bad influence. I could see it the minute she stepped in here.
SHELLY: (*To* DODGE) You were asleep!
TILDEN: (*To* SHELLY) Don't you want to cut carrots anymore?
SHELLY: Sure. Sure I do.

(SHELLY *sits back down on stool and continues cutting carrots. Pause.* VINCE *moves around, stroking his hair, staring at* DODGE *and* TILDEN. VINCE *and* SHELLY *exchange glances.* DODGE *watches T.V.*)

VINCE: Boy! This is amazing. This is truly amazing. (*Keeps moving around*) What is this anyway? Am I in a time warp or something? Have I committed an unpardonable offence? It's true, I'm not married. (SHELLY *looks at him, then back to carrots*) But I'm also not divorced. I have been known to plunge into sinful infatuation with the Alto Saxophone. Sucking on number 5 reeds deep into the wee wee hours.

SHELLY: Vince, what are you doing that for? They don't care about any of that. They just don't recognize you, that's all.

VINCE: How could they not recognize me! How in the hell could they not recognize me! I'm their son!

DODGE: (Watching T.V.) You're no son of mine. I've had sons in my time and you're not one of 'em.

(Long pause. VINCE stares at DODGE then looks at TILDEN. He turns to SHELLY.)

VINCE: Shelly, I gotta go out for a while. I just gotta go out. I'll get a bottle and I'll come right back. You'll be o.k. here. Really.

SHELLY: I don't know if I can handle this, Vince.

VINCE: I just gotta think or something. I don't know. I gotta put this all together.

SHELLY: Can't we just go?

VINCE: No! I gotta find out what's going on.

SHELLY: Look, you think you're bad off, what about me? Not only don't they recognize me but I've never seen them before in my life. I don't know who these guys are. They could be anybody!

VINCE: They're not anybody!

SHELLY: That's what you say.

VINCE: They're my family for Christ's sake! I should know who my own family is! Now give me a break. It won't take that long. I'll just go out and I'll come right back. Nothing'll happen. I promise.

(SHELLY stares at him. Pause.)

SHELLY: All right.

VINCE: Thanks. (He crosses up to DODGE) I'm gonna go out now, Grandpa and I'll pick you up a bottle. Okay?

DODGE: Change of heart huh? (Pointing off left) Money's on the table. In the kitchen.

(VINCE moves toward SHELLY.)

VINCE: (To SHELLY) You be all right?

SHELLY: (Cutting carrots) Sure. I'm fine. I'll just keep real busy while you're gone.

(VINCE looks at TILDEN who keeps staring down at SHELLY's hands.)

DODGE: Persistence see? That's what it takes. Persistence. Persistence, fortitude and determination. Those are the three virtues. You stick with those three and you can't go wrong.

VINCE: (To TILDEN) You want anything, Dad?

TILDEN: (Looks up at VINCE) Me?

VINCE: From the store? I'm gonna get grandpa a bottle.

TILDEN: He's not supposed to drink. Halie wouldn't like it.

VINCE: He wants a bottle.

TILDEN: He's not supposed to drink.

DODGE: (To VINCE) Don't negotiate with him! Don't make any transactions until you've spoken to me first! He'll steal you blind!

VINCE: (To DODGE) Tilden says you're not supposed to drink.

DODGE: Tilden's lost his marbles! Look at him! He's around the bend. Take a look at him.

(VINCE stares at TILDEN. TILDEN watches SHELLY's hands as she keeps cutting carrots.)

DODGE: Now look at me. Look here at me!

(VINCE looks back to DODGE.)

DODGE: Now, between the two of us, who do you think is more trustworthy? Him or me? Can you trust a man who keeps bringing in vegetables from out of nowhere? Take a look at him.

(VINCE looks back at TILDEN.)

SHELLY: Go get the bottle, Vince.

VINCE: (To SHELLY) You sure you'll be all right?

SHELLY: I'll be fine. I feel right at home now.

VINCE: You do?

SHELLY: I'm fine. Now that I've got the carrots everything is all right.

VINCE: I'll be right back.

(VINCE crosses stage left.)

DODGE: Where are you going?

VINCE: I'm going to get the money.

DODGE: Then where are you going?

VINCE: Liquor store.

DODGE: Don't go anyplace else. Don't go off some place and drink. Come right back here.

VINCE: I will.

(VINCE exits stage left.)

DODGE: (Calling after VINCE) You've got responsibility now! And don't go out the back way either! Come out through this way! I wanna' see you when you leave! Don't go out the back!

VINCE'S VOICE: (Off left) I won't!

(DODGE turns and looks at TILDEN and SHELLY.)

DODGE: Untrustworthy. Probably drown himself if he went out the back. Fall right in a hole. I'd never get my bottle.

SHELLY: I wouldn't worry about Vince. He can take care of himself.

DODGE: Oh he can, huh? Independent.

(VINCE comes on again from stage left with two dollars in his hand. He crosses stage right past DODGE.)

DODGE: *(To VINCE)* You got the money?

VINCE: Yeah. Two bucks.

DODGE: Two bucks. Two bucks is two bucks. Don't sneer.

VINCE: What kind do you want?

DODGE: Whiskey! Gold Star Sour Mash. Use your own discretion.

VINCE: Okay.

(VINCE crosses to stage right door. Opens it. Stops when he hears TILDEN.)

TILDEN: *(To VINCE)* You drove all the way from New Mexico?

(VINCE turns and looks at TILDEN. They stare at each other. VINCE shakes his head, goes out the door, crosses porch and exits out screen door. TILDEN watches him go. Pause.)

SHELLY: You really don't recognize him? Either one of you?

(TILDEN turns again and stares at SHELLY'S hands as she cuts carrots.)

DODGE: *(Watching T.V.)* Recognize who?

SHELLY: Vince.

DODGE: What's to recognize?

(DODGE lights a cigarette, coughs slightly and stares at T.V.)

SHELLY: It'd be cruel if you recognized him and didn't tell him. Wouldn't be fair.

(DODGE just stares at T.V., smoking.)

TILDEN: I thought I recognized him. I thought I recognized something about him.

SHELLY: You did?

TILDEN: I thought I saw a face inside his face.

SHELLY: Well it was probably that you saw what he used to look like. You haven't seen him for six years.

TILDEN: I haven't?

SHELLY: That's what he says.

(TILDEN moves around in front of her as she continues with carrots.)

TILDEN: Where was it I saw him last?

SHELLY: I don't know. I've only known him for a few months. He doesn't tell me everything.

TILDEN: He doesn't?

SHELLY: Not stuff like that.

TILDEN: What does he tell you?

SHELLY: You mean in general?

TILDEN: Yeah.

(TILDEN moves around behind her.)

SHELLY: Well he tells me all kinds of things.

TILDEN: Like what?

SHELLY: I don't know! I mean I can't just come right out and tell you how he feels.

TILDEN: How come?

(TILDEN keeps moving around her slowly in a circle.)

SHELLY: Because it's stuff he told me privately!

TILDEN: And you can't tell me?

SHELLY: I don't even know you!

DODGE: Tilden, go out in the kitchen and make me some coffee! Leave the girl alone.

SHELLY: *(To DODGE)* He's all right.

(TILDEN ignores DODGE, keeps moving around SHELLY. He stares at her hair and coat. DODGE stares at T.V.)

TILDEN: You mean you can't tell me anything?

SHELLY: I can tell you some things. I mean we can have a conversation.

TILDEN: We can?

SHELLY: Sure. We're having a conversation right now.

TILDEN: We are?

SHELLY: Yes. That's what we're doing.

TILDEN: But there's certain things you can't tell me, right?

SHELLY: Right.

TILDEN: There's certain things I can't tell you either.

SHELLY: How come?

TILDEN: I don't know. Nobody's supposed to hear it.

SHELLY: Well, you can tell me anything you want to.

TILDEN: I can?

SHELLY: Sure.

TILDEN: It might not be very nice.

SHELLY: That's all right. I've been around.

TILDEN: It might be awful.

SHELLY: Well, can't you tell me anything nice?

(TILDEN *stops in front of her and stares at her coat.* SHELLY *looks back at him. Long pause.*)

TILDEN: *(After pause)* Can I touch your coat?

SHELLY: My coat? *(She looks at her coat then back to* TILDEN *)* Sure.

TILDEN: You don't mind?

SHELLY: No. Go ahead.

(SHELLY *holds her arm out for* TILDEN *to touch.* DODGE *stays fixed on T.V.* TILDEN *moves in slowly toward* SHELLY, *staring at her arm. He reaches out very slowly and touches her arm, feels the fur gently then draws his hand back.* SHELLY *keeps her arm out.*)

SHELLY: It's rabbit.

TILDEN: Rabbit.

(*He reaches out again very slowly and touches the fur on her arm then pulls back his hand again.* SHELLY *drops her arm.*)

SHELLY: My arm was getting tired.

TILDEN: Can I hold it?

SHELLY: *(Pause)* The coat? Sure.

(SHELLY *takes off her coat and hands it to* TILDEN. TILDEN *takes it slowly, feels the fur then puts it on.* SHELLY *watches as* TILDEN *strokes the fur slowly. He smiles at her. She goes back to cutting carrots.*)

SHELLY: You can have it if you want.

TILDEN: I can?

SHELLY: Yeah. I've got a raincoat in the car. That's all I need.

TILDEN: You've got a car?

SHELLY: Vince does.

(TILDEN *walks around stroking the fur and smiling at the coat.* SHELLY *watches him when he's not looking.* DODGE *sticks with T.V., stretches out on sofa wrapped in blanket.*)

TILDEN: *(As he walks around)* I had a car once! I had a white car! I drove. I went everywhere. I went to the mountains. I drove in the snow.

SHELLY: That must've been fun.

TILDEN: *(Still moving, feeling coat)* I drove all day long sometimes. Across the desert. Way out across the desert. I drove past towns. Anywhere. Past palm trees. Lightning. Anything. I would drive through it. I would drive through it and I would stop and I would look around and I would drive on. I would get back in and drive! I loved to drive. There was nothing I loved more. Nothing I dreamed of was better than driving.

DODGE: *(Eyes on T.V.)* Pipe down would ya'!

(TILDEN *stops. Stares at* SHELLY.)

SHELLY: Do you do much driving now?

TILDEN: Now? Now? I don't drive now.

SHELLY: How come?

TILDEN: I'm grown up now.

SHELLY: Grown up?

TILDEN: I'm not a kid.

SHELLY: You don't have to be a kid to drive.

TILDEN: It wasn't driving then.

SHELLY: What was it?

TILDEN: Adventure. I went everywhere.

SHELLY: Well you can still do that.

TILDEN: Not now.

SHELLY: Why not?

TILDEN: I just told you. You don't understand anything. If I told you something you wouldn't understand it.

SHELLY: Told me what?

TILDEN: Told you something that's true.

SHELLY: Like what?

TILDEN: Like a baby. Like a little tiny baby.

SHELLY: Like when you were little?

TILDEN: If I told you you'd make me give your coat back.

SHELLY: I won't. I promise. Tell me.

TILDEN: I can't. Dodge won't let me.

SHELLY: He won't hear you. It's okay.

(*Pause.* TILDEN *stares at her. Moves slightly toward her.*)

TILDEN: We had a baby. (Motioning to DODGE) He did. Dodge did. Could pick it up with one hand. Put it in the other. Little baby. Dodge killed it.

(SHELLY stands.)

TILDEN: Don't stand up. Don't stand up!

(SHELLY sits again. DODGE sits up on sofa and looks at them.)

TILDEN: Dodge drowned it.
SHELLY: Don't tell me anymore! Okay?

(TILDEN moves closer to her. DODGE takes more interest.)

DODGE: Tilden? You leave that girl alone!
TILDEN: (Pays no attention) Never told Halie. Never told anybody. Just drowned it.
DODGE: (Shuts off T.V.) Tilden!
TILDEN: Nobody could find it. Just disappeared. Cops looked for it. Neighbors. Nobody could find it.

(DODGE struggles to get up from sofa.)

DODGE: Tilden, what're you telling her! Tilden!

(DODGE keeps struggling until he's standing.)

TILDEN: Finally everybody just gave up. Just stopped looking. Everybody had a different answer. Kidnap. Murder. Accident. Some kind of accident.

(DODGE struggles to walk toward TILDEN and falls. TILDEN ignores him.)

DODGE: Tilden you shut up! You shut up about it!

(DODGE starts coughing on the floor. SHELLY watches him from the stool.)

TILDEN: Little tiny baby just disappeared. It's not hard. It's so small. Almost invisible.

(SHELLY makes a move to help DODGE. TILDEN firmly pushes her back down on the stool. DODGE keeps coughing.)

TILDEN: He said he had his reasons. Said it went a long way back. But he wouldn't tell anybody.
DODGE: Tilden! Don't tell her anything! Don't tell her!
TILDEN: He's the only one who knows where it's buried. The only one. Like a secret buried treasure. Won't tell any of us. Won't tell me or mother or even Bradley. Especially Bradley. Bradley tried to force it out of him but he wouldn't tell. Wouldn't even tell why he did it. One night he just did it.

(DODGE'S coughing subsides. SHELLY stays on stool staring at DODGE. TILDEN slowly takes SHELLY'S coat off and holds it out to her. Long pause. SHELLY sits there trembling.)

TILDEN: You probably want your coat back now.

(SHELLY stares at coat but doesn't move to take it. The sound of BRADLEY'S leg squeaking is heard off left. The others on stage remain still. BRADLEY appears up left outside the screen door wearing a yellow rain slicker. He enters through screen door, crosses porch to stage right door and enters stage. Closes door. Takes off rain slicker and shakes it out. He sees all the others and stops. TILDEN turns to him. BRADLEY stares at SHELLY. DODGE remains on floor.)

BRADLEY: What's going on here? (Motioning to SHELLY) Who's that?

(SHELLY stands, moves back away from BRADLEY as he crosses toward her. He stops next to TILDEN. He sees coat in TILDEN'S hand and grabs it away from him.)

BRADLEY: Who's she supposed to be?
TILDEN: She's driving to New Mexico.

(BRADLEY stares at her. SHELLY is frozen. BRADLEY limps over to her with the coat in his fist. He stops in front of her.)

BRADLEY: (To SHELLY, after pause) Vacation?

(SHELLY shakes her head "no", trembling.)

BRADLEY: (To SHELLY, motioning to TILDEN) You taking him with you?

(SHELLY shakes her head "no". BRADLEY crosses back to TILDEN.)

BRADLEY: You oughta'. No use leaving him here. Doesn't do a lick a' work. Doesn't raise a finger. (Stopping, to TILDEN) Do ya'? (To SHELLY) 'Course he used to be an All-American. Quarterback or fullback or somethin'. He tell you that?

(SHELLY shakes her head "no".)

BRADLEY: Yeah, he used to be a big deal. Wore lettermen's sweaters. Had medals hanging all around his neck. Real purty. Big deal. *(He laughs to himself, notices* DODGE *on floor, crosses to him, stops)* This one too. *(To* SHELLY*)* You'd never think it to look at him would ya'? All bony and wasted away.

*(*SHELLY *shakes her head again.* BRADLEY *stares at her, crosses back to her, clenching the coat in his fist. He stops in front of* SHELLY*.)*

BRADLEY: Women like that kinda' thing don't they?
SHELLY: What?
BRADLEY: Importance. Importance in a man?
SHELLY: I don't know.
BRADLEY: Yeah. You know, you know. Don't give me that. *(Moves closer to* SHELLY*)* You're with Tilden?
SHELLY: No.
BRADLEY: *(Turning to* TILDEN*)* Tilden! She with you?

*(*TILDEN *doesn't answer. Stares at floor.)*

BRADLEY: Tilden!

*(*TILDEN *suddenly bolts and runs off up stage left.* BRADLEY *laughs. Talks to* SHELLY. DODGE *starts moving his lips silently as though talking to someone invisible on the floor.)*

BRADLEY: *(Laughing)* Scared to death! He was always scared!

*(*BRADLEY *stops laughing. Stares at* SHELLY*.)*

BRADLEY: You're scared too, right? *(Laughs again)* You're scared and you don't even know me. *(Stops laughing)* You don't gotta be scared.

*(*SHELLY *looks at* DODGE *on the floor.)*

SHELLY: Can't we do something for him?
BRADLEY: *(Looking at* DODGE*)* We could shoot him. *(Laughs)* We could drown him! What about drowning him?

SHELLY: Shut up!

*(*BRADLEY *stops laughing. Moves in closer to* SHELLY. *She freezes.* BRADLEY *speaks slowly and deliberately.)*

BRADLEY: Hey! Missus. Don't talk to me like that. Don't talk to me in that tone a' voice. There was a time when I had to take that tone a' voice from pretty near everyone. *(Motioning to* DODGE*)* Him, for one! Him and that half brain that just ran outa' here. They don't talk to me like that now. Not any more. Everything's turned around now. Full circle. Isn't that funny?
SHELLY: I'm sorry.
BRADLEY: Open your mouth.
SHELLY: What?
BRADLEY: *(Motioning for her to open her mouth)* Open up.

(She opens her mouth slightly.)

BRADLEY: Wider.

(She opens her mouth wider.)

BRADLEY: Keep it like that.

(She does. Stares at BRADLEY. *With his free hand he puts his fingers into her mouth. She tries to pull away.)*

BRADLEY: Just stay put!

(She freezes. He keeps his fingers in her mouth. Stares at her. Pause. He pulls his hand out. She closes her mouth, keeps her eyes on him. BRADLEY *smiles. He looks at* DODGE *on the floor and crosses over to him.* SHELLY *watches him closely.* BRADLEY *stands over* DODGE *and smiles at* SHELLY. *He holds her coat up in both hands over* DODGE, *keeps smiling at* SHELLY. *He looks down at* DODGE *then drops the coat so that it lands on* DODGE *and covers his head.* BRADLEY *keeps his hands up in the position of holding the coat, looks over at* SHELLY *and smiles. The lights black out.)*

ACT III

SCENE
Same set. Morning. Bright sun. No sound of rain. Everything has been cleared up again. No sign of carrots. No pail. No stool. VINCE'S *saxophone case and overcoat are still at the foot of the staircase.* BRADLEY *is asleep on the sofa under* DODGE'S *blanket. His head toward stage left.* BRADLEY'S *wooden leg is leaning against the sofa right by his head.*

The shoe is left on it. The harness hangs down. DODGE *is sitting on the floor, propped up against the T.V. set facing stage left wearing his baseball cap.* SHELLY'S *rabbit fur coat covers his chest and shoulders. He stares off toward stage left. He seems weaker and more disoriented. The lights rise slowly to the sound of birds and remain for a while in silence on the two men.* BRADLEY *sleeps very soundly.* DODGE *hardly moves.* SHELLY *appears from stage left with a big smile, slowly crossing toward* DODGE *balancing a steaming cup of broth in a saucer.* DODGE *just stares at her as she gets close to him.*

SHELLY: *(As she crosses)* This is going to make all the difference in the world, Grandpa. You don't mind me calling you Grandpa do you? I mean I know you minded when Vince called you that but you don't even know him.

DODGE: He skipped town with my money ya' know. I'm gonna hold you as collateral.

SHELLY: He'll be back. Don't you worry.

(She kneels down next to DODGE *and puts the cup and saucer in his lap.)*

DODGE: It's morning already! Not only didn't I get my bottle but he's got my two bucks!

SHELLY: Try to drink this, okay? Don't spill it.

DODGE: What is it?

SHELLY: Beef bouillon. It'll warm you up.

DODGE: Bouillon! I don't want any goddamn bouillon! Get that stuff away from me!

SHELLY: I just got through making it.

DODGE: I don't care if you just spent all week making it! I ain't drinking it!

SHELLY: Well, what am I supposed to do with it then? I'm trying to help you out. Besides, it's good for you.

DODGE: Get it away from me!

*(*SHELLY *stands up with cup and saucer.)*

DODGE: What do you know what's good for me anyway?

(She looks at DODGE *then turns away from him, crossing to staircase, sits on bottom step and drinks the bouillon.* DODGE *stares at her.)*

DODGE: You know what'd be good for me?

SHELLY: What?

DODGE: A little massage. A little contact.

SHELLY: Oh no. I've had enough contact for a while. Thanks anyway.

(She keeps sipping bouillon, stays sitting. Pause as DODGE *stares at her.)*

DODGE: Why not? You got nothing better to do. That fella's not gonna be back here. You're not expecting him to show up again are you?

SHELLY: Sure. He'll show up. He left his horn here.

DODGE: His horn? *(Laughs)* You're his horn?

SHELLY: Very funny.

DODGE: He's run off with my money! He's not coming back here.

SHELLY: He'll be back.

DODGE: You're a funny chicken, you know that?

SHELLY: Thanks.

DODGE: Full of faith. Hope. Faith and hope. You're all alike you hopers. If it's not God then it's a man. If it's not a man then it's a woman. If its not a woman then its the land or the future of some kind. Some kind of future.

(Pause.)

SHELLY: *(Looking toward porch)* I'm glad it stopped raining.

DODGE: *(Looks toward porch then back to her)* That's what I mean. See, you're glad it stopped raining. Now you think everything's gonna be different. Just 'cause the sun comes out.

SHELLY: It's already different. Last night I was scared.

DODGE: Scared a' what?

SHELLY: Just scared.

DODGE: Bradley? *(Looks at* BRADLEY*)* He's a push-over. 'Specially now. All ya' gotta' do is take his leg and throw it out the back door. Helpless. Totally helpless.

*(*SHELLY *turns and stares at* BRADLEY'S *wooden leg then looks at* DODGE. *She sips bouillon.)*

SHELLY: You'd do that?

DODGE: Me? I've hardly got the strength to breathe.

SHELLY: But you'd actually do it if you could?

DODGE: Don't be so easily shocked, girlie. There's nothing a man can't do. You dream it up and he can do it. Anything.

SHELLY: You've tried I guess.

DODGE: Don't sit there sippin' your bouillon and judging me! This is my house!

SHELLY: I forgot.

DODGE: You forgot? Whose house did you think it was?

SHELLY: Mine.

(DODGE *just stares at her. Long pause. She sips from cup.*)

SHELLY: I know it's not mine but I had that feeling.

DODGE: What feeling?

SHELLY: The feeling that nobody lives here but me. I mean everybody's gone. You're here, but it doesn't seem like you're supposed to be. *(Pointing to* BRADLEY*)* Doesn't seem like he's supposed to be here either. I don't know what it is. It's the house or something. Something familiar. Like I know my way around here. Did you ever get that feeling?

(DODGE *stares at her in silence. Pause.*)

DODGE: No. No, I never did.

(SHELLY *gets up. Moves around space holding cup.*)

SHELLY: Last night I went to sleep up there in that room.

DODGE: What room?

SHELLY: That room up there with all the pictures. All the crosses on the wall.

DODGE: Halie's room?

SHELLY: Yeah. Whoever "Halie" is.

DODGE: She's my wife.

SHELLY: So you remember her?

DODGE: Whad'ya mean! 'Course I remember her! She's only been gone for a day — half a day. However long it's been.

SHELLY: Do you remember her when her hair was bright red? Standing in front of an apple tree?

DODGE: What is this, the third degree or something! Who're you to be askin' me personal questions about my wife!

SHELLY: You never look at those pictures up there?

DODGE: What pictures!

SHELLY: Your whole life's up there hanging on the wall. Somebody who looks just like you. Somebody who looks just like you used to look.

DODGE: That isn't me! That never was me! This is me. Right here. This is it. The whole shootin' match, sittin' right in front of you.

SHELLY: So the past never happened as far as you're concerned?

DODGE: The past? Jesus Christ. The past. What do you know about the past?

SHELLY: Not much. I know there was a farm.

(*Pause.*)

DODGE: A farm?

SHELLY: There's a picture of a farm. A big farm. A bull. Wheat. Corn.

DODGE: Corn?

SHELLY: All the kids are standing out in the corn. They're all waving these big straw hats. One of them doesn't have a hat.

DODGE: Which one was that?

SHELLY: There's a baby. A baby in a woman's arms. The same woman with the red hair. She looks lost standing out there. Like she doesn't know how she got there.

DODGE: She knows! I told her a hundred times it wasn't gonna' be the city! I gave her plenty a' warning.

SHELLY: She's looking down at the baby like it was somebody else's. Like it doesn't even belong to her.

DODGE: That's about enough outa' you! You got some funny ideas. Some damn funny ideas. You think just because people propagate they have to love their offspring? You never seen a bitch eat her puppies? Where are you from anyway?

SHELLY: L. A. We already went through that.

DODGE: That's right, L.A. I remember.

SHELLY: Stupid country.

DODGE: That's right! No wonder.

(*Pause.*)

SHELLY: What's happened to this family anyway?

DODGE: You're in no position to ask! What do you care? You some kinda' Social Worker?

SHELLY: I'm Vince's friend.

DODGE: Vince's friend! That's rich. That's really rich. "Vince"! "Mr. Vince"! "Mr. Thief" is more like it! His name doesn't mean a hoot in hell to me. Not a tinkle in the well. You know how many kids I've spawned? Not to mention Grand kids and Great Grand kids and Great Great Grand kids after them?

SHELLY: And you don't remember any of them?

DODGE: What's to remember? Halie's the one with the family album. She's the one you should talk to. She'll set you straight on the heritage if that's what you're interested in. She's traced it all the way back to the grave.

SHELLY: What do you mean?

DODGE: What do you think I mean? How far back can you go? A long line of corpses! There's not a living soul behind me. Not a one. Who's holding me in their memory? Who gives a damn about bones in the ground?

SHELLY: Was Tilden telling the truth?

(DODGE stops short. Stares at SHELLY. Shakes his head. He looks off stage left.)

SHELLY: Was he?

(DODGE'S tone changes drastically.)

DODGE: Tilden? *(Turns to SHELLY, calmly)* Where is Tilden?

SHELLY: Last night. Was he telling the truth about the baby?

(Pause.)

DODGE: *(Turns toward stage left)* What's happened to Tilden? Why isn't Tilden here?

SHELLY: Bradley chased him out.

DODGE: *(Looking at BRADLEY asleep)* Bradley? Why is he on my sofa? *(Turns back to SHELLY)* Have I been here all night? On the floor?

SHELLY: He wouldn't leave. I hid outside until he fell asleep.

DODGE: Outside? Is Tilden outside? He shouldn't be out there in the rain. He'll get himself into trouble. He doesn't know his way around here anymore. Not like he used to. He went out West and got himself into trouble. Got himself into bad trouble. We don't want any of that around here.

SHELLY: What did he do?

(Pause.)

DODGE: *(Quietly stares at SHELLY)* Tilden? He got mixed up. That's what he did. We can't afford to leave him alone. Not now.

(Sound of HALIE laughing comes from off left. SHELLY stands, looking in direction of voice, holding cup and saucer, doesn't know whether to stay or run.)

DODGE: *(Motioning to SHELLY)* Sit down! Sit back down!

(SHELLY sits. Sound of HALIE'S laughter again.)

DODGE: *(To SHELLY in a heavy whisper, pulling coat up around him)* Don't leave me alone now! Promise me? Don't go off and leave me alone. I need somebody here with me. Tilden's gone now and I need someone. Don't leave me! Promise!

SHELLY: *(Sitting)* I won't.

(HALIE appears outside the screen porch door, up left with FATHER DEWIS. She is wearing a bright yellow dress, no hat, white gloves and her arms are full of yellow roses. FATHER DEWIS is dressed in traditional black suit, white clerical collar and shirt. He is a very distinguished gray-haired man in his sixties. They are both slightly drunk and feeling giddy. As they enter the porch through the screen door, DODGE pulls the rabbit fur coat over his head and hides. SHELLY stands again. DODGE drops the coat and whispers intensely to SHELLY. Neither HALIE nor FATHER DEWIS are aware of the people inside the house.)

DODGE: *(To SHELLY in a strong whisper)* You promised!

(SHELLY sits on stairs again. DODGE pulls coat back over his head. HALIE and FATHER DEWIS talk on the porch as they cross toward stage right interior door.)

HALIE: Oh Father! That's terrible! That's absolutely terrible. Aren't you afraid of being punished?

(She giggles.)

DEWIS: Not by the Italians. They're too busy punishing each other.

(They both break out in giggles.)

HALIE: What about God?

DEWIS: Well, prayerfully, God only hears what he wants to. That's just between you and me of course. In our heart of hearts we know we're every bit as wicked as the Catholics.

(They giggle again and reach the stage right door.)

HALIE: Father, I never heard you talk like this in Sunday sermon.

DEWIS: Well, I save all my best jokes for private company. Pearls before swine you know.

(They enter the room laughing and stop when they see SHELLY. SHELLY *stands.* HALIE *closes the door behind* FATHER DEWIS. DODGE'S *voice is heard under the coat, talking to* SHELLY.*)*

DODGE: *(Under coat, to* SHELLY*)* Sit down, sit down! Don't let 'em buffalo you!

*(*SHELLY *sits on stair again.* HALIE *looks at* DODGE *on the floor then looks at* BRADLEY *asleep on sofa and sees his wooden leg. She lets out a shriek of embarrassment for* FATHER DEWIS.*)*

HALIE: Oh my gracious! What in the name of Judas Priest is going on in this house!

(She hands over the roses to FATHER DEWIS.*)*

HALIE: Excuse me, Father.

*(*HALIE *crosses to* DODGE, *whips the coat off him and covers the wooden leg with it.* BRADLEY *stays asleep.)*

HALIE: You can't leave this house for a second without the Devil blowing in through the front door!

DODGE: Gimme back that coat! Gimme back the goddamn coat before I freeze to death!

HALIE: You're not going to freeze! The sun's out in case you hadn't noticed!

DODGE: Gimme back that coat! That coat's for live flesh not dead wood!

*(*HALIE *whips the blanket off* BRADLEY *and throws it on* DODGE. DODGE *covers his head again with blanket.* BRADLEY'S *amputated leg can be faked by having half of it under a cushion of the sofa. He's fully clothed.* BRADLEY *sits up with a jerk when the blanket comes off him.)*

HALIE: *(As she tosses blanket)* Here! Use this! It's yours anyway! Can't you take care of yourself for once!

BRADLEY: *(Yelling at* HALIE*)* Gimme that blanket! Gimme back that blanket! That's my blanket!

*(*HALIE *crosses back toward* FATHER DEWIS *who just stands there with the roses.* BRADLEY *thrashes helplessly on the sofa trying to reach blanket.* DODGE *hides himself deeper in blanket.* SHELLY *looks on from staircase, still holding cup and saucer.)*

HALIE: Believe me, Father, this is not what I had in mind when I invited you in.

DEWIS: Oh, no apologies please. I wouldn't be in the ministry if I couldn't face real life.

(He laughs self-consciously. HALIE *notices* SHELLY *again and crosses over to her.* SHELLY *stays sitting.* HALIE *stops and stares at her.)*

BRADLEY: I want my blanket back! Gimme my blanket!

*(*HALIE *turns toward* BRADLEY *and silences him.)*

HALIE: Shut up Bradley! Right this minute! I've had enough!

*(*BRADLEY *slowly recoils, lies back down on sofa, turns his back toward* HALIE *and whimpers softly.* HALIE *directs her attention to* SHELLY *again. Pause.)*

HALIE: *(To* SHELLY*)* What're you doing with my cup and saucer?

SHELLY: *(Looking at cup, back to* HALIE*)* I made some buillon for Dodge.

HALIE: For Dodge?

SHELLY: Yeah.

HALIE: Well, did he drink it?

SHELLY: No.

HALIE: Did you drink it?

SHELLY: Yes.

*(*HALIE *stares at her. Long pause. She turns abruptly away from* SHELLY *and crosses back to* FATHER DEWIS.*)*

HALIE: Father, there's a stranger in my house. What would you advise? What would be the Christian thing?

DEWIS: *(Squirming)* Oh, well.... I.... I really —

HALIE: We still have some whiskey, don't we?

*(*DODGE *slowly pulls the blanket down off his head and looks toward* FATHER DEWIS. SHELLY *stands.)*

SHELLY: Listen, I don't drink or anything. I just —

*(*HALIE *turns toward* SHELLY *viciously.)*

HALIE: You sit back down!

*(*SHELLY *sits again on stair.* HALIE *turns again to* DEWIS.*)*

HALIE: I think we have plenty of whiskey left! Don't we Father?

DEWIS: Well, yes. I think so. You'll have to get it. My hands are full.

(HALIE *giggles. Reaches into* DEWIS'S *pockets, searching for bottle. She smells the roses as she searches.* DEWIS *stands stiffly.* DODGE *watches* HALIE *closely as she looks for bottle.*)

HALIE: The most incredible things, roses! Aren't they incredible, Father?

DEWIS: Yes. Yes they are.

HALIE: They almost cover the stench of sin in this house. Just magnificent! The smell. We'll have to put some at the foot of Ansel's statue. On the day of the unveiling.

(HALIE *finds a silver flask of whiskey in* DEWIS'S *vest pocket. She pulls it out.* DODGE *looks on eagerly.* HALIE *crosses to* DODGE, *opens the flask and takes a sip.*)

HALIE: *(To* DODGE) Ansel's getting a statue, Dodge. Did you know that? Not a plaque but a real live statue. A full bronze. Tip to toe. A basketball in one hand and a rifle in the other.

BRADLEY: *(His back to* HALIE*)* He never played basketball!

HALIE: You shut up, Bradley! You shut up about Ansel! Ansel played basketball better than anyone! And you know it! He was an All-American! There's no reason to take the glory away from others.

(HALIE *turns away from* BRADLEY, *crosses back toward* DEWIS *sipping on the flask and smiling.*)

HALIE: *(To* DEWIS) Ansel was a great basketball player. One of the greatest.

DEWIS: I remember Ansel.

HALIE: Of course! You remember. You remember how he could play. *(She turns toward* SHELLY*)* Of course, nowadays they play a different brand of basketball. More vicious. Isn't that right, dear?

SHELLY: I don't know.

(HALIE *crosses to* SHELLY, *sipping on flask. She stops in front of* SHELLY.*)

HALIE: Much, much more vicious. They smash into each other. They knock each other's teeth out. There's blood all over the court. Savages.

(HALIE *takes the cup from* SHELLY *and pours whiskey into it.*)

HALIE: They don't train like they used to. Not at all. They allow themselves to run amuck. Drugs and women. Women mostly.

(HALIE *hands the cup of whiskey back to* SHELLEY *slowly.* SHELLY *takes it.*)

HALIE: Mostly women. Girls. Sad, pathetic little girls. *(She crosses back to* FATHER DEWIS) It's just a reflection of the times, don't you think, Father? An indication of where we stand?

DEWIS: I suppose so, yes.

HALIE: Yes. A sort of a bad omen. Our youth becoming monsters.

DEWIS: Well, I uh —

HALIE: Oh you can disagree with me if you want to, Father. I'm open to debate. I think argument only enriches both sides of the question don't you? *(She moves toward* DODGE) I suppose, in the long run, it doesn't matter. When you see the way things deteriorate before your very eyes. Everything running down hill. It's kind of silly to even think about youth.

DEWIS: No, I don't think so. I think it's important to believe in certain things.

HALIE: Yes. Yes, I know what you mean. I think that's right. I think that's true. *(She looks at* DODGE) Certain basic things. We can't shake certain basic things. We might end up crazy. Like my husband. You can see it in his eyes. You can see how mad he is.

(DODGE *covers his head with the blanket again.* HALIE *takes a single rose from* DEWIS *and moves slowly over to* DODGE.*)

HALIE: We can't not believe in something. We can't stop believing. We just end up dying if we stop. Just end up dead.

(HALIE *throws the rose gently onto* DODGE'S *blanket. It lands between his knees and stays there! Long pause as* HALIE *stares at the rose.* SHELLY *stands suddenly.* HALIE *doesn't turn to her but keeps staring at rose.*)

SHELLY: *(To* HALIE) Don't you wanna' know who I am! Don't you wanna know what I'm doing here! I'm not dead!

(SHELLY *crosses toward* HALIE. HALIE *turns slowly toward her.*)

HALIE: Did you drink your whiskey?

SHELLY: No! And I'm not going to either!

HALIE: Well that's a firm stand. It's good to have a firm stand.

SHELLY: I don't have any stand at all. I'm just trying to put all this together.

(HALIE *laughs and crosses back to* DEWIS.)

HALIE: *(To* DEWIS*)* Surprises, surprises! Did you have any idea we'd be returning to this?

SHELLY: I came here with your Grandson for a little visit! A little innocent friendly visit.

HALIE: My Grandson?

SHELLY: Yes! That's right. The one no one remembers.

HALIE: *(To* DEWIS*)* This is getting a little farfetched.

SHELLY: I told him it was stupid to come back here. To try to pick up from where he left off.

HALIE: Where was that?

SHELLY: Wherever he was when he left here! Six years ago! Ten years ago! Whenever it was. I told him nobody cares.

HALIE: Didn't he listen?

SHELLY: No! No he didn't. We had to stop off at every tiny little meatball town that he remembered from his boyhood! Every stupid little donut shop he ever kissed a girl in. Every Drive-In. Every Drag Strip. Every football field he ever broke a bone on.

HALIE: *(Suddenly alarmed, to* DODGE*)* Where's Tilden?

SHELLY: Don't ignore me!

HALIE: Dodge! Where's Tilden gone?

(SHELLY *moves violently toward* HALIE.)

SHELLY: *(To* HALIE*)* I'm talking to you!

(BRADLEY *sits up fast on the sofa,* SHELLY *backs away.)*

BRADLEY: *(To* SHELLY*)* Don't you yell at my mother!

HALIE: Dodge! *(She kicks* DODGE*)* I told you not to let Tilden out of your sight! Where's he gone to?

DODGE: Gimme a drink and I'll tell ya'.

DEWIS: Halie, maybe this isn't the right time for a visit.

(HALIE *crosses back to* DEWIS.)

HALIE: *(To* DEWIS*)* I never should've left! I never, never should've left! Tilden could be anywhere by now! Anywhere! He's not in control of his faculties. Dodge knew that. I told him when I left here. I told him specifically to watch out for Tilden.

(BRADLEY *reaches down, grabs* DODGE'S *blanket and yanks it off him. He lays down on sofa and pulls the blanket over his head.)*

DODGE: He's got my blanket again! He's got my blanket!

HALIE: *(Turning to* BRADLEY*)* Bradley! Bradley, put that blanket back!

(HALIE *moves toward* BRADLEY. SHELLY *suddenly throws the cup and saucer against the stage right door.* DEWIS *ducks. The cup and saucer smash into pieces.* HALIE *stops, turns toward* SHELLY. *Everyone freezes.* BRADLEY *slowly pulls his head out from under blanket, looks toward stage right door, then to* SHELLY. SHELLY *stares at* HALIE. DEWIS *cowers with roses.* SHELLY *moves slowly toward* HALIE. *Long pause.* SHELLY *speaks softly.)*

SHELLY: *(To* HALIE*)* I don't like being ignored. I don't like being treated like I'm not here. I didn't like it when I was a kid and I still don't like it.

BRADLEY: *(Sitting up on sofa)* We don't have to tell you anything, girl. Not a thing. You're not the police are you? You're not the government. You're just some prostitute that Tilden brought in here.

HALIE: Language! I won't have that language in my house!

SHELLY: *(To* BRADLEY*)* You stuck your hand in my mouth and you call me a prostitute!

HALIE: Bradley! Did you put your hand in her mouth? I'm ashamed of you. I can't leave you alone for a minute.

BRADLEY: I never did. She's lying!

DEWIS: Halie, I think I'll be running along now. I'll just put the roses in the kitchen.

(DEWIS *moves toward stage left.* HALIE *stops him.)*

HALIE: Don't go now, Father! Not now.

BRADLEY: I never did anything, mom! I never touched her! She propositioned me! And I turned her down. I turned her down flat!

(SHELLY *suddenly grabs her coat off the wooden leg and takes both the leg and coat down stage, away from* BRADLEY.)

BRADLEY: Mom! Mom! She's got my leg! She's taken my leg! I never did anything to her! She's stolen my leg!

(BRADLEY *reaches pathetically in the air for his leg.*
SHELLY *sets it down for a second, puts on her coat
fast and picks the leg up again.* DODGE *starts
coughing softly.)*

HALIE: *(To* SHELLY*)* I think we've had about
enough of you, young lady. Just about enough. I
don't know where you came from or what you're
doing here but you're no longer welcome in this
house.
SHELLY: *(Laughs, holds leg)* No longer
welcome!
BRADLEY: Mom! That's my leg! Get my leg
back! I can't do anything without my leg.

(BRADLEY *keeps making whimpering sounds and
reaching for his leg.)*

HALIE: Give my son back his leg. Right this
very minute!

(DODGE *starts laughing softly to himself in
between coughs.)*

HALIE: *(To* DEWIS*)* Father, do something about
this would you! I'm not about to be terrorized in my
own house!
BRADLEY: Gimme back my leg!
HALIE: Oh, shut up, Bradley! Just shut up!
You don't need your leg now! Just lay down and
shut up!

(BRADLEY *whimpers. Lays down and pulls blanket
around him. He keeps one arm outside blanket,
reaching out toward his wooden leg.* DEWIS
cautiously approaches SHELLY *with the roses in his
arms.* SHELLY *clutches the wooden leg to her chest
as though she's kidnapped it.)*

DEWIS: *(To* SHELLY*)* Now, honestly dear,
wouldn't it be better to try to talk things out? To try
to use some reason?
SHELLY: There isn't any reason here! I can't
find a reason for anything.
DEWIS: There's nothing to be afraid of. These
are all good people. All righteous people.
SHELLY: I'm not afraid!
DEWIS: But this isn't your house. You have to
have some respect.
SHELLY: You're the strangers here, not me.
HALIE: This has gone far enough!
DEWIS: Halie, please. Let me handle this.
SHELLY: Don't come near me! Don't anyone

come near me. I don't need any words from you. I'm
not threatening anybody. I don't even know what
I'm doing here. You all say you don't remember
Vince, okay, maybe you don't. Maybe it's Vince
that's crazy. Maybe he's made this whole family
thing up. I don't even care any more. I was just coming along for the ride. I thought it'd be a nice gesture. Besides, I was curious. He made all of you
sound familiar to me. Every one of you. For every
name, I had an image. Every time he'd tell me a
name, I'd see the person. In fact, each of you was so
clear in my mind that I actually believed it was you.
I really believed when I walked through that door
that the people who lived here would turn out to
be the same people in my imagination. But I don't
recognize any of you. Not one. Not even the slightest resemblance.
DEWIS: Well you can hardly blame others for
not fulfilling your hallucination.
SHELLY: It was no hallucination! It was more
like a prophecy. You believe in prophecy, don't
you?
HALIE: Father, there's no point in talking to
her any further. We're just going to have to call the
police.
BRADLEY: No! Don't get the police in here.
We don't want the police in here. This is our home.
SHELLY: That's right. Bradley's right. Don't
you usually settle your affairs in private? Don't you
usually take them out in the dark? Out in the back?
BRADLEY: You stay out of our lives! You have
no business interfering!
SHELLY: I don't have any business period. I got
nothing to lose.

(She moves around, staring at each of them.)

BRADLEY: You don't know what we've been
through. You don't know anything!
SHELLY: I know you've got a secret. You've all
got a secret. It's so secret in fact, you're all convinced
it never happened.

(HALIE moves to DEWIS)

HALIE: Oh, my God, Father!
DODGE: *(Laughing to himself)* She thinks
she's going to get it out of us. She thinks she's going
to uncover the truth of the matter. Like a detective
or something.
BRADLEY: I'm not telling her anything! Nothing's wrong here! Nothin's ever been wrong! Every-

thing's the way it's supposed to be! Nothing ever happened that's bad! Everything is all right here! We're all good people!

DODGE: She thinks she's gonna suddenly bring everything out into the open after all these years.

DEWIS: *(To* SHELLY*)* Can't you see that these people want to be left in peace? Don't you have any mercy? They haven't done anything to you.

DODGE: She wants to get to the bottom of it. *(To* SHELLY*)* That's it, isn't it? You'd like to get right down to bedrock? You want me to tell ya'? You want me to tell ya' what happened? I'll tell ya'. I might as well.

BRADLEY: No! Don't listen to him. He doesn't remember anything!

DODGE: I remember the whole thing from start to finish. I remember the day he was born.

(Pause.)

HALIE: Dodge, if you tell this thing—if you tell this, you'll be dead to me. You'll be just as good as dead.

DODGE: That won't be such a big change, Halie. See this girl, this girl here, she wants to know. She wants to know something more. And I got this feeling that it doesn't make a bit a' difference. I'd sooner tell it to a stranger than anybody else.

BRADLEY: *(To* DODGE*)* We made a pact! We made a pact between us! You can't break that now!

DODGE: I don't remember any pact.

BRADLEY: *(To* SHELLY*)* See, he doesn't remember anything. I'm the only one in the family who remembers. The only one. And I'll never tell you!

SHELLY: I'm not so sure I want to find out now.

DODGE: *(Laughing to himself)* Listen to her! Now she's runnin' scared!

SHELLY: I'm not scared!

*(*DODGE *stops laughing, long pause.* DODGE *stares at her.)*

DODGE: You're not huh? Well, that's good. Because I'm not either. See, we were a well established family once. Well established. All the boys were grown. The farm was producing enough milk to fill Lake Michigan twice over. Me and Halie here were pointed toward what looked like the middle part of our life. Everything was settled with us. All

we had to do was ride it out. Then Halie got pregnant again. Outa' the middle a' nowhere, she got pregnant. We weren't planning on havin' any more boys. We had enough boys already. In fact, we hadn't been sleepin' in the same bed for about six years.

HALIE: *(Moving toward stairs)* I'm not listening to this! I don't have to listen to this!

DODGE: *(Stops* HALIE*)* Where are you going! Upstairs! You'll just be listenin' to it upstairs! You go outside, you'll be listenin' to it outside. Might as well stay here and listen to it.

*(*HALIE *stays by stairs.)*

BRADLEY: If I had my leg you wouldn't be saying this. You'd never get away with it if I had my leg.

DODGE: *(Pointing to* SHELLY*)* She's got your leg. *(Laughs)* She's gonna keep your leg too. *(To* SHELLY*)* She wants to hear this. Don't you?

SHELLY: I don't know.

DODGE: Well even if ya' don't I'm gonna' tell ya'. *(Pause)* Halie had this kid. This baby boy. She had it. I let her have it on her own. All the other boys I had had the best doctors, best nurses, everything. This one I let her have by herself. This one hurt real bad. Almost killed her, but she had it anyway. It lived, see. It lived. It wanted to grow up in this family. It wanted to be just like us. It wanted to be a part of us. It wanted to pretend that I was its father. She wanted me to believe in it. Even when everyone around us knew. Everyone. All our boys new. Tilden knew.

HALIE: You shut up! Bradley, make him shut up!

BRADLEY: I can't.

DODGE: Tilden was the one who knew. Better than any of us. He'd walk for miles with that kid in his arms. Halie let him take it. All night sometimes. He'd walk all night out there in the pasture with it. Talkin' to it. Singin' to it. Used to hear him singing to it. He'd make up stories. He'd tell that kid all kinds a' stories. Even when he knew it couldn't understand him. Couldn't understand a word he was sayin'. Never would understand him. We couldn't let a thing like that continue. We couldn't allow that to grow up right in the middle of our lives. It made everything we'd accomplished look like it was nothin'. Everything was cancelled out by this one mistake. This one weakness.

SHELLY: So you killed him?

DODGE: I killed it. I drowned it. Just like the runt of a litter. Just drowned it.

(HALIE *moves toward* BRADLEY.)

HALIE: (*To* BRADLEY) Ansel would've stopped him! Ansel would've stopped him from telling these lies! He was a hero! A man! A whole man! What's happened to the men in this family! Where are the men!

(*Suddenly* VINCE *comes crashing through the screen porch door up left, tearing it off its hinges. Everyone but* DODGE *and* BRADLEY *back away from the porch and stare at* VINCE *who has landed on his stomach on the porch in a drunken stupor. He is singing loudly to himself and hauls himself slowly to his feet. He has a paper shopping bag full of empty booze bottles. He takes them out one at a time as he sings and smashes them at the opposite end of the porch, behind the solid interior door, stage right.* SHELLY *moves slowly toward stage right, holding wooden leg and watching* VINCE.)

VINCE: (*Singing loudly as he hurls bottles*) "From the Halls of Montezuma to the Shores of Tripoli. We will fight our country's battles on the land and on the sea."

(*He punctuates the words* "Montezuma", "Tripoli", "battles" *and* "sea" *with a smashed bottle each. He stops throwing for a second, stares toward stage right of the porch, shades his eyes with his hand as though looking across to a battle field, then cups his hands around his mouth and yells across the space of the porch to an imaginary army. The others watch in terror and expectation.*)

VINCE: (*To imagined army*) Have you had enough over there! 'Cause there's a lot more here where that came from! (*Pointing to paper bag full of bottles*) A helluva lot more! We got enough over here to blow ya' from here to Kingdomcome!

(*He takes another bottle, makes high whistling sound of a bomb and throws it toward stage right porch. Sound of bottle smashing against wall. This should be the actual smashing of bottles and not tape sound. He keeps yelling and heaving bottles one after another.*)

VINCE *stops for a while, breathing heavily from exhaustion. Long silence as the others watch him.* SHELLY *approaches tentatively in* VINCE'S *direction, still holding* BRADLEY'S *wooden leg.*)

SHELLY: (*After silence*) Vince?

(VINCE *turns toward her. Peers through screen.*)

VINCE: Who? What? Vince who? Who's that in there?

(VINCE *pushes his face against the screen from the porch and stares in at everyone.*)

DODGE: Where's my goddamn bottle!

VINCE: (*Looking in at* DODGE) What? Who is that?

DODGE: It's me! Your Grandfather! Don't play stupid with me! Where's my two bucks!

VINCE: Your two bucks?

(HALIE *moves away from* DEWIS, *upstage, peers out at* VINCE, *trying to recognize him.*)

HALIE: Vincent? Is that you, Vincent?

(SHELLY *stares at* HALIE *then looks out at* VINCE.)

VINCE: (*From porch*) Vincent who? What is this! Who are you people?

SHELLY: (*To* HALIE) Hey, wait a minute. Wait a minute! What's going on?

HALIE: (*Moving closer to porch screen*) We thought you were a murderer or something. Barging in through the door like that.

VINCE: I am a murderer! Don't underestimate me for a minute! I'm the Midnight Strangler! I devour whole families in a single gulp!

(VINCE *grabs another bottle and smashes it on the porch.* HALIE *backs away.*)

SHELLY: (*Approaching Halie*) You mean you know who he is?

HALIE: Of course I know who he is! That's more than I can say for you.

BRADLEY: (*Sitting up on sofa*) You get off our front porch, you creep! What're you doing out there breaking bottles? Who are these foreigners anyway! Where did they come from?

VINCE: Maybe I should come in there and break them!

HALIE: (*Moving toward porch*) Don't you dare! Vincent, what's got into you! Why are you acting like this?

VINCE: Maybe I should come in there and usurp your territory!

(HALIE *turns back toward* DEWIS *and crosses to him.*)

HALIE: *(To* DEWIS*)* Father, why are you just standing around here when everything's falling apart? Can't you rectify this situation?

(DODGE *laughs, coughs.*)

DEWIS: I'm just a guest here, Halie. I don't know what my position is exactly. This is outside my parish anyway.

(VINCE *starts throwing more bottles as things continue.*)

BRADLEY: If I had my leg I'd rectify it! I'd rectify him all over the goddamn highway! I'd pull his ears out if I could reach him!

(BRADLEY *sticks his fist through the screening of the porch and reaches out for* VINCE, *grabbing at him and missing.* VINCE *jumps away from* BRADLEY'S *hand.*)

VINCE: Aaaah! Our lines have been penetrated! Tentacles animals! Beasts from the deep!

(VINCE *strikes out at* BRADLEY'S *hand with a bottle.* BRADLEY *pulls his hand back inside.*)

SHELLY: Vince! Knock it off will ya'! I want to get out of here!

(VINCE *pushes his face against screen, looks in at* SHELLY.*)

VINCE: *(To* SHELLY*)* Have they got you prisoner in there, dear? Such a sweet young thing too. All her life in front of her. Nipped in the bud.

SHELLY: I'm coming out there, Vince! I'm coming out there and I want us to get in the car and drive away from here. Anywhere. Just away from here.

(SHELLY *moves toward* VINCE'S *saxophone case and overcoat. She sets down the wooden leg, downstage left and picks up the saxophone case and overcoat.* VINCE *watches her through the screen.*)

VINCE: *(To* SHELLY*)* We'll have to negotiate. Make some kind of a deal. Prisoner exchange or something. A few of theirs for one of ours. Small price to pay if you ask me.

(SHELLY *crosses toward stage right door with overcoat and case.*)

SHELLY: Just go and get the car! I'm coming out there now. We're going to leave.

VINCE: Don't come out here! Don't you dare come out here!

(SHELLY *stops short of the door, stage right.*)

SHELLY: How come?

VINCE: Off limits! Verboten! This is taboo territory. No man or woman has ever crossed the line and lived to tell the tale!

SHELLY: I'll take my chances.

(SHELLY *moves to stage right door and opens it.* VINCE *pulls out a big folding hunting knife and pulls open the blade. He jabs the blade into the screen and starts cutting a hole big enough to climb through.* BRADLEY *cowers in a corner of the sofa as* VINCE *rips at the screen.*)

VINCE: *(As he cuts screen)* Don't come out here! I'm warning you! You'll disintegrate!

(DEWIS *takes* HALIE *by the arm and pulls her toward staircase.*)

DEWIS: Halie, maybe we should go upstairs until this blows over.

HALIE: I don't understand it. I just don't understand it. He was the sweetest little boy!

(DEWIS *drops the roses beside the wooden leg at the foot of the staircase then escorts* HALIE *quickly up the stairs.* HALIE *keeps looking back at* VINCE *as they climb the stairs.*)

HALIE: There wasn't a mean bone in his body. Everyone loved Vincent. Everyone. He was the perfect baby.

DEWIS: He'll be all right after a while. He's just had a few too many that's all.

HALIE: He used to sing in his sleep. He'd sing. In the middle of the night. The sweetest voice. Like an angel. *(She stops for a moment.)* I used to lie awake listening to it. I used to lie awake thinking it was all right if I died. Because Vincent was an angel. A guardian angel. He'd watch over us. He'd watch over all of us.

(DEWIS *takes her all the way up the stairs. They disappear above.* VINCE *is now climbing through the porch screen onto the sofa.* BRADLEY *crashes off the sofa, holding tight to his blanket, keeping it wrapped around him.* SHELLY *is outside on the porch.* VINCE *holds the knife in his teeth once he gets the hole wide enough to climb through.* BRADLEY *starts crawling slowly toward his wooden leg, reaching out for it.)*

DODGE: *(To* VINCE*)* Go ahead! Take over the house! Take over the whole goddamn house! You can have it! It's yours. It's been a pain in the neck ever since the very first mortgage. I'm gonna die any second now. Any second. You won't even notice. So I'll settle my affairs once and for all.

(As DODGE *proclaims his last will and testament,* VINCE *climbs into the room, knife in mouth and strides slowly around the space, inspecting his inheritance. He casually notices* BRADLEY *as he crawls toward his leg.* VINCE *moves to the leg and keeps pushing it with his foot so that it's out of* BRADLEY'S *reach then goes on with his inspection. He picks up the roses and carries them around smelling them.* SHELLY *can be seen outside on the porch, moving slowly center and staring in at* VINCE. VINCE *ignores her.)*

DODGE: The house goes to my Grandson, Vincent. All the furnishings, accoutrements and paraphernalia therein. Everything tacked to the walls or otherwise resting under this roof. My tools—namely my band saw, my skill saw, my drill press, my chain saw, my lathe, my electric sander, all go to my eldest son, Tilden. That is, if he ever shows up again. My shed and gasoline powered equipment, namely my tractor, my dozer, my hand tiller plus all the attachments and riggings for the above mentioned machinery, namely my spring tooth harrow, my deep plows, my disk plows, my automatic fertilizing equipment, my reaper, my swathe, my seeder, my John Deere Harvester, my post hole digger, my jackhammer, my lathe—*(to himself)* Did I mention my lathe? I already mentioned my lathe—my Bennie Goodman records, my harnesses, my bits, my halters, my brace, my rough rasp, my forge, my welding equipment, my shoeing nails, my levels and bevels, my milking stool—no, not my milking stool—my hammers and chisels, my hinges, my cattle gates, my barbed wire, self-tapping augers, my horse hair ropes and all related materials are to be pushed into a gigantic heap and set ablaze in the very center of my fields. When the blaze is at its highest, preferably on a cold, windless

night, my body is to be pitched into the middle of it and burned til nothing remains but ash.

(Pause. VINCE *takes the knife out of his mouth and smells the roses. He's facing toward audience and doesn't turn around to* SHELLY. *He folds up knife and pockets it.)*

SHELLY: *(From porch)* I'm leaving, Vince. Whether you come or not, I'm leaving.
VINCE: *(Smelling roses)* Just put my horn on the couch there before you take off.
SHELLY: *(Moving toward hole in screen)* You're not coming?

*(*VINCE *stays downstage, turns and looks at her.)*

VINCE: I just inherited a house.
SHELLY: *(Through hole, from porch)* You want to stay here?
VINCE: *(As he pushes* BRADLEY'S *leg out of reach)* I've gotta carry on the line. I've gotta see to it that things keep rolling.

*(*BRADLEY *looks up at him from floor, keeps pulling himself toward his leg.* VINCE *keeps moving it.)*

SHELLY: What happened to you, Vince? You just disappeared.
VINCE: *(Pause, delivers speech front)* I was gonna run last night. I was gonna run and keep right on running. I drove all night. Clear to the Iowa border. The old man's two bucks sitting right on the seat beside me. It never stopped raining the whole time. Never stopped once. I could see myself in the windshield. My face. My eyes. I studied my face. Studied everything about it. As though I was looking at another man. As though I could see his whole race behind him. Like a mummy's face. I saw him dead and alive at the same time. In the same breath. In the windshield, I watched him breathe as though he was frozen in time. And every breath marked him. Marked him forever without him knowing. And then his face changed. His face became his father's face. Same bones. Same eyes. Same nose. Same breath. And his father's face changed to his Grandfather's face. And it went on like that. Changing. Clear on back to faces I'd never seen before but still recognized. Still recognized the bones underneath. The eyes. The breath. The mouth. I followed my family clear into Iowa. Every last one. Straight into the Corn Belt and further. Straight back as far as they'd take me. Then it all dissolved. Everything dissolved.

(SHELLY stares at him for a while then reaches through the hole in the screen and sets the saxophone case and VINCE'S overcoat on the sofa. She looks at VINCE again.)

SHELLY: Bye, Vince.

(She exits left off the porch. VINCE watches her go. BRADLEY tries to make a lunge for his wooden leg. VINCE quickly picks it up and dangles it over BRADLEY'S head like a carrot. BRADLEY keeps making desperate grabs at the leg. DEWIS comes down the staircase and stops half way, staring at VINCE and BRADLEY. VINCE looks up at DEWIS and smiles. He keeps moving backwards with the leg toward upstage left as BRADLEY crawls after him.)

VINCE: *(To DEWIS as he continues torturing BRADLEY)* Oh, excuse me, Father. Just getting rid of some of the vermin in the house. This is my house now, ya' know? All mine. Everything. Except for the power tools and stuff. I'm gonna get all new equipment anyway. New plows, new tractor, everything. All brand new. *(VINCE teases BRADLEY closer to the up left corner of the stage.)* Start right off on the ground floor.

(VINCE throws BRADLEY'S wooden leg far off stage left. BRADLEY follows his leg off stage, pulling himself along on the ground, whimpering. As BRADLEY exits VINCE pulls the blanket off him and throws it over his own shoulder. He crosses toward DEWIS with the blanket and smells the roses. DEWIS comes to the bottom of the stairs.)

DEWIS: You'd better go up and see your Grandmother.

VINCE: *(Looking up stairs, back to DEWIS)* My Grandmother? There's nobody else in this house. Except for you. And you're leaving aren't you?

(DEWIS crosses toward stage right door. He turns back to VINCE.)

DEWIS: She's going to need someone. I can't help her. I don't know what to do. I don't know what my position is. I just came in for some tea. I had no idea there was any trouble. No idea at all.

(VINCE just stares at him. DEWIS goes out the door, crosses porch and exits left. VINCE listens to him leaving. He smells roses, looks up the staircase

then smells roses again. He turns and looks upstage at DODGE. He crosses up to him and bends over looking at DODGE'S open eyes. DODGE is dead. His death should have come completely unnoticed. Vince lifts the blanket, then covers his head. He sits on the sofa, smelling roses and staring at DODGE'S body. Long pause. VINCE places the roses on DODGE'S chest then lays down on the sofa, arms folded behind his head, staring at the ceiling. His body is in the same relationship to DODGE'S. After a while HALIE'S voice is heard coming from above the staircase. The lights start to dim almost imperceptively as HALIE speaks. VINCE keeps staring at the ceiling.)

HALIE'S VOICE: Dodge? Is that you, Dodge? Tilden was right about the corn you know. I've never seen such corn. Have you taken a look at it lately? Tall as a man already. This early in the year. Carrots too. Potatoes. Peas. It's like a paradise out there, Dodge. You oughta' take a look. A miracle. I've never seen it like this. Maybe the rain did something. Maybe it was the rain.

(As HALIE keeps talking off stage, TILDEN appears from stage left, dripping with mud from the knees down. His arms and hands are covered with mud. In his hands he carries the corpse of a small child at chest level, staring down at it. The corpse mainly consists of bones wrapped in muddy, rotten cloth. He moves slowly downstage toward the staircase, ignoring VINCE on the sofa. VINCE keeps staring at the ceiling as though TILDEN wasn't there. As HALIE'S VOICE continues, TILDEN slowly makes his way up the stairs. His eyes never leave the corpse of the child. The lights keep fading.)

HALIE'S VOICE: Good hard rain. Takes everything straight down deep to the roots. The rest takes care of itself. You can't force a thing to grow. You can't interfere with it. It's all hidden. It's all unseen. You just gotta wait til it pops up out of the ground. Tiny little shoot. Tiny little white shoot. All hairy and fragile. Strong though. Strong enough to break the earth even. It's a miracle, Dodge. I've never seen a crop like this in my whole life. Maybe it's the sun. Maybe that's it. Maybe it's the sun.

(TILDEN disappears above. Silence. Lights go to black.)

On its simplest level, *Buried Child* develops a story about a family seeking to survive by denying its past. Dodge and Halie, the parents, are alienated from each other, although they continue to live in the same house; she upstairs, he downstairs. They have had three sons: Tilden, a former All-American fullback, now "burned out and displaced" like a half-witted child; Bradley, who has lost a leg to a chain saw and who vacillates between assertiveness and cowering; and Ansel, once a basketball star and soldier but who died on his honeymoon. In addition, a grandson, Vince, returns after six years' absence.

An air of mystery is created in part through the motif of the buried child, which is introduced early in the play and referred to frequently thereafter. We learn that Halie has had a fourth son but that he was killed by Dodge and buried somewhere in the backyard. Not until the end of the play does anyone acknowledge, although there have been hints earlier, that the child resulted from an incestuous relationship between Halie and Tilden. Then Dodge dies and Tilden finds the dead body and carries it upstairs to Halie.

But the play is not a mystery story, nor, despite its many realistic features, can it be adequately described as realistic, in part because so much information is withheld. We learn very little about the characters' pasts. We do not know where Dodge and Halie have come from, what their family backgrounds were, or even very much about their life together. Presumably Dodge has grown up in the heartland of America represented by the Illinois farm on which they now live; since he tells of warning Halie that life on a farm would not be easy, she apparently came from a different environment. We do not know what has turned Tilden into a seeming half-wit; Dodge says that Tilden has recently returned after 20 years in New Mexico; Tilden admits to some unnamed shameful act in New Mexico and Bradley reveals that Tilden has been in prison; and though Tilden has a son (Vince), we never hear of his wife. Of Bradley we learn little other than that he has lost a leg. Of Vince we know that he is a musician, that he has been away for six years, and that he spent part of his childhood with his grandparents. We do not even learn the family's last name.

Both this paucity of information and the motif of the buried child are related to a major theme of the play: evasion and denial of the past. None of the characters, except Vince, wants to remember the past. Dodge rejects it most completely, saying that he has no interest in genealogy: "How far back can you go? A long line of corpses! There's not a living soul behind me." Halie remembers only the pleasant things, but about even these she is vague. Tilden's memory seems to extend primarily to the dead baby, and neither he nor Dodge will acknowledge that he recognizes Vince. This desire to escape the past is embodied most fully in the buried child, and the action is resolved when the past is acknowledged and the buried child exhumed.

Evasion of the past is also related to images of barrenness and fecundity. Early in the play Tilden enters carrying an armload of corn which he swears came from the back yard, although both Dodge and Halie insist that nothing has grown there since 1935. Thus, we have simultaneous and contradictory images of fertile and fallow farmland. At the end of the play, as the buried child is acknowledged and exhumed, fertility seems to triumph over barrenness as Halie proclaims from upstairs: "I've never seen such corn. . . . Tall as a man already. . . . Carrots too.

Potatoes. Peas. It's like a paradise out there, Dodge. You oughta' take a look. A miracle."

Tied up with the idea of barrenness and fertility are others related to sexuality and sexual perversity, for which Halie is the primary focus. Even before she appears on stage, Halie reminisces about having gone to a racetrack with a horse breeder, and when she appears she is on her way "to lunch" with Father Dewis, although Dodge accepts that she will not return that day. It also seems significant that when she leaves she is dressed entirely in black, "as though in mourning," but that when she returns the next day after having spent the night with Father Dewis she is dressed in yellow and white. Such behavior is obviously typical of Halie, and it seems likely that the absence of corn in the backyard since 1935 is indicative of the estrangement that has existed between Halie and Dodge during most of their married life. Dodge's response has been to retreat inwardly—suggested visually when Tilden covers Dodge with the husks he has removed from the corn. Dodge is now merely the husk of a man, an embittered survivor who has lost all hope.

Halie's sexuality is not confined to extramarital affairs. She has also left her mark on her sons. She has been involved in incest with Tilden, whose speeches and behavior also suggest the possibility of sexual crimes and electric shock treatment in New Mexico. Halie may also have practiced incest with Ansel, who killed himself on his honeymoon: "I knew he'd never come back from his honeymoon. I kissed him and he felt like a corpse. All white. Cold. Icy blue lips. He never used to kiss like that. Never before." In the presence of his mother, Bradley is reduced to infantile behavior—whimpering, begging, and cowering. His sexual impotence is suggested when, in a kind of symbolic rape, he forces Shelly to let him put his hand in her mouth.

Given these circumstances, it is not surprising that Shelly, with her childhood storybook myths of American family life, finds her expectations of pastoral bliss transformed into cruel and frightening nightmares. But the mythic world does seem once to have existed (at least to a degree), for Shelly finds on Halie's walls pictures of a fertile landscape and happy children. It seems likely that it is Tilden's reversion to a childlike state that permits him to find corn and carrots where his parents say there are none, just as acceptance of the past at the end of the play seems to rejuvenate the land.

Despite the apparent return to fertility, the ending of the play is ambiguous. Ownership of the land has passed from the old (Dodge) to the young (Vince), but does this foretell an optimistic future or merely a new beginning for a repetitive pattern? In some ways, Vince seems merely to have replaced Dodge. He has let Shelly leave as casually as Dodge let Halie go, and at the end he is lying on the couch in precisely the same position as Dodge was at the play's beginning. Furthermore, Halie's final line, "Maybe it's the sun," recalls Dodge's earlier remark to Shelly: "You're all alike you hopers. If it's not God, then it's a man. If it's not a man, then it's a woman. If it's not a woman, then it's the land or the future of some kind. . . . See, you're glad it's stopped raining. Now you think everything's gonna be different. Just 'cause the sun comes out." Is Halie's announcement of the miraculous rejuvenation of the land merely an indication of unfounded hope?

Buried Child can be interpreted as a vision of America in a state of moral decay that can be overcome only by acknowledging and atoning for its past. Whether Shepard had such a vision in mind is unclear, but the play permits that possibility.

Overall, the dramatic power of *Buried Child* derives more from its pattern of images and symbols than from its story line. Its intensity does not grow out of issues that are faced so much as from mystery and ambiguity, which imply that a great deal more is at stake than is ever put into words.

Preface to Major Barbara

by George Bernard Shaw

First Aid to Critics

Before dealing with the deeper aspects of *Major Barbara*, let me, for the credit of English literature, make a protest against an unpatriotic habit into which many of my critics have fallen. Whenever my view strikes them as being at all outside the range of, say, an ordinary suburban churchwarden, they conclude that I am echoing Schopenhauer, Nietzsche, Ibsen, Strindberg, Tolstoy, or some other heresiarch in northern or eastern Europe.

I confess there is something flattering in this simple faith in my accomplishment as a linguist and my erudition as a philosopher. But I cannot countenance the assumption that life and literature are so poor in these islands that we must go abroad for all dramatic material that is not common and all ideas that are not superficial. I therefore venture to put my critics in possession of certain facts concerning my contact with modern ideas.

About half a century ago, an Irish novelist, Charles Lever, wrote a story entitled "A Day's Ride: A Life's Romance." It was published by Charles Dickens in *Household Words*, and proved so strange to the public taste that Dickens pressed Lever to make short work of it. I read scraps of this novel when I was a child; and it made an enduring impression on me. The hero was a very romantic hero, trying to live bravely, chivalrously, and powerfully by dint of mere romance-fed imagination, without courage, without means, without knowledge, without skill, without anything real except his bodily appetites. Even in my childhood I found in this poor devil's unsuccessful encounters with the facts of life, a poignant quality that romantic fiction lacked. The book, in spite of its first failure, is not dead: I saw its title the other day in the catalogue of Tauchnitz.

Now why is it that when I also deal in the tragicomic irony of the conflict between real life and the romantic imagination, critics never affiliate me to my countryman and immediate forerunner, Charles Lever, whilst they confidently derive me from a Norwegian author of whose language I do not know three words, and of whom I knew nothing until years after the Shavian *Anschauung* was already unequivocally declared in books full of what came, ten years later, to be perfunctorily labelled Ibsenism? I was not Ibsenist even at second hand; for Lever, though he may have read Henri Beyle, *alias* Stendhal, certainly never read Ibsen. Of the books that made Lever popular, such as *Charles O'Malley* and *Harry Lorrequer*, I know nothing but the names and some of the illustrations. But the story of the day's ride and life's romance of Potts (claiming alliance with Pozzo di Borgo) caught me and fascinated me as something strange and significant, though I already knew all about Alnaschar and Don Quixote and Simon Tappertit and many another romantic hero mocked by reality. From the plays of Aristophanes to the tales of Stevenson that mockery has been made familiar to all who are properly saturated with letters.

Where, then, was the novelty in Lever's tale? Partly, I think, in a new seriousness in dealing with Potts's disease. Formerly, the contrast between madness and sanity was deemed comic: Hogarth shews us how fashionable people went in parties to Bedlam to laugh at the lunatics. I myself have had a village idiot exhibited to me as something irresistibly funny. On the stage the madman was once a regular comic figure: that was how Hamlet got his opportunity before Shakespear touched him. The originality of Shakespear's version lay in his taking the lunatic sympathetically and seriously, and thereby making an advance towards the eastern consciousness of the fact that lunacy may be inspiration in disguise, since a man who has more brains than his fellows necessarily appears as mad to them as one who has less. But Shakespear did not do for Pistol and Parolles what he did for Hamlet. The particular sort of madman they represented, the romantic make-believer, lay outside the pale of sympathy in literature: he was pitilessly despised and ridiculed here as he was in the east under the name of Alnaschar, and was doomed to be, centuries later, under the name of Simon Tappertit. When Cervantes relented over Don Quixote, and Dickens relented over Pickwick, they did not become impartial: they simply changed sides, and became friends and apologists where they had formerly been mockers.

In Lever's story there is a real change of attitude. There is no relenting towards Potts: he never gains our affections like Don Quixote and Pickwick: he has not even the infatuate courage of Tappertit. But we dare not laugh at him, because, somehow, we recognize ourselves in Potts. We may, some of us, have enough nerve, enough muscle, enough luck, enough tact or skill or address or knowledge to carry things off better than he did; to impose on the people who saw through him; to fascinate Katinka (who cut Potts so ruthlessly at the end of the story); but for all that, we know that Potts plays an enormous part in ourselves and in the world, and that the social problem is not a problem of storybook heroes of the older pattern, but a problem of Pottses, and of how to make men of them. To fall back on my old phrase, we have the feeling — one that Alnaschar, Pistol, Parolles, and Tappertit never gave us — that Potts is a piece of really scientific natural history as distinguished from funny story telling. His author is not throwing a stone at a creature of another and inferior order, but making a confession, with the effect that the stone hits each of us full in the conscience and causes our self-esteem to smart very sorely. Hence the failure of Lever's book to please the readers of *Household Words*. That pain in the self-esteem nowadays causes critics to raise a cry of Ibsenism. I therefore assure them that the sensation first came to me from Lever and may have come to him from Beyle, or at least out of the Stendhalian atmosphere. I exclude the hypothesis of complete originality on Lever's part, because a man can no more be completely original in that sense than a tree can grow out of air.

Another mistake as to my literary ancestry is made whenever I violate the romantic convention that all woman are angels when they are not devils; that they are better looking than men; that their part in courtship is entirely passive; and that the human female form is the most beautiful object in nature. Schopenhauer wrote a splenetic essay which, as it is neither polite nor profound, was probably intended to knock this nonsense violently on the head. A sentence denouncing the idolized form as ugly has been largely quoted. The English critics have read that sentence; and I must here affirm, with as much gentleness as the implication will bear, that it has yet to be proved that they have dipped any deeper. At all events, whenever an English playwright represents a young and marriageable woman as being anything but a romantic heroine, he is disposed of without further thought as an echo of Schopenhauer. My own case is a specially hard one, because, when I implore the critics who are obsessed with the Schopenhauerian formula to remember that playwrights, like sculptors, study their figures from life, and not from philosophic essays, they reply passionately that I am not a playwright and that my stage figures do not live. But even so, I may and do ask them why, if they must give the credit of my plays to a philosopher, they do not give it to an English philosopher? Long before I ever read a word by Schopenhauer, or even knew whether he was a philosopher or a chemist, the Socialist revival of the eighteen-eighties brought me into contact, both literary and personal, with Ernest Belfort Bax, an English Socialist and philosophic essayist, whose handling of modern feminism would provoke romantic protests from Schopenhauer himself, or even Strindberg. As a matter of fact I hardly noticed Schopenhauer's disparagements of women when they came under my notice later on, so thoroughly had Bax familiarized me with the homoist attitude, and forced me to recognize the extent to which public opinion, and consequently legislation and jurisprudence, is corrupted by feminist sentiment.

Belfort Bax's essays were not confined to the Feminist question. He was a ruthless critic of current morality. Other writers have gained sympathy for dramatic criminals by eliciting the alleged "soul of goodness in things evil"; but Bax would propound some quite undramatic and apparently shabby violation of our commercial law and morality, and not merely defend it with the most disconcerting ingenuity, but actually prove it to be a positive duty that nothing but the certainty of police persecution should prevent every right-minded man from at once doing on principle. The Socialists were naturally shocked, being for the most part morbidly moral people; but at all events they were saved later on from the delusion that nobody but Nietzsche had ever challenged our mercanto-Christian morality. I first heard the name of Nietzsche from a German mathematician, Miss Borchardt, who had read my Quintessence of Ibsenism, and told me that she saw what I had been reading: namely, Nietzsche's *Jenseits von Gut und Böse*. Which I protest I had never seen, and could not have read with any comfort, for want of the necessary German, if I had seen it.

Nietzsche, like Schopenhauer, is the victim in England of a single much quoted sentence containing the phrase "big blonde beast." On the strength of this alliteration it is assumed that Nietzsche gained his European reputation by a senseless glorification of selfish bullying as the rule of life, just as it is assumed, on the strength of the single word

Superman (Übermensch) borrowed by me from Nietzsche, that I look for the salvation of society to the despotism of a single Napoleonic Superman, in spite of my careful demonstration of the folly of that outworn infatuation. But even the less recklessly superficial critics seem to believe that the modern objection to Christianity as a pernicious slave-morality was first put forward by Nietzsche. It was familiar to me before I ever heard of Nietzsche. The late Captain Wilson, author of several queer pamphlets, propagandist of a metaphysical system called Comprehensionism, and inventor of the term "Crosstianity" to distinguish the retrograde element in Christendom, was wont thirty years ago, in the discussions of the Dialectical Society, to protest earnestly against the beatitudes of the Sermon on the Mount as excuses for cowardice and servility, as destructive of our will, and consequently of our honor and manhood. Now it is true that Captain Wilson's moral criticism of Christianity was not a historical theory of it, like Nietzsche's; but this objection cannot be made to Stuart-Glennie, the successor of Buckle as a philosophic historian, who devoted his life to the elaboration and propagation of his theory that Christianity is part of an epoch (or rather an aberration, since it began as recently as 6000 B.C. and is already collapsing) produced by the necessity in which the numerically inferior white races found themselves to impose their domination on the colored races by priestcraft, making a virtue and a popular religion of drudgery and submissiveness in this world not only as a means of achieving saintliness of character but of securing a reward in heaven. Here was the slave-morality view formulated by a Scotch philosopher of my acquaintance long before we all began chattering about Nietzsche.

As Stuart-Glennie traced the evolution of society to the conflict of races, his theory made some sensation among Socialists — that is, among the only people who were seriously thinking about historical evolution at all — by its collision with the class-conflict theory of Karl Marx. Nietzsche, as I gather, regarded the slave-morality as having been invented and imposed on the world by slaves making a virtue of necessity and a religion of their servitude. Stuart-Glennie regarded the slave-morality as an invention of the superior white race to subjugate the minds of the inferior races whom they wished to exploit, and who would have destroyed them by force of numbers if their minds had not been subjugated. As this process is in operation still, and can be studied at first hand not only in our Church schools and in the struggle between our modern proprietary classes and the proletariat, but in the part played by Christian missionaries in reconciling the black races of Africa to their subjugation by European Capitalism, we can judge for ourselves whether the initiative came from above or below. My object here is not to argue the historical point, but simply to make our theatre critics ashamed of their habit of treating Britain as an intellectual void, and assuming that every philosophical idea, every historic theory, every criticism of our moral, religious and juridical institutions, must necessarily be either a foreign import, or else a fantastic sally (in rather questionable taste) totally unrelated to the existing body of thought. I urge them to remember that this body of thought is the slowest of growths and the rarest of blossomings, and that if there be such a thing on the philosophic plane as a matter of course, it is that no individual can make more than a minute contribution to it. In fact, their conception of clever persons parthenogenetically bringing forth complete original cosmogonies by dint of sheer "brilliancy" is part of that ignorant credulity which is the despair of the honest philosopher, and the opportunity of the religious imposter.

The Gospel of St. Andrew Undershaft

It is this credulity that drives me to help my critics out with Major Barbara by telling them what to say about it. In the millionaire Undershaft I have represented a man who has become intellectually and spiritually as well as practically conscious of the irresistible natural truth which we all abhor and repudiate: to wit, that the greatest of our evils, and the worst of our crimes is poverty, and that our first duty, to which every other consideration should be sacrificed, is not to be poor. "Poor but honest," "the respectable poor," and such phrases are as intolerable and as immoral as "drunken but amiable," "fraudulent but a good after-dinner speaker," "splendidly criminal," or the like. Security, the chief pretence of civilization, cannot exist where the worst of dangers, the danger of poverty, hangs over everyone's head, and where the alleged protection of our persons from violence is only an accidental result of the existence of a police force whose real business is to force the poor man to see his children starve whilst idle people overfeed pet dogs with the money that might feed and clothe them.

It is exceedingly difficult to make people realize that an evil is an evil. For instance, we seize a man and deliberately do him a malicious injury: say, imprison him for years. One would not suppose that it needed any exceptional clearness of wit to recognize in this an act of diabolical cruelty. But in England such a recognition provokes a stare of surprise, followed by an explanation that the outrage is punishment or justice or something else that is all right, or perhaps by a heated attempt to argue that we should all be robbed and murdered in our beds if such stupid villainies as sentences of imprisonment were not committed daily. It is useless to argue that even if this were true, which it is not, the alternative to adding crimes of our own to the crimes from which we suffer is not helpless submission. Chickenpox is an evil; but if I were to declare that we must either submit to it or else repress it sternly by seizing everyone who suffers from it and punishing them by inoculation with smallpox, I should be laughed at; for though nobody could deny that the result would be to prevent chickenpox to some extent by making people avoid it much more carefully, and to effect a further apparent prevention by making them conceal it very anxiously, yet people would have sense enough to see that the deliberate propagation of smallpox was a creation of evil, and must therefore be ruled out in favor of purely humane and hygienic measures. Yet in the precisely parallel case of a man breaking into my house and stealing my wife's diamonds I am expected as a matter of course to steal ten years of his life, torturing him all the time. If he tries to defeat that monstrous retaliation by shooting me, my survivors hang him. The net result suggested by the police statistics is that we inflict atrocious injuries on the burglars we catch in order to make the rest take effectual precautions against detection; so that instead of saving our wives' diamonds from burglary we only greatly decrease our chances of ever getting them back, and increase our chances of being shot by the robber if we are unlucky enough to disturb him at his work.

But the thoughtless wickedness with which we scatter sentences of imprisonment, torture in the solitary cell and on the plank bed, and flogging, on moral invalids and energetic rebels, is as nothing compared to the silly levity with which we tolerate poverty as if it were either a wholesome tonic for lazy people or else a virtue to be embraced as St Francis embraced it. If a man is indolent, let him be poor. If he is drunken, let him be poor. If he is not a gentleman, let him be poor. If he is addicted to the fine arts or to pure science instead of to trade and finance, let him be poor. If he chooses to spend his urban eighteen shillings a week or his agricultural thirteen shillings a week on his beer and his family instead of saving it up for his old age, let him be poor. Let nothing be done for "the undeserving": let him be poor. Serve him right! Also—somewhat inconsistently—blessed are the poor!

Now what does this Let Him Be Poor mean? It means let him be weak. Let him be ignorant. Let him become a nucleus of disease. Let him be a standing exhibition and example of ugliness and dirt. Let him have rickety children. Let him be cheap, and drag his fellows down to his own price by selling himself to do their work. Let his habitations turn our cities into poisonous congeries of slums. Let his daughters infect our young men with the diseases of the streets, and his sons revenge him by turning the nation's manhood into scrofula, cowardice, cruelty, hypocrisy, political imbecility, and all the other fruits of oppression and malnutrition. Let the undeserving become still less deserving; and let the deserving lay up for himself, not treasures in heaven, but horrors in hell upon earth. This being so, is it really wise to let him be poor? Would he not do ten times less harm as a prosperous burglar, incendiary, ravisher or murderer, to the utmost limits of humanity's comparatively negligible impulses in these directions? Suppose we were to abolish all penalties for such activities, and decide that poverty is the one thing we will not tolerate—that every adult with less than, say, £365 a year, shall be painlessly but inexorably killed, and every hungry half naked child forcibly fattened and clothed, would not that be an enormous improvement on our existing system, which has already destroyed so many civilizations, and is visibly destroying ours in the same way?

Is there any radicle of such legislation in our parliamentary system? Well, there are two measures just sprouting in the political soil, which may conceivably grow to something valuable. One is the institution of a Legal Minimum Wage. The other, Old Age Pensions. But there is a better plan than

either of these. Some time ago I mentioned the subject of Universal Old Age Pensions to my fellow Socialist Cobden-Sanderson, famous as an artist-craftsman in book-binding and printing. "Why not Universal Pensions for Life?" said Cobden-Sanderson. In saying this, he solved the industrial problem at a stroke. At present we say callously to each citizen "If you want money, earn it" as if his having or not having it were a matter that concerned himself alone. We do not even secure for him the opportunity of earning it: on the contrary, we allow our industry to be organized in open dependence on the maintenance of "a reserve army of unemployed" for the sake of "elasticity." The sensible course would be Cobden-Sanderson's: that is, to give every man enough to live well on, so as to guarantee the community against the possibility of a case of the malignant disease of poverty, and then (necessarily) to see that he earned it.

Undershaft, the hero of Major Barbara, is simply a man who, having grasped the fact that poverty is a crime, knows that when society offered him the alternative of poverty or a lucrative trade in death and destruction, it offered him, not a choice between opulent villainy and humble virtue, but between energetic enterprise and cowardly infamy. His conduct stands the Kantian test, which Peter Shirley's does not. Peter Shirley is what we call the honest poor man. Undershaft is what we call the wicked rich one: Shirley is Lazarus, Undershaft Dives. Well, the misery of the world is due to the fact that the great mass of men act and believe as Peter Shirley acts and believes. If they acted and believed as Undershaft acts and believes, the immediate result would be a revolution of incalculable beneficence. To be wealthy, says Undershaft, is with me a point of honor for which I am prepared to kill at the risk of my own life. This preparedness is, as he says, the final test of sincerity. Like Froissart's medieval hero, who saw that "to rob and pill was a good life" he is not the dupe of that public sentiment against killing which is propagated and endowed by people who would otherwise be killed themselves, or of the mouth-honor paid to poverty and obedience by rich and insubordinate do-nothings who want to rob the poor without courage and command them without superiority. Froissart's knight, in placing the achievement of a good life before all the other duties—which indeed are not duties at all when they conflict with it, but plain wickednesses—behaved bravely, admirably, and, in the final analysis, public-spiritedly. Medieval society, on the other hand, behaved very badly indeed in organizing itself so stupidly that a good life could be achieved by robbing and pilling. If the knight's contemporaries had been all as resolute as he, robbing and pilling would have been the shortest way to the gallows, just as, if we were all as resolute and clearsighted as Undershaft, an attempt to live by means of what is called "an independent income" would be the shortest way to the lethal chamber. But as, thanks to our political imbecility and personal cowardice (fruits of poverty, both), the best imitation of a good life now procurable is life on an independent income, all sensible people aim at securing such an income, and are, of course, careful to legalize and moralize both it and all the actions and sentiments which lead to it and support it as an institution. What else can they do? They know, of course, that they are rich because others are poor. But they cannot help that: it is for the poor to repudiate poverty when they have had enough of it. The thing can be done easily enough: the demonstrations to the contrary made by the economists, jurists, moralists and sentimentalists hired by the rich to defend them, or even doing the work gratuitously out of sheer folly and abjectness, impose only on those who want to be imposed on.

The reason why the independent income-tax payers are not solid in defence of their position is that since we are not medieval rovers through a sparsely populated country, the poverty of those we rob prevents our having the good life for which we sacrifice them. Rich men or aristocrats with a developed sense of life—men like Ruskin and William Morris and Kropotkin—have enormous social appetites and very fastidious personal ones. They are not content with handsome houses: they want handsome cities. They are not content with bediamonded wives and blooming daughters: they complain because the charwoman is badly dressed, because the laundress smells of gin, because the sempstress is anemic, because every man they meet is not a friend and every woman not a romance. They turn up their noses at their neighbor's drains, and are made ill by the architecture of their neighbor's houses. Trade patterns made to suit vulgar people do not please them (and they can get nothing else): they cannot sleep nor sit at ease upon "slaughtered" cabinet makers' furniture. The very air is not

good enough for them: there is too much factory smoke in it. The even demand abstract conditions: justice, honor, a noble moral atmosphere, a mystic nexus to replace the cash nexus. Finally they declare that though to rob and pill with your own hand on horseback and in steel coat may have been a good life, to rob and pill by the hands of the policeman, the bailiff, and the soldier, and to underpay them meanly for doing it, is not a good life, but rather fatal to all possibility of even a tolerable one. They call on the poor to revolt, and, finding the poor shocked at their ungentlemanliness, despairingly revile the proletariat for its "damned wantlessness" *(verdammte Bedürfnislosigkeit).*

So far, however, their attack on society has lacked simplicity. The poor do not share their tastes nor understand their art-criticisms. They do not want the simple life, nor the esthetic life; on the contrary, they want very much to wallow in all the costly vulgarities from which the elect souls among the rich turn away with loathing. It is by surfeit and not by abstinence that they will be cured of their hankering after unwholesome sweets. What they do dislike and despise and are ashamed of is poverty. To ask them to fight for the difference between the Christmas number of the Illustrated London News and the Kelmscott Chaucer is silly: they prefer the News. The difference between a stock-broker's cheap and dirty starched white shirt and collar and the comparatively costly and carefully dyed blue shirt of William Morris is a difference so disgraceful to Morris in their eyes that if they fought on the subject at all, they would fight in defence of the starch. "Cease to be slaves, in order that you may become cranks" is not a very inspiring call to arms; nor is it really improved by substituting saints for cranks. Both terms denote men of genius; and the common man does not want to live the life of a man of genius: he would much rather live the life of a pet collie if that were the only alternative. But he does want more money. Whatever else he may be vague about, he is clear about that. He may or may not prefer *Major Barbara* to the Drury Lane pantomime; but he always prefers five hundred pounds to five hundred shillings.

Now to deplore this preference as sordid, and teach children that it is sinful to desire money, is to strain towards the extreme possible limit of impudence in lying and corruption in hypocrisy. The universal regard for money is the one hopeful fact in our civilization, the one sound spot in our social conscience. Money is the most important thing in the world. It represents health, strength, honor, generosity and beauty as conspicuously and undeniably as the want of it represents illness, weakness, disgrace, meanness and ugliness. Not the least of its virtues is that is destroys base people as certainly as it fortifies and dignifies noble people. It is only when it is cheapened to worthlessness for some and made impossibly dear to others, that it becomes a curse. In short, it is a curse only in such foolish social conditions that life itself is a curse. For the two things are inseparable: money is the counter that enables life to be distributed socially: it *is* life as truly as sovereigns and bank notes are money. The first duty of every citizen is to insist on having money on reasonable terms; and this demand is not complied with by giving four men three shillings each for ten or twelve hours' drudgery and one man a thousand pounds for nothing. The crying need of the nation is not for better morals, cheaper bread, temperance, liberty, culture, redemption of fallen sisters and erring brothers, nor the grace, love and fellowship of the Trinity, but simply for enough money. And the evil to be attacked is not sin, suffering, greed, priestcraft, kingcraft, demagogy, monopoly, ignorance, drink, war, pestilence, nor any other of the scapegoats which reformers sacrifice, but simply poverty.

Once take your eyes from the ends of the earth and fix them on this truth just under your nose; and Andrew Undershaft's views will not perplex you in the least. Unless indeed his constant sense that he is only the instrument of a Will or Life Force which uses him for purposes wider than his own, may puzzle you. If so, that is because you are walking either in artificial Darwinian darkness, or in mere stupidity. All genuinely religious people have that consciousness. To them Undershaft the Mystic will be quite intelligible, and his perfect comprehension of his daughter the Salvationist and her lover the Euripidean republican natural and inevitable. That, however, is not new, even on the stage. What is new, as far as I know, is that article in Undershaft's religion which recognizes in Money the first need and in poverty the vilest sin of man and society.

This dramatic conception has not, of course, been attained *per saltum*. Nor has it been borrowed from Nietzsche or from any man born beyond the Channel. The late Samuel Butler, in his own department the greatest English writer of the latter half of the XIX century, steadily inculcated the necessity and morality of a conscientious Laodiceanism in religion and of an earnest and constant sense of the importance of money. It drives one almost to despair of English literature when one sees so extraordinary a study of English life as Butler's posthumous *Way of All Flesh* making so little impression that when, some years later, I produce plays in which Butler's extraordinarily fresh, free and future-piercing suggestions have an obvious share, I am met with nothing but vague cacklings about Ibsen and Nietzsche, and am only too thankful that they are not about Alfred de Musset and Georges Sand. Really, the English do not deserve to have great men. They allowed Butler to die practically unknown, whilst I, a comparatively insignificant Irish journalist, was leading them by the nose into an advertisement of me which has made my own life a burden. In Sicily there is a Via Samuele Butler. When an English tourist sees it, he either asks "Who the devil was Samuele Butler?" or wonders why the Sicilians should perpetuate the memory of the author of *Hudibras*.

Well, it cannot be denied that the English are only too anxious to recognize a man of genius if somebody will kindly point him out to them. Having pointed myself out in this manner with some success, I now point out Samuel Butler, and trust that in consequence I shall hear a little less in future of the novelty and foreign origin of the ideas which are now making their way into the English theatre through plays written by Socialists. There are living men whose originality and powers are as obvious as Butler's and when they die that fact will be discovered. Meanwhile I recommend them to insist on their own merits as an important part of their own business.

The Salvation Army

When *Major Barbara* was produced in London, the second act was reported in an important northern newspaper as a withering attack on the Salvation Army, and the despairing ejaculation of Barbara deplored by a London daily as a tasteless blasphemy. And they were set right, not by the professed critics of the theatre, but by religious and philosophical publicists like Sir Oliver Lodge and Dr Stanton Coit, and strenuous Nonconformist journalists like William Stead, who not only understood the act as well as the Salvationists themselves, but also saw it in its relation to the religious life of the nation, a life which seems to lie not only outside the sympathy of many of our theatre critics, but actually outside their knowledge of society. Indeed nothing could be more ironically curious than the confrontation Major Barbara effected of the theatre enthusiasts with the religious enthusiasts. On the one hand was the playgoer, always seeking pleasure, paying exorbitantly for it, suffering unbearable discomfots for it, and hardly ever getting it. On the other hand was the Salvationist, repudiating gaiety and courting effort and sacrifice, yet always in the wildest spirits, laughing, joking, singing, rejoicing, drumming, and tambourining; his life flying by in a flash of excitement, and his death arriving as a climax of triumph. And, if you please, the playgoer despising the Salvationist as a joyless person, shut out from the heaven of the theatre, self-condemned to a life of hideous gloom; and the Salvationist mourning over the playgoer as over a prodigal with vine leaves in his hair, careering outrageously to hell amid the popping of champagne corks and the ribald laughter of sirens! Could misunderstanding be more complete, or sympathy worse misplaced?

Fortunately, the Salvationists are more accessible to the religious character of the drama than the playgoers to the gay energy and artistic fertility of religion. They can see, when it is pointed out to them, that a theatre, as a place where two or three are gathered together, takes from that divine presence an inalienable sanctity of which the grossest and profanest farce can no more deprive it than a hypocritical sermon by a snobbish bishop can desecrate Westminster Abbey. But in our professional playgoers this indispensable preliminary conception of sanctity seems wanting. They talk of actors as mimes and mummers, and, I fear, think of dramatic authors as liars and pandars, whose main business is the voluptuous soothing of the tired city speculator when what he calls the serious business of the day is over. Passion, the life of drama, means nothing to them but primitive sexual excitement: such phrases as "impassioned poetry" or "passionate love of truth" have fallen quite out of the their vocabulary and been replaced by "passional crime" and the like. They assume, as far as I can gather, that people in whom passion has a large scope are passionless and therefore uninteresting. Consequently they come to think of religious people as people who are not interesting and not amusing. And so, when Barbara cuts the regular Salvation Army jokes, and snatches a kiss from her lover across his drum, the devotees of the theatre think they ought to appear shocked, and conclude that the whole play is an elaborate mockery of the Army. And then either hypocricially rebuke me for mocking, or foolishly take part in the supposed mockery!

Even the handful of mentally competent critics got into difficulties over my demonstration of the economic deadlock in which the Salvation Army finds itself. Some of them thought that the army would not have taken money from a distiller and a cannon founder: others thought it should not have taken it: all assumed more or less definitely that it reduced itself to absurdity or hypocrisy by taking it. On the first point the reply of the Army itself was prompt and conclusive. As one of its officers said, they would take money from the devil himself and be only too glad to get it out of his hands and into God's. They gratefully acknowledged that publicans not only give them money but allow them to collect it in the bar—sometimes even when there is a Salvation meeting outside preaching teetotalism. In fact, they questioned the verisimilitude of the play, not because Mrs Baines took the money, but because Barbara refused it.

On the point that the Army ought not to take such money, its justification is obvious. It must take the money because it cannot exist without money, and there is no other money to be had. Practically all the spare money in the country consists of a mass of rent, interest, and profit, every penny of which is bound up with crime, drink, prostitution, disease, and all the evil fruits of poverty, as inextricably as with enterprise, wealth, commercial probity, and national prosperity. The notion that you can earmark certain coins as tainted is an unpractical individualist superstition. None the less the fact that all our money is tainted gives a very severe shock to earnest young souls when some dramatic instance of the taint first makes them conscious of it. When an enthusiastic young clergyman of the Established Church first realizes that the Ecclesiastical Commissioners receive the rents of sporting public houses, brothels, and sweating dens; or that the most generous contributor at his last charity sermon was an employer trading in female labor cheapened by prostitution as unscrupulously as a hotel keeper trades in waiters' labor cheapened by tips, or commissionaires' labor cheapened by pensions; or that the only patron who can afford to rebuild his church or his schools or give his boys' brigade a gymnasium or a library is the son-in-law of a Chicago meat King, that young clergyman has, like Barbara, a very bad quarter hour. But he cannot help himself by refusing to accept money from anybody except sweet old ladies with independent incomes and gentle and lovely ways of life. He has only to follow up the income of the sweet ladies to its industrial source, and there he will find Mrs Warren's profession and the poisonous canned meat and all the rest of it. His own stipend has the same root. He must either share the world's guilt or go to another planet. He must save the world's honor if he is to save his own. That is what all the Churches find just as the Salvation Army and Barbara find it in the play. Her discovery that she is her father's accomplice; that the Salvation Army is the accomplice of the distiller and the dynamite maker; that they can no more escape one another than they can escape the air they breathe; that there is no salvation for them through personal righteousness, but only through the redemption of the whole nation from its vicious, lazy, competitive anarchy: this discovery has been made by everyone except the Pharisees and (apparently) the professional playgoers, who still wear their Tom Hood shirts and underpay their washerwomen without the slightest misgiving as to the elevation of their private characters, the purity of their private atmospheres, and their right to repudiate as foreign to themselves the coarse depravity of the garret and the slum. Not that they mean any harm: they only desire to be, in their little private way, what they call gentlemen. They do not understand Barbara's lesson because they have not, like her, learnt it by taking part in the larger life of the nation.

Barbara's Return to the Colors

Barbara's return to the colors may yet provide a subject for the dramatic historian of the future. To go back to the Salvation Army with the knowledge that even the Salvationists themselves are not saved yet; that poverty is not blessed, but a most damnable sin; and that when General Booth chose Blood and Fire for the emblem of Salvation instead of the Cross, he was perhaps better inspired than he knew: such knowledge, for the daughter of Andrew Undershaft, will clearly lead to something hopefuller than distributing bread and treacle at the expense of Bodger.

It is a very significant thing, this instinctive

choice of the military form of organization, this substitution of the drum for the organ, by the Salvation Army. Does it not suggest that the Salvationists divine that they must actually fight the devil instead of merely praying at him? At present, it is true, they have not quite ascertained his correct address. When they do, they may give a very rude shock to that sense of security which he has gained from his experience of the fact that hard words, even when uttered by eloquent essayists and lecturers, or carried unanimously at enthusiastic public meetings on the motion of eminent reformers, break no bones. It has been said that the French Revolution was the work of Voltaire, Rousseau and the Encyclopedists. It seems to me to have been the work of men who had observed that virtuous indignation, caustic criticism, conclusive argument and instructive pamphleteering, even when done by the most earnest and witty literary geniuses, were as useless as praying, things going steadily from bad to worse whilst the Social Contract and the pamphlets of Voltaire were at the height of their vogue. Eventually, as we know, perfectly respectable citizens and earnest philanthropists connived at the September massacres because hard experience had convinced them that if they contented themselves with appeals to humanity and patriotism, the aristocracy, though it would read their appeals with the greatest enjoyment and appreciation, flattering and admiring the writers, would none the less continue to conspire with foreign monarchists to undo the revolution and restore the old system with every circumstance of savage vengeance and ruthless repression of popular liberties.

The nineteenth century saw the same lesson repeated in England. It had its Utilitarians, its Christian Socialists, its Fabian (still extant): it had Bentham, Mill, Dickens, Ruskin, Carlyle, Butler, Henry George, and Morris. And the end of all their efforts is the Chicago described by Mr Upton Sinclair and the London in which the people who pay to be amused by my dramatic representation of Peter Shirley turned out to starve at forty because there are younger slaves to be had for his wages, do not take, and have not the slightest intention of taking, any effective step to organize society in such a way as to make that everyday infamy impossible. I, who have preached and pamphleteered like any Encyclopedist, have to confess that my methods are no use, and would be no use if I were Voltaire, Rousseau, Bentham, Marx, Mill, Dickens, Carlyle, Ruskin, Butler and Morris all rolled into one, with Euripides, More, Montaigne, Molière, Beaumarchais, Swift, Goethe, Ibsen, Tolstoy, Jesus and the prophets all thrown in (as indeed in some sort I actually am, standing as I do on all their shoulders). The problem being to make heroes out of cowards, we paper apostles and artist-magicians have succeeded only in giving cowards all the sensations of heroes whilst they tolerate every abomination, accept every plunder, and submit to every oppression. Christianity, in making a merit of such submission, has marked only that depth in the abyss at which the very sense of shame is lost. The Christian has been like Dickens' doctor in the debtor's prison, who tells the newcomer of its ineffable peace and security: no duns; no tyrannical collector of rates, taxes, and rent; no importunate hopes nor exacting duties; nothing but the rest and safety of having no farther to fall.

Yet in the poorest corner of this soul-destroying Christendom vitality suddenly begins to germinate again. Joyousness, a sacred gift long dethroned by the hellish laughter of derision and obscenity, rises like a flood miraculously out of the fetid dust and mud of the slums; rousing marches and impetuous dithyrambs rise to the heavens from people among whom the depressing noise called "sacred music" is a standing joke; a flag with Blood and Fire on it is unfurled, not in murderous rancor, but because fire is beautiful and blood a vital and splendid red; Fear, which we flatter by calling Self, vanishes; and transfigured men and woman carry their gospel through a transfigured world, calling their leader General, themselves captains and brigadiers, and their whole body an Army: praying, but praying only for refreshment, for strength to fight, and for needful MONEY (a notable sign, that) preaching, but not preaching submission; daring ill-usage and abuse, but not putting up with more of it than is inevitable; and practising what the world will let them practise, including soap and water, color and music. There is danger in such activity; and where there is danger there is hope. Our present security is nothing, and can be nothing, but evil made irresistible.

Weaknesses of the Salvation Army

For the present, however, it is not my business to flatter the Salvation Army. Rather must I point out to it that it has almost as many weaknesses as the Church of England itself. It is building up a business organization which will compel it eventually to see that its present staff of enthusiast-commanders shall be succeeded by a bureaucracy of men of business who will be no better than bishops, and perhaps a good deal more unscrupulous. That has always happened sooner or later to great orders founded by saints; and the order founded by St William Booth is not exempt from the same danger. It is even more dependent than the Church on rich people who would cut off supplies at once if it began to preach that indispensable revolt against poverty which must also be a revolt against riches. It is hampered by a heavy contingent of pious elders who are not really Salvationists at all, but Evangelicals of the old school. It still, as Commissioner Howard affirms, "sticks to Moses," which is flat nonsense at this time of day if the Commissioner means, as I am afraid he does, that the Book of Genesis contains a trustworthy scientific account of the origin of species, and that the god to whom Jephthah sacrificed his daughter is any less obviously a tribal idol than Dagon or Chemosh.

Further, there is still too much other-worldliness about the Army. Like Frederick's grenadier, the Salvationist wants to live for ever (the most monstrous way of crying for the moon); and though it is evident to anyone who has ever heard General Booth and his best officers that they would work as hard for human salvation as they do at present if they believed that death would be the end of them individually, they and their followers have a bad habit of talking as if the Salvationists were heroically enduring a very bad time on earth as an investment which will bring them in dividends later on in the form, not of a better life to come for the whole world, but of an eternity spent by themselves personally in a sort of bliss which would bore any active person to a second death. Surely the truth is that the Salvationists are unusually happy people. And is it not the very diagnostic of true salvation that it shall overcome the fear of death? Now the man who has come to believe that there is no such thing as death, the change so called being merely the transition to an exquisitely happy and utterly careless life, has not overcome the fear of death at all: on the contrary, it has overcome him so completely that he refuses to die on any terms whatever. I do not call a Salvationist really saved until he is ready to lie down cheerfully on the scrap heap, having paid scot and lot and something over, and let his eternal life pass on to renew its youth in the battalions of the future.

Then there is the nasty lying habit called confession, which the Army encourages because it lends itself to dramatic oratory, with plenty of thrilling incident. For my part, when I hear a convert relating the violences and oaths and blasphemies he was guilty of before he was saved, making out that he was a very terrible fellow then and is the most contrite and chastened of Christians now, I believe him no more than I believe the millionaire who says he came up to London or Chicago as a boy with only three halfpence in his pocket. Salvationists have said to me that Barbara in my play would never have been taken in by so transparent a humbug as Snobby Price; and certainly I do not think Snobby could have taken in any experienced Salvationist on a point on which the Salvationist did not wish to be taken in. But on the point of conversion all Salvationists wish to be taken in; for the more obvious the sinner the more obvious the miracle of his conversion. When you advertize a converted burglar or reclaimed drunkard as one of the attractions at an experience meeting, your burglar can hardly have been too burglarious or your drunkard too drunken. As long as such attractions are relied on, you will have your Snobbies claiming to have beaten their mothers when they were as a matter of prosaic fact habitually beaten by them, and your Rummies of the tamest respectability pretending to a past of reckless and dazzling vice. Even when confessions are sincerely autobiographic we should beware of assuming that the impulse to make them was pious or that the interest of the hearers is wholesome. As well might we assume that the poor people who insist on shewing disgusting ulcers to district visitors are convinced hygienists, or that the curiosity which sometimes welcomes such exhibitions is a pleasant and creditable one. One is often tempted to suggest that those who pester our police superintendents with confessions of murder might very wisely be taken at their word and executed, except in the few cases in which a real murderer is seeking to be relieved of his guilt by confession and expiation. For though I am not, I hope, an unmerciful person, I do not think that the inexorability of the deed once done should be disguised by any ritual, whether in the confessional or on the scaffold.

And here my disagreement with Salvation Army, and with all propagandists of the Cross (which I loathe as I loathe all gibbets), becomes deep indeed. Forgiveness, absolution, atonement, are figments: punishment is only a pretence of cancelling one crime by another; and you can no more have forgiveness without vindictiveness than you can have a cure without a disease. You will never get a high morality from people who conceive that their misdeeds are revocable and pardonable, or in a society where absolution and expiation are officially provided for us all. The demand may be very real; but the supply is spurious. Thus Bill Walker, in my play, having assaulted the Salvation Lass, presently finds himself overwhelmed with an intolerable conviction of sin under the skilled treatment of Barbara. Straightway he begins to try to unassault the lass and deruffianize his deed, first by getting punished for it in kind, and, when that relief is denied him, by fining himself a pound to compensate the girl. He is foiled both ways. He finds the Salvation Army as inexorable as fact itself. It will not punish him: it will not take his money. It will not tolerate a redeemed ruffian: it leaves him no means of salvation except ceasing to be a ruffian. In doing this, the Salvation Army instinctively grasps the central truth of Christianity and discards its central superstition: that central truth being the vanity of revenge and punishment, and that central superstition the salvation of the world by the gibbet.

For, be it noted, Bill has assaulted an old and starving woman also; and for this worse offence he feels no remorse whatever, because she makes it clear that her malice is as great as his own. "Let her have the law of me, as she said she would," says Bill: "what I done to her is no more on what you might call my conscience than sticking a pig." This shews a perfectly natural and wholesome state of mind on his part. The old woman, like the law she threatens him with, is perfectly ready to play the game of retaliation with him: to rob him if he steals, to flog him if he strikes, to murder him if he kills. By example and precept the law and public opinion teach him to impose his will on others by anger, violence, and cruelty, and to wipe off the moral score by punishment. That is sound Crosstianity. But this Crosstianity has got entangled with something which Barbara calls Christianity, and which unexpectedly causes her to refuse to play the hangman's game of Satan casting out Satan. She refuses to prosecute a drunken ruffian; she converses on equal terms with a blackguard to whom no lady should be seen speaking in the public street: in short she imitates Christ. Bill's conscience reacts to this just as naturally as it does to the old woman's threats. He is placed in a position of unbearable moral inferiority, and strives by every means in his power to escape from it, whilst he is still quite ready to meet the abuse of the old woman by attempting to smash a mug on her face. And that is the triumphant justification of Barbara's Christianity as against our system of judicial punishment and the vindictive villain-thrashings and "poetic justice" of the romantic stage.

For the credit of literature it must be pointed out that the situation is only partly novel. Victor Hugo long ago gave us the epic of the convict and the bishop's candlesticks, of the Crosstian policeman annihilated by his encounter with the Christian Valjean. But Bill Walker is not, like Valjean, romantically changed from a demon into an angel. There are millions of Bill Walkers in all classes of society today; and the point which I, as a professor of natural psychology, desire to demonstrate, is that Bill, without any change in his character or circumstances whatsoever, will react one way to one sort of treatment and another way to another.

In proof I might point to the sensational object lesson provided by our commercial millionaires today. They begin as brigands: merciless, unscrupulous, dealing out ruin and death and slavery to their competitors and employees, and facing desperately the worst that their competitors can do to them. The history of the English factories, the American Trusts, the exploitation of African gold, diamonds, ivory and rubber, outdoes in villainy the worst that has ever been imagined of the buccaneers of the Spanish Main. Captain Kidd would have marooned a modern Trust magnate for conduct unworthy of a gentleman of fortune. The law every day seizes on unsuccessful scoundrels of this type and punishes them with a cruelty worse than their own, with the result that they come out of the torture house more dangerous than they went in, and renew their evil doing (nobody will employ them at anything else) until they are again seized, again tormented, and again let loose, with the same result.

But the successful scoundrel is dealt with very differently, and very Christianly. He is not only forgiven: he is idolized, respected, made much of, all but worshipped. Society returns him good for evil in the most extravagant overmeasure. And with what result? He begins to idolize himself, to respect himself, to live up to the treatment he receives. He preaches sermons; he writes books of the most edifying advice to young men, and actually persuades himself that he got on by taking his own advice; he endows educational institutions; he supports charities; he dies finally in the odor of sanctity, leaving a will which is a monument of public spirit and bounty. And all this without any change in his character. The spots of the leopard and the stripes of the tiger are as brilliant as ever; but the conduct of the world towards him has changed; and his conduct has changed accordingly. You have only to reverse your attitude towards him — to lay hands on his property, revile him, assault him, and he will be a brigand again in a moment, as ready to crush you as you are to crush him, and quite as full of pretentious moral reasons for doing it.

In short, when Major Barbara says that there are no scoundrels, she is right: there are no absolute scoundrels, though there are impracticable people of whom I shall treat presently. Every reasonable man (and woman) is a potential scoundrel and a potential good citizen. What a man is depends on his character; but what he does, and what we think of what he does, depends on his circumstances. The characteristics that ruin a man in one class make him eminent in another. The characters that behave differently in different circumstances behave alike in similar circumstances. Take a common English character like that of Bill Walker. We meet Bill everywhere: on the judicial bench, on the episcopal bench, in the Privy Council, at the War Office and Admiralty, as well as in the Old Bailey dock or in the ranks of casual unskilled labor. And the morality of Bill's characteristics varies with these various circumstances. The faults of the burglar are the qualities of the financier: the manners and habits of a duke would cost a city clerk his situation. In short, though character is independent of circumstances, conduct is not; and our moral judgments of character are not: both are circumstantial. Take any condition of life in which the circumstances are for a mass of men practically alike: felony, the House of Lords, the factory, the stables, the gipsy encampment or where you please! In spite of diversity of character and temperament, the conduct and morals of the individuals in each group are as predictable and as alike in the main as if they were a flock of sheep, morals being mostly only social habits and circumstantial necessities. Strong people know this and count upon it. In nothing have the master-minds of the world been distinguished from the ordinary suburban season-ticket holder more than in their straightforward perception of the fact that mankind is practically a single species, and not a menagerie of gentlemen and bounders, villains and heroes, cowards and daredevils, peers and peasants, grocers and aristocrats, artisans and laborers, washerwomen and duchesses, in which all the grades of income and caste represent distinct animals who must not be introduced to one another or intermarry. Napoleon constructing a galaxy of generals and courtiers, and even of monarchs, out of his collection of social nobodies; Julius Cæsar appointing as governor of Egypt the son of a freedman—one who but a short time before would have been legally disqualified for the post even of a private soldier in the Roman army; Louis XI making his barber his privy councillor: all these had in their different ways a firm hold of the scientific fact of human equality, expressed by Barbara in the Christian formula that all men are children of one father. A man who believes that men are naturally divided into upper and lower and middle classes morally is making exactly the same mistake as the man who believes that they are naturally divided in the same way socially. And just as our persistent attempts to found political institutions on a basis of social inequality have always produced long periods of destructive friction relieved from time to time by violent explosions of revolution; so the attempt—will Americans please note—to found moral institutions on a basis of moral inequality can lead to nothing but unnatural Reigns of the Saints relieved by licentious Restorations; to Americans who have made divorce a public institution turning the face of Europe into one huge sardonic smile by refusing to stay in the same hotel with a Russian man of genius who has changed wives without the sanction of South Dakota; to grotesque hypocrisy, cruel persecution, and final utter confusion of conventions and compliances with benevolence and respectability. It is quite useless to declare that all men are born free if you deny that they are born good. Guarantee a man's goodness and his liberty will take care of itself. To guarantee his freedom on condition that you approve of his moral character is formally to abolish all freedom whatsoever, as every man's liberty is at the mercy of a moral indictment which any fool can trump up against everyone who violates custom, whether as a prophet or as a rascal. This is the lesson Democracy has to learn before it can become anything but the most oppressive of all the priesthoods.

Let us now return to Bill Walker and his case of conscience against the Salvation Army. Major Barbara, not being a modern Tetzel, or the treasurer of a hospital, refuses to sell absolution to Bill for a sovereign. Unfortunately, what the Army can afford to refuse in the case of Bill Walker, it cannot refuse in the case of Bodger. Bodger is master of the situation because he holds the purse strings. "Strive as you will," says Bodger, in effect: "me you cannot do without. You cannot save Bill Walker without my money." And the Army answers, quite rightly under the circumstances, "We will take money from the devil himself sooner than abandon the work of Salvation." So Bodger pays his conscience-money and gets the absolution that is refused to Bill. In real life Bill would perhaps never know this. But I, the dramatist whose business it is to shew the connexion between things that seem apart and unrelated in the haphazard order of events in real life, have contrived to make it known to Bill, with the result that the Salvation Army loses its hold of him at once.

But Bill may not be lost, for all that. He is still in the grip of the facts and of his own conscience, and may find his taste for blackguardism permanently spoiled. Still, I cannot guarantee that happy ending. Walk through the poorer quarters of our cities on Sunday when the men are not working, but resting and chewing the cud of their reflections. You will find one expression common to every mature face: the expression of cynicism. The discovery made by Bill Walker about the Salvation Army has been made by everyone there. They have found that every man has his price; and they have been foolishly or corruptly taught to mistrust and despise him for that necessary and salutary condition of social existence. When they learn that General Booth, too, has his price, they do not admire him because it is a high one, and admit the need of organizing society so that he shall get it in an honorable way: they conclude that his character is unsound and that all religious men are hypocrites and allies of their sweaters and oppressors. They know that the large subscriptions which help to support the

Army are endowments, not of religion, but of the wicked doctrine of docility in povery and humility under oppression; and they are rent by the most agonizing of all the doubts of the soul, the doubt whether their true salvation must not come from their most abhorrent passions, from murder, envy, greed, stubbornness, rage, and terrorism, rather than from public spirit, reasonableness, humanity, generosity, tenderness, delicacy, pity and kindness. The confirmation of that doubt, at which our newpapers have been working so hard for years past, is the morality of militarism; and the justification of militarism is that circumstances may at any time make it the true morality of the moment. It is by producing such moments that we produce violent and sanguinary revolutions, such as the one now in progress in Russia and the one which Capitalism in England and America is daily and diligently provoking.

At such moments it becomes the duty of the Churches to evoke all the powers of destruction against the existing order. But if they do this, the existing order must forcibly suppress them. Churches are suffered to exist only on condition that they preach submission to the State as at present capitalistically organized. The Church of England itself is compelled to add to the thirtysix articles in which it formulates its religious tenets, three more in which it apologetically protests that the moment any of these articles comes in conflict with the State it is to be entirely renounced, abjured, violated, abrogated and abhorred, the policeman being a much more important person than any of the Persons of the Trinity. And this is why no tolerated Church nor Salvation Army can ever win the entire confidence of the poor. It must be on the side of the police and the military, no matter what it believes or disbelieves; and as the police and the military are the instruments by which the rich rob and oppress the poor (on legal and moral principles made for the purpose), it is not possible to be on the side of the poor and of the police at the same time. Indeed the religious bodies, as the almoners of the rich, become a sort of auxiliary police, taking off the insurrectionary edge of poverty with coals and blankets, bread and treacle, and soothing and cheering the victims with hopes of immense and inexpensive happiness in another world when the process of working them to premature death in the service of the rich is complete in this.

Christianity and Anarchism

Such is the false position from which neither the Salvation Army nor the Church of England nor any other religious organization whatever can escape except through a reconstitution of society. Nor can they merely endure the State passively, washing their hands of its sins. The State is constantly forcing the consciences of men by violence and cruelty. Not content with exacting money from us for the maintenance of its soldiers and policemen, its gaolers and executioners, it forces us to take an active personal part in its proceedings on pain of becoming ourselves the victims of its violence. As I write these lines, a sensational example is given to the world. A royal marriage has been celebrated, first by sacrament in a cathedral, and then by a bullfight having for its main amusement the spectacle of horses gored and disembowelled by the bull, after which, when the bull is so exhausted as to be no longer dangerous, he is killed by a cautious matador. But the ironic contrast between the bullfight and the sacrament of marriage does not move anyone. Another contrast—that between the splendor, the happiness, the atmosphere of kindly admiration surrounding the young couple, and the price paid for it under our abominable social arrangements in the misery, squalor and degradation of millions of other young couples—is drawn at the same moment by a novelist, Mr Upton Sinclair, who chips a corner of the veneering from the huge meat-packing industries of Chicago, and shews it to us as a sample of what is going on all over the world underneath the top layer of prosperous plutocracy. One man is sufficiently moved by that contrast to pay his own life as the price of one terrible blow at the responsible parties. His poverty has left him ignorant enough to be duped by the pretence that the innocent young bride and bridegroom, put forth and crowned by plutocracy as the heads of a State in which they have less personal power than any policeman, and less influence than any Chairman of a Trust, are responsible. At them accordingly he launches his sixpennorth of fulminate, missing his mark, but scattering the bowels of as many horses as any bull in the arena, and slaying twenty-three persons, besides wounding ninety-nine. And of all these, the horses alone are innocent of the guilt he is avenging; had he blown all Madrid to atoms with every adult person in it, not one could have escaped the charge of being an accessory, before, at, and after the fact, to poverty and prostitution, to such wholesale massacre of infants as Herod never dreamt of, to plague, pestilence and famine, battle, murder and lingering death — perhaps not one who had not helped, through example, precept, connivance, and even clamor, to teach the dynamiter his well-learnt gospel of hatred and vengeance, by approving every day of sentences of years of imprisonment so infernal in their unnatural stupidity and panicstricken cruelty, that their advocates can disavow neither the dagger nor the bomb without stripping the mask of justice and humanity from themselves also.

Be it noted that at this very moment there appears the biography of one of our dukes, who, being a Scot, could argue about politics, and therefore stood out as a great brain among our aristocrats. And what, if you please, was his grace's favorite historical episode, which he declared he never read without intense satisfaction? Why, the young General Bonapart's pounding of the Paris mob to pieces in 1795, called in playful approval by our respectable classes "the whiff of grapeshot," though Napoleon, to do him justice, took a deeper view of it, and would fain have had it forgotten. And since the Duke of Argyll was not a demon, but a man of like passions with ourselves, by no means rancorous or cruel as men go, who can doubt that all over the world proletarians of the ducal kidney are now revelling in "the whiff of dynamite" (the flavor of the joke seems to evaporate a little, does it not?) because it was aimed at the class they hate even as our argute duke hated what he called the mob.

In such an atmosphere there can be only one sequel to the Madrid explosion. All Europe burns to emulate it. Vengeance! More blood! Tear "the Anarchist beast" to shreds. Drag him to the scaffold. Imprison him for life. Let all civilized States band together to drive his like off the face of the earth; and if any State refuses to join, make war on it. This time the leading London newspaper, anti-Liberal and therefore anti-Russian in politics, does not say "Serve you right" to the victims, as it did, in effect, when Bobrikoff, and De Plehve, and Grand Duke Sergius, were in the same manner unofficially fulminated into fragments. No: fulminate our rivals in Asia by all means, ye brave Russian revolutionaries; but to aim at an English princess! monstrous! hideous! hound down the wretch to his doom; and observe, please, that we are a civilized and merciful people, and, however much we may regret it, must not treat him as Ravaillac and Damiens were treated. And meanwhile, since we have not yet caught him, let us soothe our quivering nerves with the bullfight, and comment in a courtly way on the unfailing tact and good taste of the ladies of our royal houses, who, though presumably of full normal natural tenderness, have been so effectually broken in to fashionable routine that they can be taken to see the horses slaughtered as helplessly as they could no doubt be taken to a gladiator show, if that happened to be the mode just now.

Strangely enough, in the midst of this raging fire of malice, the one man who still has faith in the kindness and intelligence of human nature is the fulminator, now a hunted wretch, with nothing, apparently, to secure his triumph over all the prisons and scaffolds of infuriate Europe except the revolver in his pocket and his readiness to discharge it at a moment's notice into his own or any other head. Think of him setting out to find a gentleman and a Christian in the multitude of human wolves howling for his blood. Think also of this: that at the very first essay he finds what he seeks, a veritable grandee of Spain, a noble, high-thinking, unterrified, malice-void soul, in the guise — of all masquerades in the world! — of a modern editor. The Anarchist wolf, flying from the wolves of plutocracy, throws himself on the honor of the man. The man, not being a wolf (nor a London editor), and therefore not having enough sympathy with his exploit to be made bloodthirsty by it, does not throw him back to the pursuing wolves — gives him, instead, what help he can to escape, and sends him off acquainted at last with a force that goes deeper than dynamite, though you cannot buy so much of it for sixpence. That righteous and honorable high human deed is not wasted on Europe, let us hope, though it benefits the fugitive wolf only for a moment. The plutocratic wolves presently smell him out. The fugitive shoots the unlucky wolf whose nose is nearest; shoots himself; and then convinces the world, by his photograph, that he was no monstrous freak of reversion to the tiger, but a good looking young man with nothing abnormal about him except his appalling courage and resolution (that is why the terrified shriek Coward at him): one to whom murdering a happy young couple on their wedding morning would have been an unthinkably unnatural abomination under rational and kindly human circumstances.

Then comes the climax of irony and blind stupidity. The wolves, balked of their meal of fellow-wolf, turn on the man, and proceed to torture him, after their manner, by imprisonment, for refusing to fasten his teeth in the throat of the dynamiter and hold him down until they came to finish him.

Thus, you see, a man may not be a gentleman nowadays even if he wishes to. As to being a Christian, he is allowed some latitude in that matter, because, I repeat, Christianity has two faces. Popular Christianity has for its emblem a gibbet, for its chief sensation a sanguinary execution after torture, for its central mystery an insane vengeance bought off by a trumpery expiation. But there is a nobler and profounder Christianity which affirms the sacred mystery of Equality, and forbids the glaring futility and folly of vengeance, often politely called punishment or justice. The gibbet part of Christianity is tolerated. The other is criminal felony. Connoisseurs in irony are well aware of the fact that the only editor in England who denounces punishment as radically wrong, also repudiates Christianity; calls his paper The Freethinker; and has been imprisoned for "bad taste" under the law against blasphemy.

Sane Conclusions

And now I must ask the excited reader not to lose his head on one side or the other, but to draw a sane moral from these grim absurdities. It is not good sense to propose that laws against crime should apply to principals only and not to accessories whose consent, counsel, or silence may secure impunity to the principal. If you institute punishment as part of the law, you must punish people for refusing to punish. If you have a police, part of its duty must be to compel everybody to assist the police. No doubt if your laws are unjust, and your policemen agents of oppression, the result will be an unbearable violation of the private consciences of citizens. But that cannot be helped: the remedy is, not to license everybody to thwart the law if they please, but to make laws that will command the public assent, and not to deal cruelly and stupidly with law-breakers. Everybody disapproves of burglars; but the modern burglar, when caught and overpowered by a householder, usually appeals, and often, let us hope, with success, to his captor not to deliver him over to the useless horrors of penal servitude. In other cases the lawbreaker escapes because those who could give him up do not consider his breach of the law a guilty action. Sometimes, even, private tribunals are formed in opposition to the official tribunals; and these private tribunals employ assassins as executioners, as was done, for example, by Mahomet before he had established his power officially, and by the Ribbon lodges of Ireland in their long struggle with the landlords. Under such circumstances, the assassin goes free although everybody in the district knows who he is and what he has done. They do not betray him, partly because they justify him exactly as the regular Government justifies its official executioner, and partly because they would themselves be assassinated if they betrayed him: another method learnt from the official government. Given a tribunal, employing a slayer who has no personal quarrel with the slain; and there is clearly no moral difference between official and unofficial killing.

In short, all men are anarchists with regard to laws which are against their consciences, either in the preamble or in the penalty. In London our worst anarchists are the magistrates, because many of them are so old and ignorant that when they are called upon to administer any law that is based on ideas or knowledge less than half a century old, they disagree with it, and being mere ordinary homebred private Englishmen without any respect for law in the abstract, naïvely set the example of violating it. In this instance the man lags behind the law; but when the law lags behind the man, he becomes equally an anarchist. When some huge change in social conditions, such as the industrial revolution of the eighteenth and nineteenth centuries, throws our legal and industrial institutions out of date, Anarchism becomes almost a religion. The whole force of the most energetic geniuses of the time in philosophy, economics, and art, concentrates itself on demonstrations and reminders that morality and law are only conventions, fallible and continually obsolescing. Tragedies in which the heroes are bandits, and comedies in which law-abiding and conventionally moral folk are compelled to satirize themselves by outraging the conscience of the spectators every time they do their duty, appear simultaneously with economic treatises entitled "What is Property? Theft!" and with histories of "The Conflict between Religion and Science."

Now this is not a healthy state of things. The advantages of living in society are proportionate, not to the freedom of the individual from a code, but to the complexity and subtlety of the code he is prepared not only to accept but to uphold as a matter of such vital importance that a lawbreaker at large is hardly to be tolerated on any plea. Such an attitude becomes impossible when the only men who can make themselves heard and remembered throughout the world spend all their energy in raising our gorge against current law, current morality, current respectability, and legal property. The ordinary man, uneducated in social theory even when he is schooled in Latin verse, cannot be set against all the laws of his country and yet persuaded to regard law in the abstract as vitally necessary to society. Once he is brought to repudiate the laws and institutions he knows, he will repudiate the very conception of law and the very groundwork of institutions, ridiculing human rights, extolling brainless methods as "historical," and tolerating nothing except pure empiricism in conduct, with dynamite as the basis of politics and vivisection as the basis of science. That is hideous; but what is to be done? Here am I, for instance, by class a respectable man, by common sense a hater of waste and disorder, by intellectual constitution legally minded to the verge of pedantry, and by temperament apprehensive and economically disposed to the limit of old-maidishness; yet I am, and have always been, and shall now always be, a revolutionary writer, because our laws make law impossible; our liberties destroy all freedom; our property is organized robbery; our morality is an impudent hypocrisy; our wisdom is administered by inexperienced or malexperienced dupes, our power wielded by cowards and weaklings, and our honor false in all its points. I am an enemy of the existing order for good reasons; but that does not make my attacks any less encouraging or helpful to people who are its enemies for bad reasons. The existing order may shriek that if I tell the truth about it, some foolish person may drive it to become still worse by trying to assassinate it. I cannot help that, even if I could see what worse it could do than it is already doing. And the disadvantage of that worst even from its own point of view is that society, with all its prisons and bayonets and whips and ostracisms and starvations, is powerless in the face of the Anarchist who is prepared to sacrifice his own life in the battle with it. Our natural safety from the cheap and devastating explosives which every Russian student can make, and every Russian grenadier has learnt to handle in Manchuria, lies in the fact that brave and resolute men, when they are rascals, will not risk their skins for the good of humanity, and, when they are not, are sympathetic enough to care for humanity, abhorring murder, and never committing it until their consciences are outraged beyond endurance. The remedy is, then, simply not to outrage their consciences.

Do not be afraid that they will not make allowances. All men make very large allowances indeed before they stake their own lives in a war to the death with society. Nobody demands or expects the millennium. But there are two things that must be set right, or we shall perish, like Rome, of soul atrophy disguised as empire.

The first is, that the daily ceremony of dividing the wealth of the country among its inhabitants shall be so conducted that no crumb shall, save as a criminal's ration, go to any able-bodied adults who are not producing by their personal exertions not only a full equivalent for what they take, but a surplus sufficient to provide for their superannuation and pay back the debt due for their nurture.

The second is that the deliberate infliction of malicious injuries which now goes on under the name of punishment be abandoned; so that the thief, the ruffian, the gambler, and the beggar, may without inhumanity be handed over to the law, and made to understand that a State which is too humane to punish will also be too thrifty to waste the life of honest men in watching or restraining dishonest ones. That is why we do not imprison dogs. We even take our chance of their first bite. But if a dog delights to bark and bite, it goes to the lethal chamber. That seems to me sensible. To allow the dog to expiate his bite by a period of torment, and then let him loose in a much more savage condition (for the chain makes a dog savage) to bite again and expiate again, having meanwhile spent a great deal of human life and happiness in the task of chaining and feeding and tormenting him, seems to me idiotic and superstitious. Yet that is what we do to men who bark and bite and steal. It would be far more sensible to put up with their vices, as we put up with their illnesses, until they give more trouble than they are worth, at which point we should, with many apologies and expressions of sympathy, and some generosity in complying with their last wishes, place them in the lethal chamber and get rid of them. Under no circumstances should they be allowed to expiate their misdeeds by a manufactured penalty, to subscribe to a charity, or to compensate the victims. If there is to be no punishment there can be no forgiveness. We shall never have real moral responsibility until everyone knows that his deeds are irrevocable, and that his life depends on his usefulness. Hitherto, alas! humanity has never dared face these hard facts. We frantically scatter conscience money and invent systems of conscience banking, with expiatory penalties, atonements, redemptions, salvations, hospital subscription lists and what not, to enable us to contract-out of the moral code. Not content with the old scapegoat and sacrificial lamb, we deify human saviors, and pray to miraculous virgin intercessors. We attribute mercy to the inexorable; soothe our consciences after committing murder by throwing ourselves on the bosom of divine love; and shrink even from our own gallows because we are forced to admit that it, as least, is irrevocable—as if one hour of imprisonment were not as irrevocable as any execution!

If a man cannot look evil in the face without illusion, he will never know what it really is, or combat it effectually. The few men who have been able (relatively) to do this have been called cynics, and have sometimes had an abnormal share of evil in themselves, corresponding to the abnormal strength of their minds; but they have never done mischief unless they intended to do it. That is why great scoundrels have been beneficent rulers whilst amiable and privately harmless monarchs have ruined their countries by trusting to the hocus-pocus of innocence and guilt, reward and punishment, virtuous indignation and pardon, instead of standing up to the facts without either malice or mercy. Major Barbara stands up to Bill Walker in that way, with the result that the ruffian who cannot get hated, has to hate himself. To relieve this agony he tries to get punished; but the Salvationist whom he tries to provoke is as merciless as Barbara, and only prays for him. Then he tries to pay, but can get nobody to take his money. His doom is the doom of Cain, who, failing to find either a savior, a policeman, or an almoner to help him to pretend that his brother's blood no longer cried from the ground, had to live and die a murderer. Cain took care not to commit another murder, unlike our railway shareholders (I am one) who kill and maim

shunters by hundreds to save the cost of automatic couplings, and make atonement by annual subscriptions to deserving charities. Had Cain been allowed to pay off his score, he might possibly have killed Adam and Eve for the mere sake of a second luxurious reconciliation with God afterwards. Bodger, you may depend on it, will go on to the end of his life poisoning people with bad whisky, because he can always depend on the Salvation Army or the Church of England to negotiate a redemption for him in consideration of a trifling percentage of his profits.

There is a third condition too, which must be fulfilled before the great teachers of the world will cease to scoff at its religions. Creeds must become intellectually honest. At present there is not a single credible established religion in the world. That is perhaps the most stupendous fact in the whole world-situation. This play of mine, Major Barbara, is, I hope, both true and inspired; but whoever says that it all happened, and that faith in it and understanding of it consist in believing that it is a record of an actual occurrence, is, to speak according to Scripture, a fool and a liar, and is hereby solemnly denounced and cursed as such by me, the author, to all posterity.

London, June 1906.

Postscript 1933

In spite of the emphasis laid both in this preface and in the play on the fact that poverty is an infectious pestilence to be prevented at all costs, the lazy habit still prevails of tolerating it not only as an inevitable misfortune to be charitably patronized and relieved, but as a useful punishment for all sorts of misconduct and inefficiency that are not expressly punishable by law. Until we have a general vital hatred of poverty, and a determination to "liquidate" the underfed either by feeding them or killing them, we shall not tackle the poverty question seriously. Long ago I proposed to eradicate the dangerous disease of hunger among children by placing good bread on public supply like drinking water. No Government nor municipality has yet taken up that very sensible proposal.